LANDMARK CASES IN PUBLIC INTERNATIONAL LAW

The past two hundred years have seen the transformation of public international law from a rule-based extrusion of diplomacy into a fully-fledged legal system. *Landmark Cases in Public International Law* examines decisions that have contributed to the development of international law into an integrated whole, whilst also creating specialised sub-systems that stand alone as units of analysis. The significance of these decisions is not taken for granted, with contributors critically interrogating the cases to determine if their reputation as 'landmarks' is deserved. Emphasis is also placed on seeing each case as a diplomatic artefact, highlighting that international law, while unquestionably a legal system, remains reliant on the practice and consent of states as the prime movers of development.

The cases selected cover a broad range of subject areas including state immunity, human rights, the environment, trade and investment, international organisations, international courts and tribunals, the laws of war, international crimes, and the interface between international and municipal legal systems. A wide array of international and domestic courts are also considered, from the International Court of Justice to the European Court of Human Rights, World Trade Organization Appellate Body, US Supreme Court and other adjudicative bodies. The result is a three-dimensional picture of international law: what it was, what it is, and what it might yet become.

Landmark Cases in Public International Law

Edited by
Eirik Bjorge and Cameron Miles

·HART·

OXFORD · LONDON · NEW YORK · NEW DELHI · SYDNEY

HART PUBLISHING
Bloomsbury Publishing Plc
Kemp House, Chawley Park, Cumnor Hill, Oxford, OX2 9PH, UK

HART PUBLISHING, the Hart/Stag logo, BLOOMSBURY and the Diana logo are
trademarks of Bloomsbury Publishing Plc
First published in Great Britain 2017
First published in hardback, 2017
Paperback edition, 2020

A catalogue record for this book is available from the British Library.

Library of Congress Cataloging-in-Publication Data
a catalogue record for this book is available from the Library of Congress.

ISBN: HB: 978-1-78043-157-4
PB: 978-1-50993-770-7
ePDF: 978-1-78043-157-6
ePub: 978-1-78043-157-7

Typeset by Compuscript Ltd, shannon

To find out more about our authors and books visit www.hartpublishing.co.uk. Here you will
find extracts, author information, details of forthcoming events and the option to sign up for
our newsletters.

Foreword

BY SIR FRANK BERMAN KCMG QC

There is a particular pleasure in sitting down to write a Foreword to this imaginative collection of essays, which one hopes will have a much wider appeal than just to current scholars and practitioners of the legal discipline of international law itself. The task allows one—indeed I ought to say compels one—to do more than simply re-visit landmarks in one's own personal legal formation. It forces one irresistibly to think about the way in which international law has developed, has broadened and thickened, and about the very sizeable changes that have taken place in the functions international law is expected to perform, and in the way it performs them. It does so, too, in a manner that is particularly congenial to those from a common law background, from Pitt Cobbett in 1885 until today, by looking at how things have worked out in practice: how the key issues presented themselves in real terms, how they were dealt with, in sets of concrete circumstances, and how all that was then responded to, by acceptance, or by rejection, but most of all by further elaboration or development.

Moreover, the Landmark Cases collected in this book serve at least two other useful purposes. They remind one in the first place that no dispute going to judicial settlement ever consists of one single isolated legal issue. Indeed, one of the most striking indicators of international law as a legal <u>system</u> lies in the way in which international disputes, most especially when they are subjected to the fierce analytical discipline of forensic argument, show themselves as entailing the simultaneous application and the interplay of different legal concepts each with its relevance to particular aspects of the matter under dispute.

The second important reminder is that disputed legal issues arise out of facts on the ground. By this, I don't wish merely to restate the platitude that an important part of any tribunal's task lies in finding and stating the facts. I mean rather that each of the Landmark Cases collected in this book consists, and necessarily so, of the application of law, as found by the tribunal, to a set of facts. So that it is at one's peril that one gets into the way of thinking of any given landmark decision as having established 'a principle,' without paying the right sort of regard to how the enunciation of the principle emerged and within what context.

The particular charm of a good many of the chapters in the book is to bring us back (or at least here I speak only for myself) from the skeletal memory of a doctrine or principle to a clear understanding of just how complex and intricate a situation it had been that led to the statement of the doctrine or principle in judicial decisions that often approached the complexity of the situation that had brought them about; and then to show us which aspects of these complex decisions stood the test of international opinion, which parts of them were quietly ignored or set aside, and how that organic process led the law to what we think it may be today.

The editors, Eirik Bjorge and Cameron Miles, have had the eminently good sense not to impose any sort of rigid template on their contributors—other, that is, than the request to explore actively, and if need be sceptically, whether their Landmark deserved and still deserves what the editors delicately refer to as its 'reputation' as such. This welcome freedom has allowed the impressive range of contributors to develop, often working fruitfully in pairs, their own approaches to the task, ranging from sober appreciation to the re-fighting of old battles, but always in a way that captures the attention and seeks to hold it. It goes without saying that it would be invidious to single any of them out, though it is hard not to express admiration for Douglas Guilfoyle's elegant achievement of encapsulating, in the space of a mere 20 pages, not merely the details and consequences (deftly reassessed) of the *Lotus* case, but also the political and diplomatic history of the region and even the personalities, style and background of the two principal advocates. But this Foreword would under any circumstances be incomplete without a special mention of the chapter on the *Tyrer* case in the European Commission and Court of Human Rights by Sir Nigel Rodley, which displays all of the qualities of thoughtful care and fairmindedness which will make his sudden and premature death so great a loss to the world of international law.

Sir Frank Berman KCMG QC
London
14 August 2017

Contents

Notes on Contributors

Michael A Becker is a PhD candidate in international law at the University of Cambridge, where he is a WM Tapp Scholar at Gonville and Caius College. His doctoral research examines the contemporary role of commissions of inquiry in the international legal system. A graduate of Yale Law School, he served as an Associate Legal Officer at the International Court of Justice from 2010 to 2014. He has experience as a commercial litigator and as a federal law clerk in the United States. He is admitted to the Bar of the State of New York.

Sir Frank Berman KCMG QC joined HM Diplomatic Service in 1965 and was the Legal Adviser to the Foreign and Commonwealth Office from 1991 to 1999. Since then, he has been in practice in Essex Court Chambers in London specialising in international arbitration and advisory work in international law. He is Visiting Professor of International Law at Oxford and the University of Cape Town. He has served as a Judge *ad hoc* of the International Court of Justice and is a member of the Permanent Court of Arbitration. He has been appointed to the list of arbitrators maintained by the International Centre for Settlement of Investment Disputes.

Eirik Bjorge is Senior Lecturer in Public International Law at the University of Bristol. He has authored *The Evolutionary Interpretation of Treaties* (OUP, 2014) and *Domestic Application of the ECHR: Courts as Faithful Trustees* (OUP, 2015), and edited, and translated from the French, Bernard Stirn's *Towards a European Public Law* (OUP, 2017). With Sir Frank Berman KCMG QC, he is responsible for the law of treaties section in *Oppenheim's International Law* (10th edn, OUP, 2018), and in 2015, he was awarded the King of Norway's Gold Medal in Law.

Laurence Boisson de Chazournes has been Professor in International Law and International Organisation at the Faculty of Law of the University of Geneva since 1999. She is an Associate Member of the Institute of International Law and an adviser to various international organisations (UN, ILO and WHO), governments and law firms. In the area of dispute settlement, she advises and litigates on a wide range of international law issues. She has served as chairperson of WTO arbitration panels, has pleaded before the International Court of Justice and has been an arbitrator in investment arbitration (ICSID, ICC and PCA). She is a member of the PCA and of the Court of Arbitration for Sport in which she has also been appointed arbitrator.

Chester Brown is Professor of International Law and International Arbitration at the University of Sydney Law School, and the Co-Director of the Sydney Centre for International Law. He is also a Barrister at 7 Wentworth Selborne Chambers (Sydney) and an Overseas Associate of Essex Court Chambers (London) and Maxwell Chambers (Singapore). He teaches and researches in the fields of public and private international law, and international dispute settlement. He has been counsel in proceedings before the International Court of Justice; the Iran–US

Claims Tribunal; inter-state, investor-state and international commercial arbitral tribunals; as well as in inter-state conciliation proceedings. He is the author of *A Common Law of International Adjudication* (OUP, 2007), for which he received the ASIL Certificate of Merit, 2010. He co-authored of *The International Arbitration Act 1974: A Commentary* (2nd edn, LexisNexis, 2015), edited *Commentaries on Selected Model Investment Treaties* (OUP, 2013), and co-edited of *Evolution in Investment Treaty Law and Arbitration* (CUP, 2011). He was educated at the Universities of Melbourne, Oxford, and Cambridge.

Judge James Crawford AC is a Judge of the International Court of Justice. Previously, he was Whewell Professor of International Law at the University of Cambridge (1992–2015), and he has also held chairs in Australia and China. As a member of the International Law Commission he was responsible for the Draft Statute for an International Criminal Court (1994) and the Articles on the Responsibility of States for Internationally Wrongful Acts (2001). In addition to scholarly work on statehood, state responsibility and investment protection, he has been involved as counsel, expert or arbitrator in many international cases. In 2012, he was awarded the Hudson Medal by the American Society of International Law. In 2013, was appointed Companion of the Order of Australia.

William S Dodge is Martin Luther King, Jr Professor of Law at the University of California, Davis, School of Law. He is a co-reporter for the American Law Institute's *Restatement Fourth, the Foreign Relations Law of the United States* and a member of the US State Department's Advisory Committee on International Law. From 2011 to 2012, he served as Counselor on International Law to the Legal Adviser at the State Department. Among other publications, he is the co-author of *Transnational Business Problems* (5th edn, Foundation Press, 2014) and the co-editor of *International Law in the US Supreme Court: Continuity and Change* (CUP, 2011), which won the American Society of International Law's Certificate of Merit in 2012. He served as a law clerk for Justice Harry A Blackmun of the US Supreme Court and received his BA and JD from Yale University.

John Dugard SC is Emeritus Professor of International Law at the Universities of Leiden and the Witwatersrand, and a member of the *Institut de Droit International*. He was Director of the Lauterpacht Centre for International Law at the University of Cambridge in 1995, a member of the International Law Commission from 1997 to 2011 and UN Special Rapporteur on the Situation of Human Rights in the Occupied Palestinian Territory from 2001 to 2008. He has served as a Judge *ad hoc* of the International Court of Justice on six occasions.

Rolf Einar Fife is Ambassador of Norway to France and Monaco. He was Director-General of Legal Affairs at the Ministry of Foreign Affairs of Norway from 2002 to 2014. Prior to that, he had occupied various positions within the Ministry, including Norway's permanent mission to the United Nations, and as head of the division for the law of international organisations and the law of the sea. In the course of his career, he has represented Norway before international courts and tribunals. In 2009/10, he was elected to preside over the Committee of Legal Advisers on Public International Law of the Council of Europe. He is a member of the Permanent Court of Arbitration.

Duncan French is Professor of International Law, Head of the Law School and PGT Dean at the University of Lincoln. He has written extensively on international law and international environmental law. He was Chair of the International Law Association Study Group on Due Diligence and International Law.

Judge Giorgio Gaja is a Judge of the International Court of Justice and Emeritus Professor at the University of Florence Law School. In 2014, his general course at the Hague Academy was published under the title 'The Protection of General Interests in the International Community'.

Thomas D Grant is Fellow of Wolfson College and Senior Associate of the Lauterpacht Centre for International Law at the University of Cambridge, and an Associate Member of 3 Verulam Buildings in London. He has served as legal advisor to governments, international organisations, corporate clients, and two US presidential election campaigns. He has an extensive practice before international courts and tribunals, and is admitted to practise in the District of Columbia, New York, Massachusetts, and at the US Supreme Court. He is the author of several books, the most recent of which is *Aggression Against Ukraine: Territory, Responsibility and International Law* (Palgrave MacMillan, 2015).

Douglas Guilfoyle is Professor of Law at Monash University in Melbourne, Australia. He researches and teaches in public international law with an emphasis on the law of the sea and international criminal law. He is the author of *Shipping Interdiction and the Law of the Sea* (CUP, 2009), *International Criminal Law* (OUP, 2016) and numerous articles on maritime security, naval warfare and piracy.

Robert Kolb is Professor of Public International Law at the University of Geneva. He formerly worked for the International Commission for the Red Cross in Geneva.

Sam Luttrell is Partner in the International Arbitration Group at Clifford Chance LLP, based in Perth. His practice is focused on investor–State arbitration in the energy and resources sector. He is ranked in Band 1 for arbitration (Australia) in Chambers Global and is listed as a 'future leader' of international arbitration in *Who's Who Legal*. In addition to his work as counsel, he is a regular contributor to international law and arbitration journals, and teaches at universities and arbitral institutions around the Asia-Pacific region.

Cameron Miles is a barrister at 3 Verulam Buildings in London, specialising in public international law with a focus on state immunity, state responsibility, the procedure of international courts and tribunals, and international investment disputes. He is the author of *Provisional Measures before International Courts and Tribunals* (CUP, 2017), and numerous scholarly articles, notes and book reviews in his fields of expertise. He is admitted to practise in Australia, England and Wales, and holds an LLM and PhD from the University of Cambridge.

Makane Moïse Mbengue is Associate Professor of International Law at the Faculty of Law of the University of Geneva and Affiliated Professor at Sciences Po Paris (School of Law). He has acted, and still acts, as expert for the African Union, the United Nations Economic Commission for Africa, the United Nations Environment Programme, the World Health Organization, the World Bank, the International

Labour Organization and the International Institute for Sustainable Development among others. He also works as a professor for courses in International Law organised by the United Nations Office of Legal Affairs and by the United Nations Institute for Training and Research. He further acts as counsel in disputes before international courts and tribunals, and as advisor for governments in several fields of international law. He is the author of several publications in the field of international law.

Paul Mertenskötter is Fellow at the Institute for International Law and Justice at New York University School of Law. There, he works on the MegaReg Project, and the law and global governance of health regulation focused on diet and non-communicable diseases. He was a law clerk at the International Court of Justice from 2014 to 2015. He holds a JD, *cum laude*, from NYU, where he was a Guarini Government Service Scholar, German Academic Scholarship Foundation Scholar and recipient of the Jerome Lipper Prize for outstanding work in international law. He did his undergraduate work in philosophy, politics and economics at the Universities of York and Pennsylvania.

Callum Musto is a doctoral candidate in Public International Law at the London School of Economics and Political Science. His research spans a range of topics in international law including sources doctrine and theory, jurisdiction, international dispute settlement, law of the sea, international environmental law, and international economic law. He has taught public international law, European Union law and public law at the University of Oxford, the London School of Economics and the Australian National University. He holds a Master's degree in international law from the University of Oxford and degrees in law, history and international relations from the Australian National University. He is co-editor of the UK Materials on International Law for the *British Yearbook of International Law*.

Rowan Nicholson is a doctoral candidate in the Faculty of Law at the University of Cambridge, undertaking a dissertation on the concept of legal personality in international law. He has Bachelor's degrees in Law and Arts from the University of Adelaide and Master's degrees in International Relations and Law from Macquarie University and the University of Cambridge, respectively. Previously, he was Senior Associate to Professor James Crawford AC SC at the Lauterpacht Centre for International Law.

Sarah Nouwen is University Senior Lecturer, Co-Deputy Director of the Lauterpacht Centre for International Law and a Fellow of Pembroke College at the University of Cambridge. Prior to assuming her lectureship, she served as Senior Legal Advisor to the African Union High-Level Implementation Panel for Sudan, and as a consultant for the Netherlands Ministry of Foreign Affairs and the United Kingdom Department for International Development. She is the author of *Complementarity in the Line of Fire: The Catalysing Effect of the International Criminal Court in Uganda and Sudan* (CUP, 2013).

Katherine O'Byrne is a barrister at Doughty Street Chambers in London, specialising in international law, human rights, public law and extradition. She has been instructed as junior counsel in the Supreme Court, Court of Appeal and in public inquiries, and has represented individual and state clients before UN bodies and the International Court of Justice. She has expertise in domestic claims with international law elements, including torture, arbitrary detention and sexual abuse cases, and regularly acts on behalf of children in need. She previously practised as a solicitor at Freehills (now Herbert Smith Freehills) and was an associate to Justice Kenneth Hayne AC of the High Court of Australia. She holds an LLM from the University of Cambridge, she is the co-editor of *Surrogacy, Law and Human Rights* (Ashgate/Routledge, 2015), and has published in the areas of public law, gender, children's rights and refugee law.

Nikiforos Panagis is a doctoral candidate and Graduate Teaching Assistant in Public International Law in the Faculty of Law at the University of Oxford. He is the recipient of a doctoral grant by the Academy of Athens in Greece. He has previously studied law at the National and Kapodistrian University of Athens, where he received an LLB and LLM, and at the University of Oxford, where he obtained a MJur and MPhil.

Surabhi Ranganathan is Lecturer in International Law at the University of Cambridge, Fellow of King's College, Cambridge, and Fellow of the Lauterpacht Centre for International Law. She is the author of *Strategically Created Treaty Conflicts and the Politics of International Law* (CUP, 2014). Her research explores histories and politics of international law, with a current focus on the designation, representations and regulation of global commons, especially the deep seabed. She has written on nuclear governance, particularly in the context of the India–US nuclear deal, for law journals as well as online fora.

Catherine Redgwell is Chichele Professor of Public International Law at All Souls College, University of Oxford, having previously held posts at UCL and at the Universities of Nottingham and Manchester. She has published extensively in public international law, particularly in the areas of international environmental law, international energy law, law of the sea, and the law of treaties. She is joint general editor of the *British Yearbook of International Law* and co-editor of *Oxford Monographs in International Law* for Oxford University Press.

Sir Nigel Rodley was Emeritus Professor of Law at the University of Essex. From 1973 to 1990 he was legal adviser to Amnesty International. From 1993 to 2001 he served as Special Rapporteur on Torture on the UN Commission on Human Rights, thereafter becoming a member of the UN Human Rights Committee—serving as its president from 2013 to 2014. In 2005, he received the American Society of International Law's Golter T. Butcher Medal for distinguished work in human rights. He was the author of numerous books and articles on international human rights and humanitarian law, most notably *The Treatment of Prisoners Under International Law*, published by Oxford University Press in 1987 and now in its 3rd edition.

Philippe Sands QC is Professor of Law at University College London and Director of the Centre on International Courts and Tribunals. He has held visiting professorships at (*inter alia*) the University of Toronto (2005), the University of Melbourne (2005) and the Université de Paris I (Sorbonne). He is also a barrister and arbitrator, practicing from Matrix Chambers in London. In this capacity, he has extensive experience before a variety of international courts and tribunals, including the International Court of Justice, the International Tribunal for the Law of the Sea and the European Court of Justice. He also advises states, governments and other entities on public international law issues. He has been appointed to the list of arbitrators maintained by the International Center for Settlement of Investment Disputes and the Permanent Court of Arbitration. His most recent book, *East West Street: On the Origins of Genocide and Crimes Against Humanity* (Weidenfeld & Nicholson, 2016) won the 2017 Baillie Gifford (Samuel Johnson) Prize for Non-Fiction.

Antonios Tzanakopoulos is Associate Professor of Public International Law and Fellow of St Anne's College at the University of Oxford. He has taught as a visitor at the Universities of Paris (Paris X Nanterre), London (King's College), Athens (National and Kapodistrian), at the Interdisciplinary Center in Herzliya, and at the China University of Political Science and Law in Beijing. He was previously lecturer in international law at University College London and at the University of Glasgow. He has also delivered a special course at the Xiamen Academy of International Law in 2017 and has been invited by the Curatorium of the Hague Academy of International Law to serve as Director of Studies in 2021. He is Secretary-General of the International Law Association and Joint Secretary of its British branch.

Omri Sender is counsel for the World Bank, and a consultant and litigator in public international law. Since 2012, he assists the Special Rapporteur of the UN International Law Commission on the topic 'Identification of Customary International Law'. A graduate of Tel Aviv University (LLB, LLM) and New York University (LLM), he is currently pursuing a doctoral degree in international law (SJD) at the George Washington University Law School.

Michael Waibel is Senior Lecturer and Co-Deputy Director of the Lauterpacht Centre for International Law, and Fellow of Jesus College at the University of Cambridge. His main research interests are public international law, international economic law with a focus on finance and the settlement of international disputes.

Sir Michael Wood is a member of the UN International Law Commission, and Senior Fellow of the Lauterpacht Centre for International Law at University of Cambridge. He is a barrister at 20 Essex Street in London, where he practises in the field of public international law, including before international courts and tribunals. He was Legal Adviser to the UK's Foreign and Commonwealth Office between 1999 and 2006, having joined as an Assistant Legal Adviser in 1970.

1

Introduction

EIRIK BJORGE AND CAMERON MILES

There is some tendency on the part of English lawyers to regard that body of custom and convention which is known as International Law, as fanciful and unreal; as a collection of amiable opinions, rather than a body of legal rules. The text writers have much to answer for in this respect. Their real function is to record and collate existing usage. The function which they have striven to assume has been that of authorship. They frequently prescribe, not what is, but what they think ought to be, the practice of nations. Rules originating thus, necessarily command but scanty reverence; and perhaps nothing has tended more to lessen the esteem in which International Law is held than the misapprehension which has been begotten.[1]

I

$\mathbf{I}$N THE AUTUMN of 1885, Pitt Cobbett[2]—a barrister of Gray's Inn and a tutor at the Universities of Oxford and London—published a volume of leading cases on public international law. Books of this kind were, in an age before the *International Law Reports* and the *Max Planck Encyclopedia of Public International Law*, essential to the discipline's practice, containing excerpts of and helpful commentary on the various decisions (almost entirely of domestic courts) that had helped shape the field, such as it then was.

---

[1] P Cobbett, *Leading Cases and Opinions on International Law* (London, Stevens and Haynes, 1885) v (*Leading Cases*).

[2] Cobbett was not much of a barrister: despite having chambers at 4 King's Bench Walk in the Temple, he saw himself as an academic, and never practised. He was, however, one of the principal legal figures of early Australia. Born in Adelaide in 1853, he migrated to England with his parents in 1864, matriculating into University College, Oxford, in 1873. He took a BA in 1876, an MA and BCL in 1880, and a DCL in 1887. In 1890, he returned to Australia, where he was appointed to the Challis Professorship in the Faculty of Law at the University of Sydney and became its first Dean. *Leading Cases* ran to three editions—the second appeared in 1892 and the third (in two volumes, *Peace* and *War and Neutrality*) in 1909 and 1913. Further editions were published by others posthumously. At the time of his death in 1919, he was completing a major work on the Constitution of Australia. The manuscript was very close to completion; but in 1920, the High Court of Australia handed down judgment in *Amalgamated Society of Engineers v Adelaide Steamship Co Ltd* (1920) 28 CLR 129 (the famous *Engineers' Case*), which radically altered the nature of federalism in the Commonwealth through eradication of the doctrines of implied intergovernmental immunities and reserved state powers. The book would have required substantial revisions and was thus never published. Further: FC Hutley, 'Cobbett, William Pitt (1853–1919)' in *Australian Dictionary of Biography*, vol 8 (Melbourne, Melbourne University Press, 1981).

It is fair to say that much of Cobbett's *Leading Cases* would be unfamiliar to the modern eye—both in terms of its structure and the cases that Cobbett alighted upon as being worthy of reportage. The most recent edition of *Brownlie's Principles of Public International Law*[3] is divided into 11 parts, beginning with the sources and relations of international law, and then moving through personality and recognition, territorial sovereignty, the law of the sea, the environment, international transactions, jurisdiction, nationality, state responsibility, the protection of individuals and groups (diplomatic protection, human rights and international criminal law) before concluding, somewhat euphemistically, with disputes (encompassing the claims process, settlement of international disputes, and the use and threat of force by states). A single chapter—the last in *Brownlie's Principles*—is given over to questions relating to war, and it confines these within the four walls of the UN Charter.

Leading Cases, on the other hand, is divided into three parts: peace, war, and neutrality. 'Peace' begins with a discussion of international personality by reference to the *Cherokee Nation v State of Georgia*,[4] in which the US Supreme Court determined that whilst the Cherokee were a distinct political society, they could not be considered foreign states for the purposes of the US Constitution, likening the relation between the US and the various Native American tribes as like that of 'a ward to its guardian'. It then moves through the topics of state jurisdiction (comprising a single case, *R v Keyn*,[5] also known as *The Franconia*), before dealing with public and private vessels, foreign sovereigns, questions of nationality, ambassadors, the slave trade, and piracy. 'War' considers steps short of war, the effects of declarations of and the outbreak of hostilities, trading with the enemy, ransom contracts, capture in war, prize and booty, salvage, and the termination of hostilities. The majority of cases and incidents included in this part concern the activity of ships.[6] Less than familiar names leap out: *The Hoop*,[7] *The Vrouw Margaretha*,[8] *The Swineherd*.[9]

---

[3] J Crawford, *Brownlie's Principles of International Law*, 8th edn (Oxford, OUP, 2012).

[4] 30 US (5 Peters) 1 (1831). Surprisingly, the following year, the Court declared that the Cherokee nation was sovereign, such that Georgia state law could not be enforced in Cherokee territory: *Worcester v Georgia*, 31 US (6 Peters) 515 (1832). Further: JC Burke, 'The Cherokee Cases: A Study in Law, Politics, and Morality' (1969) 21 *Stanford LR* 500.

[5] (1876) 2 Ex D 63. It is irresponsible to suggest that this case stands for any concrete proposition: see CA Miles, 'The *Franconia* Sails On: Revisiting the Intellectual History of the Territorial Sea in the United States, Canada and Australia' (2013) 13 *OUCLJ* 347.

[6] A high number of these concern judgments given by Sir William Scott, a judge in the English High Court of Admiralty and perhaps the greatest British international lawyer of his day, during the Napoleonic Wars and in the aftermath of the American War of Independence: HJ Bourguignon, *Sir William Scott, Lord Stowell: Judge of the High Court of Admiralty, 1798–1828* (Cambridge, CUP 1987).

[7] Setting out the general rule that in times of war trading with the enemy without the permission of the Sovereign was forbidden: (1799) 1 C Rob 196.

[8] Establishing that property consigned by an enemy to a neutral vessel will be held liable for condemnation unless evidence is furnished that the consignee is the true owner of the goods: (1799) 1 C Rob 336.

[9] Establishing that war, although usually terminated via treaty of peace, can in certain situations be terminated by simple cessation of hostilities, or the conquest and submission of one of the belligerent states, in whole or in part: extracted in P-A Merlin, *Répertoire de jurisprudence, Tome XI (Prise)* (Paris, Chez Garnery, 1815) 183.

'Neutrality' follows a similar theme: neutral territory is considered at length, followed by a lengthy section on the duties of neutral states, the laws of blockade, contraband, continuous voyage, and the Rule of the War of 1759.[10] One case does prompt recognition in modern eyes: the *Alabama Claims*[11] (cited as 'the Geneva Arbitration and Award') is the subject of substantial discussion. Another familiar sight is not a case at all: *The Caroline* incident.[12] Although *Leading Cases* might today seem parochial, by the standards of its time, the fact that Cobbett's collection contained *any* genuinely international materials was nothing if not forward-looking.[13]

The overlap (or rather, the *lack* thereof) between the schema of *Leading Cases* and *Brownlie's Principles* demonstrates the 'widening and thickening'[14] that international law has experienced in the 128 years between the publication of the two books. Cobbett's international law was little more than a rule-based extrusion of international diplomacy, in which what few directives there were for the regulation of hostilities took pride of place, with the rest occupied by the corollaries of sovereignty: personality, territory, nationality, and immunity. The engine room of the lawmaking process was diplomatic interaction between the chancelleries of states awarding themselves the epithet 'civilised' and the judgments of their courts. Even temporary international tribunals were scarce, and the idea of a permanent international court impossible. Beyond bodies such as the various river commissions, international organisations did not exist in any meaningful sense. *Leading Cases*, therefore, was a fair presentation of a case law worthy of the somewhat dubious name given to it by WE Hall—'a rough jurisprudence of nations'.[15]

The international law of *Brownlie's Principles*, however, is reflective of a fully articulated legal system, complete with a distinct theory of sources, developed secondary rules of responsibility, an international organisation of plenary membership in the UN, and an ever-expanding constellation of international courts and tribunals headed informally by the International Court of Justice (ICJ) and producing hundreds of decisions, judgments, and awards annually. It regulates—and is acknowledged as regulating—the relations of states with a depth and complexity that would have been impossible when *Leading Cases* went to press. Cobbett, one suspects, would have been pleased (and possibly surprised) to see what his chosen field has become.

---

[10] Being that, on the outbreak of war, a neutral was entitled to continue trade that it had previously possessed, but was not permitted to commence new trade with either belligerent without violating the law of neutrality: *The Immanuel* (1799) 2 C Rob 186.

[11] *Alabama Claims* (US/UK) (1871) 29 RIAA 125.

[12] *The Caroline* (1840–1841) 29 BFSP 1129. Further: RY Jennings, 'The *Caroline* and *McLeod* Cases' (1938) 32 *AJIL* 82.

[13] Contemporaneous collections pertaining to international issues would contain only judgments by the domestic courts, including the prize courts, whereas the opinions on international matters which were included were by domestic Law Officers: see, eg, G Chalmers (ed), *Opinions of Eminent Lawyers* (Burlington, C Goodrich & Co, 1858); RG Marsden (ed), *Documents relating to Law and Custom of the Sea* (London, Navy Records Society, 1916).

[14] R Higgins, 'A Babel of Judicial Voices: Ruminations from the Bench' (2006) 55 *ICLQ* 791, 792.

[15] WE Hall, *A Treatise on International Law*, 8th edn (Oxford, OUP, 1924) 395.

II

The purpose of this slightly meandering introduction is to highlight that the structure, complexity, and mission of international law has evolved rather more in the past century than other systems of law. That being the case, it is appropriate to take stock, to consider how we reached this point and what cases have been—or are thought to have been—essential in bringing us here. *Landmark Cases in Public International Law* brings together 22 analyses of some of the most prominent international decisions of the past two centuries in international law with a view to interrogate critically their continued relevance. Confirming the rapid evolution of the field, only one would have been familiar to Cobbett: *The Charming Betsy*,[16] an 1804 decision of the US Supreme Court that he did not, more than 80 years later, see fit to include in his *Leading Cases*.[17] Even if one accepts that, in the normal course of events, a period of reflection is needed before a case can be considered a landmark, that seems a glaring omission.[18]

This brings us on to the question of what makes a case a 'landmark'. In its literal sense, a landmark is a point of reference on the road to somewhere else—an object that lets the traveller know that they are not the first person in that place. In a more metaphorical sense, it is something of continued significance, attesting to the progress of a particular subject. All of the cases in this volume were selected by us, as editors, for their *reputation* as landmarks of public international law. In receiving the brief, contributors were given little more guidance than this description, an assigned case (or cases), and the request that they actively question whether these judgments, awards, or opinions were still to be afforded that appellation—or, indeed, whether they had deserved it in the first place. Given the unique environment in which international law still operates, they were also asked to analyse their assigned cases as diplomatic as well as legal artefacts.

In selecting the cases, we were motivated by several considerations: (1) to prioritise the decisions of international courts and tribunals over domestic courts so as not to replicate the kind of parochialism that was forced on Cobbett and his contemporaries; (2) to ensure an even balance between international courts and tribunals; and (3) to ensure parity between different sub-systems of international law. A possible criticism of the final selection might be that it gives too much weight to the combined case-law of the Permanent Court of International Justice (PCIJ) and its successor, the ICJ. To our minds, this is defensible: as the informal apex of the system of international courts and tribunals, the Court (in both its guises) has been responsible for many of the foundational decisions of the modern system of international law, and continues to serve this function today as the only permanent international court of plenary jurisdiction. Furthermore, and notwithstanding the recent florescence of

---

[16] *Murray v The Charming Betsey*, 6 US (2 Cranch) 64 (1804). WS Dodge, this volume, ch 1.

[17] The case was granted right of berth in the third edition: *Leading Cases*, 3rd edn, vol 1 (London, Stevens and Haynes, 1909).

[18] That being said, having had ourselves to make the kind of difficult determinations that Cobbett was called on to make, however, we do not believe that all the beams are in the eyes of others: we take heart from the possibility that obvious omissions can be included in later editions or volumes.

international adjudicatory bodies, it was for most of its history the proverbial 'only game in town'.[19] To seek diversity at the expense of the Court's contribution would potentially undermine the project's mission. Nevertheless, efforts have been made to balance these competing requirements. At any rate, whilst the reader may question the inclusion of some cases rather than others, we hope they will agree that the cases selected and the insights of the individual contributors give a three-dimensional understanding of international law: what it was, what it is, and what it might yet become.

* * *

The book commences with William S Dodge's discussion of two of the foundational cases for the interaction of international and municipal law: *The Charming Betsy*; and *The Paquete Habana*.[20] Both are decisions of the US Supreme Court and represent the only municipal cases in the volume, for the reasons already given. In a nice piece of symmetry, Dodge's analysis is bookended by the final chapter, Omri Sender and Sir Michael Wood's contribution on *Jurisdictional Immunities of the State*, the ICJ's signal elaboration on the law of state immunity and its interaction with the jurisdiction of municipal courts.[21]

Although the chapters in between are arranged chronologically, distinct themes and sub-groups appear—as is often the case, however, the decisions within these groups often make significant forays into more general questions of international law. The first of these are a series of diplomatic protection cases before the PCIJ and ICJ that provided much of the grounding not only in that area of law but in diverse areas such as the definition of state acts, remedies in international law, and corporate nationality. Michael Waibel discusses the *Mavrommattis Palestine Concessions* case, a classic of diplomatic protection.[22] Chester Brown considers the various phases of the *Factory at Chorzów* saga[23] and the famous pronouncement of the PCIJ on remedies in international law. Judge Giorgio Gaja analyses the ongoing relevance of *Barcelona Traction*,[24] the decision that refined the rules on corporate nationality and

---

[19] See KJ Alter, 'The Multiplication of International Courts and Tribunals after the End of the Cold War', in CPR Romano, KJ Alter and Y Shany (eds), *The Oxford Handbook of International Adjudication* (Oxford, OUP, 2014) 63.

[20] To pre-empt an obvious criticism, the volume does not commence with a discussion of the *Alabama* Claims for two reasons. First, the decision is today cited more for the fact that it took place than for any enduring principles of law—the substantive questions raised in the arbitration were determined in accordance with certain agreed rules on the duties of neutrals that have little or no application today. (Though, we recognise that the decision is still cited as an early authority for the principles—now largely taken for granted—of *compétence de la compétence* (see, eg, *Dallah Real Estate and Tourism Holding Company v The Ministry of Religious Affairs, Government of Pakistan* [2011] 1 AC 763, [81]) and that international law prevails over domestic law (see, eg, *Applicability of the Obligation to Arbitrate under Section 21 of the United Nations Headquarters Agreement of 26 June 1947*, [1998] ICJ Rep, 12, 34)). Second, and more importantly, it would be difficult to improve on the superlative analysis of the arbitration by Lord Bingham: T Bingham, 'The *Alabama* Claims Arbitration' (2005) 54 *ICLQ* 1.

[21] O Sender and M Wood, this volume, ch 22.

[22] M Waibel, this volume, ch 3.

[23] C Brown, this volume, ch 4.

[24] G Gaja, this volume, ch 13.

formally recognised the concept of obligations *erga omnes*. The historical endpoint of this discussion is reached in Sam Luttrell's chapter on the proceedings in *Vivendi v Argentina*,[25] an episode representative of the modern system of treaty-based investor–state dispute settlement that made a significant contribution to the distinction between contract and treaty claims in international law.

Another distinct bloc contains two early cases on the law of territory. Eirik Bjorge tackles the *Island of Palmas* case,[26] and with it the modern foundation of the *lex temporis* in international law. This chapter also represents an opportunity to consider the legacy of one of the great figures of the field in the early twentieth century: Max Huber, who sat as sole arbitrator in that case. Ambassador Rolf Einar Fife then considers *Legal Status of Eastern Greenland*,[27] an early case that elaborated on the modern requirements for the assertion of sovereignty over territory and the effect of unilateral undertakings by states in international law.

Later in the book, cases begin to emerge on another significant sub-system: international law and the environment. Multiple chapters touch on this area. Duncan French addresses *Trail Smelter*,[28] the dispute between the US and Canada that begat an entirely novel tributary of law: transboundary harm. Laurence Boisson de Chazournes and Makane Moïse Mbengue consider the ICJ's decision in *Gabčíkovo-Nagymaros*,[29] the famous 'Danube Dam' case that also made significant statements on state responsibility and the law of treaties. Finally, Callum Musto and Catherine Redgwell discuss *US—Shrimp*[30] (also known as *Shrimp/Turtle*), a decision on trade and the environment that brings into play dispute settlement and the World Trade Organization.

Another later chronological appearance is international criminal law and the law of human rights. Katherine O'Byrne and Philippe Sands revisit the origins of the former field in the *Nuremberg Trials*,[31] at which the concept of an international crime was made reality and the word 'genocide' first used in open court. Sarah Nouwen and Michael Becker consider the decision in which international criminal law emerged in its modern form, the interlocutory appeal in *Tadić v Prosecutor*,[32] charting the contributions of that case to general international law, international humanitarian law, international criminal law and international legal reasoning. From the perspective of human rights, Sir Nigel Rodley opines on *Tyrer v UK*,[33] a decision of the European Court of Human Rights with much to say on the interpretation of treaties, and which crystallised the modern standard of what constitutes inhuman, cruel, and degrading treatment.

Yet another grouping is that of the law of the sea. Two chapters address this theme, although they are perhaps more significant for what they say about other areas of international law. Douglas Guilfoyle confronts the case of the *SS Lotus*[34]

---

[25] S Luttrell, this volume, ch 19.
[26] E Bjorge, this volume, ch 6.
[27] RE Fife, this volume, ch 7.
[28] D French, this volume, ch 8.
[29] L Boisson de Chazourne and MM Mbengue, this volume, ch 18.
[30] C Redgwell and C Musto, this volume, ch 20.
[31] P Sands and K O'Byrne, this volume, ch 9.
[32] SMH Nouwen and MA Becker, this volume, ch 16.
[33] N Rodley, this volume, ch 14.
[34] D Guilfoyle, this volume, ch 5.

and subjects to searching inquiry its notorious eponymous principle—that what is not expressly prohibited for states in international law must be permitted. Nikiforos Panagis and Antonios Tzanakopoulos address the *North Sea Continental Shelf* cases—formally a maritime delimitation, but also arguably the source of the modern understanding of the development of customary international law and its relationship to treaty norms.

International humanitarian law and the law concerning use of force form yet a further distinct cluster. In this context, Robert Kolb considers the various phases of *Nicaragua*,[35] a true landmark concerning both the use of force under the UN Charter and the extent to which international law and the ICJ could be used to hold a superpower such as the US to account. Surabhi Ranganathan addresses the ICJ's conclusions in the *Nuclear Weapons Advisory Opinions*,[36] and uses these as an opportunity to address the Court's troubled relationship with nuclear weapons more generally. Finally, John Dugard addresses another of the Court's advisory opinions in *Wall*,[37] and what that decision says about international humanitarian law, the law of occupation, the law of self-defence, and other areas. He also takes the opportunity to consider the wider effect of the Court's advisory jurisdiction, and to address one of the most long-running and problematic issues in international affairs, the situation of Israel–Palestine.

Finally, three chapters consider cases connected to the ICJ and its relationship with the UN as its principal judicial organ. At the broadest level, Tom Grant and Rowan Nicholson, in their chapter on the *Early United Nations Advisory Opinions*,[38] address some of the early decisions of the ICJ that set in place the administrative structure of the UN and refined its relationship with its member states, setting it on course to become the vital body it is today. In so doing, the Court also shaped the contours of the modern law of international organisations. Judge James Crawford and Paul Mertenskötter consider the *South West Africa Cases*,[39] a two-judgment and four-advisory-opinion epic that reveals important truths about the workings of the ICJ and its relationship with the other principal organs of the UN, wrapped up in the historical context of South Africa's long-running resistance to international law and public opinion in relation to its occupation of Namibia. Finally, Cameron Miles addresses the Court's role in the development of the international civil procedure through the lens of *LaGrand*,[40] a case in which the ICJ put to an end a controversy of some eight decades concerning its capacity to order binding interim relief.

III

As it is customary to remark, books of this kind would not exist without the assistance of a large number of people. With that in mind, we first extend our profound thanks to the contributors, who tolerated with charm and good humour the usual combination

---

[35] N Panagis and A Tzanakopoulos, this volume, ch 12.
[36] S Ranganathan, this volume, ch 17.
[37] J Dugard, this volume, ch 22.
[38] TD Grant and R Nicholson, this volume, ch 11.
[39] J Crawford and P Mertenskötter, this volume, ch 10.
[40] C Miles, this volume, ch 21.

of chaser emails and 'helpful' suggestions that characterise modern academic editors,[41] and despite which they produced chapters of uniformly high quality.[42]

We also thank Sir Franklin Berman KCMG QC for his gracious Foreword, produced under similar circumstances, as well as the anonymous referees to whom we sent selected chapters for review.

This project commenced with an academic seminar held at All Soul's College, Oxford, on 17 June 2015. That seminar, which was successful, would not have been possible without the good offices of Catherine Redgwell, to whom we are extremely grateful. Similar essential assistance, of a financial character, was provided by Jesus College, Oxford and Trinity Hall, Cambridge.

At Hart Publishing (now an imprint of Bloomsbury) Sinead Moloney was enthusiasm personified in receiving the original proposal for the book, and Bill Asquith and Francesca Sancarlo efficiently moved it through the publication process. Much-needed copy-editing assistance was ably provided in the first instance by Reece Lewis, a doctoral candidate in public international law at the University of Bristol. Hart's own copy-editor, Vicki Hillyard, was a model of efficiency.

Finally, a word of explanation is perhaps owed for the image that graces the cover of this book. It is the architectural drawings for the 'World Peace Centre' in The Hague, reflecting an expansion plan for the Dutch capital by the architect, urban planner and designer Hendrik Petrus Berlage (1856–1934).[43] This elaborate design would have incorporated the Peace Palace, which can be seen in the top right of the octagon that dominates the image. However, like many things in international law, despite the best will in the world, issues of cost and practicality intervened, and the *lex ferenda* never became *lex lata*.

* * *

On 25 January 2017, shortly before this volume went to press, Professor Sir Nigel Rodley died.[44] He was 75 years old. He is survived by his wife, Lyn. They were married in 1967.

---

[41] Although some older descriptions of the editorial function remain perfectly adequate. See eg A Bierce, *The Devil's Dictionary* (Oxford, OUP, 1999):

> EDITOR, n. A person who combines the judicial functions of Minos, Rhadamanthus and Aeacus, but is placable with an obolus; a severely virtuous censor, but so charitable withal that he tolerates the virtues of others and the vices of himself; who flings about him the splintering lightning and sturdy thunders of admonition till he resembles a bunch of firecrackers petulantly uttering his mind at the tail of a dog; then straightway murmurs a mild, melodious lay, soft as the cooing of a donkey intoning its prayer to the evening star. Master of mysteries and lord of law, high-pinnacled upon the throne of thought, his face suffused with the dim splendors of the Transfiguration, his legs intertwisted and his tongue a-cheek, the editor spills his will along the paper and cuts it off in lengths to suit. And at intervals from behind the veil of the temple is heard the voice of the foreman demanding three inches of wit and six lines of religious meditation, or bidding him turn off the wisdom and whack up some pathos.

[42] It should be noted that although limited opportunity was given to the authors to update their chapters during the publication process, the law as presented is generally as it was in December 2016.

[43] A Effinger, *Het Vredespaleis, 1913–1988* (The Hague, AW Sijthoff, 1988) 61.

[44] See now G Robertson and I Crewe, 'Sir Nigel Rodley obituary: Human rights lawyer committed to eradicating torture' (*The Guardian*, 2 February 2017) <www.theguardian.com/law/2017/feb/02/sir-nigel-rodley-obituary> accessed 4 April 2017; B Çali, 'In memoriam: Professor Sir Nigel Rodley' (*EJIL: Talk!*, 2 February 2017) <www.ejiltalk.org/in-memoriam-professor-sir-nigel-rodley> accessed 4 April 2017.

For most students and scholars of international law, it is considered a life well spent to have contributed to the field in a manner worthy of citation in the spirit of Article 38(1)(d) of the ICJ Statute. Giants of the discipline may, however, exceed this. Sir Nigel, in a very real sense, was one of the creators of what we now know to be the international law of human rights. Born in the West Riding of Yorkshire in 1941, he was educated initially at Clifton College, then attended the University of Leeds (LLB, 1963), Colombia University (LLM, 1965) and New York University (LLM, 1970). He was awarded a PhD from the University of Essex (1992) and an LLD from Dalhousie University (2000), where he had taken up his first teaching position as a young academic.

Sir Nigel's professional contributions to human rights commenced when in 1973 he took up a position as the legal adviser of Amnesty International, a role he held until 1990 whilst also occupying a teaching position at the London School of Economics. Whilst in these positions, he played a key role in the drafting of the UN Convention Against Torture.[45] After that time, he was appointed a Reader at the Faculty of Law at the University of Essex, and promoted to full Professor in 1994. From 1993 to 2001, he served as Special Rapporteur on Torture of the UN Commission on Human Rights, thereafter becoming a member of the UN Human Rights Committee, as established under the International Covenant on Civil and Political Rights;[46] he served as its chairperson from 2013 to 2014. His academic writings on human rights and international humanitarian law were no less essential, in particular his 1973 article (co-authored with another giant of the field, Tom Franck) in the *American Journal of International Law* on the law of unilateral humanitarian intervention,[47] his 1987 treatise on *The Treatment of Prisoners under International Law*,[48] and his 2002 contribution to *Current Legal Problems* on the definition of torture in international law,[49] produced at a time of moral crisis for practitioners in the field.

As befitted his colossal energies, Sir Nigel was made a Knight Commander of the Order of the British Empire in 1998 in recognition of his services to human rights and international law. In 2005, he received the American Society of International Law's Golter T Butcher Medal for distinguished work in human rights.

For all this, Sir Nigel was and remained an unfailingly generous and encouraging man and it was in this capacity that we knew him as a contributor to this volume. His chapter on *Tyrer v UK* is characteristic of his voice: deeply human, deeply learned and perceptive of the strengths and weaknesses of international law. We dedicate this book to his memory.

---

[45] Convention against Torture and Other Cruel, Inhuman and Degrading Treatment, 10 December 1984, 1465 UNTS 85.

[46] 16 December 1966, 99 UNTS 171.

[47] T Franck and N Rodley, 'After Bangladesh: The Law of Humanitarian Intervention by Military Force' (1973) 67 *AJIL* 275.

[48] N Rodley, *The Treatment of Prisoners under International Law* (Oxford, OUP, 1987). A second edition appeared in 1999 and a third—produced with the assistance of Matt Pollard—in 2009.

[49] NS Rodley, 'The Definition(s) of Torture in International Law' (2002) 55 *CLP* 467.

2

The *Charming Betsy* and *The Paquete Habana* (1804 and 1900)

WILLIAM S DODGE

I. INTRODUCTION

MURRAY V THE *Schooner Charming Betsy*[1] and *The Paquete Habana*[2] are two familiar landmarks along the course of the US Supreme Court's long engagement with international law. *The Charming Betsy* is best known for its statement that 'an act of Congress ought never to be construed to violate the law of nations if any other possible construction remains',[3] a principle of interpretation that may be traced to Blackstone's *Commentaries* and is known today as the *Charming Betsy* canon. *The Paquete Habana*'s significance lies in its statement that '[i]nternational law is part of our law', but also in the possibility that international law might be superseded as a rule of decision by a 'controlling executive or legislative act or judicial decision'.[4]

Although written nearly 100 years apart, each case appears to stand for similar propositions—that international law has an important place in the law of the United States, but that US domestic law should prevail in the event of conflict. What often goes unnoticed is that these decisions made their famous statements against the backdrop of very different understandings about international law and its relationship to US domestic law. Over the course of the nineteenth century, three profound shifts occurred in US thinking about customary international law. First, the theoretical foundations of customary international law shifted away from natural law towards positivism. Second, the consent requirement for making customary international law shifted from the individual consent of each state to the consent of states generally. And third, the US understanding of the relationship between international law and domestic law shifted away from monism towards dualism—away from an understanding that international law was part of US law unless displaced, towards an understanding that international law was not part of US law unless adopted.

---

[1] 6 US (2 Cranch) 64 (1804).
[2] 175 US 677 (1900).
[3] *The Charming Betsy* (n 1) 118.
[4] *The Paquete Habana* (n 2) 700.

This chapter examines *The Charming Betsy* and *The Paquete Habana* as landmarks in a changing landscape of international law. It argues that neither case changed the course of international law in the United States but that each reflects the understandings of its own time about international law and the incorporation of international law in the US legal system.

II. THE CHARMING BETSY

Today, the rule that a statute should be construed, if possible, not to violate international law is known as the *Charming Betsy* canon.[5] But the association of the case with the canon is relatively recent. Nor did the decision break new ground when it applied the rule in 1804, for this principle had been a staple of American statutory interpretation for decades. Although *The Charming Betsy* has come to be seen as a landmark for international law in the United States, it is really just a representative example of the age in which it was decided.

A. The facts

From 1797 to 1800, the United States fought an undeclared 'quasi-war' with France.[6] During the conflict, Congress passed a series of Nonintercourse Acts, including one in 1800 that prohibited commerce between 'any person resident within the United States or under their protection' and residents of French territories.[7] The 1800 act also subjected to capture and forfeiture ships in three categories: ships owned by US citizens or residents sailing to a port in French territories; ships sold by US citizens or residents to another person for the purpose of sailing to a port in French territories; and ships engaged in commerce by or for residents of French territories.[8]

On 10 April 1800, an American schooner called *The Jane* sailed from Baltimore.[9] Its captain James Phillips had orders to sell the ship and its cargo in the Caribbean—at St Bartholomew if possible, and if not, then at St Thomas. At St Thomas, Phillips sold the schooner to a resident of that island, one Jared Shattuck, who renamed the ship *The Charming Betsy*. Shattuck was born in Connecticut before the American Revolution, but had moved to the Danish island of St Thomas as a child. In 1796, Shattuck became a Danish burger, with the privileges of a Danish subject, who owed allegiance to the Danish crown.

---

[5] See, eg, CA Bradley, 'The *Charming Betsy* Canon and Separation of Powers: Rethinking the Interpretive Role of International Law' (1998) 86 *Geo LJ* 479.

[6] See A DeConde, *The Quasi-War: The Politics and Diplomacy of the Undeclared War with France, 1797–1801* (New York, Charles Scriber's Sons, 1966).

[7] An Act Further to Suspend the Commercial Intercourse between the United States and France, and the Dependencies Thereof, ch 10, § 1, 2 Stat 7, 8 (1800).

[8] ibid.

[9] The facts are taken from the district court's decree, reproduced in the report of the Supreme Court's decision, see *The Charming Betsy* (n 1) 64–70; and from an account of the case in FC Leiner, 'The *Charming Betsy* and the Marshall Court' (2001) 45 *Am J Legal Hist* 1.

On 25 June, *The Charming Betsy* sailed for the French island of Guadeloupe with a cargo owned by Shattuck. On 1 July, a French privateer took her as prize. Although Denmark was neutral in the conflict between the United States and France, the French captain claimed the ship was American, justifying its capture. Two days later, *The Charming Betsy* was captured again, this time by the American frigate *Constellation*, under the command of Captain Alexander Murray. Although *The Charming Betsy* carried Danish papers, she looked to be an American-built ship, and the French *process verbal*—an affidavit that the French privateer would have used to prove that the ship was a lawful prize—stated that the ship was American. Murray sent *The Charming Betsy* first to Martinique, to sell her cargo, and then to Philadelphia where Murray's lawyers asked the court to condemn the ship for violating the Nonintercourse Act. To Murray's dismay, the district court not only rejected his claim that *The Charming Betsy* was a lawful prize but also assessed damages against him for wrongfully seizing the ship.[10] On appeal, the circuit court affirmed that the ship was not lawfully captured, but reversed the decree for damages.[11] Both parties appealed to the Supreme Court.

B. The Supreme Court's Decision

Chief Justice John Marshall delivered the opinion of the Supreme Court on 22 February 1804. Marshall summarised Captain Murray's contentions as three: (1) that *The Charming Betsy* and her cargo were subject to confiscation under the Nonintercourse Act; (2) if not, that he was at least entitled to salvage for recapturing the vessel from the French; and (3) if not, that he at least had probable cause to seize the vessel and so should be excused from damages. The Supreme Court ruled against Murray on all three points.

First, the Court had to construe the Nonintercourse Act, and it was in the course of this analysis that Marshall wrote the line for which his decision is now famous: 'an act of Congress ought never to be construed to violate the law of nations if any other possible construction remains'.[12] It was the law of nations concerning the rights of neutrals that was relevant to the case, and the Chief Justice continued by observing that a statute 'can never be construed to violate neutral rights, or to affect neutral commerce, further than is warranted by the law of nations as understood in this country'.[13] Marshall's discussion was beside the point, however, for Murray contended that Shattuck was not a neutral but a US citizen. Whether and how a US citizen might expatriate himself was politically controversial,[14] and Marshall chose not to answer that question.[15] Instead, he held as a matter of US domestic law—not the law of nations—'that an *American* citizen may acquire in a foreign country, the

---

[10] *The Charming Betsy* (n 1) 69–70.
[11] ibid, 70.
[12] ibid, 118.
[13] ibid.
[14] Leiner, 'The *Charming Betsy*' (n 9) 12; see eg *Talbot v Jansen*, 3 US (3 Dall) 133 (1795).
[15] See *The Charming Betsy* (n 1) 120.

commercial privileges attached to his domicile, and be exempted from the operation of an act expressed in such general terms as that now under consideration.'[16]

On the second point, the Court held that Murray was not entitled to salvage for having rescued *The Charming Betsy* from the French. In reaching this conclusion, Chief Justice Marshall followed his own decision three years earlier in *Talbot v Seeman*[17] (also known as *The Amelia*), where he held that 'a neutral vessel captured by a belligerent is to be discharged without paying salvage' because 'the liberation of a clear neutral from the hand of the enemy, is no essential service rendered to him, in as much as that the same enemy would be compelled by the tribunals of his own country after he had carried the neutral into port, to release him'.[18] Marshall did not find any exception to this rule applicable in *The Charming Betsy*. She was not so armed as to 'be in a condition to annoy *American* commerce'.[19] Nor was she in 'imminent hazard of being condemned' by a French prize court determined to ignore the law of nations.[20] The captors in *Talbot* had succeeded with the latter argument because of a French decree declaring that a ship would not be considered neutral if it carried enemy cargo.[21] But Marshall apparently accepted the argument by Shattuck's counsel that the French had changed their practice and would not now condemn a neutral ship.[22]

On the third and last point, the Court rejected Murray's argument that he at least had probable cause to seize *The Charming Betsy*. She was carrying Danish papers, Chief Justice Marshall noted, which 'appear to have been perfectly correct'.[23] The French *proces verbal* stating that the ship was American was self-serving and not to be believed.[24] The American build of the ship, its recent sale, and the fact that most of its crew was not Danish did not establish probable cause because they were not unusual facts.[25] And although the common practice of giving neutral papers to American ships might have reinforced a legitimate suspicion, it could not 'be itself a motive for the seizure' for that would make all neutral vessels liable to seizure.[26]

Although Captain Murray lost on each point, the Supreme Court did find error in the determination of damages, ordering a recalculation on remand. In the end, Congress passed a private bill indemnifying Murray for the damages against him.[27]

---

[16] ibid. Marshall went on to argue that the act itself seemed to exclude Shattuck because he was not 'under the protection of the United States'. As a matter of statutory interpretation, this was questionable. The 'under the protection' language is found only in the Act's prohibition of commerce. The relevant forfeiture provision omits this language and referred expressly to 'citizens [of the United States] resident elsewhere', which is precisely what Shattuck was alleged to be. See An Act Further to Suspend the Commercial Intercourse between the United States and France, and the Dependencies Thereof, ch 10, § 1, 2 Stat 7, 8 (1800).

[17] 5 US (1 Cranch) 1 (1801).

[18] ibid, 36 (quoting *The War Onskan* (1799) 2 Rob 299, 300; 165 ER 323, 324).

[19] *The Charming Betsy* (n 1) 121.

[20] ibid.

[21] See *Talbot* (n 17) 37-43.

[22] *The Charming Betsy* (n 1) 95–105 (argument of counsel).

[23] ibid, 123.

[24] ibid, 122.

[25] ibid, 123.

[26] ibid.

[27] See An Act for the Relief of Alexander Murray, ch XII, 6 Stat 56 (1805).

C. The Significance of the Decision

The canon of construing statutes to avoid law-of-nations violations was not new to American law. In *Talbot*, the salvage case on which *The Charming Betsy* relied, Chief Justice Marshall had similarly written that 'the laws of the United States ought not, if it be avoidable, so to be construed as to infract the common principles and usages of nations'.[28] During the 1790s, the Supreme Court had decided a number of cases by reading the admiralty jurisdiction of the United States narrowly to avoid conflicts both with treaties and with the unwritten law of nations.[29] The earliest American decision applying the consistency canon appears to be *Miller v The Ship Resolution*,[30] which involved an ordinance of the Continental Congress making recaptured prizes subject to condemnation only if Great Britain had held them for at least 24 hours.[31] The Federal Court of Appeals for Prize Cases construed the ordinance to apply only to 'a legal capture' under the law of nations and not to a situation where the initial British capture had been unlawful.[32]

Perhaps the clearest articulation of the canon before *The Charming Betsy* case was New York Mayor James Duane's famous decision in *Rutgers v Waddington*, a case argued for the defendants by Alexander Hamilton,[33] which also provides clues about the origins of the canon. Mayor Duane had to construe New York's 1783 Trespass Act, authorising owners whose property had been taken during the British occupation to bring suits for damages, a statute that Hamilton argued violated the law of nations.[34] To avoid the conflict, Duane read the act not to apply during the period that the defendants occupied the property under the direct authority of the British commander.[35] 'The repeal of the law of nations, or any interference with it, could not have been in contemplation, in our opinion, when the Legislature passed this statute; and we think ourselves bound to exempt that law from its operation.'[36] Duane cited a number of reasons for this canon, including the principle that statutes should be interpreted to avoid unreasonable results and the presumption against implied repeals.[37] Both were standard principles of statutory interpretation found in William Blackstone's *Commentaries on the Law of England*.[38] Duane expressly

---

[28] *Talbot* (n 17) 43.

[29] See, eg, *United States v Peters*, 3 US (3 Dall) 121 (1795).

[30] 2 US (2 Dall) 1 (Fed Ct App 1781).

[31] See G Hunt (ed) *19 Journal of the Continental Congress 1774–1789* (GPO 1912), 315 (An ordinance relative to the capture and condemnation of prizes).

[32] *Miller* (n 30) 3–4.

[33] *Rutgers v Waddington* (NY City Mayor's Ct 1784), reprinted in Julius Goebel Jr (ed), *1 The Law Practice of Alexander Hamilton: Documents and Commentary* (New York, Columbia University Press, 1964) 392.

[34] Brief No 6, ibid, 368–73.

[35] *Rutgers* (n 33) 419.

[36] ibid, 417.

[37] See ibid, 417–18.

[38] See Sir William Blackstone, *Commentaries on the Laws of England* (Oxford, Clarendon Press, 1765–1769) vol 1, 87–92.

traced the reasonable principle to Blackstone.[39] But the presumption against implied repeals is found in the *Commentaries* too,[40] and Blackstone famously stated that 'the law of nations ... is here adopted in it's full extent by the common law, and is held to be a part of the law of the land',[41] an understanding that would make the presumption against implied repeals relevant. *Rutgers* reveals the *Charming Betsy* canon as an application of familiar English rules of statutory interpretation to the question of conflicts between statutes and international law.

In some ways, *The Charming Betsy* is an odd case after which to name this canon of statutory interpretation. In contrast to *Miller, Rutgers,* and *Talbot,* the canon did no work in *The Charming Betsy,* which Chief Justice Marshall resolved on the ground that under US domestic law a US citizen could acquire commercial privileges in another country exempting him from the Nonintercourse Act.[42] The Supreme Court would rely on *The Charming Betsy* during the nineteenth century not for this canon of construction but rather for the various points of prize law that the case had actually decided—whether a US citizen with a foreign domicile was subject to the Nonintercourse Acts,[43] whether arming a merchant vessel changed its character,[44] and whether probable cause for a seizure existed.[45] The Court also cited the decision for certain procedural questions of admiralty law.[46] In fact, the Supreme Court did not begin to cite *The Charming Betsy* for the canon of consistency with international law until the middle of the twentieth century.[47] One suspects that *The Charming Betsy* came to be associated with the consistency canon simply because its articulation of the rule is clearer and more concise than that found in any other decision of the Supreme Court.

---

[39] See *Rutgers* (n 33) 415 ('[T]his is the language of Blackstone in his celebrated commentaries'); see also Blackstone, *Commentaries* (n 38), 91 ('[W]here some collateral matter arises out of the general words, and happens to be unreasonable; there the judges are in decency to conclude that this consequence was not foreseen by the parliament').

[40] See Blackstone (n 38) 89, who states that a later law repeals an earlier one 'only when the latter statute is couched in negative terms, or by its matter necessarily implies a negative').

[41] ibid, vol 4, 67.

[42] See *The Charming Betsy* (n 1) 120; see also nn14–16 above and accompanying text.

[43] See *The Mary and Susan*, 14 US (1 Wheat) 46 (1816), 55 nf; *Maley v Shattuck*, 7 US (3 Cranch) 458 (1806), 488–89.

[44] See *The Panama*, 176 US 535 (1900), 546–47.

[45] See *Sands v Knox*, 7 US (3 Cranch) 499 (1806), 503; *Maley* (n 43) 489–90.

[46] See *The Scotland*, 105 US 24 (1881), 36 (proper rate of interest); *Manro v Almeida*, 23 US (10 Wheat) 473 (1825), 486 (availability of *in personam* remedy for maritime torts).

[47] See *Laurtizen v Larsen*, 345 US 571 (1953), 578. Justice Sutherland quoted *The Charming Betsy* in support of the consistency canon in an earlier dissenting opinion. See *Cunnard SS Co v Mellon*, 262 US 100 (1923), 132 (Judge Sutherland dissenting). Prior to this, when the Court found it necessary to articulate the consistency canon, it generally cited no case in support. See, eg, *MacLeod v US*, 229 US 416 (1913), 434 ('The statute should be construed in the light of the purpose of the government to act within the limitation of the principles of international law, the observance of which is so essential to the peace and harmony of nations'). When construing a statute to be consistent with a treaty, the Court often cited its 1884 decision in *Chew Heong*, which said that a 'court ought, if possible, to adopt that construction which recognized and saved rights secured by the treaty'. *Chew Heong v United States*, 112 US 536 (1884), 549; see, eg, *Cook v United States*, 288 US 102 (1933), 120; *United States v Payne*, 264 US 446 (1924), 449; *Lem Moon Sing v United States*, 158 US 538 (1895), 549.

But *The Charming Betsy* does reflect early American understandings of international law and its relationship to US domestic law. Consistent with Blackstone, early Americans understood that 'the law of nations ... is here adopted in it's full extent by the common law, and is held to be a part of the law of the land'.[48] In 1784, a Pennsylvania court convicted a French citizen of a common law offense for having violated the law of nations by assaulting a member of the French legation in Philadelphia.[49] '[T]he law of Nations,' wrote the Court in echo of Blackstone, 'in its full extent, is part of the law of this State'.[50] In setting up the federal courts under the new US Constitution, the First Congress assumed that violations of the law of nations could result in civil liability when it gave those courts jurisdiction 'of all causes where an alien sues for a tort only in violation of the law of nations or a treaty of the United States'.[51] The early Supreme Court regularly applied the law of nations as a rule of decision in admiralty cases.[52] As Chief Justice Marshall would later write in *The Nereide*, '[t]ill ... an act [of Congress] be passed, the Court is bound by the law of nations which is a part of the law of the land'.[53] The status of the law of nations as part of the common law was one of the foundations of the *Charming Betsy* canon for, as we have seen, the canon rested, at least in part, on the presumption against implied repeals.[54]

Marshall's famous statement in *The Charming Betsy* also assumed that Congress could override the law of nations if it chose to do so. Originally, Congress's authority to supersede the law of nations depended on which category of the law of nations was involved.[55] Just as early Americans looked to Blackstone to understand how international law fit into the common law, so they looked predominantly to the Swiss writer Emer de Vattel to understand the nature of international law

---

[48] Blackstone (n 38) vol 4, 67; see also *Heathfield v Chilton*, (1767) 4 Burr 2015, 98 ER 50 (Judge Mansfield stating that 'the law of nations ... is part of the common law of England'); *Triquet v Bath*, (1764) 3 Burr 1478, 1481; 97 ER 936, 938 (KB 1764) (Judge Mansfield stating '[t]hat the law of nations, in its full extent was part of the law of England').

[49] *Respublica v De Longchamps*, 1 US (1 Dall) 111 (Pa Ct Oyer & Terminer 1784).

[50] ibid, 116. In 1793, the federal government brought a number of common-law prosecutions for violating treaties and the unwritten law of nations with respect to US neutrality. See eg *Henfield's Case*, 11 F Cas 1099 (CCD Pa 1783) (No 6,360). Although none of the prosecutions succeeded, they illustrate the assumption that the law of nations was part of the common law in the United States. Ultimately, the Supreme Court held that there was no federal common law of crimes, see *United States v Hudson & Goodwin* 11 (7 Cranch) US 32 (1812), 34, a holding the Court later extended without discussion to cases involving the law of nations. See *United States v Coolidge*, 14 US (10 Cranch) 415 (1816).

[51] An Act to Establish the Judicial Courts of the United States (1789), ch 20, § 9, 1 Stat 72, 77; see *Sosa v Alvarez-Machain*, 542 US 692 (2004), 714 (noting that Alien Tort Statute was passed on the assumption that 'torts in violation of the law of nations would have been recognized within the common law of the time').

[52] See DL Sloss, MD Ramsey and WS Dodge, 'International Law in the Supreme Court to 1860' in DL Sloss, MD Ramsey and WS Dodge (eds), *International Law in the US Supreme Court: Continuity and Change* (Cambridge, CUP, 2011) 23–25.

[53] 13 US (9 Cranch) 388, 423 (1815).

[54] See nn 36–41 above and accompanying text.

[55] For more detailed discussion, see WS Dodge, 'Customary International Law, Congress and the Courts: Origins of the Later-in-Time Rule' in PHF Bekker, R Dolzer and M Waibel (eds), *Making Transnational Law Work in the Global Economy: Essays in Honour of Detlev Vagts* (Cambridge, CUP, 2010) 531.

itself. Vattel divided the law of nations into four categories: (1) the necessary, (2) the voluntary, (3) the conventional, and (4) the customary. The necessary law of nations was based directly on natural law; it was immutable and binding, but only internally on the conscience of the sovereign.[56] The voluntary law of nations was also based on natural law, but it created external rights and duties. It was not 'voluntary' in the modern sense, because nations were required to give their consent.[57] The conventional law of nations consisted of treaties and was based on express consent.[58] Finally, the customary law of nations consisted of state practice and was based on 'tacit consent',[59] consent that a nation could withdraw if it no longer wished to follow such a particular rule.[60] Vattel's categorisation is obviously different from the modern understandings that international law consists only of treaties and customary international law based on state practice and that nations are not free to withdraw from an established rule of customary international law.[61]

Early American cases suggested that a statute could supersede only rules belonging to the customary law of nations.[62] In *Ware v Hylton*, the US Supreme Court considered the validity of Virginia's 1777 Act confiscating debts owed to British creditors, which was alleged to violate both the treaty of peace with Britain and the unwritten law of nations. Justice Chase's overview of the law of nations clearly shows Vattel's influence:

> The law of nations may be considered of three kinds, to wit, general, conventional, or customary. The first is universal, or established by the general consent of mankind, and binds all nations. The second is founded on express consent, and is not universal, and only binds those nations that have assented to it. The third is founded on tacit consent; and is only obligatory on those nations, who have adopted it.[63]

Vattel considered the rule against confiscating debts to be part of the customary law of nations,[64] and that fact was critical to Chase's conclusion that Virginia was free to violate it. Chase wrote that the rule against confiscating private debts 'was

---

[56] E de Vattel, *The Law of Nations* (CG Fenwick tr first published 1758, Carnegie Inst 1916) Intro §§ 7–9.

[57] ibid, Intro §§ 21, 28; Book III §§ 188–92.

[58] ibid, Intro § 24.

[59] ibid, Intro § 26; Book III § 106.

[60] ibid, Intro § 25. For further discussion of the right to withdraw from the customary law of nations, see CA Bradley and M Gulati, 'Withdrawing from International Custom' (2010) 120 *Yale LJ* 202, 216–18; WS Dodge, 'Withdrawing from Customary International Law: Some Lessons from History' (2010) 120 *Yale LJ* 169, 172–75.

[61] See, eg, Restatement (Third) of Foreign Relations Law § 102 (1987) (listing sources of international law); ibid. § 102, cmt *d* ('A state that enters the international system after a practice has ripened into a rule of international law is bound by that rule.').

[62] The original understanding also seems to have been that treaties were 'beyond the lawful reach of legislation'. The Federalist No 64, at 394 (C Rossiter ed, 1961) (John Jay). For development of the so-called 'later-in-time' rule for treaties, see JT Parry, 'Congress, the Supremacy Clause, and the Implementation of Treaties' (2009) 32 *Fordham Int'l LJ* 1209; DF Vagts, 'The United States and its Treaties: Observance and Breach' (2001) 95 *AJIL* 313.

[63] *Ware v Hylton* 3 US (3 Dall) 199, 227 (1796) (Judge Chase). Chase did not mention the necessary law of nations, presumably because it did not create external rights and duties, and he referred to Vattel's voluntary law of nations as the 'general' law of nations.

[64] Vattel, *Law of Nations* (n 56) Book III § 77.

not binding on the state of Virginia, *because founded on custom only*.[65] Justice Iredell similarly expressed 'considerable doubt' that the rule was binding on Virginia, 'admitting the principle to prevail by custom only'.[66] It is instructive to compare an earlier state court decision refusing to give effect to the same Virginia law. In *Page v Pendleton*, Chancellor George Wythe viewed the rule against confiscating debts as 'depending ... on the law of nature,'[67] and on that basis, he concluded that 'the legislature could not retract their consent to observe the preacepts of the law, and conform to the usages of nations'.[68] Other early decisions involving conflicts between statutes and the law of nations similarly turned on whether a rule was part of the voluntary or customary law of nations.[69]

In sum, *The Charming Betsy* not only restated a common principle of statutory interpretation but also reflected American understandings of international law at the time. Those understandings would change significantly before *The Paquete Habana* reached the Supreme Court.

III. THE CHANGING LANDSCAPE OF INTERNATIONAL LAW

American understandings of international law and its incorporation in the US legal system shifted during the nineteenth century. When *The Charming Betsy* was decided in 1804, most international law rules were based on natural law and did not depend on state consent to give them binding force. These natural law rules were supplemented by customary rules manifested in state practice and based on tacit consent, consent each nation was free to withdraw if it wished. Both sets of rules were part of the common law in the United States, at least unless superseded by statute, something that was certainly possible for rules based on state practice, but perhaps not for rules based on natural law. When *The Paquete Habana* was decided in 1900, by contrast, all customary international law rules were based on state practice and depended on consent for their binding force. The consent required, however, was no longer the consent of each nation but instead the consent of the community of nations, which meant that individual nations were no longer free to withdraw from particular rules of customary international law. Paradoxically, at the same time that American courts acknowledged that the United States could be bound internationally to rules without its consent, they also asserted that international law was not part of domestic law unless specifically adopted by the United States. In the most general terms, then, the landscape of international law in the United States shifted during the nineteenth century away from natural law towards positivism and away from monism towards dualism.

---

[65] *Ware* (n 63) 227 (Judge Chase) (emphasis added).
[66] ibid 263 (Judge Iredell).
[67] Wythe's Rep 212 n(b) (Va Ch 1793).
[68] ibid, 213. Wythe taught law to Thomas Jefferson and John Marshall, among others, signed the Declaration of Independence in 1776, and served as a delegate to the Constitutional Convention in 1787.
[69] See Dodge, 'Customary International Law' (n 55) 536–44.

A. From Natural Law to Positivism

By the time the United States was established, the law of nations had long been understood to consist of both natural and positive law.[70] Some eighteenth-century authors emphasised natural law, and others positive law.[71] Early Americans relied most heavily on Vattel, who divided the law of nations into four categories, two based on natural law and two on positive law.[72] But natural law dominated Vattel's treatise.[73]

Vattel's system continued to influence American law into the nineteenth century. Justice Joseph Story's circuit court decision in *United States v The La Jeune Eugenie* echoed Vattel's voluntary, customary and conventional categories when he wrote that 'the law of nations may be deduced, first, from the general principles of right and justice', second, 'in things indifferent or questionable from the customary observances of civilized nations', and third, 'from the conventional or positive law'.[74] Story concluded that the African slave trade violated natural law.[75] The first edition of Henry Wheaton's *Elements of International Law*, which would become the most important American treatise on international law in the nineteenth century, similarly followed Vattel's categorisation.[76]

But while the Supreme Court continued to look to Vattel for the substance of international law rules, it tended to ignore his theoretical system. In *The Schooner Exchange v McFaddon*, for example, Chief Justice Marshall treated foreign sovereign immunity, which Vattel certainly would have viewed as part of the voluntary law of nations based on natural law,[77] as based on implied consent[78] and thus defeasible.[79] In other opinions, Marshall asserted that an act of Congress could superseded rules of prize law without regard to whether those rules were part of the voluntary or the customary law of nations.[80] The Supreme Court took a

---

[70] See, eg, H Grotius, *De Jure Belli ac Pacis* (FW Kelsey tr, first published 1646, Oxford, OUP, 1925) 9 (defining the law of nations as law 'concerned with the mutual relations among states or rulers of states, whether derived from nature, or established by divine ordinances, or having its origin in custom and tacit agreement').

[71] For an overview, see ED Dickinson, 'Changing Concepts and the Doctrine of Incorporation' (1932) 26 *AJIL* 239, 244–53.

[72] See nn 56–60 above and accompanying text.

[73] Vattel titled his work *The Law of Nations or the Principles of Natural Law Applied to the Conduct and to the Affairs of Sovereigns* and wrote in his preface that the necessary and voluntary law of nations 'will form the principal subject of my work'. Vattel (n 56) Preface, 11a. In Vattel's view, the customary law of nations was restricted to questions on which natural law was 'Indifferent', Intro. § 9, and he even doubted that it belonged 'within a systematic treatise on the Law of Nations', Intro § 25. For further discussion, see Dodge, 'Withdrawing from Customary International Law' (n 60) 172–75.

[74] *United States v The La Jeune Eugenie* 26 F Cas 832 (CCD Mass) (No 15,551) (1822), 846.

[75] ibid ('It is repugnant to the great principles of Christian duty, the dictates of natural religion, the obligations of good faith and morality, and the eternal maxims of social justice.').

[76] See H Wheaton, *Elements of International Law* (Philadelphia, Carey, Lea & Blanchard, 1836) § 14.

[77] Vattel (n 56) Book III §§ 92, 108.

[78] See *The Schooner Exchange v McFaddon* 11 US (7 Cranch) 116 (1812), 136 ('All exceptions, therefore, to the full and complete power of a nation within its own territories, must be traced up to the consent of the nation itself.').

[79] ibid 146 ('Without doubt, the sovereign of the place is capable of destroying this implication.').

[80] See *The Nereide* 13 US (9 Cranch) 388 (1815), 423 ('Till such an act be passed, the Court is bound by the law of nations which is a part of the law of the land'); *Thirty Hogsheads of Sugar v Boyle* 13 US

distinctively positivist view of the law of nations in *The Antelope*. Addressing the same question of whether the African slave trade violated the law of nations that Justice Story had earlier addressed in *The La Jeune Eugenie*, Chief Justice Marshall wrote '[w]hatever might be the answer of a moralist to this question, a jurist must search for its legal solution, in those principles of action which are sanctioned by the usages, the national acts, and the general assent, of that portion of the world of which he considers himself as a part'.[81] By this 'test of international law,' Marshall concluded, the question 'is decided in favour of the legality of the trade'.[82]

While some nineteenth century treatises continued to emphasise natural law as the basis of international law,[83] the trend was towards positivism. Wheaton, who had adopted Vattel's categories of the law of nations in the first, 1836 edition of his famous treatise, criticised that categorisation in the 1846 edition and suggested that the natural law of nations 'may more properly be called international morality'.[84] Two posthumous editions, supposedly based on changes made before Wheaton's death, omitted natural law rules deduced by reason as one of the sources of international law.[85] Richard Wildman asserted that '[t]he law of nature forms no part of international law',[86] while William Hall asserted that moral obligations could become legally binding only if 'received as positive law by the body of states'.[87] Just after the turn of the twentieth century, Lassa Oppenheim would assert that international law, like all law, was based on 'the common sense of the community'.[88]

Although the US Supreme Court sometimes mixed natural and positive idioms when discussing international law,[89] by 1872 a positivist approach had clearly prevailed. In *The Scotia*, a maritime case whose language *The Paquete Habana* would later quote, Justice Strong wrote: 'Like all the laws of nations, [the law of the sea] rests upon the common consent of civilized communities. It is of force, not because it was prescribed by any superior power, but because it has been generally accepted as a rule of conduct.'[90]

(9 Cranch) 191 (1815), 198 ('[British prize law] continued to be our prize law, so far as it was adapted to our circumstances and was not varied by the power which was capable of changing it'). In 1839, Chief Justice Roger Taney would use the phrase 'voluntary law of nations' to refer not to binding rules based on natural law but rather to discretionary acts of comity. See *Bank of Augusta v Earle* 38 US 519 (1839), 589. On the history of international comity in American law, see WS Dodge, 'International Comity in American Law' (2015) 115 *Colum L Rev* 2071, 2084–98.

[81] *The Antelope*, 23 US (10 Wheat) 66 (1825), 121.

[82] ibid.

[83] See, eg, Sir R Phillimore, *Commentaries upon International Law* (London, T & JW Johnson, 1854) vol 1, 56 ('The Primary Source ... of International Jurisprudence is Divine Law'); HW Halleck, *International Law* (San Francisco, HH Bancroft & Co, 1861) Ch 2, § 6 (quoting Phillimore).

[84] H Wheaton, *Elements of International Law*, 3rd edn (Philadephia, Lea and Blanchard, 1846) § 15.

[85] See H Wheaton, *Elements of International Law*, 6th edn (Boston, Little, Brown & Co, 1855) § 12; H Wheaton, *Elements of International Law*, 8th edn § 15 (Boston, Little, Brown & Co, 1866). For discussion see Dodge, 'Withdrawing from Customary International Law' (n 60) 180–81.

[86] R Wildman, *Institutes of International Law*, vol 2 (London, William Benning & Co, 1849).

[87] WE Hall, *International Law*, vol 4 (Oxford, Clarendon Press, 1880).

[88] L Oppenheim, *International Law: A Treatise* (London, Longmans, Green & Co, 1905) § 4.

[89] See, eg, *The Prize Cases* 67 US 635 (1863), 670 ('The law of nations is also called the law of nature; it is founded on the common consent as well as the common sense of the world'). For discussion of nineteenth-century cases, see DJ Bederman, 'Customary International Law in the Supreme Court, 1861–1900' in Sloss, Ramsey and Dodge, 'International Law' (n 52) 92–100.

[90] *The Scotia*, 81 US 170 (1872), 187.

B. From Individual to Common Consent

In Vattel's system, nations were bound by the voluntary law of nations based on natural law but were free to withdraw their consent from the customary law of nations based on state practice.[91] The shift from natural law to positivism raised the question whether nations were now free to withdraw their consent from all rules of international law. Wheaton seems to have drawn that conclusion. In his 1845 volume on the history of international law, Wheaton asserted that all rules of ambassadorial privileges 'may be disregarded by any state which chooses to incur the risk of retaliation or hostility'.[92] This position was repeated in the two editions of the *Elements* treatise published after Wheaton's death.[93]

But other nineteenth-century writers asserted that international law rested not on the individual consent of each nation but on the common consent of the community of nations. Wildman wrote that '[a]s the custom of a people forms part of their municipal law, and is binding upon all, so the custom of nations is binding on each'[94] and he denied that any nation could withdraw from customs 'established by the general practice of nations'.[95] Other writers affirmed that customary international law could be based 'general consent'[96] and expressly denied that individual nations could withdraw from such rules.[97] In 1905, Oppenheim would summarise the view that had prevailed by the end of the nineteenth century. 'Common consent' meant the consent of 'an overwhelming majority',[98] and it was 'not necessary to prove for every single rule of International Law that every single member of the Family of Nations consented to it'.[99] Thus, 'no State which is a member of the Family of Nations can at some time or another declare that it will in future no long submit to a certain recognized rule of the Law of Nations', which could 'be altered by common consent only'.[100]

This shift from individual to common consent found expression, again, in *The Scotia*. Not only did the US Supreme Court emphasise that the law of nations 'rests upon the common consent of civilized communities',[101] it pointed out repeatedly that the maritime regulations in question had become binding despite less than universal adherence.[102] The fact that the two nations whose ships were involved in the collision, Britain and the United States, had adopted the same regulations was not dispositive, for 'no statute of one or two nations can create obligations for the world'.[103] It was 'common consent' that counted.

---

[91] See nn 57–60 and accompanying text.

[92] H Wheaton, *History of the Law of Nations in Europe and America from the Earliest Times to the Treaty of Washington 1842* (New York, Gould, Banks & Co, 1845) 95–96.

[93] Dodge, 'Withdrawing from Customary International Law' (n 60) 181–82.

[94] Wildman, *Institutes* (n 86) 29.

[95] ibid, 33.

[96] Hall, *International Law* (n 87) 4.

[97] Halleck, *International Law* (n 83) ch 2, § 9.

[98] Oppenheim, *International Law* (n 88) § 11.

[99] ibid, § 12.

[100] ibid.

[101] *The Scotia* (n 90) 187

[102] ibid, 186 ('nearly all'); ibid, 187 ('almost every'); ibid, 188 ('almost all').

[103] ibid, 187.

C. From Monism to Dualism

At the beginning of the nineteenth century, Americans assumed that international law was automatically part of their law unless it had been validly superseded by statute.[104] Chief Justice Marshall captured this view in *The Nereide* when he wrote: 'Till such an act be passed, the Court is bound by the law of nations which is a part of the law of the land'.[105]

By the end of the nineteenth century, the presumption had been reversed— international law was understood to be part of American law only to the extent it had been adopted by the United States.[106] Writing in an 1875 maritime case, *The Lottawanna*, Justice Joseph Bradley said:

> [I]t is hardly necessary to argue that the maritime law is only so far operative as law in any country as it is adopted by the laws and usages of that country. In this respect it is like international law or the laws of war, which have the effect of law in no country any further than they are accepted and received as such.[107]

In most cases, reversal of the presumption made no difference because international law could be adopted not only by legislatures but also by courts.[108] The adoption theory would not, therefore, prevent a court from applying rules of international law in appropriate cases, though it might change the way in which the court characterised what it was doing. But the Court's new theory did make a difference in cases where new international law came into conflict with existing judicial precedent, which was precisely the question in *The Lottawanna*. Libellants sought to overturn an old Supreme Court decision denying the validity of their liens[109] on the ground that maritime law now recognised the validity of those liens, but the Court refused to do so. An existing precedent 'ought not to be overruled except for very

---

[104] See nn 48–69 and accompanying text.

[105] *The Nereide*, 13 US (9 Cranch) 388 (1815), 423. In another case, the Supreme Court specifically rejected the argument that international law applied only if 'the municipal law of the place has incorporated the international law as a part of itself' *Rhode Island v Massachusetts*, 37 US 657 (1838), 675 (argument of counsel). Despite the absence of legislation incorporating international law, the Court declared that it would decide the interstate border dispute 'according to the law of nations', ibid, 749.

[106] The shift may have been reinforced by parallel developments with respect to treaties. In a series of cases during the 1880s, the Supreme Court emphasised that treaties operated primarily on the international plane and that their domestic effect was subject to the control of Congress. See *The Chinese Exclusion Case*, 130 US 581 (1889), 602; *Whitney v Robertson*, 124 US 190 (1888), 194; *The Head Money Cases*, 112 US 580 (1884), 598.

[107] *The Lottawanna*, 88 US 558 (1875), 572. The court would repeat this assertion in a series of maritime cases over the next 25 years, including one authored by Justice Horace Gray, who would write *The Paquete Habana*. See *Liverpool & GW Steam Co v Phenix Ins Co*, 129 US 397 (1889), 444 (Gray, J) ('The general maritime law is in force in this country, or in any other, so far only as it has been adopted by the laws or usages thereof'). The notion that international law had to be adopted in order to become part of domestic law does not seem to have been confined to the United States. See eg *Regina v Keyn* (1876) 2 Ex D 63, 202–03 (Cockburn, CJ) ('To be binding, [international] law must have received the assent of the nations who are to be bound by it').

[108] See *The Lottawanna* (n 107) 571 (stating that a court might adopt a new rule of maritime law 'to preserve harmony and logical consistency in the general system'); see also *The John G Stevens*, 170 US 113 (1898), 126–27 ('the general maritime law is in force in this country, or in any other, so far only as administered in its courts or adopted by its own laws and usages').

[109] See *The General Smith*, 17 US (4 Wheat) 438 (1819).

cogent reasons,'[110] the Court reasoned, and a change in the practices of other countries was not 'sufficient ground' to do so.[111] It was probably cases like *The Lottawanna* that the Supreme Court had in mind when it referred in *The Paquete Habana* to international law being displaced by a 'controlling … judicial decision'.[112]

IV. THE PAQUETE HABANA

The Paquete Habana is known today both for its statement that '[i]nternational law is part of our law' and for its suggestion that international law might be superseded as a rule of decision by a 'controlling executive or legislative act or judicial decision'.[113] The former has been called the Supreme Court's 'classic utterance' on the topic of incorporation,[114] while the later has been disparaged as an 'opaque, confused, and confusing dictum'.[115] As we have seen, both the incorporation of international law into US law and the possibility that domestic law might trump international law have a long history and are reflected in *The Charming Betsy* among other decisions. The significance of *The Paquete Habana* lies not in the originality of its statements but in the way those statements reflected changes in the understanding of international law and incorporation during the nineteenth century.

A. The Facts

On 25 April 1898, the United States declared war on Spain in support of Cuba's independence.[116] The declaration was retroactive to 21 April, legitimising a blockade of Cuba's north coast that the United States had established on 21 April and proclaimed the following day. President McKinley's 22 April proclamation stated that the United States would maintain the blockade 'in pursuance of the laws of the United States and the law of nations applicable to such cases'.[117]

---

[110] *The Lottawanna* (n 107) 571.

[111] ibid, 578; see also 576 ('To ascertain, therefore, what the maritime law of this country is, it is not enough to read the French, German, Italian, and other foreign works on the subject, or the codes which they have framed; but we must have regard to our own legal history, constitution, legislation, usages, and adjudications as well').

[112] *The Paquete Habana* (n 2) 700; see nn 161–64 below and accompanying text.

[113] ibid.

[114] MW Janis, *An Introduction to International Law*, 4th edn (Aspen, Aspen Publishers, 2003) 103; see also MD Ramsey, *The Constitution's Text in Foreign Affairs* (Boston, Harvard University Press, 2007) 342 (noting that 'the case has become pivotal, almost talismanic, in modern debates over the relationship between international law and constitutional law').

[115] L Henkin, *Foreign Affairs and the United States Constitution*, 2nd edn (Oxford, Clarendon Press, 1996) 235.

[116] Act of April 25, 1898, ch 189, 30 Stat 364 (1898). For more detailed discussions of the facts of *The Paquete Habana*, see WS Dodge, 'The Paquete Habana: Customary International Law as Part of Our Law' in JE Noyes, LA Dickinson and MW Janis (eds), *International Law Stories* (New York, Foundation Press, 2007) 129; SW Stucky, 'The Paquete Habana: A Case History in the Development of International Law' (1985) 15 *U Balt L Rev* 1.

[117] Proclamation No 6, 30 Stat 1769 (1898).

He followed on 26 April with another proclamation on the capture of prizes, stating that the 'war should be conducted upon principles in harmony with the present views of nations and sanctioned by their recent practice'.[118] On 28 April, US Admiral William T Sampson reported that a large number of fishing vessels were attempting to enter Havana harbour. Because they were manned by 'excellent seamen' who might be useful to Spain, Sampson recommended that these vessels be captured and their crews detained.[119] Secretary of the Navy John Davis Long replied on 30 April, directing that 'Spanish fishing vessels attempting to violate blockade are subject, with crew, to capture, and any such vessel or crew considered likely to aid enemy may be detained'.[120]

The Paquete Habana was a 43-foot sloop with a crew of three. A US gunboat captured her on 25 April, with a cargo of fresh fish, and took her to Key West, Florida where she and her cargo were condemned as prize of war and sold for $490.[121] Her case was one of many in the lower courts involving fishing vessels.[122] And the Supreme Court's decision in this case would be just one of nine prize decisions, involving a range of issues, which the Court would hand down between 11 December 1899 and 14 May 1900[123] in its last, great elaboration of prize law.[124]

B. The Supreme Court's Decision

Justice Horace Gray delivered the Supreme Court's opinion on 8 January 1900, holding, by a vote of six to three, that coastal fishing vessels were exempt from capture under international law.[125] Justice Gray traced the rule as far back as 1403, to an order by King Henry IV of England implementing a treaty with France.[126] He found some interruption in state practice in 1798, when an English order had expressly directed the seizure of French fishing boats and the great English admiralty judge Sir William Scott had characterised the rule against capturing fishing vessels as one 'of comity only'.[127] But Gray found that international law had evolved

---

[118] Proclamation No 8, 30 Stat 1770–71 (1898).

[119] *The Paquete Habana* (n 2) 712–13 (quoting Navy Report Appendix, 178).

[120] ibid, 713 (quoting Navy Report Appendix, 178).

[121] ibid, 678–79.

[122] The appeal in *The Paquete Habana* was argued together with the appeal in *The Lola*. See ibid, 678. Claimants and the United States stipulated that the decisions in these cases would be dispositive of 10 other cases involving fishing vessels. Dodge, 'The Paquete Habana' (n 116) 132 fn 25.

[123] The others include: *The Pedro*, 175 US 354 (1899), *The Guido*, 175 US 382 (1899); *The Buena Ventura*, 175 US 384 (1899); *The Newfoundland*, 176 US 97 (1900); *The Adula*, 176 US 361 (1900); *The Panama*, 176 US 535 (1900); *The Benito Estenger*, 176 US 568 (1900); and *The Carlos F Roses*, 177 US 655 (1900). For a contemporary analysis of the prize cases by the attorney who served as counsel for the United States, see HM Holt, 'Recent Development and Tendency of the Law of Prize' (1903) 12 *Yale LJ* 306.

[124] See DJ Bederman, 'The Feigned Demise of Prize' (1995) 9 *Emory J Int'l L* 31, 37–38 (noting decline of prize cases in US courts).

[125] *The Paquete Habana* (n 2) 686.

[126] ibid.

[127] *The Young Jacob and Johanna* (1798) 1 C Rob 20, 165 ER 81. On Scott's influence as a judge, see HJ Bourguignon, *Sir William Scott, Lord Stowell: Judge of the High Court of Admiralty, 1789–1828* (Cambridge, CUP, 1987).

since then: 'the period of a hundred years which has since elapsed is amply sufficient to have enabled what originally may have rested in custom or comity, cour-
tesy or concession, to grow, by the general assent of civilized nations, into a settled
rule of international law'.[128] Gray cited nineteenth-century state practice during
the Napoleonic Wars, the Mexican–American War of 1848, the Crimean War of
1854, the Franco–Austrian War of 1859, the Franco–Prussian War of 1870, and the
Sino–Japanese War of 1894.[129] Most problematic was the Crimean War, when
England had destroyed many Russian fishing boats and storehouses, but Gray distinguished them as large businesses supplying the Russian military.[130]

The paragraph for which *The Paquete Habana* is famous came next:

> International law is part of our law, and must be ascertained and administered by the
> courts of justice of appropriate jurisdiction as often as questions of right depending upon
> it are duly presented for their determination. For this purpose, where there is no treaty and
> no controlling executive or legislative act or judicial decision, resort must be had to the
> customs and usages of civilized nations, and, as evidence of these, to the works of jurists
> and commentators who by years of labor, research, and experience have made themselves
> peculiarly well acquainted with the subjects of which they treat. Such works are resorted
> to by judicial tribunals, not for the speculations of their authors concerning what the law
> ought to be, but for trustworthy evidence of what the law really is.[131]

In large part, this paragraph simply repeated what Gray had written five years earlier in *Hilton v Guyot*, a decision on the enforcement of foreign judgments that
he cited in support.[132] *The Paquete Habana* used this paragraph to introduce the
18 scholarly works that Gray invoked in further support of the international
law rule.[133]

Finally, Justice Gray turned to consider the policy of the US Government during
the war with Spain, which he found to be 'quite in accord with the rule of international law, now generally recognized by civilized nations, in regard to coast fishing vessels'.[134] Gray quoted President McKinley's proclamations directing that the
blockade should be conducted in accordance with the law of nations.[135] He read
Admiral Sampson's report as evidence that he was 'not authorized, without express
order, to arrest coast fishermen peaceably pursuing their calling', and he read Secretary Long's answer as indicating that Sampson should not seize such vessels 'so long
as they neither attempted to violate the blockade, nor were considered likely to aid
the enemy'.[136]

Chief Justice Fuller dissented. He would have followed Sir William Scott's decision
in *The Young Jacob and Johanna* that the rule against capturing fishing vessels was

---

[128] *The Paquete Habana* (n 2) 694.
[129] See ibid, 694–700.
[130] See ibid, 699–700.
[131] ibid, 700.
[132] See *Hilton v Guyot*, 159 US 113 (1895), 163.
[133] *The Paquete Habana* (n 2) 700–08.
[134] ibid, 712.
[135] See ibid; see also nn 117–18 above and accompanying text.
[136] ibid, 713. Gray's last point was disingenuous because fishing vessels could not have returned to port
without violating the blockade.

one 'of comity only'.[137] But even if the rule were part of international law, Fuller maintained that the President was not bound by it. Quoting Chief Justice Marshall's opinion in *Brown v United States*, Fuller asserted that international law 'is a guide which the sovereign follows or abandons at his will'.[138] Thus, Fuller concluded 'that exemption from the rigors of war is in the control of the Executive. He is bound by no immutable rule on the subject. It is for him to apply, or to modify, or to deny altogether such immunity as may have been usually extended'.[139]

On remand, a commissioner assessed damages for the seizure of *The Paquete Habana* and her cargo at $4,500,[140] which the district court ordered the US Government to pay rather than the captors.[141] The United States appealed to the Supreme Court, which held that the government should indeed be liable because it had ratified the captures, but that the damages were excessive.[142] There is no record of the amount ultimately paid.[143]

C. The Significance of the Decision

The Paquete Habana was quickly hailed as a 'remarkable opinion' that settled the propositions 'that international law is law; that it is part of our municipal law; that our courts take judicial notice of it as such'.[144] In contrast to *The Charming Betsy*, the Supreme Court began to cite Justice Gray's opinion consistently for the proposition that 'International law is part of our law'.[145] Of course, the Court could as easily have cited an older opinion like *The Nereide* for the same proposition.[146] Sometimes it did, right alongside *The Paquete Habana*.[147] On the surface, Gray's opinion looked like a continuation of early American views.

---

[137] ibid, 719 (Fuller CJ, dissenting) (quoting *The Young Jacob and Johanna* (n 127) 81).

[138] ibid, 715 (quoting *Brown v United States*, 12 US (8 Cranch) 110 (1814), 128).

[139] ibid, 720.

[140] *The Paquete Habana*, 189 US 453 (1903), 467.

[141] ibid, 464.

[142] ibid, 466–67.

[143] Dodge, 'The Paquete Habana' (n 116) 157.

[144] JB Scott, 'The Legal Nature of International Law' (1907) 1 *AJIL* 831, 859–60. Scott was writing in the first volume of the American Journal of International Law, of which he was the editor. In the same volume, John Bassett Moore praised the opinion as the 'clearest and most precise application' of the principle that international law evolves through 'the general and gradual transformation of international opinion and practice'. JB Moore, 'International Law: Its Present and Future' (1907) 1 *AJIL* 11, 11. Other nations followed the rule that coastal fishing vessels were exempt from capture under international law, which was incorporated in Art 3 of Hague Convention XI. But the rule soon became obsolete, as mines and submarines made coastal blockades too dangerous. See Dodge, 'The Paquete Habana' (n 116) 157.

[145] *Kansas v Colorado*, 206 US 46 (1907), 97 (quoting *The Paquete Habana* (n 2) 700); see also *Sosa v Alvarez-Machain*, 542 US 692 (2004), 729–30; *First Nat'l City Bank v Banco Para El Comercio Exterior de Cuba*, 462 US 611 (1983), 623; *First Nat'l City Bank v Banco Nacional de Cuba*, 406 US 759 (1972), 763; *Banco Nacional de Cuba v Sabbatino*, 376 US 398 (1964), 423; *Skiriotes v Florida*, 313 US 69 (1941), 72–73.

[146] See *The Nereide*, 13 US (9 Cranch) 388 (1815), 423 ('the Court is bound by the law of nations which is a part of the law of the land').

[147] See *Sosa* (n 145) 730; *Sabbatino* (n 145) 423.

But in fact, *The Paquete Habana* reflected the shifts in American understandings of international law and its incorporation that had occurred during the nineteenth century. At the start of the nineteenth century, Americans understood the unwritten law of nations to be based primarily on natural law, supplemented on indifferent matters by state practice. At the close of the nineteenth century, the American approach to customary international law was thoroughly positivist.[148] So when *The Paquete Habana* went looking for international law to govern the capture of fishing vessels, it turned to 'the customs and usages of civilized nations'.[149] And while the opinion also looked to treatise writers, it did so not for deductions from natural law but for treatments of state practice—in Gray's words, 'not for the speculations of their authors concerning what the law ought to be, but for trustworthy evidence of what the law really is'.[150]

Another shift during the nineteenth century concerned the consent requirement for customary international law, which changed from individual consent that nations were free to withdraw to the common consent of nations that created universal obligations.[151] Like *The Scotia*, which Justice Gray quoted at length, *The Paquete Habana* asserted that the law of nations 'rests upon the common consent of civilized communities'.[152] When usages of nations became 'generally accepted', they created rules of 'universal obligation'.[153]

Finally, the American understanding of incorporation changed during the nineteenth century, away from a view that customary international law was part of domestic law unless displaced towards a view that customary international law was not part of domestic law unless adopted.[154] At first glance, *The Paquete Habana* seemed to ignore that shift when it stated that '[i]nternational law is part of our law, and must be ascertained and administered by the courts of justice of appropriate jurisdiction as often as questions of right depending upon it are duly presented for their determination'.[155] The best way to square this statement with the adoption theory is to recall that courts could adopt international law as part of domestic law too,[156] which is what Justice Gray effectively did with the international law rule on fishing vessels. But the late-nineteenth-century approach to incorporation also appears in *The Paquete Habana*'s statement that resort 'to the customs and usages of civilized nations' is necessary only 'where there is no treaty and no controlling executive or legislative act or judicial decision'.[157]

The idea that a legislative act could displace customary international law in the US system was an old one. It was implicit in *The Charming Betsy*'s statement that

---

[148] See nn 70–90 above and accompanying text.
[149] *The Paquete Habana* (n 2) 700, 686–700 (reviewing state practice from 1403 to 1894).
[150] ibid, 700, 700-09 (reviewing treatises).
[151] See nn 91–103 above and accompanying text.
[152] *The Paquete Habana* (n 2) 711 (quoting *The Scotia* (n 90) 187).
[153] ibid.
[154] See nn 104–112 above and accompanying text.
[155] *The Paquete Habana* (n 2) 700.
[156] See n 108 above and accompanying text.
[157] *The Paquete Habana* (n 2) 700. For reasons of space, I will not discuss the relationship of treaties to customary international law.

'an act of Congress ought never to be construed to violate the law of nations *if any other possible construction remains*'[158] and was explicit in *The Nereide*'s statement that '[t]ill such an act be passed, the Court is bound by the law of nations which is a part of the law of the land'.[159] *The Lottawanna* also emphasised the legislature's authority to supersede international law as a rule of decision.[160]

The influence of the adoption theory shows most clearly in *The Paquete Habana*'s reference to a 'controlling … judicial decision'. Justice Gray likely had in mind cases like *The Lottawanna* itself, in which the Supreme Court had adhered to a prior precedent rather than following later developed international practice.[161] He might also have been thinking of *The Adula*,[162] one of the eight other prize cases argued around the same time as *The Paquete Habana*, in which counsel for the ship owners asked the Court to abandon past decisions concerning the conduct of blockades because of a subsequent change in international law. The Court refused, perhaps because the international law claim seemed weak, perhaps because the precedent seemed strong, or perhaps both.[163] Justice Gray joined the dissent in *The Adula*, but the case showed that the question whether a judicial decision could prevail over a contrary rule of international law was a live one.[164]

It is *The Paquete Habana*'s reference to a 'controlling executive … act' that is most difficult to understand. The early American understanding seems to have been that the President was bound by the law of nations under his constitutional duty to 'take Care that the Laws be faithfully executed'.[165] When Chief Justice Marshall wrote in *Brown v United States* that the law of nations 'is a guide which the sovereign follows or abandon's at his will'[166]—the line Fuller quoted in his *Paquete Habana* dissent— he was referring not to the President alone but to the President and Congress acting together as sovereign. Even Justice Story, who took a more pro-executive stance in *Brown* than the Court, made it clear that the President could not violate interna-

---

[158] *The Charming Betsy* (n 1) 118 (emphasis added).

[159] *The Nereide* (n 146) 423.

[160] See *The Lottawanna* (n 107) 577 ('If, within its proper scope, any change is desired in its rules, other than those of procedure, it must be made by the legislative department').

[161] See nn 106–11 above and accompanying text.

[162] 176 US 361 (1900).

[163] ibid, 371 ('We cannot change our rulings to conform to the opinions of foreign writers as to what they suppose to be the existing law upon the subject').

[164] The question continues to arise today in various contexts. See, eg, *United States v Said*, 798 F 3d 182 (4th Cir 2015) 189–90, which followed the modern definition of piracy under international law rather than 1820 Supreme Court decision); *Trendex Trading Corp v Central Bank of Nigeria* [1977] QB 529, 553–54 (Denning MR), which followed the restrictive theory of foreign sovereign immunity despite contrary precedents. For an argument that changes in international law provide special justification for overruling past precedents, see MP Van Alstine, 'Stare Decisis and Foreign Affairs' (2012) 61 *Duke LJ* 941.

[165] US Const Art II, § 3. This was the view of both sides during the 1793 debate over President Washington's neutrality prosecutions. See A Hamilton, 'Letters of Pacificus, No 1' (1793), in HC Syrett and JE Cooke (eds), *15 The Papers of Alexander Hamilton* (New York, Columbia University Press. 1969) 33, 40 ('The Executive is charged with the execution of all laws, the law of Nations as well as the Municipal law, which recognizes and adopts those laws'); J Madison, 'Letters of Helvidius, No 2' (1793) in TA Mason, RA Rutland and JK Sisson (eds), *15 The Papers of James Madison*, 86 (Richmond, University of Virginia Press, 1985) (agreeing with Hamilton).

[166] 12 US (8 Cranch) 110 (1814), 128.

tional law: 'he cannot lawfully transcend the rules of warfare established among civilized nations'.[167] *The Lottawanna* and subsequent cases discussing the adoption of international law by the United States referred only to adoption by the legislature or the courts. Indeed, I have found no suggestion prior to *The Paquete Habana* that the President had authority to violate international law or to supersede it as a rule of decision for the courts.[168]

I have previously suggested that Justice Gray included executive acts in his list, along with legislative acts and judicial decisions, because in this case the executive's policy supported his decision.[169] President McKinley's proclamations had stated that the United States would follow the law nations in conducting the blockade,[170] a fact that Gray took care to point out.[171] Justice Gray may also have misread *Brown v United States*, like Chief Justice Fuller, as recognising presidential authority to depart from international law.[172] But even if Gray did believe that the President could authorise the seizure of fishing boats in violation of international law, he clearly did not believe that members of the armed forces could do so without such authorisation. In evaluating *The Paquete Habana*'s dictum about controlling executive acts, one must always bear in mind that the Supreme Court held the United States government liable for violating customary international law.[173] And that—by itself—is significant.

---

[167] ibid, 153 (Judge Story dissenting).

[168] For further discussion, see WS Dodge, 'After Sosa: The Future of Customary International Law in the United States' (2009) 17 *Willamette J Int'l L & Dis Res* 21, 34–38. Professor Ramsey agrees that the President cannot, consistent with the Constitution, violate international law. But Ramsey suggests that executive interpretations of international law might bind the courts. See Ramsey (n 114) 362–76. Whether or not this is best reading of the Constitution's text and history, it is probably not what Justice Gray had in mind. The executive branch did not argue for deference to its interpretation of international law in *The Paquete Habana*. See Dodge, 'The Paquete Habana' (n 116) 135 fn 50. And Justice Gray seems to have contemplated the possibility that the President could have ordered a violation of international law. See n 171 below.

[169] See Dodge, 'The Paquete Habana' (n 116) 156.

[170] See nn 117–18 above and accompanying text.

[171] See *The Paquete Habana* (n 2) 712–13. It is tempting to argue that an executive act could be 'controlling' only if it adopted international law and not if it sought to displace that law. But such an interpretation is contradicted by Justice Gray's statement elsewhere in the opinion that fishing boats were exempt from capture if 'no act of Congress or order of the President has expressly authorized [them] to be taken and confiscated,' ibid, 711, a phrase suggesting that the President might have rejected rather than adopted the international law rule.

[172] For further discussion of the readings of *Brown* in *The Paquete Habana*, see Dodge, 'The Paquete Habana' (n 116) 140–41, 154–55.

[173] The 'executive acts' dictum lay dormant until the 1980s, when a lower court used it to justify the detention of Cuban refugees in violation of international law. See *Garcia-Mir v Meese*, 788 F 2d 1446 (11th Cir 1986) 1453–55. This decision provoked a flood of commentary. See Agora: May the President Violate Customary Law? (1986) 80 AJIL 913; Agora: May the President Violate Customary Law? (Continued) (1987) 81 *AJIL* 371. The Bush administration later invoked the dictum to argue that detainees held at Guantanamo Bay, Cuba were not entitled to the protections of customary international law. See Memorandum for Alberto Gonzales, Counsel to the President, and William J Haynes II, General Counsel of the Department of Defense, from Jay S Bybee, Assistant Attorney General (22 January 2002), 35.

V. CONCLUSION

Some cases change the course of international law or the place of international law in a domestic legal system. Neither of the cases reviewed in this chapter did so. *The Charming Betsy* was just one of many decisions in the late-eighteenth and early-nineteenth centuries to construe statutes as consistent with international law, and the case did not come to be closely associated with the consistency canon until the middle of the twentieth century. *The Paquete Habana* was just one of many Supreme Court prize decisions arising from the Spanish–American War. Apart from its reference to controlling executive acts, it broke no new doctrinal ground.

To focus only on landmarks is to risk obscuring important shifts in the landscape. And when landmark decisions make superficially similar statements, one might conclude that nothing has changed in between. That is not true here. As this chapter has shown, American understandings of international law and its incorporation in the US legal system changed significantly during the nineteenth century. *The Charming Betsy* and *The Paquete Habana* are landmark cases not because they changed the course of international law in the United States but rather because they show—as landmarks often do—the contours of the ground beneath.

3

Mavrommatis Palestine Concessions (Greece v Great Britain) (1924–27)

MICHAEL WAIBEL[1]

I. INTRODUCTION

T HE *MAVROMMATIS* DISPUTE was about the fate of conflicting concessions for the supply of water and electricity and associated economic and political control over Palestine in the interwar period. Both water and electricity were essential to the aspirations of the Jewish people to create a homeland in this inhospitable part of the world. The control over water, in particular, has provoked considerable bloodshed in this region due to water scarcity,[2] and remains a central theme of the contemporary Arab–Israeli conflict.[3]

The dispute about the concessions led to the three *Mavrommatis Palestine Concessions*[4] cases before the PCIJ that are the focus of this chapter. As the sole dispute about the British Mandate in Palestine, these three cases provided a catalyst for the PCIJ to address vital constitutional questions concerning the Mandate, including the legislative powers of the Government of Palestine,[5] the conformity of such legislation with the British Mandate and the interaction of private law rights and public law from the vantage point of international law that also characterises many contemporary investment disputes.[6]

---

[1] Thanks to Hannah Dixie and Henry Moore for outstanding research assistance.

[2] N Bethell, *The Palestine triangle: the struggle for the Holy Land, 1935–48* (New York, Putnam, 1979); R El-Eini, *Mandated Landscape: British Imperial Rule in Palestine, 1929–1948* (London, Routledge, 2006); AJ Sherman, *Mandate days: British lives in Palestine, 1918–1948* (Liverpool, Johns Hopkins University Press, 2001); PL Hanna and American Council on *Public Affairs, British policy in Palestine (1942)* available at <https://babel.hathitrust.org/cgi/pt?id=mdp.39015004891787;view=1up;seq=1>.

[3] See generally E Benvenisti, *Sharing transboundary resources: international law and optimal resource use* (Cambridge, CUP, 2002).

[4] *Mavrommatis Palestine Concessions (Greece v United Kingdom)* (1924) PCIJ Ser A No 2; (1925) PCIJ Ser A No 5; (1927) Ser A No 10.

[5] According to the then Chief Justice of Palestine, '[t]he Mandate was a sort of constitution, conferring limited powers of government', TW Haycraft, 'Palestine under the Mandate' (1928) 15 *Journal of the Central Asian Society* 167, 170.

[6] N Bentwich, 'The Jurisdiction of the International Court of Justice over Concessions in a Mandated Territory' (1928) 44 *LQR* 450; M Burgis, 'Transforming (Private) Rights through (Public) International Law: Readings on a "Strange and Painful Odyssey" in the PCIJ Mavrommatis Case' (2011) 24 *LJIL* 873; H Lauterpacht, *The Function of Law in the International Community* (Oxford, Clarendon Press, 1933) 164.

II. THE HISTORICAL CONTEXT

The *Mavrommatis* dispute arose in the aftermath of World War I in a territory that was then known as Palestine, and became the State of Israel in 1948. It was the result of a state succession resulting from the dissolution of the Ottoman Empire and the temporary passing of the territory from Ottoman rule under a British mandate in the interwar period. On 9 December 1917, Great Britain occupied Jerusalem of the Ottoman Empire. Following the Treaty of Sèvres of 1920,[7] Palestine became a British Mandate.[8] Certain territories of defeated powers in World War I became mandates, assigned to particular states and with oversight by the League of Nations.[9]

On 2 November 1917, the Balfour Declaration endorsed the creation of a home for the Jewish people in Palestine.[10] Great Britain's Foreign Secretary, Arthur Balfour, pledged British support in a letter to Lord Walter Rothschild, a leading figure in the British Jewish community.[11] The declaration marks the origins of Israel. On 24 July 1922, the League of Nations incorporated it into the British mandate.[12] The British civilian administration for Palestine functioned similarly to crown colonies.[13]

The former sovereign (the Ottoman Empire) granted concessions to Mavrommatis, and the mandatory (Great Britain), after the Ottoman Empire's dissolution, granted concessions to Rutenberg. The old concessionaire, Mavrommatis, was a Greek

[7] Article 95 of the Treaty of Sèvres, 10 August 1920, provided for a mandate for Palestine: 'The High Contracting Parties agree to entrust, by application of the provisions of Article 22, the administration of Palestine, within such boundaries as may be determined by the Principal Allied Powers, to a Mandatory to be selected by the said Powers. The Mandatory will be responsible for putting into effect the declaration originally made on 2 November 1917 by the British Government, and adopted by the other Allied Powers, in favour of the establishment in Palestine of a national home for the Jewish people, it being clearly understood that nothing shall be done which may prejudice the civil and religious rights of existing non-Jewish communities in Palestine, or the rights and political status enjoyed by Jews in any other country.'

[8] Mandate for the Administration of the Former Turkish Territory of Palestine, conferred upon his Britannic Majesty, confirmed and defined by the League of Nations, 24 July 1922.

[9] Art 22 League of Nations Covenant; H Lauterpacht, 'The Mandate under International Law in the Covenant of the League of Nations' in H Lauterpacht and E Lauterpacht (eds), *International Law* (Cambridge, CUP, 1970) vol III, 29; JC Hales, 'The Creation and Application of the Mandate System. (A Study in International Colonial Supervision)' (1939) 25 *Transactions of the Grotius Society* 185.

[10] It was preceded by Herbert Samuel's Cabinet Memorandum on "The Future of Palestine" (January 1915). The memo argued that Palestine should become a British protectorate, with home rule in due course. This plan had as much to do with British imperialism as with Zionism. For the Arab Middle East, the peace settlements were the old nineteenth-century imperialism again, M MacMillan, *Paris 1919: six months that changed the world*, 1st US edn (New York, Random House, 2002) 381. Herbert Samuel later became High Commissioner for Palestine from 1920 to 1925. He formed a strong relationship with Rutenberg; see S Ronen, *Current flow: the electrification of Palestine* (Stanford, Stanford University Press, 2013) 44.

[11] The Rothschilds also provided financial support for Rutenberg's plan to electrify Palestine: N Ferguson, *The House of Rothschild: The World's Banker: 1849–1998* (New York, Penguin, 1998) vol II, 441–53.

[12] Great Britain had been the occupying power since December 1917, and had already established a civilian government in 1920, TW Haycraft, 'Palestine under the Mandate' (1928) 15 *Journal of the Central Asian Society* 167, 170.

[13] S Ronen, *Current flow: the electrification of Palestine* (Stanford, Stanford University Press, 2013) 14.

entrepreneur resident in the Ottoman Empire.[14] The new concessionaire, Rutenberg, was a Soviet national of Jewish faith who played a major role in the establishment of the state of Israel. At a time of great geopolitical upheaval, the travails of Euripides Mavrommatis with the British authorities in London and Palestine, perhaps due to his nationality, resembled the wanderings of Odysseus.[15] Perhaps Mavrommatis was simply on the wrong side of history, and Rutenberg a fortunate benefactor of Great Britain's new commitment to Zionism:

> the Rutenberg concession, which granted extraordinary monopolistic rights to exploit … natural resources and to operate public utilities, was an important milestone in the politics of the economic policy, not only in the prestige it accorded to Zionist movement but also in the violent opposition it provoked.[16]

During Britain's mandate over Palestine, relations and political and economic divisions between the Jews and Arabs steadily deteriorated,[17] culminating in the 1947–48 Civil War that led to Israel's independence. The extent to which Zionism and British policy with respect to the Mandate contributed to this deterioration is disputed.

III. THE FACTS OF *MAVROMMATIS*

In 1914, shortly prior to the outbreak of the First World War, Mavrommatis, a Greek national and public works contractor resident in the Ottoman Empire, obtained from the Ottoman authorities two sets of concessions to undertake various public works in Palestine in the cities of Jerusalem, Jaffa, and Jordan. The first set of two concessions, provided under contracts dated 27 January 1914, allowed, first, the construction and working of a system of electric tramways and, second, the distribution of electric light and power and of drinking water in the city of Jerusalem. In August 1914, due to the outbreak of World War I, the parties postponed the execution of these concessions by mutual agreement until the restoration of peace.[18] The second set of concessions concerned the city of Jaffa, similar in substance with the additional inclusion of the irrigation of the gardens of that city by means of the waters of the river El-Hodja.[19] However, while these agreements had been converted into concessions on 28 January 1916, they were not confirmed in accordance with Ottoman law. The third set of concessions, relating to the irrigation of the Jordan valley, lacked any kind of definitive contract. The Ottoman Parliament, which had adjourned once the war began, had yet to approve this set.

---

[14] Greek nationals and ethnic Greeks played a major role in the Ottoman economy in the early twentieth century; on Ottoman nationality, H Will 'What Ottoman Nationality Was and Was Not' 3 *Journal of the Ottoman and Turkish Studies Association* 2, 277–98.

[15] Burgis, 'Transforming (Private) Rights' (n 6) 897, citing Mr H Purchase, Counsel for the Greece, First Speech, Part II, Speeches and Documents Read before the Court, Series C, No 7, 1925, 41.

[16] BJ Smith, *The Roots of Separatism in Palestine: British Economic Policy 1920–1929* (Syracuse, Syracuse University Press, 1993) 118.

[17] Jews and Arabs clashed violently as early as 1921 and again in 1929.

[18] R Uerpmann-Wittzack, 'Mavrommatis Concessions Cases' (2013) *MPEPIL* 1.

[19] *Mavrommatis* Series A, No 2 (n 4) 8.

After World War I, Mavrommatis obtained renewed promises of support from his earlier backers before submitting his pre-existing concessionary claims to the Palestine administration, which forwarded them to the Colonial Office.[20] In September 1921, Britain granted two concessions for supplying and selling electricity throughout Palestine to Pinhas Rutenberg, a Soviet–Jewish engineer and businessman.[21] Rutenberg's concessions related to two schemes. The first, smaller scheme, estimated to cost Rutenberg £100,000,[22] granted him exclusive rights to use the waters of the Auja Basin and to provide power, electric light and irrigation using any type of energy in the district of Jaffa.[23] The second, larger scheme afforded him exclusive rights to exploit the waters of the Jordan River to allow a hydroelectric and irrigation scheme, on the condition that he form a company with subscribed capital of £1 million within two years.[24] It further granted Rutenberg complete rights over the supply of electric power throughout Mandatory Palestine, save for Jerusalem itself.

Britain turned to Zionism as Palestine was on the edge of an economic renaissance.[25] In the wake of the Balfour Declaration, references had begun to emerge in British policy regarding the need, as a matter of principle, to show preference to Zionist organisations in granting developmental concessions.[26] Although Rutenberg acted of his own accord as a private entrepreneur, he was a fortunate beneficiary of preferential treatment in favour of the Zionist movement.[27] The Rutenberg concessions represented 'the most practical example of the policy of setting up a National Home for the Jews'[28] and marked a milestone in Palestine economic policy.

[20] Smith, *The Roots of Separatism in Palestine* (n 16) 123.

[21] M Naor, 'An Electrifying Story' (Haartez—Israel News, 25 January 2004) <www.haaretz.com/print-edition/features/an-electrifying-story-1.111974> accessed 22 December 2016. Rutenberg founded the Palestine Electric Company. In 1961, it became the Israel Electric Corporation, of which the State of Israel owns 99.85% and which is Israel's only integrated electricity company and one of its largest companies. In January 1926, Rutenberg became the first citizen of the new Palestine, *Jewish Daily Bulletin*, 11 January 1926, New York, Vo III, No 374, A1, <pdfs.jta.org/1926/1926-01-11_374.pdf>.

[22] Circa £4 million today (calculated using MeasuringWorth).

[23] Smith (n 16) 119.

[24] ibid.

[25] ibid, 117. See also M Svirsky, *Arab-Jewish Activism in Israel-Palestine* (Farnham, Ashgate, 2012) 103.

[26] ibid. Smith goes so far as to call the concession 'nationalistic.' See also: Svirsky, *Arab-Jewish Activism* (n 25) 56, for further discussion of the preferential treatment accorded to the Zionist movement, including the granting of monopolistic concessions to allow exploitation of natural resources and operation of public services and utilities, as well as a protectionist industrial policy comprising, inter alia, tax exemptions favouring Jewish industries. *cf* J Metzer, *The Divided Economy of Mandatory Palestine* (Cambridge, CUP, 1998) 177: 'The sensitivities surrounding the delicate and always unsatisfactory—to one party or another—attempts by the government to abide by its dual obligation to the Zionist cause and the Arab case meant that any government move that could be interpreted as assisting one community (say, granting concessions to natural monopolies, devising schemes of protective tariffs, or any other area of public policy) was perceived, for that very reason, by the other community as harmful.'

[27] ibid. See also: M LeVine, 'The Discourses of Development in Mandate Palestine' (1995) 17 *Arab Studies Quarterly* (1–2) 103–04 for a possible explanation: 'Because of British financial restraints, Zionist development discourse automatically had resonance with the British ... It is clear, then, that the Mandatory not only viewed Jewish economic development as relieving them of their responsibility under the Mandate to develop the country, but moreover that the fulfilment of Zionist aims was the only way the Government could afford to rule the country'.

[28] ibid, 118. See also: K Firro, *The Druzes in the Jewish State: A Brief History* (Boston, Brill, 1999) 145–46.

By their terms, the concessions afforded Rutenberg monopolistic rights that conflicted with Mavrommatis' existing concessions and gave him a high degree of control over the economic future of Palestine.[29]

In granting the concessions to Rutenberg, Great Britain sought to achieve several objectives, namely to promote Zionist development schemes, placate Arab opposition and weaken domestic criticism of its colonial policy in Palestine:

> The agreement between the British government and Rutenberg explicitly stated that the constitution of the projected company would need the approval of the high commissioner acting on the advice of the Zionist Organization. By emphasizing that the Rutenberg concession was fundamentally a Zionist project, British officials no doubt hoped to gain some political points. The Zionists would be grateful for the preferential treatment, the Arabs would recognize the material benefits from the Jewish National Home policy, and those opposing government policy in Britain would be convinced that practical achievements were being made in Palestine and that support of the Balfour Declaration was thereby justified.[30]

In 1922, Article 11 of the Mandate for Palestine officially referenced the importance of Jewish participation in the development of the Jewish homeland.[31] However, the Zionist Organisation considered the best way to further Jewish interests was to publicly distance itself from Rutenberg, agreeing to negotiate with the administration in secret.[32] It downplayed any political affiliations between them, initially to assist in raising capital, and, later, due to 'four years of strenuous opposition to the concession and little or no benefit to the Arab population',[33] which ultimately, and undesirably, rendered the Rutenberg concession 'a symbol of Zionist aggression'.[34]

---

[29] ibid, 117–19.

[30] ibid, 119. cf Metzer, *Divided Economy* (n 26) 183: 'While I agree with Smith on the contribution of some British policies to Jewish–Arab economic separatism (largely enhanced by the attributes of Jewish economic activity), the claims that the prime beneficiaries of the tariffs in Mandatory Palestine were Jewish industrialists, and that these benefits were in any way consequential, are empirically unverified'.

[31] The British Mandate for Palestine (Council of the League of Nations, 24 July 1922) Art 11: 'The Administration of Palestine shall take all necessary measures to safeguard the interests of the community in connection with the development of the country, and, subject to any international obligations accepted by the Mandatory, shall have full power to provide for public ownership or control of any of the natural resources of the country or of the public works, services and utilities established or to be established therein. It shall introduce a land system appropriate to the needs of the country, having regard, among other things, to the desirability of promoting the close settlement and intensive cultivation of the land.

'The Administration may arrange with the Jewish agency mentioned in Article 4 to construct or operate, upon fair and equitable terms, any public works, services and utilities, and to develop any of the natural resources of the country, in so far as these matters are not directly undertaken by the Administration. Any such arrangements shall provide that no profits distributed by such agency, directly or indirectly, shall exceed a reasonable rate of interest on the capital, and any further profits shall be utilised by it for the benefit of the country in a manner approved by the Administration.'

[32] Smith (n 16) 121.

[33] ibid, 119.

[34] ibid, 121. See also LeVine, 'Discourses of Development' (n 27) 108–09: The three most important concessions in Palestine—electricity, exploiting the mineral resources of the Dead Sea, and draining the Huleh—were all granted to the Zionists soon after the British occupation, and the electricity concession, known as the Rutenberg concession, was 'singularly important' so as to be subject to debate in Parliament. This concession, which provoked violent outbursts from the Arab population, gave the Jews a monopoly on constructing the biggest electrical station in Palestine with a free hand to use the power to equip Jewish settlements. Moreover, the company could expropriate any land it deemed necessary, while

In 1921, the Palestine Zionist Executive authorised Rutenberg to answer questions relating to the establishment of the Jewish National Home for the Zionist Organisation.[35] In public, however, Chaim Weizmann, the organisation's president, expressly refuted such an idea. Instead, he professed the organisation's only interest in these affairs to be its desire that the Rutenberg concessions ran successfully and without delay. He disclaimed any direct financial interest of the Zionist Organization. He also underlined that Rutenberg was not, nor had ever been, a nominee of the Zionist Organization.[36] He described his own role as 'merely that of a friendly intermediary between M Mavrommatis and Mr Rutenberg'.[37] Before the PCIJ, the UK acknowledged that the Zionist Organization was 'anxious to see put into operation a project which would bring fertility and prosperity to large areas of Palestine',[38] but made explicit that this 'does not render Rutenberg their representative'.[39]

Mavrommatis, who had intended to resume work at the conclusion of the hostilities,[40] protested vociferously on learning of Rutenberg's conflicting concessions.[41] In 1918, Mavrommatis submitted his concessionary claims to the Palestine administration. Yet the Colonial Office in London dragged its feet. It advised him to 'come to an understanding with the Zionist organisation and with Mr Rutenberg'[42] in order to obtain his collaboration in the carrying out of the projected works, yet he endeavoured to do so without success. Lengthy negotiations ensued, over a period of four years, between Great Britain and Mavrommatis. The British Government labelled him 'slippery',[43] openly maligning Mavrommatis for his unrealistic demands for compensation regarding the expropriation of his concessions. They accused him of lacking any intention to carry out his electricity concession, alluding to his purported desire to simply make a considerable profit. Rutenberg ultimately called him a 'franchise blackmailer'.[44] When Mavrommatis realised that his claim in respect of Jaffa was futile, he focused his efforts on Jerusalem.

Efforts to reach a compromise ultimately proved fruitless. Mavrommatis 'sought assistance from every possible source in order to further his claim',[45] contacting the British press and Members of Parliament who were sympathetic to his cause. Finally, in 1924, Mavrommatis approached the Greek government to apply on his behalf to

---

no other body was permitted to distribute or sell electricity in Palestine. Thus, Arab groups were subsequently turned down for concessions to electrify Arab cities like Jaffa, and were basically forced by the British to get permission—almost never granted—from Jewish concessions to exploit their own resources.

[35] ibid, 120.

[36] TS 27/309, Statement by Dr. Chaim Weizmann, President of the Zionist Organisation (5 February, 1925) 2.

[37] ibid, 5.

[38] Speech by Sir D Hogg, Counsel for Britain, Part II, Speeches Made and Documents Read Before the Court, Series C No 7, February 1925, 128.

[39] ibid.

[40] Burgis (n 6) 888.

[41] Naor 'An Electrifying Story' (n 21).

[42] *Mavrommatis* Series A, No 2 (n 4) 19.

[43] CO 733/144/7, Government memorandum considering extension of the time of the concessions (October 1927).

[44] Naor (n 21).

[45] ibid.

the Permanent Court of International Justice (PCIJ). The Greek government accepted to exercise diplomatic protection. Greece's initial submissions were two-fold: first, the British government lacked the authority to grant the Rutenberg concessions and by doing so had infringed Mavrommatis' rights; and, second, according to the Treaty of Lausanne, the British government had taken on responsibility for all of Turkey's obligations, which included the concessions granted to Mavrommatis by the Ottoman authorities.

IV. THE PROCEEDINGS AND JUDGMENTS IN *MAVROMMATIS*

A. Judgment No 2 (1924—Jurisdiction)

The first *Mavrommatis* case concerned the jurisdiction of the Permanent Court. Greece's application contended that Britain had failed to recognise the rights of Mavrommatis, a Greek subject, under contracts and agreements concluded by him with the Ottoman authorities, in regard to concessions for certain public works to be constructed in Palestine. Greece submitted the case to the Court under Article 26 of the Mandate for Palestine, which provided for the Permanent Court's jurisdiction, as follows:

> The Mandatory agrees that, if any dispute whatever should arise between the Mandatory and another Member of the League of Nations relating to the interpretation or the applica-tion of the provisions of the Mandate, such dispute, if it cannot be settled by negotiation, shall be submitted to the Permanent Court of International Justice provided for by Article 14 of the Covenant of the League of Nations.[46]

Britain objected that the Court lacked jurisdiction over the dispute. By a narrow majority of seven to five, the Court on 30 August 1924 affirmed its jurisdiction over the Mavrommatis concessions, albeit only with respect to the Jerusalem concessions. Conversely, the Court found that the Jaffa concessions were outside its jurisdic-tion due to final approval from the Turkish government having taken place after 29 October 1914, the effective date for claiming a right of survival or succession under Protocol XII of the Treaty of Lausanne. As for the Jordan concessions, Greece aban-doned any claim in this respect during the course of proceedings, conceding it was premised simply on a verbal agreement which lacked the requisite confirmation of a definitive contract. The judgment addresses three preconditions found in Article 26, namely: (1) the existence of the dispute; (2) the prior negotiation requirement; and (3) whether the dispute concerned 'the interpretation or the application of a provision of the Mandate'.

As neither its Statute nor the Rules contained any provision on preliminary objec-tions, the Court first considered whether it had the inherent power to examine preliminary objections. The Court emphasised that it was 'at liberty to adopt the principle which it considers best calculated to ensure the administration of justice,

---

[46] British Mandate for Palestine (n 31) Art 26.

most suited to procedure before an international tribunal and most in conformity with the fundamental principles of international law'.[47]

i. Was There a Dispute Between the Mandatory and Another Member of the League of Nations?

Britain and Greece disagreed as to whether the dispute in issue was between states, or merely between a private individual and another state. Under Article 26, the Court's jurisdiction is limited to inter-state disputes. The UK firmly rejected any contention that a dispute existed between governments.[48]

The dispute in question undoubtedly began as a private one, with the alleged infringement of the concessionary rights of Mavrommatis. However, in the eyes of the Court, it was irrelevant that the dispute had originated in an injury to a private individual. In the course of its judgment, the Court endorsed a liberal approach towards diplomatic protection. In a now-famous passage, the majority held:

> It is an elementary principle of international law that a State is entitled to protect its subjects, when injured by acts contrary to international law committed by another State, from whom they have been unable to obtain satisfaction through the ordinary channels. By taking up the case of one of its subjects and by resorting to diplomatic action or international judicial proceedings on his behalf, a State is in reality asserting its own rights—its right to ensure, in the person of its subjects, respect for the rules of international law.[49]

This notion that a state is 'asserting its own right'[50] when it takes up a dispute of private origin on behalf of one of its citizens has become known as the '*Mavrommatis* fiction' or the first (of three) *Mavrommatis* formulas.

ii. Could the Dispute Be Settled by Negotiation?

The Court dealt with the second condition of negotiations similarly efficiently. The UK contended that this prior negotiating requirement referred only to negotiations between two states;[51] whereas Greece submitted that negotiations between Mavrommatis and Great Britain in 1923 satisfied this requirement.

Great Britain contended that compliance with this second jurisdictional prerequisite was a matter of great importance, since 'from the moment when there begin to be negotiations between the governments',[52] rather than simply between an individual and a government, 'it is a question which will be honoured by new men',[53] applying 'not the rule applicable to municipal matters in the particular country concerned, but the principles and standards of international law'.[54]

---

[47] *Mavrommatis* Series, A No 2 (n 4) 16; H Lauterpacht, *The Function of Law in the International Community* (Oxford, OUP, 2011).
[48] Speech by Sir C Hurst, Counsel for Britain, Part II, Speeches and Documents Read before the Court, Series C, No 5, 4 September 1924, 70.
[49] *Mavrommatis* Series A No 2 (n 4) 12.
[50] ibid.
[51] Hurst (n 48) 71.
[52] ibid, 72.
[53] ibid.
[54] ibid.

The Court found that there was no requiring that the Greek Government (as opposed to Mavrommatis) be involved in these negotiations. Rather, provided the individual on whose behalf the state was exercising diplomatic protection had previously made efforts to settle the dispute, this prerequisite for jurisdiction was met. The Court underscores the importance of flexibility.[55] The majority held that when earlier negotiations had taken place between a private individual and a government, it is 'incompatible with the flexibility which should characterize international relations'[56] to require additional discussions.

The Court conceded that new factors may enter into the diplomatic negotiations when the State enters a dispute, given that it does not act merely as a substitute claimant for its national.[57] Rather, the state asserts its own, independent right, perhaps prompting new channels of negotiation. However, it held that when earlier diplomatic negotiations between the state's national and another government had been unsuccessful and led to the involvement of the state's government, such negotiations may render further negotiations on the question which gave rise to the dispute superfluous.[58]

iii. Did the Dispute Relate to the Interpretation or Application of the Mandate?

The third requirement for jurisdiction proved the most contentious. This has been characterised as the 'major hurdle standing in the way of the Permanent Court's jurisdiction'[59] and is widely considered 'what makes the Mavrommatis case a significant example of international legal argument'.[60]

The Permanent Court was quick to acknowledge that its jurisdiction under Article 26 of the Mandate was 'limited to certain categories of disputes, which are [objectively] determined according to a legal criterion',[61] here specifically those concerning the interpretation and application of the Mandate. This approach of the Court has been influential in international dispute settlement. International courts and tribunals do not decide hypothetical disputes; the dispute must have practical relevance. The ICJ defines a dispute as a 'disagreement on a point of law or fact, a conflict of legal views or interests between two persons'.[62] This is a flexible formulation, but a party cannot create a dispute merely by asserting that one exists, nor can states simply submit disputes to the Court 'at their discretion'.[63] In Mavrommatis, the question of whether any such dispute existed was thus pivotal. Mavrommatis alleged that his rights had been undermined by the British grant of concessions to Rutenberg in spite of a British obligation to respect pre-existing concessions. The question for the

---

[55] *Mavrommatis Series*, Series A No 2 (n 4) 15.
[56] ibid.
[57] ibid.
[58] ibid.
[59] O Spiermann, *International Legal Argument in the Permanent Court of International Justice: The Rise of the International Judiciary* (Cambridge, CUP, 2004) 193.
[60] ibid.
[61] *Mavrommatis* Series A No 2 (n 4) 16–17.
[62] ibid, 11.
[63] Spiermann, *International Legal Argument* (n 59) 196–97.

Court was therefore whether the granting of concessions to Rutenberg violated the international obligations referenced in Article 11 of the Palestine Mandate.[64]

Both sides conceded that the Mavrommatis concessions themselves, granted prior to the outbreak of the war, lay outside the scope of this Article.[65] The Court thus held that Article 11 applied only to the *Mavrommatis* case if two conditions were met. First, the Rutenberg concessions must have fallen within its scope, having been granted in exercise of the Mandatory's full power to provide for public ownership or control of the natural resources of Palestine. Second, that grant must have violated Britain's international obligations.[66]

Determining the meaning of 'public ownership and control' under Article 11 was thus crucial. Whereas the French understanding of *contrôle* encompassed 'the right to grant concessions with a view to the development of the natural resources of the country or of public works, services and utilities, as also the right to annul or cancel existing concessions',[67] the English version had a more restricted meaning. Eventually, the Court decided the term public control referred to 'the various methods whereby the public administration may take over, or dictate the policy of, undertakings not publicly owned'.[68] In drawing this conclusion, the Court considered itself 'bound to adopt the more limited interpretation which can be made to harmonise with both versions ... in accordance with the common intention of the Parties'.[69]

While some minority judges sided with Great Britain in considering that public control related 'only to the governmental ownership or operation of public utilities, but not to grant of franchises to private concessionaires',[70] the majority rejected the notion that all activities not carried out by the government were private. The expression 'public control' in the English language 'covered any exercise of public authority by which private enterprise was subordinated',[71] thus extending beyond cases in which the Government takes over and itself directs an undertaking. The expression is also used to indicate certain forms of state activity regarding undertakings of a private character. It may mean measures of economic policy consisting in subordinating private enterprise to public authority. The Court held that this 'wider meaning of the English expression appears to be the only one which does not nullify the expression *contrôle public* in the French version'.[72] The Rutenberg concessions were public utilities, as the Government of Palestine supervised Rutenberg's enterprise and the companies were to be created in agreement with the Jewish Agency.[73] This character met the third jurisdictional precondition.

This exercise of control by Palestine was, however, according to Article 11 of the Mandate, subject to the Mandatory's international obligations.[74] The Court called

---

[64] E Borchard, 'The Mavrommatis Concessions Cases' (1925) 19 *AJIL* 728, 731.
[65] Bentwich (n 6) 454.
[66] ibid.
[67] *Mavrommatis* Series, Series A No 2 (n 4) 18.
[68] ibid, 19.
[69] ibid.
[70] Borchard (n 64).
[71] Bentwich (n 56) 454.
[72] *Mavrommatis* Series, Series A No 2 (n 4)
[73] Bentwich (n 6).
[74] British Mandate for Palestine (n 31) Art 11.

this limitation necessary because the international obligations of the Mandatory were not automatically the international obligations of Palestine.[75] Given the authority granted to the Palestine Administration under Article 11 of the Mandate, it was crucial that the Palestine Authority exercised this authority in a manner that was compatible with Great Britain's international obligations'.[76]

Before the Court could establish its jurisdiction, therefore, the second crucial matter was to determine the scope of Britain's international obligations referenced in Article 11. The Greek government argued that the phrase at issue in Article 11 referred to 'all international obligations in general'.[77] Meanwhile, the British view was that it referred 'only to various beneficent principles to the maintenance of which Great Britain was pledged under the Mandate, such as freedom of transit and communication and equality of commercial opportunity for all Members of the League'.[78] Accordingly, the British government contended that the dispute related not to the interpretation or application of the Mandate, but rather simply to Protocol XII of the Treaty of Lausanne. The Protocol was 'an international instrument distinct from and independent of the Palestine Mandate'[79] which dealt specifically with the kind of concessions at issue, while the Mandate did so only by implication. The Court conceded that, in the event of a conflict between the Mandate and the Protocol, the latter deserved preference 'being a special and more recent agreement'.[80]

However, holding the provisions of the Mandate applicable 'in so far as they were compatible with the Protocol',[81] the Court found no such conflict:

> The silence of Protocol XII concerning the Mandate and the jurisdiction of the Permanent Court of International Justice, does not justify the conclusion that the Parties intended to exclude such jurisdiction; for the Protocol does not only deal with mandated territories, and it includes amongst its signatories a State which is not a Member of the League of Nations.[82]

The Court thus held that the international obligations referenced in Article 11 must be understood to encompass the Protocol's requirement to maintain concessions, provided they were granted before 29 October 1914. This date, to which the Court attached considerable importance as Article 311 of the Treaty of Sèvres specified it (the essence of which later became Protocol XII) proved pivotal; it dictated that the Jerusalem concessions, but not the Jaffa concessions, were classified as obligations accepted by Great Britain under Article 11, making only the former subject to the jurisdiction of the Permanent Court. The Court stopped short of finding jurisdiction in respect of the Jaffa concessions which, granted after 29 October 1914, precluded application of Protocol XII. In the alternative, the Parties disagreed over whether 'concessions granted between 29 October 1914, and the restoration of peace in

---

[75] *Mavrommatis* Series A No 2 (n 4) 23.
[76] ibid.
[77] ibid, 24.
[78] ibid.
[79] ibid, 30.
[80] ibid, 31.
[81] ibid.
[82] ibid.

countries where Turkey continued to exercise sovereign power, hold good, in principle, as against the successor States'.[83] Supporting a theory of state succession, the Court considered the Administration of Palestine bound to honour any contracts agreed by the preceding regime, and recognise attendant concessionary rights, under 'the general principle of subrogation'.[84]

The Court paid little attention to contested nationality of Mavrommatis or to Protocol XII not yet having entered into force at seisin.[85] However, relying on the principle of effectiveness to sidestep the problem of non-retroactivity,[86] the Court concluded that the Protocol 'also granted protection against infringements anterior to the protocol's coming into force'[87] because Greece would be able to resubmit its application at any time.[88] Despite the application being premature, it was cured by the subsequent deposit of the necessary ratification.[89] Its justification for so doing was, in the words of the Permanent Court, that an International Court 'is not bound to attach to matters of form the same degree of importance which they might possess in municipal law'[90] (the second *Mavrommatis* formula).

iv. Dissenting Opinions

The majority judgment fuelled five fervent dissents, albeit to various degrees: none of the five dissenting judges was satisfied as to the existence of a dispute between two states, viewing it as merely one between Great Britain and a Greek national; Judge Bustamante refused to accept that the Court's jurisdiction could extent to a dispute predating the entry into force of Article;[91] while in the view of Judge Moore and Lord Finlay, who offered the lengthiest dissents, all three prerequisites for jurisdiction in Article 26 were not met.

On the central issue of diplomatic protection, the dissenting opinions expressed a clear preference for a more restrictive reading than that adopted by the majority judgment. Both Lord Finlay and Judge Moore emphasised the lack of any negotiation between governments.[92] Judge Moore refused to accept that a government could become a party to a dispute 'at any moment when it might see fit to intervene',[93] and was particularly concerned that a loose understanding of the need for a negotiation process encouraged governments to 'evade their obligations'[94] to use diplomacy to endeavour to settle any differences that arise. He pointed to similar provisions in general arbitration treaties which require negotiations between governments to

---

[83] ibid, 28.
[84] ibid.
[85] Burgis (n 6).
[86] Uerpmann-Wittzack 'Mavrommatis Concessions Cases' (n 18) 14.
[87] ibid, 8.
[88] ibid.
[89] *Mavrommatis* Series A No 2 (n 4) 34.
[90] ibid.
[91] Borchard (n 64) 729.
[92] Bentwich (n 6) 457.
[93] *Mavrommatis* Series A No 2 (n 4) dissenting opinion by Judge Moore, 63.
[94] ibid, 62.

reach a settlement by way of an example. Moreover, in his view, the nature of the dispute was 'eminently fit'[95] for settlement by inter-government negotiation. Until such discussions had been attempted, Judge Moore stated, 'it was not possible to say that there was a dispute as to the interpretation of the Mandate',[96] as required by the third jurisdictional condition. Meanwhile, Judge Pessôa disproved of the decision of the majority to dispense with the need for previous negotiations between two governments, considering such a requirement to be 'a tribute to the sovereignty of nations',[97] and to the principle 'that all disputes shall be settled between the nations concerned themselves'. In his view, the Court should only intervene when any likely solution 'is recognized as impossible'.[98] Similarly critical of the failure of the Greek government to make any effort to negotiate with Great Britain, Lord Finlay deemed it 'insufficient that Greece had simply espoused the claim of its national',[99] deeming it 'quite impossible to say that if the Greek Government had taken up the claim and, as a government, had pressed for a settlement, the negotiations might not have resulted in a settlement'.[100]

Regarding the third and most divisive prerequisite, he took the view that the dispute in issue fell to be considered under Article 26, refusing to accept the majority's view that the international obligations accepted by the Mandatory included provisions of Protocol XII of the Treaty of Lausanne. He contended that the Administration had not provided for the public control of the country's natural resources in a manner prohibited by Article 11 on the grounds that 'supervision of a Concession by the public authority, which is an inherent provision of nearly every Concession, is not what is contemplated by the Article of the Mandate'.[101] Such a violation would be found, Lord Finlay hypothesised, if 'the Government of Palestine had disregarded all Concessions granted by the Turks and asserted public ownership of all resources of the country'.[102] But it had not done so.

Judge Bustamante refused to accept the proposition that the Court possessed any jurisdiction to enforce unratified treaties, denying the Mandate possessed any 'retrospective effect'.[103] Judge Moore was in agreement, pointing to Article 36 of the Statute of the Court which limited its compulsory jurisdiction to matters specifically provided for 'in treaties and conventions *in force*'.[104] He was also particularly critical of the approach towards treaty interpretation by the majority, considering the French text to simply be a literal translation of the English text, 'intended to mean the same thing'.[105] However, he acknowledged the difference in opinion and that 'each clause should be interpreted in the sense which best reconciles the rights and

---

[95] Bentwich (n 6).
[96] ibid.
[97] *Mavrommatis* Series A No 2 (n 4) dissenting opinion by Judge Pessôa, 91.
[98] ibid.
[99] Uerpmann-Wittzack (n 18), 9.
[100] *Mavrommatis* Series A No 2 (n 4) dissenting opinion by Judge Finlay, 41.
[101] Bentwich (n 6) 456.
[102] ibid 457.
[103] *Mavrommatis* Series A No 2 (n 4) dissenting opinion by Judge Bustamante, 83.
[104] Judge Moore (n 93) 55.
[105] ibid, 69.

duties of the contracting Parties'.[106] More particularly, he proposed that in the case of a divergence of views on the meaning of a given term differently understood in the languages of the contracting parties, is to give preference to that country which is bound.[107]

Apart from the disagreement over whether jurisdictional conditions were satisfied, the majority and dissents in *Mavrommatis* disagreed sharply on the mandatory or consensual character of the PCIJ's jurisdiction: should a compromissory clause be dealt with simply on its terms, according to what states agreed; or 'put in the greater context of the Permanent Court as an institution and given a mainly analogical, and often extensive, interpretation in accordance with notions of what a court of justice ought to be'.[108] Judges Finlay and Moore, firm advocates of the consensual test for establishing jurisdiction in the earlier *Eastern Carelia*[109] opinion, reiterated their views in *Mavrommatis*. Indeed, Judge Moore professed to have been 'unable to grasp the majority view in a legal sense',[110] and drew attention to the fact that continental European judges seemed to favour compulsory jurisdiction, unlike judges from elsewhere.[111] Even the majority judges failed to offer a united front: while Judge Anzilotti subscribed to consensual jurisdiction, fellow majority judge, President Loder (Netherlands), issued the following warning to those who opposed compulsory jurisdiction:

> You are fighting against time; you will do so in vain ... We recognise no greatness which is raised above justice, even where it wears the mantle of sovereignty.[112]

B. Judgment No 5 (1925—Merits)

i. Nationality of Mavrommatis

Before it could establish whether any infringement of such concessions had taken place, the Court needed to rule on the validity or otherwise of the Mavrommatis concessions. The rights of non-Ottoman nationals who held concessions in Palestine were maintained, but not those of Ottoman nationals. One of the initial issues in determining the validity of the concessions was therefore whether Mavrommatis was a Greek or Ottoman national. To resolve this issue, the Court referred not only to Ottoman law but also to general principles of contract law.[113] Using such general principles, the Court dealt with the matter of Mavrommatis' nationality swiftly, finding any mistake concerned not his identity but merely his attributes. Nullity of

---

[106] ibid, 70.
[107] ibid. Judge Moore citing: A Rivier, *Principes du Droit des Gens* (1896) vol 2, 122; Bonfils, *Manuel de Droit International Public*, 7th edn (Paris, Fauchille, 1924) 571.
[108] Spiermann (n 59) 203.
[109] *Status of Eastern Carelia*, Advisory Opinion (23 July 1923) Series B, No 5.
[110] Spiermann (n 59).
[111] ibid.
[112] ibid 204. Spiermann cites BCJ Loder, *Speech Delivered by Dr BCJ Loder at the Baquest Given by the Anglo-Batavian Society* (The Hague, 1923) 19–22.
[113] *Mavrommatis* Series A, No 5 (n 4) 30.

the concessions was thus not a possibility, while annulment depended 'on the question whether Ottoman nationality was considered as a condition of the grant of the concessions'.[114] In doing so, the Court thereby rendered the nationality question irrelevant. Despite the Court's sole concern here being the validity of a concession under national law, this judgment has had some influence in the determination of a relevant error within the meaning of Article 48 of the Vienna Convention of the Law of Treaties (VCLT).[115]

ii. Expropriation of Mavrommatis' Concessions

Once the Court resolved the nationality matter, it considered whether Britain could expropriate Mavrommatis, whose prior concessions partially overlapped with those of Rutenberg in respect of electric power and tramways in Jerusalem. Unlike Article 311 of the Treaty of Sèvres which had preceded it,[116] Protocol XII to the Treaty of Lausanne maintained pre-existing concessions and gave no right to expropriate them.[117] Britain had conceded if Rutenberg's concession granted unconditionally an exclusive right to supply electric energy to Palestine, it would constitute an expropriation of Mavrommatis' concession,[118] but stressed that Rutenberg's concession does nothing of this kind.[119] In the UK's view, it was particularly telling that Mavrommatis himself did not appear to consider his concessions to be alive.[120]

However, the majority was of the view that Rutenberg's ability to request the expropriation of pre-existing concessions by the Palestine administration sufficed to constitute an interference with the rights of Mavrommatis in breach of Protocol XII.[121] This was true until, in May 1924, Rutenberg 'categorically declared'[122] that he was renouncing his right to request expropriation, leaving the Mavrommatis concessions free from potential interference. The UK addressed the Greek concerns as to Rutenberg's good faith in disclaiming his right to expropriate the concessions belonging to Mavrommatis, with Mr Hogg claiming the 'clear and unequivocal disclaimer'[123] was prompted directly by these Greek doubts.

---

[114] ibid.

[115] Uerpmann-Wittzack (n 18) [10]. An error of fact was only considered to justify annulment of a contract if the particular fact was deemed conditional for the conclusion of the contract. This idea is reflected in Art 48(1) VCLT, which states: 'A State may invoke an error in a treaty as invalidating its consent to be bound by the treaty if the error relates to a fact or situation which was assumed by that State to exist at the time when the treaty was concluded and formed an essential basis of its consent to be bound by the treaty'.

[116] On the interpretation of this provision in relation to a single concession dating back to the Ottoman period that the Government of Palestine decided to buy out, *Société du Chemin de Fer Ottoman de Jaffa à Jérusalem et Prolongements v His Britannic Majesty's Government*, Award, 4 October 1922, reproduced in Appendix I to S Rosenne, The Jaffa–Jerusalem Railway Arbitration (1992), 28 *Israel Yearbook on Human Rights*, 239–72.

[117] Borchard (n 64) 736.

[118] Hogg (n 38) 113.

[119] ibid.

[120] ibid, 124.

[121] *Mavrommatis* Series A, No 5 (n 4) 40.

[122] Borchard (n 64).

[123] Hogg (n 38) 188.

The UK reminded the Court that 'it is not really a question solely of Mr Rutenberg's intention; it is a question of the British Government's intentions',[124] which were firmly opposed to expropriation. This seemed to convince the Court, which found that, while there had previously been a clear breach of Protocol XII, this breach had occurred only between the years of 1921 and 1924, after which Rutenberg renounced the right to request expropriation.

It was therefore left for the Court to determine the extent of any compensation due to Mavrommatis during this time. Yet the Court found that Mavrommatis had suffered no loss.[125] Rather, the Court recognised that, while it had been a theoretical possibility during the time, expropriation itself had never taken place. Despite his financial difficulties, the Court found Mavrommatis had neither been inhibited in any efforts to execute his concessions, nor was he deprived of any tangible benefit attributable to the grant of concessions to Rutenberg. The Court emphasised that 'the sole subject of inquiry was the extent, if any, to which the grant of the Rutenberg concession had violated the international obligations of the Mandatory, and the losses, if any, that Mavrommatis thereby sustained'.[126] The Court agreed with British submissions that unconnected losses, or deteriorations in value attributable to the political instabilities of Palestine, fell outside the court's jurisdiction under Article 26.[127] With particular reference to Mavrommatis' accusation that the British government had caused the withdrawal of his financiers, the Court found wanting any evidence of any causal link between the two, opining instead that 'the withdrawal of his banking support was caused by many other factors, notably the uncertainty of the whole political situation due to the absence of treaty relations, and not merely by the grant of the Rutenberg concession'.[128]

Therefore, despite ruling in favour of Mavrommatis, the Permanent Court turned down his claim for compensation, and thus specifically awarded only declaratory rather than pecuniary relief, on the grounds that he had not suffered any monetary loss. Instead, the Court simply held:

> even if the clause in Article 29 of the conditions of M. Rutenberg's concession is to be regarded as contrary to the Mandatory's international obligations, in so far as it gave M. Rutenberg the right to require the expropriation of concessions conflicting with his own, this clause has not in fact either led to the expropriation or annulment of M. Mavrommatis' concessions, or caused him any loss which might justify a claim on his behalf for compensation in the present proceedings.[129]

iii. Protocol XII Treaty of Lausanne 1924

Although the majority decided that Mavrommatis, found to have suffered no loss, was unable to claim compensation, a larger majority considered that he was entitled

---

[124] ibid.
[125] *Mavrommatis* Series A, No 5 (n 4) 44.
[126] Borchard (n 64).
[127] Hogg (n 38) 100.
[128] Borchard (n 64) 736; Burgis (n 6) is highly critical of this aspect of the Court's decision, attributing Mavrommatis' struggles in implementing his concessions directly to the Mandate regime's actions, notably regarding 'the bank withdrawing its backing in the knowledge of British preferences for Rutenberg's concessions'.
[129] *Mavrommatis* Series A, No 5 (n 4) 45.

to re-adaptation of his concession in light of the new circumstances. This matter was decided not under the jurisdiction of the Court according to Article 26, but rather under a special informal agreement between the parties to decide upon which provisions of Protocol XII were applicable to the Mavrommatis concessions.[130]

The Court held that the international obligations accepted by the Mandatory under Article 11 of the Mandate incorporated by reference the provisions of Protocol XII of the Treaty of Lausanne, effective 6 August 1924. The fundamental principle of the Protocol was the maintenance of concession contracts concluded with the Ottoman Empire before 29 October 1914. The salient issue thus soon became whether Mavrommatis had begun to put his Jerusalem concessions into operation before this date, entitling him to claim the benefits of Article 4, which provided for the readaptation of concessions to conform with current economic conditions, or whether he would instead have to rely upon Article 6, which carved out an exception for concessions yet to commence.[131]

For the Court, much turned on the choice between the English and French versions of the text, and particularly with the weight accorded to the Protocol's drafting history of the latter, which included a notable linguistic change from *commencement d'éxecution* to *commencement d'application*.[132] Ultimately, the Court decided that this change was significant, and thus that putting a contract into operation included not only the execution of the contract but additionally any preliminary efforts in advance of the execution, namely the submission of surveys and designs of the works to be carried out, as Mavrommatis had done in 1914. Consequently, the Court found that Article 4 applied, which meant that Great Britain, though not liable for compensation, was obliged readapt Mavrommatis's concession to the new economic conditions.[133]

C. Judgment No 10 (1927—Readaptation)

In the wake of the 1925 judgment, which held the Rutenberg concession of 1921 to contradict British obligations as Mandatory for Palestine according to Protocol XII of the Treaty of Lausanne in conjunction with Article 11, negotiations took place to readapt and ultimately replace the 1914 concession contracts. Greece and the UK appointed experts and gave them the task of readapting the concessions for the supply of water and electricity to Jerusalem, which concluded on 25 February 1926. The new concessions contained provisions requiring that 'the Concessionaire [absolutely and] irrevocably surrendered all the rights and benefits under the Ottoman Agreements of 1914'.[134]

The High Commissioner for Palestine also conditioned the new concessions upon the concessionaire forming requisite companies within a specified timeframe, securing sufficient capital, and submitting plans for approval within three months.

---

[130] ibid, 27.
[131] Borchard (n 64) 733.
[132] *Mavrommatis* Series A, No 5 (n 4) 50.
[133] A Kuhn, 'The Mavrommatis Case on Readaptation of the Jerusalem Concessions' (1928) 22 *AJIL* 383.
[134] Bentwich (n 6) 459.

Initial efforts of Mavrommatis to wholly assign his concessionary rights to a trustee failed, having been prohibited by the terms of the contract. Subsequently, in May 1926, he submitted plans on his own behalf, the approval of which, in respect of the water concession, was not forthcoming until December 1926, considerably later than within the three months stipulated. Shortly prior to receiving such approval, Mavrommatis made apparent that 'he demurred to the refusal of the British Government to accept the deposit of the plans made by the trustee, and demanded damages for the failure to approve the plans within the time fixed in the contract itself'.[135] Such delay was purportedly attributable to opposition from Rutenberg, during which time the Rutenberg concessions were formally granted by Great Britain.

Outraged that the UK delayed the granting of these concessions, Mavrommatis turned once more to the Greek government to institute proceedings before the PCIJ on his behalf. On 28 May 1927, Greece obliged. The claim was that the British Government had breached its international obligations in granting Rutenberg's hydro-electric concession in March 1926, in light of the conflict with Mavrommatis' concession which was 'protected by international treaty'.[136] Given the hostilities Mavrommatis faced, Greece submitted, 'it was rendered materially and morally impossible for M. Mavrommatis to obtain the financing of his concessions'[137] which caused him to suffer damages.

The Court concurred with the UK, confirming that 'only where an alleged breach of the Protocol of Lausanne is the outcome of the exercise of the full power to provide for public control given by Article 11 of the Mandate that it has jurisdiction to deal with the breach',[138] thereby dismissing the Greek claims to the effect that any act whatsoever performed by the authorities concerning the grant of a public utility concession could be deemed sufficiently public.

In short, the Court determined that 'the question of readaptation fell outside the scope ... of the compromissory clause [contained in Article 26] as it had been construed in 1924'.[139] The clause thus 'did not vest the Permanent Court with jurisdiction to decide the whole dispute as defined by the applicant'.[140] Jurisdiction was held not to follow inexorably from earlier judgments No 2 and No 5.[141] Here, unlike in 1924, the Court therefore concurred with the British submissions and adopted a more conservative outlook to its jurisdictional reach, interpreting Article 26 narrowly, and ultimately declining jurisdiction. The Court's reticence is likely to have been prompted by the critical backlash that ensued its 1924 judgment. Indeed, Judge Moore considered earlier dissents to have been 'far more instructive than the principal opinion'.[142] The Court made clear that its previous decisions allowed jurisdiction only if 'the facts alleged by the Greek Government in support of its claim

---

135 ibid.
136 ibid.
137 *Mavrommatis* Series A, No 11, 6.
138 Bentwich (n 6) 461.
139 Spiermann, (n 59) 215.
140 ibid.
141 *Mavrommatis* No 11 (n 137) 14.
142 Spiermann (n 59) 225, citing Judge Moore to Hudson, 14 January 1934, Moore papers 1278 and Hudson papers 134A.1.

constitute an exercise of the full power to provide for public control under Article 11 of the Mandate'.[143] Ultimately, the Court held that it did not.

i. Dissenting Opinions

Dissents came from Judge Nyholm, Judge Altamira and, unsurprisingly, the Greek national judge, Judge Caloyanni. Those in the minority certainly favoured 'a more expansive reading of the nature of "public control" as well as the "public" role of the Jewish Agency in the development of the Mandate',[144] thereby advocating a more liberal approach to the jurisdiction of the Permanent Court. Each of these dissents is arguably premised upon the maxim *boni iudicis est ampliare iurisdictionem*, which in the past has tended to be confined to national courts.[145] Spiermann has questioned whether the majority judges may have been 'discouraged from such analogical interpretation by the meagre outcome of the previous proceedings in the judgment on the merits in 1925'.[146] This certainly could have been a factor.

Judge Caloyanni 'cautioned against relying on traditional notions of "public authority", arguing instead for flexibility in light of the *sui generis* nature of the Mandate system'.[147] In his view, the 'special *international* character of the Mandates'[148] compelled the Court to interpret its jurisdiction generally to ensure 'a degree of conformity in the exercise of the total power granted to the Mandatories'.[149] In addition, his suggestion that international obligations should require the Mandatory to 'determine its negative as well as its positive conduct so as not to infringe or impair any rights',[150] implied that any act or omission could constitute an exercise of public control under Article 11.[151] Similarly, Judge Altamira spoke of 'juridical common sense',[152] disagreeing with the narrow definition of public control adopted by the majority. He preferred to 'extend the jurisdiction of the Court by the argument that any series of acts by the Administration of Palestine which tended to set aside or to hamper certain Concessions in order to give free play to a certain economic policy of the Mandate'[153] sufficed as an exercise of public control.

The dissent of Judge Nyholm, admirably fervent in his belief that jurisdiction of the Court should be 'general, subject to specific exceptions',[154] in contrast with the majority who regarded the Court's jurisdiction as itself an exception, is particularly striking for its discussion of the implications of the majority approach. Expressing some concern, Judge Nyholm made the astute observation that the upshot of the Court's decision was, 'by the choice of his *own line of action*,

---

[143] British Mandate for Palestine (n 31) Art 11.
[144] Burgis (n 6) 895.
[145] Bentwich (n 6) 461.
[146] Spiermann (n 59) 225.
[147] Burgis (n 6).
[148] ibid.
[149] ibid.
[150] Bentwich (n 6) 462.
[151] ibid.
[152] *Mavrommatis* No 11 (n 137) dissenting opinion by Judge Altamira, 44.
[153] Bentwich (n 6).
[154] ibid.

a Mandatory may abolish the jurisdiction of the Court',[155] which he criticised as 'an inadmissible proposition'.[156] At heart, the Court's 'refusal to take jurisdiction seems to have rendered futile the carefully considered judgments rendered on the previous submissions'.[157] The breach in issue, alleged by the Greek government, was the UK's failure to comply with the re-adaptation ordered by the 1925 judgment of the Court. In 1924, the Court had found that it had jurisdiction to entertain the Mavrommatis dispute. In 1925, it determined that Great Britain was in violation of its international obligations regarding concessions belonging to Mavrommatis, who was entitled to re-adaptation provided he absolutely and irrevocably surrendered all rights to his former concessions. Mavrommatis obliged. Kuhn remarked, '*[a]nd yet* the mandatory, by failing to take the necessary steps to make the new concession definite, could annul both the old and the new concession without right of redress through the Permanent Court'.[158] Perhaps disappointingly, this appears to accurately portray the connotations of the decision of the Court in this third and final Mavrommatis judgment. Bentwich certainly believed this to be the case, suggesting the International Court will only be able to intervene exceptionally, namely, when a government act affects a concession in such a way as to violate 'some specific provision in an international agreement, to which the Mandatory is a party'.[159]

Unlike Kuhn, Bentwich believed this to be a fortunate outcome, warning of 'grave embarrassment if the opinion of the minority of the judges in the third case had prevailed, and any dispute between a pre-war Concessionaire and a Mandatory Government arising out of any action of that Government with regard to the natural resources or public utilities could form the subject of a suit in the International Court'.[160] He criticised the three dissenting judges for failing to address the British submission to the effect that jurisdiction should not be taken by the International Court 'where the complainant has a claim which can be pursued in the Municipal Courts'.[161] To demonstrate the severity of the consequences should the Court have found jurisdiction in this case, Bentwich relied upon words of the Attorney-General, who had spoken on behalf of Britain in *Mavrommatis*, and cautioned as to the long-term implications of deciding in favour of the Greek government for the existence and vitality of the Permanent Court itself:

> Nothing can be better calculated to render nations unwilling to enter into agreements submitting their cases to the decision of the Court than a consciousness that those agreements are likely to be construed in such a way as to embrace questions which were never intended when the agreement was signed. Few things can be worse for the dignity of the Court than that it should find itself involved in trying a multitude of causes which are, in effect, claims by private persons such as are dealt with in the ordinary municipal courts, but which are diverted to this tribunal because it happens that the respondent is a sovereign State and the claimant is a subject of some other Power.[162]

---

[155] *Mavrommatis* No 11 (n 137) dissenting opinion by Judge Nyholm, 31.
[156] ibid.
[157] Kuhn (n 32) 385.
[158] ibid.
[159] Bentwich (n 6) 462.
[160] ibid 463.
[161] ibid 462.
[162] Speech by Sir D Hogg, Counsel for Britain, Part II, Speeches Made in Court, Series C No 13, September 1927, 20.

This prediction, accurate or otherwise, clearly had much weight with the majority judges in the final *Mavrommatis* judgment and goes a considerable way to explaining the stark change in approach between 1924 and 1927. Spiermann broadly concurred with this statement, and asked whether the reluctance of the majority to bestow an effective interpretation upon a special agreement with limited scope in upholding jurisdiction might, borrowing words from *Chorzow Factory*, 'instead of settling a dispute once and for all, would leave open the possibility of further disputes'.[163]

V. THE LEGACY OF *MAVROMMATIS*

The *Mavrommatis* judgment is often used simply as authority for the right of states to exercise diplomatic protection. However, its significance runs deeper. It also led the Court to formulate three influential formulas in international dispute settlement generally concerning the character of diplomatic protection, flexibility in procedural matters and temporal jurisdiction and temporal reservations. For these reasons, the *Mavrommatis* case deserves the designation as a landmark.

A. Diplomatic Protection

Although disputed in 1924, the Court's concept of diplomatic protection has achieved both fame and notoriety, making the first *Mavrommatis* judgment by far the most significant. The ICJ approved the institution in the seminal cases of *Nottebohm*[164] and *Barcelona Traction*,[165] and referred to it as the 'cornerstone of diplomatic protection'.[166]

The first limb of the 'famous formula'[167] has been uncontroversial. Diplomatic protection has long been understood as a discretionary right belonging to the state whose national has been injured by another state's internationally wrongful act.[168] It is the second limb, namely, the notion that the state invokes its *own* right, which has provoked debate. In *Nottebohm*, embracing this fiction, the ICJ held accordingly: 'diplomatic protection and protection by means of international judicial proceedings constitute measures for the defence of the rights of the State'.[169]

In the 2000s, the International Law Commission (ILC) distanced itself somewhat from this so-called *Mavrommatis* fiction,[170] albeit while trying to preserve the essence

---

[163] *Case Concerning the Factory at Chorzów* (Claim for Indemnity) (Jurisdiction), Series A, No 9 (1927), 25.

[164] *Nottebohm Case (Liechtenstein v Guatemala) Second Phase* [1955] ICJ Rep 4.

[165] *Case Concerning The Barcelona Traction, Light and Power Company, Limited (New Application: 1962) (Belgium v Spain) Second Phase* [1970] ICJ Rep 3.

[166] Preliminary Report on Diplomatic Protection, International Law Commission, 50th session (1998), A/CN.4/484, 27, [1]) of the commentary on Article 2.

[167] Uerpmann-Wittzack (n 18) [14].

[168] A Pellet, 'The Second Death of Euripides Mavrommatis' (2008) 7 *LPICT* 33–38, at 35; United Nations, Draft Articles on Diplomatic Protection (2006), Art; 2.

[169] *Nottebohm* (n 164) 24.

[170] United Nations, Draft Articles on Diplomatic Protection with Commentaries (2006), Art; 4.

of diplomatic protection as established by the Permanent Court in *Mavrommatis*. The ILC hoped to 'open the door to fundamental evolution in order to put the revered institution that they claim to codify in step with international law in the 21st century'.[171]

Special Rapporteur Dugard was alert to the limited role for individuals on the international law plane, recognising that '[t]he individual may have rights under international law but remedies are few'.[172] This is evident from several international and national decisions.[173] The mechanism of diplomatic protection therefore remains an essential way for individuals to vindicate their international rights, a consideration which has been instrumental in the ILC's decision to retain the *Mavrommatis* fiction to some extent. The ILC did phrase Draft Article 1 so as to define diplomatic protection without direct reference to the *Mavrommatis* fiction. However, it was careful not to imply that the Permanent Court had wrongly decided *Mavrommatis* at the time. Rather, the ILC underlined the developments in international law since *Mavrommatis*.

After the First World War, the Court shifted in favour of states protecting the rights of individuals not through any theory of diplomatic protection, but rather 'as a distinct act of representation'.[174] Most candid in this recognition was the Arbitral Tribunal in the *Junghans* case between Germany and Romania, which held:

> The injured individual addressed his government. If the latter accepted to defend his claim, it was the State that became claimant, appearing before the arbitral tribunal *as the legal representative of its national*. Thus, the German Government appeared on behalf of the Junghans heirs *whose rights determined the extent of the claim it was bringing*.[175]

In more recent cases concerning state responsibility, the Court has acknowledged this notion that a state may appear 'for the protection of its own rights as well as for the protection of its nationals'.[176] For instance, in 1993, in *Bosnian Genocide*, the Court determined 'Bosnia and Herzegovina was entitled to receive, in its own right and as *parens patriae* for its citizens, full compensation for the damages and losses caused'.[177] Similarly, in 2005, in *Armed Activities*, it held that acts had caused injury 'to the DRC *and* to persons in its territory'.[178] It follows from this suggestion that the state has its own claim as well as a claim on behalf of its national. This change evidenced in the case law of the International Court was coupled with indications that the ILC had begun to embrace the theory of 'two rights'.[179]

---

[171] Pellet 'The Second Death of Euripides Mavrommatis' (n 168) 34.

[172] Commentary to Draft Article 1 (n 170) 26.

[173] A Vermeer-Künzli, 'As If: The Legal Fiction in Diplomatic Protection' (2007) 18 *EJIL* 37, 67. See, for example, *Jones v Ministry of Interior Al-Mamlaka Al-Arabiya AS Saudiya: Mitchell v Al-Dali and the Kingdom of Saudi Arabia* [2006] UKHL 26, where Lord Hoffman upheld state immunity in the face of serious allegations of torture.

[174] Pellet (n 168) 48.

[175] ibid 47, citing Arbitral Award of 21–29 October 1940, *second part*, 3 RIAA, 1888.

[176] ibid, 50.

[177] *The Application of the Convention on the Prevention and Punishment of the Crime of Genocide (Bosnia and Herzegovina v Serbia and Montenegro)* CR 2006/37, 24 April 2006, 60.

[178] *Armed Activities on the Territory of the Congo (Democratic Republic of the Congo v Uganda)* [2005] ICJ Rep 257, [259] (emphasis added).

[179] Pellet (n 168) 52.

Dugard pointed to human rights treaties, which 'offer foreigners only limited means to enforce the rights they are considered to have on the international plane',[180] as one reason for retaining the *Mavrommatis* fiction:

> as long as the State remains the dominant actor in international relations, the espousal of claims by States for the violation of the rights of their nationals remains the most effective remedy for the promotion of human rights. Instead of seeking to weaken this remedy by dismissing it as an obsolete fiction that has outlived its usefulness, every effort should be made to strengthen resort to diplomatic protection.[181]

Whether we view investment treaties as analogous to human rights treaties or rather to the more traditional treaties creating benefits for states only has important implications, and is not merely a theoretical debate. If the right belongs to the individual, the state's right must be purely residual, and thus may only be exercised in the absence of a remedy brought by the individual. Conversely, if the holder of the right is the state itself, as the *Mavrommatis* formula dictates, the failure of the individual to exhaust local remedies will have no impact on the ability of the state to bring its own claim.

According to the traditional *Mavrommatis* principle, whereby the right of diplomatic protection belongs to the home state, the national should not be able to prejudice its state's right to bring a claim. This means an individual is unable to waive the right as it is held by the state, and therefore removed entirely from the disposition of the individual. In the investment context, for example, if an investor contracted with the host state to waive its ability to seek diplomatic protection, the investor might be prevented from requesting diplomatic protection, but it could not prevent the home state from providing diplomatic protection. The home state could also bring and settle claims, even on unfavourable terms, without the consent, acquiescence or even knowledge of the investor. However, in *Mavrommatis* itself, the home state's ability to bring a diplomatic protection claim depended on the nature and actions of its national.[182] The state had to prove nationality both at the time of injury and when bringing the claim and demonstrate that the national had exhausted local remedies.

The *Mavrommatis* fiction has therefore arguably remained, despite some fierce criticism, to best serve the interests of the individual in international law. Without it, they would likely be worse off.

B. Jurisdiction of the International Court

Although *Mavrommatis* concerned the interpretation of a single provision, Article 11 of the British Mandate for Palestine, it provides some insight into the scope of the PCIJ's jurisdiction regarding mandates in general and more broadly, the character of the Court's jurisdiction.[183]

---

[180] ibid, 43.
[181] ibid.
[182] A Robert, 'State-to-State Investment Treaty Arbitration: A Hybrid Theory of Interdependent Rights and Shared Interpretive Authority' 2014 *Harvard International Law Journal*, 55.
[183] 4 ILR 50, in the Note, 52.

First, the ICJ consistently relies on the Permanent Court's definition of a 'dispute' given in *Mavrommatis*,[184] namely, that a dispute exists in the event of a 'disagreement on a point of law or fact, a conflict of legal views or of interests between two persons'.[185] Subsequent ICJ cases have echoed this approach.[186] In *South West Africa*,[187] South Africa objected that the conflict or disagreement alleged by Ethiopia or Liberia was not a dispute in terms of Article 7 of the Mandate for South West Africa, as it did not involve or affect any material interest of those states. There the Court held that the requirement of a dispute was satisfied where parties disagreed over points of law.

Second, the Court's treatment of Protocol XII as *lex specialis*. As we have seen, the Protocol appeared to satisfy all the conditions for overriding similar clauses in the British Mandate over Palestine: as an independent and distinct international instrument, it dealt 'specifically with the kind of concessions such as those of M. Mavrommatis',[188] unlike Article 11 of the Mandate, which did so only by implication. The Court dismissed that the Protocol would only apply insofar as it was compatible with the Mandate, emphasising that the Protocol as a special and more recent agreement prevailed.[189] Conversely, the provisions of the Mandate were held to be applicable 'in so far as they were compatible with the Protocol'.[190] Certain provisions of the Protocol clearly affected the jurisdiction of the Court, albeit without proving technically incompatible with Article 11 of the Mandate.

Third, the temporal scope of the Court's jurisdiction. In *Mavrommatis*, Great Britain objected to the PCIJ's jurisdiction on temporal grounds. It alleged that the acts forming the basis of the claim took place before the entry into force of Protocol XII to the Treaty of Lausanne.[191] The Court dismissed the objection, considering the Protocol to encompass all disputes whenever they arose, on the grounds that '[t]he reservations made in many arbitration treaties regarding disputes arising out of events previous to the conclusion of the treaty seems to prove the necessity for an explicit limitation of jurisdiction'.[192]

The Permanent Court also referred to an important systemic consideration of the treaty's effectiveness, noting that '[a]n essential characteristic therefore of Protocol XII is that its effects extend to legal situations dating from a time previous to its own existence'.[193] If that were not the case, the Court warned, the Protocol would be

---

[184] See, for instance, *Application of the International Convention on the Elimination of all Forms of Racial Discrimination (Georgia v Russian Federation) (Preliminary Objections)* [2011] ICJ Rep [30].

[185] *Mavrommatis* Series A, No 2 (n 4) 11.

[186] See for example: *Case Concerning United States Diplomatic and Consular Staff in Tehran (United States of America v Iran) (Merits)* [1980] ICJ Rep 3; *Case Concerning the Northern Cameroons (Cameroon v United Kingdom) (Preliminary Objections)* [1963] ICJ Rep 27.

[187] *South-West Africa Cases (Ethiopia v South Africa; Liberia v South Africa) (Preliminary Objections)* Judgment of 21 December 1962, [1962] ICJ Rep 327.

[188] ibid, 30.

[189] ibid, 31.

[190] ibid.

[191] *Mavrommatis* Series A, No 2 (n 4) 35; *cf* also *Phosphates in Morocco (Italy v France)* (14 June 1938), Series A/B, no 74, 24.

[192] ibid, 35.

[193] ibid, 34.

ineffective as regards the very period at which the rights in question are most in need of protection.[194]

This *Mavrommatis* principle means that a jurisdictional provision referring simply to 'disputes' applies to existing as well as new disputes, except where the jurisdictional clause is tied to the substantive operation of a treaty.[195] In the absence of temporal reservations, the only other limitation on temporal jurisdiction is the entry into force of the substantive obligation on which the claim is based.[196]

In 2008, the ICJ applied this *Mavrommatis* principle in the *Croatia Genocide* case.[197] Yugoslavia relied on the principle of non-retroactivity and submitted that the ICJ lacked jurisdiction to give effect to the Convention on the Prevention and Punishment of the Crime of Genocide with respect to acts which had occurred prior to the Genocide Convention entering into force between the parties. It submitted

> according to the rule of customary international law, the 1948 Convention on the Prevention and Punishment of the Crime of Genocide would not be operative between the parties prior to 29 December 1992 and, accordingly, this would not confer jurisdiction on the Court in respect of events occurring prior to 29 December 1992.[198]

In its famous paragraph 34, the Court said the following about its temporal jurisdiction:

> Yugoslavia, basing its contention on the principle of the non retroactivity of legal acts, has ... asserted ... that, even though the Court might have jurisdiction on the basis of the [Genocide] Convention, it could only deal with events subsequent to the different dates on which the Convention might have become applicable as between the Parties. In this regard, the Court will confine itself to the observation that the Genocide Convention—and in particular Article IX—does not contain any clause the object or effect of which is to limit in such manner the scope of its jurisdiction *ratione temporis*, and nor did the Parties themselves make any reservation to that end, either to the Convention or on [a later possible opportunity]. The Court thus finds that it has jurisdiction in this case to give effect to the Genocide Convention with regard to the relevant facts which have occurred since the beginning of the conflict which took place in Bosnia and Herzegovina.[199]

Originally conceived to overcome a procedural default in a proceeding before the PCIJ, the Court invoked but misapplied this *Mavrommatis* principle in *Croatia Genocide*.[200] The Federal Republic of Yugoslavia (FRY), then Serbia and Montenegro, did not become a Member of the United Nations until 2000 thus could not have

---

[194] ibid.

[195] See *Mondev International Ltd v United States of America* ICSID Case No ARB(AF)/99/2.

[196] *cf* Article 13 of the ILC Articles on Responsibility of States for Internationally Wrongful Acts (ARSIWA): 'An act of a State does not constitute a breach of an international obligation unless the State is bound by the obligation in question at the time the act occurs'.

[197] *Case Concerning Application of the Convention on the Prevention and Punishment of the Crime of Genocide* (Preliminary Objections) [1996] ICJ Rep. *cf* also E Bjorge, *The Evolutionary Interpretation of Treaties* (Oxford, OUP, 2014) 177; A Chua and R Hardcastle, 'Retroactive Application of Treaties Revisited: Bosnia-Herzegovina v Yugoslavia' (1997) 44 *NILR* 414.

[198] ibid, [15].

[199] ibid [34];

[200] *Case Concerning Application of the Convention on the Prevention and Punishment on the Crime of Genocide*, 3 February 2015, separate opinion, Judge Abraham, 540.

been a state-party in 1999. At the time of the ICJ's ruling, Croatia would have been unable to bring a claim against then Serbia based on the Genocide Convention given the latter's reservation to jurisdiction in this respect. Nonetheless, the Court assumed that Croatia could have validly resubmitted the case and, out of judicial economy considerations, the Court seemed to suggest that it might have jurisdiction over events prior to 27 April 1992 (but joining the determination of its jurisdiction in respect of these acts to the merits).

In its judgment on the merits, the Court adopted a more nuanced approach as regards the application of the *Mavrommatis* principle.[201] It explained that 'the absence of a temporal limitation in Article IX is not without significance but it is not, in itself, sufficient to establish jurisdiction over that part of Croatia's claim which relates to events said to have occurred before 27 April 1992'.[202] It underscored that the 'temporal scope of Article IX is necessarily linked to the temporal scope of the other provisions of the Genocide Convention'.[203] This position leaves the *Mavrommatis* principle intact, as the other limitation on temporal jurisdiction applies, namely the entry into force of the substantive obligation at issue.

C. State Succession

The *Mavrommatis* judgments have also been used in support of a rule that concessions granted by the predecessor state bind the successor state.[204] As we have seen, the dispute brought the law of state succession as it applied to state contracts to the fore. The tension between major changes in status linked to the passing of territorial sovereignty due to armed conflict and pre-existing economic agreements with private actors was at the core of the *Mavrommatis* dispute.[205]

In an earlier decision, in *German Settlers in Poland*, the Court had determined that 'private rights acquired under existing law do not cease on a change of sovereignty'.[206] Indeed, it had gone so far as to suggest that '[e]ven those who contest the existence in international law of a general principle of State succession do not go so far as to maintain that private rights including those acquired from the State as the owner of the property are invalid as against a successor in sovereignty'.[207] The first *Mavrommatis* judgment presented the Court with an occasion to develop the law on matters of State succession, having been asked to determine its jurisdiction

---

[201] *Application of the Convention on the Prevention and Punishment of the Crime of Genocide (Croatia v Serbia)*, judgment, 3 February 2015.

[202] ibid, [93].

[203] ibid.

[204] Uerpmann-Wittzack (n 18) [14].

[205] *cf* also an important arbitral award on state succession with respect to the Ottoman debt a year after the first *Mavrommatis* judgment, *Affaire de la Dette publique ottomane* (Bulgarie, Irak, Palestine, Transjordanie, Grèce, Italie et Turquie), Award, 18 April 1925. Questions of state succession increasingly arise also with respect to contemporary investment treaties. For an overview, see CJ Tams 'State Succession to Investment Treaties: Mapping the Issues' 31 *ICSID Review* 2, 314–43.

[206] *German Settlers in Poland* Series B, No 6 (1923) 36.

[207] ibid.

in respect of Mavrommatis' concessions for Jerusalem and Jaffa. The Greek Government contended that, according to the Treaty of Lausanne, Great Britain, on becoming the mandatory power for Palestine, 'assumed all of Turkey's obligations, including the electricity franchise granted to Mavrommatis'.[208] The UK disagreed, contending that the dissolution of the Ottoman Empire by the end of the First World War rendered void Mavrommatis' claims. The essence of this British submission is that such a fundamental change of circumstances, the regime change, frustrated the earlier contracts between Mavrommatis and the Ottoman authorities. If correct, later concessions granted to Rutenberg could not breach Mavrommatis' rights, since they would be deemed invalid.

The Court declined the opportunity to engage in these matters of state succession.[209] Instead, it opted to decide the matter according to the specific applicable provisions of Protocol XII, according to which it had no jurisdiction regarding the Jaffa concessions. However, the Court in *Mavrommatis* did recognise that Great Britain, succeeding Ottoman rule of Palestine, was bound to recognise certain concessionary rights that Turkey had granted under 'the general principle of subrogation'.[210] It found the Administration of Palestine was bound to recognise the Jaffa concessions based on a general principle of international law[211] which admitted no exception.

[208] Naor (n 21).
[209] Borchard (n 64) 738, lamented the Mavrommatis case as a missed opportunity for the PCIJ to contribute to the law of state succession.
[210] *Mavrommatis* Series A, No 2 (n 4) 28.
[211] ibid.

4

Factory at Chorzów (Germany v Poland) (1927–28)

CHESTER BROWN

I. INTRODUCTION

THIS VOLUME COLLECTS commentaries on 'landmark' cases in public international law, and it would not be complete without a chapter on the *Factory at Chorzów* case. For, like other contributions included in this volume, the *Factory at Chorzów* case must be among the most frequently cited judgments to have emanated from an international court or tribunal.[1] It is primarily significant for the contribution it makes to the rules of international law on issues of state responsibility, the law of reparation, and the assessment of damages, but it also deals with issues which are of contemporary concern, such as the effect of multiple or parallel proceedings, the inherent powers of international courts and tribunals concerning the consequences of an internationally wrongful act, the so-called doctrine of 'clean hands', and allegations of abusive corporate manoeuvres. It has therefore proved to be one of the more enduring international decisions and is deserving of its place in this volume.

The case concerned a claim by Germany against Poland which was brought in relation to Poland's alleged breach of its international obligations under Article 6 of the Geneva Convention of 15 May 1922,[2] and the amount of reparation that Poland owed in respect of its conduct towards two German companies—namely, the 'Oberschlesische Stickstoffwerke AG' ('the Oberschlesische') and the 'Bayerische Stickstoffwerke AG' ('the Bayrische')—at the time it took possession of the 'nitrate

---

[1] eg, in J Crawford (ed), *Brownlie's Principles of Public International Law*, 8th edn (Oxford, OUP, 2012), it is cited eight times; in D Harris and S Sivakumaran, *Cases and Materials on International Law*, 8th edn (London, Sweet & Maxwell, 2015), it is cited 15 times; in M Shaw, *International Law*, 7th edn (Cambridge, CUP, 2014), it is cited eight times; in A Zimmerman, C Tomuschat, K Oellers-Frahm and C Tams (eds), *The* Statute *of the International Court of Justice: A Commentary*, 2nd edn (Oxford, OUP, 2012), it is cited 34 times; and in G Triggs, *International Law: Contemporary Principles and Practices*, 2nd edn (London, Butterworths, 2011) it is cited nine times.

[2] Convention concerning Upper Silesia concluded at Geneva on 15 May 1922 (Germany–Poland), reproduced in Martens, *Nouveau Receuil Général des Traités*, 3rd ser, vol 16, 645 ('the Geneva Convention').

factory situated at Chorzów'.[3] The *Factory at Chorzów* case was, thus, an apparently straightforward diplomatic protection claim, albeit one in which the Permanent Court of International Justice (PCIJ or 'the Court') restated the applicable international law principles concerning the obligation on states to make reparation for an internationally wrongful act.

For a comprehensive understanding of the issues in the *Factory at Chorzów* case, it is necessary to be familiar with a number of different decisions of the Court. Indeed, the *Factory at Chorzów* litigation might also be remembered as the international proceedings which invoke thoughts of *Jarndyce v Jardyce*, the apparently endless litigation concerning a contested will before the English Courts of Chancery in Dickens's *Bleak House*.[4] The relevant decisions include both of the Court's judgments in the *Certain German Interests in Polish Upper Silesia* case (in which the underlying facts of the case are set out),[5] as well as, of course, the *Factory at Chorzów* case itself.[6] In *Certain German Interests in Polish Upper Silesia (Merits)*, the Court had declared that Poland's conduct was a breach of its obligations under Article 6 (and the following provisions) of the Geneva Convention.[7] Then on 18 October 1927, Germany sought an interpretation of the two judgments that had been issued in the *Case Concerning German Interests in Polish Upper Silesia*.[8] In its judgment of 16 December 1927, in the case titled *Interpretation of Judgment Nos 7 and 8 (The Chorzów Factory)*, the Court held that it had recognised, 'with binding effect between the Parties concerned ... amongst other things, the right of ownership of the [Oberschlesische] in the Chorzów factory under municipal law'.[9]

In the next instalment, the *Factory at Chorzów (Jurisdiction)* case, the Court enunciated what is, as James Crawford has termed it, the 'classic general statement

---

[3] *Factory at Chorzów (Merits) (Germany v Poland)*, Series A (No 17) 5 (Judgment of 13 September 1928).

[4] C Dickens, *Bleak House* (1853). The fictitious *Jarndyce v Jarndyce* litigation, which forms a central theme of Dickens's novel, involved an interminable challenge to an inheritance which played out before the English Courts of Chancery.

[5] *Certain German Interests in Polish Upper Silesia (Preliminary Objections) (Germany v Poland)*, Series A (No 6) (Judgment of 25 August 1925); *Certain German Interests in Polish Upper Silesia (Merits) (Germany v Poland)*, Series A (No 7) (Judgment of 25 May 1926). For discussion, see, eg, JHW Verzijl, *The Jurisprudence of the World Court* (Sijthoff, 1965), vol I, 145–63; A Fachiri, *The Permanent Court of International Justice: Its Constitution, Procedure and Work* (Oxford, OUP, 1932) 221–28, 234–42; M Hudson, *The World Court* (World Peace Foundation 1931) 31–35; and O Spiermann, *International Legal Argument in the Permanent Court of International Justice* (Cambridge, CUP, 2005) 215–24. This case also deals with a range of other claims brought by Germany against Poland, notably concerning Poland's liquidation of certain rural estates belonging to German private interests (see eg *Certain German Interests in Polish Upper Silesia (Preliminary Objections) (Germany v Poland)*, Series A (No 6), 6, 10–11, 22–27). This aspect of the *Certain German Interests in Polish Upper Silesia* case is not addressed in this chapter.

[6] *Factory at Chorzów (Jurisdiction) (Germany v Poland)*, Series A (No 9) (Judgment of 26 July 1927); *Factory at Chorzów (Interim Measures of Protection) (Germany v Poland)*, Series A (No 12) (Order of 21 November 1927); and *Factory at Chorzów (Merits) (Germany v Poland)*, Series A (No 17) (Judgment of 13 September 1928). For discussion, see eg Verzijl *Jurisprudence* (n 5) vol I, 163–76; Fachiri *Permanent Court* (n 5) 246–50, 263–64, 271–74, 283–88; Hudson *The World Court* (n 5) 52–55.

[7] *Certain German Interests in Polish Upper Silesia (Merits)* (n 5).

[8] *Interpretation of Judgments Nos 7 and 8 (The Chorzów Factory) (Germany v Poland)*, Series A (No 13) (Judgment of 16 December 1927).

[9] ibid, 22.

of the consequences of an internationally wrongful act',[10] as follows: '[i]t is a principle of international law that the breach of an engagement involves an obligation
to make reparation in an adequate form'.[11] After the Court disposed of a request
by Germany for interim measures of protection,[12] the proceedings culminated in the
celebrated *Factory at Chorzów (Merits)* judgment of 13 September 1928, in which
the Court issued its oft-cited dictum that:

> The essential principle contained in the actual notion of an illegal act—a principle which
> seems to be established by international practice and in particular by the decisions of arbi-
> tral tribunals—is that reparation must, as far as possible, wipe out all the consequences of
> the illegal act and reestablish the situation which would, in all probability, have existed if
> that act had not been committed. Restitution in kind, or, if this is not possible, payment of
> a sum corresponding to the value which a restitution in kind would bear; the award, if need
> be, of damages for loss sustained which would not be covered by restitution in kind or pay-
> ment in place of it—such are the principles which should serve to determine the amount of
> compensation due for an act contrary to international law.[13]

As is well known, this passage of the Court's judgment forms the basis of Article 31
of the Articles on State Responsibility of the International Law Commission (ILC),
which provides in part that: 'The responsible State is under an obligation to make
full reparation for the injury caused by the internationally wrongful act'.[14] In its
commentary, the ILC explained that:

> The obligation placed on the responsible State by article 31 is to make 'full reparation' in
> the *Factory at Chorzów* sense. In other words, the responsible State must endeavour to
> 'wipe out all the consequences of the illegal act and reestablish the situation which would,
> in all probability, have existed if that act had not been committed' through the provision of
> one or more of the forms of reparation set out in chapter II of this part.[15]

And as James Crawford has explained, the Court's definition of the obligation to
make full reparation 'has been reaffirmed on numerous occasions, by the International Court, investment tribunals, international human rights courts and committees, and other bodies'.[16]

It is perhaps ironic that despite the authoritative guidance offered by the Court
on the content of the obligation to make full reparation, the Court never issued a
judgment which implemented it. For on 6 December 1928—less than three months
after the Court had delivered its judgment on the merits—Germany notified the
Court that 'the Parties had concluded an agreement regarding the settlement

---

[10] J Crawford, *State Responsibility: The General Part* (Cambridge, CUP, 2013) 480.

[11] *Factory at Chorzów (Jurisdiction)* (n 6) 21.

[12] *Factory at Chorzów (Interim Measures of Protection)* (n 6).

[13] *Factory at Chorzów (Merits)* (n 6) 47.

[14] International Law Commission, 'Draft Articles on Responsibility of States for International Wrongful Acts, with Commentaries' (2001) *ILC Ybk*, vol II, pt II, 31, Art 31(1).

[15] ibid, 91 (Commentary to Article 31), [3] (footnotes omitted).

[16] Crawford, *State Responsibility* (n 10) 481 (footnotes omitted). See also C Brown, *A Common Law
of International Adjudication* (Oxford, OUP, 2007), 185–24.

of the dispute'.[17] On 13 December 1928, Poland issued a letter confirming that this was the case.[18] The Court thus issued an order bringing to an end the expert enquiry that had been set in train by the Court's judgment of 13 September 1928, and terminating the proceedings.[19]

Part I of this chapter sets out the background to and facts of the case, and Part II identifies the Court's conclusions on the legal issues. Part III then analyses the importance of the Court's judgment, and also notes certain limitations. It is concluded that the *Factory at Chorzów* case is one that deserves its place in the pantheon of the 'landmark cases' of international law.

II. BACKGROUND AND FACTS OF *FACTORY AT CHORZÓW*

In order to have an appreciation of the facts of the *Factory at Chorzów* case, it is necessary to be familiar with the Court's earlier judgment in *Certain German Interests in Polish Upper Silesia (Jurisdiction)*, which was handed down on 25 August 1925.[20] But before turning to that case, the broader background to the *Factory at Chorzów* case is also noteworthy. For the *Factory at Chorzów* case was but one in a series of disputes between Germany and Poland in the *interbellum*, some of which manifested themselves as inter-state disputes, whereas others became requests for an advisory opinion. The subject matter of these disputes was largely characteristic of the early case load of the Court, which frequently found itself called upon to assist in the administration of the post-World War I settlement reached (inter alia) in the Treaty of Versailles. As JHW Verzijl has said of this early period of the PCIJ's existence:

> When we try to visualise in the first place to what spheres of international law the disputes referred to the Court for a Judgment or for an Advisory Opinion belong, it appears—and this is by no means accidental—that the turmoil on the international political scene of the present day is strikingly reflected in them. The modern world is still waiting for the final settlement of the legal liquidation of World War I, and the last stubborn political struggles about it between the nations also found its echo in the Hague Court. There in refined juristic forms Poland and Czechoslovakia disputed sovereignty over the ore field of Jaworzina, Yugoslavia and Albania over a strip of land in the neighbourhood of the monastery of Saint Naoum on Lake Ochrida, Great Britain, standing up for her protégé Iraq, and (even though by a negative attitude) Turkey over the vast and valuable Mosul district.[21]

Dr Verzijl continued as follows:

> With the aid of the Court, Bulgaria tried to defend herself against an excessive burden of war reparations in favour of Greece, and the Free City of Danzig attempted to wrest itself

---

[17] *Factory at Chorzów (Indemnities) (Germany v Poland)*, Series A (No 19), 12 (Order of 25 May 1929).
[18] ibid.
[19] ibid, 13.
[20] *Certain German Interests in Polish Upper Silesia (Preliminary Objections)* (n 5).
[21] Verzijl *Jurisprudence* (n 5) vol I, 7.

free from the political grip of Poland, symbolised this time by foreign post-boxes and post-men. Also the struggle for the rights of national, religious, and linguistic minorities which flared up with unprecedented bitterness after the World War, echoed loudly before the forum of the World Court: Finland stood up energetically for oppressed kinsmen in the labour commune of Eastern Carelia, Greece fought before the supreme forum for the vital interests of her kinsmen in Constantinople, who were threatened with involvement in the radical exchange of Greek and Turkish populations and consequently with banishment from Turkey, and the Polish Republic had to defend itself there three times already against German charges that it did not accord sufficient notice to the rights of the German minorities living on its territory.[22]

The frequency with which Poland found itself before the Court during this period may reflect a tendency or desire on its part to assert its regained independence, or at least ensure that the limits of the post-World War I agreements reached with neighbouring States were properly tested. A number of these disputes concerned Poland's obligations under the Geneva Convention of 15 May 1922; other matters concerned its borders with Czechoslovakia and its relationship with the Free City of Danzig.[23] Thus, in addition to the *Certain German Interests in Polish Upper Silesia* and *Factory at Chorzów* cases, Germany also instituted proceedings against Poland in the *Rights of Minorities in Upper Silesia* case (1928),[24] the *Case Concerning the Administration of the Prince of Pless* (1933),[25] and the *Polish Agrarian Reform and German Minority* case (1933).[26] The Court was also requested to issue an advisory opinion in other matters which arose out of German–Polish relations, namely the *German Settlers in Poland* case (1923),[27] the *Acquisition of Polish Nationality* case (1923),[28] and the *Access to German Minority Schools in Upper Silesia* case (1931).[29] And as has been noted above, the Court issued a number of advisory opinions concerning Poland's rights and obligations vis-à-vis the Free City of Danzig under the Danzig—Polish Convention of 9 November 1920. These included *Polish Postal*

---

[22] ibid 7–8.

[23] See, eg, Fachiri (n 5) 189–93; M Hudson, *The Permanent Court of International Justice* (New York, Macmillan Company, 1934) 461, 463, 465.

[24] *Rights of Minorities in Upper Silesia (Minority Schools) (Germany v Poland)*, Series A (No 15) (Judgment of 26 April 1928); Fachiri (n 5) 276–80.

[25] *Case Concerning the Administration of the Prince of Pless (Germany v Poland)*, Series A/B (No 52) (Order of 4 February 1933); *Case Concerning the Administration of the Prince of Pless (Germany v Poland) (Interim Measures of Protection)*, Series A/B (No 54) (Order of 11 May 1933); and *Case Concerning the Administration of the Prince of Pless (Germany v Poland)*, Series A/B (No 57) (Order of 4 July 1933); *Case Concerning the Administration of the Prince of Pless (Germany v Poland)*, Series A/B (No 59) (Order of 2 December 1933).

[26] *Polish Agrarian Reform and German Minority (Germany v Poland) (Interim Measures of Protection)*, Series A (No 58) (Order of 29 July 1933); *Polish Agrarian Reform and German Minority (Germany v Poland)*, Series A (No 60) (Order of 4 July 1933).

[27] *German Settlers in Poland*, Series A (No 6) (Advisory Opinion of 10 September 1923); see Hudson, *Permanent Court* (n 23) 459; Fachiri (n 5) 174–83.

[28] *Acquisition of Polish Nationality*, Series B (No 7) (Advisory Opinion of 15 September 1923); see Hudson (n 23) 459; Fachiri (n 5) 183–89.

[29] *Access to German Minority Schools in Upper Silesia (Germany v Poland)*, Series A/B (No 40) (Advisory Opinion of 15 May 1931); Hudson (n 23) 464; Fachiri (n 5) 315–17.

Services in Danzig (1925),[30] *Jurisdiction of the Courts of Danzig* (1928),[31] *Access to, or Anchorage in, the Port of Danzig, of Polish War Vessels* (1931),[32] and *Treatment of Polish Nationals and Other Persons of Polish Origin or Speech in the Danzig Territory* (1932).[33] Poland's relations with its neighbours and the post-World War I political settlement in central Europe thus occupied much of the Court's attention during this period.

Returning to *Certain German Interests in Polish Upper Silesia*, the judgment in this case records that on 5 March 1915—in the first year of the First World War—the Chancellor of the German Reich had entered into a contract with the Bayrische Stickstoffwerke AG ('Bayrische') under which Bayrische agreed to 'establish for the Reich and to begin forthwith' the construction of a nitrate factory at Chorzów in Upper Silesia.[34] The German Reich was to acquire the land and ensure the registration of the land in its own name in the land register.[35] Bayrische agreed to manage the factory until 31 March 1941 and would make use of 'all patents, licences, experience gained, innovations and improvements, as also of all supply and delivery contracts of which it had the benefit'.[36] Under the contract, the Reich had the right, beginning on 31 March 1926, 'to terminate the contract for the management of the factory by the Company on March 31st of any year upon giving fifteen months' notice'.[37]

Nearly five years later, on 24 December 1919—being just after the conclusion of the First World War, including the conclusion of the Treaty of Versailles, which the Allied Powers had signed with Germany on 28 June 1919—a new company was formed, namely the Oberschlesische Stickstoffwerke AG ('Oberschlesische'), and it was agreed in a contract between the German Reich, the Oberschlesische, and the 'Stickstoff-Treuhand-Gesellschaft' which was a trust company for the nitrate factory (the 'Treuhand') that the Reich would sell the factory at Chorzów to the Oberschlesische, including 'the whole of the land, buildings and installations belonging thereto, with all accessories, reserves, raw material, equipment and stocks'.[38] Bayrische was to remain in charge of the management of the factory, and the relationship between Bayrische and Oberschlesische was confirmed in letters dated 24 December 1919 and 28 December 1919.[39] On 29 January 1920, the Oberschlesische became the registered owner of the nitrate factory at Chorzów, as was recorded by the local court ('Amtsgericht') in Koenigshuette.[40] Then, on 25 November 1920,

---

[30] *Polish Postal Services in Danzig*, Series B (No 11) (Advisory Opinion of 16 May 1925); see Hudson, (n 23) 461; Fachiri (n 5) 217–21.

[31] *Jurisdiction of the Courts of Danzig*, Series B (No 15) (Advisory Opinion of 3 March 1928); see Hudson (n 23) 463; Fachiri (n 5) 274–76.

[32] *Access to, or Anchorage in, the Port of Danzig, of Polish War Vessels*, Series A/B (No 43) (Advisory Opinion of 10 December 1931); see Hudson (n 23) 465; Fachiri (n 5) 326–29.

[33] *Treatment of Polish Nationals and Other Persons of Polish Origin or Speech in the Danzig Territory*, Series A/B (No 44) (Advisory Opinion of 4 February 1932); see Hudson (n 23) 465.

[34] *Certain German Interests in Polish Upper Silesia (Preliminary Objections)* (n 5) 8.

[35] ibid.

[36] ibid.

[37] ibid.

[38] ibid 8–9.

[39] ibid 9.

[40] ibid. Koenigshuette is the German name for Chorzów.

the Bayrische and the Treuhand (which owned all the shares of the Oberschlesische) entered into another contract which clarified the relationship between the Bayrische, the Oberschlesische, and the Treuhand.[41]

It was submitted on behalf of Germany that on 14 July 1920, Poland adopted a law which constituted a measure of liquidation as concerns property, rights and interests acquired after 11 November 1918 ('the Polish Law').[42] The principal operative provisions of the Polish Law were Article 1, 2(1), and 5. Article 1 provided that:

> In all cases where the Crown, the German Reich, the States of Germany, institutions of the Reich or States of Germany, the ex-Emperor of Germany or other members of reigning houses, are or were entered after November 11th, 1918, in the land registers of the former Prussian provinces—either as owners or as possessors of real rights—the Polish Courts shall, on the basis of the Treaty of Peace of Versailles of June 28th, 1919, in place of the above-mentioned persons or institutions, automatically enter the name of the Polish Treasury (fisc polonais) in these registers.[43]

Article 2(1) provided that:

> Should any of the above-mentioned persons or institutions have, after November 11th, 1918, either alienated or charged the landed property in question, or should a real right, registered in the name of the aforesaid persons or institutions, have been, after November 11th, 1918, either at their request or with their consent, ceded, struck out or modified in any way, the Court shall restore the entry in the land registers to the situation which would have existed if the aforesaid persons or institutions had not made any request or given the consent necessary to effect the changes in the registers.[44]

Article 5 provided that:

> The Polish Treasury (fisc), having been entered in accordance with Article 1, as owner of a landed property, may require the eviction of persons who, as a result of a contract concluded with one of the persons or institutions mentioned in Article 1, remain in occupation of such property after the coming into force of this law.[45]

Germany submitted that Article 5 constituted a liquidation of the contractual rights of the persons concerned. Germany further argued that the Polish Law was not in conformity with Articles 92 and 297 of the Treaty of Versailles.[46] Article 92 provided in part that 'the property, rights, and interests of German nationals shall not be liquidated under Article 297 by the Polish Government except in accordance with the following provisions'; those provisions included that any 'proceeds of the liquidation shall be paid direct to the owner',[47] and in addition that if an application

---

[41] *Certain German Interests in Polish Upper Silesia (Merits)* (n 5) 43.

[42] *Certain German Interests in Polish Upper Silesia (Preliminary Objections)* (n 5). The Polish Law of 14 July 1920 was called the 'Law concerning the transfer of the rights of the German Treasury and of members of reigning German Houses to the Treasury of the State of Poland'.

[43] Law of 14 July 1920, Art 1; reproduced in *Certain German Interests in Polish Upper Silesia (Merits)* (n 5) 23.

[44] Law of 14 July 1920, Art 2(1); reproduced in *Certain German Interests in Polish Upper Silesia (Merits)* (n 5) 23.

[45] Law of 14 July 1920, Art 5; reproduced in *Certain German Interests in Polish Upper Silesia (Merits)* (n 5) 23–24.

[46] *Certain German Interests in Polish Upper Silesia (Preliminary Objections)* (n 5) 5.

[47] Treaty of Versailles, Art 92.

was made to a Mixed Arbitral Tribunal established under the Treaty of Versailles, and that Tribunal considers that the conditions of the sale were 'unfairly prejudicial to the price obtained', the Tribunal 'shall have discretion to award to the owner equitable compensation to be paid by the Polish Government'.[48]

Two and a half more years passed. Then, on 1 July 1922, the Amtsgericht in Koenigshuette decided that the registration of the Oberschlesische as the owner of the factory at Chorzów was null and void and was cancelled. The Amtsgericht ordered that the pre-existing position was to be restored, and that in accordance with Article 1 of the Polish Law, the lands in question were to be registered in the name of the Polish Treasury.[49] The Amtsgericht's decision was implemented the same day.[50] On 3 July 1922, Mr Ignacy Moscicki, who was acting under the authority of a Polish ministerial decree of 24 June 1922, took possession of the factory at Chorzów and took over the management of the factory.[51]

On 10 November 1922, the Oberschlesische commenced proceedings before the Germano-Polish Mixed Arbitral Tribunal which had been established under the Treaty of Versailles,[52] asking the Tribunal (inter alia) 'to order the Polish Government, the respondent in the suit, to restore the factory, to make any other reparation which the Court may see fit to fix and to pay the costs of the action.'[53] The Polish Government contested the Tribunal's jurisdiction.[54] In addition, the Oberschlesische commenced proceedings before the Civil Courts of Kattowitz (Kattowice, Poland), in which it sought an order that the respondent 'inform the applicant as to the movable property found at the Chorzów nitrate factories at 11 am on the morning of July 3, 1922, when the working of those factories was resumed by the respondent'; that it 'state what debts it had collected' and that it 'restore to the applicant or to the [Bayrische] such movable property, or, should this be impossible, the equivalent value, and also to repay to the applicant or to the [Bayrische] the amount of the debts collected'.[55] For its part, the Bayrische also commenced proceedings before the Germano-Polish Mixed Arbitral Tribunal on 25 March 1925, 'with a view to obtaining an annual indemnity until the restitution of the factory to the Oberschlesische', and seeking 'possession and management of the factory to be restored to it'.[56] The two claims before the Mixed Arbitral Tribunal were ultimately withdrawn in June 1928 after the Court had confirmed its jurisdiction over the merits of Germany's claim for an indemnity, and the hearing of Germany's claim on the merits was concluded.[57]

In addition to the litigation commenced by the Oberschlesische, Germany filed an application instituting proceedings before the Court on 15 May 1925, essentially

---

[48] ibid.
[49] *Certain German Interests in Polish Upper Silesia (Preliminary Objections)* (n 5) 9.
[50] ibid.
[51] (No 17), 22.
[52] Treaty of Versailles, Art 304.
[53] *Certain German Interests in Polish Upper Silesia (Preliminary Objections)* (n 5) 9.
[54] ibid.
[55] ibid, 10.
[56] (No 17), 23.
[57] (No 17), 23. The hearing on the merits was held on 21–22, 25, 27, and 29 June 1928: (No 17), 6.

seeking declarations that the Polish Law of 14 July 1920 constituted 'a measure of liquidation', and as such was not in conformity with Articles 92 and 297 of the Treaty of Versailles';[58] and that 'the attitude of the Polish Government' concerning the Oberschlesische and the Bayrische was 'not in conformity with Article 6 of the Geneva Convention', and also asking that the Court declare how Poland should have behaved as regards the two companies.[59] As part of this claim, Germany also sought various declarations and compensation concerning Poland's treatment of a number of other German nationals and their property in Poland.[60] Thus commenced the claim which would ultimately give the Court the opportunity to shape the law on reparation.

III. THE PROGRESS OF GERMANY'S CLAIM

A. *Certain German Interests in Polish Upper Silesia*: Jurisdiction

Faced with Germany's quest for justice on behalf of the Oberschlesische and the Bayrische, Poland filed preliminary objections concerning Germany's claim, arguing that Germany's Application concerned a dispute 'which [was] not covered by Article 23 of the Convention of Geneva' (being the compromissory clause on which Germany based the Court's jurisdiction), and was therefore outside the Court's jurisdiction. In the alternative, Poland submitted that even if the Court had jurisdiction, the Application could not be entertained.[61]

Article 23 of the Geneva Convention provided that:

1. Should differences of opinion respecting the construction and application of Articles 6 to 22 arise between the German and Polish Governments, they shall be submitted to the Permanent Court of International Justice.

2. The jurisdiction of the Germano-Polish Mixed Arbitral Tribunal derived from the stipulations of the Treaty of Peace of Versailles shall not thereby be prejudiced.[62]

Poland's objections to the Court's jurisdiction was made on the grounds that there was no 'dispute' concerning the interpretation or application of the Geneva Convention, and that even if there was a 'dispute', it did not fall within the scope of Article 23. Poland further objected that Germany's claim was inadmissible because the same dispute had been submitted by the Oberschlesische to the Germano-Polish Mixed Arbitral Tribunal; in addition, Poland objected to an aspect of Germany's prayer for relief on the basis that it resembled a request for an advisory opinion, which Germany did not have standing to request.[63]

---

[58] *Certain German Interests in Polish Upper Silesia (Preliminary Objections)* (n 5) 5.
[59] ibid 5–6.
[60] ibid 6, 22–27.
[61] *Certain German Interests in Polish Upper Silesia (Preliminary Objections)* (n 5) 11.
[62] ibid, 13.
[63] ibid, 13, 18–19.

The Court rejected Poland's first objection, holding, consistently with its earlier decision in *Mavrommatis Palestine Concessions*, that:

> [A] difference of opinion does exist as soon as one of the Governments concerned points out that the attitude adopted by the other conflicts with its own views. Even if, under Article 23, the existence of a definite dispute were necessary, this condition could at any time be fulfilled by means of unilateral action on the part of the applicant Party. And the Court cannot allow itself to be hampered by a mere defect of form, the removal of which depends solely on the Party concerned.[64]

As for the second jurisdictional objection raised by Poland, which the Court described as its principal objection,[65] this concerned the argument that the dispute did not concern the interpretation or application of Articles 6 to 22 of the Geneva Convention, but rather concerned the Polish Law of 1920. In considering this objection, the Court analysed Article 6 of the Geneva Convention, which provided that:

> Poland may expropriate in Polish Upper Silesia in conformity with the provisions of Articles 7 to 23 undertakings belonging to the category of major industries including mineral deposits and rural estates. Except as provided in these clauses, the property, rights and interests of German nationals or of companies controlled by German nationals may not be liquidated in Polish Upper Silesia.[66]

The Court ultimately rejected this objection, concluding that 'differences of opinion contemplated by Article 23, which refers to Articles 6 to 22, may also include differences of opinion as to the extent of the sphere of application of Articles 6 to 22', which therefore covered the dispute between Germany and Poland in the present case.[67] The Court observed that Article 6 of the Geneva Convention refers to 'undertakings' of 'major industries', and the Court considered that Article 6 was 'intended to ensure the continuity of economic life', with the result that 'the factory at Chorzów must be regarded as a whole'.[68] It followed for the Court that the undertaking fell within the terms of Article 6.[69]

The Court then addressed Poland's objections which concerned the admissibility of the claim. The first of these was that Germany's application could not be entertained 'until the Germano-Polish Mixed Arbitral Tribunal in Paris has given judgment in the dispute regarding the same factory, which [the Oberschlesische] submitted to that Tribunal on November 10th, 1922'.[70] The Court explained that Poland did not formally present this objection as one based on *litispendance*, although this was a

---

[64] ibid, 14. See also *Mavrommatis Palestine Concessions*, Series A (No 2), 11, stating that 'A dispute is a disagreement on a point of law or fact, a conflict of legal views or of interests between two persons'.
[65] *Certain German Interests in Polish Upper Silesia (Preliminary Objections)* (n 5) 14.
[66] ibid, 16.
[67] ibid 16.
[68] ibid, 17
[69] ibid.
[70] ibid, 19.

'convenient expression' to describe the objection.[71] The Court rejected the objection, explaining that:

> It is a much disputed question in the teachings of legal authorities and in the jurisprudence of the principal countries whether the doctrine of *litispendance*, the object of which is to prevent the possibility of conflicting judgments, can be invoked in international relations, in the sense that the judges of one State should, in the absence of a treaty, refuse to entertain any suit already pending before the courts of another State, exactly as they would be bound to do if an action on the same subject had at some previous time been brought in due form before another court of their own country.[72]

But in any event, the Court held that there was no need for it to enter into the debate of whether *litispendance* was applicable as a general principle of law, for 'the essential elements which constitute *litispendance* [were] not present':[73]

> There is no question of two identical actions: the action still pending before the Germano-Polish Mixed Arbitral Tribunal at Paris seeks the restitution to a private Company of the factory of which the latter claims to have been wrongfully deprived; on the other hand, the Permanent Court of International Justice is asked to give an interpretation of certain clauses of the Geneva Convention. The Parties are not the same, and, finally, the Mixed Arbitral Tribunals and the Permanent Court of International Justice are not courts of the same character, and, *a fortiori*, the same might be said with regard to the Court and the Polish Civil Tribunal of Kattowitz.[74]

The Court also rejected Poland's final objection (which also concerned the admissibility of the claim) that the German application sought in part a form of advisory opinion. Poland had argued that Germany's prayer for relief, insofar as it contained the request that the Court should indicate 'the attitude which should have been adopted by the Polish Government' concerning the Bayrische and Oberschlesische in order to comply with the Geneva Convention was inadmissible.[75] The Court said that this was not a request for an advisory opinion, as had been contended by Poland, but rather a request for a decision. This was thus also rejected. The Court therefore confirmed its jurisdiction over Germany's claim in respect of the factory at Chorzów and also held that Germany's claim was admissible.[76] Germany's claim thus proceeded to the merits.

B. *Certain German Interests in Polish Upper Silesia*: Merits

The Court issued its judgment in *Certain German Interests in Polish Upper Silesia (Merits)* on 25 May 1926.[77] Noting Poland's objection regarding how its

---

[71] ibid, 19–20.
[72] ibid, 20.
[73] ibid.
[74] ibid, 20.
[75] ibid, 21.
[76] ibid, 27.
[77] *Certain German Interests in Polish Upper Silesia (Merits)* (n 5).

first claim had been formulated (namely that it seemed to deal exclusively with the Polish Law, and the relation between this law and Articles 92 and 297 of the Treaty of Versailles—rather than whether the Polish Law of 14 July 1920 was in breach of the Geneva Convention),[78] Germany had reformulated its claim such that it 'directly contemplate[d] the relation between Articles 2 and 5 of the Polish law of July 14th, 1920, and Articles 6 to 22 of the Geneva Convention'.[79] Germany's reformulated final submission was as follows:

> (1) That the application both of Article 2 and of Article 5 of the law of July 14th, 1920, in Polish Upper Silesia, decreed by the law of June 16th, 1922, constitutes a measure of liquidation within the meaning of Article 6 and the following articles of the Convention of Geneva in the sense that, in so far as the above-mentioned articles of the Convention of Geneva authorize liquidation, that application must be accompanied by the consequences attached to it by the said Convention, in particular the entry into operation of Articles 92 and 297 of the Treaty of Versailles prescribed by the said Convention, and that, in so far as those articles do not authorize liquidation, that application is illicit.

> (2) (a) That the attitude of the Polish Government in regard to the Oberschlesische Stick-stoffwerke and Bayerische Stickstoffwerke was not in conformity with Article 6 and the following articles of the Geneva Convention;

> (b) Should the decision in regard to point (a) be in the affirmative, the Court is requested to state what attitude should have been adopted by the Polish Government in regard to the Companies in question in order to conform with the above-mentioned provisions.

Although the Court had held in its Judgment of 25 August 1925 that it had juris-diction, it had added a reservation to the effect that its decision 'must in no way prejudice the question of the extent to which the Court may see fit to deal with the questions contemplated by submission No. 1 of the German Application in the proceedings on the merits'.[80] The Court thus briefly considered Poland's jurisdic-tional objections anew, and once again rejected them.

The Court then turned to consider the merits. On Germany's first submission, the Court held that it first had to consider whether, generally speaking, Articles 2 and 5 of the Polish Law were compatible with Articles 6 to 22 of the Geneva Convention.[81] The Court again considered the terms of Article 6 of the Geneva Convention, which provides that:

> Poland may expropriate in Polish Upper Silesia, in conformity with the provisions of Articles 7 to 23, undertakings belonging to the category of major industries including min-eral deposits and rural estates. Except as provided in these clauses, the property, rights and interests of German nationals or of companies controlled by German nationals may not be liquidated in Polish Upper Silesia.[82]

The Court considered the meaning of the term 'liquidation' and concluded that it was reasonable to conclude that

---

[78] ibid, 15.
[79] ibid.
[80] ibid, 16.
[81] ibid, 20.
[82] Geneva Convention, Art 6.

the intention was ... to convey the meaning that, subject to the provisions authorizing expropriation, the treatment accorded to German private property, rights and interests in Polish Upper Silesia is to be the treatment recognized by the generally accepted principles of international law.[83]

Having noted this, the Court confirmed that expropriation would only be lawful under the conditions identified in Article 7. The Court concluded, as a general matter, that:

the application of Articles 2 and 5 of the Polish law of July 14th, 1920, in Upper Silesia is not compatible with the system established by Head III of the Geneva Convention. For, on the one hand, these articles may affect private property and withdraw it from the protective *régime* instituted by Articles 6 to 22, subjecting it to more serious measures prohibited by the Convention. On the other hand, they make no provision for any investigation concerning the validity of a title, and eliminate any previous investigation of an individual case, though such investigation is necessary for a correct application of the Convention.[84]

Poland, however, had two responses: first, that the Polish Law was not contrary to the Geneva Convention but 'merely gave effect to rights which Poland derives from the Treaty of Versailles and other international instruments connected with that Treaty', which were not affected by the Geneva Convention.[85] Secondly, and in any event, even if that were wrong, Poland argued that the measures taken under Articles 2 and 5 of the Polish Law could not be regarded as 'measures of liquidation' within the meaning of Articles 6 to 22 of the Geneva Convention.[86]

Beginning with the first point, the Court reviewed Poland's obligations under the Armistice Convention of 11 November 1918, the Protocol of Spa of 1 December 1918, and the Treaty of Versailles of 28 June 1919. These provided in part that Germany was not permitted for the duration of the armistice to dissipate any of its assets,[87] and that any states to which German territory was ceded would 'acquire all property and possessions situated therein belonging to the German Empire or to the German States', with reparation being paid to Germany.[88] The Court observed that Poland was not a state party to the Armistice Convention or the Protocol of Spa, and held that 'there [had] been no subsequent tacit adherence or accession on the part of Poland to the Armistice Convention or the Protocol of Spa';[89] it further held that Poland did not have a right to reparation under the Treaty of Versailles because there had not been a state of war between Poland and Germany (Poland having of course previously been partitioned between the Kingdom of Prussia, the Russian Empire, and the Habsburg Empire until 1919.)[90] The Court thus concluded that it was not

---

[83] *Certain German Interests in Polish Upper Silesia (Merits)* (n 5) 21.
[84] ibid, 24.
[85] ibid, 25.
[86] ibid.
[87] See, eg, Protocol of Spa, Art 1, cited at *Certain German Interests in Polish Upper Silesia (Merits)* (n 5) 26.
[88] See, eg, Treaty of Versailles, Art 256(1), cited at *Certain German Interests in Polish Upper Silesia (Merits)* (n 5) 27.
[89] *Certain German Interests in Polish Upper Silesia (Merits)* (n 5) 28.
[90] ibid.

possible for Poland to rely on those treaties to displace the provisions of the Geneva Convention.[91] As the Court held:

> no title of international law has been cited by Poland which enables Articles 2 and 5 of the law of July 14th, 1920, to be regarded as the exercise of a right overriding her obligations under Head III of the Geneva Convention.[92]

The Court then turned to Poland's second argument, namely that the 'suppression of private rights' effected under Articles 2 and 5 of the Polish Law could not be regarded as 'measures of liquidation' within the meaning of Articles 6 to 22 of the Geneva Convention, because it applied to all 'property, rights, and interests' without regard to nationality, whereas the regime of liquidation only applied to German property.[93] For its part, Germany argued that 'liquidation within the meaning of the Treaty of Versailles and of the Geneva Convention includes any measure contrary to generally accepted international law which affects the property of German nationals, no matter whether such measure is authorised by a treaty provision (authorised liquidation) or whether it is not (unauthorised liquidation)'.[94] But in the end, the Court rejected Poland's submission, holding that:

> Expropriation without indemnity is certainly contrary to Head III of the Convention; and a measure prohibited by the Convention cannot become lawful under this instrument by reason of the fact that the State applies it to its own nationals.[95]

It also concluded that:

> The Court, therefore, is of opinion that the application in Upper Silesia of Articles 2 and 5 of the Polish law of July 14th 1920, is not in conformity with Articles 6–22 of the Geneva Convention, in so far as the said articles affect the persons or companies referred to in Head III of the Convention.[96]

The Court then turned to Germany's second submission, namely its request (a) for a declaration that the attitude of the Polish Government in regard to the Oberschlesische and Bayerische was not in conformity with its obligations under the Geneva Convention,[97] and (b) in the event that the answer was negative, an indication of how Poland was required to fulfill its obligations. The Court observed with respect to the second part of this submission, Germany had failed to 'formulate properly set out claims', with the result that the Court was not in a position to give judgment.[98] It therefore only considered part (a) of Germany's second submission.

Although the Court had already decided that the Polish Law was in breach of Poland's obligations under the Geneva Convention, Germany's second submission provided a separate issue to be analysed. This was 'whether the Oberschlesische

---

[91] ibid, 29.
[92] ibid, 31.
[93] ibid.
[94] ibid, 32.
[95] ibid, 33.
[96] ibid, 34.
[97] ibid, 34ff.
[98] ibid, 34–35.

and the Bayerische are really the owners of the rights which together constitute the Chorzów enterprise'.[99] If this were established, it would follow that those rights would be protected by Article 6 of the Geneva Convention, only subject to the effect of the Treaty of Versailles on the content of Poland's obligations under the Geneva Convention.[100]

In the case of the Oberschlesische, it was not disputed that it was a company controlled by German nationals.[101] Germany argued that Poland could only validly acquire the factory at Chorzów (which was the Oberschlesische's property), in accordance with Article 7 of the Geneva Convention, and in the absence of having done so, Poland must be held to be in beach of its obligations under Article 6.[102] This is because the factory was 'immune from any measure of liquidation because it possesses the character of property, rights and interests of German nationals or of companies controlled by German nationals', within the meaning of Article 6(2).[103] Poland disagreed that it was in breach of Article 6, arguing that there had been no measure of liquidation.[104]

In considering Germany's claim, the Court recalled its earlier conclusion in relation to Germany's first submission that the Polish Law was not in conformity with Poland's obligations under the Geneva Convention, and that Poland could not rely on the Armistice Convention, the Protocol of Spa, or the Treaty of Versailles to alter that.[105] The Court also considered, and rejected, an argument that there had been a 'misuse of the right possessed by [Germany] to alienate property situated in the plebiscite area, before the transfer of sovereignty'.[106] The alleged abuse was Germany's conduct in having annulled the contract between the Reich and the Bayrische of 5 March 1915 and having then replaced it on 24 December 1919 with a contract between the Reich, the nitrate trust company (the 'Stickstoff-Treuhand-Gesellschaft'), and the Oberschlesische. But the Court held that this commercial activity, far from being an abuse, had fulfilled 'a legitimate object of the administration, namely, the abandonment by the Reich of an entreprise showing a serious deficit, by means of a sale under conditions offering a reasonable guarantee that the capital invested would eventually be recovered'.[107] The Court also concluded that it could not be said that the contracts concluded in December 1919 were not 'genuine',[108] somehow 'designed to prejudice Poland's rights',[109] or were 'fictitious or fraudulent'.[110] The Court also noted that there was nothing in the Treaty of Versailles to restrain Germany from alienating property, and in any event, the

---

[99] ibid, 35.
[100] ibid.
[101] ibid.
[102] ibid, 36.
[103] ibid.
[104] ibid, 36–37.
[105] ibid, 37.
[106] ibid.
[107] ibid, 38.
[108] ibid.
[109] ibid.
[110] ibid, 42.

transaction was concluded prior to the entry into force of the Treaty of Versailles, which did not take place until 10 January 1920.[111]

Finally, the Court turned to the position of the Bayrische which had concluded the original contract with the Reich on 5 March 1915, and which, even after the contracts of 24 December 1919, was charged with 'manag[ing] the exploitation of the Chorzów factory, on behalf of the Oberschesische'.[112] It was not disputed that the Bayrische was controlled by German nationals. The question for the Court was whether Poland's act in taking possession of the Chorzów factory on 3 July 1922 amounted to an unlawful expropriation of the Bayrische's contractual rights. The Court's answer was brief and to the point:

> As these rights related to the Chorzów factory and were, so to speak, concentrated in that factory, the prohibition contained in the last sentence of Article 6 of the Geneva Convention applies in respect of them. Poland should have respected the rights held by the Bayerische under its contracts with the Oberschlesische and the Treuhand; and the attitude of Poland in regard to the Bayerische has therefore, like its attitude in regard to the Oberschlesische, been contrary to Article 6 and the following articles of the Geneva Convention.[113]

The Court therefore held as follows:

> (1) That the application both of Article 2 and of Article 5 of the law of July 14th, 1920, in Polish Upper Silesia, decreed by the law of June 16th, 1922, constitutes, in so far as it affects German nationals or companies controlled by German nationals covered by Part 1, Head III, of the Geneva Convention, a measure contrary to Article 6 and the following articles of that Convention.
>
> (2)(a) That the attitude of the Polish Government in regard to the Oberschlesische Stickstoffwerke and Bayerische Stickstoffwerke Companies was not in conformity with Article 6 and the following articles of the Geneva Convention.

However, this did not dispose of the case, even though the Court had declared Poland to be in breach of its obligations under the Geneva Convention. For Germany wanted compensation from Poland in respect of the factory at Chorzów, and in order to obtain this, it instituted separate proceedings. Thus commenced the more well-known phase of this litigation: the *Factory at Chorzów (Claim for Indemnity)* case.

C. *Factory at Chorzów (Claim for Indemnity)*: Jurisdiction

On the basis of the Court's Judgment of 25 May 1926 in *Certain German Interests in Polish Upper Silesia (Merits)*, Germany and Poland engaged in negotiations with a view to an amicable settlement of the claims of the Bayrische and the Oberschlesische for the payment of monetary compensation.[114] On 25 June 1926, Germany wrote to Poland to seek to implement the judgment, which involved:

> (1) the re-entry in the land registers of the Court of Konigshütte of the Oberschlesische as owners of the real estate constituting the Chorzów factory;

---

[111] ibid, 39.
[112] ibid, 43.
[113] ibid, 44.
[114] *Factory at Chorzów (Claim for Indemnity) (Jurisdiction)* (n 17) 15.

(2) the restoration of the factory as an industrial enterprise to the Bayerische;

(3) the payment to these two Companies of an indemnity, the amount of which to be fixed by direct negotiations between the two Governments.[115]

On 9 September 1926, Poland replied to Germany's letter, stating that for various reasons it would not be able to comply with Germany's claim for restoration of the factory, and that there would also be problems in municipal law with entering the Oberschlesische in the land register.[116] It suggested that it would be preferable for the Bayrische and Oberschlesische to approach the management of the factory directly, with limited participation by the two Governments.[117] The negotiations began on 22 November 1926, and on 19 January 1927, the German delegation sent the Polish delegation a note containing two alternative proposals concerning the amount of compensation and the method of payment. Germany also made it clear that it was prepared to take the matter back to the Court if no agreement could be reached. It is noteworthy that Germany indicated that it 'had abandoned its original claim for the restitution of the factory ... [because] it had come to the conclusion that the Chorzów factory, in its present condition, no longer corresponded to the factory as it was before the taking over in 1922'.[118] In its reply, Poland apparently agreed with the amounts of compensation claimed by Germany,[119] but disagreed with the method of payment, among other reasons because it wanted to set off the compensation against money apparently owed by Germany to Poland.[120] On 8 February 1927, Germany informed Poland that the two states' differences seemed intractable and commenced proceedings before the Court.

As in *Certain German Interests in Polish Upper Silesia*, Germany again based the jurisdiction of the Court on Article 23 of the Geneva Convention, but Germany also referred to the Germano-Polish Arbitration Treaty which had been concluded at Locarno on 16 October 1925.[121] Ultimately the Court held that Germany's claim was based on the Geneva Convention.[122] The Court also acknowledged that in considering Germany's claim,

it [could not] take account of declarations, admissions or proposals which the Parties may have made in the course of direct negotiations which have taken place between them, declarations which, moreover, have been made without prejudice in the event of the points under discussion forming the subject of judicial proceedings.[123]

Poland once again contested the Court's jurisdiction, arguing that (i) Article 23 of the Geneva Convention, which gave the Court jurisdiction over disputes concerning the interpretation or application of Articles 6 to 22 of the Geneva Convention,

---

[115] ibid, 16.
[116] ibid.
[117] ibid.
[118] ibid, 17.
[119] ibid.
[120] ibid, 18.
[121] ibid, 19.
[122] ibid.
[123] ibid.

did not confer jurisdiction on the Court over disputes relating to reparations; and (ii) even if Article 23 of the Geneva Convention did confer such jurisdiction on the Court, the Geneva Convention 'has instituted special jurisdictions' for private claims, and this jurisdiction affected the Court's jurisdiction under Article 23.[124]

With regard to its first jurisdictional objection, Poland sought to argue that the compromissory clause in Article 23 of the Geneva Convention was of a type that sought to exclude questions of compensation from the court or tribunal's jurisdiction.[125] But the Court gave Poland's jurisdictional objections relatively short shrift. As the Court explained, in stating the 'classic general statement of the consequences of an internationally wrongful act':[126]

> It is a principle of international law that the breach of an engagement involves an obligation to make reparation in an adequate form. Reparation therefore is the indispensable complement of a failure to apply a convention and there is no necessity for this to be stated in the convention itself. Differences relating to reparations, which may be due by reason of failure to apply a convention, are consequently differences relating to its application.[127]

The Court supported this view with the observation that even in treaties containing compromissory clauses which had been subjected to reservations, 'the differences concerning which [reservations] were deemed to be necessary were those relating to legal rights and obligations and not those relating to pecuniary reparation'.[128] In any event, the Court was doubtful as to whether any conclusions could be drawn from the classification of disputes in general arbitration treaties.[129] However, the Court thought that in any event, such classification supported the conclusion that the phrase 'differences of opinion resulting from the interpretation and application' in Article 23 of the Geneva Convention 'should be construed as including questions relating to reparations'.[130] Poland made the point that in another treaty concluded by Germany with the Free City of Danzig in 1921, the compromissory clause specifically included the tribunal's jurisdiction to decide questions of reparation. But the Court also rejected this, finding that:

> [T]he fact that a convention explicitly confirms the conception generally adopted in regard to arbitration clauses cannot be construed to mean that the same Parties, when employing in another convention the wording ordinarily used in conventions of this kind, have, by so doing, given evidence of an intention contrary to that which is to be presumed when interpreting an arbitration clause in a convention.[131]

The Court's conclusion was:

> It follows from the above that Article 23, paragraph 1, which constitutes a typical arbitration clause (*clause compromissoire*), contemplates all differences of opinion resulting

---

[124] ibid, 20.
[125] ibid, 21.
[126] Crawford (n 10) 480.
[127] *Factory at Chorzów (Claim for Indemnity) (Jurisdiction)* (n 17) 21.
[128] ibid, 22.
[129] ibid.
[130] ibid.
[131] ibid, 24.

from the interpretation and application of a certain number of articles of a convention. In using the expression 'differences of opinion resulting from the interpretation and application', the contracting Parties seem to have had in mind not so much the subject of such differences as their source, and this would justify the inclusion of differences relating to reparations amongst those concerning the application, even if the notion of the application of a convention did not cover reparations for possible violation.[132]

Turning to Poland's second jurisdictional objection, it argued that 'there are other tribunals before which the injured companies could assert their right to an indemnity and that, in these circumstances, the German Government cannot, by substituting itself for these companies, disturb the jurisdictional system established by the Geneva Convention'.[133] These other tribunals were the Germano-Polish Mixed Arbitral Tribunal (which was created under the Treaty of Versailles), and the Upper Silesian Arbitral Tribunal (which, under Article 5 of the Geneva Convention, had jurisdiction over claims concerning the alleged 'destruction of vested rights' arising under Part II, or 'Head II', of the Geneva Convention).[134]

As has been noted above, the Court had in an earlier phase of proceedings considered a Polish objection to admissibility on whether Germany's claim should not be entertained on the basis of *litispendance*, as proceedings were pending before the Germano-Polish Mixed Arbitral Tribunal.[135] On that earlier occasion, the Court had rejected the application of the doctrine, but here the Court reconsidered it due to the fact that Germany was now seeking compensation for Poland's breach of the Geneva Convention, rather than merely declaratory relief.[136]

The Court began by repeating its finding in the *Certain German Interests in Polish Upper Silesia* case that the seizure of the property, rights and interests of the Oberschlesische and Bayrische had been effected by the Polish Law which was in breach of 'Head III' (namely, Articles 6–22) of the Geneva Convention, and was 'not supported by some special authority having precedence over the Convention' and '[overstepped] the limits of generally accepted international law'.[137] Because the Polish Law was a breach of the provisions contained in Head III, the Court held that the Upper Silesian Arbitral Tribunal, whose jurisdiction was limited to breaches of Head II of the Geneva Convention, could not have jurisdiction over Germany's claim. As for the Germano-Polish Mixed Arbitral Tribunal, the Court recalled that Head III of the Geneva Convention had limited the liquidation regime provided for in the Treaty of Versailles, and that certain provisions of the Treaty of Versailles had been declared applicable in Polish Upper Silesia.[138] The Court considered that the jurisdiction of the Germano-Polish Mixed Arbitral Tribunal concerned 'the application' of Head III, whereas the present case arose out of 'acts contrary to' the provisions

---

[132] ibid.
[133] ibid, 25.
[134] ibid, 26. Article 5 of the Geneva Convention provided that: 'The question whether and to what extent an indemnity for the suppression or diminution of vested rights must be paid by the State, will be directly decided by the Arbitral Tribunal upon the complaint of the interested Party'.
[135] *Certain German Interests in Polish Upper Silesia (Preliminary Objections)* (n 5) 19–21.
[136] *Factory at Chorzów (Claim for Indemnity) (Jurisdiction)* (n 17) 27.
[137] ibid.
[138] ibid, 28.

of Head III.[139] The Court also explained that it was reluctant to reject jurisdiction on the basis of these provisions, as follows:

> the Court, when it has to define its jurisdiction in relation to that of another tribunal, cannot allow its own competency to give way unless confronted with a clause which it considers sufficiently clear to prevent the possibility of a negative conflict of jurisdiction involving the danger of a denial of justice.[140]

Given that the provision in the Treaty of Versailles conferring jurisdiction on the Germano-Polish Mixed Arbitral Tribunal was at least open to question, and that Poland had filed a plea to the Mixed Arbitral Tribunal's jurisdiction in the case commenced by the Oberschlesische, the Court rejected Poland's preliminary objection. It was fortified in this conclusion by noting that Poland had failed to give notice to the Oberschlesische in advance of the adoption of the Polish Law, which was in breach of the 'fundamental principles' of Head III of the Geneva Convention.[141] This had, in effect, deprived the Oberschlesische of the possibility of submitting its claim to the Mixed Arbitral Tribunal to have the Polish Law declared unlawful.[142] And the Court called in aid the doctrine that no one can be allowed to take advantage of his or her own wrong (*nullus commodum capere de sua injuria propria*) in stating that:

> It is, moreover, a principle generally accepted in the jurisprudence of international arbitration, as well as by municipal courts, that one Party cannot avail himself of the fact that the other has not fulfilled some obligation or has not had recourse to some means of redress, if the former Party has, by some illegal act, prevented the latter from fulfilling the obligation in question, or from having recourse to the tribunal which would have been open, to him.[143]

The Court therefore rejected Poland's objections to jurisdiction and admissibility. It also rejected the proposition that 'in case of doubt the Court should decline jurisdiction'; it held that '[w]hen considering whether it has jurisdiction or not, the Court's aim is always to ascertain whether an intention on the part of the Parties exists to confer jurisdiction upon it'.[144] In the present case, it had been convincingly

---

[139] ibid, 28–29.

[140] ibid, 30.

[141] ibid, 30–31.

[142] See also Bin Cheng, *General Principles of Law as Applied by International Courts and Tribunals* (Cambridge, CUP, 1953) 150.

[143] *Factory at Chorzów (Claim for Indemnity) (Jurisdiction)* (n 17) 31. As Bin Cheng explains, the *Factory at Chorzów* case provides an apt illustration of the *nullus commodum* principle: 'The Polish Government had expropriated the Chorzów Factory in virtue of her laws of July 14, 1920 and June 16, 1922, without following the procedure laid down in the Geneva Convention of 1922. As regards procedure, the Convention had provided that no dispossession should take place without prior notice to the real or apparent owner, thus affording him an opportunity of appealing to the Germano-Polish Mixed Arbitral Tribunal (Art 19). Poland, by failing to follow the procedure laid down in the Geneva Convention, had illegally deprived the other party of the opportunity of appealing to the Mixed Arbitral Tribunal. The Permanent Court held that Poland could not now prevent him or rather his home State, from applying to the Court, on the ground that the Mixed Arbitral Tribunal was competent and that, since no appeal had been made to that Tribunal, the Convention had not been complied with' (ibid, 150).

[144] ibid, 32.

demonstrated to the Court that it had jurisdiction, and the Court accordingly rejected Poland's objections to jurisdiction and reserved Germany's suit for judgment on the merits.[145]

D. Request for Interpretation of Judgments Nos 7 and 8

Before the Court could turn to the merits of the *Factory at Chorzów (Claim for Indemnity)* case, it had to deal with two requests: a request for interpretation of the two judgments in *Certain German Interests in Polish Upper Silesia*, and a request for interim measures of protection.

Germany filed its application on 18 October 1927 seeking an interpretation of the two judgments that had been issued in the *Case Concerning German Interests in Polish Upper Silesia*.[146] In its request for interpretation, Germany sought two declarations: first, that the effect of the Court's judgment in *Certain German Interests in Polish Upper Silesia (Jurisdiction)* was not that Poland had the right 'to annul by process of law, even after the rendering of that judgment, the Agreement of December 24th, 1919, and the entry, based on that agreement, of the name of the Oberschlesische as owner in the land registers'; and secondly, that the proceedings brought by Poland against the Oberschlesische before the Kattowitz Civil Court which sought to effect that annulment did not have any relevance for the proceedings before the Court.[147]

In what can only be described as a compressed timetable, Poland filed written observations on 7 November 1927, and a public hearing was held on 28 November 1927. With unusual speed—the Court issued its judgment on 16 December 1927—the Court set out the test that had to be satisfied for it to exercise its power to interpret judgments under Article 60 of its Statute: first, there had to be 'a dispute as to the meaning and scope of a judgment of the Court', and second, 'the request should have for its object an interpretation of the judgment' (rather than be, eg, a disguised attempt to reopen the case).[148] The Court considered that these conditions were satisfied,[149] and duly confirmed that it had recognised in its earlier judgments, 'with binding effect between the Parties concerned ... amongst other things, the right of ownership of the [Oberschlesische] in the Chorzów factory under municipal law'.[150]

E. *Factory at Chorzów (Claim for Indemnity)*: Interim Measures of Protection

Concurrently with its request for interpretation of the Court's judgments in *Certain German Interests in Polish Upper Silesia*, Germany also filed what was a misconceived

---

[145] ibid, 33.
[146] *Interpretation of Judgments Nos 7 and 8 (The Chorzów Factory)* (n 17).
[147] ibid, 5.
[148] ibid, 10.
[149] ibid, 10–15.
[150] ibid, 22.

Request for Interim Measures of Protection on 15 November 1927, in which it sought the payment of 30 million Reichsmarks 'within one month of the date of the Order sought'.[151] The Court rejected the German Request without even seeking observations from Poland, noting that 'the request of the German Government cannot be regarded as relating to the indication of measures of interim protection, but as designed to obtain an interim judgment in favour of a part of the claim formulated in the Application above mentioned'.[152] It followed that Germany's Request was not 'covered by the terms of the provisions of the Statute and Rules'.[153]

F. *Factory at Chorzów (Claim for Indemnity)*: Merits

Having determined Germany's request for an interpretation of the judgments in the *Certain German Interests in Polish Upper Silesia* case, and having disposed of Germany's application for interim measures of protection, the Court finally arrived at the task of deciding on Germany's claim for an indemnity.

The object of Germany's claim, as indicated in its Application of 8 February 1927, was a declaration that Poland was 'under an obligation to make good the consequent damage sustained by [the Oberschlesische and the Bayrische] from July 3rd, until the date of the judgment sought', that the amount of compensation to be paid was 59,400,000 Reichsmarks for the damage caused to the Oberschlesische, and 16,775,200 Reichsmarks for the damage caused to the Bayrische.[154] These figures were ultimately amended, and in its final submissions, Germany sought '58,400,000 Reichsmarks, plus 1,656,000 Reichsmarks in respect of the Oberschlesische, and '20,179,000 Reichsmarks' in respect of the Bayrische.[155] Germany also proposed a schedule for payment, with six per cent interest from the date of judgment.[156] In addition, Germany sought an order that 'until June 20th, 1931, no nitrated lime and no nitrate of ammonia should be exported to Germany, to the United States of America, to France or to Italy'.[157] For its part, Poland sought the dismissal of Germany's claims as regards the Oberschlesische, and Germany's claim as regards the Bayrische should be limited to 1,000,000 Reichsmarks for past loss, and that an annual rent of 250,000 Reichsmarks should be paid for the period 1 January 1928 until 31 March 1941.[158]

In its judgment of 13 September 1928, the Court first grappled with the nature of Germany's claim, and concluded that although there was nothing in international law which prevented states from conferring rights of standing on individuals to bring claims directly, the application in the instant case was 'designed to obtain, in favour

---

[151] *Factory at Chorzów (Interim Measures of Protection)* (n 6) 10.
[152] ibid.
[153] ibid.
[154] *Factory at Chorzów (Merits)* (n 6) 6.
[155] ibid, 8.
[156] ibid, 7.
[157] ibid.
[158] ibid, 15.

of Germany, reparation the amount of which is determined by the damage suffered by the Oberschlesische and Bayrische'.[159]

The Court proceeded to examine three issues: (i) 'the existence of the obligation to make reparation'; (ii) 'the existence of the damage which must serve as a basis for the calculation of the indemnity'; and (iii) 'the extent of this damage'.[160]

On the first issue, the Court confirmed its earlier conclusion that 'it is a general principle of international law, and even a general conception of law, that any breach of an engagement involves an obligation to make reparation'.[161] The Court also observed that it had already concluded that:

> [A] breach of an international engagement [had] in fact taken place in the case under consideration ... this point is *res judicata*. The non-conformity of Poland's attitude in respect of the two Companies with Article 6 and the following articles of the Geneva Convention is established by No 2 of the operative provisions of Judgment No 7. The application of the principle to the present case is therefore evident.[162]

Turning to the second issue, the Court noted that it was not common ground that damage had resulted from the wrongful act.[163] Poland denied that the Oberschlesische had suffered any damage, although it agreed that the Bayrische was entitled to an indemnity, albiet not the amount sought by Germany.[164] Poland's objection rested in part on its assertion that the Oberschesische was not the lawful owner of the factory, and so had suffered no dispossession; Poland argued further that the Oberschlesische was a company controlled by the German Government, rather than by German nationals.[165] The Court restated the principle which it said was 'accepted in the jurisprudence of arbitral tribunals', according to which 'in estimating the damage caused by an unlawful act, only the value of property, rights and interests which have been affected and the owner of which is the person on whose behalf compensation is claimed, or the damage done to whom is to serve as a means of gauging the reparation claimed, must be taken into account'.[166] This had the effect of 'excluding from the damage to be estimated, injury resulting for third parties from the unlawful act'.[167] The Court rejected Poland's submission that the Oberschlesiche was not the lawful owner of the factory, observing that it had already decided this issue in *Certain German Interests in Polish Upper Silesia*.[168] As for Poland's objection to the effect that Germany could not claim in respect of the Oberschlesische as it was government-owned, rather than owned by German nationals, the Court held that even if this issue had not already been decided in its

---

[159] ibid, 29.
[160] ibid.
[161] ibid.
[162] ibid.
[163] ibid, 30.
[164] ibid.
[165] ibid, 31, 34–35.
[166] ibid, 31.
[167] ibid.
[168] ibid, 31–33.

earlier judgments, it would be 'bound to conclude that the Oberschlesische was controlled by the Bayrische'.[169]

The Court then set down the 'guiding principles' for the assessment of compensation:

> The action of Poland which the Court had judged to be contrary to the Geneva Convention is not an expropriation—to render which lawful only the payment of fair compensation would have been wanting. It is a seizure of property, rights and interests which could not be expropriated even against compensation, save under the exceptional conditions fixed by Article 7 of the said Convention. As the Court has expressly declared in Judgment No 8, reparation is in this case the consequence not of the application of Articles 6 to 22 of the Geneva Convention, but of acts contrary to those articles.[170]

The Court then set forth its famous *dictum*:

> The essential principle contained in the actual notion of an illegal act—a principle which seems to be established by international practice and in particular by the decisions of arbitral tribunals—is that reparation must, as far as possible, wipe out all the consequences of the illegal act and reestablish the situation which would, in all probability, have existed if that act had not been committed. Restitution in kind, or, if this is not possible, payment of a sum corresponding to the value which a restitution in kind would bear; the award, if need be, of damages for loss sustained which would not be covered by restitution in kind or payment in place of it—such are the principles which should serve to determine the amount of compensation due for an act contrary to international law.[171]

It followed, for the Court, that 'the compensation due to the German Government is not necessarily limited to the value of the undertaking at the moment of dispossession, plus interest to the day of payment'. As the Court explained, '[t]his limitation would only be admissible if the Polish Government had had the right to expropriate, and if its wrongful act consisted merely in not having paid to the two Companies the just price of what was expropriated'.[172] In the present case, however, such an outcome would be 'unjust', for it might result in putting 'Germany and the interests protected by the Geneva Convention, on behalf of which interests the German Government is acting, in a situation more unfavourable than that in which Germany and these interests would have been if Poland had respected the said Convention'.[173] This passage of the Factory at Chorzów judgment is cited by the ILC in support of the proposition that in certain cases, claims for loss of profits may be appropriate.[174]

When it sought to apply this formula to the facts of the case in order to arrive at an assessment of damages, the Court was not satisfied with the material that had been submitted by the parties.[175] The Court therefore arranged for the convening

---

[169] ibid, 40.
[170] ibid, 46.
[171] ibid, 47.
[172] ibid.
[173] ibid.
[174] J Crawford, *The International Law Commission's Articles on State Responsibility* (Cambridge, CUP, 2002) 228 (Commentary to Art 36(2), [27]).
[175] *Factory at Chorzów (Merits)* (n 6) 49.

of an 'expert enquiry' under Article 50 of the Court's Statute, which had apparently been suggested by Germany.[176] It directed the expert enquiry to examine: (i) the value of the factory on the date of dispossession, being 3 July 1922; (ii) whether the factory would have made a profit between that time and the date of the present judgment, if it had remained in the hands of the Oberschlesische and the Bayrische; and (iii) what would the present value be of the factory, had it remained in the hands of the two companies.[177] The Court observed that 'the value to which the above questions relate will be sufficient to permit it with a full knowledge of the facts to fix the amount of compensation to which the German Government is entitled, on the basis of the damage suffered by the two Companies in connection with the Chorzów undertaking'.[178] The Court did not rule on all of the relief requested by Germany and Poland, preferring to wait pending the report of the expert enquiry.[179]

However as has already been noted, the matter was settled by Germany and Poland shortly after the Court rendered its judgment,[180] and, like the Court of Chancery in *Jarndyce v Jarndyce*, the Court was never able to complete its judicial task.[181] But the *Factory at Chorzów* case has left an undeniable legacy, to which the next part of this chapter turns.

IV. CONCLUSION: THE LEGACY OF *FACTORY AT CHORZÓW*

The *Factory at Chorzów* case is most well known for its authoritative statement on the law of reparation, which has been widely applied by other international courts and tribunals, forms the basis of the relevant provisions of the ILC's Articles on State Responsibility, and unquestionably reflects customary international law. But the Court's pronouncements on issues such as *lis alibi pendens*, abuse of rights in commencing multiple proceedings, the inherent powers of international courts and tribunals, and the correct approach for the Court to adopt in deciding whether it has jurisdiction, have all been the subject of much academic and judicial consideration and discussion.[182]

---

[176] ibid, 51.

[177] ibid, 51–52.

[178] ibid, 55.

[179] ibid, 59–62.

[180] *Factory at Chorzów (Indemnities)* (n 17) 12–13.

[181] The Court of Chancery in the fictitious litigation in *Jarndyce v Jarndyce*, featured in Dickens's *Bleak House*, did not issue a final judgment because the funds in the estate were ultimately consumed with the litigation costs.

[182] eg, on *lis alibi pendens* and discussion of the *Certain German Interests in Polish Upper Silesia* case, see R Kolb, *The International Court of Justice* (Oxford, Hart, 2013) 219–20; H Wehland, *The Coordination of Multiple Proceedings in Investment Treaty Arbitration* (Oxford, OUP, 2013) 135, 194 Oxford, 96; and Y Shany, *The Competing Jurisdictions of International Courts and Tribunals* (Oxford, OUP, 2003) 239–40; on the doctrine of abuse of rights (or abuse of process), see also Shany, 255–60; Brown *International Adjudication* (n 16) 245–50; and C Brown, 'The Relevance of the Doctrine of Abuse of Process in International Adjudication' [2010] *Transnational Dispute Management* 7; on inherent powers, see C Brown, 'The Inherent Powers of International Courts and Tribunals' (2005) 76 *BYIL* 195; and on the Court's approach to deciding the issue of jurisdiction, see, eg, Spiermann *International Legal Argument* (n 5) 251–24.

The impact of the *Factory at Chorzów* case has also been felt in the field of investment treaty arbitration, where uncertainty persisted until relatively recently concerning the applicable standard of compensation for an unlawful expropriation. As is well known, many investment treaties include in the provision dealing with expropriation the conditions which must be satisfied for an expropriation to be lawful; these include the payment of compensation, which is typically expressed in accordance with the Hull formula, namely that the payment of compensation must be 'prompt, adequate and effective', and most investment treaties also typically state that such compensation must represent the 'fair market value', or the 'genuine value', which is to be assessed, in the terms of the Article 6(1) of the Australia—Hong Kong BIT, 'immediately before the deprivation or before the impending deprivation became public knowledge whichever is the earlier'.[183] To similar effect, Article 4(2) of the Germany—Philippines BIT provides that '[s]uch compensation shall be equivalent to the value of the expropriated investment immediately before the date on which the actual or threatened expropriation, nationalization or comparable measure has become publicly known'.

The difficulty that arose from the interaction of such provisions with the *Factory at Chorzów* dictum was whether the date for assessing compensation stipulated in the BIT applied only in the case of a lawful expropriation (ie, one otherwise carried out in conformity with the requirements of the BIT, which are typically that the expropriation was for a public purpose, was non-discriminatory, and was made against the payment of compensation), or whether the date for assessing compensation under the BIT also applied in the case of an unlawful expropriation.[184] This issue appears to have been resolved by the ICSID tribunal in *ADC Affiliate Ltd and ADMC & ADC Management Ltd v Republic of Hungary*.[185] In that case, Hungary had issued a Ministerial Order which had the effect of terminating a series of contracts which had been entered into with the claimants concerning the refurbishment and management of Budapest International Airport, in respect of which Hungary did not pay any compensation.[186] The ICSID tribunal concluded that this was an expropriation,[187] and then turned to the issue of the standard of compensation—including the date of assessing compensation—which Hungary was obliged to pay. In contrast to many claims for expropriation, this was a material issue, since Budapest Airport had, in the time since the Ministerial Order, become a profitable enterprise, and its value had increased significantly in the intervening period.

Hungary argued that the standard of compensation set forth in the applicable BIT (Article 4(2) of the Cyprus–Hungary BIT, which provides that '[t]he amount of

---

[183] eg, Australia–Hong Kong BIT, Art 6(1).

[184] See especially A Sheppard, 'The Distinction between Lawful and Unlawful Expropriation' in C Ribeiro (ed), *Investment Arbitration and the Energy Charter Treaty* (Huntington, NY, Juris, 2006) 169–99.

[185] *ADC Affiliate Ltd and ADMC & ADC Management Ltd v Republic of Hungary* (ICSID Case No ARB/03/16, Award of 2 October 2006).

[186] The Ministerial Order was the 'Transport and Water Management Ministry Order No 45/2001 (XII.20)': *ADC Affiliate Ltd and ADMC & ADC Management Ltd v Republic of Hungary* (ICSID Case No ARB/03/16, Award of 2 October 2006), [179]–[190], [444].

[187] ibid, [423]–[455], [476].

compensation must correspond to the market value of the expropriated invest-ments at the moment of the expropriation') was a *lex specialis* to which Cyprus and Hungary had agreed, and that this ought to apply over the *Factory at Chorzów* standard.[188] But the tribunal disagreed, noting that the BIT's *lex specialis* only applied to the standard of compensation applicable in the case of a lawful expro-priation. In contrast, as the ICSID tribunal observed, 'the BIT does not contain any *lex specialis* rules that govern the issue of the standard for assessing damages in the case of an unlawful expropriation', with the result that the tribunal '[was] required to apply the default standard contained in customary international law in the pre-sent case'.[189] The tribunal proceeded to set out the Court's *dictum* from the *Factory at Chorzów* case, and explained that '[t]his statement of the customary international law standard has subsequently been affirmed and applied in a number of inter-national arbitrations relating to the expropriation of foreign owned property'.[190] Having reviewed the practice of international courts and tribunals, the ICSID tribu-nal concluded that:

> [T]here can be no doubt about the present vitality of the *Chorzów Factory* principle, its full current vigor having been repeatedly attested to by the International Court of Justice.[191]

And this directly affected the date of assessing the value of the expropriated asset, as the Court explained:

> The present case is almost unique among decided cases concerning the expropriation by States of foreign owned property, since the value of the investment after the date of expro-priation (1 January 2002) has risen very considerably while other arbitrations that apply the *Chorzów Factory* standard all invariably involve scenarios where there has been a decline in the value of the investment after regulatory interference ...

> [I]n the present, *sui generis*, type of case the application of the *Chorzów Factory* standard requires that the date of valuation should be the date of the Award and not the date of expropriation, since this is what is necessary to put the Claimants in the same position as if the expropriation had not been committed.

The impact of the Court's judgment in *Factory at Chorzów* was therefore quite material for the claimants in that case. The same applied in *Siemens AG v Argentine Republic*, a claim brought under the Germany–Argentine Republic Bilateral Invest-ment Treaty. In that case, the ICSID tribunal held that:

> Under customary international law Siemens is entitled not just to the value of its enterprise as of 18th May 2001, the date of expropriation, but also to any greater value that enterprise has gained up to the date of this award plus any consequential damages.[192]

---

[188] ibid, [480].
[189] ibid, [483].
[190] ibid, [484]–[486].
[191] ibid, [493].
[192] *Siemens AG v Argentine Republic* (ICSID Case No ARB/02/8, Award of 6 February 2007), [352]. *ADC Affiliate Ltd and ADMC & ADC Management Ltd v Republic of Hungary* (ICSID Case No ARB/03/16, Award of 2 October 2006) was not *sui generis* after all.

For the sake of completeness, it should also be noted that the international law of reparation, as based on the *Factory at Chorzów* dictum, has its limitations. The focus on restitution as the primary form of reparation can have limited application in the context of environmental damage and violations of human rights, which may not be able to be 'made good' by either of the other forms of reparation, namely compensation and satisfaction.[193] One can well imagine that the current threat of environmental degradation was not at the forefront of the PCIJ judges' minds in the 1920s, but international law need not be static; there is room for the development of new rules to cater for the challenges faced by modern international society.

The *Factory at Chorzów* case is evidently one of the Court's most important judgments. It laid the foundations for the law on state responsibility and many other issues besides, and its relevance is enduring. It is thus deserving of its place in this collection of 'landmark cases' of international law.

---

[193] See especially M Mbengue, 'A Critical Assessment of Reparation in International Law' (Paper presented at the ASIL Meeting, Washington DC, 1 April 2016). As Laura Livingston observed in the *ASIL Cable* of 3 April 2016, Professor Mbengue explains that 'most environmental damages are irreversible, precluding the possibility of ever truly restoring or reviving the *status quo ante*. This creates difficulties in transposing traditional reparations principles onto environmental issues. Though attempts have been made to enhance responsibility for environmental wrongs through imposing strict liability and strengthening liability for non-state actors, the international community still struggles to formulate effective rules regarding liability, responsibility, and compensation for environmental damages'.

5

SS Lotus (France v Turkey) (1927)

DOUGLAS GUILFOYLE

The [Lotus] dictum represents the high water mark of laissez-faire in international relations, and an era that has been significantly overtaken by other tendencies.[1]

Existe-t-il une différence entre la souveraineté turque et la souveraineté française?[2]

I. INTRODUCTION

ON THE NIGHT of 2 August 1926, a Monsieur Demons, first officer of the French mail packet *SS Lotus*, was keeping watch as his ship sailed towards Constantinople.[3] Some five or six nautical miles off Lesbos, the *SS Lotus* struck and sank the Turkish vessel *Boz-Kourt*. Somehow, neither Demons nor Hassan Bey, the captain of the *Boz-Kourt*, were sufficiently alert to prevent disaster. The Turkish vessel was cut in two and sank. The *Lotus* went to its aid, rescuing Bey and nine others; nonetheless, eight Turkish crewmen perished. On arrival at Constantinople, local authorities commenced an investigation which ended with both Demons and Bey being tried for manslaughter and convicted on 15 September 1926. Demons was sentenced to 80 days in prison and fined. History records Bey's sentence as being somewhat harsher, but omits why. France vigorously protested throughout that in a high seas collision exclusive flag state jurisdiction compelled the result that any crime committed had been committed solely aboard the *Lotus* and fell solely within French jurisdiction. The idea that a foreigner could (even if by negligence and beyond Turkish territory) kill Turkish citizens and that Turkish courts could not prosecute him sat poorly with the young Turkish republic. Indeed, Turkey had only recently escaped centuries-old capitulatory agreements limiting the jurisdiction of Turkish courts and officials over Europeans and allowing ambassadors or consuls to exercise extra-territorial criminal jurisdiction over their nationals.[4] The two states agreed by *compromis*, Turkey

---

[1] *Arrest Warrant of 1 April 2000 (Democratic Republic of the Congo v Belgium)*, ICJ Reports 2002, 3, 79 (Judges Higgins, Kooijmans and Buergenthal).

[2] PCIJ, Series C, No 13-II, 120-1 (speech of Dr Mahmut Esat, Agent for Turkey).

[3] This account draws on: *SS Lotus (France v Turkey)*, Judgment, (1927) PCIJ Reports, Series A, 3, 10–12.

[4] Not necessarily to the exclusion of local criminal jurisdiction: JB Angell, 'The Turkish Capitulations' (1901) 6 *The American Historical Review* 254, 256.

not yet being a member of the League of Nations, to submit the dispute to the Permanent Court of International Justice (PCIJ). Thus began one of the most often discussed, and perhaps most poorly understood, cases of the PCIJ.[5]

It may, in retrospect, seem surprising that the incident became a case for the PCIJ at all. Demons had escaped rather lightly. His negligence had killed eight foreign nationals and he had been sentenced only to 80 days in prison. Nonetheless, freedom of navigation through internationally regulated waters (albeit in a different context) had already been litigated before the Court in *SS Wimbledon*.[6] Then, as now, states may pursue navigational disputes simply for the principle involved. There were, however, also likely other historical and geopolitical concerns at play as discussed below.

The *Lotus* case is significant in several respects. Its principal interest arises, of course, from the greatly maligned dictum that as rules of international law binding upon independent States 'emanate from their own free will' it follows that '[r]estrictions upon the independence of States cannot therefore be presumed'.[7] This notorious 'principle of freedom' or '*Lotus* principle' has been widely condemned as erroneous or, at the least, unfortunate.[8] For all the controversy, the *Lotus* principle played little discernible role in the resolution of the *Lotus* case. Further, this passage was almost certainly not intended to outline a laissez-faire international law of coexistence founded on the proposition that all is permitted which is not prohibited. Nonetheless, as regards foundational principles or conceptions of the international legal system, generations of scholars have discussed the '*Lotus* principle', if only to disagree with it.[9]

Despite frequent disparagement of the case's contribution to the law of jurisdiction, it was at least prescient in concluding that there could be concurrent jurisdiction over events on the high seas (flag state jurisdiction notwithstanding) or, indeed, upon land.[10] It was correct on the narrow point that 'exclusive' flag state jurisdiction is no obstacle to the existence of concurrent prescriptive jurisdiction[11] and in suggesting more generally that concurrent jurisdiction might be an ordinary feature of international relations.[12] It is also notable for being the first case in which the PCIJ attempted to formulate a definition of customary international law, or at least what it is not.[13]

---

[5] Noted in: JL Brierly, 'The "Lotus" Case', (1928) 44 *LQR* 154; GW Berge, 'The Case of the SS "Lotus"' (1927–1928) 26 *Michigan LR* 361; R Ruzé, 'Affaire du Lotus' (1928) 9 *Rev Droit Int'l & Legis Comp* 3, 124; M Travers, 'Affaire du Lotus' (1928) 9 *Rev Droit Int'l & Legis Comp* 3, 400; JHW Verzijl, 'Affaire du Lotus devant la cour Permanente de Justice Internationale' (1928) 9 *Rev Droit Int'l & Legis Comp* 3, 1; and F Williams, 'L'affaire du Lotus (Trad J Ch Rousseau)' (1928) *RGDIP* 361.

[6] *SS 'Wimbledon' (United Kingdom and ors v Germany)*, Judgment, (1923) PCIJ Reports, Series A, No 1, 15.

[7] *Lotus* (n 3) 18.

[8] On the latter view: H Lauterpacht, *The Function of Law in the International Community* (Union, New Jersey, Lawbook Exchange, 2000) 94.

[9] eg, Brierly 'The "Lotus" Case' (n 5); G Fitzmaurice, 'The General Principles of International Law Considered from the Standpoint of the Rule of Law' (1957-II) 92 *Recueil des Cours* 1-277, 56–57; A Mills, 'Rethinking Jurisdiction in International Law' (2014) 84 *BYIL* 187, 190–94.

[10] *Lotus* (n 3) 27, 29 and 31.

[11] D Guilfoyle, *Shipping Interdiction and the Law of the Sea* (Cambridge, CUP, 2007), 8–10.

[12] Indeed, Mann suggested 'jurisdiction is almost always concurrent' but considered this 'a matter for regret' and evidence of the rudimentary state of development of international law. FA Mann, 'The Doctrine of Jurisdiction in International Law' (1964-I) 111 *Recueil des Cours* 9, 10.

[13] J Crawford, *Chance, Order, Change: The Course of International Law* (Leiden, Brill Nijhoff, 2014) 59, [52].

While the *Lotus* case has something to say about fundamental principles of international law, and rather more to say about jurisdiction and the formation of customary international law,[14] it is also a case about *non-liquet*.[15] What is an international court to do when it finds there is no international rule governing a case? Should judicial technique be deployed to avoid a *non-liquet*, for example, by deducing the existence of a gap-filling rule derived from more general principles? The question clearly goes to whether international law is properly conceived of as a formally complete system or is simply a wilderness of isolated primary rules.[16] If the *Lotus* principle meant what it is commonly taken to mean, it would leave the door open to (potentially frequent) findings of *non-liquet*, a possibility some scholars in the 1920s would have considered natural.[17] Instead, the reasoning of the majority appears to presume the formal completeness of international law, and leaves little space for *non-liquets*.

II. THE HISTORICAL BACKGROUND

A. Turkish–French Relations and the End of the Capitulatory Regime

Several historical and legal-political circumstances must be taken into account to appreciate how the parties themselves understood the *Lotus* case. On the Turkish side, this was not a simple dispute about the law applicable to a maritime collision. It was a litmus test for the independence and sovereignty of the new Turkish Republic, barely four years old in 1927. Further, the two states had a complex history. There had been an 'exceptionally close' diplomatic, trade and cultural relationship between the two countries from the sixteenth century until at least the end of the nineteenth century.[18] It is also worth noting that France was not a distant great power but a territorial rival actively encroaching on Turkey's borders. France retained 'extensive Levantine mandates' over areas formally under Ottoman control and both France and Turkey had claims to the Syrian province of Hatay (Alexandretta).[19] As at 1926, the status of Hatay remained unsettled and prevented 'the establishment of stable ... [French/Turkish] relations' and colored their 'attitudes towards the *Lotus* case'.[20]

Other than territorial concerns, the new Turkish Republic was a jealous guardian of the jurisdiction of its courts, having only recently ended the long (and long-resented) capitulatory regime. The capitulatory agreements of the Ottoman Empire,

---

[14] ibid.

[15] O Spiermann, *International Legal Argument in the Permanent Court Of International Justice* (Cambridge, CUP, 2005) 254; H Handeyside, 'The Lotus Principle in ICJ Jurisprudence: Was the Ship ever Afloat?' (2007) 29 *Michigan JIL* 71, 78–80.

[16] Crawford, *Chance, Order, Change* (n 13) 62–67; H Lauterpacht, 'Some Observations on the Prohibition of "Non Liquet" and Completeness of the Law' in E Lauterpacht (ed), *International Law: Selected Papers*, vol 2 (Cambridge, CUP, 1975).

[17] eg, JS Reeves, 'International Society and International Law' (1921) 15 *AJIL* 361, 371 (positing 'large areas' within which sate action is 'simply non-legal, or strictly political').

[18] U Özsu, 'De-territorializing and Re-territorializing Lotus: Sovereignty and Systematicity as Dialectical Nation-Building in Early Republican Turkey' (2009) 22 *LJIL* 29, 32.

[19] ibid.

[20] ibid; see further: M Khadduri, 'The Alexandretta Dispute' (1945) 39 *AJIL* 406.

and subsequently Turkey, lasted roughly from 1535 to 1923 (the First World War interrupting) and involved a network of concessionary treaties between Turkey and European powers. Briefly, these granted foreign nationals not only freedom of movement and freedom to practice their own religion, but a series of economic and legal privileges—notably including the establishment of consular courts with jurisdiction over disputes between foreigners.[21] These had the effect of turning the Ottoman empire into 'a virtual open and free market for Europe'.[22] Unsurprisingly, this state of affairs 'engendered resentment within the Turkish-Muslim ruling elite'.[23]

At the end of the First World War, the Ottoman Empire had concluded a disastrous peace treaty with the Allies, the 1920 Treaty of Sèvres. It had imposed 'the harsh terms of a relentless victor', resulting in the partition and occupation of Turkey as well as the re-imposition of the capitulatory regime which had been abrogated in 1914.[24] It was never accepted by the subsequent nationalist government of Mustafa Kemal (later Atatürk) and after the Turkish War of Independence against the occupying powers it was replaced with the 1923 Treaty of Lausanne.[25]

A principal objective of the Turkish negotiators of the Treaty of Lausanne was the abolition of the capitulatory regime. Indeed, its elimination had been considered by the National Forces of Mustafa Kemal as 'a non-negotiable condition for the cessation of hostilities'.[26] The new Turkish Republic sought in the Treaty a vindication of its right to be regarded as an equal sovereign under international law. Indeed, Turkey had sought an express acknowledgement in the Treaty of the competence of Turkish courts to prosecute crimes committed by foreigners beyond Turkish territory.[27] This proposal was rejected, and instead Article 16 simply provided that Turkish courts could exercise jurisdiction subject to international law. As discussed below, France relied heavily upon this drafting history in the course of the case.

B. The Treaty of Lausanne and the 1926 Special Agreement

The jurisdictional provision of the Treaty of Lausanne was crucial to the *Lotus* case, affecting the questions put to the PCIJ in the special agreement, the structure of argument adopted and possibly the formulation of the notorious *Lotus* principle. Article 15 of the Treaty of Lausanne provided that, subject to Article 16 (concerning personal status and family law): 'all questions of jurisdiction shall, as between Turkey and the other contracting Powers, be decided in accordance with the principles of international law'. Similarly, Article 17 required that Turkey afford to foreigners appearing

---

[21] Özsu, 'De-territorializing and Re-territorializing Lotus' (n 18) 38. See further: E Pears, 'Turkish capitulations and the status of British and other foreign subjects residing in Turkey' (1905) 21 *LQR* 408–25 (helpfully summarising the scholarship of the time).

[22] Özsu (n 18) 38; quoting T Naff 'The Ottoman Empire and the European State System' in H Bull and A Watson (eds), *The Expansion of International Society* (Oxford, OUP, 1984) 143, 158.

[23] ibid.

[24] P Marshall Brown, 'From Sevres to Lausanne' (1924) *AJIL* 113, 113–14.

[25] See generally: E Turlington, 'The Settlement of Lausanne', (1924) 18 *AJIL* 696–706.

[26] Özsu (n 18) 39.

[27] *Lotus* (n 3) France: Memorial, PCIJ Reports, Series C, No 13-II, 181.

before Turkish courts 'a level of protection conforming both to international law and the legal principles and procedures generally followed in other countries'.[28]

The principal question put to the PCIJ under the special agreement was:

> Has Turkey, contrary to Article 15 of the Convention of Lausanne ..., respecting ... jurisdiction, acted in conflict with the principles of international law—and if so, what principles—by instituting, following the collision ... on the high seas between the French steamer *Lotus* and the Turkish steamer *Boz- Kourt* and upon the arrival of the French steamer at Constantinople—as well as against the captain of the Turkish steamship—joint criminal proceedings ... against M. Demons ... in consequence of the loss of the Boz-Kourt [and eight lives]?

The second question was, if the first were answered in the affirmative, what compensation was due to Demons. It is, in retrospect, remarkable that France agreed to this phrasing of the question to be put. It is hard to see how asking whether Turkey had 'acted in conflict with the principles of international law—and if so, what principles' would do anything other than place the burden upon France to show that Turkey had either acted in violation of a prohibition of international law or acted in excess of the jurisdictional powers positively conferred upon States. In the event, and contrary to the common understanding of the case, the question of burdens of evidence or presumptions of law had little to do with the outcome (as discussed below).

C. Questions of Principle: The Changing Structure of International Law

The case was heard by the PCIJ under the presidency of Max Huber. It was a period in which there were relatively few experts in international law on the court. In Huber's estimation there were only himself, Moore, Anzilotti, Beichmann and (on a good day) Bustamente.[29] On Spiermann's account it was a crucial period in the international legal argument between conceptions of the State as being either a 'national sovereign' or as an 'international sovereign'.[30] The important distinction being that a conception of international law grounded in states as national sovereigns can proceed as far as a law of international coexistence delineating spheres of autonomy or self-determination but not much further. This produces a relatively static vision of a minimalist international law.[31] Alternatively, one can commence from the standpoint of a more complex and dynamic international law of cooperation in which the state is a subject of international law and in which the state as a national sovereign (enjoying complete freedom of action) is a 'residual principle'.[32] This dual character of the state, as Cheng put it, standing 'on the one hand as a supreme political institution, sovereign within its own boundaries, and on the other

---

[28] Author's translation ('d'une protection conforme au droit des gens ainsi qu'aux principes et méthodes généralement suivis dans les autres pays'). See: *Lotus* (n 3) French Memorial, Annex 4, PCIJ, Series C, No 13-III, 216.

[29] Spiermann, *International Legal Argument* (n 15) 212 fn 14.

[30] ibid, 39–40.

[31] ibid, 106–07.

[32] ibid, 106–07.

hand as a member of a society in which other equally sovereign members co-exist'[33] pervades the Turkish method of argument in the *Lotus* case (as discussed below). It was an approach which, generally, fell on receptive ears.

That is, in Spiermann's view, before the Huber Court governments continued to advance arguments which presumed the primacy of the national sovereign, and therefore involved reading down international law:

> In rejecting these and other arguments, the [PCIJ's] drafting committees eschewed arguments attractive to national lawyers and moulded an international lawyer's approach ... based on a firm hierarchy between the two structures of international legal argument. In a pure form, this approach ... [prioritized first] the international law of cooperation and [second] the international law of coexistence with the residual principle of a state freedom being applied where no international law could be discerned.[34]

While the *Lotus* case is commonly taken to have turned on a presumption of freedom, the logic of the actual decision is far more in accordance with Spiermann's view. Indeed, in the sentence preceding the Court's formulation of the *Lotus* principle it describes customary international law as consisting of:

> usages generally accepted as expressing principles of law and established in order to regulate the relations between ... co-existing independent communities or with a view to the achievement of common aims.[35]

The prioritisation of the law of co-existence or the law needed to achieve 'common aims' over any absolute presumption of freedom of action is readily apparent.

III. THE FACTS OF *SS LOTUS*

As noted above, the facts of the *Lotus* case are not especially complex.[36] On 2 August 1926, the French packet boat *SS Lotus* collided with the Turkish coal steamer *Boz-Kourt* while en route to Constantinople. The collision occurred at night, approximately five to six nautical miles north of Cape Sigri on Lesbos. Following the collision, the *Boz-Kourt* sunk. The *Lotus* rendered assistance to the shipwrecked sailors and saved 10 of the crew. Nonetheless, eight Turkish nationals perished. The following day the *SS Lotus* arrived in Constantinople, where the Turkish authorities proceeded to investigate the collision resulting in the arrest of Demons, the first officer and watch officer of the Lotus at the time of the collision as well as the captain of the Turkish vessel, Hassan Bey, who had been in charge of its navigation at the time of the collision. Both were arrested pending trial on 5 August. Despite repeated protestations from the French *chargé d'affaires* in Constantinople, both were charged with negligent homicide and the case was heard by the criminal court of Stamboul on 28 August 1926. The Turkish court rejected arguments that it lacked jurisdictional competence and on 15 September 1926 it sentenced the French lieutenant to 80 days

---

[33] B Cheng, *General Principles of Law as Applied by International Courts and Tribunals* (Cambridge, Grotius, 1987) 31.

[34] Spiermann (n 15) 213.

[35] *Lotus* (n 3) 18.

[36] This account draws on: ibid, 10–12 and Verzijl 'Affaire du Lotus devant la cour' (n 5) 1.

in prison and a fine of 22 Turkish pounds and gave the Turkish captain a slightly harsher sentence. The prosecutor entered an appeal, which had the effect of suspending the sentence pending its hearing. In the interim, Lieutenant Demons was released on bail. The episode appears to have caused considerable friction with the exchange of numerous diplomatic notes as to the competence of Turkish courts in matters of collision beyond the territorial sea involving the negligence of a foreign national aboard a foreign flagged vessel.[37] Nonetheless, the French and Turkish governments rapidly agreed to resolve their differences by arbitration and signed a compromise at Geneva on 21 October 1926 conferring jurisdiction over the conflict on the PCIJ.

IV. THE PROCEEDINGS AND JUDGMENT IN *SS LOTUS*

A. The Pleadings

The French submissions in the written and oral proceedings advanced, in essence, six arguments.[38] First, the expression 'principles of international law' as used in the Treaty of Lausanne was not to be understood as a general term, but in light of the negotiating history. That is, in the course of negotiations the Turkish delegation had expressly proposed that the Treaty refer to the jurisdiction of Turkish courts to prosecute extraterritorial crimes committed by foreigners. This was roundly rejected by participating European states. France thus proposed that the jurisdiction of Turkish courts did *not* extend to such cases, an interpretation contrary to the plain meaning of the text based on the *travaux préparatoires*.[39] As discussed below, there is good reason to consider that this was not merely tendentious argumentation but rather reflected French assumptions as to the qualified character of Turkish sovereignty. Second, France advanced the argument that international law does not permit a state to extend its criminal jurisdiction beyond its frontiers other than in cases where there has been expressed or implicit agreement to such an extension.[40] Third, and with reference to the *Franconia* case (*R v Keyn*) among others,[41] France contended that in cases of collision the exclusive jurisdiction of the flag state must mean that *only* the flag state is competent to prosecute criminal or disciplinary matters arising, if for no other reason than any offence will be defined by *national* regulations regarding safety of navigation.[42] Fourth, without much elaboration, France contended it would be 'contrary to the facts' to localise the offence as having occurred where the effects were felt; that is, aboard the Turkish vessel.[43] Fifth, France submitted that there was effectively a burden upon Turkey to show that in such a case it could point to some positive title in international law permitting it to exercise

---

[37] Reproduced in: PCIJ Reports, Series C, No 13-II, 216–23.
[38] See: Berge 'The Case of the SS "Lotus"' (n 5) 365–66.
[39] *Lotus* (n 3) France: Memorial, PCIJ Reports, Series C, No 13-II, 180–84.
[40] ibid, 192.
[41] ibid, 208; *Lotus*, France: Counter-Memorial, PCIJ Reports, Series C, No 13-II, 254. See further n 86.
[42] *Lotus* (n 3) France: Memorial, PCIJ Reports, Series C, No 13-II, 197, 208–09.
[43] *Lotus* (n 3) France: Counter-Memorial, PCIJ Reports, Series C, No 13-II, 254.

extraterritorial jurisdiction.[44] Sixth, it submitted that Article 6 of the Turkish Penal Code—permitting the prosecution of extraterritorial conduct by foreigners that affected Turkish interests—was contrary to international law.[45]

However, the French attitude to the case is perhaps more accurately captured in the Counter-Memorial's submission that:

> the substitution of the jurisdiction of the Turkish Courts for that of the foreign consular courts in criminal proceedings taken against foreigners is the outcome of the consent given by the Powers to this substitution in the Conventions signed at Lausanne on July 24th, 1923.[46]

This rather plainly puts the case on the footing not of a contest between two juridically equal sovereigns, but between a 'power' and a peripheral state which enjoyed jurisdiction not to the full extent allowed by international law but to the extent allowed by European 'powers'.[47]

Turkey had, broadly, six submissions in reply.[48] First, the plain language of Article 15 gave Turkish courts jurisdiction in accordance with international law subject only to limits imposed by Article 16 (which was not relevant to the facts). Therefore, there was no warrant to imply any further limitation to Turkish jurisdiction based on the negotiating history. Second, Article 6 of the Turkish Penal Code, which had been taken verbatim from the Italian Penal Code and was similar to provisions found in numerous other national systems, was not contrary to international law. Third, analogous cases demonstrated that an offence committed aboard a Turkish vessel could be treated as if it has occurred within Turkish territory and the same principles of criminal jurisdiction were applicable. Fourth, to the extent that the incident involved connected offences (*délits connexes*) the Turkish Code of Criminal Procedure, which had been borrowed directly *from France*, stipulated that offenders should be tried together. Thus it was appropriate and legal to try Demons and the Turkish captain together in Turkey. Fifth, even contemplating the case only from the perspective of international law applicable to collisions at sea, no principle of international criminal law debarred Turkish jurisdiction. Sixth, given that Turkey plainly had jurisdiction to prosecute Demons for manslaughter, there could be no international wrong giving rise to a requirement to pay reparations to either France or Demons.

This recitation, however, does not do full justice to the advocacy of the Turkish Agent and Minister of Justice: Dr Mahmut Esat, a dynamic Swiss-educated lawyer (and revolutionary politician) in his mid-thirties.[49] Esat was an interesting figure in the early Turkish republic, at once a fierce nationalist but also a modernising

---

[44] ibid, 246.

[45] *Lotus* (n 3) France: Memorial, PCIJ Reports, Series C, No 13-II, 186.

[46] *Lotus* (n 3) France: Counter-Memorial, PCIJ Reports, Series C, No 13-II, 282. (Author's translation: '*la substitution de la compétence des tribunaux turcs à celle des tribunaux consulaires étrangers pour connaître des actions pénales dirigées contre des étrangers a été le résultat du consentement donné par les Puissances à cette substitution dans les Conventions signées à Lausanne le 24 juillet 1923*').

[47] On international law as a system in which great powers typically enjoy special prerogatives: G Simpson, *Great Powers and Outlaw States: Unequal Sovereigns in the International Legal Order* (Cambridge, CUP, 2004).

[48] See *Lotus* (n 3) 9.

[49] Esat was so proud of his performance in *Lotus* he assumed the additional surname 'Bozkurt': Özsu (n 18) 49 fn 104.

universalist. For him, the price of creating a new and distinctly ethnically Turkish state (one which would break with the multi-ethnic Ottoman Empire) was subscription to the European standard of civilisation.[50] That is, while recognition as a 'civilised' state would entail submission to international law and adoption of European legal standards (Esat introduced the Swiss Civil Code to Turkey in 1926) it would also confer a protective cloak of sovereignty upon the young ethno-nationalist republic. As Özsu puts it, Esat advanced two parallel lines of argument: 'the one pointing in the direction of international law's binding force, the other underlining the agency or the autonomous state'. Esat thus argued that the effect of Article 15 of the Treaty of Lausanne was to recognise Turkey's complete jurisdictional competence subject only to the condition that it not contravene the principles of international law. Thus, following the abolition of the capitulations, Turkey was now 'on a footing of complete equality with other civilised and independent states, *without any restriction or difference*'.[51] Esat was thus inclined to present the French case as a 'thinly veiled attempt to reintroduce institutions of consular decentralisation'[52] and he was equally scathing of the hypocrisy implicit in France's own municipal use of the protective principle to assert criminal jurisdiction over the act of foreigners outside France affecting French interests.

The French case was presented in elegant, technical and often gently disparaging terms by the redoubtable formalist Jules Basdevant.[53] Basdevant was the older man of the two advocates, having participated in the 1919 peace conferences as a French technical expert. Now entering his fifties, he held one of very few chairs in international law in Paris and had had a distinguished academic career.[54] A frequent advocate before international arbitral tribunals and the PCIJ, he was soon to enter the Ministry for Foreign Affairs[55] and would eventually be elected to the ICJ itself in 1946 as an inaugural (and very long-serving) judge and eventual president. Very much a figure of the establishment, and a specialist in treaty law, he doggedly insisted throughout on his argument that Article 15 of the Treaty of Lausanne was the governing conventional law between the parties and had to be interpreted in light of the drafting history. Compared to Esat's fieriness he may have seemed, on this occasion, rather haughty. Maintaining his insistence, as he did even in his reply, that extra-territorial judicial competence 'had been refused to Turkey by the Allies in the negotiations at Lausanne' and one could not recognise now, by an act of treaty interpretation, a competence 'which had been clearly refused at Lausanne'[56] played

---

[50] H-L Kieser 'An ethno-nationalist revolutionary and theorist of Kemalism: Dr Mahmut Esat Bozkurt (1892-1943)' in H-L Kieser (ed), *Turkey Beyond Nationalism: Towards Post-Nationalist Identities* (London, IB Tauris, 2006) 20–27.

[51] PCIJ, Series C, No 13-II, 111-12; quoted in Özsu (n 18) 47. (Author's translation: 'sur un pied d'égalité complète avec les autres États civilisés et indépendants, *sans aucune restriction ou différence*.' Original emphasis).

[52] Özsu (n 18) 45.

[53] M Koskenniemi, *The Gentle Civilizer of Nations: The Rise and Fall of International Law 1870–1960* (Cambridge, CUP, 2001) 312.

[54] ibid.

[55] ibid.

[56] PCIJ, Series C, No 13-II, 139 (reply of Professor Basdevant, Agent for France) (author's translation).

directly to Esat's case. It found little favour with the Court which held that the words in Article 15 'principles of international law' were 'sufficiently clear' in themselves to preclude 'having regard to preparatory work'. The words could only mean, in their ordinary sense, 'international law as it is applied between all nations belonging to the community of States'.[57] His arguments to the effect that criminal jurisdiction was, absent an exception, strictly territorial found more success, albeit only among the dissenting judges.

B. The Judgment

The *Lotus* case is of lasting significance regarding at least three legal issues: whether the international legal system is to be construed as one in which everything is permitted to states unless it is prohibited; the law of jurisdiction (or more narrowly, the law of jurisdiction applicable to high seas collisions); and the rules governing the ascertainment of customary international law. First, however, something should be said as to the division of opinion within the Court.

Discussion of the case usually notes that the Court was equally divided with six votes in favour and six votes against the answers given, the final *dispositifs* following the casting vote of the President.[58] This is not entirely correct. Judge Moore dissented not on the point actually decided in answering the question posed (as discussed below) but because he considered that Turkey had in practice relied upon the passive personality jurisdiction provision of its Penal Code (which he considered impermissible as the law stood at the time) and that this should have decided the case in favour of France.[59]

The point of law finally decided in the *Lotus Case* should inform our reading of the rest of the judgment: the Court held, entirely correctly, that a ship on the high seas can be 'assimilated' to the territory of its flag state for some purposes.[60] It follows that a ship on the high seas is in the same (or no better) position as state territory for jurisdictional purposes and therefore ordinary jurisdictional principles should be applied to events on board, including objective territorial (or effects) jurisdiction. Thus:

> The act of the *Lotus* in colliding with the Turkish ship was, therefore, an act completed within the Turkish territorial jurisdiction—literally, within the Turkish ship—and accordingly liable to be prosecuted by the Turkish authorities.[61]

Nonetheless, that act was commenced by the negligence of Demons aboard the *Lotus*, itself subject to the jurisdiction of France as the flag State. France, therefore,

---

[57] *Lotus* (n 3) 16. The Court referred to the standard of civilisation only in quoting Turkey's submissions: ibid, 7.

[58] eg R Ruze, 'Affaire du Lotus' (1928) Revue de Droit International et de Législation Comparée 124, 144; C Staker, 'Jurisdiction' in MD Evans (ed) *International Law*, 4th edn (Oxford, OUP 2014) 317; A von Bogdandy and M Rau, 'The Lotus', *Max Planck Encyclopedia of Public International Law* (2006), [5]. See: Art 55, PCIJ Statute.

[59] *Lotus* (n 3) Judge Moore (dissenting opinion), 65; see also H Lauterpacht (ed), *Oppenheim's International Law*, 5th edn (London, Longmans, Green & Co, 1937) 270 fn 1.

[60] *Lotus* (n 3) 23.

[61] Staker, 'Jurisdiction' (n 58) 317.

on ordinary principles would have subjective territorial jurisdiction. The result was, in the view of the majority, that:

[i]t is only natural that each should be able to exercise jurisdiction and to do so in respect of the incident as a whole. It is therefore a case of concurrent jurisdiction.[62]

From a modern standpoint, this would appear a relatively obvious conclusion.[63] (Indeed, it was foreseen as the most likely course of reasoning for the Court in 1926 by Beckett).[64]

In such a case there is no rule of priority (let alone exclusivity) and either flag state involved will be able to exercise criminal jurisdiction if they are able to gain custody of the offender (or if national law permits trial *in absentia*).[65] This result might be thought problematic insofar as it does not preclude multiple criminal proceedings being commenced before different national courts for the same conduct. However, the same may be said of any number of transnational offences. There is no general international rule against double jeopardy:[66] though a limited version of one was introduced in the Geneva High Seas Convention to overturn this specific ruling, as discussed below.

Nevertheless, in reaching this quite narrow conclusion the PCIJ manage to render one of the most contentious decisions in its history. The controversy arises from the (in)famous passage (emphasis added):

International law governs relations between independent States. The rules of law binding upon States therefore emanate from their own free will as expressed in conventions or by usages generally accepted as expressing principles of law and established in order to regulate the relations between these co-existing independent communities or with a view to the achievement of common aims. *Restrictions upon the independence of States cannot therefore be presumed.*[67]

The final sentence has, of course, already been referred to above as the '*Lotus* principle'. One should note that, strictly, this dictum does not establish a presumption in favour of state's freedom of action: it only 'rejects a presumption against [such] freedom'.[68] Nonetheless, the usual reading of the principle suggests the court held that there is a general presumption of freedom of state action with the consequence that it is for a state denying the legality of another state's action to lead evidence of a prohibitive rule. This coincides with what Cheng or Spiermann term the 'national sovereign' approach: one which takes an essentially internal view of sovereignty, holding that a sovereign is presumptively free of any constraint. So interpreted, the principle establishes a presumption of freedom which is rebuttable, but one which necessarily commences from a proposition (or provides a technique for arriving at the conclusion) that in any given controversy between states there may not necessarily a rule governing it. This would, on its face, leave a potentially

---

[62] *Lotus*, 30–31.

[63] Guilfoyle, *Shipping Interdiction* (n 11); Mann, 'Doctrine of Jurisdiction' (n 12).

[64] WE Beckett, 'Criminal Jurisdiction Over Foreigners' (1927) 8 *BYIL* l08, 111–12.

[65] R O'Keefe, *International Criminal Law* (Oxford, OUP, 2015) 25–28.

[66] R Cryer, H Friman, D Robinson and E Wilmshurst, *An Introduction to International Criminal Law and Procedure*, 3rd edn (Cambridge, CUP, 2014) 85–87.

[67] *Lotus* (n 3) 18.

[68] Speirmann (n 15) 254.

wide scope for findings of *non-liquet*. This, however, is not the approach the Court took in substance and was one Judge Anzilotti (who drafted the judgment) ruled out early.[69]

Alternatively, the *Lotus* principle may be interpreted instead as laying out only a residual presumption: once ordinary legal technique has been exhausted in an effort to find an applicable rule, it is possible to conclude that the question is regulated by a principle of freedom.[70] On this interpretation the principle has nothing to say about burdens of proof. (And, indeed, the idea that the case set up a strict burden of proof is not compatible with the fact the Court conducted its own research into the applicable law going beyond the parties' submissions.)[71] Further, such a reading is much more compatible with the idea of (again in Cheng or Spiermann's terms) the 'international sovereign', a sovereign with legal powers which are inherently limited or circumscribed, not least by the existence of other sovereigns within a system premised on the formal and existential equality of states.[72] Obviously, in any system of formal equality the existence of other equals (especially equals claiming an immunity right in respect of a reserved domain of domestic affairs) will limit the sphere of action available to any individual. Alternatively, Crawford advances a reading of the *Lotus* principle which focuses upon the content of the word 'independence'. That is, independent sovereign states enjoy rights: of plenary competence to act on the international plane; of 'exclusive competence in their internal affairs'; not to be subject to compulsory dispute settlement without their consent; and of formal legal equality.[73] Restrictions upon these rights may exist, but are not to be presumed. While there is now much more international law which may qualify these rights 'it is still generally accurate to characterize sovereignty as a set of (rebuttable) presumptions.'[74]

Such readings are far more compatible with the paragraph which immediately followed the statement of the *Lotus* principle:

> Now the first and foremost restriction imposed by international law upon a State is that— failing the existence of a permissive rule to the contrary—it may not exercise its power in any form in the territory of another State. In this sense jurisdiction is certainly territorial; it cannot be exercised by a State outside its territory except by virtue of a permissive rule derived from international custom or from a convention.[75]

This passage, at the least, states one fundamental restrictive rule and presumes the existence of a wider corpus of well-established restrictive rules. The statement concerns, of course, only enforcement jurisdiction. However, given the great variety of

---

[69] ibid, 250 fn 209, 259.

[70] ibid, 254.

[71] ibid; *Lotus* (n 3) 31.

[72] Namely, equality of standing before international judicial organs (formal/juridical equality) and having an equal right to territorial integrity and political independence (existential equality). Neither necessarily requires legislative equality (ie equal capacity to influence law-making processes): Simpson, *Great Powers and Outlaw States* (n 46) 42–56.

[73] Crawford (n 13) 89–90, [90]–[93].

[74] ibid, 90, [95].

[75] *Lotus* (n 3) 19–20. On the significance of this paragraph for our understanding of the case see further: An Hertogen, 'Letting Lotus Bloom' (2016) 26 *EJIL* 901, 907.

national legislation attaching *civil* consequences to conduct abroad the Court went on to state:

> It does not, however, follow that international law prohibits a State from exercising juris-diction in its own territory, in respect of any case which relates to acts which have taken place abroad, *and in which it cannot rely on some permissive rule of international law* (emphasis added).[76]

This is more problematic. The first part of this sentence is uncontroversial: States do prescribe conduct which occurs abroad and clearly do not consider their jurisdiction to be strictly territorially limited. The emphasised portion supports the conventional reading of the case as setting out an unbridled positivist principle of freedom.[77] However, the picture is more complex. First, a significant part of Turkey's argu-ment was that sovereign states are free under international law to choose between a variety of national systems of jurisdiction. Following the statement above the Court was keen to emphasise that the discretion left to states by international law 'explains the great variety of rules which they have been able to adopt without objections' by other states.[78] The Court here was attempting to square a circle: the great variety of state practice on jurisdiction appeared overall to be tacitly consented to; yet the practice was not perceived as consistent enough to give rise to defined permissive rules. What we see here may also be a sign of the tensions the Court faced in attempt-ing to navigate between two conceptions of sovereignty and, indeed, towards the more modern view it is typically taken to have rejected. (A point returned to in the conclusion.)

Further, the discussion to this point in the judgment concerned civil law, and was therefore incidental. The point at hand was one of criminal jurisdiction, as the Court went on to observe:

> Nevertheless, it has to be seen whether the foregoing considerations really apply as regards criminal jurisdiction, or whether this jurisdiction is governed by a different principle ... Though it is true that in all systems of law the principle of the territorial character of crimi-nal law is fundamental, it is equally true that all or nearly all these systems of law extend ... to offences committed outside the territory of the State which adopts them, and they do so in ways which vary from State to State. The territoriality of criminal law, therefore, is not an absolute principle of international law and by no means coincides with territorial sover-eignty. This situation may be considered from two different standpoints.[79]

This passage, crucial to the final outcome, largely sets the Court's reasoning up to this point to one side. The point of departure in considering the question of criminal law prescriptive jurisdiction is not deduction from abstract principle but induction from the actual (and varied) legislative conduct of states in prescribing extra-terri-torial offences. True, the last words hint again at questions of method. One must commence from either: first, a presumption of freedom, and a restrictive rule must

---

[76] ibid.
[77] Judges Higgins, Kooijmans and Buergenthal (n 1), 79; Mills 'Rethinking Jurisdiction in Interna-tional Law' (n 9), 191.
[78] *Lotus* (n 3) 19.
[79] ibid, 20.

be proved against Turkey (the Turkish argument); or, second, a presumption of territoriality, in which case a permissive rule of extra-territorial jurisdiction must be demonstrated (the French argument). Again, we seem to be back to presumptions and burdens of proof. Critically, however, the Court did *not* choose either approach, rather it concluded that whichever approach was taken in the present case the question would be the same: whether there was a relevant rule prohibiting Turkish prescriptive jurisdiction.

One might well find this conclusion a little baffling. Part of the problem is undoubtedly caused, as noted above, by the manner in which the question was put. The special agreement between France and Turkey expressly asked whether Turkey had acted *contrary to any rule* of international law. One might thus expect it would have been difficult for the court to avoid examining whether there was a relevant prohibition. Nonetheless, in substance, that is precisely what the Court did. Instead of searching for a prohibitive rule it instead found a permissive rule. After correctly noting that the principle of exclusive flag state jurisdiction principally confers an immunity from foreign interference (ie enforcement jurisdiction) on the high seas, the Court went on to observe:

> it by no means follows that a State can never in its own territory exercise jurisdiction over acts which have occurred on board a foreign ship on the high seas. A corollary of the principle of the freedom of the seas is that a ship on the high seas is assimilated to the territory of the State the flag of which it flies, for, just as in its own territory, that State exercises its authority upon it, and no other State may do so. ... [B]y virtue of the principle of the freedom of the seas, a ship is placed in the same position as national territory; but there is nothing to support the claim according to which the rights of the State under whose flag the vessel sails may go farther ... It follows that what occurs on board a vessel on the high seas must be regarded as if it occurred on the territory of the State whose flag the ship flies. If, therefore, a guilty act committed on the high seas produces its effects on a vessel flying another flag or in foreign territory, the same principles must be applied as if the territories of two different States were concerned.[80]

That is, in holding that ships on the high seas could be in no better position that territory, the PCIJ found that they could be subject to concurrent prescriptive jurisdiction inter alia on the basis of the effects principle—which was sufficient to resolve the case at hand. To the extent that a prohibitive rule was relevant it was that of exclusive *enforcement* jurisdiction in respect of ships and territory. If one takes the Court's reasoning seriously, the implicit train of logic must be that the easiest way to demonstrate the existence or non-existence of a restrictive rule is to enquire into the existence of a permissive one. What the law permits it cannot prohibit. In this sense the majority was right: in this particular case it did not matter the approach one took to the question because the positive law already supplied an answer.

On the question of customary international law, the *Lotus* case's most obvious contribution is the introduction into the reasoning of the PCIJ (and later the ICJ) of the two-element theory of customary law. The Court took the question to

---

[80] ibid, 25.

be whether there existed a rule of international law which, in the event of a collision, reserved jurisdiction exclusively to the courts of the flag state of 'the vessel
proceeded against'.[81] Rather than proceeding on the basis that it already knew the
law (*jura novit curia*), the Court instead required evidence of the rule.[82] Thus it was
not enough for France and to show that cases concerning (disputed or concurrent)
criminal jurisdiction in the event of a collision were rare and that this was consistent
with a duty upon states other than the flag state not to prosecute. Even if the rarity
of reported cases proved the factual point alleged by the French agent:

> it would merely show that states had often, in practice, abstained from instituting criminal
> proceedings, and not that they recognized themselves as being obliged to do so; for only if
> such abstention were based on their being *conscious of having a duty to abstain* would it be
> possible to speak of an international custom.[83]

While a strict two-element formulation of custom has become a staple of the
written judgments of the ICJ, the extent to which it is applied in practice is, at best,
dubious.[84]

C. The Dissenting Opinions

Six dissents were appended to the Court's judgment. Of these, as noted, Judge
Moore was actually in agreement with the majority on the question decided.
His 'dissenting' opinion makes an eloquent case that every 'law-governed' state,
including France, asserted the right in some cases to punish crimes occurring in
its territory even though committed 'by a person at the time corporeally present
in another state'.[85] He further concludes that 'there was nothing in the law or in
the reason of the thing' compelling a conclusion that this principle should operate
differently in respect of ships at sea than on land.[86] This and his dissection of the
various cases lead in support of the contrary conclusion was enough to lead him to
agree with the majority.[87] His dissent went only to the question of legality of passive
personality jurisdiction at international law.[88] (That is, while he considered that
Turkey could have taken jurisdiction as a flag state over the incident, he considered
that in practice it had relied on Article 6 of its Penal Code, which was not in conformity with international law as he understood it.) The dissent of Judges Loder,
Weiss, Finlay, Nyholm and Altamira are considered in turn below.

---

[81] ibid, 25–26.
[82] Crawford (n 13) 66.
[83] *Lotus* (n 3) 28 (emphasis added).
[84] S Talmon, 'Determining Customary International Law: The ICJ's Methodology between Induction,
Deduction and Assertion' (2015) 26 *EJIL* 417–443; A Roberts, 'Traditional and Modern Approaches to
Customary International Law: A Reconciliation' (2001) 95 *AJIL* 757–91.
[85] *Lotus* (n 3) Judge Moore (dissenting opinion), 69–70.
[86] ibid, 69.
[87] National case law as to whether a flag State may prosecute the death of a national aboard its flag
vessel where caused by a foreigner aboard a foreign vessel was contradictory. See eg Beckett 'Criminal
Jurisdiction Over Foreigners' (n 64) on the difference in reasoning and result between *R v Keyn* (1876) 2
ExD 63 and *US v Davis* (1837) 2 Sumn 482.
[88] ibid, 89–93.

Judge Loder disagreed with the proposition that 'every door is open unless it is closed by treaty or by established custom' and thought rather that international law rested on 'a general consensus of opinion' among states.[89] More concretely, Judge Loder prioritised territoriality, holding that exceptions to the principle should be proven and strictly construed.[90]

> The criminal law of a state may extend to crimes and offences committed abroad by its nationals, since such nationals are subject to the law of their own country; but it cannot extend to offences committed by a foreigner in foreign territory, without infringing the sovereign rights of the foreign State concerned, since in that State the State enacting the law has no jurisdiction.[91]

Further, this jurisdiction could not be extended by the 'subsequent presence' of the accused in the territory of the prescribing state.[92] He considered objective territoriality a legal fiction justified only in the case of intentional transboundary effects and disapproved entirely of any passive personality or protective doctrine.[93]

Judge Weiss also placed a paramount importance upon territoriality, holding that once the frontier is traversed 'the right of states to exercise police duties and jurisdiction ceases to exist'.[94] A state's criminal jurisdiction is thus 'based on *and limited by*' territory.[95] Further, he took the freedom of the high seas to warrant treating a ship as 'a detached and floating portion of the national territory' of its flag state with the consequence of excluding 'any jurisdiction other than that of the flag' other than in 'certain exceptional cases'.[96]

Lord Finlay considered the application of the objective territorial principle to events having their effects aboard a vessel 'a new and startling application of [the] metaphor' that flag State jurisdiction could be analogised to territory.[97] Without much reasoned explanation, though with some reference to authority, he considered it natural that maritime law would dictate in the event of a collision jurisdiction should rest with the flag state of the negligently navigated vessel or alternatively the state of nationality of the person responsible.[98] He also disapproved of any argument based on protective jurisdiction.[99]

Judge Nyholm, proceeded from a similarly strict conception of territoriality as the other dissenters. In his view, the principle of exclusive flag state jurisdiction collapsed in the case of a collision and the ordinary principle of territorial jurisdiction applied.[100] However, no positive rule permitting an exercise of extra-territorial jurisdiction in

---

[89] *Lotus* (n 3) Judge Loder (dissenting opinion), 34.
[90] ibid 34–35.
[91] ibid, 35.
[92] ibid.
[93] ibid, 36–37.
[94] *Lotus* (n 3) Judge Weiss (dissenting opinion), 44.
[95] ibid, 45.
[96] ibid, 46.
[97] ibid, 52.
[98] ibid, 53.
[99] ibid, 56–57.
[100] *Lotus* (n 3) Judge Nyholm (dissenting opinion), 62–63.

such cases had yet emerged, though he conceded there was a 'tendency towards a relaxation in the strict application' of territoriality of criminal jurisdiction.[101] As to the existence of a rule of international custom, Judge Nyholm took a somewhat more relaxed view than the majority holding that custom could be:

> a manifestation of international legal ethics which takes place through the continual recurrence of events with an innate consciousness of their being necessary.[102]

Judge Altamira proceeded from the proposition that 'the jurisdiction of a state is territorial in character and that in respect of its nationals a state has preferential, if not sole jurisdiction', and that exceptions to these principles had only been recognised in 'extreme cases'.[103] He was unpersuaded that the fact that a number of states had adopted similar legislation regarding the prosecution of offences committed extra-territorially could prove a rule of customary international law. At best, he considered that it might be evidence of the opinion of states on a question;[104] the existence of a general agreement among states being the critical issue. Judge Altamira conducted a forensic review of relevant case law and national legislation to content himself that states generally only asserted extra-territorial criminal jurisdiction in particularly serious cases but held that there was insufficient uniformity to demonstrate the existence of an agreed rule. He found the 'preponderating opinion' of states to be against the assertion of jurisdiction in a case such as the *Lotus* and appeared to accord significant weight to the protests of France as evidence that it had not consented to any such rule.[105] Such a strict version of positivism has not subsequently found favour in the case law of the ICJ where the consent or non-consent of the state 'contesting the existence of [a] rule is not as decisive as we might expect' in an ostensibly consent-based system.[106]

V. THE AFTERMATH OF SS LOTUS

It would be an understatement to say the PCIJ's judgment in Lotus was not well received, either in practice or in the academy.[107] As noted, the narrowest ground for the decision was that the collision had 'taken place' on the Turkish ship and was therefore an event within the jurisdiction of the flag state (by analogy with the objective territorial or effects principle).[108] The decision 'produced alarm among seafarers, and a long campaign against the rule',[109] which was thought to create the risk of multiple prosecutions for the same offence.

---

[101] ibid, 63.
[102] ibid, 60.
[103] *Lotus* (n 3) Judge Altamira (dissenting opinion), 95.
[104] ibid, 96.
[105] ibid, 103.
[106] Crawford (n 13) 69, [65].
[107] See ibid 40 and 458; von Bogdandy and Rau 'The Lotus' (n 58) [1].
[108] RR Churchill and AV Lowe, *The Law of the Sea*, 3rd edn (Manchester, Manchester University Press, 1999), 208; *cf* DP O'Connell (I Sheared, ed), *The International Law of the Sea*, vol II (Oxford, Clarendon, 1984), 800.
[109] P Malanczuk, *Akehurst's Modern Introduction to International Law* (London, Routledge, 1997), 109.

This resulted first in the International Convention for the Unification of Certain Rules relating to Penal Jurisdiction in matters of Collisions and Other Incidents of Navigation 1952 (Brussels Penal Jurisdiction Convention).[110] This provided in Article 1:

> In the event of a collision or any other incident of navigation concerning a sea-going ship and involving the penal or disciplinary responsibility of the master or of any other person in the service of the ship, criminal or disciplinary proceedings may be instituted only before the judicial or administrative authorities of the State of which the ship was flying the flag at the time ...

Article 2 prohibited measures of arrest or detention of the vessel in such cases being taken by any authority other than the flag state.

With only very minor amendments to the wording, these provisions were adopted in 1956 as Article 35 of the International Law Commission's (ILC) Articles concerning the Law of the Sea.[111] The ILC drafting was modified slightly in Article 11(1) of the 1958 Geneva Convention on the High Seas (High Seas Convention), in particular by further treating the question of disciplinary proceedings in an additional paragraph which also acknowledged the jurisdiction of licence issuing authorities over non-nationals.[112] Article 11(1) of the High Seas Convention was subsequently reproduced almost verbatim as Article 97 of the UN Convention on the Law of the Sea.[113] There appears to have been no significant debate on this point during either UNCLOS I or UNCLOS III.[114] Given that the rule has been re-enacted in successive widely-adhered-to treaties—and without, it would appear, any debate on the principle involved—one may conclude that it now represents customary international law[115] in respect of collisions, incidents of navigation and disciplinary matters. In other cases of criminal jurisdiction the rule enunciated in the *Lotus* case (events occurring aboard a ship are within the flag state's criminal jurisdiction, even if those events commenced outside the ship) presumably remains unaffected.

As noted throughout this chapter, academic commentary has tended to focus upon the 'principle of freedom' or '*Lotus* presumption' and has often been scathing. Shortly after the case was decided Brierly rather acidly dismissed it as a:

> highly contentious metaphysical proposition of the extreme positivist school that the law emanates from the free will of sovereign independent States, and from this premiss ... that restrictions on the independence of States cannot be presumed. Neither ... can the absence of restrictions; for we are not able to deduce the law applicable to a specific state of facts from the mere fact of sovereignty or independence.[116]

---

[110] International Convention for the Unification of Certain Rules relating to Penal Jurisdiction in Matters of Collision and Other Incidents of Navigation, 10 May 1952, 439 UNTS 233.

[111] ILC, Report of the International Law Commission: Articles Concerning the Law of the Sea, UN Doc A/3159 (1956), GAOR 11th Sess Suppl 9, 8.

[112] Resulting from a French proposal: UN Conference on the Law of the Sea I, Report of the Second Committee, UN Doc A/CONF.13/L.17 (1958), OR II, 96 [29].

[113] On the drafting history, see ibid [30].

[114] See: MH Nordquist, SN Nandan, S Rosenne (eds), *United Nations Convention on the Law of the Sea 1982: A Commentary*, vol III (The Hague, Nijhoff, 1995) 167–68.

[115] Following: ICJ, *North Sea Continental Shelf Cases (Federal Republic of Germany v. Netherlands/ Denmark)*, [1969] ICJ Rep 3, [71]–[74].

[116] Brierly 'The "Lotus" Case' (n 5) 155.

Thus the general view of the *Lotus* case is that it represents the last gasp of an 'old' vision of international law based on the mere coexistence of sovereigns relatively unencumbered by legal relations in their dealings with each other, a view barely apposite in the 1920s and completely unsustainable now.[117] This is the received wisdom; and it is, in part at least, wrong. Critics do not always appear to have considered the *Lotus* principle either in its immediate textual context or framed against the wider circumstances of the case. Indeed, given that the majority launch straight from formulating the *Lotus* principle into a discussion of the first-principle restrictions imposed upon states' sovereign powers,[118] it can hardly be concluded that the Court considered that the 'principle of freedom' was to be taken as a starting point in all cases. Indeed, if the *Lotus* principle means what it literally says, then the PCIJ in *Lotus* failed to apply it.

As discussed above, other more satisfactory readings are available. In context, it may be construed as articulating either a residual principle to address *non-liquets* or as a proposition that sovereignty under international law (a state's 'independence') consists of a bundle of rebuttable presumptions derogations from which may be proven but not assumed. This is not to say the *Lotus* presumption is actually in some revisionist sense good law or an early statement compatible with the modern 'heads' or 'principles' of jurisdiction approach. It is not. Nor, however, does it necessarily embody the dated two-dimensional vision of positivism for which it is commonly made the whipping boy.

VI. *SS LOTUS* AND THE DEVELOPMENT OF INTERNATIONAL LAW

It would be bold to suggest that *Lotus* has had any crucial role in the subsequent development of public international law.[119] Nonetheless, a number of propositions of law which the PCIJ outlined in *Lotus* were broadly correct and remain recognisable. Certainly as regards the law of jurisdiction it was in error when it said:

> Far from laying down a general prohibition to the effect that states may not extend the application of their laws and the jurisdiction of their courts to persons, property and acts outside their territory, it leaves them in this respect a wide measure of discretion which is only limited in certain cases by prohibitive rules; as regards other cases, every state remains free to adopt the principles which it regards as best and most suitable.[120]

The error, however, was largely one of emphasis and overstatement. It must be remembered that Turkey had pleaded that as a sovereign state it had a free choice as between several equally valid systems of criminal jurisdiction which it might adopt.[121]

---

[117] eg Judges Higgins, Kooijmans and Buergenthal (n 1).
[118] *Lotus* (n 3) 18.
[119] It has occasionally found favour: *Case Concerning Right of Passage over Indian Territory (Merits)*, ICJ Reports 1960, 6, Judge Moreno Quintana (dissenting opinion) 91; *North Sea Continental Shelf* [1969] ICJ Rep 3, Judge Amoun (Sep Op) 101; *Fisheries Jurisdiction (United Kingdom v. Iceland)*, [1974] ICJ Rep 3, Judge Dillard (Sep Op) 59; and in *Legality of the Threat or Use of Nuclear Weapons*, [1996] ICJ Rep 220 see: Judge Guillaume (Sep Op) 291–2, President Bedjaoui (Declaration) 271, and Judge Shahabuddeen (dissenting opinion) 426. See further: Spiermann (n 15) 253 fn 218. Note also: *Arrest Warrant* (n 1) Belgium: Counter-Memorial [3.3.29].
[120] *Lotus* (n 3) 19.
[121] Esat (n 2) 116.

These included at one end of the spectrum the system of strict territoriality and at the other the more controversial 'protective' system of jurisdiction (which it attributed to France). It also does an injustice to the Court to read the quote above without reading the passage which follows, emphasising that in practice states have adopted a great variety of systems of criminal law based on different principles of jurisdiction and have done so without protest. The Court further noted that various law reform and treaty drafting efforts to simplify or eliminate the 'conflicting jurisdictions arising from the diversity of the principles adopted by the various states' had not generally met with any success.[122] In a sense, the PCIJ was refreshingly modern (or postmodern) in its willingness to accept the possibility of multiple concurrent jurisdictions as an inevitable feature of a system of law regulating the co-existence of sovereigns. The idea that international law must contain some rule to resolve questions of concurrent jurisdiction decisively in favour of one state or another remains illusory.[123] The Court was thus on firm ground, and remains entirely right, when it stated:

> In these circumstances, all that can be required of a State is that it should not overstep the limits which international law places upon its jurisdiction; within these limits, its title to exercise jurisdiction rests in its sovereignty.[124]

As Crawford has noted, following the *Arrest Warrant Case* it is possible to suggest that the general rule is now that a state must be able to point to a permissive title in international law supporting an exercise of jurisdiction. However, he has accurately characterised this as a 'shift in focus' which is 'largely cosmetic'.[125] As discussed above, the method actually adopted by the PCIJ in *Lotus* was to enquire first into the existence of a permissive rule. Having found that the principle of territoriality applied by analogy, the more theoretical discussion to which a general presumption of freedom might have been relevant simply fell away.

VII. CONCLUSIONS

How should we now assess the *Lotus* case? As already observed, there are effectively two *Lotus* cases: the most discussed version of the case, dealing with first principle understandings of international law; and, second, the case regarding the law of jurisdiction on the high seas, and criminal jurisdiction more generally. It is widely accepted that the *Lotus* principle is bad law. Attempts to suggest otherwise than that the PCIJ literally meant what it said (restrictions upon States' independence cannot be presumed) are apt to be dismissed as revisionism.[126] Nonetheless, this chapter has suggested those criticisms are somewhat overstated. Rather than being the high water mark of old-fashioned positivism, in the *Lotus* case we may see instead a turning point. It displays an earnest attempt to revise the dominant theory

---

[122] *Lotus* (n 3) 19.
[123] Cryer et al, *Introduction to International Criminal Law* (n 66).
[124] *Lotus* (n 3) 19.
[125] J Crawford, *Brownlie's Principles of Public International Law*, 8th edn (Oxford, OUP, 2012) 458.
[126] Mills 'Rethinking Jurisdiction in International Law' (n 9), 190.

of international law (one increasingly at variance with the facts) and construct a law not merely of coexistence but cooperation. This much is plain on the bare text of the Court's judgment. Further, it is worth noting that the *Lotus* principle was not actually applied in the *Lotus* case, or at least not in any decisive fashion.

The driver of the decision was instead the proposition that the foremost restriction upon the sovereign power of the state is that it may not exercise jurisdictional power in another state's territory absent a permissive rule. This is clearly not only still a good statement of law, but the cornerstone of the modern international system. It is present, for example, in the non-intervention principle and the prohibition on the use of force in the UN Charter.[127]

Further, the Court's approach to the discernment of custom has clearly been influential in the development of the jurisprudence of the International Court of Justice. The two-element theory of custom has never been formally resiled from, even if it is open to debate whether it is a formula more honoured in the breach than the observance.[128]

As regards the Court's conclusion that there could be concurrent jurisdiction on the high seas in matters of collusion, it has been noted that this is one of the few rules of custom—possibly the only one—discerned by the PCIJ or the ICJ which has been subsequently overturned in treaty law.[129] This, however, tends to obscure the fact that absent the special rule introduced to deal with collisions the proposition remains good law. There are numerous instances in which states may have concurrent jurisdiction over events occurring upon the high seas going well beyond cases of universal jurisdiction such as piracy. These are usually explicitly created by treaty, drug interdiction and (historically) unauthorised radio broadcasting being clear examples.[130] However, it is established that a flag state may waive its jurisdiction ad hoc in order to allow another state to prosecute offences discovered aboard its vessel irrespective of an underlying treaty arrangement.[131] This strongly suggests that the correct understanding of exclusive jurisdiction on the high seas is not that it excludes other states from exercising prescriptive jurisdiction, but rather it is a guarantee against interference by foreign government vessels (enforcement jurisdiction).[132] The conclusions of the PCIJ on point were, and remain, correct.

Finally, however, it is worth noting the modernity of the Court's conclusion that concurrent jurisdiction could exist as part of the natural state of affairs in the international order. In a sense, this conclusion is what caused the most alarm at the time. It still finds echoes in unjustified alarm over universal jurisdiction. Nonetheless, among numerous changes to the international legal order since 1927 we increasingly 'live in a world of interpenetrating jurisdictional orders not [always] closely tied to territory'.[133] In the latter, the PCIJ was, at the very least, prescient.

---

[127] Bogdandy and Rau (n 58), 19.

[128] ibid.

[129] Crawford (n 13), 66 [60].

[130] Guilfoyle (n 11) Chs 5 and 7.

[131] ibid 72, 84, 119, 121, 248, 256, 287; see eg: *Mevedyev v France*, Application No 3394/03, Judgment of the Grand Chamber, 29 March 2010 [96].

[132] *Arrest Warrant* (n 1) Judge ad hoc Van Den Wyngaert (dissenting opinion) 169, [49].

[133] D Guilfoyle, 'Reading *The City and the City* as an International Lawyer: Reflections on Territoriality, Jurisdiction And Transnationality' (2015) 4 *London Review of International Law* 195, 207.

6

Island of Palmas (Netherlands v United States of America) (1928)

EIRIK BJORGE

A T ISSUE IN *Island of Palmas*[1] was the sovereignty over a miniscule island called the Island of Palmas, or the Island of Miangas,[2] in the north of the archipelago which today constitutes Indonesia. The 700 inhabitants of the coconut-palm-strewn island mainly exported dried coconut kernels and mats.[3] From a commercial, as well as military, point of view the island's value was, like the island itself, small.[4]

Nonetheless, when on 21 January 1906 General Leonard Wood, US Governor of the Province of Moro, made landfall on the island, he was dismayed to find there a Dutch flag flying on the shore as well as on the dinghy that came out to greet him. 'As far as I could ascertain,' reported General Wood when he had later left the island for Zamboanga in the Philippines, 'the Dutch flag has been there for the past fifteen years'; indeed 'one man said he thought it had always been there'.[5]

Although it surfaced only in 1906, the dispute as to the sovereignty over the island had a long backstory. Spain had claimed to have discovered the Island of Palmas in the sixteenth century, possibly as early as 1526, the island having at that time been 'seen' by a Spanish explorer.[6] The Spaniards never landed or made any contact with the inhabitants of the island; indeed, no signs of taking possession or of administration by Spain had been shown or even alleged to have existed on the part of Spain. Having discovered the island, Spain had then, by virtue of the Treaty of Paris of 10 December 1898,[7] ceded the island to the United States. The United States, by reason of the Treaty of 1898, founded its argument on the Spanish discovery of the island in the sixteenth century. The sovereign rights of Spain over the island were,

---

[1] *Island of Palmas (Netherlands, United States of America)* (1928) 2 RIAA 829, (1928) 4 ILR 3.

[2] Having chosen English as the language of the arbitration, the sole arbitrator elected to use English geographical names, 'as shown on the British Admiralty Chart 2575'; the name of the case, therefore, is *Palmas* rather than *Miangas*.

[3] WJB Versfelt, *The Miangas Arbitration* (Utrecht, Kemink, 1933) 1–2.

[4] ibid 2; FK Nielsen, *The Island of Palmas Arbitration before the Permanent Court of Arbitration at the Hague* (Washington, DC, Government Printing Office, 1928) 1.

[5] Versfelt, *The Miangas Arbitration* (n 3) 4.

[6] *Island of Palmas (Netherlands, United States of America)* (1928) 2 RIAA 829, 844–45.

[7] Treaty of Peace between Spain and the United States, 10 December 1898, 187 CTS 100.

in the submission of the United States, confirmed by the Treaty of Munster of 1648.[8] Nothing had, in the view of the United States, occurred which operated to invalidate the title thus acquired by Spain which was later ceded to the United States in the 1898 Treaty.[9] Against this background, the United States argued that it did not need to prove itself that it had exercised sovereignty over the island. As to the question of the intertemporal law, that is, whether the law to be applied was that of the sixteenth century or that of later centuries, the United States had argued that only the law as understood when the island was first discovered could be taken into account, citing a communication by Secretary of State Upshur to Mr Everett, American Minister to Great Britain, of 9 October 1843:

> How far the mere discovery of a territory which is either unsettled, or settled only by savages, gives a right to it, is a question which neither the law nor the usages of nations has yet definitely settled. The opinions of mankind, upon this point, have undergone very great changes with the progress of knowledge and civilization. Yet it will scarcely be denied that rights acquired by the general consent of civilized nations, even under the erroneous views of an unenlightened age, are protected against the changes of opinion resulting merely from the more liberal, or the more just, of after time. The rights of nations to countries discovered in the sixteenth century is to be determined by the law of nations as understood *at that time*, and not by the improved and more enlightened opinion of three centuries later.[10]

The United States furthermore made reference to what Hall observed in his *Treatise of International Law*, that is, that '[i]n the early days of European exploration it was held, or at least every state maintained with respect to territories discovered by itself, that the discovery of previously unknown land conferred *an absolute title* to it upon the state by whose agents the discovery was made'.[11] The argument was that Spain's title should, against this background, not be judged by the view of a later date as to the necessity of exacting more solid ground for title than those sanctioned in the past, that is, the view that discovery would give only an inchoate title, to be perfected by permanent occupation and administration.[12] Furthermore, the United States argued that since the island formed a geographical unity with the archipelago of the Philippines, it was unnecessary to impose on the sovereign of the totality of that territory to prove that it had exercised effective sovereignty of so small a unit. Without relying in terms on the principle of contiguity as a means by which to establish its title, the United States seemed to try to lighten its burden of proof as to the sovereignty over the island by reference to this somewhat nebulous concept.[13]

---

[8] Treaty of Peace between Spain and the Netherlands, 30 January 1648, 1 CTS 1.

[9] Nielsen, *Island of Palmas Arbitration* (n 4) 2–3.

[10] JB Moore, *Digest Vol I*, 259; cited in Memorandum of the United States 52–53; Nielsen (n 4) 3.

[11] A Pearce Higgins, *Hall's Treatise on International Law*, 7th edn (Oxford, Clarendon Press, 1917) 104 (emphasis added).

[12] Nielsen (n 4) 30.

[13] F de Visscher, 'L'arbitrage de l'Île de Palmas (Miangas)' (1929) 10 *Revue du droit international et de législation comparée* 735, 737.

The Netherlands, for its part, claimed that it had exercised sovereignty on the island up until the time at which the dispute crystallised between the parties. The Dutch Government contested the titles of acquisition on which the United States founded its argument, arguing that the Spanish discovery had never in the first place been proved; if Spain had indeed had a title, such title had been lost. It also expressed profound disagreement with the principle of contiguity. Represented in the period in question by the Dutch East India Company, the Netherlands argued that, by reason of agreements entered into with certain local chieftains of the Sangi Islands, establishing Dutch suzerainty over the territories of these chieftains, including the Island of Miangas, it had acquired and possessed rights of sovereignty over the island since at least 1677, probably as far back as 1648. On the Dutch argument, its claim to title, founded on a continuous and peaceful display of state authority over the island, must prevail over a title of acquisition of sovereignty which had not been followed by actual display of state authority.[14]

As foreshadowed above, up until 1906 no dispute had arisen between the United States and Spain on the one hand and the Netherlands on the other in connection with the Island of Palmas.[15] On the heels of General Wood's landfall, the United States' Ambassador at The Hague, on 31 March 1906, asked of the Dutch Government what its understanding was as to the status of the Island of Palmas. The Netherlands Ministry of Foreign Affairs, in a note of 17 October 1906, replied, stating that on several grounds the island, referred to as Miangas rather than Island of Palmas by the Dutch, formed a part of Dutch possessions.[16]

This diplomatic exchange continued fruitlessly for almost 20 years. On 23 January 1925, the two governments, on the basis of a bilateral arbitration convention from 1908,[17] signed a *compromis* in which they agreed to refer to settlement by a sole arbitrator the intractable question of the sovereignty over the island.[18] The parties agreed on Max Huber, the then president of the Permanent Court of International Justice, as sole arbitrator of a tribunal set up under the auspices of the Permanent Court of Arbitration. It was agreed that: '[t]he sole duty of the arbitrator shall be to determine whether the Island of Palmas (or Miangas) in its entirety forms a part of territory belonging to the United States of America or of Netherlands territory'.[19] All of the proceedings would be in writing: no oral hearing would take place.[20]

I. CLAIMS TO LANDMARK STATUS

As one Dutch commentator observed shortly after the award had been handed down, '[i]t cannot be denied that the material importance of the Island of Miangas

---

[14] Versfelt, *The Miangas Arbitration* (n 3) 6.
[15] *Island of Palmas* (n 6) 836.
[16] Versfelt (n 3) 5.
[17] Arbitration Convention between the Netherlands and the United States, 2 May 1908, 207 CTS 7.
[18] MA Mathews, 'Chronicle of International Events for the Period November 16, 1924–February 15, 1925' (1925) 19 *AJIL* 382, 389.
[19] *Island of Palmas* (n 6) 832.
[20] MO Hudson, 'The Permanent Court of Arbitration' (1933) 27 *AJIL* 440, 457.

is by no means in proportion to the trouble taken by the litigating Powers and to the time taken to settle the dispute'.[21] In international law, as in other fields, great things come from small beginnings:[22] *Island of Palmas* has justly been referred to as 'one of the most influential arbitral decisions ever'.[23] Handed down in 1928, 'the celebrated Award of Judge Huber in the *Island of Palmas* case'[24] in short order became a classic of international law, and has remained so in the jurisprudence of international courts and tribunals.[25] This was because Sole Arbitrator Huber, having been invited in the pleadings of the two parties to address certain fundamental questions of international law, missed no opportunity to set out his view of them in a way which clearly shaped the contours of a number of principles which at the beginning of the twentieth century had no more than been limned by other international courts and tribunals. Indeed, according to Fernand de Visscher, the Sole Arbitrator's account of the concept of territorial sovereignty, the conditions of acquisition and of conservation, and the burden of proof, amounted to nothing less than a remarkable feat of doctrinal exposition.[26] The two propositions to which the Award gives expression in its doctrinal frontispiece—one concerning the nature of sovereignty; the other, the intertemporal law—have both taken their rightful place in the mainstay of international law. They could also both be thought to be paradoxical. The chapter will deal with them in turn, seeking to shed light on the paradoxes which they contain within them.

II. SOVEREIGNTY

First, the Award establishes that state sovereignty 'signifies independence' and 'exclusive competence', such that in international law sovereignty is 'the point of departure in settling most questions that concern international relations'.[27] From the fact that sovereignty is a signifier rather than a legal norm or institution, it follows that appeals to sovereignty, for the settlement of legal disputes, must be

---

[21] Versfelt (n 3) 147.

[22] cf *Zechariah* 4:10.

[23] O Diggelmann, 'Max Huber (1874–1960)' in B Fassbender and A Peters (eds), *The Oxford Handbook of the History of International Law* (Oxford, OUP, 2012) 1157.

[24] R Jennings and A Watts, *Oppenheim's International Law Vol I*, 9th edn (London, Longman, 1992) 708–09.

[25] See, eg, *Legal Status of Eastern Greenland, Judgment* (1933) PCIJ Series A/B No 53, 45; *Rann of Kutch (India/Pakistan)* (1968) 27 RIAA 1, 554–55; *Canton of Valais v Canton of Tessin* (1980) 75 ILR 114, 117; *Eritrea v Yemen (Phase One: Territorial Sovereignty and Scope of the Dispute)* (1998) 114 ILR 1, 117–18, [450]–[454]; *Territorial and Maritime Dispute between Nicaragua and Honduras in the Caribbean Sea (Nicaragua v Honduras)* [2007] ICJ Rep 659, 723, [214]; *Sovereignty over Pedra Branca/Pulau Batu Puteh, Middle Rocks and South Ledge (Malaysia/Singapore)* [2008] ICJ Rep 12, 36–37, [67].

[26] de Visscher 'L'arbitrage de l' Île de Palmas (Miangas)' (n 13) 738.

[27] *Island of Palmas* (n 6) 838. See also: *Status of Eastern Carelia* (1923) PCIJ Series B No 5, 27; United Nations Declaration on Principles of International Law Concerning Friendly Relations and Cooperation among States, Section 3 Res 2625 (XXV); reprinted in (1970) 9 ILM 1292, 1296; *Military and Paramilitary Activities in and against Nicaragua (Nicaragua v United States of America)*, Merits, Judgment, [1986] ICJ Rep 14, 106–7, [202]–[203].

accompanied by careful examinations of what exactly sovereignty signifies.[28] Yet the Award also brings out the importance of coexistence, stressing that international law 'has the object of assuring the coexistence of different interests which are worthy of legal protection'.[29] Thus, on the one hand, there is sovereignty:

> Sovereignty in the relations between States signifies independence. Independence in regard to a portion of the globe is the right to exercise therein, to the exclusion of any other State, the functions of a State. The development of the national organisation of States during the last few centuries and, as a corollary, the development of international law, have established this principle of the exclusive competence of the State in regard to its own territory in such a way as to make it the point of departure in settling most questions that concern international relations.[30]

Thus conceived, the requirement of effectiveness is not only a logical consequence of the nature of territorial sovereignty: it is also a requisite element of any mode of acquisition of territorial sovereignty and its maintenance.[31]

On the other, there is the coexistence of sovereign states: 'International law, like law in general, has the object of assuring the coexistence of different interests which are worthy of legal protection'.[32] A leading international law writer such as Guggenheim made of this statement the centrepiece of his theory of international law, stating at the outset of his treatise on public international law that: 'the original core of public international law is constituted by the rights and obligations which follow therefrom'.[33]

Island of Palmas makes plain that with sovereignty, as that concept is understood in international law, comes not only certain rights and freedoms for states—but also obligations.[34]

A similar change was occurring in the domestic law of especially continental legal systems, where in the 1910–20s what could be termed a *positive* concept of the sovereignty of the state was crystallising.[35] It is clear, for example, in the French law of the inter-war period, as exemplified by the work of Léon Blum, who left an indelible mark on French public law first as a judge for more than 20 years in the Conseil d'État, and later as a parliamentarian and prime minister in charge of several legislative reforms. Following the conclusions of then *commissaire du gouvernement* Blum, the Conseil d'État[36] in *Compagnie générale française des*

---

[28] V Lowe, 'Sovereignty and International Economic Law' in W Shan, P Simons and D Singh (eds), *Redefining Sovereignty in International Economic Law* (Oxford, Hart, 2008) 77.

[29] *Island of Palmas* (n 6) 870.

[30] ibid, 838.

[31] R Ago, *Il requisito dell'effettività dell occupazione in Diritto internazionale* (Rome, Anonima Romana Editorale, 1934) 25–26.

[32] ibid, 870.

[33] P Guggenheim, *Traité de Droit international public tome I* (Geneva, Librairie de l'Université, 1953) 2 ('*Le noyau original du droit des gens est constitué par les droits et devoirs qui en résultent.*').

[34] M Giuliano, *I diritti e gli obblighi degli stati* (Milan, CEDAM, 1956) 79; V Lowe, 'Regulation or Expropriation?' (2002) 55 CLP 447, 451.

[35] The development was a slower one in English law: S Sedley, *Lions under the Throne: Essays on the History of English Public Law* (Cambridge, CUP, 2015) 23–69.

[36] Supreme Court for administrative law matters, as well as legal advisor to the Executive.

tramways held that,[37] although the Government had entered into certain concession contracts with a tramway company, the Government nevertheless retained a residual inalienable sovereignty (*'pouvoir de souveraineté'*), certain police powers (*'pouvoir de police'*) to make changes to the contracts in light of the needs of society.[38] The Government could not be taken to have abandoned its right to regulate, as 'the state remains the guarantor of the execution of the provision of the service vis-à-vis the whole citizenry'.[39] Its rights to make unilateral changes to the concession contracts was found in the general interest.[40] Therefore, on this conception of the sovereignty of the state, the obverse to these powers of the Government, or to this particular *negative* aspect of sovereignty, was that the state was conceived of 'as a public service, an agency providing services rather than exercising sovereignty' only in the negative sense.[41] Thus *Compagnie générale française des tramways* exemplifies the move from a private law to a public law conception of state contracts within domestic law. The domestic law governing railway concessions was more than the synallagmatic law of contract. It was a law that, going beyond the concept of the night-watchman state of the nineteenth century, took into consideration the exigencies of providing, in a positive sense, state services to the individuals over whom the state exercises sovereignty.

This was prefigured too in the Dissenting Opinion of Judge Moore in *SS Lotus*,[42] where Judge Moore observed that: 'a nation possesses and exercises within its own territory an absolute and exclusive jurisdiction'; '[t]he benefit of this principle equally enures to all independent and sovereign States, and is attended with a corresponding responsibility for what takes place within the national territory'.[43]

Thus, in *Island of Palmas*, sovereignty involves not merely the exclusive right to engage in the activities of a state within a given territory, but also, as a corollary, the obligation to protect within that territory the rights of nationals of other states:

> Territorial sovereignty cannot limit itself to its negative side, ie to excluding the activities of other States; for it serves to divide between nations the space upon which human activities are employed, in order to assure them at all points the minimum protection of which international law is the guardian.[44]

---

[37] L Blum, 'Conclusions' in Conseil d'Etat 11 March 1910 *Compagnie générale française des tramways* Case No 16178, reported in (1910) 17 *Revue du droit public* 274–84.

[38] The *commissaire du gouvernement* entered the following caveat in relation to the concept of police powers as an expression of state sovereignty, however: *'quand il s'agit de services publics de transports, ce pouvoir n'est pas seulement le commandement vague général, indéterminé, variable suivant les cas et les nécessites qu'on appelle le pouvoir de police. C'est bien un droit de règlementation très précis, très défini, qui est conféré par des textes et repose sur des textes'*: ibid, 275.

[39] ibid.

[40] Conseil d'Etat 11 March 1910 *Compagnie générale française des tramways* Case No 16178 (*'l'intérêt du public'*); Conseil d'Etat 2 February 1987 *Société TV 6* (*'des motifs d'intérêt général'*).

[41] P Birnbaum, *Léon Blum: Prime Minister, Socialist, Zionist* (New Haven, Yale University Press, 2015) 75–76.

[42] *SS Lotus* PCIJ (1927) Series A No 10, 68.

[43] See Giuliano, *I diritti e gli obblighi degli stati* (n 34) 79.

[44] *Island of Palmas* (n 6) 839.

This dichotomy is what was also developed by the majority of the Permanent Court in *Lotus* (decided by the casting vote of President Huber), when it stressed that international law governs relations between independent states and that, equally importantly, the rules of international law are established 'in order to regulate the relations between these co-existing independent communities or with a view to the achievement of common aims'.[45] Huber seems to have taken these aspects of sovereignty into consideration in making his determination:

> If, as in the present instance, only one of two conflicting interests is to prevail, because sovereignty can be orientated to but one of the Parties, the interest which involves the maintenance of a state of things having offered at the critical time to the inhabitants of the disputed territory and to other States a certain guarantee for the respect of their rights ought, in doubt, to prevail over an interest which—supposing it to be recognized in international law—has not yet received any concrete form of development.[46]

Transfer of sovereignty thus has little in common with transfer of property in domestic private law.[47] The Award brings out the importance in international law of the contribution which a state actually makes to a stable and constructive order of affairs as against the negative insistence on a historic right, dating back to a period in history when the purely proprietary conception of sovereignty prevailed.[48]

This theme has become a part of the grammar of international law. The Tribunal in *Rann of Kutch* held that:

> Territorial sovereignty implies, as observed by Judge Huber in the *Island of Palmas* case, certain exclusive rights which have as their corollary certain duties. In adjudicating conflicting claims by rival sovereigns to a territory, all available evidence relating to the exercise of such rights, and to the discharge of such duties, must be carefully evaluated with a view to establishing in whom the conglomerate of sovereign functions has exclusively or predominantly [been] vested.[49]

This meant that, in determining whether the Rann of Kutch belonged to India or Pakistan, the Tribunal would look to which of those two states, or their forerunners, had on the one hand, 'in actual fact enjoyed the rights of sovereignty over the disputed territory' and, on the other, 'which of them carried out the burden of discharging the duties inherent in sovereignty in that territory at each relevant period of time'.[50] Similarly, the ICSID Tribunal in *Antoine Goetz* referred, in relation to the concept of sovereignty, to '*le principe, énoncé par Max Huber dans la sentence arbitrale relative à l' Île de Palmas, selon lequel la souveraineté territorial ne comporte pas seulement le droit exclusive de l'exercice des activités étatiques mais aussi le corollaire de l'obligation de protéger sur le territoire étatique les droit des nationaux des autres Etats*'.[51]

---

[45] *SS Lotus* (n 42) 18.

[46] *Island of Palmas* (n 6) 870.

[47] de Visscher (n 13) 754 ('*la notion de souveraineté n'est plus celle de jadis*').

[48] Memorial of the United Kingdom of 3 March 1952, *Minquiers & Ecrehous*, 105; Giuliano, *I diritti e gli obblighi degli stati* (n 34) 147.

[49] *Rann of Kutch* (n 25) 554.

[50] ibid, 554–55.

[51] *Antoine Goetz & Others v Republic of Burundi* ICSID ARB/95/3 (Weil, President; Bedjaoui; Bredin) [65].

It is part of the legacy of *Island of Palmas* that it showed clearly how international law looks to whether a state has in fact discharged the duties inherent in sovereignty. '[I]nternational arbitral jurisprudence in disputes on territorial sovereignty,' observed the Sole Arbitrator, 'would seem to attribute greater weight to—even isolated—acts of display of sovereignty than to continuity of territory, even if such continuity is combined with the existence of natural boundaries'.[52]

In this regard, he cited in terms the case of *Alpe di Craivarola*[53] where, in 1874, Sole Arbitrator Marsh, adjudicating on whether the alpine border area of the Alp of Craivarola belonged to Switzerland or to Italy, referred to the effective use of the land by villagers from certain Italian communes. Amongst other things, the villagers could show that they had, as private individuals, purchased the pastureland in question as far back as 1554; that they, together with their officials, had planted border marks around the pastureland; and that they 'had the incontestable possession and use of certain parts of the Alp of Cravairola for nearly four centuries, and of other parts of the same period of much longer still'.[54] In the aggregate these acts amounted to display of sovereignty that was held to be more important than the continuity of territory and alleged principle according to which territorial limitation in mountainous regions should follow the watershed of rivers in the region, to which Switzerland, in its submissions, was able to point.

Another case which could be thought to have been covered by 'international arbitral jurisprudence in disputes on territorial sovereignty',[55] but which was not mentioned by the Sole Arbitrator in terms, is the *Meerauge* award,[56] where, dealing with the issue of possession from time immemorial, the Tribunal observed that: '[p]ossession from time immemorial is understood as the form of possession where no evidence can be adduced that the situation was ever different and no living person has ever heard of a different state of affairs'.[57] Importantly, however, the Tribunal went on to observe that: '[s]uch possession must also be unbroken and uncontested, and it is self-evident that possession so defined must have continued up to the present—that is, up to the time at which the dispute leading to the conclusion of an arbitration agreement occurred.'[58] By positing that possession—'*Besitz*' in the German original—must continue, the *Meerauge* award arguably prefigured the conclusion in *Island of Palmas* in so far as the position set out by Sole Arbitrator Huber was beginning to crystallise already in *Meerauge* that an initial claim to title is somehow not good enough if 'possession' is not continued up to the present.

---

[52] *Island of Palmas* (n 6) 855.

[53] *Alpe di Craivarola* in H La Fontaine, *Pasicrisie internationale: histoire documentaire des arbitrages internationaux* (Berne, Stämpfli, 1902) 201–9 (Sole Arbitrator GP Marsh); translation printed in *Decision of arbitration concerning the definite fixing of the Italian–Swiss frontier at the place called Alpe de Cravairola* (1874) 28 RIAA 141.

[54] (1874) 28 RIAA 141, 147; *Pasicrisie internationale* 201, 204.

[55] *Island of Palmas* (n 6) 855.

[56] *Meerauge Arbitral Award (Austria/Hungary)* (1902) 3 *Nouveau recueil général de traités*, 3rd Series, 71; (1902) 28 RIAA 379 (see *Sovereignty over Pedra Branca/Pulau Batu Puteh, Middle Rocks and South Ledge* (n 25) 32; *cf* Sep Op Judge ad hoc Sreenivasa Rao, 157, [9]).

[57] (1902) 3 *Nouveau recueil général de traités*, 3rd Series, 71, 80; (1902) 28 RIAA 379, 391.

[58] ibid.

By making the point about effective possession so clearly, Huber brought out a broader principle which was crystallising in the jurisprudence of international courts and tribunals;[59] but he went further, in that he would also point up the importance of the activities of the state vis-à-vis the individuals living on the territory over which the state claims to have sovereignty. Shortly after the Award in *Island of Palmas* had been handed down, Lauterpacht observed that any international court or tribunal has at its disposal

> that source of judicial activity which consists in the realization of the purpose of the law, namely, in finding, in case of doubt, solutions most conducive to the benefit of the community as a whole and to the necessity of stable and effective legal relations between its members.[60]

The operation of this method, he continued, is illustrated by the principal reasons which caused international tribunals to recognise extinctive and acquisitive prescription, that is, considerations of stability, of the necessity for maintaining, so far as possible and equitable, the established order of things, and of discouraging endless litigation. It was against this background, Lauterpacht argued, that the arbitrator in *Island of Palmas*, when stressing the importance of peaceful, continuous, and effective display of state activity as a title of acquisition of sovereignty, expressed the view that the recognition of the effect of prescription is necessary in view of the particular needs of international society.[61] Strikingly similar reasoning had informed the determination in 1909 by the Permanent Court of Arbitration in *Grisbadarna*,[62] where the Tribunal observed that: '[i]t is a settled principle of the law of nations that a state of things *which actually exists* and has existed for a long time should be changed as little as possible'.[63] What the Tribunal then went on to say was of no less importance,[64] namely, that this was all the more so when individuals and their rights vis-à-vis the state were involved:

> [t]his rule is specially applicable in a case of private interests which, if once neglected, can not be effectively safeguarded by any manner of sacrifice on the part of the Government of which the interested parties are subjects.[65]

---

[59] H Lauterpacht, *The Development of International Law by the International Court* (Cambridge, CUP, 1958) 241; JHW Verzijl, *International Law in Historical Perspective VIII: Inter-State Disputes and Their Settlement* (Leyden, AW Sijthoff, 1976) 307.

[60] H Lauterpacht, *The Function of Law in the international Community* (Oxford, Clarendon Press, 1933) 131.

[61] ibid.

[62] *Affaire des Grisbadarna (Norvège/Suède)* (1909) 11 RIAA 147; *Grisbadarna (Maritime Boundary Dispute between Norway and Sweden)* (1910) 4 AJIL 204.

[63] *Grisbadarna (Maritime Boundary Dispute)* (n 62) 233 (emphasis added). (original: '*dans le droit des gens, c'est un principe bien établi, qu'il faut s'abstenir autant que possible de modifier l'état des choses existant de fait et depuis longtemps*'—*Affaire des Grisbadarna* (n 62) 161). See H Lauterpacht, *Private Law Analogies and Sources of International Law* (London, Longman, 1927) 264; Lauterpacht, *The Function of Law* (n 60) 131.

[64] Lauterpacht failed to mention this important point: H Lauterpacht, *The Function of Law* (n 60) 131; he focused on the private law aspects of international law rather than the public law ones: cf Lauterpacht's *Private Law Analogies* (n 63).

[65] *Grisbadarna (Maritime Boundary Dispute)* (n 62) 234.

This was exactly the point which would take on such importance in *Island of Palmas*, where, distancing himself from a private law concept of sovereignty-as-ownership, negative sovereignty, the Sole Arbitrator considered himself bound to conceive of sovereignty as a fundamentally concrete concept, positive sovereignty:

> Although municipal law, thanks to its complete judicial system, is able to recognize abstract rights of property as existing apart from any material display of them, it has none the less limited their effect by the principles of prescription and the protection of possession. International law, the structure of which is not based on any super-State organisation, cannot be presumed to reduce a right such as territorial sovereignty, with which almost all international relations are bound up, to the category of an abstract right, without concrete manifestations.[66]

Already in the late 1920s sovereignty could no longer be conceived as a pure juridical abstraction, as a prerogative that did no more than to confer on a state the right to exclude the activity of every other state in a given region.[67] It must instead be conceived of as a positive function the raison d'être of which is to be found in the general interest.[68] As the Sole Arbitrator in *Island of Palmas* put it:

> Territorial sovereignty cannot limit itself to its negative side, i.e. to excluding the activities of other States; for it serves to divide between nations the space upon human activities are employed, in order to assure them at all points the minimum of protection of which international law is the guardian.[69]

If this anthropocentric view of the concept of state sovereignty did not quite match the Lauterpachtian proposition that '[t]he individual is the ultimate unit of all law, international and municipal',[70] it did delineate with unmatched clarity the new—positive—concept of sovereignty that had been taking shape in the international law of the nineteenth and fledgling twentieth century.

Furthermore, the *Island of Palmas* dictum according to which a state could not expect to benefit from negative sovereignty if it had not shown itself to be prepared to exercise positive sovereignty arguably finds expression in the jurisprudence of the European Court of Human Rights, which in *Al-Skeini*[71] set out the rules governing extraterritorial application of the European Convention on Human Rights.[72] The concepts of negative and positive sovereignty are closely interlinked and mutually dependent on one another. It is clear from *Al-Skeini* that a state cannot expect to be allowed to show, or purport to show, positive sovereignty (to the extent that the United Kingdom visited upon the Iraqi population certain human rights abuses),

---

[66] *Island of Palmas* (n 6), 839.
[67] de Visscher (n 13) 740.
[68] See also *Compagnie générale française des tramways* (n 37).
[69] *Island of Palmas* (n 6) 839.
[70] H Lauterpacht, 'The Grotian Tradition in International Law' (1946) 23 BYIL 1, 27. Criticised in LC Green, 'Book Review, International Law and Human Rights. By H. Lauterpacht' (1951) 4 ILQ 126, 126–28; M McDougal, 'Book Review, International Law and Human Rights. By H. Lauterpacht' (1951) 60 Yale LJ 1051; J Crawford and CA Miles, 'Four Ways of Thinking about the History of International Law' in JC Sainz-Borgo and others (eds), *Liber Amicorum in Honour of a Modern Renaissance Man, His Excellency Gudmundur Eiriksson* (New Dehli, Universal Law Publishing 2017) 265, 287.
[71] *Al-Skeini v United Kingdom* (App No 55721/07) 7 July 2011, (2011) 147 ILR 181.
[72] 4 November 1950, 213 UNTS 222.

without international law also imposing upon it the duties that come with such displays of sovereignty. In *Island of Palmas* Spain, desirous of sovereignty over the territory in question, had not been prepared to exercise positive sovereignty and therefore was not in law granted sovereignty over it. In *Al-Skeini*, conversely, the United Kingdom, which did not want to be held to exercise jurisdiction over the territory in question, had been nothing if not prepared to exercise positive sovereignty, and therefore in law was held to exercise jurisdiction over the impugned acts taking place at its hands in the territory.[73] This, too, serves to bring out the premium put by Huber's approach on the human beings on the territory in question, 'in order to assure them at all points the minimum of protection of which international law is the guardian'.[74]

III. THE INTERTEMPORAL LAW

Secondly, as was seen above, the existence of the rights of Spain, and its successor, to title would have to follow the conditions required by the evolution of law. *Island of Palmas* establishes that 'a juridical fact must be appreciated in the light of the law contemporary with it'.[75] Nonetheless, '[t]he same principle which subjects the act creative of a right to the law in force at the time the right arises, demands that the existence of the right, in other words its continued manifestations, shall follow the conditions required by the evolution of law'.[76]

---

[73] Further: C McLachlan, *Foreign Relations Law* (Cambridge, CUP, 2014) 333–36.

[74] *Island of Palmas* (n 6) 839.

[75] ibid 845. Also: *Enterprize* in A de Lapradelle and N Politis, *Recueil des arbitrages internationaux I* (Paris, Pedone, 1905) 703; *Hermosa* and *Créole* in de Lapradelle and Politis (ibid) 703–04; *Lawrence* in de Lapradelle and Politis (ibid) 740–41; *Volusia* in de Lapradelle and Politis (ibid) 741; *The Pious Fund Case (United States v Mexico)* (1902) 9 RIAA 1, 11–14; *Cape Horn Pigeon (USA v Russia)* (1902) 9 RIAA 63, 64; *James Hamilton Lewis (USA v Russia)* (1902) 9 RIAA 66, 67 and 69; *CH White (USA v Russia)* (1902) 9 RIAA 71, 72; *Kate & Anna (USA v Russia)* (1902) 9 RIAA 76, 77; *Pelletier* in JB Moore, *History and Digest of International Arbitrations to which the United States has been a Party II* (Washington, DC, Government Printing Office, 1898) 1750; *SS Lisman (USA v United Kingdom)* (1937) 3 RIAA 1767, 1771; *Mixed Claims Commission: Sambaggio case (Italy v Venezuela)* (1903) 10 RIAA 499, 522; *Case concerning Right of Passage over Indian Territory (Merits) Judgment* [1960] ICJ Rep 6, 37; *Société Générale in respect of DR Energy Holdings Limited and Empresa Distribuidora de Electricidad del Esta SA v Dominican Republic* Award on Preliminary Objections to Jurisdiction (LCIA Case No UN 7927) (Orrego Vicuna, President; Doak Bishop; Cremades), [86]; *Ping AN Life Insurance Company of China, Ltd v Belgium* (ICSID Case No ARB/12/29) Award (Lord Collins, President; Sands; Williams), [135]; *Jan de Nul NV v Arab Republic of Egypt* (ICSID Case No ARB/04/13) Award (Kaufmann-Kohler, President; Mayer; Stern), [132].

[76] ibid 845. Also: *Portendick* in de Lapradelle and Politis, (ibid), 530–31; *Sentence arbitrale relative aux requêtes de la Grande-Bretagne et du Portugal sur certains territoires de la côte Est de l'Afrique appartenant autrefois aux Rois de Tembe et Mapoota, incluant les îles de Inyack et Éléphant (Baie de Delagoa ou Lorenzo Marques)* (1875) 28 RIAA 157, 160; *Carolines* arbitration, 22 October 1885, printed in MC Calvo, *Le droit international: théorique et pratique*, 6th edn (Paris, Pedone 1888) 420–21; *Veloz-Mariana* in H La Fontaine, *Pasicrisie internationale: histoire documentaire des arbitrages internationaux* (Berne, Stämpfli, 1902) 26; *Guiana Boundary case (Brazil/Great Britain)* (1904) 11 RIAA 11, 21–22; *Nationality Decrees Issued in Tunis and Morocco* (1923) PCIJ Series B No 4, 24; *Island of Clipperton (Mexico v France)* (1931) 2 RIAA 1105; *Minquiers & Ecrehos Case (France/United Kingdom), Judgment* [1953] ICJ Rep 47; *Western Sahara, Advisory Opinion* [1975] ICJ Rep 12, 68; *Kasikili/Sedudu Island (Botswana/Namibia), Judgment* [1999] ICJ Rep 1045, [25] and [89].

In Reuter's words, *Island of Palmas* gave expression to the rule generally recognised in domestic law that legal situations come into being validly in accordance with rules that are in operation at a certain given point in time but depend, for their continued existence, on rules which later come into existence.[77] The Sole Arbitrator explicitly tempered the second limb of its test by adding the rider that the second limb would not be brought to bear in the case of 'territories in which there is already an established order of things'.[78] This may obviously be a difficult question of degree.

As Crawford would later observe, 'the two elements of the *Island of Palmas* case are less antithetical than they may seem; stability due to the creation, and flexibility due to evolution in the existence of rights, should be conceived as complementary principles'.[79] The Permanent Court of International Justice in *Eastern Greenland* treated continuity of display of state authority as an integral element in the Danish title to the territory.[80] The Court did not regard it as sufficient that Denmark established its sovereignty at a particular moment in history. Instead it traced the exercise of sovereignty through successive periods until the critical date.[81]

The two-limbed principle of intertemporality was not a new one. Early arbitrations settled on the heels of the gradual development of the customary rules concerning discovery and occupation showed the gradual evolution of international law in respect of the acquisition of sovereignty from the original legal sufficiency of discovery or symbolic occupation to the requirement of the effectiveness of the occupation.[82]

The early jurisprudence of international tribunals, and the writings of the most highly qualified publicists, hesitated at first as to how to grapple with the passage of time and intertemporality. Westlake for example observed that 'titles must be judged by the state of international law at the time when, if at all, they arose'.[83]

It would be wrong, however, to think that the rule enunciated in *Island of Palmas* was new. In the *Carolines* arbitration,[84] something very much akin to the principle of intertemporal law had been relied on.[85] The particular pertinence of this case stems from the fact that the parties had presented the arbitrator with almost exactly the same question as would arise *Island of Palmas*. The *Carolines* arbitrator, Pope Leo XIII, decided in almost the exact same vein as Sole Arbitrator Huber would do

---

[77] P Reuter, 'Cours générale de droit international public' (1961) 103 *Hague Recueil* 554 ('*la règle (généralement admise dans les droits nationaux) que les situations juridiques se créent validement suivant les règles en vigueur à un moment donné, mais qu'elles doivent pour se perpétuer satisfaire ultérieurement à de nouvelles règles qui seraient établies*').

[78] *Island of Palmas* (n 6) 839.

[79] J Crawford, *State Responsibility: The General Part* (Cambridge, CUP, 2013) 242.

[80] *Legal Status of Eastern Greenland* (n 25) 22.

[81] H Waldock, 'Disputed Sovereignty in the Falklands Islands Dependencies' (1948) 25 *BYIL* 311, 321. Also: *Minquiers & Ecrehos Case* (n 76).

[82] Verzijl, *International Law* (n 59) 307.

[83] J Westlake, *International Law I*, 2nd edn (Cambridge, CUP, 1910) 114.

[84] *Carolines* arbitration, 22 October 1885, printed in MC Calvo, *Le droit international: théorique et pratique*, 6th edn (Paris, Pedone, 1888) 420.

[85] ibid, 420–21.

later in *Island of Palmas*: Spain had in the sixteenth century discovered the islands making up the Carolines and Palaos archipelago; it had founded its sovereignty over the islands by the principles of international law then in force. It was uncontested that only Spain had at the time acted so as to obtain the right to title according to the sixteenth-century rules. On the other hand, Germany—as well as the United Kingdom—had declared expressly, in 1875, to the Spanish government that they did not recognise the sovereignty of Spain over the islands. Germany averred that it was effective occupation of a territory which gave rise to sovereignty over it, and that Spain had never occupied the archipelago in the fashion required. The arbitrator in his ruling affirmed the sovereignty of Spain over the archipelago, but this was tempered in three important ways. First, the Spanish government must, 'in order to render effective its sovereignty', establish on the islands a regular administration which would be capable of safeguarding order and guaranteed rights. Secondly, Spain must offer to Germany full liberty of commerce, navigation, and fishery in the archipelago, as well as the right to establish there a naval station and a coal depot. And, thirdly, Germany was to be given the right to establish plantations and agriculture on an equal footing with Spanish nationals. The *Carolines* arbitration is therefore, as Basdevant observed, an early precedent for the proposition that '*la reconnaissance de la souveraineté acquise selon le droit ancien est ... tempérée par l'engagement de la rendre plus active selon le vœu du droit moderne*'.[86]

Nonetheless, the rule came in for criticism. The United States Agent Nielsen's comment to the Tribunal's conclusions as to intertemporality was that:

> It would seem difficult to perceive how an international title, so to speak, acquired under law definitively accepted as a certain period of time, or a domestic title to land acquired under rules regulating the acquisition of title the time of acquisition, could be regarded as an absolute title, if the title acquired, in order to continue to exist, must 'follow the conditions required by the evolution of law.' It would seem that the 'evolution of law' could only affect titles acquired contemporaneously with the stages of evolution. If this were not so, there could be no acquisition of a title subject to alteration or destruction by the 'evolution of law'.[87]

In a similar vein, several academic authors took issue with the way in which *Island of Palmas* dealt with the intertemporal law.[88] The principle of intertemporality was most famously criticised by Jessup. He attempted in his criticism to take the

---

[86] J Basdevant, '*Efficacité des Règles générales du droit de la paix*' in (1936) 58 Hague *Recueil* 537. This solution was, in material terms, also the one codified in the General Act of the Berlin Conference of 26 February 1885, and later reiterated in the Convention of Saint-Germain of 10 September 1919. Article 10 of the Convention of Saint-Germain provided that: '*les Hautes Parties contractantes reconnaissant l'obligation de* maintenir, *dans les régions relevant de le leur autorité, l'existence d'un pouvoir et des moyens de police suffisants pour assurer la protection des personnes et des biens et, le cas échéant, la liberté du commerce et du transit*'. Further: M Kohen, *Possession contesté et souveraineté territoriale* (Paris, Presses universitaires de France, 1997) 184.

[87] Nielsen (n 4) 31.

[88] Giuliano, *I diritti e gli obblighi degli stati* (n 34) 192; R Jennings, *The Acquisition of Territory in International Law* (Manchester, MUP, 1963) 29–30; K Doehring, 'Die Wirkung des Zeitablaufs auf den Bestand völkerrechtlicher Regeln' [1964] Max Planck *Jahrbuch* 70, 88.

axe to the very root of the ruling in *Island of Palmas*, the effects of which he saw as highly disturbing.[89] Jessup in his criticism gave an example in order to bear out the to his mind deleterious effects which would follow in the wake of the principle on which *Island of Palmas* was based:

> Assume that State A in a certain year acquires Island X from State B by a treaty of peace after a war in which A is the victor. Assume Island X is a barren rocky place, uninhabited and desired by A only for strategic reasons to prevent its fortification by another Power. Assume that A holds Island X, but without making direct use of it, for two hundred years. At the end of that time suppose that the development of international morality has so far progressed as to change the previous rule of international law and that the new rule is that no territory may be acquired by a victor from a vanquished at the close of a war. Under the theory of 'intertemporal law' as expounded, it would appear that A would no longer have good title to Island X but must secure a new title upon some other basis or in accordance with the new rule. Such a retroactive effect of law would be highly disturbing.[90]

The argument put forward by Jessup in his example is open to criticism, and that criticism seems logically to fall in four parts.

First, Jessup's case in point is different from the legal situation in *Island of Palmas*. While the norm relied on by Huber related only to the facts obtaining at the time of the coming into force of the norm itself, the norm in Jessup's example bears on the way in which the territory was acquired in the first place. Thus A's right to Island X in Jessup's example could be extinguished only if it was applied to the acquisition which took place 200 years before the norm's coming into force.[91] This was, however, exactly that which the tribunal was at pains to avoid in *Island of Palmas*; it made very clear that the effects of the new rule was that 'discovery alone, without any subsequent act, cannot *at the present time* suffice to prove sovereignty over the Island of Palmas'.[92] It is thus far from clear that the effect here described is actually retroactive. Rather the case is that the change of law prompts a change *ex nunc* as opposed to *ex tunc*. This has parenthetically led one commentator to argue not only that Jessup had misunderstood the difference between nullity *ex nunc* and *ex tunc* but also that his was an outright misreading of the whole *Island of Palmas* case.[93] In the light of the above, this criticism of Jessup's stance seems fair.

Secondly, counter examples to Jessup's example could be imagined that would make very clear the necessity of the rule of intertemporality. One could think of examples bearing on colonialism. It could hardly be disputed that colonialism was central to the development of international law;[94] *Island of Palmas* is a case in point.

---

[89] P Jessup, 'The Palmas Island Arbitration' (1928) 22 *AJIL* 735, 740.
[90] ibid, 740.
[91] W Krause-Ablaß, *Intertemporales Völkerrecht* (Hamburg, Forschungsstelle für Völkerrecht und ausländisches Recht der Universität Hamburg, 1969) 27–28; HW Baade, 'Intertemporales Völkerrecht' (1957) 7 Jahrbuch für internationals Recht 229, 242.
[92] *Island of Palmas* (n 6) 846 (emphasis added).
[93] Krause-Ablaß, *Intertemporales Völkerrecht* (n 81) 28.
[94] A Anghie, *Imperialism, Sovereignty and the Making of International Law* (Cambridge, CUP, 2004) 2–3.

It is possible therefore to imagine examples to do with slavery, exploitation, and the rights of peoples to self-determination which would furnish us with situations in which that which was once in conformity with international law at a later point is singularly in breach of a newly emerged rule because, to use Jessup's words, 'the development of international morality has so far progressed as to change the previous rule of international law'.[95]

Suffice it here to give one example, from the jurisprudence of the International Court.

In *Western Sahara*,[96] one pressing question was, which law applied, the old one of the nineteenth century or the new twentieth-century one of self-determination? The International Court began by observing that the questions before it must be addressed 'by reference to the law in force at that period'.[97] The Court had found that there existed, at the time of Spanish colonisation, 'legal ties of allegiance between the Sultan of Morocco and some of the tribes living in the territory of Western Sahara'.[98] The materials and information presented to the Court had also shown the existence of rights, including some rights relating to the land, which constituted legal ties between the Mauritanian entity and the territory of Western Sahara. The Court made clear that its ruling was one which took into account both limbs of the principle of intertemporality when it commented on its own conclusion that the materials and information presented to it did not establish any tie of territorial sovereignty between the territory of Western Sahara and the Kingdom of Morocco or the Mauritanian entity:

> Thus the Court has not found legal ties of such a nature as might affect the application of resolution 1514 (XV) in the decolonization of Western Sahara and, in particular, of the principle of self-determination through the free and genuine expression of the will of the peoples of the Territory.[99]

This was in line with the argument of Algeria and went against the grain of the argument presented by Morocco. This final sentence of the Court's ruling is essential in that it shows that the Court was concerned not to address only the old law but also to take into account the present law, reflected in the Charter and in the resolutions on self-determination.[100] In that sense the Court correctly applied both limbs of the principle of the intertemporal law enunciated in *Island of Palmas*.

Morocco in fact made the same mistake in its criticism of intertemporal law as Jessup had done in his criticism of *Island of Palmas*: in its pleadings Morocco had

---

[95] Jessup 'The Palmas Island Arbitration' (n 89) 740.
[96] *Western Sahara, Advisory Opinion* (n 76).
[97] ibid, 38–39.
[98] ibid, 68.
[99] ibid. This point seems to be lost on some authors, who claim that the Court did not fully engage with the intertemporal issues, and instead adopted a 'conservative' approach: M Shaw, 'The *Western Sahara* Case' (1978) 49 BYIL 119, 152; M Koskenniemi, *From Apology to Utopia*, 2nd edn (Cambridge, CUP, 2005) 456–57.
[100] P Tavernier, 'Observations sur le droit intertemporal dans l'affaire de l'île de *Kasikili/Sedudu (Botswana/Namibie)*' (2000) *RGDIP* 429, 441–42.

assumed that the second limb of the intertemporal rule would mean that the title was invalid retroactively. This was based on a two-fold misconception: first, the new norm did not in point of fact reopen the question of the title acquired at the date of colonisation, it rather demanded its cessation and just possibly eroded it; secondly, the new norm did not operate on the basis of re-examining old titles but based itself on the rights of the inhabitants of the colonially defined territory to self-determination.[101]

If one sees the rule of intertemporality under the angle of colonialism and the right of peoples to self-determination, as the International Court did in *Western Sahara*, its soundness becomes very clear, even clearer than was in the case of the two colonial powers vying for imperium over a faraway territory in *Island of Palmas*.

A third criticism levelled at the principle relied on by the tribunal in *Island of Palmas* by Jessup was that the application of Huber's principle would mean chaos if such a principle were to be applied to private law and private titles in national law.[102] It is in this regard apposite to mention that the tribunal in *Island of Palmas* probably took some inspiration from European national law, where the principle already was well developed. This seems to have been entirely overlooked by Jessup in his criticism.

In Germany the principle, or an early cognate, may be traced back to as early as in the end of the nineteenth century.[103] One German scholar dated it back to 1897, when the term '*intertemporales Recht*' had been used to describe the law determining the period to which legislation applies.[104] By 1908 at the latest it had, under the names '*droit transitoire*' as well as '*droit intertemporel*', made an appearance in French private law doctrine.[105] Furthermore the principle was highly developed in Swiss law;[106] in fact the Swiss civil code of 1907, in Article 17 of its last chapter, codifies the principle.[107] These examples seem to go some way in giving the lie to Jessup's argument that the result would have been chaos had the principle been imported into national law. The issue may have been under-researched in the common law, and that may go some way in explaining this lack of understanding of what, to Jessup, clearly seemed a very strange proposition indeed.[108]

The intertemporal law, like other branches of international law, 'does not operate in a vacuum'; rather it operates in 'relation to facts and in the context of a wider

---

[101] Shaw 'The *Western Sahara* Case' (n 99) 153.

[102] P Jessup 'The Palmas Island Arbitration' (n 89) 740.

[103] A Rodger, 'A Time for Everything under the Law: Some Reflections on Retrospectivity' (2005) 121 *LQR* 57, 60–62.

[104] FX Affolter, *Geschichte des intertemporalen Privatrechts* (Leipzig, Veit, 1902) 1.

[105] M Popoviliev, 'Le droit civil transitoire ou intertemporel (sa nature, sa règle générale et sa place dans la législation)' (1908) 3 *Revue trimestrielle de droit civil* 462.

[106] HW Baade 'Intertemporales Völkerrecht' (1957) 7 *GYIL* 229, 242.

[107] Article 17 of the last chapter of the Swiss civil code provides that: '1. *Les droits réels existant lors de l'entrée en vigueur du code civil sont maintenus, sous réserve des règles concernant le registre foncier. 2. Si une exception n'est pas faite dans le présent code, l'étendue de la propriété et des autres droits réels est néanmoins régie par la loi nouvelle dès son entrée en vigueur. 3. Les droits réels dont la constitution n'est plus possible à teneur de la loi nouvelle continuent à être régis par la loi ancienne.*'

[108] Rodger 'A Time for Everything under the Law' (n 103) 60–61.

framework of legal rules of which it forms only a part'.[109] The impact of the inter-temporal law will be reduced by the effect of other principles of international law. These include the effect of recognition, acquiescence, and the rule that abandonment is not to be presumed.[110] An example of this may be found in *Pedra Branca*, where the historic title of the Sultanate of Johore to the disputed territories survived despite the fact that the Sultanate had exercised little or no governmental authority over them.[111]

The principle of the *Island of Palmas* rule has become an article of faith in inter-national law. Yet the chaos foreshadowed by Jessup seems somehow not to have come to pass. This is partly because of the flexibility of the rule. It is also partly because other principles of interpretation and application of intertemporal law such as acquiescence, prescription, and desuetude would operate to make it impossible for the second element of the principle to work injustices.[112]

But the success of the principle is also precisely the fact that it reflects the evolu-tion of law. There is no surprise in the fact that states follow international law, for it is the states themselves who will have made the law which they are following. The reason why states do comply, and always have complied, with international law is that they make the rules to suit themselves.[113] That which is seen by some as the very problem of the intertemporal rule is in fact its saving grace.

We should not forget that the jurist who—while he did not invent it—brought the intertemporal law into the mainstream of international law was himself known for his sociological approach to law. The author of *Die soziologischen Grundlagen des Völkerrechts*,[114] Huber took a view of international law which was in no way blind to what states *actually* do. This is a point of some significance. If the system of territorial title internationally has not collapsed as a result of the adoption by inter-national law of the principle of intertemporality that is partly because the changing requirements of the law with which the rights must be kept up in accordance, will be a reflection of the development of state practice.

It bears mention therefore that the principle on which the *Island of Palmas* tribu-nal based its decision had, in material terms, been codified by the world powers in the General Act of the Berlin Conference of 26 February 1885, and later reiterated in the Convention of Saint-Germain of 10 September 1919. Article 10 of the Conven-tion of Saint-Germain provided that: '*les Hautes Parties contractantes reconnaissant*

---

[109] *Interpretation of the Agreement of 25 March 1951 between the WHO and Egypt* [1980] ICJ Rep 73, 76 [10].

[110] J Crawford, *Brownlie's Principles of Public International Law*, 8th edn (Oxford, OUP, 2012) 218–19.

[111] *Sovereignty over Pedra Branca/Pulau Batu Puteh, Middle Rocks and South Ledge* (n 25).

[112] TO Elias, 'The Doctrine of Intertemporal Law' (1980) 74 *AJIL* 285, 286–87; I Brownlie, *Principles of Public International Law*, 2nd edn (Oxford, OUP 1973) 132–33.

[113] See AV Lowe, *International Law* (Oxford, OUP, 2007) 19.

[114] M Huber, *Die soziologischen Grundlagen des Völkerrechts* (Berlin, Verlag für Recht und Gesells-chaft, 1928). Further: J Delbrück, 'Max Huber's Sociological Approach to International Law Revisited' (2007) 18 *EJIL* 97, 102–10; O Spiermann, 'Judge Max Huber at the Permanent Court of International Justice' (2007) 18 *EJIL* 115, 116–19; O Diggelmann, 'Max Huber (1874–1960)' in Fassbender and Peters *History of International Law* (n 23) 1156–51.

l'obligation de maintenir, dans les régions relevant de le leur autorité, l'existence d'un pouvoir et des moyens de police suffisants pour assurer la protection des personnes et des biens et, le cas échéant, la liberté du commerce et du transit'.[115]

It seems important to point out, however, that it is not the case that all territories acquired by way of methods now deemed unacceptable should be taken away from the states in issue. In most cases, such as those where title was acquired by conquest, the latter-day criterion of effective occupation will anyway later be fulfilled. This ties in with the sociological point: it is no surprise that states should in fact be acting in conformity with a rule which flows from state practice.

These points seem to bear out the correctness, in normative terms, of the principle of intertemporal law. The same conclusions may be drawn from the vicissitudes to be found in international jurisprudence and doctrine. The issues are there sometimes simplified but the time related matters which in their bearing on the law seem at first so simple may on further examination prove to be very difficult indeed.

Sometimes, not least in cases where the tribunal seems to have been unaware of the principle of intertemporality, one can detect a tendency in the argument of the tribunal away from the 'old law' in direction surreptitiously of the 'new law'.

The *Carolines* arbitration has already been dealt with above. This can be seen in classic cases such as *Clipperton*,[116] *Veloz-Mariana*,[117] *Delagoa Bay*,[118] and the *Guiana Boundary Case*.[119] The same surreptitious slippage from old to new law may be observed in modern international jurisprudence too. The International Court in *Kasikili/Sedudu* had to interpret an 1890 treaty between Germany and the United Kingdom, the foundation of the rights of Botswana and Namibia as successor states, that fixed the spheres of influence in Africa of Germany and the United Kingdom as colonial powers. Article III delimited 'the sphere in which the exercise of influence is reserved to Germany' to the east by a line which 'descends the centre of the main channel' of the river Chobe 'to its junction with the Zambesi, where it terminates'.[120] The Court noted that 'at the time of the conclusion of the 1890 Treaty, it may be that the terms "centre of the [main] channel" and *"Thalweg" des Hauptlaufes* were used interchangeably'.[121] It went on to hold that 'although, as explained above the parties in 1890 used the terms "thalweg" and "centre of the channel" interchangeably, the former reflects more accurately the common intention to exploit navigation than does the latter. Accordingly, this is the term that the Court will consider determinative'.[122] The boundary thus followed the line of deepest soundings in the

[115] C Rousseau, *Principes généraux du droit international public* (Paris, Pedone, 1944) 32–33.

[116] *Island of Clipperton* (n 76).

[117] Veloz-Mariana in H La Fontaine, *Pasicrisie internationale: histoire documentaire des arbitrages internationaux* (Berne, Stämpfli, 1902) 26.

[118] *Sentence arbitrale relative aux requêtes de la Grande-Bretagne et du Portugal sur certains territoires de la côte Est de l'Afrique appartenant autrefois aux Rois de Tembe et Mapoota, incluant les îles de Inyack et Éléphant (Baie de Delagoa ou Lorenzo Marques)* (1875) 28 RIAA 157, 160.

[119] *Guiana Boundary Case (Brazil/Great Britain)* (1904) 11 RIAA 11, 21–22.

[120] German original: '*setzt sich dann im Thalweg des Hauptlaufes dieses Flusses fort*'.

[121] *Kasikili/Sedudu Island* (n 76) [25].

[122] ibid, [89].

northern channel around the Kasikili/Sedudu Island. The authors who have studied the meaning concept of thalweg in the nineteenth and twentieth century have, however, underlined the considerable uncertainty that obtained as to its content.[123] Namibia in this vein insisted that there was not in general international law in 1890 a principle according to which river frontiers followed the thalweg. This the Court did not take into account, choosing instead to have recourse to the definitions of the thalweg which had crystallised after the 1890s.

Arbitrators and international judges, in spite of their best efforts to the contrary, have difficulty stepping back in time. This of course has cogent reasons, and could only with difficulty be criticised. In fact, the Sole Arbitrator's judgment in *Island of Palmas* inadvertently exemplifies this. For around the time when *Island of Palmas* was handed down, but clearly too late for any of the parties, or the Tribunal, to have noticed, scholarship came to light which incontrovertibly showed that it was in fact never the case that the sixteenth century rules of international law on discovery were such that the mere discovery of a new land could give rights of sovereignty.[124] The position already at that early period was the one set out by Grotius, that is, that 'to discover a thing is not only to seize it with the eyes but to take real possession of it'.[125] To the extent, therefore, that *Island of Palmas* tried to come to grips with the old law, the law of the sixteenth century, by getting it so wrong the Sole Arbitrator brought out one of the difficulties of relying for its application in the modern period on ancient law.

This leads us to an important conclusion when it comes to the soundness of the application of the principle of intertemporality. Against this background a plea for a two-limbed principle of intertemporality becomes something like a plea for transparency in international adjudication, and in fact also an argument for predictability. As international tribunals—on the clear evidence of the international law reports from their very first volumes all the way up to present times—will tend to apply modern conceptions of law, or apply an old law which looks very much like the new law, when on their own admission they are simply applying the old law, then surely the solution in *Island of Palmas*, with its attendant complexities, is preferable if for no other reason than that it leads to a more transparent form of international adjudication.

It may be so difficult to grasp this spirit of the past that at times international tribunals have failed to understand and to apply the old law, instead dressing up contemporaneous law as old and applying that in lieu of the old one. This fact, as was seen above, leaps from the pages of international law reports old and new. The double helix of intertemporality recognises that it is very difficult, when one is interpreting a

[123] P La Pradelle, *La frontière: étude de droit international* (Paris, Les Éditions internationales, 1928); E Lauterpacht, 'River Boundaries: Legal Aspects of the Shatt-al-Arab Frontier' (1960) 9 *ICLQ* 208; P Tavernier, 'Le conflit frontalier entre l'Irak et l'Iran et la guerre du Chatt-el-Arab' [1981] Arès Défense et Sécurité 333, 341; F Schroetter, 'Les systèmes de délimitation dans les fleuves internationaux' (1992) 38 *Annuaire français de droit international* 948, 959–64.

[124] J Goebel, *The Struggle for the Falkland Islands* (New Haven, Yale University Press, 1927); de Visscher (n 13) 741–42.

[125] ibid, 117.

treaty, not to view it from the perspective of the time of interpretation.[126] This is one reason why application in international arbitration of the two limbs of the principle from *Island of Palmas* may lead to more transparency and in the final analysis also more predictability. The principle of intertemporality seems to have been designed to govern a situation in which the necessary stability in relations between states is to be preserved, while at the same time the necessity for evolution in those relations and in the law regulating them is recognised. There is no real antithesis between the first and second element, and the more we have regard to this consideration the better we can appreciate the delicate balance aimed at in the formulation of the doctrine as now generally accepted. The analysis above, however, commands the conclusion that the solution reached in *Island of Palmas* is the best proffered yet.

The intertemporal principle to which *Island of Palmas* gives expression has taken on importance within treaty interpretation.[127] Perhaps the clearest example of how the principle in *Island of Palmas* continues to operate within the law of treaties was given by the International Court in *Aegean Sea*, where Huber's words are mirrored closely: in certain cases, the interpretation of the treaty must 'follow the evolution of the law and ... correspond with the meaning attached to the expression by the law in force at any given time'.[128]

IV. OTHER ISSUES SETTLED BY THE AWARD

Two other issues settled by the Award merit mention. First, as the International Court observed in *Land and Maritime Boundary*, the Award is authority for the proposition that agreements between states and local chieftains are not treaties, the Court referring to Arbitrator Huber's determination that such an instrument 'is not an agreement between equals; it is rather a form of internal organisation of a colonial territory, on the basis of autonomy of the natives'.[129] As Judge Al Khasawneh pointed out in his Separate Opinion, however, *Island of Palmas* was on this score clearly wrong: the fact that the agreement is not one between equals does not mean that it cannot be valid as a matter of the law of treaties. Judge Al Khasawneh observed that 'Such an approach is a confusion of inequality in status on the one hand and inequality in power on the other. That local rulers and chiefs were weak is apparent from their agreeing to enter into treaties of protection, but this does not detract from the fact that they had the capacity to enter into treaty relations'.[130] A generous view might be to say that this part of Huber's award is no more than an instance of Homer nodding; but, as Mamadou Hébié has observed, the reality of the matter is that 'Max Huber ruled that some local political entities in South-East Asia

---

[126] D Greig, *Intertemporality and the Law of Treaties* (London, BIICL, 2001) 138.

[127] E Bjorge, *The Evolutionary Interpretation of Treaties* (Oxford, OUP, 2014).

[128] *Aegean Sea Continental Shelf (Greece v Turkey) (Judgment)* [1978] ICJ Rep 3, 32 at [77].

[129] *Land and Maritime Boundary between Cameroon and Nigeria (Cameroon v Nigeria: Equatorial Guinea Intervening)* [2002] ICJ Rep 303, 405 at [205].

[130] ibid, 495–96 at [5].

could not conclude real treaties because they were outside the European Family of Nations'.[131]

Secondly, and less controversially, *Island of Palmas* is authority for the evidentiary rule that maps are to be handled with great care. As the Sole Arbitrator observed in a passage which has been cited on many occasions by international courts and tribunals:

> only with the greatest caution can account be taken of maps in deciding a question of sovereignty ... Any maps which do not precisely indicate the political distribution of territories ... clearly marked as such, must be rejected forthwith ... The first condition required of maps that are to serve as evidence on points of law it their geographical accuracy. It must here be pointed out that not only maps of ancient date, but also modern, even official or semi-official maps seem wanting in accuracy.[132]

V. CONCLUSION

Though the disputed territory in question was all but miniscule, the Award settling which state had sovereignty over it is nothing if not a landmark of public international law. In fact, as this chapter has sought to show, *Island of Palmas* is one of the first cases which made public international law a *public* law as opposed to being only, as one leading nineteenth-century work would have it, 'private law writ large'.[133] As the Sole Arbitrator showed, private law concepts of ownership were not sufficient to inspire the international law of sovereignty over land. *Island of Palmas* thus took a small but decisive step away from a conception of international law in which sovereignty had been modelled on transfer of property in domestic private law. Small, because it was founded on already existing international law, as set out in numerous awards and judgments. Important, because, by leaving behind the negatively conceived private law concept of sovereignty-as-ownership, Sole Arbitrator Huber in *Island of Palmas* considered himself bound to conceive of sovereignty as a fundamentally concrete concept, positively conceived, and one which gave importance to the individuals who actually lived on the territory in question. According to the orthodox conception of international law, individuals were classed as objects of international law on a par with rivers and canals;[134] *Island of Palmas*, through the concept of sovereignty that it promulgated, effected a jurisprudential dent in this age-old conception. As will have been seen, the Award in *Island of Palmas* built on

---

[131] M Hébié, 'The Role of the Agreements Concluded with Local Political Entities in the Course of French Colonial Expansion in West Africa' (2015) 85 *BYIL* 21, 25. See, more generally, M Hébié, *Souveraineté territoriale par traité* (Paris, Presses universitaires de France, 2015).

[132] *Island of Palmas* (n 6) 852–53. Quoted in, eg *Territorial and Maritime Dispute between Nicaragua and Honduras* (n 25) 723, [214]; *Case concerning the Temple of Preah Vihear (Cambodia v Thailand)* dissenting opinion Judge Moreno Quintana ICJ Rep 1962, 69–70; *Eritrea v Yemen* (n 25) 100, [388].

[133] TE Holland, *Studies in International Law and Diplomacy* (Oxford, Clarendon Press, 1898) 152.

[134] L Oppenheim, *International Law* (London, Longmans, 1905) 344–45.

precedents such as *Alpe di Cravairola*,[135] in which the point was explicitly made that human activity could, in the determination of which state enjoyed sovereignty, take precedence over the importance of the watershed of a river, and *Grisbadarna*, which stressed the importance 'of private interests which, if once neglected, cannot be effectively safeguarded by any manner of sacrifice on the part of the Government of which the interested parties are subjects'.[136] In this way *Island of Palmas* can be seen to have laid the groundwork for later developments of international law which would recognise individuals as subjects and no longer only objects of international law. This should be seen as being closely connected with that which the Award says about the intertemporal law. The second limb of the intertemporal rule was no more than a natural corollary to the modern doctrine according to which sovereignty involves the provision of guarantees for the observance of minimum standards of international law in the territory.[137]

---

[135] *Alpe di Craivarola* in H La Fontaine, *Pasicrisie internationale: histoire documentaire des arbitrages internationaux* (Berne, Stämpfli, 1902) 201.

[136] *Grisbadarna (Maritime Boundary Dispute)* (n 62) 234.

[137] Waldock, *Disputed Sovereignty* (n 81) 321.

7

Legal Status of Eastern Greenland (Denmark v Norway) (1933)

ROLF EINAR FIFE

I. INTRODUCTION

IN 1933 A contentious issue between Denmark and Norway concerning sovereignty over a swathe of Eastern Greenland was successfully resolved through international dispute settlement.[1] This was the first time that a dispute over acquisition of territorial sovereignty was settled by the Permanent Court of International Justice in The Hague (PCIJ), the predecessor of the present International Court of Justice (ICJ).[2] In fact, this also proved to be the only time that it did so.[3] As distinct from earlier arbitral awards, such international adjudication by a standing court is in itself a historic landmark. Moreover, the judgment has later been relied upon as a building-block for the international jurisprudence in this field, as will be seen in Part IV.

The parties swiftly complied with the judgment. It helped 'clear the air' between them and provides a case study of the potential role of law and legal process in international politics.[4] Nevertheless, *Eastern Greenland* is rarely mentioned in surveys of the interplay between law and international politics, or even in treatises on international relations for the period between the First and Second World Wars.[5]

---

[1] *Legal Status of Eastern Greenland (Denmark v Norway)*, Judgment of 5 April 1933, PCIJ, Series A/B, No 53.

[2] For an overview of the precursors, the creation and the procedures of the Permanent Court of International Justice, see MO Hudson, *The Permanent Court of International Justice 1920–1942* (New York, Macmillan, 1943). Five years before the *Eastern Greenland* judgment a notable arbitral award was issued with *Island of Palmas (Netherlands, United States of America)* (1928) 2 RIAA 829. Two years before *Eastern Greenland*, and a few months before Norway proclaimed its occupation of the territory, an arbitral award concerning an uninhabited territory was delivered by the King of Italy on 28 January 1931, in the case *Island of Clipperton (Mexico v France)* (1931) 2 RIAA 1105.

[3] As opposed to a frontier dispute, see R Dollot, 'Le Droit international des espaces polaires' (1949) 75 *Hague Recueil* 1949, 121, 162; O Spiermann, *International Legal Argument in the Permanent Court of International Justice—The Rise of the International Judiciary* (Cambridge, CUP, 2005) 344.

[4] The expression 'clear the air' was used by one of the protagonists, Professor Frede Castberg; see the quotation at the end of the article.

[5] No reference was made to *Eastern Greenland* in the classic and regularly revised JB Duroselle, *Histoire des Relations internationales de 1919 à 1945, Vol 1*, 12th edn (Paris, Armand Colin, 2001); nor is any reference made to it, for instance, in M Byers (ed), *The Role of Law in International Politics—Essays in International Relations and International Law* (Oxford, OUP, 2000).

Even recognised handbooks of the history of international law happen to avoid references to the judgment.[6]

This stands in sharp contrast to the frequent references in later jurisprudence and in manuals of international law.[7] There may be several reasons for such excessive sobriety. The rapidly deteriorating international climate in 1933 may have led to a general shift in focus over to other, decidedly more worrying, political issues than those related to remote and uninhabited Arctic territories. Admittedly, 1933 is not widely remembered for *Eastern Greenland*, or as the year of the first international adjudication by a world court of a contentious territorial sovereignty dispute and its successful legal and political resolution.[8] Instead, it remains associated with Hitler's rise to power in Berlin as chancellor in January, against a backdrop of global economic recession and social disruption. In March of the same year, Japan left the League of Nations, to be followed by Germany in October.

The judgment having 'cleared the air', the parties themselves did not have any incentives to make frequent references to it. On the Norwegian side, the occupation of Eastern Greenland on 10 July 1931 came instead increasingly to be seen as a questionable episode, not least in a domestic political and constitutional law perspective.[9] As an experience that few would like to be reminded of it came to be relegated to a parenthesis in Norway's political history.[10]

For students of international law, the judgment came to signify two pithy propositions. As regards acquisition of territorial sovereignty, the principle of effectiveness requires little in terms of evidence of display of state authority if the territory in question is inhospitable. In addition, the phenomenon known as the 'Ihlen Declaration' came to signify that a unilateral declaration of a foreign minister may become legally binding for a state under international law.

---

[6] No reference is provided in the otherwise thorough B Fassbender and A Peters (eds), *The Oxford Handbook of the History of International Law* (Oxford, OUP, 2012).

[7] G Alfredsson, 'Eastern Greenland Case' *Max Planck Encyclopedia of Public International Law* (2007) 267, 268 noted no fewer than 26 references to the case in I Brownlie, *Principles of Public International Law*, 5th edn (Oxford and New York, Clarendon 1998); the number remains the same in J Crawford, *Brownlie's Principles of Public International Law*, 8th edn (Oxford, OUP, 2012).

[8] The general decline of the order established after the First World War is key to P Krüger's chapter 'From the Paris Peace Treaties to the End of the Second World War' in Fassbender and Peters *History of International Law* (n 6) 679, 693.

[9] An example of an even-handed, though characteristically short, narrative is provided by B Furre, *Norsk Historie 1905–1990* (Oslo, Det norske samlaget, 1992) 140–41. In recent years, detailed analyses of political and economic history related to Eastern Greenland have been carried out. The most comprehensive survey to date is covered in the three-volume EA Drivenes & HD Jølle (eds), *Norsk Polarhistorie* (Oslo, Gyldendal, 2004), in particular vol 2 at 215–44; and vol 3 at 188 and 266–71. The present contribution draws heavily on the backgrounds provided by Drivenes and Jølle. A single-volume English edition was published in 1996: EA Drivenes and HD Jølle (eds), *Into the Ice—The History of Norway and the Polar Regions* (Oslo, Gyldendal, 2006) 296–306. The impact of the dispute between Denmark and Norway in shaping Norwegian foreign policy was discussed in OB Fure, *Mellomkrigstid 1920–1940*, vol 3 of *Norsk Utenrikspolitisk Historie* ('History of Norwegian foreign policy') (Oslo, Universitetsforlaget, 1996) 121–32.

[10] Some protagonists were later associated with the Nazi party during the Second World War, which contributed to their discreditation. They included Gustav Smedal (1888–1951) (see n 121 below), who had worked as a lawyer in the Norwegian Foreign Ministry from 1920 to 1923. His doctoral thesis at the University of Oslo in 1930 (*Ervervelse av statshøihet over polarområder*) proved highly influential for the formulation of the legal basis for the Norwegian claim over Eastern Greenland in 1931. It was

More recently, the judgment has been considered by some as representing decidedly classical inter-state international law, notably without analysing issues pertaining to indigenous populations.[11] Its continued relevance as a keystone of the jurisprudence pertaining to the establishment of territorial sovereignty has nevertheless both been proven and richly analysed.[12]

The object of this contribution is to highlight the 1933 judgment's continued importance and interest in several perspectives, and possibly help unshackle such mental brackets as might still surround it.[13]

II. SETTING THE STAGE: GEOGRAPHY, THE PARTIES AND THEIR CLAIMS

A. Geography

An aphorism commonly attributed to Napoleon is that the foreign policy of a state follows from its geography.[14] In addition to promoting a keener understanding of the parties' interests, claims and arguments, placing *Eastern Greenland* in its wider geographical context may also benefit its legal analysis.

Greenland (in Greenlandic, *Kalaallit Nunaat*) covers 2.2 million km², with population concentrated largely in settlements on the west coast. These could not easily be linked by transport over land, and the latter remains difficult today. *Eastern Greenland* concerned a disputed territory covering a part of the east coast situated north of the Arctic Circle, at latitudes between 71°30'N and 75°40'N. The Court emphasised the Arctic climate and character of the territory. In its own words, 'only a narrow strip of varying width along the coasts is free of permanent ice'.[15] Moreover,

---

published in English in 1931 as *Acquisition of Sovereignty over Polar Areas* (C Meyer tr) and remained an important reference in international law; see for example CHM Waldock, 'Disputed Sovereignty in the Falklands Islands Dependencies' (1948) 25 BYBIL 311 at 315–36; R Ago, *Il requisito dell'effettività dell'occupazione in diritto internazionale* (Rome, Anonima Romana Editoriale, 1934). In 1931, Smedal also published *Oppgjør og forståelse med Danmark* ('Resolution and understanding with Denmark'), which became politically influential in activist circles in connection with the *Eastern Greenland* case.

[11] Alfredsson 'Eastern Greenland Case' (n 7) 268, [10].

[12] There is no scope here for a survey of this rich literature. For a brief but elegant introduction, see V Lowe, *International Law* (Oxford, OUP, 2007) 136–48. For a readable overview of acquisition and transfer of territorial sovereignty, see J Crawford, *Brownlie's Principles of Public International Law*, 8th edn (Oxford, OUP, 2012) 215–44. For a foundational discussion of legal method, with frequent references to Eastern Greenland, see M Kohen, *Possession contestée et souveraineté territoriale* (Paris, Presses Universitaires de France, 1997). For the normative significance of statehood and its international law conditions, including effectiveness, see J Crawford, *The Creation of States in International Law*, 2nd edn (Oxford, OUP, 2006).

[13] A summary of the 1933 judgment is provided in *Summaries of Judgments, Advisory Opinions and Orders of the Permanent Court of International Justice* (United Nations, New York, 2012) (ST/LEG/SER.F/1/Add.4) 306–18. A synopsis is provided in Part III below.

[14] 'Tout Etat fait la politique de sa géographie', as quoted by A Defay, *La géopolitique* (Paris, Presses Universitaires de France, 2005) 4.

[15] *Eastern Greenland* (n 1) 26. This characteristic has become subject to climate change. For an overview of Greenland's physical and economic geography see C Berthelsen, IH Mortensen and E Mortensen, *Kalaallit Nunaat Greenland Atlas* (Nuuk, Greenland, Pilersuiffik, 1990), with overall maps of regions and settlements at 18 and 51.

not only the vast Greenland ice sheet, in the judgment referred to as the 'inland ice', but also parts of the coast were deemed difficult to access. Such difficulties were seasonally compounded on the east coast 'owing to the influence of the Polar current and the stormy winds on the icebergs and the floe ice and owing to the frequent spells of bad weather'.[16]

The coastal region concerned extended between Carlsberg Fjord in the south and Bessel Fjord in the north. Economic interests in the area related to traditional marine activities, namely fishing and hunting. The coastal front faced the Greenland Sea and the island of Jan Mayen. This island had recently been annexed by Norway (1929). Incidentally, such long-standing interests seemed to re-emerge again later, in a case between Denmark and Norway that led to the 1993 ICJ judgment concerning the maritime delimitation between Greenland and Jan Mayen.[17] This judgment concerned a maritime area facing the coast of Eastern Greenland.[18]

A careful consideration of the wider geographical context of *Eastern Greenland* may also bring to the fore what Neil MacCormick would have called 'consequentialist arguments', ie consequences of various alternative rulings as to the types of decision which would have to be given in other hypothetical cases.[19] The landward limits of the area covered the Norwegian act of occupation in 1931, and thus the landward extent of the disputed area, had not been defined, other than by reference to the 'inland ice'.[20] If the area had ultimately been found to be *terra nullius* and thus open to occupation, there would be pause to reflect on what consequences this would have had for the definition of landward limits and beyond, but not solely. Consequential issues would have arisen for other unsettled parts of Greenland.

In fact, this proved to be more than a purely hypothetical question. In 1932, in the course of these proceedings, Norway brought a case against Denmark before the PCIJ concerning a different part of Greenland, the *South-Eastern Territory of Greenland*.[21] This case followed from a second act of occupation made by Norway on 12 July 1932, further south on the eastern coast of Greenland.[22] Both parties had sent hunting expeditions to this area, and both had nationals invested with police powers.[23] On 18 July 1932, Norway instituted proceedings before the PCIJ requesting the Court to order interim measures of protection, alleging a 'serious reason to

---

[16] *Eastern Greenland* (n 1) 27. Recent developments of climate change have led to dramatic decreases of the ice sheet, but also to a high incidence of drift ice at sea and continued seasonal challenges for navigation and other forms of communication.

[17] *Maritime Delimitation in the Area between Greenland and Jan Mayen, Judgment* [1993] ICJ Rep 38. On treaty-making in the wake of the ICJ judgment, RE Fife, 'Les accords faisant suite à l'arrêt rendu par la Cour internationale de Justice en 1993 dans l'affaire entre le Danemark et la Norvège concernant la délimitation maritime dans la région située entre le Groenland et Jan Mayen' (1999) 4 *Annuaire du droit de la mer* 199.

[18] This maritime area is situated at latitudes between 69°54′N and 74°21′N, thus largely coinciding with the latitudes defining *Eastern Greenland*.

[19] N MacCormick, *Legal Reasoning and Legal Theory* (Oxford, Clarendon Press, 1978) 129ff.

[20] *Eastern Greenland* (n 1) 26.

[21] *Legal Status of the South-Eastern Territory of Greenland*, Order 3 August 1932, PCIJ, General list, Nos 52 and 53, 276. See *Summaries of Judgments*, etc 320–21.

[22] Between the latitudes 63°40′N and 60°30′N.

[23] *South Eastern Territory of Greenland* (n 21) 283.

fear ... acts of violence against Norwegian nationals'.[24] The request was dismissed in an order on 3 August, while the Court reserved its right subsequently to consider whether new circumstances would require the indication of such provisional measures. The case was ultimately removed from the Court's list in 1933 following the withdrawal of both acts of occupation by Norway after the *Eastern Greenland* judgment. However, the question as to what other parts of Greenland might have been deemed open to occupation, had the Court instead found in favour of Norway in that case, has rarely been the object of a sharpened focus in legal or other commentaries.

This is not to say that Eastern Greenland hinges on such consequentialist arguments, nor that the state of international law was so indeterminate as to pave the way for more subjective influences. However, it may be useful to underline a geographical context that helps explain that the core issue in *Eastern Greenland* was not whether Denmark had territorial sovereignty in Greenland—that was undisputed. The issue, in its pithiest form, was instead whether that sovereignty covered Greenland as a whole or whether instead there could remain *terrae nullius* areas open to occupation.

B. Background to the Norwegian Occupation in 1931 of Erik Raudes Land

Since the end of the nineteenth century Norwegian hunters and fishers had been operating in the waters adjacent to Eastern Greenland and Jan Mayen, sometimes using bases on the Greenlandic shore.[25] The establishment of a Danish trade monopoly for all Greenland led to a fear within such circles that it would drive out Norwegian interests. Protests ignited parts of Norwegian public opinion, particularly in coastal areas of the Norwegian mainland dependent on fishing and trapping. Greenland associations were formed. They organised rallies claiming that Norway had been subjected to historic injustice, when Greenland and other overseas territories had been handed over to Denmark at the end of the Napoleonic wars in 1814, and recalling that Norwegians had continued making a living in these Arctic areas. As a consequence, demands were made that the Norwegian Government occupy an unsettled area on the East coast of Greenland, on the assumption that it was *terra nullius*.

Such demands were first resisted by the Government. They also led to a sharp cleavage between political parties. These demands met with opposition either to so-called 'polar imperialism' or to unilateralist action. Considering that the core issue concerned the extension of a trade monopoly detrimental to vested Norwegian economic interests, the Government favoured negotiations with Denmark with a view to securing equal fishing and hunting rights.

Nevertheless, both states increased their activity in Eastern Greenland to bolster their claims. Private hunting and scientific expeditions were invested with police authority, on both sides. In the spring of 1931, an advisory council for polar affairs

---

[24] The request was made in accordance with Art 41 of the Statute of the Court; ibid, 278.
[25] The following summary of factual developments draws heavily on authors referred to in n 9, in particular Drivenes and Jølle.

of the Norwegian Government (*Ishavsrådet*), comprising representatives of hunting and scientific interests, demanded that the Government occupy a part of Greenland. Not having received the approval of the Government, the council's chairman, the international lawyer Gustav Smedal organised the hoisting of the Norwegian flag on the territory by a private expedition on 26 June 1931.[26] This 'private occupation' proclaimed Erik Raudes Land to be Norwegian.

Under swiftly mounting political pressure, the Government ultimately relented. On 10 July 1931, it associated itself with these private acts and declared sovereignty over this part of Eastern Greenland. This declaration triggered the Court case. On 12 July 1931, Denmark submitted its application instituting proceedings on the basis of the optional clause contained in Article 36 (2) of the Court's statute.

At the same time, political tensions between Denmark and Norway should not be exaggerated. Thus, in the *South-Eastern Territory of Greenland* case brought the subsequent year, the Court characterised the attitude and conduct of the parties in the following way:[27]

> even in this form, these declarations, taken together, are indicative of the existence in responsible circles in both countries of a state of mind and of intentions which are eminently reassuring.

To reach this conclusion, the Court took into consideration internal instructions issued to a Norwegian national invested with police powers, which emphasised the need to display 'the utmost tact' and required 'avoiding complications'.[28] Furthermore, no obstacles were to be placed in the way of Danish expeditions operating within the framework of a bilateral Convention of 9 July 1924 between Denmark and Norway concerning Eastern Greenland. This allowed fishers and hunters from both countries to continue their activities subject to the legislation of their respective countries. The two governments could not be presumed to act otherwise than in conformity with the intentions expressed before the Court. In any case, the Court considered that the sovereignty rights in question at the time could not be affected by the expeditions.[29] Relying on a presumption of good faith of the parties, the Court therefore dismissed the Norwegian request. It reserved its right to subsequently consider whether new circumstances could arise requiring a different stance.[30] The conduct of the parties was deemed 'eminently reassuring', and characterises more broadly the relations between them.

C. Key Claims

Denmark disputed the 1931 proclamation by Norway, stating that it had sovereignty over the whole of Greenland. Thus, the declaration of occupation and any steps taken in this connection by the Norwegian Government were deemed to

---

[26] n 10.
[27] *South Eastern Territory of Greenland* (n 21) 286.
[28] ibid.
[29] ibid, 287.
[30] ibid, 289.

constitute a violation of the existing legal situation and were, accordingly, unlawful and invalid. Norway claimed that Denmark had no sovereignty over the area named Eirik Raudes land, which was considered *terra nullius*—no man's land—at the critical date, ie the date of proclamation of Norwegian sovereignty in 1931, and that Norway had acquired the sovereignty over the territory.

Considerable amounts of evidence were presented in the written and oral pleadings, with public hearings held from November 1932 to February 1933. Arguments presented by the Danish side, including its counsel Charles de Visscher, claimed actual exercise of sovereignty over time, but also general recognition and acquiescence by other states.[31] Denmark maintained that the legal status of a given region depends on community recognition of other states (*communis opinio*). This spoke in favour of considering references to Greenland in various domestic legal acts and international instruments and documents as including the whole of Greenland.[32]

Among Norway's arguments were a lack of sufficient display of state authority by Denmark in the area concerned, ie insufficient evidence of effective Danish possession, which spoke in favour of considering it *terra nullius* in 1931. Any bilateral recognition of Danish sovereignty by others was not deemed to engage Norway.[33] Norway claimed that references to Greenland in a variety of instruments, domestic as well as international, included only the colonised parts of the island. It was maintained that they did not comprise the isolated and more inaccessible east coast. As stated by Norway's counsel Gilbert Gidel, with the exception of Denmark none of 24 states that had been notified by Norway of the occupation of Eirik Raudes Land, had objected to it.[34]

III. THE DECISION: SYNOPSIS OF KEY FINDINGS

With a majority of 10 judges against two, the Court concluded that on 10 July 1931 Denmark possessed a valid title to the sovereignty over all Greenland.[35] Also dissenting, Judge Anzilotti found in favour of Denmark, albeit on different grounds. The synopsis reveals a thorough consideration of treaties, displays of governmental authority and diplomatic correspondence, following a chronological structure:

a   The Court gave a detailed account of historical and constitutional developments, based on the information provided by the parties. The first colonisation of Greenland was assumed to have taken place around 1000 AD. Two settlements on the south-west coast of Greenland became tributary to the kingdom of Norway in the thirteenth century. In 1380, the kingdoms of Norway and Denmark were united under the same Crown. In so far as it constituted a

---

[31] Pleadings, Denmark's Memorial, 101.
[32] Pleading, Denmark's Reply. 712.
[33] Pleadings, Norway's Counter-Memorial, 538.
[34] Pleadings, Norway, Gidel, No 66, 3185–280. See Dollot, *Le Droit international* (n 3) 161.
[35] The two dissenting opinions were of Judge Anzilotti (Italian) and the Norwegian judge ad hoc Vogt; howeverJudge Anzilotti reached the same conclusion as the majority.

dependency of the Crown, Greenland continued to be regarded as a Norwegian possession.[36] The colonies in Greenland disappeared before 1500, but this did not put an end to the King's pretensions to sovereignty over it.[37] Under King Christian IV in the seventeenth century these pretensions were displayed in the form of a concession for a navigation and trade monopoly and in some contacts with foreign states. In 1723 and 1734 concessions for monopolies were granted for the whole of Greenland and exclusive privileges for their holders were enforced. There were also periods, intermittently, where the monopoly was directly exercised by the state. In 1776 Greenland trade became a monopoly of the state of Denmark by Ordinance of the King. Further regulations issued in 1781 divided the island into two administrative districts.[38] While the Court recognised that the King's claims 'amounted merely to pretensions', it found that 'in the absence of any competing claim the King's pretensions to be the sovereign of Greenland subsisted'. Furthermore, the Court considered that 'Legislation is one of the most obvious forms of the exercise of sovereign power', and that its enactment had in principle not been limited to the colonies, but concerned all Greenland.[39] Legislative acts and administrative acts, including ordinances related to concessions, indicated that references to the word 'Greenland' had been made in the geographical sense, rather than meaning only the colonised area on the west coast. The Court relied on the 'ordinary meaning of the word' and stated that '(i)f it is alleged by one of the Parties that some unusual or exceptional meaning is to be attributed to it, it lies on that Party to establish its contention'.[40] The burden of proof thus lied on Norway. The evidence provided did not support that the word 'Greenland' was to be interpreted in a restricted sense. Moreover, in the absence of any claim to sovereignty by another Power, and due to the Arctic and inaccessible character of the uncolonised parts of Greenland, the King of Denmark and Norway was found to have exercised his authority to an extent that was sufficient to establish a valid claim to sovereignty over all Greenland. Up to 1814, the rights which the King possessed over Greenland had been enjoyed by him as King of Norway. Summing up, no part of Greenland was to be considered 'terra nullius' in 1814.

b   Thereafter, the Court attached 'special importance' to events between 1814 and 1819.[41] Norway had up to 1814 been united to Denmark, which had supported France in the Napoleonic wars. Napoleon's defeat made it possible for Sweden to obtain the cession of the Kingdom of Norway. The Kiel Peace Treaty of 14 January 1814 became significant in this context, as its Article 4 explicitly

---

[36] *Eastern Greenland* (n 1) 27.

[37] ibid. Among others, Waldock, 'Disputed Sovereignty' (n 10) 321 has noted that the Court treated continuity of display of state authority as an integral element in the Danish title, irrespective of the fact that it did not emphasise the requirement of continuity as regards display of state activity to the same extent as Judge Huber in *Island of Palmas (Netherlands, United States of America)* (1928) 2 RIAA 829, (1928) 4 ILR 3 876.

[38] ibid, 29.

[39] ibid, 48.

[40] ibid, 49.

[41] ibid, 31.

excluded Greenland, the Faroe Islands and Iceland from the cession—thereby also signifying that Greenland would thereafter be delinked from Norway. Subsequently, and as a reaction to the Kiel treaty, Norway declared independence, but was ultimately forced into union with Sweden in the autumn of 1814. A Stockholm Convention of 1 September 1819 between Norway and Denmark effected the 'complete liquidation of all matters arising out of the Union between Denmark and Norway'. The PCIJ considered a Norwegian attempt in the negotiations to formally claim the restitution of the Faroes, Iceland and Greenland at that time. The claim met with a Danish refusal, was withdrawn by Norway and formally renounced in a note to Denmark of 28 May 1819.[42] In addition, the Court interpreted the Stockholm Convention as amounting to a renunciation of any further claims.[43] Using modern legal classifications, state succession as regards a territory was thus an important issue in *Eastern Greenland*. While Norwegian circles may have perceived the forced cession as coercive and unjust, ultimately contributing to the chain of events that led to the occupation in 1931, there could be no doubt as to the clarity of the Norwegian renunciation of any residual claims to sovereignty in Greenland.

c   The Court considered thereafter the period between 1819 and 1915, scrutinising displays of public authority, in particular treaty practice and concessions granted. It found that Denmark had continued to display its authority over the uncolonised part of Greenland to a degree sufficient to confer a valid title of sovereignty.[44] The same applied to its exercise of governmental functions in the years leading up to 1931.[45]

d   The Court considered Norwegian claims that Denmark during and after the First World War, particularly in 1919, had attempted to 'extend' her sovereignty to the whole of Greenland. However, the use of the word 'extension' in Danish correspondence was not deemed decisive.[46] Moreover, Denmark was not found to be estopped from claiming that Denmark possessed an old established sovereignty over all Greenland.[47] Danish efforts to gain recognition that all Greenland was under Danish sovereignty, had been supported by the United states and other powers.

e   A separate question was whether also the Norwegian Foreign Minister, Niels Claus Ihlen,[48] had made a binding engagement to this effect when making an oral 'declaration' in 1919 that Norway would not oppose Danish claims. The PCIJ first considered more generally, and in detail, whether Norway had made any legally binding undertakings that recognised Danish sovereignty over all Greenland, or whether such undertakings only concerned the colonised

---

[42] ibid, 65–66.
[43] ibid, 66–68.
[44] ibid, 54.
[45] ibid, 62–63.
[46] ibid, 60.
[47] ibid, 62.
[48] Nils Claus Ihlen (1855–1925) was the Foreign Minister of Norway from 1913 to 1920.

parts of Greenland. The Court concluded that the Norwegian renunciation of claims in the 1819 Convention implied a recognition of Danish sovereignty over all Greenland.[49] Moreover, the PCIJ found on the basis of a bilateral treaty of 1826, as well as multilateral postal conventions in 1920, 1924 and 1929, that Norway had reaffirmed that it had recognised the whole of Greenland as Danish.[50] Finally, the Court considered in depth the assurance given by Foreign Minister Ihlen on 22 July 1919 to the Danish head of the diplomatic mission in Norway.[51] This undertaking had been made in response to Denmark's stated intention to obtain recognition of its sovereignty over the whole of Greenland at the 1919 Peace Conference in Paris after the First World War. It declared 'that the Norwegian Government would not make any difficulties in the settlement of this question'. Significantly, the PCIJ found that Denmark and Norway had made two declarations of an equivalent nature concerning Greenland and Spitsbergen respectively.[52] Denmark had, for its part, stated a week earlier, on 14 July 1919, that it was prepared to renew at the Peace Conference an unofficial assurance already given to the Norwegian Government on 2 April 1919 that, having no special interests at stake in Spitsbergen, it would raise no objection to Norway's claims upon that archipelago. Accordingly, the Danish Government counted on the Norwegian Government not making any difficulties with regard to Danish intentions as to Greenland.[53] Even if the Danish attitude to the Spitsbergen question and the Norwegian attitude in the Greenland question were not to be regarded as 'interdependent' and thus creating a bilateral engagement, the Court found that it could hardly be denied that the two declarations were of an 'equivalent nature'.[54] Consequently, Norway was also 'under an obligation to refrain from contesting Danish sovereignty over Greenland as a whole and *a fortiori* to refrain from occupying a part of Greenland'.[55] The Ihlen Declaration was found to be binding upon Norway.

The majority view thus considered a variety of legal arguments to be relevant, with the collateral academic advantage of providing an analysis of a wealth of legal instruments throughout history—and an interesting account of diplomatic history and of domestic constitutional developments in Denmark and Norway.

As regards the acquisition of territorial sovereignty, the judgment recalled that a claim of sovereignty not based upon some particular act or title such as a treaty

---

[49] *Eastern Greenland* (n 1) 68.

[50] ibid, 69.

[51] ibid, 69–73.

[52] The archipelago of Svalbard was formerly known as Spitsbergen. Since 1925 the latter name has been reserved for the main island, while the whole archipelago, including Bear Island, bears the name Svalbard. The summary that follows is drawn from RE Fife, 'Denmark/Greenland–Norway (Svalbard)', Report 9–25, in DA Colson and RW Smith (eds), *International Maritime Boundaries* (Leiden and Boston, MA, Martinus Nijhoff, 2011) 4513–31, which analyses the background and contents of the 2006 maritime delimitation agreement between Denmark and Norway for the area between Greenland and Svalbard.

[53] ibid, 36–37 and 57–58.

[54] ibid, 70–71.

[55] ibid, 73.

of cession but merely upon continued display of authority, must involve both the intention and will to act as sovereign, and some actual exercise or display of such authority.[56] The judgment established that in thinly populated and inhospitable areas such as the Arctic and inaccessible territory concerned, a court may be satisfied with very little in the way of the actual exercise of sovereign rights, provided that the other state could not make out a superior claim.[57] Such exercise of sovereign rights has to rely on display of state authority, or acts *à titre de souverain*, by a state.[58] When confronted with a competing claim by another state, a limited display of authority was found to be sufficient to give rise to a valid claim to sovereignty.

The judgment's consideration of the requirement of effective exercise of sovereignty was criticised by Judge Dionisio Anzilotti in his dissenting opinion, noting 'the disproportion between the claim to sovereignty over all Greenland and the effective exercise of that sovereignty'.[59] On the other hand, Anzilotti held that the Danish request in 1919 and the declaration made in response thereto constituted the only agreement between the two countries that concerned the question submitted to the Court.[60] On this account, he reached the same conclusion as the majority.[61] The Norwegian ad hoc judge Vogt did not question that Denmark had an intention and will to act as a sovereign, ie *animus possidendi*, as regards the entirety of Greenland. He was however of the view that it had not provided sufficient evidence of a *corpus possidendi*, ie actual administration. Nor did Vogt question the, in principle, binding nature of the Ihlen Declaration. He held instead that the declaration had been given under conditions that had not later been met by the Danish side.

IV. ENDURING INFLUENCE OF *EASTERN GREENLAND*

A. Acquisition of Territorial Sovereignty

The 1933 judgment is indisputably part of classical international law, allocating territory, power and rights to states, as referred to by *Crawford*, with little concern for distributive justice or other considerations.[62] While one has to exercise caution

---

[56] *Eastern Greenland* (n 1) 45–6. The first element is often referred to as *animus*, the second to *corpus*.

[57] ibid, 46.

[58] ibid, 45–46, 51, 54.

[59] Dissenting opinion of Anzilotti, 83.

[60] ibid 76, 94.

[61] Judges Schücking (German) and Wang (Chinese) concurred with the majority. However, they issued jointly observations to the effect that Denmark's diplomatic overtures toward other States between 1915 and 1921 proved that Denmark herself did not maintain towards those states the theory of an already existing Danish sovereignty over the whole island. In their view, Denmark sought instead to extend her sovereignty to it, with the assent of the states chiefly interested.

[62] J Crawford, *Chance, Order, Change: The Course of International Law, General Course on Public International Law* (2013) 365 Hague Recueil 344, [607], fn 1260. For a distinction between classic coexistence law and modern cooperation law, see W Friedmann, *The Changing Structure of International Law* (New York, Columbia University Press, 1964) 60–64. See also the distinction between relational and institutional law ('Le droit de la société relationnelle' and 'Le droit de la société institutionnelle') in RJ Dupuy, *Le droit international Que Sais-je?*, 11th edn (Paris, Presses Universitaires de France, 2001); cf C Leben, 'The Changing Structure of International Law Revisited

in reifying rules or treating them as discrete units,[63] it should also be noted that key propositions in the 1933 judgment continue to resonate vibrantly in the legal arguments of international court-rooms and the jurisprudence concerning territorial sovereignty.[64] They have become building-blocks in the reasoning of later judgments and arbitral awards concerning territorial sovereignty in less accessible or inhospitable territories, in regions as diverse as the Red Sea, the South China Sea and the Caribbean Sea.[65]

An illustration in this regard is provided by the 1998 arbitral award between Eritrea and Yemen. It concerned Red Sea islands and islets at the opposite end of the thermometer scales, as compared to Eastern Greenland. After having described these small or tiny islands as inhospitable, 'waterless and habitable only with great difficulty',[66] the tribunal stated:

> It is well known that the standard of the requirements of such activity may have to be modified when one is dealing, as in the present case, with difficult or inhospitable territory. As the Permanent Court of International Justice said in the *Legal Status of Eastern Greenland* case, '[I]t is impossible to read the records of the decisions in cases as to territorial sovereignty without observing that in many cases the tribunal has been satisfied with very little in the way of the actual exercise of sovereign rights, provided that the other state could not make a superior claim'.[67]

Another example is provided by the 2002 ICJ judgment in the case between Indonesia and Malaysia concerning sovereignty over the 'very small islands which are uninhabited or not permanently inhabited' of Ligitan and Sipadan (Pulau Ligitan and Pulau Sipadan).[68] Yet another was provided by the ICJ in the 2008 case between Malaysia and Singapore concerning the small island Pedra Branca/Pulau Batu Puteh at the point where the Straits of Singapore open up into the South China Sea.[69] The *Eastern Greenland* reasoning related to thinly populated or unsettled territories has also shown its continued relevance in the geographic setting of the Caribbean Sea, as in the 2012 ICJ judgment in a case between Nicaragua and Colombia.[70]

By Way of Introduction' (1997) 3 EJIL 399–408, and Spiermann, *International Legal Argument* (n 3) 48–49. Drawing on Anzilotti, *Droit international*, 44–45, Alf Ross referred to international law as a 'law of coordination' rather than of subordination: A Ross, *Lærebog i Folkeræt*, 5th edn (Copenhagen, Nyt Nordisk Forlag, 1980) 25–26.

[63] W Twining and D Miers, *How to Do Things with Rules*, 5th edn (Cambridge, CUP, 2010) 102–07.

[64] The importance of the *Eastern Greenland* judgment and of other developments in the Arctic for the development, unity and universality of international law is considered in RE Fife, 'Arctic Reflections Among Receding Sea-ice' in *International Law of the Sea—Essays in memory of Anatoly L Kolodkin* (Moscow, Statut, 2014) 206–21.

[65] Award of the Arbitral Tribunal in the first stage of the proceedings between Eritrea and Yemen (*Territorial Sovereignty and Scope of the Dispute* (1998), 114 ILR 1, 118 [452]; *Sovereignty over Pulau Ligitan and Pulau Sipadan (Indonesia/Malaysia), Judgment*, [2002] ICJ Rep 625, 682, [134]; *Sovereignty over Pedra Branca/Pulau Batu Puteh, Middle Rocks and South Ledge (Malaysia/Singapore), Judgment* [2008] ICJ Rep 12, 35–36, [63]–[67]; *Territorial and Maritime Dispute (Nicaragua v Colombia), Judgment* [2012] ICJ Rep 624, [80].

[66] *Eritrea/Yemen* (n 67) 31, [93] and 69, [239].

[67] ibid, 118, [452].

[68] *Sovereignty over Pulau Ligitan and Pulau Sipadan* (n 67) 682, [134].

[69] *Sovereignty over Pedra Branca /Pulau Batu Puteh, Middle Rocks and South Ledge* (n 67) 16, [22], 35–36, [63]–[67].

[70] *Territorial and Maritime Dispute (Nicaragua v Colombia)* (n 65) [80].

B. Unilateral Declarations of States

In addition, *Eastern Greenland* triggered a doctrinal debate concerning unilateral declarations of states and its key dicta were later confirmed by the jurisprudence. The judgment found that an unconditional and definitive declaration made by the Minister of Foreign Affairs on behalf of his government in response to a request by the diplomatic representative of a foreign state, in regard to a question falling within his province, is binding upon the state to which the minister belongs.[71] The Court itself referred to it as the 'Ihlen Declaration', which later became a familiar notion for students of international law and contributed to a debate on the role of unilateral declarations.[72] As to whether domestic Norwegian law authorised Ihlen to make such a declaration, the court rejected the Norwegian argument that he was constitutionally incompetent under domestic law to issue it.

The Court held that the oral declaration made on 22 July 1919 by Norway's Foreign Minister constituted an 'undertaking' that obliged Norway 'to refrain from contesting Danish sovereignty over Greenland as a whole, and *a fortiori* to refrain from occupying a part of Greenland'.[73] This was not as such a Norwegian recognition of Danish sovereignty over the island in its entirety. It signified, however, an obligation to refrain from contesting the Danish position in this regard.[74] The Court found that a foreign minister under the concrete circumstances was presumed to have authority to bind the state:[75]

> The Court considers it beyond dispute that a reply of this nature given by the Minister for Foreign Affairs on behalf of his Government in response to a request by the diplomatic representative of a foreign Power, in regard to a question falling within his province, is binding upon the country to which the Minister belongs.

There may be reason to pause before extrapolating this presumption without discernment. First, the Court undertook a thorough analysis of the circumstances at hand, which were closely related to a multilateral event, the Paris Peace Conference after the First World War, and a sequence of concrete diplomatic exchanges that made it clear that the declaration was 'unconditional and definitive'.[76] Second, the Court identified a Danish declaration of a similar nature, which was 'interdependent' with the Ihlen declaration.[77] Thirdly, it is interesting to note *Rousseau's* emphasis on the particular circumstances of an oral statement thereafter consigned

---

[71] *Eastern Greenland* (n 1) 71.

[72] For example JG Campos, LS Rodríguez and PA Sáenz de Santa Maria, *Curso de Derecho Internacional Público*, 2nd edn (Madrid, Civitas, 2002) 140; Crawford, *Brownlie's Principles* (n 12) 416; P Daillier, M Forteau and A Pellet, *Droit international public*, 8th edn (Paris, LGDJ, 2009) 395–36, [236]–[237]; R Kolb, *Interprétation et création du droit international* (Brussels, Bruylant, 2006) 246–47.

[73] *Eastern Greenland* (n 1) 73.

[74] The Court had incidentally also found that Norway previously had recognised Danish sovereignty over all Greenland, inter alia on the basis of the 1819 Treaty referred to above.

[75] ibid, 71.

[76] ibid, 72. Further guidance may be drawn from Anzilotti's dissenting opinion, which placed additional emphasis on the existence of what, in his view, amounts to an accord between Denmark and Norway.

[77] ibid, 70.

in written form and taken note of in the other representative's presence. In his view, this 'must have exercised a decisive influence on the Court's decision'.[78] This seems to be confirmed by the Court's references to the way the Danish request and Mr Ihlen's reply were recorded by him in a minute.[79] There was therefore no possible basis for disputing or questioning the statement's authenticity. This may contribute to explaining why the Court did not follow the approach of the 1927 Arbitral Award of the Mixed Romanian–Hungarian Arbitral Tribunal in *Kulin*, which decided not to attach decisive weight to oral statements of a Hungarian delegate in Brussels in 1923.[80]

Anzilotti came to the same result in his dissenting opinion.[81] In his view, no international legal rule required that such a declaration be made in written form. As already noted, he held that the Danish request in 1919 and the declaration made in response thereto constituted the only agreement between the two countries that concerned the question submitted to the Court.[82] This had also an influence on McNair, who considered the arrangement as an 'informal agreement'.[83] While there has been no disagreement as to whether Norway had made a legally binding undertaking, views have thus been more divided as to the purely unilateral nature of the declaration and whether the circumstances in Eastern Greenland really made the Ihlen Declaration a classic case of autonomous unilateral engagement. For this reason, later legal theory and jurisprudence has instead relied heavily on the 1974 Judgments in *Nuclear Tests*.[84] Nevertheless, it is fair to say that *Eastern Greenland* provided a seminal development that triggered the emergence of this topic in international law and its main tenets were confirmed by later jurisprudence. In 2006, the International Law Commission adopted its 'Guiding Principles applicable to unilateral declarations of states capable of creating legal obligations', reflecting this jurisprudence.[85]

It is thus on the above two accounts that the judgment has contributed to shaping classic international law, in the sense of the law essentially concerned with the inter-state rules of mutual respect for state sovereignty and abstention from interference in such sovereignty.[86] The jurisprudence confirms that the 1933 judgment not only is part of *classical* international law, as related to a key historical period of the legal system's development, but also of *classic* international law, in the broader sense of having a lasting and enduring systemic significance.

---

[78] C Rousseau, *Droit international public* (Paris, Sirey, 1970) vol 1, 419.

[79] *Eastern Greenland* (n 1) 69, 70.

[80] *Affaire des optants hongrois (Emeric Kulin père c État roumain)* (1927) 7 TAM 138; see also Decisions of the 50th session, 1998, *ILC Ybk*, vol 2, part 1, 329, [86].

[81] *Eastern Greenland* (n 1) Anzilotti, dissenting opinion, 91–92.

[82] ibid, 76 and 94.

[83] McNair, *The Law of Treaties* (Oxford, OUP, 1961) 10.

[84] See *Nuclear Tests (Australia v France), Judgment* [1974] ICJ Rep 253. *Nuclear Tests (New Zealand v France), Judgment* [1974] ICJ Rep 457.

[85] Report of the International Law Commission, 58th session, 2006 (A/CN.4/L.703), [176]. The Guiding Principles were taken note of by the United Nations General Assembly on 4 December 2006 with resolution A/RES/61/34.

[86] Friedmann (n 62); Spiermann, *International Legal Argument* (n 3) 48.

V. CRITICAL REFLECTIONS: THE NATURE OF INTERNATIONAL LEGAL ARGUMENT

The dissenting opinion of Anzilotti and his criticism of the majority's legal arguments concerning acquisition of territorial sovereignty were influential in legal doctrine. The Court's handling of the test of effectiveness was thus summarised by Hyde as[87]

> deference for the value of ancient claims as the foundation of rights of sovereignty over an unpossessed and unexplored territory, unwillingness to derive abandonment thereof from a mere cessation of any visible connection between the claimant sovereign an such territory for some two centuries, and a readiness to accept as tests of the limits of territorial pretensions over a vast area remaining unoccupied even in the twentieth century, something other and less than actual administrative control throughout the same.

Anzilotti's argument was also largely echoed by Alf Ross, arguably the most influential Danish international lawyer in the period after the Second World War. He asserted that mere legislation over a territory without any authority of enforcement amounts to 'empty pretensions'.[88] In his view, the judgment meant that the Court in this situation had in reality given up asserting any real requirement of effectiveness. In the context of a lasting and effective occupation within a given larger, naturally defined area, within which no other state had carried out any colonisation, a mere will to extend the occupation to the entire area would then prove sufficient to create a legal entitlement that had to be respected by other states. This he referred to as being, in reality, a theory of geographical unity. However, instead of stating as much in plain words, the Court had in his view sought to achieve a result in conformity with the rule of occupation. In his view, this undermined the very contents of the principle of effectiveness and represented an act of dissimulation. Such an act was unhelpful since it easily could lend itself to arbitrary conclusions as to what would generally be required in terms of effective occupation.

These arguments rested in fact on the view that Court had applied a doctrine of continuity or geographical unity. This also seems to have had some influence, at least among Nordic lawyers.[89] They have, however, been effectively rebutted by Waldock, who recalled that 'effective occupation' does not mean physical settlement of the territory but effective display of state activity. This the Court found that Denmark had displayed in regard to the whole of Greenland, slight though the impact of that authority might have been in the contested part of the island.[90] He observed that the geographical unity of Greenland was an important fact in assessing the limits of Denmark's state activity. Nevertheless, geographical continuity would have been to no avail if Denmark had not established some state activity displayed in regard to the whole island. Thus, the Court's judgment did not conflict with the views of Judge Huber in Island of Palmas.[91]

---

[87] C Cheney Hyde, *International Law Chiefly as Interpreted and Applied by the United States* vol I, 2nd edn (1945) 336, quoted by H Briggs, *The Law of Nations—Cases, Documents and Notes*, 2nd edn (London, Stevens & Sons, 1953) 250–51.

[88] A Ross, *A Textbook of International Law* (London, Longmans, Green and Co, 1947) 146–47.

[89] See Alfredsson (n 7) 268, [11].

[90] Waldock (n 10) 343–44.

[91] ibid.

If one follows Anzilotti's broader criticism, which was largely echoed by Alf Ross, one might also be tempted to consider that the Court's majority did not draw its main inspiration from 'Ockham's Razor', or a principle of simplicity, according to which the better explanations can do with fewer, instead of multiplying hypotheses. An understandable and laudable inclination towards Ockham's ideal might possibly have contributed to later legal theory often being less than kind as to the quality of the majority's legal reasoning.

Koskenniemi has used the judgment as an illustration of the general substantial indeterminacy of international law. He had held that '[t]he embarrassing dilemma is that by failing to indicate a preference between fact (possession) and views about fact (recognition), dispute-solution fails to be guided by any rule at all'.[92] As regards *Eastern Greenland*, he observed that:[93]

> Every argument was interpreted so as to point in the same direction: the conduct of third states implied recognition of Danish sovereignty; Danish conduct constituted effective possession; Norway had recognized Danish sovereignty; as it had recognized Danish sovereignty, its own acts could not amount to effective possession.

And, as the razor-sharp Ockham might have done, he added that:

> The decision was overdetermined. The same conclusion was drawn from conflicting premises. The embarrassing dilemmas involved in an effort to make a preference were awarded by presuming that there was no conflict.[94]

While stimulating, these categorisations made in 1989 are at least debatable. This concerns, for instance, the amalgamation of acquiescence, recognition and various other forms of consent, but also the question as to what was really in issue. As already mentioned, in its pithiest form, the question was not whether Denmark had sovereignty in Greenland, but whether that sovereignty covered Greenland as a whole or there could instead remain *terrae nullius* open to occupation. This also explains why the meaning of the term 'Greenland' as either the colonised area or the island as a whole, emerged as a key object of interpretation in several contexts. These contexts include the assessment of evidence of an actual display of state authority, as documented by legal acts and instruments of a domestic or international nature, as well as the documented attitude of other states in this regard.[95] It is also debatable whether this can be reduced to a tension between pure facts and a legal approach to sovereignty.[96]

Significantly, the PCIJ applied principles of interpretation as regards treaties, unilateral declarations and domestic administrative or legislative acts, for the purpose

---

[92] M Koskenniemi, *From Apology to Utopia—The Structure of International Legal Argument* (Cambridge, CUP, 1989, with epilogue 2005) 288.

[93] ibid, 293.

[94] ibid, 293. Reference is also made in the 2005 epilogue, ibid 578, to this judgment together with an increasingly fact-focused and contextual territorial jurisprudence of the ICJ in the 1990s.

[95] For a general rebuttal of Koskenniemi's substantive indeterminacy, see Crawford, *Chance, Order, Change* (n 62) 123–35.

[96] On the relationship between title and *effectivités*, see Kohen, *Possession contestée* (n 12) 209–10.

of ascertaining the actual use or ordinary meaning of the term 'Greenland' in various contexts.[97] More than three decades before the adoption of the 1969 Vienna Convention on the Law of Treaties—and long before Wittgenstein followed by Oxford philosophers of language had delved into the notion of 'ordinary meaning' and the relationship between rule-following and practice—the Court signified, in a nutshell, that the meaning of the word was its use in language.[98] Acting, in a way, as harbinger for the principle later codified in the Vienna Convention Article 31(4), the Court established that Norway had the burden of proof for any unusual or exceptional meaning of the term:[99]

> The geographical meaning of the word 'Greenland', i.e. the name which is habitually used in the maps to denominate the whole island, must be regarded as the ordinary meaning of the word. If it is alleged by one of the Parties that some unusual or exceptional meaning is to be attributed to it, it lies on that Party to establish its contention.

Moreover, Koskenniemi held that the Court's role in *Eastern Greenland* largely amounted to an effort to reduce the scope of the dispute, to the extent of verging towards a conclusion that there actually existed no disagreement whatsoever between the parties.[100] Careful consideration of the possibilities of reducing the scope of a dispute is however not entirely foreign to the process of peaceful settlement of disputes. The PCIJ thoroughly considered the conduct of the parties and identifiable patterns, reflecting a particular interest for any expressions of consent in its various forms as a traditional cornerstone in the production of rules in international law, as well as acquiescence in its broadest possible sense. Moreover, this was the first time ever a standing international court considered a dispute of acquisition of territorial sovereignty. As shown by Waldock, the Court confirmed legal consistency with clear authority provided by recent arbitral decisions in *Island of Palmas* (1931) and *Clipperton Island* (1932) as regards requirements of continued display of state authority in particular geographical contexts.[101]

While this may be a sociological observation rather than a normative assessment related to the quality of the legal argument, it may be useful to consider not only what the Court was *saying*, but what it was *doing*. From an institutional vantage point, it was still in the phase of establishing its credentials as the first World Court, in the first contentious case concerning the basic structure of legal argument pertaining to the establishment of territorial sovereignty. It is also worthwhile noting the composition of the Court. It was presided over by the Japanese lawyer Mineichiro

---

[97] *Eastern Greenland* (n 1) 49, 52 and 58.
[98] See the general rule of interpretation contained in the Vienna Convention on the Law of Treaties of 23 May 1969, Art 31, in particular paras 1 and 4. As regards philosophy of language, see in particular L Wittgenstein (GEM Anscombe and R Rhees (eds), GEM Anscombe (tr), *Philosophical Investigations* (Oxford, Blackwell, 1953) 43. Among the Oxford philosophers' turn to ordinary language, see for example G Ryle, *Ordinary Language* (1953) in *Collected Papers II* (London, Hutchinson, 1971), 316.
[99] *Eastern Greenland* (n 1) 49. The same principle was applied by the Court to treaties (52) and unilateral declarations (59).
[100] Koskenniemi (n 92) 293.
[101] Waldock (n 10) 315, 321, 335 and 337.

Adachi (also spelled Adatci), known for his considerable diplomatic experience, in addition to his legal skills. The court's vice-president was the Salvadoran jurist Gustavo Guerrero, who had been foreign minister 1927/28 and later succeeded Adachi as president of the PCIJ, and ultimately became the first president of the ICJ. The court included other prominent national lawyers, notably the former Chinese Minister of Justice Wang Ch'ung-hui, who later became foreign minister.[102] It may be worthwhile to consider how the Court brought together experiential knowledge relevant for delicate international dispute settlement, in addition to what is sometimes referred to as textual knowledge, as represented by prominent legal professors such as Dionisio Anzilotti. There is a challenge in rendering commensurable different traditions or, in short, producing commensurability.[103] The identification of building-blocks of consensus may have required turning a number of stones. If the decision was 'overdetermined', thus sacrificing Ockham's ideal of simplicity, this may have appeared as a small sacrifice, if the effect was to build a broad majority and quasi-unanimity of result.

The majority appears to have sought to identify the existence of consensual bases in the form of instruments or engagements that would lend themselves to interpretation. In the case of Anzilotti, this resulted in narrowing down on the engagements made in 1919, which were deemed to amount to an accord, whose breach by Norway constituted what we today would have termed an *internationally wrongful act* entailing state responsibility. The majority considered a range of other engagements as relevant, but laid considerable emphasis on the 1819 liquidation agreement between Denmark and Norway as being a settlement of what we today would have called a *state succession*. In both cases, as well as in the case of judge *ad hoc* Vogt, the judgment sheds light on basic principles of interpretation of agreements and of unilateral declarations. As already noted, the general rule that was applied, including the appurtenant burden of proof that was established, appear familiar today in light of the relevant provisions of the 1969 Vienna Convention on the Law of Treaties and customary international law.

The painstaking analysis of different legal bases might be linked to a *legitimation effect*, in order to enhance acceptability along several competing world views

---

[102] President Adachi had previously inter alia participated in the negotiations ending the Russo-Japanese war in 1905, the Paris Peace Conference in 1919, represented Japan as ambassador in Brussels 1920–27 and in Paris 1927–30 and presided the Council of the League of Nations. While engaged in various capacities in work for the Council he was inter alia its rapporteur in 1923 in conciliation efforts pertaining to the Hungaro-Romanian land reform, which led to the 1927 arbitral award in the *Kulin* case: n 80 above). See F Castberg, *Excès de pouvoir en justice international* (1931) 35 *Hague Recueil* 37; A Mandelstam, 'Conciliation internationale' (1931) 35 *Hague Recueil*, 534. As regards the prominent Chinese judge Wang, see Ole Spiermann, 'Judge Wang Chung-hui at the Permanent Court of International Justice' (2006) 5 *Chinese Journal of International Law* 1, 115–28.

[103] I owe this expression and perspective to Sanjay Subrahamanyam: see inter alia his 'Par-delà l'incommensurabilité: Pour une histoire connectée des empires aux temps modernes' (2007) 54 *Revue d'histoire moderne et contemporaine* 34, which appeared in an early electronic version in English: 'Beyond Incommensurability: Understanding Inter-Imperial Dynamics, Theory and Research in Comparative Social Analysis', Paper 32, Department of Sociology (UCLA, Los Angeles, 2005).

and interests, based on common principles of interpretation.[104] The requirements of negotiating a broad common platform included considering, weighing and absorbing several perspectives and legal bases. Ockham's ideal of simplicity thus might have to be relegated to a dissenting opinion, as compared to the establishment of an overwhelmingly clear majority. It may have reappeared in the court's formulation of the applicable principles of interpretation.

This leads to a brief digression on the merits of Vaughan Lowe's reminder that 'International law has always owed more to bricolage and pragmatism than to the cold logic of bloodless scholarship'.[105]

Bricolage is a word often intuitively associated with improvisation. In a legal context, it might appear to be at variance with substantive determinacy or enhanced legal security and predictability. However, the metaphor of the 'bricoleur' takes on a different and inspiring form in Levi-Strauss' anthropology, and might also be helpful in this context:[106]

> The example of the 'bricoleur' helps to bring out the differences and similarities. Consider him at work and excited by his project. His first practical step is retrospective. He has to turn back to an already existent set made up of tools and materials, to consider or reconsider what it contains and, finally and above all, to engage in a sort of dialogue with it and, before choosing between them, to index the possible answers which the whole set can offer to his problem ... But the possibilities always remain limited by the particular history of each piece and by those of its features which are already determined by the use for which it was originally intended or the modifications it has undergone for other purposes.

The PCIJ was dealing, in essence, with problem-solving and had to make do with what was at hand—it may be suggested that it did so respectably.[107] And, as observed by Levi-Strauss, the totality of means at the disposal of the 'bricoleur' cannot easily be defined as a project.[108] Similarly, when Lowe referred to *pragmatism*, in addition to bricolage, one may reflect on John Dewey's conception of inquiry, which provides an understanding of the nature of pragmatism:[109]

> He sees inquiry as beginning with a problem; we are involved in 'an indeterminate situation'. And inquiry aims for 'the controlled or directed transformation of an indeterminate situation into one that is so determinate in its constituent distinctions and relations as to convert the elements of the original situation into a unified whole'.[110]

---

[104] The legitimation effect originally analysed by Max Weber, has undergone various transformations in regard to legal theory, see for instance D Kennedy, *A Critique of Adjudication (fin de siècle)* (Cambridge, MA, HUP, 1997) 236ff, 398ff.

[105] Lowe, *International Law* (n 12) 142.

[106] C Lévi–Strauss, *La pensée sauvage*, in *Oeuvres* (Paris, Gallimard, 2008) 576–77; translated from the French by George Weidenfield and Nicholson Ltd, *The Savage Mind* (Chicago, University of Chicago Press, 1966), based on *La Pensée savage* (Paris, Librarie Plon, 1962); http://web.mit.edu/allanmc/www/levistrauss.pdf.

[107] In Lévi-Strauss's parlance (n 106), 'les "moyens de bord"'.

[108] ibid, 'L'ensemble des moyens du bricoleur n'est donc pas définissable par un projet'.

[109] J Dewey, 'Logic: the Theory of Inquiry' in L Hickman and T Alexander (eds), *The Essential Dewey* Vol 2 (Bloomington and Indianapolis, Indiana University Press, 1998) 169–79.

[110] ibid, 171.

Both approaches are compatible with a strive for systemic coherence in international law.[111] This requires a painstaking analysis, which is also be advocated by Anzilotti:[112]

> The best way of appreciating these overtures is, in my view, to allow the documents relating to them to speak for themselves. Though the attitude adopted by the Danish Government is, in a sense, the most important factor, the answer given by the foreign governments must also be noted, either because it shows how the Danish request was understood, or because the Danish Government, in accepting these answers without observations or reservations, showed that it accepted the interpretation placed by the other Government upon its request.

The cumulation of alternative legal bases and reasoning in *Eastern Greenland* may therefore not only be linked to a desired legitimation effect, it may also reflect problem-solving and promote systemic coherence. As highlighted by Marcelo Kohen, the rules pertaining to acquisition of territorial sovereignty have a bearing on international peace and security—and related requirements of stability have today to be considered as part of the broader framework of the law of the United Nations Charter.[113]

Alfredsson has implied that the judgment has lost its relevance as regards the consideration of 'disputes of a colonial character', because it did not consider decolonisation or issues of indigenous peoples' rights, in spite of an acknowledgement in the judgment of Inuit presence.[114] Thus, he asserted[115]

> Today, the right of colonized peoples to external self-determination would be of paramount consideration ... As to acquisition of territory and effective occupation, therefore, the applicable law has undergone substantial changes when it comes to the fate of separate and overseas territories that are inhabited by non-European or non-Western peoples and administered by European or Western Powers.

No reference was made in the judgment to later developments concerning indigenous populations or peoples, nor for instance to the status of non-self-governing territories under the United Nations Charter. This may hardly be surprising in 1933. The core question raised in the application by Denmark in *Eastern Greenland* was whether the declaration of occupation promulgated by Norway on 10 July 1931 was unlawful, to which the Court replied in the affirmative.

Legal theory has later debated whether indigenous communities not regarded as states could be regarded as occupants of their territory, with the effect of precluding *terra nullius* status and the possibility of occupation, or whether only state sovereignty was sufficient to preclude occupation.[116] The ICJ advisory opinion in *Western Sahara* 1975 affirmed a restrictive concept of *terra nullius*, and excluded from it territories inhabited by peoples having a social and political organisation.[117]

---

[111] MacCormick, *Legal Reasoning* (n 19) 106–08 and 119–218.
[112] *Eastern Greenland* (n 1) Dissenting Opinion of Anzilotti, 77 [3].
[113] Kohen (n 12); see also the preface of George Abi-Saab in this regard.
[114] See Alfredsson (n 7); 'Greenland and the Law of Political Decolonization' (1982) 25 *GYIL* 290–308.
[115] Alfredsson (n 7) 268 [10].
[116] Crawford, *Creation of States* (n 12) 263ff.
[117] *Western Sahara* [1975] ICJ Rep 12, 39 [79]–[80].

While passing reference has been made in the debate to *Eastern Greenland*'s mention of the Inuit inhabitants of Greenland, this case was decided on other grounds. The position of original inhabitants, moreover concentrated in Western Greenland and not in the territory in issue, was not discussed in argument.[118]

In *Eastern Greenland* the Court found that international agreements concluded in 1814 and 1819 amounted, in reality, to state succession. Sovereignty over Greenland had been transferred in its totality from Norway to Denmark. A later question could have been to what extent the principle of *uti possidetis juris* would have had any bearing on Greenland. Yet a separate perspective under international law is the development of obligations pertaining to the rights of indigenous peoples, as Denmark and Norway are parties to ILO Convention 169 of 27 June 1989 no 169 concerning Indigenous and Tribal Peoples in Independent Countries, which require the adoption of measures not raising the issue of external self-determination.[119]

VI. BEHIND THE SCENES

History has a marvellous way sometimes of providing hindsight. What actually happened in 1931? What was the role of government and that of private actors, and for those especially interested: what role did international lawyers play?

Recent historiography has contributed new perspectives on what happened behind the scenes on the Norwegian side. The 'Greenland case' has often been interpreted within a broader context of polar colonisation, in addition to the specific economic interests of fishers and seal hunters.[120] The concrete chain of events that ultimately triggered the filing of the court case started out, in fact, as part of a private conspiracy, involving even a tale of 'cloak and dagger'.

To ensure secrecy, a key activist supporter of Norwegian sovereignty in Eastern Greenland, Carl Marstrander, travelled on 26 June 1931 from Oslo to Gothenburg.

---

[118] Crawford (n 12), 267–68 fn 66, as compared to LC Green and OP Dickason, *The Law of Nations and the New World* (Edmonton, University of Alberta Press, 1989).

[119] For an overview of the Greenland Inuit (the *kalaallit*), see the statement of Finn Lynge on behalf of Denmark in the Oral Pleadings of the ICJ Greenland Jan Mayen case, CR 93/2, *Public sitting, held on Tuesday 12 January 1993*.

[120] This was brought to an extreme in Gustav Smedal, *Grönland und die Monroe-Doktrin*, Monatshefte für Auswärtige Politik, 7 July 1941, 521–31. Smedal (*Oppgjør og forståelse*, n 10), had established himself as a key strategist for an aggressive, nationalist brand of territorial activists, speaking in favour of occupation of East Greenland, organising the private occupation in 1931 and ultimately taking part in the legal team before the Court. After the judgment in 1933, he continued, however, as an irredentist. He was drawn to membership in Quisling's National Socialist (NS) party and, after the Nazi invasion in 1940 of Denmark and Norway and the ensuing US occupation of Greenland, he sought to mobilise German support to re-open the issue of sovereignty in Norway's favour, this time claiming Norwegian sovereignty over all Greenland, allegedly to thereby restore immemorial links between the territory and the Kingdom. The above article in German is thus premised with a reference to 'the ties that link the history of the Norwegian population from time immemorial to Greenland' and to 'the strong and lively interest in Norway for the polar regions' (*Norwegen, wo die Bevölkerung von den ältesten Zeiten ihrer Geschichte an mit Grönland verbunden gewesen und wo das Interesse für die Polargebiete stark und lebendig ist*). Nevertheless, Smedal did not succeed in persuading Berlin. After the Second World War he was sentenced for his NS activities. His 1930 doctoral thesis remains however an important source in the legal history of territorial acquisition in the Arctic, see inter alia references in n 10 above.

Marstrander was a prominent professor of Celtic languages at the University of Oslo, but acted now under cover of being a pastor Jonas Dahl. Under that fictitious name, he sent the following coded message to the leader of a hunting expedition in Greenland: 'The gospel is proclaimed across the city of Oslo, pastor Dahl'.[121] This happened to be the order activating a plan to carry out the occupation of Eastern Greenland.

At the receiving end of that message was Hallvard Devold. He had led an expedition to Greenland between 1926 and 1928 and started out on a new one in 1929, with a team of trappers and scientific researchers. He was deeply convinced that Denmark was determined to drive the Norwegians out of Greenland and he was intent on protecting Norwegian interests in Eastern Greenland. Upon receiving the coded message, he proceeded to carry out the ceremony of hoisting the Norwegian flag and declaring an occupation of the territory named Erik the Red's Land (Eirik Raudes Land).[122] This name was evocative of early Viking exploits in North America. Nevertheless, that name was less firmly grounded in reality than that of the site chosen for the hoisting of the flag, less romantically named Mosquito Bay.[123]

On the same day, 26 June, the Foreign Affairs Committee of the Norwegian Parliament (Storting) had actually staked out a different course of events. It had recommended that Norway should engage in negotiations with Denmark with a view to finding a satisfactory solution to a long-standing dispute concerning hunting and fishing rights in Greenland.[124] The private occupation was perceived as a direct challenge to both Government and Parliament, particularly as it was combined with the launch of a carefully orchestrated press campaign.[125] It came after a protracted series of events that had pitted a group of activists, whose views were in part supported by the legal adviser to the Foreign Ministry, Professor Frede Castberg, against the Government. The group called for a more forceful defence of Norwegian interests in the Arctic, since these had increasingly been threatened by the Danish hunting and fishing monopoly over the whole of Greenland, the 1921 enlargement of Soviet territorial waters to 12 nautical miles and closure of the White Sea to Norwegian trappers and the 1926 Soviet proclamation of the Sector principle, which declared sovereignty over all Arctic areas north of Russia.

What followed was not politicians setting aside cautious advice from international law experts. On the contrary, an almost unanimous international legal expertise in Norway supported a rapidly growing extra-parliamentary movement. This coalition caused the government to take a different course—in the teeth of a parliamentary majority.

Professor Frede Castberg was legal adviser to the Norwegian Foreign Ministry and later became rector of the University of Oslo, and was a key adviser as regards

---

[121] Drivenes and Jølle (eds), *Into the Ice* (n 9) 296.

[122] ibid, 297.

[123] In Norwegian: *Myggbukta*.

[124] An approach that received full support in the plenary of the Parliament, in a closed session held on 24 June 1931, see Fure, *Mellomkrigstid* (n 9) 130.

[125] Various newspapers carried the news on 29 June, leading to great popular interest. The Government responded nevertheless to a question from the Danish diplomatic mission in Norway on that day that it would not be swayed by the private occupation, though not condemning it: see ibid 130–31.

events in 1931. He recounts in his memoirs a nuanced narrative.[126] He referred to
a unanimous assessment amid international lawyers in Norway that Eastern
Greenland was 'no man's land and that it would be permissible for Norway to
occupy it'. Castberg did however not advocate the course proposed by the newly
appointed minister of defence, Vidkun Quisling.[127] In a ministerial meeting where
Castberg was present, Quisling had allegedly spoken in favour of a state occupation. In his view, 'such a policy would conform to a general contemporary trend of
assertive and energetic conduct, which could create a fait accompli' and referred
to the 1922 coup by the polish general Zeligowski, that had led to Polish control
over Vilnius.[128] Castberg marked sharp opposition to 'such a military operation and
favoured instead a course of action limited to enhancing the legal basis for a possible
case before an international court'. The only aim of such action would be to prevent
Denmark pre-empting Norway with acts of occupation on her own. Castberg regretted the belated consideration of such action, since a Danish expedition under the
leadership of Knud Rasmussen was already on its way to the territory. Undoubtedly
stung by criticisms of constitutional irregularities by the Government, Castberg
discarded as totally unwarranted any analogy between 'international judicial policy'
of this kind and a 'policy amounting to a military coup'.[129]

A newly appointed Norwegian government was in May 1931 taken aback by
the mounting popular campaign in favour of occupation. Prime Minister Kolstad
characterised it as an 'unwarranted intrusion into our foreign policy'.[130] A fortnight
later, however, on 10 July 1931, the Government relented. It proclaimed a formal
(state) occupation of Eirik Raudes Land.[131] The next day, Denmark brought the case
before the PCIJ.

The Norwegian Parliament subsequently became the foremost critic in Norway of
the 1931 occupation and of its consequences.[132] As regards the policy that led to the
occupation of Eastern Greenland in the first place, later historiography has revealed
how private initiatives actually had undercut policy, and how foreign policy came
to follow as a function of these initiatives. In addition, the evidence does not reveal
a case of politicians willing to take risks in side-stepping caution recommended by
international legal advisers, but rather lawyers driving policy, albeit for reasons
that now appear more circumspect and respectable than some would have it in the
aftermath.

It should be noted, however, that the decisive legal advice actually provided by
Castberg contained both a dose of activism and circumspection on 2 July 1931, less

---

[126] F Castberg, *Minner—om politikk og vitenskap fra årene 1900–1970* (Oslo, Universitetsforlaget,
1971) 20–24 and 29–35.

[127] At the time, Quisling was not yet member of the National Socialist party and this was before his
name became associated with the Nazi occupation of Norway.

[128] Castberg, *Minner* (n 126) 29.

[129] ibid, 30.

[130] Drivenes and Jølle (eds) (n 9) 300.

[131] Fure (n 9) 131.

[132] In spite of stinging parliamentary criticism, constitutional lawyers have not deemed it necessary
under the Norwegian constitution to seek prior parliamentary approval before proceeding to an act of
occupation. This includes F Castberg, *Norges Statsforfatning*, 2nd edn (Oslo, Arbeidernes aktietrykkeri,
1947) vol II, 178; J Andenæs, *Statsforfatningen i Norge*, 7th edn (Oslo, Tano, 1990) 301.

than a week after the private occupation had been announced and a week before the Government decided to issue its proclamation:[133]

> In my opinion, bringing land in Eastern Greenland under Norwegian sovereignty does not create a better basis for handling an international legal dispute than if no Norwegian occupation takes place. Should Norway not undertake an occupation, the claim in dispute settlement would have to be based on Eastern Greenland being no-man's land. Even if a judgment would find in favour of Norway in this regard, this would however not be satisfactory for Norway. Should a judgment decide that the territory is no-man's land, for instance at the time when proceedings should be instigated, this would not prevent Denmark from afterwards taking steps to acquire sovereignty.

> Naturally there is no way one can predict with absolute certainty the outcome of an international dispute settlement in such a case. International legal rules in this field are too vague to provide such an answer. However, it would be quite unacceptable to portray the occupation by a state of no-man's land, which another state claims to be entitled to, as contempt for modern international justice and a modern policy based on the League of Nations. Support for efforts to strengthen international justice does of course not mean that one will waive or renounce one's national interest within the limits of one's assumed entitlement. The latest developments in international justice are precisely what makes it possible in so many cases to make national claims without any real risk of triggering warfare or unfriendly relations between nations.

> When a Norwegian occupation in Eastern Greenland among others in the Swedish press has been compared to the Polish occupation of Vilna or the Italian one in Fiume,[134] we can only observe that there are in practice almost no similarities between the military occupation of densely populated cities and land areas that are in another state's possession and, on the other hand, the peaceful inclusion under national sovereignty of an almost uninhabited territory, in conformity with international legal rules pertaining to no-man's land. The only thing in common between a military occupation and occupation of terra nullius under international law is the word 'occupation'.

VII. THE AFTERMATH

As already indicated, the judgment settled not only a legal issue, but also a major political controversy. The judgment was accepted with 'dignity' by the parties.[135] Arguably, it even helped shaping Norwegian foreign as well as domestic policies in the aftermath.

The Norwegian Government repealed the two resolutions of 1931 and 1932 proclaiming sovereignty over parts of Eastern Greenland. The Norwegian Parliament issued a strong criticism of the treatment of the whole issue of occupations. With a broad majority the Foreign Affairs Committee noted that Denmark had contributed to activating traumatic elements and a feeling of injustice in the collective recollection of Norwegians, but it added:[136]

---

[133] Translation to English by the author. F Castberg, 'PM Okkupasjonsspørsmålets stilling i dag' in *Utredninger om Folkerettsspørsmål 1922–1941* (Oslo, Thronsen, 1950) 237–38.

[134] This actually reflected Quisling's argument in the cabinet (n 127).

[135] Dollot (n 3) 161; Waldock (n 10) 350.

[136] Author's translation. Parliamentary Archives (Stortingets arkiv), *Innst S nr 166 (1933:72)*, quoted by Fure (n 9) 131.

The Committee has found it paramount on its part to do whatever it can to ensure that what we have experienced during these years never be repeated. We must effectively prevent that important decisions be ripped out of the hands of the competent authorities, that loose agitation become a substitute for calm assessment and objective deliberation, and that one act behind the back of Parliament.

One can only speculate whether this experience was later instrumental in strengthening the role of the Norwegian Parliament in foreign affairs. If so, the issues raised by Eastern Greenland have had a lasting domestic impact in Norway.

According to Waldock and Dollot the Court had established principles that would be applicable to Antarctica.[137] International cooperation as regards the latter continent led, however, to the adoption in 1959 of the Antarctica Treaty whereby all territorial claims and protests were frozen in Article IV. The judgment's major impact was therefore in the Arctic, including a significant contribution to understanding of the collateral legal history and status of Svalbard (Spitsbergen) and related engagements.[138] In Part IV we have seen how the judgment also became a building block in the reasoning of later judgments and arbitral awards concerning territorial sovereignty in inhospitable territories.

In the aftermath, the court case led to recriminations on the Norwegian side, including by Professor Jon Skeie, who had participated in the Norwegian legal team before the Court. He published stinging criticisms against individual members of the team and politicians who had been involved.[139]

In sharp contrast to such recriminations, and foreshadowing that *Eastern Greenland* would become a landmark case, professor Castberg held a lecture in Stockholm while the proceedings were still ongoing, where he stated sentences that may stand as a conclusion:[140]

I believe that the judgment that will be issued next year at The Hague may in some respects become a landmark in the development of international law. This is due to the important questions of legal principle that the judgment will have to decide as regards certain disputed areas of international law but also to the fact that this court case sets a precedent in that a state institutes proceedings against another before an international court in a case that concerns important, national questions.

As for Norway and Denmark this case and the judgment will undoubtedly—and whatever the outcome—clear the air like a thunder storm and leave behind a fresher, healthier atmosphere in the relations between two peoples that—in spite of everything—are bound to each other through so many and strong bonds.

---

[137] Waldock (n 10) 350; Dollot (n 3) 162.

[138] See above nn 17 and 65.

[139] J Skeie, *Politikere og diplomater i Grønlandssaken* (Oslo, Olaf Norli Forlag, 1933).

[140] Translated by the author from the Norwegian quotation in Castberg, *Minner* 35 from a lecture before the Norwegian Association (*Det norske samfunn*) in Stockholm 1932.

8

Trail Smelter (United States of America/Canada) (1938 and 1941)

DUNCAN FRENCH

It is an awkward fit with other rules of international environmental law, and ... it is at the same time a cornerstone of that law.[1]

I. INTRODUCTION

THE *TRAIL SMELTER Arbitration (United States/Canada)*[2] would undoubtedly be characterised as a landmark case, particularly if the principal criterion for such status is subsequent repetition leading to widespread and near-universal endorsement. As a pivotal—and indeed foundational—moment in the development of international environmental law, *Trail Smelter* (as it is invariably reduced to in metonymic form to represent cumulatively the facts, the judgment and, most prominently, the international legal principle enunciated therein) has received significant attention, if not something approaching legal veneration. No discussion of the history, formulation or gradual hardening of this particular area of international law would be complete without citation, usually positive, of this particular case.[3] In addition to its specific focus on responsibility for transboundary air pollution—which has subsequently developed into a more general rule of customary international environmental law—it is also pointed to as an early intergovernmental environmental dispute (and a successfully resolved one at that),[4] as well as, more generally, being one of a series of original moments in the emergence of the

---

[1] J Ellis, 'Has International Law outgrown Trail Smelter?' in R Bratspies and R Miller (eds), *Transboundary Harm in International Law: Lessons from the Trail Smelter Arbitration* (Cambridge, CUP, 2006) 64.

[2] Reports of International Arbitral Awards, 16 April 1938 and 11 March 1941, vol III, 1905–82.

[3] See, for instance, P Sands and J Peel, *Principles of International Environmental Law*, 3rd edn (Cambridge, CUP, 2012) 26: 'The award ... and its finding on the state of international law on air pollution in the 1930s has come to represent a crystallising moment for international environmental law' and R Barnes, *Property Rights and Natural Resources* (Oxford, Hart, 2009), which describes the award as the '*locus classicus* of this rule'.

[4] *cf* T Stephens, *International Courts and Environmental Protection* (Cambridge, CUP, 2009) 124.

dominant politico-legal environmental narrative, such as the publication in 1962 of Rachel Carson's *Silent Spring*[5] or the reaction to the high profile *Torrey Canyon* marine pollution incident in 1969;[6] such is its perceived, and projected, importance.

There were, of course, earlier legal (and judicial) precursors on environmental matters than *Trail Smelter*, which are equally worthy of reference—take for instance the 1893 Award arising from the *Bering Sea Fur Seals Arbitration*[7]—but, as a defining point in the formulation of general legal principle, it is *Trail Smelter* that attracts much of the normative attention. This has, of course, a lot to do with the context and timing of the award (an initial decision in 1938 and a final award in 1941) on an issue of increasing relevance, namely the transboundary impact of industrialisation, and the paucity until even relatively recently of international environmental case law. But more than that—and in a way this differentiates the earlier *Bering Sea Fur Seals* arbitration—*Trail Smelter* has remained influential because of the apparent clarity of the principle stated. It remains the only decided international case that is squarely on the issue of transboundary air pollution; with the *Aerial Herbicide (Ecuador v Colombia)* case—which concerned, not atmospheric industrial pollution, but the transboundary drift of herbicide spraying—being settled in 2013 before the International Court had the opportunity to rule on the merits.[8]

This chapter therefore seeks to achieve a rather difficult balance. It would be churlish in a collection on landmark cases not to laud *Trail Smelter* as an important arbitration and award; as deserving a place in the pantheon of singularly remarkable, even historic, international cases. Would it not be slightly curious for a case, which is generally accepted as providing a foundation for an entire sub-discipline of international law, to not be worthy of such attention? But as the quotation from Ellis above indicates, and as this chapter explores, much about *Trail Smelter* is not what it seems. Despite frequent citation across the standard array of normative outlets—court decisions, pleadings, by academics, in the work of the International Law Commission (ILC) inter alia—the complexity of the dispute is often ignored, instead replaced by focusing attention on just one sentence (or indeed only part thereof)[9] in the final award:

> under the principles of international law, as well as of the law of the United States, no state has the right to use or permit the use of its territory in such a manner as to cause injury by fumes in or to the territory of another or the properties or persons therein, when the case is of serious consequence and the injury is established by clear and convincing evidence.[10]

---

[5] On the role of prominent individuals in the development of international environmental consciousness, see M Drumbl, 'Actors and Law-Making in International Environmental Law' in M Fitzmaurice, D Ong and P Merkouris (eds), *Research Handbook on International Environmental Law* (Cheltenham, Edward Elgar, 2010) 13.

[6] For detail, see Sands and Peel, *Principles of International Environmental Law* (n 3) 391.

[7] *Great Britain v United States* (1893) Moore's International Arbitration 755.

[8] See Application Instituting Proceedings (31 March 2008) and Order of 13 September 2013 (Removal from List).

[9] See K Mickelson, 'Rereading Trail Smelter' (1993) 31 *Canadian Yearbook of International Law* 219, 226: 'the discussion tends to focus on this single celebrated (or denigrated) passage'.

[10] Reports (n 2) 1965.

The chapter will return to how these words have been understood—and misunderstood—later, but it is equally interesting to reflect on how far a case becomes important less because of itself but because of how even a very small part of it is subsequently taken up, used and repeated. In thinking about the invariably 'landmark-ed' nature of this particular dispute, it has been useful to reflect on a timeline of four epochs in the development of such a case. These are not chronological per se—though to a large extent there is a semblance with time passed—but rather they indicate a process by which a case (and certainly this arbitration), subsequent to it being handing down, might thereafter evolve.[11] The first epoch is repetition and endorsement; a case becomes significant because it is adopted—not necessarily through citation by other courts and tribunals (though that may be an element of this)—but equally because it is included in legal argumentation and the development of state practice, policy and doctrine. Importantly, this is not about a case becoming a formal legal precedent, nor necessarily is it about the strength of its reasoning (though one always hopes that might be a consideration). As the history of *Trail Smelter* reveals, the apparent enunciation within the decision of a putative general(-ised) principle can be a particularly influential reason for its wider adoption. The second epoch is myth-making. The case becomes relied upon and incessantly quoted, rarely with reference to the circumstances in which it occurred, and primarily for the establishment of a general principle. It is used to justify a legal norm that is broader than the court or tribunal, which gave the ruling, envisaged. At this stage, the risk of over-simplification is significant. The third epoch is deconstruction; either dismissal of the significance of the Award or, much more likely, an attempt to reconnect the principle with the particularities (both substantive and procedural) of the case itself. Either way, it is often a critical attempt to reanalyse, perhaps in some cases even relegate, the generality of its relevance and application. This has certainly occurred with *Trail Smelter*,[12] with one commentator—to whom I will return—seeing the importance of the arbitration more in terms of it being a 'case-study' in environmental dispute settlement, than as a landmark 'case'. Finally, the fourth epoch is re-evaluation; seeking to rebalance the myth of the case with the criticism, which it has received. How can a case that has been so widely used, referenced and endorsed now be understood when placed against such (usually very incisive) criticism? With *Trail Smelter*, this is where the debate arguably now stands.

Thus, this chapter is structured as follows. Part II will set out in some detail the background to the dispute, the procedure of the arbitration and the award itself. Not only is the case itself worth significant attention, but such examination reveals a number of under-researched and under-reported facets of the dispute, which are lost through a narrow filtering of its meaning. While not undermining the viewpoint that *Trail Smelter* is deserving of inclusion as a landmark case, the chapter reveals

---

[11] There is indeed a parallel with the literary criticism of *la mort de l'auteur*, which indicates that once published, the writing takes on an independence unrelated to, and detached from, its creator. The original argument arose from an essay by R Barthes, 'The Death of the Author' (1967) *Aspen* 5–6.

[12] See various contributions to Bratspies and Miller, *Transboundary Harm* (n 1). As the editors say in their introduction, 'There are important lessons to be learned from a modern engagement with *Trail Smelter*—including both novel applications with the arbitration and a real sense of its limitations' 10.

features that both contextualise and particularise the original dispute. Part III then explores the assumed significance of *Trail Smelter*; how it has indeed become that foundational case, principally centred around the quoted sentence above. Within this discussion, there will be a review of the development of international environmental law as a discipline comprising soft law, conventional regimes and, increasingly, case law, as well as how that complex interplay of sources has itself provided normative justification for what then became known as the 'no harm' principle. Part III then moves on to summarise an array of criticisms of *Trail Smelter*; questioning its right to be viewed as a 'great' case whilst concurrently suggesting that there are alternative models of analysis still worthy of exploration in relation to either the award or, more broadly, the dispute. Such criticisms are manifold but can be divided largely into two types: analysis of how the case has been subject to over-simplification and mis-interpretation over the decades (without necessarily criticising the arbitration itself); and, more fundamentally, criticism of the reasoning of the arbitral tribunal. Part IV, in conclusion, in seeking to bridge the gap between the arbitration's acquired status and such criticism will provide a re-evaluation of the case and tentatively conclude that questions over its normative significance tells us as much about the structural development of international law as it does about the subject matter of this particular case. Moreover, whilst one cannot predetermine how a case will be subsequently interpreted, reimagined and refined, there is equally value in not extracting general principle at the expense of, or perhaps more precisely without consideration of, the factual circumstances that led to that point.

II. *TRAIL SMELTER*: THE DISPUTE, ARBITRATION AND AWARD

The beginning of the timeline of the *Trail Smelter* dispute—as with many disputes which are prompted by something other than a discrete, or one-off, event—is invariably subject to some contention. The Award itself provides as authoritative a summary of the history of the dispute as one is likely to find.[13] As the Tribunal noted, a smelter factory was established in Trail in British Columbia, Canada in 1896, which since 1906 had been owned and operated by the Consolidated Mining and Smelting Company of Canada, Limited. The proximity, and geographical lie of the land, between Trail and the Canadian/United States border was of particular relevance; 'The distance from Trail to the boundary line is about seven miles as the crow flies or about eleven miles, following the course of the river (and possibly a slightly shorter distance by following the contour of the valley'.[14] As will be seen, the Tribunal found it extremely necessary to study the topographical and climatic conditions between the smelter and the affected parts of the United States, in this case the northern reaches of the State of Washington, in significant—arguably unprecedented—detail. Thus, this part will consider the background to the dispute, the arbitration and the Award, as each provides a complexity and a richness invariably lost in the subsequent repetition of a singular phrase or principle, often in abstraction.

[13] See, in particular, Reports (n 2) 1913–19.
[14] ibid, 1913.

A. The Dispute

The factory was involved in the smelting of zinc and lead ores in significant quanti-ties, leading it to become 'one of the best and largest equipped smelting plants on this continent'.[15] In particular, the development of the smelter between 1925 and 1927 through the erection of two high chimney stacks of approximately 410 feet not only increased still further its level of production but increased the quantity and concentration of sulphur dioxide emitted as a consequence. As the Tribunal noted, 'it is claimed by one government (though denied by the other) that the added height of the stacks increased the area of damage in the United States'.[16] Nevertheless, it seems beyond dispute—and certainly accepted by the Tribunal—that the tonnage of sulphur emitted from the smelter rose substantially over the first three decades of the twentieth century, with an important factual finding in the Award that 'From 1925, at least, to the end of 1931, damage occurred in the State of Washington, resulting from the sulphur dioxide emitted from the Trail Smelter'.[17]

The arbitral Tribunal was established by means of an international agreement, the *Convention for Settlement of Difficulties arising from Operation of Smelter at Trail, BC*, signed and ratified in 1935. The highly specific nature of the 'difficulties'—a term I will return to—cannot be lost. This was essentially a *compromis* (if somewhat of an unusual sort) between two governments relating exclusively to the operation of a private business in the territory of one, causing harm to the other. Some of the pro-visions of the Convention will be considered momentarily, though it is worth not-ing three aspects of the wider context to the dispute. First, this was not the earliest attempt at settlement in relation to the smelter's emissions. Back in 1927, the United States had proposed to Canada that the International Joint Commission (IJC)—established in 1909 by the Boundary Waters Treaty[18]—should investigate the matter. The IJC had authority under Article IX of the 1909 Treaty to investigate and report on 'any other questions or matters of difference arising between them involving the rights, obligations, or interests of either in relation to the other or to the inhabitants of the other, along the common frontier between the United States and the Dominion of Canada'. Significantly, such a report by the IJC 'shall in no way have the character of an arbitral award'. On the acceptance of Canada to make such a reference to the IJC, and following a detailed investigation which included evidence of both witnesses and scientific experts, the IJC issued its report in February 1931. In the report, the IJC proposed that an 'indemnity [be paid] that will compensate United States inter-ests in respect of such fumes, up to and including the first day of January, 1932 ... the sum of $350,000'.[19] Thereafter, the IJC recommended that if damage were to continue after this date—something which the IJC sought to minimise by proposing various technical measures to reduce the emission of sulphur dioxide—the two gov-ernments were to agree on the level of indemnity '"in the event of"' such a private

---

[15] ibid, 1917.
[16] ibid.
[17] ibid.
[18] 10 IPE 5158.
[19] Reports (n 2) 1918.

claim of harm '"not being adjusted by the company within a reasonable time"'.[20] The IJC report—despite its analytical rigour—proved not acceptable, particularly to the United States, and subsequent correspondence between the governments eventually led to the 1935 convention to establish the Tribunal.

The second aspect of the wider context, often ignored, was that the owner of the smelter itself recognised the potential damaging nature of its operations and the likelihood of harm across the border. As the Award noted, it 'took the matter up seriously and made a more or less thorough and complete investigation'.[21] Indeed, the smelter company negotiated with a number of property owners in the State of Washington and concluded settlements in a number of instances. This occurred in the period 1926–28. However, these bilateral negotiations (primarily with farmers) came to end with the establishment of a 'Citizens' Protective Association'—a non-governmental organisation—which included within its Articles a prohibition of individual settlements without the majority consent of its board of directors, something which then did not occur.[22]

Thirdly, and something which will be discussed later when considering both the myth of *Trail Smelter* and the critique of the arbitration, what is often lost is that the intergovernmental dispute arose principally because of perceived weaknesses in the domestic legal system of both countries. The law of the State of Washington provided limited opportunity for the Canadian company, which owned the smelter to resolve the dispute, either through the purchase of affected property or the purchase of so-called smoke easements.[23] The Tribunal recognised the legal limitations on the company's ability to settle the dispute at a local level, but noted that both as a matter of 'fact or as to the law, the Tribunal expresses no opinion and makes no ruling'.[24] Likewise, Canadian law was viewed as unsupportive of the private interests of American claimants. As Read notes:

> It was the general opinion of the lawyers concerned at the time that the British Columbia courts would be compelled to refuse to accept jurisdiction in suits based on damage to land situated outside of the province. Apart, therefore, from the practical difficulty confronting some hundreds of claimants in bringing suits in a foreign forum, there was the moral certainty that they would lose.[25]

Thus, just as it is a misrepresentation of the Award in *Trail Smelter* to view it in reductionist form as only an enunciation of the principle of state liability for transboundary harm, it is also a simplification of the dispute to view it purely on the intergovernmental plane, setting to one side the interests of both the smelter company and those private actors whose interests were harmed, or were allegedly harmed. True, the dispute was between the two governments—and indeed, the Tribunal was very

---

[20] ibid, 1919.
[21] ibid, 1917.
[22] ibid.
[23] On the use of such easements, see J Read, 'The Trail Smelter Dispute' (1963) 1 *Canadian Yearbook of International Law* 213, 223.
[24] Reports (n 2) 1918.
[25] Read, 'The Trail Smelter Dispute' (n 23) 222.

clear that the United States was acting in its own sovereign capacity and not as agent for a claim of diplomatic protection[26]—but the identification of a single polluter and the causal link between the emissions and the harm caused meant that this was much more than just a standard intergovernmental bilateral arbitration. Read, who was involved in the proceedings on the Canadian side, perhaps describes it best (if a little ambiguously) as 'transmuting the claims by individuals against the Trail Smelter into claims sounding in international tort by the United States against Canada'.[27] In the intervening years, there has been progress on principles of transboundary civil justice to support private actions in such instances, though there is much that could still be achieved, and there is by no means uniformity in approach.[28]

B. The Arbitration

To fully appreciate the complexity of the dispute, one needs to consider some of the essential features of the 1935 convention, which established the arbitration. First, whilst not endorsing the IJC report, Article I nevertheless required the Canadian Government to pay the United States $350,000 'in payment of all damage which occurred in the United States, prior to the first day of January, 1932'. Importantly, the Article is silent on the legal basis for this, something of a stumbling block for subsequent comment in seeking to elucidate from the case a general rule on historic responsibility. Secondly, Article IV of the convention sets out both the applicable law and the overall object of the arbitration, as follows:

> The Tribunal shall apply the law and practice followed in dealing with cognate questions in the United States of America as well as international law and practice, and shall give consideration to the desire of the high contracting parties to reach a solution just to all parties concerned.

Article IV thus embedded the parameters, but also highlighted the peculiarities, of the arbitration, namely, the requirement to consider both US and international law and practice; recognition of both governmental and private interests; and an apparent synergy between legal settlement (narrowly conceived) and broader dispute resolution. Whereas the first of these three characteristics—the applicable law—is perhaps obvious from the face of the wording of Article IV, though no less significant for that, the other two are worth further consideration. First, it is quite clear that though Canada and the United States are the 'high contracting parties', the reference to 'all parties concerned' is intended to be wider and includes (not only them) but both the smelter and those potentially harmed by the sulphur emissions. It is arguable that it also included those impacted by the economic opportunities that the

---

[26] Reports (n 2) 1912: 'The Tribunal is not sitting to pass upon claims presented by individuals or on behalf of one or more individuals by the Government, although individuals may come within the meaning of "parties concerned"'.

[27] Read (n 23) 223.

[28] See, for instance, 2006 Toronto Report of the International Law Association Committee on Transnational Enforcement of Environmental Law (www.ila-hq.org/en/committees/index.cfm/cid/31).

smelter created in terms of employment, and which would be impacted by too puni-tive or restrictive a final award. Secondly, as the Tribunal makes clear particularly in the 1941 Award, its role is to balance legal adjudication—respecting the usual rules and expectations arising therefrom—with ensuring a just solution[29] captured, in the view of the Tribunal, by the reference in the Convention's preamble to reaching a 'permanent settlement'. Not appreciating the particularity of this mandate has again resulted in a subsequent over-generalisation of the arbitration, as well as perpetuat-ing confusion as to the role, significance, and meaning of equitable considerations in transfrontier harm disputes.

To recognise that there is indeed this tension between what the Tribunal achieved and what it is often believed to have achieved, one only needs to review the questions, which it was asked to 'finally decide' upon. Article III sets out the four questions, worth quoting in full:

1   Whether damage caused in the Trail Smelter in the State of Washington has occurred since the first day of January, 1932 and, if so, what indemnity should be paid therefor?
2   In the event of the answer to the first part of the preceding Question being in the affirmative, whether the Trail Smelter should be required to refrain from causing damage in the State of Washington in the future, and, if so, to what extent?
3   In the light of the answer to the preceding Question, what measures or régime, if any, should be adopted or maintained by the Trail Smelter?
4   What indemnity or compensation, if any, should be paid on account of any decision or decisions rendered by the Tribunal pursuant to the next two preceding Questions?

It is important to note on what issues the Tribunal was not asked to decide. It was not asked to rule on historical damage up to 1932; as noted above, Article I having already settled this by the transfer of monies from the Canadian government to United States, though notably without any specific statement as to the legal basis as to why, or if indeed this was because of any liability on the part of the Canadian state. Moreover, if one reads closely, the Tribunal was also not asked to rule on Canadian responsibility, either subsequently to 1932 or prospectively. Rather the question relates to what is expected of Trail Smelter, and what 'indemnity or compensation' should be paid. In this regard, there was recognition—in questions 2 and 3—that damage might be ongoing and thus what measures should be adopted to ameliorate such harm and—in question 4—what indemnity should be paid 'on account of any decision or decisions rendered'.[30] There is very little in these questions pointing the Tribunal towards making legal determinations, or taking an explicitly normative approach, to state responsibility and liability under international law. Of course, putting oneself in the shoes of those drafting the convention, these were neither principal nor pragmatic considerations. As Read notes, 'at the time of nego-tiation, those who were concerned were thinking in terms of smoke damage caused

---

[29] See JG Merrills, *International Dispute Settlement*, 5th edn (Cambridge, CUP, 2011) 96.
[30] The framing of questions 1 and 4 on the payment of indemnity might, paradoxically, allow for the elaboration of contrary arguments that this was both an acceptance (and a rejection) of strict liability in international law. In truth, neither position is sustainable, nor can a general principle be inferred from this bilateral convention.

by a Canadian corporation to a very large number of private interests, mostly farmers and owners of wood lots, in Washington'.[31] This arbitration was not about the application (never mind the development) of abstract rules of customary international law—as it is sometimes retrospectively portrayed—but resolving the dispute in the most effective manner, relying primarily on the rules of US negligence as the principal means of settlement.[32]

Following the appointment of the three-member Tribunal, chaired by the third-party jurist Jan Frans Hostie of Belgium, it was supported in its work by two scientists, one designated by each government, who were 'to assist the Tribunal' as permitted under the convention.[33] As will be noted below, this scientific expertise is clearly evident in the depth of the scientific analysis in the Award, as well as helping the Tribunal to devise the 'measures or régime' envisaged under question 3. The Tribunal undertook its work through the usual steps of adopting its rules of procedure, exchange of pleadings, as well as a detailed site visit, and various sessions for the hearing of evidence from the governments, interested parties and experts—all of which occurred during the summer and autumn of 1937. Read was particularly complimentary of the arbitrators on this point; 'When the members of the Tribunal inspected the area involved … it was no casual survey. They made a close examination of many of the farms and orchards and cruised the forests. When they heard the evidence, the witnesses and experts were talking about places and conditions familiar to them'.[34]

On completion of this stage of the proceedings, the Tribunal began the difficult task of seeking to answer the questions asked of it. It is at this point that what might have been a relatively straightforward arbitral award—at last from a procedural perspective—became something much more interesting. Again, this is something which is rarely picked up when the dispute is viewed singularly in terms of fixating on a particular principle, and divorced from the broader context. Under Article XI of the 1935 Convention, the Tribunal was required to report its final decision within three months of conclusion of the proceedings, unless such period was extended by agreement of the two governments. As the agents of both governments jointly informed the Tribunal on 2 January 1938 that they had nothing else to present, that three-month clock would have required the publication of the final Award by 2 April of the same year. The Tribunal informed the governments that it could indeed provide such an award by then, but that it would be 'on the basis of data which it considered inadequate and unsatisfactory'.[35] The governments agreed to a time extension of three months from 1 October 1940, which was eventually extended again until 12 March 1941; the final Award ultimately being delivered a day before that deadline.

---

[31] Read (n 23) 222.

[32] Somewhat ironically, the Canadian Government would have been more concerned by any reliance by the Tribunal on Canadian law; 'Those precedents were unfavourable to industrial enterprise, and, if applied, might be disastrous to the Smelter' (ibid, 227).

[33] Art II, para 4 of 1935 Convention.

[34] Read (n 23) 215.

[35] Reports (n 2) 1912.

The Tribunal nevertheless did issue an Award on 16 April 1938, which it said at the time was a 'final decision' on question 1, and a temporary decision under questions 2 and 3. The apparent finality of question 1 became a significant feature of the 1941 Award. Significantly, the preliminary decision to question 3 was to establish a temporary (if nonetheless innovative and complex) regime for a trial period to allow the Tribunal to 'predict, with some degree of assurance, that a permanent régime based on a more adequate and intensive study and knowledge of meteorological conditions in the valley ... will effectively prevent future significant fumigations in the United States, without unreasonably restricting the output of the plant'.[36] The Tribunal justified this need for a temporary regime quite clearly on what it viewed as the 'primary purpose of the Convention', namely to ensure that the final outcome was a just solution and a permanent settlement.

C. The Award

In discussing the Award of the *Trail Smelter* arbitration it is important to recognise both the separateness of the two decisions, as well as the unity of the Award as a whole. True, there is significant repetition of the facts within the two decisions—as the Tribunal refers to them[37]—but there is also value in each. Stylistically and, to some extent, as regards content, there is a distinction between the two decisions. There are noticeably few references to international law in the 1938 Decision, focusing substantially on the scientific and technical information, as well as US tort law. On the other hand, in the 1941 Decision—despite also containing significant detail on the scientific and technical information, particularly in establishing the permanent regime—there is much more discussion of international law, not only to the (in) famous reference to Canada's responsibility in international law cited in the introduction, but also on matters such as *res judicata* and whether judicial decisions are open to revision and reconsideration. The geographical narrowness of the 1938 Decision—unsurprising given the nature of the dispute—also gives way to a more policy-attuned approach in the 1941 Decision.

> As between the two countries involved, each has an equal interest that if a nuisance is proved, the indemnity to damaged parties for proven damage shall be just and adequate and each also has an equal interest that unproven or unwarranted claims shall not be allowed. For, while the United States' interests may now be claimed to be injured ... it is equally possible that at some time in the future Canadian interests might be claimed to be injured by an American corporation ...

> The Tribunal should endeavour to adjust the conflicting interests by some 'just solution' which would allow the continuance of the operation of the Trail Smelter but under such restrictions and limitations as would, as far as foreseeable, prevent damage ... and as would

---

[36] ibid, 1934.
[37] For the remainder of this part, they will be referred to as the '1938 Decision' and the '1941 Decision'. Elsewhere in the chapter, unless otherwise specified, they will be referred—as they have been up to this point—collectively as the 'Award'.

enable indemnity to be obtained, if in spite of such restrictions and limitations, damage should occur in the future in the United States.[38]

The Tribunal in answering the questions asked of it—in particular, in devising the permanent regime for the Trail Smelter—was acutely aware not only of the economic consequences of measures that would impose undue burdens, even potential closure, upon a key industry (which would 'exaggerate ... the interests of the agricultural community'), whilst at the same time ensuring a balance with other interests ('the agricultural community should [not] be oppressed to advance the interest of industry').[39] Thus, returning to the title of the 1935 convention—'difficulties arising from operation of smelter at Trail'—it is apparent that the Tribunal viewed its role as principally prospective in finding a meaningful—and agreed—way forward for both governments, which was in the interests of all parties, rather than adjudicate per se on legal wrongs. A perhaps alternative perspective would be to say that the law—both domestic (US) and international—was used as a meaningful framework for the construction of a balancing of interests, satisfactory to all parties.

This chapter is unable to provide a detailed analysis of the Tribunal's answers to each of the four questions. In particular, it is unable to examine the Tribunal's approach to the US law of nuisance or trespass, or to set out the scope and complexity of either the temporary or permanent regime established. What is important to note however is that the Tribunal was guided to—and did indeed establish—such a regime, within the context of the questions asked of it. Recognising the establishment of this regime as a fundamental feature of the decision also underlines the argument that 'A "contextualised" analysis is both more accurate and more useful than the standard invocation of abstract principles'.[40]

If it is impossible to consider the Award in detail, several aspects are nevertheless worth drawing out. First, while much has been made of the fact that the Tribunal awarded damages in respect of 'owned' property (agricultural land and forestry) but not in respect of damage to unowned land[41]—thus positing the argument that *Trail Smelter* is precedent against damage for pure environmental harm—this is a simplification of the reasoning of the Tribunal on two counts. First, to my mind, the Tribunal does not rule out expressly the award of damages for environmental harm per se though admittedly the focus of the Award is for damages based on loss of use or rental value. Many of the claims failed because of a lack of direct causal evidence of harm. For instance, the Tribunal noted that 'it is impossible to determine whether such damage has been due to fires or to mortality of trees and shrubs caused by fumigation'.[42] Similarly, the Tribunal rules out awarding damages for a failure

---

[38] Reports (n 2) 1938–39.
[39] ibid, 1939.
[40] Mickelson, 'Rereading Trail Smelter' (n 9) 232.
[41] *Aerial Herbicide Spraying (Ecuador v Colombia)*: Written Memorial of Ecuador, Volume I (28 April 2009), para 10.17: 'The two awards of the Arbitral Tribunal [in Trail Smelter] did not deal with pure environmental damage per se, and did not assess damages in respect of injurious consequences to the Colombia River'. See also A Boyle, 'Reparation for Environmental Damage in International Law: Some Preliminary Problems' in M Bowman and A Boyle (eds), *Environmental Damage in International and Comparative Law: Problems of Definition and Valuation* (Oxford, OUP, 2002) 19.
[42] Reports (n 2) 1926.

of reproduction of fir trees near the boundary for a lack of scientific evidence.[43] There remain, of course, valid arguments as to whether, and how far, pure ecological damage outside private ownership would have been compensable in US law at the time in any event, but the case is beyond a singular general principle, one way or the other.[44] Secondly, it also clear that the Tribunal does not award damages in all cases of 'owned' property; claims of indemnity for alleged damage to livestock, urban property and reduced profitability of business enterprises were all denied— for lack of evidence in the first two cases, and for reasons also of remoteness in the last instance.[45] Moreover, in the 1941 Decision, the Tribunal also refused to award further damages (to cover the period between the decisions) for alleged harm to crops and forestry, on the basis of lack of evidence.[46] Such analysis of what was— and what was not—compensated, and for what reasons, is often lost in summary discussions of the Award.

Secondly, in what now might seem a curious argument arising from the 1938 Decision, the United States sought to argue before the Tribunal that it should reconsider that part of the 1938 Decision where the Tribunal had decided that 'damage' under question 1 did not include the cost of the investigations that the United States had undertaken in assessing whether the smelter had caused damage in the State of Washington. As the Tribunal had noted in the 1938 Decision, this was the only costs the United States had set next to its claim for damages in respect of violation of its own sovereignty. The Tribunal concluded that such investigatory costs were not within the definition of damage as intended by both governments in drafting the 1935 Convention, nor could they be awarded as incidental to the other damages which were. In something of a mild rebuke, the Tribunal noted that such costs are likely in an international dispute 'where each government has incurred expenses and where it is to the mutual advantage of the two governments that a just conclusion and permanent disposition of an international controversy should be reached'.[47] Unsurprisingly, such an approach to costs has become characteristic of international arbitration, though as recently as 2015, the Tribunal in *Arctic Sunrise (Netherlands v Russian Federation)* (2015) had occasion to rule that the Dutch claim for, inter alia, survey expenses and incidental fees were to be borne by the party presenting its own case.[48]

Nevertheless, despite the relative small amount in question—$89,655: small compared not only to that claimed overall, but particularly when contrasted with the size

---

[43] ibid, 1930.

[44] Significantly, there was indeed limited indemnity for damage which might now be viewed as pure environmental harm. See ibid, 1926: 'As regards these lands in their use as pasture lands, the Tribunal is of opinion that there is no evidence of any marked susceptibility of wild grasses to fumigations, and very little evidence to prove the respective amounts of uncleared land devoted to wild grazing grass and barren or shrub land, or to prove the value thereof, which would be necessary in order to estimate the value of the reduction of the use of such land. *The Tribunal, however, has awarded a small indemnity for damage to about 200 acres of such lands in the immediate neighborhood of the boundary*' (emphasis added).

[45] ibid, 1931.

[46] ibid, 1959.

[47] ibid, 1933.

[48] Award of 14 October 2015 [396], [400].

of the other claims rejected—it was this failed claim, which the United States asked the Tribunal to reopen and reconsider. The argument of the United States raised two distinct legal questions; was the 1938 Decision on question 1 *res judicata* and, even if it was, did the Tribunal have the authority to review its previous decision in light of a material error of law. To an international lawyer, these are demonstrably questions of international law, though the Tribunal was faced with the initial question as to whether the provision in the 1935 Convention on applicable law—which included both US and international law—applied and, if so, how. It is at this point, one can arguably see a discreet 'turn to' international law in the overall Award. The Tribunal was adamant; these were issues of international law: that it 'shall proceed as international law, justice and equity may require'.[49] This is significant, not only for its reasoning but because it allowed the Tribunal to assert its autonomy from both governments and to allow it to access a body of general principle not bound within the confines of either the 1935 Convention, or US law and practice.

The Tribunal, though already having asserted that its answer in the 1938 Decision to question 1 was final, nevertheless considered previous cases where *res judicata* had been raised by arbitral tribunals and the Permanent Court of International Justice (PCIJ). Relying on this jurisprudence, the Tribunal comes decisively to the view that as 'The three traditional elements for identification: parties, object and cause ... are the same',[50] there was no doubt that there was *res judicata* on this particular issue. This, of course, did not deal with the issue entirely as the United States had also claimed an error in law by the Tribunal. In a particularly interesting and informative section of the 1941 Decision, the Tribunal first considers its authority to review a decision (outside of any provision of the *compromis*), before considering earlier awards and judgments which had touched upon revision, including the PCIJ cases of *Saint Naoum Monastery*,[51] as well as the 1907 Hague Convention for the Pacific Settlement of Disputes. The authority on this issue was significantly less settled than on the matter of *res judicata* and the Tribunal is left to determine for itself the appropriate test. In an important ruling that 'mere error in law is no sufficient ground for a petition',[52] and that the terminology of 'essential error' is mistaken, the Tribunal finds the true test 'on the strength of precedents and practice' was whether the Tribunal had made a 'manifest error',[53] in this case in the interpretation of the 1935 Convention, which the Tribunal moreover finds has not been made out. This aspect of the Tribunal's Award—much overlooked in favour of its contribution to environmental jurisprudence—is nevertheless a notable contribution to the development of the administration of this particular aspect of international justice.[54]

---

[49] Reports (n 2) 1950, referring to Art 16 of its own Rules of Procedures (adopted at its hearing on 21–22 June 1937).

[50] ibid, 1952.

[51] Advisory Opinions, Series B, No 9, 21.

[52] Reports (n 2) 1957.

[53] ibid.

[54] See C Brown, *A Common Law of International Adjudication* (Oxford, OUP, 2007) 167.

D. Responsibility for Transboundary Harm

The aspect of the Award that requires most attention, and the one for which it is most renowned, is its answer in the 1941 Decision to question 2: '... whether the Trail Smelter should be required to refrain from causing damage in the State of Washington in the future and, if so, to what extent?'. As noted above, on its face this is not a question demanding an answer in international law. Moreover, as the Tribunal makes clear in its opening remarks on this question—the principal issue before it was one of disagreement between Canada and United States as to what precisely constituted damage. Canada supported the International Joint Commission view in its earlier report that damage—at least damage that might prompt a duty on the smelter to respond—did not include 'occasional damage ... [including] by reason of unusual atmospheric conditions'.[55] One might suggest this is the application of a *de minimis* test. The United States, on the other hand, refused to accept a definition which might exclude injury 'regardless of the remedial works ... and regardless of the effect of those works'.[56] This would seem to approach something close to a strict liability rule. It was of course this disagreement that had, inter alia, led to the conclusion of the 1935 Convention and the arbitration.

Part—but only part—of the answer to this disagreement was determined by the Tribunal in what would become its most famous sentence, set out again for ease of reference: 'under the principles of international law, as well as of the law of the United States, no State has the right to use or permit the use of its territory in such a manner as to cause injury by fumes in or to the territory of another or the properties or persons therein, when the case is of serious consequence and the injury is established by clear and convincing evidence'. But considering this sentence alone, viewed in abstraction, and outside of the context of how the Tribunal reasoned both up to this point and then how it finalised its answer to question 2 thereafter, fails to reflect the more nuanced, and arguably controversial, approach taken by the Tribunal. In fact, there is overall very little recognition or reference to placing Canada's obligations within a general international law frame. Thus, it might prompt one to ask whether the discussion of Canada's customary responsibility is but a rhetorical flourish or, in legal terms, obiter?

Notably the Tribunal assimilates to no small degree the law of the United States and international law. It does so, in part, by reasoning that the factual nature of the relations between federal states is sufficiently similar to that of sovereign states.[57] As the Tribunal notes at separate points:

—   The law followed in the United States in dealing with the quasi-sovereign rights of the States of the Union, in the matter of air pollution, whilst more definite, is in conformity with the general rules of international law.[58]

---

[55]   Reports (n 2) 1962.
[56]   ibid, 1963.
[57]   The Tribunal (ibid, 1963) also relies on an unnamed, though cited, Swiss case, involving two of its cantons concerning transfrontier aspects of a shooting establishment, analogising again that the situation is similar as the matter involves 'territorial relations'.
[58]   ibid, 1963.

— For it is reasonable to follow by analogy, in international cases, precedents established by [the Supreme Court] in dealing with controversies between States of the Union ... where no contrary rule prevails in international law.[59]

— What the Supreme Court says ... under the Constitution equally applies to the extraordinary power granted this Tribunal under the Convention. What is true between States of the Union is, at least, equally true concerning the relations between the United States and the Dominion of Canada.[60]

In particular, the Tribunal notes the absence of international case law on transfrontier harm, be it air or water pollution, but adds that 'certain decisions of the Supreme Court of the United States which may legitimately be taken as a guide in this field of international law'.[61] It is unclear if the Tribunal was thinking of Article 38(1)(d) of the PCIJ Statute—identical to the present ICJ Statute—so that domestic 'judicial decisions ... as subsidiary means for the determination of rules of law' [sic], or whether its reference to 'guide' was jurisprudentially disconnected from and/or looser than the reference set out in the World Court Statute. The Tribunal cites a number of US cases, including *State of Missouri v State of Illinois*,[62] *State of New York v State of New Jersey*[63]—both water pollution cases—and *State of Georgia v Tennessee Copper Company and Ducktown Sulphur, Copper and Iron Company, Limited*[64]—which concerned atmospheric pollution—to assist it in its reasoning. The *New York v New Jersey* case seems particularly apposite as language from that case referencing harm that is of 'serious magnitude ... established by clear and convincing evidence' finds its way into the Tribunal's own reasoning. Separately, the *Georgia v Tennessee Copper* case is equally important in highlighting a feature of the Tribunal's own approach. The Tribunal both quotes the US Supreme Court in its belief that Georgia is entitled to 'stand [...] upon her extreme rights' (assumingly a demand that it receives unpolluted air from Tennessee) but also notes, that at a later stage, the actual injunction framed (which set out an annual compensation arrangement) only required emissions to be reduced 'adequate[ly] to diminish materially the present probability of damage',[65] thus suggesting something more in conformity with an approach to the matter focused on harm minimisation.

This focus on US case law isn't of course to suggest that the Tribunal didn't consider international law; the Tribunal makes mention of previous precedents—though only the *Alabama Claims*[66] is actually named—as well as Eagleton's 1928 work on *Responsibility of States in International Law*, which is cited with approval, where he states 'A state owes at all times a duty to protect other states against injurious acts by individuals from within its jurisdiction',[67] a principle the Tribunal says both countries, notably Canada, did not question at the hearing. Thus, it is not surprising

---

[59] ibid, 1964.
[60] ibid.
[61] ibid.
[62] 200 US 496, 521.
[63] 256 US 296, 309.
[64] 206 US 230.
[65] Reports (n 2) 1965 referencing 237 US 474, 477.
[66] *Great Britain v United States* (1872) 1 Moore's International Arbitration 45.
[67] New York, New York University Press, 1928, 80.

that the Tribunal concluded as it did, namely that both US law and international law imposes an obligation on states not to use or allow the use of its territory 'in such a manner as to cause injury'. It goes on to say that such injury may not cause harm to another state's territory or to 'property or persons therein' so long as it is of 'serious consequence' and evidenced clearly. When set next to the 1938 Decision on quantum awarded (under principles of US tort law), one can perceive how the principle as thus enunciated had already played out in the Tribunal's own application of legal principles, where not all harm is considered sufficiently evidenced or connected to the original source.

Particularly unclear is on what basis a state owes this responsibility—purely because harm occurred (a form of strict liability) or because it has failed to adequately prevent it (the idea of a failure of due diligence upon the state). The Tribunal itself confuses this question by going on to note that 'Canada is responsible in international law for the conduct of the Trail Smelter';[68] an unfortunate statement that in later decades would similarly cause ambiguity in the work of the International Law Commission on state liability for 'acts not prohibited by international law'.[69]

If the reasoning of the Tribunal leading up to the famous dictum reveals a wide array of issues, what is often missed is its disposition of question 2, which raises even broader uncertainty as to what precisely is the scope of the ruling identified, as well as the status (and purpose) of the pronouncement on the existence of a rule of international law. The Tribunal stated the following disposition:

> So long as the present conditions in the Columbia River Valley prevail, the Trail Smelter shall be required to refrain from causing any damage through fumes in the State of Washington; the damage herein referred to and its extent being such as would be recoverable under the decisions of the courts of the United States in suits between private individuals. The indemnity for such damage should be fixed in such manner as the Governments, acting under Article XI of the Convention, shall agree upon.[70]

As an answer to question 2—guided, as the Tribunal says, by the objective of achieving a just solution—this might be perfectly satisfactory, though the conflation of a requirement not to cause 'any damage' and then stating damage is only 'recoverable under the decisions' of the US courts highlights the very conceptual confusion that this chapter has identified. But in response to how this disposition links to the Tribunal's previous reasoning on international law, it is merely question-begging? Where is the reference to international law? How does Canada's responsibility interrelate to that of the requirements on the smelter? Does the obligation on the smelter provide a basis for the responsibility of the former, and if so how and of what kind? How indeed can the Tribunal impose a requirement on the smelter directly? Is there an expectation that Canada regulates to ensure this?

---

[68] Reports (n 2) 1965. *cf Responsibilities and obligations of states sponsoring persons and entities with respect to activities in the Area* ITLOS Reports (2011) 10, 60: 'Under international law, the acts of private entities are not directly attributable to States except where the entity in question is empowered to act as a State organ ... or where its conduct is acknowledged and adopted by a State as its own'.

[69] A Boyle, 'State Responsibility and International Liability for Injurious Consequences of Acts Not Prohibited by International Law: A Necessary Distinction' (1990) 39 *ICLQ* 1, 12–14.

[70] Reports (n 2) 1966.

Such uncertainty resurfaces in the Tribunal's answer to question 4 on future indemnity. The particular issue, from the perspective of the modern law, was whether indemnity was payable on any damage caused (subject to the evidential thresholds already mentioned) or whether it was only payable if the damage was beyond or incapable of being regulated by the established regulatory regime. Again, future commentators have scrutinised too intently the scant language in the Award on this issue. The Tribunal rather cursorily—and without relying on authority—noted that indemnity was payable 'whether through failure on the part of the Smelter to comply with the regulations ... or notwithstanding the maintenance of the regime'.[71] This might again be interpreted as justifying a form of strict liability in international law. Alternatively, as the International Law Commission finally decided, this is not principally about the liability of states but rather should centre on the fair allocation of loss between transboundary private actors. Of course, those who search the language of the Award will largely search in vain, though those who continue to read on will discover the real relevance of future indemnity. It will only occur 'when and if the two governments shall make arrangements for the disposition of the claims'.[72] In other words, this is not customary law, but a negotiation process driven by the particular provisions of the 1935 convention.

It is thus unsurprising that the *Trail Smelter* arbitration provides little elucidation on the key principles for which it arguably stands. Arguably it provides little more than guidance on the importance equitable considerations can play in resolving transboundary environmental disputes. Indeed, returning to the disposition of question 2, what does 'so long as the present conditions in the Columbia River Valley prevail' mean? It seems hopelessly vague from a legal perspective, as any requirement imposed dependent on conditions outside the governments' control surely would be. It does, however, make a little more sense if the Tribunal saw its role, as I have argued, as primarily about finding a permanent settlement to the particular 'difficulties' between the governments. Certainly, when one considers the regulatory regime established, its complexity is tailored for the sulphur dioxide emissions of those particular climatic conditions. As Read notes, 'by far the most difficult part of the case consisted of issues of fact, highly technical in character, and dependent for their solution on scientific experiment and testimony'.[73]

It is arguable that the Tribunal, guided by its scientific experts, took an almost utopian belief in the role of science and technology in the settlement of this dispute. Thus, by relating the resolution of the dispute so closely to the geographical and climatic conditions of the valley, the Tribunal moves not only away from reliance on abstract principle, but reveals that its principal purpose, and achievement, was the establishment of the control regime. Perhaps it is no surprise that the Tribunal found reason to comment on the US Supreme Court judgments, to which it had cause to cite, that they were 'decisions in equity'.[74] At the very least, it affirms this chapter's

---

[71] Reports (n 2) 1980.
[72] ibid.
[73] Read (n 23) 225.
[74] Reports (n 2) 1965.

argument that the recourse to international law in *Trail Smelter* is ultimately tangential to the bespoke arrangements that the Tribunal put in place as a response to the particular set of circumstances confronting it.

III. *TRAIL SMELTER*: EMERGENCE—AND CRITIQUE—OF THE MYTH

Despite the previous discussion of the richness of the arbitration and Award, the enduring significance of *Trail Smelter* has undoubtedly been how its decision has subsequently been narrowed so as to represent a singular 'landmark', and universalising, rule of customary international environmental law.[75] Part of this must rest on the paucity of other case law in this field; a general lack which only recently began to change since the mid-1990s, perhaps even later. Thus, *Trail Smelter* stands out, not only as an early case, but one with an apparently clear enunciation of a general principle. This perhaps distinguishes the case from other early decisions, such as the *Bering Sea Fur Seals Arbitration*, where the ruling was—from the standpoint of environmental law at least—more complicated. In that case, the principal ruling was in fact against the environmental argument; namely that the traditional freedom of all states to fish in the high seas (made by the United Kingdom on behalf of Canada) was upheld in the face of unilateral conservation measures (argued by the United States).[76] Though, like *Trail Smelter*, a regulatory regime was instigated as part of the arbitral award (thus again indicating a complexity often lost in subsequent discussion), the case is nevertheless more nuanced and it is significantly less easy to attribute any form of environmentally progressive general obligation. Moreover, whilst the atmosphere is generally (though not wholly) regarded as a common, or shared, resource deserving of protection,[77] the balance between exploitation and sustainable use of marine resources remains substantially more contested.[78] Thus it is the apparent simplicity—and ubiquity—of the *Trail Smelter* principle, which has carried its reputation.

A. Repetition and Myth-making

But what invariably helped to translate *Trail Smelter* from being a bilateral award to (admittedly in the early period) a putative global norm was its apparent relevance to and, for at least one member of the International Court, persuasive force in helping to decide a broader issue of environmental harm. As is well known, the

---

[75] Stephens, *International Courts* (n 4) 133: 'The longevity of the dictum is a consequence of the flexible and negotiable standard articulated by the tribunal'. As regards its impact on non-environmental forms of transboundary harm, see the chapters in Part 3 of Bratspies and Miller (n 1).

[76] See V Lowe, *International Law* (Oxford, Clarendon, 2007) 236.

[77] See Report of the International Law Commission (Sixty-seventh session) (4 May–5 June and 6 July–7 August 2015) ILC Report, A/70/10, 2015, ch V (Protection of the Atmosphere) [54].

[78] For recent clarification on the importance of cooperation between coastal and flag states in the matter of fisheries, see *Request for an Advisory Opinion Submitted by the Sub-Regional Fisheries Commission (SRFC)*, Advisory Opinion of 2 April 2015, [213].

matter confronting the International Court in the 1974 *Nuclear Tests Cases* concerned the radioactive fall-out from French atmospheric nuclear tests in the South Pacific. Despite the majority of the Court accepting France's unilateral declaration as disposing of the case,[79] nevertheless the subject matter of the dispute meant it was one of a very few environmentally cognate cases considered by any international tribunal between 1945 and the 1990s. More specifically, the inclusion of a reference to *Trail Smelter* in this case, noticeably in the dissenting opinion of Judge de Castro,[80] is arguably one of a number of key moments that assisted in the juridical development of Trail Smelter's global reach, as well as revealing the possibility of its scope beyond cross-boundary fume pollution. The *erga omnes* arguments raised in this case have been well scrutinised,[81] but it is perhaps also worth noting the seemingly unproblematic assertion of the *Trail Smelter* principle to disputes beyond territorial boundaries.

Judge de Castro, in an almost exemplary example of my criticism of how the case has been reduced to an atomised form, summarises *Trail Smelter* with almost no reference to the facts, quotes only part of the pertinent sentence—even capitalises the start of his quote when in fact it is mid-sentence[82]—and then determines that 'the consequence must be drawn, by an obvious analogy' that the general principle enunciated in Trail Smelter can be applied in other situations, to include a general obligation not to cause harm in non-sovereign areas, in this case, radioactive fall-out onto the high seas.[83] Thus, by 1974, it is apparent that the value of the Award had already begun to morph from a 'right to demand prohibition of the emission by neighbouring properties of noxious fumes'[84] into a wider prohibition on other forms of atmospheric harm. Judge de Castro goes further and notes that 'This award marks the abandonment of the theory of Harmon (absolute sovereignty of each state in its territory with regard to all others)'.[85]

There is, of course, a risk of appearing contradictory and retrospectively churlish to criticise the use of *Trail Smelter* in this way. The reliance by Judge de Castro of an earlier arbitral decision to build up his own reasoning is *per se* not unusual and indeed if one takes the view that international environmental law cannot operate without a 'Trail Smelter' principle, its evolution from the specific to the general is both inevitable and to be viewed positively. Nevertheless, there is room for discussion. Should a principle moulded for the particular circumstances of bilateral, and presumably reciprocal, relations be applied wholly and unquestionably to a very different situation? More specifically, in light of the specific difficulties around enforcement for harm to common areas,[86] is the universal application of one generalised rule

---

[79] *Nuclear Tests (Australia v France)* [1974] ICJ Rep 253, 270; *Nuclear Tests (New Zealand v France)* [1974] ICJ Rep 457, 475.

[80] ibid, 372, 389.

[81] M Ragazzi, *The Concept of International Obligations Erga Omnes* (Oxford, OUP, 1997) 175–81.

[82] Judge De Castro does include a footnote which references the earlier part of the sentence, particularly that the principle draws on both international and US law, but it isn't made clear how the two phrases fit together.

[83] See n 80.

[84] ibid.

[85] ibid, fn 2.

[86] *cf Responsibilities and Obligations of States* (n 68) 59.

necessarily to be encouraged? Judge de Castro in his approach, of course, is merely mirroring what has happened to the principle in diplomatic fora, but nevertheless as revealed in the later work of the International Law Commission, which limited its investigations in this area to the prevention of, and liability for, the occurrence of *transboundary* harm, there is—whether one likes it or not—significant divergence in approach and efficacy of rule enforcement when harm happens to sovereign, in contrast to non-sovereign, areas.[87]

What is also particularly noticeable is how de Castro, followed invariably by academic treatises, makes a link between Trail Smelter and the International Court's first case, *Corfu Channel*, and its general dicta that 'every state's obligation not to allow knowingly its territory to be used for acts contrary to the rights of other states.[88] The intention of making this connection is premised upon linking Trail Smelter to general international law and thus its relevance, I'd suggest, is two-fold. First, *Trail Smelter* as an emerging rule of international law can be seen as reflective of—and supportive of the formation of—a much more foundational principle in international law. Secondly, by making a connection between *Trail Smelter* and *Corfu Channel*, it has the undisputed effect of normalising and mainstreaming international environmental law.[89] The prohibition of transboundary harm thus becomes less an esoteric and 'green' (invariably viewed as a soft) commitment, and more of a legally binding rule, which is merely one manifestation of the wider obligation espoused by the Court in *Corfu Channel*. Retrospectively, it might now be wondered why *Corfu Channel* is so readily mentioned in early textbooks on international environmental law, but as a link to both a general principle of international law and, more specifically, as a precise dictum of the International Court, *Trail Smelter* is thus associated very closely within the accepted body of international law. Thus, even where the majority of Court refused to engage in environmental considerations—in *Nuclear Tests Cases*—nevertheless, academic treatises on environmental law can make a chronological narrative from bilateralism towards global acceptance, with implicit endorsement by the International Court.

Within this process, two diplomatic events are especially important; the adoption, already by 1972, of the UN Declaration on the Human Environment and the conclusion of the negotiations of the 1982 UN Convention on the Law of the Sea (UNCLOS). Through these two seminal texts, the *Trail Smelter* rule is thus codified

---

[87] D French, 'Common Concern, Common Heritage and other Global(-ising) Concepts: Rhetorical Devices, Legal Principles or a Fundamental Challenge?' in M Bowman, P Davies and E Goodwin (eds), *Research Handbook on Biodiversity and Law* (Cheltenham, Edward Elgar, 2016) 336–37: 'no distinction is made between the responsibility for transboundary impact and the negative effects of harm caused in areas beyond national jurisdiction. It has thus justified the evolution of a single meta-norm (the singularly inappropriately-named 'no harm' principle) to come into existence, notwithstanding the very significant legal and practical differences that exist between these two scenarios'.

[88] *Corfu Channel (United Kingdom v Albania) Merits*, [1949] ICJ Rep 4, 22.

[89] J Viñuales, 'The Contribution of the International Court of Justice to the Development of International Environmental Law: A Contemporary Assessment' (2008) 32 *Fordham Journal of International Law* 232, 238: '*Corfu Channel* ... came as a confirmation of this narrow view ... confirmed and linked to general international law'. *cf* J Crawford, *Brownlie's Principles of Public International Law*, 8th edn (Oxford, OUP, 2012) 353.

into something more precise and, in the latter case, conventional. It is useful to place excerpts from each, side by side:

Principle 21 of the 1972 UN Stockholm Declaration[90]

States have, in accordance with the Charter of the United Nations and the principles of international law, the sovereign right to exploit their own resources pursuant to their own environmental policies, and the responsibility to ensure that activities within their jurisdiction or control do not cause damage to the environment of other States or of areas beyond the limits of national jurisdiction.

Articles 192–194(2) UNCLOS[91]

Article 192: States have the obligation to protect and preserve the marine environment.

Article 193: States have the sovereign right to exploit their natural resources pursuant to their environmental policies and in accordance with their duty to protect and preserve the marine environment.

Article 194(1) ...

Article 194(2): States shall take all measures necessary to ensure that activities under their jurisdiction or control are so conducted as not to cause damage by pollution to other States and their environment, and that pollution arising from incidents or activities under their jurisdiction or control does not spread beyond the areas where they exercise sovereign rights in accordance with this Convention.

This is *Trail Smelter* writ large, stripped of context and applied as a general principle, or rule, of international law—to the extent that it becomes known, more than a little erroneously, as the 'no harm' principle.[92] Indeed, no longer is it limited to atmospheric harm. Several points are worthy of note. Principle 21 is remarkable both for its brevity and its ambition. Unlike almost all of the rest of the Declaration, this is placed not in aspirational terms but drafted in the language of international law. Unsurprisingly, following 1972, a flurry of legal agreements sought to give effect to Principle 21 on a broad array of environmental matters; including marine pollution,[93] atmospheric pollution,[94] and ozone pollution.[95] Even the later 1992 (so-called 'Rio') treaties on climate change and biodiversity reference the principle,[96] as do many others almost as a matter of ritual.[97] It is for that reason—above almost all others—that 1972 is often said to be the 'birth' of international environmental law.

---

[90] UN Doc A/CONF.48/14/Rev.1.

[91] 21 ILM (1982) 1261.

[92] P Birnie, A Boyle and C Redgwell, *International Law and the Environment*, 3rd edn (Oxford, OUP, 2009) 137.

[93] 1972 Convention for the Prevention of Marine Pollution by Dumping of Wastes and other Matter (11 ILM (1972) 1294), preamble.

[94] 1979 Convention on Long-Range Transboundary Air Pollution (18 ILM (1979) 1442), preamble.

[95] 1985 Vienna Convention for the Protection of the Ozone Layer (26 ILM (1987) 1529), preamble.

[96] 1992 UN Framework Convention on Climate Change (31 ILM (1992) 851), preamble and 1992 Convention on Biological Diversity (31 ILM (1992) 818) Art 3.

[97] D French, 'A Reappraisal of Sovereignty in the light of Global Environmental Concerns' (2001) 21 *Legal Studies* 376, 383.

Principle 21 of course encapsulates two rather separate principles; permanent sovereignty over natural resources (itself still very much controversial at the time) and secondly, the essence of the rule—if not quite the language—of *Trail Smelter*. The extent to which these are discrete rules, operationally independent, or the extent to which the one might constrain the application of the other, are fundamental questions with which the international community continues to grapple.[98] Diplomatically, of course, the combination of the two principles was to elicit consensus amongst the states present in Stockholm, representing the developed and developing perspectives. Nevertheless, notwithstanding the politics inherent within the principle, there is also a legal tension at play. It is therefore unsurprisingly that states elected to develop specific conventional regimes as the most effective way of applying it to particular environmental problems.

As well as prompting regulatory action, the 1972 Declaration sets out the beginnings of a framework for state responsibility for environmental harm, though without the answers to several key questions. Much of the subsequent discussion since then has therefore been on the precise scope of such responsibility. In particular, queries as to the nature of the obligation of the state (as one of conduct or of result?), the necessity of loss before action (which now raises the related matter of the relevance and status of the precautionary principle)[99] and the accepted compensable heads of damage have, inter alia, come to dominate both academic and juridical debate. Though states were willing to establish primary rules of conduct through the adoption of regulatory conventions, they rarely specified, in clear terms, express rules of liability. As will be noted, the ILC's work was especially problematic in this regard. And as Principle 13 of the 1992 Rio Declaration on Environment and Development indicates, 20 years after the Stockholm Declaration, little progress had been, or seemingly could be, made on liability.[100] The lack of case law also ensured courts and tribunals had relatively few cases to develop general rules of international law on liability in this area.

Moreover, as rather subtle differences in the wording of the Stockholm Declaration and the cited provisions on UNCLOS reveal, there was a broader jurisprudential debate as to whether the 'no harm' principle was a negative obligation on states not to cause (or allow the causation of) harm, or whether it was a positive, more extensive, obligation to protect the environment. The Stockholm Declaration was notably muted in this respect; UNCLOS on the other hand seemed more progressive (at Article 192), though its subsequent obligation to 'prevent, reduce and control pollution' itself raised questions as to the actual commitment required of states.

---

[98] See generally N Schrijver, *Sovereignty over Natural Resources: Balancing Rights and Duties* (Cambridge, CUP, 1997).

[99] Principle 15 of 1992 Rio Declaration on Environment and Development (UN Doc A/CONF.151/26/Rev.1): 'In order to protect the environment, the precautionary approach shall be widely applied by States according to their capabilities. Where there are threats of serious or irreversible damage, lack of full scientific certainty shall not be used as a reason for postponing cost-effective measures to prevent environmental degradation'.

[100] 'States shall also cooperate in an expeditious and more determined manner to develop further international law regarding liability and compensation for adverse effects of environmental damage caused by activities within their jurisdiction or control to areas beyond their jurisdiction'.

Thus, even at the early stages in the global acceptance of 'no harm' principle, there lacked precision and specificity at the heart of the fundamental rule. Moreover, as the principle had now become detached from the very case from which it had closest resonance, namely *Trail Smelter*, reference to that particular arbitral decision was to provide little in the way of clarity. Commentators would search in vain for answers as to the relevant standard of care (often converted into a simple binary division between strict liability and due diligence), and the severity of the harm required.

Nevertheless, the progressive advance of the principle into an accepted rule of custom was inevitable. As Judge Weeramantry noted in his dissent against the Order of 22 September 1995 in *Request for an Examination of the Situation in Accordance with Paragraph 63 of the Court's Judgment of 20 December 1974 in the Nuclear Tests (New Zealand v France) Case*, the principle 'is well entrenched in international law and goes as far back as the *Trail Smelter* case … and perhaps beyond'.[101] A year later, the International Court finally accepted the principle as part of the canon of customary law in its Advisory Opinion on *Legality of the Threat or Use of Nuclear Weapons*. Stylistically, if less so in terms of substance, there is significant impact in the wording of the Court, when it notes (without reference to its sister clause of sovereignty over resources) that 'the general obligation of states to ensure that activities within their jurisdiction and control respect the environment of other states or of areas beyond national control is now part of the corpus of international law relating to the environment'.[102] From an environmental perspective, there is significant advantage in transforming an essentially negatively framed obligation into a more positively worded commitment. But, as an aside, one might wonder about the reasoning here. Certainly, it seems to fit aptly into Talmon's discussion of the methodology of the International Court in determining customary international law, where inductive and deductive reasoning models both fail to capture adequately the judicial process of the Court, but rather 'In the large majority of cases, the Court does not offer any … reasoning but simply asserts the law as it sees fit'.[103]

B. Limitations and Deconstruction

There is, however, a paradox. Notwithstanding this move towards being accepted as a general norm of international law, it has remained elusive in terms of its scope and obligation. This is perhaps no more evident that in the work of the ILC. The ILC has struggled to conceptualise, and to balance, a rule-based approach to transboundary responsibility with a more permissive approach to regulating lawful activity on state territory, encapsulated in what it now terms an equitable balancing of interests.[104]

---

[101] [1995] ICJ Rep 317, 346.

[102] [1996] ICJ Rep 226, 242.

[103] S Talmon, 'Determining Customary International Law: The ICJ's Methodology between Induction, Deduction and Assertion' (2015) 26 *EJIL* 417, 434.

[104] See, for instance, Art 10 of the 2001 draft Articles on Prevention of Transboundary Harm from Hazardous Activities: 'factors involved in an equitable balance of interests' (for details, see n 108 below).

This attempt to reconcile respecting sovereign rights, on the one hand, with responsibility for harm, on the other has been at the heart of the ILC's work programme—
some would suggest has been its perennial woe—in this area since it started its work
on this topic in the late 1970s. In attempting to address the issue of liability, the
very title of the ILC's original project—'international liability for injurious consequences arising out of acts not prohibited by international law'—highlighted the
complexity that the ILC was to soon find itself in on whether a state could be liable
for transboundary harm caused by lawful acts without a consequential violation
of international law by the state itself. Doctrinal confusion within the ILC on this
matter provoked significant criticism.[105]

The decision in 1997 to divide the ILC's work into the identification of rules of
international law on the prevention on transboundary harm, on the one hand, and
international liability in case of loss arising therefrom, on the other, was to prove the
turning point.[106] On the first part, the ILC focused on the due diligence obligations
on states to seek to minimise transboundary harm, focusing primarily on domestic
regulatory and enforcement measures and international obligations of notification
and consultation.[107] On the second part, the ILC more adventurously looked at
the prospects for access to justice at the cross-jurisdictional level,[108] recognising the
limitations—to private victims—of the first approach of an international obligation
premised on due diligence. This divide, whilst not wholly satisfactory, nonetheless
allowed the ILC to bring its work in this area to a close. In the ILC's commentaries
to both final products, namely the 2001 Draft Articles on Prevention of Transboundary Harm from Hazardous Activities[109] and the 2006 Draft Principles on Allocation
of Loss in the Case of Transboundary Harm arising out of Hazardous Activities,[110]
there are numerous references to *Trail Smelter*, though these are invariably limited—
in the usual way—to a reductionist form.

In some instances, where there are references to the case, there is often some difficulty in making the necessary conceptual link. For instance, in finding support in
Trail Smelter for the 2001 draft Article 7 (assessment of risk), the ILC is nevertheless
forced to admit that 'Although the assessment of risk in the Trail Smelter case may
not directly relate to liability for risk, it nevertheless emphasized the importance of
an assessment of the consequences of an activity causing significant risk'.[111] The ILC
goes on to note, quoting the Tribunal: 'The tribunal in that case indicated that the
study undertaken by well-established and known scientists was 'probably the most
thorough [one] ever made of any area subject to atmospheric pollution by industrial
smoke'.[112] Though it does not try to conceal it, the ILC nevertheless conflates post

---

[105] See generally Boyle 'State Responsibility' (n 69).

[106] For discussion of the ILC Working Group on this matter, see Document A/CN.4/L.536 as
mentioned in ILC Ybk 1997, vol II (Part Two), [165]–[167].

[107] For further discussion, see Birnie, Boyle and Redgwell, *International Law* (n 92) 137–88, *passim*.

[108] See A Boyle, 'Globalising Environmental Liability: The Interplay of National and International
Law' (2005) 17 *Journal of Environmental Law* 3.

[109] To be found in ILC Ybk 2001, vol II, Part Two, 148–70.

[110] To be found in ILC Ybk 2006, vol II, Part Two, 110–82.

[111] ILC Ybk 2001 (n 109) 158.

[112] ibid.

hoc scientific assessment for the purposes of devising a regulatory regime (on which the Tribunal was commenting) with ante hoc assessment for the purposes of assessing risk as part of the due diligence obligation (on which the Tribunal had little to say). Needless to say, this is an attribution by the ILC seemingly out of necessity, which is actually deeply problematic from a conceptual perspective.

What is also noticeable—certainly not in every reference but at various points throughout the two commentaries—is a conflation between the *Trail Smelter* arbitration and the development of subsequent principles, where the former is viewed both as the antecedent of, as well as justification, for the latter, but usually without reference to its particularities and nuanced factual circumstances. Thus, for instance, in the commentaries on the 2006 Draft Principles, the ILC notes that:

> the notion of prompt and adequate compensation ... reflects the understanding and the desire that victims of transboundary damage should not have to wait long in order to be compensated. The importance of ensuring prompt and adequate compensation to victims of transboundary damage has its underlying premise in the Trail Smelter arbitration and the Corfu Channel case, as further elaborated and encapsulated in Principle 21 of the Stockholm Declaration.[113]

This is a particularly unsatisfactory statement; not only does it grossly oversimplify each of these key precedents, but it blatantly ignores that neither specifically prioritises the adoption of domestic rules for the administration of justice in respect of transboundary harm based on a system of strict liability (as envisaged by the 2006 Draft Principles) in contrast to international responsibility for harm caused (accepted in the 2001 Draft Articles as an obligation of due diligence). As the ILC's commentaries reveal, it is noticeable how little is gleaned by the ILC for either project from an in-depth reading of *Trail Smelter* on either the issue of due diligence or strict liability. For those that have held *Trail Smelter* in such high regard as an enduring principle on environmental law, this must be of concern. But in light of the limited role international law played in the arbitration, this must be considered far from surprising.

Despite a general lack of case law on transboundary pollution, it would be remiss to suggest that there has been no discussion of *Trail Smelter* at various points, though the history here is one of selectivity. For instance, in the *Pulp Mills on the River Uruguay (Argentina v Uruguay)* (2010), concerning pollution of a shared watercourse, despite referencing the 'no harm' principle (seen by the Court as 'the principle of prevention, as a customary rule [which] has its origins in the due diligence that is required of a State in its territory')[114] there was no mention of *Trail Smelter* but relying instead on its own case of *Corfu Channel*, an internal stylistic technique often used by the Court.[115] Recent cases are also noticeable for their elaboration of

---

[113] ILC Ybk 2006 (n 110) 141.
[114] [2010] ICJ Rep 14, 55.
[115] See also *Certain Activities Carried out by Nicaragua in the Border Area (Costa Rica v Nicaragua) / Construction of a Road in Costa Rica along the San Juan River (Nicaragua v Costa Rica)* [2015] ICJ Rep 665, [104].

a customary obligation to undertake transboundary environmental impact assessment where there is risk of harm, thus advancing the procedural aspects of the obligation.[116]

Perhaps most interesting in terms of the usage of *Trail Smelter* is to be found in the pleadings of *Aerial Herbicide (Ecuador v Colombia)*, which also related to atmospheric pollution. In its written memorial, Ecuador gives credence to the historical relevance of the arbitration,[117] though it also seeks to engage with the detail of the Award to support its own position, where relevant, but also to identify what it considers is its limitations.[118] This seems to be a more analytical, and justifiable, approach to the decision than has often previously been the case. Colombia in its own way also relies on *Trail Smelter*—perhaps in less detail—but no less relevantly for that, when it seeks to defend itself against what it perceives as a tendency in international adjudication for aspirational argumentation: 'New and aspirational instruments ... are combined, higgledy-piggledy, with established propositions such as that of the Trail Smelter arbitration'.[119] As previously noted, the dispute was settled, and the International Court was not afforded the opportunity to consider such arguments.[120] However, the reliance by the parties in their written memorials on the Award is not insignificant. It highlights once again the underlying paradox that the arbitral Award is both universally endorsed, and yet equally enigmatic in its application. As Ellis had cause to note, 'it is an awkward fit with other rules of international environmental law, and ... it is at the same time a cornerstone of that law'.[121]

Thus, in turning to some of the criticism of *Trail Smelter*, it is useful to demarcate between critique of the over-use and subsequent reliance on the case, and critique of the case itself. Mickelson, for example, in her article entitled *Rereading Trail Smelter*, highlights a range of scholars who have over the years criticised the over-use and misrepresentation of the importance of Trail Smelter. She quotes Handl, for instance, who remarked that the case as being a 'much cited, and with regard to its international legal relevance also often over-estimated, decision'.[122] Similarly,

---

[116] Sands and Peel (n 3) 620–21.

[117] Written Memorial of Ecuador (n 41) [8.4]: 'The law on this subject is rooted in the well-known decision in the Trail Smelter Arbitration which, like the present case, was concerned with air pollution'.

[118] ibid, [10.17]: 'The case is largely of historical interest, applying the approach to compensation that pertained in the early part of the twentieth century, which approach has been significantly developed in recent years'.

[119] *Aerial Herbicide Spraying (Ecuador v. Colombia)*: Written Counter-Memorial of Colombia, Vol I (29 March 2010) [8.1].

[120] Nevertheless, the recital in the Order of 13 September 2013 (Removal from List) referencing the agreement between the Parties is of substantial interest concerning how the dispute was settled in practice, reflecting some of the key procedural techniques utilised in international environmental law: 'the Agreement of 9 September 2013 establishes, inter alia, an exclusion zone, in which Colombia will not conduct aerial spraying operations, creates a Joint Commission to ensure that spraying operations outside that zone have not caused herbicides to drift into Ecuador and, so long as they have not, provides a mechanism for the gradual reduction in the width of the said zone; and whereas, according to the letters, the Agreement sets out operational parameters for Colombia's spraying programme, records the agreement of the two Governments to ongoing exchanges of information in that regard, and establishes a dispute settlement mechanism'.

[121] Ellis, 'Has International Law Outgrown Trail Smelter?' (n 1).

[122] G Handl, 'Balancing of Interests and International Liability for the Pollution of International Watercourses: Customary Principles of Law Revisited' (1975) 13 Canadian Yearbook of International Law 156, 167–68 in Mickelson (n 9) 230, fn 31.

Munton is noted as saying that the award 'has become accepted—and, to a certain extent, mythologised—as a landmark case in international law'.[123] Reflecting the themes of this chapter, such scholars are pointing to the temptation of over-simplification and the invariable error that will result therefrom. As Rubin notes— referring specifically to Trail Smelter—'heavy reliance on a single precedent breeds overstatement ... the precedent can be applied only by raising it to a level of abstraction far beyond the range of its logic'.[124] For Mickelson, such criticism focuses invariably on how *Trail Smelter* has been put to use since its Award in the 1940s, rather than criticism of the case itself. As she notes, 'it is more an object of reverence than a subject of analysis'.[125]

On the other hand, for Ellis, it is not only the legacy of the dispute that is problematic but the legal reasoning of the Award; its long-term 'persuasiveness is compromised by a lack of clarity in the Tribunal's reasoning'.[126] Thus, such criticism is not purely retrospective—premised on misunderstanding and misapplication in later cases—but also on the coherence of the Award itself. Ellis, in particular, points out that the Tribunal's own understanding on state responsibility is ultimately flawed; for though it relied on the work of Eagleton to justify the maxim of responsibility to which it refers, 'His reasoning is not adopted by the Tribunal'.[127] Nowhere does the Tribunal conclude on what precise grounds Canada is responsible for the trans-boundary pollution, but merely asserts it as such. As Ellis notes, 'the Tribunal did not identify the nature of the international legal obligation that Canada breached in this case'.[128] Thus, not only does *Trail Smelter* not have the precedential value that many believe it to have, but it perhaps fails to convince on its own merit as regards its own reasoning as the law stood in 1941.

A third criticism is to suggest increasing irrelevance for *Trail Smelter*; that the focus of international law in the area of environmental harm has changed. Drumbl, for instance, notes that if the primary obligation of *Trail Smelter* is—as has been explained, an 'obligation not to cause serious environmental harm'—there was also always a secondary obligation in operation, namely the provision of reparation and compensation. As he notes, 'I see an important distinction in terms of the currency of Trail Smelter's primary rule ... and the currency of Trail Smelter's secondary obligation'.[129] Relying in part on the work of Dinah Shelton, he argues that

> despite the ILC's clarification of the rules regarding state responsibility, Trail Smelter may continue to lead a somewhat lonely existence. Shelton observes that 'the Trail Smelter arbitration is almost alone today in being cited for state responsibility and reparations in the

---

[123] D Munton, 'Dependence and Interdepedence in Transboundary Environmental Relations' (1980–81) 36 *International Journal* 139, 140 in Mickelson (n 9) 223, fn 13.

[124] A Rubin, 'Pollution by Analogy: The Trail Smelter Arbitration' (1971) 50 *Oregon Law Review* 259.

[125] Mickelson (n 9) 220.

[126] Ellis (n 1) 59.

[127] ibid.

[128] ibid, 60.

[129] M Drumbl, 'Trail Smelter and the International Law Commission's work on State Responsibility for Internationally Wrongful Acts' in Bratspies and Miller (n 1) 93.

field of environmental protection, because virtually no interstate cases have been brought in the decades since it was decided'[130]

On the other hand, of course, it is not all about formal dispute settlement. The work of the ILC—and international law more generally—is to structure the peaceful settlement of disputes, not to govern legal procedures alone. There is scope for recognising the importance of inter-state negotiation, inter alia, as a key means to reconcile the competing interests of States. As the Tribunal recognised, equity invariably plays a central part in such a settlement. The 2001 Draft Articles on Prevention of Transboundary Harm themselves list a range of factors that contribute to an equitable balancing of interests. Though this might undermine the certainty of law, in matters such as these where harm is pervasive, ongoing and to be controlled rather than to be strictly prohibited (as with a one-off disaster, say), finding appropriate solutions must be part-legal/part-policy. To the extent that *Trail Smelter* is viewed as providing for a general principle—in contrast to a framework for inter-State resolution—then it may rightly be perceived as unhelpful.

Thus, criticism of *Trail Smelter* has ranged from the intrinsic to the consequential. As this chapter has identified throughout, there is a paradox to the Award. It would seem to be both relevant and irrelevant to the structure and operation of modern-day international environmental law. As time has passed, its stature has waned as other disputes have been decided, conventions have been adopted and processes of codification and progressive development have reviewed which rules and principles of international environmental law are necessary and required. Nevertheless, *Trail Smelter* retains an almost mystical presence that won't be ignored. Referring generally, though there is a pertinence to the issue under discussion, D'Aspremont frames it thus:

> the practice of taking refuge in judicial validation and the judicialization of international legal thought that comes with it ... is not to repudiate international lawyers' practice of taking refuge in judicial validation of argumentative structures. It may be that such short-cuts are necessary to preserve the possibility of legal argumentation ... Yet, accepting the inevitability of the phenomenon does not mean that one should not take a hard look at the practice.[131]

IV. *TRAIL SMELTER* IN CONCLUSION: RE-EVALUATION AS A LANDMARK DISPUTE SETTLEMENT?

There is a significant risk when discussing a dispute such as *Trail Smelter*—viewed latterly as a 'landmark' judgment—that one can generalise to an unreasonable extent. Usually, and undoubtedly at the initial stages, this over-generalisation is often an uncritical, and uncriticised, process to elaborate on its importance. This may be

---

[130] ibid, 94 referencing D Shelton, 'Righting Wrongs: Reparations in the Articles on State Responsibility' (2002) 96 *AJIL* 833, 854–55.

[131] J D'Aspremont, 'If International Judges Say So, It Must Be True: Empiricism or Fetishism?' (2015) 4 *ESIL Reflections* 9, 5.

a necessary part of its development, but it is during this stage that the case and the general rule/principle, which it is said to stand for begin to converge. As noted in the introduction, very often this is most clearly reflected by a metonymic synthesis between the name of the case and the said rule/principle. When we discuss such well-known cases as *Wimbledon*, *Lotus* and *Chorzów Factory*, what are we actually referring to? Almost invariably, the dominant rule/principle arising from the case and very little else. And as such cases become generalised both in terms of their acceptance and their application, they broaden in scope, harden in normativity and yet, paradoxically, narrow into a singular rule capable of easy citation and repetition.

What is perhaps more novel about *Trail Smelter* is that its evolution into a general principle has relied as much—if not more so—on diplomatic initiatives and soft law than it has on judicial endorsement. And though the mechanisms are far from identical, they are not wholly separate. As Talmon noted in a paper on the methodology of judicial determination of customary international law, 'judicial deduction is not the same as logical deduction ... logical reasoning is replaced by legal reasoning, which has its basis in the traditions of the legal system'.[132] Nevertheless, though each has its own internal structure and values, they are sufficiently linked to be supplementary and mutually supportive in the development of international law. *Trail Smelter* has come to represent something very different from that which it actually concerned. At this juncture, it is perhaps worth restating an obvious; there is nothing wrong per se with the principle attributed to the case—there is arguably even good reason for the Tribunal to have relied on an early iteration of it in this particular dispute. What however, has happened, and which is problematic, is that the principle has absorbed all else about the dispute. Consequently when one looks at the case through the prism of the general principle (still most easily referenced as) 'no harm', one loses the importance and the rigour of context. Moreover, as the principle was relevant, yet tangential, to the determination of the case, the case itself does not answer key questions on the general application of the principle; causation, level of harm, nature of liability, compensable heads of damage, etc.

It is thus not surprising that many have queried the case and contested its long-term significance. This rush to re-read the case is, of course, not without merit, and the insights brought by such critiques are invaluable and long overdue. It has allowed a less reverential, and more analytical, approach to be brought to a 'landmark-ed' case. What has emerged is a case stripped of much of the rhetoric that surrounded it. More generally, it has highlighted the importance of referring back to the original text. Nevertheless, in moving towards a fourth epoch of re-evaluation, perhaps we need not go so far. Notwithstanding the veracity of the criticism, it cannot be denied that the case was instrumental in the development of international environmental law. As McCaffrey concludes, 'Whether praised as bold and visionary or dismissed as narrow and compromising ... This was a remarkable decision'.[133] It would be as ahistorical to deny this as it would be to give it a substance and meaning that it

---

[132] Talmon, 'Determining Customary International Law (n 103) 420.

[133] S McCaffrey, 'Of Paradoxes, Precedents and Progeny: The *Trail Smelter* Arbitration 65 Years Later' in Bratspies and Miller (n 1) 45.

does not deserve. The Tribunal, by positioning its answer within the rubric of international law, did so intentionally; as did Judge de Castro and others who relied on it subsequently. It is not that the abstract principle was given undue prominence in later developments, but that the case in its totality—the principle, innovative procedural aspects (use of scientific experts), the Tribunal's reasoning at other points (eg. *res judicata* and the revision of awards), as well as the establishment of the regulatory regime (both in the first and the final decisions)—has not been considered worthy of further, and deeper, exploration and endorsement. As Mickelson notes, '*Trail Smelter* would remain a landmark, although its usefulness is not so much as a "case", but as a "case study"'.[134] If indeed that had occurred, rather than undermining its status, such analysis would have revealed much earlier the importance of dispute settlement in international environmental law. It also provides a salutary lesson against rushing to reduce any case to a singular, abstract, principle.

---

[134] Mickelson (n 9) 232.

9

Trial Before the International Military Tribunal at Nuremberg (1945–46)

KATHERINE O'BYRNE AND PHILIPPE SANDS[1]

I. INTRODUCTION

OVER SEVEN DECADES ago, on 21 November 1945, US Chief Prosecutor Robert H Jackson gave his opening address[2] at the trial of major Nazi war criminals before the International Military Tribunal ('IMT' or 'the Tribunal') at Nuremberg.[3] Jackson told the eight judges:

> The privilege of opening the first trial in history for crimes against the peace of the world imposes a grave responsibility. The wrongs which we seek to condemn and punish have been so calculated, so malignant, and so devastating, that civilization cannot tolerate their being ignored, because it cannot survive their being repeated. That four great nations, flushed with victory and stung with injury stay the hand of vengeance and voluntarily submit their captive enemies to the judgment of the law is one of the most significant tributes that Power has ever paid to reason.[4]

On 30 September and 1 October 1946, for the first time in history, an international tribunal convicted individuals of international crimes, including crimes against peace (waging aggressive war), war crimes and crimes against humanity. The principles of international law recognised in the Charter[5] and Judgment[6] of the Nuremberg Tribunal were later affirmed by the UN General Assembly,[7] and the

---

[1] Thanks to Megan Hirst and Ailsa McKeon for their editorial assistance on previous drafts of this chapter.

[2] Given on Day 2, 21 November 1945, the Indictment having been read on Day 1.

[3] This chapter deals only with the trial of major war criminals before the IMT, and not the subsequent trials of lower-level functionaries and private citizens before the Nuremberg Military Tribunals 1946–49. As to the subsequent trials, see the comprehensive analysis in KJ Heller, *The Nuremberg Military Tribunals and the Origins of International Criminal Law* (Oxford, OUP, 2012).

[4] Nuremberg Trial Proceedings, Volume 2, Day 2, Wednesday 21 November 1945, Transcript 97–98. The Proceedings Volumes, including full transcripts, are available online via Yale Law School at the Avalon Project: <http://avalon.law.yale.edu/subject_menus/imt.asp>.

[5] United Kingdom of Great Britain and Northern Ireland, United States of America, France and Union of Soviet Socialist Republics, *Agreement for the Prosecution and Punishment of the Major War Criminals of the European Axis* ('London Agreement'), *and Charter of the International Military Tribunal* ('Nuremberg Charter'), 82 UNTS 280 (entered into force 8 August 1945).

[6] *France v Göring*, Judgment and Sentence [1946] 22 IMT 203, (1946) 41 AJIL 172, (1946) 13 ILR 203, ICL 243 (IMTN 1946) (1 October 1946) ('Nuremberg Judgment').

[7] UNGA Res 95(I), 'Affirmation of the Principles of International Law Recognized by the Charter of the Nürnberg Tribunal', adopted on 11 December 1946.

seven key principles established at Nuremberg were codified by the International Law Commission.[8]

At the time of the trial itself, many individuals closely involved recognised it to be a landmark. In his closing address before the Tribunal, Sir Hartley Shawcross, the chief British prosecutor, stated:

> This Trial must form a milestone in the history of civilization, not only bringing retribution to these guilty men, not only marking that right shall in the end triumph over evil, but also that the ordinary people of the world—and I make no distinction now between friend or foe—are now determined that the individual must transcend the state.[9]

The judges presiding over the trial were no less convinced of the trial's significance. Norman Birkett (later Lord Birkett), the associate British judge, called it 'the greatest trial in history'.[10] US prosecutor Telford Taylor, even more involved in later cases, wrote that Nuremberg was conceived as 'an episode that would leave an enduring judicial monument, to mark as a giant step in the growth of international law'.[11] US Secretary of War Henry Stimson, one of the architects of the Tribunal, concluded: 'The surviving leaders of the Nazi conspiracy against mankind have been indicted, tried, and judged in a proceeding whose magnitude and quality make it a landmark in the history of international law'.[12] Even Nuremberg's defence lawyers, while criticising aspects of the trial's legitimacy, admitted to its landmark qualities. Otto Kranzbühler, representing Hitler's successor Admiral Karl Dönitz, wrote: 'Nuremberg was conceived, and can only be understood, as a revolutionary event in the development of international law ... One was fully aware that a step forward was being ventured'.[13]

As significant as that step was, for a time it seemed as though it might be the only footfall along the path to realising international criminal justice. Certainly, the answer to the question whether Nuremberg is a landmark may have been different prior to the establishment of the ad hoc international criminal tribunals for Rwanda and Yugoslavia in 1993. Then, it may have been seen as a point of interest in the landscape, a postscript to a war that devastated the world, but otherwise as a failed or infertile model. During the second half of the twentieth century, crimes against humanity and mass killings abounded: not only in Yugoslavia and Rwanda, but in Cambodia, Bangladesh, Kenya, Zimbabwe, South Africa, Sudan, Indonesia, Iran, Iraq, East Timor, China, Chile and Argentina; revolutions, conflicts and repressions

---

[8] Pursuant to General Assembly Resolution 177 (II), paragraph (a); see International Law Commission, *Principles of International Law Recognized in the Charter of the Nürnberg Tribunal and in the Judgment of the Tribunal* (1950), adopted by the International Law Commission at its second session in 1950 and submitted to the General Assembly as a part of the Commission's report covering the work of that session, including the commentaries of the Commission on the Principles, (1950) 2 ILC Ybk 374. The seven principles are: individual criminal responsibility for international crimes; internal law cannot relieve responsibility under international law; official position does not relieve responsibility; superior orders are not a defence; the right to a fair trial; crimes against peace, war crimes and crimes against humanity are punishable; and complicity is a crime.

[9] Nuremberg Trial Proceedings, Volume 19, Day 188, Saturday, 27 July 1946, Transcript 527–28.

[10] MR Marrus, 'The Nuremberg Trial: Fifty Years After' (1997) 66 *The American Scholar* 563, 563.

[11] T Taylor, *Nuremberg and Vietnam: An American Tragedy* (New York, New York Times Books, 1970) 80.

[12] HL Stimson, 'The Nuremberg Trial: Landmark in Law' (1947) 25 *Foreign Affairs* 179, 179.

[13] O Kranzbühler, 'Nuremberg Eighteen Years Afterwards' (1965) 14 *DePaul Law Review* 333, 335.

rising from the disintegration of pre-war colonisation, opportunistic power grabs and age-old enmities. Most went unattended by judicial responses. Only after the end of the Cold War did international criminal law begin to flourish, with the establishment of the ad hoc tribunals, various hybrid mechanisms, and the International Criminal Court (ICC). Through the work of these institutions, the indictment and prosecution of warlords, military commanders, and former and serving heads of state gave new life to the principles established at Nuremberg. But for Nuremberg (and the proceedings in Tokyo,[14] themselves catalysed by Nuremberg), it is unlikely that these subsequent developments would have occurred at all, or in the form they did.

Today, Nuremberg's status and reputation as a landmark in the topography of international law, particularly international criminal law, is not in doubt. All roads lead to Nuremberg, it may be said. But despite this legacy, the grand aspirations expressed during the Nuremberg trial have been fulfilled only to a limited extent, and serious questions remain as to the commitment of the international community to the role of international criminal courts. Seventy years after the trial, a vicious civil war rages in Syria, which international courts have so far failed to reach. Longstanding conflicts and repressive regimes continue to provide fertile ground for international crimes and impunity in the Middle East, Africa, Central Asia, and elsewhere. Meanwhile, in Libya, Sudan, the Democratic Republic of the Congo, the Central African Republic, Rwanda, Cambodia, and other states touched by the work of international criminal mechanisms, accountability continues to be the exception and the power of deterrence remains highly questionable. Western powers—including the United Kingdom and United States—appear to remain beyond the reach of international criminal courts, even where jurisdictional grounds are clear (as in the case of Afghanistan) or plausible (as in the case of allegations of involvement in 'extraordinary rendition'). Thinking about Nuremberg at this juncture raises fundamental questions. If Nuremberg is a landmark, what makes it so? What did it signify at the time, how have its principles been deployed and developed, and what does it mean for us today?

Nuremberg is a landmark for multiple legal, political, historical, and social reasons, all of which form the basis of extensive analysis elsewhere, and not all of which can be explored here. Much writing and discussion has been dedicated to analysing the context, precursors, progress, outcomes, and legacies of the trial. As well as creating a record of Nazi crimes, Nuremberg provided a model for new institutions of international law and an approximation of due process to the captured leaders of a totalitarian regime. Of course, the concept of a landmark does not necessarily carry normative content. The trial continues to be controversial,[15] which is not surprising given that it was born of a compromised, experimental, and highly political process.

---

[14] See International Military Tribunal for the Far East, Judgment of 12 November 1948, in J Pritchard and SM Zaide (eds), *The Tokyo War Crimes Trial* (New York, Garland, 1981), vol 22.

[15] See, eg, Georg Schwarzenberger, 'The Judgment of Nuremberg', in G Mettraux, *Perspectives on the Nuremberg Trial* (Oxford, OUP, 2008) 167; E Borchard, 'The Impracticality of 'Enforcing' Peace' (1946) 55 *Yale LJ* 966; G Finch, 'The Nuremberg Trial and International Law' (1947) 41 *AJIL* 20; F Schick, 'The Nuremberg Trial and the International Law of the Future' (1947) 41 *AJIL* 770; D Luban, 'The Legacies of Nuremberg', in Mettraux, 638; K Sellars, 'Imperfect Justice at Nuremberg and Tokyo' (2010) 21 *EJIL* 1085.

The focus of this chapter is on three major themes which can be said to have established Nuremberg as a legal landmark. The first of these is the foundation of the Tribunal itself to create a new institution of international law. While not entirely without precedent, Nuremberg was for its time the most successful example of an international war crimes tribunal, which created a model for further international tribunals and trials.

The second major theme is the creation and development of new and distinct categories of international criminal liability in the Nuremberg Charter, Indictment and Judgment. The lawyers and judges involved in the Nuremberg trial formed the foundation for our modern conceptions of aggression (crimes against peace), crimes against humanity and genocide.[16] Crimes against peace, made for the first time the subject of formal criminal sanctions in the Nuremberg Charter, were the predecessors of the crime of aggression in the Statute of the International Criminal Court, finally defined at Kampala in June 2010. The concept of crimes against humanity, first articulated in the Nuremberg Charter, has since developed to provide more concrete protection to individuals in civilian populations in times of war or peace. It is also necessary to say something of the role of Nuremberg as a platform for the development of Raphael Lemkin's concept of 'genocide', despite the fact that genocide was not mentioned in the Charter or Judgment of the Tribunal.

The third major theme, that of the individual in international law, runs as an undercurrent through the institutional and substantive legal aspects of the trial. Nuremberg, for the first time in history, gave effect to international accountability for individual leaders and contributed to the provision of international protection to individual civilians. Nuremberg and its principles, alongside the advent of international human rights law, played a part in effecting a shift in the focus of international law on state-to-state relations towards a complex and ever-evolving exchange between individuals, groups, and states.[17]

Part II of this chapter briefly traverses the well-known history leading up to the establishment in 1945 of the IMT as a new international legal institution, the genesis of the trial, models and precedents, and its basic factual parameters. Part III examines the three key developments in international criminal law precipitated by Nuremberg, explains how they came to be, and analyses their developments since the trial. The chapter concludes in Part IV with a reflection on legacy, how Nuremberg cemented the place of individuals at the forefront of the international legal framework, and how it continues to serve as a foundational and imperfect model for international tribunals and prosecutions today.

---

[16] In the limited space available, this chapter does not attempt to cover Nuremberg's contribution to the concept of war crimes, which, while one of the pillars of international criminal law, existed previously in the law of armed conflict and was not subject to major innovation at Nuremberg. Similarly, the chapter does not explore the concept in the Charter of conspiracy or common plan.

[17] For a detailed treatment of these themes, and of the lives and contributions of Sir Hersch Lauterpacht and Raphael Lemkin in particular, see P Sands, *East West Street: On the Origins of Genocide and Crimes Against Humanity* (London, Weidenfeld & Nicolson, 2016); P Sands, *My Nazi Legacy: What Our Fathers Did* (London, Wildgaze Films, 2015); P Sands, *A Song of Good and Evil* (various performances around the UK and Europe, 2014–16).

II. FOUNDATIONS FOR AN INTERNATIONAL TRIBUNAL

A. Fall and Capture of the Nazi Leadership

The horrors committed by the Nazi regime in Europe are well known. Sir Hartley Shawcross, in his closing speech at Nuremberg on 26 July 1946, described the ten million needless deaths of soldiers, sailors and other combatants in aggressive wars waged by Hitler in Poland, Denmark, Norway, Belgium, the Netherlands, Luxembourg, Yugoslavia, Greece, and the Soviet Union.[18] He lamented the deaths of civilians:

> 12 million men, women, and children ... in the cold, calculated, deliberate attempt to destroy nations and races ... Two-thirds of the Jews in Europe exterminated, more than 6 million of them on the killers' own figures. Murder conducted like some mass production industry in the gas chambers and the ovens of Auschwitz, Dachau, Treblinka, Buchenwald, Mauthausen, Maidanek, and Oranienburg.

The foundations for Nuremberg were laid swiftly in the months following the fall of the Nazi leadership in Spring 1945. On 30 April 1945 in Berlin, Hitler, having announced to his generals that the war was lost, committed suicide with his wife, Eva Braun, inside the *Führerbunker*. The Battle of Berlin raged outside as the Soviet Red Army approached. The next day, Goebbels and his wife committed suicide, having killed their six children.[19] Himmler followed suit after his capture and detention in British custody.

Those Nazi ringleaders who had survived the war were arrested by the Allied forces in the days and weeks following Hitler's demise. On 3 May 1945, Hans Frank, Hitler's chief lawyer and Governor General of occupied Poland, was captured by American troops near his home in Bavaria.[20] Hermann Göring, former Commander of the Luftwaffe, had been expelled from the Nazi Party after offering to take over as Führer, an overture perceived by Hitler as traitorous. On 6 May 1945, he made his way to American lines and was taken into custody. On 7 May 1945 in Rheims, France, Alfred Jodl, Chief of the Operations Staff of the Armed Forces High Command, signed an unconditional surrender to the Allies. On 23 May 1945, Karl Dönitz, named in Hitler's will as *Reichspräsident* and Supreme Commander of the Armed Forces, surrendered to British troops with the rest of the Flensburg Government.

---

[18] Nuremberg Trial Proceedings, Volume 19, Day 186, Friday 26 July 1946, Transcript 432.

[19] See, eg, WL Shirer, *The Rise and Fall of the Third Reich: A History of Nazi Germany* (New York, Simon & Schuster, 1960) ch 31: 'Goetterdaemmerung: The Last Days', 1016–17, 1019.

[20] Frank was arrested along with an extensive art collection and 42 volumes of his diaries, which were later used as evidence against him at trial. He had notated an address to his colleagues with the words: 'We must remember that we, who are gathered together here, figure on Mr Roosevelt's list of war criminals. I have the honour of being Number One'. The documents were prosecution exhibits at the proceedings of the IMT against Frank: Document 2233-AA-PS: Frank Diary, Official Meetings, 1943: Warsaw, 21/25/1943, in *Nazi Conspiracy and Aggression*, Volume IV: Documents 1409-PS-2373-PS (US Government Printing Office 1946) 916–17. See generally Sands, *East West Street* (n 17) 209–63.

B. Options for Dealing with the Nazi Leaders

The British judge at Nuremberg, Geoffrey Lawrence (Lord Oaksey), later posited: 'There were, I suppose, three possible courses: to let the atrocities which had been committed go unpunished; to put the perpetrators to death or punish them by executive action; or to try them. Which was it to be?'[21] Contemporaneous records reveal discussion of various approaches, but show that the decision to try the senior Nazi leadership was initially motivated primarily by politics, propaganda, and posterity, rather than a desire to develop or enforce international law.

During the war, at the Moscow Conference of October 1943, the UK, the US, and the Soviet Union, on behalf of 32 nations, issued a 'Statement on Atrocities' intended as both a plan for the delivery of summary justice post-war and as an undisguised warning to the Nazis, whom the Allies regarded as responsible for 'government by terror', 'ruthless cruelties', and 'monstrous crimes'.[22] Local trials were the proposed option for foot-soldiers, lower-level officers and regular party members, who would be 'judged and punished' in the countries where atrocities had been committed.[23] 'Let those who have hitherto not imbrued their hands with innocent blood beware lest they join the ranks of the guilty,' the Statement threatened, 'for most assuredly the three Allied powers will pursue them to the uttermost ends of the earth'.[24]

At that early stage, the attitude towards the Nazi leadership was more perfunctory, and envisaged a summary form of joint punishment without judgment: 'German criminals whose offenses have no particular geographical localization ... will be punished by joint decision of the government of the Allies'.[25] The Morgenthau Plan of 1944,[26] initially supported by Roosevelt and Secretary Stimson, recommended that Nazi 'Arch Criminals' be identified, apprehended and 'put to death forthwith by firing squads made up of soldiers of the United Nations'.[27] This met with public disapproval, particularly from Jewish groups in the US.[28] Stimson changed his mind, writing to the US President on 9 September 1944: 'the very punishment of these

---

[21] G Lawrence, 'The Nuremberg Trial' (1947) 23 *International Affairs* 151, 152–53. See further Stimson, 'The Nuremberg Trial' (n 12): 'There were three different courses open to us when the Nazi leaders were captured: release, summary punishment, or trial'.

[22] The Statement on Atrocities was appended to the *Joint Four-Nation Declaration* (30 October 1943) between the US, UK, the Soviet Union and China. Note that the Statement itself was agreed to only between the US, UK and the Soviet Union, not China.

[23] ibid. Over dinner at the Soviet Embassy in Tehran on 29 November 1943, Prime Minister Churchill, Marshal Joseph Stalin and President Franklin D Roosevelt discussed what was to be done with the German forces. While Stalin advocated their liquidation in large numbers, Churchill 'took strong exception to what he termed the cold-blooded execution of soldiers who fought for their country'. Churchill said that 'war criminals must pay for their crimes and individuals who had committed barbarous acts, and in accordance with the Moscow Document, which he himself had written, they must stand trial at the places where the crimes were committed. He objected vigorously, however, to executions for political purposes.': Bohlen Minutes, Tehran Conference: Tripartite Dinner Meeting, November 29, 1943, Soviet Embassy, 8.30 pm.

[24] ibid.

[25] HJ Morgenthau, Memorandum to the President: 'Treasury Plan for the Treatment of Germany' (4 September 1944), in BF Smith, *The American Road to Nuremberg: The Documentary Record 1944–1945* (Stanford, Hoover Institution Press, 1982) 27–28.

[26] ibid.

[27] ibid.

[28] See, eg, American Jewish Conference, 'Statement on Punishment of War Criminals', 18 August 1944.

men in a dignified manner consistent with the advance of civilization will have the greater effect on posterity ... I am disposed to believe that at least as to the chief Nazi officials, we should participate in an international tribunal constituted to try them'.[29]

Churchill, on the other hand, initially favoured dealing with the Nazi leadership by political means. In November 1943, Churchill proposed to his Cabinet that a list should be compiled 'of all major criminals', namely 'the Hitler and Mussolini gangs' and 'the Japanese War Lords', that they should 'be declared world outlaws' and that once captured and identified, should be 'shot to death within six hours and without reference to higher authority ... By this means we should avoid all the tangles of legal procedure'.[30] The recently declassified diaries of Guy Liddell, then head of counter-espionage at MI5, reveal that Churchill proposed at the Yalta Conference in February 1945 that 'a fact-finding committee should come to the conclusion that certain people should be bumped off and that others should receive varying terms of imprisonment',[31] with punishment to be implemented by military bodies. Roosevelt and Stalin preferred that the Nazis should be tried before a court: Roosevelt favoured this course of action because 'Americans would want a trial'; Stalin, 'on the perfectly frank grounds that Russians liked public trials for propaganda purposes'.[32]

What the historical documents make clear is that the establishment of the IMT was not initially driven, at least at the highest level, by an appetite for a legal process per se or any sort of commitment to the elaboration of a new and broader model of international criminal justice—indeed, leaders including Churchill wished to avoid overcomplicated legalism. Their priority was not the creation of a new legal institution, but how to extend their military might to ensure that the Nazis were penalised and permanently vanquished. The Allied occupation of Germany has been characterised as an *occupatio sui generis* enabling war crimes proceedings based on Germany's unconditional surrender and the assumption of supreme authority by the four powers.[33] It was judges, lawyers and legal philosophers, whose contribution is discussed below, who pressed the argument that the world needed new legal rules and instruments to demonstrate abhorrence and to guard against the recurrence of such atrocities, and who devised the legal principles on which the Tribunal was based. The IMT managed to unite, though imperfectly, both principled and pragmatic aims.

The British eventually acquiesced in the plan for a trial under pressure from the Americans. President Roosevelt had died on 12 April 1945, and was replaced by the more vociferously pro-trial President Harry Truman.[34] No doubt the decision

---

[29] Cited in GJ Bass, *Stay the Hand of Vengeance: The Politics of War Crimes Tribunals* (New Jersey, Princeton University Press, 2000) 165.

[30] ibid, 186, 188.

[31] See I Cobain, 'Britain favoured execution over Nuremberg trials for Nazi leaders', *The Guardian* (26 October 2012).

[32] ibid.

[33] See RK Woetzel, *The Nuremberg Trials in International Law* (London, Stevens & Sons Limited, 1962) 58–95, esp 89.

[34] The British turnaround appeared to have been prompted by a statement on 2 May 1945 by President Truman, announcing America's commitment to a trial: 'It is our objective to establish as soon as possible an international military tribunal; and to provide a trial procedure which will be expeditious in nature and which will permit no evasion or delay—but one which is in keeping with our tradition of fairness toward those accused of crime': see E Stover, V Peskin and A Koenig, *Hiding in Plain Sight: The Pursuit of War Criminals from Nuremberg to the War on Terror* (Berkeley, University of California Press, 2016) 29.

to proceed with a trial was also influenced by the fact that the distasteful prospect of affording a manifestly evil leader a platform to mount a defence was obviated by events at the close of the war. Hitler, Himmler, Goebbels and Mussolini, the ring-leading 'gangsters' most likely to make a trial both unpalatable and unmanageable,[35] were all dead by the end of the spring of 1945.

C. Models for the Tribunal

Although there was no concrete model for an international trial for wartime crimes of military leaders captured by a victorious enemy, some precedents did exist. The examples most often cited include the trial in 1474 by judges of Austria and a number of Swiss cities of Peter von Hagenbach, the former Governor of Breisach on the Upper Rhine, for atrocities including rape and murder;[36] the executive action taken against Napoleon Bonaparte by the Congress of Vienna following his escape from Elba in 1815; and the arrest and trial at Leipzig of German war criminals in 1921, following World War I, under Articles 227–30 of the Treaty of Versailles.[37] This included a failed attempt to extradite ex-Kaiser Wilhelm von Hohenzollern from the Netherlands for a 'supreme offence against international morality and the sanctity of treaties', resisted by the Netherlands on the basis that no such crime existed in international law.[38]

The uncovering of previously buried historical materials means that comparators continue to accumulate. In early 2017, the Wiener Library in London opened the archive of the UN War Crimes Commission, closed since the late 1940s. The archive contains documents relating to thousands of prosecutions, by member states of the Commission, of Axis leaders including Hitler, including evidence and charges compiled while the concentration camps were in operation.[39]

Commentators have debated whether such examples constitute true precedents for Nuremberg, and distinctions are frequently drawn based on the nature of each forum, the crimes tried, the law applied, and the relationship between trial

---

[35] T Taylor, *The Anatomy of the Nuremberg Trials: A Personal Memoir* (New York, Skyhorse Publishing, 1993) 32.

[36] See, eg, G Gordon, 'The Trial of Peter von Hagenbach: Reconciling History, Historiography and International Criminal Law', in KJ Heller and G Simpson (eds), *The Hidden Histories of War Crimes Trials* (Oxford, OUP, 2013); T McCormack, 'From Sun Tzu to the Sixth Committee: The Evolution of an International Criminal Law Regime' in T McCormack and G Simpson (eds), *The Law of War Crimes: National and International Approaches* (The Hague, Kluwer Law International, 1997) 31–63.

[37] Treaty of Versailles, 1919 (225 CTS 188), Art 227.

[38] See M Cherif Bassiouni, 'An Appraisal of the Growth and Developing Trends of International Criminal Law' in J Dugard and C Van den Wyngaert (eds), *International Criminal Law and Procedure* (Aldershot, Dartmouth, 1996) 79–95.

[39] See Wiener Library, United Nations War Crimes Commission: records, available at <http://wiener. soutron.net/Portal/Default/en-GB/RecordView/Index/92681>; O Bowcott, 'Opening files on Holocaust will "rewrite chapters of history"', *The Guardian* (18 April 2017). For the first academic analysis of this material, see D Plesch, *Human Rights After Hitler—The Lost History of Prosecuting Axis War Crimes* (Washington DC, Georgetown University Press, 2017).

and armed conflict.[40] Looking back, from a perspective informed by the modern proliferation of war crimes tribunals with a variety of jurisdictional set-ups and by prosecutions at the domestic level of international crimes, it may be argued that such distinctions serve to illustrate the forward movement of international prosecutions in various forms. It cannot, however, be said that any provides a parallel; Nuremberg was in a class of its own in virtually every respect.

In addition to its innovations of procedure and principle, it is arguable that Nuremberg represented the first tribunal that could properly be called 'international' in character. This argument has been based primarily on two forms of international sanction:[41] first, that 23 nations signed up to the London Agreement and the Charter, representing a significant proportion of the international community of states at the time; and, second, that the international community through the General Assembly of the United Nations later endorsed the principles applied at Nuremberg[42] and confirmed the understanding that the Charter and Judgment were instruments of international law.[43]

In late 1944, a new plan, drafted primarily in the form of a six-page memorandum by US War Department lawyer Lieutenant Colonel Murray C Bernays entitled 'Trial of European War Criminals',[44] was presented to the US Secretary of State. Bernays' plan contained a number of innovations, particularly in the area of collective criminality, sowing seeds that developed into what we now view as some of Nuremberg's most significant legacies.

First, Bernays developed the notion of criminal liability for 'conspiracy or common plan', which allowed the Nuremberg indictment to reach individuals at the top of the Nazi power structures and the authors of Nazi political doctrine for acts prior to 1939, not just those who carried out orders and implemented policies. Second, the plan supported prosecution of crimes committed against German and Axis-territory nationals on religious, racial or political grounds, which, because they were not committed against enemy populations, were not traditional war crimes (ie what became the concept of crimes against humanity). Third, Bernays recommended the collective criminalisation of organisations including the SA, the SS, the Gestapo, the Nazi Government, and the Nazi Party.

Meanwhile, the Soviet lawyer, legal academic and head of the Soviet Extraordinary State Commission for the Investigation of German War Crimes, Professor Aron Trainin, put forward two further major innovations in the Soviet plan: trying the Germans for waging aggressive war (crimes against peace) and doing so with

---

[40] See, eg, Woetzel, *The Nuremberg Trials* (n 33) 17–39.

[41] ibid, 49–57.

[42] UNGA Res 95(I) (n 7).

[43] See International Law Commission (n 8). The Commentaries state at paragraph 96 that 'since the Nürnberg principles had been affirmed by the General Assembly, the task entrusted to the Commission ... was not to express any appreciation of these principles as principles of international law but merely to formulate them'.

[44] Secretary of War to Secretary of State, Annex: Trial of European War Criminals (memorandum dated 15 September 1944), 27 October 1944. See MC Bernays, 'Legal Basis of the Nuremberg Trials' (1946) 35 *Survey Graphic* 5; Smith, The American Road to Nuremberg (n 25).

premeditated brutality (crimes against the laws of war).[45] Bernays' proposals became the basis of the US plan for a war crimes trial[46] and the foundation for negotiations between Britain, the US, the Soviet Union and France for the establishment of an international tribunal. Together the proposals set the stage for the design of the Tribunal and its principles at the London Conference in Summer 1945.

D. Overview of the Proceedings

On 8 August 1945, following several months of negotiations, the Charter of the Tribunal was agreed in London by four nations (Britain, the US, the Soviet Union and France).[47] The London Agreement was ratified by 19 other states. It gave the Tribunal jurisdiction in respect of three substantive crimes (crimes against peace, war crimes, crimes against humanity), via two modes of responsibility: commission of a defined crime, regardless of superiority ('individual responsibility'), and 'common plan or conspiracy'. The offences appeared in Article 6 of the Charter as follows:

> The following acts, or any of them, are crimes coming within the jurisdiction of the Tribunal for which there shall be individual responsibility:
>
> (a) *'Crimes against peace'*: namely, planning, preparation, initiation or waging of a war of aggression, or a war in violation of international treaties, agreements or assurances, or participation in a common plan or conspiracy for the accomplishment of any of the foregoing.
>
> (b) *'War crimes'*: namely, violations of the laws or customs of war. Such violations shall include, but not be limited to, murder, ill-treatment or deportation to slave labour or for any other purpose of civilian population of or in occupied territory, murder or ill-treatment of prisoners of war or persons on the seas, killing of hostages, plunder of public or private property, wanton destruction of cities, towns or villages, or devastation not justified by military necessity.
>
> (c) *'Crimes against humanity'*: namely, murder, extermination, enslavement, deportation, and other inhumane acts committed against any civilian population, before or during the war, or persecutions on political, racial or religious grounds in execution of or in connection with any crime within the jurisdiction of the Tribunal, whether or not in violation of the domestic law of the country where perpetrated.

Article 6 went on to provide that criminal responsibility could arise from a conspiracy or common plan:

> Leaders, organizers, instigators and accomplices participating in the formulation or execution of a common plan or conspiracy to commit any of the foregoing crimes are responsible for all acts performed by any persons in execution of such plan.

Articles 7 and 8 respectively provided that the official position of a defendant could not be invoked in defence or mitigation, and that superior orders could be considered

---

[45] See AN Trainin and AY Vishinsky (eds), A Rothstein (tr), *Hitlerite Responsibility Under Criminal Law* (London, Hutchinson & Co, 1945).

[46] As approved at meeting at the Pentagon on 9 November 1944.

[47] See above (n 5).

not as a defence but as a mitigating factor in respect of punishment. Article 9 provided that:

At the trial of any individual member of any group or organization the Tribunal may declare (in connection with any act of which the individual may be convicted) that the group or organization of which the individual was a member was a criminal organization.

The Article allowed for an individual member of the organisation to apply to be heard on the question of its criminality.

Each of the four Allied powers named one judge and one alternate judge, eight judges in all.[48] Prosecutors were nominated from each of the four countries, including several leading lawyers. Among them were Jackson, a former Attorney-General and serving Supreme Court Justice, for the US, and Sir David Maxwell-Fyfe, assisting Sir Hartley Shawcross, for Britain. Assisting the British team was an Austro-Hungarian-born lawyer, then the Whewell Chair of International Law at the University of Cambridge, Hersch Lauterpacht. Lauterpacht was instrumental in drafting aspects of Article 6 of the Charter and in catalysing the recognition in international law of crimes against individuals. A Polish lawyer, Raphael Lemkin, also born in East Central Europe, travelled from Washington DC to Nuremberg where he clung to the periphery of the American team, but waged his own campaign: having failed to get the concept of genocide included in the Charter, he managed to get it inserted into the Indictment.[49]

Twenty-four accused were named on the Indictment[50] as having been charged with various combinations of the Charter crimes; 23 were arrested and 21 appeared at trial.[51] The trial began in Courtroom 600 at the Nuremberg Palace of Justice on 20 November 1945, and ran until 1 September 1946. The Tribunal handed down its Judgment on 30 September 1946; individual convictions and sentences were read out on 1 October 1946. Nineteen accused were convicted,[52] 12 sentenced to death and seven to prison sentences ranging from 10 years to life imprisonment. Ten accused were executed by hanging on 16 October 1946.[53] Martin Bormann, Hitler's private secretary, was never captured and was convicted and sentenced *in absentia*. Hermann Goering committed suicide in his cell by biting into a smuggled cyanide pill the night before he was due to be hanged.

---

[48] They were: Lord Justice Colonel Sir Geoffrey Lawrence, President of the Tribunal (United Kingdom); Sir Norman Birkett (British alternate); Francis Biddle (United States); John J Parker (American alternate); Professor Henri Donnedieu de Vabres (France); Robert Falco (French alternate); Major General Iona Nikitchenko (Soviet Union); Lieutenant Colonel Alexander Volchkov (Soviet alternate).

[49] Sands (n 16) 188–89.

[50] Nuremberg Trial Proceedings, Volume 1, Indictment, Defendants, [I].

[51] They were Hermann Göring, Karl Dönitz, Hans Frank, Wilhelm Frick, Hans Fritzsche, Walther Funk, Rudolf Hess, Alfred Jodl, Ernst Kaltenbrunner, Wilhelm Keitel, Konstantin von Neurath, Franz von Papen, Erich Raeder, Joachim von Ribbentrop, Alfred Rosenberg, Fritz Sauckel, Hjalmar Schacht, Baldur von Schirach, Arthur Seyss-Inquart, Albert Speer and Julius Streicher. Robert Ley, Head of the German Labour Front, committed suicide before the trial began. Gustav Krupp von Bohlen und Halbach, a leading industrialist, was found medically unfit for trial. Martin Bormann, Hitler's private secretary, was not captured and tried *in absentia*, as noted below.

[52] Fritzsche, von Papen and Schacht were acquitted.

[53] Frank, Frick, Jodl, Kaltenbrunner, Keitel, Ribbentrop, Rosenberg, Sauckel, Seyss-Inquart and Streicher.

III. LAWS FOR A NEW WORLD

A. Drafting the Charter

A second respect in which the Nuremberg trial constituted a landmark was its role in the conception and development of new substantive rules of international law. Alongside the design and establishment of the Tribunal itself, those who drafted the Nuremberg Charter made a number of formative contributions to substantive international law, which were applied in the Judgment of the Tribunal and created a legacy that shapes international criminal law today. The core contents of the Charter of the Tribunal, the opening and closing speeches and many of the legal and factual arguments made over the course of the proceedings, as well as the Tribunal's Judgment in 1946, enshrined soon thereafter by the UN General Assembly in the Nuremberg Principles,[54] changed the landscape and shaped the future direction of international law.

Of all the substantive innovations in the Charter, the drafting, use at trial, and subsequent development of the two most significant concepts are discussed in detail below: crimes against peace (Article 6(a)) and crimes against humanity (Article 6(c)). Also discussed is an international crime that did not make it into the Nuremberg Charter, but which nonetheless has been one of the most significant legacies of the trial: the crime of genocide, or acts intended to destroy groups.

From 26 June to 8 August 1945, representatives of the four victorious powers— the US, France, UK, and the Soviet Union—met in London to draft the Agreement and Charter that would establish the architecture of the Tribunal and the crimes to be tried. There was disagreement on the content of the Charter, and negotiations were difficult.

Some key individuals influenced the inclusion and articulation in the Charter of crimes against peace and crimes against humanity. Robert Jackson, then a former Attorney-General and US Supreme Court Justice known for championing individual liberties, was appointed as US chief counsel in May 1945, and proved a vigorous force during the negotiations on the Charter in London during Summer 1945.[55] Jackson described the Nuremberg Charter itself as 'something of a landmark, both as a substantive code defining crimes against the international community and also as an instrument establishing a procedure for prosecution and trial of such crimes before an international court'.[56] He saw as particularly significant the fact that the

---

[54] UNGA Res 95(I) (n 7).

[55] Sellars explains that he nearly walked out several times: (n 15), 84–85. As a prosecutor, Jackson was regarded as less effective than others in some respects: Telford Taylor recalls that he was criticised for his 'disappointing' cross-examination of Goering: Taylor, *Nuremberg and Vietnam* (n 11), 335–47. Maxwell-Fyfe wrote to his wife on 21 March 1946 about his own cross-examination of Goering: 'Jackson had not only made no impression but actually built up the fat boy further. I think I knocked him reasonably off his perch': A Topping, 'Bringing a Nazi to justice: how I cross-examined "fat boy" Göring', *The Guardian* (20 March 2009); correspondence of Sir David Maxwell-Fyfe available in The Papers of Lord Kilmuir, GBR/0014/KLMR, Churchill Archives Centre at the University of Cambridge. See further D Maxwell-Fyfe, *Political Adventure: The Memoirs of the Earl of Kilmuir* (London, Weidenfeld & Nicholson, 1964).

[56] Report of Robert H Jackson, United States Representative to the International Conference on Military Trials (Washington DC, US Government Printing Office, 1945) ('Jackson Report'), viii.

Charter resulted from the collective efforts of individuals from vastly different legal backgrounds:

> The significance of the charter's procedural provisions is emphasised by the fact that they represent the first tried and successful effort by lawyers from nations having profoundly different legal systems, philosophies, and traditions to amalgamate their ideas of fair procedure so as to permit a joint inquiry of judicial character into criminal charges.[57]

In negotiating the content of the Charter, Jackson, a pragmatist, relied little on legal theorising; but he did credit the advice and insights of Professor Lauterpacht, with whom he personally consulted in relation to both crimes against peace and crimes against humanity. Lauterpacht had by that time been appointed to the Whewell Chair of International Law at Cambridge. He was personally affected by the subject matter of the Nuremberg trial: his family remained in the ghettos of Zolkiew and Polish Lvov (formerly Lemberg, soon to become Soviet Lviv),[58] detained as Jews by the Nazis following Operation Barbarossa and placed under the governorship of Hans Frank, one of the Nuremberg accused.[59] With the exception of Lauterpacht's niece, Inka, they did not survive.[60]

Lauterpacht was engaged by the Foreign Office to work on Anglo-American matters, and in September 1945 was appointed to the British War Crimes Executive, charged with the preparation and presentation of the prosecution of German war criminals.[61] Jackson consulted Lauterpacht on the intricacies of drafting the Charter during the London Conference, and Lauterpacht was instrumental in advising on the terminology and format for the list of crimes. 'I do hope', Jackson wrote in May 1945, 'that we can get together and that I can have the benefit of your good judgment and learning on the difficult subjects with which we must deal'.[62] On 29 July 1945, Jackson visited Lauterpacht's house in Cranmer Road, Cambridge.[63] Elihu Lauterpacht recalled: 'It was at these meetings that Hersch put forward the idea of presenting the case against the major war criminals under three principal headings: crimes against the peace; war crimes; and crimes against humanity'.[64] That was almost exactly how they were reflected in the Charter.

As will be seen, of all the legal dilemmas faced by the drafters of the Charter, the question of retroactivity of crimes was perhaps the most challenging. In respect of crimes against peace and crimes against humanity, whether the delegates were codifying generally accepted principles of positive law or creating sources of criminal

---

[57]   ibid, viii–x, quoted in Mettraux, *Nuremberg Trial* (n 15) xiv.

[58]   Polish–Soviet Border Agreement, signed 16 August 1945, entry into force 5 February 1946.

[59]   Sands (n 17) 219–20.

[60]   ibid, 102–05, 299–301.

[61]   Sir Hartley Shawcross also drew extensively on Lauterpacht's expertise in preparing for Nuremberg, asking him to draft substantial sections of his speeches for both the opening and closing of the trial. Lauterpacht's drafts were published in full for the first time in H Lauterpacht, 'Draft Nuremberg Speeches' (2012) 1 *CJICL* 45.

[62]   Letter from Robert H Jackson to Hersch Lauterpacht (30 May 1945), quoted in E Lauterpacht, *The Life of Hersch Lauterpacht* (Cambridge, CUP, 2010) 272.

[63]   Lauterpacht (n 62) 271 fn 18, 272.

[64]   Jackson subsequently attributed this formulation to 'an eminent scholar of international law' (Jackson Report (n 56) 416), whom William E Jackson later identified as Lauterpacht: (n 62) 272 fn 20. See further on this point Sands (n 17) 110–11.

liability ex post facto was a vexed question. That the drafters engaged in some innovation is not in doubt, and is part of what makes Nuremberg so significant. In this respect, Nuremberg was a sign of things to come. The issue of retroactivity is an ongoing challenge in international criminal law today: even where the substantive law is established, it is problematic that many of the international tribunals (although not the ICC)[65] have been established during or after the events they are designed to charge and try.[66] In respect of individual accused, the willingness to overlook or de-emphasise the *nullum crimen sine lege* and *nulla poena sine lege* principles is a reflection of the wider tension between international criminal law and the right to a fair trial under international human rights law.

Tragically—some may say ironically[67]—the signing of the London Agreement was bookended by two cataclysmic acts of war. Two days beforehand, on 6 August 1945, the US dropped an atomic bomb on Hiroshima. Nagasaki followed one day after the signing, on 9 August 1945.

B. Crimes Against Peace

The term 'crimes against peace' derived from the work of Aron Trainin,[68] who attended the London Conference on behalf of the Soviet Union. The British negotiator, Lord Chancellor William Jowitt, suggested:

> I think Professor Trainin's book treats aggression not as the crime of war but as a crime against peace, and I do think that if you do have a nomenclature it would be well to have a nomenclature that comes from his book, and instead of calling it 'crime of war', call it 'crime against peace'.[69]

---

[65] As to which see Rome Statute of the International Criminal Court, UN Doc A/CONF 183/9, 2187 UNTS 90, opened for signature 17 July 1998, (entered into force 1 July 2002) ('Rome Statute'), Art 24.

[66] See, eg, D Luban, 'Fairness to Rightness: Jurisdiction, Legality, and the Legitimacy of International Criminal Law', in S Besson and J Tasioulas (eds), *The Philosophy of International Law* (Oxford, OUP, 2010) ch 28.

[67] Note the remarks of Justice Pal in dissent at the International Military Tribunal for the Far East regarding the Allied powers' use of the atomic bomb: 'History will say whether ... it has become legitimate by such indiscriminate slaughter to win the victory by breaking the will of the whole nation to continue to fight ... This policy of indiscriminate murder to shorten the war was considered to be a crime. In the Pacific war under our consideration, if there was anything approaching what is indicated in the above letter of the German Emperor, it is the decision coming from the Allied powers to use the bomb. Future generations will judge this dire decision ... It would be sufficient for my present purpose to say that if any indiscriminate destruction of civilian life and property is still illegitimate in warfare, then, in the Pacific war, this decision to use the atom bomb is the only near approach to the directives of the German Emperor during the first world war and of the Nazi leaders during the second world war': Pal's dissent was 1,235 pages long and is available at 'Dissentient Judgment of Justice RB Pal, Tokyo Tribunal' (12 November 1948) (Tokyo, Kokusho-Kankokai, 1999), at www.cwporter.com/pal10.htm. See also R Falk, 'The Shimoda Case: A Legal Appraisal of the Atomic Attacks Upon Hiroshima and Nagasaki' (1965) 59 AJIL 759; Y Tanaka and R Falk, 'The Atomic Bombing, The Tokyo War Crimes Tribunal and the Shimoda Case: Lessons for Anti-Nuclear Legal Movements' and Comment (2009) 44 *The Asia-Pacific Journal* 1, esp at 19; CL Blakesley, 'Acting out against terrorism, torture and other atrocious crimes: contemplating morality, law and history', in LN Sadat and MP Scharf, *The Theory and Practice of International Criminal Law: Essays in Honor of M. Cherif Bassiouni* (Leiden, Martinus Nijhoff, 2008) 164–67.

[68] Trainin and Vishinsky, *Hitlerite Responsibility* (n 45).

[69] Jackson Report (n 56) 416–17.

The question of retroactivity of crimes reared its head in relation to crimes against peace. Did a crime of waging aggressive war exist as a matter of customary international law at the time the Nazis invaded and instigated conflicts in countries across Europe, such that it could give rise to individual criminal responsibility and be made the subject of a criminal charge? And did it matter? If the principle was not so recognised, could it simply be asserted that the Charter was making new law which could legitimately be applied?

It was clear that, by the start of World War II, waging aggressive war was regarded as *unlawful* under international law, and that the Axis powers themselves had subscribed to this view, but it was not yet recognised as a source of individual criminal responsibility. Attempts to curtail the exercise by states of aggressive military force date back to antiquity, but the first codification of a prohibition on aggression at the international level was in the Covenant of the League of Nations, signed by its original parties at Versailles in 1919.[70] Following World War I, a Commission was formed by the Preliminary Peace Conference to consider the possible criminality of the acts that had provoked the conflict. The Commission concluded that deliberate violations of international law—specifically, breaches of binding treaty obligations—were culpable acts and, on that basis, recommended that the Conference formally condemn such acts. The Commission concluded, however, that no criminal charge could be laid against the responsible authorities or individuals, on the basis of institutional limitations and difficulties of proof, and thought it 'desirable that, for the future, penal sanctions should be provided for such grave outrages against the elementary principles of international law'.[71] As Lord Birkenhead, British Attorney-General, said at the time:

> It is necessary for all time to teach the lesson that failure is not the only risk which a man possessing at the moment in any country despotic powers and taking the awful decision between Peace and War, has to fear. If ever again that decision should be suspended in nicely balanced equipoise, at the disposition of an individual, let the ruler who decides upon war know that he is gambling, amongst other hazards, with his own personal safety.[72]

The Commission's recommendation went unheeded. In September 1927, the League of Nations published a Declaration Concerning Wars of Aggression, adopted by roll call of its members,[73] which included Germany, Italy and Japan. The Assembly noted its conviction that 'a war of aggression can never serve as a means of settling international disputes and is, in consequence, an international crime', and declared that 'all wars of aggression are, and shall always be, prohibited' and that 'the States

---

[70] *Treaty of Peace Between Allied and Associated Powers and Germany*, signed 28 June 1919 (entered into force 10 January 1920), Part 1. See further S Glaser, 'The Charter of the Nuremberg Tribunal and New Principles of International Law', in Mettraux (n 15); S Glueck, *The Nuremberg Trial and Aggressive War* (New York, Knopf, 1946) 25–34.

[71] 'Commission on the Responsibility of the Authors of the War and the Enforcement of Penalties' (1920) 14 *AJIL* 95, 118.

[72] D Lloyd George, *Memoirs of the Peace Conference* (New Haven, Yale University Press, 1939) 60.

[73] *Declaration Concerning Wars of Aggression*, Special Supplement No 53, *League of Nations Official Journal*, 22 (24 September 1927) 22. This document is reproduced as Document No 5 in BB Ferencz's work, *Defining International Aggression—The Search for World Peace* (Dobbs Ferry, Oceana Publications, 1975), vol 1, and available at www.derechos.org/peace/dia.

Members of the League are under an obligation to conform to these principles'.[74] In 1928, Germany, Italy and Japan were all original signatories to the Kellogg–Briand Pact,[75] declaring 'that they condemn recourse to war for the solution of international controversies, and renounce it as an instrument of national policy in their relations with one another'.[76] Germany had also concluded non-aggression treaties with numerous countries including England,[77] France,[78] the Soviet Union[79] and Poland.[80]

Despite, however, the ambiguous reference to 'an international crime', these instruments did not explicitly make aggression a source of individual, as opposed to state, responsibility which could be prosecuted under international law. If a law, it was a law without a sanction capable of being incurred by individuals. Lauterpacht had in the early 1940s expressed the view that the punishment by legal means of aggressive war was a social necessity:

> There appear to be compelling reasons for the establishment in the future of an International Criminal Court having jurisdiction to try the crime of war (i.e. resort to war in violation of international law) ... In this matter the position is now different from that which obtained in 1914 and which prompted the Commission of Responsibilities set up in 1919 by the Paris Conference to declare that 'by reason of the purely oppositional character of the institutions at The Hague for the maintenance of peace (International Commissions of Enquiry, Mediation and Arbitration) a war of aggression may not be considered as an act directly contrary to positive law.' The law of any international society worthy of the name must reject with approbation the view that between nations there can be no aggression calling for punishment. It must consider the responsibility for the premeditated violation of the General Treaty for the Renunciation of War as lying within the sphere of criminal law.[81]

Views of participants at the London Conference were split over whether the Charter could, or more to the point whether it should, declare that crimes against peace could attract individual criminal responsibility.[82] Jackson and the US delegation answered both questions firmly in the affirmative:

> International Law is more than a scholarly collection of abstract and immutable principles. It is an outgrowth of treaties or agreements between nations and of accepted customs ... Innovations and revisions in International Law are brought about by the action of

---

[74] ibid.

[75] General Treaty for Renunciation of War as an Instrument of National Policy, signed 27 August 1928, 94 LNTS 57 (entered into force 24 July 1929).

[76] ibid.

[77] German–British Non-Aggression Pact (30 September 1938).

[78] German–French Declaration ('Die deutsch-französische Erklärung') (6 December 1938).

[79] Molotov–Ribbentrop Pact (23 August 1939).

[80] German–Polish Non-Aggression Pact (26 January 1934).

[81] H Lauterpacht, 'The Law of Nations and the Punishment of War Crimes' (1944) 21 BYIL 58, 81 and fn 1; also published in E Lauterpacht (ed), *International Law: Collected Papers* (Cambridge, CUP, 2004), vol 5, 519 and fn 42.

[82] See S Glueck, 'The Nuernberg Trial and Aggressive War', in Mettraux (n 15), for an exposition of the positions by an attendee at the London Conference. Glueck, for his part, had not been convinced of the idea in 1944 but came around based on the argument that the Pact of Paris together with other treaties and resolutions was sufficiently developed custom: see ibid, fn 3.

governments designed to meet a change in circumstances. It grows, as did the Common-law, through decisions reached from time to time in adapting settled principles to new situations.[83]

Jackson therefore was 'not disturbed by the lack of precedent for the inquiry we propose to conduct'. In his view, by the time the Nazis came to power it was established that launching an aggressive war was illegal and the defence of legitimate warfare was unavailable. 'It is high time that we act on the juridical principle that aggressive war-making is illegal *and criminal*'.[84]

The French delegation had concerns, however, that designating aggression as a criminal charge was neither principled nor wise. On 19 July 1945, Professor André Gros voiced his objections to the American draft:

We do not consider as a criminal violation the launching of a war of aggression. If we declare war a criminal act of individuals, we are going farther than the actual law ... We do not want criticism in later years of punishing something that was not actually criminal ... It is said very often that a war of aggression is an international crime, as a consequence of which it is the obligation of the aggressor to repair the damages caused by his actions. But there is no criminal sanction ... We think it will turn out that nobody can say that launching a war of aggression is an international crime—you are actually inventing the sanction.[85]

Interestingly, Gros' objections derived at least in part from his belief that the parties were engaged in the building of a landmark, and that therefore the legal principles contained in the Charter must be robust. 'The statute of the International Tribunal will stand as a landmark which will be examined for many years to come', he said, 'and we want to try to avoid any criticisms'.[86]

Lauterpacht, as ever, analysed the applicable principles in detail, and in doing so assisted in assuaging the concerns about a lack of precedent. In his role on the British War Crimes Executive, he wrote to the Foreign Office after the signing of the Charter on 20 August 1945:

The main criticism which the Government will have to meet in this matter will be that [Article 6(a)] is an innovation. The paragraph which I am sending you shows that it is not so ... The General Treaty for the Renunciation of War not only rendered aggressive war unlawful; it <u>condemned</u> it and thus created the basis for a declaration that aggressive war is not only unlawful, but also criminal. It is very important that full use should be made in this connection of the General Treaty for the Renunciation of War—a universal treaty solemnly ascribed to by Germany, Italy and Japan. The legislative character, if any, of the Agreement of August 8, 1945, consists in the acceptance of the principle—which is an unavoidable principle if the law is not to be reduced to an absurdity—that the agency which commits a criminal act is not the abstract mystical entity of the State, but human beings who plan and execute the crime. There is, therefore, on sound principle no element of retroactivity either

---

[83] Jackson Report (n 56) 51–52.
[84] ibid, 52 (emphasis added). In a letter to Sir Stephen Schwebel in May 1999, Jackson's son William recalled that Lauterpacht agreed with this analysis when they consulted together in Cambridge. William Jackson had accompanied his father on the trip from London. 'The subject of discussion, as I recall, was whether a war of aggression was a crime under international law (which was central to my father's position during the London negotiations). I believe that Professor Lauterpacht shared and supported my father's position': quoted in Lauterpacht (n 62) 271 fn 18.
[85] Jackson Report (n 56) 295.
[86] ibid.

in expressly declaring an aggressive war to be a criminal act or in fixing that responsibility upon the individual human agents.[87]

Lauterpacht knew that convincing the Tribunal would not be easy. In drafting Shawcross's opening speech, Lauterpacht took care to demonstrate that the criminalisation of waging of aggressive war was 'not in any way an innovation'.[88] Lauterpacht devoted pages to identifying legal sources establishing the illegality of aggression, then again took the further step of arguing that the criminal prosecution of individuals for such conduct was not the retrospective operation of new law. Rather, it amounted to holding the individuals representing the 'controlling minds' of the state responsible, rather than permitting them to hide behind the 'veil' of the state. The mental energy Lauterpacht dedicated to this issue, however, demonstrates that the question exercised him greatly. When it came to Shawcross's closing speech, Lauterpacht was even more emphatic, asserting that, 'in a very real sense, the crime of war had become the parent of and the opportunity for the war crimes'.[89]

The Tribunal agreed. On 1 October 1946, in the Judgment, aggression was declared the 'supreme international crime'.[90] The Tribunal had preceded this assessment by describing the charges of planning and waging aggressive war as 'charges of the utmost gravity. War is essentially an evil thing. Its consequences are not confined to the belligerent States alone, but affect the whole world'.[91]

The legal theorist Hans Kelsen, who taught Lauterpacht in Vienna in the early 1920s, later reflected that it was the Charter, and not the Judgment, that created aggression as an international crime:

> The rules created by this Treaty and applied by the Nuremberg Tribunal, but not created by it, represent certainly a new law, especially by establishing individual criminal responsibility for violations of rules of international law prohibiting resort to war.[92]

The legacy created by the Charter and the Judgment in recognising the crime of aggression has reverberated through international legal history, and ultimately come full circle. It is striking that such significant advances, culminating in criminal convictions, were made at Nuremberg when, 50 years later, in negotiating the Rome Statute of the International Criminal Court, state parties still could not agree on the definition of the crime. Some states disputed whether the Court should have jurisdiction over aggression at all. As a compromise measure, it was agreed that aggression should be included in the Court's subject matter jurisdiction, but its definition, and the exercise by the Court of that jurisdiction, would be postponed.[93]

---

[87] Hersch Lauterpacht to Patrick Dean, Foreign Office legal adviser, 20 August 1945, quoted in Lauterpacht (n 62) 273.

[88] H Lauterpacht, *Draft Opening Speech—Part I* (typed foolscap, 1945) 17, quoted in P Sands, 'Twin Peaks: The Hersch Lauterpacht Draft Nuremberg Speeches' (2012) 1 *CJICL* 37, 39.

[89] H Lauterpacht, *Draft Closing Speech* (typed foolscap, 1946) 35, quoted in Sands, *Twin Peaks* (n 88) 41.

[90] Nuremberg Trial Proceedings, Volume 22, Day 217, 30 September 1946, 426.

[91] ibid.

[92] H Kelsen, 'Will the Judgment in the Nuremberg Trial Constitute a Precedent in International Law?', in Mettraux (n 15) 275.

[93] See discussion of the debates surrounding the inclusion of the crime of aggression in the Rome Statute in WA Schabas, *The International Criminal Court: A Commentary on the Rome Statute*, 2nd edn (Oxford, OUP, 2010) 303–05. Schabas notes that it was 'literally on the final day of the Conference,

That task was accomplished[94] at the Review Conference of the Rome Statute in May and June 2010, in Kampala, Uganda, within the framework established by the Assembly of States Parties to the Rome Statute. Stefan Barriga and Claus Kreß describe the mood amongst those individuals present on the final evening of the conference at Kampala on 11 June 2010:

> After two weeks of intense consultations, the endgame was as dramatic as anyone could have imagined. After the President of the Conference had tabled his last attempt to reach consensus shortly before midnight on the final day of the Conference, delegates held their breaths as one delegation raised its flag to voice a number of concerns. A collective sigh of relief filled the room as it became clear that, despite these concerns, no delegation was willing to stand in the way of consensus. Moments later, thunderous applause erupted as the President declared the Kampala compromise on the crime of aggression adopted. That night, the terrace of the vast Munyonyo Commonwealth Resort, with its splendid view of Lake Victoria, was transformed into the place where delegates from the world over celebrated the conclusion of an almost century-long process of trying to define the crime.[95]

The crime of aggression has thus been brought into the twenty-first century and defined to reflect modern warfare. But the conviction of individuals at Nuremberg for waging aggressive war is yet to be replicated. The amendments require two further conditions to be fulfilled for the International Criminal Court to exercise jurisdiction. The jurisdiction of the Court may begin one year after the 30th ratification of the amendment, but not before the Assembly of States Parties has approved the commencement of jurisdiction after 1 January 2017. While 32 states have now ratified the amendments, the approval of commencement of jurisdiction has yet to occur. In addition, the amendments only come into force for parties that have ratified the amendments. Germany has done so. Other powerful parties to the Rome Statute, including the United Kingdom, France, Canada, Japan, South Korea and Australia, have not. Non-party states, including the United States and Russia, as well as Israel, India and China, have chosen not be bound by principles similar to those that bound the German defendants at Nuremberg. The jurisdictional requirements for the prosecution of aggression, in Article 15 *bis* of the Rome Statute, have the effect that the ICC will only have jurisdiction over an act of aggression committed by a state party which has accepted that jurisdiction, and only when that act is also committed against a state party.[96]

[that] agreement was reached that authorized the Court to exercise jurisdiction over aggression once the crime was defined and its scope designated in a manner consistent with the purposes of the *Statute* and the ideals of the United Nations': 305.

[94] Article 8 *bis* of the Rome Statute now defines the crime of aggression as 'the planning, preparation, initiation or execution, by a person in a position effectively to exercise control over or to direct the political or military action of a State, of an act of aggression': (1). An 'act of aggression' is 'the use of armed force by a State against the sovereignty, territorial integrity or political independence of another State, or in any other manner inconsistent with the Charter of the United Nations': (2). Article 15 *bis* provides for jurisdiction over aggression. The Court will not exercise such jurisdiction over a State that has declared that it does not accept jurisdiction: (4) or a State that is not party to the Rome Statute: (5).

[95] S Barriga and C Kreß (eds), *The Travaus Préparatoires of the Crime of Aggression* (Cambridge, CUP, 2012) xv. See further C McDougall, *The Crime of Aggression under the Rome Statute* (Cambridge, CUP, 2013).

[96] See KJ Heller, 'The Sadly Neutered Crime of Aggression', *Opinio Juris* (13 June 2010) available at <http://opiniojuris.org/2010/06/13/the-sadly-neutered-crime-of-aggression>.

Despite the painstaking development of a complex legal framework over a period of a century, in which Nuremberg was undoubtedly a landmark, the legacy remains imperfect. It remains the fact that the instigators of wars that may be characterised as aggressive may never be prosecuted as such. In any event, even in addition to the restrictive jurisdictional requirements, the crime of aggression is likely to be very difficult to apply in practice. The idea that in every inter-state conflict one or both sides must be a wrongdoer is arguably unrealistic, when the concept of whether a war is legitimate is usually a subjective and partisan one.[97] Nor can it be said, in many cases, that a decision whether to go to war is 'suspended in nicely balanced equipoise',[98] even if ultimately the final decision is taken by an individual or a group of individuals.

C. Crimes Against Humanity

The concept of crimes against humanity, ultimately defined in Article 6(c) of the Charter, crystallised against the backdrop of the Charter's drafters being faced with the problem that traditional principles of international humanitarian law left a gap. 'War crimes' did not cover acts of atrocity committed by a state against its own people. Essentially, as Sir Hartley Shawcross explained in his closing speech during the trial, crimes against humanity were intended to cover atrocities 'which the Criminal Law of all countries would normally stigmatise as crimes: murder, extermination, enslavement, persecution on political, racial or economic grounds'[99] when committed against a civilian population, as well as discriminatory persecution of the kind that was rife during the Nazi regime. In substance, therefore, the crimes were similar to war crimes; but their legal foundation differed.

On the questions of legal innovation and retroactivity, it appears clear that the concept of individual criminal responsibility for crimes against humanity was novel. In older documents, the terms 'humanity', 'laws of humanity', 'dictates of human-ity' and the like had been used non-technically—for example, in the Fourth Hague Convention of 1907.[100] In May 1915, the Allies used the term in a joint declaration on the massacre of Armenians:

> In view of these new crimes of Turkey against humanity and civilization the Allied govern-ments announce publicly ... that they will hold personally responsible ... all members of the Ottoman government ... who are implicated in such massacres.[101]

The inclusion of the term in the Charter, however, marked its first appearance in an instrument of international law using the formulation 'crimes against humanity' as

---

[97] See, eg, the critical perspective offered by M Walzer, 'The Crime of Aggressive War' (2007) 6 *Washington University Global Studies Law Review* 635.

[98] See above (n 72).

[99] Nuremberg Trial Proceedings, Volume 19, Day 186, 26 July 1946, Transcript 470.

[100] Laws and Customs of War on Land (Hague IV) (18 October 1907), Preamble.

[101] United States Department of State, *Papers relating to the foreign relations of the United States, 1915, Supplement, The World War* (1915), Part IV: Other problems and responsibilities, 981, 'The Ambassador in France (Sharp) to the Secretary of State [Telegram], Paris, May 28, 1915'.

a source of individual criminal liability. In 1947, the principal French IMT judge, Professor Henri Donnedieu de Vabres, frankly observed in hindsight that, in contrast to war crimes, 'the concept of "crimes against humanity" is a new one. It had probably been conceptualised by some authors for a certain time, but only with the Nuremberg trial did this notion enter into judicial practice'.[102]

Lauterpacht was of a similar view, and (privately at least) did not seek to make a case against retroactivity. He explained to the Foreign Office that the concept of 'crimes against humanity' was 'clearly an innovation':

> It is a fundamental piece of international legislation affirming that international law is not only the law between States but also the law of mankind and that those who transgress against it cannot shield themselves behind the law of their State or the procedural limitations of international law ... It will be as well if the four Governments frankly admit that—notwithstanding the doctrine and the various historical instances of humanitarian intervention—all this is an innovation which the outraged conscience of the world and an enlightened conception of the true purposes of the law of nations impel them to make immediately operative.[103]

It will be recalled that Article 6(c) of the Charter defined crimes against humanity as 'murder, extermination, enslavement, deportation, and other inhumane acts committed against any civilian population, *before or during the war*, *or* persecutions on political, racial or religious grounds *in execution of or in connection with any crime within the jurisdiction of the Tribunal*' (emphasis added). The French and English texts of the Charter originally contained a semi-colon after the phrase 'before or during the war'. This was thought to create two different types of crimes against humanity, one encompassing any of the enumerated acts against a civilian population, and one comprising persecutions with a connection (or 'nexus') to crimes against peace, war crimes or common plan. As Lauterpacht explained, 'The principle part of paragraph (c), namely; its first sentence[104] is very wide indeed; it is not limited by the somewhat vague qualifications to which the crimes enumerated in the second sentence are subject'.[105] It was, however, later discovered that the Russian text contained a comma in place of the semi-colon in the definition, creating a drafting ambiguity as to whether the 'nexus' requirement applied to the whole of Article 6(c), or only to its second phrase.[106] On 6 October 1945, the prosecutors from all four nations signed the Berlin Protocol agreeing that the Russian text was correct.[107]

---

[102] H Donnedieu de Vabres, 'The Nuremberg Trials and the modern principles of international criminal law' in Mettraux (n 15) 227. Egon Schwelb, in 'Crimes against Humanity' (1946) 23 *BYIL* 178, 179, similarly described crimes against humanity as a 'novel' concept in law, while Hannah Arendt, writing after the trial in Israel of Adolf Eichmann, called it 'new and unprecedented': *Eichmann in Jerusalem: A Report on the Banality of Evil* (first published 1963; New York, Penguin, 2006) 255, 257.

[103] Letter from Hersch Lauterpacht to Patrick Dean, FO371/51034 (20 August 1945), quoted in Lauterpacht (n 62) 274.

[104] It may have been that Lauterpacht meant the first 'phrase' of Article 6(c), before the semi-colon, rather than the first sentence, as Article 6(c) did not contain more than one sentence.

[105] Letter from Hersch Lauterpacht to Patrick Dean, FO371/51034 (20 August 1945), quoted in Lauterpacht (n 62) 274.

[106] For a full discussion of this issue see C Fournet, *Genocide and Crimes Against Humanity: Misconceptions and Confusion in French Law and Practice* (Oxford, Hart, 2013) 21–22.

[107] Berlin Protocol signed on 6 October 1945, available at <http://avalon.law.yale.edu/imt/jack61.asp>.

Nevertheless, the Indictment, signed on the same day, charged crimes pursuant to Article 6(c) under two headings. Part X(A) mirrored the language of the first phrase of Article 6(c): 'murder, extermination, enslavement, deportation, and other inhumane acts committed against civilian populations *before and during the war*' (emphasis added) in relation to civilians believed to be hostile or potentially hostile to the Nazis, including the operation of concentration camps since 1933.[108] Part X(B) mirrored the second phrase, charging 'persecution on political, racial, and religious grounds *in execution of and in connection with the common plan mentioned in count one*' (emphasis added) in relation to the Jews, including internment at concentration camps, murder and ill-treatment, also dating back to 1933. This bipartite division of the concept, with nexus to the common plan applying only to the second part, would suggest that the Allies did not intend at an early stage for the nexus requirement to apply to the whole of Article 6(c), or to exclude crimes occurring before 1939 from the jurisdiction of the Tribunal. It is unlikely, however, that the parties would have gone to the effort to sign the Berlin Protocol for the sake of a comma if they had not considered that it altered the scope of Article 6(c).[109]

Ultimately, the Tribunal found the charges of crimes against humanity substantiated. It declined, however, to find that crimes against humanity were carried out before the war, in the years between 1933 and 1939, because it interpreted the nexus requirement in the second phrase of Article 6(c) as applying to the whole paragraph. The Tribunal observed that:

> To constitute crimes against humanity, the acts relied on before the outbreak of war *must have been in execution of, or in connection with, any crime within the jurisdiction of the Tribunal*. The Tribunal is of the opinion that revolting and horrible as many of these crimes were, it has not been satisfactorily proved that they were done in execution of, or in connection with, any such crime. The Tribunal therefore cannot make a general declaration that the acts before 1939 were crimes against humanity within the meaning of the Charter.[110]

Nonetheless, the Tribunal went on to make the first findings of crimes against humanity, stating that

> from the beginning of the war in 1939 war crimes were committed on a vast scale, which were also crimes against humanity; and insofar as the inhumane acts charged in the Indictment, and committed after the beginning of the war, did not constitute war crimes, they were all committed in execution of, or in connection with, the aggressive war, and therefore constituted crimes against humanity.[111]

The significance of the convictions for crimes against humanity was later identified by Hannah Arendt, in her Epilogue to *Eichmann in Jerusalem: The Banality of Evil*.[112]

---

[108] Nuremberg Trial Proceedings, Volume 1, Indictment, Count Four—Crimes Against Humanity.

[109] For a contemporaneous view see E Schwelb, 'Crimes Against Humanity' (1946) 23 *BYIL* 178; see also the extensive analysis in M Cherif Bassiouni, *Crimes Against Humanity in International* Law, 2nd edn (Kluwer Law International, 1999) 25–30.

[110] Nuremberg Judgment (n 6) 'The Law Relating to War Crimes and Crimes Against Humanity', available at <http://avalon.law.yale.edu/imt/judlawre.asp>.

[111] ibid.

[112] Arendt (n 102).

There, she argued that while the Nuremberg judges appeared more comfortable with convicting the accused of the more readily recognisable war crimes, they reserved crimes against humanity for the most egregious cases. Arendt added: 'they revealed their true sentiment by meting out their most severe punishment, the death penalty, only to those who had been found guilty of those quite uncommon atrocities that actually constituted a "crime against humanity"'.[113] Indeed, without exception, all those sentenced to death had been convicted of crimes against humanity.[114] This priority given to protecting individuals including German citizens as well as those of other nationalities was what Schwelb later described as a 'radical inroad ... into the sphere of the domestic jurisdiction of sovereign states'.[115]

The single most significant development in the concept of crimes against humanity since Nuremberg has been its liberation from the 'nexus' requirement linking it to armed conflict.[116] In fact, the requirement was not mentioned in Allied Control Council Law No 10, under which the Allies supervised the subsequent trials of lower-level functionaries and private citizens before the Nuremberg Military Tribunals from 1946 to 1949.[117] In 1947, the UN General Assembly requested the International Law Commission to draft a code of offences against the peace and security of mankind based on the Nuremberg Principles. The Draft Code was not completed for 50 years, but significantly, its 1996 iteration omitted the requirement for inhumane acts to be committed 'before or during the war'.[118] While the Statute of the International Criminal Tribunal for the former Yugoslavia retained a requirement that crimes against humanity be committed 'within armed conflict',[119] whether international or non-international, the Statute of the International Criminal Tribunal for Rwanda omitted the formal nexus with armed conflict but instead required that the inhumane acts must be part of a 'systematic or widespread attack against any civilian population on national, political, ethnic, racial or religious grounds'.[120] The Rome Statute similarly mandates that 'murder, extermination, torture, rape,

---

[113] ibid, 257.

[114] The converse was almost true: with only a few exceptions, a conviction of crimes against humanity resulted in a death sentence. The exceptions were Walther Funk (life imprisonment), Baron Konstantin von Neurath (15 years), Baldur von Schirach (20 years) and Albert Speer, the only defendant to plead guilty (20 years).

[115] Schwelb, 'Crimes Against Humanity' (n 109) 179.

[116] K Ambos and S Wirth, 'The current law of Crimes against Humanity: an analysis of UNTAET Regulation 15/2000' (2002) 13 Criminal Law Forum 1, 3–13; Antonio Cassese, International Law (2nd edn, Oxford, OUP, 2005), 442; and see generally Beth van Schaack, 'The Definition of Crimes against Humanity: Resolving the incoherence' (1998) 37 Columbia Journal of Transnational Law 787.

[117] Allied Control Council Law No 10, Article II(1)(c).

[118] International Law Commission, Draft Code of Crimes against the Peace and Security of Mankind with commentaries (1996), adopted by the International Law Commission at its 48th session, in 1996, and submitted to the General Assembly as a part of the Commission's report covering the work of that session [50]. The report, which also contains commentaries on the draft articles, appears in (1996) ILC Ybk, vol II, Part Two.

[119] UN Security Council, Statute of the International Criminal Tribunal for the Former Yugoslavia (as amended), 25 May 1993 (as established by UNSC Res 808/1993, 827/1993 and amended by UNSC Res 1166/1998, 1329/2000, 114/2002) ('ICTY Statute'), Art 5.

[120] UN Security Council, Statute of the International Criminal Tribunal for Rwanda (as amended), 8 November 1994 (as established by UNSC Res 955 (1994) of 8 November 1994 and last amended by UNSC Res 1717 (2006) of 13 October 2006) ('ICTR Statute'), Art 3.

political, racial, or religious persecution and other inhumane acts' reach the threshold of crimes against humanity only if they are 'part of a widespread or systematic attack directed against any civilian population'.[121]

While crimes against humanity are not yet the subject of their own specific convention (the ILC is currently elaborating a draft convention under the stewardship of Professor Sean Murphy),[122] their flexibility has enabled them to embrace developing conceptions of inhumanity, such as torture, rape and sexual assault.[123] Although protections against gender-based violence were not a feature at Nuremberg,[124] they have become a fundamental aspect of modern international humanitarian and criminal law, which Lauterpacht's conception of crimes against humanity has been sufficiently wide to embrace. As David Luban has put it, the phrase 'has acquired enormous resonance in the legal and moral imaginations of the post–World War II world' in two senses, being crimes that aggrieve all human beings as well as violating the core value of our shared humanity.[125] In May 1999, Serbian President Slobodan Milošević became the first serving head of state to be indicted for crimes against humanity, for alleged acts in Kosovo. In April 2012, Charles Taylor was the first head of state to be convicted of crimes against humanity. A few months later he was sentenced to 50 years in prison.

The unshackling of crimes against humanity has not only allowed for successful prosecutions, but has gone further. For example, in 2013 the UN Human Rights Council established a Commission of Inquiry on Human Rights in the Democratic People's Republic of Korea.[126] The Commission's mandate was to investigate 'systematic, widespread and grave violations of human rights ... with a view to ensuring full accountability, in particular where these violations may amount to crimes against humanity'.[127] In its final report in 2014, the Commission considered that

---

[121] Rome Statute (n 65), Art 7.

[122] At its 66th session in 2014, the International Law Commission decided to include 'crimes against humanity' in its programme of work, and to appoint Professor Sean Murphy as Special Rapporteur for the topic: Report of the International Law Commission, 66th session (5 May–6 June and 7 July–8 August 2014), UN GAOR, 69th session, Supplement No 10, UN Doc A/69/10, Ch XIV, s A.1. For a summary of the Commission's ongoing work on crimes against humanity, with links to the relevant texts and instruments, see ILC, Summaries of the Work of the International Law Commission, Crimes against humanity, available at <http://legal.un.org/ilc/summaries/7_7.shtml>.

[123] Although the concept of crimes against humanity in the Charter did not refer to gender-based crimes, it has in later years become a useful tool for prosecuting them. Allied Control Council Law No 10 outlawed rape as a crime against humanity (Art II(1)(c)), though no rapes were prosecuted. Note the resolution adopted by UN Security Council in 2008, which noted that 'rape and other forms of sexual violence can constitute war crimes, crimes against humanity or a constitutive act with respect to genocide': UNSC Res 1820, UN SCOR, 63rd session, UN Doc S/Res/1820 (19 June 2008), [18].

[124] Indeed, there were hardly any women present at Nuremberg, the notable exception being Katherine B Fite, a US lawyer who was involved in the preparations for and proceedings of the IMT. See generally JQ Barrett, 'Katherine B Fite: The Leading Female Lawyer at London & Nuremberg, 1945' (Paper presented at the Robert H Jackson Third Annual International Humanitarian Law Dialogs, Chautauqua Institution, 31 August 2009). Katherine Fite was the staff lawyer who travelled with Jackson to meet Lauterpacht in Cambridge on 29 July 1945: Sands (n 17) 111.

[125] David Luban, 'A Theory of Crimes Against Humanity', (2004) 29 *Yale JIL* 85, 86.

[126] Human Rights Committee, *Situation of human rights in the Democratic People's Republic of Korea*, 22nd session, UN Doc A/HRC/RES/22/13 (9 April 2013).

[127] ibid [5].

its basic factual findings (including findings of murder, rape, forced disappearances, population transfers, persecution, and the particular inhumane act of knowingly causing prolonged starvation) could constitute reasonable grounds establishing the commission of crimes against humanity, warranting domestic or international criminal investigation.[128] The Commission's conclusions demonstrate the existence of a widespread and systematic attack on the civilian population, the relevant conduct occurring throughout and beyond the DPRK over an extended period, and being perpetrated 'pursuant to policies established at the highest level of the State'.[129]

As the experience of the Commission shows, the absence of a war nexus requirement raises violations of basic human rights to a level equal with that of breaches of humanitarian law. The concept of crimes against humanity permits a state to be held responsible for grave failures in upholding the human rights of its own nationals, even in times of peace. Despite Nuremberg's more conservative approach, the articulation of crimes against humanity in the Charter and in the Judgment were crucial precursors to these more modern developments.

D. Genocide

Today, the mass killing of Jews, gypsies, Poles, homosexuals, and other minorities in the Holocaust, broadly defined, is the most obvious and frequently cited example of what we now regard as genocide. Yet the astute reader will note that genocide was not one of the crimes enumerated in the Nuremberg Charter, and nor was it mentioned in the Tribunal's Judgment. An analysis of Nuremberg's significance and legacy, however, would not be complete without making mention of the crime of genocide.

The recognition of genocide was initially an individual project. At and around the time of Nuremberg, genocide was the sole obsession of one individual, Raphael Lemkin. Born in what is now Belarus, Lemkin, like Lauterpacht, studied law at the University of Lwow where be obtained a doctorate in criminal law. He then worked as a public prosecutor in Warsaw.[130] At a conference in Madrid in 1933, his first paper was circulated, proposing that a new international law was needed to prohibit barbarism and repression against racial and religious groups.[131] Lemkin cited examples: the Huguenots in France; the Protestants in Bohemia; the Hottentots in German West Africa; the Armenians in Turkey. He also warned about Hitler's recent rise to power in Germany.

---

[128] Human Rights Committee, *Report of the commission of inquiry on human rights in the Democratic People's Republic of Korea*, 25th session, UN Doc A/HRC/RES/25/63 (7 February 2014), [74].

[129] ibid [75].

[130] R Lemkin and D-L Frieze (ed), *Totally Unofficial: The Autobiography of Raphael Lemkin* (New Haven, Yale UP, 2013) 20–21. See generally D Irvin-Erickson, *Raphael Lemkin and the Concept of Genocide* (Philadelphia, University of Pennsylvania Press, 2017); JQ Barrett, 'Raphael Lemkin and "Genocide" at Nuremberg', in C Safferling and E Conze, *The Genocide Convention Sixty Years After Its Adoption* (The Hague, Asser, 2010); J Cooper, *Raphael Lemkin and the Struggle for the Genocide Convention* (New York, Palgrave Macmillan, 2008); S Power, *'A Problem from Hell': America and the Age of Genocide* (New York, Basic Books, 2002).

[131] Sands (n 17) 157, 175.

In the early 1940s, Europe was in the grips of what Churchill described as 'the crime without a name'.[132] Lemkin escaped Europe as an academic refugee, taking up a post at Duke University in North Carolina, USA, carrying with him suitcases full of Nazi decrees and ordinances which he believed showed Hitler's underlying aims. Lemkin's analysis of German rule in occupied countries, *Axis Rule in Occupied Europe*, was published in November 1944.[133] In Chapter IX, he named the crime 'genocide', defined as the 'extermination of racial and religious groups'.[134] In Summer 1945, he was appointed as an advisor to the War Department and to Robert Jackson.

Lemkin's ideas were controversial and were resisted by the legal teams at Nuremberg, for both legal and political reasons. Lauterpacht considered the crime of genocide to be unsupported by past practice, and had previously been rather dismissive of Lemkin's work.[135] In the US, conservatives were anxious about whether African-Americans could invoke the term 'genocide' to seek redress from the state.[136] British and other colonial powers may well have had the same concerns about past acts directed at the elimination or assimilation of cultural groups.[137]

Lemkin campaigned for the German leaders to be charged with the crime of 'genocide', but was disappointed to learn late in the summer that the Nuremberg Charter made no reference to the word. But, having flown to London to press for

---

[132] *BBC*, 'Prime Minister Winston Churchill's broadcast to the world about the meeting with President Roosevelt' (24 August 1941), available at www.ibiblio.org/pha/policy/1941/410824a.html.

[133] Cited by the International Court of Justice when defining the protected group in *Application of the Convention on the Prevention and Punishment of the Crime of Genocide (Bosnia and Herzegovina v Serbia and Montenegro)* (2007) *ICJ Reports* 43, [193].

[134] Sands (n 17) 179.

[135] ibid, 107, 108.

[136] Obstructionism also from conservatives prevented Congress's assent to the Genocide Convention in 1948: DT Critchlow and N MacLean, *Debating the American Conservative Movement: 1945 to the Present* (Lanham MD, Rowman & Littlefield, 2009), 138. Similar tactics had been used in relation to the inclusion of a non-discrimination clause in the Universal Declaration of Human Rights: A de Conde, *Ethnicity, Race, and American Foreign Policy: A History* (New Hampshire, UPNE, 1992) 129. Such fears proved to some degree well founded as, between 1946 and 1951, three American civil rights organisations directly petitioned the UN to obtain assistance in combatting racial discrimination in the United States. The third petition, submitted by the Civil Rights Congress in 1951, made specific allegations based on the newly adopted Genocide Convention that each level of US administration, from local to federal, was engaged in genocide against the black populace: see CH Martin, 'Internationalizing "the American dilemma": the Civil Rights Congress and the 1951 Genocide Petition to the United Nations' (1997) 16 *Journal of American Ethnic History* 35, 36. Nonetheless, redress was not forthcoming.

[137] See discussion of these objections in M Lewis, *The Birth of the New Justice: The Internationalization of Crime and Punishment, 1919–1950* (Oxford, OUP, 2014), 202–03. Indeed, Lemkin had conducted a detailed case study of the Tasmanian Aboriginal peoples as part of an unfinished work on genocide written in the 1940s–50s: see generally A Curthoys, 'Raphael Lemkin's "Tasmania": An Introduction' in D Moses and D Stone (eds), *Colonialism and Genocide* (Abingdon, Routledge, 2013). Nonetheless, prior to the UK's ratification of the Genocide Convention (delayed by concerns about the extradition obligation under Art 7), the British Conservative Government felt no qualms in 'giving an unqualified assurance that Her Majesty's Government would never themselves violate the principles embodied in the Convention': United Kingdom, *Parliamentary Debates*, House of Commons, 18 July 1962, 423–4 (Edward Heath). Similarly, despite advertence to Genocide Convention's applicability to treatment of indigenous peoples, it was apparently not considered at the time of Australia's ratification that the Genocide Convention might be relied upon by its Aboriginal and Torres Strait Islander peoples: Commonwealth, *Parliamentary Debates*, Senate, 6 July 1949, 2004–05 (Reginald Murray).

the inclusion of 'genocide' in the Nuremberg Indictment, Lemkin was in the end successful.[138] Count Three of the Indictment, on war crimes, under the heading 'Murder and ill-treatment of civilian populations of or in occupied territory and on the high seas', stated as follows:

> Throughout the period of their occupation of territories overrun by their armed forces the defendants, for the purpose of systematically terrorizing the inhabitants, murdered and tortured civilians, and ill-treated them, and imprisoned them without legal process.

> The murders and ill-treatment were carried out by divers means ... [The defendants] *conducted deliberate and systematic genocide, viz, the extermination of racial and national groups*, against the civilian populations of certain occupied territories in order to destroy particular races and classes of people and national, racial, or religious groups, particularly Jews, Poles, and Gypsies and others.

In the closing arguments for each of the prosecuting states at the end of the trial, the concept of 'genocide' was again used by the Soviet, French and British lawyers.[139] All three states supported a conviction for genocide. Sir Hartley Shawcross's closing speech,[140] as drafted by Lauterpacht, did not mention the word. Nor did Robert Jackson in his closing speech for the US. Nor, in the end, did the Tribunal's Judgment. Lemkin later recorded the day of the Judgment as 'the blackest' of his life.[141]

Lemkin redoubled his efforts before the United Nations. By the end of 1946, he had convinced the General Assembly to pass a resolution recognising genocide as a crime under international law.[142] His efforts eventually led to the adoption of the Genocide Convention at the UN on 9 December 1948.[143] Article 2 defines genocide as 'any of the following acts committed with intent to destroy, in whole or in part, a national, ethnical, racial or religious group', namely, killings, serious bodily or mental harm, deliberately inflicting conditions of life calculated to cause physical destruction, preventing births and forcibly transferring children. In 1951, the ICJ confirmed that the Convention has *jus cogens* force.[144]

In this respect, Nuremberg is a landmark not in the sense of being the site of recognition of the crime of genocide, but as a gateway to recognition. Nuremberg saw the first mention of 'genocide' in a formal international legal document, the

---

[138] In his unpublished autobiography, Lemkin speaks of having gone to London in 1945, as the Nuremberg Charter was concluded, and 'succeeded in having inscribed the charge of genocide against the Nazi war criminals in Nuremberg. Everything seemed to progress successfully with the genocide charge against the Nazis until things started to be spoiled at Nuremberg': R Lemkin, 'Totally Unofficial Man' in S Totten and SL Jacobs (eds), *Pioneers of Genocide Studies* (New Brunswick, New Jersey, Transaction Publishers, 2013) 375.

[139] Nuremberg Trial Proceedings, Volume 19, Day 186, 26 July 1946, Transcript 493, 496, 497, 508, 514 (Sir Hartley Shawcross); 530, 549, 550, 561, 563 (Auguste Champetier de Ribes); 569 (General Roman Rudenko).

[140] ibid, Transcript 432–528.

[141] W Korey, *An Epitaph for Raphael Lemkin* (New York, Jacob Blaustein Institute for the Advancement Human Rights, 2001) 25.

[142] *The Crime of Genocide*, UNGA Res 96(1), UN GAOR, 6th Comm, 1st session, UN Doc A/RES/96(I) (11 December 1946). Lemkin described the process of getting the resolution before the UN General Assembly in 'Genocide as a Crime under International Law' (1947) 41 *AJIL* 145, 148–50.

[143] *Convention on the Prevention and Punishment of the Crime of Genocide*, opened for signature 9 December 1948, 78 UNTS 277 (entered into force 12 January 1951).

[144] *Reservations to the Genocide Convention (Advisory Opinion)* (1951) *ICJ Reports* 15, 23.

Nuremberg Indictment. The proceedings raised the profile of the concept of genocide on the international stage. Somewhat paradoxically, its necessity was affirmed by the gap left in the Nuremberg Judgment by linking crimes against humanity to aggressive war or war crimes: acts directed at the extermination of groups during peacetime were excluded, as pointed out by Lemkin in an article for the *United Nations Bulletin*.[145] Again the determination of an individual and his ability to influence others both at Nuremberg and before other bodies on the international stage (albeit in a way that was not always entirely welcome), was critical in the development of international law.

The legacy of Nuremberg, and of Lemkin, has been in recognition rather than prevention of genocide. In the intervening period, there have been what have been recognised in law as more genocides (Rwanda, Bosnia, Cambodia, Darfur). While the Nuremberg defendants were not convicted of genocide, others have been. In 1968, Adolf Eichmann was convicted under an Israeli law reflecting the Convention definition of genocide.[146] The International Criminal Tribunal for Rwanda (ICTR) in *Akayesu*[147] handed down the first genocide verdict in modern international criminal law, and recognised for the first time that mass rape could amount to genocide. This was followed in the International Criminal Tribunal for the former Yugoslavia (ICTY) by the convictions of Radislav Krstić in 2004 for aiding and abetting genocide[148] and of Radovan Karadžić in 2016 for committing genocide as part of a joint criminal enterprise.[149] In September 2007, the International Court of Justice in The Hague ruled[150] that Serbia had violated the obligation to prevent genocide in Srebrenica. This was the first time that a state has been condemned for violating the Genocide Convention. In July 2010, President Omar al-Bashir of Sudan became the first serving Head of State to be indicted for genocide by the ICC.

Of course, genocide has been the subject of critique. The post-Nuremberg emancipation of crimes against humanity from the requirement of a nexus to armed conflict means that any act that meets the definition of genocide is also now likely to constitute a crime against humanity, whether committed in time of war or peace. Arguably this does not create total overlap or make genocide redundant, as the reverse is not true: the specific *mens rea* for genocide makes it notoriously difficult to establish.[151]

---

[145] Korey, *Epitaph for Raphael Lemkin* (n 141).

[146] *Attorney-General v Eichmann* (1968) 36 ILR 5 (District Court of Jerusalem), para 80. Section 1(b) of the *Nazis and Nazi Collaborators (Punishment) Law 1950* 4 LSI 154 (Isr) is drafted to reflect the definition in Art 2 of the Genocide Convention, but is slightly wider than that insofar as it also includes destroying or desecrating Jewish religious or cultural assets or values, and inciting hatred of Jews. The *Eichmann* court observed, however, that those subsections had no relevance to his case: [16].

[147] *Prosecutor v Akayesu*, Trial Judgment (ICTR-96-4-T), 2 September 1998. This conviction was not disturbed on appeal.

[148] Judgment, *Prosecutor v Krstić*, Appeal Judgment (IT-98-33-A), 19 April 2004. Krstić had been convicted at trial of committing genocide as part of a joint criminal enterprise. However, his appeal against that finding was successful, leading to a substituted conviction on the accessorial basis of aiding and abetting.

[149] *Prosecutor v Karadžić*, Trial Judgment (IT-95-5/18-T), 24 March 2016.

[150] *Application of the Convention on the Prevention and Punishment of the Crime of Genocide (Bosnia and Herzegovina v Serbia and Montenegro)* (2007) ICJ Reports 43.

[151] See, eg, *Application of the Convention on the Prevention and Punishment of the Crime of Genocide (Croatia v Serbia)* (2008) ICJ Reports 412.

Its characterisation, however, as 'the crime of crimes',[152] which is singled out for 'special condemnation' by international courts,[153] regularly leaves victims of atrocities feeling cheated if they can make out only a 'lesser' offence, and risks devaluing other international crimes. Ultimately, however, genocide has been absorbed into the canon of international criminal law along with the fundamental principles established at the Nuremberg trial.

IV. CONCLUSIONS

Writing about the meaning of Nuremberg as a landmark, Secretary Stimson said:

> A single landmark of justice and honor does not make a world of peace ... But the sins of others do not make the Nazi leaders less guilty, and the importance of Nuremberg lies not in any claim that by itself it clears the board, but rather in the pattern it has set.[154]

Those words, written 70 years ago, are no less true today. Nuremberg was, from a legal perspective at least, a moment of crystallisation following a period of unspeakable horrors. In the context of the early plans for summary executions, it was notable that the Nuremberg trial occurred at all. Courtroom 600 is rightly regarded as the birthplace of the modern system of international criminal justice: the conception of a novel (if not entirely unprecedented) kind of international court, a fresh legal jurisdiction, and a new way of holding to account some of those responsible for atrocities against both individuals and groups, albeit in a way that was lopsided and left unpunished certain other crimes—including those committed by the Allies. Nuremberg reflects the marriage of pragmatism and principle. It has not altered the reality of war and law; attempts to deliver post-conflict justice remain flawed, insufficient and uneven. What Nuremberg did achieve was to set a framework or expectation that the consequences of conflict could be dealt with in a particular way, according to what are now recognised as fundamental international principles. Those principles have been deployed time and again, and have developed in ways that were not anticipated at the time of their conception.

The example set by Nuremberg would stand alone for 50 years before bearing fruit, but would ultimately be taken up in successor tribunals of various forms. The tribunals for the former Yugoslavia, Rwanda, Sierra Leone, Cambodia and Lebanon have drawn on the Nuremberg model in crafting hybrid jurisdictional arrangements.[155] In July 1998, more than 150 states adopted the Statute for an International Criminal Court. These tribunals have indicted, convicted and

---

[152] *Prosecutor v Kambanda*, Judgment and Sentence (ICTR-97-23-S), 4 September 1998, [16].

[153] *Krstić* (n 148) [36].

[154] Stimson (n 12) 188.

[155] ICTY Statute (n 119); ICTR Statute (n 120); UN Security Council, Statute of the Special Court for Sierra Leone, 16 January 2002; United Nations, Agreement between the United Nations and the Royal Government of Cambodia Concerning the Prosecution under Cambodian Law of Crimes Committed During the Period of Democratic Kampuchea, 6 June 2003; UN Security Council, Security Council resolution 1757 (2007) on the establishment of a Special Tribunal for Lebanon, UN Doc S/RES/1757 (30 May 2007).

sentenced some former and sitting heads of state. There is no doubt, however, that the institutional legacy of Nuremberg remains flawed and unevenly applied. The notion of lopsided justice—a system used by the strong against the weak—is hard to refute. In a statement to the press on 9 August 1945, Robert Jackson said: 'however unfortunate it may be, there seems no way of doing anything about the crimes against peace or against humanity except that the victors judge the vanquished'.[156] That observation, and its legacy, perpetuates today.[157]

As well as Nuremberg's contribution as a matter of substantive law, it has been an underpinning theme of this chapter that one of the key features of the Nuremberg trial was its recognition of individuals as subjects, as well as authors, of international law.[158] As seen in this chapter, the contributions of certain key individuals, rather than the anonymous acts of states, shaped the definition of crimes and the course of the trial, and ultimately mapped the landscape of international law.

As subjects of that law, individuals are given rights and obligated to abide by certain responsibilities, the breach of which results in criminal liability. Nuremberg established that rampant individualism, and the subordination of the group to the whims and totalitarian agenda of one individual, will be a matter of concern to the whole international community. As confirmed by Articles 7 and 8 of the Charter, the individual cannot hide from responsibility for his acts on the grounds that they were authorised by a state or by the order of a superior. The ruling of the Tribunal assisted in chipping away at the invincibility of the state as the supreme being of international law, concluding that '[c]rimes against international law are committed by men, not by abstract entities and only by punishing individuals who commit such crimes can the provisions of international law be enforced'.[159]

We might ask whether the concept of individual criminal liability in international law has been taken too far. Over-emphasis on individual criminal liability may obscure egregious acts of states committed by arms of government that cannot be pinned to one particular individual, or which may be more systemic. All three crimes analysed in this chapter illustrate the underlying paradox that, although they are the subjects of individual criminal responsibility, in reality they are generally committed only pursuant to some form of collective deliberation, related to either a 'widespread and systematic attack', an 'intent to destroy, in whole or in part, a group', or 'the planning, preparation, initiation or execution of an act of aggression' of sufficient character, gravity and scale to constitute a manifest violation of the UN Charter.[160]

---

[156] 'The Texts of the War Crimes Committee Report and the Jackson Statement' *New York Times* (9 August 1945).

[157] See, eg, D Zolo, *Victors' Justice: From Nuremberg to Baghdad* (London, Verso, 2009); F Barr Lebo, 'Proposing a new framework: Including China on the crossroads of transitional justice and reconciliation' (2016) 1 *Asian Journal of Comparative Politics* 171, 181–82.

[158] See, eg, K Parlett, *The Individual in the International Legal System: Continuity and Change in International Law* (Cambridge, CUP, 2013) ch 4.

[159] Nuremberg Judgment (n 6) 'The Law of the Charter', available at <http://avalon.law.yale.edu/imt/judlawch.asp>.

[160] See Trainin and Vishinsky (n 45) 79: 'as distinct from common crimes, international crimes are almost always committed not by one person, but by several or many persons—a group, a band, a clique'.

This was to some extent reflected at Nuremberg in the specific criminalisation of certain organisations as a means of targeting the whole group and not allowing its members to escape criminal liability. Modern international criminal prosecutions are in practice very often directed at groups of wrongdoers, even if not formally pursuant to a joint criminal enterprise. This is illustrative of the ongoing interplay between the individual and the group in international legal systems: through the Nuremberg trial, international law embraced both liability and protection of both the individual and the group.

Nuremberg remains the standard-bearer. It is a place and a process to which those who advocate for individual and collective rights in times of upheaval can point in order to demonstrate that the international community will not—or at least should not—allow impunity and injustice to prevail. In a time of ongoing turmoil on the international stage, safeguarding that legacy, however imperfect, remains important.

10

The Early *United Nations* Advisory Opinions (1948–62)

THOMAS D GRANT AND ROWAN NICHOLSON

I. INTRODUCTION

FITZMAURICE, WRITING IN 1952, observed that the advisory practice of the International Court of Justice (ICJ) was rather sparse.[1] Though the Court would remain less active in this regard than its predecessor, the Permanent Court of International Justice, it was by no means dormant. By 1962, the Court had received 12 advisory requests and delivered 13 advisory opinions. The jurisprudence that took shape during this period helped consolidate a particular conception of the international community, both as organised around a central institution—the United Nations (UN)—and as expressed through law-making performed by states in multilateral treaties.

On three occasions the Court addressed rules that govern participation in international organisations. The first advisory opinion of the Court, on *Conditions of Admission of a State to Membership in the United Nations* (1948), led it into the deep end of the international politics of the day, the two Cold War blocs having fallen into deadlock over requests by states for admission to the UN. The Court considered the constitution of the UN again in 1950, when a question arose as to the competence of the General Assembly in respect of the admission of a state as a UN member. In 1959, another question about the constitution of an international organisation arose, this time concerning a specialised organisation, the Maritime Consultative Committee of the Inter-Governmental Maritime Consultative Organization. The Maritime Consultative Committee was not a flashpoint of East–West tensions; the Advisory Opinion holds some general interest nevertheless. How the Court treated the then new practice of registering ships in states of convenience, far from the effective ownership of the world's fleets, presaged a world of evermore fluid transactions and legal relations across borders. We address these three opinions together in Part II of this chapter.

The Advisory Opinion on *Reparation for Injuries* (1949) merits treatment as a landmark in its own right, establishing, as it finally did, that states may constitute an organisation among themselves as an international legal person having a legal character opposable against all states. If *Reparation for Injuries* affirmed that the

---

[1] GG Fitzmaurice, 'The United Nations and the Rule of Law' (1952) 38 *Transactions of the Grotius Society* 135, 138.

UN had the capacity to engage in legal relations at the international level, then *Certain Expenses*, adopted in 1962—at the opposite end of the period considered in this chapter—affirmed that the UN had the power to secure from its members the funds necessary to impart practical effects to those relations. Both were a logical corollary of the increased willingness of states after World War II to vest broadened competence in a multilateral institution. We address these advisory opinions in Part III.

The two advisory opinions on *Interpretation of Peace Treaties* (1950) illustrate that the search for a dispute settlement apparatus to apply rules and principles of international human rights began almost at the outset of the UN era; it also affirmed the role of the Court as principal judicial organ of the UN and tested the Court as a supervisory mechanism for international arbitration. The opinion as delivered was more qualified than human rights advocates would have liked. The Court here nevertheless affirmed its own role in the international organisation of which it is part, and it made clear that the substantive protections and procedural machinery of the Peace Treaties had a binding character. *Reservations to the Convention on the Prevention and Punishment of the Crime of Genocide* (1951) concerned the relations *inter partes* of the parties to a multilateral convention to which different states have adopted different reservations and different objections. The community-building impetus here was clear: divergent reservations practice does not interrupt the coalescence of general international law rules where these reflect values of central importance to the community. We consider these two advisory opinions in Parts IV and V.

This period also saw the first advisory opinions arising out of labour disputes within the UN, disputes ostensibly having little significance to international law as a whole, but which were entwined with international (and national) politics and with legal principles as well. The advisory opinions on *Effect of Awards of Compensation Made by the United Nations Administrative Tribunal* (1954) and *Judgments of the Administrative Tribunal of the ILO upon Complaints Made against UNESCO* (*ILOAT UNESCO Judgments*) (1956) addressed concerns that have persisted in various forms to this day, including legal controls over the principal organs of the UN and the standing of individuals in an international dispute settlement apparatus (Part VI). If a community composed of states is to have a central institution, then the ultimate purpose of the community—to protect and enhance the dignity of the individual human being—will be served only if its institution is held to account.

II. WHOSE INTERNATIONAL ORGANISATION? THE ADVISORY OPINIONS ON MEMBERSHIP

A. *Conditions of Admission of a State to Membership in the United Nations, 28 May 1948*

The Court's first advisory opinion, *Conditions of Admission*,[2] arose out of an impasse between the Western and Eastern blocs into which states were split during the Cold War.

---

[2] *Conditions of Admission of a State to Membership in the United Nations (Article 4 of the Charter)*, Advisory Opinion [1948] ICJ Rep 57.

When the United Nations came into being in 1945, it had 50 original members.[3] Article 4(1) of the Charter provides that membership is additionally 'open to all other peace-loving states which accept the obligations contained in the present Charter and, in the judgment of the Organization, are able and willing to carry out these obligations'. In 1947, applications for membership from five former Axis states came before the Security Council, of which three were supported by the Soviet Union (Bulgaria, Hungary and Romania) and two by the West (Finland and Italy). Poland and the Soviet Union proposed that all five be voted on together, as a package; otherwise, they would oppose the admission of Italy.[4] This proposal was rebuffed. The result was that all five applications were rejected, the Soviet-supported ones by majority vote of the Security Council and the Western-supported ones by exercise of the Soviet veto.[5]

This conduct by the Soviet Union was what the General Assembly had in mind when it requested the Advisory Opinion from the Court. But it is worth noting that the attitudes of each camp were more a function of politics than of consistently held interpretations of Article 4(1). The previous year, it had been the United States that had proposed that the Security Council recommend the admission of all eight applicants under consideration, and the Soviets (along with a Western state, Australia) that had objected that each had to be considered separately.[6]

The question posed to the Court was this:

> Is a Member of the United Nations which is called upon, in virtue of Article 4 of the Charter, to pronounce itself by its vote, either in the Security Council or in the General Assembly, on the admission of a State to membership in the United Nations, juridically entitled to make its consent to the admission dependent on conditions not expressly provided by paragraph 1 of the said Article? In particular, can such a Member, while it recognizes the conditions set forth in that provision to be fulfilled by the State concerned, subject its affirmative vote to the additional condition that other States be admitted to membership in the United Nations together with that State?[7]

At first sight, this looked like a political question. But the Court wasted little time in finding that it was a *legal* question, and hence one on which the Court was competent to give an advisory opinion under Article 65 of the Statute. The thrust of the question was whether the conditions in Article 4(1) were 'exhaustive in character' in the sense that 'a Member is not legally entitled to make admission dependent' on other conditions.[8] This was a matter of treaty interpretation, and there was nothing

---

[3] UN Charter, Art 3.

[4] Admission of New Members: Special Report of the Security Council, 9 October 1947, UN Doc A/406, 2–3. Further: Y-L Liang, 'Conditions of Admission of a State to Membership in the United Nations' (1949) 43 *AJIL* 288, 289–91; T Franck, 'Admission of a State to Membership in the United Nations (Advisory Opinions)', last updated 2006, *Max Planck Encyclopedia of Public International Law*, www.mpepil.com; T Grant, *Admission to the United Nations, Charter Article 4 and the Rise of Universal Organization* (Leiden, Brill, 2009) 27–44.

[5] Admission of New Members: Special Report of the Security Council, 9 October 1947, UN Doc A/406, 6–7.

[6] Liang, 'Conditions' (n 4) 289–90.

[7] UNGA Res 113B (II), 17 November 1947.

[8] *Conditions of Admission* (n 2) 61.

to stop the Court from exercising in regard to the Charter 'an interpretative function which falls within the normal exercise of its judicial powers'.[9]

The Court extracted five conditions from Article 4(1), each of which was subject to the judgment of the existing members: that an applicant be a 'State'; be 'peace-loving'; accept the obligations of the Charter; be able to carry out these obligations; and be willing to do so.[10] It held that these conditions *were* exhaustive—both necessary and sufficient. To hold otherwise 'would lead to conferring upon Members an indefinite and practically unlimited power of discretion in the imposition of new conditions'.[11] That would be inconsistent with the character of Article 4, 'which, by reason of the close connexion which it establishes between membership and the observance of the principles and obligations of the Charter, clearly constitutes a legal regulation of the question of the admission of new States'.[12] This is not quite as inflexible as it might seem, in that it 'does not forbid the taking into account of any factor which it is possible reasonably and in good faith to connect with the conditions'.[13] But the Court rejected arguments that Article 4(2), which empowered the General Assembly and the Security Council to judge whether the conditions were fulfilled, thereby permitted regard to be had to 'considerations of political expediency' by reason of the political responsibilities of those organs.[14]

The Court went on to find that making consent to admission dependent on the admission of other applicants 'clearly constitutes a new condition ... entirely unconnected with those' in Article 4(1).[15] Each application had to be voted on separately, on its own merits.

A dissent by Judges Basdevant, Winiarski, McNair, and Read highlighted a problem with a distinction drawn in the plurality opinion. The plurality of the Court thought that since the question concerned 'conditions on which a Member "makes its consent dependent"', it could 'only relate to the statements made by a Member concerning the vote it proposes to give' rather than 'to the reasons which, in the mind of a Member, may prompt its vote'.[16] The dissenters noted the strangeness of giving 'a Member freedom to base its vote upon a certain consideration and at the same time' forbidding 'it to invoke that consideration in the discussion preceding the vote'; that interpretation of the Charter 'would not conduce to that frank exchange of views which is an essential condition of the healthy functioning of an international organization'.[17] They held that the conditions in Article 4(1) were necessary but not sufficient; a Member was free to introduce into the discussion 'a political factor' that it considered of importance.[18]

The dissenters had a point. Merely by precluding states from offering extraneous reasons for their votes about admission, without being able to stop them from actually voting in accordance with those reasons, the advisory opinion could not

[9] ibid, 61.
[10] ibid, 62.
[11] ibid, 63.
[12] ibid.
[13] ibid.
[14] ibid, 64.
[15] ibid, 65.
[16] ibid, 60.
[17] ibid, 82–83 (Judges Basdevant, Winiarski, McNair, and Read dissenting).
[18] ibid, 90–91 (Judges Basdevant, Winiarski, McNair, and Read dissenting).

offer a way out of the impasse. As Pakistan's representative put it in the General Assembly, 'the only way to resolve the deadlock was for the permanent members of the Security Council to reach agreement among themselves'.[19]

Invoking divisions within the Court itself, the Soviet Union denied that an advisory opinion had been adopted. The seven authors of the plurality opinion plus the two who gave concurring opinions (Judges Alvarez and Azevado) outnumbered the six dissenters (those already mentioned plus Judges Zoričić and Krylov). But the Soviet argument was that the concurring opinions 'differed ... on the most important issue of whether political considerations could be invoked in addition to the legal conditions' in Article 4(1), so the supposed majority was really in the minority: seven judges to eight.[20] This argument was questionable. Judge Azevedo, for instance, whatever reasoning led him to his conclusions, summed them up by saying 'I agree with the findings of the Court'.[21] The General Assembly, in any event, adopted a resolution recommending that the Advisory Opinion be complied with.[22]

B. *Competence of the General Assembly for the Admission of a State to the United Nations*, 3 March 1950

In 1949, the General Assembly made a second attempt to escape the impasse by requesting an advisory opinion. *Competence of the General Assembly*[23] concerned the paragraph of the Charter immediately following that considered in the earlier opinion, Article 4(2), according to which the 'admission of any such State to membership of the United Nations will be effected by a decision of the General Assembly upon the recommendation of the Security Council'.[24]

The question was whether the admission of a State under Article 4(2) can be

effected by a decision of the General Assembly when the Security Council has made no recommendation for admission by reason of the candidate failing to obtain the requisite majority or of the negative vote of a permanent Member.[25]

Recalling its reasoning in its earlier opinion, the Court held that this was a legal question.[26]

Admission, it held, requires two steps: 'a "recommendation" of the Security Council and a "decision" of the General Assembly'; both steps are 'indispensable'.[27] Nor can the General Assembly 'attribute to a vote of the Security Council the character of a recommendation when the Council itself considers that no such recommendation has been made'.[28] The text of Article 4(2) was clear enough to enable the Court to form this view without much discussion.

---

[19] UN Doc A/AC.24/SR.9, 3–5.
[20] UN Doc A/AC.24/SR.7, 5–6.
[21] *Conditions of Admission* (n 2) 73 (Judge Azevedo).
[22] UNGA Res 197A (III), 8 December 1948. Further Liang, 'Conditions' (n 4) 295–98.
[23] *Competence of the General Assembly for the Admission of a State to the United Nations*, Advisory Opinion [1950] ICJ Rep 4.
[24] UN Charter, Art 4(2).
[25] UNGA Res 296A (IV), 22 November 1949.
[26] *Competence of the General Assembly* (n 23) 6–7.
[27] ibid, 8.
[28] ibid, 10.

The Court nonetheless went on to make some observations about the roles of the political organs of the United Nations that reinforced its conclusions and may also have wider significance. The 'Charter does not place the Security Council in a subordinate position' to the General Assembly but 'confers upon it "primary responsibility for the maintenance of international peace and security"'.[29] Among its powers relevant to membership, the Security Council has the sole power to reinstate a Member that has been suspended.[30] To decide that the General Assembly acting alone could admit a state to membership 'would almost nullify the role of the Security Council in the exercise of one of the essential functions of the Organization'.[31]

So the impasse remained. In the end, a way out was provided not by the Court but by a diplomatic bargain that resembled in substance the package deal the Soviet Union had proposed in 1947. In 1955, following receipt of a report from a committee of good offices established for the purpose, the General Assembly requested that the Security Council reconsider 18 applicants for admission.[32] Shortly afterwards, both organs voted to admit 16 of these (including those rejected in 1947: Bulgaria, Hungary, Romania, Finland and Italy).[33]

C. *Constitution of the Maritime Safety Committee of the Inter-Governmental Maritime Consultative Organization*, 8 June 1960

Like the earlier opinions, *Maritime Safety Committee*[34] required the Court to interpret a membership provision in a treaty establishing an international organisation, though this time the organisation was the Inter-Governmental Maritime Consultative Organization (which has since been renamed the International Maritime Organization).[35]

Article 28(a) of the treaty provided:

> The Maritime Safety Committee shall consist of fourteen Members elected by the Assembly [of the Inter-Governmental Maritime Consultative Organization] from the Members, governments of those nations having an important interest in maritime safety, of which not less than eight shall be the largest ship-owning nations, and the remainder shall be elected so as to ensure adequate representation of Members, governments of other nations with an important interest in maritime safety, such as nations interested in the supply of large numbers of crews or in the carriage of large numbers of berthed and unberthed passengers, and of major geographical areas.[36]

---

[29] ibid, 8–9, quoting UN Charter, Art 24.
[30] UN Charter, Art 5.
[31] *Competence of the General Assembly* (n 23) 9.
[32] UNGA Res 918 (X), 8 December 1955.
[33] UNSC Res 109 (1955), 14 December 1955; UNGGA Res 995 (X), 14 December 1955. The two applicants from among the 18 that were excluded were Japan, which was vetoed by the Soviet Union but admitted in 1956, and Mongolia, which was vetoed by the Republic of China (Taiwan) but admitted in 1961. Further: Grant, *Admission to the United Nations* (n 4) 85–86.
[34] *Constitution of the Maritime Safety Committee of the Inter-Governmental Maritime Consultative Organization, Advisory Opinion* [1960] ICJ Rep 150.
[35] IMCO Assembly Res A.358 (IX) (14 November 1975); IMCO Assembly Res A.371 (X) (9 November 1977).
[36] Convention on the Inter-Governmental Maritime Consultative Organization, 6 March 1948, 289 UNTS 48.

If the eight 'largest ship-owning nations' meant the eight states with the largest tonnage registered to their flags, then they included Liberia and Panama. But Liberia and Panama were flags of convenience: the majority of their registered tonnage was beneficially owned by nationals of other states. The Assembly accepted a proposal by Britain that a separate vote be taken to fill each of the eight places reserved for the largest ship-owning nations and that states be voted on in the order in which they appeared on a list of the states with the largest registered tonnage.[37] When the Assembly proceeded to do this, it voted down Liberia and Panama and instead elected the states with the ninth and 10th largest registered tonnage.[38] Liberia and Panama objected. The Assembly requested an advisory opinion to say whether the Committee had been 'constituted in accordance with' the treaty establishing the Organization.[39]

This was a straightforward question of treaty interpretation. It raised two problems.

The first was whether the Assembly had a discretion *not* to elect one of the eight largest ship-owning nations. One argument supporting this conclusion was that the word *elected* in Article 28(a) connoted 'a notion of choice' implying 'an individual judgment on each member to be elected and a free appraisal of the qualifications of that member'.[40] Another argument was that 'having an important interest in maritime safety' was a distinct qualification for election, taking precedence over the qualification of being among the eight largest ship-owning nations, and that the Assembly had a discretion to choose from among states with that overriding qualification.[41] The Court rejected both arguments. If discretion were the 'supreme rule for the constitution' of the Committee, that would 'render superfluous' most of Article 28(a).[42] The reference to election was to be read in light of the mandatory statement that at least eight members 'shall be' the largest ship-owning nations.[43] So was the requirement of an important interest in maritime safety: being one of the largest ship-owning nations necessarily constituted the required interest.[44]

The second problem was how the eight largest ship-owning nations were to be identified. Practice and analogies with comparable treaty provisions indicated that the sole test applied was registered tonnage, not the nationality of the beneficial owners, which in any event 'would be difficult to catalogue, to ascertain and to measure'.[45] The relevant practice included the fact that the Assembly had simply elected the states with the largest registered tonnage minus Liberia and Panama; it had not identified eight states by reference to some other calculation.[46]

The Assembly was divided about how to respond to the Court's opinion, fearing the effect that invalidating the existing Committee would have on work already done and in progress.[47] In the end, it adopted a British–Liberian resolution that

---

[37] *Maritime Safety Committee* (n 34) 150, 155. Further KR Simmonds, 'The Constitution of the Maritime Safety Committee of IMCO' (1963) 12 *ICLQ* 56, 61–62.

[38] ibid, 154–56, 169.

[39] ibid, 151. Further Simmonds, 'Constitution' (n 37).

[40] *Maritime Safety Committee* (n 34) 158–59.

[41] ibid, 159.

[42] ibid, 161.

[43] ibid, 159.

[44] ibid, 160.

[45] ibid, 169, further 165–71.

[46] ibid.

[47] Simmonds, 'Constitution' (n 37) 78–9.

dissolved the existing Committee with an amendment that confirmed the measures the Committee had taken since being elected in 1959.[48] It then adopted a proposal to declare elected the eight states with the largest registered tonnage and to elect afresh the other six members of the Committee provided for by Article 28(a). The result was that Liberia joined the eight, dislodging the Netherlands. The Netherlands in turn was elected as one of the six in place of the United Arab Republic.[49]

D. Commentary and Assessment

The importance of the questions discussed in these opinions may seem to have faded.

Maritime Safety Committee, now seldom cited, arose from a dispute that was localised in time and political context. A concern expressed at the time by KR Simmonds, in an article critical of the opinion, was that the 'Court's decision to accept without question the exclusiveness of the registered tonnage criterion may … only serve to exacerbate existing high feelings on this matter'.[50] The opinion has nonetheless influenced the interpretation of the requirement, codified in the Convention on the Law of the Sea, that there 'exist a genuine link' between a ship and the state to whose flag it is registered.[51] Simone Borg remarks that it ultimately contributed to a 'shifting away from attempts to use the genuine link so as to limit reflagging of ships to open registries' towards an emphasis on 'the need to ensure a genuine link by calling for the adoption of more stringent international norms for safety of ships and vessel-source pollution'.[52]

The opinion foreshadowed debates about arrangements made by multinational companies to minimise their exposure to domestic taxes and regulations. Just as ships selected Liberia and Panama as flags of convenience, companies shift or attribute activities to convenient jurisdictions. And as in *Maritime Safety Committee*, international courts and tribunals will sometimes hesitate to look behind the legal form of a transaction to its real economic substance. A contrast might be drawn with a case in which the Court *did* look behind form. In *Nottebohm*, it declined to admit an application by Liechtenstein to exercise diplomatic protection over a national, originally German, whose connection to Liechtenstein was tenuous[53]—Liechtenstein was, as it were, a nationality of convenience. *Nottebohm* was in fact raised in the pleadings in *Maritime Safety Committee*: Norway cited the decision for the proposition that a state's rights could not be allowed to depend entirely on facts that it was within that state's power to create.[54]

---

[48] IMCO Assembly Res A.21 (II) (6 April 1961).

[49] Simmonds (n 37) 80–81.

[50] ibid, 85.

[51] United Nations Convention on the Law of the Sea, 10 December 1982, 1833 UNTS 3, Art 91(2).

[52] S Borg, 'The Influence of International Case Law on Aspects of International Law Relating to the Conservation of Living Marine Resources Beyond National Jurisdiction' (2012) 23 *Yearbook of International Environmental Law* 44, 56 fn 68.

[53] *Nottebohm (Liechtenstein v Guatemala)*, Second Phase [1955] ICJ Rep 4.

[54] Oral Statement of Mr Seyersted (Norway), *Constitution of the Maritime Safety Committee of the Inter-Governmental Maritime Consultative Organization*, ICJ Pleadings 360, 365. Compare Oral Statement of Mr Riphagen (Netherlands), *Constitution of the Maritime Safety Committee of the Inter-Governmental Maritime Consultative Organization*, ICJ Pleadings 351, 357.

Equally, the diplomatic impasse out of which the UN admission opinions arose was rooted in the geopolitics of the Cold War. Today, unlike in its early years as a political project of the victors of the Second World War, and especially since the Cold War ended in 1991, the United Nations aspires to universality. And leaving aside the anomaly of the Vatican City and a few contested cases (notably Palestine, Taiwan and Kosovo) universality has been achieved. New states are admitted without much enquiry into whether they meet the conditions identified in *Conditions of Admission.* Still, the conditions come up occasionally. An argument made by Greece in 1993 against admitting Macedonia was that its name and symbols, which it shared with a wider region, 'undermines the sovereignty of neighbouring states'.[55] Thomas Franck interprets this as an argument that it failed the condition of being 'peace-loving'.[56] It was admitted with the caveat that it be 'provisionally' referred to as 'the former Yugoslav Republic of Macedonia'.[57]

What about the wider importance of the opinions on membership?

Both of the treaty provisions interpreted in the opinions—Article 4 of the Charter and Article 28(a) of the Convention on the Inter-Governmental Maritime Consultative Organization—have been cited to illustrate how the drafters of a treaty may forge a compromise by omitting reference to a disputed point.[58] That makes them good examples of how the Court might step in and, through treaty interpretation abstracted from the politics, fill the gaps left by the drafters. As will be seen below with the incomplete Treaty Commissions in *Interpretation of Peace Treaties,* the Court does not in all cases step in.

On one hand, as Franck points out, since the opinions on UN admission did not in the end actually resolve anything, they pose 'in near-textbook fashion the question of the limits of adjudication in what is essentially a politico-diplomatic dispute'.[59]

On the other hand, those limits did not prevent the opinions from influencing the law of treaty interpretation. For instance, all three opinions dealt with the role of drafting history. In *Maritime Safety Committee,* the Court cited *Competence of the General Assembly* for the proposition that it is only if the natural and ordinary meaning of words leads to ambiguity 'that resort need be had to other methods of construction'.[60] The Court does not seem to have treated *Maritime Safety Committee* as a case of ambiguity; it apparently thought that the words of Article 28(a) were already clear enough on their own. It nonetheless went on to analyse the drafting history, which corroborated its conclusions: the concern of the drafters had been that the Committee be controlled by the largest ship-owning nations, which were

---

[55] Letter from Greece to the United Nations, 25 January 1993, UN Doc A/47/877, appendix [10].

[56] Franck, 'Admission of a State to Membership' (n 4) § 11.

[57] UNSC Res 817 (1993), 7 April 1993; UNGA Res 47/225, 8 April 1993. A sequel to the UN admission controversy played out in NATO, which has its own substantive admission rules and decision-making procedures, about which see *Interim Accord of 13 September 1995 (the former Yugoslav Republic of Macedonia v Greece)* [2011] ICJ Rep 633, 659–61 and Greece, Counter-Memorial, *Interim Accord* (19 January 2010), [1.5]–[1.6], [5.9]–[5.15], [5.48]–[5.55].

[58] C Brown, 'The Inherent Powers of International Courts and Tribunals' (2005) 76 *BYIL* 195, 203 fn 40.

[59] Franck, 'Admission of a State to Membership' (n 4) § 7.

[60] *Maritime Safety Committee* (n 34) 159–60.

originally to be 'selected' (the word *elected* had been substituted at the last moment, seemingly without discussion).[61] So in *Maritime Safety Committee* the Court seems to have assumed that, although it is not *necessary* to consider the drafting history in a case where words lack ambiguity, it is still *permissible*. Despite the Court's reference to *Competence*, this approach actually departed from, or at least refined, what the Court had said in that earlier opinion. There it had said that if words

> in their natural and ordinary meaning are ambiguous or lead to an unreasonable result, then, *and then only*, must the Court, by resort to other methods of interpretation, seek to ascertain what the parties really did mean when they used these words.[62]

The Court had clarified that if there is no problem with the natural and ordinary meaning, it is not 'permissible … to resort to *travaux préparatoires*'.[63] It appears, then, that in *Maritime Safety Committee* the Court took a more flexible view of drafting history than it had taken in *Competence*.

In any event, since the Court used the drafting history merely for corroboration, the opinion was based on the text. Indeed, *Maritime Safety Committee* is significant because, as Jan Klabbers has observed, the Court essentially took a textual approach rather than one based on the purpose of the drafters. He suggests that a purposive approach would most likely have led to 'the opposite result': 'flag of convenience' states were 'not known for their scrupulous adherence to safety standards', the topic dealt with by the Committee.[64] He adds that the opinion is also remarkable in being the only occasion on which the Court suggested that a decision by an international organisation might be invalid until 1996[65] (when the Court rejected as beyond power a request for an advisory opinion made by the World Health Organization).[66]

Finally, the opinions raise tangentially a question that is relevant to the next pair of opinions that we will discuss. Klabbers notes that in *Conditions of Admission* the Court interpreted Article 4(1) as creating an obligation to treat the conditions therein as exhaustive. But

> does [this obligation] rest upon the organs concerned [the Security Council and General Assembly]? Or rather upon the member states comprising those organs? [T]he first option stresses the separate identity of the organization and its organs, whereas the second seems to relegate the organization to a mere vehicle for its member states.[67]

The Court a year after *Conditions of Admission* would deal directly with the separate identity of the United Nations. This would be in the Advisory Opinion on *Reparation for Injuries*, to which we now turn.

---

[61] ibid, 165, further 161–65.
[62] Emphasis added. *Competence of the General Assembly* (n 23) 8. Compare *Conditions of Admission* (n 2) 63; Vienna Convention on the Law of Treaties, 23 May 1969, 1155 UNTS 331, Art 32.
[63] ibid, 8.
[64] J Klabbers, 'The Life and Times of the Law of International Organizations' (2001) 70 *NJIL* 287, 305.
[65] ibid.
[66] *Legality of the Use by a State of Nuclear Weapons in Armed Conflict*, Advisory Opinion Requested by the World Health Organization [1996] ICJ Rep 66.
[67] Klabbers, 'Life and Times' (n 64) 304.

III. THE ORGANISATION'S CAPACITY TO ACT: *REPARATION FOR INJURIES* AND *CERTAIN EXPENSES*

A. *Reparation for Injuries Suffered in the Service of the United Nations,* 11 April 1949

The International Court's second advisory opinion, *Reparation for Injuries*,[68] arose out of events following the establishment of the state of Israel in the former British mandate of Palestine. On 17 September 1948, Folke Bernadotte, a Swedish diplomat recently appointed as the UN mediator in Palestine, was assassinated by an Israeli paramilitary group, Lehi.[69] Colonel André Sérot, a UN observer from France, was also assassinated. The United Nations paid expenses and indemnities to their heirs.[70] With a view to claiming reparation from Israel, the General Assembly posed two questions to the Court, of which the first was this:

> In the event of an agent of the United Nations in the performance of his duties suffering injury in circumstances involving the responsibility of a State, has the United Nations, as an Organization, the capacity to bring an international claim against the responsible *de jure* or *de facto* government with a view to obtaining the reparation due in respect of the damage caused (*a*) to the United Nations, (*b*) to the victim or to persons entitled through him?[71]

One source of doubt about whether the United Nations could claim reparation was that at that time there was no consensus that international organisations had international legal personality in their own right. The character of its predecessor, the League of Nations, had been unclear.[72] That the framers of the Charter had made provision for the legal personality of the United Nations in *domestic* law,[73] while not conclusive as to relations on the international plane, established that personality was possible in principle. Before the opinion was requested, the Secretary-General had said that he had no doubt that the United Nations had the capacity to present claims.[74] Nor was the international legal personality of the United Nations disputed in the proceedings or in any of the dissenting opinions.[75] In affirming that it did have international legal personality, the Court at last resolved the point and provided the closest thing to an authoritative definition of the concept. Describing the United Nations as 'an international person', the Court remarked, is

> not the same thing as saying that it is a State, which it certainly is not, or that its legal personality and rights and duties are the same as those of a State. Still less is it the same thing as saying that it is 'a super-State', whatever that expression may mean. It does not even

---

[68] *Reparation for Injuries suffered in the Service of the United Nations*, Advisory Opinion [1949] ICJ Rep 174.

[69] Y-L Liang, 'Reparation for Injuries Suffered in the Service of the United Nations' (1949) 43 *AJIL* 460, 460–61.

[70] UN Doc A/674, 7 October 1948.

[71] UNGA Res 258 (III), 3 December 1948.

[72] Further: JL Brierly, 'The Covenant and the Charter' (1946) 23 *BYIL* 83.

[73] UN Charter, Art 104.

[74] UN Doc A/674, 7 October 1948, 5. Further on views expressed before the opinion: Liang, 'Reparation' (n 69) 461–72.

[75] Liang, 'Reparation' (n 69) 472.

imply that all its rights and duties must be upon the international plane, any more than all the rights and duties of a State must be upon that plane. What it does mean is that it is a subject of international law and capable of possessing international rights and duties, and that it has capacity to maintain its rights by bringing international claims.[76]

Capacity meant 'capacity to resort to the customary methods recognized by international law for the establishment, the presentation and the settlement of claims', among them 'protest, request for an enquiry, negotiation, and request for submission to an arbitral tribunal or to the Court'.[77]

The Court drew this conclusion from the nature of the functions entrusted to the United Nations, which could not have been carried out 'if it was devoid of international personality'.[78] Of course, to have legal personality does not in itself mean that an entity has standing to submit to a given tribunal or court. There are, if anything, even more international legal persons today—and yet still only limited opportunities for them to submit claims. As we will relate below, the Court would later give opinions touching on access to justice and the accountability of organs from which justice might be sought.

The *Reparation* opinion also holds interest for its consideration of the general opposability of legal personality. The assassinations that had motivated the request for the opinion had occurred after Israel's declaration of independence on 14 May 1948 but before it had been admitted to the United Nations. The Court dealt with this complication only in brief terms, by observing that

fifty States, representing the vast majority of the members of the international community, had the power, in conformity with international law, to bring into being an entity possessing objective international personality, and not merely personality recognized by them alone, together with capacity to bring international claims.[79]

The United Nations thus had international legal personality even relative to non-members.

A corollary of the Court's definition of international legal personality was that it did not imply that the United Nations had the *specific* right to bring a claim of the sort contemplated. International legal persons 'are not necessarily identical in their nature or in the extent of their rights': whereas 'a State possesses the totality of international rights and duties recognized by international law, the rights and duties' of the United Nations 'must depend upon its purposes and functions as specified or implied in its constituent documents and developed in practice'.[80] The Court nevertheless readily found that the United Nations could bring a claim for damage exclusively caused by a breach of a duty owed to it, to its own interests, administration, property, or assets, or to 'the interests of which it is the guardian'.[81] The Court also went further by articulating an entirely new doctrine of *functional protection*, analogous with the right of states to exercise diplomatic protection over

---

[76] *Reparation for Injuries* (n 68) 179.
[77] ibid, 177.
[78] ibid, 179.
[79] ibid, 185.
[80] ibid, 178, 180.
[81] ibid, 180.

their nationals. This followed from an 'examination of the character of the functions entrusted to the Organization and of the nature of the missions of its agents', who must know that in the performance of their duties they are 'under the protection of the Organization'.[82] Functional protection meant that damage suffered by agents of the United Nations, which were under its protection, could be included in the reparation to which it was entitled.[83]

That answered the first question that the General Assembly had put to the Court.

The second question was how this answer could 'be reconciled with such rights as may be possessed by the State of which the victim is a national',[84] that is to say, with the established doctrine of diplomatic protection. In the absence of a rule assigning priority either to the state or to the United Nations in bringing an international claim, the Court merely expressed confidence that parties could 'find solutions inspired by goodwill and common sense' and that 'in due course a practice will be developed'.[85] A defendant state could not, however, be compelled to make reparation twice for the same damage.[86]

In the event, Bernadotte's widow did not press for a claim, and the United Nations claimed against Israel solely for damage suffered to itself from the assassination of Bernadotte. It asked Israel to apologise, to arrest the assassins, and for an indemnity of $54,628.[87] Although Israel duly paid the sum and expressed regret, it was not able to apprehend the assassins and considered that without new evidence further efforts were unlikely to succeed. The Secretary-General accepted that this was 'substantial compliance'.[88]

B. *Certain Expenses of the United Nations*, 20 July 1962

Where *Reparation for Injuries* concerned the legal capacity of the United Nations, *Certain Expenses* concerned how to give that capacity effect through actions on the ground. What right, if any, did the UN have to obtain funds from its member states to cover expenses its actions incurred?[89]

Article 17(2) of the Charter provides that the 'expenses of the Organization shall be borne by the Members as apportioned by the General Assembly'. The General Assembly asked the Court whether certain expenditures that the Assembly had

[82] ibid, 184, further 181–84.

[83] As a matter of principle, this entitlement to reparation for injuries suffered by its agents would imply that the organisation can hold legal responsibility for injuries that its agents cause. The Court eventually affirmed that point: *Difference Relating to Immunity from Legal Process of a Special Rapporteur of the Commission on Human Rights*, Advisory Opinion [1999] ICJ Rep 62, 89, [66].

[84] UNGA Res 258 (III), 3 December 1948.

[85] *Reparation for Injuries* (n 68) 186.

[86] ibid. Compare Articles on Responsibility of States for Internationally Wrongful Acts [2001] 2(2) *ILC Ybk* 26, Art 46 (Plurality of injured States); commentary to Art 46, [3]–[4] and fn 705.

[87] UNGA Res 365 (IV), 1 December 1949; Annual Report of the Secretary-General on the Work of the Organization, 1 July 1949–30 June 1950, UN Doc A/1287, 124–5.

[88] ibid, 125.

[89] *Certain Expenses of the United Nations (Article 17, Paragraph 2, of the Charter)*, Advisory Opinion [1962] ICJ Rep 151.

authorised and sought to apportion really constituted 'expenses of the Organization' within Article 17(2).[90] The expenditures related to the peacekeeping operation deployed in the Congo,[91] in pursuance of resolutions of the General Assembly and Security Council, and to the United Nations Emergency Force deployed in the Middle East at the end of the Suez crisis, in pursuance of General Assembly resolutions. Some states had refused to pay the amounts apportioned to them. In particular, the Soviet Union argued that the operations in the Congo and the Middle East violated the Charter and were therefore not valid expenses.[92] Not only allies of the Soviet Union but also many other states—for example, Argentina, Saudi Arabia, and Spain—had paid nothing towards the operations. Since the expenses of the operations amounted to almost two-thirds of its annual budget, this put the United Nations in financial difficulties.[93] In December 1961, the acting Secretary-General, U Thant, warned that it would 'soon be facing imminent bankruptcy'.[94]

Underlying the advisory request was a dispute with the Soviet Union over the role of the General Assembly in the maintenance of international peace and security. In 1950, in response to the impasse between the Eastern and Western blocs that had paralysed the Security Council, the Assembly adopted the Uniting for Peace resolution asserting that it could make recommendations in regard to the maintenance of international peace and security—including, possibly, recommendations for collective military action.[95] The operations in the Congo and the Middle East were novel in that they were supervised by the General Assembly (though they were deployed with Congolese and Egyptian consent).[96] The United States—by far the largest contributor to the budget—was, in contrast to the Soviet Union, 'the strongest advocate of virtually unlimited budgetary powers for the Assembly'.[97]

The Court said little about this background, merely reaffirming that questions about the Charter were ultimately questions of treaty interpretation, whatever their political significance. The Court's view was that 'on its face' Article 17(2) referred to *all* expenses, not just 'regular expenses'.[98] But it had been argued that expenses 'resulting from operations for the maintenance of international peace and security ... fall to be dealt with exclusively by the Security Council, and more especially through agreements negotiated in accordance with Article 43'.[99] Under Article 43, member

---

[90] UNGA Res 1731 (XVI), 20 December 1961.

[91] Officially what is here called the Congo was, at the time, the Republic of the Congo (capital: Léopoldville) and after multiple name changes is now the Democratic Republic of the Congo (capital: Kinshasa).

[92] The Soviet Union pursued this argument in the pleadings: Memorandum of the USSR Government, *Certain Expenses* (n 89) 270. Further on the pleadings: KR Simmonds, 'The UN Assessments Advisory Opinion' (1964) 13 ICLQ 854, 861–69.

[93] JF Hogg, 'Peace-keeping Costs and Charter Obligations: Implications of the International Court of Justice Decision on *Certain Expenses of the United Nations*' (1962) 62 *Columbia LR* 1230, 1231–32.

[94] Statement by the Acting Secretary-General at the 899th Meeting of the Fifth Committee, 11 December 1961, UN Doc A/C.5/907, [14]. Further on the political background to the case: Simmonds, 'Assessments' (n 92) 855–61.

[95] Uniting for Peace, UNGA Res 377 (V), 3 November 1950.

[96] Hogg, 'Peace-keeping Costs and Charter Obligations' (n 93) 1235.

[97] L Gross, 'Expenses of the United Nations for Peace-keeping Operations: The Advisory Opinion of the International Court of Justice' (1963) 17 *International Organization* 1, 8.

[98] *Certain Expenses* (n 89) 161, further 158–62.

[99] ibid, 162.

states undertake to contribute to the maintenance of peace and security, including by making armed forces and other assistance available in accordance with special agreements. The Court firmly rejected this argument. The Security Council's responsibility for the maintenance of international peace and security was 'primary',[100] not 'exclusive'; although the General Assembly could not authorise coercive action, it could still concern itself with those matters.[101] Nor did Article 43 constitute a *lex specialis* derogating from the general rule in Article 17.[102] In fact, the Court went further than it needed to go to answer the question before it: the operations in the Congo and the Middle East had not been authorised under Chapter VII, but even if they had been, the Court said its answer would have been the same. Among other considerations there was this: if such expenses were to be borne solely by states that negotiated agreements under Article 43, that would limit the Security Council's discretion in negotiating agreements and would leave it 'impotent in the face of an emergency situation when agreements under Article 43 have not been concluded'.[103]

The Court did hold that 'expenditures must be tested by their relationship to the purposes of the United Nations', in that an expenditure not made for one of those purposes 'could not be considered an "expense of the Organization"'. It muted the impact of this limitation, however, by observing that when the United Nations 'takes action which warrants the assertion that it was appropriate for the fulfilment of one of the stated purposes ..., the presumption is that such action is not ultra vires the Organization'; each organ of the United Nations 'must, in the first place at least, determine its own jurisdiction'.[104] Thus if an 'action was taken by the wrong organ ...', this would not necessarily mean that the expense incurred was not an expense of the Organization'.[105] In short, the only allowable expenses are those incurred for the purposes of the United Nations, but if an organ adopts a resolution ostensibly for one of those purposes and the Secretary-General consequently incurs financial obligations, they 'must be presumed to constitute "expenses of the Organization"'. This was enough to found a conclusion that the expenditures fell under Article 17(2).[106]

The President of the Court, Winiarski, criticised this approach in a dissenting opinion. His objection was that the resolutions authorising the operations were merely recommendations, not binding decisions, and that it 'is difficult to see by what process of reasoning recommendations could be held to be binding on States which have not accepted them' or to be 'partially binding' insofar as they imposed financial obligations on such states.[107]

Despite indicating that it did not need to do so, the Court went on to consider whether the operations were within the power of the General Assembly, along with how the Assembly had dealt with the expenses in its own practice.[108] The Court

---

[100] UN Charter, Art 24.
[101] *Certain Expenses* (n 89) 162–65.
[102] ibid, 165–67.
[103] ibid, 166–67.
[104] ibid, 167–68.
[105] ibid, 168.
[106] ibid, 170.
[107] ibid, 234 (President Winiarski dissenting).
[108] ibid, 170–79.

confirmed the conclusion already reached. Some of the judges criticised the Court for having considered the validity of the operations.[109] The Assembly had rejected a proposal by France to ask the Court whether the expenses were 'decided on in conformity with' the Charter, but the Court denied that the point was beyond its reach.[110] Judges Spender and Fitzmaurice also objected to this part of the plurality opinion on the ground that the practice of the General Assembly to which the Court referred did not necessarily reflect an agreement of the parties to the Charter and therefore ought not to be relied upon in interpreting it.[111] The Vienna Convention on the Law of Treaties, signed a few years after *Certain Expenses*, might be cited in support of this criticism: it describes 'subsequent practice' as part of the context for interpreting a treaty where it 'establishes the agreement of the parties regarding its interpretation'.[112]

Leo Gross pointed out that although the Court 'refrained from declaring it explicitly, the opinion had the effect of holding that Members of the UN were legally bound to pay the assessments made by the Assembly to defray the costs of the two operations'.[113] He speculated that in effect 'this may well amount to a revision of the Charter', especially 'if it is adopted and acted upon by the General Assembly'.[114] The Assembly did adopt it and at the same time re-established a working group on budgetary procedures.[115] The Soviet Union and its allies, for their part, maintained their position that the operations in the Middle East and the Congo had been ultra vires and thus imposed no financial obligations on members.[116]

C. Commentary and Assessment

Yuen-Li Liang anticipated at the time that *Reparation for Injuries*, being the first case in which the Court had been 'asked to pass on the basic question of the status of a general world organization in international law', 'should have far-reaching consequences, many of which may not be immediately evident'.[117] The same is true of *Certain Expenses*. The two opinions helped to open new fields of law relating to international organisations.

First, the events surrounding *Reparation for Injuries* foreshadowed later efforts to protect UN agents, not only through functional protection but also through treaties such as the Convention on the Safety of United Nations and Associated Personnel.[118] It also established the doctrine of implied powers of international organisations. The Court found that the United Nations 'must be deemed to have those powers which, though not expressly provided in the Charter, are conferred upon it by

---

[109] eg, ibid, 181 (Judge Spiropoulos declaration), 182, 197 (Judge Spender).
[110] ibid, 156–57.
[111] ibid, 187–92 (Judge Spender), 201 (Judge Fitzmaurice). Further: Hogg (n 93) 1241–45.
[112] Vienna Convention on the Law of Treaties, 23 May 1969, 1155 UNTS 331, Art 31(3)(b).
[113] Gross, 'Expenses of the United Nations for Peace-keeping Operations' (n 97) 1.
[114] ibid, 27.
[115] UNGA Res 1854 A–B (XVII), 19 December 1962.
[116] Simmonds, 'Assessments' (n 92) 882–88.
[117] Liang, 'Reparation' (n 69) 477.
[118] Convention on the Safety of United Nations and Associated Personnel, 9 December 1994, 2051 UNTS 363.

necessary implication as being essential to the performance of its duties'.[119] This idea finds an echo in the presumption, identified in *Certain Expenses*, that the United Nations is empowered to perform an action if that action 'was appropriate for the fulfilment' of one of the United Nations' purposes.[120] In the *Nuclear Weapons* opinion for the World Health Organization, the Court cited *Reparation for Injuries* for the proposition that 'the necessities of international life may point to the need for organisations, in order to achieve their objectives, to possess subsidiary powers which are not expressly provided for in the basic instruments which govern their activities'.[121] This reference to 'objectives' accords more closely with the emphasis in *Certain Expenses* on the purposes of an organisation than with the suggestion in *Reparation for Injuries* that implied powers must be 'essential to the performance of its duties'.

Secondly, as Pierre d'Argent observes, *Reparation for Injuries* 'has become standard reference in any textbook addressing the legal personality, capacity and competences ... of international organizations'.[122] The focus of the opinion on the United Nations, however, complicates its application to other international organisations. Since the Court's explanation of why the United Nations' international personality was 'objective' was that it had been brought into being by 'the vast majority of the members of the international community',[123] it remains debatable whether organisations with more limited membership necessarily also have objective international personality, as distinct from personality solely relative to their own members.[124]

Thirdly, *Certain Expenses* has contributed to the debate about the division of powers between organs of the UN. The Court interpreted the exclusive competence of the Security Council narrowly.[125] The Court thereby left open the possibility that the General Assembly could make recommendations in specific cases or organise its own peacekeeping operations. In doing so it rejected the view, expressed by President Winiarski, that the

> intention of those who drafted [the Charter] was clearly to abandon the possibility of useful action rather than to sacrifice the balance of carefully established fields of competence ... It may be that the United Nations is sometimes not in a position to undertake action which

---

[119] *Reparation for Injuries* (n 68) 182.

[120] *Certain Expenses* (n 89) 168.

[121] *Nuclear Weapons*, Advisory Opinion Requested by WHO (n 66) 79.

[122] P d'Argent, 'Reparation for Injuries Suffered in the Service of the United Nations (Advisory Opinion)', last updated 2006, MPEPIL, www.mpepil.com, § 11.

[123] *Reparation for Injuries* (n 68) 185.

[124] eg, H Schermers and N Blokker, *International Institutional Law: Unity within Diversity*, 5th edn (Leiden, Nijhoff, 2011) § 1568 restrict 'objective' legal personality to organisations 'of a universal character'; American Law Institute, *Restatement of the Law: The Foreign Relations Law of the United States*, 3rd edn (St Paul, American Law Institute Publishers, 1987) § 223 comment *e*, restricts it to those with a 'substantial' membership; C Amerasinghe, *Principles of the Institutional Law of International Organizations*, 2nd edn (Cambridge, CUP 2004) 87, 89–90 takes a more liberal view. The ILC has remarked that although the Court 'has not identified particular prerequisites, its dicta on the legal personality of international organisations do not appear to set stringent requirements'; in *Reparation for Injuries* (n 68) and other opinions, it 'appeared to favour the view' that an organisation's personality 'is an "objective" personality': Articles on Responsibility of International Organizations [2011] 2 *ILC Ybk* 2, commentary to Art 2, [8], [9]. The other opinions concerned the World Health Organization: *Interpretation of the Agreement of 25 March 1951 between the WHO and Egypt*, Advisory Opinion [1980] ICJ Rep 73, 89–90; *Nuclear Weapons*, Advisory Opinion Requested by WHO (n 66) 8–9.

[125] *Certain Expenses* (n 89) 165.

would be useful for the maintenance of the international peace and security or for one or another of the purposes indicated in Article 1 of the Charter, but that is the way in which the Organization was conceived and brought into being.[126]

The rejection of President Winiarski's view placed the fulfilment of the purposes of the United Nations ahead of the 'balance of ... fields of competence'. This was not to be the final word on the matter. The Court would clarify in 1996 that particular organs have their limits: 'international organizations are subjects of international law which do not, unlike States, possess a general competence ... they are invested by the States which create them with powers, the limits of which are a function of the common interests whose promotion those States entrust to them'.[127]

France warned that the Advisory Opinion might lead to a global legislative power; the Court was imposing on member states an obligation to bring their parliaments to vote for the contributions fixed by the General Assembly and the taxes necessary to pay for them.[128] The United States, however, 'believe[d] referral [of the question of expenses] to the ICJ [was] essential for future of UN as effective instrument [of] world peace'.[129] The US actively lobbied non-aligned states (such as India) in the hope of building support for that view in connection with ICJ proceedings.[130] Since the United Nations has continued to face difficulties in persuading states to pay their dues, and since it is as often accused of being impotent as of imposing its will on states, France's concern now seems overblown. Nevertheless, *Certain Expenses*, along with *Reparation for Injuries*, helped to make the United Nations more effective and enabled it to remain active despite the impasses of the Cold War.

IV. HUMAN RIGHTS, ARBITRATION, AND THE COURT AS ORGAN OF THE UNITED NATIONS: *INTERPRETATION OF PEACE TREATIES*

A. The Advisory Opinions of 30 March and 18 July 1950

The advisory opinions on *Interpretation of Peace Treaties with Bulgaria, Hungary and Romania* arose from one of the first major skirmishes of the Cold War concerning human rights. A number of Western Allies had set out 'grave accusations ... against the Governments of Bulgaria and Hungary regarding the suppression of human rights and fundamental freedoms in those countries'.[131] Romania was included subsequently. The legal provision that addressed these matters, which was contained *mutatis mutandis* in all three Peace Treaties, read as follows:

> Bulgaria shall take all measures necessary to secure to all persons under Bulgarian jurisdiction, without distinction as to race, sex, language or religion, the enjoyment of human rights and of the fundamental freedoms, including freedom of expression, of press and publication, of religious worship, of political opinion and of public meeting.

---

[126] *Certain Expenses* (n 89) 230 (President Winiarski dissenting).
[127] *Nuclear Weapons*, Advisory Opinion Requested by WHO (n 66) 78.
[128] Lettre de la République Française, *Certain Expenses* (n 89) 134. Further: Gross (n 97) 6.
[129] Telegram from US Department of State to US Embassy, New Delhi, 17 November 1961, NND 949637; RG 59; CDF 1960-63; Box 575.
[130] ibid.
[131] UNGA Res 272 (III), 30 April 1949, [1].

Accusations of breaches of obligations such as these would vex East–West relations for decades. The basic lines of argument were exposed at the time of the *Peace Treaties* opinion. Albeit with somewhat different protagonists, those lines are still visible today. A group of Western states alleged that a group of other states had breached international human rights obligations, and the latter asserted that, under UN Charter Article 2(7), such matters belong to the protected domain of domestic jurisdiction and thus are not appropriate matters for others to address.[132] The East–West divide traversed much the same ground, for example, in the negotiations leading to the Helsinki Final Act[133] and in the debates of the late 1970s and early 1980s over the definition of intervention and interference.[134]

After having sought but failed to discuss the matter of human rights and fundamental freedoms with the governments in Sofia, Budapest and Bucharest, the Allied Governments called upon Bulgaria, Hungary and Romania to 'join in appointing Commissions pursuant to the provisions of the respective Treaties of Peace for the settlement of dispute concerning the interpretation or execution of these Treaties'.[135] The three Eastern bloc states refused to appoint their representatives and maintained that they were under no legal obligation to do so.[136]

The General Assembly, in a resolution of 22 October 1949,[137] asked the Court four questions, which may be summarised as follows:

I.   whether certain diplomatic exchanges between Bulgaria, Hungary, and Romania and the Western Allies disclosed disputes concerning the human rights provisions of the treaties;

II. in the event of an affirmative reply to Question I, whether those three Eastern bloc states were obliged to appoint their representatives to Treaty Commissions called for under the dispute settlement provisions of the Peace Treaties;

III. in the event of an affirmative reply to Question II and a failure by one of those states to notify the UN Secretary-General that it had appointed a representative, whether the Secretary-General was authorized to appoint the missing member to the Treaty Commission;

IV. in the event of an affirmative reply to Question III, whether a Treaty Commission composed only of a representative of one party and a third member appointed by the Secretary-General would constitute a Commission within the meaning of the relevant Peace Treaty articles competent to make a definitive and binding decision in settlement of a dispute.

---

[132] See Letter from the Chargé d'Affaires AI of the USSR in the Netherlands to the Registrar of the ICJ, 14 January 1950, *Interpretation of Peace Treaties with Bulgaria, Hungary and Romania* [1950] ICJ Pleadings 199.

[133] A Bloed and P van Dijk, 'Human Rights and Non-Intervention' in A Bloed and P van Dijk (eds), *Essays on Human Rights in the Helsinki Process* (Dordrecht, Nijhoff, 1985) 57, 66–71. See also SB Snyder, *Human Rights Activism and the End of the Cold War* (Cambridge, CUP, 2011) 15–32.

[134] See, eg, Mr Flitan (Romania), First Committee, 3 December 1981, UN Doc A/C.1/36/PV.50, 11, arguing that the definition of 'interference' should encompass 'more subtle forms', including criticisms by one state of another's human rights practice.

[135] UNGA Res 294 (IV), 22 October 1949, preambular [7]–[8].

[136] ibid, preambular [9].

[137] ibid, as transmitted by the Secretary-General of the United Nations to the President of the International Court of Justice, 31 October 1949.

Though the human rights clauses of the peace treaties were the wellspring of the difficulty leading to the advisory request in 1949,[138] the Court did not understand the General Assembly to have asked it 'to deal with the [human rights] charges brought before the General Assembly'.[139] Instead, according to the Court, the questions put to the Court related 'solely to obtaining from the Court certain clarifications of a legal nature regarding the applicability of the procedure for the settlement of disputes by the Commissions provided for' under the dispute settlement provisions of each of the three Peace Treaties.[140] The Court summarily dismissed the argument that Charter Article 2(7) deprived the Court of competence over the matter.[141] The Court similarly dismissed the objection that the requested advisory procedure would replace the procedure contemplated under the Peace Treaties; it would not; it would only 'facilitate it by seeking information for the General Assembly as to its applicability to the circumstances of the present case'.[142]

The Court gave more consideration to the Eastern bloc objection invoking the Permanent Court's Advisory Opinion on the *Status of Eastern Carelia* (1923). The Council of the League of Nations had asked whether the autonomy and self-determination provisions of the Treaty of Peace between Russia and Finland (1920) and related declarations 'constitute engagements of an international character which place Russia under an obligation to Finland'.[143] Though this was an advisory request, the Permanent Court laid emphasis on the contentions of the two states parties to the instruments for which interpretation had been requested. The Permanent Court perceived Finland's contentions to have been that the provisions were 'executory obligations' and that Russia 'ha[d] not carried out those obligations',[144] contentions which Russia did not accept. Having described the matter in that way, the Permanent Court denied that it was considering the question whether 'an advisory opinion, if [relating] to matters which form the subject of a pending dispute between nations, should be put to the Court without the consent of the parties'.[145] Party consent[146] and the 'integrity of the Court's judicial function',[147] however, are the principles with which *Eastern Carelia* came widely, if rather imprecisely, to be associated.[148] This is perhaps because the PCIJ went on to say that 'the opinion which the Court has been

---

[138] See UNGA Res 272 (III), 30 April 1949.
[139] *Interpretation of Peace Treaties* (n 132) 70.
[140] ibid.
[141] ibid, 71.
[142] ibid.
[143] LN Council Res (21 April 1923), transmitted by the Secretary-General to the Permanent Court of International Justice, 27 April 1923.
[144] *Status of Eastern Carelia*, Advisory Opinion, PCIJ Ser B No 5, 25.
[145] ibid, 27.
[146] See, eg, *Maritime Delimitation in the Area between Greenland and Jan Mayen (Denmark v Norway)* [1993] ICJ Rep 38, 208–09 (Judge Shahabuddeen); Written Submission of Spain, 26 March 1975, *Western Sahara*, ICJ Pleadings 1975, vol I, 186 [299].
[147] See, eg, *Accordance with International Law of the Unilateral Declaration of Independence in Respect of Kosovo*, Advisory Opinion [2010] ICJ Rep 403, 416.
[148] See also investment practice, where *Eastern Carelia* (n 144) has been cited in respect of party consent: eg, *Wintershall AG v Argentine Republic*, ICSID Case No ARB/04/14 (Nariman, President; Torres Bernárdez and Bernardini, Members), 8 December 2008, [160] n 135; *Daimler Financial Services AG v Argentine Republic*, ICSID Case No ARB/05/1 (Dupuy, President; Brower and Bello Janeiro, Members), Award, 22 August 2012, [174]; *Koza LLP v Turkmenistan*, ICSID Case No ARB/11/20 (Townsend, President; Lambrou and Boisson de Chazournes, Members), Jurisdiction, 3 July 2013, [21] fn 21.

requested to give bears on an actual dispute between Finland and Russia' and then concluded, in view of Russia's non-participation in the League and explicit exclusion of differences with Finland from League settlement, that it was 'impossible to give its opinion on a dispute of this kind'.[149] Also in view was the difference between Finland and Russia over whether the autonomy provisions were international obligations; the Permanent Court said that this difference was 'really one of fact'.[150]

The objections to the *Interpretation of Peace Treaties* request, then, were that the request in truth called on the Court to settle a dispute between states, not all of which had consented to the jurisdiction of the Court, and that the request was a roundabout way to place the human rights claims of the Western Allies before the Court.[151] The Court, unlike its predecessor, did not find the objections convincing. It concluded that 'the present Request ... is solely concerned with the applicability to certain disputes of the procedure for settlement instituted by the Peace Treaties, and it is justifiable to conclude that it in no way touches the merits of those disputes'.[152] In reaching that conclusion, the Court observed that an advisory opinion 'is given not to the States, but to the organ which is entitled to request it'.[153]

It also observed that, in *Eastern Carelia,* the Permanent Court had been concerned that the question put to it 'raised a question of fact which could not be elucidated without hearing both parties'.[154] The Western Allies had highlighted this as a central distinction. The United States, for example, when arguing in favour of the exercise of jurisdiction in 1949–50, placed emphasis on the factual dimension, which had 'deterred the Court from giving an advisory opinion on the *Status of Eastern Carelia*' but which (it said) was absent in the *Peace Treaties* request.[155] On these considerations, the Court accepted that it could address the questions put to it.

In reply to Question I, the Court stated that whether 'there exists an international dispute is a matter for objective determination'.[156] Considering the positions of the two groups of states, East and West, the Court concluded: 'There has ... arisen a situation in which the two sides hold clearly opposite views concerning the question of the performance or non-performance of certain treaty obligations. Confronted with such a situation, the Court must conclude that international disputes have arisen'.[157]

Having answered Question I in the affirmative, the Court turned to Question II. The General Assembly's request had asked whether the three states are obliged 'to carry out the provisions of the articles referred to in Question I, including the provisions for the appointment of their representatives to the Treaty Commissions'.

---

[149] *Eastern Carelia* (n 144) 27–28.

[150] ibid, 28. South Africa in its pleadings in *Namibia* placed weight on the 'fact' strand of *Eastern Carelia,* a stratagem that met with no greater success than Spain's in *Western Sahara* four years later. See Written Statement of South Africa, *Namibia,* ICJ Pleadings 1971 vol I, 448, [44].

[151] See, eg, Telegram from Minister of Foreign Affairs of the People's Republic of Bulgaria addressed to the President of the Court, 14 January 1950, *Interpretation of Peace Treaties* (n 132) 196.

[152] *Interpretation of Peace Treaties* (n 132) 72.

[153] ibid.

[154] ibid.

[155] Written Statement of the United States, *Interpretation of Peace Treaties* (n 132) 135. See also Written Statement of the United Kingdom, *Interpretation Peace Treaties* (n 132) 169, [7].

[156] *Interpretation of Peace Treaties* (n 132) 74.

[157] ibid.

This form of words suggests that Question II concerned provisions in addition to the appointment provisions. Indeed, Question I referred to the substantive human rights provisions as well. The Court, however, did 'not think that the General Assembly would have asked it whether Bulgaria, Hungary and Romania are obligated to carry out the articles concerning human rights'.[158] The Court observed that those states had not denied that they were subject to the human rights articles.[159] The Court thus took the question to concern the dispute settlement articles only.

The dispute settlement articles of the Treaties provided that any dispute not settled by direct diplomatic negotiations or reference to the Heads of Mission shall be referred at the request of either party to a Commission, appointment to which the Treaties contained provisions addressing. Those antecedent processes having failed, the door was open to settlement by means of the Treaty Commissions—and the Western Allies took advantage of the opportunity—that is to say, they appointed their Treaty Commissioners. In turn, 'Bulgaria, Hungary and Romania [were] obligated to carry out the [appointment] provisions' and appoint their own Treaty Commissioners.[160] The Court in these terms answered Question II in the affirmative as well and delivered its Advisory Opinion on Questions I and II on 30 March 1950.

Thirty days elapsed after the delivery of the Advisory Opinion on Questions I and II without any of the Eastern bloc states having made an appointment to the Treaty Commissions. The Court then turned to Questions III and IV.[161] The US, UK and head of the UN Legal Department made written and oral submissions in this second phase; the Eastern bloc states did not.[162]

The crux of Question III was this. Articles 36, 40, and 38 of the Peace Treaties (Bulgaria, Hungary and Romania) provided that, in the event that the two parties have 'failed to agree within a period of one month upon the appointment of the third member [of the Treaty Commission], the Secretary-General may be requested by either party to make the appointment'. The Western states contended that it was open to one party to request the Secretary-General to appoint the missing neutral when the other party had not appointed its own member. Their contention implied that a Commission would be validly constituted in this way—notwithstanding the failure of the respondent state to appoint and the resultant empanelment of only two, not three, Commissioners. The Court did not accept the Western states' contention. In considering the matter, the Court placed emphasis on the sequence of events identified in the dispute settlement clause:

> While the text in its literal sense does not completely exclude the possibility of the appointment of the third member before the appointment of both national Commissioners it is nevertheless true that according to the natural and ordinary meaning of the terms it was intended that the appointment of both the national Commissioners should precede that of the third member.[163]

---

[158] ibid, 76.
[159] ibid.
[160] ibid, 77.
[161] *Interpretation of Peace Treaties* (n 132) 225.
[162] ibid, 225–26.
[163] ibid, 227.

The Court drew further support from 'the practice of arbitration', in which 'this is the normal order followed'.[164]

Unremarkable in itself, the dispute settlement provision in the Peace Treaties assured that failure of the primary mechanism of appointment would not result in a failure to appoint. Well-drafted dispute settlement clauses contain provisions to similar effect. However, this particular clause addressed only a failure to appoint the third member; it was silent in respect of a failure by one of the parties to appoint its 'national commissioner'. The Court concluded that 'the refusal by the Governments of Bulgaria, Hungary and Romania to appoint their own Commissioners has made the constitution of [a Treaty Commission] impossible'.[165] In reaching this conclusion, the Court suggested that the Peace Treaties effectively defined the Commission to be a body comprised of three members: 'A Commission consisting of two members is not the kind of commission for which the Treaties have provided'.[166] The dispute settlement clause did not explicitly state that the Commission could come into being only if both parties appointed, but that was the practical effect. States, when crafting arbitral mechanisms in other treaties, in a number of notable instances would take steps to avoid the problem that had arisen from the respondents' refusal to appoint under the Peace Treaties.[167]

The Court made clear that its conclusion on this point did not mean that the three states were at liberty not to appoint: they were 'under an obligation to appoint ... and it is clear that refusal to fulfil a treaty obligation involves international responsibility'.[168] International responsibility for breach of an obligation does not, however, in itself mean jurisdiction exists to settle a dispute, nor does the rule of effectiveness (*ut res magis valeat quam pereat*) revise a treaty in favour of creating an effective dispute settlement organ. The Court said, in a phrase to be frequently repeated (in dissents as much as in judgments and awards), it 'is the duty of the Court to interpret the Treaties, not to revise them'.[169]

---

[164] ibid.

[165] ibid, 228.

[166] ibid. The US and UK had noted that in the *Lena Goldfields* arbitration, an incomplete tribunal had functioned and produced an award. However, that had been a fully constituted tribunal in which one arbitrator refused to participate. It would appear from this practice that non-appearance of an arbitrator who had been duly appointed is to be treated like non-appearance of a party, but a failure to constitute the decision-making body in the first place is a different category of problem. See JJ Veeder, 'The Lena Goldfields Arbitration: The Historical Roots of Three Ideas' (1998) 47(4) *ICLQ* 747, 752–53.

[167] See especially UN Convention on the Law of the Sea, 10 December 1982, 1833 UNTS 571, Annex VII, Art 3, for application of which see *Philippines v China*, PCA Case No 2013-19 (Mensah, President; Cot, Pawlak, Soons and Wolfrum, Members), Jurisdiction and Admissibility, 29 October 2015, [29]–[31].

[168] *Interpretation of Peace Treaties*, Second Phase (n 132) 228.

[169] ibid, 229. See *Navigational and Related Rights (Costa Rica v Nicaragua)* [2009] ICJ Rep 214, 286 (Judge Skotnikov); *Anglo-Iranian Oil Co (United Kingdom v Iran)*, Preliminary Objections [1952] ICJ Rep 93, 142 (Judge Read dissenting); *South West Africa (Ethiopia v South Africa; Liberia v South Africa)*, Preliminary Objections [1962] ICJ Rep 319, 583 Judge ad hoc van Wyk dissenting). See also *Rights of Nationals of the United States of America in Morocco (France/USA)* [1952] ICJ Rep 176, 196. From arbitral practice, see *Venezuela US, SRI v Bolivarian Republic of Venezuela*, PCA Case No 2013-34 (Tomka, President; Fortier and Kohen, Members), Jurisdiction, 26 July 2016, [59] fn 29 (in respondent's objection to jurisdiction, which the Tribunal rejected); *Wintershall AG v Argentine Republic*, ICSID Case No ARB/04/14 (Nariman, President; Torres Bernárdez and Bernardini, Members), 8 December 2008, [84] ('If this be the duty of an international court, the duty of an ICSID Tribunal is no different'). And from national court practice (in the High Court of Australia), *Minister for Immigration and Multicultural Affairs v Respondents* (2004) 222 CLR 1, [109] (Judge Kirby).

B. Commentary and Assessment

Some 40 years after *Interpretation of Peace Treaties*, in the *Arbitral Award of 31 July 1989*, a contentious case, the Court referred to *Interpretation of Peace Treaties* to support its interpretation of an Arbitration Agreement between Guinea-Bissau and Senegal to define their maritime boundary.[170] In their joint dissenting opinion Judges Aguilar-Mawdsley and Ranjeva invoked the advisory, as distinct from contentious, character of the opinion on which the Court relied, in order to support their view that that opinion furnished no guidance.[171] This is a familiar refrain, but it has not prevented the Court from tapping its advisory jurisprudence when helpful. *Interpretation of Peace Treaties* is one of the advisory opinions that the Court frequently has referred to, including in its judgments in contentious cases.

Interpretation of Peace Treaties also, unsurprisingly, has surfaced in the Court's subsequent advisory practice. This, perhaps, was the fork in the road between *Eastern Carelia* and its modern approach, under which the Court will not decline to exercise its advisory jurisdiction solely because a state party to a dispute that is relevant to the advisory request has not consented to adjudication.[172] Nor will an advisory opinion necessarily be declined because the questions put to the Court require an evaluation and interpretation of facts.[173] It is difficult to reconcile *Eastern Carelia* and *Peace Treaties* with a single *jurisprudence constante*;[174] jurists indeed have described the later case as a progressive step in international advisory practice,[175] the earlier as anomalous or archaic, even a 'red herring'.[176] Reisman described *Peace Treaties* as making 'a good deal of far-reaching international constitutional law and international arbitral law'.[177]

In affirming that it will proceed to give an advisory opinion notwithstanding the presence of an interstate dispute, the Court recalled that its reply to the competent UN organ 'is only of an advisory character: as such, it has no binding force'. Indeed, the non-binding character of advisory opinions was the premise from which the

---

[170] *Arbitral Award of 31 July 1989 (Guinea-Bissau v Senegal)* [1991] ICJ Rep 53, 70.

[171] ibid, 127 (Judges Aguilar-Mawdsley and Ranjeva dissenting).

[172] See K Keith, 'The Advisory Jurisdiction of the International Court of Justice: Some Comparative Reflections' (1996) 17 *Australian YBIL* 39, 43–44.

[173] *Legal Consequences of the Construction of a Wall in the Occupied Palestinian Territory*, Advisory Opinion [2004] ICJ Rep 136, 160–62.

[174] For a brave, and not wholly unconvincing, attempt, see G Abi-Saab's statement (for Egypt) in the two *Nuclear Test* advisory proceedings: 1 November 1995, CR 1995/23, 19–23.

[175] Maurice Kamto, for example, contrasted *Eastern Carelia* (n 144) with 'a trend in international law for each multilateral instrument to be viewed as a kind of legal subsystem, with its own dispute settlement procedure': ILC 2622nd mtg, 17 May 2000 [2000] 1 *ILC Ybk* 78. Judge Owada (ICJ President at the time) described it as belonging to an earlier stage in the 'historical evolution of the advisory opinion procedure': ILC 3100th mtg, 7 July 2011, UN Doc A/CN.4/SR.3100, 10. For Pierre Marie-Dupuy's account of the change from *Eastern Carelia* to *Interpretation of Peace Treaties* fn 132, see Exposé Oral de M Dupuy (for Morocco), 15 May 1975, *Western Sahara*, ICJ Pleadings 1975 vol IV p 95, 97–98. Compare K Oellers-Frahm, 'Lawmaking through Advisory Opinions?' (2011) 12 *German LJ* 1033, 1050–51 and fn 83.

[176] JE Alvarez, 'Legal Remedies and the United Nations *à la Carte* Problem' (1991) 12 *Michigan JIL* 229, 293.

[177] WM Reisman, 'The Supervisory Jurisdiction of the International Court of Justice: International Arbitration and International Adjudication' (1996) 258 *Hague Recueil* 1, 160.

Court concluded that the absence of a state's consent does not prevent the exercise of jurisdiction:

> It follows that no State, whether a Member of the United Nations or not, can prevent the giving of an Advisory Opinion which the United Nations considers to be desirable in order to obtain enlightenment as to the course of action it should take. The Court's Opinion is given not to the States, but to the organ which is entitled to request it; the reply of the Court, itself an 'organ of the United Nations,' represents its participation in the activities of the Organization, and, in principle, should not be refused.[178]

The Court might be taken to task here for having given with one hand (affirming advisory jurisdiction) only to have taken away with the other (recalling the non-binding character of advisory opinions). For states that worried that advisory practice was creeping towards a binding general power (as some did),[179] the Court's observations here perhaps gave comfort, but to have said that advisory opinions are advisory was to state the obvious. The scope of jurisdiction when a concerned state objected, by contrast, in light of the practice of the PCIJ, was a real question. The net result of the advisory opinions in 1950 was to reinforce the Court's position as an 'organ of the United Nations'.[180] Mindful of that position, only for 'compelling reasons' would the Court after *Peace Treaties* decline to give an opinion in response to a request falling within its jurisdiction.[181] The ICJ indeed (from 1946 to 2017) has not declined to give an advisory opinion on discretionary grounds.[182] Its refusal to answer the WHO's request concerning nuclear weapons resulted not from the Court exercising discretion but from an organ making a request that it did not have the competence to make.[183]

The influence of *Peace Treaties* can be seen in the ILC's Model Rules and draft convention on arbitral procedure as well. Draft Article 1, paragraph 1, in the Model Rules (Article 2, paragraph 1, in the draft convention), provided as follows:

> If, before the constitution of the arbitral tribunal, the parties to an undertaking to arbitrate disagree as to the existence of a dispute, or as to whether the existing dispute is wholly or

---

[178] *Peace Treaties,* First Phase (n 132) 71.

[179] In instructions to the 'USSR Representative' [sic] at the ILC, the Politburo in draft Protocol No 68 of March 1949 (whether the Protocol was adopted is not clear from the archive sources made available to the present writers) advised that the USSR representative 'proceed from the premise that we are not interested in the development of the activity of this Commission, since the purpose of the Anglo-American majority is [inter alia ...] with the assistance of this Commission and as a result of its work, to strengthen the role of the International Court and in the process to undermine the influence and significance of the Security Council by making the interpretations and the so-called advisory opinions of the Court on legal issues compulsory': File 1523 / former Fond 3, op 4, file 986, AP RF; PB Prot No 68 from 17/03–10/05/49, 60; Point 166 (from 9 April 1949); On the instructions [*direktivy*] for the representative of the USSR in the UN ILC.

[180] See on this point A Pellet, 'Strengthening the Role of the International Court of Justice as the Principal Judicial Organ of the United Nations' (2004) 3 *Law and Practice of International Courts and Tribunals* 159, 162.

[181] *Judgments of the Administrative Tribunal of the ILO upon Complaints Made against UNESCO,* Advisory Opinion [1956] ICJ Rep 77, 86; *Immunity from Legal Process* (n 83) 78; *Wall* (n 173); *Kosovo* (n 147) 416.

[182] *Legality of the Threat or Use of Nuclear Weapons,* Advisory Opinion Requested by the General Assembly [1996] ICJ Rep 226, 235.

[183] *Nuclear Weapons,* Advisory Opinion Requested by WHO (n 66) 84.

partly within the scope of the obligation to go to arbitration, such preliminary question shall, at the request of any of the parties and failing agreement between them upon the adoption of another procedure, be brought before the International Court of Justice for decision by means of its summary procedure.

This provision 'ha[d] as its aim to address situations like that which was presented in the case of *Interpretation of Peace Treaties*'[184]—that is to say, in particular as related to Question I.

So too was the concern raised that when 'account is taken of the considerable number of international arbitration clauses and agreements ... negative answers to Questions III and IV would have wide effects'.[185] *Peace Treaties* was not the first time that the ICJ or its predecessor had been asked to consider a disputed arbitration clause, nor would it be the last. We noted *Arbitral Award of 31 July 1989* above. Already in 1953, the *Ambatielos* case called upon the Court to say whether or not a Declaration of 1926, referring to an 1886 Treaty of Commerce and Navigation between Great Britain and Greece, obliged those parties to constitute a Commission of Arbitration to deal with a private claim.[186] The Permanent Court, in 1928, had addressed a (somewhat) similar question of interpretation in respect of the Greco-Turkish Agreement of 1926.[187] Some ILC members thought it unwise to 'set up the International Court of Justice as a sort of super-tribunal not subordinate to the agreement of the parties', but the prevailing opinion accepted, in principle, that the Court, subject to the terms of a jurisdictional instrument, might yet perform a role like that it was asked to (and, partly, did) in *Peace Treaties*.[188]

The Court was evidently mindful that its interpretation of the dispute settlement clause in the Peace Treaties might have a ripple effect in arbitral practice. It considered the concern that because 'of the very large number of existing treaties and other international agreements which contain arbitration clauses similar or analogous to [these] ... the basic issue ... in the present advisory case is one of general and wide significance'.[189] Examining the practice of arbitration, the Court noted that the existence of treaty provisions that do address default of appointment illustrate that states 'felt the impossibility of remedying this situation simply by way of interpretation'.[190] The Court perhaps can be heard (faintly) to have suggested that the Peace Treaties harboured a pathology in their incomplete default provisions,[191] but the Court did not accept it to be a proper exercise of the judicial function to 'remedy ... a default

---

[184] Commentary on the Project on Arbitral Procedure Prepared by the Secretariat, 5 May 1953, UN Doc A/CN.4/L.40, 14 (commentary on draft Art 2).

[185] Written Statement of the United States, 22 October 1949, *Peace Treaties*, Second Phase (n 32) 239.

[186] *Ambatielos (Greece v United Kingdom)* [1953] ICJ Rep 10, 26.

[187] *Interpretation of the Greco-Turkish Agreement of 1 December 1926* (Final Protocol, Article IV), Advisory Opinion, PCIJ Ser B No 16.

[188] ILC Model Rules on Arbitral Procedure, General Commentary, Article 1 [1958] 2 *ILC Ybk* 87, [25].

[189] Written Statement of the United States, 22 October 1949, *Peace Treaties*, Second Phase (n 132) 215.

[190] *Peace Treaties*, Second Phase (n 132) 229.

[191] Reisman addresses *Peace Treaties* under the title 'inoperable clauses': Reisman, 'Supervisory Jurisdiction' (n 177) 158–64. On its significance for the role of the ICJ in supervising arbitral jurisdiction, see ibid, 129–45.

for the occurrence of which the Treaties have made no provision'.[192] Interstate arbitration is 'still hardly a central feature of international politics',[193] but it is a recurrent phenomenon, and *Peace Treaties* is the starting point of the ICJ's involvement with it.

Peace Treaties also has joined the standard citation list for the definition of 'legal dispute'. Permanent Court in *Mavrommatis Palestine Concessions* already had identified a dispute as 'a disagreement on a point of law or fact, a conflict of legal views or of interests between two persons'.[194] This, the *locus classicus* on the point, was in 1924—that is, nearly 30 years before *Interpretation of Peace Treaties*. And, yet, the dispute over the Peace Treaties in the late 1940s exposed unsettled questions as to the juristic character of disputes and their impact on agreed dispute settlement procedures. The Advisory Opinion was a significant step towards settling those questions, and it seems to have been one factor that provoked the ILC to attempt to settle them definitively. Though it would prove premature (as it remains) to invest a general function of determining matters of jurisdiction in the ICJ, the 1950 Advisory Opinion nevertheless further clarified that, whoever decides the matter, the existence of a dispute is an 'objective determination'.[195] The Court has referred to the Advisory Opinion for this principle, including in numerous contentious proceedings.[196] As a requirement that a party instituting proceedings must meet,[197] the existence of a dispute would seem an unlikely one not to be satisfied; the Marshall Islands in 2016 gained the distinction of being the first not to satisfy it, though the Court was heavily divided on the point.[198]

Placing the 1950 Advisory Opinion in its wider setting, this was only three months before the invasion of South Korea by the forces of the North. The Advisory Opinion was adopted on 30 March 1950; the resolution of the Security Council recommending that the member states 'furnish such assistance to the Republic of Korea as may be necessary to repel the armed attack' was passed on 27 June 1950, famously in

---

[192] *Peace Treaties*, Second Phase (n 132) 229–30.

[193] Reisman (n 177) 41.

[194] *Mavrommatis Palestine Concessions (Hellenic Republic v Great Britain)*, Jurisdiction, PCIJ Ser A, No 2, 11. And see M Waibel, this volume, ch 3.

[195] *Peace Treaties*, First Phase (n 132) 74.

[196] See, eg, *East Timor (Portugal v Australia)* [1995] ICJ Rep 90, 101; *Questions of Interpretation and Application of the 1971 Montreal Convention arising from the Aerial Incident at Lockerbie (Libya v United States)*, Preliminary Objections [1998] ICJ Rep 115, 123; *Armed Activities on the Territory of the Congo (New Application: 2002) (Democratic Republic of the Congo v Rwanda)*, Jurisdiction and Admissibility [2006] ICJ Rep 6, 40; *Application of the International Convention on the Elimination of All Forms of Racial Discrimination (Georgia v Russia, Preliminary Objections* [2011] ICJ Reports 70, 84. Making that determination 'is an integral part of the Court's judicial function', and it may require the Court to determine whether a putative legal dispute has already been settled, as it had been in respect of sovereignty over San Andrés, Providencia and Santa Catalina: *Territorial and Maritime Dispute (Nicaragua v Colombia)*, Preliminary Objections [2007] ICJ Rep 833, 874. See also *Nuclear Tests (New Zealand v France)* [1974] ICJ Rep 457, 476: 'The dispute brought before it must … continue to exist at the time when the Court makes its decision'.

[197] ICJ Statute, Art 36(2).

[198] *Marshall Islands v Pakistan*, Jurisdiction and Admissibility, 5 October 2016, [34]–[55], about which see FI Paddeu, 'Multilateral Disputes in Bilateral Settings: International Practice Lags behind Theory' (2017) 76 *CLJ* 1, 1–2.

the absence of the Soviet Union.[199] Jurists, Kelsen and Stone among them, doubted whether, lacking the participation of one of the permanent members, the Security Council had adopted a binding resolution for an enforcement action.[200] *Interpretation of Peace Treaties*—itself instigated by non-participation of Eastern bloc states— was one of a number of political, military and legal incidents that indicated the entrenchment of opposing Cold War camps. Archive sources indeed suggest the role that the Soviet Union played in directing the main lines of Eastern bloc response to the advisory request: the Soviet Foreign Ministry, unselfconsciously it would seem, advised Stalin that it would be 'reasonable to advise the Hungarians … to make it clear that … this issue is entirely the subject matter of Hungary's domestic jurisdiction'.[201] Scholars of Soviet approaches to international law described the position taken by Hungary, Bulgaria, and Romania in the advisory proceedings as reflecting the 'socialist view' which 'extends domestic concepts of jurisdiction and of national sovereignty to include even the situations covered by international agreements'.[202] The 40 years following *Interpretation of Peace Treaties* would bring considerable challenges to international adjudication. Nevertheless, the Advisory Opinion made clear that a request concerning a legal question falls within the proper bounds of an advisory opinion, even when the legal question is politically sensitive. That political matters do not in themselves oust the Court's advisory jurisdiction has been a guiding consideration ever since.[203]

V. THE COURT AS GENERAL LAW-MAKER: *RESERVATIONS TO THE GENOCIDE CONVENTION*

A. *Reservations to the Genocide Convention*, 28 May 1951

Reservations to the Genocide Convention gave the Court another opportunity to express itself on an aspect of the law of treaties.[204] The Genocide Convention, signed in 1948, was to enter into force on a date after 20 states had ratified or acceded to it.[205] Nothing was said in the treaty about reservations. Eight of the states that

---

[199] UNSC Res 83 (1950), 27 June 1950.

[200] See DHN Johnson, 'The Korean Question and the United Nations' (1956) 26 *Nordisk Tidsskirft Int'l Ret* 25.

[201] RGASPI (Russian State Archive of Social and Political History), Fond 82 (Lichnyi arkhiv VM Molotova [VM Molotov Papers]), op 2 (The activities of VM Molotov as head of the Soviet Foreign Policy), 13 June 1949: 5/5/15 3:40–4:20, 174.

[202] K Grzybowski, 'Socialist Judges in the International Court of Justice' [1964] *Duke Law Journal* 536, 541.

[203] See, eg, *Legal Consequences for States of the Continued Presence of South Africa in Namibia (South West Africa) Notwithstanding Security Council Resolution 276 (1970)*, Advisory Opinion [1971] ICJ Rep 16, 171 (Judge de Castro).

[204] *Reservations to the Convention on the Prevention and Punishment of the Crime of Genocide*, Advisory Opinion [1951] ICJ Rep 15.

[205] Convention on the Prevention and Punishment of the Crime of Genocide, 9 December 1948, 78 UNTS 277, Art XIII.

ratified it—for example, the Philippines and Bulgaria—did so with reservations that other parties to the treaty objected to. All eight reserving states made reservations concerning Article IX, which provided for the compulsory jurisdiction of the ICJ; some of them also made reservations concerning other provisions.[206] The question this raised was whether the reserving states were parties to the treaty (and hence counted toward the threshold of 20 for purposes of entry into force).[207]

The General Assembly asked the Court three questions, of which the first was this:

> Can the reserving State be regarded as being a party to the [Genocide] Convention while still maintaining its reservation if the reservation is objected to by one or more of the parties to the Convention but not by others?[208]

The traditional rule, based on the principle that 'in its treaty relations a State cannot be bound without its consent', was that 'no reservation was valid unless it was accepted by all of the contracting parties'. But the Court abandoned this strict approach, noting among other relevant circumstances 'the very wide degree of participation' envisaged by the Genocide Convention.[209] It was also significant that in a treaty, such as the Genocide Convention,

> manifestly adopted for a purely humanitarian and civilizing purpose ... the contracting States do not have any interests of their own; they merely have, one and all, a common interest, namely, the accomplishment of those high purposes which are the *raison d'être* of the convention .... The high ideals which inspired the Convention provide, by virtue of the common will of the parties, the foundation and measure of all its provisions.[210]

This memorable language should not obscure that the Court was treading carefully between competing considerations. On the one hand, it was 'inconceivable that the contracting parties readily contemplated that an objection to a minor reservation' would completely exclude the reserving state. On the other hand, they could not 'have intended to sacrifice the very object of the Convention in favour of a vain desire to secure as many participants as possible'.[211] From this, the Court concluded that

> it is the compatibility of a reservation with the object and purpose of the Convention that must furnish the criterion for the attitude of a State in making the reservation on accession as well as for the appraisal by a State in objecting to the reservation.[212]

---

[206] *Reservations to the Genocide Convention* (n 204) 31 (Vice-President Guerrero and Judges McNair, Read, and Hsu Mo dissenting). Further on the background to the opinion: GG Fitzmaurice, 'Reservations to Multilateral Conventions' (1953) 2 *ICLQ* 1; C Redgwell 'Universality or Integrity? Some Reflections on Reservations to General Multilateral Treaties' (1993) 64 *BYIL* 245, 247–50.

[207] On the practice of the Secretary-General as depository and, in effect, accountant for tabulating treaty ratifications, see S Rosenne, *Developments in the Law of Treaties, 1945–1986* (Cambridge, CUP, 1989) 424–36; PTB Kohona 'Some Notable Developments in the Practice of the UN Secretary-General as Depository of Multilateral Treaties: Reservations and Declarations' (2005) 99 *AJIL* 433.

[208] UNGA Res 1731 (XVI), 20 December 1961.

[209] *Reservations to the Genocide Convention* (n 204) 21.

[210] ibid, 23.

[211] ibid, 24.

[212] ibid.

The second question before the Court proceeded from the premise that a reserving state *could* be regarded as a party despite an objection to its reservation. The question was this:

> what is the effect of the reservation as between the reserving State and:
>
> (a)   the parties which object to the reservation?
> (b)   those which accept it?[213]

In reply, the Court reaffirmed the underlying principle of consent. Each objecting state 'will or will not, on the basis of its individual appraisal within the limits of the criterion of the object and purpose ..., consider the reserving State to be a party to the Convention'.[214] In other words, a reserving state would be considered to be a party to the Convention relative to states that accepted the reservation, *and* relative to states that objected to the reservation but still consented to treating the reserving state as a party, *but not* relative to objecting states that did not so consent. The Court thought that the disadvantages of this relativity were 'mitigated by the common duty of the contracting states' to be guided by compatibility with the object and purpose of the treaty.[215]

The third question before the Court concerned whether it mattered if an objection to a reservation was made by a state that was not yet a party to the treaty.[216] The Court held that if an objection was made by a signatory to the treaty that had not yet ratified it, the objection could serve as notice but would have its full legal effect only on ratification; an objection by a state that was entitled to sign or accede but that had not yet done so would have no legal effect at all.[217]

At the same time as the General Assembly had requested the Advisory Opinion from the Court, it had asked the ILC, which was conducting the study that would lead to the Vienna Convention on the Law of Treaties, to provide a report on reservations and to give priority to the topic.[218] In its report to the Assembly, the ILC hewed more closely to the traditional approach and expressed the view that 'the criterion of the compatibility of a reservation with the objects and purposes of a multilateral convention ... is not suitable for application to multilateral conventions in general'.[219] But the General Assembly (and on its instructions the Secretary-General) adopted the Court's view.[220] It later extended the approach to 'all conventions concluded under the auspices of the United Nations which do not contain provisions to the contrary'.[221] The ILC came round and incorporated elements of the Court's

---

[213] UNGA Res 1731 (XVI), 20 December 1961.
[214] *Reservations to the Genocide Convention* (n 204) 26.
[215] ibid.
[216] UNGA Res 1731 (XVI), 20 December 1961.
[217] *Reservations to the Genocide Convention* (n 204) 27–29.
[218] UNGA Res 1731 (XVI), 20 December 1961.
[219] Report of the International Law Commission Covering the Work of Its Third Session, 16 May–27 July 1951 [1951] 2 *ILC Ybk* 123, [24]. Further: Report on Reservations to Multilateral Conventions [1951] 2 *ILC Ybk* 1.
[220] UNGA Res 598 (VI), 12 January 1952.
[221] UNGA Res 1452 B (XIV), 7 December 1959, [1].

view into the Vienna Convention, which was signed in 1969 and came into force in 1980.[222] In particular, under Article 19(c), a state may not make a reservation that 'is incompatible with the object and purpose of the treaty'. Note that, according to both the Court and the Vienna Convention, this rule applies only where a treaty does not already make express provision for the effect of reservations.

The ILC was not alone in its reluctance to abandon the traditional approach. In a joint dissenting opinion, Vice-President Guerrero and Judges McNair, Read, and Hsu Mo denied that there was a new test of compatibility with the object and purpose of the treaty. In the dissenting judges' view, without the consent of all other parties, a reserving state could not become a party. The dissenters concluded 'that the parties entered into the Convention on the basis of the existing law and practice' and saw no reason to 'impute to them the intention to adopt a new and different rule'.[223] They warned that the test of compatibility with object and purpose would be difficult to apply and would invite more states to adopt reservations.[224] The ILC, 60 years later, remarked that 'international jurisprudence [does not] enable us to define it', and thought the 'helpful hints' as to the meaning of the expression 'object and purpose' still to be those found in *Reservations*.[225]

B. Commentary and Assessment

Writers at the time, Fitzmaurice among them, shared the dissenting judges' apprehension that *Reservations* would set off a chain reaction—of reservations.[226] It would be going too far to say that subsequent practice in respect of reservations is attributable to the Advisory Opinion alone, but reservations there were and in significant number. *Reservations to the Genocide Convention* would be central to the debate about reservations to human rights treaties in general that peaked in the 1990s.[227]

The Court itself returned to the question of reservations to the Genocide Convention in 1999. It dismissed the *Legality of Use of Force* cases brought against Spain and the United states by the Federal Republic of Yugoslavia (Serbia and Montenegro) on the ground that the respondents had made reservations to the dispute settlement clause, Article IX[228] (a provision that Fitzmaurice, 'obviously inspired by the cold

---

[222] Vienna Convention on the Law of Treaties, 23 May 1969, 1155 UNTS 331, Arts 19–23.

[223] *Reservations to the Genocide Convention* (n 204) 44 (Vice-President Guerrero and Judges McNair, Read, and Hsu Mo dissenting).

[224] ibid, 47 (Vice-President Guerrero and Judges McNair, Read, and Hsu Mo dissenting).

[225] ILC Guide to Practice on Reservations to Treaties, ILC 63rd session (2011), UN Doc A/66/10/Add.1, 34, 355 (commentary to § 3.1.5, [7]).

[226] Fitzmaurice, 'Reservations' (n 206).

[227] See further Y Tyagi 'The Conflict of Law and Policy on Reservations to Human Rights Treaties' (2000) 71 *BYIL* 181.

[228] *Legality of Use of Force (Federal Republic of Yugoslavia v Spain)*, Provisional Measures [1999] ICJ Rep 761, 772; *Legality of Use of Force (Federal Republic of Yugoslavia v United States)*, Provisional Measures [1999] ICJ Rep 916, 923–24.

war debate',[229] thought incapable of reservation).[230] Similarly, in *Armed Activities on the Territory of the Congo*, in 2006, it accepted that Rwanda's reservation to Article IX was compatible with the object and purpose of the Convention.[231]

The question of reservations to another human rights treaty, the International Covenant on Civil and Political Rights,[232] was considered by the United Nations Human Rights Committee in a general comment in 1994.[233] It held that 'the object and purpose test ... governs the matter of interpretation and acceptability of reservations' and gave a number of examples of reservations that would fail the test.[234] These included reservations to provisions that reflect customary norms binding on states regardless of the treaty; reservations 'denying peoples the right to determine their own political status and to pursue their economic, social and cultural development'; and reservations to the obligation to respect rights on a non-discriminatory basis.[235] The Committee also affirmed that the 'normal consequence of an unacceptable reservation is not that the Covenant will not be in effect at all for the reserving party' but that it 'will be operative for the reserving party without benefit of the reservation'.[236] The European Court of Human Rights has taken the same view of the European Convention of Human Rights[237] (though in other respects the European Convention makes express provision for the effect of reservations).[238]

Though an exercise of advisory jurisdiction, *Reservations to the Genocide Convention* came to influence the International Law Commission, the drafters of the Vienna Convention, and decisions by other international courts. Fitzmaurice said that the traditional rule on reservations had had 'almost the entire weight of previous international authority behind it'.[239] This ignores the substantially different practice of Latin American states, to which the Court referred, but, even considering that regional exception to the 'weight of ... authority', the influence of the opinion is remarkable. Insofar as the Court articulated a new approach to reservations that departed from the traditional rule, it was engaging in what is sometimes called 'the progressive development of international law'—a term that the General Assembly used in requesting the Advisory Opinion, albeit in the part of the resolution addressed to the Commission rather than to the Court.[240] Hersch Lauterpacht described the Advisory Opinion as judicial legislation.[241]

---

[229] ILC Guide to Practice on Reservations to Treaties, ILC 63rd session (2011), UN Doc A/66/10/Add.1, 34, 388 (commentary to § 3.1.5.7, [1]).

[230] GG Fitzmaurice, Report on the Law of Treaties, 14 March 1956 [1956] 1 *ILC Ybk* 104, 127.

[231] *Congo v Rwanda* (n 196) 32–33.

[232] International Covenant on Civil and Political Rights, 16 December 1966, 999 UNTS 1.

[233] CCPR General Comment No 24: Issues Relating to Reservations, UN Doc CCPR/C/21/Rev.1/Add.6.

[234] ibid, [6].

[235] ibid, [8]–[11].

[236] ibid, [18].

[237] *Belilos v Switzerland*, ECtHR App No 10328/83, 29 April 1988, [60].

[238] European Convention for the Protection of Human Rights and Fundamental Freedoms, 4 November 1950, ETS 5, Art 57.

[239] Fitzmaurice, 'Reservations' (n 206) 11.

[240] UNGA Res 1731 (XVI), 20 December 1961.

[241] H Lauterpacht, *The Development of International Law by the International Court* (Cambridge, CUP, 1958) 189–90.

VI. HOLDING INTERNATIONAL ORGANS TO ACCOUNT: *EFFECT OF AWARDS OF COMPENSATION (UNAT)* AND *JUDGMENTS OF THE ADMINISTRATIVE TRIBUNAL OF THE ILO UPON COMPLAINTS MADE AGAINST UNESCO*

Unsurprisingly, an organisation with the personnel, budget, activities and politics of the United Nations encountered questions about the interpretation and application of its own rules. As we already have related, the earliest advisory opinions of the ICJ addressed basic questions about how the UN is constituted (*Conditions of Admission*) and about its character as a legal person (*Reparation for Injuries*). Also in the first decade of its operation, the ICJ addressed questions arising out of disputes between the Organization (or one of its specialised agencies) and its personnel. The disputes themselves, at first blush, were matters that might arise in any large bureaucracy—allegations of unfair dismissal and unfair refusal to renew contracts of employment. On further inspection, the questions posed to the Court went to fundamental aspects of international organisation and international law, including equality of parties in legal proceedings, accountability and judicial independence, separation of powers within the UN, and the relation between legal responsibility of the organisation and legal responsibility of the member states. The present section will briefly summarise the questions and holdings in the advisory opinions on *Effect of Awards of Compensation Made by the United Nations Administrative Tribunal* (1954) and *Judgments of the Administrative Tribunal of the ILO upon Complaints Made against UNESCO* (1956). We then will assess the wider significance of these early landmarks in the Court's treatment of intramural matters of the system of which it is 'the principal judicial organ'.

A. *Effect of Awards of Compensation,* 13 July 1954

Controversies over financial contributions to the UN have surfaced from time to time since early in the UN era. A major early episode erupted out of concerns in the United States that persons with communist sympathies had infiltrated the UN civil service. Having intensified scrutiny of its own civil service personnel, the United States in 1953 brought US nationals employed by the UN under its Civil Service Commission program of loyalty screening.[242] A number of UN personnel of US nationality were then dismissed from UN service. Ten dismissed personnel brought 11 cases before the Administrative Tribunal of the United Nations (UNAT). Not all resulted in compensatory awards in favour of the dismissed personnel,[243] but six did, which equated to favourable judgments for five out of 10 claimants, requiring

---

[242] See LRY Storrs, 'McCarthyism and the Second Red Scare' in *Oxford Encyclopedia of American History* (Oxford, OUP, 2015).

[243] See, eg, Judgment No 26 (Case No 34: *Marjorie L Zap v Secretary-General of the United Nations*), 21 August 1953; Judgment No 46 (Case No 53: *Lyman Cromwell White v Secretary-General of the United Nations*) (Bastid, President; Lord Crook, Vice-President; Petrén, Vice-President; Loutfi and Abdoh, alternates), 11 December 1953.

an appropriation by the General Assembly of $179,420.[244] To give one example, Jane Reed, a member of the Secretariat Library staff, appeared as a witness before the Internal Security Sub-Committee of the US Senate (which seems to have been in a competitive posture toward the US House Un-American Activities Committee). Ms Reed had invoked the privilege under the Fifth Amendment to the US Constitution and refused to reply to certain questions that the Sub-Committee had posed. This was on 15 October 1952. The Secretary-General of the United Nations told her that 'he was very much concerned about this matter' and placed her on leave on 22 October 1952. The Secretary-General on 1 December told Ms Reed that he would terminate her employment if she did not waive her Fifth Amendment privilege and return to testify to the US Senate Sub-Committee. She refused. The Secretary-General terminated Ms Reed's employment on 5 December. She brought a claim for compensation before UNAT, which resulted in an award of money damages.[245]

A public outcry ensued in the United States in opposition to financing the General Assembly appropriations required to satisfy the UNAT awards. Pressure was brought to bear at the UN to refuse to satisfy the awards.

The General Assembly on 9 December 1953 presented the following questions to the ICJ for an advisory opinion:

(1)   Having regard to the Statute of the United Nations Administrative Tribunal and to any other relevant instruments and to the relevant records, has the General Assembly the right on any grounds to refuse to give effect to an award of compensation made by that Tribunal in favour of a staff member of the United Nations whose contract of service has been terminated without his assent?

(2)   If the answer given by the Court to question (1) is in the affirmative, what are the principal grounds upon which the General Assembly could lawfully exercise such a right?

This, then, was not a call to review the UNAT awards. There was, in any event, no provision for appeal or review in the UNAT Statute. The request instead concerned the powers of one of the principal organs in respect of a dispute settlement mechanism that that organ had itself constituted. The Court answered the first question categorically in the negative: 'the General Assembly has not the right on any grounds to refuse to give effect to an award of compensation' such as that in the UNAT judgments.[246] The second question accordingly did not call for consideration.

The Advisory Opinion provoked further objection in the United States. A Joint Resolution of the US House and Senate (Resolution 262) expressed the sense of Congress that no part of the awards should be settled from funds provided by the United States.[247] This in turn spurred the United States to call for a judicial review procedure of UNAT awards. John Foster Dulles, the Secretary of State, did affirm that

---

[244] The sum was given in UNGA Res 785 A (VIII), 9 December 1953, preambular [1], by which the advisory request was made.

[245] Judgment No 37 (Case No 45: *Jane Reed v Secretary-General*), 21 August 1953.

[246] *Effect of Awards of Compensation Made by the United Nations Administrative Tribunal*, Advisory Opinion [1954] ICJ Rep 47, 62.

[247] Adopted 10 August 1954 (House); 20 August 1954 (Senate), for which see Congressional Record, vol 100, part II, 13949, 15386.

the United States would, owing to 'our traditional respect [for] judicial opinions ... abide by [the] Court's finding despite our sharp disagreement'.[248] A certain degree of damage nevertheless appears to have been done on the US domestic scene to the prestige of the Organization.

B. *ILOAT UNESCO Judgments*, 23 October 1956

A further advisory opinion arose out of much the same political circumstances. Both chambers of the United States legislative branch having set up loyalty screening procedures, as noted above, the executive branch did the same. Four US nationals employed by UNESCO found themselves called to testify to the International Organizations Employees Loyalty Board of the United States Civil Service Commission.[249] Mr Peter Duberg, a representative example of the four UNESCO employees, refused to appear before the Board. Having informed the Director-General of UNESCO on 13 July 1954 of his refusal, Mr Duberg was informed by letter of 13 August 1954 that his appointment as a UNESCO employee would not be renewed.[250] Mr Duberg sought compensation from UNESCO before the Administrative Tribunal of the International Labour Organization (ILOAT). ILOAT found that UNESCO's decision should be rescinded and declared that that decision 'constitutes an abuse of rights'. ILOAT awarded $15,500 and other allowances to Duberg in the event UNESCO did not renew his appointment.[251]

Article II, paragraph 5, of the Statute of ILOAT provided (and still provides) that the Tribunal has competence to hear certain complaints from personnel of an international organisation other than the ILO, where the organisation has declared its recognition of the jurisdiction of the ILOAT for that purpose. Article XII of the ILOAT Statute as it was in 1956 provided that an organisation having declared such recognition may submit certain questions of the validity of an ILOAT decision to the ICJ for an advisory opinion, that opinion to be binding. The questions must concern either (or both) a challenge to the ILOAT's jurisdiction or the contention that the ILOAT's decision 'is vitiated by a fundamental fault in procedure'. UNESCO, which recognised ILOAT jurisdiction in accordance with Article II, paragraph 5, invoked Article XII, in effect for the purpose of challenging the ILOAT judgment in

---

[248] Secretary of State to Certain Diplomatic Missions, 11 December 1954, reprinted in *Foreign Relations of the United States, 1952–1954*, vol III (United Nations Affairs) (Office of the Historian, US Department of State) 410–11.

[249] Interestingly, the Department of State officers who fleshed out the operating practice of the Loyalty Board identified UNESCO as an example of the specialised agencies upon which the board should focus. They also recognised—as would the Court (*ILOAT UNESCO Judgments* [1956] ICJ Rep 77, 92)—that applicants for employment would have no standing to complain to the tribunals but that 'in taking action against an employee the Secretary General of an international organisation had to consider decisions reached by administrative tribunals ... and in some instances he was bound by them': Memorandum by William L Franklin (Office of Security), Subject: Transmission of Information under Executive Orders 10422 and 10459 by the Civil Service Commission's International Organizations Employees Loyalty Board, 11 August 1953, reprinted in *Foreign Relations of the United States, 1952–1954*, vol III (United Nations Affairs) (Office of the Historian, US Department of State) document 127.

[250] *ILOAT UNESCO Judgments* (n 250) 81–82.

[251] *In re Duberg*, ILOAT, Judgment No 17, 26 April 1955.

the Duberg case and the other three American UNESCO employee cases. UNESCO contended that ILOAT had exceeded its jurisdiction; it did not contend that ILOAT's judgments were 'vitiated by a fundamental fault in procedure'.

The ICJ noted that Article XII of the ILOAT Statute, in establishing the binding effect of an advisory opinion on the requesting organ, 'goes beyond the scope attributed by the Charter and by the Statute of the Court to an Advisory Opinion'.[252] According to the Court, this extension of the opinion's effect 'provides no reason why the Request for an Opinion should not be complied with'.[253] That was not the end of the matter, however. Considering the purpose for which UNESCO requested the opinion, a problem arose. UNESCO requested the opinion in order to challenge four Judgments of ILOAT in favour of four UNESCO officials. As reflected in the written submissions, certain member states wished to overturn, nullify or otherwise avoid the results of those judgments. Notwithstanding formal qualifications to distinguish the advisory proceedings from an appeal, the Court could not avoid the observation that the 'advisory procedure thus brought into being appears as serving, in a way, the object of an appeal'.[254] Moreover, as the Court acknowledged, Article XII envisaged advisory proceedings as a substitute for contentious proceedings for the reason that the latter are open only to states, and so a contentious case between an international organisation and an individual would have doubly failed.[255] The problem was that placing the matter under advisory procedure still left one party out. Articles 66 and 67 of the Court's Statute provide for states and international organisations to participate in advisory proceedings, not for individuals. The particular terms of UNESCO's consent to ILOAT jurisdiction and to the possibility of advisory recourse to the ICJ did nothing to remedy the omission. As the Court observed, UNESCO, 'in challenging the four Judgments and applying to the Court ... availed itself of a legal remedy which was open to it alone'.[256] The individual claimant, whose rights under the ILOAT Judgment the judgment debtor now challenged, had no independent standing before the Court. Suggesting a certain anxiety about the matter, the Court repeatedly offered assurances that the problem was not a problem at all. The Court said that the use to which the Advisory Opinion would be put under ILOAT Statute Article XII 'in no wise affects the way in which the Court functions' or its reasoning;[257] it said that 'the inequality ... does not in fact constitute an inequality before the Court'.[258]

The (supposed) balm for the inequality of the parties was a procedural sleight of hand. The Court denied that it was changing the way it conducted its proceedings ('the inequality ... does not affect the manner in which the Court undertakes the examination'), but it lay emphasis on the fact that UNESCO transmitted to the Court supplementary observations 'formulated on behalf of the persons in whose

---

[252] *ILOAT UNESCO Judgments* (n 250) 84.
[253] ibid. The Court since has made clear that, when agreed, binding effects can be attributed to an advisory opinion in respect of a State as well: *Immunity from Legal Process* (n 83) 77, [25].
[254] ibid, 84.
[255] ibid, 85.
[256] ibid.
[257] ibid, 84.
[258] ibid, 85.

favour [the] Judgments ... were given'.[259] In this way—*via* the organisation that was now seeking to undermine their earlier success in proceedings against that organisation—the individual claimants were said to enjoy all due procedural protection. Judge Córdova, dissenting, fairly described this as a 'very unusual procedure'.[260] He took it to be unacceptable that the individual parties 'had to depend upon the goodwill of their opponents to act as an intermediary for the presentation of their views'.[261] He would have declared the Court incompetent to give the opinion.[262] In short, speaking from behind a screen is not the same thing as speaking face to face. The point would resurface from time to time and, for a time, it occasioned no great disquiet.[263] However, as will be seen below, it eventually presaged the end of ILOAT Article XII and the form of advisory recourse that provision enabled.

C. Commentary and Assessment

Effect of Awards of Compensation and *ILOAT UNESCO Judgments,* quite apart from the fraught politics surrounding them, would hold continuing interest for their legal content.

Particular attention was drawn to *Effects of Awards* during discussions at the ILC in connection with the draft Articles on Responsibility of International Organizations. Alain Pellet proposed that, from the Advisory Opinion, it 'followed that international organizations [are] legally obliged to discharge their financial obligations arising in the context of reparation *and that member States had no choice but to enable them to do so*'.[264] This was in reference to the Advisory Opinion, where the Court had said that 'the assignment of the budgetary function to the General Assembly cannot be regarded as conferring upon it the right to refuse to give effect to the obligation arising out of the award of the Administrative Tribunal'[265] and that the 'General Assembly has not the right on any grounds to refuse to give effect to [such] an award'.[266] ILC members agreed that the risk that an international organisation would lack (or be deprived of) the resources to satisfy its obligations presents a problem; they had difficulty agreeing to a solution.[267] Nolte saw *Effect of Awards of Compensation* as concerning one constitutive treaty (the UN Charter) and thus as saying little about general international law. As such, it did not, in his view, 'postulate an obligation on the part of the Member States ... but only on the part of the General Assembly'.[268] It had to do with a 'special case of the effects of a final judgment *within a constitutional*

---

[259] ibid, 80.
[260] ibid, 166.
[261] ibid.
[262] ibid, 168.
[263] See *Review of Judgment No 158 of the United Nations Administrative Tribunal,* Advisory Opinion [1973] ICJ Rep 166, 172.
[264] A Pellet, ILC 2935th mtg, 12 July 2007 [2007] 1 *ILC Ybk* 145 [76].
[265] *Effect of Awards* (n 246) 59.
[266] ibid, 62.
[267] Pellet (n 264) [70].
[268] G Nolte, ILC 2935th mtg, 12 July 2007, [2007] 1 *ILC Ybk* 159 [50].

system', but not the general system of international law.[269] *Effect of Awards of Compensation* in light of these divergent views can be seen as an early page in the search for a solution to the problem of responsibility of organisations constituted under multilateral treaties—and, in particular, the problem of giving their responsibility practical effect.[270]

Article 40, paragraph 2, of the Articles as eventually adopted provides:

> The members of a responsible international organization shall take all the appropriate measures that may be required *by the rules of the organization* in order to enable the organization to fulfil its obligations under this Chapter.[271]

The ILC Commentary added:

> While the rules of the organization do not necessarily deal with the matter expressly, an obligation for members to finance the organization as part of the general duty to cooperate with the organization may be implied under the relevant rules.[272]

The Commentary referred to Fitzmaurice's separate opinion in *Certain Expenses* in support of the (possible) 'general duty'.[273] The Commentary thus suggested, though not with much conviction, that the obligations of member states for giving an organisation the funds to satisfy its debts might have something to do with rules outside those of the organisation. The matter in the main is contained within each organisation's particular legal framework.

Distinct from the question of legal responsibility of member states for the finances of and other conduct of an international organisation, there is a question of mechanisms to hold an international organisation to account. *Effect of Awards of Compensation* by no means imposed a general international law obligation on member states. But it did amount to an early, if halting, step towards accountability of international organisations.[274] It is true that the Court drew attention to the power of the General Assembly to revoke the Statute that gave UNAT the power to adopt awards binding on the General Assembly.[275] Such a power of revocation would seem to diminish, not enhance, accountability. At the same time, in drawing attention to this power, the Court dismissed the contention that the Assembly could not have conferred such power on a tribunal;[276] it noted, by domestic law analogy, that national legislatures 'create courts with the capacity to render decisions legally binding on the legislatures which brought them into being'.[277] Moreover, the Court

---

[269] ibid (emphasis added).

[270] Compare *JH Rayner (Mincing Lane) Ltd v Department of Trade and Industry (International Tin Council Case)* (1990) 81 ILR 670, 678–80 (Lord Templeman), 683–84 (Lord Griffiths).

[271] Articles on Responsibility of International Organizations [2011] 2 *ILC Ybk* 2, Art 40 (emphasis added).

[272] ibid, commentary to Art 4, [5].

[273] *Certain Expenses* (n 89) 208 (Judge Fitzmaurice).

[274] Klabbers notes that the Court's analysis of its role in judicial review of the General Assembly's conduct was scanty: J Klabbers, 'Checks and Balances in the Law of International Organizations' (2007) 13 *Ius Gentium* 141, 160.

[275] *Effect of Awards* (n 246) 56.

[276] The Court referred in this connection to *Reparation for Injuries* (n 68) 182 ('the Organization must be deemed to have those powers which, though not expressly provided in the Charter, are conferred upon it by necessary implication'). See *Effect of Awards* (n 246) 56.

[277] *Effect of Awards* (n 246) 61.

expressed the opinion that, if the General Assembly ever were to change the UNAT Statute, for example by setting up an appellate instance, 'the General Assembly itself, in view of its composition and functions, could hardly act as a judicial organ ... all the more so as one party to the disputes is the United Nations Organization itself'.[278] This was a directive (or at least a suggestion) to the legislator: feel free to adopt a different procedure, but you cannot be your own judge. The Court here can be heard to have affirmed judicial independence as a principle applicable within the constellation of UN rules and procedures. It was by General Assembly act that 'an independent and truly judicial body' had been constituted.[279] Taking the Advisory Opinion as a whole, it appears that the Court would not accept any approach that lacked those properties.

As to the role of the ICJ in the wider institutional framework, the 1950s advisory opinions might have invited further recourse to the Court for settlement of differences relating to tribunal awards. Indeed, administrative tribunal cases did lead to a succession of advisory proceedings,[280] but by no means did a floodgate open. Other institutions that might have provided for recourse to the ICJ did not do so. The World Bank, for example, when establishing its own Administrative Tribunal, considered the practice of the UN and ILO tribunals but on several grounds declined to include a mechanism for ICJ advisory opinions. For one thing, 'the mechanism itself has been criticised by the ICJ and a similar attempt at the Bank to channel cases to the ICJ may present similar difficulties'. For another, in the Bank's view, 'there appears to be no compelling reason to have a stage beyond a properly constituted tribunal'.[281] From the early administrative tribunal advisory opinions, one thus can trace still-live questions of international law. The question remains unsettled how to hold an international organisation to account. And, so too, the question continues to concern states and jurists whether—and if so to what extent and in what form—agreed dispute settlement procedures need higher instances as a control.[282]

For the UN administrative system, at any rate, the question whether to have such a control was, at length, addressed in the affirmative. The General Assembly—in 2007–8, which is to say over half a century after John Foster Dulles had suggested it—abolished UNAT and replaced it with a two-tier system. A UN Dispute Tribunal now deals with staff cases, and a UN Appeals Tribunal receives appeals from its decisions,[283] which are binding upon the parties.[284]

---

[278] ibid, 56.

[279] ibid, 53.

[280] *Review of Judgment No 158* [1973] ICJ Rep 166; *Review of Judgment No 273 of the United Nations Administrative Tribunal*, Advisory Opinion [1982] ICJ Rep 325; *Review of Judgment No 333 of the United Nations Administrative Tribunal*, Advisory Opinion [1987] ICJ Rep 18; *Judgment No 2867 of the Administrative Tribunal of the International Labour Organization upon a Complaint Filed against the International Fund for Agricultural Development*, Advisory Opinion [2012] ICJ Rep 10.

[281] Memorandum relating to draft Statute for Bank Administrative Tribunal, 1 November 1979, 5. From World Bank Group Archives, Administrative Tribunal—Correspondence 01; Folder ID: 1201400; ISAD(G) Reference Code: WB/IBRD/IDA 03 Exc-10-4539S.

[282] Consider the European Commission's proposal of 12 November 2015 for an 'investment court system' for the Transatlantic Trade and Investment Partnership, about which see SW Schill, 'The European Commission's Proposal of an "Investment Court System" for TTIP: Stepping Stone or Stumbling Block for Multilateralizing International Investment Law?' (2016) 20 *ASIL Insights* 9.

[283] UNGA Res 61/261, 4 April 2007; 62/228, 22 December 2007; 63/253, 24 December 2008.

[284] Statute of the United Nations Appeals Tribunal, Art 10(5).

That by no means implies that the only impact of the 1950s advisory opinions on administrative tribunals was in the remote future. They had near-term effects as well. In particular, they helped to settle questions about the management of the UN and legal relations within it. The advisory opinions of the Court are not binding. However, Article XII of the Statute of the Administrative Tribunal of the ILO[285] provided that an advisory opinion of the ICJ resulting from a request made by an agency that accepts the jurisdiction of the ILO Administrative Tribunal will be binding. This was 'nothing but a rule of conduct for the Executive Board [of UNESCO in the case at hand]'.[286] It was nonetheless a rule for that body.

There were six organisations recognising the jurisdiction of the ILO Tribunal at the time (WHO, ITU, UNESCO, WMO, FAO, and CERN).[287] There are over 60 today.[288] The ILO itself, after consultation with the organisations recognising the ILO Administrative Tribunal's jurisdiction, in 2016 amended the Statute of the ILO Administrative Tribunal, deleting Article XII.[289] A similar amendment to the UNAT Statute had removed the ICJ advisory provision in 1995. This might be seen as another long-term effect of the 1956 Advisory Opinion, telegraphed through more recent practice. In particular, the Advisory Opinion concerning *Judgment No 2867 of the Administrative Tribunal of the ILO upon a Complaint Filed against the International Fund for Agricultural Development* (2012) had returned to the problem of equality of parties.[290] Judge Greenwood's separate opinion drew pointed attention to it:

> [I]n the circumstances of the present case, the Court was right to comply with the request for an advisory opinion but I have reached that conclusion with considerable reluctance and only because of the particular circumstances of the case. The Opinion highlights—rightly, in my view—the unsatisfactory nature of the provision for recourse to the Court laid down in Article XII of the Annex to the Statute of the Administrative Tribunal ... As the Court makes clear, the procedure created by that provision is open to serious criticisms in that it falls well short of modern standards on equality of the parties in legal proceedings ... The need for reform of Article XII of the ILOAT Statute is urgent and it is very much to be hoped that a new procedure for challenging judgments of the Tribunal can be put in place within a short period of time.[291]

The ILO itself, when in due course it deleted Article XII, expressed concern over 'equality of access to justice and equality of arms'.[292]

As binding decisions under the rules of the tribunals concerned, the ICJ's early statements on the powers of the administrative tribunals contributed to

---

[285] Statute of the Administrative Tribunal of the ILO, 9 October 1946, amended 29 June 1949, Art XII.

[286] *ILOAT UNESCO Judgments* (n 250) 84.

[287] ibid, 79.

[288] For a list of cases by organisation, see www.ilo.org/dyn/triblex/triblexmain.byOrg.

[289] International Labour Conference, 105th session (June 2016); ILO Governing Body, 326th session (March 2016).

[290] Advisory Opinion [2012] ICJ Rep 10, 26 ('any review procedure should enable the staff member to participate on an equitable basis in such procedure, which should ensure substantial equality').

[291] ibid, 93–94 (Judge Greenwood).

[292] 'Amendments to the Statute of the ILO Administrative Tribunal adopted', 14 June 2016, <www.ilo.org/global/about-the-ilo/how-the-ilo-works/departments-and-offices/jur/legal-instruments/WCMS_498369/lang--en/index.htm>.

the jurisprudence of these organs and have influenced their conduct since. Other tribunals, like the World Bank Administrative Tribunal, have referred to the ICJ's advisory practice for guidance.[293] The core of an international administrative law— or at least an administrative law for international organisations—in this way began to emerge.[294]

VII. CONCLUSION

The present chapter has considered a series of advisory opinions delivered in the first decade and a half of the International Court of Justice, which is to say in the opening years of the era of the UN Charter. States in the period from the Charter's adoption in 1945 to the Court's delivery of the *Certain Expenses* Advisory Opinion in 1962 took steps towards implementing a new understanding of sovereignty. They placed an array of technical functions in the hands of international institutions and adopted new multilateral instruments of general subscription. Yet in the same period, deep fissures opened in international society—with the Cold War, between East and West; and, with decolonisation, between North and South. The early advisory practice of the ICJ was part of the community-building enterprise of the day, with all the cross-currents and challenges that that enterprise entailed.

In view of the circumstances, it comes as little surprise that the impact of this advisory practice was not uniform. Surprising, perhaps, is that legal developments would emerge from the practice over such substantial lengths of time. It is not obvious, for example, that one court would have affirmed that the main international organisation could hold the right to receive reparation for injuries done *to* its agents (*Reparation for Injuries*); remain essentially silent for half a century as to the *obligation* of that organisation for injuries done *by* its agent; and then—with only modest intervening hints as to what eventually would come—affirm the obligation in plain language (*Immunity from Legal Process of a Special Rapporteur*). Then there was the accountability of this sprawling machinery of international governance to the individuals sometimes caught up in its wheels. It was in 1956 that the Court first confronted the problem of equality of access to justice (*ILOAT UNESCO Judgments*); it was in 2012 that the Court threw down the gauntlet to the other organs of the international system and thus helped instigate corrective steps (*Judgment No 2867*). Slow though it may be, this is a court with institutional memory. The jurisprudence, as expounded in the advisory opinions of the ICJ, might not have looked like it was on a course of inexorable progress—nevertheless, it progressed.

Perhaps the sharpest challenge against the particular conception of international community emerging during this time came from South Africa. The challenge took form both in South Africa's internal policy of *apartheid* and in its administration of South West Africa (Namibia), a territory that had been entrusted to it by the League of Nations. The Court gave three advisory opinions during the period considered

---

[293] See JI Charney (1998) 271 *Hague Recueil* 1, 225–27.
[294] See E Benvenisti, 'The Interplay between Actors as a Determinant of the Evolution of Administrative Law in International Institutions' (2005) 68 *Law and Contemporary Problems* 319, 325–31.

in this chapter addressing different aspects of the problem of South West Africa—
International Status of South-West Africa (1950),[295] *Voting Procedure on Questions
Relating to Reports and Petitions Concerning the Territory of South-West Africa*
(1955),[296] and *Admissibility of Hearings of Petitioners by the Committee on South
West Africa* (1956).[297] The contentious proceedings instituted against South Africa
by Liberia and Ethiopia in 1960 are better known,[298] and the judicial culmination
came in 1971 with the Advisory Opinion on Namibia.[299] South Africa was generally dismissive of the Court, seeing the South West Africa cases at most as a useful
distraction that afforded 'a further breathing space to decide what is to be done
about the territory'.[300] Decades indeed would elapse before Namibia's independence
in 1990, but the 'breathing space' brought South Africa no closer to the result its
apartheid rulers desired. To the contrary, the successive advisory and contentious
proceedings at the Court traced the accelerating collapse of South Africa's credibility
and resilience in world affairs. Like the other main developments that the advisory
practice of the period advanced, the full impact of the South Africa advisory opinions took time to emerge.

For a court whose effectiveness in international relations is sometimes questioned,
the early advisory opinions remind us that time indeed may have to pass before we
can take its full measure.

---

[295] Advisory Opinion [1950] ICJ Rep 128.
[296] Advisory Opinion [1955] ICJ Rep 67.
[297] Advisory Opinion [1956] ICJ Rep 23.
[298] *South West Africa (Ethiopia v South Africa; Liberia v South Africa)*, Preliminary Objections [1962]
ICJ Rep 319; Second Phase [1966] ICJ Rep 6.
[299] *Legal Consequences for States of the Continued Presence of South Africa in Namibia (South West
Africa) notwithstanding Security Council Resolution 276 (1970)*, Advisory Opinion [1971] ICJ Rep 16.
The *Namibia* Advisory Opinion and the 1950s advisory opinions concerning South West Africa are
treated in the next chapter.
[300] US Embassy (Pretoria) to Department of State, 8 November 1960, report by Philip K Crowe of conversation with Minister of External Affairs of South Africa, Eric Louw: Dispatch No 264; 360/11-860.

11

The *South West Africa Cases* (1949 to 1971)

JAMES CRAWFORD* AND PAUL MERTENSKÖTTER

I. INTRODUCTION

FOUR ADVISORY OPINIONS, two judgments, the most litigated territory before the International Court of Justice (ICJ). The *South West Africa Cases* carry important lessons both about the workings of the Court with its changing composition and about its interaction with the other principal organs of the United Nations.[1] As Solomon Slonim pointed out in 1973, this 'notable intermeshing of law and politics ... must be reckoned among the distinctive features of the entire dispute'.[2] It is this interplay of legal judgment and political affairs in the face of a clear public policy need—the fight against apartheid in a mandated territory—that provides the theme for this contribution.

Part II provides the historical context necessary to understand the *South West Africa Cases*: the struggle over ultimate authority goes back to Versailles.[3] Part III recounts the three advisory opinions handed down between 1950 and 1956. Part IV examines the 1962 and 1966 judgments in the contentious proceedings between Ethiopia and Liberia as Applicants and South Africa as Respondent. Part V traces the highly critical reactions to the 1966 judgment and analyses the Court's own counterpoise in the form of the 1971 advisory opinion.

---

* The views expressed are those of the authors.

[1] *South West Africa Cases* refers to the following six decisions: *International Status of South-West Africa*, (Advisory Opinion) [1950] ICJ Rep 128; *South-West Africa—Voting Procedure* (Advisory Opinion) [1955] ICJ Rep 67; *Admissibility of Hearings of Petitioners by the Committee on South West Africa* (Advisory Opinion) [1956] ICJ Rep 23; *South West Africa Cases (Ethiopia v South Africa; Liberia v South Africa* (Preliminary Objections) [1962] ICJ Rep 319; *South West Africa Cases, Second Phase*, [1966] ICJ Reports 6; *Legal Consequences for States of the Continued Presence of South Africa in Namibia (South West Africa) Notwithstanding Security Council Resolution 276 (1970)* (Advisory Opinion) [1971] ICJ Rep 16.

[2] S Slonim, *South West Africa and the United Nations: An International Mandate in Dispute* (Baltimore, John Hopkins University Press, 1973) 5.

[3] For a useful account of the history see S Pederson, *The Guardians. The League of Nations and the Crisis of Empire* (Oxford, OUP, 2015) esp Chs 4, 7.

II. THE MANDATE OVER SOUTH WEST AFRICA, 1919–50

Article 22 of the Covenant inaugurated the mandates system, giving the League a supervisory role over the territorial administration of former German and Ottoman territories detached by the Peace Treaties. Article 22 was subject to long and heated negotiations, with the United States insisting on League supervision over all mandates, while South Africa and Australia pushed for the annexation of former German South West Africa and New Guinea respectively.[4] The final language sacrificed clarity for an ambiguity acceptable to all.[5] It read:

(1)   To those colonies and territories which as a consequence of the late war have ceased to be under the sovereignty of the States which formerly governed them and which are inhabited by peoples not yet able to stand by themselves under the strenuous conditions of the modern world, there should be applied the principle that the well-being and development of such peoples form a sacred trust of civilisation and that securities for the performance of this trust should be embodied in this Covenant.

(2)   The best method of giving practical effect to this principle is that the tutelage of such peoples should be entrusted to advanced nations who by reason of their resources, their experience or their geographical position can best undertake this responsibility, and who are willing to accept it, and that this tutelage should be exercised by them as Mandatories on behalf of the League.

(3)   The character of the mandate must differ according to the stage of the development of the people, the geographical situation of the territory, its economic conditions and other similar circumstances.

(4)   Certain communities formerly belonging to the Turkish Empire have reached a stage of development where their existence as independent nations can be provisionally recognised subject to the rendering of administrative advice and assistance by a Mandatory until such time as they are able to stand alone. The wishes of these communities must be a principal consideration in the selection of the Mandatory.

(5)   Other peoples, especially those of Central Africa, are at such a stage that the Mandatory must be responsible for the administration of the territory under conditions which will guarantee freedom of conscience and religion, subject only to the maintenance of public order and morals, the prohibition of abuses such as the slave trade, the arms traffic and the liquor traffic, and the prevention of the establishment of fortifications or military and naval bases and of military training of the natives for other than police purposes and the defence of territory, and will also secure equal opportunities for the trade and commerce of other Members of the League.

(6)   There are territories, such as South-West Africa and certain of the South Pacific Islands, which, owing to the sparseness of their population, or their small size, or their remoteness from the centres of civilisation, or their geographical contiguity to the territory of the Mandatory, and other circumstances, can be best administered under the laws of the Mandatory as integral portions of its territory, subject to the safeguards above mentioned in the interests of the indigenous population.

(7)   In every case of mandate, the Mandatory shall render to the Council an annual report in reference to the territory committed to its charge.

---

[4] For a general historical introduction, see Slonim, *South West Africa* (n 2) 11–38.
[5] MO Hudson, *The Permanent Court of International Justice, 1920–1942* (New York, Macmillan, 1943) 229.

(8) The degree of authority, control, or administration to be exercised by the Mandatory shall, if not previously agreed upon by the Members of the League, be explicitly defined in each case by the Council.

(9) A permanent Commission shall be constituted to receive and examine the annual reports of the Mandatories and to advise the Council on all matters relating to the observance of the mandates.

While Article 22 established the mandate system and defined the 'primary and substantive obligation undertaken by the mandatory', its implementation required further agreements between the League and the mandatory to settle the specific 'degree of authority, control, or administration'.[6] The agreement for South West Africa was confirmed by the League Council in December 1920.[7] Article 2 provided that:

(1) The Mandatory shall have full power of administration and legislation over the territory subject to the present Mandate as an integral portion of the Union of South Africa to the territory, and may apply the laws of the Union of South Africa to the territory, subject to such local modifications as circumstances may require.

(2) The Mandatory shall promote to the utmost the material and moral well-being and the social progress of the inhabitants of the territory subject to the present Mandate.

Article 6 provided for an annual report by the Mandatory to the Council. Article 7 provided:

(1) The consent of the Council of the League of Nations is required for any modification of the terms of the present Mandate.

(2) The Mandatory agrees that, if any dispute whatever should arise between the Mandatory and another Member of the League of Nations relating to the interpretation or the application of the provisions of the Mandate, such dispute, if it cannot be settled by negotiation, shall be submitted to the Permanent Court of International Justice.

The fundamental question, which neither the Covenant nor the Mandate Agreement clearly answered, concerned the location of ultimate authority over the mandate: did it lie with the League or with the Mandatory?[8] This question was at issue, expressly or by implication, in all the cases before the Court.

III. THE FIRST THREE ADVISORY OPINIONS: STATUS, VOTING PROCEDURE, HEARING OF PETITIONERS

The UN came into being in October 1945 and the League was dissolved shortly after. Under Article 37 of the Statute of the International Court of Justice (an integral part of the UN Charter) the Permanent Court of International Justice was replaced by the new Court in existing jurisdictional clauses, including Article 7(2) of the Mandate for South West Africa. But the Court's initial involvement took the form not of proceedings under Article 7(2) but of a series of advisory opinions.

---

[6] A Anghie, *Imperialism, Sovereignty and the Making of International Law* (Cambridge, CUP, 2004) 2; Art 22 [8] of the Covenant.

[7] Slonim (n 2) 40.

[8] See J Crawford, *The Creation of States in International Law*, 2nd edn (Oxford, OUP, 2006) 568.

A. *International Status of South West Africa* (1950)

In December 1949, the General Assembly requested an advisory opinion as to 'the international status of the Territory of South West Africa' and 'the international obligations of the Union of South Africa arising therefrom'.[9] The request concerned Article 77 of the Charter which did not firmly establish whether former mandated territories (if not already independent) would necessarily become part of the new Trusteeship System. South Africa denied any obligation to convert South West Africa to a trusteeship, and indeed sought approval to annex the territory.

The institutional locus for the debate was the Fourth Committee, which received information about the indigenous population's terrible living conditions through the efforts of Michael Scott, an Anglican clergyman in Johannesburg, the International League for Human Rights, the National Association for the Advancement of Colored People (NAACP), and the Government of India.[10] Following the National Party's 1948 electoral victory on an 'apartheid' platform, the passage of the South West Africa Affairs Amendment Act 1949 signaled a move toward annexation.[11] Over the vehement opposition of South Africa, the debate led to a resolution requesting an advisory opinion about South West Africa's international status.[12] The first and most important question for the Court was whether 'South Africa continue[s] to have international obligations under the Mandate for South-West Africa and, if so, what ... those obligations are'.[13]

The Court began by affirming two principles of 'paramount importance' for the creators of the mandate system, 'non-annexation' and the 'sacred trust of civilisation' for the well-being and development of peoples not yet able to assume a full measure of self-government.[14] Article 22 and the Mandate Agreement required South Africa 'to exercise an international function of administration on behalf of the League, with the object of promoting the well-being and development of its inhabitants'.[15] Authority over South West Africa rested on the mandate. 'If the Mandate lapsed,' so the Court held, South Africa's 'authority would equally have lapsed. To retain the rights derived from the Mandate and deny the obligations thereunder could not be justified'.[16] This was to become the bedrock of the Court's stand on the fundamental question of authority implicit in subsequent cases, with the exception only of the 1966 Judgment.[17]

---

[9] UNGA Res 338 (IV) (6 December 1949).

[10] RS Clark, 'The International League for Human Rights and South West Africa 1947–1957: The Human Rights NGO as Catalyst in the International Legal Process' (1981) 3 *HRQ* 101, 114.

[11] J Dugard (ed), *The South West Africa/Namibia Dispute: Documents and Scholarly Writings on the Controversy Between South Africa and the United Nations* (Berkeley, University of California Press, 1973), 119–27.

[12] UNGA Res 338 (n 9).

[13] ibid.

[14] *International Status of South-West Africa* (n 1) 131.

[15] ibid, 132.

[16] ibid.

[17] *South West Africa Cases* (Preliminary Objections) (n 1) 333 (citing the same language); *Legal Consequences for States of the Continued Presence of South Africa in Namibia* (n 1) 42 (citing the same language).

Because realising the fundamental purposes of the Mandate did not depend on the existence of the League, the winding-up of the League did not put an end to the mandate or to South Africa's obligations under it.[18] The Court confirmed this view with reference to Article 80(1) of the Charter and the League's final resolution on the question of mandates, which made it clear that the mandates themselves did not come to an end.[19] But it also relied on South Africa's own acknowledgment of continuing 'obligations under the Mandate', implying that the substantive obligations continued.[20]

This led to the corollary institutional question: what now, with the disappearance of the League, was the 'machinery for implementation' of the Mandatory's obligations?[21] The Court could not discern in the language of Articles 75 and 77(1) any obligation to conclude a trusteeship agreement, but Article 10 of the Charter gave the General Assembly analogous functions. The subsequent practice of the General Assembly as well as the League's own final resolution on the topic confirmed that South Africa had an 'obligation to submit to supervision and control of the General Assembly and to render annual reports to it'.[22]

This institutional transfer logic enabled the Court to find that the League Council's procedural innovation as to petitions also carried over to the UN. During its operation, the League Council had adopted rules requiring the mandatory to forward petitions to the League from people living in the mandate. South Africa now had to forward these petitions to the GA.[23] This procedural aspect had become politically salient, because of Michael Scott's attempts to have his own views as well as that of the South West African indigenous groups—the Herero in particular—heard at the UN.[24] The Court's institutional logic is sound in light of the basic principle that the mandatory did not have ultimate authority over the mandate. An institution was needed to maintain accountability. Legally, the transfer conception and the emphasis on maintaining the 'special legal status' created by Article 22 overcame the problem of South Africa's not having consented to the new set-up.[25] Consent was not necessary as no new legal relation was entered into, whereas conceiving of it as a novation would make lack of consent problematic.[26] But the Court qualified its finding to some degree with a limiting principle, holding that:

> The degree of supervision to be exercised by the General Assembly should not ... exceed that which applied under the Mandates System, and should conform as far as possible to the procedure followed in this respect by the Council of the League of Nations.[27]

[18] *International Status of South-West Africa* (n 1) 133.
[19] UN Charter, Art 80(1); ibid, 134.
[20] ibid, 134–36.
[21] ibid, 136.
[22] ibid.
[23] ibid, 138. Art 22(9) of the Covenant had not provided for individual petitioning.
[24] Clark, 'Human Rights and South West Africa' (n 10) 114.
[25] *International Status of South-West Africa* (n 1) separate opinion of Judge McNair, 154.
[26] *Legal Consequences for States of the Continued Presence of South Africa in Namibia* (n 1) dissenting opinion of Judge Fitzmaurice, 267; see also, Crawford (n 8) 592.
[27] ibid, 138.

The General Assembly's second sub-question was 'whether the Charter imposes upon the Union of South Africa an obligation to place the Territory under the Trusteeship System by means of a Trusteeship Agreement'.[28] A narrow majority of eight judges relied on the voluntary language in Articles 75 and 77 to conclude that the Charter did not require South Africa to submit to the trusteeship system. By contrast Judge de Visscher, with whom three other judges agreed,[29] thought that the object and purpose of the UN read with the language of Article 80(2) established an obligation to negotiate with a view to bringing South West Africa under trusteeship.

It was again the logic of institutional transfer from the League to the General Assembly that provided the basis for the Court's unanimous answer to the third sub-question, concerning the 'competence to modify the international status of the Territory of South-West Africa'.[30] Here the Court more strongly emphasised South Africa's consent to the General Assembly as the 'competent international organ'.[31]

The General Assembly accepted the Court's opinion but continued to call on South Africa to place South West Africa under trusteeship.[32] It also established an ad hoc committee to implement the Opinion:[33] three years later that Committee was replaced by the permanent Committee on South West Africa,[34] whose work would trigger two further advisory opinions.

B. *Voting Procedure on Questions Relating to Reports and Petitions Concerning the Territory of South-West Africa* (1955)

When establishing the Committee on South West Africa, the General Assembly passed Special Rule F which established that its decisions needed a two-thirds majority.[35] Since during League times voting had been by consensus, the question was raised whether the new procedure was consistent with the 1950 Opinion.[36]

The Court first analysed its 1950 statement that 'the degree of supervision to be exercised by the General Assembly should not therefore exceed that which applied under the Mandates System'. But this qualification only related to substance, not procedure.[37] This conclusion was forcefully questioned by Judge Lauterpacht in his separate opinion.[38] As to the statement that the General Assembly's supervision 'should conform as far as possible to the procedure' used by the League's Council,[39]

---

[28] ibid, 139.
[29] *International Status of South-West Africa* (n 1) 188.
[30] ibid, 141.
[31] ibid, 142.
[32] UNGA Res 449A (V) (13 December 1950) (accepting the advisory opinion); UNGA Res 449B (V) (13 December 1950) (reiterating that 'the normal way' for South West Africa was to be placed under trusteeship).
[33] UNGA Res 449A (n 32).
[34] UNGA Res 749A (VIII) (28 November 1953).
[35] UNGA Res 844 (IX) (11 October 1954).
[36] *International Status of South-West Africa* (n 1) 138.
[37] *South-West Africa—Voting Procedure* (n 1) 72–73, citing ibid, 138.
[38] See ibid, 94.
[39] ibid, 72, citing *International Status of South-West Africa* (n 1) 138.

this did not require the Assembly to change its own constitutional arrangements—of which the voting procedure under Article 18 of the Charter was one.[40] In the Court's words: 'one system cannot be substituted for another without constitutional amendment.'[41] What is 'possible' in terms of transformation for purposes of the saving clause is determined by the receiving institution's own constitution.[42]

C. *Admissibility of Hearings of Petitioners by the Committee on South West Africa* (1956)

Three months after the *Voting Procedure* opinion, a university student claiming to be 'the only native born from South West Africa in America'[43] sought an oral hearing before the Committee on South West Africa. It was argued that South Africa's refusal to cooperate, including its failure to transmit petitions, left an informational lacuna.

As rephrased by the Court, the question to be answered was 'whether it was legally open to the General Assembly to authorise the Committee to grant oral hearings to petitioners'.[44] The reasoning of the Court, again, was guided by what Judge Lauterpacht called 'the method of pure construction'.[45] The Court recalled its principle requiring an unchanging 'degree of supervision' in conformity 'as far as possible with the procedure' followed by the League.[46] But it was not the case that more information made available to the Committee by way of oral hearings would 'add to the obligations of the Mandatory':[47] information was a means to effective supervision, not supervision in itself. Rather, the Court said, 'it is in the interest of the mandatory, as well as of the proper working of the Mandates System, that the exercise of supervision by the General Assembly should be based upon material which has been tested as far as possible, rather than upon material which has not been subjected to proper scrutiny'.[48]

Thus the limiting principle of 1950 allowed for flexibility of methods, but the Court then reached a more politically sensitive issue: South Africa's refusal to transmit petitions from South West Africans.[49] It was this that had made the previous procedure impracticable and the direct petition process to the Committee necessary in the first place.[50] For South Africa now to contend that the Committee was not

---

[40] ibid, 75.
[41] ibid.
[42] ibid, separate opinion of Judge Lauterpacht, 92.
[43] UN Doc/A/2913/Add.2, Annex I(a) (Letter dated 20 September 1955 from Mr E Mburumba Getzen, Lincoln University, Pennsylvania, to the Chairman of the Fourth Committee).
[44] *Admissibility of Hearings* (n 1) 23.
[45] *South-West Africa—Voting Procedure* (n 1) 90.
[46] *Admissibility of Hearings* (n 1) 30.
[47] ibid.
[48] ibid.
[49] ibid, 31.
[50] ibid. The dissenting opinion criticised consideration of this factor. See dissenting opinion of Vice-President Badawi and Judges Basdevant, Hsu Mo, Armand-Ugon and Moreno Quintana, 61.

maintaining 'as far as possible' the League's procedures was an attempt, so the Court implied, to benefit from its own wrongdoing. The vote here was eight to five. The majority opinion did not rely as heavily on the institutional transfer logic as it had done in 1950 and 1955. Reading the dissent makes clear why: the logic of transfer implied reference back to League practice.[51] If no constitutional problem arose, as it did in 1955 with Article 18 of the Charter, the old system of inadmissibility of oral petitions should be maintained.[52]

Ten years after the end of the League the Court was drawn toward a legal conclusion going beyond the mandates system as it had existed in practice. The trusteeship system, the spirit of human rights at the UN and rising voices against apartheid encouraged the Court to be more progressive. South Africa's frustration of the League's petitioning process provided the legal hook for the majority. From South Africa's perspective, refusal to cooperate with the League's system had led to a more drastic qualification of its claimed sovereignty. And that still-unrenounced South African claim provided the subtext for the next episode of Court involvement. In 1950, the Court held that while the League had disappeared, the mandate had not. In 1966, after its narrow decision of 1962 in favour of jurisdiction, it effectively reversed itself, holding the mandate obligations unenforceable *in limine* because even African members of the League lacked a legal interest in their enforcement.

IV. THE 1962 AND 1966 JUDGMENTS

THE COURT, by the President's casting vote—the votes being equally divided, decides to reject the claims of the Empire of Ethiopia and the Republic of Liberia.[53]

This single-sentence *dispositif* of the 1966 Judgment caused singular damage to the Court's relations with the General Assembly and with developing states. After the claims had been argued on the merits, their rejection on purely technical grounds was seen as evasive and legalistic and as implying that mandatory obligations were in effect non-justiciable.[54] This reaction was exacerbated by the fact of the 1966 decision being taken on the casting vote of the President (Sir Percy Spender), after he had earlier provoked the recusal of Judge Zafrullah Khan on a questionable basis.[55] Had Judge Zafrullah Khan participated, the decision would no doubt have gone the other way: the 1966 'majority' thus seemed not merely technical but manipulated.

A. Leading up to 1962

Following South Africa's refusal to meet its reporting obligations, the General Assembly asked the Committee on South West Africa to study 'what legal action

---

[51] ibid, dissenting opinion of Vice-President Badawi and Judges Basdevant, Hsu Mo, Armand-Ugon and Moreno Quintana, 65.
[52] ibid, 68–69.
[53] *South West Africa, Second Phase* (n 1) 51, [100].
[54] Dugard, *The South West Africa / Namibia Dispute* (n 11) 216–375.
[55] See S Rosenne, *The Law and Practice of the International Court 1920–2005*, vol II, 4th edn (The Hague, Martinus Nijhoff, 2005), 1058–59 and references.

is open' against South Africa.[56] The most promising suggestion was for a former Member of the League to bring a case to the Court on the basis 'that a dispute concerning the supervision functions themselves could properly exist, as well as a dispute relating to the administration or the status of the Territory'.[57] The General Assembly welcomed the Committee's report and in June 1960 Ethiopia and Liberia announced their intention to follow the sketched course.[58]

The lead-up to the contentious proceedings demonstrates how the Court had, through its three advisory opinions in the 1950s, not only taken a central place in the institutional machinery of the UN but was seen as a place of progressive potential. It was the Court that the Member States looked to for the next step toward resolution, and it was 'legal action' that was seen to be effective rather than, or at least in conjunction with, the politics at the General Assembly. The Court had accumulated significant institutional and social capital, and it was seen to be organisationally located between the General Assembly and enforcement at the Security Council.

B. The 1962 Judgment

On 21 December 1962, the Court, by a vote of eight to seven, rejected all of South Africa's objections to jurisdiction.[59] South Africa made four objections: (1) the Mandate for South West Africa was no longer 'a treaty or convention in force' as required by Article 37 of the Court's Statute; (2) the applicants were no longer Members of the League as required by Article 7 of the Mandate Agreement; (3) the relief sought could not constitute a dispute for purposes of Article 7, because the applicants did not have 'material interests' at stake; and (4) the claims were not capable of a negotiated settlement.[60]

i. The First and Second Preliminary Objections

The Court rejected the first two objections, relying on the institutional transfer rationale that had guided it in the Advisory Opinions. It stated that 'the unanimous holding of the Court in 1950 on the survival and continuing effect of Article 7 of the Mandate, continues to reflect its opinion today'.[61] South Africa's obligation to submit to jurisdiction was 'effectively transferred' to the Court by Article 37 and remained in force.[62] League Members' ability to bring claims was a necessary check on a Mandatory which could otherwise block a Council decision due to the unanimity requirement.[63] This made 'judicial protection of the sacred trust in each Mandate [...] an essential feature of the Mandates System'.[64]

---

[56] UNGA Res 1060 (XI) (26 February 1957).
[57] UNGAOR, Twelfth Session, Suppl No A (A/3625), 5–6, cited in Dugard (n 11) 212–13.
[58] UNGA Res 1142 (XII) (25 October 1957); Slonim (n 2) 180.
[59] *South West Africa Cases* (Preliminary Objections) (n 1) 347.
[60] ibid, 326–27.
[61] ibid, 334.
[62] ibid.
[63] ibid, 319, 337.
[64] ibid, 336.

In a lengthy joint dissent, Judges Spender and Fitzmaurice entirely disavowed the institutional transfer rationale. In response to the question whether Ethiopia and Liberia could still be considered Members of the League the dissent spoke of the 'transformation or metamorphosis involved'[65] for the 'carry-over' to work.[66] Such a transformation would only be legally possible if the aspect transferred 'was of so fundamental and essential a character that the instrument or institution could not function without it'.[67] But Article 7 'could not have not been regarded as having this character'.[68] The unanimity rule deprived the mandate system of any overriding effect:

> [T]here is no conceivable warrant for supposing that it was ever intended to be a part of the Mandates System that the Council of the League should be able to impose its own view on the Mandatory. The existence of the unanimity rule shows the exact reverse.[69]

According to the dissent, the Council's voting procedure thus rendered South Africa invulnerable to direction, whatever substantive obligations it had undertaken, and Article 7 could not have been intended to change this situation.

ii. The Third and Fourth Preliminary Objections

The Court rejected the third preliminary objection on the basis that under Article 7 the Members of the League had a 'legal right or interest' in the Mandatory observing its obligations toward the inhabitants of the Mandate.[70] Article 7 could not be limited to individual rights such as those under the 'open door' (which in any event had no application to South West Africa): 'the well-being and development of the inhabitants of the Mandated territory are not less important' than the Members' own material interests.[71]

The fourth objection concerned the possibility of resolving the dispute by negotiation, the impossibility of which was required for the Court's jurisdiction of the compromissory clause in Article 7. The Court focused on the evident 'deadlock' that had long existed at the United Nations, which showed that negotiations were impossible.[72]

C. The Judicial Philosophy of Judges Fitzmaurice and Spender

The 99-page joint dissent of Judges Spender and Fitzmaurice was the harbinger of the 1966 Judgment. Two major features are its legal technique, and their conception of the United Nations and the Court's role. The dissent features a positivism that

---

[65] ibid, dissenting opinion of Sir Percy Spender and Sir Gerald Fitzmaurice, 506.
[66] ibid, 516, see generally 516–18 (discussing the institutional transfer question and its two fallacies).
[67] ibid, 518.
[68] ibid, 519.
[69] ibid, 520.
[70] ibid, 343.
[71] ibid, 344.
[72] ibid, 346.

presumes international law to exist in freedom from politics. The dissenters claimed in dual double negatives to be

> not unmindful of nor ... insensible to the various considerations of a non-juridical character, social, humanitarian and other, which underlie this case; but these are matters for the political rather than the legal arena. They cannot be allowed to deflect us from our duty of reaching a conclusion strictly on the basis of what we believe to be the correct legal view.[73]

This categorisation of humanitarian considerations as by definition 'non-juridical' begs the question, especially when the relevant texts were drafted with humanitarian considerations in mind. According to the dissenters, the requirement in Article 22 of the Covenant that the Mandatory 'promote to its utmost the material and moral well-being and the social progress of the inhabitants of the territory' gave the Judges 'serious misgivings as to the legal basis on which the necessary objective criteria could be found'.[74] To them the Court was not the proper forum for the merits, and this normative consideration 'strongly reinforce[d]' their negative conclusion on jurisdiction.

The dissenters subscribed to a formalist conception in which the sources of international law would work to keep law and politics separate. Legal technique should keep the law distant from inherently normative determinations, such as those apparently entailed by Article 2 of the Mandate.[75] Though artfully presented as positivist, their interpretative stance was as value laden as that of the judges now in dissent in 1966.[76] The Judgment's repeated insistence on the framing of the Mandate in 1920 as the critical date for analysis[77] was likewise positivist in form but void in substance. The Wilsonian ideals underpinning the mandate system were present at the creation, though the contingency of the dissolution of the League was not addressed. The mandate gave authority to the Council and the Permanent Mandates Commission but nowhere stated or inferred that they were the only implementing authorities. To impose that meaning on Article 7 was as unjustified in 1966 as it would have been in 1920.

These criticisms were made at the time. Thus, Michael Reisman wrote in 1966 of the Court's analysis

> A jurisprudence which fabricates a distinction between law and policy and proceeds to apply the desiccated results of the distinction without judicial cognizance of the most intense expectations and demands of the vast majority of the world is a retreat into mysticism. A jurisprudence which has so little confidence in the vigor of law that it must concern itself first with the purity of its own 'discipline' rather than the functional and instrumental

---

[73] ibid, dissenting opinion of Sir Percy Spender and Sir Gerald Fitzmaurice, 466.

[74] ibid, 466–67.

[75] S Besson, 'Legal Philosophical Issues of International Adjudication' in Cesare Romano, Karen Alter and Yuval Shany (eds), *The Oxford Handbook of International Adjudication* (Oxford, OUP, 2014) 426–28.

[76] See also, *South West Africa Cases, Second Phase* (n 1) 34, [50] (the Court again stating that even if a treaty, ie the UN Charter, includes humanitarian considerations, they do not 'themselves amount to rules of law.'); *cf* ibid, dissenting opinion of Judge Padilla Nervo, 453 ('The sacred trust is not only a moral idea, it has also a legal character and significance; it is in fact a legal principle').

[77] See also ibid 23, [16].

character of law in social progress can hardly serve the needs of a rapidly changing world community. A jurisprudence that can, in the name of law, reach a conclusion which is against the moral and humanitarian principles that it itself concedes, is disquieting. A jurisprudence, which cannot grasp the inevitable, subjective, policy-choice element in legal decision but shuttles through the corridors of Aristotelean logic in order to be "forced" to a conclusion which is non consonant with community policy, lacks the spleen which the modern world may properly demand of theories of law.[78]

As his dissent in the *Temple* case showed, Sir Percy Spender (who by 1966 had been elected president of the Court) was well aware of the dynamics of colonialism.[79] But he was a conservative who was suspicious of international organisations such as the UN, which he felt might 'contain those who are working to disrupt the order we believe in'.[80] In this he was no doubt influenced by the 'strict and complete legalism' of Sir Owen Dixon, the leading Australian jurist of the time.[81] But this legalism is not to be conflated with an approach to adjudication that regards political questions as beyond judicial resolution. 'It is not,' Dixon said, 'a question whether the considerations are political, for nearly every consideration arising from the Constitution can be so described, but whether they are compelling'.[82] In contrast to the approach implicit in the 1962 dissent, and the 1966 Judgment, Dixon had faith in the law as a progressive force:

> [I]t is an error, if it is believed that the technique of the common law cannot meet the demands which changing conceptions of justice and convenience make. The demands made in the name of justice must not be arbitrary or fanciful. They must proceed, not from political or sociological propensities, but from deeper, more ordered, more philosophical and perhaps more enduring conceptions of justice.[83]

The same should apply to international law.

i. The 1966 Judgment

In 1965, the Court heard long and detailed argument about South Africa's policies toward South West Africa's indigenous inhabitants and its policy of apartheid. The outcome was a complete surprise.[84] In July 1966, on President Spender's casting vote, the majority (comprising judges from Australia, Poland, Greece, the United

---

[78] WM Reisman, 'Revision of the South West Africa Cases' (1966) 7 *Va L R* 1, 87–88.

[79] See *Case concerning the Temple of Preah Vihear (Cambodia v Thailand)* [1962] ICJ Rep 101, dissenting opinion of Sir Percy Spender,139–42.

[80] D Lowe, 'Percy Spender, Minister and Ambassador' in J Beaumont, C Waters and D Lowe (eds), *Ministers, Mandarins and Diplomats: Australian Foreign Policy Making, 1941–1969* (Melbourne, Melbourne University Press, 2003) 62, 70; see also J Crawford, '"Dreamers of the Day": Australia and the International Court of Justice' (2013) 14 *MJIL* 1, 11.

[81] O Dixon, 'Upon Taking the Oath of Office as Chief Justice' in J Woinarski (ed), *Jesting Pilate and Other Papers and Addresses* (Melbourne, Law Book Co, 1965) 245, at 247.

[82] *Melbourne Corporation v The Commonwealth* (1947) 74 CLR 31, 82; see generally D Dawson and M Nicholls, 'Sir Owen Dixon and Judicial Method' (1985–1986) 15 *MULR* 543, 545.

[83] O Dixon, 'Concerning Judicial Method' (1956) 29 *ALJ* 468, 479.

[84] South Africa had not even pleaded the standing objection at the Merits Phase.

Kingdom, Italy, France and South Africa, over the dissent of the judges from China, the USSR, Japan, the United States, Mexico, Senegal and Nigeria) overruled the 1962 majority and dismissed the case for lack of standing.

The first question that arises is whether the 1962 Judgment had not foreclosed this possibility—was it not *res judicata*? The Court in 1966, conscious of what had been decided in 1962, introduced a distinction. It said:

> [T]here was one matter that appertained to the merits of the case but which had an ante-cedent character, namely the question of the Applicants' standing in the present phase of the proceedings, not, that is to say, of their standing before the Court itself, which was the subject of the Court's decision in 1962, but the question, as a matter of the merits of the case, of their legal right or interest regarding the subject-matter of their claim, as set out in their final submissions.[85]

This approach to standing was perhaps best criticised by Rosalyn Higgins:

> [I]n 1966, the Court sought to explain this effective reversal by saying: 'To hold that the parties in any given case belong to the category of State specified in the Clause—that the dispute has the specified character—and the forum is the one specified—is not the same as finding the existence of a legal right or interest relative to the merits of the claim'.[86] But it *must* be the same thing—for the categories of States specified in the clause are presumably those who *do* have a legal interest in the carrying of the Mandate. Moreover, the Court in 1962 classified the Applicants as falling within that category, not as an abstract proposition but in relation to an already existing and formulated set of claims.[87]

This must be the correct view, otherwise the Court cannot *decide* any preliminary objection that has an admissibility component, despite the terms of Article 79(9) of the Rules. It is confirmed by the Court's application of *res judicata* to its preliminary objections phase in *Bosnian Genocide*.[88]

The more consequential part of the 1966 Judgment was, however, the question of substance on which the dismissal was based. Why were there no legal interests or rights of Liberia and Ethiopia at issue? Two main arguments were relied on.

ii.   'Conduct' and 'Rights and Interests' Provisions

The distinction between 'conduct' and 'rights and interests' provisions was the first of these, already foreshadowed in the 1962 joint dissent. Conduct provisions were those, like Article 22 of the Covenant, which required the Mandatory to act a certain way toward the people living in the Mandate. These requirements as to conduct

---

[85]   See also, *South West Africa Cases, Second Phase* (n 1) 18, [4].

[86]   ibid, 37, [60].

[87]   R Higgins, 'The International Court and South West Africa: the Implications of the Judgment' (1966) 42 *Int'l Aff.* 573, 580; for a different view see Slonim (n 2) 296–98 (concluding that the legal basis of the 1966 Judgment was pure non-justiciability because of the inherently political character of the dispute).

[88]   *Application of the Convention on the Prevention and Punishment of the Crime of Genocide (Bosnia and Herzegovina v. Serbia and Montenegro)* (Preliminary Objections) [2007] ICJ Rep 49, 93–101, [121]–[139].

derived, so the argument ran, from the 'sacred trust'. 'Rights and interests' provisions, on the other hand, were clauses like Article 5 of the Mandate Agreement, which protected certain *material* interests of the other Members of the League, such as missionary activities (if such can be considered material).[89]

In 1966, the Court took the view that, in contrast to the 'rights and interests' provisions, which all Members of the League could attempt to enforce through the international legal process, the conduct provisions 'appertained exclusively to the League itself'.[90] The conduct provisions created no 'legal tie between the mandatories and other individual members'.[91] The 1966 Judgment further denied that the Mandate Agreements created rights *erga omnes partes* by implication. The Members of the League could derive only those rights from the Mandate Agreements which were 'unequivocally conferred, directly or by a clearly necessary implication. The existence of such rights could not be presumed or merely inferred or postulated'.[92] But no such rights of policing the conduct provisions—neither in their own name nor as agents of the League—had been explicitly conferred on the League's Members.[93] In direct contrast was Judge Tanaka, who wrote in his 1966 dissent:

> [T]here is no reason why an immaterial, intangible interest, particularly one inspired by the lofty humanitarian idea of a 'sacred trust of civilization' cannot be called 'interest'. In short, the interest possessed by the member States of the League as its Members is corporate and, at the same time, idealistic. However, this does not prevent it from being 'interest'.[94]

The idea that there could be 'humanitarian considerations' justifying such general legal rights and obligations was rejected by the Court as lying outside the law.[95] But to take the view that 'conduct provisions' create legal rights only if they expressly confer rights 'in the same way' that 'special interest provisions' do is a debilitating assumption, especially given the different types of legal rights involved.[96] Moreover, and to the same end, the Court interpreted Article 7(2) restrictively. The Court could

> see nothing in it that would take the clause outside the normal rule that, in a dispute causing the activation of a jurisdictional clause, the substantive rights themselves which the dispute is about, must be sought for elsewhere than in this clause, or in some element apart from it—and must therefore be established *aliunde vel aliter*.[97]

---

[89] Mandate for German South West Africa, Art 5 ('The Mandatory shall ensure in the territory freedom of conscience and the free exercise of all forms of worship, and shall allow all missionaries, nationals of any State Member of the League of Nations, to enter into, travel, and reside in the territory for purpose of prosecuting their calling').

[90] See also *South West Africa Cases, Second Phase* (n 1) 22, [14].

[91] ibid, 26, [25].

[92] ibid, 28, [32].

[93] ibid; 29, [33], 35, [54].

[94] ibid, dissenting opinion of Judge Tanaka, 252.

[95] See also, ibid, 34, [49].

[96] ibid, 39, [66].

[97] See also ibid, 39, [65].

This limiting approach to compromissory clauses has not been followed by the Court,[98] and does not reflect the modern law.[99]

iii. The Role of Institutions in the International Legal Order

The Judgment and the separate and dissenting opinions take very different approaches to the role of institutions in the international legal order. The 1966 Judgment, as Slonim put it, 'rent asunder ... the entire fabric of Assembly-Court cooperation—developed and woven through the advisory opinions of 1950, 1955, and 1956 and the Judgment of 1962.'[100]

In 1962, Judges Fitzmaurice and Spender thought the issue was one between South Africa and the General Assembly exclusively. Liberia and Ethiopia were only appearing in 'representational capacity', because Article 34 precluded the United Nations from appearing as a party before the Court.[101] They did not consider that a dispute conducted 'solely within the framework of an international organization' could constitute an interstate dispute for the purposes of compromissory clauses, especially where the applicant has only participated through its membership in the organisation.[102] This position maintains a radical division between the activities of international organisations and politics among states. The same logic of division between international organisation and member state carried over into the 1966 Judgment.[103]

One response to this institutional distinction came from Judge Koretsky who framed the contentious proceeding not as an instance of inter-state dispute, but as a process by which the alternative control organ of the Mandates, the Court, could be brought into action. On this view, the State was 'endowed with a right ... of judicial initiative within the limits defined by Article 7(2)'.[104] The state plays an initiating role in the *process* but no dichotomy is maintained as between the legal relationship between the League and Mandatory on the one side, and Member of the League and Mandatory on the other side. For Koretsky, the 'real interest of the Applicants in

---

[98] See, eg, *Application of the Convention on the Prevention and Punishment of the Crime of Genocide (Croatia v Serbia)* [2015] ICJ Rep [114] (in dealing with the possibility of state succession to responsibility, the Court referred to the compromissory clause of the Genocide Convention, Article IX, and noted that it 'speaks generally of the responsibility of a State and contains no limitation regarding the manner in which that responsibility might be engaged.' In this sense, the Court was focusing on a part of the compromissory clause to imply the possibility of finding an extension of the obligations within it).

[99] M Papadaki, 'Compromissory Clauses as the Gatekeepers of the Law to be "Used" in the ICJ and PCIJ' (2014) 5 *JIDS* 560; E Cannizzaro and B Bonafé, 'Fragmenting International Law through Compromissory Clauses? Some Remarks on the Decision of the ICJ in the Oil Platforms Case' (2005) 16 *EJIL* 481.

[100] Slonim (n 2) 313.

[101] *South West Africa Cases* (Preliminary Objections) (n 1) dissenting opinion of Sir Percy Spender and Sir Gerald Fitzmaurice, 547–48.

[102] ibid, 549.

[103] See also, *South West Africa Cases, Second Phase* (n 1) 30, [37].

[104] See, eg, ibid, dissenting opinion of Judge Koretsky, 246.

these cases' was for them to 'exercise this judicial initiative'.[105] Judge Tanaka wrote in the same spirit of institutional innovation when he said:

> [T]he existence of the Council as a supervisory organ of the Mandate cannot be considered as contradictory to the existence of the Court as an organ of judicial protection of the Mandate. The former, being in charge of the policies and administration of the Mandatory and the latter, being in charge of the legal aspects of the Mandate, they cannot be substituted the one for the other and their activities need not necessarily overlap or contradict each other. They belong to different planes. The one cannot be regarded as exercising appellate jurisdiction over the other.[106]

Another reflection on the institutional issue came from Judge Jessup who started his discussion of the issue with a quotation from Arnold McNair:

> There was perhaps no part of the Covenant that called forth more derision from the cynical and the worldly-wise than the Mandates System contained in Article XXII ... The Mandates System represents the irruption of the idealist into one of the periodical world settlements which have in the past lain too much in the hands of so-called 'practical men'.[107]

Judge Jessup went on to provide examples of cases brought by multiple states and in the context of shared League membership.[108] In such cases individual member states did not need to show another 'legal interest' beyond a disagreement about 'a constitutional or other basic treaty provision'.[109] He further noted the institutional innovation created by the League through the 'inter-relation of the function of the Permanent Court of International Justice and of the political organs of the League of Nations, [which was] frequently illustrated in connection with the peace settlements after World War I'.[110]

V. POLITICAL FALL-OUT FROM 1966 AND THE 1971 ADVISORY OPINION

The 1966 Judgment lost the Court trust among large parts of the international community, notably the G77. As a direct result the Court's composition became an issue. In the following year, the General Assembly 'made sure that no white Commonwealth judge was elected'.[111] The Court was also institutionally sidelined in the United Nations system. The Court responded in its turn, at least tacitly. The famous *erga omnes* passage in *Barcelona Traction* may be seen as recompense for 1966, if not an outright acknowledgement of error. In a passage that clearly implied a reconsideration of the 1966 distinction between an applicant state's interest in the Mandates 'conduct' and 'legal rights and interest' provision, the Court declared:

> [A]n essential distinction should be drawn between the obligations of a State towards the international community as a whole, and those arising vis-à-vis another State in the field

---

[105] ibid, 248.
[106] ibid, dissenting opinion of Judge Tanaka, 257.
[107] Editor's Preface to J Stoyanovsky, *The Mandate for Palestine* (London, Longmans, 1928) v.
[108] *South West Africa Cases, Second Phase* (n 1) dissenting opinion of Judge Jessup, 413–14.
[109] ibid, 414.
[110] ibid, 423.
[111] Dugard (n 11) 378.

of diplomatic protections. By their very nature the former are the concern of all States. In view of the importance of the rights involved, all States can be held to have a legal interest in their protection; they are obligations *erga omnes*.

...

Such obligations derive, for example, in contemporary international law, from the outlawing of acts of aggression, and of genocide, as also from the principles and rules concerning the basic rights of the human person, including protection from slavery and racial discrimination.[112]

For South West Africa itself, events moved more swiftly. On 27 October 1966, by 114 votes to two (Portugal and South Africa) and with three abstentions (France, Malawi and the United Kingdom) the General Assembly adopted Resolution 2145(XXI) terminating the Mandate for South West Africa. The Resolution remarked that the General Assembly was '*[g]ravely concerned* at the situation in the Mandated Territory, which has seriously deteriorated following the judgment of the International Court of Justice of 18 July 1966'.[113] As a result, South West Africa came under the 'direct responsibility of the United Nations'.[114]

In a logical next step, the General Assembly set up a Council for South West Africa to administer the territory in May 1967.[115] The Council was given legislative authority over South West Africa and there was to be a Commissioner for South West Africa to hold executive powers.[116] South Africa denied the validity of these acts and continued its presence in South West Africa, making it impossible for the Council and Commissioner to discharge their functions.

The aftermath of the 1966 Judgment brought into play a further institutional dimension of the United Nations system—the relationship between the General Assembly and the Security Council. Whereas the idea behind contentious proceedings in 1960 had been for the Court to create the institutional link between the Assembly and the Council, the 1966 Judgment had foreclosed that path. The institutions now needed to find another route.

South Africa having ignored the resolution terminating the mandate, the Assembly turned to the Council for help. Initially the Council was reluctant: it was only the passing of drastic legislation by South Africa that prompted action.[117] After South Africa rebuffed its first resolution, the Security Council adopted a sharper tone and called upon South Africa 'to withdraw its administration from the territory immediately and in any case before 4 October 1969'.[118] South Africa refused again.[119] The Security Council passed a resolution aimed at isolating South Africa internationally,[120] and a further resolution requesting an advisory opinion from the

---

[112] *Barcelona Traction, Light and Power Company, Limited (Belgium v Spain), Second Phase* [1970] ICJ Rep 3, 32, [33]–[34].
[113] UNGA Res 2145(XXI) (27 October 1966).
[114] ibid, [4]; see also Crawford, *Creation of States* (n 8) 589.
[115] Dugard (n 11) 409–13, reproducing in full UNGA Res 2248 (S-V) (19 May 1967).
[116] UNGA Res 2248 (n 115) [1(b)], [3].
[117] Slonim (n 2) 322–26; Dugard (n 11), 438; UNSC Res 264 (20 March 1969) UN Doc S/RES/264.
[118] UNSC Res 269 (12 August 1969) UN Doc S/RES/269, [5].
[119] Dugard (n 11) 441.
[120] UNSC Res 283 (29 July 1970) UN Doc S/RES/283.

ICJ as to 'the legal consequences for States of the continued presence of South Africa in Namibia, notwithstanding Security Council resolution 276 (1970)'.[121] The Court was back in the game.[122]

A. The 1971 Advisory Opinion

The Court's Advisory Opinion was delivered in June 1971, more than 20 years after its Opinion on the *International Status of South West Africa*. By 13 votes to two, the Court upheld the validity of the various resolutions and spelled out the legal consequences of the termination of the mandate. While the Opinion raises a number of legal issues,[123] we will again focus on the Court's approach to the institutional questions; foremost the Court's understanding of the power of the Assembly and Council to create international obligations for states.

In determining the legal consequences of South Africa's continuing presence in South West Africa, the central question was whether the United Nations had validly terminated South Africa's Mandate thereby making the latter's continuing presence there unlawful. The two relevant acts were General Assembly Resolution 2145 and Security Council Resolution 276.[124]

General Assembly resolutions are generally not binding.[125] But the Advisory Opinion held that in 'specific cases' such resolutions can 'make determinations or have operative design'.[126] It also held that '[b]y resolution 2145 (XXI) the General Assembly terminated the Mandate'.[127] Evidently this was one of those 'specific cases'. The basis for this, according to Judges Zafrullah Khan, Petrén, Oneyeama and Dillard was the institutional transfer logic developed in the 1950 Opinion.[128] If the General Assembly was the effective successor to the League Council, and the latter had the power to revoke the mandate in the face of a serious breach as a 'necessary part of its supervisory powers', so did the General Assembly.[129]

---

[121] UNSC Res 284 (29 July 1970) UN Doc S/RES/284.

[122] Afro-Asian States remained unenthusiastic about bringing the matter back to the Court. See Dugard (n 11) 493.

[123] See eg Crawford, *Creation of States* (n 8) 162–68 (addressing the Opinion's approach to the duty of non-recognition).

[124] See Dugard (n 11) 487.

[125] UN Charter, Art 10 (the General Assembly 'may make recommendations to the Members of the United Nations or the Security Council'); *South-West Africa—Voting Procedure* (n 1) separate opinion of Judge Lauterpacht, 92 ('the absence of full legal binding force in the resolutions of the GA is a ... fundamental and ... rudimentary proposition'); see generally E Klein and S Schmahl, 'Article 10' in B Simma, D-E Khan, G Nolte and A Paulus (eds), *The Charter of the United Nations*, 3rd edn (Oxford, OUP, 2012) 468, 479–87.

[126] *Legal Consequences for States of the Continued Presence of South Africa in Namibia* (n 1) 16, [50].

[127] ibid, [51].

[128] *International Status of South-West Africa* (n 1) 137.

[129] *Legal Consequences for States of the Continued Presence of South Africa in Namibia* (n 1), Declaration of President Khan, 61; separate opinion of Judge Petrén, 131–33; separate opinion of Judge Oneyama, 146–47; separate opinion of Judge Dillard, 163–65.

But the Opinion was not unequivocal: elsewhere it suggested that it was only the Security Council that converted the General Assembly's recommendation into an international obligation binding on States. Thus the Assembly was 'lacking the necessary powers to ensure the withdrawal of South Africa from the Territory' and consequently 'enlisted' the co-operation of the Security Council'.[130]

But how could the Security Council resolution, not adopted under Chapter VII, be binding upon states? Here the Court relied on Article 25 of the Charter, which states that 'the Members of the United Nations agree to accept and carry out the decisions of the Security Council in accordance with the present Charter'.[131] While 'revolutionary' at the time,[132] the accepted view today is that this provides a basis for the Security Council's power to make binding decisions outside Chapter VII in certain limited circumstances.[133] In these respects the 1971 Opinion seems to have developed the law toward more institutional power of the Security Council.

A final point to make about the Advisory Opinion, also institutional in a sense, goes to the Court's apparent adjudication of the underling merits of the dispute it had declined to decide in 1966. The Advisory Opinion includes the following passage:

> Under the Charter of the United Nations, the former Mandatory had pledged itself to observe and respect, in a territory having an international status, human rights and funda-mental freedoms for all without distinction as to race. To establish instead, and to enforce, distinctions, exclusions, restrictions and limitations exclusively based on grounds of race, colour, descent or national or ethnic origin which constitute a denial of fundamental human rights is a flagrant violation of the purposes and principles of the Charter.[134]

It is doubtful whether this question was actually before the Court. It is also unclear why the Court decided to address this question when it had earlier stated that it was for the General Assembly to make the determination.[135] Perhaps most importantly, it is unclear why the Court was willing to make such a substantive finding without having heard or examined any evidence. The Opinion seems to rest on the principle of non-discrimination alone, which was controversial as a matter of *lex lata* at the time, and remains so today.[136] It has even been suggested that it was the applicants' move toward this legal strategy that had a significant effect on the outcome of the 1966 case. The question of international law's position toward apartheid had been squarely before the Court in the contentious proceedings, but was never resolved.

---

[130] ibid, [51].

[131] UN Charter, Art 25.

[132] Dugard (n 11) 488.

[133] A Peters, 'Article 25' in Simma et al (n 125) §§ 11–12.

[134] *Legal Consequences for States of the Continued Presence of South Africa in Namibia* (n 1) 16, [131].

[135] ibid, [103]; see also Dugard (n 11) 489–90.

[136] Slonim (n 2) 245–49; AA D'Amato, 'Legal and Political Strategies of the South West Africa Litigation' (1967) 4 *Law Transition Quarterly* 8, 32–39. Of the seven dissenting judges, only Judge Tanaka seems to have found the applicants' case, as argued, persuasive, see Slonim (n 2) 299–302.

In a way, and this is the institutional point, this finding suggests another attempt by the Court to re-establish its standing as a guardian of fundamental rights.

VI. CONCLUSION

Notwithstanding the Advisory Opinion, South Africa held out against an increasing international consensus on South West Africa for nearly two decades. Eventually a negotiated solution led to the independence of the territory following elections under UN auspices, a process described elsewhere.[137] Namibia was admitted to the United Nations on 23 April 1990.

---

[137] Crawford, *Creation of States* (n 8) 596.

12

North Sea Continental Shelf (Federal Republic of Germany v Netherlands; Federal Republic of Germany v Denmark) (1969)

NIKIFOROS PANAGIS AND ANTONIOS TZANAKOPOULOS

I. INTRODUCTION

THE NORTH SEA, a marginal sea lying between the eastern coast of Great Britain and the north-western part of continental Europe, has featured prominently in European history as the source of crucial battles fought not only with Viking longships but also with law books since the days of Grotius.[1] It should therefore be of no surprise that the North Sea provided the setting for the first judicial decision by the International Court of Justice (ICJ) concerning the delimitation of maritime zones beyond the territorial sea.[2] Somewhat ironically, the judgment was not particularly illuminating on matters of maritime delimitation, even though it has had some (nominal) impact on this front. It is a *cause célèbre*, however, for its articulation of important principles relating to the sources of international law and their interaction. Indeed, most students of international law will come across the case not because of whatever it said about the continental shelf and its delimitation, but for its analysis of the elements of custom, its description of the relationship between treaty and custom, and perhaps for its resort to a rule or principle of law requiring the application of largely undefined equitable principles. This chapter will first provide an overview of the historical and legal context in which the legal dispute arose (Part II). It will then focus on the issues on which the ICJ pronounced (Part III), and discuss subsequent developments (Part IV).

---

[1] On the so-called 'battle of the books' see D Bederman, 'The Sea' in B Fassbender and A Peters (eds), *The Oxford Handbook of the History of International Law* (Oxford, OUP, 2012) 364–69. See also H Grotius, *The Free Sea* (D Armitage ed and intro, R Hakluyt tr) (Indianapolis, Liberty Fund, 2004) xi.

[2] *North Sea Continental Shelf (Federal Republic of Germany/Netherlands; Federal Republic of Germany/Denmark)* [1969] ICJ Rep 3 (hereinafter *NSCS*).

II. THE SETTING OF THE DISPUTE

A. Developing the Legal Concept of the Continental Shelf

In geological terms, the continental shelf is the part of the seabed on which the continent rests; it is adjacent to the coast and it slopes down gradually from the shore. Usually at an average depth of 130 metres the downward slope of the seabed becomes steeper, and at this point the continental shelf is followed by another section of the seabed, the continental slope.[3] While the coastal state enjoys sovereignty over the section of the continental shelf lying under its territorial sea, until the Second World War claims of jurisdiction over the seabed beyond the territorial sea were rather scarce.[4] Upon the discovery that the continental shelf is particularly rich in natural resources (it contains almost 90 per cent of the total value of minerals extracted from the seabed),[5] the legal concept of the continental shelf was 'discovered' as well.[6] A 1942 bilateral treaty between the UK and Venezuela relating to the submarine areas of the Gulf of Paria[7] and the 1945 Proclamation by US President Truman[8] are only two notable examples of a rapidly emerging trend since the 1940s, whereby coastal states claimed jurisdiction over the resources found in the continental shelf adjacent to their coast.[9]

The International Law Commission (ILC) considered the topic as part of its work on the law of the sea between 1949 and 1956, and its Articles[10] served as the basis for the adoption, among three other treaties, of the 1958 Convention on the Continental Shelf.[11] This was the first international treaty to outline the regime applicable to the continental shelf. According to the (legal) definition of the concept, the seaward limit of the continental shelf was placed at the point where the waters reach a depth of 200 metres or, beyond that limit, where the depth of the waters permits exploitation of the natural resources of the seabed and subsoil.[12] Notably, neither depth nor exploitability reflected any scientific (geological) benchmarks, and in this sense this first legal definition of the continental shelf was different from the scientific (geological) definition.[13]

Further, the 1958 Convention provided for the delimitation of a continental shelf that is adjacent to the territories of two or more states, distinguishing cases where the said states have 'opposite' coasts from cases where the coasts of the relevant

---

[3] UNESCO Secretariat, 'Scientific Considerations Relating to the Continental Shelf' (Document A/CONF.13/2 and Add.1 in UNCLOS Official Records vol I, 1958) [6] and [14].

[4] See, for example, the UK claims in C Hurst, 'Whose is the Bed of the Sea? Sedentary Fisheries outside the Three-Mile Limit' (1923) 4 *BYIL* 34, esp 39–42.

[5] RR Churchill and AV Lowe, *The Law of the Sea*, 3rd edn (Manchester, MUP, 1999) 141.

[6] René-Jean Dupuy, *L'océan partagé* (Paris, Pedone, 1979) 104–05.

[7] British Treaty Series No 10 (1942) (British Command Paper 6400); 1 UN Leg Series 44.

[8] Presidential Proclamation No 2667, (1945) 10 Federal Register 12303; 1 UN Leg Series 38.

[9] For a compilation of state practice until 1951 see (1951) 1 UN Leg Series 3–44.

[10] Articles concerning the Law of the Sea with commentaries [1956]-II ILC Ybk 256.

[11] Convention on the Continental Shelf (signed 29 April 1958, entered into force 10 June 1964) 499 UNTS 311 (hereinafter 1958 Convention).

[12] 1958 Convention, Art 1.

[13] BB Jia, 'The Notion of Natural Prolongation in the Current Regime of the Continental Shelf: An Afterlife?' (2013) 12 *Chin JIL* 79, 84–85.

states are 'adjacent' to each other.[14] Interestingly, the method of delimitation is essentially identical in both cases:[15] priority is given to delimitation by agreement between the states and, if agreement cannot be reached, the boundary will be a line equidistant from the nearest points of the baselines of the parties, unless special circumstances warrant drawing a different delimitation line.[16] Both in the case of states with 'opposite' and in the case of states with 'adjacent' coasts, the equidistant line (called 'median' and 'lateral' line, respectively) results in leaving to each of the states concerned all those portions of the continental shelf that are nearer to a point on its own coast than they are to any point on the coast of the other party.[17]

B. The Attempts to Delimit the North Sea Continental Shelf

The North Sea, surrounded by the shores of Norway, Denmark, the Federal Republic of Germany, the Netherlands, Belgium, France and the United Kingdom (Great Britain, Orkney and Shetlands), has the general look of an enclosed (or semi-enclosed) sea.[18] The seabed of the North Sea essentially consists of a single continental shelf at a depth of less than 200 metres (except for a somewhat deeper narrow belt of water off the south-western coast of Norway).[19] The discovery of oil and natural gas in its seabed in the 1960s[20] motivated the states surrounding it to seek to delimit their respective continental shelves. Given the legal definition of the continental shelf in the 1958 Convention, the coastal states held overlapping claims over the same North Sea continental shelf. Within a few years, Denmark, the United Kingdom and the Netherlands became parties to the 1958 Convention, and a series of bilateral continental shelf delimitation agreements were concluded between Denmark, the Netherlands, Norway (which became a party rather later, in 1971) and the United Kingdom, on the basis of the equidistance principle provided for in Article 6 of the Convention.[21] By way of contrast, Germany signed but never ratified the 1958 Convention, although it had declared in a public Proclamation of 1964 its intention to do so, acknowledging that the Convention expressed the development of general international law.[22]

---

[14] The 1958 Convention provided no definition for the two concepts; indeed, this distinction has been heavily criticised: M Evans, *Relevant Circumstances and Maritime Delimitation* (Oxford, Clarendon, 1989) 124; P Weil, *The Law of Maritime Delimitation—Reflections* (M MacGlashan tr) (Cambridge, Grotius Publications, 1989) 246.

[15] *Delimitation of the Continental Shelf (UK and France)* (1979) 54 ILR 6, [238] (hereinafter *Anglo-French Continental Shelf*); Weil, *Maritime Delimitation* (n 14) 247.

[16] Art 6(1) and (2).

[17] *NSCS* (n 2) [6].

[18] Note that this term is used here in the legal sense reflected in Part IX of the UN Convention on the Law of the Sea 1982; in oceanographic terms the North Sea, like the South China Sea, is a 'semi-open' sea: see generally JCJ Nihoul, 'Oceanography of Semi-Enclosed Seas' in JCJ Nihoul (ed), *Hydrodynamics of Semi-Enclosed Seas* (Liège, Elsevier, 1982) 1.

[19] *NSCS* (n 2) [4].

[20] F Eustache, 'L'affaire du Plateau continental de la mer du Nord devant la Cour internationale de justice' (1970) 74 *RGDIP* 590, 591, with further references.

[21] F Monconduit, 'Affaire du Plateau continental de la mer du Nord' (1969) 15 *AFDI* 213, 215–16.

[22] Promulgation of the Proclamation of the Federal Government concerning the Exploration and Exploitation of the German Continental Shelf of 22 January 1964, reproduced in Counter-memorial submitted by the Government of the Kingdom of Denmark (ICJ Pleadings vol I 157, 244).

Unsurprisingly, the delimitation of the continental shelf between Germany and its adjacent states (Denmark and the Netherlands) was more problematic. Germany accepted the principle of equidistance for the establishment of a partial boundary between each of its neighbours but it refused to draw an equidistance line through-out the course of the continental shelf boundary.[23] In fact, Germany did not consider itself bound by the delimitation method enshrined in Article 6 of the 1958 Conven-tion, as it was not party to the latter, and argued that the principle of equidistance should be departed from when it would yield an 'inequitable result'. As the German North Sea coast forms a concave near the Elbe estuary, the German continental shelf would be 'boxed in'[24] by the shelves of Denmark and the Netherlands, preventing Germany from accessing the seabed in the centre of the North Sea (up to the median line with the United Kingdom).[25] Instead, Germany argued that delimitation in such instances should be governed by the principle that each coastal state is entitled to a 'just and equitable share'.[26] Denmark and the Netherlands, on the other hand, con-tended that Germany was obligated to abide by the delimitation method provided for in Article 6 of the 1958 Convention and that, in the absence of any special cir-cumstances, an equidistance line ought to be drawn between the continental shelf of Germany and that of each of the two states.[27]

Following new rounds of trilateral negotiations, the three states agreed to sub-mit the dispute to the ICJ on the basis of two essentially identical special agree-ments between Germany and Denmark, and between Germany and the Netherlands, respectively.[28] Pursuant to a request by the parties, the Court joined the two cases, as it found that Denmark and the Netherlands were in the same interest.[29] In neither case was the Court tasked with delimiting the continental shelf boundary; rather, it was requested merely to declare the principles and rules of international law applica-ble to the delimitation of the continental shelf, while the three states undertook the obligation to effect the delimitation pursuant to the Court's decision subsequently.[30]

III. THE JUDGMENT AND ITS AFTERMATH

A. The Issue Before the Court

The Court was faced with two 'fundamentally different' positions:[31] Denmark and the Netherlands argued that the delimitation method provided for in Article 6 of

---

[23] See generally I Foigel, 'The North Sea Continental Shelf case' (1969) 39 *NJIL* 109, 111–12.
[24] The illustrative expression is borrowed from JG Merrills, 'Images and Models in the World Court: The Individual Opinions in the North Sea Continental Shelf Cases' (1978) 41 *MLR* 638, 639.
[25] *NSCS* (n 2) [8].
[26] ibid, [11].
[27] ibid, [12].
[28] Appearing in [1968] ICJ Pleadings vol I 6 and 8.
[29] *North Sea Continental Shelf cases* (Order) [1968] ICJ Rep 9, 10. Acting in concert, the two states appointed the same ad hoc judge (Sørensen).
[30] Art 1 of the Special Agreement(s); *NSCS* (n 2) [2].
[31] *NSCS* (n 2) [13].

the 1958 Convention expressed a legal rule that was binding on Germany, either by virtue of the Convention itself, or by virtue of general (ie customary) international law. The rule would thus require adopting equidistance lines for the continental shelf boundaries of Germany with both states, because the configuration of the German coast did not constitute 'special circumstances' allowing deviation from the principle of equidistance. Similarly, the continental shelf boundaries drawn between Denmark and the Netherlands were opposable to Germany, precisely because they were drawn pursuant to a rule (the rule in Article 6) binding on that state too.[32]

Germany, for its part, did not consider itself bound by the rule contained in Article 6 of the 1958 Convention, whether as a matter of treaty or as a matter of customary international law. While recognising the utility of equidistance as a method of delimitation, Germany argued that this method should be used only if it would achieve a just and equitable apportionment of the continental shelf among the states concerned. According to Germany, the principle that each state be accorded a 'just and equitable share' was not a principle of equity, which would be applicable by the Court only if expressly so requested by the parties,[33] but rather a general principle of law. Alternatively, Germany contended that even if the rule of Article 6 were applicable in this case, the configuration of the German coast would constitute 'special circumstances' excluding the use of an equidistance line.[34]

Clearly, the Court was in no way required to uphold one of the two opposing arguments,[35] and in fact it eventually rejected both of them.

B. The Legal Nature of the Continental Shelf

Three paragraphs were all it took for the Court to dismiss the German contentions. By referring to an 'apportionment' of the continental shelf in a way that awards a just and equitable 'share' to all states concerned, Germany seemed to suggest that the continental shelf in areas like that of the North Sea consisted of an integral or even undivided whole, which ought to be 'shared' or 'apportioned' between the littoral states through the performance of particular legal acts. As the Court held, this conception ran contrary to the rule

> that the rights of the coastal State in respect of the area of continental shelf that constitutes a natural prolongation of its land territory into and under the sea exist *ipso facto* and *ab initio*, by virtue of its sovereignty over the land, and as an extension of it in an exercise of sovereign rights for the purpose of exploring the seabed and exploiting its natural resources.[36]

In other words, the sovereign rights of the coastal state over the continental shelf were an attribute that the state already possessed by virtue of merely having

---

[32] ibid, [13]–[14].

[33] Art 38(2) ICJ Statute.

[34] *NSCS* (n 2) [15]–[17].

[35] See *Free Zones of Upper Savoy and the District of Gex* (1929) PCIJ Series A No 22, 15; *Diversion of Water from the Meuse* (1937) PCIJ Series A/B No 70, 123.

[36] *NSCS* (n 2) [19].

a coast; they need not be constituted through a particular procedure, and even less so be awarded through some process of apportionment—they were 'inherent'. This rule, stressed the Court, was 'the most fundamental of all the rules of law relating to the continental shelf, enshrined in Article 2 of the 1958 Geneva Convention, though quite independent of it'.[37]

On the basis of this definition, the Court also dismissed the Danish and Dutch argument that equidistance was a 'juristic inevitability', a delimitation method inherent in the concept of continental shelf rights itself. The Court began by acknowledging that delimitation on the basis of equidistance combines unparalleled practical convenience and certainty of application, but this did not mean that it was the only method of delimitation conceivable.[38] As the Court explained, the principle of equidistance is based on the notion of proximity, namely the notion that to a coastal state appertain all those parts of the shelf that are (but only if they are) closer to it than they are to any point on the coast of another state.[39] Proximity, however, was not fundamental to the concept of continental shelf; rather, what defined the continental shelf was its continuity with the land territory of the coastal state in a way that classified the shelf as a 'natural prolongation' of the latter.[40] The Court accepted that the continental shelf area of states with coasts lying opposite each other can be claimed by each state as a natural prolongation of its territory, and that therefore an equidistance (median) line was the only means to divide equally the area in question.[41] The same, however, was not necessarily true for states with adjacent coasts: in such cases the continental shelf of a state might extend to an area lying closer to another state; therefore drawing an equidistance (lateral) line would deprive the former state of its inherent rights to its shelf.[42] Consequently, the principle of equidistance could not be regarded as the only principle thinkable, as if logically necessary, for the delimitation of overlapping continental shelf areas, at least for states with adjacent coasts.[43]

C. Estoppel

The question that would have to be answered then was whether this principle, although not inescapably applicable, had become obligatory through the operation of legal rules. The first point for the Court to examine was whether Germany had consented to be bound by the relevant provision of the 1958 Convention, as Denmark and the Netherlands contended. If the treaty rule was binding on all parties to the dispute, it would prevail over any contrary rules of general customary international law (save, of course, for peremptory norms).[44] The Court accepted

---

[37] ibid, [19].
[38] ibid, [23]–[24].
[39] ibid, [39].
[40] ibid, [43].
[41] ibid, [57].
[42] ibid, [44] and [58].
[43] ibid, [46].
[44] ibid, [25]; *cf* [72].

the principle on which the argument by Denmark and the Netherlands was based, namely that the conduct of a state could evidence that the state accepted a rule in a treaty despite not having ratified the treaty in question. At the same time, the Court noted that such an intention of the state to be bound should not be presumed lightly. A very definite, very consistent course of conduct to this effect was required, precisely because the fact that a state refrains from carrying out the prescribed formalities strongly indicates lack of consent.[45] This was corroborated in the instance by the fact that the treaty itself permitted states to tailor their obligations through making reservations to the provision in question, yet Germany had preferred to refrain from ratifying the treaty altogether.[46] The Court rejected that Germany was estopped from denying the applicability of the treaty. Giving the 'most precise definition of the conditions for invoking the doctrine of estoppel',[47] the Court held that clearly and consistently evinced acceptance of the treaty rule by Germany was a necessary but not sufficient element. Denmark and the Netherlands would have to show that they were induced to detrimentally change their position or suffer some prejudice, which in this case they had failed to do.[48]

D. Customary International Law

The Court then sought to ascertain whether the provision of Article 6 of the 1958 Convention reflected a rule of customary international law. In the Court's opinion, there were three ways in which the treaty provision could have come to reflect custom. First, a rule of customary international law of the same content might have pre-dated the 1958 Convention, and the states merely wrote the rule down in the Convention (codification). Second, the rule might have emerged by and through the process of drawing up the 1958 Convention. In other words, the process of drawing up the Convention might have crystallised a customary rule (crystallisation). Third, a customary rule might have emerged in the light of state practice subsequent to the Convention, ie the Convention rule might have served as a basis for the development of a new customary rule in the image of the Convention rule (development).[49] The first option (which was not actively supported by Denmark and the Netherlands) was summarily dismissed by the Court.[50] The Court then found that a customary rule had not emerged through the drafting process of the 1958 Convention,

---

[45] ibid, [28]; see also H Lauterpacht, 'Decisions of Municipal Courts as a Source of International Law' (1929) 10 *BYIL* 65, 89.

[46] *NSCS* (n 2) [29].

[47] *Delimitation of the Maritime Boundary in the Gulf of Maine* [1984] ICJ Rep 246, [145].

[48] *NSCS* (n 2) [30]. The restrictive approach to estoppel established here was followed in subsequent cases: see I Sinclair, 'Estoppel and Acquiescence' in V Lowe and M Fitzmaurice (eds), *Fifty Years of the International Court of Justice: Essays in Honour of Sir Robert Jennings* (Cambridge, CUP, 1996) 111–15.

[49] *NSCS* (n 2) [60]. *cf* ILC, 'Identification of Customary International Law' (2015) UN Doc A/CN.4/L.869, Draft Conclusion 11 [12], [1]. E Jiménez de Aréchaga, 'The Work and the Jurisprudence of the International Court of Justice 1947–1986' (1987) 58 *BYIL* 1, 32–33 notes thus that treaties have respectively either a 'declaratory', a 'crystallising', or a 'generating' effect on customary international law.

[50] *NSCS* (n 2) [61].

being consolidated through the works of the Geneva Conference and the reaction of states to the drafting proposals of the ILC. The delimitation method in question was rather included on an experimental and certainly on an optional basis (the Convention permitted states to opt-out from that method through reservations), which indicated that there could not be a mandatory equivalent rule of customary international law.[51]

Finally, the Court inquired whether the provision of Article 6 had passed into customary international law since the adoption of the Convention. In order for this to be possible, the conventional rule in question would have to be 'of a fundamentally norm-creating character'.[52] But the principle of equidistance as couched in Article 6 did not possess this feature: the fact that its use was subordinated to the option of a different agreement by the parties concerned, the fact that it was coupled with the obscure notion of 'special circumstances', and the fact that it could be avoided by states through reservations all pointed to that conclusion.[53] More importantly, the Court was not satisfied that the two elements for the formation of custom were present. With respect to practice, the Court considered that it could not draw inferences from the practice of states that were or shortly became parties to the 1958 Convention, since their practice was justified by the operation of the conventional rule.[54] Similarly, the delimitation of continental shelves between opposite states (ie through the use of median lines) was considered irrelevant for the purposes of establishing the legal status of (lateral) equidistance lines between adjacent states.[55] Regarding the 'subjective element' for the determination of rules of customary law, the Court unsuccessfully sought evidence that states, when agreeing to draw boundaries on the basis of equidistance, 'felt' compelled to do so pursuant to some legal obligation, rather than being motivated by other factors.[56]

The Court held that the parties were not obligated to use any particular method, including equidistance, for the delimitation of the continental shelf areas concerned.[57] Rather, they were obligated to enter into negotiations with a view to reaching an agreement based on equitable principles.[58] In the Court's view, what mattered was that the result achieved be equitable[59] and for this purpose the principle of equidistance might or might not be suitable, depending on the circumstances.[60] Indeed, several factors ought to be taken into account in the process of delimitation, including the geographical configuration of the coasts, physical and geological features, the unity of any deposits of natural resources, as well as a degree of proportionality between the length of the coastline and the extent of the continental shelf.[61]

---

[51] ibid, [61]–[63].
[52] ibid, [72].
[53] ibid.
[54] ibid, [76].
[55] ibid, [79].
[56] ibid, [77]–[78].
[57] ibid, [83].
[58] ibid, [85].
[59] ibid, [88]; *cf Continental Shelf (Tunisia/Libya)* [1982] ICJ Rep 18, [70].
[60] NSCS (n 2) [89]–[90].
[61] ibid, [92]–[99].

The Court referred to a 'rule' requiring the application of equitable principles, and even to '*opinio juris*' of states in that regard,[62] so that it may be presumed that this rule, vague as it is, is one of customary international law—though its references also to 'principles' of law may cause some confusion as to whether we are dealing here with general principles under Article 38(1)(c) of the ICJ Statute.[63]

E. Aftermath of the Case

Although the Court rejected the arguments of both parties to the dispute, the judgment was arguably a victory for Germany, to the extent that it obligated the other parties to the dispute to negotiate with view to reaching an agreement. In fact, the parties sat at the negotiating table no fewer than nine times.[64] Denmark emphasised the need to establish elaborately the geological criteria alluded to in the judgment,[65] while the Netherlands, like Germany, was interested in reaching a speedy conclusion in optional terms, even if this meant ignoring the judgment[66] or breaking ties with Denmark.[67] On the opposite front, Germany clearly arrived with an upper hand, sometimes claiming a share between 38,000 and 50,000km² , ie an area significantly larger than the 36,7000km² claimed before the Court.[68] Ultimately, however, it refrained from maintaining a very assertive stance against its counterparts, for fear of raising the spectres of some not-too-distant claims of *Lebensraum*.[69]

The negotiations culminated in a set of two bilateral agreements:[70] Germany contracted to an area of 35,600km²,[71] but was given access to the centre line of the North Sea, ie the continental shelf boundary with the United Kingdom, while Denmark and the Netherlands made equivalent concessions to Germany as compared to the areas that would have been drawn on the basis of equidistance.[72] The outcome reached through the so-called Copenhagen Agreements has been

---

[62] ibid, [85]–[86].

[63] ibid, [84]–[85].

[64] S Fietta and R Cleverly, *A Practitioner's Guide to Maritime Boundary Delimitation* (Oxford, OUP, 2016) 172.

[65] AG Oude Elferink, *The Delimitation of the Continental Shelf between Denmark, Germany and the Netherlands: Arguing Law, Practicing Politics?* (Cambridge, CUP, 2013) 359–64 *cf* 379.

[66] ibid, 396–97.

[67] ibid, 373–74.

[68] ibid, 414.

[69] ibid, 445.

[70] Treaty between the Kingdom of Denmark and the Federal Republic of Germany concerning the delimitation of the continental shelf under the North Sea (with annexes and exchange of letters) (signed 28 January 1971, entered into force 7 December 1972) 857 UNTS 119; Treaty between the Kingdom of the Netherlands and the Federal Republic of Germany concerning the delimitation of the continental shelf under the North Sea (with annexes and exchange of letters) (signed 28 January 1971, entered into force 7 December 1972) 857 UNTS 142.

[71] This was still an area larger than the one that would have appertained to Germany on the basis of equidistance, namely 24,600km²; see C Gloria, 'Seegebiete mit küstenstaatlichen Nutzungsvorrechten' in Knut Ipsen (ed), *Völkerrecht*, 4th edn (München, CH Beck, 1999) 759–60, [55].

[72] Fietta and Cleverly, *Maritime Boundary Delimitation* (n 64) 172.

characterised as a 'pragmatic solution'.[73] Despite purportedly being based on the ICJ judgment, the Agreements rest on considerations unconnected with the legal guidelines provided by the Court, in particular the obscure concept of 'natural prolongation'.[74]

IV. LANDMARK OR HIGH WATERMARK?

The most significant part of the Court's inquiry in *NSCS* in terms of general international law is undoubtedly the one focusing on the sources of international law and the way in which rules stemming from different sources emerge and relate to one another (see A below). The part of the judgment that relates to the nature of the continental shelf and the principles of its delimitation is somewhat underwhelming and has not stood the test of time, except by habitual incantation (see B below).

A. The Sources of International Law and Their Relations

The nature of the question posed before the Court invited it to engage with the sources of international law and their relationship, and to produce a judgment which was considered at the time unprecedented in terms of its analytical rigour.[75] The issues discussed by the Court had already been raised both in academic doctrine and in legal practice. Still, this was an opportunity for the Court to elaborate on them in a coherent and systematic manner, and so it did.

i. The Building Blocks of Custom: A Matter of Principle

The *NSCS* judgment is considered to contain one of the classic statements of the Court on the processes of formation and the evidence of rules of customary international law.[76] Reference to it is made by domestic[77] and international[78] courts

---

[73] D Anderson, 'Denmark–Federal Republic of Germany: Report Number 9–8' in J Charney and L Alexander (eds), *International Maritime Boundaries*, vol I (Dordrecht, Martinus Nijhoff, 1993) 1805; *cf* D Anderson, 'Federal Republic of Germany–The Netherlands: Report Number 9–11' in Charney and Alexander, 1839.

[74] Weil (n 14) 112–13.

[75] K Marek, 'Problème des sources du droit international dans l'arrêt sur le plateau continental de la Mer du Nord' (1970) 6 *RBDI* 44, 45.

[76] M Wood, 'First Report on formation and evidence of customary international law' (2013) UN Doc A/CN.4/663, [57]; similarly, it has been characterised 'unquestionably the leading case relating to proof of the existence of a customary rule' (A Pellet, 'Article 38' in A Zimmerman, C Tomuschat, K Oellers-Farm and C Tams (eds), *The Statute of the International Court of Justice: A Commentary*, 2nd edn (Oxford, OUP, 2012) [229]).

[77] *Flores and ors v Southern Peru Copper Corporation* (29 August 2003) ILDC 303 (US 2003) (Court of Appeals) [39]; *Bayan v Romulo, Muna v Romulo and Ople* (1 February 2011) ILDC 2059 (PH 2011) (Supreme Court) [90]–[91]; *War Crimes Act case, Polyukhovich v Australia and Commonwealth Director of Public Prosecutions* (14 August 1991) ILDC 2726 (AU 1991) (High Court) (Judge Brennan) [28].

[78] *Baena Ricardo and ors v Panama*, Competence (28 November 2003), IACHR Series C no 104, IHRL 1487 (IACHR 2003) (Inter-American Court of Human Rights), [102]–[104]; *Article 55 of the American Convention on Human Rights* (29 September 2009), IACHR Series A no 20, OC–20/09, [48];

and tribunals alike—not least so by the ICJ itself[79]—when they seek to ascertain the establishment of a rule of customary international law. This is because, besides reaffirming the two constituent elements of custom (general practice and *opinio juris*), the judgment articulates specific criteria for the assessment of evidence regarding the existence of each of the two elements.

a. General Practice

With respect to the element of practice, the Court affirmed the principle already alluded to by its predecessor[80] that a short time span of practice could suffice for the formation of custom. Very few years had elapsed since the first references to the concept of the continental shelf under international law, still fewer since the adoption of the 1958 Convention; but this would not preclude the creation of customary rules on the continental shelf.[81] Several judges writing individually also insisted that the formation of customary law should not be impeded by time requirements, especially in the light of the exigencies of contemporary reality.[82] If circumstances called for speedy legal regulation and states engaged in the relevant practice, the short duration of that practice should not bar the formulation of a legal rule.[83] This is eminently sensible; as is to consider that no *longa usus* is required when states have expressed clear *opinio juris* with respect to a particular rule.[84]

What is crucial according to the Court is not the passage of considerable time, but rather that the practice be 'extensive and virtually uniform'.[85] This standard has

---

Prosecutor v Rwamakuba (André), Decision on appropriate remedy (31 January 2007) Case no ICTR–98–44C–T, ICL 81 (ICTR 2007) (International Criminal Tribunal for Rwanda), [22]; *Erdemović*, Judgment (7 October 1997) Case no IT–96–22–Tbis, ICL 47 (ICTY 1997) (International Criminal Tribunal for the former Yugoslavia), Separate Opinion McDonald and Vohrah, [49]; *Galić*, Judgment (30 November 2006) Case no IT–98–29–A, ICL 510 (ICTY 2006) (International Criminal Tribunal for the former Yugoslavia), Separate and Partially Dissenting Opinion of Judge Schomburg, [10n24]; *Prosecutor v. Fofana and Kondewa*, Judgment (28 May 2008) Case no SCSL–04–14–A–829 (Special Court for Sierra Leone), [405]; *Interlocutory Decision on the Applicable Law: Terrorism, Conspiracy, Homicide, Perpetration, Cumulative Charging* (16 February 2011) STL–11–01/I (Special Tribunal for Lebanon), [102].

[79] See, most recently, *Jurisdictional Immunities of the State (Germany v Italy: Greece intervening)* [2012] ICJ Rep 99, [55]. On this case, see further this volume, ch 23.

[80] *Free City of Danzig and International Labour Organization* (Advisory Opinion) (1930) PCIJ Ser B No 18, at 12–13, on practice of less than 10 years.

[81] NSCS (n 2) [73]. The fact that the element of time is not necessary does not mean that it is completely irrelevant as a factor evidencing the generality of practice; thus, the ICJ has occasionally relied on the element of time to establish rules of customary law: *Right of Passage* [1960] ICJ Rep 6, 40, on practice 'having continued over a period extending beyond a century and a quarter unaffected' by other factors; cf *Anglo–Norwegian Fisheries* [1951] ICJ Rep 116, 138, where a practice was followed 'consistently and uninterruptedly' for roughly eighty years, although what was sought there was the objection of a state to the formation of a customary rule.

[82] NSCS (n 2) 177 (dissenting opinion Tanaka); 230 (dissenting opinion Lachs).

[83] G Fitzmaurice, 'The Law and Procedure of the International Court of Justice, 1951–54: General Principles and Sources of Law' (1953) 30 BYIL 1, 31; JL Brierly, *The Law of Nations*, 4th edn (Oxford, Clarendon, 1949) 63; see also H Lauterpacht, 'Sovereignty over Submarine Areas' (1950) 27 BYIL 376, 393.

[84] See V Lowe, *International Law* (Oxford, OUP, 2007) 42.

[85] NSCS (n 2) [74].

been characterised as very demanding,[86] even though the Court had already stressed in the past that practice must be 'constant and uniform' for customary rules to be formed.[87] Nonetheless, the demand appears less stringent when interpreted against the background of the case. In particular, it would make sense for more extensive and uniform practice to be required in circumstances where the length of time is shorter (except in cases where there is clearly expressed *opinio juris*). By contrast, the Court has found in other cases that absolute consistency in the practice of states is not required, as long as contrary practice can be explained away or has been treated as being in breach of the customary rule.[88]

The Court insisted that practice leading to the emergence of a customary rule must include that of states 'whose interests are specially affected'.[89] It has thus been asserted that, for the purposes of customary law formation, some states are 'more equal' than others by virtue of their size, volume of international relations and—by way of rather circular reasoning—the 'contribution that [they make] to the development of international law'.[90] The Court's finding, however, can be seen as merely restating the obvious point that, although not all states need to uphold the rule in their practice,[91] certain states are in a position concretely to contribute to the creation of different customary rules,[92] depending on their content. The practice of states which engage intensively with the subject matter of the putative rule will thus be important.[93] Other tribunals[94] and the ICJ itself[95] in later practice dropped the reference to 'specially affected states', seeking instead to establish a consensus among states with varying or conflicting interests as to the existence of a putative rule of customary law. The ILC Special Rapporteur on the matter also noted that the identification of states specially affected with respect to each putative rule might be difficult, or even irrelevant,[96] but has maintained the importance of the practice to be reflective of a wide and representative group of states.[97] Put differently, although

---

[86] J Crawford, *Brownlie's Principles of Public International Law*, 8th edn (Oxford, OUP, 2012) 25; *cf* LDM Nelson, 'The North Sea Continental Shelf cases and Law-Making Conventions' (1972) 35 *MLR* 52, 54.

[87] *Asylum case (Colombia/Peru)* [1950] ICJ Rep 266, 276.

[88] See *Anglo–Norwegian Fisheries* (n 81) 138; more clearly in *Military and Paramilitary Activities in and against Nicaragua (Nicaragua v USA)* (Merits) [1986] ICJ Rep 14, [186].

[89] *NSCS* (n 2) [74]; also [73].

[90] RR Baxter, 'Treaties and custom' (1970) 129 *RdC* 27, 66.

[91] *NSCS* (n 2) 104 (separate opinion Ammoun); 229 (dissenting opinion Lachs); J Kunz, 'The Nature of Customary International Law' (1953) 47 *AJIL* 662, 666; *South West Africa (2nd phase)* [1966] ICJ Rep 6, 291 (dissenting opinion Tanaka).

[92] M Sørensen, 'Principes de droit international public: cours général' (1960) 101 *RdC* 1, 40; A Verdross, 'Entstehungsweisen und Geltungsgrund des universellen völkerrechtlichen Gewohnheitsrechts' (1969) 29 *ZaöRV* 635, 650; P Daillier, M Forteau and A Pellet, *Droit international public*, 8th edn (Paris, LGDJ, 2009) 360, [211].

[93] P de Visscher, 'Cours général de droit international public' (1972) 136 *RdC* 1, 67; J-P Quéneudec, 'La notion d'État intéressé en droit international' (1995) 255 *RdC* 339, 408.

[94] *Texaco v Libya* (1978) 53 ILR 389, [84] and [86]–[87].

[95] *Legality of the Threat or Use of Nuclear Weapons (Advisory Opinion)* [1996] ICJ Rep 226, [67]–[71]; see P Tomka, 'Custom and the International Court of Justice' (2013) 12 *LPICT* 195, 211–12.

[96] M Wood, 'Second Report on identification of customary international law' (2014) UN Doc A/CN.4/672, [54].

[97] ibid, [52]–[53].

no customary rule may be formed without general practice, no customary law may be 'vetoed' by a particular state, even if its interests are 'specially affected' by the putative rule.[98]

b. Accepted as Law

The Court also discussed the 'subjective element' of customary rules, ie what it called state 'belief that this practice is rendered obligatory by the existence of a rule of law requiring it'.[99] In insisting that the conduct of states must be of such quality as to manifest a particular legal view of these states, the Court stressed the distinction between legal rules and other rules of habitual conduct.[100] At the same time, it set a particularly rigorous test for the creation of custom.[101] Aside from the fact that states as fictional (legal) entities should not be anthropomorphised so as to be said to harbour 'beliefs' or 'opinions',[102] they rarely express the motivations or intentions behind their conduct.[103] The creation of custom really rests on a rebuttable presumption whereby practice is to be regarded as evidencing *opinio juris*, at least with respect to permissive (and, less so, prescriptive) rules.[104] It is impracticable to demand positive proof of legal conviction in such cases, while it is feasible and desirable to demand proof for the lack of a legal conviction enveloping the practice.[105] The practice is presumed to go hand in hand with a legal claim that what is being done is at least allowed (permissive rules) or may even be required, as indicated by context (prescriptive rules). On the other hand, proscriptive rules would require practice to reflect the 'not doing of something', ie doing nothing, and as has been rightly noted, 'states often do nothing, and for a wide variety of reasons'.[106] In those cases it is the existence of *opinio juris* that will highlight the importance of the not doing of something, that will in other words shed light on the relevant practice of omitting that which is seen as prohibited by international law.[107]

The Court itself has rarely followed such a rigorous approach as indicated in *NSCS* regarding proof of *opinio juris* for permissive or prescriptive rules in its own practice. Often the Court infers the requisite *opinio juris* from other material (such as general practice itself,[108] or from scholarly opinion, most notably that

---

[98] Y Dinstein, 'The interaction between customary international law and treaties' (2007) 322 *RdC* 243, 289.

[99] *NSCS* (n 2) [77].

[100] J Verhoeven, *Droit international public* (Bruxelles, Larcier, 2000) 330–31.

[101] Nelson, 'North Sea Continental Shelf' (n 86) 56; Crawford, *Brownlie's Principles* (n 86) 26.

[102] See Lowe, *International Law* (n 84) 51.

[103] Baxter, 'Treaties and custom' (n 90) 68.

[104] See Lowe (n 84) 51–53. cf S Séfériades, 'Aperçus sur la coutume juridique internationale notamment sur son fondement' (1936) 43 *RGDIP* 129, 144.

[105] H Lauterpacht, *The Development of International Law by the International Court* (London, Stevens and Sons, 1958) 380; similarly Crawford (n 86) 27.

[106] Lowe (n 84) 41.

[107] See also ch 15 in this volume, fn 71, which refers to J Verhoeven, 'Le droit, le juge et la violence: les arrêts Nicaragua c Etats-Unis' (1987) 91 *RGDIP* 1159, 1205.

[108] FL Kirgis, 'Custom on a Sliding Scale' (1987) 81 *AJIL* 146, 149.

of the ILC),[109] or—according to more sceptical views—simply asserts its existence.[110] What was important in this case was not so much the reaffirmation, in the abstract, that a sense of legal conviction is in principle necessary for the establishment of custom. Rather, the matter was here one of evidence, namely what evidentiary weight ought to be attached to treaty rules and to the practice of states bound by those rules in the process of ascertaining whether equivalent rules exist under customary international law.[111] It is to this matter that we now turn.

ii. The Interplay Between Custom and Treaty: A Matter of Evidence

Before *NSCS* it was not disputed in principle that a treaty may embody existing rules of customary law,[112] and it was also widely assumed that a treaty rule may contribute to the subsequent formation of a customary rule in its image.[113] As the ILC had noted a few years before the judgment, 'the role played by custom in sometimes extending the application of rules contained in a treaty beyond the contracting States [was] well recognised'.[114] The ICJ itself, as well as its predecessor, had in several cases examined treaties that were not binding on (at least one of) the parties before it, with a view to inferring the existence of general rules of international law binding on those parties.[115] What was novel about *NSCS* was the elaborate articulation by the Court of factors that would determine the evidentiary value of treaties for the identification of rules of customary international law.[116] Some of the factors put forward by the Court were not wholly uncontroversial. Still they have been highly influential in subsequent international legal practice.

---

[109] An emerging trend was already noticed in S Schwebel, 'The Inter-active Influence of the International Court of Justice and the International Law Commission' in CA Armas Barea, JA Barberis, J Barboza, H Caminos, E Candioti, E de La Guardia, HDT Gutiérez Posse, G Moncayo, EJ Rey Caro, RE Vinuesa (eds), *Liber Amicorum 'In Memoriam' of Judge José María Ruda* (London, Kluwer, 2000) 485–86; see also Pellet, 'Article 38' (n 76) [230].

[110] S Talmon, 'Determining Customary International Law: the ICJ's Methodology between Induction, Deduction and Assertion' (2015) 26 *EJIL* 417, 434–40.

[111] Similarly, T Meron, 'The Geneva Conventions as Customary Law' (1987) 88 *AJIL* 348, 367.

[112] International Military Tribunal Judgment and Sentences (*France and ors v Göring and ors*) (1946) 41 *AJIL* 172, 219 and 248–49; H Lauterpacht, 'Règles générales du droit de la paix' (1937) 62 *RdC* 100, 156; RY Jennings, 'The Progressive Development of International Law and Its Codification' (1947) 24 *BYIL* 301, 304; GG Fitzmaurice, 'Some Problems regarding the Formal Sources of International Law' in *Symbolae Verzijl* (La Haye, Martinus Nijhoff, 1958) 159.

[113] See already J Kosters, 'Les fondements du droit des gens: contribution à la théorie générale du droit des gens' (1925) 4 *Bibliotheca Visseriana* (Lugduni Batavorum, Brill) 221; Lauterpacht, 'Règles générales du droit de la paix' (n 112) 156–57; A Ulloa, *Derecho Internacional Publico*, vol I, 4th edn (Madrid, Ediciones Iberoamericanas, 1957) 52 [49c]; *cf NSCS* (n 2) 225 (dissenting opinion Lachs).

[114] ILC, 'Draft Articles on the Law of Treaties with commentaries' in ILC 'Report of the International Law Commission on the work of its eighteenth session' [1966]-II ILC Ybk 187, commentary to draft Art 34 (230), [1].

[115] See already *SS Wimbledon* (1923) PCIJ Rep Series A No 1, 25; *Factory at Chorzow (Claim for Indemnity) (Jurisdiction)* (1927) PCIJ Rep Series A No 9, 22; *Territorial Jurisdiction of the International Commission of the River Oder* (1929) PCIJ Rep Series A No 23, 27; *Asylum case* (n 87) 277; *Nottebohm* [1955] ICJ Rep 4, 22–23.

[116] See to that effect *Perinçek v Switzerland* (2016) 63 EHRR 6, [266]; *R (European Roma Rights Centre and Others) v Immigration Officer at Prague Airport and Another (United Nations High Commissioner for Refugees intervening)* [2004] UKHL 55, [23] (Lord Bingham).

For example, the fact that the treaty provision in question was open to reservations by parties to the 1958 Convention was heavily relied on by the Court as strong evidence against the conclusion that this provision codified or crystallised or was 'potentially possible' (sic) to develop identical rules of customary rules.[117] This reasoning, however, is problematic, at least to the extent that it refers to codification of existing or crystallisation of emerging customary rules. As was pointed out both by dissenting judges and by scholarly opinion, the faculty of reservations (and even the submission of reservations, as long as they are not so numerous as to negate the customary character of the rule) by states on the contractual plane has no effect on the plane of customary law.[118] While states may exempt themselves from the application of a particular rule in their relations with other parties to a treaty, they may not exempt themselves from the application of an identical rule under customary law in situations where that treaty is not applicable (ie essentially in their relations with states not parties to that treaty). In fact, the Court itself accepted this proposition in *NSCS*, when it held that any reservations in the 1958 Convention would not release states from obligations existing 'outside and independently of the Convention'.[119]

Consequently, the fact that states are permitted to exempt themselves from the treaty provision cannot in itself serve as proof that there does (not) exist an identical rule under customary law.[120] Or conversely, in the words of the ILC, 'The fact that a treaty provision reflects a rule of customary international law does not in itself constitute an obstacle to the formulation of a reservation to that provision'.[121] This after all makes sense, since treaties also constitute the instrument *par excellence* for contracting out of customary international law.[122] In this latter context, the *Diallo* case is instructive: even if states have contracted out of the general rules of diplomatic protection by way of many treaties, this has not necessarily affected the status of the relevant customary rules.[123]

The Court also noted that a treaty provision should possess a 'fundamentally norm-creating character' in order to develop a customary counterpart.[124] Taken at face value, the Court's remark alludes to the old distinction between 'law-making' and 'purely contractual' treaties (and accordingly provisions), a distinction which

---

[117] See above, text to nn 51–53.

[118] *NSCS* (n 2) 198 (dissenting opinion Morelli); 224 (dissenting opinion Lachs); 248 (dissenting opinion Sørensen); K Skubiszewski, 'Elements of Custom and The Hague Court' (1971) 31 *ZaöRV* 810, 848.

[119] ibid, [65]; as it has been noted, the Court might thus be considered as contradicting itself: K Zemanek, 'Bedeutung der Kodifizierung des Völkerrechts' in R Marcic, H Mosler, E Suy, and K Zemanek (eds), *Internationale Festschrift für Alfred Verdross zum 80. Geburtstag* (München, Wilhelm Fink, 1971) 584.

[120] GM Danilenko, *Law-Making in the International Community* (Dordrecht, Martinus Nijhoff, 1993) 154; M Villiger, *Customary International Law and Treaties: A Manual on the Theory and Practice of the Interrelation of Sources*, 2nd edn (The Hague, Kluwer, 1997) 258, [406].

[121] ILC, 'Guide to Practice on Reservations to Treaties' (2011) UN Doc A/66/10/Add.1, guideline 3.1.5.3; see also commentary thereto, esp [3]–[7].

[122] Dinstein, 'Interaction' (n 98) 406.

[123] *Ahmadou Sadio Diallo (Guinea v DR Congo)* (Preliminary Objections) [2007] ICJ Rep 582, [90].

[124] See above, text to n 53.

had long been dismissed as legally irrelevant.[125] Indeed, whether a rule enshrined in a treaty subsequently passes into customary law is a question of fact, namely a question of the attitude of states vis-à-vis the legal status of that rule,[126] and there is no reason of principle why a very specific, technical, or sophisticated provision should not be able to attain the status of customary law.[127] That said, such a provision may be more unlikely to pass into customary international law.[128] Therefore, the 'norm-creating' character of certain treaty provisions might be useful from a methodological perspective,[129] as a further piece of evidence regarding the likelihood of customary status. Indeed, the Special Rapporteur on identification of customary international law has also noted that some treaty provisions are 'unlikely', rather than unable, to form the basis of customary rules.[130]

The Court further indicated that the evidence potentially relevant to confirming the putative rule as one of customary law lies outside the treaty. With respect to pre-existing rules, the declaration in the treaty itself that it codifies pre-existing custom is relevant only to the extent that it expresses the *opinio juris* of the ratifying states,[131] and ought to be assessed together with evidence preceding the entry into force of the treaty—most importantly, the (lack of) practice and *opinio juris* of other states.

When it comes to treaty rules purportedly forming the basis for subsequent customary law, on the other hand, the conduct of states parties to the treaty between themselves constitutes conduct in compliance to the treaty rule, therefore evidence must be sought in the practice of parties with third states, or of third states between themselves.[132] In what appears as somewhat of a paradox, then, lack of participation of states in a multilateral treaty might indicate that states do not consider the rules enshrined therein as part of customary law,[133] whereas wide participation of states in a treaty diminishes the instances of practice and *opinio juris* where the

---

[125] H Lauterpacht, 'Report on the Law of Treaties' UN Doc A/CN.4/63 [1953]-II ILC Ybk 90, 99; GG Fitzmaurice, 'Report on the Law of Treaties' UN Doc A/CN.4/101 [1956]-II ILC Ybk 104, 108 (draft Art 8).

[126] M Akehurst, 'Custom as a Source of International Law' (1975) 47 *BYIL* 1, 50; MH Mendelson, 'The Formation of Customary International Law' (1998) 272 *RdC* 155, 320–21.

[127] See H Waldock, 'Third Report on the Law of Treaties' UN Doc A/CN.4/167 and Add.1–3 [1964]-II ILC Ybk 5, 34 (commentary to draft Art 64); similarly R Kolb, 'Selected Problems in the Theory of Customary International Law' (2003) 50 *NILR* 119, 148; J Crawford, 'Chance, Order, Change: The Course of International Law' (2013) 365 *RdC* 9, 97.

[128] Kolb, 'Selected Problems' (n 127) 148.

[129] For the descriptive or methodological, as opposed to the legal, value of the distinction between 'law-making' and 'purely contractual' treaties and provisions see C Rousseau, *Principes généraux du droit international public*, vol I (Paris, Pedone, 1944) 136 [66].

[130] M Wood, 'Third Report on identification of customary international law' (2015) UN Doc A/CN.4/682, [39].

[131] I Shihata, 'The Treaty as a Law-Declaring and Custom-Making Instrument' (1966) 22 *Revue égyptienne de droit international* 51, 65.

[132] Dinstein (n 98) 376–77; C Rozakis, 'Treaties and Third States: A Study in the Reinforcement of the Consensual Standards in International Law' (1975) 35 *ZaöRV* 1, 33.

[133] See to that effect *NSCS* (n 2) [73]; Baxter (n 90) 95–96.

application of rules of custom (rather than the treaty) might be affirmed.[134] This has also been called the 'Baxter Paradox'.[135]

These questions of evidence raised by *NSCS* have generated more trouble in theory than they have in practice. At the same time, the judgment illustrated a relationship 'replete with paradoxes' between treaties and custom.[136] The Court subsequently held that non-binding instruments, such as Resolutions by the General Assembly of the United Nations, might be relevant evidence for the identification of customary law.[137] Perhaps more importantly, the earlier trend of the ILC encouraging the adoption of treaties on the basis of its completed projects has been reduced. Instead, the ILC (and the UN General Assembly as its supervisory body) has opted for more flexible avenues, that would avoid the 'decodifying effect' to which unsuccessful (or even very successful) treaties are susceptible.[138] The example of the Articles on the Responsibility of States for Internationally Wrongful Acts[139] showcases how *the lack* of binding force of written rules may be catalytic for the formation of identical rules under customary international law[140]—another aspect of the paradoxical relationship between treaty and custom.

B. The Regime of the Continental Shelf

i. The Continental Shelf Defined

By emphasising that the continental shelf delimitation was a process of drawing boundaries between areas already appertaining to the states involved, the Court primarily addressed the German contention that the North Sea continental shelf should be shared equitably among the disputing parties. The Court's proposition, however, had several wider implications. To begin with, the Court held that the rights of coastal states over the continental shelf existed 'quite independent[ly]' of the 1958 Convention', ie under customary international law. This finding was arguably not controversial in the context of that particular case, because all three states accepted the binding nature of the provisions of the 1958 Convention relating to the content of the rights over the continental shelf. Denmark and the Netherlands were parties to the Convention, and Germany had essentially reproduced its Article 2 in a 1964

---

[134] See to that effect *NSCS* (n 2) [76]; A D'Amato, 'Treaties as a Source of General Rules of International Law' (1962) 3 *Harvard International Law Club Bulletin* 1, 8; Baxter (n 90) 64.

[135] See Crawford, 'Chance, Order, Change' (n 127) 90ff, and his proposed solution at 109ff.

[136] Kolb (n 127) 145.

[137] *Military and Paramilitary Activities* (n 88) [188]; *Nuclear Weapons* (n 95) [70].

[138] See most notably J Crawford, 'Fourth Report on State Responsibility' (2001) UN Doc A/CN.4/517 and Add.1, [23], with respect to the (Draft) Articles on the Responsibility of States for Internationally Wrongful Acts.

[139] UNGA Res 56/83 (28 January 2002) UN Doc A/RES/56/83.

[140] The resulting rules have been considered 'customary international law by stealth': Crawford (n 127) 108. See also D Caron, 'The ILC Articles on State Responsibility: The Paradoxical Relationship between Form and Authority' (2002) 96 *AJIL* 857, 867–68.

governmental proclamation.[141] This, however, does not seem to justify the absence of scrutiny, on the part of the Court, regarding the existence of such rights under customary international law.[142] As the Court observed several years later, 'the shared view of the Parties as to the content of what they regard as the rule is not enough. The Court must satisfy itself that the existence of the rule in the *opinio juris* of States is confirmed by practice'.[143]

When placed in a broader context, this statement proves to be even bolder than it first appears. The existence of continental shelf rights under customary international law had been affirmed in academic literature before the adoption of the 1958 Convention,[144] but they had been equally (if not more strongly) denied.[145] Further, the umpire of the *Abu Dhabi* arbitration in the early 1950s opined that the purported 'doctrine' (ie the claim) regarding the continental shelf had not yet solidified into an established rule of international law,[146] while the ILC in its 1956 Report to the UN General Assembly had been rather equivocal as to the legal basis of the sovereign rights that were later enshrined in the 1958 Convention,[147] reflecting, as it were, the 'immaturity of the legal regime'.[148] The relatively scarce academic literature since the adoption of the Convention had been rather sceptical (or at least inconclusive) about the existence of such a rule under customary international law.[149] Seen in this light, the pronouncement of the Court might not have intended to rewrite legal history,[150] but it appears less elementary than it is sometimes presented.[151]

What was arguably more innovative in the Court's approach was the conceptualisation of the continental shelf as the 'natural prolongation' of the coastal state's land territory. This proposition was central both to the finding that the rights of

---

[141] Monconduit, 'Affaire du plateau continental' (n 21) 222.

[142] In a subsequent part of the judgment, the ICJ noted that 'it [was] clear' that the first three Articles of the 1958 Convention (stipulating the nature of the rights exercisable, the limits of the continental shelf etc) were 'regarded [at the 1958 Geneva Conference] as reflecting, or as crystallizing, received or at least emergent rules of customary international law', but it did not elaborate this assertion further: *NSCS* (n 2) [63].

[143] *Military and Paramilitary Activities* (n 88) [184].

[144] Lauterpacht, 'Sovereignty' (n 83) 393–98.

[145] MW Mouton, 'The Continental Shelf' (1954) 85 *RdC* 343, 430–32; H Thirlway, 'The Law and Procedure of the International Court of Justice 1960–1989: Part Five' (1993) 64 *BYIL* 1, 8 fn 23; *cf* J Symonides, 'Geographically disadvantaged states under the 1982 Convention on the Law of the Sea' (1988) 208 *RdC* 283, 340.

[146] *Arbitration between Petroleum Development (Trucial Coast) Ltd and the Sheikh of Abu Dhabi* (1951) 18 ILR 144, 155.

[147] Articles concerning the Law of the Sea with commentaries (n 10) 298 (commentary to Art 68, para 8).

[148] I Brownlie, *Principles of Public International Law*, 7th edn (Oxford, OUP, 2008) 207.

[149] BBL Auguste, *The Continental Shelf: The Practice and Policy of the Latin American States with Special Reference to Chile, Ecuador and Peru* (Genève, Droz, 1960) 101–03; ZJ Slouka, *International Custom and the Continental Shelf: A Study in the Dynamics of Customary Rules of International Law* (The Hague, Martinus Nijhoff, 1968) 165; *cf* UNGA Res 2574 A (XXIV) (15 December 1969); see however W Burke, 'Law and the New Technologies' in L Alexander (ed), *The Law of the Sea: Offshore Boundaries and Zones* (Columbus, Ohio State University Press, 1967) 209.

[150] Churchill and Lowe, *The Law of the Sea* (n 5) 144–45.

[151] RY Jennings, 'The Limits of the Continental Shelf Jurisdiction: Some Possible Implications of the North Sea Case Judgment' (1969) 18 *ICLQ* 819, 819.

the continental shelf existed 'inherently' under customary international law, and to the treatment of continental shelf delimitation. The basis of the coastal state's entitlement over the continental shelf, according to the Court, is its entitlement—its title of sovereignty—over the territory lying above the sea. To the extent that the state enjoys sovereignty over land territory, it enjoys title over the areas which, although covered by seawater, 'may be deemed to be actually part of [that] territory', in the sense that they are an extension—a prolongation—of that territory under the sea.[152] The rights to the continental shelf are a mere application of the principle that the land dominates the sea.[153] This in turn suggests that the rights are not contingent on the establishment of a particular legal framework. The sole determinant factors for their establishment are the sovereignty over land territory and the geomorphological continuity between that territory and the submarine area in question, irrespective of the fact that the nature and extent of such rights had been perceived in the light of then recent technological developments.[154]

Such a clear emphasis by the Court on geomorphology for the definition—and, consequently, for the delimitation—of the continental shelf was not unheard of. It echoed the Truman Proclamation, whose preamble characterised the continental shelf as 'an extension of the land-mass of the coastal nation and thus naturally appurtenant to it'.[155] At the same time, it stood in stark contrast with the definition of the continental shelf provided for in Article 1 of the 1958 Convention. There it was preferred to uncouple the legal definition of the continental shelf from geological criteria in order to avoid discrimination among coastal states.[156] The Court can thus be seen as accepting the general concept of the continental shelf reflected in the 1958 Convention,[157] but at the same time reintroducing geological factors.[158]

The judgment has greatly influenced our thinking about the nature and definition of the continental shelf.[159] It still serves as a point of reference for the conceptualisation of the source and nature of the rights enjoyed by the coastal state over its continental shelf.[160] A Chamber of the ICJ did not hesitate to comment later that the

---

[152] *NSCS* (n 2) [43].

[153] ibid, [96]; see also subsequent references in the case law (n 160). This is one of the most ancient principles of the law of the sea; see H Grotius, *De jure belli et pacis libri tres*, vol I (originally published 1625, W Whewell tr) (Cambridge, John Parker, 1853) ch III, para VIII.

[154] DP O'Connell, *The International Law of the Sea*, vol I (Oxford, Clarendon, 1982) 483–84.

[155] Truman Proclamation (n 8).

[156] R-J Dupuy and D Vignes, *A Handbook on the Law of the Sea*, vol I (Leiden, Brill, 1991) 336.

[157] It is worth noting that the Court's language does not unequivocally support that Arts 1–3 of the 1958 Convention reflect customary international law: see O'Connell, *International Law* (n 154) 475; Dupuy and Vignes, *Handbook* (n 156) 338–39.

[158] See generally Jennings, 'The Limits of the Continental Shelf Jurisdiction' (n 151) 828–29; Dupuy and Vignes, *Handbook* (n 156) 130. For a different explanation see *Continental shelf (Tunisia/Libya)* (n 59) [46] (separate opinion Jiménez de Aréchaga). See further SC Chaturvedi, 'The North Sea Continental Shelf cases analysed' (1973) 13 *IndianJIL* 481, 492.

[159] RY Jennings and Arthur Watts, *Oppenheim's International Law*, vol I, 9th edn (Oxford, OUP, 1996) 771.

[160] See, among others, *Aegean Sea Continental Shelf (Greece v Turkey)* [1978] ICJ Rep 3, [86]; *Maritime Delimitation and Territorial Questions (Qatar v Bahrain) (Merits)* [2001] ICJ Rep 40, [185]; *Territorial and Maritime Dispute between Nicaragua and Honduras in the Caribbean Sea (Nicaragua v Honduras)* [2007] ICJ Rep 659, [113]; *Maritime Delimitation in the Black Sea (Romania v Ukraine)*

NSCS judgment 'has made the greatest contribution to the formation of customary law' in the field of the continental shelf.[161] While this statement might have been true at the time when it was made, it probably does not hold water nowadays.

The propositions of the Court with respect to the nature of the continental shelf did lend support to the process of revision of the continental shelf definition during the Third UN Conference on the Law of the Sea.[162] And yet, the definition in the 1958 Convention was in many respects problematic anyway.[163] The *NSCS* judgment merely catalysed a process which was already underway. According to the new definition, the continental shelf extends throughout the natural prolongation of the coastal state's land territory to the outer edge of the continental margin, or to a distance of 200nm from the baselines.[164] In other words, while the concept of 'natural prolongation' was eventually inserted in the new definition of the continental shelf, it was coupled with a distance criterion, which provided a new legal basis for the entitlement to continental shelf rights.[165] Soon after the adoption of UNCLOS in 1982 (and before its entry into force) the ICJ acknowledged that title over areas of the continental shelf situated at a distance of under 200nm from the coast depend solely on distance. The geomorphological characteristics of such areas are completely immaterial. The geophysical factors on which the *NSCS* judgment relied 'now [belong] to the past, in so far as sea-bed areas less than 200 miles from the coast are concerned'.[166] Natural prolongation, at least for narrow-margined states or states whose coasts are fewer than 400nm apart, was dead.[167]

It has been suggested that the geological criteria stemming from the concept of natural prolongation as propounded by the ICJ in *NSCS* might still be relevant for the determination of the so-called 'outer continental shelf',[168] ie the area of the continental shelf extending beyond 200nm.[169] Ironically, while the concept of 'natural prolongation' was initially employed to extend the coastal state's jurisdiction over areas beyond its territorial waters, it could thus be relied on to deny claims over

[2009] ICJ Rep 61, [77] and [99]; *Territorial and Maritime Dispute (Nicaragua v Colombia)* [2012] ICJ Rep 624, [140]; C–37/00 *Weber v Universal Ogden Services Ltd* ECLI:EU:C:2002:122, 27 February 2002, [34]; C–347/10 *Salemink v Raad* ECLI:EU:C:2012:17, 17 January 2012, [32].

[161] *Delimitation of the Maritime Boundary in the Gulf of Maine Area* [1984] ICJ Rep 246, [91].

[162] For the invocation of the judgment by several states (starting with China) see MH Nordquist, SN Nandan and S Rosenne (eds), *United Nations Convention on the Law of the Sea 1982— A Commentary*, vol II (The Hague, Martinus Nijhoff, 1993) [76.4]–[76.5].

[163] For the general problems of the 1958 Convention definition see O'Connell, *International Law* (n 154) 492–96.

[164] Article 76 UNCLOS (signed 10 December 1982, entered into force 16 November 1994) 1833 UNTS 397.

[165] *Continental Shelf (Tunisia/Libya)* (n 59) [48].

[166] *Continental Shelf (Libya/Malta)* [1985] ICJ Rep 13, [39]–[40].

[167] I Brownlie, *The Rule of Law in International Affairs* (The Hague, Martinus Nijhoff, 1998) 169–70; DA Colson, 'The Delimitation of the Outer Continental Shelf between Neighboring States' (2003) 97 *AJIL* 91, 101.

[168] This term is nowhere to be found in UNCLOS, but it is often used for reasons of simplification; see B Már Magnússon, 'Outer Continental Shelf Boundary Agreements' (2013) 62 *ICLQ* 345, 345 fn 2.

[169] D Anderson, 'Some Recent Developments in the Law Relating to the Continental Shelf' (1988) 6 *Journal of Energy and Natural Resources Law* 95, 96–97; Brownlie, *The Rule of Law* (n 167) 170; Colson, 'Delimitation' (n 167) 107.

the seabed beyond 200nm from the coast, if these are not justified by geological criteria.[170] However, this does not seem to have been the case. The International Tribunal for the Law of the Sea has rejected that natural prolongation constitutes a separate and independent criterion that a coastal state must satisfy in order to be entitled to a continental shelf beyond 200nm.[171] After noting that the concept of natural prolongation has not been defined since NSCS,[172] the Tribunal opined that it ought to be read in the light of the other provisions of the (quite complex) definition in Article 76 of UNCLOS.[173] These provisions essentially flesh out a legal, rather than a geological, concept of the continental shelf, providing artificial formulae for its demarcation.[174] In short, despite having been heralded by the ICJ in the NSCS case, the concept of 'natural prolongation' is, for all practical purposes, irrelevant.[175]

ii. The Continental Shelf Delimited

The definition of the continental shelf provided by the Court in NSCS had an impact on the method of its delimitation when neighbouring states made claims over the same submarine area. The delimitation line was conceptualised as a physical line separating the overlapping natural prolongations into the sea, a line somehow already 'engraved' in the seabed[176] to be discovered not through the application of equidistance but by the operation of 'equitable principles'. The judgment's proposition as to continental shelf delimitation exerted significant influence in the drafting process of UNCLOS. Unlike its 1958 predecessor, the 1982 Convention is silent as to the use of particular delimitation methods, emphasising instead the obligation of neighbouring states to reach an 'equitable solution' when delimiting their continental shelves.[177] As such, UNCLOS comes close to requiring delimitation based on 'equitable principles'.[178] The difficult question, of course, is the identification of such 'equitable principles', a matter on which the Court gave little guidance in NSCS. The classification of equitable principles as part of general international law was an important finding on principle—and it has repeatedly been recognised as such.[179]

---

[170] Dupuy and Vignes, Handbook (n 156) 339–40; Y Huang and X Liao, 'Natural Prolongation and Delimitation of the Continental Shelf Beyond 200 nm: Implications of the Bangladesh/Myanmar Case' (2014) 4 Asian JIL 281, 305.

[171] Delimitation of the maritime boundary in the Bay of Bengal (Bangladesh/Myanmar) [2012] ITLOS Rep 4, [435].

[172] ibid, [432].

[173] ibid, [437].

[174] S Suarez, The Outer Limits of the Continental Shelf: Legal Aspects of their Establishment (Berlin, Springer, 2008) 241.

[175] H Jung Kim, 'Natural Prolongation: A Living Myth in the Regime of the Continental Shelf?' (2012) 45 ODIL 374, 381; cf Colson, 'Delimitation' (n 167) 101 (with reference to the 'inner' continental shelf).

[176] J Lilje-Jensen and M Thamsborg, 'The Role of Natural Prolongation in Relation to Shelf Delimitation beyond 200 Nautical Miles' (1995) 64 Nordic JIL 619, 621.

[177] Article 83 UNCLOS; see also Art 76 on the exclusive economic zone.

[178] Nordquist, Nandan and Rosenne, United Nations Convention (n 162) [83.3]; DP O'Connell, The International Law of the Sea, vol II (Oxford, OUP, 1988) 689.

[179] Jennings and Watts, Oppenheim (n 159) 44; Daillier, Forteau and Pellet, Droit international public (n 92) 389–90, [232]–[233]; A Verdross and B Simma, Universelles Völkerrecht: Theorie und Praxis, 3rd

However, it is not clear how the application of such principles would lead to delimitation which is not *ex aequo et bono*.[180] Further, the identification of principles by reference to the result they yield[181] is a truism,[182] or simply suggests that the process of delimitation involves a direct balancing act on a case-by-case basis, either by the states themselves or by the court seised.[183] The risks of this approach were pointed out by several dissenting judges in *NSCS*. These stressed that such an approach was at once susceptible to arbitrariness[184] and unhelpful for the resolution of disputes between neighbouring states who disagreed precisely on what an equitable delimitation would or should look like.[185]

Several members of the bench also criticised the Court for limiting its analysis on the customary status of the rule of equidistance. Instead, the appropriate rule whose customary status ought to be ascertained (and affirmed, according to these judges) was the rule combining the elements of equidistance and special circumstances, precisely as provided for in Article 6 of the 1958 Convention. That rule, according to dissenting judges, lived up to the standards of equity and reflected customary law.[186]

The latter approach was apparently adopted by the arbitral tribunal in the *Anglo–French Continental Shelf* case. While endorsing the finding in *NSCS* that equidistance was not obligatory under customary international law, it observed that the combined operation of the principle of equidistance and the provision for special circumstances (as enshrined in Article 6 of the 1958 Convention) amounted to a delimitation of the continental shelf on the basis of equitable principles: in other words, the rule 'equidistance–special circumstances' had the same effect as the rule on 'equitable principles'.[187] This ruling was, in turn, endorsed by the ICJ itself, which applied the rule of Article 6 as a matter of customary international law first in relation to states with opposite[188] and then with adjacent[189] coasts. It is now settled practice of the Court to adopt the equidistance–special circumstances method as the presumptive method of delimitation, then refining corrective principles in order

edn (Berlin, Duncker & Humbolt, 1984) 422–23, [658]; P-M Dupuy and Y Kerbrat, *Droit international public*, 10th edn (Paris, Dalloz, 2010) 394, [362].

[180] See to that effect *Continental Shelf (Tunisia/Libya)* (n 59) [1] (dissenting opinion Oda); JI Charney, 'Is International Law Threatened by Multiple Tribunals?' (1998) 271 *RdC* 101, 321–22.

[181] *Continental Shelf (Tunisia/Libya)* (n 59) [70].

[182] ibid, [155] (dissenting opinion Oda).

[183] *Continental Shelf (Libya/Malta)* (n 166) [28]; see also Y Tanaka, *Predictability and Flexibility in the Law of Maritime Delimitation* (Oxford, Hart, 2006) 123–25.

[184] *NSCS* (n 2) 166 (dissenting opinion Koretsky); *cf* 257 (dissenting opinion Sørensen).

[185] ibid, 195–96 (dissenting opinion Tanaka).

[186] See ibid, 186 (dissenting opinion Tanaka); 162–63 (dissenting opinion Koretsky); *cf* 151 [56] (separate opinion Ammoun).

[187] *Anglo–French Continental Shelf* (n 15) [70]; *cf* [75].

[188] *Maritime Delimitation in the Area between Greenland and Jan Mayen (Denmark v Norway)* [1993] ICJ Rep 38, [46].

[189] *Maritime Delimitation and Territorial Questions (Qatar/Bahrain)* (n 160) [230].

to achieve an equitable result,[190] including the lack of disproportionality between the ratio of the coastal lengths and that of the maritime areas divided.[191] This is the so-called 'three-stage approach' or 'test'.

While it has been noted that recent delimitation cases before international courts and tribunals seem to signal a return to 'equitable principles' by wavering on the so-called 'three-stage test' that has been dominating delimitation decisions for the last decades,[192] this may be a bit overstated. There is nothing binding about the practice of the ICJ and other tribunals in the aftermath of NSCS in elaborating and adopting the 'three-stage test'. Given the relevant provisions of UNCLOS which codify the meaningless dictum of the Court in NSCS, the 'three-stage test' is merely a practice that offers some predictability, indeed some content, to the exercise of achieving an equitable result.[193] As we noted above, describing an exercise by reference to its ultimate goal is circular, and in fact does not describe the exercise at all. This does not mean that the 'three-stage test' cannot be diverged from (as indeed it had been also during its supposed heyday).[194] Rather, the test provides a settled method for reaching an equitable result,[195] and any departure from it will require 'compelling reasons',[196] or at least some justification. Whether that justification is convincing or not is another matter altogether. As is the question of whether maritime delimitation can ever be subject to mechanistic application of rigid rules without some possibility of flexible adjustment.[197] Be that as it may, NSCS is now remembered precisely because it contains little worth remembering under the contemporary international law of the sea.

V. CONCLUSION

The NSCS cases will invariably be cited in textbooks, as they have been, for years to come. And rightly so, but mainly for the principled elaboration of the sources of

---

[190] See V Lowe and A Tzanakopoulos, 'The Development of the Law of the Sea by the International Court of Justice' in CJ Tams and J Sloan (eds), *The Development of International Law by the International Court of Justice* (Oxford, OUP, 2013) 177, 189.

[191] *Maritime Delimitation in the Black Sea (Romania v Ukraine)* (n 160) [115]–[122].

[192] See generally MD Evans, 'Maritime Boundary Delimitation: Whatever Next?' in J Barrett and R Barnes (eds), *Law of the Sea: UNCLOS as a Living Treaty* (London, BIICL, 2016) 41ff.

[193] Y Tanaka, *The International Law of the* Sea, 2nd edn (Cambridge, CUP, 2015) 207–08.

[194] See *Territorial and Maritime Dispute between Nicaragua and Honduras in the Caribbean Sea (Nicaragua v Honduras)* (n 160), [280]–[281].

[195] DH Anderson, 'Recent Judicial Decisions Concerning Maritime Delimitation' in L del Castillo (ed), *Law of the Sea, From Grotius to the International Tribunal for the Law of the Sea: Liber Amicorum Judge Hugo Caminos* (Leiden, Brill, 2015) 500–01.

[196] *Maritime Delimitation in the Black Sea (Romania v Ukraine)* (n 160), [116]; *Territorial and Maritime Dispute (Nicaragua v Colombia)* (n 160) 191; *Maritime Dispute (Peru v Chile)* [2014] ICJ Rep 3, [180].

[197] For a critical take on the judicial leeway afforded by the three-stage test see generally F Olorundami, 'Objectivity versus Subjectivity in the Context of the ICJ's Three-stage Methodology of Maritime Boundary Delimitation' (2017) 32 *IJMCL* 36, 49–51.

international law and their relationship, rather than for any significant contribution they may have made with respect to the law of the sea. Habitual incantation of natural prolongation and equitable principles will no doubt also retain their positions in textbooks and judicial decisions, but the law has progressed so as to render them practically irrelevant. As such, the *NSCS* cases are definitely a landmark rather than a high watermark; or they are indeed a high watermark for the geomorphological approaches to the continental shelf and for principles of equity whose vagueness prevent them from having any meaningful practical application.

13

Barcelona Traction, Light and Power Company (Belgium v Spain) (1970)

GIORGIO GAJA

I. INTRODUCTION

DURING HIS HIGHLY successful pleadings in the *Barcelona Traction* case,[1] Roberto Ago used a metaphor that would not be acceptable today. When he was referring to the *Delagoa Bay* case, he said that Delagoa was an old lady whose veil it was not advisable to lift.[2] One could say that now Barcelona Traction has also become an old lady.

The long time that has passed since the Court's judgments, and my limited role in the pleadings, assisting Roberto Ago and Antonio Malintoppi, may allow me to revisit the case with the eyes of a scholar, in the context of the present study of landmark decisions on international law.

Barcelona Traction was a holding company which controlled a number of companies producing electricity in Catalonia. It was declared bankrupt in 1948 by the Court of Reus, in Spain, because it had failed to pay interest on some bonds issued in sterling. The sum was a small amount of money and Barcelona Traction had not paid interest because the Spanish monetary authorities had refused to allow the company to export profits that it had made in Spain. As can happen in civil law countries, the bankruptcy judgment was given without hearing the company concerned, which could have subsequently filed an opposition with the same Court. However, Barcelona Traction did not make use of this remedy. The bankruptcy proceedings continued and Barcelona Traction lost control of its subsidiary companies. As a result of the bankruptcy, Barcelona Traction's assets were transferred to a Spanish company, Fuerzas Eléctricas de Cataluña SA (FECSA).

There was a suspicion that the Spanish authorities had contrived Barcelona Traction's bankruptcy. The strong man in FECSA was Juan March. He was closely linked to General Francisco Franco, whom he had aided in the Spanish Civil War, especially by providing him with air transport from the Canary Islands at the beginning of the war.[3] On the other hand, there was no evidence of corruption concerning

---

[1] The full title is *Case Concerning the Barcelona Traction, Light and Power Company, Limited (New Application: 1962) (Belgium v Spain)*.

[2] *Pleadings*, Vol III, 858–59.

[3] For a detailed account see J Brooks, 'Barcelona Traction', *The New Yorker*, 21 May 1979, 41–101, and 26 May 1979, 42–91.

the judge who had declared the bankruptcy. Also the accounting firm Peat and Marwick found, on consultation by Spain, that the evaluation of Barcelona Traction's assets in the bankruptcy proceedings had been fair.[4]

Belgium contended that various Spanish authorities had acted in breach of Spain's obligations under international law and requested reparation. After years of diplomatic exchanges, which involved also Canada, the United Kingdom and the United States, Belgium made an application to the ICJ. The case concerned a huge sum of money and involved an unprecedented number of lawyers, some of them with the role of monitoring the work of other lawyers. The representatives of the private interests played an important part. The principal actors were FECSA on the Spanish side and SOFINA on the Belgian side.

Belgium first applied to the ICJ on 23 September 1958. The claim concerned reparation for the injury caused to the company Barcelona Traction and was espoused by Belgium because of the alleged Belgian nationality of the shareholders of the company. Belgium filed a Memorial and Spain Preliminary Objections. The proceedings were discontinued by Belgium on 23 March 1961 pending negotiations for a settlement between representatives of the private interests. Spain declared that it did not object to the discontinuance of the proceedings and the Court recorded the discontinuance in an order of 10 April 1961.[5]

After the negotiations broke down, Belgium filed a new application on 19 June 1962, this time seeking reparation for the 'damage suffered by Belgian nationals, individuals or legal persons, being shareholders of Barcelona Traction'.

II. THE 1964 JUDGMENT ON PRELIMINARY OBJECTIONS

With regard to this new claim, Spain raised four preliminary objections. The first one was that the discontinuance affected the admissibility of the new application. The discussion of this objection turned on whether there had been an understanding between the parties that discontinuance involved a final waiver. The Court rejected Spain's objection mainly because it found that the various exchanges between the parties were 'wholly inconclusive'[6] and that one could not reasonably 'suppose that on the eve of difficult negotiations, the success of which must be uncertain, there could have been any intention on the Belgian side to forgo the advantage represented by the possibility of renewed proceedings'.[7]

The second preliminary objection concerned jurisdiction. A bilateral Treaty of 1927 provided for compulsory adjudication of disputes, which had to be submitted to the PCIJ. Belgium maintained that the present Court's jurisdiction rested on those treaty provisions and on Article 37 of the Court's Statute, according to which

---

[4] *Pleadings*, Vol VI, 31, and Vol VII, 673.
[5] *Barcelona Traction, Light and Power Company, Limited (Belgium v Spain)*, Removal from the List [1961] ICJ Rep 9.
[6] *Barcelona Traction, Light and Power Company, Limited (Belgium v Spain)*, Preliminary Objections [1964] ICJ Rep 6, 23.
[7] ibid.

'Whenever a treaty or convention in force provides for reference of a matter ... to the Permanent Court of Justice, the matter shall, as between the parties to the present Statute, be referred to the International Court of Justice'. Spain contended that there could not have been a transfer of jurisdiction from the Permanent Court to the present Court because Spain was not a party to the ICJ Statute when the Permanent Court was dissolved. The Court distinguished the interpretation of Article 37 from that which had been previously given to the transfer of jurisdiction based on declarations under the optional clause. It found that the dissolution of the PCIJ could not be 'a cause of lapse or abrogation of any of the jurisdictional clauses concerned'[8] and rejected the second preliminary objection.

Spain's third and fourth preliminary objections respectively concerned Belgium's *jus standi* and the exhaustion of local remedies. They were both extensively discussed but the Court joined them to the merits. Spain argued that Barcelona Traction had failed to exhaust local remedies mainly because it had omitted to use the remedy of opposition to the declaration of bankruptcy. According to the Court, this question was 'inextricably interwoven with the issues of denial of justice which constitute the major part of the merits'.[9]

The question of the exhaustion of local remedies was the object of further written and oral pleadings, but also in its 1970 judgment the Court did not find it necessary to examine it. This judgment was focused on the third preliminary objection, which led to the rejection of Belgium's claim.

III. THE 1970 JUDGMENT

A. The Dicta on Obligations *Erga Omnes*

The most famous passages in the 1970 judgment concern obligations *erga omnes*, defined as those for which 'all States can be held to have a legal interest in their protection'.[10] These passages have often been viewed as obiter dicta, since the Court distinguished obligations *erga omnes* from 'those arising vis-à-vis another State in the field of diplomatic protection' (ibid) and only the latter were considered by the Court to be at stake in *Barcelona Traction*. The Court said that 'Obligations the performance of which is the subject of diplomatic protection are not of the same category'[11] as obligations *erga omnes*. The Court could not have signalled more clearly that in referring to the latter obligations it was deviating from its course.

The most likely reason for these obiter dicta, the drafting of which has been attributed to Judge Lachs, was to send a signal to the international community that the Court was ready to take a different approach from the one followed in the *South*

---

[8] ibid, 34.
[9] ibid, 46.
[10] *Barcelona Traction, Light and Power Company, Limited (Belgium v Spain)*, Merits, Second Phase [1970] ICJ Rep 3, 32, [33].
[11] ibid, 32, [35].

West Africa cases.[12] The Court did not say that any state would have been entitled to invoke another state's responsibility in case of breach of an obligation *erga omnes*, but this conclusion could be taken as implied.[13] However, the implications of the existence of obligations *erga omnes* were outlined by the Court only some 40 years later, in its judgment in *Questions relating to the Obligation to Prosecute or Extradite (Belgium v Senegal)*, when the 'common interest in compliance with the relevant obligations under the Convention against Torture' was said to imply that 'any State party to the Convention may invoke the responsibility of another State party with a view to ascertaining the alleged failure to comply with its obligations *erga omnes partes*'.[14]

In *Barcelona Traction* the Court named as examples of obligations *erga omnes* those resulting 'from the outlawing of acts of aggression, and of genocide, as also from the principles and rules concerning the basic rights of the human person, including protection from slavery and racial discrimination'.[15] The Court also specified that, 'With regard more particularly to human rights, to which reference has already been made in paragraph 34 of this Judgment, it should be noted that these also include protection against denial of justice'.[16] However, the Court considered that protection against denial of justice as a human right applied only at a 'regional level' and moreover was not relevant in the case at hand, because Spain was then not a member of the Council of Europe and therefore not a party to the European Convention on Human Rights.[17] Had the Court found that protection against denial of justice was a human right under customary international law, it would have had to consider the claim alleging a denial of justice irrespective of the nationality of the legal or natural persons concerned.

In *Barcelona Traction* the Court did not consider the question whether diplomatic protection also covers claims for the breach of human rights. Only in *Ahmadou Sadio Diallo (Republic of Guinea v Democratic Republic of the Congo)* did the Court state that 'the scope *ratione materiae* of diplomatic protection, originally limited to alleged violations of the minimum standard of treatment of aliens, has subsequently

---

[12] This point was made by several commentators. See J Charpentier, 'L'affaire de la Barcelona Traction devant la Cour internationale de Justice (arrêt du 5 février 1970)' (1970) 16 *Annuaire français de droit international* 307, 312; VS Mani, 'The Barcelona Traction Case' (1971) 11 *Indian Journal of International Law* 112 at 123; W Karl, 'Menschenrechtliches jus cogens—Eine Analyse von "Barcelona Traction" und nachfolgender Entwicklungen' in E Klein (ed), *Menschenrechtsschutz durch Gewohnheitsrecht* (Berlin, Berliner Wissenschafts-Verlag, 2003) 102, 103; CJ Tams and A Tzanakopoulos, '*Barcelona Traction* at 40: The ICJ as an Agent of Legal Development' (2010) 23 *LJIL* 781, 792 and 799.

[13] In a comment on the *Barcelona Traction* judgment, R Higgins, 'Aspects of the Case Concerning the Barcelona Traction, Light and Power Company, Ltd' (1970–1971) 11 *Virginia Journal of International Law* 327, 329–30 observed: 'Is it really correct, as the Court seems to imply, that obligations *erga omnes* entitle any state to claim against the alleged wrongdoer? ... It seems bizarre for the Court to be suggesting this when in 1966 it declined to pronounce on whether racial discrimination was prohibited under general international law'.

[14] *Questions relating to the Obligation to Prosecute or Extradite (Belgium v Senegal)* [2012] ICJ Rep 450, [69].

[15] *Barcelona Traction* (n 10) 32 [34].

[16] ibid, 47, [91].

[17] ibid.

widened to include, inter alia, internationally guaranteed human rights'.[18] This does not imply that, when a state is entitled to exercise diplomatic protection, other states cannot invoke responsibility for a breach of an obligation concerning human rights. The latter obligation retains its character of obligation *erga omnes*.

B. The Distinction Between Rights of a Company and Rights of Its Shareholders

The key question of international law that was before the Court in *Barcelona Traction* was whether the state of nationality of the shareholders of a company was entitled to exercise diplomatic protection on behalf of these shareholders in relation to the alleged breach of an obligation under international law that caused harm to the company, irrespective of the place of incorporation of the company or of the location of its *siège social*.

Literature generally favoured the possibility of exercising diplomatic protection for the benefit of the shareholders, taking an approach that was sometimes termed substantive rather than formalistic, because it allowed the protection of the real interests at stake. The trend prevailing in bilateral investment treaties was to give protection to shareholders. The case law was less certain, although there were some indications that a claim could be preferred in favour of the shareholders if the harm was caused to a company having the nationality of the host state.

Scholars generally expected the Court to contribute to modernising diplomatic protection by asserting that the state of nationality of the shareholders could exercise it in view of its economic interests. One commentator recalls that at a debate held at the American Society of International Law in 1969 'the eleven panelists ... all anticipated, incorrectly, that the then-forthcoming Barcelona Traction Case would develop the law and allow a right of judicial intervention by the shareholder's national state'.[19]

The joining of the third preliminary objection to the merits could also have been taken as a sign that the Court was reluctant to conclude that only the state of nationality of the company was entitled under the circumstances to exercise diplomatic protection.

Notwithstanding these expectations the Court upheld Spain's third preliminary objection and 'reject[ed] the Belgian Government's claim'[20] by an almost unanimous vote, with only the judge ad hoc selected by Belgium expressing his dissent.

---

[18] *Ahmadou Sadio Diallo (Republic of Guinea v Democratic Republic of the Congo)*, Preliminary Objections [2007] ICJ Rep 599, [39].

[19] Higgins, 'Aspects of the Case' (n 13) 331, fn 43.

[20] *Barcelona Traction* (n 10) 51, [103]. Some commentators maintained that the Court should instead have declared the application inadmissible. See HW Briggs, 'Barcelona Traction: The *Jus Standi* of Belgium' (1971) 65 *AJIL* 327, 344–45; E Grisel, 'L'arrêt de la Cour internationale de Justice dans l'affaire de la Barcelona Traction (seconde phase): problèmes de procédure et de fond' (1971) 27 *Schweizerisches Jahrbuch für internationales Recht* 31, 48. While the choice of the wording of the *dispositif* was probably due to the wish to record a larger majority, the objection retained could be characterized as raising a preliminary question relating to the merits.

This outcome caused great surprise to both parties. It is true that the *dispositif* specified that 'twelve votes of the majority [were] based on the reasons set out in the present Judgment'.[21] This leaves out the position of three judges holding different views from those expressed by the majority. They may be identified as Judges Tanaka, Jessup and Gros, each of whom appended a lengthy separate opinion. Moreover, a long separate opinion was contributed also by Judge Fitzmaurice, who pointed to the possible 'recognition of Belgian capacity to claim on behalf of any person or entity who, at the material times, was both of Belgian nationality and a shareholder in the Barcelona company'.[22] Judge Tanaka concluded on this point that 'Belgium ha[d] an independent right to protect the Belgian shareholders in Barcelona Traction in conformity with the interpretation of customary international law concerning the diplomatic protection of nationals'.[23] Judge Jessup defended inter alia the 'primacy of the general economic interest of the State in protecting private investments abroad'.[24] Also according to Judge Gros, what was relevant was whether an investment was 'connected with a particular national economy'.[25] The reason why Judges Gros and Jessup voted in favour of the rejection of the Belgian claim related to what they considered an insufficiency of evidence concerning the Belgian nationality of Barcelona Traction's shareholders.[26]

The main separate opinions were much appreciated in the subsequent literature, which prevailingly found the line of argument reflecting the majority view disappointing.[27]

For the majority of the Court, the key element was the distinction between the rights of a company and those of its shareholders. For the purpose of diplomatic protection,

> international law has had to recognize the corporate entity as an institution created by States in a domain essentially within their domestic jurisdiction. This in turn requires that, whenever legal issues arise concerning the rights of States with regard to the treatment of companies and shareholders, as to which rights international law has not established its own rules, it has to refer to the relevant rules of municipal law.[28]

The Court noted that 'The concept and structure of the company are founded on and determined by a firm distinction between the separate entity of the company and that of the shareholder, each with a distinct set of rights'.[29] This point was decisive

---

[21] ibid.
[22] ibid, 81–82, [30].
[23] ibid, 135.
[24] ibid, 196–97, [61].
[25] ibid, 283, [27].
[26] ibid, 282–83; 202–20.
[27] See in particular RB Lillich, 'The Rigidity of Barcelona' (1971) 65 *AJIL* 522, 531–32; SP Metzger, 'Nationality of Corporate Investment under Investment Guaranty Schemes—The Relevance of Barcelona Traction' (1971) 65 *AJIL* 532, 541; I Seidl-Hohenveldern, 'Der Barcelona-Traction-Fall' (1971) 22 *ÖzöRV* 255, 275 and 295–96. Criticism was also expressed by one of Belgium's counsel, FA Mann, 'The Protection of Shareholders' Interests in the Light of the Barcelona Traction Case' (1973) 67 *AJIL* 259.
[28] *Barcelona Traction* (n 10) 33–34, [38].
[29] ibid, 34, [41].

because 'Not a mere interest affected, but solely a right infringed involves responsibility, so that an act directed against and infringing only the company's rights does not involve responsibility towards the shareholders, even if their interests are affected'.[30]

The Court gave as examples of rights of shareholders, which were considered 'distinct from those of the company', the following: 'the right to any declared dividend, the right to attend and vote at general meetings, the right to share in the residual assets of the company on liquidation'.[31] None of these rights concerned 'difficulties or financial losses to which [the shareholders] may be exposed as the result of the situation of the company'.[32]

The distinction between rights of shareholders and their interests is not always outlined in municipal law in a way that would justify the significant consequences that follow according to the Court.[33] The use of the term 'interests' instead of 'rights' does not necessarily signify a different legal situation. Reference is often made to 'rights and interests' without a clear dividing line.

The Court did not focus on any particular system of municipal law. It referred to 'rules generally accepted by municipal legal systems'[34] and held that, in making such a reference, 'the Court cannot modify, still less deform' rules of municipal law.[35]

While there may be a convergence among many systems of municipal law on identifying the entitlements of shareholders, shareholders' rights are not necessarily identical under the different laws. It may be questionable why the Court did not identify the relevant system of municipal law under which one should determine which rights pertain to a shareholder.[36] Similar criticism may be addressed to the Court's failure in the same context to identify the system under which the rights of a company are established. There may also conceivably be instances where the rights of shareholders overlap with those of their company.[37]

The Court's reluctance to specify which law applies may reflect a more general attitude of reluctance to address issues of conflict of laws and to go into the details of the municipal law held to be applicable. However, a more detailed analysis of the issues of municipal law appears to be often a necessary step towards a decision concerning diplomatic protection. For instance, how could the Court assess

---

[30] ibid, 36, [46].

[31] ibid, 36, [47].

[32] ibid.

[33] This point was stressed by W Lewald, 'Die Stellung der juristischen Person des Handelsrechts im Völkerrecht' in *Multitudo Legum Ius Unum. Festschrift für Wilhelm Wengler zu seinem 65. Geburtstag* (Berlin, Interrecht, 1973) 245, 254–56.

[34] *Barcelona Traction* (n 10) 37, [50].

[35] ibid.

[36] The reference to generally accepted rules of municipal law rather than to a specific municipal law was criticised particularly by Grisel (n 20) 45; by G Perrin, 'Les rapports entre le droit international et le droit interne, en particulier dans l'arrêt Barcelona Traction' Liber Amicorum BCH Aubin (Kehl am Rhein/Strasbourg, Engel, 1979) 107, 118–20; and more recently by D Müller, *La protection de l'actionnaire en droit international. L'héritage de la Barcelona Traction* (Paris, Pedone, 2015) 244–45. According to the last author, one should apply the law governing the statute of the company, which however cannot always be determined univocally.

[37] This was observed by G Sacerdoti, 'Barcelona Traction Revisited: Foreign Owned and Controlled Companies in International Law', in Y Dinstein (ed), *International Law at a Time of Perplexity. Essays in Honour of Shabtai Rosenne* (The Hague, Martinus Nijhoff, 1989) 699, 705.

that a certain expropriation is unlawful, without first ascertaining which is the law applicable to the ownership of the property concerned and then applying that law to the case at hand?

It is noteworthy that, in reaching its conclusion under customary international law, the Court relied on general statements concerning the nature of the claims that a state may put forward on behalf of a company or its shareholders when harm is caused to the company. It did not refer to state practice or even mention the various arbitral decisions which had been extensively discussed by the parties.[38] The Court noted only that:

> in most cases the decisions cited rested upon the terms of instruments establishing the jurisdiction of the tribunal or claims commission and determining what rights might enjoy protection; they cannot therefore give rise to generalization going beyond the special circumstances of each case.[39]

With regard to the protection of shareholders, the Court even referred to 'the silence of international law'.[40]

One of the arguments developed by the Court for justifying its conclusion was based on the observation that shareholders could have many different nationalities, possibly each with few shares. According to the Court, 'the adoption of the theory of diplomatic protection of shareholders as such, by opening the door to competing diplomatic claims, could create an atmosphere of confusion and insecurity in international economic relations'.[41] Judge Fitzmaurice observed in his separate opinion that this objection 'would only go to the *quantum* of reparation recoverable by the various governments'.[42] It cannot in fact be a decisive objection and was not offered by the Court as such. However, given that transfers of shares occur frequently and without any publicity, it would often be problematic to determine who the shareholders of a company are at any given time. The host state would have to face claims under international law with regard to harm caused to a local company even if that state was unaware of the presence of foreign shareholders when the harm occurred.

The approach taken by the Court in *Barcelona Traction* with regard to the protection of shareholders in relation to harm caused to a company has not been followed by the Chamber that decided the case of *Elettronica Sicula SpA (ELSI) (United States of America v Italy)*. The United States exercised diplomatic protection on behalf of two United States corporations which owned the totality of the shares of a company constituted under Italian law in relation to harm caused to that company. The claims rested on a bilateral Treaty of Friendship, Commerce and Navigation (FCN). Italy gave a more restrictive interpretation to the relevant treaty clauses.

---

[38] S Beyer, *Der diplomatische Schutz der Aktionäre im Völkerrecht* (Berlin, Nomos Verlagsgesellschaft, 1977) 49, criticised this attitude, but after an analysis of arbitral decisions stated that the Court's conclusion was correct (126).

[39] *Barcelona Traction* (n 10) 40, [63].

[40] ibid, 38, [52].

[41] ibid, 49, [96].

[42] ibid, 77, fn 21.

All the issues raised in the *ELSI* case were examined only on the basis of the FCN Treaty. In view of the facts, the Chamber always concluded that a choice between the opposing readings of the relevant treaty provisions was not called for.

In order to illustrate the Chamber's approach, it may be sufficient to refer to what the Chamber said with regard to two treaty provisions. With regard to the taking of property, the Chamber considered whether the United States could bring a claim on behalf of the shareholders of a company the property of which had been taken. The Chamber quoted the first paragraph of the Protocol to the FCN Treaty, which reads as follows:

The provisions of paragraph 2 of Article V [of the FCN Treaty], providing for the payment of compensation, shall extend to interests held directly or indirectly ... by nationals, corporations and associations of either High Contracting Party in property which is taken within the territories of the other High Contracting Party.

The Chamber observed that 'the English text of this provision suggests that it was designed precisely to resolve the doubts just described'. It recalled that Italy had suggested that the Italian text, which is also authoritative, had a narrower meaning, but did not find it necessary to dwell on this question of interpretation given the facts to which the quoted provision had to be applied.[43] One can see that the Chamber rather favoured a reading of the treaty provision which would allow the exercise of diplomatic protection of the shareholders for the harm indirectly suffered, when the property of their company has been taken.

A similar approach was taken by the Chamber with regard to Article VII of the FCN Treaty. According to its English text, this provision conferred on nationals of the parties the right 'to acquire, own and dispose of immovable property or interests therein'. The United States contended that the phrase was 'sufficiently broad to include indirect ownership of property rights held through a subsidiary that is not a United States corporation'. Italy relied on the Italian text of the provision, which referred to '*diritti reali*' instead of '*interessi* (interests)'. The Chamber expressed 'some sympathy with the contention of the United States, as being more in accord with the general purpose of the FCN Treaty'.[44] However, the Chamber concluded that no breach of this treaty provision had occurred.[45]

In *ELSI* the Chamber could not take a decision on the protection of the two United States companies under customary international law, because this would have been outside the Court's jurisdiction.[46] However, the Chamber would not have been prevented from examining the treaty provisions in the context of customary rules. It could then have incidentally reconsidered the approach taken in *Barcelona Traction* with regard to the protection of shareholders, but this was probably viewed as a task that would have been more appropriate for the full Court.

---

[43] *Elettronica Sicula SpA (ELSI) (United States of America v Italy)* [1989] ICJ Rep 15, 70–71, [118].
[44] ibid, 79, [132].
[45] ibid, 80–81, [133]–[135].
[46] This made it unnecessary for the Chamber to specify that it had to apply the treaty provisions instead of the customary rules concerning the diplomatic protection of companies and shareholders. Criticism of the lack of analysis of customary rules in the Chamber's judgment was voiced by B Stern, 'La protection diplomatique des investissements internationaux. De Barcelona Traction à Elettronica Sicula ou les glissements progressifs de l'analyse' (1990) 117 *Journal du Droit International* 897, 927–35.

The relevance of the distinction between conduct affecting the direct rights of shareholders and conduct affecting the rights of the company was endorsed by the ILC in Article 12 of its draft articles on Diplomatic Protection. The Commission expressed the following rule:

> To the extent that an internationally wrongful act of a State causes direct injury to the rights of shareholders as such, as distinct from those of the corporation itself, the State of nationality of any such shareholders is entitled to exercise diplomatic protection in respect of its nationals.[47]

This rule has to be read in the context of another rule contained in the draft articles which, as we shall see,[48] tends to widen the protection of shareholders for harm caused to their company.

The Court addressed again the question of the protection of shareholders from the viewpoint of customary international law in *Ahmadou Sadio Diallo (Republic of Guinea v Democratic Republic of the Congo)*. The case concerned harm caused to Africom-Zaire and Africontainers-Zaire, two companies (*sociétés privées à responsabilité limitée*, SPRL) incorporated in the Democratic Republic of the Congo, and its legal consequences for Mr Diallo, an '*associé*' of those companies.

In the proceedings relating to preliminary objections, Guinea argued that 'the direct rights of Mr Diallo as a shareholder of Africom-Zaire and Africontainers-Zaire' had been affected, in particular his 'right to control, supervise and manage the companies'.[49] In their pleadings, the Parties frequently referred to the *Barcelona Traction* judgment.[50] According to the Court:

> Conferring independent corporate personality on a company implies granting it rights over its own property, rights which it alone is capable of protecting. As a result, only the State of nationality may exercise diplomatic protection on behalf of the company when its rights are injured by a wrongful act of another State. In determining whether a company possesses independent and distinct legal personality, international law looks to the rules of the relevant domestic law.[51]

The Court referred to 'the domestic law of the Democratic Republic of the Congo' for establishing 'the precise legal nature' of the two companies involved[52] and concluded on this point:

> what amounts to the internationally wrongful act, in the case of *associés* or shareholders, is the violation by the respondent State of their direct rights that are defined by the domestic law of that State, as accepted by both Parties, moreover.[53]

---

[47] *ILC Ybk* 2006/II(2), 42. Also this text does not specify under which law the rights of shareholders are to be identified. Para 4 of the commentary refers to 'municipal law of the State of incorporation', but notes that 'Where the company is incorporated in the wrongdoing State ... there may be a case for the invocation of general principles of company law in order to ensure that the rights of foreign shareholders are not subjected to discriminatory treatment' (ibid, 43).

[48] See below, section C.

[49] *Diallo* (n 18) 604, [55].

[50] ibid, 605, [60].

[51] ibid, 605, [61].

[52] ibid, 605, [62].

[53] ibid, 606, [64].

The *dispositif* stated that Guinea's application was admissible 'in so far as it concern[ed] protection of Mr. Diallo's direct rights as *associé* in the State of incorporation of the companies'.[54]

The Court considered that the judgment on preliminary objections was not the stage of the proceedings at which it had to determine 'which specific rights appertain to the status of *associé* and which to the position of *gérant* of an SPRL under Congolese law'.[55] This was left to a later decision, to be given following pleadings on the merits.

In its judgment on the merits, the Court quoted para 38 of the *Barcelona Traction* judgment[56] and then proceeded to identify more specifically Mr Diallo's direct rights as *associé* of the two companies under the law of the Democratic Republic of the Congo.[57] The Court examined whether any of these rights had been infringed. In particular, with regard to property, the Court observed that:

> international law has repeatedly acknowledged the principle of domestic law that a company has a legal personality distinct from that of the shareholders. This remains true even in a case of a SPRL which may have become unipersonal in the present case. Therefore, the rights and assets of a company must be distinguished from the rights and assets of an *associé*.[58]

In sum, the Court followed the same approach taken in *Barcelona Traction*,[59] but, rather than referring to principles held to be common to municipal laws, applied the law of the state of incorporation of the companies in order to identify the 'direct rights' of *associés* or shareholders.

C. The Determination of the Nationality of the Company

It has already been noted that the Court in *Barcelona Traction*, when it was discussing the distinction between the rights of shareholders and those of their company, did not consider it necessary to specify under which municipal law these rights had to be determined. The judgment contains, however, some remarks on the nationality of corporations and gives an indication that in the Court's view Barcelona Traction had Canadian nationality.

The declared purpose of that analysis was to consider the consequences 'of the lack of capacity of the company's national State to act on its behalf'.[60] Leaving those consequences aside for the moment, let us consider the criteria that the Court

---

[54] ibid, 617–18, [98].

[55] ibid, 606, [66].

[56] *Barcelona Traction* (n 10) 33–34 [38].

[57] *Ahmadou Sadio Diallo (Republic of Guinea v Democratic Republic of the Congo)*, Merits [2010] ICJ Rep 639, 675, [104].

[58] ibid, 689, [155].

[59] The view that the *Diallo* judgment reaffirmed what the Court had stated in *Barcelona Traction* was expressed by CJ Tams and A Tzanakopoulos (n 12) 790–91, and by L Ngobeni, '*Barcelona Traction* and *Nottebohm Revisited*: Nationality as a requirement for diplomatic protection of shareholders in South African law' (2012) 37 *South African Yearbook of International Law* 169, 181.

[60] *Barcelona Traction* (n 10) 41, [69].

used for defining the nationality of the company for the purpose of the exercise of diplomatic protection on its behalf by the state of nationality.

The Court first stated what it defined as a 'traditional rule', which 'attributes the right of diplomatic protection of a corporate entity to the State under the laws of which it is incorporated and in whose territory it has its registered office'.[61] However, the Court also noted that 'it has been the practice of some States to give a company incorporated under their law diplomatic protection solely when it has its seat (*siège social*) or management or centre of control in their territory'.[62] Given that incorporation is mentioned again in this passage, the location of the seat or management or centre of control seems to be an additional requirement. Within the limits outlined in the passages quoted above, the Court seems to leave it within each state's discretion to establish the criteria which are relevant for exercising diplomatic protection on behalf of a company. However, this would run counter to the practice of those states which consider the *siège social* rather than incorporation the decisive criterion for attributing nationality.

For the purposes of the *Barcelona Traction* case, the Court did not find it necessary to discuss further this issue. The Court noted that it was 'not disputed that the company was incorporated in Canada and ha[d] its registered office in that country'.[63] Thus Barcelona Traction had to be considered a Canadian company under what the Court had called a 'traditional rule'. The Court assumed that no further requirements were set forth under Canadian law.

The *Nottebohm* judgment had raised the question whether the nationality of an individual on behalf of whom a state exercised its diplomatic protection could be regarded as sufficient or whether some kind of genuine connection was required. The applicability of a similar approach to the diplomatic protection of companies gave rise to ample discussion in the pleadings, with Belgium contesting the existence of a genuine connection between Canada and the Barcelona Traction.

The Court briefly addressed the issue. It observed that 'in the particular field of the diplomatic protection of corporate entities, no absolute test of the "genuine connection" has found general acceptance'. The Court referred to the *Nottebohm* case and said that 'given both the legal and factual aspects of protection in the present case the Court is of the opinion that there can be no analogy with the issues raised or the decision given in that case'.[64]

With these brief remarks, the Court did not reject the idea that a State, in order to exercise diplomatic protection on behalf of a company having its nationality, should have a genuine connection with the company which would make nationality effective.[65] However, the Court did not specify what kind of links would be required,

---

[61] ibid, 42, [70].
[62] ibid.
[63] ibid, 42, [71].
[64] ibid, 42, [70].
[65] This point was made particularly by A Gianelli, 'La protezione diplomatica di società dopo la sentenza concernente la *Barcelona Traction*' (1986) 69 *Rivista di Diritto Internazionale* 762, 768. G Abi-Saab, 'The International Law of Multinational Corporations: A Critique of American Legal Doctrine' (1971) 2 *Annals of International Studies* 97, 115 expressed on the contrary the view that the Court implied that 'no "genuine link" is required for the diplomatic protection of corporations'.

because it considered that, in any event, those links existed between Canada and Barcelona Traction. Apart from Canada being the country of incorporation and that where the company's 'registered office, its accounts and its share registers' were located, the Court also referred to Canada as the place where 'board meetings were held ... for many years'[66] and to the fact of the listing of the company 'in the records of the Canadian tax authorities'. The Court concluded on this point:

> Thus a close and permanent connection has been established, fortified by the passage of over half a century. This connection is in no way weakened by the fact that the company engaged from the very outset in commercial activities outside Canada, for this was its declared object. Barcelona Traction's links with Canada are thus manifold.[67]

The Court did not give any weight, for establishing the existence of a genuine connection, to the nationality of shareholders. Nor did the Court consider the links of the company with the host state, the weight of which had been decisive for the conclusion reached in *Nottebohm*.[68]

Given that, according to the Court, there existed a genuine connection between Canada and Barcelona Traction, there was no need for the Court to dwell on the consequences of the disqualification of a state from exercising diplomatic protection because of the absence of those links.

The International Law Commission also did not address this question in its draft articles on Diplomatic Protection, but for the different reason that the Commission did not endorse the requirement of a genuine connection for the exercise of diplomatic protection, whether on behalf of a natural or of a legal person. Partly following the view expressed by Judge Jessup in his separate opinion, the Commission stated a criterion of nationality based on the nationality of the controlling shareholders. When certain conditions are fulfilled, this replaces the general criterion based on the law under which the company was incorporated.[69] According to Article 9 of the draft articles,

> when the corporation is controlled by nationals of another State or States and has no substantial business activities in the State of incorporation, and the seat of management and the financial control of the corporation are both located in another State, that State shall be regarded as the State of nationality.

D. The Possible Exceptions Allowing for the Protection of Shareholders

In *Barcelona Traction* the Court discussed whether there were some exceptional cases that would allow a state to exercise diplomatic protection on behalf of its

---

[66] In his separate opinion Judge Jessup came to the different conclusion that 'Barcelona Traction's management was not centred in Toronto' (*Barcelona Traction* (n 10) 190, [49]).

[67] ibid, 42, [71].

[68] The need for a further analysis of this aspect was stressed by Judge Fitzmaurice in his separate opinion (ibid, 80–82, [28]–[30]).

[69] Although Art 9 of the draft on Diplomatic Protection may suggest that the criterion quoted below in the text provides an additional criterion for determining nationality, the commentary makes it clear that, when the exceptional conditions are fulfilled, only the alternative criterion applies. *ILC Ybk* (n 47) 38.

nationals who are shareholders of a foreign company for harm caused to the company. The Court noted that, from this perspective, 'protection by the national State of the shareholders can hardly be graduated according to the absolute or relative size of the shareholding involved'.[70] The assertion of these exceptions is not in harmony with the general approach taken by the Court to the effect that diplomatic protection of the shareholders may concern only their rights.[71]

The Court did not find it necessary to take a position on any of these exceptions because they were considered inapplicable to the case at hand. However, the attitude of the Court appears to be somewhat favourable to the existence of some exceptions extending the protection of shareholders. This is reflected in the general statement that:

> The process of lifting the veil, being an exceptional one admitted by municipal law in respect of an institution of its own making, is equally admissible to play a similar role in international law. It follows that on the international plane also there may in principle be special circumstances which justify the lifting of the veil in the interest of shareholders.[72]

Considering the issue on the basis of equity, the Court referred to 'a theory ... developed to the effect that the State of the shareholders has a right of diplomatic protection when the State whose responsibility is invoked is the national State of the company'.[73] This exception is intended to provide some protection under international law to foreign investments when they take the form of shares in a company having the nationality of the host state. It is reflected in a wide number of treaty provisions and has found acceptance in some arbitral decisions, to none of which the Court specifically referred.

In Article 11 of its draft articles on Diplomatic Protection, the ILC expressed the opinion that the state of nationality of shareholders in a corporation would be entitled to exercise diplomatic protection if '(b) the corporation had, at the date of injury, the nationality of the State alleged to be responsible for causing the injury, and incorporation in that State was required by it as a precondition for doing business there'.[74] This exception is based on the assumption that, when the host state requires the establishment of a local company, it does so in order to diminish the risk that diplomatic protection be exercised or that the investors resort to international arbitration. The requirement bears similarities with the Calvo clause.[75]

The scope of this exception was discussed in the *Diallo* case. Guinea had invoked the possibility of exercising diplomatic protection 'by substitution'. According to Guinea, 'the shareholders of a company can enjoy the diplomatic protection of their own national State as regards the national State of the company when the State is responsible for an internationally wrongful act against it'.[76] The Court stated that,

> having carefully examined State practice and decisions of international courts and tribunals in respect of diplomatic protection of *associés* and shareholders, it [was] of the opinion that

---

[70] *Barcelona Traction* (n 10) 48, [94].
[71] This point was made by Judge Jessup in his separate opinion (ibid, 192–93, [53]).
[72] ibid, 39, [58].
[73] ibid, 48, [92].
[74] *ILC Ybk* (n 47) 39.
[75] This was observed by the Commission in its commentary to Art 11 (ibid, 42).
[76] As quoted by the Court, *Diallo* (n 18) 613, [83].

these do not reveal—at least at the present time—an exception in customary international law allowing for protection by substitution, such as is relied on by Guinea.[77]

The Court did not produce any analysis of state practice or of judicial or arbitral decisions, except for observing that 'The arbitrations relied on by Guinea are ... special cases, whether based on specific international agreements between two or more States, including the one responsible for the allegedly unlawful acts regarding the companies concerned ... or based on agreements concluded directly between a company and the State allegedly responsible for the prejudice to it.[78]

The Court then noted that 'It is a separate question whether customary international law contains a more limited rule of protection by substitution, such as that set out by the ILC in its draft Articles on Diplomatic Protection ...'.[79] The Court referred to Article 11(b), quoted above. The Court did not find it necessary to address this question, since 'the companies, Africom-Zaire and Africontainers-Zaire, were not incorporated in such a way that they would fall within the scope of protection by substitution in the sense of Article 11, paragraph (b), of the ILC draft Articles'.[80]

Another exception envisaged by the Court in *Barcelona Traction* concerns the case of the company having ceased to exist.[81] According to the Court:

> Only in the event of the legal demise of the company are the shareholders deprived of the possibility of a remedy available through the company; it is only if they became deprived of all such possibility that an independent right of action for them and their government could arise.[82]

The Court did not dwell on the issue whether in the case of a legal demise of the company, the state of nationality of the shareholders was entitled to protect them in relation to harm caused to the company, because it found that Barcelona Traction was 'in receivership in the country of incorporation' but 'continue[d] to exist'.[83]

Article 11(a) of the draft articles of the International Law Commission on Diplomatic Protection considers that the state of nationality of shareholders is 'entitled to exercise diplomatic protection in respect of such shareholders in the case of an injury to the corporation' when 'the corporation has ceased to exist according to the law of the State of incorporation for a reason unrelated to the injury'.[84]

This provision was not examined in the *Diallo* case, because it was clearly not relevant.

In *Barcelona Traction* the Court referred as a possible exception also to 'the lack of capacity of the company's national State to act on its behalf'.[85] The scope of this exception and its consequences were not clearly spelled out. What seems implied in this reference is that if the state of nationality of the company was not entitled to exercise diplomatic protection towards the host state, for instance because of the

---

[77] ibid, 615, [89].
[78] ibid, 615, [90].
[79] ibid, 615, [91].
[80] ibid, 616, [93].
[81] *Barcelona Traction* (n 10) 40, [64].
[82] ibid, 41, [66].
[83] ibid, 41, [67].
[84] *ILC Ybk* (n 47) 39.
[85] *Barcelona Traction* (n 10) 41, [69].

lack of a genuine connection with the company, the state of nationality of the shareholders would be able to protect them in relation to a harm indirectly caused to them.

The Court did not find it necessary to analyse the exception any further. It concluded on this point that

> the record shows that, from 1948 onwards the Canadian Government made to the Spanish Government numerous representations which cannot be viewed otherwise than as the exercise of diplomatic protection in respect of the Barcelona Traction company. Therefore this was not a case where diplomatic protection was refused or remained in the sphere of fiction.[86]

E. The Exercise of Diplomatic Protection

After examining the preconditions for the exercise of diplomatic protection with regard to a company and to its shareholders, the Court considered the role of the state in that exercise. The apparent purpose of this analysis was to make it clear that Barcelona Traction had not been deprived of the possibility that its state of nationality exercised diplomatic protection.

The Court observed that, 'within the limits prescribed by international law, a State may exercise diplomatic protection by whatever means and to whatever extent it thinks fit, for it is its own right that the State is asserting'.[87] The Court thus held that a state's exercise of diplomatic protection is an exercise of its own right. This means that the state enjoys discretion in deciding whether or not to exercise diplomatic protection and, when it is exercised, whether to discontinue it. The Court said:

> The State must be viewed as the sole judge to decide whether its protection will be granted, to what extent it is granted, and when it will cease. It retains in this respect a discretionary power the exercise of which may be determined by considerations of a political or other nature, unrelated to the particular case.[88]

These passages implicitly endorse the definition of diplomatic protection that the PCIJ had famously expressed in the *Mavrommatis* case.[89] A different definition, which seeks to enhance the position of the individual or entity for whose benefit the diplomatic protection is exercised, was given by the Court in *Diallo*. The Court then noted that:

> under customary international law, as reflected in Article 1 of the draft Articles on Diplomatic Protection of the International Law Commission ... 'diplomatic protection consists of the invocation by a State, through diplomatic action or other means of dispute settlement, of the responsibility of another State for an injury caused by an internationally wrongful act of that State to a natural or legal person that is a national of the former State with a view to the implementation of such responsibility'.[90]

---

[86] ibid, 43–44, [76].

[87] ibid, 44, [78].

[88] ibid, 44, [79].

[89] *Mavrommatis Palestine Concessions (Greece v UK)* (1924) PCIJ, Series A, No 2, 12. According to this judgment, 'by resorting to diplomatic action or international judicial proceedings on his behalf, a State is in reality asserting its own rights—its right to ensure, in the person of its subjects, respect for the rules of international law'.

[90] *Diallo* (n 18) 599, [39].

This definition considers that the relevant injury is that caused to the natural or legal person. Moreover, it does not enunciate that the exercise of diplomatic protection is a right of the state. However, also according to the draft articles on Diplomatic Protection, the state of nationality has discretion whether or not to exercise diplomatic protection. Article 2 sets forth that state's 'right to exercise diplomatic protection',[91] which implies discretion, subject only to the recommendation set forth in Article 19.[92]

The Court noted that the Canadian Government had exercised diplomatic protection on behalf of Barcelona Traction[93] and that 'the Spanish Government ha[d] not questioned Canada's right to protect the company'.[94] In his separate opinion Judge Fitzmaurice did not find that a conclusion that Spain was precluded from raising the question of Canada's *jus standi* would have been 'self-evidently well-founded'. This because 'diplomatic representations—which need not necessarily be based on or imply a claim of right, but are often admitted or received in the absence of any such claim or pretension to it—belong to a different order of international act from the presentation of a formal claim before an international tribunal'.[95] It is reasonable to consider that the preclusion of a host state from raising an objection to *jus standi* may depend on the nature of the claims previously addressed to that state. However, preclusion could rest also on the fact that, as the Court observed, 'The Spanish Government ... never challenged the Canadian nationality of the company, either in the diplomatic correspondence with the Canadian Government or before the Court' and 'unreservedly recognized Canada as the national State of Barcelona Traction in both written pleadings and oral statements made in the course' of the judicial proceedings.[96]

IV. CONCLUSION

Already at the time when the *Barcelona Traction* judgments were delivered, the importance of the entitlement under customary international law to exercise diplomatic protection on behalf of a company or of its shareholders was limited by the presence of many international agreements for the protection of foreign investments. These have in the meantime multiplied and, as the Court observed in *Diallo*, 'the role of diplomatic protection somewhat faded, as in practice recourse is only made to it in rare cases where treaty régimes do not exist or have proved inoperative'.[97]

Customary international law on diplomatic protection could have developed following the prevailing trends in investment agreements. This has occurred according

---

[91] *ILC Ybk* (n 47) 28.
[92] ibid, 53. Art 19 sets forth that 'A State entitled to exercise diplomatic protection according to the present draft articles, should (a) give due consideration to the possibility of exercising diplomatic protection, especially when a significant injury has occurred'.
[93] *Barcelona Traction* (n 10) 43–44, [76].
[94] ibid, 45, [83].
[95] ibid, 82, [31].
[96] ibid, 45, [83].
[97] *Diallo* (n 18) 614, [88].

to some authors,[98] but not in the opinion of others[99] or of the Court, which followed in *Diallo* an approach consistent with that adopted in *Barcelona Traction*. One element that has limited the impact of investment treaties on customary international law is the great variety of treaty provisions concerning investments in the form of shares in a foreign company.[100] Other factors are the attitudes of states where the investment takes place, which do not favour extending the protection of foreign investments, and also the policy of some major investor states, which are reluctant to let other states reap the benefits of the regime consigned in the investment treaties that the former states concluded.

---

[98] See F Orrego Vicuña, *International Dispute Settlement in an Evolving Global Society—Constitutionalization, Accessibility, Privatization* (Cambridge, CUP, 2004) 42; C Schreuer, 'Shareholder Protection in International Investment Law' in: PM Dupuy, B Fassbender, MN Shaw and KP Sommermann (eds), *Völkerrecht als Wertordnung. Common Values in International Law. Festschrift für Christian Tomuschat* (Kehl, Engel, 2006) 603–04.

[99] See in particular M Paparinskis, 'Barcelona Traction: A Friend of Investment Protection Law' (2008) 8 *Baltic Yearbook of International Law* 105, 131–33; and D Müller (n 36) 435ff, who stresses the variety of criteria used in investment treaties.

[100] This is illustrated by P Peters, 'Some Serendipitous Findings in BITs: the Barcelona Traction Case and the Reach of Bilateral Investment Treaties' in E Denters and N Schrijver (eds), *Reflections in International Law from the Low Countries in Honour of Paul de Waart* (The Hague, Martinus Nijhoff, 1998) 27.

14

Tyrer v United Kingdom (1978)

NIGEL RODLEY

I. INTRODUCTION

ANTHONY TYRER WAS a 15-year-old boy, from the Isle of Man, convicted in 1972 of violent assault on another boy from his school. He had pleaded guilty and was sentenced by the trial court to three strokes of the birch. He appealed unsuccessfully and the punishment was inflicted. Another boy, Andrew Hays, convicted at the same time for the same offence, did not appeal. The sentence was promptly carried out. The National Council for Civil Liberties (NCCL, later rebranded Liberty), a British human rights NGO, sprang into action. It had long campaigned against corporal punishment and had been waiting for a test case to challenge under the European Convention of Human Rights (ECHR) the last bastion of corporal punishment in the UK.

The late Larry Grant, the first Legal Officer of NCCL, was a solicitor. Unfamiliar with international law, he turned to the author of this chapter for advice on submitting the application. The nub of the case was that the infliction of corporal punishment violated the ECHR Article 3 prohibition of 'torture or inhuman or degrading treatment or punishment'. The European Commission of Human Rights ('the Commission') found Hays' application inadmissible for non-exhaustion of domestic remedies. The UK did not contest the admissibility of Tyrer's complaint and the Commission found that the UK had violated ECHR Article 3. It did so despite Tyrer's request to withdraw the case. It then referred the case to the European Court of Human Rights ('the Court') which upheld the Commission's view, confirming the Article 3 violation.

This was the first authoritative international decision to find corporal punishment as such to be unlawful under international human rights law (IHRL). Most of what follows is based on the official public records of the European Court of Human Rights. The proceedings before the Commission have been archived for an exorbitant 70 years from the dissolution of the Commission and are not available for consultation. This is justified by the fact that proceedings before the Commission were confidential. While respecting that confidentiality, the present writer's memory, supplemented by a file held by Larry Grant's successor as NCCL Legal Officer, solicitor William Nash, have assisted in providing useful contextual background.

II. HISTORICAL BACKGROUND

Until the first half of the twentieth century, the UK had officially espoused corporal punishment as a criminal sanction and as a disciplinary punishment for prisoners. It had exported this institution, that it no doubt considered civilised, throughout the British Empire. Like capital punishment, corporal punishment was retained by most British colonies on independence by means of the 'savings clause' of the new states' constitutions.[1]

However, the United Kingdom was reviewing its policy even before World War II. It commissioned what became known as the Cadogan Report,[2] published in 1938. The Report recommended abolishing the punishment. Perhaps due to the intervening conflict, it took until 1948 for abolition to be effected in Great Britain and until 1968 in Northern Ireland. As with capital punishment, public opinion lagged behind abolition[3] and demands for the restoration of corporal punishment led to another report, the Barry Report,[4] which confirmed the findings of Cadogan. The government of the day accepted these findings and left abolition intact.

By a constitutional quirk, the Isle of Man was not considered as an integral part of the UK. The UK was responsible for its defence and international relations, but its internal legal workings were a matter for its own parliament, the Tynwald. Under a constitutional convention, the UK considered itself able to legislate over the heads of the houses of the Tynwald, only if it were necessary to do so to implement an international obligation. Probably in the light of vigorous Manx opinion in relation to retaining corporal punishment and the relative novelty of an international law of human rights creating obligations in relation to such 'internal' matters, the UK was not minded to enact the legislation required to bring the Isle of Man into line with the UK proper.

Meanwhile, some brave Manx people took on local public opinion and campaigned for abolition. In this, they were supported by NCCL. One such person was Angela Kneale who, as part of the campaigning work, wrote a book entitled *Against Birching: Judicial Corporal Punishment in the Isle of Man.*[5] The book, published by NCCL, provided valuable information about the practice of corporal punishment in the Isle of Man, including its applicability for offences other than violent ones, such as larceny.

---

[1] By which existing punishments provided by the criminal law of the time were insulated against being ruled unconstitutional: see generally on corporal punishment in international human rights law, NS Rodley and M Pollard, *The Treatment of Prisoners under International Law*, 3rd edn (Oxford, OUP, 2009) ch 10.

[2] Report of the Departmental Committee on Corporal Punishment (Cmnd 5684, March 1938).

[3] FE Zimring and G Hawkins, *Capital Punishment and the American Agenda* (Cambridge, CUP, 1960).

[4] Report of the Advisory Council on the Treatment of Offenders, 'Corporal Punishment' (Cmnd Report 1213, November 1960).

[5] (National Council for Civil Liberties 1973).

III. THE FACTS

The facts of the case are uncomplicated. Anthony Tyrer was one of several boys who violently attacked a school prefect. The prefect had apparently been responsible for reporting some of them for bringing beer into the school, leading to their being, ironically, caned by the school. The attack was in retaliation for their having been reported. On 7 March 1972 Hays and Tyrer were convicted of unlawful assault occasioning actual bodily harm. Hays, aged 14 at the time, was held to be the ring-leader and so sentenced to five strokes of the birch. Tyrer, aged 15 at the time, was sentenced to three strokes. Three days later, Hays was given three strokes before the attending doctor advised against continuing the flogging for the full five strokes. Tyrer appealed unsuccessfully against the sentence and on the 28 April 1972, the day of the appeal, he received the full three-stroke punishment. In both cases the strokes were administered on the bare buttocks, an indignity reserved for young persons between 14 and 21 years of age. Had they been under 14 or adults they would have been able to keep their buttocks covered.

IV. EUROPEAN COMMISSION OF HUMAN RIGHTS—ADMISSIBILITY

The applications for Hays and Tyrer complaining of a violation of the ECHR were introduced on 5 and 21 September 1972 respectively. In the case of Hays, the application was just within the six-month time limit set by Article 26 (now Article 35(1)) of the ECHR. NCCL asked that the cases be joined and the Commission agreed. The original applications were relatively sketchy, mainly to meet the time limit, but also because the facts almost seemed to speak for themselves. The details of the execution of the sentences were self-evidently prurient; Angela Kneale's book, which was submitted in evidence, demonstrated the general practice of corporal punishment in the Isle of Man which had not been restricted to violent criminality, and the official UK Cadogan and Barry Reports, also submitted in evidence, providing an authoritative debunking of any possible legitimate penal justification for the penalty, including the absence of any demonstrable special deterrent effect. There would be time to develop and refine the arguments later.

The Commission found the application of Hays, who had not appealed against sentence, to be inadmissible under Article 26 for non-exhaustion of domestic remedies. He had argued that any appeal would have been ineffective. The application of the penalty was current in the island (his brother had been subjected to it two years earlier), it was provided for by law and so akin to an administrative practice that rendered exhaustion of domestic remedies unnecessary[6] and, as evidenced by the fate of the unsuccessful appeal of Tyrer, who had been less culpable, any appeal would have been futile. However, the Commission, without addressing these facts,

---

[6] Where an administrative practice exists it was held unnecessary to show exhaustion of domestic remedies in respect of each of the individuals who have been victims of the practice: *Ireland v United Kingdom (No 18/01/1978)* (1979) Series A no 25, [159].

simply concluded that its examination of the case 'does not disclose the existence of any special circumstances which might have absolved the applicant ... from exhausting the domestic remedies at his disposal'.[7]

This was a setback for NCCL, as well as a disappointment for Andrew Hays. The details of his flagellation were more harrowing, with the doctor being moved to interrupt the process, than those of Tyrer.[8] The Commission proceeded to deal with Tyrer's complaint. Since the Government had not contested admissibility in respect of Article 3, the Commission had no difficulty finding the complaint admissible. It dismissed, harmlessly, a make-weight claim of a violation of Article 1 (general obligation to secure the Convention's rights) by virtue of a violation of Article 3. It also dismissed a similar claim of a violation of Article 13 (absence of domestic remedies). It further dismissed summarily a claim of a violation of Article 8 (respect for private and family life), which had argued the very punishment was destructive of family well-being.

Both applicants had originally claimed a violation of Article 14, together with Article 3, asserting that the punishment was primarily imposed on persons from financially and socially deprived homes. They had withdrawn the complaint before the Commission's consideration of admissibility, presumably because of an inability to marshal the necessary supporting evidence.

On the other hand, the Commission of its own motion decided to declare the case admissible in respect of Article 3 in conjunction with Article 14 on the grounds of possible discrimination on grounds of age and/or sex.

At the time of the original application, it was not clear that corporal punishment was reserved for children and young persons, not adults, and indeed the Government would later deny precisely that.[9] However, it is unclear why the applicant did not invoke discrimination on grounds of sex. A possible explanation may be a wish to avoid the risk of equalising 'down'. In other words, it could be feared that the Manx addiction to corporal punishment could lead to legislation to extend it to both sexes.[10]

V. THE EUROPEAN COMMISSION OF HUMAN RIGHTS—MERITS

Thus, when it came to the pleadings on the merits, the only substantive issues at stake were whether the punishment had violated Article 3 and/or Article 3 together with Article 14. The position of the Government was that it did not.

---

[7] *X and Y v United Kingdom*, 17 *Yearbook of the European Convention on Human Rights* 356, 366 (1976) (hereafter 'Commission Admissibility Decision').

[8] Albeit Tyrer's father had to be restrained when he 'went for' one of the attending police officers: *Tyrer v United Kingdom (No 2856/72)*, Report of the European Commission of Human Rights, 14 December 1976: European Court of Human Rights, Series B, No 24 (1981) 10, [8].

[9] ibid.

[10] As would occur in *Abdulaziz, Cabales and Balkandili v United Kingdom* when the UK responded to an Art 14 violation because the UK only granted automatic nationality to spouses of male UK citizens by denying automatic nationality to any foreign spouses.

The applicants originally claimed that their punishment was degrading treatment within the meaning of Article 3.[11] By the time of the examination on the merits, Tyrer's team was arguing that any or all of the limbs of Article 3 ('torture', 'inhuman treatment or punishment' or 'degrading treatment or punishment' would apply.[12] The thrust of the argument was that the indignity and pain he himself had been subjected to violated Article 3. It was not explicitly a claim against all corporal punishment. It was open to the Commission to conclude, for example, that the dimension of the infliction of the strokes on the bare buttocks raised what might have been a permissible punishment to the level of an impermissible one.

Nevertheless, there was also an invitation to the Commission to address the system as a whole, given that there was no evidence of its continuing existence in the European countries, nor any demonstrable penological justification for the penalty. Thus, he emphasised the Cadogan and Barry Reports that indeed addressed corporal punishment as such.[13] He also drew attention to Angela Kneale's book which focused on corporal punishment as applied in the Isle of Man.[14] Also, Tyrer had been the first ever to take advantage of his right of appeal. According to the book, juvenile offenders were often not informed of the right to appeal, the punishment had been used for offences of dishonesty and sometimes it resulted in laceration of the skin.[15]

The Government, for its part, denied that the punishment was sufficiently cruel or barbaric to be classed as inhuman and asserted that it did not meet either a dictionary definition of degrading, or the Commission's own definition. The former required that the treatment be 'such as to lower in estimation, character or quality, or to debase morally'.[16] The latter contemplated that the treatment 'grossly humiliates' or drives the person 'to act against his will or conscience'.[17] Having stressed that this implied a certain relativity, it also pointed out that 'corporal punishment existed in many countries at [the] time' of the adoption of the Convention.[18] Here the Government was both addressing the challenge of the applicant concerning the by then anomalous nature of the penalty, but also seemingly making an originalist, founding fathers argument about how to interpret the Convention.

The Commission had little difficulty in concluding that the case did not raise issues that could amount to torture or to inhuman treatment. On the other hand, it seems similarly to have had little difficulty in finding the notion of 'degrading' both relevant and indeed applicable. While not necessarily espousing the perhaps-too-wide dictionary definition, nor was a 'restrictive interpretation' called for.

---

[11] Commission Report (n 8) [1].
[12] ibid, [10].
[13] ibid [12].
[14] ibid, [13].
[15] ibid, [16]; in Tyrer's case the skin had been raised but not broken: [8].
[16] ibid, [23].
[17] ibid.
[18] ibid.

The key paragraphs of the Commission's conclusion are succinct enough to merit reproduction in full:

> 35. Judicial birching humiliates and disgraces the offender and can therefore be said to be degrading treatment or punishment. This is particularly evident in the procedure used for birching in the present case, including the fact that persons between 14 and 21 years of age have to strip off their trousers when being birched.
>
> ...
>
> 39. The Commission is of the opinion that birching as a punishment ordered by a court and administered as provided for in the Isle of Man is an assault on human dignity which humiliates and disgraces the offender without any redeeming social value. Furthermore the Commission observes that other persons involved may be humiliated or disgraced by the whole procedure.
>
> 40. For these reasons the Commission concludes that judicial corporal punishment constitutes a breach of Art. 3 of the Convention and, consequently, its infliction on the applicant was in violation of this provision of the Convention.

It seems the Commission, which voted 14 to one for the finding of a violation, had as much difficulty as the applicant and his team in understanding how the punishment was *not* degrading. Particularly notable was the clear condemnation in paragraph 35 of corporal punishment as such. On the other hand, the strong language in paragraph 39 is qualified by the words 'administered as provided for in the Isle of Man' could at first sight seem to be read as leaving the door open for some more sanitised form. However, the operative language of paragraph 40, by which the Commission 'concludes that judicial corporal punishment constitutes a breach of Art. 3' seems to throw a bucket of cold water on that interpretation.

As to the Article 14 issue, as raised at admissibility by the Commission *ex officio*, the Commission decided that, having found a violation of Article 3, it did not need to examine separately the Article 14 dimension.[19]

There remained the question of the Isle of Man's status as a dependent territory? As such a territory—that is, a territory for whose international relations the UK is responsible—Article 63(3) was applicable.[20] This provided for application of the Convention 'in such territories with due regard ... to local requirements'. For the Government, the specific local requirements seemed to boil down to the firm belief of the local population in the deterrent effect of the punishment. Tyrer's team[21] at the oral hearings held by the Commission pointed out that the *travaux préparatoires* of the provision suggested that it was included because 'the state of civilization of certain overseas territories does not permit the application of fundamental

---

[19] ibid, [44].

[20] Now Art 56(3).

[21] The team consisted of William Nash, NCCL; Cedric Thornberry, Barrister-at-law; and the present writer, then legal officer of Amnesty International, but acting in his personal capacity: Commission Report, Appendix 1.

rights under the same conditions as for European territories'.[22] They invited the Attorney-General of the Isle of Man, JW (Jack) Corrin, a member of the Government's delegation, to inform the Commission of the respect in which the state of civilisation in Isle of Man fell short of European standards. When Mr Corrin took the floor he began by insisting that the island was 'a civilised place with an excellent health service, very low unemployment, very few poor people'.[23] He went on to insist on how in some respects, such as gender equality and female suffrage, it was in advance of the UK and other European countries. This exchange presumably explains the cursory treatment that the Commission afforded the Article 63(3) issue, notably the following single sentence paragraph:

> As to the local requirements mentioned in Art. 63(3), the Commission does not find any significant social or cultural differences between the Isle of Man and the United Kingdom which would be relevant to the application of Art. 3 in this case.[24]

The one dissent, that of Mr Mangan (Irish member), will not be the subject of substantial analysis. It boils down to his failure to be persuaded that what was obviously degrading to his colleagues was not to him. His starting point is seemingly the fact that he received slaps at home and at school and had, in turn, delivered such to his own children. The only observation this wisdom may be permitted to elicit is that he is equating judicially administered corporal punishment with the wholly different context of family and community in a school setting. The Cadogan Report had addressed this issue, not least in a paragraph quoted at length by the Commission.[25] Mr Mangan took no account of it. The continuing relevance of the distinction will be reverted to later.

A final procedural point needs to be made at this stage. In January 1976, three months after the Commission held its oral hearings, the applicant through a firm of solicitors sought to withdraw the application. This raised an issue as to whether the Commission could or should continue with the case. The withdrawal was certainly not pursuant to any friendly settlement that the Commission might have sought to reach pursuant to ECHR Article 28. In a laconic sentence, the Commission indicated that it considered the notification on 9 March 1976 and 'decided it could not accede to the applicant's demand since the case raised questions of a general character affecting the observance of the Convention which necessitated a further examination of the issues involved'.[26]

The authority for this course of action appears to have been Rule 47 of the Commission's Rules of Procedure.[27] Nowadays, the Convention itself would offer

---

[22] Council of Europe, *Collected Edition of the 'Travaux Préparatoires' of the European Convention on Human Rights*, Vol. III, Committee of Experts 2 February–10 March 1950 (Leiden, Martinus Nijhoff, 1976) 266; author's recollection; it would later be taken up by the Court: see below.

[23] Cited by the Commission's delegate before the Court quoting from the verbatim records of the Commission's hearing: Series B, No 24 (1981) 59.

[24] Commission Report (n 8) [47].

[25] Cadogan Report (n 2) [30]: ibid, [38].

[26] Commission Report (n 8) [2].

[27] *Tyrer v United Kingdom* (no 5856/72) (1978) Series A no 26 [hereafter 'Judgment'].

sufficient authority. Article 37(1) provides for striking out applications if 'the applicant does not intend to pursue his [sic] application'. However, the Court is required to continue its consideration of the case, 'if respect for human rights as defined in the Convention and the Protocols so requires'.[28] The 'purported' withdrawal[29] would surface again at the level of the Court.

VI. THE EUROPEAN COURT OF HUMAN RIGHTS

The Commission referred the case to the Court on 11 March 1977, that is, within the three-month time limit required by former ECHR Article 31. A number of factual developments since the application to the Commission was made led to certain procedural issues demanding the attention of the Court.

One flowed from the fact that the UK's declaration accepting the compulsory jurisdiction of the Court in respect of the Isle of Man had expired on 13 January 1976, some 14 months before the Commission referred to the case to the Court. The failure to renew the jurisdiction can only be explained by the fact that the Government had succumbed to pressure from the island to avoid an adverse decision of the Court. In fact, the Commission argued that, as long as the compulsory jurisdiction existed at the time of the application to the Commission, it should remain available for the full ECHR process. In the end, the Government did not contest the jurisdiction.[30] It would be surprising if the Isle of Man authorities were happy with this decision. It may even have been that the government was signalling that it was contesting the case for internal political reasons, rather than because of a genuine wish to challenge the Commission's finding of a violation of Article 3.

It would not have been the first time. It had resisted evidently necessary changes to the Prison Rules restricting prisoners' communication with counsel and others, despite convincing findings of ECHR violations by the Commission.[31] This was doubtless to show the influential Prisoners Officers Association, which opposed the change, that the Government had done all it could, but it had to abide by the Court's rulings.

Another procedural issue arose from the purported withdrawal of the case by Mr Tyrer. The Attorney-General for the Isle of Man, Jack Corrin, moved that the Court strike the case out of its list. The Court comprehensively dismissed the motion. It noted that the Attorney-General seemed not to be contesting the regularity of the Commission's decision and that neither the Commission nor the Court had ever examined or been given the reasons for 'and circumstances surrounding' the applicant's request to withdraw the case.[32] The quoted words seemed like a signal that

---

[28] This text originated in Protocol 8, adopted 1985, providing a new Art 30.

[29] See Commission Report, Appendix 1, referring to 'the applicant's purported withdrawal of application' (emphasis added).

[30] *Tyrer* (n 27) [23].

[31] *Golder v United Kingdom (no 4451/70)* (1975) series A, No 18 (preventing correspondence with legal advisers); *Silver v United Kingdom (no 5947/72)* (1983), series A No 61 (censorship of correspondence).

[32] *Tyrer* (n 27) [24].

the Commission and the Court had doubts about the propriety of the context that led to Mr Tyrer's withdrawal of his case. Could it be excluded, for example, that the withdrawal was made in the absence of improper threats or inducements?[33]

Accordingly, if the Commission's decision to proceed despite the withdrawal of the application could not be impugned, then it only remained to be seen if the Court should do so under its own Rules of Procedure. However, since it was not the applicant, but the Commission, that had referred the case to the Court and, as a result of the withdrawal, neither the applicant nor his legal team could be involved in the proceedings, the withdrawal could 'not entail the effects of a discontinuance'. Only a party that had brought the case before the Court could take advantage of the relevant rule (Rule 47).[34] Driving home the nail in the coffin of the Attorney-General's motion, the Court pointed out that only a friendly settlement could justify a discontinuance of the proceedings.

Mr Corrin also moved to strike out the case on more substantive grounds, namely that there was a legislative proposal to remove corporal punishment as a penalty for assault occasioning actual bodily harm. The principal Commission delegate, Mr Love Kellberg (Danish member) took the view that 'nothing short of total abolition of judicial corporal punishment would in the view of the Commission be acceptable as a 'act of a kind to provide a solution of the matter" in the context of Rule 47(2).'[35] The Court pointed out that the proposed legislation could not be such a fact, because whether or when the law would actually be adopted was uncertain. Nor could it 'erase a punishment already inflicted'. Also, it did not go to 'the substance of the issue, which was 'whether judicial corporal punishment as inflicted on the applicant in accordance with Manx legislation is contrary to the Convention'.[36] Meanwhile the Commission's delegate had confirmed the absolutist interpretation of the Commission's finding suggested earlier. Another procedural issue raised by Mr Corrin for the Isle of Man put the Court in a position to give some indication of its view of at least part of the case. He invited the Court to visit the island for an on-the-spot investigation.[37] The Court deferred its decision until after completion of the oral proceedings. It then concluded that 'the very full information that had [already] been supplied ... rendered it unnecessary to carry out the investigation requested'.[38] This could well have reflected at least the Court's view that there were no special local circumstances that would affect its view of the relevance of Article 3. Indeed, it was probably also a signal that the Court was going to focus on corporal punishment as such, not the manner of its application, as proved to be the case.

---

[33] This was the obvious implication of a 21 March 1977 letter from Mr Thornberry to the Court, indicating the need for 'enlightenment as to whether there might have been any question of breach by local authorities of Mr Tyrer's right (or, at least, the United Kingdom obligation) under Article 25 of the Convention': Series B, No 24 (1981) 40.

[34] *Tyrer* (n 27) [25].

[35] ibid, [26].

[36] ibid.

[37] ibid, [6] and [7].

[38] ibid, [8].

Before considering the Court's treatment of the substance, a parenthetical observation regarding the presentation of the Government's case may be made here. First,
only two members of the Government's delegation to the proceedings participated,
namely, the Attorney-General for the Isle of Man and a distinguished Queen's Counsel, Mr Louis Blom-Cooper, a well-known campaigner for the abolition of the death
penalty and penal reformer. Neither the agent for the government, David Anderson
(Legal Counsellor of the Foreign and Commonwealth Office), nor Mr Andrew
Collins, the barrister who had sustained the burden of defending the government's
case before the Commission took the floor before the Court.[39]

Mr Blom-Cooper was responsible for the Article 3 and 14 issues. On Article 3,
he maintained that the absolute prohibition contained in the Article 'argues ... in
favour of a high threshold' for an act to be violative of it.[40] Yet at no point did he
actually assert that corporal punishment did not reach that threshold. Moreover, he
virtually invited the Court not to focus on the method of inflicting the punishment,
as the government did not wish to 'put forward any special considerations applicable to the present case as having relevance in this context'.[41] He also would not even
provide support for the Attorney-General's issues under Article 63(3), announcing
that the Government 'desire to express no view' as to whether 'the provisions of
Article 63(3) affect the Court's ruling'.[42] In other words, it fell to Mr Corrin, the
Attorney-General, to do the heavy lifting on the whole Government defence. The
Government must have seemed to the Court to be washing its hands of the case.

VII. CORPORAL PUNISHMENT UNDER ARTICLE 3

The Court treated the issue of whether the punishment violated Article 3 at greater
length than the Commission, though not, it must be admitted, with substantially
greater clarity. The Court agreed with the Commission that the punishment was
neither torture, nor inhuman treatment. It was not torture because the applicant
did not undergo suffering of the level it had required in the Northern Ireland
case, notably that the treatment be an aggravated and deliberate form of inhuman
treatment.[43] It was not inhuman treatment because 'the suffering occasioned must
attain a particular level' to be so categorised and that level was not attained in the
present case.[44]

It then went on to address the notion of 'degrading'. Here it focused on the element of humiliation that it treated as the central characteristic of the notion. It
ruled out, as it had to, the level of humiliation inherent in any judicial punishment.
In fact, 'the humiliation or debasement involved must attain a particular level'.[45]

---

[39] ibid, [7].
[40] Series B No 24 (1981) 62.
[41] ibid, 63.
[42] ibid.
[43] *Tyrer* (n 27) [30], referring to *Northern Ireland case* (n 6), [163].
[44] ibid, [29].
[45] ibid, [30].

To the implicit question thus begged, namely, 'what is that particular level?', the Court could only respond that the 'assessment is, in the nature of things, relative: it depends on all the circumstances of the case and, in particular, on the nature and context of the punishment itself and the manner and method of its execution'.[46] This definition was, as pointed out by the dissent, somewhat tautologous.[47] On the other hand, case-by-case application of value judgements is not unknown to the law, whether it be found in the wisdom of the legendary reasonable man on the Clapham omnibus or that of the judge who says (of obscenity) 'I know it when I see it'.[48] That was, after all, how—as noted—the applicants' original legal team had seen it.

In any event, the Court then proceeded to address a number of points raised by the Isle of Man Attorney-General. He had insisted that the punishment was not degrading because it did not outrage public opinion. With evident doubt that public opinion could be relevant ('even assuming that local public opinion can have an incidence on the interpretation of [the notion]'), the Court provocatively noted that 'it might well be that one of the reasons why they view the penalty as an effective deterrent is precisely the element of degradation that it involves'.[49] As to the issue of deterrence itself, even if a particular punishment were a deterrent, 'it is never permissible to have recourse to punishments which are contrary to [Article 3], whatever their deterrent effect may be'.[50]

It was at this point that the Court articulated its living instrument doctrine:

> The Court must also recall that the Convention is a living instrument which, as the Commission rightly stressed, must be interpreted in the light of present-day conditions. In the case before it the Court cannot but be influenced by the developments and commonly accepted standards in the penal policy of the member States of the Council of Europe in this field.[51]

As will be noted later, this doctrine has been of real interpretative significance for the Court, especially, but not only in relation to Article 3. At this point, it suffices to note that it amounts to a clear rejection of any originalist argument, such as that advanced by the UK at the Commission stage.

The Court then proceeded to address arguments relating to the 'manner and method' of execution of the birching. Thus, the Attorney-General had argued that the punishment was not degrading by virtue of being conducted in private and without publication of the offender's name. However, for the Court, the absence of publicity was not determinative, as 'it may well suffice that the victim is humiliated

---

[46] ibid.

[47] ibid, Separate Opinion of Judge Sir Gerald Fitzmaurice; Professor Zellick was similarly critical of the Court's reasoning: G Zellick, 'Corporal Punishment in the Isle of Man' (1978) 27 ICLQ 665.

[48] Per Associate Justice Potter Stewart, in *Jacobellis v Ohio*, 378 US 184 (1964).

[49] *Tyrer* (n 27) [31].

[50] ibid. Earlier, Mr Kellberg had referred to Andrew Hays' inadmissible application before the Commission, pointing out that Hays' brother had previously been birched and that hadn't deterred him: Series B No 24 (1981) 84.

[51] ibid. While the Commission report had not addressed the matter, Mr Kellberg argued before the Court that the Convention should not be interpreted 'simply by reference to the intentions of the High Contracting Parties'; rather a 'dynamic interpretation' was called for, whereby meaning must be given to notions of fundamental rights in present-day circumstances': Series B No 24 (1981) 57.

in his own eyes, even if not in the eyes of others'.[52] The use of the word 'victim' for someone convicted of an offence is also telling!

The Court acknowledged the safeguards in place, such as the already referred to role of the medical doctor, but then proceeded to stress the elements conducing to an evaluation that the punishment was degrading. For the Court, the punishment consisted of the infliction of 'physical violence' that was 'institutionalised', involving treating the victim 'as an object in the power of the authorities'. The violence was itself 'an assault on precisely that which is one of the main purposes of Article 3 to protect, namely, a person's dignity and physical integrity'.[53] Implicitly making the point that judicial corporal punishment is distinct from that sometimes inflicted in schools or at home, it considered that the institutionalised violence was 'compounded by the whole aura of official procedure attending the punishment and by the fact that those inflicting it were total strangers to the offender'.[54] In addition, that was the delay of over seven weeks between sentence and execution that were a source of 'mental anguish'.[55] Evidently, such a delay is inevitable, as pointed out by the dissent, if an appeal is undertaken. Presumably, for the Court, this was implicit confirmation that the punishment was irredeemably degrading. Finally, addressing an implicit proportionality argument, the Court considered that the punishment was not saved from being degrading by virtue of the fact that it was imposed for a crime of violence.[56]

Accordingly, the humiliation element of the punishment had altogether 'attained the level inherent in the notion of "degrading punishment"'.[57] Stressing that the Court was addressing the degrading nature of corporal punishment as such, it evaluated the relevance of the beating having taken place without the protection of trousers thus: 'The indignity of having the punishment administered over the bare posterior aggravated to some extent the degrading character of the applicant's punishment but it was not the only or the determining factor'.[58] This conclusion also may explain the Court's ignoring of the island's recent change of law 'in the light of the Commission's report', putting an end to the practice of removing trousers.[59]

While at first it seemed that the Court was adopting a case-by-case approach whereby it substituted its own assessment for that of the jurisdiction in question, in fact what it was doing was taking a punishment-by-punishment approach. While certain factors could aggravate the violation, this punishment was irredeemably degrading.

In fact, it is precisely this approach that is challenged by the dissent of Judge Sir Gerald Fitzmaurice. His arguments largely track those of Mr Mangan in the Commission (not excluding reference to his experience of corporal punishment at school).

[52] *Tyrer* (n 27) [32].
[53] ibid, [33].
[54] ibid.
[55] ibid, [34].
[56] ibid.
[57] ibid, [35].
[58] ibid.
[59] ibid, [12].

His basic case is narrow: even if corporal punishment, accepted over the ages, but now considered undesirable, were also to be considered degrading for adults, this was not the case for children. In fact, his own assertions are no more and arguably less supported than those of the Commission and the Court. Indeed, they ignore evidence to the contrary from the Cadogan Report and other material referred to by the Commission. The dissent also fails, as did Mr Mangan's, to distinguish between judicial corporal punishment and that inflicted in schools in assessing the sense of debasement that may be involved. Ultimately, what was evident to the majority in the Commission and the Court was not evident to the dissenters. There was simply a conflict of subjectivities.

VIII. ARTICLE 63(3): LOCAL CIRCUMSTANCES

Like the Commission finding the corporal punishment degrading, the Court proceeded to consider whether local conditions affected its conclusion. Inevitably the arguments were effectively a re-run of those in the Commission. Despite having been effectively cut adrift by Mr Blom-Cooper, Mr Corrin rose vigorously to the challenge.[60] His basic affirmation in terms of relevant local conditions was that public opinion was powerfully supportive of it, as evidenced by a recent 'privately organised' petition supporting retention which had gathered 31,000 signatures from among the some 45,000 islanders entitled to vote (ie over 75%).[61] He also insisted on the deterrent effect of the penalty (inflicted on average about twice a year in the previous 12 years) with a relatively small number of violent crimes (averaging just over 55% over the same period).[62] Again, he felt obliged to undermine his own case, by defending the level of civilisation in the island, which was 'not a stagnant backwater, but a progressive society'.[63]

The Commission's principal delegate, Mr Kellberg, made a strong preliminary point that it was difficult to conceive of any local conditions that would justify a breach of Article 3, albeit this was not on its face entirely consistent with its words about 'slaps and blows' in the *Greek* case.[64] He also indicated that the Commission's view was that there were no significant cultural differences between the UK and the Isle of Man. For the Court, 'the beliefs and local public opinion' could not amount to a 'requirement' within the meaning of Article 63(3). Taking up the point made by the applicant at the Commission, he referred to the presence in the *travaux préparatoires* of 'talk of bringing a state of civilisation to overseas territories'.[65] Particularly uncompromisingly, the Court affirmed that even if public opinion were

---

[60] Series B No 24 (1981) 64–82.
[61] Tyrer (n 27) [15].
[62] ibid, [18].
[63] Series B No 24 (1981) 66–67.
[64] Judgment para 37. In the Greek case the Commission had opined that 'a certain roughness of treatment' in the form of 'slaps and blows' might be consistent with what would tolerated 'in different societies': *The Greek case* (1969) 12 *Yearbook of the European Convention on Human Rights* 501, [11].
[65] Series B No 24 (1981) 88.

correct about the punishment's advantages, there was no evidence to show that law and order 'could not be maintained without recourse to that punishment'.[66] Most, if not all, other European countries had either done without it or been able to dispense with it, while maintaining law and order. Then, effectively recalling the point made by the applicant before the Commission the Court noted that the Article 63(3) provision was designed to accommodate the fact that, at the time of the Convention's drafting, there were still 'colonial territories whose state of civilization did not, it was thought, permit the full application of the Convention'.[67] This clearly was not relevant to the Isle of Man, which 'historically, geographically and culturally ... has always been included in the European family of nations'.[68]

Finally, the Court rallied to the absolutist position staked out by the Commission: 'even if law and order in the Isle of Man could not be maintained without recourse to judicial corporal punishment, this would not render its use compatible with the European Convention'.[69] This was because of the 'absolute' nature of the Article 3 prohibition as a whole, from which no derogation was permitted.[70]

* * *

Having found a violation of Article 3, the Court followed the Commission in considering it unnecessary to address the Article 14 issues.[71] It then turned to the question of 'just satisfaction' under Article 50. In the absence of an applicant, there could be no award, which could otherwise have consisted of damages.

In those days, the Court did not address possible institutional measures, such as requiring repeal of offending legislation. Nevertheless, it fell to the Committee of Ministers to supervise execution of the Court's judgments. The UK did not legislate to repeal the punishment. Rather, it formally notified the Manx authorities that the judgment means that the island's judicial corporal punishment 'must now be held to be in breach of' the Convention. This message was accordingly passed on by the Chief Justice of the Isle of Man (First Deemster) to the relevant judicial authorities.[72]

IX. AFTERMATH

For several years it seemed that abolition of corporal punishment in the Isle of Man had been achieved de facto, since the judiciary were not imposing it. However, a magistrate did hand down a birching sentence for a serious act of violence committed on the island by Hugh O'Callaghan, a Scottish youth.[73] Mr O'Callaghan appealed and this time the appeal was upheld. The judge delivering the Court of

---

[66] *Tyrer* (n 27) [38].
[67] ibid.
[68] ibid.
[69] ibid.
[70] ibid.
[71] ibid [41]–[42].
[72] Council of Europe, Committee of Ministers res (78) 39 (1978).
[73] S McGregor, 'Scots youth sentenced to the birch', *Glasgow Herald*, 21 July 1981.

Appeal's decision, a visiting judge from the UK, Mr Benet Hytner QC, was reported as saying that the Court considered that the European Court of Human Rights decision was 'binding' on it. 'Sentences of birching, if carried out, would render the United Kingdom and the Isle of Man in breach of an international obligation'.[74] The fact that the magistrates at trial were merely applying the law represented 'a most unsatisfactory state of affairs'.[75] Yet it was to be another 12 years before the island in 1993 formally repealed legislation providing for judicial corporal punishment.

No doubt, the British political establishment preferred to let sleeping dogs lie, since the dog had roused itself from its slumbers only once, without biting. Meanwhile, in 1988, a grateful Isle of Man would appoint Jack Corrin—the Attorney-General who defended the punishment in Strasbourg—as First Deemster, the island's equivalent of Chief Justice. In fact, he was the immediate successor of Arthur Luft, the second judge on the Court of Appeal that upheld Hugh O'Callaghan's appeal in 1981.

Thus, the case effectively created a corporal-punishment-free zone across the 47 countries of Europe, east and west. For when the countries of Eastern Europe joined the Convention, corporal punishment was already unknown to them.

X. IMPACT OF THE CASE

The *Tyrer* case may be considered a landmark case from a number of perspectives beyond terminating its last vestige in Europe. First, it was the first judicial finding that corporal punishment violated the prohibition of torture or inhuman or degrading punishment. Second, it was the case in which the Court articulated its 'living instrument' approach to interpretation of the ECHR. Third, it was an early case to have been brought by an NGO on behalf of an applicant.

A. A Precedent for Outlawing Corporal Punishment

There were some minor antecedents of international concern about corporal punishment, notably, that of the UN Trusteeship Council (supported by the General Assembly) in respect of its use in a number of UN Trust Territories, that is, colonial territories under UN supervision.[76] Its particularly brutal and arbitrary use by 'tribal authorities' set up in South West Africa by South Africa, in the period before it finally ceded independence to Namibia, caused outrage and was roundly condemned by the UN Commission on Human Rights.[77] This was while the *Tyrer* case was proceeding before the European Court of Human Rights. However, the UN Commission's focus on the excesses of the application of the penalty in the territory made it of limited relevance.

---

[74] C Gillies, '"Birch"' youth held for third hearing', *Glasgow Herald*, 7 October 1981.
[75] ibid.
[76] See Rodley, *Treatment of Prisoners* (n 1) 429–30.
[77] UN Commission on Human Rights, Resolution 5 (XXXI) (1975); also Rodley, *Treatment of Prisoners* (n 1) 430–31.

In fact, none of these UN activities seems to have played a role in the *Tyrer* case. Perhaps more important was the fact that international humanitarian law made provision against corporal punishment. Thus, corporal punishment is prohibited in respect of prisoners of war under the Third Geneva Convention and protected civilian persons under the Fourth Geneva Convention.[78] These were cited to the Commission, although not the Court.[79] Of course, these 1949 Conventions applied only in international armed conflict. It was not until 1977 that Additional Protocol II made clear that the punishment was also prohibited in armed conflicts not of an international character.[80] Also referred to in the Commission proceedings was Article 31 of the UN Standard Minimum Rules for the Treatment of Prisoners (SMR).[81] Neither the Commission nor the Court referred to these instruments in their analyses, but they may have eased the decision-making.

It was natural for the Court to look to European practice in reaching its conclusion: the ECHR was, after all, an instrument adopted within (then) Western Europe. That could, however, have limited its precedential value in other parts of the world. This has not proven to be the case.

The UN Human Rights Committee first pronounced itself on the matter in 1982 General Comment 7 ('the prohibition must extend to corporal punishment').[82] Consistently with the Committee's practice at the time, the text itself cites no authority. However, it can be presumed that the Committee was well aware of the case, as one of its then members, the late Professor Torkel Opsahl of Norway, was a member, both of the Committee (and its working group that prepared the first draft of the General Comment) and of the Commission when it dealt with *Tyrer*.[83] In fact, it was evident that the Committee was also influenced in taking an absolutist line by its contemporaneous consideration of the report of Iran less than three years after the 1979 revolution that overthrew the Shah. The new regime's use of the most barbaric forms of corporal punishment had apparently shocked Committee members.[84]

Tyrer was cited to the Committee in its first individual case of corporal punishment, *Osbourne v Jamaica*, brought under the Optional Protocol to the ICCPR. Without citing any authority or indeed, giving any reasons, the Committee merely insisted that 'corporal punishment constitutes cruel, inhuman and degrading treatment or punishment contrary to Article 7 of the Covenant'.[85] The Committee's own General Comments would doubtless have been relevant in the Committee's conclusion, but with substantial new membership over the years, the confirmation in an

---

[78] Geneva Convention relative to the Treatment of Prisoners of War, 12 August 1949 (Geneva Convention III), Art 87; Geneva Convention relative to the Protection of Civilian Persons in Time of War, 12 August 1949 (Geneva Convention IV), Art 32.

[79] Commission Report (n 8) [18].

[80] Protocol Additional to the Geneva Conventions of 12 August 1949, and relating to the Protection of Victims of Non-International Armed Conflicts (Additional Protocol II), Art 4(2)(a).

[81] Commission Report (n 8) [8].

[82] Human Rights Committee, General Comment No 7 (16) (1982), UN Doc HRI/GEN/1/Rev1 (1994) [2]; now replaced by General Comment 20: Art 7 Prohibition of torture, or other cruel, inhuman or degrading treatment or punishment) (1992); ibid, [5], addressing corporal punishment in the same terms.

[83] UN Human Rights Committee, Annual Report, UN Doc A/36/40 (1981), [15].

[84] See UN Doc CCPR/C/SR.371 (1982) [9]; also Rodley, *Treatment of Prisoners* (n 1) 440–41.

[85] UN Doc CCPR/C/68/D/759/1997 (2000) [9.1].

individual case would not have been a foregone conclusion. It would certainly have been difficult for the Committee not to follow the regional court's precedent.

Successive UN Special Rapporteurs on the question of torture and other cruel, inhuman or degrading treatment or punishment have taken the view that corporal punishment must violate their mandate. The first, the late Professor Peter Kooijmans (later Judge of the International Court of Justice) did so in his first report to the UN Commission on Human Rights, quoting with approval Human Rights Committee General Comment 7.[86] His successor, the present writer, developed the point in his 1997 annual report responding to a challenge from Saudi Arabia to his having sent an urgent appeal aimed at preventing the execution of a sentence of corporal punishment in that country.[87] More recently, the mandate's stance was confirmed by the fourth Special Rapporteur, Professor Manfred Nowak, who explicitly referred to Tyrer as 'a landmark judgment'.[88]

In 2005, the Inter-American Court of Human Rights also dealt with a corporal punishment case, against Trinidad and Tobago. The description of the flogging of Mr Caesar, a stripped adult, tied to a wheel, until he was unconscious—in the presence of a doctor—would certainly have justified the Court's addressing the case-specific use of the penalty.[89] However, neither the Inter-American Commission on Human Rights which referred the case to the Court, nor the Court itself seem to have had any doubt that all judicial corporal punishment violated the prohibition of torture or cruel, inhuman or degrading treatment or punishment contained in Article 5 of the Inter-American Convention on Human Rights. For the Court the relevance of the brutality of the application of the penalty seems to have been in the level of reparation.[90] It may also have been relevant in its conclusion that this was a case not only of degrading punishment, but of torture.

Typically of this Court, it carefully canvassed all relevant international instruments, the practice of the UN Human Rights Committee and, of course, the Tyrer judgment from its regional counterpart, of whose jurisprudence it is always respectful. Trinidad and Tobago may have encouraged the Court to adopt an uncompromising line, as it did not participate in the proceedings, having denounced the Convention in 1998 after losing a death penalty case before the Court. They Court rightly took the view that the denunciation could not affect its jurisdiction over matters that had occurred before the denunciation.[91]

The African Commission on Human and Peoples' Rights has also found corporal punishment to violate Article 5 of the African Charter on Human and Peoples' Rights, prohibiting torture or cruel, inhuman or degrading treatment or punishment. The case, against Sudan, involved a sentence of 25 to 40 lashes for improper dress and immorality (consisting of a mixed-gender picnic). Specifically citing Tyrer, the Commission declared that there was 'no right for … the government of a country to

---

[86] E/CN.4/1986/15, [14].
[87] E/CN.4/1997/71, [3]–[11].
[88] A/HRC/10/44 (2009), [35].
[89] Caesar v Trinidad and Tobago, Inter-American Court of Human Rights, Series C No 123 (2005).
[90] ibid, [49(27)] and [49(28)].
[91] ibid, [6].

apply physical violence to individuals for offences'; any such right 'would be tantamount to sanctioning State-sponsored torture under the Charter'.[92]

Also, a number of African cases have found corporal punishment to violate their constitutions, with at least the first of them, the Zimbabwean Supreme Court case of *The State v Ncube* referring to *Tyrer* and each of the others building on earlier ones.[93] In brief, while it would be extravagant to suggest that the unanimity of the relevant regional and universal bodies depend on the *Tyrer* case, it would be implausible to conclude that this unanimity was not significantly facilitated the by judgment.

B. Living Instrument Doctrine

The Court's invocation in *Tyrer* of a 'living instrument' doctrine, as a basis for interpretation of the scope of ECHR obligations, heralded a clear style to be followed by the Court itself and other bodies. The doctrine is understood to be a refutation of a 'founding fathers' or 'originalist' interpretation that purports to give effect to the 'original intentions' of the parties.[94] A particularly vivid example is to be found in the 1999 case of *Selmouni* v *France*. In that case, the applicant had been beaten with blunt objects and subjected to threats and sexual humiliation while being interrogated by French security personnel. The beatings were of the sort that had led the Court a decade earlier in the *Northern Ireland* case to conclude that such treatment was 'inhuman' within the meaning of Article 3, but was not sufficiently grave to be categorised as torture.

The Court reversed its position in *Selmouni*, precisely basing itself on the 'living instrument' doctrine. This approach permitted it to affirm that:

> certain acts which were classified in the past as 'inhuman and degrading treatment' as opposed to 'torture' could be classified differently in the future. It takes the view that the increasingly high standard being required in the area of the protection of human rights and fundamental liberties correspondingly and inevitably requires greater firmness in assessing breaches of fundamental values of democratic societies.[95]

Accordingly, the beating and other ill-treatment inflicted on the applicant constituted torture, in violation of Article 3.[96] It is likely that the Court was also signalling its dissociation from its more controversial conclusion in the *Northern Ireland* case. The UK had resorted to certain interrogation techniques that, together, the

---

[92] *Curtis Francis Doebbler v Sudan*, Communication 236/2000, African Commission on Human and Peoples' Rights, 16th Activity Report, 2002–2003, Annex VII (2003), [42].

[93] *The State v Ncube* [1987] (2) ZLR 246 (SC) 267 B–C; [1988] (20 SA 702 (ZSC), 717 B–D; the decision was adopted despite Zimbabwe's Constitution having a savings clause as regards existing punishments; see Rodley, *Treatment of Prisoners* (n 1) 443 for later cases.

[94] See generally E Bjorge, *The Evolutionary Interpretation of Treaties* (Oxford, OUP, 2014).

[95] *Selmouni v France* [GC] (no 25803/94) ECHR 1995-V, [101].

[96] ibid, [105].

European Commission of Human Rights had found to be torture.[97] The Court found, without any argument from the parties—the UK had accepted the Commission's assessment—that the techniques should be considered inhuman, rather than torture.

The Inter-American Court of Human Rights has, in adopting an 'evolutionary' approach to interpretation, invoked the practice of its European counterpart in its advisory opinion on *Consular Assistance*. Referring to guidance offered by Article 31(3) of the Vienna Convention on the Law of Treaties, which speaks of subsequent state practice, the Court said:

> This guidance is particularly relevant in the case of international human rights law, which has made great headway thanks to an evolutive interpretation of international instruments of protection. That evolutive interpretation is consistent with the general rules of treaty interpretation established in the 1969 Vienna Convention. Both this Court, in the Advisory Opinion on the Interpretation of the American Declaration of the Rights and Duties of Man (1989), and the European Court of Human Rights in *Tyrer v. United Kingdom* (1978), *Marckx v. Belgium* (1979), *Loizidou v Turkey* (1995), among others, have held that human rights treaties are living instruments whose interpretation must consider the changes over time and present-day conditions.[98]

Perhaps superfluously, the Court invoked this approach finding violations of the rights of the child in two cases of extreme violation of the rights to life, to humane treatment and to freedom from arbitrary arrest and detention.[99] The invocation was to justify a finding that each state had failed to take positive means of protection of children as required by Article 19.

In one case, dealing with property rights of indigenous groups, the African Commission on Human and Peoples' Rights has also cited the doctrine approvingly. It specifically quoted a passage from the Inter-American Court case, *The Indigenous Community of Yakye Axa*: 'Previously this Court as well as the European Court of Human Rights have asserted that human rights are live *[sic]* instruments, whose interpretation must go hand in hand with evolution of the times and of current living conditions'.[100]

In at least one case the Human Rights Committee availed itself of the doctrine. It is the one case in which the Committee has expressly reversed itself. The case was *Judge v Canada*, involving the extradition to the Commonwealth of Pennsylvania

---

[97] *Northern Ireland case* (n 6) [167]–[168]; the techniques were wall-standing, hooding, subjection to noise, sleep deprivation; deprivation of food and drink [96].

[98] I/A Court HR, *The Right to Information on Consular Assistance in the Framework of the Guarantees of the due Process of Law*. Advisory Opinion OC-16/99 of October 1, 1999. Series A No 16, [114]; footnotes removed.

[99] I/A Court HR, *Case of the 'Street Children' (Villagrán-Morales et al.) v Guatemala*. Merits. Judgment of November 19, 1999. Series C No 63 (84 dead) [93]; I/A Court HR, *Case of the Gómez Paquiyauri Brothers v Peru*. Merits, Reparations and Costs. Judgment of 8 July 2004. Series C No 110 (two dead), [165].

[100] African Commission on Human and Peoples Rights, 276/2003 (2009) *Centre for Minority Rights Development (Kenya) and Minority Rights Group International on behalf of Endorois Welfare Council v Kenya*, fn 115, www.achpr.org/files/sessions/46th/comunications/276.03/achpr46_276_03_eng.pdf (accessed 6 January 2016).

in the United States of a person suspected of a capital crime. In a 1993 case, *Kindler v Canada,* the Committee held, over five dissents, that there was no violation. In *Judge* it decided the contrary, on the grounds that an abolitionist state could not thus expose a person to the risk of execution. The Committee justified its switch of position by reference to a 'broadening international consensus in favour of abolition of the death penalty, and in states which have retained the death penalty, a broadening consensus not to carry it out'.[101] It also referred to a subsequent change in Canada's internal jurisprudence on the issue. The relevance of this was because the Committee considered 'that the Covenant should be interpreted as a living instrument and the rights protected under it should be applied in context and in the light of present-day conditions'.[102]

C. The Role of NGOs and Individuals

While not the first case of its kind, *Tyrer* could in some ways to be said to be a classic illustration of a stage in the developing power of individuals to hold the state to account. The case preceded the current situation, pioneered in the ECHR system, of allowing individuals to haul states directly before a court in respect of alleged human rights violations. At the time such a radical reversal of state sovereignty inhibitions was unthinkable. Even now, it is the only human-rights-specific regime permitting individuals to challenge all states parties before a court *as of right.* Even access to the Commission was optional at the time. Nor, as is common with, seemingly distant, international machinery was it generally familiar or accessible to ordinary people or even ordinary practising lawyers.

Yet here was a case of two young individuals having access to a quasi-judicial body, the Commission, and able to put their government 'in the dock', even if one would not get the substance of his complaint determined. This was no mean thing. Predictably, it required a NGO, aware of at least, the existence of the Commission and concerned about the human rights problem in question.[103] Merely getting the application to the Commission secretariat within the excessively strict six-month time-limit required specialist knowledge.

Normally when the Commission referred case to the Court, it associated the applicant and his or her representatives with its delegation. This, as has been seen, was not possible in *Tyrer* because of the purported withdrawal of the applicant. Fortunately, this proved to be no obstacle to the service the system was able to afford, not just to the applicants, but to any Isle of Man resident or any other citizens or others within the jurisdiction of the Council of Europe region.

---

[101] *Judge v Canada,* UN Doc CCPR/C/78/D/829/1998 (2003), [10.3].
[102] ibid.
[103] For more on the important role of NGOs in protecting human rights, see N Rodley, 'The Contribution of British NGOs to the Development of International Law', in R McCorquodale and J-P Gauci (eds), *British Influences on International Law, 1915–2015* (London, British Institute of International and Comparative Law, 2016).

XI. PROFESSIONAL ETHICS—A CODA

One issue that was not considered in the *Tyrer* proceedings was the question of professional ethics. Most evidently, the role of doctors in the process of corporal punishment raises such questions. The participation of doctors was hailed by the UK as an important guarantee protecting the individual.[104] While there is no explicit international standard of professional medical ethics relating to corporal punishment, the World Medical Association's Declaration of Tokyo requires doctors not to 'countenance, condone or participate in the practice of torture or other forms of cruel, inhuman or degrading procedures'.[105] The WMA considers corporal punishment covered by this.[106] The UN Principles of Medical Ethics specifically consider a contravention of medical ethics that a doctor would 'certify, or participate in the certification of, the fitness of prisoners or detainees for any form of treatment or punishment that may adversely affect their physical or mental health'.[107] Neither document was in existence at the time that Tyrer's team appeared before the Commission. Even though the WMA declaration was adopted two days later, on 10 October 1975, it was not thereafter raised in the proceedings. The UN instrument was adopted only six years after the judgment.

By contrast, the Inter-American Commission on Human Rights in *Caesar* certainly did raise the issue, manifestly affected by the attending doctor's certification of an already sick man as fit for the punishment by the attendant doctor to prevent the lashings leading to Mr Caesar's becoming unconscious and requiring hospitalisation for five weeks.[108] The Court responded to this by maintaining that its function was not to 'assess individual responsibilities'.[109]

Medical ethical concern has now further developed. Thus, while the original UN Standard Minimum Rules for the Treatment of Prisoners (SMR) required doctors to certify the fitness of prisoners to undergo solitary confinement, that provision has been removed from the revised Nelson Mandela Rules. Indeed, the Rules now provide that health care personnel 'shall not have any role in the imposition of disciplinary sanctions or other restrictive measures'.[110] This was at the urging of medical experts.[111]

---

[104] Commission Report (n 8) [23].

[105] Declaration of Tokyo of the World Medical Association—Guidelines for Medical Doctors Concerning Torture and other Cruel, Inhuman or Degrading Treatment or Punishment in relation to Detention and Imprisonment, adopted at the 29th World Medical Assembly, Tokyo, Japan, 10 October 1975, [1].

[106] Thus, the WMA intervened in respect of doctor participation in amputation of hands in Mauritania: (1981) 28 *World Medical Journal* 2, 21; see Rodley, *Treatment of Prisoners* (n 1) 518 and 522.

[107] Principles of Medical Ethics relevant to the role of health personnel, particularly physicians, in the protection of prisoners and detainees against torture and other cruel, inhuman or degrading treatment or punishment, UN General Assembly resolution 37/194 (1982), Annex; see Rodley, *Treatment of Prisoners* (n 1) 515–18, on some interpretative issues regarding the scope of the Principles.

[108] *Caesar* (n 89) [50(j)].

[109] ibid, [80]–[81].

[110] Rule 46. The Nelson Mandela Rules were adopted by the UN General Assembly on 17 December 2015, as an updating of the original 1957 SMR, from a text finalised by an intergovernmental expert group meeting in Cape Town in March 2015: General Assembly resolution 70/175 (2015), Annex.

[111] An influential recommendation from an expert meeting, including medical ethical professionals, convened by the University of Essex Human Rights Centre on the revision process, was that healthcare

Another area of professional ethics that could have been relevant is that of the judiciary.[112] There is limited black-letter international material to invoke. Nevertheless, there should be limits to what the legislator can demand of the judge in applying the law. There is a hint of this in the 2003 Bangalore Principles of Judicial Conduct which require a judge to 'keep himself or herself informed about relevant developments of international law, including ... human rights norms'.[113] While verbally keeping to its declared role of not dealing with individual responsibility, the Inter-American Court, perhaps out of a sense of professional pride, did feel obliged

> to put on record its profound regret that the presiding office in the State's High Court saw fit to exercise any option which would manifestly have the effect of inflicting a punishment that is not merely in blatant violation of the State's international obligations, but also is universally stigmatized as cruel, inhuman and degrading.[114]

The issue did not, understandably, figure in the *Tyrer* case. However, when Hugh O'Callaghan in 1981 appealed his sentence, the Court of Appeal judges were reported as observing that they were 'surprised that the magistrates ordered birching after four and a half years [since the *Tyrer* judgment] without considering all the consequences'.[115]

XII. CONCLUSION

Evidently the *Tyrer* case was the landmark judicial decision on the progressive realisation that if corporal punishment did not qualify as cruel, inhuman or degrading punishment, then it was hard to conceive of any lawful sanction that would. Now it is no longer a question only of treaty body decisions, but also of intergovernmental political bodies. The UN Commission on Human Rights and its successor Human Rights Council have endorsed the understanding.[116] The fact that a small number of countries continue to use corporal punishment—and in much more brutal forms, such as amputation of limbs and flagellation to death—must now be seen not as a failure of the norm but as resulting from the limits of international law.

The case was also a fine example of a person of no social or political influence in his society having the opportunity to find redress against his government beyond the jurisdiction of his own government. And it was a step on the way to the growing international judicialisation of human rights grievances, which, at least in the greater Europe (minus Belarus!) is now available as of right.

---

professionals 'shall not perform medical duties or engage in medical interventions for any security or disciplinary purposes': Expert Meeting at the University of Essex on the Standard Minimum Rules for the Treatment of Prisoners Review—Summary, 20 November 2012, 9; at Cape Town, the present writer, who was an invited international expert, recalls the representative of the World Health Organization supporting the revised text.

[112] See C Foley, *Combating Torture—A Manual for Judges and Prosecutors* (Colchester, University of Essex Human Rights Centre, with the Foreign and Commonwealth Office, 2003).

[113] The Bangalore Principles of Judicial Conduct (2002), UN Doc E/CN.4/2003/65, Principle 6.4.

[114] *Caesar* (n 89) [74].

[115] *Glasgow Herald*, 7 October 1981 (n 74).

[116] See Rodley, *Treatment of Prisoners* (n 1) 432.

The interpretative technique used by the Court, the living instrument doctrine, was a clear articulation of a mode that was still unfamiliar to many governments. It was to take some time before their thinking caught up with the language of the 1969 Vienna Convention on the Law of Treaties, Article 31 of which demanded interpretation according to the plain language of the text, in its context and 'in the light of the object and purpose of the treaty'. It should have required less effort to understand that the enhancement of human dignity—the principal goal of human rights treaties—would hardly be reconcilable with an originalist approach. It took the coining of the term 'living instrument' to give a boost to the required change of awareness.

A tangential, but perhaps especially significant consequence of the development of this evolutionary approach, is that international judicial and quasi-judicial bodies are able to contribute to the evolution of customary or general international human rights law. This is because most of the substantive human rights treaty provisions in fact reflect norms of general or customary international law. As old wisdom has it, 'from small acorns mighty oaks may grow'.

15

Military and Paramilitary Activities in and against Nicaragua (Nicaragua v United States of America) (1984 to 1986)

ROBERT KOLB

I. INTRODUCTION

THE JUDGMENTS OF the International Court of Justice (ICJ) delivered in *Military and Paramilitary Activities in and against Nicaragua (Nicaragua v United States of America) (Nicaragua)*,[1] in the mid-1980s, are among the most important ever issued by the Court. This is so for at least three reasons:

(1) For the first time, the question of the use of force and aggression was squarely put before the Court and considered in a most sweeping way. This subject matter was of great political and legal importance, belonging as it did to a sphere which, up to that time, had been regarded in some circles as not fully suitable for adjudication (*de maximis non curat praetor*).

(2) The dispute concerned the relations between a 'great power', a permanent member of the Security Council of the United Nations, and a small state, situated in a 'sphere of influence' of the former. Ultimately, the great power was condemned for having committed unlawful acts. This could have happened only at a court of justice and not in dispute settlement schemes of a political nature.

(3) Finally, the judgments are striking in their scope and detail. The Court treated with great care a host of questions of international law, placing *Military and Paramilitary Activities in and against Nicaragua* amongst the most densely reasoned and extensive analytical tools issued by the Court.

---

[1] Four decisions of significance were issued by the Court: the first was the Order of 10 May 1984 concerning provisional measures of protection (*Nicaragua*, Provisional Measures [1984] ICJ Rep 169); the second was the Order of 4 October 1984 concerning El Salvador's application to intervene in the proceedings (*Nicaragua*, Declaration of Intervention [1984] ICJ Rep 215); the third was the Court's judgment of 26 November 1984 concerning the jurisdiction of the Court and the admissibility of Nicaragua's application (*Nicaragua*, Jurisdiction and Admissibility [1984] ICJ Rep 392); finally, the Court issued its Judgment of 28 June 1986 on the merits, bringing the proceedings to a close (*Nicaragua*, Merits [1986] ICJ Rep 14).

II. BACKGROUND OF THE DISPUTE

From the point of view of Nicaragua as claimant, the background of the dispute was rooted in the recurrent policy of intervention of the United States in Central America—in particular the anti-Communist interventionism during the Cold War—which found its ultimate expression in the 'Reagan doctrine'.[2] The plea of Nicaragua was that the US, through the CIA, unlawfully intervened by force on its territory with a view to overthrowing a government of which the US disapproved. From the point of view of the US as respondent, the background of the dispute is rooted in the Communist expansionism in Central America, which had destabilised allied governments by covert subversion and intervention.[3] The age-old policy of intervention in Central America to safeguard US interests, to protect US citizens and to ensure friendly governments (as pioneered in the foreign policy of Presidents James Monroe and Theodore Roosevelt) was here concentrated on the issue of defence of the 'free world' against Communist subversion. The US thus argued that Nicaragua had intervened itself by force in El Salvador through trans-border military incursions provision of assistance for the Communist rebels operating there. Their plea was that the US could exercise, on behalf of El Salvador, the right of collective self-defence.[4]

The recent history of Nicaragua was heavily influenced by persistent political instability and no less persistent US interventionism.[5] In 1909, US Secretary of State, PC Knox, sustained a group of conservative Nicaraguans in their fight against President José Santos Zelaya. The latter was forced to resign, and was succeeded by his foreign minister, José Madriz, who in turn was replaced through a successful insurgency conducted by General Juan Estrada with the support of the US. The newly established regime subjected itself to the policy priorities of the US as conveyed by Thomas Dawson, a Special Commissioner who had previously overseen American intervention in the Dominican Republic. In 1912, local insurrections against the Government thus established took place, resulting in the deployment of a detachment of US marines, who established a tight political and financial control over Nicaragua. In 1914, the US and Nicaragua signed the Bryan–Chamorro Treaty,[6] granting the US the right to build a trans-oceanic canal across Nicaragua territory by way of the San Juan River.

---

[2] See R Charvin, 'La doctrine américaine de la "souveraineté limitée"' (1987) 20 *RBDI* 5. On the interaction of the Reagan administration with international law more generally, see JK Gamble Jr , 'International Law in the Reagan Years: How Much of an Outlier?' (1990) 26 *Akron LR* 351.

[3] A detailed expression of this view can be found in JN Moore, 'The Secret War in Central America and the Future of World Order' (1987) 81 *AJIL* 160. For a study espousing the Nicaraguan point of view, see P Harrison, *Etats-Unis contre Nicaragua* (Geneva, Centre Europe-Tiers Monde, 1988). Both studies are less than even-handed.

[4] See, eg, N Rostow, 'Nicaragua and the Law of Self-Defence Revisited' (1986) 11 *Yale JIL* 437.

[5] See C Lang, *L'affaire Nicaragua / Etats-Unis devant la Cour internationale de Justice* (Paris, Librairie générale de droit et de jurisprudence, 1990) 2–3.

[6] Treaty concerning the Construction of an Interoceanic Canal Through the Territory of the Republic of Nicaragua, 5 August 1918, 1 IELR 554. Further: GA Finch, 'The Treaty with Nicaragua granting Canal and Other Rights to the United States' (1916) 10 *AJIL* 344.

With a stable, friendly government in Nicaragua, the marines could withdraw in 1925, but they were back in 1929 owing to Nicaraguan resistance to certain US objectives in the region. The US now contributed to a revolt against the established government, leading to the seizure of power by General Anastasio Somoza García in 1937, opening a long phase of dynastic rule that lasted until 1979. The Somoza family was a direct ally of the US and even played the role of proxy policeman in Central America, though its dictatorial bent ultimately lead to opposition and insurrection. This movement brought to power the *Frente Sandinista de Liberación Nacional* (in the guise of the *Junta de Gobierno de Reconstrucción Nacional*) and President Daniel Ortega. After an initial phase of collaboration with the administration of US President James Carter, Nicaragua–US relations rapidly deteriorated under that of President Ronald Reagan. The 'Communist against Free World' dichotomy and its attendant system of proxy warfare were thus initiated.

III. CONTENT OF THE JUDGMENTS

It may be useful to recall the main points that the Court was required to address.[7] The case was based on the filing of a complaint by Nicaragua against the US in a dispute concerning the responsibility of the latter for military and paramilitary activities directed against the former by direct action through the CIA (eg the mining of ports) or by indirect action sustaining the so-called *contras*.[8] Nicaragua based the jurisdiction of the Court on the optional clause jurisdiction provided by Article 36(2) of the Statute, and later also on a compromissory clause contained in the bilateral 1956 Treaty of Friendship, Commerce and Navigation[9] (FCN Treaty) under Article 36(1) of the Statute.

A. The Incidental Proceedings

There were two incidental proceedings. First, the Court indicated, under Article 41 of the Statute, *provisional measures of protection* by an Order of 10 May 1984, requiring the US to abstain from mining and sabotaging Nicaragua's ports and to respect the sovereignty and independence of Nicaragua. It further imposed on both parties the duty not to aggravate the dispute.[10] To some extent, these measures

---

[7] For a more detailed summary, see: UN Doc ST/LEG/SER.E/1 (1992). Further: J Crawford, 'Military and Paramilitary Activities in and against Nicaragua Case (Nicaragua v United States)' in R Wolfrum (ed), *Max Planck Encyclopedia of Public International Law*, vol 7 (Oxford, OUP, 2012) 173; PM Eisemann and P Pazartzis, *La jurisprudence de la Cour internationale de Justice* (Paris, Pedone, 2008) 238.

[8] Being the various rebel groups that were active in opposing the Sandinistas from 1979 to the early 1990s. The foremost of these was the *Fuerza Democrática Nicaragüense*. From the mid-1980s, these groups unified to form various umbrella organizations such as the *Unidad Nicaragüense Opositora* and, later, the *Resistencia Nicaragüense*. Further: G Prevost, 'The "Contra" War in Nicaragua' (1987) 7 JCS 3, 5.

[9] 21 January 1956, 367 UNTS 3.

[10] *Nicaragua*, Provisional Measures (n 1) 186–88.

anticipated the merits,[11] but it was impossible entirely to disentangle the provisional demands from the final result, as some irreparable harm could be done to the object of the dispute by those very activities complained of at the provisional and at the merits stage. The jurisprudence of the Court developed in the direction of indicating provisional measures to some extent co-substantive with the rights invoked on the merits. It must also be noted that the criticism[12] according to which the Court ought to have indicated measures for both sides in dispute is unfounded. The Court indeed said that both parties must refrain from action aggravating the dispute and impairing the rights at stake. Conversely, it could urge only the US not to intervene in Nicaragua. Had the US wished provisional measures against Nicaraguan action in Salvador, it should have formulated its own request for provisional measures.

Second, the Court, in a very short Order of 4 October 1984, rejected the Salvadorian request for *intervention* under Article 63 of the Statute.[13] This Order has been often criticised,[14] inter alia for displaying bias. Reasonable minds can certainly differ as to whether El Salvador should have been granted an oral hearing. But there remains the fact that the request for intervention was so vaguely expressed that it hardly fulfilled the procedural requirements for being accepted under Article 82 of the Court's Rules. Moreover, the intervention concerned multilateral conventions on which the Court could not at this preliminary stage assume jurisdiction, due to the Vandenberg Reservation contained in the optional clause declaration of the US. Finally, it has to be noted that intervention under Article 63 is designed for intervention on the interpretation of a multilateral convention on the merits, not for arguing the lack of jurisdiction of the Court while purporting to intervene on the correct interpretation of the Statute (where the Court will in any case ensure a 'uniform interpretation' to which all parties to the Statute are automatically 'bound', since the Statute is mainly interpreted by itself).[15] If it were otherwise, all parties to the Statute could intervene in every contentious case, since the interpretation of the Statute is always at stake in proceedings before the Court. The Court accepted, however, that El Salvador could intervene during the merits stage if the interpretation

---

[11] J Verhoeven, 'Le Droit, le Juge et la Violence, Les arrêts Nicaragua c. Etats-Unis' (1987) 91 *RGDIP* 1159, 1166–68.

[12] TM Franck, 'Icy Day at the ICJ' (1985) 79 *AJIL* 379, 381.

[13] *Nicaragua*, Declaration of Intervention (n 1) 217.

[14] JN Moore, 'The Nicaragua Case and the Deterioration of World Order' (1987) 81 *AJIL* 151, 158; WM Reisman, 'Has the International Court Exceeded its Jurisdiction?' (1986) 80 *AJIL* 128, 132; T-H Cheng, *When International Law Works: Realistic Idealism after 9/11 and the Global Recession* (Oxford, OUP, 2012) 147. Even the authors who agree with the rejection of the request for intervention often affirm that the Court ought to have granted El Salvador a hearing: see eg Crawford, 'Nicaragua' (n 7) 174–75. The question is not whether an oral hearing could have served any useful purpose on the legal issues, which remains more than doubtful—but it might have served, at least, to obviate any impression of bias. The Court rejected the declaration essentially on account of the clear inadequacy of its object at that stage of the proceedings, the Court's possession of all the necessary elements to decide the matter and of the tight time limits in the principal case.

[15] See S Torres Bernardez, 'L'intervention dans la procédure de la Cour internationale de Justice' (1995) 256 *RdC* 392; C Chinkin, 'Article 63', in A Zimmermann, C Tomuschat, K Oellers-Frahm and CJ Tams (eds), *The Statute of the International Court of Justice: A Commentary*, 2nd edn (Oxford, OUP, 2012) 1580; R Kolb, *The International Court of Justice* (Oxford, Hart, 2013) 736–37.

of some multilateral convention would be at stake there (subject to the fate of the Vandenberg Reservation, addressed below). El Salvador abstained from doing so.

B. Jurisdiction and Admissibility

The Court made several further rulings in its judgment concerning jurisdiction and admissibility of 26 November 1984.[16] The Nicaraguan optional declaration of 1929 was technically invalid, since the instrument of ratification of the Statute of the PCIJ (more precisely the 'Protocol of Signature' of the Statute) had never been received by the Court. Nicaragua, however, announced itself to have complied with that formality, as the law of the PCIJ allowed the deposit of an optional declaration before the ratification of the Statute. Hence the declaration had a potential effect, to be perfected by the incumbent ratification. The latter occurred when Nicaragua became a member of the United Nations per Article 92 of the UN Charter, in the process becoming a party to the ICJ Statute. This perfected the old declaration's potential effect by virtue of Article 36(5) the later Statute, which transfers the optional declarations under the PCIJ to the ICJ. Moreover, the Court noted that Nicaragua had always considered itself bound by the optional clause and was mentioned as a state party to the system in the Court's *Yearbook*, albeit with a footnote recalling the lack of receipt of the instrument of ratification. This, it was held, was sufficient to indicate that Nicaragua was bound to the Court's jurisdiction by way of acquiescence.

The Court then turned its attention towards the letter sent by US Secretary of State George Schultz to UN Secretary General Javier Pérez de Cuéllar on 6 April 1984. This had been sent in anticipation of the proceedings, three days before Nicaragua had deposited its application with the Court. In the relevant part, this provided that the US's declaration under Article 36(2) of the Statute:

> [S]hall not apply to disputes with any Central American state or arising out of or related to events in Central America, any of which disputes shall be settled in such a matter as the parties to them may agree ... Not withstanding the terms of the aforesaid Declaration, this proviso shall take effect immediately and shall remain in force for two years, so as to foster the continuing regional dispute settlement process.[17]

The Court held that this denunciation by the US of its own optional clause declaration could not deprive the Court of jurisdiction. It was performed directly prior to and with knowledge of the deposit of the Nicaraguan request, and was further contrary to the US declaration of 1946, whereby the US had bound itself to a notice period of six months with respect to any modification of consent.[18] The Court further dismissed the US argument whereby it alleged to be able to avail itself

---

[16] *Nicaragua*, Jurisdiction and Admissibility (n 1) 392ff.

[17] Letter from Secretary Schultz to Secretary-General Pérez de Cuéllar, 6 April 1984, extracted in 23 ILM 670.

[18] Acceptance of Compulsory Jurisdiction of the International Court of Justice, 26 August 1946, TIAS 1596.

of reciprocity with the optional clause declarations by Nicaragua or third states in order to benefit, on an equal footing with them, from a right to denounce with immediate effect. The Court recalled that the principle of reciprocity in this context related only to the substance of the declarations and not to the formal conditions for their entry into force and their denunciation. It further noted that reciprocity could be invoked only by the state having accepted more broadly the jurisdiction of the Court in order to avoid being placed at a disadvantage with respect to another state having qualified its acceptance of the jurisdiction by reservations—it could not be invoked by a state that wished to flout the terms of its own declaration freely assumed. Finally, the Court said, there was no such thing as 'pre-seisin' reciprocity: reciprocity existed only between the parties to a case before the ICJ, not against all the optional declarations outside the context of a proceeding. The Court noted that the Nicaraguan declaration did not contain any period of notice for withdrawal, but the US supposition that it could be denounced with immediate effect was legally wrong. Nicaragua, by analogy with the law of treaties, and in accordance with the principle of good faith, was bound to flag any modification to consent within a reasonable time before it could take effect.

A further US objection to jurisdiction concerned the so-called 'Vandenberg Reservation', inserted into its 1946 declaration by Senator Arthur H Vandenberg of Michigan. This excluded from the jurisdiction of the Court 'disputes arising under a multilateral treaty, unless (1) all parties to the treaty affected by the decision are also parties to the case before the Court, or (2) the United States of America specially agrees to jurisdiction'.[19] The Court held this reservation to be prima facie applicable to the proceedings, but not sufficient to vitiate at that point in time the US's consent to jurisdiction, as the extent to which third states to the proceedings could be 'affected' by the Court's final ruling depended on certain determinations inextricably linked to issues on the merits. The question was not, therefore, of an exclusively preliminary nature and was accordingly referred to the merits stage. The Court then considered and affirmed a further basis of jurisdiction, that is, the compromissory clause contained in Article XXIV(2) of the FCN Treaty, certain provisions of which Nicaragua alleged had been breached.

The Court also considered various US objections pertaining to the admissibility of the Nicaraguan claim. In the first place, it pointed out that third parties, potentially affected by the decision, were not indispensable to the proceedings within the meaning of the Court's pronouncement in the *Monetary Gold* case.[20] The ruling of the Court would not consider in the first place the rights and duties of third states, which could at best be indirectly affected by the judgment of the Court. Thus, the protection of Article 59 of the Statute, providing that any decision of the Court was binding only on the parties to the dispute, was sufficient to protect their interests.[21] In the

---

[19] Further: A D'Amato, 'The United States Should Accept, by a New Declaration, the General Compulsory Jurisdiction of the World Court' (1986) 80 *AJIL* 331.

[20] *Monetary Gold Removed from Rome in 1943 (Italy v France, UK & US)*, Preliminary Question [1954] ICJ Rep 19, 32.

[21] This principle was later refined in *Certain Phosphate Lands in Nauru (Nauru v Australia)*, Preliminary Objections [1992] ICJ Rep 240, 255ff. See also *East Timor (Portugal v Australia)* [1995] ICJ Rep 90, 102.

second, the Court held that its jurisdiction was not hampered by the parallel seisin of the Security Council. Under Article 24(1) of the UN Charter, the Security Council had only a primary competence on matters concerning the maintenance of peace; such competence was not exclusive. Moreover, Article 12(1) of the Charter did not contain any limitation on parallel activities as between the Security Council and the Court, in contrast to the relationship between the Security Council and the General Assembly. Consequently, under the division of powers set out in the UN Charter, the Council was authorised to deal with the political aspects of international disputes and the Court with legal ones, an arrangement confirmed as appropriate by the Court in the *Tehran Hostages* case.[22] In the third, the Court rejected the US argument that the matter was non-justiciable, holding that it would apply only the rules governing the use of force and non-intervention under international law and in so doing would not exceed its judicial function. If some facts are difficult to establish in an ongoing conflict, it was said, the situation would be dealt with under the rules of evidence. Finally, the Court held that the parties were not bound to exhaust any political procedures for the settlement of the dispute before seizing the Court, most notably the so-called 'Contadora Process'.[23] Ongoing negotiations did not deprive the Court of its jurisdiction or lead otherwise to the inadmissibility of the claim.

On the basis of the foregoing, the Court therefore found by 11 votes to five that it possessed jurisdiction to hear the case under the optional clause, and by 14 votes to two that it possessed jurisdiction under the FCN Treaty. All arguments concerning the inadmissibility of the claim were rejected unanimously.

C. Judgment on the Merits

In its judgment on the merits of 27 June 1986,[24] the Court again had to determine certain preliminary points. First, the US, aggrieved by the Court's findings on jurisdiction, refused to appear on the merits,[25] leading to the application of Article 53 of the ICJ Statute. Second, there was the issue of the Vandenberg Reservation, which had been held over by the Court from the jurisdictional phase. The Court considered that the Reservation functioned to exclude jurisdiction over multilateral treaties: El Salvador would clearly be 'affected' by a decision of the Court on the claimed right of the US to exercise collective self-defence on its behalf—as it was not

---

[22] That is not to say, however, that Security Council seisin cannot affect other elements of the Court's procedure: cf *Questions of Interpretation and Application of the 1971 Montreal Convention arising from the Aerial Incident at Lockerbie (Libya v UK)*, Provisional Measures [1992] ICJ Rep 3, 14–16; *in passim (Libya v US)*, Provisional Measures [1992] ICJ Rep 114, 126–28.

[23] The Contadora Process was launched in the early 1980s by the Foreign Ministers of Colombia, Mexico, Panama and Venezuela in order to deal with the persistent military conflicts in El Salvador, Nicaragua and Guatemala, which were threatening to destablilize the region. Further: HD Sims and V Petrash, 'The Contadora Peace Process' (1987) 7 *JCS* 4, 5.

[24] *Nicaragua*, Merits (n 1) 14ff.

[25] See G Fitzmaurice, 'The Problem of the Non-Appearing Defendant Government' (1980) 51 *BYIL* 89; J Elkind, *Non-Appearance before the International Court of Justice: Factual and Comparative Analysis* (The Hague Martinus Nijhoff, 1984); HWA Thirlway, *Non-Appearance before the International Court of Justice* (Cambridge, CUP, 1985).

a party to the proceedings, the US via its optional clause declaration could be said to have consented to the jurisdiction of the ICJ in this respect. This determination, however, did not preclude the Court's exercise of jurisdiction with regard to customary international law. Third, the Court considered how to ascertain the relevant facts of the dispute, and ventured into a careful determination to this effect, devising the following principles:

— press articles and book extracts have to be treated with great caution. They do not prove a fact in themselves but they may corroborate a fact;
— certain facts can constitute public knowledge;
— declarations by a state representative can have a strong evidentiary value when they are unfavourable to the interests of the state on whose behalf the representative appears. Such declarations may be considered a form of admission. Otherwise, great caution must to be exercised with respect to representative declarations;
— witnesses may have certain importance when stating facts of first-hand knowledge, in particular if the statements are unfavourable to the state on whose behalf they testify; and official state publications have a significant probative value.

The Court then proceeded to make its findings of fact, eg as to the mining of certain Nicaraguan ports or the violation of the Nicaraguan airspace. In this context, the Court found that the actions of the *contras* could not be attributed to the US: the insurgents were not de facto organs of the US, nor could they be considered to be within its capacity to direct, as the US did not display 'effective control' over the rebels. As to the facts imputable to Nicaragua, the Court found that there had been assistance to the rebels in El Salvador, especially before 1981, but also sporadically thereafter. It also found that a number of trans-border incursions took place.

The Court then moved to consider these findings in light of the customary international law concerning the use of force, to the exclusion of multilateral treaty law. Although the customary and conventional law and the subject remained formally distinct, their substantive norms are largely similar. Accordingly, the danger that the Court would express on rights and duties not concretely applicable between the parties (the latter being bound by multilateral treaties as *lex specialis*) was non-existent. The Court then affirmed that international practice did not have to be virtually uniform to locate a customary rule: it is sufficient that the practice generally conformed to the rule and that states treated non-compliant conduct as violations of the law, rather than as exceptions to the old rule or forerunners of a new rule. In the present case, the Court analysed the customary status of the law on the use of force, relying heavily on *opinio juris* as expressed in various UN resolutions. In particular, the Court affirmed that Article 3(g) of General Assembly Resolution 3314, relating to 'indirect aggression', constituted a norm of customary international law.[26]

---

[26] UNGA Res 3314(XXIX) (14 December 1974) Art 3(g): 'The sending by or on behalf of a State of armed bands, groups, irregulars or mercenaries, which carry out acts of armed force against another State of such gravity as to amount to the acts listed above, or its substantial involvement therein'.

Conversely, the Court held that the mere assistance of the rebels, eg by supply of weapons, did not reach the threshold of an armed attack or aggression giving rise to a right of self-defence. In order to exercise collective self-defence, the state victim of the aggression had to declare itself attacked and call for foreign assistance.

The Court then moved on to define and determine the customary status of the principle of non-intervention in internal affairs. It denied that in case of violation of the principle of non-intervention, third states could have recourse to forcible coun-ter-measures. The Court then addressed to the customary principle of sovereignty, which guaranteed the inviolability of a state's territory by the forces of another state. This was followed by consideration of international humanitarian law (IHL). The Court found that the main customary principles of IHL were conveniently summa-rized in common Article 3 of the Geneva Conventions of 1949, and corresponded to the 'elementary considerations of humanity' that to which the Court had referred in its judgment in *Corfu Channel*.[27] Finally, there remained the FCN Treaty, which due to its bilateral character fell outside the Vandenberg Reservation. It further fell to the Court to determine whether the conditions for applying the saving clause on vital interests in Article XXI of the FCN Treaty were met or not. In this connection, it noted that the clause was formulated objectively and not subjectively, and that the Court was consequently capable of determining whether the measures presented by the US as being designed to protect its 'essential security interests' were to be consid-ered 'necessary', or merely useful.

In addressing the above issues, the Court first found that that the customary prin-ciple of non-use of force has been breached by the US through several acts, such as the mining of ports and certain direct military attacks. It further found that there was no extant situation of collective self-defence vis-à-vis El Salvador which would have precluded the wrongfulness of the acts—Nicaragua's assistance of insurgents within El Salvador via the provision of weapons did not give rise to an armed attack. As to the alleged trans-border incursions by Nicaragua, the affected states had not claimed to be the victim of an armed attack, did not call the US for armed assistance and the US itself had never notified the Security Council of an exercise of self-defence, as required under Article 51 of the UN Charter. Moreover, the measures taken by the US were not 'necessary' in the sense required by the law on self-defence: the US actions occurred months after the Salvadorian rebels had been largely pushed back, depriving the situation of any real immediacy. Nor was the principle of proportion-ality respected, eg by the mining of ports or by the fact that the action was pursued for a long time after the trans-border armed attacks of Nicaragua. Second, the Court found that the principle of non-intervention had been breached by the coercion exercised by the US on matters which should have remained for the free choice of Nicaragua, notably through assistance given to the *contras*. Conversely, it was said, mere humanitarian assistance did not prima facie constitute an unlawful intervention, but to remain lawful must be distributed without discrimination to all victims. The Court also pointed out that opposition forces within a state cannot invite a foreign state to intervene—were that allowed, the principle of non-intervention would be

---

[27] *Corfu Channel (UK v Albania)* [1949] ICJ Rep 4, 22.

utterly compromised, perhaps to vanishing point. Alternatively, to the extent that intervention could be considered a collective countermeasure, such countermeasures could not imply the use of force and could, moreover, have been adopted only by the affected states, that is, El Salvador, Honduras or Costa Rica. Third, the Court declared that the US had violated Nicaragua's sovereignty, not only through the acts already condemned as unlawful by the Court, but also by unauthorised overflights. Finally, the Court confirmed that IHL has been violated, notably through the distribution amongst the *contras* of a CIA manual on psychological warfare (*Operaciones sicológicas en guerra de guerrillas*). This called for some fundamental breaches of the principles of IHL in the context of terror warfare.

The Court separately considered the fact that Nicaragua had given certain assurances to the Organization of American States (OAS) with regards to demilitarisation, democratisation, rule of law and respect for human rights. These assurances notwithstanding, the Court held that Nicaragua had not assumed a legal obligation in this regard—these were only policy statements, and even if they achieved greater statute, the obligations would have been assumed towards the OAS and not the US. The latter were thus not even entitled to enforce the promises, let alone by force. The fact that a government is a 'communist dictatorship', so-called, does not entitle another government that happens to disagree with this policy choice to intervene by force. Furthermore, the Court said, any violation of human rights must be sanctioned by the ordinary control mechanisms for the implementation of those rights, not by the use of force. Finally, the Court noted that there are no general rules of customary law which would prohibit a certain degree of militarisation of a given state.

With respect to the FCN Treaty, the Court held that it was impossible to hold that all acts contrary to the general object and purpose of a treaty of 'friendship'—ie all acts that are to some degree 'unfriendly'—are *ipso jure* violations of that treaty. Rather, unfriendly acts contravene the treaty only when they relate to specific matters regulated therein. In the present case, the activities of the US were contrary to the very spirit of the treaty *and* to specific provisions, eg through direct attacks, mining of ports, and also the abrupt embargo—though not through the freezing of voluntary aid. Further, the vital interest exception in Article XXI could not be invoked successfully by the US, since the measures taken could hardly be objectively termed 'necessary' for national security.

Finally, Nicaragua's claim for reparation of the wrongful acts committed by the US was referred to a later phase of the proceedings, in which Nicaragua would have to show the exact extent of the losses suffered. An occasion was offered to the US to take position on the issue in the hope that, eventually, a negotiated agreement could be reached.

At the conclusion of its judgment, the Court adopted a very elaborate operative part with majorities ranging from unanimity (regards the reminder of the duty to settle the dispute peacefully), to 11 votes against four (on the fate of the Vandenberg Reservation). The three main dissenters were Judges Jennings of the UK, Oda of Japan and Schwebel of the US. Judges Jennings and Oda dissented mainly on jurisdictional issues, with Judge Schwebel additionally dissenting on merits issues. The sometimes acerbic and aggressive tone of Judge Schwebel's dissent was unfortunate, and additional self-reflection and possibly self-restraint would have been welcome, all the more since no other judge shared his substantive concerns and—his fellow dissenters aside—the other Western judges (Judge Mosler of the Federal Republic of Germany and Judge Ago of Italy) voted with the majority. This should have been a reason for a touch of humility.

IV. CRITICISM OF THE COURT'S PRONOUNCEMENTS

The judgments in the *Nicaragua* case have been lauded by a great part of legal doctrine.[28] Third World and European writers generally hailed the Court's pronouncements in the case. In the US, however, opinion was highly split. The jurisdiction and admissibility judgment of 1984 gave rise to significant doubts.[29] The treatment of the optional clause in such an atypical setting and with the unavoidable legal gymnastics gave rise to some understandable puzzlement. The merits judgment was considered overdue.[30] The Court had no choice but to condemn actions which fell afoul of the most elementary rules of international law. It may be useful at this juncture to consider a certain number of important criticisms which have been levelled against the two decisions.

A. The Court Should Have Considered a Wider Range of Issues at the Provisional Measures Phase[31]

Two preliminary considerations may be considered together. First, the Court ought to have addressed the arguments of the US according to which the present dispute

---

[28] Generally, see Lang, *L'affaire Nicaragua* (n 5); PM Eisemann, 'L'arrêt de la CIJ du 27 juin 1986 (fond) dans l'affaire des activitiés militaires et paramilitaires au Nicaragua et contre celui-ci' (1986) 32 *AFDI* 153. In the US, see, eg, HW Briggs, 'Nicaragua v United States: Jurisdiction and Admissability' (1985) 79 *AJIL* 373, 373ff and HW Briggs, 'The ICJ Lives Up to its Name' (1987) 81 *AJIL* 78, 78ff; or K Highet, 'Evidence, the Court and the Nicaragua Case' (1987) 81 *AJIL* 1, 1ff.

[29] See, eg, PM Eisemann, 'L'arrêt de la CIJ du 26 novembre 1984 (Compétence et recevabilité) dans l'affaire des activitiés militaires et paramilitaires au Nicaragua et contre celui-ci' (1984) 30 *AFDI* 373; Crawford, 'Nicaragua' (n 7) 175; Verhoeven, 'Le Droit' (n 11) 1168–73. Some writers insist at least that the findings of the Court are 'hardly arbitrary': Franck 'Icy Day' (n 12) 382. For a view generally supportive of the ICJ, see DW Greig 'Nicaragua and the United States: Confrontation over the Jurisdiction of the ICJ' (1991) 62 *BYIL* 119, 123ff.

[30] See, eg, Eisemann, 'L'arrêt (fond)' (n 28) 153–55, 188–89; BS Chimni, 'The International Court and the Maintenance of Peace and Security: The Nicaragua Decision and the US Response' (1986) 35 *ICLQ* 960, 964ff; A Chayes, 'Nicaragua, the United States and the World Court' (1985) 85 *Col LR* 1445; PW Kahn, 'From Nuremberg to The Hague: the United States Position in Nicaragua' (1987) 12 *Yale JIL* 1; Briggs, 'The ICJ' (n 28) 85–86; FA Boyle, 'Determining US Responsibility for Contra Operations under International Law' (1987) 81 *AJIL* 86; R Falk, 'The World Court's Achievement' (1987) 81 *AJIL* 106; T Farer, 'Drawing the Right Line' (1987) 81 *AJIL* 112, 113; Verhoeven, 'Le Droit' (n 11) 1159ff, 1237–39. Contra TM Franck, 'Some Observations on the ICJ's Procedural and Substantive Obligations' (1987) 81 *AJIL* 116; JL Hargrove, 'The Nicaragua Judgment and the Future of the Law of Force and Self-Defense' (1987) 81 *AJIL* 135; Moore, 'The Nicaragua Case' (n 14); WM Reisman, 'The Other Shoe Falls: The Future of Article 36(1) Jurisdiction in the Light of Nicaragua' (1987) 81 *AJIL* 166; PM Norton, 'The Nicaragua Case: Political Questions before the ICJ' (1987) 27 *Va JIL* 459.

[31] Cheng, *When International Law Works* (n 14) 145–46.

was part of a large complex of interrelated political, social, economic, and security matters in the Central American Region. Second, the Court ought to have stated the reasons for deciding in favour of Nicaragua. Article 56 states that judgments shall be reasoned (arguably, it may is added, an 'order' is not a 'judgment', but that is too literal a reading of Article 56).

The criticism is not warranted. First, the Court does not address the merits in the provisional measures stage. This is an urgent procedure which is concerned only with the preservation of the object of the dispute (or the rights the claimant puts to fore) and/or the non-aggravation of the dispute as a whole. Nor was the Court at this early stage in a position to express itself on the merit arguments; it did not yet possess the necessary elements to that effect. It has to be stressed that the jurisprudence of the Court, since the times of the PCIJ, bears uninterrupted testimony to such an approach to the issues arising at the provisional measures stage. Second, the argument that the Court would have to express on the 'wider context' of the dispute seems particularly contrived, since the Court has always—rightly—rejected such arguments. Just a handful of years before the provisional measures order in *Nicaragua*, the Court had rejected, at the merits stage, exactly the same argument made by Iran against the US in the *Tehran Hostages* case of 1980.[32] The Court is not divested of its competence on a certain issue simply because a legal dispute is part of a larger context; if that were so, the Court's jurisdiction could in almost every case be stultified, since the legal dispute brought to the Court will always be part of a larger political context. Finally, the reference to Article 56 is astonishing. The orders of the Court are always reasoned in a less fulsome way than judgments; they are only provisional and express exclusively on issues relevant during the proceedings at the Court (from the seizin to the merits judgment, if any). This has been so since the first order on provisional measures by the PCIJ, in the *Sino-Belgian Treaty* case in 1927.[33] The Court did exactly the same, incidentally, in 1979, when it issued an order benefiting the US in the *Tehran Hostages* case.[34] It is moreover strange to proffer an argument that the Court has not been legalistic in not reasoning the order as if it had been a judgment (contrary to its consolidated practice), but to claim on the other hand legalism for the own argument, which openly misreads the wording of Article 56 of the Statute by including 'orders' in a provision covering only 'judgments'.

B. The Court Had No Jurisdiction

The argument that the Court lacked jurisdiction was presented in different shades. First, it has been claimed that since the Nicaraguan optional declaration had never been formally 'in force', it could not be valid under Article 36(2) of the Statute.

---

[32] *United States Diplomatic and Consular Staff in Tehran (US v Iran)* [1980] ICJ Rep 3, 19–20.
[33] *Denunciation of the Treaty of 2 November 1865 between China and Belgium (China v Belgium)* (1927) PCIJ Ser A No 8, 6.
[34] *Tehran Hostages*, Provisional Measures [1979] ICJ Rep 7, 20–21.

Thus it could not be transferred from the old to the new Court by virtue of Article 36(5) of the Statute.[35] Second, it has been affirmed that the cause of action was so inextricably linked with multilateral conventional law—that is, the UN Charter—that the Court ought to have declined jurisdiction because of the Vandenberg Reservation.[36] The cause of action should not be confused with the applicable law. Third, it has been pointed out that the Court did not have jurisdiction under the FCN Treaty's compromissory clause because of the exception on national security contained in Article XXI of the Treaty.[37]

The first argument has a certain weight but is not necessarily convincing, especially if account is taken of the unique situation of Nicaragua. In the law of the PCIJ, it was possible to issue an optional declaration before having ratified the Protocol of Signature. This declaration had then a 'potential' effect to be perfected by the deposit of the instrument of ratification of the Protocol. For many years this did not occur: Nicaragua was under foreign occupation and suffered from instability. Later it was indicated that the instrument had been sent to Geneva; it may have been lost at sea during World War II. When Nicaragua became a member of the UN, it thereby became a party to the Statute. The manifest object and purpose of Article 36(5) of the Statute was to keep intact as much as feasible the *acquis* of jurisdictional titles in respect of the PCIJ, so that the change from the PCIJ to the ICJ would not in any way impair the legal position. It is consequently understandable that the majority of judges considered that the *potential effect* (to be perfected by becoming a party to the Statute) could be transferred to the new Court, there to be perfected by the State becoming a party to the new Statute. Certainly, the wording of Article 36(5) in the English version—declarations 'still in force'—may be incompatible with such an interpretation. But it must be taken into account that: (i) the letter of the law is not always determinative of its true meaning; (ii) the drafters of the new Statute could have in mind only the normal occurrence of declarations which had not lapsed, and not unusual situations as the one of Nicaragua; (iii) in consequence, the latter situation has to be regarded as legally non-regulated by Article 36(5) of the Statute; (iv) in any case, an application by analogy of that provision to the 'potential effect' was warranted in regard of its general aim; (v) finally, the French text contains the words *'pour une durée qui n'est pas encore expirée'*, a wording that is more open than the English. It seems to refer to the idea that the declaration shall not have temporally lapsed (which the Nicaraguan declaration could not, because it had no limitation in time).

---

[35] This argument is shared by a significant number of authors. See already the various separate opinions in Nicaragua, Jurisdiction and Admissibility, [1984] ICJ Rep 392, 473ff (Judge Oda), 533ff (Judge Jennings), 563 (Judge Schwebel, dissenting). In scholarship, see, eg, Reisman, 'Exceeded Jurisdiction' (n 14) 132; Eisemann, 'L'arrêt (Competence)' (n 30) 373ff; Crawford, 'Nicaragua' (n 7) 175; Verhoeven, 'Le Droit' (n 11) 1168ff; Cheng, *When International Law Works* (n 14) 149.

[36] Moore, 'The Nicaragua Case' (n 14) 155–6; Crawford, 'Nicaragua' (n 7) 176; J Crawford, 'Chance, Order, Change: The Course of International Law' (2013) 356 *RdC* 9, 59. *cf* Lang, *L'affaire Nicaragua* (n 5) 103ff; Verhoeven, 'Le Droit' (n 11) 1175ff.

[37] Reisman, 'The Other Shoe Falls' (n 31) 166ff. *cf* Franck, 'Icy Day' (n 12) 383; Eisemann, 'L'arrêt (Compétence)' (n 35) 382.

The second argument cannot either be fully accepted. The cause of action was not a multilateral treaty: neither the UN Charter, nor the OAS Charter, nor for that matter any other. It was the unlawful use of force. The law applicable was conventional and customary. It can be argued that the two legal limbs were so closely intertwined in the present case that the Court could not meaningfully have separated them. The Court did consider this argument and concluded that the applicable rules were sufficiently similar, so that its legal findings would not remain in a legal limbo. However that may be, the argument is that, if the applicable rules are so closely linked to one another, it must have been the intention of the reserving state to except the totality of the dispute. The argument is not entirely compelling. A reservation is a unilateral act interpreted according to the text and the intention of the reserving state. The Vandenberg Declaration's text is obscure. The intent of the US seems to have been based on a legal misunderstanding. The aim of the reservation was apparently to avoid the compulsory jurisdiction of the ICJ in cases where other parties to the proceedings had not accepted the same optional clause jurisdiction.[38] However, this result flows already from Article 36(2) of the Statute: it concedes jurisdiction only among States having made an optional declaration. If that was the true aim of the reservation, the Court is right not to give it the meaning of excluding customary law jurisdiction in the present case. Moreover, since the text of the reservation is obscure,[39] the Court could have interpreted it *contra proferentem* so as not to curtail its jurisdiction.[40] If the reservation really requires the presence of all parties to a multilateral convention at the ICJ in a particular case to be able of apply that convention, this would raise the question of the compatibility of the declaration with the Statute.[41]

As to the third argument, related to the FCN Treaty, the application of the exception clause of Article XXI depends on the appreciation of the measures taken. It cannot be seriously argued that the fact that a state adopts some measures and subjectively claims that these measures are necessary for its security would suffice to deprive the Court of jurisdiction. If this were true, the compromissory clause would be deprived of efficacy and the compulsory jurisdiction of the Court would be turned into *forum prorogatum*. Since the concrete measures taken must be appreciated in the light of the exception clause, the issue is not one of jurisdiction but one of the merits. If the action of the US was allowed under the clause, this would not go to denying jurisdiction but to reject the claim of the violation of the treaty. In other words, the compromissory clause also covers the application and interpretation of the saving clause contained in Article XXI: the Court has jurisdiction to adjudge whether its conditions are fulfilled (Article 36(6) of the Statute). That is what the Court had done already in the *Tehran Hostages* case in 1980.[42]

---

[38] See the references in Lang, *L'affaire Nicaragua* (n 5) 108–09. See also A D'Amato, 'Modifying US Acceptance of the Compulsory Jurisdiction of the World Court' (1985) 79 *AJIL* 394.

[39] There is a general agreement on this point: see eg Briggs, 'Nicaragua v US' (n 28) 378; Verhoeven, 'Le Droit' (n 11) 1175ff.

[40] ibid, 1179.

[41] Briggs, 'Nicaragua v US' (n 28) 378 concludes that the reservation is not compatible with the Statute. The present author contends for the same view.

[42] *Tehran Hostages* (n 32) 18ff (especially 28).

C. The Schulz Letter Vitiated US Consent to Jurisdiction

It has been said that the Court should not have applied the six-month notice for denunciation of the optional declaration by the US. That would be unfair to states that have committed to no obligation under the optional system, and also to Nicaragua which could withdraw with immediate effect from its own declaration (lack of reciprocity).[43]

The optional declaration of the US contained a stipulation entitling it to withdraw the declaration on six months' notice. The optional declaration of the applicant, Nicaragua, contained no such clause. The US argued that, absent any restrictive wording, Nicaragua could withdraw its declaration with immediate effect. Consequently, by operation of reciprocity, the US claimed the benefit of the same right to withdraw its own declaration with immediate effect. This reasoning is defective in several ways. First, it confuses a condition as to the duration of the optional declaration with a subject-matter reservation. Second, it presupposes that an optional declaration containing no provision as to time-notice of withdrawal could be denounced with immediate effect. The Court had no difficulty in showing that this was not true and that the rule of a 'reasonable period of time' applied.[44] Third, the argument ran counter to the fact that reciprocity is applicable only once the Court is seized and between parties to a concrete case. There is no 'pre-seizin' reciprocity. At the pre-seizin stage, reciprocity would have to be multilateral and inchoate. A state could pick and choose in all other optional declarations (with no link to a case to be brought to the Court) the conditions most favourable in order to manipulate, or to withdraw from, its declaration so as to sterilise the jurisdiction of the Court. Fourth, the USA was claiming to rely on a 'reservation' against a state which had not accepted the Court's jurisdiction in terms narrower than its own. The Court stated, by way of reminder, that:

> It appears clearly that reciprocity cannot be invoked in order to excuse departure from the terms of a State's own declaration, whatever its scope, limitations or conditions ... Reciprocity enables a State which has made the wider acceptance of the jurisdiction of the Court to rely upon the reservations to the acceptance laid down by the other party. There the effect of reciprocity ends.[45]

Thus, it seems astonishing that the Court is encouraged simply to ignore a black letter condition for the denunciation of the US optional declaration. The US has freely chosen to insert this limitation: it should honour its own pledge. There is no unfairness here. The comparison of states within the optional system and states not bound by it is unheard of. It would be tantamount to compare the situation of someone bound by a contract and someone else not bound by a contract saying that it is unfair to hold the first to its contractual obligations since the second is not bound by the same obligations. According to that logic, states that are parties to

---

[43] Cheng, *When International Law Works* (n 14) 150–51.
[44] *Nicaragua*, Jurisdiction and Admissibility (n 1) 419–20.
[45] ibid, 419.

the optional system would have to be allowed to do anything they wished, simply because other states, not parties to the system, are free in relation to the Court. This would seem to project reciprocity not just onto all states parties to the system of the optional clause but onto all the states of the world. Finally, the statement that the unfairness stems from the fact that Nicaragua could withdraw with immediate effect, whereas the US could not, is unwarranted and frankly unfair. Indeed, the Court affirms exactly the opposite:[46] it affirms that Nicaragua could not denounce with immediate effect.

D. The Central Issue of the Case Was Non-justiciable

Many arguments have been raised with regard to justiciability:[47]

(i)   the Security Council was alone competent to make determinations as to the use of force under Chapter VII of the UN Charter. The ICJ should not interfere in such matters;

(ii)   it is improper to intervene in an ongoing armed conflict where the Court will have difficulties in ascertaining the facts and where many indispensable actors will be absent from the fore;

(iii)   the dispute is already pending in the Contadora political negotiation process. The Court should not interfere.

It is not necessary to refute such arguments at length. They were unanimously rejected by all judges when determining the Court's jurisdiction in 1984, including Judge Schwebel. Suffice it to say that:

(i)   the Court did not enter into qualifications under Chapter VII of the Charter that are reserved to the Security Council; neither does it review a decision of the Security Council acting under its Chapter VII powers. Rather, the Court applies the content of Articles 2(4) and 51 under customary international law.[48] There is no rule that some norms under general international law are the exclusive competence of one institutional organ. This parallel competence

---

[46] ibid, 420.

[47] See mainly Norton, 'The Nicaragua Case' (n 30) 1449ff; Kahn, 'From Nuremberg to The Hague' (n 30) 1ff; Verhoeven, 'Le Droit' (n 11) 1183ff; Eisemann, 'L'arrêt (Compétence)' (n 35) 385ff.

[48] The argument of Norton, 'The Nicaragua Case' (n 30) 471, that contrary to *Tehran Hostages*, where the US has asked the Court to rule on Iran's compliance with treaty and customary law on issues that did not fall squarely into the competence of the Security Council, the *Nicaragua* proceedings raised exactly such points, is misconceived. Nicaragua asked the Court to rule on treaty and customary positions, and further asked the Court to consider the issue under international law, not under the lens of Security Council powers. The fact that the ICJ and the Security Council can act in parallel has been accepted as a matter of jurisprudence since *Aegean Sea Continental Shelf (Greece v Turkey)*, Jurisdiction and Admissibility [1978] ICJ Rep 3. This jurisprudence has been made all the more sound by the considerable extension of the powers of the Security Council since then (most recently in relation to terrorism). It would be absurd to speculate in each case on what are the 'core powers' of that organ. The Security Council exercises its political function, the Court its judicial equivalent.

has been the constant jurisprudence of the Court also since 1986, eg in *Armed Activities (DRC v Uganda)*[49] and in the *Wall.*[50]

(ii)   The difficulties in ascertaining the facts cannot be a reason to refuse to exercise jurisdiction.[51] There are rules of evidence, and they have to be applied. These rules are of a 'private' litigation type, and this is helpful in this regard: the Court does not seek the material truth as in a criminal procedure; it decides by formal truth on the evidence as presented by the parties. If in a particular case the Court is faced with factual deficiencies so grave as not to allow it to act compatibly with judicial integrity, it could and should declare inadmissibility. Such difficulties did not arise here. Further, there are no 'indispensable parties' in a case at the ICJ. The Court will refuse to exercise jurisdiction only where the rights or obligations of a non-consenting third party have logically to be determined *before* the issue submitted in the proceedings can be decided (*Monetary Gold* principle).[52] This was not the case here.

(iii)   The fact that negotiation is pursued by the parties while the case is pending is not a reason to decline admissibility.[53] The Court often invites the parties, during the proceedings, to continue negotiation. It could hardly engage in that course if it were thereby divested of its jurisdiction. Only the claimant may decide to what extent it wishes to stay or discontinue the case on account of negotiations. Any different solution would mean that the political means to solve the dispute would automatically have the precedence over the legal one. Such a rule does not exist in international law.

It can be added that international society does not know of a 'political question' doctrine for questions on the use of force. This is true not only because there is no separation of powers and no real government in international affairs (but rather cooperation between sovereign states and therefore overlapping competencies).[54] It is also true since for municipal law tribunals issues on the use of force in international relations belong to a highly political sphere, reserved to the executive. For an international court or tribunal, rules on the use of force are extensively codified in the applicable law and pertain to the cornerstone provisions of the international legal order. It would be astonishing if the ICJ should shy away from applying the most important rules of its legal order of reference—perhaps comparable to the due process clause in US Constitutional law.

---

[49] *Armed Activities on the Territory of the Congo (DRC v Uganda)* [2005] ICJ Rep 168, 221ff.

[50] *Legal Consequences of the Construction of a Wall in the Occupied Palestinian Territory* [2004] ICJ Rep 136, 164ff. See further John Dugard, this volume, chapter 22.

[51] If that were so, the respondent could conceivably, simply by withholding facts, defeat the power of the Court to decide the dispute and thus, by extension, frustrate its compulsory jurisdiction.

[52] *Monetary Gold* (n 20) 32.

[53] Norton, 'The Nicaragua Case' (n 30) 485–86, makes a distinction between the multilateral negotiations in *Nicaragua*, where the Court should have declared inadmissibility, and the bilateral negotiations in *Tehran Hostages*, where the Court could thus proceed. The argument is manifestly self-serving and devoid of any merit: the rationale for declining to exercise jurisdiction would in both cases be exactly the same: primacy to the political process *pendente lite*. It could even be said that bilateral arrangements are statistically more promising and that the greater chance of their success should lead the Court to declare inadmissibility more readily.

[54] Chayes, 'Nicaragua' (n 30) 1474ff; Verhoeven, 'Le Droit' (n 11) 1191.

E. The Court Twisted the Evidence to Suit Nicaragua's Position

It has been contended that the Court biased the facts, in particular on aggressive actions of Nicaragua in the neighbouring states.[55]

The main problem connected with this statement is that the US, by not appearing at the merits stage and by denying certain information to the Court under the guise of national security, produced itself the situation it later complained of.[56] The information relied on by Judge Schwebel and by JN Moore is unfortunately essentially contained in *ex post facto* statements and secondary publications. It is generally of a highly partisan nature.[57] The truth is that the issue had never been considered by the Reagan administration under the legal lens of self-defence. The international legal case was mounted after the fact with hard strain. This state of affairs is not astonishing when it was common in the 1980s to hear US Secretaries of State discussing the use of force as a tool to be used discretionarily to further US interests, thereby completely ignoring the UN Charter. The debate concerned only whether the US Congress should have its say or whether the President had a free hand.[58] It is equally well known that in many interviews President Reagan had been frank enough to admit that the policy aim he pursued was to overthrow the communist government in Managua.[59] It may be possible to bring some of that action within the four corners of self-defence, but it is not easy. Moreover, contrary to what has been suggested, the Court clearly recognised aggressive action by Nicaragua.[60] But it denied that it gave rise to self-defence (no armed attack through assistance by weapons) or that the conditions for self-defence were fulfilled (on the account of timing or necessity/proportionality). Overall, the judgment of Eisemann,[61] scarcely a left-wing commentator, considering that the fact-finding of the Court was equilibrated, prudent and exact, can be approbated. It may be added that a series of authors considered that the ICJ favoured the US too much, notably in the context of the responsibility for the acts of the *contras*.[62] It may finally be recalled that all judges but one accepted the facts as the Court espoused them.

It may be asked why the US withdrew from the proceedings and omitted to present evidence at the merits stage if that evidence was, as it claims, so incredibly

---

[55] Moore, 'The Nicaragua Case' (n 14) 153. See also *Nicaragua*, Merits (n 1) 272–73 (Judge Schwebel, dissenting). *cf* Verhoeven, 'Le Droit' (n 11) 1225–26.

[56] This is fairly stated by Highet, 'Evidence' (n 28). See also Chayes, 'Nicaragua' (n 30) 1447.

[57] See Falk, 'World Court' (n 30) 111.

[58] See the debate between Secretary George Shultz and Secretary Caspar Weinberger: Chayes, 'Nicaragua' (n 30) 1480.

[59] See the quotes in ibid, 1468 fn 110.

[60] Thus, the surreptitious and suggestive insinuations in S Rosenne, *The World Court: What It Is and How It Works*, 5th edn (The Hague, Martinus Nijhoff, 1995) 152–53, recalling that in 1993 weapons were found in Managua testifying to the assistance of the Sandinistas for the rebels in El Salvador, do not prove anything new. First, the Court could not possess this piece of evidence in 1986. Second, the Court did not deny such assistance. Third, the Court recalled that the mere assistance by weapons is not an armed attack giving rise to self-defence. The discovery of 1993 thus does not change any fundamental tenet of the Court's reasoning in Nicaragua.

[61] Eisemann, 'L'arrêt (fond)' (n 28) 188.

[62] Boyle, 'US Responsibility' (n 30) 86.

overwhelming. This would have been a grave strategic error. If the evidence was not so overwhelming, the choice is easier to explain.

F. The Court Misconstrued the Law on the Use of Force

There are several criticisms here. The three main ones were as follows. First,[63] the ICJ applied too high a threshold for self-defence. In order not to tie the hands of the victim, the threshold of the armed attack should have been be lowered to include any type of armed action. The principle of proportionality should therefore be the lodestar for deciding on lawfulness or excess. Second,[64] the Court erred when it held that the assistance of rebels with weapons does not constitute an armed attack. Third,[65] the Court was overly formalistic in requiring the request of assistance by the attacked government in the exercise of collective self-defence.

The first criticism (which is not devoid of merit) has flavours of a debate of old standing.[66] The choice of the Court conformed to the reading of the UN Charter by the overwhelming majority of the members of the UN: a rule of non-use of force writ large and a self-defence exception interpreted narrowly.[67] Only the Great Powers and some other states (eg Israel) depart markedly from this view. The Court can hardly be castigated for having chosen the interpretation which corresponds to the wishes of the drafters of the Charter, is borne out by the text of the Charter ('use of force' in Article 2(4) and 'armed attack'/'agression armée' in Article 51), is endorsed in Resolutions 2625 and 3314 of the General Assembly and is preferred by the great majority of states of the international community. Even Anglo-American dominated arbitral commissions have favoured this interpretation. Thus, in the *Jus Ad Bellum* Award of the Eritrea–Ethiopia Claims Commission, it is stated: 'Localized border encounters between small infantry units, even those involving the loss of life, do not constitute an armed attack for the purposes of the Charter'.[68] This reading implies a certain sacrifice of the aggrieved state, which is not allowed to respond by force. But it avoids the spiralling down of violence and counter-violence.

Second, the Court was right to affirm that the mere assistance with weapons (without involvement on the spot as required by Article 3(g) of Resolution 3314) does not cross the threshold of an armed attack. If it were otherwise, a great number of states (a number made even greater by collective self-defence) could have taken

---

[63] See, eg, Franck, 'Some Observations' (n 30) 120; Hargrove, 'The Nicaragua Judgment' (n 30) 139. *cf* Farer, 'Drawing' (n 30) 112ff.

[64] Hargrove'The Nicaragua Judgment' (n 30) 139–40; Moore, 'The Nicaragua Case' (n 14) 154 ('flatly wrong in international law'); Cheng, *When International Law Works* (n 14) 152. *cf* Verhoeven, 'Le Droit' (n 11) 1233.

[65] Moore, 'The Nicaragua Case' (n 14) 155. See also *Nicaragua, Merits* (n 1) 544–46 (Judge Jennings, dissenting).

[66] A Randelzhofer and G Nolte, 'Article 51', in B Simma (ed), *The Charter of the United Nations: A Commentary*, 3rd edn (Oxford, OUP, 2012) vol, 2 1406ff. See also T Ruys, *Armed Attack and Article 51 of the UN Charter* (Cambridge, CUP, 2010).

[67] See O Corten, *Le droit contre la guerre*, 2nd edn (Brussels, Bruylant, 2014) 88ff, 657ff.

[68] *Partial Award: Jus Ad Bellum—Ethiopia's Claims 1–8* (2005) 26 RIAA 459, 465.

forcible measures in self-defence against the US and on the latter's territory in reaction to the massive weapons supply directed to rebels of its own obedience, eg in Angola. This can hardly be a sound legal proposition in the context of a law attempting to secure the maintenance of international peace.

Third, the request for assistance is essential for the exercise of self-defence, lest a state decide to use force in the name of some other without, or even against, the latter's will. It is unwarranted to criticise a court of justice for upholding a requirement of public order. The secrecy of the subversive war is no decisive contrary argument. The request may not have been made publicly; but there must be some trace of it. It is also of no avail to say that President Duarte had claimed to be the victim of an armed attack in press conferences; this is manifestly no demand for assistance. The assistance request was constructed after the fact. It is an indicator that the action was initially considered only in terms of policy ('overthrowing a hostile Government') and not in terms of law—even more than that: in derision and contempt for the UN Charter.

G. The Court Misconstrued Customary International Law

Some authors considered that the Court misunderstood customary international law.[69] Their main contention is that *opinio juris* cannot constitute customary law unconnected from actual behaviour in the real world. In particular, the mere voting behaviour in the context of UN resolutions is insufficient. Aspirational positions are not enough, all the more since the non-use of force rule has been so often violated since the end of World War II.

This is not the place to get entangled in a discussion on the sliding or monolithic scales of customary international law.[70] Two remarks must suffice. First,[71] the ICJ had to deal in Nicaragua essentially with negative rules, ie rules requiring an abstention: *non*-use of force; *non*-intervention; etc. In this context, the element of practice loses weight. The relevant practice would be the abstention to use force, ie the fact that State A does not attack State B now, and does not attack one second later, and again one second later, and so on; and the same for all other states.[72] This exercise is too contrived. It is therefore understandable that *opinio juris* gains ground as the only palpable element. Second,[73] the ICJ was concerned more with the identification of *existing* rules of customary international law (the *opinio juris* being the main evidence for that) rather than with the identification of *new* rules of customary

---

[69] A D'Amato, 'Trashing Customary International Law' (1987) 81 *AJIL* 101; Franck, 'Some Observations' (n 30) 119. See in response FL Kirgis Jr, 'Custom on a Sliding Scale' (1987) 81 *AJIL* 146.

[70] For a general analysis, see M Mendelson, 'The Formation of Customary International Law' (1998) 272 *RdC* 155.

[71] This was correctly foreshadowed by Verhoeven, 'Le Droit' (n 11) 1205.

[72] Contrary to what Franck ('Some Observations' (n 30) 119) suggests, 'violations' do not constitute the practice, since most of them were either simple breaches (which do not create new law) or were clothed as self-defence (thus confirming rather than denying the existing legal rules).

[73] Eisemann, 'L'arrêt (fond)' (n 28) 173–74.

international law though the process of law-creation (practice having a priori more weight in such a context).

H. The Court Went Too Far in Interpreting the Principle of Non-intervention

It has been stated[74] that the Court interpreted too broadly the principle of non-intervention. It could not be said under international law that the choice of a totalitarian dictatorship violating human rights is an internal matter. The violation of human rights runs precisely against generally accepted norms of international law, and in this case even against unilateral promises Nicaragua had assumed towards the OAS.

This criticism is only partially pertinent. The Court did not deny that the matters discussed are of international concern. It only denied that the US could intervene by coercive means on Nicaragua (the coercion is one definitional element of most patterns of prohibited intervention) in order to produce a change. Whether the Court used 'overblown' and 'antiquated worship of sovereignty'[75] is essentially a matter of personal taste. For a US observer of a certain background this may be the case, for a 'receiver' of regular US interventions the perspective may well look wholly different.

I. The Court Interpreted Certain Norms in a Manner Too Deferential to the US

There are also some reverse criticisms, ie that the Court was too deferent to the US. The argument has been made especially with regard to the attribution of acts of the *contras*,[76] through the devising of a wholly unprecedented restrictive 'effective control' criterion.[77] Another argument was that the Court should have condemned the US for the acts of the *contras* because President Reagan had publicly endorsed them by statements such as 'Their combat is our combat'. Why did the Court not apply the same standard as in *Tehran Hostages*, where Iran was held responsible in the second phase of the events for the reason that its highest authorities has endorsed by public statements the acts of the students?[78]

The Court can hardly be blamed for having been prudent on these issues of a potentially great effect on current and future affairs. The criticism on the 'endorsement' is,

---

[74] FR Tesón, 'Le Peuple, c'est moi! The World Court and Human Rights' (1987) 81 *AJIL* 173.

[75] ibid, 183.

[76] See, eg, Lang, *L'affaire Nicaragua* (n 5) 217ff; Boyle, 'US Responsibility' (n 30) 86ff. The latter's criteria of superior responsibility and criminal international law standards may well not be fully applicable to state responsibility issues.

[77] This criterion has been sharply contested in later legal debates: see, eg, the interesting but very committed article by A Cassese, 'The Nicaragua and Tadic Tests revisited in the Light of the ICJ Judgment on Genocide in Bosnia' (2007) 18 *EJIL* 649. For a different view: M Milanovic, 'State Responsibility for Genocide: A Follow-Up' (2007) 18 *EJIL* 694.

[78] Lang, *L'affaire Nicaragua* (n 5) 223.

however, more difficult to rebut. Be that as it may, it has been said not without reason that the ICJ gave the US every reasonable benefit of doubt.[79]

J. Minor Criticisms

Only three such further criticisms will be dealt with here. First, the interview of the President of the ICJ when the procedure was pending. Second, the choice of the title of the case. Third, Nicaragua's unclean hands as a reason to dismiss jurisdiction.

The first aspect was raised among others by Judge Schwebel in his dissent.[80] He complained that the then President of the ICJ, TO Elias, had given an interview to Associated Press in which he took certain positions which were scarcely compatible with even-handedness. For example: that the question was one of aggression; that certain US behaviour (such as the invasion of Grenada) was contrary to the rule of law; that modern international law could not tolerate gunboat diplomacy, etc. President Elias regretted that his words were taken out of context (a common occurrence with journalists, interested not in analysis but in strong statements). He emphasised, however, that the Court, under a new president, had condemned the US.[81]

The statements of President Elias were not contrary to the law. But it must be considered highly unfortunate for a judge of the Court to give interviews during a procedure (or even thereafter) and to take clear positions on issues under consideration.

The second aspect is also pointed out by Judge Schwebel.[82] The title chosen sounds to him like a pre-condemnation of the US. It shows that the Court has not properly understood the case. The title, framed in the sole perspective of the claimant, could be compared unfavourably with the neutral formula in *Corfu Channel*.

The criticism is not entirely sound. The object of the dispute is fixed by the claimant in its request; it can be enlarged or altered by a counter-claim of the defendant. In the *Corfu Channel* case the responsibility for the mining activity was not the central issue; the central point was the legal consequences for non-warning of the presence of the mines, as well as some related issues (eg the sweeping of the mines). At a push, the case might have been called *Mines in the Corfu Channel* case. Here, by contrast, Nicaragua complained exactly of what is in the title of the case: the military and paramilitary activities in and against Nicaragua. If the US wished to enlarge the object to the armed activities in El Salvador it should have brought a counter-claim. Nevertheless, it can be conceded that neutral titles are better, as the ones the Court used later for such affairs: *Armed Activities in the Territory of—*...

The last aspect is also canvassed in the opinion of Judge Schwebel.[83] Nicaragua had, in his view, come to the ICJ with terribly dirty hands. Since it is the true

---

[79] Falk, 'World Court' (n 30)106.
[80] *Nicaragua*, Merits (n 1) 315 (Judge Schwebel, dissenting).
[81] ibid, 179–90 (Judge Elias).
[82] ibid, 320–21 (Judge Schwebel, dissenting).
[83] ibid, 392ff.

aggressor, the Court ought to have declared its submissions inadmissible. He who seeks equity must come in equity; *ex dolo malo non oritur actio*.

This last criticism is legally unfounded. International law knows of the doctrine of estoppel (which applies under quite exacting conditions) but not of a doctrine of clean hands as a condition of admissibility for judicial claims.[84] The doctrine could in any event not apply at the admissibility level: if a state comes with dirty hands, this should not mean that its claims are to be barred in entirety, but rather that possible damages will be partially set off in regard to previous torts on the merits stage. If it where otherwise, any equitable apportionment of the torts would become impossible, since the inadmissibility operates *in limie litis* and *en bloc*. Why should the judge rebut one state completely when its dirty hands are only partial or when the other party also has dirty hands? Moreover, the discussion on the 'degree of cleanness' of hands could emerge in almost every case. The relations between nations are complex. One of the arguments of Iran in the *Tehran Personnel* case of 1980 was precisely that the US had unclean hands in relation to Iran and that the Court should therefore dismiss it claim; two judges endorsed this argument.[85] It is better not to open the Pandora's Box of political quibbling and moralist undertones in this regard. Indeed, judicial practice has refused to venture into such a slippery avenue.

* * *

For JN Moore, counsel to the US in the proceedings, the merits judgment was a 'tragedy for world order'. It allows secret war by the totalitarians and at the same time curtails democratic response.[86] Along the same lines, T Franck affirms that the merits judgment would have unfortunate implications for the rule of law.[87] At the other end of the spectrum, it has been contended that the Court lived up to its judicial responsibility through a judgment that will remain in the annals.[88] It has been added that 'anyone with even a 25% open mind is likely to be convinced by the majority opinion'.[89] It may not be too much to say that the Court upheld the international *rule* of law by its judgments; it is even more certain that it was steadfast on the *rules* of law. The true test for intellectual fairness is to reverse the situation or to mask it behind a veil of ignorance: what would the position be if Nicaragua had intervened on US territory in the way the US had done on Nicaraguan territory, in order to react to massive US anti-communist intervention in Central America in order to overthrow the Government? Or: how should the situation be judged if the issue were presented as a contention between States A and B, whose ideological sidings we ignore?

---

[84] See R Kolb, *La bonne foi en droit international public* (Paris, PUF, 2000) 568ff.

[85] *Tehran Hostages* (n 32) 53–55 (Judge Morozo, dissenting), 62–63 (Judge Tarazi, dissenting).

[86] Moore, 'The Nicaragua Case' (n 14) 152. *cf* Verhoeven, 'Le Droit' (n 11) 1237.

[87] Franck, 'Some Observations' (n 30) 121.

[88] Eisemann, 'L'arrêt (fond)' (n 28) 153–55; Lang, *L'affaire Nicaragua* (n 5) 1; Briggs, 'The ICJ' (n 28) 78–79, 86; G Abi-Saab, 'Cours général de droit international public' (1987) 207 *RdC* 9, 272–74.

[89] Falk, 'World Court' (n 30) 112.

V. AFTERMATH OF THE CASE

The follow-up of the *Nicaragua* judgments is characterised by two contradictory wings. First, the rejection of the judgments by the US and the fact that the merits judgment was never implemented. Second, the importance of the judgments for the determination and development of international law, as well as for the Court itself. It overcame its crisis of the 1970s through the drum roll of these double C Major utterances. The first point will be developed in this section, while the second will be developed in the next.

A. Rejection of the Judgments by the US

After the Court had issued its 1984 Judgment on jurisdiction and admissibility, the US State Department, in a declaration dated 18 January 1985, pointed out that it would not participate in the further proceedings in this case.[90] In October 1985, the US withdrew its optional declaration under Article 36(2) of the ICJ Statute. The Court was accused of anti-Western bias; the dispute was termed as political and not suitable for adjudication. After the Court had rendered its merits judgment, the US persisted in an attitude of open defiance. The issue of reparation for the damages caused remained open for negotiation, according to the ruling of the ICJ in the 1986 Judgment. However, the cessation of the unlawful intervention in Nicaragua was the main aspect on which the implementation of the judgment was sought by the claimant. True, the judgment produced some indirect material effect: the US Congress became progressively more active in curbing the Nicaraguan activities of the Reagan administration.[91] But on the formal plane the non-compliance remained.

B. Follow-up of the Proceedings Before the Security Council and General Assembly[92]

By a letter dated 17 October 1986, Nicaragua seized the Security Council of the UN under Article 94(2) of the UN Charter in order to demand consideration of the non-compliance by the US with the judgment of the Court.[93] A draft resolution by Third World states provided for the full and immediate implementation of the

---

[90] For the reaction of the US, see the document extracted at (1986) 80 *AJIL* 423.

[91] See Lang, *L'affaire Nicaragua* (n 5) 274; A Azar, *L'exécution des décisions de la Cour internationale de Justice* (Brussels, Bruylant, 2003) 100.

[92] On this issue, see A Tanzi, 'Problems of Enforcement of Decisions of the International Court of Justice and the Law of the United Nations' (1995) 6 *EJIL* 539ff, particularly 544ff; A Tanzi, 'Diritto ed esecuzione della sentenza della Corte internazionale di Giustizia tra Nicaragua e Stati Uniti' (1970) 70 *RDI* 293ff. See also C Schulte, *Compliance with Decisions of the International Court of Justice* (Oxford, OUP, 2004) 184ff; A Azar, *L'exécution des décisions de la Cour internationale de Justice* (Brussels, Bruylant, 2003), at various pages mentioned in the index at 322.

[93] UN Doc S/18414 (10 November 1986).

judgment. It was vetoed by the US[94]—a course regretted by certain members of the Security Council. The US was the sole state to vote against the draft; France and the UK abstained. Nicaragua considered that the veto should not have impeached the triggering of the resolution: (i) first, because the US as the directly interested party would have had to abstain (*nemo judex in causa sua*); (ii) second, since according to Resolution 267(III), sponsored by the US itself, decisions to remind members of the UN of their obligations under the UN Charter were to be considered procedural questions to which Article 27(2) of the Charter applied (no veto). A legal analysis of these arguments is beyond the scope of this chapter.[95]

After this rebuffing, Nicaragua presented the same draft resolution defeated in the Security Council to the UN General Assembly.[96] The draft resolution was adopted by 94 votes against three (El Salvador, Israel and the US), with 47 abstentions.[97] The power of the General Assembly to express on this matter rested on Article 10 of the Charter. The resolution of the General Assembly was a mere recommendation. It could not add anything to the obligation of the US under Article 94(1) of the UN Charter and Article 59 of the ICJ Statute.

Finally, elections were held in Nicaragua and the opposition won. The newly elected Government, with V Chamorro at its head, tried to normalise the relations with the US.[98] The deal was to drop the implementation of the *Nicaragua* judgment and to abandon any interventionist policy against the resumption of friendly relations with the US. In the context of this deal, the case was withdrawn from the Court.[99]

It can thus be said that the merits judgment was never implemented. In particular, no indemnity was ever paid. Formally, however, damages were not due any more since Nicaragua had withdrawn its demand. Materially speaking, the US awarded Nicaragua's new Government important sums for reconstruction. In this informal sense, it can be considered that the US paid for the losses it had caused through the armed activities the Court condemned in the 1986 judgment. Overall, this Judgment remains one of the rare stubbornly non-implemented substantive pronouncements of the ICJ.

VI. IMPORTANCE OF THE JUDGMENTS

In the US (and to some extent in the Western) literature immediately after the decisions, the fear was expressed that the bold course of the Court—which dared to condemn a great power basing itself on a not wholly solid jurisdictional basis—would

---

[94] UN Doc S/PV.2718 (28 October 1986) 51.
[95] See however Tanzi, 'Diritto ed esecuzione della sentenza' (n 92) 296ff.
[96] UN Doc A/41/L.22 (1986).
[97] UN Doc A/41/PV.53 (15 November 1999) 92.
[98] B Stern, *20 ans de jurisprudence de la Cour internationale de Justice* (The Hague, Martinus Nijhoff, 1998) 406.
[99] *Nicaragua*, Order of 26 September 1991 [1991] ICJ Rep 47, 47–48.

lead to a decline of the optional clause jurisdiction and more generally to a decline of the ICJ.[100] Those apprehensions proved not be be warranted. They corresponded to an excessively self-referred conception of the surrounding reality. The US or the West are not the world; the Court is not successful or unsuccessful only against the rod of what a commentator thinks to be a proper course within his ideological framework—and times change. In reality, the *Nicaragua* judgments turned out to be among the most important judgments the Court ever delivered. They have to this day remained benchmarks and cornerstones in the jurisprudence of the Court. This was so on two accounts: it was so on the law; and it was so for the role of the Court.

A. Significance of *Nicaragua* for International Law Generally

On the determination and development of international law, the judgments are of paramount importance. They clarified many issues of international law and are con-stantly quoted as authority on these points: the denunciation of optional clauses; their legal nature (applicability of the law of treaties by analogy); the scope of Article 36(5) of the Statute in the transfer of jurisdiction from the PCIJ to the ICJ; the role of conduct in the jurisdiction of the Court; the interpretation of compromissory clauses and in particular the objective or self-judging construction of saving clauses; the Vandenberg reservation's scope; issues of justiciability in the context of ongoing armed conflicts and of politically loaded disputes; the scope of Article 53 of the Statute (non-appearance); the main rules on fact-finding; the issue of attribution of acts by armed groups; the role and complexion of customary international law (especially the role of *opinio juris*); the scope and construction of the rules on the use of force (non-use of force, self-defence); the issue of 'indirect aggression' through the assistance to armed bands; the scope and interpretation of necessity and propor-tionality in self-defence; the importance of a call for assistance of the victim state in the exercise of collective self-defence; the reach and definition of the principle of non-intervention in internal affairs (the most important definition of the principle in the whole case-law is to be found in the merits case); the reach and conditions for counter-measures; the definition of core principles of IHL and the role of common Article 1 of the Geneva Conventions of 1949; the principles of humanitarian assis-tance; the conditions for the binding character of unilateral promises; the permis-sible reactions to human rights violations by a third State; the issue of armaments; the question of the object and purpose of the treaty as an autonomous title of breach of the treaty, etc.

Never had a judgment of the ICJ spanned such a rich array of international law questions. The ICJ's rulings have been confirmed as good law in many instances thereafter. Thus, for example, the attribution test of 'effective control' was adopted

---

[100] See, eg, MJ Glennon, 'Protecting the Court's Institutional Interests: Why not the Marbury Approach' (1987) 81 *AJIL* 116, 121; Reisman, 'Exceeded Jurisdiction' (n 14) 134; Norton, 'The Nicaragua Case' (n 30) 526; *Nicaragua*, Merits (n 1) 297 (Judge Schwebel, dissenting).

by the ILC in its codification of the Law of State Responsibility.[101] The Court itself reiterated it and gave it further refinement in the *Bosnian Genocide* case of 2007.[102] The law on the use of force was also crystallised by the 1986 Judgment. It constitutes to this day the leading case of the ICJ on the matter. All the following judgments on the same subject matter having built on it.[103] Indeed, the very fact that the Court was seized of such a high-level dispute has been saluted by some authors as an important progress of international law in world affairs.[104]

B. Institutional Significance of Nicaragua

On the life of the Court, all the predictions that the Nicaragua judgments would inaugurate a phase of decline have proven to be wrong. The Court had indeed suffered from a crisis after the 1966 *South-West Africa* cases,[105] especially towards the growing number of Third World states. In 1986 the tide had turned. The Nicaragua judgments reconciled many new states with the Court, which was seen as courageous and steadfast. Since that time, the flow of cases at the Court would see a constant increase. In particular African states and later states from all over the world began to litigate regularly at the ICJ. Western states also returned. As has been aptly observed, the Nicaragua judgments constitute a watershed: they increased the credibility of the ICJ in the eyes of most states.[106] The same can be said of the prediction of decline of the optional clause. The truth is that this decline has been halted since 1986. Thus, for example, all the new cases of 2014 were based on the optional declarations.[107]

---

[101] ILC *Ybk* 2001/II(2), 20ff. The same principle has been heeded in the context of the responsibility of international organisations, see the ILC's Draft Articles on the Responsibility of International Organizations: see *Official Records of the General Assembly, Sixty-sixth Session, Supplement No 10*, UN Doc A/66/10, §§77ff.

[102] *Application of the Convention on the Prevention and Punishment of the Crime of Genocide (Bosnia and Herzegovina v Serbia and Montenegro)* [2007] ICJ Rep 43, 206ff.

[103] See, eg, *Armed Activities (DRC v Uganda)* (n 49).

[104] M Bedjaoui, 'L'humanité en quête de paix et de développement, Cours général de droit international public' (2006) 325 *RdC* 9, 90–92. Fore a more sceptical view on this type of disputes, see L Caflisch, 'Cent Ans de règlement pacifique des différends interétatiques' (2001) 288 *RdC* 357, 441.

[105] RJ Dupuy, 'L'adaptation de la Cour internationale de Justice au monde d'aujourd'hui' (1972) 18 *AFDI* 265; H Golsong, 'Role and Functioning of the International Court of Justice' (1971) 31 *ZaöRV* 673; L Gross, 'The International Court of Justice: Consideration of Requirements for Enhancing its Role in the International Legal Order' (1971) 65 *AJIL* 253; M Lachs, 'La Cour internationale de Justice dans le monde d'aujourd'hui' (1975) 11 *RBDI* 548; S Petrén, 'Some Thoughts on the Future of the International Court of Justice' (1975) 6 *NYIL* 59; M Scerni, 'Considerazioni su la crisi della Corte internazionale di giustizia' (1975) 14 *CeS* 777; L Gross (ed), *The Future of the International Court of Justice* (Dobbs Ferry, Oceana, 1976); L Gross, 'Underutilization of the International Court of Justice' (1986) 27 *Harv ILJ* 571; RA Falk, Reviving the World Court (Charlottesville, University Press of Virginia, 1986). See also RP Anand, 'Attitude of the 'New' Asian-African Countries Towards the International Court of Justice' (1962) 4 *Int'l Stud* 119; JA De Yturriaga Barbesan, 'Atitud de los nuevos Estados ante el Tribunal internacional de justicia' (1965) 18 *REDI* 175; WL Williams (ed), *Attitudes of the Lesser Developed Countries Toward the International Court of Justice* (Washington, World Association of Lawyers, 1976).

[106] G Abi-Saab, 'Cours général de droit international public' (1987) 207 *RdC* 9, 274.

[107] See R Kolb, 'Chronique de la jurisprudence de la Cour internationale de Justice en 2014' (2015) 25 *RSDIE* 121.

The majority of the cases on the docket of the Court are now based on the optional clause-title of jurisdiction, ie the so-called 'compulsory jurisdiction'. Overall, the *Nicaragua* judgments proved healthy for the Court. Rather than being confined to uttering a series of minor judgments on secondary disputes, the pronouncement in this important proceeding produced a symbolic upshot and inaugurated a new phase in the venerable story of the International Court. There exist drum-roll symphonies—and also drum-roll judgments.

16

Tadić v Prosecutor (1995)

SARAH MH NOUWEN AND MICHAEL A BECKER[1]

I. INTRODUCTION: WHEN I SAY TADIĆ, YOU SAY ...

S AY 'TADIĆ' TO a group of international lawyers, and you'll receive a wide-range of responses: 'joint criminal enterprise', 'primacy', 'Cassese'. The international humanitarian lawyer's first association could well be 'war crimes in non-international armed conflicts' or 'sexual violence'; the generalist may think of 'judicial review of the Security Council' or 'effective control'. This is but a partial list; the case of *Tadić v Prosecutor* stands for many things in international law. No matter how small Duško Tadić may be, physically or figuratively, he is a giant in international law because of the landmark case law that bears his name.

If a landmark is a distinguishing feature in the landscape, we can consider at least two types of landmarks: signposts for other travellers, indicating the direction to be followed, or high-water points, relics of a particular moment in time. Against that background, we can consider whether *Tadić* stands as a signpost that has directed legal travellers down new paths, or whether *Tadić* reflects a mere stopping-off point, since abandoned by international lawyers.

This chapter considers the significance of the *Tadić* case in both senses of landmark. It does so first by reflecting upon the case as a matter of diplomatic and legal history (Part II). It then analyses one decision from the *Tadić* case—the interlocutory appeal decided by the Appeals Chamber on 2 October 1995[2]—as a landmark with respect to three areas of international law (Part III): general international law; international humanitarian law; and international criminal law. It concludes with a perspective on the significance of the interlocutory appeal for legal reasoning in international law (Part IV).

[1] This work was supported by the Economic and Social Research Council (Grant Number ES/L010976/1), the Leverhulme Trust (PLP-2014-067), and the Isaac Newton Trust (RG79578).
[2] *Prosecutor v Tadić* (Decision on Defence Motion for Interlocutory Appeal on Jurisdiction) IT-94-1-AR72 (2 October 1995) (hereinafter *Tadić* (Interlocutory Appeal)). Electronic versions of the court documents from the *Tadić* proceedings are available on the ICTY website at <www.icty.org/case/tadic/4> accessed 21 February 2017.

II. *TO BE A TADIĆ*: THE SIGNIFICANCE OF *TADIĆ* IN DIPLOMATIC AND LEGAL HISTORY

Tadić is a landmark in simplest terms because it was the first case before the International Criminal Tribunal for the former Yugoslavia (ICTY or the Tribunal)—the first international criminal tribunal since Nuremberg and Tokyo. His horrible acts notwithstanding, Tadić was not among those most responsible for the crimes in the context of the Balkan wars. He was prosecuted because the opportunity to do so presented itself and this gave the Tribunal the chance to mobilise its machinery. In that way, too, *Tadić* is a landmark: *to be a Tadić*—to be the first defendant, even if one's relative importance to the precipitating events is low and one's trial is a prosecution of opportunity—has become a regular feature in international criminal law.

A. A Prosecution of Historic Significance

On 25 May 1993, the United Nations Security Council decided 'to establish an international tribunal for the sole purpose of prosecuting persons responsible for serious violations of international humanitarian law committed in the territory of the former Yugoslavia' after 1 January 1991.[3] The Security Council took this step approximately two years after the chaotic dissolution of the former Yugoslavia had begun. By this point, media coverage and an expert commission created by the UN had publicised wide-scale atrocities that evoked the horrors of the Second World War.[4]

The ICTY was the first international criminal tribunal ever established by the UN Security Council. No longer constrained by Cold War-era politics, and without any of the permanent members directly involved in the conflict, the Security Council acted unanimously. Using its Chapter VII powers, the Council created the Tribunal as an instrument of international peace and security, but its members did not present a unified theory as to how an international criminal tribunal would serve this aim. Instead, members provided diverging justifications, ranging from retribution to prevention, from securing respect for international law to encouraging a peace process.[5] The transcripts of the relevant Security Council meetings create the impression that Council members, under pressure to act and frustrated with the disrespect for its previous resolutions concerning the violence, wanted to be seen as taking a forceful measure, short of military action.[6]

---

[3] UNSC Res 827 (25 May 1993) UN Doc S/RES/827. The Security Council had already decided in February 1993 that a tribunal would be established and had directed the Secretary-General to produce a report aimed at operationalising that decision. UNSC Res 808 (22 February 1993) UN Doc S/RES/808. The Secretary-General's report (UN Doc S/25704 (3 May 1993)) contained the proposed statute for the tribunal ('the Statute'), which the Security Council adopted in Resolution 827.

[4] The Secretary-General established the Commission of Experts pursuant to a request by the Security Council set forth in UNSC Res 780 (6 October 1992) UN Doc S/RES/780 [2].

[5] See UNSC Verbatim Record (22 February 1993) UN Doc S/PV.3175; UNSC Verbatim Record (25 May 1993) UN Doc S/PV.3217.

[6] ibid. See, for instance, the statement by the President of the Council, speaking in his capacity as representative of Morocco: 'In establishing the principle of a war crimes tribunal, the Council is responding to the unanimous wish of the international community, which for almost two years has been deploring the acts in question and strongly calling for punishment and action'. (S/PV.3175 (22 February 1993) 27).

Whilst its significance for the former Yugoslavia has been debated,[7] the ICTY's establishment was a watershed moment for international lawyers. It revitalised the field of international criminal law. Even if the Tribunal had not gone on to indict and try far more significant figures—Milosević, Karadzić, Mladić—Tadić's trial stood for the *possibility* of prosecuting individual perpetrators under international law in an international court. As it has turned out, the *Tadić* case was not just a high-water point, but a signpost: the first of many such prosecutions over the past quarter century—a grim record of accomplishment.

B. A Prosecution of Opportunity

In its early days, the Tribunal faced lukewarm support from states, including the permanent members of the Security Council. The appointment of a prosecutor was delayed, budgets were insufficient, and the cooperation needed to secure evidence and arrest alleged perpetrators was lacking. Not a single suspect had been apprehended and transported to The Hague a year after its establishment, and the war in Bosnia raged on. The ICTY seemed expensive and ineffective. And then came Duško Tadić.

On 12 February 1994, German police arrested Tadić in Munich, where he had been living for several months, on suspicion of having committed offences at the notorious Omarska camp in the former Yugoslavia in June 1992.[8] German prosecutors intended to prosecute Tadić on the basis of universal jurisdiction over war crimes. However, on 8 November 1994 the Tribunal formally requested that Germany instead defer to the ICTY and transfer Tadić to its custody.[9] While that request was pending, the Tribunal indicted Tadić in February 1995. A few months later the defendant found himself standing in the dock at The Hague.[10]

The final amended indictment contained charges relating to the rape, unlawful killing, torture and cruel treatment of Bosnian Muslims and Bosnian Croats, involving 13 deaths and the torture and abuse of at least 18 people.[11] Following a 79-day trial in 1996, Tadić was convicted of crimes against humanity and war crimes under customary law, but acquitted on the charges relating to grave breaches of the Geneva

---

[7] *cf* WM Reisman, 'Institutions and Practices for Restoring and Maintaining Public Order (1995–96) 6 *Duke J Comp & Int'l L* 175, 182–83 with RJ Goldstone, 'Justice as a Tool for Peace-Making: Truth Commissions and International Criminal Tribunals' (1995–96) 28 *NYU J Int'l L & Pol* 485, 488–90 and M Milanovic, 'The Impact of the ICTY on the Former Yugoslavia: An Anticipatory Postmortem' (2016) 110 *AJIL* 233.

[8] S Kinzer, 'Germans Arrest Serb as Balkan War Criminal' *New York Times* (16 February 1994) <www.nytimes.com/1994/02/16/world/germans-arrest-serb-as-balkan-war-criminal.html> accessed 21 February 2017; *Prosecutor v Tadić* (Judgment) IT-94-I-T, T Ch II (7 May 1997) [6]. The amended indictment on which Tadić faced trial included an expanded list of alleged offences, beyond those alleged to have taken place at Omarska.

[9] *Prosecutor v Tadić* (Decision of the Trial Chamber on the Application by the Prosecutor for a Formal Request for Deferral) IT-94-1-D, T Ch I (8 November 1994).

[10] Tadić made his initial appearance before the Tribunal on 26 April 1995. *Tadić Case*, Transcript (26 April 1995).

[11] *Prosecutor v Tadić*, Second Amended Indictment (14 December 1995).

Conventions. The Appeals Chamber overturned the acquittal, however, and found Tadić also guilty of grave breaches and of additional war crimes and crimes against humanity.[12] He was sentenced to 25 years' imprisonment,[13] which was reduced on appeal to 20 years.[14] After serving most of his post-trial sentence in Germany, Tadić was granted early release in 2008.[15]

In the grand scheme of the Balkan wars, Tadić was 'small fry'.[16] A café owner, karate instructor and former president of the local board of the Serb Democratic Party in the town of Kozarac, 10 km east of Prijedor in north-western Bosnia, Tadić was at most a 'savage pawn in the Bosnian Serb forces' and not a leading figure on the level of the Nazi defendants at Nuremberg.[17] Richard Goldstone, the Tribunal's first prosecutor, later observed that it was 'highly unsatisfactory that someone at the level of Duško Tadić'—as opposed to a higher profile defendant—'should face trial and that those who incited and facilitated his conduct should escape justice', but he also explained that there had been no real choice: 'Tadić was the only accused available to bring before the Tribunal at a time when the judges, the media, and the international community were clamoring for us to begin prosecutions.'[18]

Yet there were certain advantages to the Tribunal cutting its teeth on a low-level figure. It began the accumulation and evaluation of evidence that established a foundation for more complicated trials—the 'big fish'. It also informed victims that the ICTY would pursue 'their' perpetrators, those with blood on their hands, and signaled to negotiating parties that the Tribunal's work need not threaten the peace process. And most of all, *Tadić* gave the Tribunal an occasion to assert its competence, in multiple senses.

This history suggests one landmark aspect of the *Tadić* case—the idea of the initial test case: the defendant who may be 'small fry' but whose presence in the dock, whether by design or chance, provides the opportunity for a court or tribunal to mobilise its machinery. Thus 'to be a Tadić'—to be the first defendant, even if one's relative importance to the conflict is low—is a phenomenon that has reappeared in other international and domestic contexts (for example, Thomas Lubanga at the International Criminal Court (ICC)[19] or Thomas Kwoyelo at the Ugandan War Crimes Court).[20]

---

[12] *Prosecutor v Tadić* (Judgment) ICTY-41-1-A, A Ch (15 July 1999).

[13] *Prosecutor v Tadić* (Sentencing Judgment) IT-94-1-T, T Ch (14 July 1997); *Prosecutor v Tadić* (Sentencing Judgment) IT-94-1-Tbis-R177, T Ch (11 November 1999).

[14] *Prosecutor v Tadić* (Judgment) IT-94-1-A, IT-94-1-Abis, A Ch (26 January 2000).

[15] *Prosecutor v Tadić* (Decision of the President on the Application for Pardon or Commutation of Sentence of Dusko Tadić) IT-94-1-ES (17 July 2008).

[16] For instance, neither Misha Glenny's journalistic account of the Balkan Crisis (*The Fall of Yugoslavia*, 3rd edn (London, Penguin Books, 1996)) nor Richard Holbrooke's memoire of the negotiations leading up to Dayton (*To End a War* (New York, Random House, 1998)) mention Tadić.

[17] GJ Bass, *Stay the Hand of Vengeance: The Politics of War Crimes Tribunals* (Princeton, Princeton University Press, 2000) 206.

[18] Interview with Richard Goldstone, cited in M Scharf, 'The Prosecutor v Dusko Tadić: An Appraisal of the First International War Crimes Trial Since Nuremberg' (1997) 60 *Albany LR* 861, 876.

[19] *Prosecutor v Lubanga* (Judgment pursuant to Article 74 of the Statute) ICC-01/04-01/06-2842, ICC Trial Chamber (14 March 2012).

[20] The International Crimes Division of the High Court of Uganda was established pursuant to the Juba peace negotiations between Uganda and the Lord's Resistance Army. Its intended first case, against Kwoyelo, however, has faced multiple obstacles. See *Thomas Kwoyelo v Uganda* High Court-001-ICD

The remainder of this chapter is limited to only one of many legal decisions gener-ated by the *Tadić* proceedings: *Tadić v Prosecutor, Decision on the Defence Motion for Interlocutory Appeal on Jurisdiction* that was decided by the Appeals Chamber in October 1995. Our observations on the landmark status of the *Tadić* case thus do not address well-known and important pronouncements in, for instance, the Appeals Chamber judgment of 15 July 1999 on the concept of 'joint criminal enter-prise', the criterion of 'overall control' as opposed to 'effective control', and whether discriminatory intent is an element of crimes against humanity.[21]

III. THE CONTRIBUTION OF THE INTERLOCUTORY APPEAL TO INTERNATIONAL LAW

The Appeal Chamber's decision addressed the defence motion that the Tribunal lacked jurisdiction to try the case (or, in fact, any case). Tadić challenged the Tribu-nal's jurisdiction on three main grounds: (i) that the establishment of the Tribunal was unlawful; (ii) that the Tribunal lacked primacy over national courts; and (iii) that the Tribunal lacked subject-matter jurisdiction.[22] The Trial Chamber had held that it lacked competence to consider the lawfulness of the decision by the Security Council to establish the ICTY and dismissed the claims relating to primacy and subject-matter jurisdiction.[23] The Appeals Chamber affirmed the result, but on different grounds. The expansive, ground-breaking, and controversial reasoning and conclusions of the Appeals Chamber are what has made this *Tadić* decision a legal landmark.

A. Contributions to General International Law

Tadić's first set of objections focused on whether the Security Council could establish an international criminal tribunal and whether the ICTY was established 'by law' and could lawfully exert 'primacy' over national courts. These objections raised two preliminary questions: (1) whether the Appeals Chamber had the jurisdiction to entertain these claims as an interlocutory appeal given that Rule 72(b) of the ICTY Rules of Procedure and Evidence limited interlocutory appeal to cases 'of dismissal of an objection based on lack of jurisdiction'; and (2) whether the Tribunal had the authority to consider a challenge to the validity of its establishment, as a matter of jurisdiction or otherwise.

Case no 02/2010, 22 September 2011 (Constitutional Court of Uganda), *Uganda v Thomas Kwoyelo* [2015] UGSC 5, 8 April 2015 (Supreme Court of Uganda), and SMH Nouwen, *Complementarity in the Line of Fire: The Catalysing Effect of the International Criminal Court in Uganda and Sudan* (Cambridge, CUP, 2013) 215–27.

[21] *Prosecutor v Tadić* (Judgment) (n 12).
[22] *Tadić* (Interlocutory Appeal) (n 2) [2].
[23] *Prosecutor v Tadić* (Decision on the Defence Motion on Jurisdiction) IT-94-I-T, T Ch (10 August 1995) (hereinafter Trial Chamber Decision on Jurisdiction).

i. Did the Appeals Chamber Have the Jurisdiction to Entertain These Claims as an Interlocutory Appeal?

The Prosecutor argued that Tadić's claims about the Tribunal's establishment and primacy over national courts were not issues of 'jurisdiction', and therefore not subject to interlocutory appeal. The Appeals Chamber rejected a 'narrow interpretation of the concept of jurisdiction' that would 'fall foul of a modern vision of the administration of justice'. As argument it advanced mostly 'common sense', to which it referred directly and through rhetorical questions:

> All the grounds of contestation relied upon by Appellant result, in the final analysis, in an assessment of the legal capability of the International Tribunal to try his case. What is this, if not in the end a question of jurisdiction? And what body is legally authorized to pass on that issue, if not the Appeals Chamber of the International Tribunal?

The Appeals Chamber concluded that it was 'indisputable' that Tadić's objection to the legality of the Tribunal's creation was a jurisdictional matter.[24]

If that decision amounts to a landmark, it is probably a high-water point, a relic of a particular moment in time. The ICTY judges themselves turned the tide in 2000 by amending the Rules of Procedure to exclude challenges to the Tribunal's legality from an exhaustive list of possible motions on jurisdiction.[25] Whereas the ICTY, and subsequently, the International Criminal Tribunal for Rwanda (ICTR) excluded such challenges only after they had at least once been litigated,[26] the Special Tribunal for Lebanon (STL) incorporated similar limitations in their Rules of Procedure and Evidence from the outset.[27] Nonetheless, the STL Appeals Chamber in *El Sayed* found a right to interlocutory appeal even where the Rules of the STL limited this right. That Chamber happened to be presided over by the same jurist that presided over the Appeals Chamber in *Tadić*: Judge Antonio Cassese. In his Scheduling Order in *El Sayed*, Cassese acknowledged the limitations on interlocutory appeal, but considered that 'in case of ambiguity, the Tribunal shall interpret the Rules inter alia in a manner consistent with the spirit of the Statute and the general principles of international criminal procedure'.[28] The subject matter of the appeal was different than in *Tadić* (namely whether the STL had jurisdiction over a request for evidence from a non-defendant who alleged that he had been unlawfully imprisoned, including briefly in the custody of the STL), but *El Sayed* reads as an effort by Cassese to consolidate the approach in *Tadić* which it expressly recalls.[29] However, after

---

[24] *Tadić* (Interlocutory Appeal) (n 2) [6].

[25] See RPE Rule 72(D). *See Prosecutor v Tolimir* (Decision on Zdravko Tolimir's Appeal Against the Decision on Submissions of the Accused Concerning Legality of Arrest) IT-05-SS/2-AR72.2 (12 March 2009) [11]–[12], with further references in fn 23; see also *Prosecutor v Karadzic* (Decision on the Accused's Motion Challenging the Legal Validity and Legitimacy of the Tribunal) IT-95-5/1S-T (7 December 2009) [8]. But see *Prosecutor v Milosevic* (Decision on Preliminary Motions) IT-02-54, T Ch (8 November 2001) [5]–[17].

[26] As noted below (n 46), the ICTR addressed an initial challenge to its legality in *Prosecutor v Kanyabashi* (Decision on the Defence Motion on Jurisdiction) ICTR-96-15-T (18 June 1997). The ICTR amended its rules in 2003 to narrow the grounds on which a defendant could challenge jurisdiction.

[27] Special Tribunal for Lebanon, Rules of Procedure and Evidence, 10 June 2009, STL/BD/2009/01/Rev.1 (adopted on 20 March 2009) (amended on 5 June 2009), Rule 90.

[28] Special Tribunal for Lebanon, the President, Scheduling Order, Ch/Pres/2010/02 (1 October 2010) 2.

[29] Special Tribunal for Lebanon, *El Sayed* (Decision on Appeal of Pre-Trial Judge's Order Regarding Jurisdiction and Standing) CH/AC/2010/02, Appeals Chamber (10 November 2010) [41].

Judge Cassese passed away in 2011, a differently constituted STL Appeals Chamber in another case, *Ayyash et al*, expressly disavowed the reasoning of the Appeals Chamber in *Tadić* and found that the broad scope given to jurisdictional challenges at the time of *Tadić* was justifiable only because the ICTY's Rules of Procedure and Evidence had not then defined the term jurisdiction.[30]

ii. Did the Tribunal Have Jurisdiction to Review the Legality of Its Own Creation?

In *Tadić*, the Prosecutor took the position that the ICTY could not review the legality of its establishment. The Trial Chamber agreed, finding that the question of the validity of the Tribunal's creation was not a matter of 'jurisdiction',[31] that the Tribunal was 'not a constitutional court set up to scrutinize the actions of organs of the United Nations' and had 'no authority to investigate the legality of its creation by the Security Council'.[32]

The Appeals Chamber, however, rejected 'a distinction between the validity of the creation of the International Tribunal and its jurisdiction'.[33] It reasoned that 'A narrow concept of jurisdiction may, perhaps, be warranted in a national context but not in international law' and that the challenge to the validity of the Tribunal's establishment went 'to the very essence of jurisdiction as a power to exercise the judicial function within any ambit'.[34] The Appeals Chamber drew a distinction between, on the one hand, its 'original', 'primary' or 'substantive' jurisdiction (ie its jurisdiction as set forth in the Statute), and on the other, its 'incidental' or 'inherent' jurisdiction, 'which derives automatically from the exercise of the judicial function'.[35] The Chamber stressed that the Tribunal was not an ordinary 'subsidiary organ' of the Security Council—'a "creation" totally fashioned to the smallest detail by its "creator" and remaining totally in its power and at its mercy'.[36] Instead, it was a judicial tribunal, which is 'a special kind of "subsidiary organ"',[37] that necessarily had residual powers based on 'the requirements of the "judicial function" itself'.[38] One of these powers was, according to the Appeals Chamber, *Kompetenz-Kompetenz*, or *compétence de la compétence*—the 'jurisdiction to determine its own jurisdiction'.[39]

---

[30] *Ayyash and others* (Decision on the Defence Appeals Against the Trial Chamber's 'Decision on the Defence Challenges to the Jurisdiction and Legality of the Tribunal') STL-11-O1/PT/AC/AR90.1, Appeals Chamber (24 October 2012) [14] [hereinafter *Ayyash* (Appeals Chamber)].

[31] *Tadić* (Trial Chamber Decision on Jurisdiction) (n 23) [4].

[32] ibid [5]. The Trial Chamber nonetheless commented on the legality of the Tribunal's establishment and concluded that the 'broad discretion given to the Security Council in the exercise of its Chapter VII authority itself suggests that decisions taken under this head are not reviewable' (ibid [8]). It also engaged extensively with whether that exercise of discretion by the Security Council was lawful (ibid [7]–[39]). It explained that because the ICTY marked the first time that 'the international community has created a court with criminal jurisdiction', it was appropriate to do so given the need to ensure that the Tribunal itself be viewed as a legitimate body (ibid [6]).

[33] *Tadić* (Interlocutory Appeal) (n 2) [5].

[34] ibid, [12].

[35] ibid, [14].

[36] ibid, [15].

[37] ibid, [15].

[38] ibid, [14].

[39] ibid, [18].

While acknowledging that reviewing the legality of its establishment by the Security Council was outside its primary jurisdiction, it emphasised that the issue was whether it could assess this question in exercising its incidental jurisdiction, 'solely for the purpose of ascertaining its own "primary" jurisdiction over the case before it'.[40] Relying on a few brief sentences from two advisory opinions of the International Court of Justice (ICJ), the Appeals Chamber concluded that ICJ practice did not contradict its theory of 'incidental jurisdiction'[41] (even though the ICJ, as a principal organ of the UN, had a different position vis-à-vis the Security Council than did the ICTY, a subsidiary organ). On this basis, the Appeals Chamber concluded that it had jurisdiction to examine the plea.

Tadić's challenge to the legality of the Tribunal's creation was the first in a long line of cases in which defendants before the ICTY and other international criminal tribunals have sought to challenge the legal validity of those bodies. The ICTR Trial Chamber in *Kanyabashi* 'respect[ed] the persuasive authority' of the ICTY's *Tadić*, so much so that it immediately addressed the defence's substantive arguments, without pausing to ask whether it had the authority to review the legality of its own creation.[42] The Special Court for Sierra Leone (SCSL), established by agreement between the UN and Sierra Leone, also followed the ICTY Appeals Chamber when it had its *Tadić* moment on the legality of its establishment. In *Kallon and others*, the SCSL Appeals Chamber cited the *Tadić* interlocutory appeal to confirm its jurisdiction to hear that challenge, similarly finding it 'indisputable' and a matter of 'common sense' that its competence to determine its jurisdiction includes reviewing the lawfulness and validity of its creation.[43]

However, the STL Trial Chamber in *Ayyash et al* explicitly rejected the view of the *Tadić* Appeals Chamber that a court has the inherent jurisdiction to review its own legality,[44] finding instead that the Trial Chamber in *Tadić* (and a dissenting judge in the Appeals Chamber) had correctly found that a challenge to the legality of the creation of the Tribunal was not a jurisdictional matter.[45] The STL Appeals Chamber rejected the idea that it had inherent jurisdiction to entertain the appeal[46] and affirmed the non-reviewability of Security Council action.[47] In a striking set of paragraphs, the STL Appeals Chamber in *Ayyash et al* made the case, in essence, that the decision of the Appeals Chamber in *Tadić* was an outlier, and that its reasoning—including the reliance on advisory opinions of the ICJ to make the case for

---

[40] ibid, [20]–[22].

[41] ibid, [21].

[42] *Prosecutor v Kanyabashi* (Decision on the Defence Motion on Jurisdiction) (n 26) [8]. The ICTR Trial Chamber in *Karemera*, however, stated *obiter* that it did not have the authority 'to review or assess the legality of Security Council decisions' (*Prosecutor v Karemera* (Decision on the Defence Motion pertaining to lack of jurisdiction and defects in the form of the Indictment) ICTR-98-44-T, ICTR, Trial Chamber II (25 April 2001) [25]).

[43] *Kallon and others* (Decision on Constitutionality and Lack of Jurisdiction) SCSL-04-15-PT-060, SCSL, Appeals Chamber (13 March 2004) [34]–[37].

[44] *Ayyash and others* (Decision on the Defence Challenges to the Jurisdiction and Legality of the Tribunal) STL-11-01/PT/TC, STL, Trial Chamber (27 July 2012) [28] [hereinafter *Ayyash* STL Trial Chamber].

[45] ibid, [29].

[46] Ayyash (Appeals Chamber) (n 30) [16].

[47] ibid, [35].

an inherent or incidental jurisdiction—was not persuasive.[48] In the view of the STL Appeals Chamber, it would be an impossibly speculative exercise to subject Security Council determinations on the existence of a threat to international peace and security to judicial scrutiny, and the Security Council alone would have the prerogative to decide upon what measures to take under Article 41 of the Charter.[49] For these reasons, the STL Trial Chamber had been correct in holding that it did not possess the authority to review the Security Council's actions when creating the Tribunal. Indeed, according to the STL Appeals Chamber this meant that the Trial Chamber should not have continued to engage with the substance of the defence arguments in this regard, as it had done (not unlike the Trial Chamber had in *Tadić*).[50]

So the lasting significance of *Tadić*'s affirmation of an inherent jurisdiction implicit to the judicial function and the presumptive reviewability of Security Council decision-making is subject to some doubt. Where *Tadić* had opened the route to international courts and tribunals reviewing Security Council decisions, *Ayyash et al* has closed the door. Neither decision is binding on other courts and tribunals, but in dismissing the *Tadić* reasoning, *Ayyash et al* may have transformed this aspect of *Tadić* from a signpost into a high-water point.

iii. Was the Establishment of the Tribunal by the Security Council in Accordance with International Law?

After dismissing, in line with established case law of the ICJ, the argument that the lawfulness of the Tribunal's establishment was a 'political question' and as such non-justiciable,[51] the ICTY Appeals Chamber took up the challenge on substance. This marked the first time that review by an international court of the conformity of a Security Council decision with international law threatened to invalidate that decision as a matter of law, or at least, to treat it as unlawful.[52]

---

[48] ibid, [40]–[50].

[49] ibid, [51]–[52].

[50] ibid, [54]. In a partial dissent, the lone voice of Judge Baragwanath—Judge Cassese's successor as President of the STL—made the opposite case and asserted that the rule of law gave the STL the implicit and inherent jurisdiction to examine the legality of its own creation: *Ayyash* (Appeals Chamber) (Judge Baragwanath, dissenting) (n 30) [45]–[81].

[51] *Tadić* (Interlocutory Appeal) (n 2) [23]–[25].

[52] In exercising its advisory jurisdiction, the ICJ had examined Security Council resolutions, but not affirmed the authority to engage in 'judicial review' of Security Council decisions. For example, in *Certain Expenses*, the Court remarked that the powers conferred upon UN organs to advance the broad purposes of the Organization are not unlimited, but that the Court lacked the 'ultimate authority' to determine the conformity of Security Council decisions with the Charter: *Certain Expenses of the United Nations* [1962] ICJ Rep 151 (Advisory Opinion) (20 July 1962) 168. In the *Namibia* advisory opinion, the Court disavowed a power of 'judicial review or appeal in respect of the decisions taken by the United Nations organs concerned': *Legal Consequences for States of the Continued Presence of South Africa in Namibia (South West Africa) Notwithstanding Security Council Resolution 276 (1970)* [1971] ICJ Rep 16 (Advisory Opinion) (21 June 1971) [89]. Shortly before *Tadić*, Libya challenged the conformity of a Security Council resolution with international law in two related contentious cases, but the Court did not address that question at the provisional measures phase: *Interpretation and Application of the 1971 Montreal Convention Arising from the Aerial Incident at Lockerbie* (Libya v United States) (Provisional Measures) (14 April 1992) [39], [43]; *Interpretation and Application of the 1971 Montreal Convention Arising from the Aerial Incident at Lockerbie* [1992] ICJ Rep 114 (Libya v United Kingdom) (Provisional Measures) (14 April 1992) [36], [40].

The Appeals Chamber began by noting that the broad powers entrusted to the Security Council by Article 39 of the UN Charter were subject to 'constitutional limitations' and that the Security Council was not *legibus solutus* (unbound by law).[53] In particular, the Security Council 'shall act in accordance with the Purposes and Principles of the United Nations' and was granted 'specific powers', not 'absolute fiat'.[54] The Appeals Chamber then emphasised that the Charter expressly empowered the Security Council to make the threshold determination that there exists 'any threat to the peace, breach of the peace, or act of aggression', the necessary precondition for enforcement measures under Articles 41 or 42 'to maintain or restore international peace and security'.[55] In the case of the dissolution of the former Yugoslavia, the Appeals Chamber found it obvious that this threshold had been met as of 1993.[56]

Tadić conceded this point on appeal, but continued to challenge the legality and appropriateness of the ICTY as an enforcement measure under Chapter VII of the UN Charter. In particular, he argued that the drafters of the Charter had never envisioned a criminal tribunal as a Chapter VII measure, that the Security Council was 'constitutionally or inherently incapable of creating a judicial organ' and that the Tribunal could not constitute an instrument to promote peace and security.[57]

The Appeals Chamber found that the Security Council enjoyed a 'wide margin of discretion' and 'very broad and exceptional powers' under Chapter VII.[58] The authority of the Security Council to establish a criminal tribunal could be found within Article 41, which authorised 'measures not involving the use of armed force ... to give effect' to Security Council decisions. The Appeals Chamber affirmed the view that Article 41 was illustrative and non-exhaustive, and thus could encompass judicial, as well as economic and political, measures of enforcement.[59] It was irrelevant that the Security Council itself was not a judicial body. The establishment of the Tribunal was not a delegation of the Security Council's own powers; rather, the Tribunal was an 'instrument for the Security Council's exercise of its own principal function to maintain peace and security' and the decision to establish a criminal tribunal fell squarely within the wide discretionary powers of the Security Council.[60] Whether it was a wise or prudent decision—and would in fact contribute to restoring peace in the former Yugoslavia—did not bear on the validity in law of that decision.[61]

The Appeals Chamber thus held that the Security Council had not acted ultra vires or otherwise unlawfully in its decision to establish the ICTY. This was obviously

---

[53] *Tadić* (Interlocutory Appeal) (n 2) [28].

[54] ibid.

[55] ibid [29].

[56] The Appeals Chamber noted that whether the conflict(s) were considered international or internal, the situation 'would still constitute a "threat to the peace" according to the settled practice of the Security Council and the common understanding of the United Nations membership in general': ibid, [30].

[57] ibid, [32].

[58] ibid, [31].

[59] ibid, [35].

[60] ibid, [38].

[61] ibid, [39]. Oddly, it was the Trial Chamber—which emphasised the non-justiciability of the question—that engaged in the closer analysis of the proffered justifications for establishing an international criminal tribunal to advance peace and security: *Tadić* (Trial Chamber Decision on Jurisdiction) (n 23) [30]–[31].

essential to allowing the *Tadić* case to move forward. But it was also a key moment—indeed, a landmark event—with respect to the role of the Security Council. The interlocutory appeal stands for the principle that even the Security Council is subject to legal constraints.[62] Yet the decision also served to *legitimize* the Council's exceptional powers under Chapter VII. The Appeals Chamber stressed repeatedly the broad discretion invested in the Security Council, including when making a threshold determination under Article 39. While *Tadić* tells us that such a determination is reviewable in principle, it left unclear how such a review could be meaningfully exercised.[63] In the end, by arguing that the Security Council is bound by law and that the Tribunal itself is independent from the organ that created it, the Appeals Chamber's decision has bestowed the Council's exercise of its executive powers, including in the realm of international criminal justice, with more legitimacy. The finding that the Security Council—a political body—could establish a judicial body was not a landmark. As the Appeals Chamber pointed out, the ICJ had upheld the power of the General Assembly to create an administrative tribunal in the *Effect of Awards* advisory opinion. However, the portrayal of international criminal tribunals as instruments of peace and security was of landmark significance. The Appeals Chamber in *Tadić* did not have to concern itself with empirical evidence on the actual contribution of international criminal law or the ICTY to peace and security, assessing as it did only the powers under which the Security Council had acted. Since *Tadić* the narrative of justice in the interest of peace has been often repeated, by other tribunals, scholars and international criminal justice proponents, even radicalising it to the claim of 'no peace without justice'.[64] The possibility—if not the imperative—of creating international criminal justice mechanisms in response to nearly any conflict involving mass civilian casualties has become 'deeply ingrained'.[65] The Security Council's willingness to employ international criminal justice in the absence of clear theories as to how it contributes to peace and security, let alone empirical evidence to that effect, suggests that it may view accountability as an end in itself: if we cannot prevent or halt these crimes, then at least we do not condone. The October 1995 decision in *Tadić* can lay claim to serving as a key signpost along this path.

iv. Was the Tribunal 'Established by Law'?

Tadić asserted that the Tribunal was not 'established by law', whereas Article 14, paragraph 1, of the International Covenant on Civil and Political Rights (ICCPR) entitles 'everyone', in the context of a criminal trial, to 'a fair and public hearing by

---

[62] The Trial Chamber in *Kanyabashi* departed from the reasoning of the Appeals Chamber in *Tadić* in finding that the Security Council's discretion to determine whether there exists a threat to international peace and security is 'not justiciable': *Prosecutor v Kanyabashi* (n 26) [20]–[21], [26].

[63] Subsequent to this *Tadić* decision, however, there have been legal efforts to defy, but explicitly not review, Security Council resolutions in some cases. The *Kadi* case before the European Court of Justice may be the most well-known example: Case C-402/05 P and C-415/05, *Kadi v Council and Commission* [2008] ECR I–6351.

[64] See for instance *Kanyabashi* (n 26) [26]: 'peace and security cannot be said to be re-established adequately without justice being done'.

[65] See F Mégret, 'A Special Tribunal for Lebanon: The UN Security Council and the Emancipation of International Criminal Justice' (2008) 21 *LJIL* 485, 485.

a competent, independent and impartial tribunal *established by law*'.[66] Remarkably for a Chamber that presented itself as a protector of human rights, as we will see below, the Appeals Chamber found that the requirement that a criminal tribunal be 'established by law' constituted 'an international obligation which only applies to the administration of criminal justice in a municipal setting'.[67] Possibly wanting to safeguard the idea of an international rule of law,[68] the Appeals Chamber nonetheless considered that an international criminal tribunal could not be lawfully established 'at the mere whim of governments', but 'ought to be rooted in the rule of law and offer all guarantees embodied in the relevant international instruments'.[69]

The Appeals Chamber rejected two interpretations of 'established by law' ('established by a legislature' or established by a body which is explicitly authorised to do so)[70] before it adopted a third: 'in accordance with the rule of law'.[71] It interpreted this to mean that a tribunal 'must be established in accordance with the proper international standards; it must provide all the guarantees of fairness, justice and even-handedness, in full conformity with internationally recognized human rights standards'.[72] The Appeals Chamber did not, however, require that criminal courts be 'pre-established' (thus precluding post hoc criminal tribunals). It then found, in a brief paragraph, that the Tribunal satisfied, at least on paper, the fair trial guarantees and requirements of procedural fairness mandated in a domestic context by the ICCPR.[73] By redefining 'established by law' into 'in accordance with the rule of law', and assessing that criterion through an exclusive focus on fair trial rights—as opposed to approaching that requirement by also examining the legal basis on which the tribunal was created—the Chamber effectively read the 'established by law' requirement out of Article 14(1).[74]

This understanding of 'established by law' has been followed by other international tribunals. For instance, the Trial Chamber in *Kanyabashi* explicitly endorsed *Tadić* and equated the 'established by law' requirement with guarantees of procedural fairness.[75] The SCSL Appeals Chamber in *Kallon* held (remarkably without a reference to *Tadić*) that 'it is a norm of international law that for it to be "established by law", its establishment must accord with the rule of law'.[76] As in *Tadić*, it assessed

---

[66] International Covenant on Civil and Political Rights (adopted 16 December 1966, entered into force 23 March 1976) 999 *UNTS* 171, Art 14(1) (emphasis added). The European Convention on Human Rights and the American Convention on Human Rights contain similar provisions: European Convention for the Protection of Human Rights and Fundamental Freedoms (adopted 4 November 1950, entered into force 3 September 1953) 213 *UNTS* 221, Art 6(1); American Convention on Human Rights (adopted 2 November 1969, entered into force 18 July 1978) OAS Treaty Series No 36, Art 8(1); Tadić's written submissions did not frame the 'established by law' requirement as a matter of international human rights law, but the idea was raised during the hearing. See *Prosecutor v Tadić* (Transcript of the Hearing of the Interlocutory Appeal on Jurisdiction) IT-94-1-AR72 (7 September 1995), 18, 25–27, 30–35. See also *Tadić* (Trial Chamber Decision on Jurisdiction) (n 23) [8].

[67] *Tadić* (Interlocutory Appeal) (n 2) [42].
[68] See J Crawford, 'International Law and the Rule of Law' (2003) 24 *Adelaide LR* 3, 8–9.
[69] *Tadić* (Interlocutory Appeal) (n 2) [42].
[70] ibid, [43]–[44].
[71] ibid, [45].
[72] ibid, [45].
[73] ibid, [46].
[74] See also J Alvarez, 'Nuremburg Revisited: The *Tadić* Case' (1996) 7 *EJIL* 245, 258.
[75] *Kanyabashi* (n 26) [43]–[44].
[76] *Kallon* (n 43), [55].

this standard on the basis of the applicable fair trial rights.[77] It was again the STL Trial Chamber in *Ayyash* that broke the chain. The STL Trial Chamber seemed to accept the *Tadić* reasoning on whether the Tribunal was 'established by law', but it disguised that agreement by citing *Kallon* and referring to the *Tadić* decision only through a mere 'See also' in a footnote.[78] Moreover, in applying the test, the STL Trial Chamber actually departed from *Tadić* by assessing not merely whether fair trial rights applied, but also whether the STL had been created by legal instruments that fell within the constitutional authority of the body creating it. In doing so, it indirectly reviewed the legality of the Security Council's actions after all,[79] the only point on which it was criticised by the STL Appeals Chamber.[80]

v. Could the Tribunal Lawfully Exercise 'Primacy' over Domestic Courts?

Challenging the legal basis on which Germany had transferred him to the ICTY, Tadić argued that the Tribunal's 'primacy' over national courts infringed the sovereignty of any state affected by a deferral request.[81] Article 9(1) of the ICTY Statute provided that the Tribunal and national courts 'shall have concurrent jurisdiction to prosecute persons' for serious violations of international humanitarian law committed in the former Yugoslavia.[82] Article 9(2) specified that the ICTY 'shall have primacy over national courts' and may direct national courts 'to defer to the competence' of the ICTY.[83]

The Trial Chamber found that Tadić lacked standing to make a sovereignty argument.[84] The Appeals Chamber found differently, by simultaneously playing up and playing down the importance of state sovereignty. On the one hand it held that sovereignty, once 'a sacrosanct and unassailable attribute of statehood', had 'suffered progressive erosion at the hands of more liberal forces at work in the democratic societies, particularly in the field of human rights'. On the other hand, it established that the defendant's right to a fair trial must include the right to raise a violation of state sovereignty: 'an accused, being entitled to a full defence, cannot be deprived of a plea so intimately connected with, and grounded in, international law as a defence based on violation of State sovereignty'.[85]

The Appeals Chamber's relaxed approach to the rules of standing in this instance may have been strategic—a means to legitimise the rule of primacy by addressing the challenge on the merits. This was made possible by the existence of several grounds on which to dismiss the argument substantively.[86]

---

[77] ibid, [56]–[58].
[78] ibid [67].
[79] ibid, [69]–[73].
[80] *Ayyash* (Appeals Chamber) (n 30) [54].
[81] *Tadić* (Interlocutory Appeal) [50].
[82] Statute of the International Criminal Tribunal for the Former Yugoslavia, UN Doc S/25704 (ICTY Statute), Art 9(1).
[83] ibid, Art 9(2).
[84] *Tadić* (Trial Chamber Decision on Jurisdiction) [41].
[85] *Tadić* (Interlocutory Appeal) (n 2) [55].
[86] The ICTR in *Kanyabashi* followed the *Tadić* Appeals Chamber's approach by affirming the defendant's standing to invoke a violation of sovereignty, and then subsequently dismissing that argument. *Prosecutor v Kanyabashi* (n 26) [12]–[15]. The STL Trial Chamber, however, again took the opposite view, arguing that *Tadić* had 'depart[ed] from prevailing legal precedents in 1995'. (*Ayyash* STL Trial Chamber (n 44) [59]–[60]).

First, the Appeals Chamber pointed out that enforcement measures taken by the Security Council under Chapter VII were excluded from the rule of non-interference in domestic affairs prescribed by Article 2(7) of the Charter. Secondly, it emphasised that Bosnia and Herzegovina had 'not contested' the Tribunal's jurisdiction and, in fact, had 'actually approved, and collaborated with' the Tribunal. Germany, too, had cooperated with the Tribunal.[87] Thirdly, the Appeals Chamber suggested that the nature of the alleged offences—which 'shock the conscience of mankind'—provided a further reason to reject the invocation of sovereignty as an argument against the primacy of the Tribunal.[88] Treating the enforcement of international criminal law as a human rights imperative, the Appeals Chamber stated (rather than reasoned):

> It would be a travesty of law and a betrayal of the universal need for justice, should the concept of State sovereignty be allowed to be raised successfully against human rights. Borders should not be considered as a shield against the reach of the law and as a protection for those who trample underfoot the most elementary rights of humanity.[89]

The Appeals Chamber then took this general juxtaposition of sovereignty and human rights to formulate a more specific finding with respect to primacy:

> Indeed, when an international tribunal such as the present one is created, it must be endowed with primacy over national courts. Otherwise, human nature being what it is, there would be a perennial danger of international crimes being characterised as 'ordinary crimes' ... or proceedings being 'designed to shield the accused' or cases not being diligently prosecuted ... If not effectively countered by the principle of primacy, any of those strategems might be used to defeat the very purpose of the creation of an international criminal jurisdiction, to the benefit of the very people whom it has been designed to prosecute.[90]

On these three grounds, the Appeals Chamber dismissed the appeal on the question of primacy.[91] The Chamber did not discuss the fact that the ICTY Statute,[92] unlike that of the Rwanda Tribunal,[93] was ambiguous as to whether the Tribunal enjoyed primacy only vis-à-vis the former Yugoslav states, as some statements in the Security Council debates suggested,[94] or vis-à-vis all states, that is to say, including Germany. However, after *Tadić*, this was no longer in question.[95]

On the matter of primacy, *Tadic* was a high-water point. It is true that the constituent documents of subsequent international criminal tribunals—namely the ICTR, the SCSL and the STL—also provided for primacy over national courts (although the primacy of the SCSL and the STL extended only to the states in which the crimes

---

[87] *Tadić* (Interlocutory Appeal) (n 2) [56].

[88] ibid, [57].

[89] ibid, [58].

[90] ibid.

[91] ibid [59].

[92] ICTY Statute (n 82), Art 9(2) ('The International Tribunal shall have primacy over national courts').

[93] Statute of the International Criminal Tribunal for Rwanda, annexed to UNSC Res 955 (1994) UN Doc S/RES/955, Art 8(2) (stating that the tribunal has primacy 'over the national courts of all States').

[94] See, for instance, UNSC Verbatim Record UN Doc (25 May 1993) S/PV.3217, 18–19 (Sir David Hannay).

[95] See more elaborately, S Nouwen and D Lewis, 'Jurisdictional Arrangements and International Criminal Procedure', in G Sluiter, H Friman, S Linton, S Vasiliev and S Zappalà (eds), *International Criminal Procedure: Principles and Rules* (Oxford, OUP, 2013) 116, 119.

were committed, Sierra Leone and Lebanon).[96] However, without any change in 'human nature', the idea that an international criminal tribunal 'must be endowed with primacy over national courts'[97] was abandoned explicitly and intentionally by the drafters of the Rome Statute establishing the ICC. The Rome Statute provides for the so-called principle of 'complementarity', according to which a case shall be inadmissible if it is being, or has been, genuinely investigated or prosecuted by a state which has jurisdiction over it.[98] The Rome Statute's indicators of a lack of genuineness, encapsulated by the notions of 'unwillingness' and 'inability', contain some of the scenarios that the *Tadić* Appeals Chamber envisaged, particularly domestic proceedings designed to shield the accused. However, one of the scenarios that the Appeals Chamber mentioned explicitly as a justification for primacy—'a perennial danger of international crimes being characterised as "ordinary crimes"'—was not included as a ground for admissibility in the Rome Statute.[99] In other words, unlike the Appeals Chamber in *Tadić*, the drafters of the Rome Statute did not consider it a problem for an offence to be prosecuted as an ordinary crime (eg 1,000 counts of murder) rather than an international crime that might encompass the same conduct (eg a crime against humanity).

Finally, the ICTY Appeals Chamber also affirmed the Trial Chamber's dismissal of the related objection under the heading *jus de non evocando*, which according to Tadić entitled him to be tried by national courts under national laws. The Appeals Chamber concurred with the Trial Chamber that a defendant had no right to be tried exclusively before his own country's domestic courts.[100] In the Appeals Chamber's view, the principle in question aimed to prevent criminal defendants from facing trial for political offences before specially constituted national courts that do not guarantee a fair trial. Arguing there was no such risk in the case of a transfer of jurisdiction to 'an international tribunal created by the Security Council acting on behalf of the community of nations',[101] the Appeals Chamber again used the opportunity to set out what it perceived as its own strengths:

No rights of accused are thereby infringed or threatened; quite to the contrary, they are all specifically spelt out and protected under the Statute of the International Tribunal. No accused can complain. True, he will be removed from his 'natural' national forum; but he will be brought before a tribunal at least equally fair, more distanced from the facts of the case and taking a broader view of the matter.

[96] The Trial Chamber in *Kanyabashi* based its defence of primacy on the fact that the Security Council had exercised its powers under Chapter VII; it did not refer to the sweeping assertions from *Tadić* about the functional necessity of primacy. *Prosecutor v Kanyabashi* (n 26) [32].

[97] *Tadić* (Interlocutory Appeal) (n 2) [58].

[98] Rome Statute of the International Criminal Court (opened for signature 17 July 1998, entered into force 1 July 2002) 2187 UNTS 90 (Rome Statute), Art 17(1).

[99] See also *Prosecutor v Saif Al-Islam Gaddafi and Abdullah Al-Senussi* (Judgment on the Appeal of Mr Abdullah Al-Senussi against the Decision of Pre-Trial Chamber I of 11 October 2013 Entitled Decision on the Admissibility of the Case against Abdullah Al-Senussi) ICC-01/11-01/11-565, ICC, Appeals Chamber (24 July 2014) [119]: 'it is the alleged conduct, as opposed to its legal characterisation, that matters'.

[100] *Tadić* (Interlocutory Appeal) (n 2) [63].

[101] ibid, [62].

Furthermore, one cannot but rejoice at the thought that, universal jurisdiction being nowadays acknowledged in the case of international crimes, a person suspected of such offences may finally be brought before an international judicial body for a dispassionate consideration of his indictment by impartial, independent and disinterested judges coming, as it happens here, from all continents of the world.[102]

The Chamber's reasoning to justify its primacy is indicative of its lack of trust in the state, including domestic courts, and its faith in international institutions, including international courts.[103] However, the Chamber did not shy away from also emphasizing state consent to the Tribunal's activities (whether via Chapter VII or the individual consent of states) to validate the Tribunal's primacy.[104]

B. Contributions to International Humanitarian Law

Tadić's most permanent signpost landmarks are probably in the terrain of international humanitarian law (IHL), and in particular its definition of armed conflict and its findings on the applicable humanitarian law in internal armed conflict. Tadić raised separate arguments relating to the existence and classification of armed conflict. These arguments gave the Appeals Chamber a significant opportunity to pronounce on IHL.

i. The Existence of an Armed Conflict

Before the Trial Chamber, Tadić had argued that the alleged crimes, if proven, had taken place during an internal armed conflict over which the Tribunal lacked jurisdiction,[105] but on appeal he made the alternative argument that there was no armed conflict of any type in the Prijedor region where the alleged crimes had taken place.[106] The Appeals Chamber rejected that argument and held that 'the temporal and geographic scope' of an armed conflict, whether internal or international, 'extends beyond the exact time and place of hostilities'.[107] On the basis of a textual analysis of several provisions in the Geneva Conventions, the Appeals Chamber offered the following definition of 'armed conflict' for the purpose of determining the applicability of IHL:

> An armed conflict exists whenever there is a resort to armed force between States or protracted armed violence between governmental authorities and organized armed groups or between such groups within a State. International humanitarian law applies from the initiation of such armed conflicts and extends beyond the cessation of hostilities until a general conclusion of peace is reached; or, in the case of internal conflicts, a peaceful settlement is achieved. Until that moment, international humanitarian law continues to apply in the

---

[102] ibid.
[103] See also ibid, [36].
[104] *Tadić* (Interlocutory Appeal) (n 2) [56].
[105] The ICTY Statute uses the term 'internal armed conflict" rather than "non-international armed conflict', which might be deemed slightly broader.
[106] *Tadić* (Interlocutory Appeal) (n 2) [65].
[107] ibid, [67].

whole territory of the warring States or, in the case of internal conflicts, the whole territory under the control of a party, whether or not actual combat takes place there.[108]

The *Tadić* definition of armed conflict for the purposes of the applicability of IHL (which establishes different tests for international and non-international armed conflict) has had a lasting impact. The ICTY, other ad hoc international criminal tribunals, international commissions of inquiry, UN special rapporteurs, and various military manuals on the law of armed conflict have all relied upon this definition, particularly for purposes of defining non-international armed conflict.[109] It was also incorporated into the Rome Statute.[110] However, the definition also raises questions. For instance, 'protracted armed violence' leaves open the requisite intensity needed to transform a discrete incident into a situation of armed conflict covered by IHL.[111] The definition has also been criticised for broadening the definitions of armed conflict set forth in the Additional Protocols to the Geneva Conventions—language that had been 'painstakingly negotiated by states in the Diplomatic Conference'.[112]

Applying its own definition, the Appeals Chamber found that there had undoubtedly been an armed conflict in the former Yugoslavia since 1991, prior to the incidents from the summer of 1992 set forth in the indictment, and that therefore IHL applied.[113]

ii. Classification of an Armed Conflict as 'International' or 'Internal'

The Appeals Chamber then addressed the thorny question of how to classify that conflict and what this would mean for the Tribunal's subject-matter jurisdiction. Article 2 of the ICTY Statute referred to 'grave breaches' of the Geneva Conventions of 1949, which could mean that such crimes might fall within the Tribunal's jurisdiction only if committed during an international armed conflict because such breaches were 'widely understood to be committed only in international armed conflicts'.[114] By contrast, Article 5 (crimes against humanity) expressly referred to internal and international armed conflicts. Article 3 (violations of the laws or customs of war) was silent on the matter, which could have suggested that it was not intended to apply to internal armed conflicts (in light of the more specific wording in Article 5).[115]

---

[108] *Tadić* (Interlocutory Appeal) (n 2) [70].

[109] See A Cullen, *The Concept of Non-International Armed Conflict in International Humanitarian Law* (Cambridge, CUP, 2010) 120–21, 137–38; A Bianchi and Y Naqvi, 'Terrorism' in A Clapham and P Gaeta (eds), *The Oxford Handbook of International Law in Armed Conflict* (Oxford, OUP, 2014) 575, 585.

[110] Rome Statute (n 98), Art 8(2)(f).

[111] See E David, 'Internal (Non-International) Armed Conflict' in A Clapham and P Gaeta (eds), *The Oxford Handbook of International Law in Armed Conflict* (Oxford, OUP, 2014) 353, 358 (describing different interpretations of the 'protracted armed violence' requirement, including the approach of the Inter-American Court of Human Rights which has focused more on 'the nature and level of violence, even within a short duration'). See also Bianchi and Naqvi (n 109) 574, 584–85.

[112] AM Danner, 'When Courts Make Law: How the International Criminal Tribunals Recast the Laws of War' (2006) 59 *Vand LR* 1, 30. Danner notes that the definition of armed conflict in *Tadić* in fact resembles a proposal made by the ICRC for Additional Protocol II that was rejected.

[113] *Tadić* (Interlocutory Appeal) (n 2) [70].

[114] ibid [71].

[115] ibid.

To address the question of classification, the Appeals Chamber focused on the Security Council's stated goal of 'bringing to justice persons responsible for serious violations of international humanitarian law in the former Yugoslavia, thereby deterring future violations and contributing to the re-establishment of peace and security in the region'. In the view of the Appeals Chamber, the Security Council 'intended to achieve this purpose without reference to whether the conflicts in the former Yugoslavia were internal or international'.[116] It was 'preoccupied' with bringing the perpetrators of alleged atrocities to justice, 'regardless of context'.[117]

The Appeals Chamber concluded that 'the conflicts in the former Yugoslavia have both internal and international aspects'[118] and that the Security Council 'intended that, to the extent possible, the subject-matter jurisdiction of the International Tribunal should extend to both internal and international armed conflicts'.[119] The Appeals Chamber specifically credited the Report of the Secretary-General of 3 May 1993 and statements by Security Council members regarding the ICTY Statute.[120] Throughout, the Appeals Chamber was at pains to emphasise that limiting its subject-matter jurisdiction to crimes committed only in an international armed conflict would defeat the underlying purpose of the Tribunal, since many of the alleged offenses had taken place in situations of internal armed conflict.[121]

It arguably would have been far easier for the Appeals Chamber to have classified the entire situation an international armed conflict, thus eliminating the need to consider the content and scope of international humanitarian law applicable to internal armed conflicts.[122] This was the approach of the UN Commission of Experts.[123] It would have also prevented future ICTY prosecutions from getting bogged down in classification disputes. But the weight of scholarly opinion has praised the decision of the Appeals Chamber to acknowledge the complexity of the situation and to leave it open to the Trial Chamber in each case to assess the applicable law.[124] Moreover, a decision to classify the entire conflict as international would have deprived the Appeals Chamber of the opportunity to reshape the common understanding of what

---

[116] ibid, [72].

[117] ibid, [74].

[118] ibid, [77]. The Appeals Chamber considered the agreements reached by various parties to the conflict 'to abide by certain rules of humanitarian law', the position taken by the International Committee of the Red Cross, and various statements by the Security Council: ibid, [73]–[75].

[119] ibid, [78].

[120] ibid, [75].

[121] ibid, [78].

[122] See, eg, G Aldrich, 'Jurisdiction of the International Criminal Tribunal for the Former Yugoslavia' (1996) 90 *AJIL* 64, 67–69; T Meron, 'Cassese's *Tadić* and the Law of Non-International Armed Conflict' in L Chand Vohrah, F Pocar, Y Featherstone, O Fourmy, C Graham, J Hocking and N Robson (eds), *Man's Inhumanity to Man: Essays on International Law in Honour of Antonio Cassese* (The Hague, Kluwer, 2003) 533, 534; T Hoffman, 'The Gentle Humanizer of Humanitarian Law—Antonio Cassese and the Creation of the Customary Law of Non-International Armed Conflicts' in C Stahn and L van den Herik (eds), *Future Perspectives on International Criminal Justice* (The Hague, TMC Asser Press, 2010) 58, 64, 68.

[123] UNSC 'Final Report of the Commission of Experts Established Pursuant to Security Council Resolution 780 (1992)' (27 May 1994) UN Doc S/1994/674, Annex, [44]. The Commission of Experts found that because 'the content of customary law applicable to internal armed conflict is debatable', universal jurisdiction over offences committed in an internal armed conflict would generally be limited to crimes against humanity and genocide: [42].

[124] See, eg, C Greenwood, 'International Humanitarian Law and the *Tadic* Case' (1996) 7 *EJIL* 265, 270.

rules of IHL apply to an internal armed conflict—the section of the judgment to which we now turn.

iii. Grave Breaches, Crimes Against Humanity and 'Violations of the Laws and Customs of War' in Non-International Armed Conflict

a. Article 2 (Grave Breaches)

On grave breaches the Appeals Chamber found that the reference in Article 2 of the ICTY Statute to the 1949 Geneva Conventions implied that grave breaches could be committed only in international armed conflicts. The Trial Chamber had interpreted Article 2 as identifying conduct that could be prosecuted before the Tribunal regardless of whether the armed conflict was international or internal.[125] But the Appeals Chamber explained that the 'grave breaches' regime was the product of a compromise during the drafting of the 1949 Geneva Conventions to limit intentionally the obligation to prosecute grave breaches to international armed conflict; states at that time 'did not want to give other States jurisdiction over serious violations of international humanitarian law committed in their internal armed conflicts'.[126] The Appeals Chamber focused closely on the text of Article 2, which referred to the Tribunal having jurisdiction in relation to grave breaches that constituted 'acts against persons or property protected under the provisions of the relevant Geneva Conventions'. In its view, the reference to the 'strict conditions set out by the Conventions themselves' necessarily limited the scope of the Tribunal's jurisdiction under Article 2 to grave breaches against 'persons or objects protected only to the extent that they are caught up in an international armed conflict'.[127]

The Appeals Chamber was cognizant of the fact that its cautious approach to Article 2 might seem at odds with its pronouncements elsewhere in the judgment about the blurring of 'the traditional dichotomy between international wars and civil strife'—and it noted that *opinio juris* appeared to be evolving.[128] It highlighted the position of the United States (set forth in an *amicus curiae* brief) that the grave breaches regime was applicable to all types of armed conflict, and it pointed to a few other examples of then-recent practice that pointed in this direction.[129] But for the Appeals Chamber, this evidence was insufficient to demonstrate new customary international law on the application of the grave breaches regime to internal armed conflicts. However, the Appeals Chamber's strict or formalist approach to the identification of rules of custom here may have been meant to compensate for the more liberal approach taken to that same exercise on other points (as discussed below).[130]

---

[125] *Tadić* (Trial Chamber Decision on Jurisdiction) (n 23) [49]–[53].
[126] *Tadić* (Interlocutory Appeal) (n 2) [80].
[127] ibid, [81].
[128] ibid, [83]. In Part IV of his separate opinion, Judge Abi-Saab argued that a strong case existed for also finding that the grave breaches regime applied regardless of the classification of the conflict.
[129] *Tadić* (Interlocutory Appeal) (n 2) [83].
[130] Its decision that the Tribunal had jurisdiction over the crimes in Article 2 only in international armed conflicts led to Tadić's acquittal of grave breaches by the Trial Chamber, because the Trial Chamber found that his crimes took place in an internal armed conflict. The Appeals Chamber, however, overturned this acquittal, finding that because of the FRY's 'overall control' of the Bosnian Serbs, the conflict was international (see *Tadić* (n 12) 33ff).

b. Article 5 (Crimes Against Humanity)

Article 5 expressly grants the Tribunal jurisdiction over crimes against human-ity whether committed in an international or internal armed conflict. According to Tadić, however, this provision violated the principle of *nullum crimen sine lege* because under customary international law crimes against humanity could be com-mitted only in an international armed conflict.[131] In response, the Appeals Chamber confirmed the Security Council's view on the status of crimes against humanity by finding that 'It is by now a settled rule of customary international law that crimes against humanity do not require a connection to international armed conflict'.[132] It went further, beyond what it had to do to establish its jurisdiction over crimes against humanity in the present case, by finding that the Security Council's defini-tion of crimes against humanity was in fact narrower than what international law provides, since 'customary international law may not require a connection between crimes against humanity and any conflict at all'.[133] In this respect, too, *Tadić* fulfilled a signpost function: the definition of crimes against humanity in the Rome Statute includes no reference to armed conflict.[134]

c. Article 3 (Violations of the Laws or Customs of War)

The Appeals Chamber's most revolutionary interpretation concerned Article 3, which established the Tribunal's jurisdiction over violations of 'the laws or cus-toms of war' and provided a non-exhaustive list of such offences. The provision was based, at least in part, on the 1907 Hague Convention IV.[135] Tadić argued that because the Hague Convention IV regulated only international armed conflict, the Tribunal lacked jurisdiction under Article 3 if the alleged offences had taken place during an internal armed conflict.[136]

Rejecting that argument, the Appeals Chamber held that the scope of offences covered by Article 3 of the Statute was unrestricted by the international or internal nature of the conflict. Leaning heavily on statements made by the American, British and French representatives to the Security Council in connection with the adop-tion of the Tribunal's Statute, the Appeals Chamber held that Article 3 'confers on the International Tribunal jurisdiction over *any* serious offence against international humanitarian law not covered by Article 2, 4, or 5'.[137] With the goal of making the Tribunal's jurisdiction 'watertight and inescapable', the Security Council had fashioned Article 3 as 'a residual clause designed to ensure that no serious violation of international humanitarian law' fell beyond the Tribunal's jurisdiction.[138]

---

[131] *Tadić* (Interlocutory Appeal) (n 2) [139].
[132] ibid, [141].
[133] ibid.
[134] Rome Statute (n 98), Art 7.
[135] Convention Respecting the Laws and Customs of War on Land (Hague Convention IV) (signed 18 October 1907, entered into force 26 January 1910).
[136] *Tadić* (Interlocutory Appeal) (n 2) [86].
[137] ibid, [91].
[138] ibid.

The Tribunal next articulated a set of requirements to determine whether any particular alleged offence could be subject to prosecution under Article 3: (i) that the violation infringe a rule of IHL; (ii) that the rule constitute customary international law or derive from a treaty in force upon the relevant party at the relevant time; (iii) that the violation be 'serious'; and (iv) that the violation entail individual criminal responsibility under customary or conventional law.[139] These requirements—not the classification of the armed conflict in question—controlled the question of subject-matter jurisdiction under Article 3.

Having noted 'the paucity of authoritative judicial pronouncements and legal literature' on the existence of customary rules governing internal armed conflicts,[140] the Appeals Chamber went beyond analysing what was necessary for the case at hand, where charges were limited to violations of common Article 3 of the Geneva Conventions, and embarked on a detailed legal-historical analysis of the evolution of the law of armed conflict. Taking the Spanish Civil War as a key turning point, the Appeals Chamber described a transition since the 1930s from a strict dichotomy between inter-state war (ie, belligerency, which was subject to international law) and internal strife (ie, insurgency, which was not) to a less sovereignty-oriented paradigm that placed a greater focus on human rights and community interests.[141] Four factors explained this transition: (i) the increasing frequency of civil wars (facilitated by technological progress that gives insurgents greater access to weaponry); (ii) the fact that civil wars more often were 'cruel and protracted' and might involve an 'all-out resort to armed violence' that diminishes any qualitative distinction between internal and international armed conflict; (iii) that the 'increasing interdependence of States in the world community' (ie, globalisation) means that third states were more likely to have their interests affected by large-scale civil strife; and (iv) the 'impetuous development and propagation' of international human rights law.[142] As a result, according to the Appeals Chamber, 'a State-sovereignty-oriented approach has been gradually supplanted by a human being-oriented approach' as to when and where international law regulates hostilities:

> Gradually the maxim of Roman law *hominem causa omne jus constitutum est* (all law is created for the benefit for human beings) has gained a firm foothold in the international community. It follows that in the area of armed conflict the distinction between interstate wars and civil wars is losing its value as far as human beings are concerned. Why protect civilians from belligerent violence, or ban rape, torture or the wanton destruction of hospitals, churches, museums or private property, as well as proscribe weapons causing unnecessary suffering when two sovereign States are engaged in war, and yet refrain from enacting the same bans or providing the same protection when armed violence has erupted 'only' within the territory of a sovereign State? If international law, while of course duly safeguarding the legitimate interests of States, must gradually turn to the protection of human beings, it is only natural that the aforementioned dichotomy should gradually lose its weight.[143]

[139] ibid, [94].
[140] ibid, [95].
[141] ibid, [96]–[97].
[142] ibid, [97].
[143] ibid.

Having justified its impending conclusion on the basis of natural-law style reasoning, the Chamber then dedicated several pages to developments in state practice that were meant to demonstrate, in a positivist style, the emergence of various principles and rules of customary law applicable to internal armed conflict.[144] To identify that custom, the Appeals Chamber explained that it relied primarily on 'official pronouncements of States, military manuals and judicial decisions', rather than the 'actual behavior of troops in the field', which was far more difficult to ascertain.[145]

On the basis of a selection of such 'practice', ranging from the Spanish Civil War and the 1967 conflict in Yemen to conflicts in the Democratic Republic of the Congo, Nigeria and El Salvador, and on the work of the International Committee of the Red Cross (ICRC) and some General Assembly resolutions, the Appeals Chamber concluded that a significant number of general principles applicable to internal armed conflict had emerged, in particular rules aimed at protecting civilian populations or more generally, those who are *hors de combat*. The Appeals Chamber further concluded that general principles relating to the 'means and methods of warfare' had emerged with respect to internal armed conflict, although these principles were not directly relevant to the charges against Tadić. The Chamber emphasised that it was not endorsing 'a full and mechanical transplant' of the entire law of armed conflict to internal conflict; 'rather, the general essence of those rules, and not the detailed regulation they may contain, has become applicable to internal conflicts'.[146]

The evidence relied upon by the Appeals Chamber in 1995 was probably not robust enough to support all of its findings on the applicability of IHL rules to internal armed conflict as a matter of custom,[147] but other practice soon reflected the Appeals Chamber's move to apply the rules normally applicable in international armed conflict to internal armed conflict. To give but a few examples, subsequent case law of the ICTY construed the decision 'to authorize the importation not only of common Article 3, but of the entirety of customary international law applicable in non-international armed conduct, and thus even of offences not explicitly mentioned in common Article 3, such as rape' (notwithstanding the warning against a 'full and mechanical' transplant).[148] Neither a 1993 draft treaty for an international criminal court nor the 1995 International Law Commission draft Code of Crimes Against the Peace and Security of Mankind included provisions relating to internal armed conflict, but new drafts that were produced shortly after the interlocutory appeal in *Tadić* did so.[149] In addition, key treaties regulating the use of particular types of

---

[144] ibid, [98]–[99].
[145] ibid, [99].
[146] ibid, [126].
[147] See, eg, Greenwood, 'International Humanitarian Law' (n 124) 278 (questioning reliance on a lone Nigerian case to establish that perfidy constituted a violation of IHL in an internal armed conflict). See also D Akande, 'Nwaoga' in Antonio Cassese (ed), *The Oxford Companion to International Criminal Justice* (Oxford, OUP, 2009) 856.
[148] Meron, 'Cassese's *Tadić*' (n 122) 534–35.
[149] Hoffman, 'Gentle Humanizer' (n 122) 70.

weapons were amended in the wake of *Tadić* to extend the scope of their protections to non-international armed conflicts.[150] Since *Tadić*, some national militaries have also taken the position that the same rules of IHL apply in international and non-international armed conflicts,[151] and the standards applied to UN peacekeeping forces make no distinction about the applicability of IHL rules based on the classification of the conflict.[152] The 2005 ICRC study on the rules of customary humanitarian law reflects the diminishing gap between the rules applicable to international and non-international armed conflicts—and the Appeals Chamber's conclusion that the customary rules of IHL applicable to internal armed conflict extend beyond the provisions of Additional Protocol II to the Geneva Conventions.[153] Echoing the language of *Tadić*, the ICRC study appeals expressly to 'common sense' for the proposition that the principles of distinction and proportionality 'should be equally applicable in international and non-international armed conflict'.[154] The Rome Statute of the ICC also reflects the approach of *Tadić* in that it enumerates, in Article 8(2)(d), a long list of violations of the laws and customs applicable to internal armed conflict.[155] At the same time, the states negotiating the Statute were not willing to let go of the distinction between international and non-international armed conflict all together: the war crimes listed in Article 8 are organised per the international or non-international character of the conflict.

The very novelty of the ICTY Appeals Chamber's pronouncements—and their rapid incorporation by a variety of actors—undermines the central proposition (or myth?) of *Tadić*: that the law as described by the Appeals Chamber satisfied the requirements of custom. In fact, the Appeals Chamber was pushing the law in a new direction.

C. Contributions to International Criminal Law

Tadić argued that even if customary rules of IHL applied to internal armed conflicts, this did not mean that the violation of those rules triggered individual criminal responsibility.[156]

---

[150] For example, states parties to the 1980 Convention on Prohibitions or Restrictions on the Use of Certain Conventional Weapons Which May Be Deemed to Be Excessively Injurious or to Have Indiscriminate Effects (adopted 10 October 1980, entered into force 2 December 1983) 1342 UNTS 137 amended article 1 of that treaty in 2001 to expand its scope to all common Article 3 situations. See United Nations Office for Disarmament Affairs, 'The Convention on Certain Conventional Weapons', www. un.org/disarmament/geneva/ccw (accessed 21 February 2017). See also the Second Protocol to the Hague Convention of 1954 for the Protection of Cultural Property in the Event of Armed Conflict (adopted 26 March 1999, entered into force 9 March 2004) 2253 UNTS 212, Art 22 (expanding the scope of the 1954 treaty to conflicts not of an international character).

[151] Meron (n 122) 536.

[152] United Nations Secretary-General, Bulletin on the Observance by United Nations Forces of International Humanitarian Law, UN Doc ST/SGB/1999/13, reprinted in 38 *ILM* 1656 (1999).

[153] See J-M Henckaerts and L Doswald-Beck, *Customary International Humanitarian Law, Volume 1: Rules* (Cambridge, CUP, 2005) xxix, 40, 554; Meron (n 122) 536.

[154] Henckaerts and Doswald-Beck, *Customary International Humanitarian Law* (n 153) xxix.

[155] Rome Statute (n 98), Art 8(2)(d).

[156] *Tadić* (Interlocutory Appeal) (n 2) [128].

The Appeals Chamber again broke new ground by holding that 'customary international law imposes criminal liability for serious violations of common Article 3, as supplemented by other general principles and rules on the protection of victims of internal armed conflict, and for breaching certain fundamental principles and rules regarding means and methods of combat in civil strife.'[157] There was no precedent for this pronouncement.[158] Conventional law regulating internal armed conflict— ie, common Article 3 of the Geneva Conventions and Additional Protocol II—did not require prosecution or establish universal jurisdiction in a manner equivalent to the regime for grave breaches in an international armed conflict; indeed, it did not even refer to criminal liability. The Appeals Chamber instead referred to the criteria that the Nuremberg tribunal had considered for establishing the existence of individual criminal responsibility for violations of international humanitarian law (albeit in international armed conflict): 'the clear and unequivocal recognition of the rules of warfare in international law and State practice indicating an intention to criminalise the prohibition, including statements by government officials and international organizations, as well as punishment of violations by national courts and military tribunals'.[159] Applying these criteria, the Appeals Chamber again combined an eclectic selection of state practice (as evidenced by military manuals, some national legislation implementing the Geneva Conventions, and Security Council resolutions)[160] with morality and, as the Appeals Chamber saw it, common sense, to support the conclusion 'that states intend to criminalise serious breaches of customary rules and principles on internal conflicts'.[161] It did not discuss all the contrary practice: the instances in which states had *not* treated violations of common Article 3 as incurring individual criminal responsibility.[162] Yet the Appeals Chamber offered that its conclusions were 'fully warranted from the point of view of substantive justice and equity' because serious violations of IHL were already punishable under the domestic law of the former Yugoslavia and had been made punishable in Bosnia and Herzegovina by an April 1992 decree-law.[163] Accordingly, nationals 'were therefore aware, or should have been aware, that they were amenable to the jurisdiction of the national criminal courts' in cases of violation of IHL.[164] As if to add an additional layer of security to this conclusion, the Appeals Chamber also found that the 1 October 1992 agreement among the parties to the conflict clearly contemplated criminal prosecution for IHL violations, including in internal armed conflict.[165]

---

[157] ibid, [134].
[158] Greenwood, 'International Humanitarian Law' (n 124) 281; T Meron, 'The Continuing Role of Custom in the Formation of International Humanitarian Law' (1996) 90 *AJIL* 235, 244.
[159] *Tadić* (Interlocutory Appeal) (n 2) [128].
[160] ibid [131]–[133]. The Appeals Chamber referred to Security Council Resolutions 794 (3 December 1992) and 814 (26 March 1993) regarding Somalia in which the Security Council had demanded that the perpetrators of various breaches of IHL be held 'individually responsible': ibid [133].
[161] *Tadić* (Interlocutory Appeal) (n 2) [129].
[162] See Greenwood, 'International Humanitarian Law' (n 124) 280 and Akande, 'Nwaoga' (n 147) 856.
[163] *Tadić* (Interlocutory Appeal) (n 2) [135].
[164] ibid, [136].
[165] ibid, [136].

Finally, the Appeals Chamber held that the Tribunal's jurisdiction over 'violations of the laws or customs of war' also covered any IHL obligations set forth in agreements between the conflicting parties. It reasoned that because the drafters of the ICTY Statute had purposefully directed the Tribunal to apply well established rules of international customary law in order to avoid running into problems with the prohibition on retrospective criminal laws, there could be no obstacle to the Tribunal also applying treaty-based rules governing armed conflict.[166] This finding, however, 'neglect[ed] the fact that the relevant international treaties [did] not in and of themselves establish individual criminal responsibility'.[167]

But the most pointed criticism of these 'revolutionary'[168] findings on individual criminal liability for violations of customary and conventional law may be that the Appeals Chamber disregarded the unambiguous instructions set forth in the Secretary-General's report on the establishment of the ICTY: that 'the international tribunal should apply rules of international humanitarian law *which are beyond any doubt* part of customary law'.[169] Some commentators have endorsed the sentiment expressed by Judge Li in his dissenting opinion: that the holding that criminal liability attached to violations of IHL norms in non-international armed conflict failed to meet the test for establishing custom (state practice and *opinio juris*) and thus amounted to 'an unwarranted assumption of legislative power'.[170] Yet after *Tadić*, there was suddenly wide acceptance that individual criminal responsibility existed for violations of international humanitarian law in internal armed conflict—and that this had been the case even before *Tadić*.[171] Thus, as Tamás Hoffman explains, by identifying putatively pre-existing custom, 'The *Tadić* judgment changed forever not only the future but even the past'.[172] *Tadić* is thus not only a 'signpost' landmark of international law, in that the 'audacity' of the Appeals Chamber's decision opened up a new pathway for IHL in an era of non-international armed conflicts. It is also a 'high-water point' landmark in the way it achieved this result—through a particularly potent exercise of judicial law-making.

IV. 'TO DO A *TADIĆ*' : THE SIGNIFICANCE OF *TADIĆ* FOR LAW-MAKING AND LEGAL REASONING IN INTERNATIONAL LAW

Tadić provided an opportunity for the ICTY to set its machinery in motion, but also for the judges and, in particular, the judge who authored the decision, to change the law.

---

[166] ibid, [143]–[144].

[167] C Kress, 'International Criminal Law', *Max Planck Encyclopedia of Public International Law* (2009) [12].

[168] Hoffman (n 122) 65.

[169] Report of the Secretary-General pursuant to Paragraph 2 of Security Council Resolution 808 (1993) (3 May 1993) UN Doc S/25704 [34] (emphasis added). See also many of the interventions in the Security Council debates to that effect.

[170] Interlocutory Appeal, Separate Opinion of Judge Li [10]–[13]. See E La Haye, *War Crimes in Internal Armed Conflicts* (Cambridge, CUP, 2008) 152–53, 160, 170–71.

[171] Hoffman (n 122) 69–72.

[172] ibid, 73.

When later asked 'What was the most important case that you sat on?', the President of the *Tadić* Appeals Chamber, Judge Antonio Cassese, responded:

> Probably *Tadić*. Because I pushed so much and we exploited the *Tadić* case to draw as much as possible from a minor defendant to launch new ideas, and be creative. Actually, *Tadić* offered us the opportunity to pronounce on the legality of the Tribunal, whether the Tribunal had been set up in conformity with the law, the question of whether it would be appropriate to make a distinction between war crimes committed in internal or civil war and international conflict, and also the question of the extent to which a civil war may turn into an international war.[173]

As noted above, it would not have been surprising for the Appeals Chamber to have decided that the situation in the former Yugoslavia was an international armed conflict, full stop, for purposes of identifying the applicable law. But this would have deprived Cassese of the chance to address a topic on which he had spent much of the previous 20 years as a scholar and an advocate—the disparity between the scope of IHL, and corresponding individual criminal liability, applicable to international versus internal armed conflict.[174] As Tamás Hoffman has set out, already during a renowned scholarly career (including posts at the University of Pisa, the University of Florence, and the European University Institute, in addition to leading positions on Council of Europe bodies on human rights and the prevention of torture) then Professor Cassese had argued for filling gaps in the international regulation of non-international armed conflict. Characteristically, he did not have much faith in states to do so, and called upon public opinion and non-governmental organisations to bring 'moral authority' to bear 'where the law is silent'.[175] Cassese realised that his decisions from the bench could, in Hoffman's words, 'support his own scholarly theories' and create 'a mutually re-enforcing cycle' of scholarship and judicial decisions.[176] Accordingly, as Cassese reported in the above-cited interview:

> I said to my colleagues, should we stick to the traditional concept that war crimes can only be committed in international armed conflict? This to me is crazy! A rape is a rape; a murder is a murder, whether it is committed within the framework of an international armed conflict, a war proper, or a civil war. The doctrine that had been upheld by everybody, including the International Committee of the Red Cross, was that if you kill civilians, you rape women, you murder wounded POWs in an internal armed conflict—this is not a war crime ... So I said 'why don't we jettison this stupid distinction?' My colleagues said 'yes we agree with what you are saying, it's very nice, but how can you create this criminal offence? Nino, if you can show that there is some custom in international law supporting

---

[173] 'To Be an International Criminal Court Judge: Conversation with Antonio Cassese', Distinguished Fellows Lecture Series, 4 September 2003, Hauser Global Law School Program, NYU School of Law, 15, reprinted in JHH Weiler, 'Editorial' (2011) 22 *EJIL* 931, 942.

[174] Hoffman (n 122) 63.

[175] ibid, 58 (quoting A Cassese, 'La Guerre Civile et le Droit International' (1986) 90 *RGDIP* 553, 578.

[176] ibid, 79–80. Cassese's post-ICTY career included other influential positions in which he reinforced not just earlier scholarship, but also elements of *Tadić*, for instance, as Chairman of the International Commission of Inquiry on Darfur and, as discussed above, as President of the Special Tribunal for Lebanon. See the references to *Tadić* in *El Sayed* (n 29), and in the Report of the International Commission of Inquiry on Darfur to the United Nations Secretary-General, pursuant to Security Council Resolution 1564 of 18 September 2004 (25 January 2005), UN Doc S/2005/60.

your views, we will go along with it. But try to find some sort of evidence.' So I took six months, and set up a team. … [W]e came up with a lot of evidence … well some evidence.[177]

This is what can be considered 'doing a *Tadić*': an attempt to revolutionise the law through a judicial decision.[178]

For all of the decision's substantive contributions, the most striking characteristic of the *Tadić* decision may be its approach to judicial reasoning in the service of this goal. That approach reflected strong views about the international order and creatively applied sources of international law to change that order.

The Appeals Chamber situated the question of jurisdiction at the crossroads of a fundamental struggle between the state (conceptualised as sovereignty) and the individual (conceptualised as human rights). The not-so-subtle *leitmotif* of the *Tadić* decision is the idea that the state cannot be trusted and that it is for international judges to remake international law in the name of humanity. Hence the imperative that an international tribunal 'be endowed with primacy over national courts', which cannot be trusted to do the right thing.[179] It is the international judge who will be 'at least equally fair' and 'more distanced from the facts of the case' than a domestic judge, but who will also benefit the community, as well as the accused, by 'taking a broader view of the matter'.[180] This thinking also animated the sidestep by the Appeals Chamber on the meaning of 'established by law', in which the Appeals Chamber displaced the more literal interpretation of the term, which suggested the need for the consent of states through a law-making process, with a right to procedural fairness.[181]

This theme also comes to the fore in the analysis of the extent to which the customary rules of IHL governed internal armed conflicts. The decision is a sustained assault on the notion that policy—and thus law—can justify a distinction in the applicable law based on classification of the conflict. Thus we have the powerful assertions that the concept of sovereignty 'recently has suffered progressive erosion at the hands of more liberal forces at work in the democratic societies, particularly in the field of human rights',[182] that 'A State sovereignty-oriented approach has been gradually supplanted by a human-being-oriented approach' and that the maxim that 'all law is created for the benefit of human beings' finds itself with a 'firm foothold in the international community'.[183]

---

[177] 'To Be an International Criminal Court Judge' (n 173).

[178] Introducing the concept, Robert Cryer used the term 'to do a *Tadić*' more narrowly, namely to refer to the way in which the ICTY had expanded its subject-matter jurisdiction. See R Cryer, Lauterpacht Centre for International Law, Friday Lecture 'On the Siren Song of Sui Generis: Customary law, humanitarian law, and the ILC' (16 January 2015) (minute 41) <www.lcil.cam.ac.uk/events/lcil-friday-lecture-siren-song-sui-generis-customary-law-humanitarian-law-and-ilc-professor-r> accessed 21 February 2017.

[179] *Tadić* (Interlocutory Appeal) (n 2) [58].

[180] ibid, [62].

[181] There is an irony in the fact that the Appeals Chamber simultaneously rejected the notion that the requirements placed by international human rights law on domestic judiciaries apply to international tribunals: ibid, [42].

[182] ibid, [55].

[183] ibid, [97].

However, the Appeals Chamber's strike against sovereignty was not unambiguous. As indicated above, it chipped away at sovereignty by empowering a mere individual to assert an objection to primacy that might otherwise have been seen as falling within the exclusive purview of the state, but in justifying this it emphasised the importance of state sovereignty within the international system. The Appeals Chamber also reinforced the centrality of sovereignty to international law by seeking to support its overtly moralist reasoning with the positivist sources of international law, grounded in state consent. This style of reasoning was strategic. Robert Cryer explains that Cassese 'understood the necessity of bringing states along with him by using the language, and, to a fair extent, methods of positivism', an approach that Cryer labels 'presentational positivism'.[184] The Appeals Chamber's effort to eviscerate the barrier between international and internal armed conflict as to prohibited means and methods of warfare exemplifies the technique. The seven paragraphs dedicated to establishing that the customary rules concerning these prohibitions in international armed conflict were also applicable to internal armed conflict contain only two examples of state practice: Iraq's use of chemical weapons against the Kurds in 1988, an act that was widely condemned by states as contrary to international law;[185] and a decision by the Supreme Court of Nigeria regarding perfidy.[186] This limited discussion of state practice is framed, however, by a more basic call to fundamental notions of justice:

> Indeed, elementary considerations of humanity and common sense make it preposterous that the use by States of weapons prohibited in armed conflicts between themselves be allowed when States try to put down rebellion by their own nationals on their own territory. What is inhumane, and consequently proscribed, in international wars, cannot but be inhumane and inadmissible in civil strife.[187]

This is the *Tadić* (or Cassese?) approach in a nutshell: a judgment that, in Cryer's words, is 'largely clothed in positivist garb', but which 'reads with more than a hint of the law of nature'.[188] We see this play on positivist sources as well in the reliance on statements, rather than battlefield practice, to identify customary international law.[189] Cassese sought 'to hold states up to the standards they claimed to live up to, rather than what their practice may imply'.[190] This was prudent and tactical, as states may be disinclined to condemn a tribunal's declaration of custom that reflects their 'avowed position', if not the reality.[191] But the actual evidence relied upon to demonstrate the existence of customary international law applicable to internal armed

---

[184] R Cryer, 'International Criminal Tribunals and Sources of International Law: Antonio Cassese's Contribution to the Canon' (2012) 10 *JICJ* 1045, 1048.

[185] *Tadić* (Interlocutory Appeal) (n 2) [120]–[124].

[186] ibid, [125]. The reliance placed on this example has been criticized. See Greenwood, 'International Humanitarian Law' (n 124) 278.

[187] *Tadić* (Interlocutory Appeal) (n 2) [119].

[188] R Cryer, 'The Philosophy of International Criminal Law' in A Orakhelashvili (ed), *Research Handbook on the Theory and History of International Law* (Cheltenham, Edward Elgar, 2011) 232, 246.

[189] T Meron, 'The Continuing Role of Custom in the Formation of International Humanitarian Law' (1996) 90 *AJIL* 235, 239–40.

[190] Cryer, 'International Criminal Tribunals' (n 184) 1050.

[191] ibid, 1050.

conflict probably did not meet the traditional threshold. In Cassese's own words, the Appeals Chamber came up with 'some' custom, 'some' evidence: not exactly evidence of 'settled practice'[192] or conduct that is 'widespread and uniform'.[193] But for Cassese, it seems, formal sources doctrine was ill-suited to the situation that faced the Tribunal given the 'object and purpose behind the enactment of the Statute'.[194] Taking a teleological approach to interpretation of the Statute, the Appeals Chamber emphasised that the Tribunal's purpose was to deter further atrocities and to contribute to the re-establishment of peace and security.[195] For Cassese, this was a situation in which, in his own words, 'you go beyond the black letter of the law because you look at the spirit of the law'.[196] At times, this seems to turn interpretation on its head: rather than taking the text, ie what the Security Council actually provided in the Statute, as the starting point, the judge starts with the Council's purported 'purpose' and what it therefore must have wanted to provide.[197] The judicial reasoning in *Tadić* reflects the handiwork of a careful legal strategist: a considered approach, attuned to the language and vocabulary of international law, that works hard to make a certain 'humanising' impulse acceptable to the community of states.

Despite the paucity of practice on which it relies, the decision functioned as a catalyst for the formation of 'high speed custom'[198] and has been hugely influential in changing and shaping the *opinio juris* that it claimed to be affirming. Whatever one's qualms may be about the methodology,[199] it is difficult not to conclude on the basis of subsequent practice that this 'interweaving of naturalist sentiment and positivist proof' has been successful:[200] post-*Tadić* the distinctions in the rules applicable to international and internal armed conflict have generally been reduced. Nor did the legitimacy of the Tribunal appear to suffer; the opposite may be true. The outcome may have been widely accepted, and indeed embraced, because the Chamber had 'identified a transformation that was indeed already well under way'.[201] In any event, the legitimacy of international criminal courts does not seem to turn on

---

[192] North Sea Continental Shelf (Federal Republic of Germany/Denmark; Federal Republic of Germany/Netherlands) (Merits) [1969] ICJ Rep 1, 44, [77].

[193] Maritime Delimitation and Territorial Questions Between Qatar and Bahrain (Merits) [2001] ICJ Rep 40, 102, [205].

[194] *Tadić* (Interlocutory Appeal) (n 2) [71].

[195] ibid, [72].

[196] H Verrijn Stuart and M Simons, *The Prosecutor and the Judge: Benjamin Ferencz and Antonio Cassese, Interviews and Writings* (Amsterdam, Amsterdam University Press, 2009) 52–53. Note how this style of reasoning was followed by Judge Baragwanath, the only dissenting judge in the *Ayyash* decision by the STL, where he stated: 'interpretation is not confined to the literal language of any text'.

[197] See, for instance, *Tadić* (Interlocutory Appeal) (n 2) [78]: 'the Security Council's object in enacting the Statute—to prosecute and punish persons responsible for certain condemned acts being committed in a conflict understood to contain both internal and international aspects—suggests that the Security Council intended that, to the extent possible, the subject-matter jurisdiction of the International Tribunal should extend to both internal and international armed conflicts'.

[198] Hoffman (n 122) 69.

[199] For example, Hoffman's identification of the risk of 'a special kind of "meta-international" law' that takes root in the doctrine, but deviates from the preferences of 'the primary law-makers, the states': ibid, 80.

[200] Cryer, 'Philosophy of International Criminal Law' (n 188) 247.

[201] D Robinson and G MacNeil, 'The Tribunals and the Renaissance of International Criminal Law: Three Themes' (2016) 110 *AJIL* 191, 201.

respect for the principle of legality.[202] As Payam Akhavan has observed, in the field of international criminal law, 'no one wins prizes for strict interpretation'.[203]

However, this is not to say that the legal reasoning and judicial innovation of *Tadić* are a landmark in the sense of signpost: *Tadić* is as much a product of its time (post-Cold War and pre-9/11) as of Cassese. The Tribunal's establishment signaled an unusual, if not unique, moment in which the P-5 members of the Security Council were acting in concert and could proceed with little fear that their own nationals would face prosecution.[204] They were therefore willing to vest an extraordinary amount of power and discretion in the judges at The Hague.[205] With the tribunal having been created as an enforcement measure under Chapter VII, there was also no risk of 'exit' by states in reaction to judicial overreach.[206] This free-wheeling approach to the grant of judicial authority in the case of the ICTY, of course, stands in marked contrast with the approach taken in the Rome Statute of the ICC, for most states a less 'safe' tribunal,[207] which seems designed to rein in any progressive tendencies on the part of judges, and where, if judges go beyond what states are willing to accept, threat of exit has proven a very real option.[208] Thus the decision on the interlocutory appeal in *Tadić* is more a high-water point landmark than a signpost in terms of its judicial reasoning and innovation. There is little question that states have made some effort to place limits on the possibility of what we might call the 'Cassese approach',[209] or 'doing a Tadić'.

V. CONCLUSION

The *Tadić* Interlocutory Appeal is thus a landmark of public international law in the sense of both signpost and high-water point. It has functioned significantly as a signpost in its validation of the power of the Security Council to pursue the project of international criminal law and of developments in international humanitarian law, particularly the diminishing relevance of the distinction between international and non-international armed conflict. It is in this latter respect, however, primarily a signpost on paper; the bombs that are being dropped on civilians in Syria and Yemen

---

[202] See Alvarez, 'Nuremburg Revisited' (n 74) 264 (noting that 'For those who support prosecutions of these horrible crimes, the fulfillment of particularistic legal niceties may not be the sole test of legitimacy' and that 'justice may not always comply strictly with law').

[203] Comment during the workshop 'Landmark Cases in Public International Law', All Souls College, Oxford, 17 June 2015.

[204] Hoffman (n 122) 75.

[205] During the negotiations to establish the ICTY, the United States viewed it as 'desirable to give the Tribunal wide latitude' because this was likely to produce 'a more expansive definition' of IHL than negotiations would have generated: MJ Matheson and D Scheffer, 'The Creation of the Tribunals' (2016) 110 *AJIL* 173, 185.

[206] Hoffman (n 122) 76.

[207] R Cryer, Prosecuting International Crimes: Selectivity and the International Criminal Law Regime (Cambridge, CUP, 2005) 232ff.

[208] See, for example, South Africa's instrument of withdrawal from the ICC, available at <www.capetalk.co.za/articles/193225/south-africa-to-begin-exit-process-from-icc> accessed 21 February 2017.

[209] Cassese, in his own words, described this as a perception of the judge 'overdoing it, becoming dangerous by say, producing judgments that can be innovative': Verrijn Stuart and Simons (n 196) 52–53.

at the time of writing provide only the latest indication that states remain unwilling to implement—or to enforce—the robust image of IHL in internal armed conflict that *Tadić* announced. In other areas, *Tadić* is better viewed as a high-water mark, including as a case study in judicial law-making and legal reasoning that invokes natural law or appeals to morality to overcome perceived shortcomings in the positive law. That said, even in areas where its approach has subsequently not been uniformly followed, for instance on the possibility of a Security Council-created tribunal reviewing the legality of its own creation, the precedents established by *Tadić* remain part of the landscape of international law. In terms of the landmark status of the Interlocutory Appeal, the aspects of that decision that appear to be high-water marks today may yet turn out to be signposts in the future.

17

The *Nuclear Weapons* Advisory Opinions (1996)

SURABHI RANGANATHAN

I. INTRODUCTION

ON 8 JULY 1996, the International Court of Justice (ICJ or 'the Court') delivered two advisory opinions. The first, *Legality of the Use by a State of Nuclear Weapons in Armed Conflict*,[1] was in response to a request by the World Health Organization (WHO). The second, *Legality of the Threat or Use of Nuclear Weapons*,[2] was in response to a request by the United Nations General Assembly (UNGA).

In the first advisory opinion, the Court found it had no jurisdiction to answer the question asked, which was: 'In view of the health and environmental effects, would the use of nuclear weapons by a state in war or other armed conflict be a breach of its obligations under international law including the WHO Constitution?'[3] According to the Court, this question concerned a matter beyond the competence of the organisation. In the second advisory opinion, the Court had no difficulty in dismissing a challenge to its jurisdiction; but was unable to offer a conclusive answer to the question asked, which was: 'Is the threat or use of nuclear weapons in any circumstance permitted under international law?'[4] Following an extensive review of international law, the Court offered a number of conclusions, the most prominent of which were the two sentences that constituted operative paragraph 2E:

> It follows from the above-mentioned requirements that the threat or use of nuclear weapons would generally be contrary to the rules of international law applicable in armed conflict, and in particular the principles and rules of humanitarian law;

> However, in view of the current state of international law, and of the elements of fact at its disposal, the Court cannot conclude definitively whether the threat or use of nuclear weapons would be lawful or unlawful in an extreme circumstance of self-defence, in which the very survival of a State would be at stake;[5]

---

[1] [1996] ICJ Rep 66. Hereafter '*Legality of Nuclear Weapons in Armed Conflict*'.
[2] [1996] ICJ Rep 226. Hereafter '*Legality of Nuclear Weapons*'.
[3] Res WHA46.40 (14 May 1993).
[4] UNGA Res 49/75 K (15 December 1994).
[5] *Legality of Nuclear Weapons* (n 2) 266, [105].

The Court's meaning in respect of this operative paragraph has remained a matter of debate, with the popular view being that the Court here confessed to a *non liquet.*[6]

The two advisory opinions have been prominent in the Court's body of jurisprudence, and it is appropriate also to classify them as landmarks in international law. As to the Court's jurisprudence, they represent a number of 'firsts': the WHO advisory opinion was the first occasion on which the Court declined to answer the question put to it;[7] the UNGA advisory opinion was the first occasion on which all 14 judges wrote opinions,[8] although it was certainly not the first occasion on which the casting vote of the President determined the answer given by the Court.[9] Most importantly, as some judges noted,[10] this was first occasion on which questions of a general nature were asked of the Court—previous requests for advisory opinions related to specific factual situations[11]—and this factor prompted the Court to reflect upon its own advisory function, and place within the scheme of the United Nations Organisation. The opinions were also significant in the political trajectory of the Court. For, although the requests for the advisory opinions were formally made by the WHO and the UNGA, they were initiated by Third World states, and were a sign, perhaps, of the Court's success in its endeavour to rebuild the confidence amongst these constituents that had been gravely undermined by the 1966 *South West Africa* judgment. At the historical juncture at which the two questions were posed to the Court, amidst expansive claims that with the end of the Cold War the era of international law and the values represented by it could truly begin, the requests were perhaps also an effort to recruit the Court in the struggle for complete nuclear disarmament.

As to international law, setting aside for the moment the novelty of the Court's finding of a *non liquet,* the two opinions also provided clarity on a number of important basic questions about international law: the relationship between international human rights law and international humanitarian law, the law of international organisations and inter-institutional relations within the UN, the significance of General Assembly resolutions in the development of international law, the development of environmental law and its relationship to the law of armed conflict, and the constraints imposed by the law of armed conflict on the use of force in self-defence.[12] Its final, uncertainly formed conclusion in the *Legality of Nuclear Weapons* was itself significant, for by this formulation, the court put on display, perhaps for the first (and only) time, *both* its resistance to the view that difficult questions were

---

[6] P Weil, '"The Court Cannot Conclude Definitively …": *Non Liquet* Revisited' (1997) 36 *Columbia Journal of Transnational Law* 109.

[7] The Permanent Court of International Justice had declined the Council of the League of Nations' request for an advisory opinion in *Status of Eastern Carelia* (1923) PCIJ (series B) No 5, 7.

[8] As Akande notes, this speaks both to the 'difficulty of the decision the Court faced but also to the seriousness with which the task was carried out': D Akande 'Nuclear Weapons, Unclear Law: Deciphering the Nuclear Weapons Advisory Opinions of the International Court' (1998) 68 *BYIL* 165, 168.

[9] Nor the most notorious: *South West Africa, Second Phase, Judgment* (1966) ICJ Rep 6. See this volume, ch 11.

[10] See, eg, *Legality of Nuclear Weapons* (n 2) Judge Oda dissenting, 371–72, [50]–[51].

[11] See chs 10, 11 and 22 in this volume.

[12] In these respects the Court strengthened the *bedrock* of international law: See this volume, ch 16.

incapable of a judicial answer, and its discomfort with taking an approach that would effectively reduce a horrifying situation of mass killing to measurements of necessity and proportionality.[13] Operative paragraph 2E is disappointing in its drafting, but at the same time, together with the advisory opinion as a whole, it is a remarkable dual assertion, both of international law as the medium for political and military assessments, and of that which remains unsayable within it.

This chapter will explore specific aspects of the two Advisory Opinions. These are indicated in the following section, which first provides an overview of the Court's conclusions in both cases. The chapter is by no means a comprehensive treatment of the two cases; indeed, such a treatment would be impossible within the framework of a short chapter. Fortunately, it would also be superfluous in the literature, for this chapter is neither the first word on these cases, nor likely the last; those interested should refer to the several rich commentaries and critiques that have been published in the past years.[14]

II. THE TWO ADVISORY OPINIONS, AND KEY THEMES

In *Legality of Nuclear Weapons in Armed Conflict*, the Court determined that it had no jurisdiction to answer the question posed to it by the WHO. The Court noted that its advisory jurisdiction is governed by Article 65(1) of its Statute, which provides that the Court may opine on 'any legal question at the request of whatever body may be authorized by or in accordance with the Charter of the United Nations to make such a request'. The relevant provision of the UN Charter, Article 96(b), states: 'Other organs of the United Nations [besides the UNGA and the Security Council] and specialised agencies, which may at any time be so authorised by the General Assembly, may also request advisory opinions of the Court on legal questions arising within the scope of their activities'. Cumulatively, in deciding upon its jurisdiction to respond to a question asked by a specialised agency like the WHO, the Court must consider whether it is duly authorised to seek advisory opinions, the question asked is of a legal nature, and falls within the scope of activities of that agency.

The Court accepted that the WHO was authorised to seek advisory opinions from the Court.[15] Moreover it was not perturbed by allegations that the request had a

---

[13] See M Koskenniemi, 'The Silence of Law/The Voice of Justice' in L Boisson de Chazournes and P Sands (eds), *International Law, the International Court of Justice and Nuclear Weapons* (Cambridge, CUP, 1999) 488.

[14] A brief selection includes: Boisson de Chazournes and Sands, *International Law* (n 13) Akande, 'Nuclear Weapons' (n 8); R Falk, 'Nuclear Weapons, International Law and the World Court: A Historic Encounter' (1997) 91 *AJIL* 64; P Weiss, R Falk, MJ Matheson, BH Weston, S Mendlovitz, M Datan, G Abi-Saab and A Chayes, 'Nuclear Weapons, the World Court and Global Security: Symposium' (1997) 7 *Transnational Law and Contemporary Problems* 313–486; G Herczegh, Y Sandoz, L Condorelli, E David, L Doswald-Beck, H Fujita, C Greenwood, TLH McCormack, M Mohr, JH McNeill and ICRC, 'The Advisory Opinion of the International Court of Justice on the legality of nuclear weapons and international humanitarian law: Special Issue 316', (1997) 37 *International Review of the Red Cross* 6–119.

[15] *Legality of Nuclear Weapons in Armed Conflict* (n 1) 72, [11]–[12]. The WHO had obtained an advisory opinion in *Interpretation of the Agreement of 25 March 1951 between the WHO and Egypt* [1980] ICJ Rep 73.

political aspect. It held that question was of a legal nature, asking the Court to 'identify the obligations of States under the rules of law invoked, and assess whether the behaviour in question conforms to those obligations'. Satisfied on this point, the Court would not refuse to answer a question simply because it also had a political aspect; it was unconcerned with the political motives that had inspired the request, and the possible political implications of its opinion.[16]

The Court's decision to decline jurisdiction turned on the third consideration. It found that the question asked by the WHO fell outside the scope of the activities of that agency. Although the WHO request referred to the health effects of nuclear weapons and—the Court agreed—the WHO was authorised to take preventive measures to protect against such effects, the Court considered that the status in law of nuclear weapons was irrelevant to the WHO's performance of its functions. The Court reasoned that the health effects of nuclear weapons, the WHO's duty to deal with these health effects, and the measures that it would take in doing so, would remain unchanged whether the weapons were used legally or illegally. Therefore, it did not seem to the Court that the WHO Constitution conferred upon it the competence to address the question of legality of the use of nuclear weapons, nor to direct that question to the Court.[17] The Court further pointed out that the WHO did not possess a general competence; its powers were outlined in its constituent treaty. Although it was possible to infer certain additional powers necessary for the fulfilment of the WHO's stated purposes, the question of legality of nuclear weapons— more properly a concern of other bodies within the UN system—could not be judged as falling within its express or implied powers.[18]

In contrast, in the *Legality of Nuclear Weapons*, the Court was satisfied as to all three considerations for the exercise of its jurisdiction. The UNGA's competence to seek advisory opinions is provided in Article 96(a) of the UN Charter, which states that it 'may request the International Court of Justice to give an advisory opinion on any legal question'. Although the contrast with the language used in Article 96(b) suggests that the UNGA is not limited by the condition that the request must concern a question falling with the scope of its activities, the Court did not rely on this distinction, preferring to note that 'in the present case, the General Assembly has competence in any event to seise the Court', for the request fell well within the scope of its activities.[19] The Court also rejected the proposition that is should use its discretion to decline the request because the question asked was vague and abstract; addressed complex issues that were being considered by interested states and within other UN bodies with an express mandate to address them; the opinion would provide no practical assistance to the UNGA in carrying out its functions; and could undermine political progress on a sensitive subject.[20]

---

[16] *Legality of Nuclear Weapons in Armed Conflict* (n 1) 73–74, [15]–[17].
[17] ibid, 75–77, [20]–[22].
[18] ibid, 78–81, [25]–[26].
[19] *Legality of Nuclear Weapons* (n 2) 233 [11]–[12]. Some states had urged the Court to interpret paragraph (a) of Article 96 in line with paragraph (b), notwithstanding the difference in wording; see, ibid, 232–33 [10]; it appears that the Court was neither willing to endorse this restrictive interpretation nor reject it.
[20] ibid, 236, [15].

Some of the Court's particular answers are of interest in revealing how it views its judicial function, and will be discussed in later sections; here it may be noted that the Court asserted that as 'the principal judicial organ' of the UN, 'it should not, in principle, refuse to give an advisory opinion', and only compelling reasons would lead it to such a refusal once it had established that it had jurisdiction.[21]

The Court then proceeded to the merits of the question, examining states' obligations under international human rights law,[22] law prohibiting genocide,[23] international environmental law,[24] law on the use of force,[25] and law of armed conflict including specific treaty and customary law obligations relating to nuclear weapons,[26] international humanitarian law,[27] and the principle of neutrality.[28] It reached the following conclusions.[29] First, neither conventional nor customary international law afforded any specific authorisation of the threat or use of nuclear weapons. Second, nor did either body of law afford any comprehensive or universal prohibition of the threat or use of nuclear weapons.[30] Third, any threat or use of force by means of nuclear weapons that was contrary to Article 2(4) of the UN Charter, or failed to meet the requirements of Article 51, would be unlawful. Fourth, any threat or use of nuclear weapons should also satisfy the requirements of the law of armed conflict, especially the rules and principles of international humanitarian law and the express obligations relating to nuclear weapons provided for in treaties and other undertakings. Fifth, the controversial operative paragraph 2E. And sixth, an also controversial, if unanimous observation that states were obliged 'to pursue in good faith and bring to a conclusion negotiations leading to nuclear disarmament in all its aspects under strict and effective international control'.[31] To be clear, this observation was more controversial for the fact that it was offered at all—outside the terms of reference of the question asked to the Court—than for its content, which clarified the meaning of the obligation provided for under Article VI of the Nuclear Non Proliferation Treaty (NPT).[32]

In what follows, I discuss the two opinions under five heads, which, although not adding up to a comprehensive engagement with either text, illuminate the work of the Court in two contexts: the Court's institutional context; and the context of

---

[21] ibid, 235, [14].
[22] ibid, 239–40, [24]–[25].
[23] ibid, 240, [26].
[24] ibid, 241–43, [27]–[33].
[25] ibid, 244–47, [37]–[49].
[26] ibid, 247–55, [52]–[73].
[27] ibid, 256–60, [75]–[87] and 261–63, [90]–[96].
[28] ibid, 260–61, [88]–[96].
[29] ibid, 266–67, [105].
[30] The Court rejected the interesting argument that, given the scale of their effects, the very use of nuclear weapons would permit the inference of an intent to destroy the group against which they were used. The Court considered that a specific genocidal intent could only be determined in the specific context of each case, it could not be located in the fact of the use of nuclear weapons. Here, as elsewhere, the Court seemed influenced by the limits of its own knowledge as to whether it was technically feasible to use nuclear weapons in such a way as to limit the damage caused by them. See ibid, 240, [26].
[31] ibid, 267, [105 (2F)].
[32] Adopted 1 July 1968, entered into force 5 March 1970, 729 UNTS 161.

nuclear governance. Of the five, the first two speak particularly to the first context, and the remaining three to the second, but there are, inevitably, spillovers. The five heads are: firstly, the politics of the two requests and the Court's own response; secondly, the Court's view of intra-institutional relations within the UN; third, the meaning(s) given to the controversial operative paragraph 2E; fourth, the choice of a *non liquet* formulation; and fifth, a brief review of the developments in nuclear governance since the two opinions.

III. THE POLITICS UNDERLYING THE REQUESTS, AND THE COURT'S RESPONSE

In his review of the two opinions, Dapo Akande had observed that '[t]he history of the requests for the advisory opinions on the question of the legality of the threat or use of nuclear weapons is unique and filled with intrigue'.[33] And, although in both cases, the Court took the formal position that it would not concern itself with the 'political nature of the motives which may be said to have inspired the request and the political implications that the opinion given might have',[34] it seems fair to assume that the political context to the requests did influence the Court to some extent. At least one judge, Oda, focused his opinions entirely on this context, making it clear that his opposition to the Court delivering an opinion in *either* case arose from his reluctance to see it being used as an instrument to advance a specific political aim— of obtainment of a judicial declaration of the illegality of nuclear weapons in the bid to advance the goal of complete nuclear disarmament.[35] Judge Guillaume too noted that the circumstances of the *seisin* were such as could have justified the Court in also declining the General Assembly's request, although he did not vote against the Court's finding of jurisdiction.[36] Other judges, notably Koroma and Weeramantry, took the opposite view, expressing sympathy with the underlying object of the two requests and noting that the Court's response was called for precisely because of the fundamental political importance of the issue placed before it.[37]

The precise circumstance that Judges Oda and Guillaume mentioned as a concern was that the requests had been catalysed by the lobbying activity of non-governmental organisations keen to press nuclear weapons-possessing states towards expeditious disarmament. They noted the role played by organisations such as the International Association of Lawyers against Nuclear Arms, International Physicians for the Prevention of Nuclear War and the International Peace Bureau,

---

[33] Akande (n 8) 169.

[34] *Legality of Nuclear Weapons* (n 2) 234, [13]; *Legality of Nuclear Weapons in Armed Conflict* (n 1) 74, [17].

[35] *Legality of Nuclear Weapons* (n 2) Judge Oda dissenting, 330–74, [1]–[55]; *Legality of Nuclear Weapons in Armed Conflict* (n 1) Judge Oda dissenting, 88–96, [1]–[16].

[36] *Legality of Nuclear Weapons* (n 2) Judge Guillaume separate opinion, 287, [2].

[37] ibid, Judge Weeramantry dissenting, 429–554; Judge Koroma dissenting, 556–82; *Legality of Nuclear Weapons in Armed Conflict* (n 1) Judge Weeramantry dissenting, 101–71; Judge Koroma dissenting, 172–224.

which, having jointly established the World Court Project in mid-1992,[38] sought 'to obtain from the Court a proclamation of the illegality of the threat or use of nuclear weapons'.[39] Judge Oda's opinions offered detailed accounts of influence of NGO activity on the formulation of the two requests for advisory opinions; while Judge Guillaume, although not entering into similar details 'wondered whether, in such circumstances, the requests for opinions could still be regarded as coming from the Assemblies which had adopted them or whether, piercing the veil, the Court should not have dismissed them as inadmissible'.[40] Ultimately, however, he was satisfied that 'Governments and intergovernmental institutions still retain sufficient independence of decision to resist the powerful pressure groups which besiege them'.[41] To Judge Oda, the split in the votes taken at both the World Health Assembly (WHA) and the UNGA on making the requests was also significant, because he saw it as reflecting the opposition between those who wished to recruit the Court as an ally in a political struggle and those who were more mindful of the distinctive competence both of the forum within which they were acting, and of the Court itself.

The parties ranged on either side of the votes at the WHA and the UNGA were the same: *de jure* nuclear weapons states (NWS, identified as such by the NPT Art IX(3)) and their allies on the one hand, and most members of the Non Aligned Movement (NAM) on the other. Judge Oda recognised this of course, but characterised the position of the NWS and their allies as solely concerned with the appropriateness of the *seisin*. In relation to the WHO request, he noted that even the WHO Legal Counsel 'was fully aware of and actually asserted the Organization's lack of competence to request an advisory opinion of the Court'[42] (although this is reading too much into the statements of the Counsel);[43] and described the discussions as wholly focused on whether the request would fall within the competence of the WHO, and not on the substance of the question.[44] In relation to the UNGA request, he endorsed the arguments of the NWS and their allies that the question asked was a political one that could damage the credibility of the Court as well as undermine negotiations at other forums, and observed that the partisans of the resolution failed to offer an explanation as to why the '*lex lata* concerning the "threat or use of nuclear weapons" should, as of 1994, require clarification by the International Court of Justice'.[45]

Nevertheless, there was more, both to the propagation and opposition of the two requests. Judge Oda's dismissive criticism that 'no positive argument in support of

---

[38] See <http://lcnp.org/wcourt > accessed 14 July 2017.

[39] *Legality of Nuclear Weapons* (n 2) Judge Guillaume separate opinion, 287, [2].

[40] ibid, 287–88, [2].

[41] ibid, 288, [2].

[42] *Legality of Nuclear Weapons in Armed Conflict* (n 1) Judge Oda dissenting, 96, [16].

[43] On this point, see V Leary, 'The WHO case: Implications for Specialised Agencies', in Boisson de Chazournes and Sands, *International Law* (n 13) 122–26. As Leary notes, the WHO Counsel adopted a posture of neutrality on the basis that this was enforced upon him by the division in the WHO membership—he could not take a position that would uphold one of the competing attitudes; Judge Weeramantry, however, expressed discomfort with the neutral and detached way in which the WHO presented its position, noting that it did not accord with the fact that a large majority of the WHA had supported the request: ibid, Judge Weeramantry dissenting, 112–13.

[44] ibid, Judge Oda dissenting, 94, [12].

[45] *Legality of Nuclear Weapons* (n 2) Judge Oda dissenting, 337–40, [10]–[12].

the request was heard from any delegate ... Rather, the statements ... appear for the most part to have been no more than appeals for the elimination of nuclear weapons' and emphasis on the vulnerability of NAM states to NGO lobbying, undervalue the importance of the disarmament cause at the time, and the importance of the question of legality to the cause. The issue of legality, of clarifying the *lex lata*, was critical in 1994 because it was at that time that the balance of obligations, between NWS and other states was being reassessed. The NPT, famously encapsulating the bargain that the NWS would work towards the elimination of their arsenals while others would refrain from developing nuclear weapons, was due for a review in 1995, on which occasion a decision as to its longevity would also be taken.[46] Meanwhile, the bargain had begun to chafe. It was apparent, not least from the 564-page dossier submitted to the Court by the UNGA as part of its request, that there had been a lack of progress on disarmament negotiations at multilateral forums.[47] The previous years had witnessed diminishing support for a series of UNGA resolutions titled 'Non-use of nuclear weapons and the prevention of nuclear war', which called for the adoption of a binding agreement to prohibit the threat or use of nuclear weapons; and impediments to the conclusion of a comprehensive nuclear test ban treaty (the CTBT, now adopted, remains not in force).[48,49] A slew of measures, including the strengthening of export control frameworks (including resuscitation of the Nuclear Suppliers Group[50] (NSG)), expansion of the International Atomic Energy Agency's (IAEA) verification mechanisms,[51] and the United States' adoption of the Nuclear Non Proliferation Act[52]—although important for securing non-proliferation—also seemed to tilt the focus wholly in that direction, and away from the parallel goal of disarmament.

Paradoxically, these very measures served as fodder for arguments of nuclear discrimination, by states that had either refused to sign the NPT for that reason (India, Pakistan), or were trying to exit from it (North Korea), or were undermining it in fact (Iraq). NAM states' perception that Israel was able to circumvent the non-proliferation regime altogether also did not help matters. Although none of these

---

[46] NPT Article X (2).

[47] Request for Advisory Opinion (including the dossier of documents), 6 January 1995, <www.icj-cij. org/docket/files/95/7646.pdf>. I discuss some of the points made here, in this chapter, more briefly in S Ranganathan, 'Nuclear Weapons and the Court', Symposium on the Marshall Islands case (2017) 111 *AJIL Unbound* 88.

[48] The CTBT was adopted on 10 September 1996, but is yet to be ratified by eight of the 44 nuclear capable states identified by it. It cannot enter into force until these ratifications are received.

[49] Judge Oda recounts these developments in detail in his *Legality of Nuclear Weapons* opinion.

[50] <www.nuclearsuppliersgroup.org/en> accessed 14 July 2017; 'The Nuclear Suppliers Group: Its Origins, Role and Activities', Background document, INFCIRC/539/Rev 3 (2005).

[51] The IAEA reports that following proliferation concerns vis-à-vis Iraq and North Korea, it launched 'Programme 93+2' in late 1993 to strengthen its safeguards mechanisms. Its objective was to improve its capacity to detect undeclared nuclear material and activities. Some of the relevant improvements were achieved under the existing framework of comprehensive safeguards (INFCIRC/153 (corr), for others the IAEA sought additional legal authority by asking states to conclude an Additional Protocol (INFCIRC/540(corr),1997):<www.iaea.org/safeguards/safeguards-legal-framework/additional-protocol> accessed 14 July 2017.

[52] Public Law 103–236, 30 April 1994.

developments were expected to obstruct the extension of the NPT (and indeed the timing of the requests was such that the Court could not be reasonably expected to answer the questions posed prior to the extension conference), it was hoped that the Court, in pronouncing that the threat or use of nuclear weapons was totally prohibited, would restore the balance between the two objectives and provide fresh impetus for the disarmament movement. It is worth noting the observation of the delegate from Vanuatu that progress in obtaining a ban on atmospheric nuclear testing in the Pacific (with its brutal costs to the health of Pacific Islanders) was only achieved once the matter was taken to the Court.[53] As her speech made clear, she was indeed seeking to recruit the Court, but to a cause that seemed insurmountable without its intervention.

All of this was perfectly clear to Judge Oda. Indeed, he observed that in seeking an opinion on the legality of the threat or use of nuclear weapons, some states were effectively hoping to obtain a pronouncement on the illegality of possession or production of nuclear weapons ... 'thus laterally achieving agreement on the Convention which would establish the illegality of nuclear weapons themselves'.[54] Such an engagement appeared to him an act of *lawfare* (although he did not use the term)—'commissioning the sanction of the court to make claims for resources, recognition, voice, integrity, sovereignty'[55]—and entirely out of keeping with the advisory function of the Court. Particularly of concern to him was the challenge implied to the NPT, which he considered 'a necessary evil in the context of scrutiny', further placing on record that he thought it 'most unlikely that ... nuclear-weapon States will use those weapons, even among themselves, but the possibility of the use

---

[53] World Health Assembly, 46th Meeting 3–14 May 1993, Verbatim Records of Plenary Meetings, WHA46/1993/REC2, 275. The cases referred to were *Nuclear Tests (New Zealand v France)* (1974) ICJ Rep 457 and *(Australia v France)*, (1974) ICJ Rep 253. In 1995, New Zealand instituted an application inviting the Court to re-examine the situation described in its previous judgment: *Request for an Examination of the Situation in Accordance with Paragraph 63 of the Court's Judgment of 20 December 1974 in the Nuclear Tests (New Zealand v France)*, Application, 21 August 1995. New Zealand noted that the basis for the previous judgment had been France's unilateral undertaking that it would cease atmospheric nuclear testing; France had since continued underground nuclear testing for several years, agreeing finally to impose a moratorium in 1992, but which it now proposed to lift (just months after the NPT was indefinitely extended). According to New Zealand, it lacked, in the period between 1974 and 1992 the necessary scientific evidence to contest France's underground tests, but it had now become clear that they were as deleterious as atmospheric tests. It asked the Court to declare that the proposed tests would violate the rights of New Zealand and other states, and could not be lawfully undertaken without an Environmental Impact Assessment establishing that they would not contaminate the marine environment. Although the Court dismissed the case as not falling properly under the indicated paragraph 63 of its previous judgment ([1995] ICJ Rep 288), the episode further illustrates the imbalance in the actions taken by NWS in pursuit of horizontal non-proliferation on the one hand (relevant to the non-proliferation element of the NPT bargain), and vertical proliferation to enhance their own arsenals on the other (relevant to the disarmament element).

[54] *Legality of Nuclear Weapons* (n 2) Judge Oda dissenting, 350, [25].

[55] J Comaroff and JL Comaroff, 'An Introduction', in J Comaroff and JL Comaroff (eds), *Law and Disorder in the Postcolony* (Chicago, University of Chicago Press, 2006) 31; in other contexts, bringing matters to the Court for advisory opinion (eg *Wall* [2004] ICJ Rep 136) has been described as lawfare: LN Sadat and J Geng, 'On Legal Subterfuge and the So-called "Lawfare" Debate' (2010) *Case Western Reserve Journal of International Law* 153, 154. In the present context, the evident attempt to use a legal mechanism to coerce a prohibition on the threat or use of nuclear weapons makes the application of the concept all the more apposite.

of those weapons cannot be totally excluded in certain special circumstances [under the logic of nuclear deterrence]', and that both these facts holding true, there was no need, in 1994, to raise the question of the legality or illegality of nuclear weapons.[56]

There is something rather poignant in the *Japanese* judge taking the above position.[57] Perhaps Judge Oda—who has elsewhere noted the fact of Japan's experience with nuclear weapons in appealing for the discontinuance of nuclear testing[58]— would have been less concerned about lawfare had he recognised that the position taken by the NWS and their allies was also a form of lawfare. Their preferred political and military position, the ability to threaten with the use of nuclear weapons—a threat that acquires resonance precisely because the devastation wrought by the use of such weapons is well known—had been dressed up as a *legal* position, preserved by the NPT and the doctrine of deterrence, while the attempt to have the Court merely assess the continuing validity of the position was represented as a political quest.

The Court, fortunately, was unconcerned about being used as a tool of lawfare. It dismissed objections as the political nature of the requests, finding that they had a sufficiently legal core, which permitted the Court to carry out its routine judicial task of assessing 'the legality of the possible conduct of States with regard to the obligations imposed upon them by international law'.[59] In case of the UNGA request, the Court also demonstrated its awareness that 'legality' could be a prize for either side, in firstly recalling that 'in situations in which political considerations are prominent it may be particularly necessary for an international organization to obtain an advisory opinion from the Court as to the legal principles applicable with respect to the matter under debate'[60] and that 'no matter what might be its conclusions ... they would ... present an additional element in the negotiations on the matter'[61] and then proceeding to pronounce, *ultra petita*,[62] on the scope of the disarmament obligation of the NWS. The Court's discussion on this point is no doubt partly a gesture of mitigation following its pronouncement of a *non liquet*;[63] but it is also, as much, a

---

[56] *Legality of Nuclear Weapons* (n 2) Judge Oda dissenting, 364, [41]; also 368–69, [45]–[46].

[57] It has been noted that the Japanese Government, falling within the US nuclear umbrella also took an ambivalent approach to nuclear weapons, with its official view that 'it is difficult to conclude that the use of nuclear weapons is necessarily contrary to current positive international law' being deleted its written submissions because of strongly opposed public opinion (and the unequivocal view of the mayors of Hiroshima and Nagasaki that the use of nuclear weapons was illegal): Y Shigeta, 'The Perspective of Japanese International Lawyers' in Boisson de Chazournes and Sands, *International Law* (n 13) 435–36.

[58] *Request for an Examination of the Situation* (n 53) Judge Oda separate opinion, 310.

[59] *Legality of Nuclear Weapons* (n 2) 234, [13].

[60] ibid.

[61] ibid, 237, [17].

[62] ibid, Judge Guillaume separate opinion, 293, [13]; Vice President Schwebel separate opinion, 329; see also Decl President Bedjaoui, 274, [23] (insisting that the finding with respect to the disarmament obligation was not ultra petita, 'The Court patently had to say [it]'), and Judge Weeramantry dissenting, 437 (noting that operative paragraph 2F was strictly outside the terms of reference of the question, but 'in the overall context of the nuclear weapons problem' a useful reminder of state obligations).

[63] The Court has been known to perform such gestures in other contexts, eg *Arrest Warrant (DRC v Belgium)* [2002] ICJ Rep 3, 25–26, [61].

seizing of occasion to intervene in support of an ongoing campaign. The Court evidently, is not just unafraid of lawfare, but willing to engage in it, albeit to the limited extent made possible by its concern for propriety, non-legislation, and other such factors by which it defines the appropriate scope of its judicial function.

IV. INTRA-INSTITUTIONAL RELATIONS WITHIN THE UN

Although overshadowed its *Legality of Nuclear Weapons* Opinion, the Court's refusal to give an opinion in *Legality of Nuclear Weapons in Armed Conflict* has attracted commentary in relation to its findings that the legality or illegality of nuclear weapons in armed conflict was irrelevant to the WHO's performance of its obligations, and that the request violated the rule of speciality.[64] To that literature, I would like to add only brief observations on how the Court described interinstitutional relations between the WHO, the UNGA, and itself.

That the above-mentioned findings were questionable emerges from the discussion in the previous section: it is not self-evident that the legal or illegal status of nuclear weapons is irrelevant to the WHO's work; and, in such case, the question placed by it before the Court could not be said to violate the rule of speciality, which limits the powers enjoyed by an international organisation to the functions entrusted to them by states.[65]

Nevertheless, although one might disagree with the substance of the Court's findings, the approach taken—judicial determination of the scope of the WHO's powers, and by reference to the idea that its competence is functional, not general— was unexceptionable. Although the Court does not claim to exercise judicial review with respect to UN organs and special agencies, it has been called upon to determine the extent of their powers on a number of occasions.[66] Furthermore, the Court acknowledged that it was for the WHA to determine its own competence to submit a request for an advisory opinion, asserting that the Court was merely pronouncing upon its own competence to give the opinion requested and its review of the WHO constitution followed by necessary implication.[67] And its assertion of the WHO's functional, rather than general competence, reiterates a well-established position in international law.

However, as the Court went on to suggest, its construction of the WHO's competence seemed informed by a further factor:

> [T]he Charter of the United Nations laid the basis of a 'system' designed to organize international co-operation in a coherent fashion by bringing the United Nations, invested with powers of general scope, into relationship with various autonomous and complementary

---

[64] See M Bothe, 'The WHO Request', and Leary, 'The WHO case' in Boisson de Chazournes and Sands, *International Law* (n 13) 103–27.

[65] The Court defines the rule in *Legality of Nuclear Weapons in Armed Conflict* (n 1) 78, [25].

[66] E Lauterpacht, 'Judicial Review of the Acts of International Organisations' in Boisson de Chazournes and Sands (n 13) 92–102, 98.

[67] *Legality of Nuclear Weapons in Armed Conflict* (n 1) 82–83, [29].

organizations, invested with sectorial powers ... the WHO Constitution can only be interpreted, as far as the powers conferred upon that Organization are concerned, by taking due account not only of the general principle of speciality, but also of the logic of the overall system contemplated by the Charter.[68]

The Court thus wished to construe the WHO's powers not only by reference to its specific functions, but also the functions of the other parts of the UN system. Moreover, it seemed that the latter criterion was the more important one, as the Court observed 'it is difficult to imagine what other meaning that notion [of specialized agency] could have if such an organization need only show that the use of certain weapons could affect its objectives in order to be empowered to concern itself with the legality of such use'.[69] The Court described the subject matter of the request—'concerning the use of force, the regulation of armaments and disarmament'[70]—as one peculiarly of concern to the United Nations, not the specialised agencies. Presumably, the indication here was that only the UNGA (whose competence passed without question in *Legality of Nuclear Weapons*), or the Security Council could have placed such a request before the Court; the WHO's request 'encroached'[71] upon their functions.

It has been noted that Court's implied suggestion that there could be no overlap between the functions of the 'members of the UN family' reflects too narrow a view,[72] and one that seems at variance with UN practice, in which we have often seen overlap between the functions of different organs and specialised agencies. Judge Weeramantry specifically noted this, stating that it was 'in the nature of a complex organization like the United Nations that there will be, owing to the multiplicity and complexity of its functions, some areas of overlap between the legitimate spheres of authority of its constituent entities' and emphasising that the Court itself had given expression to the principle of complementarity between the functions of the organisations making up the UN family.[73]

Moreover, if *encroachment* was the concern, then it seems strange that the Court chose not to place any value upon the support expressed for the WHO's request by the UNGA, a body competent not only to seek an opinion of the question, but also, as per Article 96(2) of the UN Charter, the body competent to authorize the WHO to seek advisory opinions. In resolution 49/75 K, containing its own request to the Court for an advisory opinion, the UNGA 'welcome[d]' the WHO request, 'clearly reflect[ing]' (to use the Court's own words), 'the wish of a majority of States that the Assembly should lend its political support to the action taken by the WHO'.[74] Resolution 49/75 K would appear to confirm not only the UNGA's grant of a general

---

[68] ibid, 80, [26].

[69] ibid, 80–81, [26].

[70] ibid, 80, [26].

[71] ibid.

[72] Lauterpacht, 'Judicial Review' (n 66) 100–01.

[73] *Legality of Nuclear Weapons in Armed Conflict* (n 1) Judge Weeramantry dissenting, 150. The case he referred to was *Military and Paramilitary Activities in and against Nicaragua (Nicaragua v USA), Jurisdiction and Admissibility* [1984] ICJ Rep 392, 435, [95].

[74] *Legality of Nuclear Weapons in Armed Conflict* (n 1) 83, [30].

authorisation to seek advisory opinions to the WHO, but its assessment that the present request was in conformity with that general authorisation and complementary to the UNGA's own request. The Court, however, did not draw this conclusion. It stated that it did not consider that 'the General Assembly meant to pass upon the competence of the WHO to request an opinion on the question raised' and further that 'General Assembly could evidently not have intended to disregard the limits within which Article 96, paragraph 2, of the Charter allows it to authorize the specialized agencies to request opinions from the Court'.[75]

In this passage (which Sir Elihu Lauterpacht has described as the most interesting of the opinion from the jurisprudential perspective)[76] the Court gently delivered a double rap on the knuckles of the UNGA;[77] suggesting, in effect, that the UNGA was in danger of exceeding its competence both in seeming to pronounce upon the competence of the WHO; and in the event that it sought to confirm that it had conferred on the WHO an authorisation broad enough to encompass the question asked. The Court, which disclaims any capacity to undertake judicial review, here in fact does review the actions of a principal UN organ, and offers the assessment (albeit in indirect terms) perhaps for the first time, that it has exceeded its powers. Putting to one side its pronouncement on the WHO's competence, this was an interesting position for the Court to have taken vis-à-vis the UNGA.

V. OPERATIVE PARAGRAPH 2E

Let us now turn to the Court's famous pronouncement in *Legality of Nuclear Weapons*. As noted above, the conclusion in operative paragraph 2E consists of two sentences. In the first, the Court notes that 'the threat or use or nuclear weapons would generally be contrary to the rules of international law applicable in armed conflict, and in particular the principles and rules of humanitarian law'. In this sentence, the Court's use of the word 'generally' has produced much confusion.

It is not clear whether the Court is implying, in just this first sentence, that there may be exceptional circumstances—left unelaborated—in which the threat or use of nuclear weapons would not be contrary to the law of armed conflict; or, whether this sentence serves a purely contrapuntal function, throwing into sharp relief that observation in the second sentence, that 'in view of the current state of international law, and of the elements of fact at its disposal, the Court cannot conclude definitively whether the threat or use of nuclear weapons would be lawful or unlawful in an extreme circumstance of self-defence, in which the very survival of a State would be at stake'.

---

[75] ibid, 83–84, [30].

[76] Lauterpacht (n 66) 101–02. Inter alia, Lauterpacht makes the point that the Court seemed to ignore the UNGA's practice is regarded, by the Court itself, to have a law modifying effect, and here could have been settling the interpretation of the scope of the WHO's competence to seek the relevant advisory opinion.

[77] An anthropomorphic idiom seems indicated by the Court's emphasis on the UNGA's *intentions*.

The latter reading is indicated by the use of the word 'however' at the beginning of the second sentence; and if valid, would suggest that the circumstance indicated in that sentence is the only one which might constitute a *possible* exception to the illegality of nuclear weapons. It is also the better reading for many reasons. For one, it makes sense of phrasing (the use of 'however') that could be described as sloppy otherwise. Second, it excludes the possibility that the Court has rather lazily elaborated only one of many possible exceptional circumstances in which the threat or use of nuclear weapons may or may not be illegal.[78] Third, it excludes the even more dangerous possibility that the two sentences outline different orders of exception: the first refers to exceptional circumstances where a nuclear weapon may be used compatibly with the law of armed conflict; the second to exceptional circumstances where the legality of its use need not be evaluated by reference to the law of armed conflict.

Yet the former reading, in which the first sentence conveys a meaning on its own, also finds support in the literature. And that it does is reason for criticism of the Court's drafting. As I show below, the Court itself was divided on what precisely it had said in paragraph 2E. Amongst the judges who appended declarations or separate opinions (and therefore presumably saw their own readings as compatible with the Court's) some judges took the view that the Opinion had confirmed the legality of the threat or use of nuclear weapons; others that it had confirmed the illegality; and yet others that it had endorsed neither legality nor illegality. They also took quite different views on what paragraph 2E provided with respect to the need for compatibility with the law of armed conflict.

A. Legal, Illegal, Neither

Judge Guillaume is amongst those who read paragraph 2E as confirming the legality of the threat or use of nuclear weapons under certain circumstances.[79] He noted that the wording of the first sentence was 'vague but ... nevertheless implies that the threat or use of nuclear weapons are not prohibited "in any circumstance" by the law applicable in armed conflict'. And he pointed out that the Court had stated as much in the text of the advisory opinion.[80] Effectively, he offered the first of the two

---

[78] On this point, see also Akande (n 8) 210.

[79] Although Judge Guillaume voted against the paragraph 2E, he wrote a separate, and not a dissenting opinion. He explained that although he voted against the paragraph because it did not explicitly acknowledge the legality of the threat or use of nuclear weapons under certain circumstances, he was convinced that it did so implicitly. In short, the Advisory Opinion was in line with, and not opposed to his own view of the matter. See *Legality of Nuclear Weapons* (n 2) Judge Guillaume separate opinion, 291, [8].

[80] ibid, 290, [7]. Judge Guillaume referred to para 95 of the Advisory Opinion, in which the Court has noted that it could not 'make a determination on the validity of the view that the recourse to nuclear weapons would be illegal in any circumstance owing to their inherent and total incompatibility with the law applicable in armed conflict.' Although, 'in view of the unique characteristics of nuclear weapons', their used seemed 'scarcely reconcilable with respect for [the law of armed conflict's] requirements', the Court considered that 'it does not have sufficient elements to enable it to conclude with certainty that the use of nuclear weapons would necessarily be at variance with the principles and rules of law applicable in armed conflict in any circumstance.'

interpretations of that sentence: that its use of 'generally' indicates that there are circumstances in which the use of nuclear weapons may be compatible with the law of armed conflict. Judge Guillaume further read the second sentence as implicitly confirming the existence of 'a kind of "absolute defence" (*"excuse absolutoire"*) similar to the one which exists in all systems of criminal law' that would justify a state's use of nuclear weapons in self-defence where its survival was under threat.[81] In such cases, the law of armed conflict would not operate as a bar: Judge Guillaume suggested this conclusion followed from two propositions. First, that the '*jus ad bellum*' should provide 'some clarification of the rules of the *jus in bello*'[82]—a delicately-phrased assertion to the effect that the law of armed conflict applied differently in different circumstances of the use of force, and would not impede necessary and proportionate action in self-defence. And second, the *Lotus* principle, that in the absence of a prohibition states remained free to act as they intend, which was applicable here because the Court clearly stated that it was unable to definitively conclude that the threat or use of nuclear weapons would be unlawful in extreme circumstances of self-defence.[83] Judge Guillaume only regretted that paragraph 2E had not 'explicitly recognized the legality of deterrence for defence of the vital interests of States'; had it contained this additional element, he would have voted in favour of it.[84]

Judges Herczegh and Ranjeva took the opposite view, that paragraph 2E effectively confirmed the illegality of the threat or use of nuclear weapons. Judge Herczegh's brief declaration noted that the paragraph could have 'summarized more accurately the current state of international law regarding the question of the threat or use of nuclear weapons "in any circumstance"'.[85] Nevertheless, he voted in favour because to have voted against 'would have meant adopting a negative stance on certain essential conclusions—also set forth in this Opinion and alluded to in paragraph 2E—which I fully endorse.'[86] Amongst these conclusions, was presumably that 'The fundamental principles of international humanitarian law, rightly emphasized in the reasons of the Advisory Opinion, categorically and unequivocally prohibit the use of weapons of mass destruction, including nuclear weapons. International humanitarian law does not recognize any exceptions to these principles'.[87] Judge Herczegh suggested that the principles of international humanitarian law could have been the basis for the Court to state in more specific terms the conclusion it advances implicitly in operative paragraphs 2C and 2E, of the illegality of the threat or use of nuclear weapons.[88]

---

[81] ibid, 290, [8].
[82] ibid.
[83] ibid, 291, [9]–[10]. See *The SS Lotus* (1927) *PCIJ*, Series A, 10, 3. The case is discussed in ch 5.
[84] ibid.
[85] *Legality of Nuclear Weapons* (n 2) Decl Judge Herczegh, 276.
[86] ibid.
[87] ibid, 275.
[88] ibid, 275–76. Paragraph 2C notes that a use of force in self-defence must comply with the requirements of Article 51 of the UN Charter. And, as the Court had noted in para 42 of the Advisory Opinion: 'a use of force that is proportionate under the law of self-defence, must, in order to be lawful, also meet the requirements of the law applicable in armed conflict which comprise in particular the principles and rules of humanitarian law'.

Judge Ranjeva also read the first sentence of paragraph 2E as confirming 'the principle of the illegality of the threat or use of nuclear weapons'.[89] With respect to the use of the word 'generally', he noted, 'in the majority of cases and in the doctrine; its grammatical function is to determine with emphasis the statement made in the main proposition'.[90] Contrasting its 'determinative effect' with the dubitative effect that another adverb such as 'apparently', 'perhaps' or even 'no doubt' would have produced, he was clear that 'The wording of the first clause of operative paragraph 2E excludes any limitation to the general principle of illegality'.[91] He conceded that the clear rule stated in the first sentence was however challenged by the second sentence of paragraph 2E, for this sentence was open to multiple readings.[92] On the one hand, it could be read as providing for an exceptional case of self-defence in which a state need not comply with the law of armed conflict; on the other hand, no such exceptional case was known to international law, and the reference to self-defence must be read as self-defence in compliance with the requirements of the *jus ad bello*. Judge Ranjeva favoured the latter reading and, noting that 'no evidence of the existence of a "clean nuclear weapon" was presented to the Court', considered that the exception of 'extreme circumstance of self-defence' was effectively inoperative: 'strip[ped] ... of all logical and juridical foundation'.[93]

Both judges cleaved to the view that the first sentence of paragraph 2E states the general proposition of the illegality of the threat or use of nuclear weapons. They recognised that the second sentence identifies a possible exception, but both were sceptical as to its utility, for they doubted that—as a matter of fact—nuclear weapons could be used compatibly with the law of armed conflict.

The middle position, that paragraph 2E confirms neither legality nor illegality is reflected in President Bedjaoui's declaration. In contrast with Judge Guillaume, who invoked the *Lotus* principle, President Bedjaoui was at pains to clarify that that principle was inapplicable to the present case.[94] He insisted that *Lotus* reflected a particular temporal and judicial context, in which international law had been the law of co-existence; the present case concerned a far more important question, and at a time when international law had evolved into the law of cooperation. The mere absence of the 'red light of prohibition' did not imply the presence of the 'green light of authorization'; the Court 'd[id] not feel able to give a signal either way'.[95] Nevertheless, his declaration appeared to imply that to the extent that an argument could be made for the legality of nuclear weapons in extreme circumstances of self-defence, this argument would be made *despite* the law of armed conflict. For, he was persuaded that in the present state of technology, 'Atomic warfare and humanitarian law ... appear to be mutually exclusive, the existence of the one

---

[89]   ibid, Judge Ranjeva separate opinion, 294.
[90]   ibid.
[91]   ibid.
[92]   ibid, 294, 301–04.
[93]   ibid, 303.
[94]   ibid, Decl President Bedjaoui, 270–71, [12]–[15].
[95]   ibid, 271, [14].

automatically implying the non-existence of the other'.[96] But, holding firm to the *non liquet* approach, he did not state whether such an argument would be acceptable, only noting that the threat or use of nuclear weapons in extreme circumstances of self-defence would place two sets of fundamental principles—those of international humanitarian law and that of a state's right to survival—into relentless opposition with each other.[97] (His own preference was for giving priority to international humanitarian law. He noted that to set the survival of a state above all other considerations could be foolhardy and, given the threat of escalation, endangered the survival of all mankind.)[98]

It emerges from Judge Bedjaoui's discussion that he too cleaved to the view that the first sentence of paragraph 2E states the general principle of illegality of the threat or use of nuclear weapons; unlike Judges Ranjeva or Herczegh, however, he did not feel able to state with conviction that the exception noted in the second sentence can only apply to threats or uses that are compatible with the law of armed conflict. As we will see, his was perhaps the dominant voice on this highly contested point.

B. Self-defence and International Humanitarian Law

As the previous section begins to highlight, paragraph 2E lends itself to a variety of interpretations. In this respect, the second sentence is particularly open-textured, and there has been much debate on the precise relationship it indicates between the use of force in self-defence and the application of the law of armed conflict, particularly international humanitarian law. Two broad positions may be defined. The first is that to be lawful, the threat or use of nuclear weapons in self-defence must comply with the law of armed conflict; this position was endorsed both in the advisory opinion and in the written and oral statements of the many states participating in the proceedings.[99] The second position, that in exceptional circumstances force may be lawfully used in self-defence even if it is not compatible with international humanitarian law, is implied by Judge Guillaume, and conceded as a grey area in the law by Judge Bedjaoui. It was more or less explicitly endorsed by Judge Fleischhauer.

Judge Fleischhauer's opinion reiterated the sense expressed by many judges that nuclear weapons were 'scarcely reconcilable' with the rules and principles of international humanitarian law.[100] As they noted, the large-scale effects of nuclear weapons would violate two fundamental principles of international humanitarian law: the principle of distinction (between combatants and civilians) and the prohibition on

---

[96] ibid, 273, [20].

[97] ibid, 273, [22].

[98] ibid.

[99] ibid, 245, [42]; Written Statement of the USA, 20 June 1995, 21, <www.icj-cij.org/docket/files/95/8700.pdf>; see also Statement of the UK, June 1995, <www.icj-cij.org/docket/files/95/8802.pdf>.

[100] ibid, Judge Fleischhauer separate opinion, 305. The judge was quoting the language used in para 95 of the Advisory Opinion.

causing unnecessary suffering. As Judge Fleischhauer succinctly stated 'The nuclear weapon cannot distinguish between civilian and military targets. It causes immeasurable suffering'.[101] For many judges, including, as discussed above, Herczegh and Ranjeva, and dissenting judges such as Koroma and Weeramantry,[102] this meant in effect that the threat or use of nuclear weapons would be illegal in all circumstances. Judge Fleischhauer, however, took the opposite view: that in exceptional circumstances, a state's right of self-defence would overcome its obligations under international humanitarian law. He observed that:

> To end the matter with the simple statement that recourse to nuclear weapons would be contrary to international law applicable in armed conflict … would have meant that the law applicable in armed conflict … was given precedence over the inherent right of individual or collective self-defence which every State possesses as a matter of sovereign equality and which is expressly preserved in Article 51 of the Charter.[103]

This would be an incorrect allocation of priority; instead, recourse to nuclear weapons must be considered justified 'in an extreme situation of individual or collective self-defence in which the threat or use of nuclear weapons is the last resort against an attack with nuclear, chemical or bacteriological weapons or otherwise threatening the very existence of the victimized State'.[104]

Judge Fleischhauer's approach, explicitly placing the threat or use of nuclear weapons above the law of armed conflict in certain circumstances, represents a possible interpretation of paragraph 2E, but it is not an attractive one. Commentators have preferred to read this paragraph as embracing only the possibility that in some circumstances the threat or use of nuclear weapons may conform to the rules and principles of international humanitarian law.[105] This possibility, which in legal terms would imply no conflict at all between the right to self-defence and international humanitarian law, was also the one embraced by several judges who took the position that the Court should have avoided stating a *non liquet*.

Judge Schwebel's dissent turned on this point. He dismissed the suggestion that a state's interests, including its right to survival, were above the law. Rather he examined instances in which nuclear weapons could be used tactically so as to avoid any contravention of the law of armed conflict.[106] One of his examples was Operation Desert Storm, where the threat of use of nuclear weapons by the United States had forestalled Iraq from using chemical, as well bacteriological and nuclear weapons

---

[101] ibid, 306, [2].

[102] ibid, Judge Koroma dissenting, 562–63; Judge Weeramantry dissenting, 435, 472, 476–77.

[103] ibid, Judge Fleischhauer separate opinion, 306, [3].

[104] ibid, 308, [5].

[105] See, eg, C Greenwood, '*Jus ad bellum* and *jus in bello* in the *Nuclear Weapons* Advisory Opinion', in Boisson de Chazournes and Sands, *International Law* (n 13) 247–66 (noting also that Judge Fleischhauer's approach had several dangers).

[106] *Legality of Nuclear Weapons* (n 2) Vice President Schwebel dissenting, 322 ('When it comes to the supreme interests of State, the Court discards the legal progress of the twentieth century, puts aside the provisions of the Charter of the United Nations of which it is "the principal judicial organ", and proclaims, in terms redolent of Realpolitik, its ambivalence about the most important provisions of modern international law. If this was to be its ultimate holding, the Court would have done better to have drawn on its undoubted discretion not to render an opinion at all').

against opposing forces.[107] Another, hypothetical example, in which the decision would be fairly simple, was the use of nuclear weapon to destroy a nuclear submarine; such an action would produce much less radiation than on land, would not cause immediate civilian casualties, and would meet the test of proportionality.[108] A more complicated judgment would be required in case of the 'use of nuclear weapons to destroy an enemy army situated in a desert', for 'In certain circumstances, such a use of nuclear weapons might meet the tests of discrimination and proportionality; in others not'.[109] In such cases, proportionality would have to be carefully calibrated by reference to the threat sought to be avoided; no answer could be given in the abstract.

As were Judges Herczegh, Ranjeva, Koroma and Weeramantry, Judge Schwebel was guided by an appreciation of the technological possibilities of nuclear weapons. However, unlike those other judges, who were persuaded that the present state of technology did not afford the possibility of tactical or limited-effect uses of nuclear weapons, Judge Schwebel evidently had a different appreciation. And this in part determined his view of the legality of the threat or use of nuclear weapons (it must be said though that Desert Storm or other uses of nuclear deterrence did not impress the other judges as indicating the legality of the threat or use of nuclear weapons).

However, as Judge Higgins' dissent—perhaps the most incisive of the individual opinions—indicates, the debate at its core was not simply about the factual state of nuclear technology.[110] The UNGA's request in fact offered the Court an opportunity to elaborate on the meanings to be given to fundamental principles of international humanitarian law, which would have also clarified the occasions on which a state could lawfully threaten or use nuclear weapons in self-defence. For example, the Court could have explained what is implied in the prohibition of *unnecessary* suffering of combatants, and elaborated upon the balance that must be drawn between the necessity of attacking a legitimate military target and the suffering thereby produced. It could have considered what military necessity could justify the horrendous degree of suffering nuclear weapons could produce, and addressed whether extreme circumstances ('defence against untold suffering or the obliteration of a State or peoples') could recalibrate the balance between necessity and suffering.[111] Similarly, in relation to the principle of distinction, the Court could have explained how to determine whether the collateral harm caused to civilians as the result of attacking a military target would be so disproportionate as to violate that principle, and again whether a situation implicating 'the very survival of a State or the avoidance of infliction of vast and severe suffering on its population' would lead to a more generous assessment of proportionality of a nuclear attack. It could have considered whether nuclear weapons must be considered as incapable of discriminating between military and civilian targets.[112]

---

[107] ibid, 323–29.
[108] ibid, 320–21.
[109] ibid, 321.
[110] ibid, Judge Higgins dissenting, 583–93.
[111] ibid, 585–87, [11]–[18].
[112] ibid, 587–89, [19]–[24].

Judge Higgins did not suggest that the Court could give specific or comprehensive answers on all these points, merely that the Court might have done more to advance our understanding of the tests that may be used in the application of the general principles of international humanitarian law to concrete situations, especially those posing an exceptional threat to a state or its people. The Court, however, did not do so. It simply held to the position that, in view of technological uncertainties, it could not say with certainty that all threats or uses of nuclear weapons would violate the law of armed conflict. It might have logically proceeded from that point to note that a threat or use of nuclear weapons could be justified if (and only if) compatible with the law on the use of force and the law of armed conflict. However, it chose instead the vaguer formula of paragraph 2E—on the basis that this spoke neither to the legality nor illegality of the use of nuclear weapons in extreme situation (as explained by Judge Bedjaoui); but with the danger of opening the way to an interpretation that placed nuclear weapons above the law of armed conflict.

VI. CHOOSING *NON LIQUET*

Paragraph 2E, adopted on the casting vote of the President, embraced what we might call the 'Bedjaoui approach', in preference to the 'Higgins approach', which would have been to elaborate on the scope and application of the relevant principles of humanitarian law, in the context of the limit case presented by nuclear weapons. In other words, the Court preferred to state that there was a *non liquet*—a gap in the law—rather than explaining the legal standards according to which the legality of any specific threat or use of nuclear weapons would be evaluated. Of course, had the Court taken the latter approach, it might have still made the point that it did not have sufficient facts at its disposal to state whether all threats or uses would violate the law of armed conflict.

The question to be pondered is why did the Court not adopt the Higgins approach? One possible answer is provided by Martti Koskenniemi, who reasons that this approach would have led the Court onto precisely the terrain that it wished to avoid.[113] For one, it would have led the Court to concede, in express terms, the legality of the threat or use of nuclear weapons. And, secondly, it would have required the Court to yet again redescribe pure horror—mass killings at the press of a button—in a normalising legal-technical language, of proportionality calculation. To put this in Koskenniemi's words, (although he does not refer particularly to the Higgins approach), the Court

> would have instituted a public, technical discourse for the defence of the killing of the innocent. By lifting the matter onto the level of judicial reason, the Court would have broken the taboo against any use of nuclear weapons. It would have opened a professionally honourable and perhaps even a tragically pleasurable way of addressing the unaddressable. The (massive) killing of the innocent would have become another contextual determinant, a

---

[113] Koskenniemi, 'The Silence of Law' (n 13) 488–510.

banal 'factor' in an overall balancing of the utilities, to be compared with the equally banal factors of sovereignty, military objectives, and so on.[114]

By remaining silent, the Court was able to 'leave room for the workings of the moral impulse, the a-rational, non-foundational appeal against the killing of the innocent'.[115] Koskenniemi here challenges the view that the completeness of the law demands that it must always afford an answer to a difficult moral question. He notes that in entering into a discussion of the standards according to which a nuclear weapon may be used compatibly with international humanitarian law, the Court would trivialise the decision to be made, and lift the weight of the ethical responsibility from the decision-maker.

While Koskenniemi offers perhaps the subtext to the Advisory Opinion, at least two of the individual opinions also provided an express justification for the choice of a *non liquet* formulation. President Bedjaoui noted that such a formulation was an honest reflection of the state of the relevant international law, which was in 'a very advanced process of change ... or, in other words, of a current trend towards the replacement of one rule of international law by another, where the first is already defunct and its successor does not yet exist'.[116] Particularly with reference to the second sentence of paragraph 2E, the *non liquet* conveyed this state of flux in the law. The Court could signal that it had 'reached a point in its reasoning beyond which it cannot proceed without running the risk of adopting a conclusion which would go beyond what seems to it to be legitimate'.[117] This approach served to highlight the 'imperfections' in the law, and call upon 'international society to correct them'.[118] It was in this context that the Court also offered its observations in relation to the nature of the disarmament obligation provided for in the NPT.[119]

Judge Vereschetin further elaborated on the possible benefit of declaring a *non liquet*. As a preliminary point, he noted that in an advisory procedure, the Court is not concerned with proving the completeness of the legal system, for it is not called upon to resolve 'an actual dispute between actual parties, but to state the law as it finds it at the present stage of its development'.[120] Not only did nothing in

---

[114] ibid, 496–97. It may be noted that Judge Higgins herself had flagged a similar concern, noting: 'It may well be asked of a judge whether, in engaging in legal analysis of such concepts as "unnecessary suffering", "collateral damage" and "entitlement to self-defence", one has not lost sight of the real human circumstances involved'. (*Legality of Nuclear Weapons* (n 2) Judge Higgins dissenting, 592, [41]). Her response was: 'The judicial lodestar, whether in difficult questions of interpretation of humanitarian law, or in resolving claimed tensions between competing norms, must be those values that international law seeks to promote and protect. In the present case, it is the physical survival of peoples that we must constantly have in view. [Given current realities] ... It is not clear to me that either a pronouncement of illegality in all circumstances of the use of nuclear weapons or the answers formulated by the Court in paragraph 2E best serve to protect mankind against that unimaginable suffering that we all fear' (ibid, 592–93, [41]).

[115] Koskenniemi (n 13) 497–98. To be clear, Koskenniemi also explains why a position holding the illegality of the threat or use of nuclear weapons in all circumstances would also give way to a similar result of the normalisation of the use of nuclear weapons: ibid, 490–94.

[116] *Legality of Nuclear Weapons* (n 2) Decl President Bedjaoui, 272, [16].

[117] ibid, 272, [18].

[118] ibid, 269, [8].

[119] ibid, 274, [23].

[120] ibid, Decl Judge Vereschetin, 279.

the UNGA request ask the Court to fill any gaps in the law, but also several states, in their submissions, specifically asked the Court not to act as a legislator.[121] More generally, it was not part of the judicial function for the Court to undertake law-creation in the course of rendering an advisory opinion; where the law was inconclusive, the Court simply had to state as much.[122]

He then discussed the benefit of a *non liquet*, noting, by reference to Sir Hersch Lauterpacht,[123] that 'apparent indecision [of the Court], which leaves room for discretion on the part of the organ which requested the Opinion, may—both *as a matter of development of the law and as a guide to action*—be preferable to a deceptive clarity which fails to give an indication of the inherent complexities of the issue'.[124] He cautioned against the Court's taking on the role of law-making on such a fraught issue, asking what would be the 'authority and effectiveness of [a] "deduced" general rule with respect to [a] matter on which the States are so fundamentally divided'.[125] Instead, the Court's 'partial "apparent indecision"' could have a positive effect in nudging states towards completing the process of 'construction of the solid edifice for the total prohibition on the use of nuclear weapons'.[126] The Court had done its job in showing that this edifice was 'being constructed and a great deal ha[d] already been achieved'; it had also 'shown that the most appropriate means for putting an end to the existence of any "grey areas" in the legal status of nuclear weapons would be "nuclear disarmament in all its aspects under strict and effective international control"'.[127] The rest must be left to states.

In sum, whereas judicial legislation could evoke antagonism on the part of states, a *non liquet* coupled with clarification of the NPT's disarmament obligation might lead them to further develop the law prohibiting threat or use of nuclear weapons.

VII. NUCLEAR WEAPONS, TWO DECADES ON

Two decades later, it is difficult to say that Judge Vereschetin was justified in his expectations of the potential impact of the Advisory Opinion. Of course, the past years have seen major achievements with respect to nuclear disarmament. A number of regional nuclear weapons-free zones treaties have been concluded: Treaty of Bangkok, covering Southeast Asia;[128] Treaty of Pelindaba, covering Africa;[129]

---

[121] ibid, 280.

[122] ibid.

[123] Lauterpacht, as Judge Vereschetin noted, was 'a strong proponent of the "completeness" of international law and the inadmissibility of non liquet' (ibid, 281). He is the standard authority cited by those who have criticised the Court for reaching a *non liquet*.

[124] ibid (citing H Lauterpacht, *The Development of International Law by the International Court* (Cambridge, CUP, 1982) 152; emphasis added by Judge Vereschetin).

[125] ibid, 280–81.

[126] ibid, 281.

[127] ibid.

[128] Adopted 15 December 1995, entered into force 27 March 1997.

[129] Adopted 11 April 1996, entered into force 15 July 2009.

and Treaty of Semipalatinsk, covering Central Asia;[130] these add to the previously concluded Treaty of Tlatelolco (Latin America and the Caribbean),[131] and Treaty of Rarotonga (South Pacific).[132] A similar treaty with respect to the Middle East has also been proposed, though it remains an unlikely prospect.[133] Altogether, 89 states are parties to these treaties and the five NWS have ratified protocols committing not to threaten or use nuclear weapons in these zones. The United States and Russia have also bilaterally concluded treaties to reduce their nuclear weapons arsenals, most recently the 'New START' which entered into force in February 2011.[134] Other NWS have initiated meetings to discuss confidence building measures towards nuclear disarmament.[135] As to treaties of universal scope, 1996 saw the adoption of the CTBT, which is yet to enter into force. A fissile material cut-off treaty (FMCT) has been proposed to prohibit production of weapons-grade nuclear fuel, but remains in the pre-negotiation phase.[136] Most recently, in July 2017, 122 non-nuclear weapons states adopted a Treaty on the Prohibition of Nuclear Weapons, in negotiations marked by the absence of all NWS; the treaty will be opened for signature later in the year.

However, a series of developments confirm that complete nuclear disarmament remains a distant, if not illusory goal. In terms of the individual practice of states, both India and Pakistan conducted multiple nuclear tests in 1998, thus overtly announcing their nuclear weapons programmes. North Korea has since also claimed nuclear weapons capability. And Iran, although never actually proved to be developing nuclear weapons, has failed to explain its nuclear enrichment programmes to the satisfaction of the IAEA. But the issue is not just the deviant (or, in the case of Iran, allegedly deviant) practice of a few states. The 2000s saw a virtual rewriting of the nuclear governance regime underpinned by the NPT. The imbalance between the goals of horizontal non-proliferation and disarmament, already seen in the early 1990s, was further exacerbated.[137] A shift of focus—from actions to actors, and from formal NPT rules and IAEA verification processes to informal United States-led networks such as the NSG, Proliferation Security Initiative,[138] Missile Technology Control Regime,[139] and the Global Nuclear Energy Partnership,[140] permitted arbitrary treatment of states based on political friendships and enmities. For example,

---

[130] Adopted 8 September 2006, entered into force 21 March 2009.

[131] Adopted 14 February 1967, entered into force 23 October 2002.

[132] Adopted 6 August 1985, entered into force 11 December 1986.

[133] First proposed in UNGA Res 3236 (9 December 1974), calls for such a treaty was renewed at the 1995 and 2010 NPT Review Conferences. However, a proposal to convene a drafting conference failed at the 2015 Conference.

[134] Measures for the Further Reduction and Limitation of Strategic Offensive Arms, adopted 8 April 2010, entered into force 5 February 2011.

[135] See, eg, 2010 Review Conference of the Parties to the Treaty on the Non-Proliferation of Nuclear Weapons, Final Document, NPT/CONF 2010/50 (Vol I), 13, [93].

[136] The FMCT was first proposed in 2002. For an overview, see <www.nti.org/learn/treaties-and-regimes/proposed-fissile-material-cut-off-treaty> accessed 14 July 2017.

[137] See D Joyner, *Interpreting the Nuclear Non-Proliferation Treaty* (Oxford, OUP, 2011) 35–108.

[138] <www.psi-online.info> accessed 14 July 2017.

[139] <http://mtcr.info/deutsch-ziele> accessed 14 July 2017.

[140] <www.ifnec.org> accessed 14 July 2017.

India entered into a full civil nuclear deal with the United States. This deal, endorsed by the NSG, more or less explicitly recognised it as a nuclear weapons state, imposing on it conditions designed not to interfere with its nuclear weapons programme (and different from those imposed on other states that the NPT classifies as *de jure* non-nuclear weapons states).[141] On the other hand, Iran, whose transgressions remain unproven, was subjected to weighty sanctions. While an argument may be made that the overall approach has (perhaps fortuitously) consolidated the nuclear governance regime in some respects,[142] it cannot by any stretch be described as in pursuit of a clear principle (and most certainly not the principle of disarmament). And, although some of the NPT Review Conferences (notably 1995, 2000 and 2010) have provided occasions for renewal of disarmament commitments, their record has been a mixed one; the most recent of these conferences—of 2015—failed to generate a final document.

Moreover, the sources of threat have multiplied. As the revelation of the AQ Khan nuclear smuggling network, stretching from Pakistan to Iran, Libya and North Korea showed, non-state actors could be agents of nuclear proliferation, whether acting on their own or in concert with governments. We have since seen the rise of a succession of well-resourced multinational terrorist groups who have enjoyed a level of access to strategic information and weaponry that was not perhaps foreseen even in 1996 when the Court delivered its opinions.

And, we are losing our capacity for horror. The various wars on terror fought since 9/11, one of them indeed invoking the spectre of weapons of mass destruction, and the further conflicts that they have catalysed, have seen an escalation both in 'spectacular' and 'ordinary' forms of violence: the use of chemical weapons by a state against its own citizens, mass displacement to the order of millions of refugees living in makeshift camps, deprived of livelihoods, and—a spectacle that has become agonisingly ordinary—drowning in boatloads as they seek to make their escape into a more secure environment. The massive killing of the innocent has indeed become just another contextual determinant, a banal 'factor' in an overall balancing of the utilities, to quote Koskenniemi; the unsayable has become the quotidian. If the use of a nuclear weapon still—perhaps—remains unimaginable, it is only because such use seems superfluous given the increasing efficacy of our other means, military and not, of destroying the globe.

But I do not want to end this chapter on a bleak note. For, recently a brave new move was made to engage the Court in the fight against nuclear weapons. The Marshall Islands, victim both of nuclear testing and climate change, instituted applications against the United Kingdom, India and Pakistan, seeking declarations that these states are in breach of their obligations of cessation of the nuclear arms race and disarmament, and asking the Court to order that they take immediate steps

---

[141] I examine the India-US Nuclear Deal, and its impact on the nuclear governance regime in *Strategically Created Treaty Conflicts and the Politics of International Law* (Cambridge, CUP, 2014) ch 6.
[142] For a version of this argument in respect of the India–US nuclear deal, see ibid.

towards fulfilment of these obligations.[143] The Court here had the opportunity to build on its *Legality of Nuclear Weapons* finding that NPT disarmament obligations were obligations of result, not merely conduct[144]—a finding that was surely intended to give ballast to flagging disarmament negotiations then, and worth a judicial determination now for the same reason. The Court however chose to decline jurisdiction, on rather formalistic reasoning.[145] This was a disappointing result, and one that raises questions about the Court's ability to play a constructive role with respect to nuclear weapons, or indeed other issues involving community interests.[146] Nevertheless, the *fact* that these applications were brought by the Marshall Islands is important in itself—they were are an oddly hopeful act, reminding us, that amidst all the destruction (for the applicant state total and near-inevitable, as they sink into the Pacific) that looms all around us, campaigns such as that for complete nuclear disarmament remain worthwhile goals, not least because they restore to us the awareness that the realities we accept as normal are actually scandalous

---

[143] *Obligations concerning Negotiations relating to Cessation of the Nuclear Arms Race and to Nuclear Disarmament (Marshall Islands v India)*, Application, 24 April 2014, <www.icj-cij.org/files/case-related/158/18292.pdf>; *(Marshall Islands v Pakistan)*, Application, 24 April 2014, <www.icj-cij.org/files/case-related/159/18294.pdf>; *(Marshall Islands v United Kingdom)*, Application, 24 April 2014, <www.icj-cij.org/files/case-related/160/18296.pdf> (all accessed 24 March 2016).

[144] See fns 62, 63.

[145] *Obligations concerning Negotiations relating to the Cessation of the Nuclear Arms Race and to Nuclear Disarmament (Marshall Islands v United Kingdom)*, Preliminary Objections (ICJ October 5, 2016); *Obligations concerning Negotiations relating to the Cessation of the Nuclear Arms Race and to Nuclear Disarmament (Marshall Islands v India)*, Preliminary Objections (ICJ October 5, 2016); *Obligations concerning Negotiations relating to the Cessation of the Nuclear Arms Race and to Nuclear Disarmament (Marshall Islands v Pakistan)*, Preliminary Objections (ICJ October 5, 2016).

[146] For a discussion see, Ranganathan, 'Nuclear Weapons and the Court' (n 47). See also the other papers in the symposium: (2017) 111 *AJIL Unbound* 62–101.

18

Gabčíkovo-Nagymaros Project (Hungary/Slovakia) (1997)

LAURENCE BOISSON DE CHAZOURNES*
AND MAKANE MOÏSE MBENGUE

I. INTRODUCTION

THE *GABČÍKOVO-NAGYMAROS PROJECT (Hungary/Slovakia)* case (hereinafter, the *Gabčíkovo-Nagymaros* case or *Gabčíkovo-Nagymaros*)[1] has, like a prism, refracted the international law on environmental protection as well as on fundamental fields of general international law such as state responsibility, the law of treaties and the law of international watercourses. It is a landmark decision. Its reach in terms of subject matter is very wide indeed. At the time of its handing down by the International Court of Justice (ICJ), the President of the Court said that the case 'proved to be compendious in terms of the range of legal issues it summoned up: the law of treaties, of state responsibility, of international watercourses, of state succession and environmental law'.[2] This is the reason why it may be considered all things to all people.

Gabčíkovo-Nagymaros was the first case before the ICJ to be concerned with international environmental law in such a comprehensive manner, and in many ways the ICJ clarified this field of law. Notwithstanding, while the Court had occasion to consider a broad spectrum of issues in the light of international environmental law, one cannot escape the conclusion that it could have done more, as the ICJ ultimately founded many of its holdings in this case on the basis of more 'traditional' grounds, such as the law of treaties and state responsibility.[3] Moreover, after the

---

* The authors are greatly indebted to Jason Rudall, PhD candidate in International Law at the Graduate Institute of International and Development Studies, Geneva and Researcher at the Law Faculty of the University of Geneva, for his assistance in the preparation of this contribution.

[1] *Case Concerning the Gabčíkovo-Nagymaros Project (Hungary/Slovakia)*, [1997] ICJ Rep 7.

[2] S Schwebel, 'The influence of the International Court of Justice on the work of the International Law Commission and the influence of the Commission on the work of the Court', keynote address, United Nations Colloquium on Progressive Development and Codification of International law to Commemorate the Fiftieth Anniversary of the International Law Commission, United Nations, New York, 28 October 1997, cited in M Fitzmaurice, 'The Gabčíkovo-Nagymaros Case: The Law of Treaties' (1998) 11 *LJIL* 2, 321, 344.

[3] J Klabbers, 'The Substance of Form: The Case Concerning the Gabčíkovo-Nagymaros Project, Environmental Law, and the Law of Treaties' (1997) 8 *Yearbook of International Environmental Law* 32, 34.

Court weighed and balanced all aspects of the dispute, neither of the parties can be said to have won or lost the case, as the Court found both parties to be at fault on various grounds.

Much like looking through a kaleidoscope, this chapter will consider the major issues of international law that were at stake in the *Gabčíkovo-Nagymaros* case, from international environmental law and sustainable development to state responsibility and the law of treaties. Before we turn to those, however, let us reconsider the situation in which the ICJ found itself.

II. ONCE UPON A TIME...

Under the 1977 Treaty Concerning the Construction and Operation of the Gabčíkovo-Nagymaros System of Locks, Hungary and Czechoslovakia (as it was before it was broken up into the Czech Republic and Slovakia in 1993) had agreed to construct and operate a system of locks, a dam, a reservoir, a hydroelectric power plant and flood controls along the Danube River. Subsequent to this treaty, both countries experienced significant changes to their internal political and economic systems, more especially at the end of the 1980s with the fall of the Berlin Wall and circumstances surrounding this event. In Hungary, a significant environmental lobby began to grow and oppose the planned works on the Danube. Following these events, Hungary stopped its part of the works and ultimately sought to terminate the 1977 treaty. In 1992, Czechoslovakia began works to divert the Danube River into a power canal, controlling 80–90 per cent of its flow, under an alternative project (known as Variant C) to that which had been agreed between the two countries. Slovakia and Hungary decided to submit the dispute for resolution by the ICJ.

An important context to this case is the timing of its submission to the ICJ. Indeed, it was submitted shortly after the fall of the Berlin Wall and the demise of communism in Eastern Europe. The EU Commission had attempted to broker an agreement to appease tensions between Slovakia and Hungary that would ultimately become new members of the EU. As a subsequent step, the two countries agreed to bring their case before the ICJ. Moreover, the landscape of international environmental law was beginning to change. The Conference on Environment and Development held in Rio de Janeiro in June 1992 gave significant momentum to the shaping and development of the international legal order. Instruments such as the Rio Declaration on Environment and Development,[4] the Program of Action Agenda 21[5] and the Conventions on Climate Change[6] and on Biological Diversity[7] entrenched notions and principles, such as 'sustainable development' and the 'precautionary principle'. One ongoing problem, however, was and remains the definition of these notions and principles. Since the 1972 United Nations Conference on the Human Environment held at Stockholm—which marked the birth of international environmental

---

[4] Reproduced in (1992) 31 ILM 874.
[5] UN Conference on Environment and Development: Agenda 21, UN Doc A/CONF.15/4 (1992).
[6] Framework Convention on Climate Change (9 May 1992), reproduced in (1992) 31 ILM 849.
[7] Convention on Biological Diversity (5 June 1992), reproduced in (1992) 31 ILM 849.

law[8]—the degree of importance to be given to environmental protection has been a source of dissension between developing and developed states. The pressing need for economic development was in tension with the development of an environmental ethic.[9] Twenty years later at the United Nations Conference on Environment and Development in Rio, the same conflict resurfaced. There was little consensus on the real environmental issues, the significance of the terms 'environment' and 'development' and indeed the nature of the 'environment-development' interaction.[10]

In this context, when the *Gabčíkovo-Nagymaros* case came before the ICJ, the Court tipped its hat to these emerging concepts and principles. However, it ultimately founded its decision on more traditional bases of international law. Placing an emphasis on *pacta sunt servanda*, it held that a fundamental change of circumstances may justify the termination of a treaty but these must have been unforeseen and the pre-existing circumstances should have been critical to the consent offered by the parties. In this case, the changed political and economic circumstances were not an essential basis of the consent of the parties, and could not be considered to constitute a fundamental change of circumstances. The Court also clarified that a state of necessity which would suspend treaty obligations can only be temporary, although it did not rule out the possibility that a state of ecological necessity could exist.[11] On the other hand, the unilateral action taken by Czechoslovakia to divert 80–90 per cent of the flow of the Danube was an internationally wrongful act. Moreover, while the Court accepted that the 1977 Treaty had not been terminated, it also did not order Hungary to perform its obligations under the 1977 Treaty. Instead, the parties were encouraged to negotiate an agreement that was consistent with both the 1977 Treaty's object and purpose as well as contemporary international environmental law.

III. ENVIRONMENTAL PRINCIPLES IN THE WAKE OF THE RIO CONFERENCE ON ENVIRONMENT AND DEVELOPMENT

As alluded to, the timing of the case before the Court was significant in light of the developments in the field of international environmental law leading up to the

[8] See *Arbitration Regarding the Iron Rhine Railway (Belgium v. Netherlands)* ICGJ 373 (PCA 2005), [59] ('Since the Stockholm Conference on the Environment in 1972 there has been a marked development of international law relating to the protection of the environment').

[9] The Report of the UN Conference on the Human Environment reads in part as follows: 'Considerable emphasis was placed by speakers from developing countries upon the fact that for two-thirds of the world's population the human environment was dominated by poverty, malnutrition, illiteracy and misery ... The priority of developing countries was development. Until the gap between the rich and the poor countries was substantially narrowed, little if any progress could be made ... support for environmental action must not be an excuse for reducing development'. UN Doc A/CONF.48/14 and Corr 1 (1972), reproduced in (1972) 11 ILM 1416.

[10] A Najam, 'The South in International Environmental Negotiations' (1994) 31 *International Studies* 4, 427, 441. While the industrialised countries sought progress on climate change, biodiversity, forest loss and fishery issues, developing states placed more emphasis on market access, trade, technology transfer, development assistance and capacity building.

[11] See L Boisson de Chazournes, 'Unilateralism and Environmental Protection: Issues of Perception and Reality of Issues' (2000) 2 *EJIL* 315.

proceedings. After the Stockholm Conference of 1972, several other milestones facilitated the elaboration of environmental principles, including the Vienna Convention for the Protection of the Ozone Layer in 1985, the Montreal Protocol of 1987 and the Convention on Biodiversity in 1992. The Rio Declaration following the Conference of 1992 was a particularly important conduit through which environmental principles would crystallise. A brief appraisal of the state of environmental principles at the time of the *Gabčíkovo-Nagymaros* case, as well as the way in which they were argued by the parties, is helpful to understand better the new tools that the Court had to deal with. Those principles make reference to notions of prevention and of sustainable development, and protection for future generations.

Turning first to prevention, this principle has always played a central role in the life of international environmental law. Indeed, prevention is often better than a cure when it comes to environmental protection.[12] This centrality of prevention was recognised not least in the Espoo Convention of 1991. It is also manifested in Principle 17 of the Rio Declaration, which envisages the evaluation of risks through an environmental impact assessment. As such, it was necessary for states to take into account the impact of activities conducted on their territory, including in respect of the environment.

In the *Gabčíkovo-Nagymaros* proceedings, Hungary connected prevention to precaution in its arguments by urging that 'The previously existing obligation not to cause substantive damage to the territory of another State had ... evolved into an *erga omnes* obligation of prevention of damage pursuant to the "precautionary principle"'[13]

As with the principle of prevention, the principle of precaution also constitutes a lynchpin of international environmental law.[14] The latter principle in fact often extends and completes the spirit of the former principle.[15] The principle of precaution found its primary expression in Principle 15 of the Rio Declaration, which provides that 'in order to protect the environment, the precautionary approach shall be widely applied by states according to their capabilities. Where there are threats of serious or irreversible damage, lack of full scientific certainty shall not be used as a reason for postponing cost-effective measures to prevent environmental degradation'. Moreover, expressions of the principle can be found in the preamble of the Convention on Biodiversity and its Cartagena Protocol (Articles 9 and 10), the Convention on Climate Change of 1992, as well as the Vienna Convention for the Protection of the Ozone Layer of 1985 and its 1987 Montreal Protocol, which both referred to precautionary measures, and the Convention on the Protection and Use of Transboundary Watercourses and International Lakes of 1992.

This principle requires decision-makers to consider the risks of environmental damage and to take measures that will minimise the risks of events harmful to

---

[12] L Boisson de Chazournes and S Maljean-Dubois, 'Principes du Droit International de l'Environnment' (2011) *Jurisclasseur Environnement et Développement Durable* [60].

[13] *Case Concerning the Gabčíkovo-Nagymaros Project* (n 1) [97].

[14] Boisson de Chazournes and Maljean-Dubois, 'Principes du Droit International' (n 12) [64].

[15] ibid.

the environment occurring. It imposes both obligations of means and of results. Just as with the principle of prevention, the principle of precaution is concerned with the evaluation of risk. In this way, both principles are closely intertwined with the requirement to conduct an environmental impact assessment, which is now provided for in both conventional and customary international law.

Hungary invoked the precautionary principle to justify the impossibility of respecting a treaty by which it was bound to Czechoslovakia. In this way Hungary claimed 'that subsequently imposed requirements of international law in relation to the protection of the environment precluded performance of the Treaty' and that it was 'forced (to terminate the Treaty) by the other party's refusal to suspend work on Variant C'.[16] Moreover, Hungary pleaded that states were required by international law to 'take measures to anticipate, prevent or minimise damage to their transboundary resources and mitigate adverse effects. Where there are threats of serious or irreversible damage, lack of full scientific certainty should not be used as a reason for postponing such measures'.[17] Overall, the parties had agreed on the need to adopt a precautionary approach, but they disagreed on whether it was necessary to know if the conditions for the implementation of the concept were present in that specific situation.

The Court evoked the appearance of new norms which must be taken into account in the field of environmental protection, without however resorting to the qualification of the precautionary principle as a legal principle.[18] Judge Weeramantry, in his separate opinion, stressed the necessity of taking into account *erga omnes* obligations in international judicial proceedings. The precautionary principle would belong to this category of obligations. As Judge Weeramantry said:

> We have entered an era of international law in which international law subserves not only the interests of individual States, but looks beyond them and their parochial concerns to the greater interests of humanity and planetary welfare. In addressing such problems, which transcend the individual rights and obligations of the litigating States, international law will need to look beyond procedural rules fashioned for purely *inter partes* litigation. When we enter the arena of obligations which operate *erga omnes* rather than *inter partes*, rules based on individual fairness and procedural compliance may be inadequate. The great ecological questions now surfacing will call for thought upon this matter. International environmental law will need to proceed beyond weighing the rights and obligations of parties within a closed compartment of individual State self-interest, unrelated to the global concerns of humanity as a whole.[19]

In the end, the precautionary principle did not play as significant a role as might have been expected in this case. It was not mentioned explicitly by the majority.

---

[16] *Case Concerning the Gabčíkovo-Nagymaros Project* (n 1) [97].

[17] *Application of the Republic of Hungary v The Czech and Slovak Republic on the Diversion of the Danube River*, [31]

[18] *Case Concerning the Gabčíkovo-Nagymaros Project* (n 1) [140]. On the precautionary principle, see, MM Mbengue, *Essai sur une théorie du risque en droit international: L'anticipation du risque environnemental et sanitaire* (Paris, Pedone, 2009); L Boisson de Chazournes, 'Precaution in International Law: Reflection on its Composite Nature', in TM Ndiaye and R Wolfrum (eds), *Law of the Sea, Environmental Law and Settlement of Disputes* (Leiden, Brill, 2007), 21–34.

[19] *Case Concerning the Gabčíkovo-Nagymaros Project* (n 1) Judge Weeramantry separate opinion, 118–19.

While the Court did not refer to precaution, it did accept that 'vigilance and prevention' were to be exercised in the area of the protection of the environment.[20]

Turning to another environmental principle that was relevant in this case, inter-generational equity purports to extend the universal application of rights to individuals not yet born. Inter-generational equity aims to ensure equity between generations. It is in this sense a principle of distributive justice.[21] The spirit of the principle was expressed by the Brundtland Commission as follows:

> Sustainable development is development that meets the needs of the present without compromising the ability of future generations to meet their own needs.[22]

It is evident from this expression that inter-generational equity is integral to sustainable development. Principle 2 of the 1972 Stockholm Declaration of the United Nations Conference on the Human Environment also provided that 'The natural resources of the earth ... must be safeguarded for the benefit of present and future generations ...'. Principle 5 of the Stockholm Declaration provided that 'The non-renewable resources of the earth must be employed in such a way as to guard against the danger of their future exhaustion...' In its Advisory Opinion in *Legality of the Threat or Use of Nuclear Weapons,* the ICJ had recognised that 'the environment is not an abstraction but represents the living space, the quality of life and the very health of human beings, including generations unborn'.[23]

In *Gabčíkovo-Nagymaros,* the ICJ appeared to lend its support to the principle of inter-generational equity. It did so by restating what it had said in *Legality of the Threat or Use of Nuclear Weapons.* Also, in that case it had been considered that

> in order correctly to apply to the present case the Charter law on the use of force and the law applicable in armed conflict, in particular humanitarian law, it is imperative for the Court to take account of the unique characteristics of nuclear weapons, and in particular their destructive capacity, their capacity to cause untold human suffering, and their ability to cause damage to generations to come.[24]

Judge Weeramantry's dissenting opinion in the *Nuclear Weapons* advisory opinion recognised that 'the rights of future generations have passed the stage when they were

---

[20] ibid [140]: 'The Court is mindful that, in the field of environmental protection, vigilance and prevention are required on account of the often irreversible character of damage to the environment and of the limitations inherent in the very mechanism of reparation of this type of damage'. It should be noted that a year later in the *Hormones* case, the Appellate Body of the World Trade Organization (WTO), following in the footsteps of the ICJ, refused to take a position on the customary status of the precautionary principle. The Appellate Body noted 'that the Court did not identify the precautionary principle as one of those recently developed norms. It also declined to declare that such principle could override the obligations of the Treaty between Czechoslovakia and Hungary of 16 September 1977 concerning the construction and operation of the Gabcíkovo/Nagymaros System of Locks' (see European Communities—Measures Concerning Meat and Meat Products (Hormones), Report of the Appellate Body, WT/DS48/AB/R, 16 January 1998, [123] and fn 93.

[21] D Shelton, 'Intergenerational Equity' in R Wolfrum and C Kojima (eds), *Solidarity: A Structural Principle of International Law* (Heidelberg, Springer, 2010).

[22] *The World Commission on Environment and Development, Our Common Future* (Oxford, OUP, 1987) 43.

[23] *Legality of the Threat or Use of Nuclear Weapons* [1996] ICJ Rep 226, [29]; *Case Concerning the Gabčíkovo-Nagymaros Project* (n 1) [112].

[24] *Legality of the Threat or Use of Nuclear Weapons* (n 23) [36].

merely an embryonic right struggling for recognition. They have woven themselves into international law through major treaties, through juristic opinion and through general principles of law recognised by civilized nations'.[25] Moreover, in placing an emphasis in *Gabčíkovo-Nagymaros* on sustainable development as embodying the 'need to reconcile economic development with protection of the environment',[26] a place for intergenerational equity was recognised. Indeed, intergenerational equity has been described in the literature as forming a part of sustainable development.[27]

Despite the differences that had arisen on the issues of the environment and development in the period prior to the case, a consensus had nevertheless culminated around the concept of 'sustainable development' at the time of this dispute. Defined as development that meets the needs of the present without compromising the ability of future generations to meet their own needs,[28] sustainable development has acquired a rhetorical power for bridging gaps, at least at a preliminary level. Subsequent practice has shown the virtue of the concept of sustainable development for reconciling different interests and for establishing links between different areas of international regulation.[29]

Even though the issues of the environment and development were considered as incompatible at the time of the Stockholm Conference in 1972, the concept of eco-development was nevertheless an observable feature of the debate at that time.[30] It was, however, at the Rio Conference of 1992 that the concept of sustainable development emerged in earnest. Principle 4 of the Rio Declaration had recognised the existence of sustainable development (emphasising that 'environmental protection shall constitute an integral part of the development process and cannot be considered in isolation from it'), while Principle 3 provides that 'developmental and environmental needs of present and future generations' must be met in an equitable manner and Principle 27 calls for cooperation on elaborating sustainable development under international law. Article 3(4) of the Climate Change Convention of 1992 stipulates that 'the parties have a right to, and should, promote sustainable development' and the Biodiversity Convention also makes reference to 'sustainable use'. The principle can of course be observed in a variety of contexts, including the preamble of the Agreement establishing the World Trade Organization (WTO). While its precise content and obligations remain somewhat unclear, the concept envisages that the requirements of the environment are taken into account in policy-making along with other economic and social considerations. The environment cannot be considered in isolation.[31]

Hungary had argued that new environmental norms should be taken into consideration in the interpretation of the 1977 Treaty and also noted that, as regards

---

[25] ibid, Judge Weeramantry dissenting, 455.

[26] *Case Concerning the Gabčíkovo-Nagymaros Project* (n 1) [140].

[27] See, for example, P Sands and J Peel, *Principles of International Environmental Law* (Cambridge, CUP, 2012); S Bell and D McGillivray, *Environmental Law*, 7th edn (Oxford, OUP, 2008).

[28] See Principles 3 and 4 of the Rio Declaration on Environment and Development.

[29] P Sands, 'International Courts and the Application of the Concept of "Sustainable Development"' (1999) 3 *Max Planck Yearbook of United Nations Law* 363.

[30] Boisson de Chazournes and Maljean-Dubois (n 12) [29].

[31] ibid [34].

'future relations between the Parties … "a joint environmental impact assessment of the region and of the future of Variant C structures in the context of the sustainable development of the region" should be carried out'.[32] The Court referred to sustainable development in recognising the 'need to reconcile economic development with protection of the environment'.[33] Moreover, 'The awareness of the vulnerability of the environment and the recognition that environmental risks have to be assessed on a continuous basis have become much stronger in the years since the treaty's conclusion'.[34] This is evidence that environmental considerations should be part and parcel of decisions taken by parties on development projects.

The Court simply referred to sustainable development as a concept and did not seem to attach any legal value to it. It was only Judge Weeramantry who recognised this principle as having an *erga omnes* character. In this respect, questions as to how such an obligation may be actionable can rightly be asked.[35] Judge Weeramantry also described the principle of sustainable development as taking into account 'the needs of development and the necessity to protect the environment'. Moreover, consistent with *Legality of the Threat or Use of Nuclear Weapons*, it was affirmed that whatever agreement the parties came to under the Treaty to pursue development works, the latter had to be consistent with the obligation of continuing environmental assessment.

Overall, it would seem that the ICJ considers it had a role to play in adjudicating not only the immediate dispute before it but the wider issues of interest to the international community, such as the development and application of emerging principles of environmental protection, even if this was done in a relatively nuanced way in the present case. Nevertheless, in this context, it should also be noted that this was in fact the first contentious case before the ICJ in which non-governmental organisations requested the filing of an *amicus* brief, an indication of the broader interests that the ICJ was willing to consider.

IV. THE GREENING EFFECT OF INTERPRETATION

It should not be forgotten that the progressive inroads on environmental principles were made through more conservative means in this case. While the Court never abandoned the treaty that had been agreed by the parties in place of newly developed principles of environmental protection, it nevertheless sought to interpret the 1977 treaty in light of those new principles. Indeed, the Court clarified that individual treaties are not to be interpreted in isolation but rather in the context of an evolving international law. The development of the international legal regime over

---

[32] *Case Concerning the Gabčíkovo-Nagymaros Project* (n 1) [125].
[33] ibid [140].
[34] ibid [112].
[35] A Koe, 'Damming the Danube: The International Court of Justice and the Gabčikovo-Nagymaros Project (*Hungary v Slovakia*)' (1998) 20 *Sydney Law Review* 4, 612.

time can have a bearing on the interpretation and application of existing treaties and thus the parties are called upon to take these developments into account:

> The Court does not consider that new developments in the state of environmental knowl-edge and of environmental law can be said to have been completely unforeseen. What is more, the formulation of Articles 15, 19 and 20, designed to accommodate change, made it possible for the parties to take account of such developments and to apply them when implementing those treaty provisions.[36]

Moreover, it was underlined that 'the Treaty is not static, and is open to adapt to emerging norms of international law'.[37] This evolutive interpretation found favour with the tribunal in the *Iron Rhine Arbitration*. There, drawing support from the ICJ's approach in *Gabčíkovo-Nagymaros*, it was affirmed that 'an evolutive inter-pretation, which would ensure an application of the treaty that would be effective in terms of its object and purpose, will be preferred to a strict application of the intertemporal rule'.[38] The Tribunal cited Article 31(3)(c) of the Vienna Convention on the Law of Treaties as a legal base for a contemporaneous interpretation of the treaties at issue. According to this provision 'any relevant rules of international law applicable in the relations between the Parties' shall be taken into account in inter-preting international agreements. The Tribunal therefore considered principles of international environmental law in their current form as relevant to its decision.[39] The Arbitration Court in the *Indus Waters Kishenganga Arbitration* followed the same pattern of reasoning as the ICJ and the *Iron Rhine* Tribunal (which was in its majority composed of ICJ judges). It said:

> It is established that principles of international environmental law must be taken into account even when (unlike the present case) interpreting treaties concluded before the development of that body of law. The *Iron Rhine* Tribunal applied concepts of custom-ary international environmental law to treaties dating back to the mid-nineteenth century, when principles of environmental protection were rarely if ever considered in international agreements and did not form any part of customary international law. Similarly, the Inter-national Court of Justice in *Gabčíkovo-Nagymaros* ruled that, whenever necessary for the application of a treaty, "new norms have to be taken into consideration, and ... new stand-ards given proper weight." It is therefore incumbent upon this Court to interpret and apply this 1960 Treaty in light of the customary international principles for the protection of the environment in force today.[40]

Similarly, the ICJ had suggested that no explicit treaty provision was required to apply new environmental norms in the *Gabčíkovo-Nagymaros* case.[41] This has been commended as a sensible approach given that where treaties do not provide for obligations under customary international law—such as environmental impact

[36] *Case Concerning the Gabčíkovo-Nagymaros Project* (n 1) [104].
[37] ibid [112].
[38] *Arbitration Regarding the Iron Rhine Railway (Belgium v Netherlands)* ICGJ 373 (PCA 2005), [80].
[39] ibid [58].
[40] *Indus Waters Kishenganga Arbitration (Pakistan v India)*, Partial Award (PCA 2013), [452] (original footnotes omitted).
[41] *Case Concerning the Gabčíkovo-Nagymaros Project* (n 1) [140].

assessments—the latter should in any event apply.[42] This interpretative approach has been followed in subsequent cases, such as *Pulp Mills*, in which the Court interpreted the 1975 Statute of the River Uruguay at issue in that case as follows:

> Article 41(a) distinguishes between applicable international agreements and the guidelines and recommendations of international technical bodies. While the former are legally binding and therefore the domestic rules and regulations enacted and the measures adopted by the State have to comply with them, the latter, not being formally binding, are, to the extent they are relevant, to be taken into account by the State so that the domestic rules and regulations and the measures it adopts are compatible ('con adecuación') with those guidelines and recommendations.[43]

One of the most important aspects of this judgment was the recognition of the concept of sustainable development, which has been described as something of an interstitial norm.[44] Some international tribunals have since relied on the Court's decision in this respect. For instance, in the *Iron Rhine Arbitration*, the tribunal noted that sustainable development was an acknowledgment that environment and development were 'mutually reinforcing, integral concepts'.[45]

A significant contribution to international environmental law was also made through the recognition of 'ecological necessity', even though this did not arise on the facts in this case. Moreover, environmental impact assessment, to be conducted on an ongoing basis throughout the project, is another important take-away from this judgment.

V. INTERNATIONAL WATERCOURSES: ON EQUITY AND SUSTAINABILITY

As for the Court's indication that the international community has an interest in sustainable development, it also clarified that this is a further aspect to be considered when balancing the interests of the parties to a dispute over a particular watercourse. In this way, the decision in *Gabčíkovo-Nagymaros* had an important impact on the law of international watercourses. The Court connected the two concepts of equitable and sustainable utilisation of an international watercourse, emphasising that the former had to be interpreted in light of the latter. While Hungary had violated its obligations under the Treaty, the ICJ noted 'that cannot mean that Hungary forfeited its basic right to an equitable and reasonable sharing of the resources of an international watercourse'.[46]

---

[42] A Boyle, '*Gabčíkovo-Nagymaros* Case: New Law in Old Bottles' (1997) 8 *Yearbook of International Environmental Law* 13, 15.

[43] *Case Concerning Pulp Mills on the River Uruguay (Argentina v Uruguay)* [2010] ICJ Rep 14, [62].

[44] V Lowe, 'Sustainable Development and Unsustainable Arguments' in A Boyle and D Freestone (eds) *International Law and Sustainable Development: Past Achievements and Future Challenges* (Oxford, OUP, 1999).

[45] *Arbitration Regarding the Iron Rhine Railway (Belgium v Netherlands)* ICGJ 373 (PCA 2005), [59]. The Tribunal also referred to the decision of the ICJ case in *Gabčíkovo-Nagymaros*: The Tribunal would recall the observation of the International Court of Justice in the Gabčíkovo-Nagymaros case that 'This need to reconcile economic development with protection of the environment is aptly expressed in the concept of sustainable development' [59].

[46] *Case Concerning the Gabčíkovo-Nagymaros Project* (n 1) [190].

The Court, in applying the principle of equitable utilisation, found that the alternative works that Slovakia sought to implement were a violation of Hungary's right to a share of the Danube that was equitable and reasonable. In making reference to the principle of equitable and reasonable utilisation enshrined in the 1997 UN Watercourses Convention, Hungary's 'basic right' to 'an equitable and reasonable sharing of the resources of an international watercourse' was affirmed.[47] Hungary had a right to equitable and reasonable use of the watercourse, and Slovakia had violated this right.

As regards the interaction between the principle of equitable utilisation (Article 5, UN Watercourses Convention) and the obligation not to cause significant harm (Article 7, UN Watercourses Convention), Stephen McCaffrey has argued that the decision showed that the former has precedence over the latter under the UN Watercourses Convention.[48] While the Court referred to the equitable utilisation principle on a number of occasions in the *Gabčíkovo* case, McCaffrey has noted the absence of a reference to the 'no-harm' principle in the Court's judgment, despite Hungary's reliance on it during the pleadings.[49] McCaffrey goes on to suggest: 'I do not believe that means the "no-harm" rule has been weakened; but it suggests that the Court views the principle of equitable utilization to be the more important of the two'.[50] However, is it not the case that the UN Watercourses Convention provides for an integrated approach to water management at the international level? Article 6 of the UN Watercourses Convention in fact favours a mutual and supportive application of the principles laid down in Articles 5 and 7, as they include taking into consideration 'the effects of the use or uses of the watercourse in one watercourse State on other watercourse States'.[51]

In its discussion of countermeasures, and particularly whether the internationally wrongful act committed by Czechoslovakia in implementing Variant C could be characterised as a countermeasure, the Court noted that an important consideration in this context was the effect of the countermeasure and that the latter was proportionate to the harm originally suffered. The judgment of the Permanent Court of International Justice in the *River Oder Case* was recited as follows: '(the) community of interest in a navigable river becomes the basis of a common legal right, the essential features of which are the perfect equality of all riparian States in the user of the whole course of the river and the exclusion of any preferential privilege of any one riparian State in relation to others'.[52] The majority then went on to note

---

[47] ibid [47].
[48] S McCaffrey, 'The UN Convention on the Law of the Non-Navigational Uses of International Watercourses: Prospects and Pitfalls', in L Boisson de Chazournes and S Salman (eds), *International Watercourses: Enhancing Co-Operation and Managing Conflicts* (World Bank Technical Paper No 414, 1998), 22.
[49] ibid, 27.
[50] ibid.
[51] Art 6(1)(d), *Convention on the Law of the Non-navigational Uses of International Watercourses*, 1997, 36 ILM 700. See L Boisson de Chazournes, *Fresh Water in International Law* (Oxford, OUP, 2013), 29–30.
[52] Territorial Jurisdiction of the International Commission of the River Oder (1929) PCIJ Series A No 23, 27.

that 'Modern development of international law has strengthened this principle for non-navigational uses of international watercourses as well, as evidenced by the adoption of the Convention of 21 May 1997 on the Law of the Non-Navigational Uses of International Watercourses by the United Nations General Assembly'.[53] This is one of the many illustrations of the dialogue and mutual crystallisation that takes place between the International Law Commission and the ICJ in the law-making process.

Interestingly, while Article 50 of the Articles on the Responsibility of States for Internationally Wrongful Acts makes no mention of the possible illegality of countermeasures by reason of potential damage to the environment, the *Gabčíkovo-Nagymaros case* has shed light on some aspects of the question.[54] During the course of proceedings before the Court, Slovakia argued that Hungary's decision to suspend, then to abandon, the construction of the works had made it impossible for Czechoslovakia to carry out the construction work as originally envisaged by the 1977 Treaty, and that the latter thus was entitled to resort to a solution as close as possible to the original design.[55] Slovakia equally maintained that Czechoslovakia had been under an obligation to mitigate the damage resulting from Hungary's illegal acts. It argued that a state which is confronted by the illegal act of another state is bound to minimise its losses, and thus reduce the damages claimable from the responsible state.[56] The damages claimed by Slovakia were nonetheless considerable, taking into account the investments made and the extra damage, economic as much as ecological, which would have resulted from leaving the works at Dunakiliti/Gabčíkovo unfinished and from the non-operation of the system; on this basis it was argued that Czechoslovakia had not only a right, but was even under an obligation, to put Variant C into action. Although Slovakia had asserted that Czechoslovakia's conduct had been lawful, it maintained, as a secondary argument, that, even were the Court to find otherwise, the putting into action of Variant C could be justified as a countermeasure.

Was such a 'countermeasure' lawful? In answering that question, the Court enumerated the conditions to be satisfied in relation to the recourse to countermeasures, including the condition according to which the 'effects of a countermeasure must be commensurate with the injury suffered, taking account of the rights in question'.[57] It concluded that the countermeasure was unlawful by reason of the fact that it deprived Hungary of its right to a fair and reasonable share of the natural resources of the Danube. An economic approach was thereby favoured, without attaching much importance to an ecological approach to proportionality.[58] It was

---

[53] *Case Concerning the Gabčíkovo-Nagymaros Project* (n 1) [85].

[54] L Boisson de Chazournes, 'Other non-derogable obligations', in J Crawford, A Pellet and S Olleson (eds), *The Law of International Responsibility* (Oxford, OUP, 2010).

[55] *Case Concerning the Gabčíkovo-Nagymaros Project* (n 1) [67].

[56] ibid [68]–[69].

[57] ibid [85].

[58] See also the Separate Opinion of Judge Bedjaoui: 'In any event ... Variant C is not a countermeasure capable of excusing its unlawfulness. Nor indeed is it proportionate, since from the outset it deprives Hungary of the waters of the Danube as a shared resource and also of any control over a joint investment laid down in the 1977 Treaty'. *Case Concerning the Gabčíkovo-Nagymaros Project* (n 1) [52].

only in an incidental and rather timid manner that the unilateral diversion of the Danube was considered to have continuing effects on the ecology of the riparian region of Szigetköz.[59] The judicial body adopted a classic approach to the assessment of the impact of countermeasures, one which is certainly important, but nevertheless is somewhat limited, given the way in which international environmental law is currently developing and taking root in the international legal system.

Could it nevertheless be argued that countermeasures disturbing the ecological and eco-systemic balance of a given area are prohibited? Can countermeasures be permitted to have negative repercussions on the environment? In other words, above and beyond the issue of proportionality or potential reversibility, could it not be envisaged that there are measures prone to damage the environment which cannot be taken in any circumstances?

Having found Slovakia's countermeasure to be illegal by reason of its disproportionate character, the Court saw it as unnecessary to rule on further conditions on which the legality of countermeasures depends, namely that the latter must have the aim of encouraging the responsible state to carry out its obligations under international law, and that the measure must consequently be 'reversible'.[60] However, the issue of 'reversibility' could have provided an opportunity to hold that countermeasures having an impact on the environment are unlawful. After all, the particular and substantial characteristic of much environmental damage is its irreversibility as the Court noted itself in its judgment.[61]

In its guidance to the parties, the Court stressed once more the importance of the principle of equitable and reasonable utilisation of an international watercourse and asserted that the re-implementation of the joint regime would 'reflect in an optional way the concept of common utilization of shared water resources for the achievement of several objectives in the Treaty'[62] and noted that this was in accordance with Article 5(2) of the Convention on the Law of the Non-Navigational Uses of International Watercourses, which provides 'Watercourse States shall participate in the use, development and protection of an international watercourse in an equitable and reasonable manner. Such participation includes both the right to utilise the watercourse and the duty to cooperate in the protection and development thereof, as provided in the present Convention'.[63]

VI. THE LAW OF STATE RESPONSIBILITY AS A PROTECTED FORTRESS

Another major area of law to be considered in the *Gabčíkovo-Nagymaros* case was the law of state responsibility, under which umbrella a variety of issues arose. While different circumstances precluding wrongfulness had been pleaded by both

[59] ibid [85].
[60] ibid [87].
[61] ibid [140].
[62] ibid [147].
[63] ibid.

Hungary and Slovakia, the ICJ ultimately held that there were intersecting wrongs.[64] In terminating the project, Hungary had committed an internationally wrongful act and Slovakia had similarly done so by its unilateral implementation of a modified version of the 1977 agreement. Moreover, this implementation of the so-called Variant C, an alternative to the works proposed under the 1977 Treaty, violated Hungary's territorial integrity and sovereign independence.[65]

The most prominent aspect of state responsibility that was discussed in the case was that of necessity. In fact, one commentator has observed that 'It is an incontrovertible fact that the *Gabčíkovo-Nagymaros* case has proven to be the most prominent in contributing to the clarification [of] issues raised regarding the plea of necessity in international environmental law'.[66] In response to Hungary's plea that a state of ecological necessity existed, the Court noted that the state of necessity must be concerned with an essential interest of a state, that this interest must be under grave and imminent peril and there would have been no other measure to prevent this threat to the interest. While it was recognised that a state of ecological necessity could indeed exist, in this case the peril was not sufficiently imminent and there were other means available for Hungary to protect the essential interest of its natural environment. Notwithstanding, the International Law Commission noted in the Draft Articles on State Responsibility that 'safeguarding the ecological balance has come to be considered an "essential interest" of all States'.[67]

The ICJ left the door open for a plea of ecological necessity to be accepted under Article 33 of the Draft Articles on State Responsibility, but noted that in this case such a situation did not arise. However, it should be noted that the Court has been criticised for this finding on the facts since it did not actually evaluate in any detail the scientific data and research findings suggesting the environmental risk. It has been stated that the failure to engage in this analysis 'failed to respect the precautionary principle in international environmental law and neglected consideration of ramifications that present uncertainties may have upon the future'.[68] Notwithstanding, the Court did not rule out the potential for ecological necessity to justify an otherwise wrongful act was significant. In addition, the Court was also conscious of the ecological effects caused by Slovakia's actions.

The invocation of the protection of essential interests and the 'urgent need to safeguard essential interests' is often used as a reason for justifying the resort to unilateral measures. This is especially the case today, a time of increased awareness of the scarcity of natural resources as well as a perceived increase in vulnerability due to developments in science and technology. This raises the question of the

---

[64] For a detailed critique of the ICJ's handling of the state responsibility issues in this case, see R Lefeber, '*The Gabčíkovo-Nagymaros Project* and the Law of State Responsibility' (1998) 11 *LJIL* 3, 609.

[65] *Case Concerning the Gabčíkovo-Nagymaros Project* (n 1) [88].

[66] M Fitzmaurice, 'Necessity in International Environmental Law' (2010) 41 *NYIL: Necessity Across International Law* 159, 179.

[67] International Law Commission, *Draft Articles on State Responsibility*, Art 33, Comment 14, *Report of the International Law Commission on the Work of its Thirty-Second* Session (1980) 2 *ILC Ybk* 30, 39.

[68] Koe, 'Damming the Danube' (n 35) 612.

legality of measures taken for such reasons. 'State of necessity' as envisaged by the International Law Commission in its Draft Articles on State Responsibility for wrongful acts has been referred to in this context. International practice in this area is long-standing and the ICJ has pronounced on the matter. However, one may question the potential of this legal concept to meet new environmental challenges adequately. If there is, as the arbitral tribunal stated in the *Lake Lanoux* case, no rule of general international law 'that forbids one state, acting to safeguard its legitimate interests, *to put itself in a situation which would in fact permit it*, in violation of international pledges, seriously to injure a neighbouring state',[69] it remains to be seen whether a state can be excused for actually going beyond the threshold of legality in unilaterally safeguarding environmental interests.

In the *Gabčíkovo-Nagymaros Project* case, a state of necessity as embodied in draft Article 33 of the ILC Draft Articles on State Responsibility was held to be a norm of customary international law.[70] In approving verbatim the ILC's formulation of the state of necessity, and in considering the conditions attaching to the draft Article, the Court commented that the safeguarding of the environment was indeed an 'essential interest' for the purposes of that provision, even if on the facts of the case, Hungary could not avail itself of the defence.

If a 'state of necessity' was to be available to safeguard environmental interests,[71] the ILC had in its commentary in 1980 nonetheless stressed the need to distance the possibility of the plea being raised in circumstances which could be associated with historical notions of necessity that did not form a part of positive international law; such as the natural law inspired 'doctrine of fundamental rights', from which stemmed a purported inherent right of self-preservation.[72] In the past, it had been claimed that self-preservation was a right before which all other things had to yield in the event of conflict. In the nineteenth century in particular, this doctrine had provided one allegedly theoretical underpinning for action taken ostensibly under the cover of necessity, but in reality in contravention of international law. To emphasise that the necessity referred to in draft Article 33 is not a right, fundamental or otherwise, on the basis of which a state may make a claim on others, draft Article 33 is entitled '*state* of necessity'.[73] Thus, necessity is merely a situation which may temporarily exempt a state from complying with an otherwise binding obligation.

To avoid the possibility of abuse, draft Article 33 was cast in particularly strict terms. In the *Gabčíkovo-Nagymaros* case, the ICJ was also particularly strict in that it applied the notion of the state of necessity in a rather literal manner. The ICJ appeared to say that for the purposes of draft Article 33, the uncertainties surrounding the peril in that case, meant that the risk was insufficiently imminent to satisfy the requirements of the draft Article.[74]

---

[69] *Lake Lanoux Arbitration (France v Spain)* (1957) 24 ILR 101, 126 (emphasis added).
[70] *Case Concerning the Gabčíkovo-Nagymaros Project* (n 1) [50].
[71] *ILC Ybk* vol II, Part 2 (1980), 39, [14].
[72] ibid, 17–18, [7]–[8] and [35], [4]. See also to the same effect in Roberto Ago's report, *ILC Ybk* vol I (1980), 154, [41]–[45].
[73] Emphasis added.
[74] *Case Concerning the Gabčíkovo-Nagymaros Project* (n 1) [54].

The peril, according to the Court, must be 'duly established at the relevant point in time'. It seems that the Court in fact came close to saying that for a peril to be 'imminent' it has to be 'certain'. In his Second Report on State Responsibility, Special Rapporteur James Crawford considered that the Court recognised 'the existence of scientific uncertainty was not enough, of itself, to establish the existence of an imminent peril'.[75] Yet, in the environmental field, risks may not be certain and states may, in order to act in conformity with the precautionary principle, need to take action before the risk is as 'imminent' as the International Court would seem to require. In his report to the Commission in 1999, the Special Rapporteur considered the possibility that the current provision in Article 33, be relaxed to accommodate the precautionary principle. He stated: 'in questions relating, for example, to conservation and the environment or to the safety of large structures, there will often be substantial areas of scientific uncertainty, and different views may be taken by different experts on whether there is a peril, how grave or imminent it is and whether the means proposed are the only ones available in the circumstances'.[76] Were the precautionary principle accommodated within Article 33, there would be greater scope for unilateral action to safeguard the environment. However, the Special Rapporteur decided against such an amendment, on the basis of the possibility of abuse of the Article.[77]

In *Gabčíkovo-Nagymaros*, it was accepted that a state of necessity was an exceptional circumstance precluding wrongfulness, as provided for in customary international law and under Article 33 of the 1980 ILC Draft Articles on the Responsibility of States, and this approach was followed in *Legal Consequences of the Construction of a Wall in the Occupied Palestinian Territory*.[78]

Hungary had also argued that Slovakia's insistence on the implementation of Variant C meant that a temporary state of necessity was converted into a permanent state of necessity, which in turn should terminate the treaty. On this point, the Court clarified that a permanent state of necessity cannot exist to terminate a treaty since a state of necessity must always be temporary in nature and this can only suspend a treaty until the state of necessity disappears. This, the ICJ observed, was the intention of the drafters of Article 61 of the Vienna Convention on the Law of Treaties.[79]

VII. THE SANCTITY OF TREATIES

In another major area of international law that arose in this case, the ICJ turned its attention to the law of treaties. In fact, while certain doors were opened, the

---

[75] *Second Report on State Responsibility*, Addendum, UN Doc A/CN.4/498/Add.2 of 30 April 1999, 32, [289].

[76] ibid.

[77] ibid; Boisson de Chazournes, 'Unilateralism' (n 11).

[78] *Advisory Opinion Concerning Legal Consequences of the Construction of a Wall in the Occupied Palestinian Territory* [2004] ICJ Rep 136.

[79] *Case Concerning the Gabčíkovo-Nagymaros Project* (n 1) [102].

sanctity of the treaty was also very carefully preserved. Hungary had argued that a fundamental change of circumstances justified the termination of the treaty. This argument was, however, rejected on the facts of this case. The political situation was not closely connected to the object and purpose of the 1977 Treaty and could not be considered an essential basis of the consent underlying the treaty, which had fundamentally changed since the conclusion of the 1977 Treaty. The same reasoning was applied to the economic conditions as well as to environmental considerations.[80] According to the Court, a fundamental change of circumstances must 'have been unforeseen; the existence of the circumstances at the time of the Treaty's conclusion must have constituted an essential basis of the consent of the parties to be bound by the Treaty'.[81] In this way—and following a similar line of reasoning to that made in respect of the state of ecological necessity—the door was left open for environmental considerations to constitute the basis for a fundamental change in circumstances.[82]

As for the claim that there had been a material breach of the treaty by Slovakia, as had been alleged by Hungary, while the violation of a treaty provision or treaty provisions may justify resort to certain countermeasures by an injured state, termination of the treaty was held not to be justified by such a violation. Countermeasures should in fact be distinguished from the concept of material breach under Article 60 of the Vienna Convention on the Law of Treaties. In this respect, the Court took the opportunity to clarify that the law of state responsibility and the law of treaties are separate branches of international law whose scope is also distinct. As such,

[a] determination of whether a convention is or is not in force, and whether it has or has not been properly suspended or denounced, is to be made pursuant to the law of treaties. On the other hand, an evaluation of the extent to which the suspension or denunciation of a convention, seen as incompatible with the law of treaties, involves the responsibility of the State which proceeded to it, is to be made under the law of State responsibility.[83]

Consequently, 'when it invoked the state of necessity in an effort to justify [its] conduct, Hungary chose to place itself from the outset within the ambit of the law of state responsibility, thereby implying that, in the absence of such a circumstance, its conduct would have been unlawful'.[84]

Overall, the Court underlined that it was only 'a material breach of the treaty itself, by a State party to that treaty, which entitles the other party to rely on it as a ground for terminating the treaty', as is provided for under Article 60 of the Vienna Convention.[85] There was also an incongruence in the timing given that the breach of the 1977 Treaty by Slovakia, namely the operation of the Variant C works, was

---

[80] Fitzmaurice, 'The Gabčikovo-Nagymaros Case' (n 2) 333–34.
[81] *Case Concerning the Gabčíkovo-Nagymaros Project* (n 1) [104].
[82] Klabbers, 'The Substance of Form' (n 3).
[83] *Case Concerning the Gabčíkovo-Nagymaros Project* (n 1) [47].
[84] ibid [48].
[85] ibid [106].

not until October 1992, which was after Hungary's notification of its intention to terminate the treaty in May 1992. Hungary was therefore unable to avail of material breach as a ground on which to terminate the 1977 Treaty.

The principle of *pacta sunt servanda* was ensured and preserved, even though both parties to the treaty had not complied with the treaty. Almost alarmingly, the Court noted that it would set a dangerous precedent for the principle of *pacta sunt servanda* 'if it were to conclude that a treaty in force between States, which the parties have implemented in considerable measure and at a great cost over a period of years, might be unilaterally set aside on grounds of reciprocal non-compliance'.[86] The Court also noted that, even if there was a state of necessity, this was not a ground for the permanent termination of a treaty. Once the state of necessity has passed, regular treaty obligations are restored.

The treaty had been concluded and all efforts should be made to keep it alive. This was emphasised with the Court ultimately asking the parties to negotiate in the context of the treaty. The ICJ clarified that Hungary and Slovakia were free to agree upon and incorporate into the 1977 Treaty 'newly developed norms of environmental law', albeit that a situation under Article 64 of the Vienna Convention on the Law of Treaties arose.[87]

Ultimately relying on the parties' judgment, the ICJ (as the Permanent Court of International Justice did in the *Diversion of the River Meuse*[88] dispute) left the parties to negotiate an agreement that would put an end to their dispute on the basis of the Court's decision:

> It is not for the Court to determine what shall be the final result of these negotiations to be conducted by the Parties. It is for the Parties themselves to find an agreed solution that takes account of the objectives of the Treaty, which must be pursued in a joint and integrated way, as well as the norms of international environmental law and the principles of the law of international watercourses ... What is required in the present case by the rule *pacta sunt servanda*, as reflected in Article 26 of the Vienna Convention of 1969 on the Law of Treaties, is that the Parties find an agreed solution within the co-operative context of the Treaty.[89]

VIII. CONCLUSION

The *Gabčíkovo-Nagymaros Project (Hungary/Slovakia)* case is undoubtedly a landmark case. Not only does it deal with an impressive array of legal disciplines, it also breaks new ground in many respects. This is particularly with regard to the principle of sustainable development and ecological necessity. However, while the Court opened the doors to these newly emerging principles and concepts in

---

[86] ibid [114].
[87] ibid [112].
[88] *Diversion of Water from the River Meuse (Netherlands v Belgium)* (1937) PCIJ Series A/B No 4.
[89] *Case Concerning the Gabčíkovo-Nagymaros Project* (n 1) [141]–[142].

international law, we must remember that it ultimately held on the basis of more traditional precepts. With the benefit of hindsight, we now know that the opening of those doors was in and of itself significant. Although one swallow does not make a summer, this case has become a foundation stone for the ongoing emergence and consolidation of international environmental law. Indeed, developments since its rendering, such as the evolution of evidence in environmental cases, the *Pulp Mills* case,[90] the *Whaling* case,[91] and the role of experts, all represent further swallows.

---

[90] *Pulp Mills on the River Uruguay (Argentina v Uruguay)* [2010] ICJ Rep 14.
[91] *Whaling in the Antarctic (Australia v Japan: New Zealand intervening)* [2014] ICJ Rep 226.

19

Vivendi v Argentina (1997–2010)

SAM LUTTRELL*

Contracts have such binding force that most of the everyday transactions of life, whether of Greeks or Foreigners, arise through them. Because we can rely on them we can go among strangers and get what each of us needs.

Isocrates, *Against Callimachus* (402 BC)[1]

No issue in the field of investment arbitration is more fundamental, more disputed, than the distinction between treaty and contract.

Professor James Crawford AC SC (2008)[2]

I. INTRODUCTION

W HAT HAPPENS WHEN a company accepts an offer of arbitration made to it by a country? Where the offer is made in a contract, nothing extraordinary. But where the offer is made in a *treaty*, it may get complicated. An arbitration agreement is formed, that is for sure. The scope of that agreement is fixed by the treaty, but that does not make the arbitration agreement a treaty itself; indeed, the arbitration agreement cannot be a treaty because not all of the parties to it are states. But the agreement—or at least some terms of it—*originates* from a treaty, and it is normally formed for the determination of claims for breach of that treaty. The subject

* The writer is grateful to Ishbel McLachlan for her considerable assistance in researching and writing this chapter. The writer also thanks Cameron Miles, Romesh Weeramantry, Olga Boltenko and Ben Love for their comments on earlier drafts of this chapter (needless to say, any errors are for the writer's account). Of course, the views expressed in this chapter are the author's alone and do not necessarily reflect the views of Clifford Chance LLP.

[1] Isocrates, *Against Callimachus*, 18.27-28; cited in D Roebuck, *Disputes and Differences: Comparisons in Law, Language and History* (Oxford, HOLO Books: The Arbitration Press, 2010) 320.

[2] J Crawford, 'Treaty and Contract in Investment Arbitration' (2008) 24 *Arbitration International* 3, 351.

matter of the dispute (the *ratione materiae*), meaning the assets or rights of the investor that have been affected by the state's conduct, will depend on the case. Whether a particular asset or right that has been affected can actually be brought into the arbitration will depend on the treaty: if the treaty says that the investments that qualify for protection under it include contracts between the investor and the state, then claims in relation to such contracts will be within the scope of the agreement to arbitrate. And, in this situation, the dispute submitted to arbitration will include things that contract lawyers would call treaty and things that public international lawyers would call contract.

That is what happened in *Vivendi v Argentina*: a claim was made under an investment treaty in relation to measures the state took against a water-services concession contract between a French company and an Argentine Province. That contract contained an exclusive jurisdiction clause in favour of local courts (the courts of the Argentine Province of Tucumán). The French company (Compagnie Générale des Eaux, which would later become Vivendi Universal) and its affiliates commenced arbitration at the International Centre for Settlement of Investment Disputes (ICSID) under the 1991 Agreement between the Argentine Republic and the Republic of France for the Promotion and Reciprocal Protection of Investments (the Argentine-France BIT or the BIT).[3] But the ICSID tribunal got into difficulty: it upheld jurisdiction *notwithstanding* the exclusive jurisdiction clause, but then declined to exercise that jurisdiction *because of* the exclusive jurisdiction clause. Essentially, the Tribunal found that the exclusive jurisdiction clause acted as a bar to the interpretation and application of the concession contract, and that it was impossible to decide Vivendi's claims without engaging in such an exercise. Having lost on the merits, Vivendi sought annulment of the Tribunal's award. And, in deciding Vivendi's request, the ICSID Annulment Committee made one of the most important decisions in the history of international investment law—a decision which held wider implications for the system of international law as a whole.

The ad hoc Annulment Committee was composed of Yves Fortier CC QC (formerly Canada's Ambassador and Permanent Representative to the United Nations), Professor James Crawford SC (now a judge of the International Court of Justice) and Professor José Carlos Fernández Rozas (an eminent Spanish academic). The Committee held that the Tribunal had made an annullable error (*infra petita*) in failing to decide those of Vivendi's claims that related to the concession contract. The panel observed that the concession contract and the BIT each set an independent standard, noting—in dicta quoted many times since—that 'A state may breach a treaty without breaching a contract, and vice versa'.[4] For the Committee, whether there had been a breach of the BIT and whether there had been a breach of the contract were 'different questions',[5] each to be determined by reference to its own

---

[3] *Accord sur l'Encouragement et la Protection Réciproques des Investissements* ('Agreement on the Reciprocal Promotion and Protection of Investments') (France-Argentina) (signed 3 July 1991, entered into force 3 March 1993) 1728 UNTS 281.

[4] *Compañía de Aguas del Aconquija SA and Compagnie Générale des Eaux/Vivendi Universal v Argentine Republic*, ICSID Case No ARB/97/3, Decision on Annulment (3 July 2002) (2004) 19 ICSID Rev—FILJ 89, ('*Vivendi I*') [95].

[5] ibid [96].

applicable law (international law in respect of BIT claims and the proper law of the contract in respect of contract claims).[6]

Critically, the panel held that, under the broadly worded or 'generic' dispute resolution clause of the BIT (which extended to 'dispute[s] relating to investments', the definition of the latter including contracts), the Tribunal had jurisdiction to base its decision upon the Concession Contract—*at least* insofar as it was necessary in order to determine whether there had been a breach of the substantive standards of the BIT. Not only did the Committee uphold the Tribunal's jurisdiction, but, in what is arguably the most important part of the decision, the Committee gave an indication of how that jurisdiction should have been exercised:

> [I]t is one thing to exercise contractual jurisdiction (arguably exclusively vested in the administrative tribunals of Tucumán by virtue of the Concession Contract) and another to take into account the terms of a contract in determining whether there has been a breach of a distinct standard of international law, such as that reflected in [the fair and equitable treatment provision] of the BIT.[7]

For the panel, the terms of the arbitration agreement (namely the definition of 'dispute' contained in it) made Vivendi's contract-related claims admissible and the Tribunal was bound to determine them, notwithstanding the exclusive jurisdiction clause of the Concession. The annullable error lay in the Tribunal's failure to exercise jurisdiction over this admissible subject matter.

The decision of the panel (hereinafter referred to as '*Vivendi I*') attracted a great deal of attention at the time it was handed down, and remains the subject of debate today. According to leading ICSID scholar Professor Christoph Schreuer, who gave expert evidence in the annulment proceeding, *Vivendi I* is 'the most important case on the relationship between claims based on a treaty and claims based on a contract'.[8] As Antonio Parra has noted in his *History of the ICSID Convention*, 'the distinction [between treaty and contract claims], first articulated in *Vivendi v Argentina*, was important in many of the BIT cases brought to ICSID after 2000'.[9] Fundamentally, what the *Vivendi I* decision did was not to announce the non-existence of the gulf between national and international law, or the existence of a bridge between the two systems, but rather to map a new continent: *international investment law*. To be sure, the coasts of this continent had been sighted—even explored—by other tribunals in the past, but it was not until *Vivendi I* that we gained an understanding of its true shape and scale. In jurisprudential terms, *Vivendi I* marks the birth of what Judge Crawford would later call the 'integrationist' school of investment-treaty theory and the beginning of a process (which continues today) in which investment

---

[6] ibid.

[7] ibid [105].

[8] C Schreuer, 'Investment Treaty Arbitration and Jurisdiction over Contract Claims: the Vivendi I Case Considered', in T Weiler (ed), *International Investment Law and Arbitration: Leading Cases from the ICSID, NAFTA Bilateral Treaties and Customary International Law* (London, Cameron May, 2005) 281, 281.

[9] AR Parra, *History of the ICSID Convention* (Oxford, OUP, 2012) 285.

treaty tribunals would move away from the 'dominant dualist theory of relations between national and international law'.[10] As he would later say:

> No doubt distinctions between legal systems should be observed, but not at the expense of appropriate connections between them. There is a distinction between treaty and contract, but they are part of the same one world with many legal systems that international arbitrators have long inhabited.[11]

For Crawford, there was and is 'no great gulf fixed' between treaties and contracts.[12]

Today, with the benefit of *Vivendi I* and its many successor authorities (only a small handful of which are discussed in this chapter), it is now widely understood that investment treaty actions involve '"hybrid" claims, with both national and international law potentially relevant'.[13] But it bears emphasising that this was far from conventional wisdom at the time. Stanimir Alexandrov, one of Vivendi's lawyers, later wrote that the *Vivendi I* panel signalled that 'The BIT and ICSID dispute settlement system requires arbitrators to work comfortably in both fields', teaching that the task of arbitrators in treaty cases is 'to engage in a detailed analysis of a tangle of claims, including, if necessary, claims relating to contractual performance, in order to assess them on the basis of [the] BIT standard'.[14]

That the *Vivendi* case is a landmark is evident from the fact that, 14 years after the seminal decision of the first Annulment Committee, *Vivendi I* is still cited in almost every case in which the treaty/contract interface is relevant. Those active in the field of international investment law will know that this particular 14 year period was, in jurisprudential terms, a most formative era, in which the volume of investment treaty disputes (and resulting arbitral awards) went from a trickle to a torrent. Where many decisions from the 'early days' have lost their currency, *Vivendi I* has stood the test of time—even if the main proposition for which it stands remains controversial in the eyes of many.

While the case is most valuable as an exposition of the treaty/contract nexus, and that aspect is the focus of this chapter, it must be acknowledged that a number of other contributions were made, and not just by the first Annulment Committee. Like many of the cases discussed in this volume, *Vivendi v Argentina* was a drawn-out affair, spanning 13 years and entailing two full procedural cycles: arbitration to annulment and back around again. The stage described as Act One in the account below began with the initiation of arbitration at ICSID in 1997 and ended with the decision of the first Annulment Committee in 2002 (*Vivendi I*, which decision is the focus of this chapter); Act Two began with the filing of the resubmitted case in 2003 and ended with the decision of the second Annulment Committee in 2010. In the course of these two cycles, lessons were learned in a range of areas, from how the annulment grounds and mechanics of the ICSID Convention work to the threshold for the disqualification of arbitrators.

---

[10] Crawford, 'Treaty and Contract in Investment Arbitration' (n 2) 352.

[11] ibid, 373–74.

[12] ibid, 373.

[13] J Crawford, *Brownlie's Principles of Public International Law* (Oxford, OUP, 2012) 717.

[14] SA Alexandrov, 'The Vivendi Decision and the Lessons for Future ICSID Arbitrations: The Applicants' Perspective' in E Gaillard (ed), *Annulment of ICSID Awards* (New York, Juris Publishing, 2004) 97, 116.

II. ACT ONE

A. The Concession

In terms of its social and political context, the Vivendi case can be situated in what have colourfully been referred to as the 'Water Wars'—the series of disputes (a number of which were referred to international arbitration) that arose out of the privatisation programmes that certain Latin American countries undertook in the area of water services during the 1990s. In Vivendi, the privatisation programme at issue was that implemented by the Argentine Province of Tucumán.

Before privatisation, most residents of Tucumán received their water and sewage facilities from a provincial entity.[15] Over time, this entity encountered a number of challenges and ultimately fell into a state of disrepair.[16] By the early 1990s, its revenues only covered 30 per cent of its expenses, the delta being met by state subsidies.[17] Attempts to raise water tariffs were unsuccessful and, without adequate funding, the physical water-distribution infrastructure in Tucumán was deteriorating. Faced with inadequate (or non-existent) services, a number of communities not served by the provincial entity transitioned to self-reliance, establishing (and funding) their own water municipal utilities.[18]

The situation with water services in Tucumán was not unique: at this time, essential services were poor in many other parts of Argentina, due to a combination of mismanagement by the responsible government authorities and a general lack of investment in the country. Over time, popular dissatisfaction translated into political mandate and an investment liberalisation movement emerged. Up until this time, almost all public services in Argentina were state-owned and operated. However, the Menem administration, which began in 1989, set out to reform the economy, the reform measures including an extensive privatisation programme.[19] On 17 January 1993 the Tucumán provincial government, lead by Governor Ortega, declared its intention to privatise its water and sewage facilities.[20] Governor Ortega invited national and international companies to submit bids for the provision of water and sewage services in Tucumán.[21] Unsurprisingly, not everybody shared Ortega's enthusiasm for privatisation, and the tender process was shadowed by intense political debate.[22]

Aguas del Aconquija, later to become Compañía de Aguas del Aconquija SA (CAA), was the only consortium to bid for the Tucumán concession.[23] At the time, the consortium consisted of a French corporation, Compagnie Générale des Eaux

---

[15] *Compañía de Aguas del Aconquija SA and Compagnie Générale des Eaux/Vivendi Universal v Argentine Republic*, ICSID Case No ARB/97/3, Award (15 August 2007) [4.2.2].
[16] ibid [4.2.3].
[17] ibid.
[18] ibid.
[19] ibid [4.2.1].
[20] ibid [4.2.4].
[21] ibid.
[22] ibid [4.8.1].
[23] ibid [4.3.1].

(CGE, which would later become Vivendi Universal) and three partners.[24] CGE and its partners analysed market conditions in Tucumán before preparing their bid.[25] After revisions were made to the initial bid, the relevant government entities in Tucumán approved the consortium's offer.[26] Governor Ortega formally awarded the concession on 26 December 1994.[27] Pursuant to the Bid Conditions, CAA was incorporated as an Argentine company,[28] and the Province executed the Concession Agreement on 18 May 1995.[29]

After a delay in the takeover, CGE commenced operations under the Concession on 22 July 1995.[30] However, owing to the serious technical deficiencies in the Tucumán water and sewer system at the time of the CGE takeover,[31] disputes arose between CGE and the authorities of Tucumán almost as soon as the Concession Agreement took effect.[32] The detail of the disputes will be apparent from the discussion that follows.

B. The ICSID Arbitration

On 26 December 1996, CGE and CAA filed a request for arbitration at ICSID.[33] The request invoked the provisions of the France-Argentina BIT. ICSID registered the request on 19 February 1997.[34] The claimants named Peter D Trooboff (a distinguished American lawyer) as their party-appointed arbitrator; Argentina did not nominate an arbitrator, and so the Chairman of the ICSID Administrative Council designated Judge Thomas Buergenthal (a US national and judge of the International Court of Justice (ICJ)) as the state's wing; as President of the Tribunal, ICSID designated Judge José Francisco Rezek (a former justice of the Supreme Court of Brazil and, at the time, also a judge of the ICJ).

Three facts bear emphasis at the outset: first, the Republic of Argentina was not a party to the Concession, nor did the central Government of the Republic play any role in negotiating or concluding the Concession.[35] Second, the Concession made no reference to the remedies available to CGE under the BIT or the ICSID Convention.[36] Third, and most significantly, the Concession included a forum-selection clause, Article 16.4, in the following terms: 'For purposes of interpretation and application of this Contract the parties submit themselves to the exclusive jurisdiction of the Contentious Administrative Tribunals of Tucumán'.

---

[24] ibid.
[25] ibid [4.3.2].
[26] ibid [4.3.9].
[27] ibid [4.3.13].
[28] ibid [4.4.2].
[29] ibid [4.4.3].
[30] ibid [4.4.6].
[31] *Compañía de Aguas del Aconquija SA and Compagnie Générale des Eaux/Vivendi Universal v Argentine Republic*, ICSID Case No ARB/97/3, Award (21 November 2000) [28].
[32] ibid [29].
[33] ibid [1].
[34] ibid [5].
[35] ibid [25].
[36] ibid [26].

The arbitration quickly evolved to include questions of jurisdiction, to which this clause would be central. The claimants submitted that the Tribunal had jurisdiction on the basis of Article 25 of the ICSID Convention and Article 8 of the BIT,[37] the latter of which provided that an investor in the Republic of Argentina is entitled to submit to ICSID a 'dispute relating to investments, within the meaning of this agreement'. Article 1(1) of the BIT defined 'investments' to include 'Concessions granted by law or by virtue of an agreement'—language the claimants contended plainly captured the Concession Contract between CGE and Tucumán.[38]

Argentina argued that the Tribunal lacked jurisdiction because: first, the dispute arose under and related exclusively to the Concession, to which the Argentine Republic was a stranger; second, without Argentina's consent and designation of Tucumán, paragraphs (1) and (3) of Article 25 of the ICSID Convention precluded the claimants from asserting against Argentina a claim based on the actions of the Province of Tucumán; and third, that the only claims presented by the claimants related to rights and obligations of the parties under the Concession, Article 16.4 of which required those claims be submitted to the contentious administrative tribunals of Tucumán.[39] In reply, the claimants argued that, notwithstanding Article 16.4 of the Concession, the BIT imposed no requirement that covered investors pursue local remedies prior to bringing a treaty claim. The claimants argued that, if indeed they had gone to the Argentine courts, they would have taken a 'fork in the road' under Article 8 of the BIT and thus waived their right to ICSID arbitration.[40]

On the merits, the principal contention advanced by the claimants was that Argentina violated two of the substantive protections accorded to them under the BIT: Article 3 (fair and equitable treatment, FET)[41] and Article 5(2) (expropriation).[42] The claimants' substantive case boiled down to two legal submissions: first, that the actions of the officials of Tucumán were attributable to the Argentine Republic and could, therefore, serve as the basis for a finding that the Argentine Republic had expropriated their rights under the Concession and denied the claimants FET; second, that the inaction of the Federal Government constituted a violation of a legal duty that the Argentine Republic owed to covered investors under the BIT and international law.[43] Within this frame, the claimants enumerated four categories of

---

[37] ibid [40]; Art 25(1) of the ICSID Convention provides that the jurisdiction of ICSID extends to 'any legal dispute arising directly out of an investment' provided that the parties consent to submit their dispute to the Centre.

[38] ibid [45].

[39] ibid [41].

[40] ibid [42].

[41] Art 3 of the BIT provides as follows: 'Each of the Contracting Parties undertakes to grant within its territory and its maritime area, fair and equitable treatment according to the principles of international law to investments made by investors of the other Party, and to do it in such a way that the exercise of the right this recognised is not obstructed de jure or de facto'.

[42] Art 5(2) of the BIT provides as follows: 'The Contracting Parties shall not adopt, directly or indirectly, measures of expropriation or nationalisation or any other equivalent measure having an effect similar to dispossession, except for public purpose and provided that such measures are not discriminatory or contrary to a specific commitment'. 'Such measures referred to above which could be adopted, shall allow the payment of a prompt and adequate compensation, the amount of which, computed on the basis of the actual value of the investments affected, shall be evaluated in relation to the normal economic situation, and prior to any threat of dispossession'.

[43] *Compañía de Aguas del Aconquija*, Award (21 November 2000) (n 31) [44].

acts or omissions by the provincial authorities that they said engaged the Republic's responsibility under the BIT: (i) 'Acts that resulted in a fall in the recovery rate'; (ii) 'Acts that unilaterally reduced the tariff rate'; (iii) 'Abuses of regulatory authority'; and (iv) 'Dealings in bad faith'.[44]

Argentina argued that, as an 'utter stranger' to the Concession,[45] it owed no legal duty to the claimants and that there was no basis in international law to attribute the actions of the provincial authorities of Tucumán to the Argentine Republic. Further, Argentina argued that the scope of its duty to the claimant was affected not only by Article 16.4 of the Concession but also by the provisions of the Argentine Constitution that established and governed the federal relationship between the central government and the provinces.[46] In other words, Argentina sought to invoke the exclusive jurisdiction clause of the Concession as a barrier to jurisdiction, and its internal constitutional order as a barrier to both jurisdiction and substantive liability.

C. The First Award

The Tribunal ruled against Argentina on jurisdiction. First, the Tribunal held that the claimants' claims regarding both the acts of the central government and the acts of the provincial authorities were treaty claims, not contract claims.[47] Second, the Tribunal held that, under international law, the acts of a subdivision of a federal state—such as the Province of Tucumán in the federal structure of the Argentine Republic—are attributable to the central government, and that in no circumstances can a state rely on its internal constitutional structure to limit the scope of its international obligations.[48] Third, the Tribunal held that the designation mechanism in Article 25(3) of the ICSID Convention was irrelevant, as that mechanism is intended to allow for agencies or subdivisions of contracting states to be parties to ICSID proceedings in their own right;[49] in the case at hand, the claimants were not suing Tucumán so no issue of designation arose. Fourth, and most significantly, the Tribunal held that Article 16.4 of the Concession did not deprive it of jurisdiction to hear the claimants' claims because that clause was neither a waiver of CGE's rights nor a provision contemplating legal action of a kind that would trigger the 'fork in the road' in Article 8 of the BIT.[50] Thus, Argentina's objections to jurisdiction were dismissed.

On the merits, the Tribunal found against the claimants, dismissing all of their claims against the state. In reaching this conclusion, the Tribunal first analysed the relationship between the alleged violations of the BIT by Argentina with the allegations of non-performance under the Concession. As none of the claimants' four categories of acts and omissions by the Tucumán authorities included any act or

---

[44] ibid [63].
[45] Alexandrov, 'The Vivendi Decision' (n 14) 99.
[46] *Compañía de Aguas del Aconquija*, Award (21 November 2000) (n 31) [44].
[47] ibid [50].
[48] ibid [49].
[49] ibid [51]–[52].
[50] ibid [53]–[55].

omission by officials of the Argentine Republic, the Tribunal held that the Argentine Republic could only be held liable if the actions of the Tucumán authorities were attributed to it.[51] The Tribunal held that the acts in each of these four categories arose from disputes between the claimants and Tucumán concerning performance/non-performance of the Concession and, in each case, the claimants had failed to challenge any of those acts in the contentious administrative tribunals of Tucumán, the agreed forum.[52]

The Tribunal then considered the relationship between state responsibility (ie the Republic's international legal responsibility for the acts of the Tucumán authorities) and the terms of the Concession, particularly its forum-selection provision.[53] The Tribunal held that because of the 'crucial connection' between the terms of the Concession and the alleged BIT violations, the Argentine Republic could not be held liable unless and until claimants had—as required by Article 16.4 of the Concession—asserted their rights in proceedings before the contentious administrative courts of Tucumán and had been denied their rights in that forum, either 'procedurally or substantively'.[54]

For present purposes, the key aspect of the Tribunal's reasoning was its finding regarding the 'Tucumán claims'.[55] In what would prove to be the fatal flaw of its reasoning, the Tribunal held that, due to the nature of the dispute, it was 'not possible ... to determine which acts of the Province were taken in exercise of its sovereign authority and which were taken in the exercise of its rights as a party to the Concession'. In the Tribunal's view, to make such a determination it would have had to 'undertake a detailed interpretation and application of the Concession Contract, a task left by the parties to that contract to the exclusive jurisdiction of the administrative courts of Tucumán'.[56] As the claimants failed to seek relief in the Tucumán courts, and there was no evidence that the claimants would be 'denied procedural or substantive justice' if they did,[57] the Tribunal decided that there was no basis on which to hold the Republic liable under the BIT.[58] As part of this, the Tribunal

---

[51] ibid [64].

[52] ibid [65]–[76].

[53] ibid [77].

[54] ibid [78].

[55] In respect of the 'federal claims', the core question was whether the Argentine Republic was liable under the BIT for failing to respond to the actions of Tucuman officials. The record contained no evidence that Argentine officials ever failed to take any specific action that the claimants requested, and the claimants did not present as evidence any document in which they put the central government on notice regarding what action the Argentine governmental authorities had taken that constituted a violation of the BIT or what action, if not taken by the Argentine Republic, would have constituted a breach of the BIT. Therefore, the Tribunal concluded that there was no basis for holding that the Argentine Republic failed to respond to the situation in Tucuman and the requests of the claimants in accordance with the obligations of the Argentine government under the BIT.

[56] *Compañía de Aguas del Aconquija*, Award (21 November 2000) (n 31) [79]. A further indication of the Tribunal's 'impossibility' reasoning can be found in paragraph 81 of the award, which deals with the fork in the road under the BIT: 'In this case, the obligation to resort to the local courts is compelled by the express terms of Article 16.4 of the private contract between claimants and the Province of Tucumán and the impossibility, on the facts of the instant case, of separating potential breaches of contract claims from BIT violations without interpreting and applying the Concession Contract, a task that the contract assigns expressly to the local courts', [81].

[57] ibid [80].

[58] ibid.

also rejected the claimants' argument that, if they had taken action in the Tucumán courts, they would have waived their right to ICSID arbitration by taking the fork in the road in the BIT.[59]

The claimants requested annulment of the award pursuant to Article 52 of the ICSID Convention. However, the claimants framed their application as a request for *partial* annulment. In accordance with Article 52(3) of the ICSID Convention, the chairman of the Administrative Council appointed three members of the Panel of Arbitrators to serve as members of the ad hoc Annulment Committee: Mr Fortier; Professor Crawford; and Professor Rozas. The three members agreed that Mr Fortier would serve as president of the Committee.

D. Argentina's Challenge to the President of the Annulment Committee

Upon acceptance of their appointments, the three members of the panel gave the usual Rule 6 declarations of independence. However, Mr Fortier qualified his declaration in one respect, this relating to work done by one of his partners for an affiliate of Vivendi. It was on this factual basis that Argentina made a proposal for his disqualification—the first time a challenge had ever been made to a member of an ICSID Annulment Committee.

The threshold issue was whether the disqualification procedure of the ICSID Arbitration Rules was applicable in annulment proceedings. Exercising *kompetenz-kompetenz* on this point, the two unchallenged members of the panel—Professor Crawford and Professor Rozas—determined that they were competent to rule on the challenge to Mr Fortier. The basis for this finding was Rule 53, which says that the provisions of the ICSID Rules to apply *mutatis mutandis* to any procedure relating to the interpretation, revision or annulment of an award and to the decision of the Tribunal or Committee. Relying on Rule 53, Professors Crawford and Rozas found that the arbitrator-disqualification procedure in Rule 9 applies *mutatis mutandis* to proposals to disqualify any member of an Annulment Committee.[60] Thus, because under Rule 9 unchallenged arbitrators are entitled to rule on challenges to their fellows, so are members of Annulment Committees.

Professors Crawford and Rozas then turned to consider the substance of the challenge.[61] The principal legal question was the standard for disqualification.[62] Under Article 14(1) of the ICSID Convention, persons designated to serve on 'panels' (Tribunal and Annulment Committee members) must have certain qualities, one of

---

[59] ibid [81].

[60] *Compañía de Aguas del Aconquija SA and Compagnie Générale des Eaux/Vivendi Universal v Argentine Republic*, ICSID Case No ARB/97/3, Decision on the Challenge to the President of the Committee (3 October 2001) (2002) 17 ICSID Rev—FILJ 168, [3].

[61] The material facts of the challenge were not disputed: Mr Fortier's firm had advised an affiliate of Vivendi on tax issues in Quebec; at the time of Mr Fortier's disclosure in the annulment proceeding, most of the work was already completed; further, the work was unrelated to the dispute with Argentina and Mr Fortier was not involved.

[62] *Compañía de Aguas del Aconquija*, Decision on the Challenge to the President of the Committee (n 60) [20].

which is that they 'may be relied upon to exercise independent judgment'.[63] Under Article 57, disqualification is only called for where there is a 'manifest lack' of any of the qualities required under Article 14(1). The interpretive task for Professors Crawford and Rozas was to ascertain what work the term 'manifest' does in Article 57.

While today we have the benefit of a vast (and expanding) body of challenge juris-prudence, at the time of the first annulment proceeding in *Vivendi*, there was only one reported ICSID challenge decision, this being the challenge to Seymour Rubin in *Amco Asia v Indonesia*.[64] There, the Tribunal dismissed the challenge, holding that the ICSID Convention term 'manifest' required 'not a possible lack of the qual-ity, but ... a highly probable one'.[65] But Professors Crawford and Rozas were not enamoured of *Amco Asia*, noting that the decision had been 'strongly criticised' and adding that, as 'a lawyer–client relationship existed between the claimant and [Arbitrator Rubin] personally during the pendency of the arbitration, there must surely have been 'a sufficient basis for a reasonable concern as to independence'.[66] Rather than require that the lack of impartiality or independence be highly probable, Professors Crawford and Rozas preferred to formulate the Article 57 test in terms of *real risk*: whether, based on the facts there is a real risk that a lack of impar-tiality could reasonably be apprehended.[67] In terms of the evidence required, Professors Crawford and Rozas said that the 'circumstances actually established (and not merely supposed or inferred) must negate or place in *clear doubt* the appear-ance of impartiality' for the challenge to be upheld.[68] Thus, for Professors Craw-ford and Rozas, the function of the word 'manifest' in Article 57 was not to make the lack of the challenged member's lack of the capacity for independent judgment a 'matter of degree",[69] but rather to exclude 'reliance on speculative assumptions or arguments'.[70] As Professor Crawford would later put it, the conclusion he and Professor Rozas reached was that '"manifest" applies to the evidence'.[71]

Applying their interpretation of Article 57 to the facts at hand, Professors Crawford and Rozas found that there were no grounds for concluding that Mr Fortier's independence was impaired.[72] They noted that 'the mere existence of

[63] ibid [14].

[64] *Amco Asia Corporation and others v Republic of Indonesia*, ICSID Case No ARB/81/1, Challenge Decision (24 June 1982). At the time of the *Vivendi I* challenge, a second challenge decision was pending in another ICSID case, *Zhinvali Development Ltd v Republic of Georgia*, ICSID Case No ARB/00/1.

[65] ibid [21].

[66] ibid.

[67] ibid [25].

[68] ibid.

[69] J Crawford, 'Challenges to Arbitrators in ICSID Arbitrations' (Confronting Global Challenges: From Gunboat Diplomacy to Investor-State Arbitration, PCA Peace Palace Centenary Seminar, The Hague, 11 October 2013) 2.

[70] *Compañía de Aguas del Aconquija*, Decision on the Challenge to the President of the Committee (n 60) [25].

[71] Crawford, 'Challenges to Arbitrators' (n 69) 2.

[72] ibid [27]. In reaching this conclusion, Professors Crawford and Rozas gave most weight to the following points: (a) the relationship in question was immediately and fully disclosed by Mr Fortier, further information was given on request and full transparency was thus maintained; (b) Mr Fortier had no personal lawyer-client relationship with Vivendi or those of its affiliates that received the relevant legal services (Quebec tax law advice); (c) the legal work done by Mr Fortier's colleague had nothing to do with the Argentina case; (d) the work was not general legal or strategic advice, rather it only concerned a specific transaction; and (e) the lawyer–client relationship was nearing completion (ibid [26]).

some professional relationship with the party is not an automatic basis for disqualification of an arbitrator or Committee member',[73] and that it would only be where the relationship is sufficiently significant to raise reasonable doubts as to the impartiality of the arbitrator that he or she could be disqualified.[74] In obiter remarks that have been relied upon in subsequent challenges, Professors Crawford and Rozas noted that, while in this case there was no need to rely on *de minimis*, that rule would have re-enforced their conclusion.[75]

E. Annulment: The *Vivendi I* Decision

The claimants' request for partial annulment invoked three of the five grounds set out in Article 52(1) of the ICSID Convention, specifically that there had been a serious departure from a fundamental rule of procedure (Article 52(1)(d)),[76] that the Tribunal had manifestly exceeded its powers (Article 52(1)(b))[77] and that the award failed to state the reasons on which it was based (Article 52(1)(e)).[78]

On the point of manifest excess of powers, the core issue was whether the Tribunal was able to uphold jurisdiction over the claims relating to the Concession on the one hand, but then decline to decide the merits of those claims on the other. The claimants argued that if the Tribunal was wrong in declining to decide the merits of their claims (on the basis that doing so would have entailed an invasion of the exclusive jurisdiction of the Tucumán courts), then the Tribunal manifestly failed to exercise jurisdiction.[79]

Somewhat controversially, the state also sought annulment, arguing that there was a contradiction between the reasons that the Tribunal gave for upholding its jurisdiction and the reasons it gave for its decision on the merits, and that the Tribunal lacked jurisdiction in any event, with the result that the Tribunal committed a manifest excess of power by proceeding to determine the merits at all. On these grounds, Argentina said that the award should be annulled *in toto*.[80]

In what are now (for good reason) almost template features of ICSID annulment decisions, the panel observed that it was not a court of appeal and that it was under an obligation to 'guard against the annulment of awards for trivial cause'.[81] However, the panel noted that the power and procedure grounds of Article 52,

---

[73] ibid [28].
[74] ibid.
[75] ibid [27].
[76] *Vivendi I* (n 4) [82].
[77] ibid [86].
[78] ibid [116].
[79] ibid [87].
[80] ibid [72]. The claimants characterised the state's position as a late annulment application by way of a counterclaim—a procedure not contemplated by Article 52 of the ICSID Convention. The Committee ultimately rejected this characterisation and found rather that the state was validly arguing that if claimants' position on the merits were to be upheld—either under Art 52(1)(b) or 52(1)(e)—the effect must necessarily be to bring down the whole Award. So, in the eyes of the Committee members, the state was not making a counter-claim, but rather a responsive argument that was within the scope of the Committee's mandate as framed by the claimants' application.
[81] ibid [63].

which posit internal thresholds in the terms 'manifest' and 'serious', are by definition *not trivial*.[82]

In the substance, the panel first addressed the state's request for annulment of the Tribunal's jurisdictional finding. In this part of the decision, the panel discussed the earlier case of *Lanco v Argentina*.[83] In *Lanco*, the contract in issue involved an agency of the federal government of Argentina, and contained an exclusive jurisdiction clause which referred contractual disputes to a federal contentious administrative tribunal.[84] The Tribunal concluded that the exclusive jurisdiction clause in Lanco's contract did not exclude ICSID jurisdiction.[85] The *Vivendi I* panel agreed with the conclusion in *Lanco*,[86] albeit for different reasons. In any event, because the Committee disagreed with the state's arguments on the impact of the exclusive jurisdiction clause, it saw no defect—let alone an *annullable* defect—in the decision that the Tribunal reached on jurisdiction. Thus, the Committee rejected the state's request for annulment.[87]

The panel then turned to the claimants' three grounds for annulment. The panel gave short shrift to the claimants' contention that there had been a departure from a fundamental rule of procedure.[88] That head was dismissed. The claimants' arguments on the 'failure to give reasons' ground were also disposed of in relatively short order, although, as discussed below, the Committee provided useful guidance on the scope and operation of this ground. The Committee then turned to the question of manifest excess of powers.

The panel set out the two ways in which an ICSID tribunal may commit an excess of powers: if the tribunal exercises a jurisdiction which it *does not have* under the relevant instrument—be it a law, agreement or treaty—and the ICSID Convention, read together (*ultra petita*); and, more interestingly, if the Tribunal *fails* to exercise jurisdiction which it *does have* under those instruments (*infra petita*).[89] This was the first time *infra petita* had been recognised in the ICSID system. Significantly, the panel also said that, for a failure to exercise jurisdiction to be considered a manifest excess of power, the failure must relate to a point that was 'clearly capable of making a difference to the result'.[90] In other words, the Committee linked the 'manifest' threshold to the substantive outcome of the case, rather than the quasi-evidential question of whether, on the face of the award, any part of the dispute submitted to the Tribunal has obviously been left undecided. As Doak Bishop and Silvia Marchili have observed in their survey of ICSID annulment practice, in reading the term 'manifest' to mean 'outcome determinative', the *Vivendi I* panel distanced itself from

---

[82] ibid.

[83] *Lanco International Inc v The Argentine Republic*, ICSID Case No ARB/97/6, Jurisdiction of the Arbitral Tribunal (8 December 1998).

[84] *Vivendi I* (n 4) [77].

[85] We get a glimpse of the role this authority played in the parties' arguments from the account of the Annulment Committee's decision that Stanimir Alexandrov, who was one of the lawyers representing Vivendi, wrote in 2008. According to Alexandrov, the '*Lanco* rule' is that investors' treaty-based right to turn to the neutral forum of ICSID arbitration cannot be thwarted by provisions in underlying contracts that would consign them to domestic fora. See Alexandrov, 'The Vivendi Decision' (n 14) 114.

[86] *Vivendi I* (n 4) [78].

[87] ibid [80].

[88] ibid [85].

[89] ibid [86].

[90] ibid.

the 'reasonable consensus in the case law regarding the meaning of the "manifest" requirement as "easy to perceive"'.[91]

Applying these principles, the panel rejected the claimants' request for partial annulment of the award as it related to the Tribunal's determination of the federal claims.[92] That portion of the award survived, and was therefore *res judicata*.[93] However, the Committee upheld the claimants' request for partial annulment of that part of the award that related to the Tucumán claims. The Committee held that the Tribunal had acted *infra petita* by not examining the merits of the Tucumán claims.[94]

Arriving at this conclusion, the panel considered the relationship between Argentina's responsibility (to French investors) under the BIT and the rights and obligations of the parties to the Concession.[95] It must be said that this part of the decision clearly displays the influence of Professor Crawford, whose work in the field of state responsibility is well known. The Committee held that the treaty (the BIT) and the contract (the Concession) each set an independent standard. Referring to Article 3 of the ILC Articles on State Responsibility, the Committee observed that 'A state may breach a treaty without breaching a contract, and vice versa',[96] noting that whether there has been a breach of the BIT and whether there has been a breach of the contract are different questions,[97] each to be determined by reference to its own proper or applicable law (international law in respect of BIT claims and the proper law of the contract in respect of contract claims).[98]

In the seminal part of its decision, the panel then elaborated on the distinction between contract claims and treaty claims. According to the panel, where the 'essential basis' of a claim brought before an international tribunal is a breach of contract, the treaty tribunal will give effect to any valid choice of forum made in that contract. The Committee referred at this point to the *Woodruff* case,[99] in which a claim was brought before an international tribunal (the US–Venezuela Mixed Claims Commission) for breach of a contract that contained a forum selection clause in favour of the 'ordinary tribunals of Venezuela'.[100] The Mixed Claims Commission found that Mr Woodruff was bound by that clause not to refer his contractual claim to any other tribunal—international tribunals included.[101] But the *Vivendi I* panel saw a difference between Mr Woodruff's situation and the situation at hand, noting that where the fundamental basis of the claim is a treaty, 'the existence of an exclusive jurisdiction clause in a contract between the claimant and the Respondent State or one of its subdivisions cannot operate as a bar to the application of the treaty standard'.[102]

Again, the panel drew support for its conclusion from Article 3 of the ILC Articles on State Responsibility, under which the characterisation of an act of state

---

[91] D Bishop and S M Marchili, *Annulment under the ICSID Convention* (Oxford, OUP, 2012) 67.
[92] *Vivendi I* (n 4) [92].
[93] ibid [119].
[94] ibid.
[95] ibid [94].
[96] ibid [95].
[97] ibid [96].
[98] ibid.
[99] *Woodruff Case*, US-Venezuelan Mixed Claims Commission (1903), IX RIAA 213.
[100] *Vivendi I* (n 4) [98].
[101] ibid [99].
[102] ibid [101].

as internationally wrongful is governed by international law, and such characterisa-tion is 'not affected by the characterization of the same act as lawful by internal law'.[103] Essentially, as it owed its existence to an Argentine-law-governed contract, the forum selection clause was *internal* law and could not, therefore, displace the international standard by which the actions of Argentina and its Province were to be judged under the BIT. For the *Vivendi I* members, the exclusive jurisdiction clause could be relevant to the determination of whether the treaty had been breached, but nothing more.[104]

In a critical elucidation, the panel then explained that exercising contractual jurisdic-tion is quite different to taking into account terms of a contract to determine whether there was a breach of a distinct standard of international law, such as a provision of a relevant BIT: while the former was arguably within the exclusive jurisdiction of the administrative tribunals of Tucumán (as per Article 16.4 of the Concession), the latter was within the ambit of an international tribunal *regardless* of any contractual forum-selection clause.[105] Applying this reasoning, the Committee concluded that, by declining to decide important parts of the claimants' BIT claims on the grounds that they turned on the performance (*vel non*) of the Concession contract, the Tribunal actually failed to decide whether or not the conduct in question amounted to a breach of the BIT. This, the members found, amounted to a manifest excess of power by *infra petita*.[106] The Tribunal's award was, therefore, partially annulled.

Finally, it is worth noting how the Committee approached the 'fork in the road'. At first instance, the Tribunal found that, if the claimants had gone to the Tucumán courts, they would *not* have taken the 'fork in the road' at Article 8(2) of the BIT—a decision that informed the Tribunal's merits finding that the claimants should go (or should *have gone*) to those courts. The panel disagreed. The members observed that the dispute resolution clause of the BIT dealt generally with disputes 'relating to investments'. Under the dispute resolution scheme of the treaty, the investor had a choice whether to submit such disputes to domestic or international adjudication. Consequently, the panel found that:

> [I]f a claim brought by an investor before a national court concerned 'a dispute relating to investments made under [the BIT]' within the meaning of Article 8(1) [of the BIT], then Article 8(2) [i.e. the fork in the road] will apply. In the Committee's view, a claim by CAA against the Province of Tucumán for breach of the Concession Contract, brought before the contentious administrative courts of Tucumán, would prima facie fall within Article 8(2) and constitute a 'final' choice of forum and jurisdiction, if that claim was coextensive with a dispute relating to investments made under the BIT.[107]

Thus, the Committee held that, by commencing ICSID arbitration, CAA took the risk of a tribunal holding that the acts complained of neither individually nor collectively rose to the level of a breach of the BIT—a finding that, if made, would have meant CAA lost both its treaty claim and its contract claim.[108] This scope-for-scope reasoning

---

[103] International Law Commission, *Articles on the Responsibility of States for Internationally Wrongful Acts* (2001), Art 3.
[104] *Vivendi I* (n 4) [101].
[105] ibid [105].
[106] ibid [111].
[107] ibid [55].
[108] ibid [113].

seems to have been informed by the Committee's literalist approach: because the definition of 'dispute' in Article 8(1) of the BIT applied across both procedural options in Article 8(2) (domestic courts and international arbitration), there could only be one trigger for the fork in the road (ie submission of 'the dispute', meaning submission of 'Any dispute relating to investments' to either a court or an arbitral tribunal).

F. Argentina's Request for Supplementation and Rectification

The first procedural cycle of the *Vivendi* case closed with a skirmish. Following the decision on annulment, Argentina submitted a request for a supplementary decision and rectification. The basis of the Argentine request was Article 49(2) of the ICSID Convention.[109] Argentina argued that the panel failed in its analysis of one aspect of the Tribunal's jurisdictional finding (Argentina requested a supplementary decision on this issue)[110] and made seven material errors in its decision (errors which, Argentina said, related to the Committee's description of its arguments and legal position). The panel denied Argentina's request for supplementation, characterising it as an attempt to 'reopen a substantive debate' that was resolved during the earlier merits phase of the annulment proceeding—something the panel said it could not and would not do.[111] Of the seven material errors in respect of which rectification was sought, the panel denied all but two.[112]

III. ACT TWO

Whilst not uneventful, the second procedural cycle of the case—Act Two—was a relatively straightforward affair. Before the newly constituted ICSID tribunal, Argentina challenged jurisdiction again, but its efforts to skirt the *res judicata* of the first award were in vain. The only real intrigue occurred when, in the second round of annulment proceedings that followed, Argentina alleged a lack of independence on the part of one of the arbitrators, Professor Kaufmann-Kohler. This development, and the way it was handled by the second Annulment Committee, triggered debate within the international arbitration community.

A. The Resubmitted Case

The second cycle began on 29 August 2003, when the claimants—CAA and Vivendi Universal SA—resubmitted the dispute to ICSID pursuant to Article 55(1) of the

---

[109] *Compañía de Aguas del Aconquija SA and Compagnie Générale des Eaux/Vivendi Universal v Argentine Republic*, ICSID Case No ARB/97/3, Decision of the *ad hoc* Committee on the Request for Supplementation and Rectification of its Decision Concerning Annulment of the Award, (28 May 2003) (2004) 19 *ICSID Rev—FILJ* 139, [2].

[110] ibid [6]. Under this ground, Argentina said the Committee failed to consider whether the Tribunal's failure to account for the fact that the transfer of CAA's shares from DyCASA to CGE—which was not authorised by the Government of Tucumán—undermined its decision on jurisdiction.

[111] *Compañía de Aguas del Aconquija*, Decision of the ad hoc Committee on the Request for Supplementation and Rectification of its Decision Concerning Annulment of the Award (n 109), [19].

[112] ibid [45].

ICSID Arbitration Rules. The first Tribunal's dismissal of the 'federal claims' having been upheld by the panel, the claimants only sought the adjudication of their BIT claims arising out of the alleged acts and omissions of the Tucumán authorities (what the first Annulment Committee had compartmentalised as the 'Tucumán claims').[113] In the second round arbitration, the claimants' causes of action were the same: FET[114] and expropriation.[115]

B. Jurisdiction

Argentina raised five objections to the jurisdiction and competence of the new Tribunal,[116] all of which were dismissed by the Tribunal.[117] The doctrine of *res judicata* was of central importance.[118]

---

[113] *Compañía de Aguas del Aconquija SA and Compagnie Générale des Eaux/Vivendi Universal v Argentine Republic*, ICSID Case No ARB/97/3, Decision on Jurisdiction (14 November 2005) [5].

[114] The parties disagreed as to the content and scope of the fair and equitable treatment obligation expressed in Art 3. The state contended that on the facts there was no unfair or inequitable treatment in violation of Art 3 of the BIT, asserting that it contains only an international minimum standard. Whereas the claimants argued that the fair and equitable treatment standard had evolved and includes: (i) refraining from arbitrary or discriminatory conduct; (ii) providing transparency and due process; (iii) acting in good faith; and (iv) providing security for reasonable, investment-backed expectations. The claimants asserted that the Tucumán authorities' actions deprived Vivendi/CAA of FET in the form of protection and full security and that Art 5(1) (protection and full security) requires more than physical security, rather it includes an obligation on the host State to provide security against any harassment that impairs the normal functioning of an investor's business. The state opposed the claimants' contention on this point, arguing rather that the standard is limited to physical security.

[115] The claimants contended that the Tucumán authorities expropriated their investment without compensation in breach of Art 5(2) of the BIT. They relied on six principal arguments in support of their case: (i) the BIT's guarantee against uncompensated expropriation was broad; (ii) Art 5 barred the expropriation of concession and contract rights; (iii) the Tucumán authorities' deprivation of claimants' reasonably expected economic benefit constituted expropriation; (iv) whether taken singly or cumulatively, the Province's acts and omissions constituted expropriation (v) the forced provision of services during the alleged 'hostage period' constituted expropriation; and (vi) the effects of the Tucumán authorities' actions were determinative. The state argued that the actions of the Tucumán authorities were reasonable and proportionate, and that the claimants' property was not expropriated within the meaning of the BIT.

[116] *Compañía de Aguas del Aconquija*, Decision on Jurisdiction (n 113) [10]. The state's five jurisdictional objections were as follows: (i) Vivendi Universal lacked *ius standi* to sue, not having established itself as the successor to CGE; (ii) Vivendi Universal's claim constituted a derivative claim forbidden by Argentine and international law; (iii) CAA did not acquire French 'nationality' under the protection of the BIT; (iv) CAA and Vivendi Universal failed to comply with essential preconditions to instituting an ICSID arbitration proceeding; and (v) the claimants' claims were prohibited under the terms of the Annulment Committee's decision.

[117] ibid [129].

[118] For example, in rejecting the state's first objection, the second Tribunal explained that the first Tribunal established jurisdiction under the ICSID Convention and the BIT, and the Annulment Committee affirmed that the first Tribunal had rightly done so. Thus, according to the doctrine of *res judicata*, the second Tribunal was bound by the decision of the first Tribunal if the two actions involved the same parties and the same cause of action. The second Tribunal found that Vivendi Universal was the successor of CGE and shareholder of CAA, therefore the decision of the first Tribunal involved the same parties and the same claims as that before the second Tribunal, with the result that the conditions for the application of the doctrine of *res judicata* were present. The second Tribunal was therefore precluded from reconsidering the jurisdictional determination of the first Tribunal.

C. The Second Award

The second Tribunal issued its final award on 20 August 2007. In the context of this chapter, the only part of the second Tribunal's award that warrants particular attention is that in which the Tribunal considered its competence to consider alleged breaches of contract. In an illustration of what Professor Schreuer has identified as the 'educat[ing]' role that an Annulment Committee can play in the ICSID system,[119] the Tribunal distinguished breach of contract from breach of treaty, and expressed the view that:

> A state may breach a treaty without breaching a contract; it may also breach a treaty at the same time as it breached a contract. In the latter case it is permissible for the Tribunal to consider such alleged contractual breaches, not for the purpose of determining whether a party has incurred liability under domestic law, but to the extent necessary to analyse and determine whether there has been a breach of the Treaty.[120]

But, with a caveat that reveals the still-evolving state of the law at the time, the Tribunal emphasised that:

> In doing so the Tribunal would in no way be exercising jurisdiction over the contract, it would simply be taking into account the parties' behaviour under and in relation to the terms of the contract in determining whether there has been a breach of a distinct standard of international law, as reflected in Articles 3 and 5 of the BIT.[121]

We will return to this issue, within which lies the thorny question of whether an investment treaty tribunal can exercise 'pure' contractual jurisdiction (meaning jurisdiction over contract claims that do not implicate the state's substantive obligations under the treaty). For the second Tribunal, it was not necessary to come to a definitive view as to whether either party had or had not breached the Concession.[122] The arbitrators concluded that the provincial authorities of Tucumán had violated the FET standard,[123] and the prohibition against unlawful expropriation,[124] and held that the Argentine Republic was responsible for these breaches.[125]

---

[119] C Schreuer, 'From ICSID Annulment to Appeal: Half Way Down the Slippery Slope' (2011) 10 *The Law and Practice of International Courts and Tribunals* 211, 223.

[120] *Compañía de Aguas del Aconquija*, Award (15 August 2007) (n 31) [7.3.10].

[121] ibid.

[122] ibid [7.3.11].

[123] In reaching this conclusion, the second Tribunal interpreting the FET provision of the BIT in accordance with Art 31(1) of the *Vienna Convention*. The arbitrators rejected the state's submission that it ought to be equated to the minimum standard of treatment, preferring FA Mann's formulation of the FET standard: 'A Tribunal will not be concerned with a minimum, maximum, or average standard. It will have to decide whether in all circumstances the conduct in issue is fair and equitable or unfair and inequitable'.

[124] Regarding the claim under Art 5 of the BIT (expropriation), the second Tribunal held that contractual rights are capable of being expropriated and that it is not infrequent in cases of indirect expropriation that the investor suffers a substantial deprivation of value of its investment. The arbitrators rejected the state's proposition that an act of state must be presumed to be regulatory—and thus not expropriatory—absent proof of bad faith. The arbitrators found that the claimants were 'radically deprived of the economic use and enjoyment of their investment, the benefits of which (ie the right to be paid for services provided) had been effectively neutralised and rendered useless. Under these circumstances, rescission of the Concession Agreement represented the only rational alternative for claimants. By leaving claimants no other rational choice, we conclude that the Province thus expropriated claimant's right of use and enjoyment of their investment under the Concession Agreement'.

[125] *Compañía de Aguas del Aconquija*, Award (15 August 2007) (n 15) [7.6.2].

D. The Second Round of Annulment Proceedings: *Vivendi II*

On 13 December 2007, Argentina requested annulment of the second award. The state sought annulment on the grounds set out in Article 52(1)(a),(b),(d) and (e) of the ICSID Convention,[126] including that the Tribunal was not properly constituted and that the award was annullable for other reasons.[127] Argentina also sought a stay of enforcement of the second award pending determination of the annulment request.[128] The *Vivendi II* panel was composed of Dr Ahmed S El Kosheri, Professor Jan Hendrick Dalhuisen and Ambassador Andreas J Jacovides.

Argentina's request for annulment was ultimately denied. In terms of contributions to the development of international law, the main point of interest lay in how the second Committee approached Argentina's argument that the Tribunal was not properly constituted because one of the arbitrators, Professor Kaufmann-Kohler, did not fulfil the independence requirement of the ICSID Convention and should (in Argentina's submission) have been disqualified during the proceedings.

The issue arose out of Professor Kaufmann-Kohler's April 2006 appointment to the board of Swiss bank UBS. The facts and circumstances that Argentina alleged affected Professor Kaufmann-Kohler's ability to serve as an arbitrator were 'only discovered' after the second award had already been rendered; they were not known to the parties during the arbitral proceedings and could not be considered public knowledge.[129] Argentina's challenge raised two main issues: whether directorship in a major international bank was compatible with the function of international arbitrator;[130] and, if there was a basic failure (on the part of the challenged arbitrator) to investigate, disclose, or inform, what the consequences of that failure would be in an annulment context.[131]

As to the compatibility of functions point, the *Vivendi II* panel noted that a director's fiduciary duty to shareholders is to further the interests of the company,[132] and considered that this fiduciary duty was fundamentally at odds with an arbitrator's duty of independence.[133] The Committee considered that prima facie this conflict made the two functions incompatible[134] and that, given this obvious conflict, an arbitrator who seeks to combine such functions is under a duty to exercise great care—care that, in the view of the Committee, correlated to a duty of continuous investigation.[135]

---

[126] *Compañía de Aguas del Aconquija SA and Compagnie Générale des Eaux/Vivendi Universal v Argentine Republic*, ICSID Case No ARB/97/3, 2010, Decision on the Argentine Republic's Request for Annulment of the Award rendered on 20 August 2007 (10 August 2010) ('*Vivendi II*') [17].

[127] The other grounds were: (i) the Tribunal manifestly exceeded its powers; (ii) the award failed to state the reasons on which it is based and the Tribunal departed from a fundamental rule of procedure (Art 52(1)(d) and (e)); and (iii) issues concerning the award of damages. Initially, Argentina's request for annulment also invoked Art 52(1)(c) (corruption on the part of a member of the Tribunal), but this ground was later dropped (see Schreuer, 'From ICSID Annulment to Appeal' (n 119) 214).

[128] *Vivendi II* (n 126) [3].

[129] ibid [202].

[130] ibid [204].

[131] ibid [205].

[132] ibid [217].

[133] ibid [218].

[134] ibid.

[135] ibid [221]–[222].

The panel considered whether the acts and omissions of Professor Kaufmann-Kohler constituted sufficient grounds to annul the second award.[136] The Committee found that, in the circumstances, Professor Kauffmann-Kohler's independent judgment under Article 14 of the ICSID Convention was *not* impaired, with the result that there were no sufficient grounds to annul the second award.[137] However, in reaching this conclusion, the Committee criticised Professor Kauffmann-Kohler in fairly strong terms.

Addressing the state's other grounds for annulment, the *Vivendi II* panel noted the distinction between annulment and appeal,[138] emphasising the availability of judicial economy by saying that not all arguments have to be addressed, only the fundamental ones.[139] The Committee found that none of the objections raised by Argentina could be elevated to a ground for annulment under Article 52(1) of the ICSID Convention.[140] Consequently, Argentina's request was denied, thereby completing the second procedural cycle of the case and drawing the curtains on Act Two of the *Vivendi* saga.

IV. DISCUSSION

Over the course of the two acts of *Vivendi v Argentina*, contributions were made to a number of discrete areas of international investment law. By far the most significant was the *Vivendi I* panel's decision on the interpretation of the jurisdictional offer that Argentina made through the applicable BIT—a species of treaty that was, at the time of *Vivendi I*, widely distributed but not yet well understood. The discussion below is intended to analyse this part of the case and, in so doing, demonstrate that it contains a number of individual lessons for arbitrators and counsel. After identifying these lessons, the discussion turns to the other advances made over the course of the two acts of the case, which pertain to the annulment mechanism and the threshold for disqualification of arbitrators under the ICSID Convention.

---

[136] ibid [233].

[137] ibid [238]–[239].

[138] Schreuer, 'From ICSID Annulment to Appeal' (n 119) 215–16.

[139] *Vivendi II* (n 126) [248].

[140] ibid [267]. In brief, the *Vivendi II* Committee held that a failure to express specific reasons in respect of interest and its calculation is not a sufficient ground for annulment, the reasons stated within the context of the Tribunal's approach to the evaluation of the damages to be compensated may be understood to cover also the issue of interest. On the issue of the nationality of CAA, which the state raised under Art 51(1)(b), the Annulment Committee found that this was already considered by the first Tribunal and the first *ad hoc* Committee, thus the second Tribunal did not manifestly exceed its power in confirming the views of those bodies. The *Vivendi II* Annulment Committee also clarified the meaning of Art 42 of the ICSID Convention in dealing with the issue of the applicable law, noting that 'at the time the ICSID Convention was concluded the normal dispute resolution facility was based on a contractual arbitration clause. In cases based on BITs, the emphasis is essentially on international law violation in the sense that the host state is alleged to have breached the standards of treatment provided for the foreign investor under the BIT in question. The result was a distinction between contract and treaty claims. As to the latter, international law applies'. Regarding the jurisdictional issue raised under Art 52(1)(b) and (e), the second Tribunal considered the jurisdiction issues *res judicata*, and so the Annulment Committee found that there was neither manifest excess of power nor insufficient reasoning. On the issue of whether the actions of the Province of Tucumán were properly considered, a point the state raised under Art 52(1) (b),(d) and (e), the Annulment Committee found that the second Tribunal acted within its powers.

A. Terra Nova

In the introduction to this chapter, it was said that the *Vivendi I* decision mapped a new continent: international investment law. It was, however, acknowledged that the coasts of this land had been sighted before. The most significant of these earlier sightings occurred in cases concerning state responsibility for contracts and measures taken against foreign-held contractual rights. At least since the *Norwegian Shipowners' Claims*,[141] it has been accepted that, where a state takes foreign-held contractual rights, international principles of expropriation and restitution may be brought into operation. Indeed, as Professor Crawford noted (writing six years after *Vivendi I*), 'investment contracts have always coexisted with international law standards for the protection of investments, so [the] tension [between treaty and contract] is not novel, as students of the old mixed arbitral tribunal decisions will not need reminding'.[142]

What gave *Vivendi I* the quality of a discovery was that it identified the arbitration agreement as the medium of integration: the precise location at which public international law and municipal (contract) law meet in an investment treaty case. Thus, the *terra nova* mapped by the *Vivendi I* panel can be imagined as landscape comprising all of the generic dispute resolution clauses contained in all of the investment treaties that make up the global BIT complex—the interior of a land where the traditional dualist relationship between international law and municipal law has evolved to produce the 'hybrid' body of law that we now see applied in investment treaty cases every day. To understand the true value of this discovery, it is important to note that, at the time of the *Vivendi I* decision, the investment treaty system was established but not yet in widespread use: states had been signing arbitration-backed BITs since the 1960s,[143] but it was not until 1987 that a claim under a BIT was actually taken to ICSID arbitration (in *AAPL v Sri Lanka*).[144] In fact, it was only after 2000 that the BIT caseload actually took off, the cause of the surge being the Argentine Financial Crisis of 1999–2002, as a consequence of which a diverse group of foreign investors brought treaty claims against the State. The *Vivendi I* decision was handed down just as this group of BIT claims was moving into the ICSID system—optimal timing in jurisprudential terms. It is therefore in the historical context of the investment treaty system, which today regulates billions in cross-border capital flows, that the *Vivendi I* discovery must be placed. Ultimately, it was the device of the BIT that caused the *terra nova* of international investment law to break away from the Pangaea of public international law.

B. Interpretation of the Jurisdictional Offer

Writing extra-curially in 2008, Professor Crawford observed that the implication of the *Vivendi I* decision was that, subject to certain qualifications, 'contractual

---

[141] *Norwegian Shipowners' Claims (Norway v United States)*, Award, Permanent Court of Arbitration (13 October 1922) (1922) I RIAA 307.

[142] Crawford, 'Treaty and Contract in Investment Arbitration' (n 2) 352.

[143] A R Parra, *History of the ICSID Convention* (Oxford, OUP, 2012) 199.

[144] *Asian Agricultural Products Ltd v Republic of Sri Lanka*, ICSID Case No ARB/87/3.

jurisdiction can be invoked under any sufficiently clear generic dispute settlement clause in a BIT'.[145] While there is now a trend towards narrower jurisdictional offers (especially in the new generation of multilateral investment treaties), the architecture of international investment law is still very much dominated by BITs. As was widely noted by commentators after the *Vivendi I* decision was handed down, many BITs—including the model BITs of a number of capital-exporting states—contain jurisdictional offers couched in broad terms similar to offer in the Argentina–France BIT.[146] Ultimately, the prevalence of the 'relating to/concerning/regarding investments' drafting pattern in the global BIT complex was (and is) the structural amplifier of *Vivendi I*: the systemic feature that enabled the decision to acquire the status of a landmark in the field of international investment law specifically, and, in international law generally.

Turning to the interpretive lesson of the case, unlike the agreement that is formed when the investor accepts the state's offer of arbitration, the offer itself is part of a treaty. And, as part of a treaty, the language of the offer must be interpreted in accordance with international law: applying the general rule in Article 31(1) of the Vienna Convention on the Law of Treaties, the words of the offer must be given their natural and ordinary meaning, in light of the object and purpose of the treaty in which they are contained. Adhering to this interpretive scheme, a broadly worded or 'generic' dispute resolution clause can be read in one of two ways: *literally*, such that the clause encompasses both treaty *and* contract claims, provided the claims 'relat[e] to investments'; or *restrictively* such that, absent express words to extend the Tribunal's jurisdiction to contractual claims, such jurisdiction is not to be inferred.[147] The *Vivendi I* Committee preferred the literal approach, observing that the jurisdictional offer did 'not use a narrow formulation, requiring that the investor's claim allege a breach of the BIT itself'.[148]

Subsequent tribunals have disagreed with the literal approach of *Vivendi I*, or have at least displayed caution. For example, in *SGS v Pakistan*, the ICSID tribunal held that the wording of the generic dispute resolution clause of the applicable BIT ('dispute[s] with respect to investments') was merely intended to describe the subject matter of disputes that could be submitted to arbitration under the treaty, rather than to have any special legal import.[149] Although the Tribunal in *SGS v Pakistan* accepted the generic clause of the BIT gave it jurisdiction over contract claims, the arbitrators held that such jurisdiction was conditional upon the alleged breach of contract also constituting a breach of the substantive standards of the BIT.[150]

[145] Crawford, 'Treaty and Contract in Investment Arbitration' (n 2) 362.

[146] See, for example, A Sinclair, 'Bridging the Contract/Treaty Divide' in C Binder, U Kriebaum, A Reinisch and S Wittich (eds), *International Investment Law for the 21st Century: Essays in Honour of Christoph Schreuer* (Oxford, Oxford Scholarship Online, 2009) 2, noting that generic dispute resolution clauses feature in the Model BITs of the UK, the Netherlands, Germany and Switzerland.

[147] E Gaillard, 'Treaty-Based Jurisdiction: Broad Dispute Resolution Clauses' (6 October 2005) 234(68) *New York Law Journal* 1, 2.

[148] *Vivendi I* (n 4) [55].

[149] *SGS Société Générale de Surveillance SA v Islamic Republic of Pakistan*, ICSID Case No ARB/01/13 Decision of the Tribunal on Objections of 6 August 2003 (2003) 18 ICSID Rev—FILJ 307.

[150] ibid.

Similarly, in *LESI-DIPENTA v Algeria*, the Tribunal read into the generic dispute resolution clause of the applicable BIT a requirement of simultaneous breach: the claimant had to demonstrate that the breach of contract also constituted a breach of the BIT.[151]

Ultimately, regardless of whether the literal or restrictive approach is taken, the word 'dispute' is the fulcrum of jurisdiction in an investment treaty case: ascertained using the interpretive scheme of international law, it is the meaning of 'dispute' that determines the scope of the jurisdictional offer made by the state in the treaty, and thus the scope of the arbitration agreement that is formed when the investor accepts. If, as in the Argentina–France BIT, the term 'dispute' can be read to include disputes *relating to* contracts, then the Tribunal will have jurisdiction to hear such claims.

However, as Professor Crawford later noted, contractual jurisdiction is subject to a number of qualifications which 'significantly limit its scope'.[152] First, the contract must qualify as an 'investment' under the treaty and, if the arbitration is taking place at ICSID, the contract must also qualify as an 'investment' for the purposes of Article 25 of the ICSID Convention—meaning, in practice, that it must be an *investment contract* (and not, for example, a short-term contract for the supply of goods or services).[153] This qualification did not arise in *Vivendi*, because the qualification of the Concession Contract as an 'investment' was not disputed. Second, the contract must be a contract 'with the state itself'—a point that *did* arise in Vivendi and which caused the first Tribunal considerable difficulty, in part because the arbitrators seem to have approached it (sub-consciously or sub-textually) as a question of admissibility rather than jurisdiction.[154] The third qualification—and the one where by far the most ink has been spilt since—arises where the contract in question contains an exclusive jurisdiction clause.[155] As Professor Schreuer has said, 'The central point in *Vivendi I* was the decision that the forum selection clause in the Concession Contract did not oust the ICSID's jurisdiction based on the BIT'.[156]

C. How to Approach an Exclusive Jurisdiction Clause in a Treaty Case

Looking at *Vivendi I* and subsequent cases, it can be said that, in the context of an investment treaty arbitration, there are (at least) two ways to approach an exclusive jurisdiction clause in a state agreement: first, the clause can be treated as a waiver of the investor's right (under the treaty) to arbitrate contract claims in a treaty forum

---

[151] *Consortium Groupment LESI-DIPENTA v République Algérienne Démocratique et Populaire*, ICSID Case No ARB/03/08, Award (10 January 2005).

[152] Crawford, 'Treaty and Contract in Investment Arbitration' (n 2) 362.

[153] ibid.

[154] ibid 363. In Professor Crawford's words: 'The issue of attribution arises when it is sought to hold the State responsible for some breach of an international obligation, including one arising under a substantive provision of a BIT. The problem here concerns jurisdiction, not merits; the formation of a secondary agreement to arbitrate, not the breach of a primary obligation concerning the protection of investments. In short, the question is one of interpretation of the jurisdictional offer, not attribution of conduct to the state'.

[155] ibid, 363.

[156] Schreuer, 'Investment Treaty Arbitration' (n 8) 288.

(a point in which the treaty/contract distinction is operative); second, the investor's contractual obligation to resolve contract disputes in another forum can be seen as an obligation that bears on the *admissibility* of its claims before a treaty tribunal. Professor Crawford has suggested the jurisdictional vantage is preferable,[157] but like most jurisdictional/admissibility debates this is a matter on which eminent and reasonable minds disagree.

Undoubtedly the best example of disagreement is *SGS v Philippines*,[158] the jurisdictional decision of which was handed down less than two years after *Vivendi I*. That dispute arose out of a contract for the provision of pre-shipment customs inspection services. The contract contained an exclusive jurisdiction clause in favour of the local courts. The contractor-investor, SGS, commenced arbitration under the Switzerland–Philippines BIT, making treaty and contract claims. The ICSID Tribunal found that it had jurisdiction over both SGS's treaty claims and its contract claims. However, the Tribunal declined to proceed to the merits, instead referring to the parties to the agreed local court for the determination of the amount due under the disputed contract. Critically, the arbitrators framed their decision in terms of the inadmissibility of the investor's claims—rather than the 'impossibility' of separating contract claims from treaty claims (the merits finding that exposed the first *Vivendi* tribunal to annulment). As Professor Schreuer observed of *SGS v Philippines*, 'the Tribunal's introduction of the concept of admissibility' was the 'most important part' of the decision;[159] indeed, Jan Paulsson has identified the case as 'the most illuminating precedent' on the point of admissibility in investment arbitration.[160] In effect, the then-novel frame of admissibility allowed the *SGS v Philippines* tribunal to reach a conclusion that was (as Schreuer wryly observed) 'strongly reminiscent' of the decision of the first Tribunal in *Vivendi*.[161] This begs the question of whether the award of the first *Vivendi* Tribunal might have survived annulment if the arbitrators had framed their finding of impossibility (of separating contract claims from treaty claims) as a decision that the claims were inadmissible. Quite possibly, it would seem.

D. The Role of the Jurisdiction/Admissibility Distinction

Although the line between admissibility and jurisdiction is far from bright, the different outcomes in *Vivendi I* and *SGS v Philippines* show that admissibility has a

---

[157] Crawford, 'Treaty and Contract in Investment Arbitration' (n 2) 363: 'it is arguable that under a generic dispute settlement clause [in a BIT] this issue [the existence of an exclusive jurisdiction clause in a contract] should be classified as an issuer of jurisdictional properly so-called, and not one of admissibility. Whatever answer may be given to the question whether an investor can by contract in advance renounce the right to arbitrate treaty claims, there cannot be any doubt that it can renounce the right to arbitrate contract claims in a treaty forum. An exclusive jurisdiction clause in a contract is surely intended to do just that'.

[158] *SGS Société Générale de Surveillance SA v Republic of the Philippines*, ICSID Case No ARB/02/6, Decision of the Tribunal on Objections to Jurisdiction (29 January 2004).

[159] Schreuer, 'Investment Treaty Arbitration' (n 8) 294.

[160] J Paulsson, *The Idea of Arbitration* (Oxford, OUP, 2013) 86.

[161] Schreuer, 'Investment Treaty Arbitration' (n 8) 294.

useful—in some cases even critical—role to play where contract (or contract-related) claims are brought before investment treaty tribunals.

Comparing the two cases, it might be said that approaching an exclusive jurisdiction clause as a matter of admissibility entails the analysis of the clause from the perspective of *compliance*. Using this compliance perspective, the Tribunal in *SGS v Philippines* found that SGS could not approbate and reprobate: if SGS wanted to make contract claims, it had to comply with the contract itself and this meant suing in the agreed forum. Thus, it was the (unsatisfied) substantive obligation created by the exclusive jurisdiction clause that barred the claim, not the mere *presence* of the exclusive jurisdiction clause in the underlying contract.

In contrast, when the exclusive jurisdiction clause is approached as a waiver (in Professor Crawford's words, as a clause that 'renounce[s] the [investor's] right to arbitrate contract claims in a treaty forum'),[162] it is more the *existence* of the clause that is at issue, rather than compliance with the rule it creates. From this vantage— what could be termed the 'existence perspective'—the exclusive jurisdiction clause is (or is at least arguably) a matter of jurisdiction, if for no other reason that, with the merits issue of compliance excised from the analysis, jurisdiction is all it could logically be.

To reduce it further, the existence perspective focuses on the investor's entry into the contract that contains the exclusive jurisdiction clause, whereas the compliance perspective focuses on the investor's subsequent conduct under that contract. To a large extent, which perspective is more appropriate will depend on the claims over which the Tribunal is asked to exercise jurisdiction, the determination of which will involve a preliminary question as to whether the Tribunal should analyse the claims as formulated by the claimant (the approach taken by the first *Vivendi* Tribunal,[163] and at least tacitly approved by the first Annulment Committee),[164] or whether an objective analysis is appropriate (this being the view expressed by a number of sub-sequent ICSID tribunals).[165] If, as in *Vivendi*, the investor makes no claim for breach of the contract, and rather claims only that the state took measures in relation to the contract that were violative of the treaty, then the case for interpreting the exclu-sive jurisdiction clause from the existence perspective will be stronger; if, as in *SGS v Philippines*, the investor makes a claim for breach of contract, the compliance perspective may make more sense, although there will be arguments for and against both perspectives.

---

[162] Crawford, 'Treaty and Contract in Investment Arbitration' (n 2) 363.

[163] *Compañía de Aguas del Aconquija SA and Compagnie Générale des Eaux/Vivendi Universal v Argentine Republic*, ICSID Case No ARB/97/3, Award (21 November 2000) [50]. ('As formulated, these claims against the Argentine Republic are not subject to the jurisdiction of the contentious adminis-trative tribunals of Tucuman, if only because, ex hypothesi, those claims are not based on the Concession Contract but allege a cause of action under the BIT').

[164] *Vivendi I* (n 4) [74]. However, as Schreuer has observed, the *Vivendi I* Committee appears to have accepted an element of objectivity in the assessment of the investor's claims for jurisdictional purposes. In this regard, Schreuer points to the following part of the annulment committee's decision: 'In a case where the essential basis of a claim brought before an international tribunal is a breach of contract, the tribunal will give effect to any valid choice of forum clause in the contract'; Schreuer, 'Investment Treaty Arbitration' (n 8) 315–16.

[165] See, for example, *Joy Mining Machinery Limited v Arab Republic of Egypt*, ICSID Case No ARB/03/11 Award on Jurisdiction (6 August 2004).

E. 'Mere Relation' Versus 'Pure Contract' Jurisdiction

As noted in the introduction to this chapter, arguably the most important advance made in the whole course of the *Vivendi* case was that, having identified the contractual jurisdiction of a tribunal constituted under a generic dispute resolution clause, the *Vivendi I* panel gave an indication of how this jurisdiction could be exercised, namely by 'tak[ing] into account the terms of a contract in determining whether there has been a breach of a distinct standard of international law'.[166] This can be thought of as 'mere relation' jurisdiction—jurisdiction over treaty claims that merely *relate to* contracts, either as a matter of law or fact, but which do not necessarily entail claims that a contract has been *breached*. This was the case that Vivendi ran against Argentina: that the state took measures in relation to the Concession that violated the BIT. Since *Vivendi I*, this area of jurisdiction has proven relatively uncontroversial. As noted above, the middle—where 'simultaneous claims' are made—has seen more debate, especially as it is where the jurisdiction/admissibility distinction becomes relevant (as illustrated by *SGS v Philippines*). But it is in the area of 'pure contract' claims that the debate inspired by *Vivendi I* is most intense.[167] The Venn diagram below is intended to illustrate these three fields of jurisdiction and their spatial relations *inter se*.

Jurisdiction of a Tribunal Under a Generic Dispute Resolution Clause

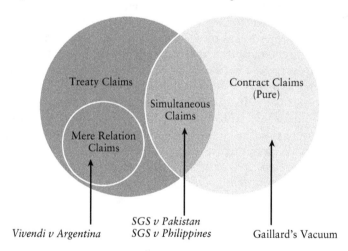

Where 'pure' contract jurisdiction is concerned, the core question is whether an investment treaty tribunal hear a claim in which no violation of the substantive

---

[166] *Vivendi I* (n 4) [105].

[167] As a frame to this debate, it is worth remembering that public international law has long recognised that tribunals can be vested with pure contractual jurisdiction. In *Oppenheim's International Law*, the position of contracts in international law is summarised as follows: 'either by virtue of a term in the contract itself or of an agreement between the state and the alien, or by virtue of an agreement between

standards of the treaty is alleged. In obiter, the *Vivendi I* panel suggested this would be possible under a generic dispute resolution clause.[168] Schreuer agrees: 'The view that a jurisdictional clause [in a treaty] referring all investment disputes to international arbitration vests the tribunal also with competence over pure contract claims is clearly the better one'.[169] On the other hand, Emmanuel Gaillard—one of the arbitrators in the *LESI-DIPENTA* case (in which the tribunal opposed the literalist approach of the *Vivendi I* panel) has advocated caution on the pure contractual jurisdiction of treaty tribunals, pointing to the 'danger in divorcing the jurisdictional provisions from the substantive terms of the same treaty' and the risk that the recognition of pure contractual jurisdiction 'may suggest that the treaty-based tribunal has jurisdiction but is invited to rule on a vacuum'.[170]

Anthony Sinclair's response to Gaillard is that 'A tribunal that upheld its jurisdiction to adjudicate contractual disputes would not be called upon 'to rule in a vacuum', since under most applicable arbitration rules, tribunals are competent to determine the applicable law or rules of law to govern the merits of the dispute', Sinclair's conclusion being that 'The applicable law or rules of law would, in the first place at least, be the proper law of the contract'.[171] As appealing as Sinclair's response is, it does leave intact Gaillard's starting premise, which is that it would be 'odd to interpret a treaty as creating a jurisdictional basis for a treaty-based tribunal in cases where it is not called upon to rule on alleged violations of that treaty'.[172]

In his analysis, Sinclair also notes the view of Jörn Griebel, who has attached significance to whether or not the treaty contains an umbrella clause, his view being that if it does *not*, then that suggests 'a conscious decision against the protection of contract claims under an investment treaty'.[173] Of course, the more evidence there was for this 'conscious decision' having been made by the states when they negotiated the treaty, the stronger Griebel's argument will be (conversely, where the *travaux préparatoires* are silent or non-existent—as is often the case for BITs of the older generations—the more readily Griebel's argument could be opposed).

As yet, there is no reported case in which an investment treaty tribunal has exercised pure contractual jurisdiction. There have, however, been a number of cases in which 'mere relation' jurisdiction has been exercised, and also cases in which

---

the state allegedly in breach of its contractual obligations and the state of which the alien is a national, disputes as to compliance with the terms of contracts may be referred to an internationally composed tribunal, applying, at least in part, international law'. R Jennings and A Watts (eds), *Oppenheim's International Law*, vol 1, 9th edn (Oxford, OUP, 1996) 927.

[168] *Vivendi I* (n 4) [55]. ('Read literally, the requirements for arbitral jurisdiction under Article 8 [of the BIT] do not necessitate that the claimant allege a breach of the BIT itself: it is sufficient that the dispute relate to an investment made under the BIT').

[169] Schreuer, 'Investment Treaty Arbitration' (n 8) 299.

[170] Gaillard, 'Treaty-Based Jurisdiction' (n 147) 3.

[171] Sinclair, 'Bridging the Contract/Treaty Divide' (n 146) 10.

[172] Gaillard, 'Treaty-Based Jurisdiction' (n 147) 3.

[173] J Griebel, 'Jurisdiction over "Contract Claims" in Treaty-Based Investment Arbitration on the Basis of the Wide Dispute Settlement Clauses in Investment Agreements' (2007) 4 *Transnational Dispute Management* 5, 14.

simultaneous treaty/contract claims have been determined. While we wait for the Black Swan, the debate on 'pure' contract jurisdiction will continue, with the themes summarised above in its foreground. But a number of issues lie in the background. One is the investment treaty system itself—which, having been constructed quickly and quietly towards the end of the twentieth century, has exposed states to responsibility in areas in which they have traditionally enjoyed immunity or at least considerable freedom of action. A related issue is the general concern that the jurisdiction granted to arbitrators under investment treaties is already excessive—a concern that is at the heart of the wider debate around the virtues and vices of investor-state dispute settlement (ISDS) provisions in the new generation of trade and investment treaties, of which the Trans-Pacific Partnership is the most recent example. There is also the issue of the effect that the investment treaty complex has had (and is having) on the international legal order: in Francisco Orrego Vicuna words, 'treaties are becoming privatized'.[174] As he has observed 'At a time when transactions were largely domestic international rules were applied as subsidiary, while today, where transactions are mostly international, it is the national rules that are applied in the subsidiary'.[175] Ultimately, in all of these background issues, the common politico-legal theme is state sovereignty.

F. Annulment Lessons

The *Vivendi* case included two rounds of annulment proceedings, the seven-year gap between which was a formative period for international investment law. The two cycles of case therefore contain a number of lessons on how the annulment mechanism of the ICSID Convention operates. The first annulment decision—which Schreuer has placed in the welcome 'third generation' of ICSID annulment jurisprudence—is by far the more important of the two,[176] it being an authority for the interpretation and application of two of the five grounds for annulment under the ICSID Convention: manifest excess of powers and failure to give reasons. As noted above, *Vivendi I* was also where the educating role of an Annulment Committee was demonstrated. Although the second annulment decision was primarily concerned with the State's 'challenge' to one of the arbitrators of the second Tribunal, it too shows that, in certain circumstances, Annulment Committees can play a useful role as educators in the ICSID system.

i. Infra petita

As was noted by the Annulment Committee in *Caratube v Kazakhstan*, *Vivendi I* is authority for a somewhat paradoxical proposition: a manifest *shortfall* in the

---

[174] F Orrego Vicuña, 'Of Contracts and Treaties in the Global Market' (2004) 8 *Max Planck Yearbook of United Nations Law* 341, 357.

[175] ibid, 343.

[176] C Schreuer, 'Three Generations of ICSID Annulment Proceedings' in E Gaillard (ed), *Annulment of ICSID Awards* (New York, Juris Publishing, 2004) 17, 18.

exercise of jurisdiction may also constitute a manifest *excess* of power and lead to annulment of the award.[177] *Vivendi I* was the first of only three instances in the history of ICSID where committees have used their power to annul awards on the ground that the tribunal failed to exercise jurisdiction.[178] The second was *Helnan International Hotels A/S v Arab Republic of Egypt*,[179] in which the applicant relied on *Vivendi I* in its submissions on *infra petita*.[180] In circumstances similar to *Vivendi I*, the *Helnan* award was partially annulled, due to the Tribunal's failure to exercise jurisdiction: the *Helnan* Tribunal had imposed the requirement that before an administrative decision could be construed as a treaty breach, it had to be challenged in local courts.[181] The third instance was the well-known case of *Malaysian Historical Salvors v Government of Malaysia*,[182] in which the applicant relied on *Vivendi I* as a basis for its argument that the Tribunal's failure to exercise the jurisdiction which it possessed, constituted an excess of power within the meaning of Article 52(1)(b).[183] In that case the ad hoc Committee annulled the award on jurisdiction on the basis that the sole arbitrator manifestly exceeded his powers by failing to exercise jurisdiction over a treaty dispute.[184]

ii. Failure to State Reasons

Article 52(1)(e) of the ICSID Convention provides that an award may be annulled if it has 'failed to state the reasons on which it was based'. As the *Vivendi I* panel observed, unlike the grounds in Article 52(1)(b) ('manifest excess of powers') and (d) ('serious departure from a fundamental rule of procedure'), Article 52(1)(e) does not contain an internal qualifier (such as 'manifest' or 'serious'). Thus, it was necessary for the members of the *Vivendi I* panel to interpret Article 52(1)(e) to ascertain its threshold. Distancing itself from the status of an appellate court, the *Vivendi I* panel said 'Provided that the reasons given by a tribunal can be followed and relate to the issues that were before the tribunal, their correctness is beside the point'.[185] The Committee also referred to Schreuer's treatise on the ICSID Convention, stating that it is 'well accepted both in the cases and the literature that Article 52(1)(e) concerns a failure to state any reasons with respect to all or part of an award, not the

---

[177] *Caratube International Oil Company LLP v Republic of Kazakhstan*, ICSID Case No ARB/08/12, Decision on the Annulment Application of Caratube International Oil Company LLP (21 February 2014) [75].

[178] ibid [76].

[179] *Helnan International Hotels A/S v Arab Republic of Egypt*, ICSID Case No ARB/05/19, Decision of the ad hoc Committee (14 June 2010).

[180] ibid [31].

[181] ibid [28]–[57].

[182] *Malaysian Historical Salvors Sdn Bhd v Government of Malaysia*, ICSID Case No ARB/05/10, Decision on the Application for Annulment (16 April 2009).

[183] ibid [27].

[184] ibid [56]–[82]. The principal issue in *Malaysian Historical Salvors* was whether the requirement that an investment represent a contribution to the economic development of the host State was a condition for jurisdiction under Article 25(1) of the ICSID Convention. The sole arbitrator found that it was, but the majority of the Annulment Committee disagreed and annulled the award on jurisdiction.

[185] *Vivendi I* (n 4) [64].

failure to state correct or convincing reasons'.[186] The Committee then formulated the test for annulment under this ground as follows:

> In the Committee's view, annulment under Article 52(1)(e) should only occur in a clear case. This entails two conditions: first, the failure to state reasons must leave the decision on a particular point essentially lacking in any expressed rationale; and second, that point must itself be necessary to the tribunal's decision.[187]

The claimants relied on Article 52(1)(e) to allege that in dismissing the claim the Tribunal failed to state the reasons on which its decision was based. The panel found that, for the Federal claims, the Tribunal had given reasons for dismissal; as to the Tucumán claims, the panel found that the Tribunal gave 'very full reasons for the steps it took, viz, the dismissal of those claims without any overall consideration of their merits'.[188]

The issue of 'contradictory reasons' formed an important part of the panel's decision. This ground is often argued, the contention of applicants normally being that true contradiction amounts to total absence. While the *Vivendi I* panel did acknowledge that, in some circumstances, it could be said that 'contradictory reasons cancel each other out', the members stressed that an Annulment Committee must not confuse 'conflicting considerations', which can be balanced, with 'genuinely contradictory' reasons.[189] This has proven to be valuable dicta, because 'contradictory reasons' arguments involve (or invite) qualitative analysis of the award—an exercise that, if conducted by an Annulment Committee, has the potential to give the process the character of cassation.

Given the relative brevity with which the panel dealt with this ground, it is perhaps surprising that *Vivendi I* has assumed the status of an authority on 'failure to state reasons' as a ground of annulment.[190] But, because the points above were traversed

---

[186] ibid. C Schreuer with L Malintoppi, A Reinisch and A Sinclair, *The ICSID Convention: A Commentary*, 2nd edn (Cambridge, CUP, 2009).

[187] *Vivendi I* (n 4) [65].

[188] ibid [116].

[189] ibid [65] ('an ad hoc committee should be careful not to discern contradiction when what is actually expressed in a tribunal's reasons could more truly be said to be but a reflection of such conflicting considerations').

[190] Examples of cases in which *Vivendi I* has been cited as authority for the 'failure to state reasons' ground include *MTD Equity Sdn Bhd and MTD Chile SA v Republic of Chile*, ICSID Case No ARB/01/7, Decision on Annulment (21 March 2007) [50], [78]; *Hussein Nuaman Soufraki v United Arab Emirates*, ICSID Case No ARB/02/7, Decision of the Ad Hoc Committee on the Application for Annulment of Mr Soufraki (5 June 2007) [124]; *Industria Nacional de Alimentos, SA and Indalsa Perú, SA v Republic of Peru*, ICSID Case No ARB/03/4, Decision on Annulment (5 September 2007) [128]; *CMS Gas Transmission Company v Argentine Republic*, ICSID Case No ARB/01/8, Decision of the Ad Hoc Committee on the Application for Annulment of the Argentine Republic (25 September 2007) [54]; *Azurix Corp v the Argentine Republic*, ICSID Case No ARB/01/12, Decision on the Application for Annulment of the Argentine Republic (1 September 2009) [55], [178], [364]–[365]; *MCI Power Group, LC and New Turbine, Inc v Republic of Ecuador*, ICSID Case No ARB/03/6, Decision on Annulment (19 October 2009) [81], [85]; *Rumeli Telekom AS and Telsim Mobil Telekomunikasyon Hizmetleri AS v Republic of Kazakhstan*, ICSID Case No ARB/05/16, Decision of the ad hoc Committee (25 March 2010) [82], [137]; *Enron Creditors Recovery Corporation (formerly Enron Corporation) and Ponderosa Assets, LP v Argentine Republic*, ICSID Case No ARB/01/3, Decision on the Application for Annulment of the Argentine Republic (30 July 2010) [76]; *Fraport AG Frankfurt Airport Services Worldwide v Republic of the Philippines [I]*, ICSID Case No ARB/03/25, Decision on the Application for Annulment of Fraport AG Frankfurt

by the members at a time when ICSID annulment practice was limited, the *Vivendi I* decision is rightly considered authoritative on this point.

iii. Annulment Committees as 'Educators'

Annulment is a limited exception to the principle of arbitral finality, concerned only with the legitimacy of the decision-making *process* and not the substantive correctness of the decision.[191] The powers of an Annulment Committee are limited to *annulment*: the Committee may not amend or replace the award by its own decision.[192] That said, annulment is the apex of the ICSID system, and ICSID arbitration is the main method by which investment disputes are resolved. So there is at least a structural argument that an Annulment Committee has a role beyond merely determining whether or not an arbitral award should stand. An early and indeed controversial example of a Committee exercising a pedagogical function can be seen in the decision of the very first ICSID Annulment Committee, constituted in *Klöckner v Cameroon* (also known as '*Klöckner I*').[193] A better example is *Malaysian Historical Salvors v Government of Malaysia*,[194] where the panel provided useful guidance on how to determine whether or not an investment exists for the purposes of Article 25 of the ICSID Convention (and the relationship between that article and the definition of 'investment' in the applicable BIT). As the discussion above shows, the *Vivendi I* panel also played the role of educator, primarily on the treaty/contract distinction. What is interesting—and, with respect, commendable—is that the panel did so in a succinct, sparing fashion.

Other Annulment Committees have been more overt, and have attracted criticism as a result. For example, Aron Broches, father of the ICSID Convention, criticised

Airport Services Worldwide (23 December 2010) [272], [274], [277]; *Continental Casualty Company v Argentine Republic*, ICSID Case No ARB/03/9, Decision on the Application for Partial Annulment of Continental Casualty Company and the Application for Partial Annulment of the Argentine Republic (16 September 2011) [102]; *AES Summit Generation Limited and AES-Tisza Erömü Kft v Republic of Hungary*, ICSID Case No ARB/07/22, Decision of the ad hoc Committee on the Application for Annulment (29 June 2012) [53]; *Victor Pey Casado and President Allende Foundation v Republic of Chile*, ICSID Case No ARB/98/2, Decision on the Application for Annulment of the Republic of Chile (18 December 2012) [83], [85]; *Libananco Holdings Co Limited v Republic of Turkey*, ICSID Case No ARB/06/8, Excerpts of Decision on Annulment (2 May 2013) [applied ICSID Arbitration Rules (2006)] [94]; *Malicorp Limited v Arab Republic of Egypt*, ICSID Case No ARB/08/18, Decision on Annulment (3 July 2013) [43]; *SGS Société Générale de Surveillance SA v Republic of Paraguay*, ICSID Case No ARB/07/29, Decision on Annulment (19 May 2014) [140]; *Alapli Elektrik BV v Republic of Turkey*, ICSID Case No ARB/08/13, Decision on Annulment (10 July 2014) [200]; *El Paso Energy International Company v Argentine Republic*, ICSID Case No ARB/03/15, Decision on Application for Annulment (22 September 2014) [applied ICSID Arbitration Rules (2006)] [217], [220]; *Daimler Financial Services AG v Argentine Republic*, ICSID Case No ARB/05/1, Decision on Annulment (7 January 2015) [77]; *Tza Yap Shum v Republic of Peru*, ICSID Case No ARB/07/6, Decision on Annulment (12 February 2015) [102], [172].

[191] *Vivendi I* (n 4) [64].

[192] ibid [62].

[193] *Klöckner Industrie-Analgen GmbH and others v United Republic of Cameroon and Société Camerounaise des Engrais*, ICSID Case No ARB/81/2 Decision on Annulment (3 May 1985) para 82; Schreuer, 'From ICSID Annulment to Appeal' (n 119) 223.

[194] *Malaysian Historical Salvors Sdn Bhd v Government of Malaysia*, ICSID Case No ARB/05/10, Decision on the Application for Annulment (16 April 2009).

Klöckner I for its 'exorbitant' pronouncements;[195] similar criticisms were made of the annulment decision in *Fraport v Philippines*,[196] where the panel offered guidance on treaty interpretation (guidance that, according to Schreurer, was incorrect in substance).[197] Writing in 2011, Schreuer observed that:

> It has become common for *ad hoc* committees to offer gratuitous advice and criticism. Even if the award survives, the criticism may act as a consolation prize to the losing party. At the same time this makes compliance with the award more difficult.[198]

The *Vivendi* case provides an example of this too: in the part of *Vivendi II* that concerned Professor Kaufmann-Kohler's conflict of interest and independence, the Annulment Committee did not limit itself to determining whether this meant that the Tribunal was not properly constituted (Article 52(1)(a)) or whether a serious departure from a fundamental rule of procedure had occurred (under Article 52(1)(d)); rather, the *Vivendi II* panel castigated Professor Kaufmann-Kohler, the members declaring their 'opinion on conflicts of interest and how they should have been handled'.[199] In Schreuer's view, the *Vivendi II* panel exercised a function akin to that of 'a supreme court judge',[200] the 'major part of the Decision deal[ing] with what the panel thought would have been the proper way to handle disclosures in cases of possible conflicts of interest and not with the decision on whether to annul'.[201]

Considering the two annulment decisions in the *Vivendi case*, it could be said that they show the educational or pedagogical function is best reserved for situations where annulment is granted. The primary justification for this approach would be that annulment is draconian, and arbitrators, as the first-instance decision-makers (and, in professional/reputational terms, 'risk-takers') in the ICSID system, need to understand why an award has been vacated in order to avoid making the same mistake themselves. On any view, where hazards are clearly marked, accidents are less likely to occur. A narrowly crafted annulment decision may not be sufficient for this purpose, and so some obiter may be necessary—especially where the point is clearly one of wider significance, as was the case in *Vivendi I*. However, as Hans Van Houtte has cautioned, where an Annulment Committee does this it must take care to avoid creating the impression that its members have better minds than the arbitrators whose award they are reviewing, the risk being that the 'whole review process could be depicted as mere academic rivalry'.[202]

---

[195] A Broches, 'Observations on the Finality of ICSID Awards' (1991) 6 *ICSID Rev-FILJ* 324, 376.

[196] *Fraport AG Frankfurt Airport Services Worldwide v Republic of the Philippines [I]*, ICSID Case No ARB/03/25, Decision on the Application for Annulment of Fraport AG Frankfurt Airport Services Worldwide (23 December 2010).

[197] Schreuer, 'From ICSID Annulment to Appeal' (n 119) 224.

[198] ibid [225].

[199] *Vivendi II* (n 126) [242].

[200] Schreuer, 'From ICSID Annulment to Appeal' (n 119) 223.

[201] ibid, 224.

[202] H Van Houtte, 'Article 52 of the Washington Convention: A Brief Introduction' in E Gaillard (ed), *Annulment of ICSID Awards* (New York, Juris Publishing, 2004) 11, 15.

G. Standard for Disqualification of ICSID Arbitrators

The final lesson of the *Vivendi* case concerns the standard for disqualification of arbitrators—and members of Annulment Committees—under the ICSID Convention. In the overall scheme of the case, the challenge to Mr Fortier was a side show. However, as noted above, the decision Professors Crawford and Rozas made (as the unchallenged members of the *Vivendi I* panel) was significant in the area of challenge jurisprudence, in which the recurring question is what the word 'manifest' means for the standard for disqualification.

Professors Crawford and Rozas considered that the effect of the word 'manifest' was to introduce an evidentiary threshold for challenges, rather than to posit a margin of tolerance for conflicts; in their view, the word 'manifest' in Article 57 functions to exclude 'reliance on speculative assumptions or arguments' and not to permit conflicts that exist but which are not serious enough to warrant disqualification.[203] In their criticism of the threshold for disqualification set in the *Amco Asia* case (what the writer has called the first high of the two 'tides' that can now be observed in ICSID challenge jurisprudence),[204] Professors Crawford and Rozas effectively aligned the ICSID disqualification threshold with that which prevails in international commercial arbitration, noting that 'in light of the object and purpose of Article 57', it would not be a 'correct interpretation' to conclude that the ICSID Convention sets a lower standard for arbitrator independence and bias than other international instruments (such as the International Bar Association Code of Ethics).[205]

From where we stand today, in a world in which challenges to treaty arbitrators are a regular occurrence, it is now possible to identify the challenge to Mr Fortier as the beginning of a period in which a lower ('reasonable apprehension' or 'reasonable doubt') threshold was recognised at ICSID, the ebb of the first tide of ICSID challenge jurisprudence.[206] Although the tide rose again for a period (the second

---

[203] *Compañía de Aguas del Aconquija SA and Compagnie Générale des Eaux/Vivendi Universal v Argentine Republic*, ICSID Case No ARB/97/3, Decision on the Challenge to the President of the Committee (3 October 2001) (2002) 17 *ICSID Rev—FILJ* 168, [25].

[204] S Luttrell, 'Beware the Blue Bank: the Implications of a Lower Threshold for ICSID Arbitrator Disqualification for International Arbitration in Asia' (October 2014) *Asian Dispute Review* 172, 173. For a more detailed discussion of the development of ICSID challenge law and practice, readers are referred to the two books have been written on the topic of arbitrators' challenges: one by the writer (*Bias Challenges in International Commercial Arbitration: the Need for a 'Real Danger' Test* (The Netherlands, Kluwer Law International, 2009)) and the other by Karel Daele (*Challenge and Disqualification of Arbitrators in International Arbitration* (The Netherlands, Kluwer Law International, 2012)). See also A Sheppard, 'Arbitrator Independence in ICSID Arbitration' in C Binder, U Kriebaum, A Reinisch and S Wittich (eds), *International Investment Law for the 21st Century* (Oxford, OUP, 2009) 237. For a more recent discussion of the challenge mechanics of the ICSID Convention, see S Luttrell, 'Testing the ICSID Framework for Arbitrator Challenges' (Fall 2016) 31(3) *ICSID Rev—FILJ* 597, 597-621.

[205] *Compañía de Aguas del Aconquija SA and Compagnie Générale des Eaux/Vivendi Universal v Argentine Republic*, ICSID Case No ARB/97/3, Decision on the Challenge to the President of the Committee (3 October 2001) (2002) 17 *ICSID Rev—FILJ* 168, [20].

[206] Luttrell, 'Beware the Blue Bank' (n 204) 173.

high occurring in another treaty action against Argentina),[207] the 2014 challenge decision in *Blue Bank International v Venezuela*[208]—in which a standard equivalent to 'reasonable doubt' was applied by the Chairman of the ICSID Administrative Counsel—shows that the views expressed by Professors Crawford and Rozas remain persuasive today.

V. CONCLUSION

What the *Vivendi* case teaches is that an international tribunal confronted with a contract-related claim made under an investment treaty must take great care in interpreting the jurisdictional offer made by the host state under the applicable treaty and, where the relevant contract contains an exclusive jurisdiction clause, this interpretive exercise must be sensitive to two main distinctions: the distinction between treaty and contract claims, and the distinction between jurisdiction and admissibility. If care is not taken, the tribunal may sail straight past the *terra nova* of international investment law mapped by the *Vivendi I* panel.

As we have seen, the context was unique: the *Vivendi I* decision was handed down at the beginning of a period in which the boom in BIT arbitrations (many of which were brought against Argentina) occurred and ICSID's caseload took off; in other words, it was a case of right issue, right time. But that does not mean the value of the decision has declined over time. The lessons of *Vivendi I* remain highly relevant today, in large part because the system of international investment law is still underpinned by the global web of BITs, within which generic dispute resolution clauses like that at issue in the *Vivendi* case are common. Even in a more multilateral future, in which the architecture of international investment law is less reliant on broadly worded BITs, the lessons of the *Vivendi* case will still remain valuable because—much like Isocrates noted in his arguments against Callimachus—foreign investments will continue to be made through contracts, and the use of investment treaties is now entrenched in international business practice.

---

[207] *Suez, Sociedad General de Aguas de Barcelona SA and Interagua Servicios Integrales de Agua SA v Argentine Republic*, ICSID Case No ARB/03/11, and *Suez, Sociedad General de Aguas de Barcelona SA and Vivendi Universal SA v Argentine Republic*, ICSID Case No ARB/03/19, Decision on the Proposal for the Disqualification of a Member of the Arbitral Tribunal (22 October 2007), where it was held (at para 41) that 'The challenging party must prove not only facts indicating the lack of independence, but also that the lack is "manifest" or "highly probable", not just "possible" or "quasi-certain"'.

[208] *Blue Bank International & Trusts (Barbados) v Bolivarian Republic of Venezuela*, ICSID Case No ARB/12/20, Decision of the Parties' Proposals to Disqualify a Majority of the Tribunal (12 November 2013).

20

US—Import Prohibition of Certain Shrimp and Shrimp Products (1998)

CALLUM MUSTO AND CATHERINE REDGWELL

I. INTRODUCTION

O N 30 NOVEMBER 1999 hundreds of people donned sea turtle costumes and marched through the streets of Seattle. They, and thousands of others, were there during the World Trade Organization's (WTO) Third Ministerial Conference to protest against the impacts of liberalised global trade on the environment and particularly the Appellate Body's (AB) recently published decision in *US—Shrimp*.[1] These scenes underscore the perceived tension between trade and other concerns, including the environment[2] and are testament to the impact the AB's decision in *US—Shrimp* had outside the trade law community.

US—Shrimp was the first case to come before the newly created WTO Dispute Settlement Body (DSB)[3] in which the AB was required to consider the compatibility with GATT 1994 of unilateral trade measures for the protection of global environmental concerns.[4] It was also the fifth dispute in less than a decade concerning the United States' environmental measures brought before a GATT panel or the WTO DSB,[5] and the second time in two years for such a dispute to be considered

---

[1] *United States—Import Prohibition of Certain Shrimp and Shrimp Products*, Report of the AB (12 October 1998) WT/DS58/AB/R, '*US–Shrimp*' or 'AB Report'.

[2] See D Esty, 'An environmental perspective on Seattle' (2000) 3 *JIEL* 1, 176–78 and ibid, 'Environment and the Trading System: Picking up the Post-Seattle Pieces' in J Schott (ed), *The WTO After Seattle* (Washington DC, Institute for Economics, 2000) 1501. See also P Galizzi, 'Globalisation, Trade and Environment: Broadening the Agenda after Seattle?' [2000] 4 *Env'l Liab* 106.

[3] 1994 WTO Agreement and Dispute Settlement Understanding (DSU), in force 1 January 1995.

[4] These are shared concerns in so far as certain species of endangered sea turtle are found in US waters, as well as on the high seas and in the waters of third states. The constellation of interests at stake, domestically and globally, are discussed further in section II. For brief discussion of sea turtles as a 'shared global resource' see Panel Report [7.53].

[5] *US—Restrictions on Imports of Tuna (Mexico)*, GATT Panel Report (unadopted) BISD 39S/155 (3 September 1991) DS21/R; *US—Restrictions on Imports of Tuna (EEC)*, GATT Panel Report (unadopted) (16 June 1994) DS29/R; *US—Taxes on Automobiles*, GATT Panel Report (unadopted) (11 October 1994) DS31/R; *US—Reformulated Gasoline-Report of the Panel* (29 January 1996) WT/DS2/R; *US-Reformulated Gasoline-Report of the AB* (29 April 1996) WT/DS2/AB/R.

by the AB.[6] *US—Shrimp* was also the first time a claim was brought by a coalition of developing country members against a developed WTO member.[7]

India, Malaysia, Pakistan and Thailand initiated their complaint against the US in consequence of unilateral measures pursuant to the US Endangered Species Act of 1973 which prohibited the import of shrimp harvested outside US waters and in a manner incompatible with US standards for endangered sea turtle protection. As we shall discuss below, the case is significant for its findings on the scope of justification for trade restrictive environmental measures under GATT 1994 and for the AB's approach to treaty interpretation.

II. BACKGROUND TO THE CASE

Shrimp is one of the most important globally traded fishery commodities;[8] yet shrimp harvesting contributes to large-scale drowning or killing of non-target species, notably of sea turtles,[9] seven endangered species listed globally for protection under Appendix I of the 1973 Convention on International Trade in Endangered Species (CITES).[10] CITES is, however, concerned with limiting or prohibiting trade in species threatened with extinction and does not mandate specific measures for sea turtle protection and conservation. Indeed, as noted by the AB in this regard, there is no global sea turtle conservation agreement[11] and only one regional agreement, the 1996 Inter-American Convention for the Protection and Conservation of Sea Turtles,[12] which in any event was not applicable in the harvesting areas of the complainants' shrimp fisheries.

Domestically, US research programmes had concluded that the incidental capture and drowning of sea turtles in shrimp trawl nets was a significant source of sea

---

[6] The first—and the first case before the newly created AB—was *United States—Standards for Reformulated and Conventional Gasoline (Venezuela and Brazil)* Report of the AB (29 April 1996) WT/DS2/AB/R, 'US—Gasoline'.

[7] The proceedings in *US—Shrimp* spanned five years and involved 17 WTO members. In addition to the disputing members, 12 participated as third parties in the Panel, AB and/or subsequent Article 21.5 compliance proceedings (Australia, Ecuador, El Salvador, the EC, Guatemala, Hong Kong, Japan, Mexico, Nigeria, The Philippines, Singapore and Venezuela).

[8] According to the FAO *Global Study of Shrimp Fisheries* (2008).

[9] See WWF, 'Fact Sheet—Sea Turtle By-Catch—a Global Issue' (2017). Dolphins, seahorses, dugongs, albatrosses, and penguins also perish: ibid. For general discussion of the background to *US—Shrimp* see MA Young, *Trading Fish, Saving Fish: The Interaction between Regimes in International Law* (Cambridge, CUP, 2011) Ch 4.

[10] 993 UNTS 243, in force 1 July 1975. At the time of these proceedings, all seven species of sea turtle were listed under Appendix I as species threatened with extinction, all but two of which occurred in US waters.

[11] In 2009, the FAO produced non-binding global *Guidelines to Reduce Sea Turtle Mortality in Fishery Operations* (Rome, FAO, 2009).

[12] Concluded in 1996, but did not enter into force until 2001 upon the eighth ratification. Apart from this agreement, noted the AB, the record before the Panel 'does not indicate any serious, substantial efforts [by the US Secretary of State] to carry out [the] express directions of Congress' under Section 609(a) to negotiate bilateral or multilateral agreements ... for the protection and conservation of ... sea turtles': AB Report (n 1) [167].

turtle mortality.[13] In response, the US National Marine Fisheries Service (NMFS) developed a turtle excluder device (TED) for shrimp trawler nets which provided a 'trapdoor' for turtles to escape from the net. When a programme encouraging voluntary use of TEDs proved ineffective, legislative steps were taken requiring all US shrimp trawl vessels to use approved TEDs in specified areas where there was significant turtle mortality in shrimp trawls.[14] This was followed in 1989 by Section 609 of Public Law 101–102,[15] implemented through Guidelines, and which ultimately led to the WTO proceedings.[16]

Section 609 provided for an import ban on shrimp harvested with commercial fishing technology which may adversely affect sea turtles protected under US law. Harvesting states could escape the ban only through a certification process further specified in the subsequent Guidelines.[17] These required demonstration that a regulatory programme comparable to the US programme was in place regarding the incidental taking of sea turtles *and* that the average rate of incidental taking of sea turtles was comparable to that in the US.[18] For certification it was not sufficient to demonstrate that shrimp harvesting methods were comparable in effectiveness to those required under US law; ie what was required was a country-based measure, not merely a process-based measure (or 'how-to' restrictions).[19] Initially limited in its geographic application to the wider Caribbean/western Atlantic region, in 1996 the ban was made global.[20]

---

[13] LD Jenkins, 'Reducing Sea Turtle Bycatch in Trawl Nets: A History of NFMS Turtle Excluder Device ([by the TED) Research' (2012) 74 *Marine Fisheries Review* 2, 26.

[14] 52 Fed Reg 24244, 29 June 1987.

[15] 16 USC 1537.

[16] There was considerable resistance to these measures from US shrimpers, leading inter alia to the 'first successful blockade of US harbors since the War of 1812': M Donnelly, 'The History and Politics of Turtle Device Regulations' (1989) 6 *Endangered Species UPDATE* 11, 1; see also P Cressick, 'Explaining US Policy on *Shrimp—Turtle*' in E Brown Weiss, JH Jackson and N Bernasconi-Osterwalder (eds), *Reconciling Environment and Trade* (The Hague, Nijhoff, 2001) 504 and AV Margavio and CJ Forsyth, *Caught in the Net: The Conflict between Shrimpers and Conservationists* (Texas, Texas A&M University Press, 1996). Constitutional challenges were made to the legislation and unsuccessful attempts to use state law to block the measures: see eg *State of Louisiana, ex rel Guste v Verity* (29 February 1988) [US District Court, ED LA] 681 F Supp 1178 and *State of Louisiana, ex rel Guste v Verity* (15 August 1988) [US Court of Appeals, 5th Cir] 853 F.2d 322. The regulations were finally reinstated on 15 October 1989 as the result of environmental NGOs litigation seeking effective turtle protection under the Endangered Species Act: see *National Wildlife Federation, et al v Mosbacher* (11 August 1989) [US District Court, ED LA] Civ A No 89-2089.

[17] Guidelines were issued in 1991 (56 Fed Reg 1051) and revised in 1993 (58 Fed Reg 9015) and 1996 (61 Fed Reg 17342). For the record of certifications as of 1 January 1998, see Panel Report [2.16].

[18] Or that the 'fishing environment of the harvesting country did not pose a threat of incidental taking of sea turtles in the course of shrimp harvesting'.

[19] B Cooreman, 'Addressing Environmental Concerns Through Trade: A Case for Extraterritoriality?' (2016) 65 *ICLQ* 229, 244, drawing on Charnovitz's similar distinction between government policy and 'how to' restrictions: S Charnovitz, 'The Law of "PPMs" in the WTO: Debunking the Myth of Illegality' (2002) 27 *Yale JIL* 59. For the AB this was 'proof' that 'the measure in application was more concerned with effectively influencing other WTO Members to adopt the same policy, rather than inquiring into the appropriateness of different comparable programs to protect the concern at issue'. ibid 244 fn 78.

[20] This was in response to a ruling by the US Court of International Trade (CIT) that the initial 1991 Guidelines' restricted application to the wider Caribbean/Western Atlantic region violated Section 609, with a direction to the Department of State to extend the ban worldwide by 1 May 1996: *Earth Institute v Warren Christopher*, 913 F Supp 559 (CIT, 1995).

The ban had serious impacts on the complainant states where fishing for domestic consumption and for export contributes significantly to their economies.[21] Together, they produced almost a quarter of the world's wild-caught shrimp, with much of this production exported and for which the US was a key market[22] as one of the world's biggest consumers of shrimp.[23] Thus the US market was, and continues to be, extremely important for shrimp-exporting countries. For example, according to Malaysia, 'exports of shrimp to the US market ... constituted about 5.6 per cent of its total export of shrimp in 1995. Malaysia contended that the enforcement by the US of Section 609 had significantly affected the shrimp export industry in Malaysia' and that its exports to the US had fallen by 38 percent as a result.[24] In its arguments before the Panel, Pakistan similarly complained that the US ban had 'decimated Pakistan's exports to the United States', with the value of exports falling by around 65 per cent.[25]

III. THE PROCEEDINGS

India, Malaysia, Pakistan and Thailand[26] complained that the US measures pursuant to the Endangered Species Act of 1973 were contrary to Article XI GATT 1994 which prohibits quantitative restrictions on trade.[27] The Panel found that the US did not dispute that 'with respect to countries not certified under Section 609, [the ban] amounted to a restriction on the importation of shrimp within the meaning of Article XI:1'.[28] The US sought to justify the inconsistent measures under the general exceptions contained in Article XX GATT 1994, specifically paragraph (b) 'necessary to protect human, animal or plant life or health' and paragraph (g) 'relating to the conservation of exhaustible natural resources if such measures are made effective in conjunction with restrictions on domestic production or consumption'. The Panel found violation of Article XI without saving by Article XX, but (erroneously) commenced its consideration of the latter with an analysis of the chapeau[29] leaving

---

[21] See fisheries statistics by country at www.fao.org.

[22] In 1995 Thailand's shrimp exports (including fresh, frozen, wild and farmed shrimp and shrimp products) amounted to over 25% of global shrimp exports by value, India's 6.5%, Malaysia 1.5% and Pakistan about 1%: FAO, Fisheries and Aquaculture Information and Statistics Service, available at www.fao.org.

[23] ibid.

[24] Panel Report [3.120].

[25] ibid [3.121].

[26] Pursuant to Article 4 DSU and Article XXII:1 GATT 1994, the complainants had first requested consultations with the US concerning Section 609 and the 1996 Guidelines, but these failed to arrive at a satisfactory solution: ibid [1.1].

[27] Article 1 and Article XIII GATT were also included in their claim, but not considered further by the Panel given its findings on GATT Article XI: Panel Report [7.22]–[7.23].

[28] ibid [7.13], [7.15], [7.17]. The Panel stressed that this finding was also buttressed by sufficient evidence that such restriction had been imposed: ibid [7.17].

[29] The chapeau to Article XX reads: 'Subject to the requirement that such measures are not applied in a manner that would constitute *a means of arbitrary or unjustifiable discrimination between countries where the same conditions prevail,* or a *disguised restriction on international trade,* nothing in this Agreement shall be construed to prevent the adoption or enforcement by any contracting party of measures' (emphasis added).

prima facie consideration of saving under Article XX(b) or (g) to the second stage of analysis. It found unjustified discrimination between countries where similar conditions prevail and thus held that the US measure at issue 'is not within the scope of measures permitted under Article XX'.[30] Moreover, in interpreting the chapeau to Article XX the Panel placed great emphasis on protection of the world trading system, employing a 'slippery slope' type of argument:

> We are of the opinion that the chapeau of Article XX, interpreted within its context and in the light of the object and purpose of GATT and of the WTO Agreement, only allows Members to derogate from GATT provisions, so long as, in doing so, they do not undermine the WTO multilateral trading system, thus also abusing the exceptions contained in Article XX ... We consequently find that when considering a measure under Article XX, we must determine not only whether the measure on its own undermines the WTO multilateral trading system, *but also whether such type of measure, if it were to be adopted by other Members, would threaten the security and predictability of the multilateral trading system.*[31]

As in the *Tuna/Dolphin* cases,[32] the US legislation was operating in the absence of multilateral rules agreed for the protection of the species in question. The Panel in *US—Shrimp* was at pains to address the international environmental law context, stressing the need 'to reach co-operative agreement on integrated conservation strategies ... taking into account the specific conditions of the different geographical areas concerned'. Sustainable development, one of the objectives of the WTO set forth in the Preamble, is expressly referred to by the Panel in exhorting such multilateral cooperation in order to protect sea turtles 'in a manner consistent with WTO objectives'.[33] Furthermore, it observed that:

> General international law and international environmental law clearly favour the use of negotiated instruments rather than unilateral measures when addressing transboundary or global environmental problems, particularly when developing countries are concerned. Hence a negotiated solution is clearly to be preferred, both from a WTO and an international environmental law perspective.[34]

This comes close to suggesting that not only is protection of the multilateral trading system at the core of the Panel's concern, but that it will be a rare unilateral measure indeed which satisfies not only the conditions of Article XX(b) and (g) but also (as interpreted by the Panel) the chapeau. This lack of balance in addressing trade and environment issues was severely criticised.[35]

The US appealed against the Panel's decision, affording the AB the opportunity to reconsider the balance between trade and environment within the GATT. In particular, it reviewed the rules of general international law relating to treaty interpretation and their application by the Panel in the instant case. Relying on language

---

[30] Panel Report [7.48]–[7.49].
[31] ibid [7.44] emphasis added. This reasoning was held by the AB to constitute an error in legal interpretation and was reversed: see further below.
[32] Above n 5.
[33] Panel Report [7.42], [7.52] and [9.1].
[34] ibid [7.61]
[35] See, eg, R Howse, 'The Turtles Panel: Another Environmental Disaster in Geneva' (1998) 32 *JWT* 73.

drawn implicitly from Article 31 of the Vienna Convention on the Law of Treaties (VCLT),[36] the AB stated the relevant rules to require an 'examination of the ordinary meaning of the words of a treaty, read in their context and in the light of the object and purpose of the treaty involved'.[37] So far, so good. The AB went on, however, to observe, in a misapplication of the requirements of Article 31(1) VCLT, that:

> A treaty interpreter must begin with, and focus upon, the text of the particular provision to be interpreted. It is in the words constituting the provision, read in their context, that the object and purpose of the states parties to the treaty must first be sought. Where the meaning imparted by the text itself is equivocal or inconclusive, or where confirmation of the correctness of the reading of the text itself is desired, light from the object and purpose of the treaty as a whole may usefully be sought.[38]

As Gardiner rightly observes, this is a misreading of Sinclair and the VCLT because the second and third sentences do not reflect the 'proper approach to the first part of the general rule of treaty interpretation, even if they may follow a typical or logical process of thought',[39] in seeking the object and purpose by reference to the particular treaty provision, and then linking recourse to the object and purpose of the treaty with the ordinary meaning of the terms being equivocal or conclusive (a test found in Article 32 VCLT).[40]

Applying this interpretative approach, the AB considered that the Panel had demonstrably failed to give the chapeau of Article XX its 'ordinary meaning'—in particular, by disregarding the reference to the *manner* in which the measures sought to be justified are applied. In *US—Gasoline* the AB had stressed the need to examine not the measure and its specified contents as such, but rather the manner of its application. Here, the Panel had failed properly to consider how the manner of the application of Section 609 constituted 'a means of arbitrary or unjustifiable discrimination between countries where the same conditions prevail, or a disguised restriction on trade' within the meaning of the chapeau. This is a crucial distinction because the Panel's stress upon the nature of the unilateral measures in question,[41] combined with its broad interpretative approach whereby measures which 'undermine the WTO multilateral trading system' fall outside those measures permitted under the chapeau of Article XX, set a virtually inevitable collision course between environmental measures and Article XX. In contrast, the AB took a more nuanced approach: maintaining the multilateral trading system is not an interpretative rule

---

[36] Article 3.2 DSU requires the application of 'customary rules of interpretation of public international law' of which Art 31(1) VCLT is a general reflection. In addition to its own case law, the AB relies on I Sinclair, *The Vienna Convention on the Law of Treaties*, 2nd edn (MUP, 1984) for the general rule of interpretation set forth in Art 31(1), in particular the application of the object and purpose test: [114] n 82.

[37] AB Report (n 1) [114].

[38] ibid, citing Sinclair 130–31.

[39] R Gardiner, *Treaty Interpretation*, 2nd edn (Oxford, OUP, 2015) 133.

[40] ibid 133–34; see also D Shanker, 'The Vienna Convention on the Law of Treaties, the Dispute Settlement System of the WTO and the Doha Declaration on the TRIPs Agreement' (2002) 36 *JWT* 721, 741–42.

[41] AB Report [115], referred to also by the AB as 'the design of the measure itself'.

to be applied in interpreting specific provisions of the GATT but rather 'a fundamental and pervasive premise underlying the WTO Agreement'.[42] Indeed, the purpose of the chapeau had been identified in the *US—Gasoline* case where the AB
indicated that its purpose 'is generally the prevention of abuse of exceptions of
[Article XX]'.[43]

Not only was its interpretative approach flawed, but the Panel had also ignored
the careful two-step process enunciated in earlier case law whereby the specific paragraphs of Article XX are examined before reviewing the applicability of the conditions set forth in the chapeau.[44] The AB reversed the Panel's finding that Section 609
fell outside the scope of measures permitted under Article XX and thus found it
necessary to conduct the two-stage legal analysis eschewed by the Panel, namely, to
consider whether the US could claim justification for Section 609 under Article XX(g)
and then to test such justification, if made, by the conditions of the chapeau.[45] The
first question for the AB was whether Section 609 is a measure concerned with the
conservation of 'exhaustible natural resources' within the meaning of Article XX(g),
a phrase it considered 'is not "static" in its content or reference but is rather "by
definition, evolutionary"'.[46] Accordingly, the AB explicitly adopted an evolutive
approach[47] to interpretation of Article XX(g) 'in the light of contemporary concerns of the community of nations about the protection and conservation of the
environment'.[48] Though Article XX was not amended in the Uruguay Round, the
AB drew inspiration for this evolutive approach from the preamble to the WTO
Agreement which refers, inter alia, to 'the objective of sustainable development,
seeking both to protect and preserve the environment and to enhance the means for
doing so', which demonstrates that the states parties to the WTO Agreement were
'fully aware of the importance and legitimacy of environmental protection as a goal
of national and international policy'.[49] Such language 'demonstrates a recognition
by WTO negotiators that optimal use of the world's resources should be made in
accordance with the objective of sustainable development'.[50] It adds 'colour, texture and shading to the rights and obligations of members under the WTO Agreement, generally, and under the GATT 1994, in particular'.[51] The AB then relied on a

---

[42] ibid [116].

[43] Above (n 5) [22].

[44] The Panel expressly seeks to justify such express departure at [7.28]. For criticism of this two-stage
approach, see L Bartels, 'The Chapeau of the General Exceptions in the WTO GATT and GATS Agreements: A Reconstruction' (2015) 109 *AJIL* 95.

[45] Article XX(b) was also invoked by the US, but only in the alternative should the Article XX(g)
justification fail.

[46] AB Report [130] citing general international law sources including the *Namibia (Legal Consequences) Advisory Opinion* [1971] ICJ Rep 31 and the *Aegean Sea Continental Shelf Case* [1978] ICJ
Rep 3.

[47] ibid [130].

[48] ibid [129].

[49] ibid.

[50] ibid [153]. The AB also notes there is no evidence of the intention of the original drafters of
Article XX to exclude living resources from the ambit of Article XX(g) ([131] n 81) and that earlier
adopted panel reports had found fish to be an 'exhaustible natural resource' within the meaning of
Article XX(g) [131].

[51] ibid [155]. In addition, the AB noted the creation of the WTO Committee on Trade and Environment (CTE) in 1994 and the preamble to the Ministerial Decision on Trade and Environment which

number of 'modern international conventions and declarations [which] make frequent reference to natural resources as embracing both living and non-living resources'[52] to support its conclusion that 'living resources are just as "finite" as petroleum, iron ore and other non-living resources'.[53] At the end of this part of its analysis the AB also cites the principle of effectiveness in support of this conclusion on the interpretation of Article XX(g).[54]

Turning to the specific issue of whether the sea turtles in particular are 'exhaustible', the AB swiftly concluded that they are, not least since all seven species of sea turtle are listed in Appendix I of CITES. All the participants in the appeal were parties to CITES, which continues to enjoy widespread support.[55] Whether there is any jurisdictional limitation on the scope of Article XX(g) was *not* expressly considered since sea turtles are highly migratory species and occur, inter alia, within US waters over which it clearly has jurisdiction. The AB thus found 'sufficient nexus' between the sea turtles and the US.[56]

The AB then examined the question of whether the measure sought to be justified 'relates to' the conservation of exhaustible natural resources. Once again, the interpretative methodology of the AB is clearly expressed: 'In making this determination, the treaty interpreter essentially looks into the relationship between the measure at stake and the legitimate policy of conserving exhaustible natural resources'.[57] The widespread participation of all states, including the participants in the present dispute, in CITES underscores the legitimacy of the concern. More particularly, however, the AB considered it necessary to 'examine the relationship between the general structure and design of the measure here at stake, Section 609, and the policy goal it purposes to serve, that is, the conservation of sea turtles',[58] adopting

states, inter alia, 'that there should not be, nor need be, any policy contradiction between upholding and safeguarding an open, non-discriminatory and equitable multilateral trading system on the one hand, and acting for the protection of the environment, and the promotion of sustainable development, on the other'.

[52] It refers to the 1982 UN Convention on the Law of the Sea (UNCLOS), the 1992 Convention on Biological Diversity (CBD), and the 1979 Convention on the Conservation of Migratory Species of Wild Animals (CMS), in each case simply noting in a footnote the extent of participation by the parties to the dispute, and to Agenda 21: [130]. For discussion of how the Panel and AB in *US-Shrimp* acquired information about these other regimes, see Young (n 9) 206–24. There is no explicit interpretative justification for relying on these instruments which appear to be provided as context in evidencing a shift in legal opinion since the adoption of GATT 1947: see below text to n 117. On the use of other international law as context, see I Van Damme, *Treaty Interpretation by the WTO Appellate Body* (Oxford, OUP, 2009) 258–59.

[53] AB Report [128].

[54] ibid [131], citing previous AB Reports including *US—Gasoline* and *Japan—Alcoholic Beverages*, and a range of general international law authorities including *Oppenheim* and *Sinclair*.

[55] See further <www.cites.org>. At the time of the AB's decision, there were 144 states parties to CITES.

[56] AB Report (n 1) [133]. Nor was the matter explored further in the recent *EC—Seals* case owing to lack of argument on this point by the parties, leaving the question open whether trade measures aimed to address environmental concerns outside the territory of the regulating State are justifiable: WTO, AB Report, *European Communities—Measures Prohibiting the Importation and Marketing of Seal Products* (2014) WT/DS401/AB/R [5.173]. For critique and a proposed 'extraterritoriality decision tree' see Cooreman, 'Addressing Environmental Concerns' (n 19).

[57] AB Report (n 1) [135].

[58] ibid [37].

the methodology employed in examining the baseline regulation of the Clean Air Act in *US—Gasoline*. Here the design of the measure *is* relevant. The AB found 'The means and end relationship between Section 609 and the legitimate policy of conserving an exhaustible, and in fact, endangered species, is observably a close and real one, a relationship every bit as substantial as that which we found in *US—Gasoline* between the EPA baseline establishment rules and the conservation of clean air in the United States'.[59] It also determined that such measures were made effective 'in conjunction with' restrictions on US shrimp trawl vessels ('in principle, Section 609 is an even-handed measure'), thus leaving only the hurdle of satisfaction of the chapeau conditions for the US measure to be a justifiable exception under Article XX.

The AB's characterisation of Section 609 as a 'legitimate' environmental measure should be contrasted with the later finding of the US Court of Appeals for the Federal Circuit in reviewing the Court of International Trade's decision in *Turtle Island*,[60] when it held that its 'legislative history' showed that Section 609 was primarily 'focused on protecting the domestic shrimp industry, not the sea turtle'.[61] Although invited to do so in the parties' pleadings, the AB was seemingly reluctant to pierce the sovereign veil to consider the legislative history of the import ban and whether Section 609 constituted a 'disguised restriction' on trade.

The general interpretative approach of the AB to the chapeau has already been detailed above. In its light, the exceptions of (a) to (j) of Article XX are revealed as *limited* and *conditional* exceptions from substantive GATT obligations, subject to compliance with the chapeau. Indeed, the AB likens the chapeau conditions to an obligation of good faith in the exercise of rights under the GATT.[62] It thus considers whether the application of the measure provisionally justified under Article XX(g) constitutes 'unjustifiable discrimination ... or a disguised restriction on trade' within the meaning of the chapeau. As in *US—Gasoline* the measure fell at this final hurdle, for the AB held that in its application Section 609 had 'intended an actual coercive effect on the specific policy decisions made by foreign governments, Members of the WTO'.[63] Any flexibility intended in the primary legislation was swept aside by the 1996 Guidelines and the practical administration of the certification scheme which required a demonstration that the regulatory programme requires the use of turtle extractor device or a requirement falling within the extremely limited exceptions available to US shrimp trawlers. 'Other measures the harvesting nation undertakes to protect sea turtles' referred to in the Guidelines were of little relevance in administrative practice. In sum, the AB found 'the effect of the application of Section 609 is to establish a rigid and unbending standard' requiring other WTO members to adopt a regulatory program that is not merely comparable, but rather *essentially the same*, as that applied to the United States shrimp trawl vessels'.[64]

---

[59] ibid [141].

[60] *Turtle Island Restoration Network v Mallett* (19 Jul 2000) 110 F.Supp.2d 1005.

[61] *Turtle Island Restoration Network v Evans* (21 March 2002) 284 F.3d 1282, 1295.

[62] AB Report (n 1) [158], as both a general principle of law and a general principle of international law.

[63] ibid [161].

[64] ibid [163] (emphasis in original).

The final obstacle to success in meeting the conditions of the chapeau was the evidence that even states complying with the regulatory conditions of the scheme, ie shrimp caught using methods identical to those in the US, would be subject to the import ban if the shrimp were caught in the waters of a non-certified state. This suggests to the AB 'that this measure, in its application, is more concerned with effectively influencing WTO members to adopt essentially the same comprehensive regulatory regime as that applied by the United States to its domestic shrimp trawlers, even though many of those Members may be differently situated'.[65] Coupled with the failure to respond vigorously to the exhortation in the legislation to seek bilateral and multilateral agreements for sea turtle conservation,[66] the AB had little difficulty in determining that the measure had been applied in an unjustifiably discriminatory fashion. It also found the discrimination to be arbitrary, thus depriving the measure of Article XX protection and rendering unnecessary consideration of the final limb of the chapeau (disguised restriction on trade).[67]

Both the language and methodology of the AB is a striking departure from the wording and the approach of the Panel Report, and demonstrates a willingness to strike a more even balance between trade and environment concerns. Of particular note is the acceptance of an unsolicited NGO brief, a move consonant with general measures within the WTO to improve transparency and access for, though not the direct participation of, NGOs.[68] In *US—Shrimp* the AB took the view that the Panel erred in its legal interpretation that accepting non-requested information from non-governmental sources was incompatible with the DSU.[69] However, in a 'practical disposition of the matter' endorsed by the AB, the Panel permitted the parties to put forward the documents, or parts thereof, and the US duly attached part of an NGO brief as an annex to its second submission to the Panel.[70] This was not the first time such 'practical disposition' was adopted by a dispute settlement body: there is no provision for *amicus* briefs in the ICJ's Statute yet it permitted Hungary to adopt NGO material as part of its submission in the *Gabčíkovo—Nagymaros* case.[71]

---

[65] ibid [165].

[66] Only one agreement had been concluded, the 1996 Inter-American Convention for the Protection and Conservation of Sea Turtles (n 12). See further www.seaturtle.org.

[67] This limb of the chapeau has been relatively unexplored: Bartels, 'A Reconstruction' (n 44).

[68] As part of this initiative see <www.wto.org/wto/ngo/contact.htm>. The WTO's Committee on Trade and Environment has a number of observers from intergovernmental bodies, including representatives of the Secretariat of the CBD and CITES.

[69] This was one of the issues raised in the United States appeal: *US–Shrimp* [98 et seq]. The Panel received a brief from the Center for Marine Conservation (CMC) and the Center for International Environmental Law (CIEL), and one from the World Wide Fund for Nature: ibid [99]. The CMC also played a domestic role, threatening legal proceedings against the Secretary of Commerce for failing to fulfil his mandate under the ESA and indicating that it would call for a moratorium on all shrimp fishing in waters in which sea turtles are present: see further Donnelly, 'History and Politics' (n 16) 2; Margavio and Forsyth, *Caught in the Net* (n 16) 8.

[70] Section III of the CMC/CIEL brief: ibid [110]. See generally G Umbricht, 'An "Amicus Curiae Brief" on Amicus Curiae Briefs at the WTO' (2001) 4 *JIEL* 773.

[71] [1997] ICJ Rep 7; see currently Practice Direction XII. See generally A-K Lindblom, *Non-Governmental Organisations and International Law* (Cambridge, CUP, 2005). ITLOS has similarly grappled with the introduction of *amicus* briefs in the absence of express authority to do so in its Statute, through its Rules of Procedure and judicial practice: see for example *The Arctic Sunrise Case (Kingdom of the Netherlands v Russian Federation)* Case No 22, Order of 22 November 2013 and, generally, A Dolidze, 'The Arctic Sunrise and NGOs in International Judicial Proceedings' (2014) 18 *ASIL Insights* 1.

This introduction of external views into a 'members only' WTO dispute settlement procedure has, however, proved controversial,[72] though in practice panels and the AB have been 'very restrained in actually considering them'.[73]

More generally, the reliance by the AB in *US—Shrimp* on general international law principles, as well as general principles of international environmental law, is striking. Most telling is the AB's awareness of its wider audience, for it concludes, inter alia, with what the appeal has *not* decided:

> We have *not* decided that the protection and preservation of the environment is of no significance to the Members of the WTO. Clearly, it is. We have *not* decided that the sovereign nations that are Members of the WTO cannot adopt effective measures to protect endangered species, such as sea turtles. Clearly, they can and should. And we have *not* decided that sovereign states should not act together bilaterally, plurilaterally or multilaterally, either within the WTO or in other international fora, to protect endangered species or otherwise protect the environment. Clearly, they should and do.[74]

As it transpired, this did not prove to be the AB's final word on the matter. The AB Report adopted by the WTO's DSB on 6 November 1998 was accompanied by the recommendation that the US bring the import prohibition into conformity with its obligations under the WTO Agreement. However, in implementing the decision and recommendations the US did not amend Section 609—with the import prohibition on uncertified states remaining intact—but instead issued Revised Guidelines under which a state might seek certification on the basis that it has implemented and enforced a 'comparably effective' regulatory programme to protect sea turtles without the use of TEDs. On 12 October 2000 Malaysia, one of the original complainants, requested the matter be remitted back to the original panel as it is entitled to do under the DSU where non-compliance with a DSB ruling is alleged. It argued that the US had failed to lift the import prohibition and had not taken 'the necessary measures to allow the importation of certain shrimp and shrimp products in an unrestrictive manner' and challenged the Revised Guidelines as insufficiently flexible to meet the requirements of the Article XX chapeau.[75] Malaysia also argued that the US had failed to take adequate steps to negotiate and conclude an international agreement on sea turtle protection before imposing the unilateral import ban. In justifying its steps regarding compliance, the US stressed, inter alia, its continuing efforts to secure agreement with Governments in the Indian Ocean region on the protection of sea

---

[72] See further R Howse, 'Membership and its Privileges: The WTO, Civil Society, and the *Amicus* Brief Controversy' (2003) 9 *EJIL* 496 and P Mavroidis, '*Amicus curiae* Briefs Before the WTO: Much Ado About Nothing' in A von Bogdandy, P Mavroidis and Y Meny (eds), *European Integration and International Co-ordination, Studies in Transnational Economic Law in Honour of Claus-Dieter Ehlermann* (The Hague, Kluwer, 2002) 317. Opposition was exacerbated by the special procedures for *amicus* briefs adopted in the subsequent *US-Asbestos* where the AB anticipated a high volume of brief from public interest NGOs (see further Young (n 9) 221) and by the perception that briefs from environmental and labour NGOs in particular would argue against the interests of developing countries and their right to exploit their own resources: see further J Bhagwati, 'Afterword: The Question of Linkage' (2002) 96 *AJIL* 126.

[73] Young (n 9) 221–24.

[74] AB Report (n 1) [185].

[75] *United States—Import Prohibition on Certain Shrimp and Shrimp Products*, Recourse to Article 21.5 of the DSU by Malaysia, Report of the AB, 22 October 2001, WT/DS58/AB/RW, [6], '*Malaysia Recourse*'.

turtles in that region.[76] The Panel noted these ongoing 'serious good faith efforts', as did the AB, which stressed that requiring the conclusion of an agreement would be unreasonable and that the mere failure to do so did not constitute 'arbitrary or unjustifiable discrimination' under the Article XX chapeau solely because agreement was reached with some parties but not with others.[77] As for the Revised Guidelines, the AB rejected the Malaysian argument that once again the measures unilaterally imposed US domestic standards on exporters, since on application for certification US authorities were permitted to take into account the specific conditions of Malaysian shrimp production and of its sea turtle conservation programme.[78]

IV. *US—SHRIMP* AS A LANDMARK

A. *US—Shrimp's* Legacy Within the WTO

We could consider *US—Shrimp* a landmark merely because of its impact within trade law and on the 'trade and environment' debate.[79] Subsequent panels and the AB routinely cite the AB Report in *US—Shrimp*—usually alongside *US—Gasoline*—as the starting point for any analysis under Article XX. The AB's decision in *US—Shrimp* is also frequently cited in disputes concerning Articles 2 of the SPS and TBT Agreements.[80] This is unsurprising given the preambles to both Agreements repeat the wording of the chapeau of Article XX GATT.

In this context *US—Shrimp* is generally cited as authority for five main points. First, that the interpretation and application of Article XX requires a 'two-tiered' approach under which a measure must be shown to be provisionally justified by a paragraph (a) to (j) exception before its chapeau-compliance is assessed.[81] Second, that both as a requirement of and expression of the principles of 'good faith' and '*abus de droit*' a panel or the AB assessing a measure under Article XX must seek to 'balance' or find 'equilibrium' between Members' right to invoke the exceptions and other Members' substantive rights under the WTO Agreement.[82] Third, that an assessment under the substantive paragraphs of Article XX requires the completion of a 'means–ends' inquiry. The standard of connection required under each individual exception is considered to shift along a sliding scale depending on the language employed—whether a measure must be 'necessary' for or merely 'relate

---

[76] ibid [115].

[77] ibid [123].

[78] ibid [148].

[79] See, eg, the contributions to 9 *Ybk IEL* (1998) by Brack, Mann and Wirth; R Howse, 'The AB Rulings in the Shrimp/Turtle Case: A New Legal Baseline for the Trade and Environment Debate?' (2002) 27 *Columbia JEL* 491; and JH Knox, 'The Judicial Resolution of Conflicts Between Trade and Environment' (2004) 28 *Harv ELR* 1.

[80] See, eg: *India—Agricultural Products*, Panel Report (14 October 2014) WT/DS430/R, [7.432], [7.434]; *US–Tuna II*, AB Report (16 May 2012) WT/DS381/AB/R, [226], [339] et seq.

[81] *China—Raw Materials*, AB Report [354]; *China—Rare Earths*, AB Report [5.87]–[5.89]; *EC—Seal Products*, AB Report [5.169].

[82] *Brazil—Tyres*, AB Report [224]; *EC—Seal Products*, AB Report [5.297]; see also the EC's arguments in *EC—Asbestos*, Panel Report [3.499].

to' its intended purpose.[83] Fourth, subsequent panels and the AB have reaffirmed
US—Shrimp's distinction between a measure's 'design and structure' and its 'application',
reiterating that a measure may comply with Article XX on its face, be provisionally
justified under a valid exception, and yet be *applied* in a manner that breaches the
chapeau requirements.[84] As per the AB decision in *US—Shrimp* subsequent decision makers have focused on the institutions, processes and procedures involved in
application.[85] Fifth, *US—Shrimp* is frequently cited in support of the view that discrimination may arise where countries in which *different* conditions prevail (or may
prevail) are treated the *same*, as well as when countries in which the *same conditions
prevail* are treated differently, or the 'discrimination-as-inflexibility' thesis.[86]

US—Shrimp has thus been described as marking the beginning of a 'procedural
turn' in WTO jurisprudence on Article XX.[87] As Lang notes, the AB made significant efforts to focus, not on the environmental purpose of the measure, nor whether
it was a disguised restriction on trade, but on 'the institutions, structures and procedures through which' the Section 609 import ban was applied:

> Conceptually, then, the key move in this case was to determine the legitimacy of the US
> measure in question not by reference to some technically defined ideal of an optimally
> regulated market, nor through the application of a balancing or proportionality test, but
> rather by reference to the administrative ideal of good governance articulated as due pro-
> cess, or procedurally proper administration. What was subject to scrutiny were the proce-
> dures, structures and institutions forming the context in which the regulatory measure was
> applied, not the substantive legitimacy or efficacy of its content.[88]

In *US—Shrimp* the AB continued its move, begun in *US—Gasoline*, toward establishing Article XX's chapeau as essentially a good governance provision. But what
conception of good governance and what assumptions, legal and conceptual, underpin its assessment? As academic discussion since *US—Shrimp* was decided has illu-
minated, the AB left space for a variety of approaches.[89] On one view, focus on
the procedural aspects allows both for appropriate scrutiny of domestic (generally

---

[83] *EC—Biotech*, Panel Report [7.94]; *Thailand—Cigarettes*, AB Report (17 June 2011) WT/DS371/
AB/R, [194]; *China—Raw Materials*, AB Report [355]; *China—Rare Earths* [5.90], [5.105], [5.111];
US–Tuna II, Art 21.5 Panel Report (14 April 2015) WT/DS381/RW, [7.513], [7.531].

[84] *China-Rare Earths* [5.96]; *US-Animals*, Panel Report [7.573], [7.620]–[7.621].

[85] See also the AB's use of *US-Shrimp* in support of the view that Article X(3) GATT 'establishes certain
minimum standards for transparency and procedural fairness in Members' administration of their trade
regulations': *Thailand-Cigarettes*, AB Report [202].

[86] See, eg: *India—Agricultural Products*, Panel Report (14 October 2014) WT/DS430/R, [7.432],
[7.434]; *US—Animals*, Panel Report (WT/DS447/R [7.620]; *US–Poultry*, Panel Report (29 September
2010) WT/DS392/R, [7.292]; See too the US's arguments in: *US—Tuna II*, AB Report (20 November
2015) WT/DS381/AB/R [7.311], [7.327]; However, *cf: US–Tuna II*, Art 21.5 Panel Report (14 April
2015) WT/DS381/RW, [7.574], where the panel re-emphasised that the chapeau requires the '*same*
conditions' to prevail for a finding of discrimination.

[87] A Lang, *World Trade Law after Neoliberalism: Reimagining the Global Economic Order* (Oxford,
OUP, 2011), 326.

[88] ibid.

[89] ibid, 239–41; see more generally E Fisher, *Risk Regulation and Administrative Constitutionalism*
(Oxford, Hart, 2007) and B Rigod, *Optimal Regulation and the Law of International Trade* (Cambridge,
CUP, 2015).

regulatory) measures, and appropriate deference to domestic decision-making.[90] But we could also see this shift as the AB shying away from making *explicit* judgments regarding the substantive aims of a measure, in favour of doing so *implicitly* or indirectly through construing the chapeau as giving rise to minimum (but often vague) good governance standards.

US—Shrimp's language of 'balancing' and 'equilibrium', and the view decision-makers must interpret Article XX and police its invocation so as to prevent its 'abuse' now strongly pervades subsequent Panels' and the AB's decisions. This is particularly true of decisions dealing with the exceptions in inter alia paragraphs (a), (b), and (d) that employ the language of 'necessity', where Panels and the AB frequently employ the language of 'weighing and balancing' in assessing the Article XX consistency of measures.[91] Some have even gone so far as to suggest that Panels and the AB have adopted a proportionality standard in assessing measures' compliance under Article XX.[92]

B. *US—Shrimp's* Legacy in General International Law

i. *International Dispute Settlement*

US—Shrimp is clearly regarded as a landmark—or at least a point of departure—in several contexts in WTO jurisprudence. It is difficult, however, to say the same of its influence in other areas of international dispute settlement. By way of illustration, the ICJ has not made reference to the case in any judgment to date, although Ecuador expressly relied upon the WTO's decision in *US—Shrimp* in support of the 'principle' of 'evolutionary interpretation' in its memorial in the *Aerial Spraying* case before the ICJ.[93] Further, and in spite of a clear—and arguably growing—tendency on the part of parties and tribunals to refer to WTO cases in the context of investment dispute settlement, *US—Shrimp* appears to have been referred to only a handful of times in investment arbitration: by the tribunals in *ADF v US*[94] and

---

[90] M Andenas and S Zleptnig, 'Proportionality: WTO Law in Comparative Perspective' (2006–2007) 42 *Tex ILJ* 371, 412

[91] See, eg: *Korea—Beef*, AB Report (11 December 2000) WT/ DS161/AB/R, [164]; *China—Rare Earths*, AB Report, [5.116]; and *India—Solar Cells*, Panel Report (24 February 2016) WT/DS456/R, [7.349]; *Argentina—Goods and Services*, AB Report (14 April 2016) WT/DS453/AB/R [6.221].

[92] See, eg, M Hilf, 'Power, rules and principles—which orientation for WTO/GATT law?' (2001) 4 *JIEL* 111, 120 et seq; Andenas and Zleptnig (n 90) 421; E Vranes, *Trade and the Environment: Fundamental Issues in International Law, WTO Law, and Legal Theory* (Oxford, OUP, 2009) 283; G Bücheler, *Proportionality in Investor-State Arbitration* (Oxford, OUP, 2015) 70–71.

[93] Memorial of Ecuador (Vol I) (28 April 2009) *Case Concerning Aerial Herbicide Spraying (Ecuador v Colombia*, ICJ, [8.76].

[94] For the proposition that the object and purpose of treaty parties is to be 'found, in the first instance, in the words in fact used by the parties': *ADF v US* [Award] (9 January 2003) ICSID Case No ARB(AF)/00/1, [147].

Venezuela Holdings v Venezuela,[95] and by the complainant investors in *Merrill & Ring v Canada*[96] and *SD Myers v Canada*.[97]

US—Shrimp was however relied upon by the tribunal in the *Iron Rhine* arbitration which cited the AB's reasoning to support the general proposition that some 'generic' treaty terms require the interpreter to take into account developments that occurred subsequent to the treaty's completion.[98] And it was cited by Judge Pinto de Albuquerque in his separate opinion in *Hermann v Germany* for the existence of 'a broad concept of environment balance which includes animal life and welfare' as having 'been repeatedly enshrined in international environmental law' when considering the extent to which animals are protected under the European Convention on Human Rights in the context of conscientious objection to hunting.[99]

The scarcity of express references to *US—Shrimp* in dispute settlement outside trade law is somewhat surprising, given the AB's reliance on the general principles of '*abus de droit*' and 'good faith'[100] in developing its interpretation of 'unjustifiable discrimination' as generating general duties of cooperation, flexibility and procedural fairness. Arguably the AB's reasoning in giving effect to these principles could have reached further than the chapeau of Article XX GATT, especially as a core element of the AB's reasoning was based on the concept that all treaty (and by logic also customary) rights must be exercised 'bona fide, that is to say, reasonably'.[101] Perhaps this is explained because, as Howse noted in 2002, the AB does not appear to have been elaborating a general, 'self-standing duty to cooperate',[102] but rather used the general principles and the 'duties' to cooperate in the environmental agreements cited to support a particular reading of the express terms of Article XX.[103]

---

[95] *Mobil Corp, Venezuela Holdings BV & ors v Venezuela* [Decision on Jurisdiction] (10 Jun 2010) ICSID Case No ARB /07/27, [175]. The tribunal, which included former ICJ President Judge Guillaume, quoted the AB's discussion of the principles of good faith and *abus de droit*.

[96] The claimant referred to the AB's interpretation of 'arbitrary' and 'unjustifiable discrimination' in its fair and equitable treatment claim under Article 1105 NAFTA: *Merrill & Ring v Canada* [Award] (31 March 2010) UNCITRAL, [156].

[97] *SD Myers Inc v Canada* [Separate Opinion of B P Schwartz to Partial Award] (12 Nov 2000) NAFTA, UNCTRAL, [241]. Schwartz accepted the claimant's arguments that the AB's approach to transparency and due process under Art X:3 GATT was relevant in interpreting Art 1108 NAFTA's publication requirements.

[98] *Arbitration regarding the Iron Rhine Railway between the Kingdom of Belgium and the Kingdom of the Netherlands* Award] (24 May 2005) XXVII *UNRIAA* 35, 73, [79], citing the AB Report at [130].

[99] Partly Concurring and Partly Dissenting Opinion of Judge Pinto de Albuquerque, *Case of Herrmann v Germany* App No 9300/07 (ECtHR Grand Chamber, 26 June 2012) 34–35. This use seems to stretch the AB's findings quite thin.

[100] AB Report (n 1) [158]; see analysis by M Fitzmaurice, 'Canons of Treaty Interpretation: Selected Case Studies from the World Trade Organization and the North American Free Trade Agreement' (2007) 10 *Austrian RIEL* 41.

[101] ibid.

[102] Howse, 'Membership and its Privileges' (n 72) 508.

[103] On general duties to cooperate see eg: P-M Dupuy, 'The place and role of unilateralism in contemporary international law' (2000) 11 *EJIL* 19, 22ff; R Briese, 'Precaution and Cooperation in the World Trade Organization: An Environmental Perspective' (2002) 22 *Austrian Yearbook of International Law* 113, esp 127, 151; R Pavoni, 'Mutual Supportiveness as a Principle of Interpretation and Law-Making: A Watershed for the 'WTO-and-Competing-Regimes' Debate?' (2010) 21 *EJIL* 649, 666; and P Sands, '"Unilateralism", values, and international law' (2000) 11 *EJIL* 291, 300.

ii. Treaty Interpretation

Undoubtedly the most enduring legacy of *US—Shrimp* in general international law is the AB's approach to treaty interpretation.[104] In a distinct break with pre-1994 GATT jurisprudence, and following its own lead in *US—Gasoline*,[105] the AB interpreted GATT 1994 in accordance with international law on the interpretation of treaties, as codified in Articles 31–33 VCLT, and not in accordance with specific GATT canons of interpretation.[106] This facilitated a more nuanced environmental jurisprudence[107] in particular, because 'the very decision to follow these general public international law interpretative norms enhances the legitimacy of the dispute settlement organs in adjudicating competing values—because these norms are common to international law generally, including regimes that give priority to very different values, and are not specific to a regime that has traditionally privileged a single value, that of free trade'.[108] There are three related aspects of the 'treaty interpretative legacy' of *US—Shrimp*: the principle of mutual supportiveness, the principle of integration, and the evolutive interpretation of treaties.

a. Mutual Supportiveness

Agenda 21 stresses the need to make trade and environment 'mutually supportive' as does Principle 12 of the Rio Declaration.[109] Both are cited by the AB in *US—Shrimp*; indeed, the AB Report and the follow-up compliance report are the

---

[104] For general discussion of 'Who Interprets Treaties?' in the context of the WTO DSU, see Gardiner, *Treaty Interpretation* (n 39) 131–34; for a case study of *US—Shrimp*, inter alia, see Fitzmaurice, 'Canons of Treaty Interpretation' (n 100) 53. On the role of the AB, inter alia, as a distinct epistemic and interpretative community see M Waibel, 'Interpretative Communities in International Law' in A Bianchi, D Peat and M Windsor (eds), *Interpretation in International Law* (Oxford, OUP, 2015) 147. He concludes at 164 that 'Beneath the veneer of uniformity of the VCLT's interpretative principles, distinct interpretative communities have contributed to diverse interpretative approaches in international law'. This chimes with Abi Saab's view that while Panels and the AB make reference to the customary rules on treaty interpretation, their method and underlying assumptions are different to other international legal fora because the WTO 'constitutes a legal universe quite different from the others': G Abi-Saab, 'The AB and Treaty Interpretation' in M Fitzmaurice, OA Elias and P Merkouris (eds), *Issues of Treaty Interpretation and the Vienna Convention on the Law of Treaties: 30 Years On* (Leiden, Nijhoff, 2009) 106.

[105] AB Report (n 1) [16].

[106] It will be recalled that Art 3(2) DSU expressly provides that the existing provisions of the WTO covered agreements are to be clarified 'in accordance with customary rules of interpretation of public international law'. In *US—Gasoline* the AB followed the jurisprudence of the ICJ in determining that the rules of treaty interpretation in the VCLT reflect customary international law and as such are binding on all members: (n 5) [16]–[17].

[107] There is no provision in the DSU for panels adjudicating environmental cases to have specific environmental expertise. However, Charnovitz notes that the presiding judge in the AB which reversed WTO panel decisions that 'threatened to render the environmental exceptions unusable' in *US—Gasoline, Shrimp-Turtle*, and the *EC—Asbestos Cases* was Florentino Feliciano: S Charnovitz, 'The WTO's Environmental Progress' (2007) 10 *JIEL* 685, fn 53.

[108] Howse in J Weiler (ed), *The EU, the WTO and the NAFTA* (Oxford, OUP, 2000), 54.

[109] Agenda 21, 13 June 1992, ch 2. Principle 12 of the 1992 Rio Declaration is analysed by MA Young in J Viñuales (ed), *The Rio Declaration on Environment and Development. A Commentary* (Oxford, OUP, 2015) 325–49. 'Mutual supportiveness' was a key theme in the contributions to the influential trade and environment Agora in the (2002) 96 *AJIL* 1.

only AB decisions to refer directly to Principle 12.[110] It has been argued that similar considerations underpin the reference in the first paragraph of the WTO Agreement preamble to 'the objective of sustainable development'.[111] It reflects a 'synergistic' rather than 'conflict' model of, inter alia, the relationship between environmental protection and trade disciplines.[112] The legal implications of 'mutual supportiveness' are, however, far from clear: is it merely a policy statement, an interpretative guideline or 'principle', a conflict clause allocating hierarchy, or a legal principle?[113] That it may play at least an interpretative role in trade disputes, alongside other principles of treaty interpretation, is illustrated by US—Shrimp which remains the 'high water mark' for such an approach.[114]

b. 'Systemic Integration'

As noted above, the AB referred both to the preamble to the WTO Agreement and to exogenous agreements including the 1982 UNCLOS, CITES, the CBD, and the CMS in the interpretation of 'exhaustible natural resources' in Article XX(g).[115] This was putting into practice what the AB had famously stated in US—Gasoline, viz that the GATT (and by logical inference the other covered agreements) was 'not to be read in clinical isolation from public international law'.[116] However, for each instrument cited the AB merely footnotes the extent of participation by the complainants and the US, from which it is clear that CITES is the only agreement cited to which all five members were party. There is no explicit interpretative justification for relying on these instruments which appear to be provided as context in evidencing a shift in legal opinion since the adoption of GATT 1947.[117] Indeed, McLachlan considers US—Shrimp an example of interpretation of 'general and open-textured' treaty provisions with reference to other areas of international law as context.[118]

On the face of it, then, the AB Report provides only limited support for an interpretation of Article 31(3)(c) VCLT that 'applicable in relations between the parties' can be satisfied by looking to other treaties to which the treaty parties in the

---

[110] Young, ibid, 345.

[111] P-M Dupuy and JE Viñuales, *International Environmental Law* (Cambridge, CUP, 2015) 393. In his overview of the Rio Declaration, Viñuales emphasises the principle of integration as the main expression of the concept of sustainable development, and highlights its influence on treaty practice citing as an example the influence of the preamble to the WTO Agreement in integrating environmental considerations: above (n 109) 25.

[112] For discussion see Pavoni, 'Mutual Supportiveness' (n 103).

[113] Dupuy and Viñuales, *International Environmental Law* (n 111), 394.

[114] This approach was foreshadowed in *US—Gasoline* where the AB recognised the importance of coordinating trade and environmental policies and considered that the language of the Preamble added 'colour, texture and shading' to the interpretation of the WTO covered agreements, a phrase repeated by the AB in *US—Shrimp* [153].

[115] Though in the case of UNCLOS noting specifically that the US considers the relevant living resource provisions to reflect customary international law: *US—Shrimp* [130] fn 77.

[116] *US—Gasoline* (n 5) 17. See generally G Marceau, 'A Call for Coherence in International Law: Praises for the Prohibition Against "Clinical Isolation" in WTO Dispute Settlement' (1999) 33 *JWT* 120.

[117] See above (n 53).

[118] C McLachlan, 'The Principle of Systemic Integration and Article 31(3)(c) of the Vienna Convention' (2005) 54 *ICLQ* 279, 302.

dispute are also parties.[119] In contrast, these references were expressly noted by the Panel in *Malaysia Recourse*, which went on explicitly to cite Article 31(3)(c) VCLT, stating 'the juxtaposition making it appear that the test for the provision's application was whether the parties to the dispute (rather than to the treaty under interpretation) were parties to the other instruments'.[120] Gardiner, however, considers that *US—Shrimp* gives 'scant support' for such interpretation, particularly bearing in mind that in this later phase in proceedings the principal parties had accepted, or committed to accept, all but one of the instruments cited in the early proceedings.[121] Moreover, in later disputes the DSB's approach has been more limited. For example, in *Chile—Price Band* the Panel explicitly parked the question of whether a rule of international law under Article 31(3)(c) VCLT should be applicable in the relations between all WTO members to play a role in interpretation.[122] And in *China—Raw Materials*[123] the Panel explicitly followed the 2006 panel report in *EC—Biotech* in adopting a much narrower understanding of systemic integration, interpreting Article 31(3)(c) to require that another treaty must be applicable to all WTO members in order to be relevant for the purposes of interpretation.[124]

In academic commentary some caution has been expressed regarding the AB's approach to exogenous rules in *US—Shrimp*. For example, Pauwelyn argues that

> Opening the door to rules not legally binding on all WTO members, not even on the disputing parties, may be permissible, but it remains a risky step: When and how will the AB decide that something rises to the level of a 'contemporary concern of the community of nations', 'a widely recognised principle' or a 'broad-based recognition of a particular need'? Any such explanation should not be reached lightly and must be explained.'[125]

As Dunoff puts it more broadly, 'the central challenge posed by the *Shrimp-Turtle* dispute is whether certain people, ideas, doctrines, and policy measures would be permitted within the borders of the international trade regime'.[126]

c. Evolutive Interpretation

The AB explicitly adopted the approach taken by the ICJ in its *Namibia* Advisory Opinion[127] that where the concepts embodied in a treaty are evolutive, their

---

[119] ibid, 314.
[120] *Malaysian Recourse* [5.57]. The Panel did not address the issue whether the other WTO members were parties to these instruments.
[121] Gardiner, *Treaty Interpretation* (n 39) 315.
[122] *Chile—Chile Price Bank System* WT/DS207/R (2002), [7.85] (no relevant rule of international law yielded by the other agreement invoked).
[123] *China—Measures relating to the Exportation of Various Raw Materials* WT/DS394/R, WT/DS395/R, WT/DS398/R (5 July 2011) (Panel Reports) [7.364].
[124] Thus limiting the interpretative effect of the CBD and its Cartagena Protocol on the applicable trade disciplines: *European Communities—Measures affecting the Approval and Marketing of Biotech Products* WT/DS291/R, WT/DS292/R, WT/DS293/R (9 September 2006) [7.68]–[7.70] and [7.74]–[7.75].
[125] J Pauwelyn, 'The Use of Experts in WTO Dispute Settlement' (2002) 51 *ICLQ* 926–27.
[126] JL Dunoff, 'Border Patrol at the World Trade Organization' (1999) 9 *Ybk IEL* 20.
[127] *Legal Consequences for States of the Continued Presence of South Africa in Namibia (South West Africa) notwithstanding UNSC Res 276 (1970)*, Advisory Opinion 21 June 1971, [1971] ICJ Rep 16, 31.

interpretation has to conform with the subsequent development of law.[128] Following in the footsteps of *US—Gasoline*, the AB's approach was grounded in the inclusion of 'sustainable development' as an objective in the preamble to the WTO Agreement[129] and in the 'principle of effectiveness'.[130] As recalled above, the AB considered the term 'exhaustible natural resources' in Article XX(g) 'is not "static" in its content or reference but is rather "by definition evolutionary"'[131] and had to be interpreted 'in the light of contemporary concerns of the community of nations about the protection and conservation of the environment'.[132] It is a generic term.[133]

Subsequently, *US—Shrimp* has been widely cited as an example of the evolutive approach to treaty interpretation. For example, Ecuador relied upon it in support of the 'principle' of 'evolutionary interpretation' in its memorial in the case of *Aerial Spraying* before the ICJ:

> The WTO AB has given a similarly evolutionary interpretation [as that of the ICJ in *Oil Platforms*] to certain terms in the 1947 GATT Agreement. In the *Shrimp-Turtle* decision, for example, it referred inter alia to the 1992 Rio Declaration on Environment and Development, the 1982 UNCLOS, the 1973 CITES Convention, the 1979 Convention on Conservation of Migratory Species and the 1992 Convention on Biological Diversity in order to determine the present meaning of 'exhaustible natural resources'.[134]

There remains significant controversy around what is permissible under an 'evolutionary interpretation' of treaty terms, and what 'law' can permissibly be referred to under Article 31(3)(c) VCLT, a distinction Judge Bedjaoui emphasised in his Separate Opinion in *Gabčíkovo—Nagymaros*.[135] The distinction between interpretation and revision has again recently surfaced in the parties' arguments before the ICJ in *Navigational and Related Rights* regarding the appropriate interpretation of the term 'commerce' in the 1858 Treaty of Limits between Costa Rica and Nicaragua,[136] and in *Aerial Spraying*, concerning the interpretation to be given to Article 14(2) of the 1988 UN Narcotics Convention.[137]

A final observation is that object and purpose is essential to the analysis of interpretation over time but is not in itself a complete guide 'for determining when and

---

[128] This approach was confirmed by the ICJ in the *Gabčíkovo-Nagymaros Project (Hungary v Slovakia)*, Judgment of 25 September 1997, [1997] ICJ Rep 7 [112], in which the Court said that 'Consequently, the Treaty is not static, and is open to adapt to emerging norms of international law'.

[129] AB Report (n 1) [129]–[130].

[130] ibid [131].

[131] ibid [130].

[132] ibid [129]–[132].

[133] On the interpretation of generic terms, see further E Bjorge, *The Evolutionary Interpretation of Treaties* (Oxford, OUP, 2014) 125–27.

[134] Memorial of Ecuador (Vol I) (28 April 2009) *Case Concerning Aerial Herbicide Spraying (Ecuador v Colombia*, ICJ, [8.76].

[135] Above (n 128).

[136] *Dispute Concerning Navigational and Related Rights (Costa Rica v Nicaragua)* [2009] ICJ Rep 213; see, eg, Counter-Memorial of Nicaragua, Vol I (29 May 2007), [4.3.17]–[4.3.18]; Rejoinder of Nicaragua, Vol I (15 July 2008) [1.11], [3.5], [3.96]–[3.98].

[137] *Case Concerning Aerial Herbicide Spraying (Ecuador v Colombia)* ICJ; Memorial of Ecuador (Vol I) (28 April 2009), [8.76]; Counter-Memorial of Colombia, Vol I (29 March 2010), [8.16], [8.80].

how a treaty should be capable of change over time'.[138] One problem is the 'multiple object and purpose' debate. Sir Ian Sinclair—whose work was repeatedly relied upon by the AB in *US—Shrimp*—observed that 'most treaties have no single, undiluted object and purpose but a variety of differing and possibly conflicting objects and purposes'.[139] This doubtless underlies the AB's approach in assessing the purposes of the (dynamic, evolutive) general exceptions clause in Article XX separately from the (static) trade liberalisation object and purpose of the GATT as a whole. Indeed, Arato considers *US—Shrimp* 'usefully illustrates why the question of one or several object(s) and purpose(s) matters'.[140] In acknowledging 'different provisions are included for different reasons, and these reasons should not be subsumed into the general goals of the treaty', the AB paved the way for the 'lonely, but important provision incorporating environmental protection', Article XX(g), 'in a treaty otherwise mostly dedicated to trade liberalisation', to form the evolutive hook for dynamic interpretation of the whole.[141]

V. CONCLUSION

US—Shrimp was a pivotal case for the fledgling dispute settlement system of the WTO, building on the decision in *US—Gasoline* and consolidating a more nuanced approach to the balancing of trade and environment than had been evident under the GATT 1947. It is widely portrayed in the trade law literature as a 'well-reasoned decision of great importance for the trade/environment controversy' with the AB going 'out of its way to emphasise concern for protection of the environment and respect for both general environmental law and international environmental agreements'.[142] While some view it as providing the foundation for justifying trade restrictive measures pursuant to such an agreement under Article XX(b) or (g), a less sanguine view is that the possibility of normative conflict, of competing or even conflicting obligations and objectives, persists within and without the WTO. Nonetheless, from a general international law perspective, the use by the AB of such agreements not binding on the parties as an aid to the interpretation of existing WTO provisions, and the explicit adoption of an evolutive approach to treaty interpretation, remain its most enduring legacy.

---

[138] J Arato, 'Accounting for Difference in Treaty Interpretation Over Time' in A Bianchi, D Peat and M Windsor (eds), *Interpretation in International Law* (Oxford, OUP, 2015) 205, 213.

[139] AB Report (n 1) [130]. See discussion above, text accompanying nn 38–40.

[140] Above (n 138) 214.

[141] ibid.

[142] TJ Schoenbaum, 'International Trade and Environmental Protection' in P Birnie, A Boyle and C Redgwell, *International Law and the Environment*, 2nd edn (Oxford, OUP, 2002) 712.

21

LaGrand (Germany v United States of America) (2001)

CAMERON MILES

One has the suspicion that [*LaGrand*] will hardly prove to be a major contribution to the main stream of World Court jurisprudence.[1]

Throughout [*LaGrand*], the whole question [of the binding character of provisional measures] was bathed in a mysterious and disquieting half-light, provoking such a strange sense of nervous expectation that the only true comparison is with feelings aroused by certain artistic movements by, for example, the opening bars of Beethoven's Ninth Symphony.[2]

I. INTRODUCTION

O N THE MORNING of 7 January 1982, a man was killed and a woman seriously injured during a botched attempt to rob the Valley National Bank in Marana, Arizona.[3] By that evening, two brothers, Karl and Walter LaGrand, were in custody. They were charged with murder and attempted murder in the first degree, as well as attempted armed robbery and two counts of kidnapping. Following a trial before the Arizona Superior Court for Pima County, both men were sentenced to death on 14 December 1984. The jury deliberated for 45 minutes before rejecting the brothers' defence that the murder was unpremeditated.[4]

One might be forgiven for thinking that from the matter would end there—or, more likely, after the seemingly endless series of state and federal appeals that accompany death penalty cases in the United States. It did not. Instead, the conviction and sentencing of the brothers triggered an international incident that was only resolved

---

[1] R Jennings, 'The *LaGrand* Case' (2002) 1 *LPICT* 13, 55. Sir Robert sat on the bench of the ICJ from 1982 to 1995. He served as President from 1991 to 1994.

[2] R Kolb, *The International Court of Justice* (Oxford, Hart, 2013) 638.

[3] Marana is today an incorporated suburb of the city of Tucson, Arizona. The town itself was named for the Spanish word *maraña*—meaning 'thicket'—by railway workers clearing tracks through the area in the nineteenth century. Given the dense tangle of judicial decisions that the *LaGrand* episode produced, this might be considered oddly appropriate.

[4] The facts and procedural history of the criminal prosecution are set out in detail in *State v LaGrand (Karl)*, 733 P.2d 1066 (Ariz 1987); *State v LaGrand (Walter)*, 734 P.2d 563 (Ariz 1987).

by the International Court of Justice (ICJ) in 2001.[5] By then, both of the brothers were dead. Arizona executed Karl LaGrand by lethal injection on 24 February 1999. Walter LaGrand followed on 4 March 1999, electing to die by the gas chamber.

The inter-state aspects of the case did not arise directly from international opposition to the death penalty—though this certainly exacerbated the situation.[6] Rather, it emerged from the brothers' German nationality[7] and the fact that, on arrest, they were entitled to consular assistance under Article 36 of the Vienna Convention on Consular Relations[8] (VCCR). It was the Arizonan authorities' failure to notify the brothers of the availability of assistance that led Germany to file suit before the ICJ in 1999, less than 24 hours before Walter LaGrand was due to be executed.

The significance of *LaGrand* arises not from the Court's conclusions regarding application of the VCCR,[9] but from the Court's decision to settle a long-running debate over whether provisional measures ordered under Article 41 of its Statute were binding. A finding in the affirmative prompted the Court to elaborate, in a series of subsequent decisions, its jurisprudence on interim relief, such that the state of the art today is considerably more complex than that which would have confronted a litigant 15-odd years ago. Furthermore, the fact that other international courts and tribunals look to the ICJ to provide guidance on provisional measures has resulted in a wider dissemination of these ideas than might otherwise be expected.

---

[5] *LaGrand (Germany v US)* [2001] ICJ Rep 466. Noted: X Yang (2001) 60 *CLJ* 441; WJ Aceves (2002) 96 *AJIL* 210; M Mennecke and CJ Tams (2002) 51 *ICLQ* 449; T Stephens (2002) 3 *MJIL* 173. All written and oral submissions pertaining to ICJ cases may be found at www.icj-cij.org (accessed 14 May 2015).

[6] *cf* WA Schabas, 'ICJ Ruling against the United States: It Is Really about the Death Penalty' (2002) 27 *Yale JIL* 445.

[7] Though the execution of foreign nationals by the US is not in itself unusual: as of 2017, 32 foreign nationals have been executed by various states since 1976 and 139 are on 'death row': 'Foreign Nationals and the Death Penalty in the US' (*Death Penalty Information Centre*, 10 February 2015), www.death-penaltyinfo.org/foreign-nationals-and-death-penalty-us (accessed 30 March 2017). After a period of constitutional uncertainty following its decision in *Furman v Georgia*, 408 US 238 (1972), the US Supreme Court in *Gregg v Georgia*, 428 US 153 (1976), *Jurek v Texas*, 428 US 262 (1976) and *Proffitt v Florida*, 428 US 242 (1976) affirmed the constitutionality of death penalty statutes in the three respondent states and, by extension, the death penalty itself.

[8] 24 April 1963, 596 UNTS 261. The precise content of the provision need not detain us overly—it was on the facts of *LaGrand* clearly breached and the US acknowledged as much. For further information, see LT Lee and J Quigley, *Consular Law and Practice* (Oxford, OUP, 2008) 139–85; I Roberts, *Satow's Diplomatic Practice*, 6th edn (Oxford, OUP, 2009) 279–82.

[9] Though that was, in its own way, significant. The Court determined that certain obligations arising under the VCCR could be invoked directly by individuals, the Convention's status as an inter-state agreement notwithstanding: see §IV.D. *cf* SD Murphy, 'Does International Law Obligate States to Open their National Courts to Persons for the Invocation of Treaty Norms that Protect or Benefit Persons?' in D Sloss (ed), *The Role of Domestic Courts in Treaty Enforcement: A Comparative Study* (Cambridge, CUP, 2009) 61. This finding also had a material impact on the way in which capital punishment cases are litigated in the US: HS Schiffman, 'The *LaGrand* Decision: The Evolving Legal Landscape of the Vienna Convention on Consular Relations in US Death Penalty Cases' (2002) 42 *Santa Clara LR* 1099; S Babcock, 'The Limits of International Law: Efforts to Enforce Rulings of the International Court of Justice in US Death Penalty Cases' (2012) 62 *Syracuse LR* 183. The potential for the VCCR to provide a systematic basis of appeal in US criminal cases first recognised in 1994: GD Grisvold, 'Strangers in a Strange Land: Assessing the Fate of Foreign Nationals Arrested in the United States by State and Local Authorities' (1994) 78 *Minn LR* 771. For a *vade mecum* of consular law and practice, see Lee and Quigley, *Consular Law and Practice* (n 8).

To appreciate the seismic character of this determination, we must look first at the historical background of the problem, which began with the drafting of the Statute of the ICJ's predecessor institution, the Permanent Court of International Justice, in 1920.[10]

II. THE HISTORICAL BACKGROUND

A. The Problem Stated

Provisional measures of protection serve a vital function in international litigation,[11] viz to prevent one or both of the parties from taking steps or doing something which would render the final judgment or award nugatory in whole or in part.[12] Such orders may be divided into two distinct species: (a) measures for the protection of rights *pendente lite*; and (b) measures prohibiting any act that would aggravate or otherwise extend the dispute. These concepts were reflected in Article 41 of the PCIJ Statute as follows:

> The Court shall have the power to indicate, if it considers that the circumstances so require, any provisional measures which ought to be taken to reserve the respective rights of either party. Pending the final decision, notice of the measures suggested shall forthwith be given to the parties and the Council [of the League of Nations].

But this rendering of Article 41 was not a happy one. In the first place, the printer's error 'reserve' was introduced in place of 'preserve'.[13] In the second, the English and French versions of the text were 'not in total harmony',[14] with the latter (considered to be the original) reading:

> *La Cour a le pouvoir d'indiquer, si elle estime que les circonstances l'exigent, quelles mesures conservatoires du droit de chacun doivent être prises à titre provisoire. En attendant l'arrêt définitive, l'indication de ces mesures est immédiatement notifiée aux parties et au Conseil.*

This version of Article 41 differs in several vital respects from the English text. The phrase *'doivent être prises'* is not the precise equivalent of the words 'ought to be taken', with the former on the whole bearing a more normative or mandatory

---

[10] For a history of the law of provisional measures up to 1939, see CA Miles, 'The Origins of the Law of Provisional Measures before International Courts and Tribunals' (2013) 73 ZaöRV 615; C Miles, *Provisional Measures before International Courts and Tribunals* (Cambridge, CUP, 2017) ch 2.

[11] Further: J Elkind, *Interim Protection: A Functional Approach* (Deventer, Kluwer, 1981); J Sztucki, *Interim Measures in the Hague Court: An Attempt at a Scrutiny* (The Hague, Kluwer, 1983); S Rosenne, *Provisional Measures in International Law: The International Court of Justice and the International Tribunal for the Law of the Sea* (Oxford, OUP, 2005); M Semih Gemelmaz, *Provisional Measures of Protection in International Law, 1907–2010* (Istanbul, Legal Kitapevi, 2011); C Miles, *Provisional Measures* (n 10). In this chapter, 'provisional measures' is used interchangeably with the term 'interim relief'.

[12] In domestic litigation, a similar effect would be achieved by asking for an interlocutory or interim injunction: see, eg, *American Cyanamid Co v Ethicon Ltd* [1975] AC 396.

[13] MO Hudson, *The Permanent Court of International Justice, 1920–1942* (New York, Macmillan, 1943) 199.

[14] *LaGrand* [2001] ICJ Rep 466, 502. Also: *Arbitral Award of 31 July 1989 (Guinea-Bissau v Senegal)*, Provisional Measures [1990] ICJ Rep 78 (Judge ad hoc Thierry, dissenting).

character than the latter. Furthermore, the English phrase 'the measures suggested' is rendered in French as simply '*ces mesures*', excluding the vital adjective.

Article 41 of the PCIJ Statute was copied almost word for word by the drafters of Article 41 of the ICJ Statute, and whilst the printer's error was removed and a reference to the Security Council inserted, the discrepancy between English and French remained. Accordingly, from the outset, the shared text of Article 41 contained a fundamental ambiguity: could the Court order binding interim relief under the terms of the provision, or could it only 'suggest' measures that 'ought' to be taken pending judgment?[15]

B. The Textual Argument

The debate over the binding quality (*vel non*) of provisional measures proceeded on several fronts. The first concerned the text of Article 41 itself. The use of less than mandatory language (eg 'indicate' and 'suggest') in the provision prompted a number of commentators (including the PCIJ's long-serving Registrar, Åke Hammarskjöld)[16] to conclude that orders made under the provision were, at best, hortatory.[17] Hammarskjöld also made note of the fact that Article 41 was placed in Chapter III of the PCIJ Statute, which dealt with procedural rather than substantive matters.[18]

This position was apparently supported by the *travaux préparatoires* of Article 41. The provision first appeared in the report of the Advisory Committee of Jurists to the Council of the League of Nations on the proposed PCIJ Statute. In relation to then-Article 39 of the Draft Statute, the Advisory Committee put forth the view that measures ordered under this provision would not be binding

---

[15] The literature on the debate is vast, but is summarized by the following: PJ Bernhardt, 'The Provisional Measures Procedure of the International Court of Justice through *US Staff in Tehran: Fiat Iusticia, Pereat Curia?*' (1980–1981) 20 *Va JIL* 556, 604–09; Sztucki, *Interim Measures in the Hague Court* (n 11) 280–87; J Kammerhofer, 'The Binding Nature of Provisional Measures in the International Court of Justice: The "Settlement" of the Issue in the *LaGrand* Case' (2003) 16 *LJIL* 67, 68–72; A Tzanakopoulos, 'Provisional Measures Indicated by International Courts and Tribunals: Emergence of a General Principle of International Law' (2004) 57 *RHDI* 53, 56–69. A useful bibliography is provided by Kolb, *International Court* (n 2) 644–45.

[16] Å Hammarskjöld, 'Quelques aspects de la question des mesures conservatoires en droit international positif' (1935) 15 *ZaöRV* 5, 20. Hammarskjöld served as Registrar from 1922 to 1936. In 1936 he was elected as a judge, but served only nine months before his untimely death. His brother, Dag Hammarskjöld, was the second UN Secretary-General, serving from 1953 to 1961.

[17] See, eg, P Goldsworthy, 'Interim Measures of Protection in the International Court of Justice' (1974) 68 *AJIL* 258, 273–74; L Gross, 'Some Observations on Provisional Measures', in Y Dinstein (ed), *International Law in a Time of Complexity: Essays in Honour of Shabtai Rosenne* (The Hague, Martinus Nijhoff, 1989) 307, 307; L Collins, 'Provisional and Protective Measures in International Litigation' (1992) 234 *RdC* 19, 216–20; HWA Thirlway, 'Indication of Provisional Measures by the International Court of Justice', in R Bernhardt (ed), *Interim Measures Indicated by International Courts* (Berlin, Springer, 1994) 1, 28–29; E Szabó, 'Provisional Measures in the World Court: Binding or Bound to be Ineffective?' (1998) 10 *LJIL* 477–48; J Collier and V Lowe, *The Settlement of Disputes in International Law: Institutions and Procedures* (Oxford, OUP, 1999) 174–75.

[18] Hammarskjöld, 'Des mesures conservatoires' (n 16) 25–27. *cf* also the PCIJ's pronouncement in *Free Zones of Upper Savoy and the District of Gex* (1929) PCIJ Series A No 2, 13 that its order had no final force or binding effect 'in deciding the dispute brought ... before the Court'. This position, however, only applies *to the Court*, and has no wider bearing on whether orders may be binding on the parties *pendente lite*.

on the parties.[19] This view also seems to have prevailed within the PCIJ itself follow-ing adoption of the Statute. During its internal deliberations regarding amendment of its procedural rules in 1931, the members of the Court appear to have considered it uncontroversial that measures ordered under Article 41 of the Statute were not binding on the parties.[20] Seen in such a light, commentators argued, it was clear that Article 41 was at most capable of imposing a moral obligation of compliance on the parties, but that this diminished position was not without force. Edward Dumbauld, the most astute early observer of the topic, described provisional measures as 'a spe-cial form of advisory opinion' which while 'not formally binding' represented 'the solemn pronouncement of a learned and august tribunal'.[21]

This view, however, was not shared by another group of scholars, who noted that such analyses did not take into account the French text of Article 41 and its seemingly mandatory language.[22] With respect to Hammarskjöld's argument regarding the placement of Article 41 in the Statute, it was noted that Chapter III in fact contained several important provisions with binding effect on proceedings—including Article 60, which provided that judgment would be final and without appeal.[23] Alternatively, it was argued, the mere fact that a provision of the Statute was located in Chapter III did not justify imposing an artificial separation from Chapter II concerning the (mandatory) competence of the Court.[24] It was also pointed out that domestic analogies were invariably considered compulsory, procedural character notwithstanding.[25] As for Dumbauld's argument that the moral overtones of Article 41 provided sufficient impetus for compliance, Hersch Lauterpacht—whilst not committing completely to the alternative view—noted that:

> It cannot be lightly assumed that the Statute of the Court—a legal instrument—contains provisions relating to any merely moral obligations of States and that the Court weighs minutely the circumstances which permit it to issue what is no more than an appeal to the moral sense of the parties.[26]

---

[19] *Procès-Verbaux of the Proceedings of the Committee* (The Hague, Van Langenhuysen Brothers, 1920) 735. Further: Miles (n 10) 642–45.

[20] Modification of the Rules (1931) PCIJ Series D No 2, 183 (Registrar Hammarskjöld), 183 (Judge Fromageot), 183 (Judge Schücking), 184 (Vice-President Guerrero), 184 (Judge van Eysinga). Further: Miles (n 10) 647–49.

[21] E Dumbauld, *Interim Measures of Protection in International Controversies* (The Hague, Martinus Nijhoff, 1932) 164.

[22] See, eg, H Gerd Niemeyer, *Einstweilige Verfügungen des Weltgerichtshof, ihr Wesen und ihre Grenzen* (Leipzig, R Noske, 1932) 29–35; Sztucki (n 11) 263–64. *cf* K Oellers-Frahm, 'Article 41', in A Zimmermann, K Oellers-Frahm, C Tomuschat and CJ Tams (eds), *The Statute of the International Court of Justice: A Commentary*, 2nd edn (Oxford, OUP, 2012) 1026, 1063–64, arguing that the term 'indicate' or '*indiquer*' was given greater weight during the drafting process than 'measures suggested' or '*doivent être prises*' and therefore that, that despite the more mandatory wording of the French text, provisional measures under Article 41 were still intended to be non-binding.

[23] E Hambro, 'The Binding Character of Provisional Measures Indicated by the International Court of Justice' in W Schätzel and H-J Schlochauer (eds), *Rechtsfragen der internationalen Organisation. Fest-schrift für Hans Wehberg zu seinem 70 Geburtstag* (Frankfurt am Main, V Klostermann, 1956) 152, 164.

[24] DW Greig, 'The Balancing of Interests and the Granting of Interim Protection by the International Court' (1987) 11 *Australian YIL* 108, 131.

[25] Elkind, *Interim Protection* (n 11) 155–56.

[26] H Lauterpacht, *The Development of International Law by the International Court of Justice*, revised edn (London, Stevens & Sons, 1958) 234. This appears to be a qualified reversal or development of his

When the ICJ succeeded the PCIJ, a new front opened. As the new Court was considered to be 'the principal judicial organ of the United Nations',[27] the UN Charter included a number of new provisions designed to give effect to that relationship. Article 94(1) of the Charter provided that member states were obliged to comply with 'any decision of the [ICJ] in any case to which it was a party', with the obvious question being whether an order made under Article 41 could be considered a 'decision'. One view argued that the term as it appeared was synonymous with the term 'judgment', excluding interim relief by implication.[28] On another view, however, 'decision' as it appeared in Article 94(1) referred to all orders of the Court, with 'judgments' given special treatment only insofar as a failure to comply could entail recourse to the Security Council under Article 94(2).[29]

C. Questions of Principle

The text of Article 41 was not the only source of controversy. Running parallel to this argument was a debate about whether the power to order binding interim relief was a general principle of law within the meaning of Article 38(1)(c) of the Statute. This discussion—though it centred on the PCIJ and ICJ—held wider implications for the settlement of international disputes, being applicable to the practice of international courts and tribunals generally.[30] This view was originally propounded by Hans Niemeyer, who engaged in a comparative analysis of interim relief across a variety of municipal jurisdictions before arriving at the general conclusion that the power of an international court or tribunal to award binding interim relief was a general principle of international law.[31] He further saw the principle as arising from the proposition that parties, once a dispute had been submitted to adjudication, should be expected to refrain from any act or omission which would prejudice the decision of a court or tribunal or prevent its full execution.[32] Echoes of this,

---

earlier views in *The Function of Law in the International Community* (n 1) 208: 'It will be noted that the Orders of the Court under Article 41 have no binding effect: they merely *indicate* provisional measures'.

[27] ICJ Statute, Art 1; UN Charter, Art 92.

[28] Szabó, 'Provisional Measures in the World Court' (n 17) 489–80.

[29] VS Mani, 'Interim Measures of Protection: Article 41 of the ICJ Statute and Article 94 of the UN Charter' (1970) 10 *Indian JIL* 359, 367–72; H Mosler, 'Article 94', in B Simma, *The Charter of the United Nations: A Commentary* (Oxford, OUP, 1994) 1003, 1003–04.

[30] C Brown, *A Common Law of International Adjudication* (Oxford, OUP, 2004) 146–50.

[31] Niemeyer, *Einstweilige Verfügungen des Weltgerichtshof* (n 21) 22–24.

[32] ibid, 11–16. cf *Ungarische Erdgas A-G v Romania* (1925) 3 ILR 412, 413 (Romania–Hungary MAT). Other commentators also adopted this purposive view, though their reasoning on occasion differed: see, eg, Hambro (n 22) 166–68; J Stone, *Legal Controls of International Conflict* (London, Stevens & Sons, 1954) 132; Mani, 'Interim Measures of Protection' (n 29) 360–67; Elkind (n 11) 162; BH Oxman, 'Jurisdiction and the Power to Indicate Provisional Measures', in LF Damrosch (ed), *The International Court of Justice at the Crossroads* (Dobbs Ferry, Transnational Publishers, 1987) 323, 332. Others agreed that the power to order interim relief was a general principle of law, but denied that this automatically entailed binding effect: Dumbauld, *Interim Measures of Protection* (n 21) 180; Collins, 'Provisional and Protective Measures' (n 17) 214, 216.

arguably, could be seen in the PCIJ's pronouncement in *Electricity Company* that provisional measures reflected:

> [The] principle generally accepted by international tribunals ... to the effect that the parties to a case must abstain from any measures capable of exercising a prejudicial effect in regard to the execution of the decision to be given and, in general, not allow any step of any kind to be taken which might aggravate and extend the dispute.[33]

The view that Article 41 merely reflected a more general principle of international law had prominent supporters within the ICJ. Writing extra-curially, Sir Gerald Fitzmaurice argued that binding force was a logical corollary of provisional measures:

> [F]or this jurisdiction is based on the absolute necessity, when the circumstances call for it, of being able to preserve, and to avoid prejudice to, the right of the parties, as determined by the final judgment of the Court.[34]

In respect of other courts and tribunals, Fitzmaurice stated that binding interim relief was a principle of international law, such that the textual debate surrounding Article 41—which was to Fitzmaurice the sole source of doubt on the question—assumed an 'iron[ic] and unsatisfactory character'.[35]

This view, however, was rejected by commentators such as Hugh Thirlway, who saw the general principle so identified as going no further than that propounded by the PCIJ in *Electricity Company* that parties should, in general, refrain from taking action that would aggravate or extend the dispute: the notion that the Court could give more specific directions to a party to do or refrain from doing a certain action was another thing entirely.[36]

D. Judicial Practice

It will not have escaped the reader's attention that the above debate was conducted almost entirely in the pages of academic publications. With one or two exceptions—more Delphic than oracular—the Court maintained a stony disposition towards the question for eight decades. This did not, however, prevent the question from arising before the Court, particularly in light of parties' breach of provisional measures in a variety of cases.[37]

The first serious discussion concerning the binding nature of provisional measures under Article 41 was not judicial, but institutional. In *Anglo-Iranian Oil*, the ICJ ordered a suite of measures designed to ensure that the Anglo-Iranian Oil Company

---

[33] *Electricity Company of Sofia and Bulgaria (Belgium v Bulgaria)* (1939) PCIJ Series A/B No 79, 199.

[34] G Fitzmaurice, *The Law and Procedure of the International Court of Justice*, vol 1 (Cambridge, Grotius Publications, 1986) 548.

[35] ibid, 549.

[36] Thirlway 'Indication of Provisional Measures' (n 17) 30.

[37] See, eg, *Anglo-Iranian Oil Co (UK v Iran)*, Provisional Measures [1951] ICJ Rep 89; *Fisheries Jurisdiction (UK v Iceland)*, Provisional Measures [1972] ICJ Rep 12; *Fisheries Jurisdiction (FRG v Iceland)*, Provisional Measures 1972 ICJ Rep 30; *Application of the Convention for the Prevention and Punishment of the Crime of Genocide (Bosnia & Herzegovina v Serbia & Montenegro)*, Provisional Measures [1993] ICJ 3; *in passim*, Further Request for Provisional Measures [1993] ICJ Rep 325.

could operate effectively pending resolution of the dispute.[38] These were promptly ignored by the non-appearing Iran, which continued with its nationalisation of the Company on the basis that the Court, in its view, had jurisdiction to neither hear the dispute nor order provisional measures.[39] The measures having been communicated to the Security Council pursuant to Article 41(2) of the Statute,[40] the UK representative requested that the Council force Iran to comply with the Court's Order, arguing that provisional measures under Article 41 could be considered a 'decision' within the meaning of Article 94(1) of the Charter, and binding on the parties as a result.[41]

The Iranian representative, conversely, took the view that provisional measures could not be the subject of Security Council jurisdiction under Article 94, and that furthermore, such measures could only be binding if states 'were bound by an arbitration treaty expressly obligating them to respect such measures'.[42] Beyond this, however, the Council's discussions moved away from interim relief to the question of whether the situation was within the domestic jurisdiction of Iran, and it was not required to revisit the issue. In a way this was unfortunate, with commentators assuming that this failed attempt to enforce an order for provisional measures was in some way a comment on whether it was legally binding—a separate and antecedent question.[43]

Beyond occasionally making mention of the fact that its provisional measures had been breached,[44] no item of the Court's practice caused any of its judges to consider whether parties were obliged to follow its indications on interim relief, and no party ventured to ask the court to so rule.[45] In *Bosnian Genocide*, however, the Court ordered provisional measures to prevent the genocide of Bosnia's Muslim population by Serbian paramilitaries allegedly under the control of Yugoslavia (later Serbia and

---

[38] *Anglo-Iranian Oil* [1951] ICJ Rep 89, 94. Further: BF Brown, 'The Juridical Implications of the Anglo-Iranian Oil Company Case' (1952) 32 *Wash ULQ* 384, 393–95; Y Liang, 'The Question of Domestic Jurisdiction in the Anglo-Iranian Oil Dispute before the Security Council' (1952) 46 *AJIL* 272; AW Ford, *The Anglo-Iranian Oil Dispute of 1951–1952: A Study of the Role of Law in the Relations of States* (Berkeley, University of California Press, 1954) Part II, §8; WM Reisman, *Nullity and Revision: The Review and Enforcement of International Judgments and Awards* (New Haven, Yale University Press, 1971) 720–28; Sztucki (n 11) 276–77.

[39] Liang, 'The Question of Domestic Jurisdiction' (n 38) 273.

[40] UN Doc S/2239 (11 July 1951).

[41] UN Doc S/P.V.559 (1 October 1951) 79–81.

[42] UN Doc S/P.V.560 (15 October 1951) 34–36. *cf* the remarks of the representative of Ecuador: UN Doc S/P.V. 562 (16 October 1951) 13–14.

[43] CH Crockett, 'The Effects of Interim Measures of Protection in the International Court of Justice' (1977) 7 *Ca West JIL* 348, 376–77. *cf Anglo-Iranian Oil* [1951] ICJ Rep 89, 91, noting that provisional measures 'retain their own authority' independent of enforcement.

[44] See, eg, *Fisheries Jurisdiction (UK v Iceland)*, Provisional Measures [1973] ICJ Rep 302, 305 (Judge Ignacio-Pinto); *Fisheries Jurisdiction (Federal Republic of Germany v Iceland)*, Provisional Measures [1973] ICJ Rep 313, 316 (Judge Ignacio-Pinto), *in passim*, [1974] ICJ Rep 175, 226 (Judge de Castro); *Nuclear Tests (Australia v France)* [1974] ICJ Rep 253, 451 (Judge ad hoc Barwick, dissenting). Further: Sztucki (n 11) 274–75.

[45] *cf Military and Paramilitary Activities in and Against Nicaragua (Nicaragua v US)* [1986] ICJ Rep 14, 144: 'When the Court finds that the situation requires [provisional measures], it is incumbent on each party to take the Court's indications seriously into account, and not to direct its conduct solely by reference to what it believes to be its rights'. Judge Shahabuddeen opined that this statement 'could bear the interpretation that the measures themselves are not binding, a party merely having a duty to take account of the Court's indication of them': *Bosnian Genocide* [1993] ICJ Rep 325, 365.

Montenegro). When the killings continued unabated, the Court reaffirmed its earlier decision on interim relief.[46] Whilst the majority made no comment on the binding character of its earlier order, Vice-President Weeramantry attached a separate opinion setting out the arguments in favour of such a reading of Article 41.[47] He began by setting out the distinction between the binding character of an order for interim relief on the one hand, and its enforcement on the other, noting that the mere fact that an order could not be enforced directly by the Court did not *ipso facto* deprive it of mandatory effect.[48] He argued that it followed from the binding character of the Court's final judgment that interim measures designed to preserve that judgment were also binding—the principle of 'institutional effectiveness'.[49] He addressed the text of Article 41 of the Statute and Article 98 of the Charter, concluding that despite the ambiguity of each, it was possible to infer an obligation of compliance with respect to provisional measures.[50] Finally, he examined the scraps of information available on the question from the Court's earlier jurisprudence, and the extra-curial writings of its judges.[51] This, he said, led to the conclusion that as a matter of construction and principle, orders made under Article 41 were binding: 'To view [such an order] as anything less than binding so long as it stands would weaken the regime of international law in the very circumstances in which its restraining influence is most needed'.[52]

III. THE FACTS OF *LAGRAND*

A. The Domestic Proceedings

Although they lived virtually their entire lives in the United States, Karl and Walter LaGrand brothers were not US citizens. They were born in Germany in 1962 to a German mother to whom neither of their fathers—two US servicemen—was married. A third American soldier later married the mother and brought the family to live in the United States when the boys were aged five and six. Despite this, they never formally relinquished their German nationality.

VCCR Article 36(1)(b) provides that, with a view to facilitating the exercise of consular functions by individuals, receiving states must inform the relevant consular post of the sending state if one of its nationals is 'arrested or committed to prison or to custody pending trial or is detailed in any other matters'. Consular notification is to be given at the request of the national in question, but in all events the authorities 'shall inform the person concerned without delay of his rights'. Under subparagraph (c) of the same, consular authorities, once notified, are able to

---

[46] ibid, 349–50.
[47] ibid, 370ff.
[48] ibid, 374.
[49] ibid, 376–79, citing Mani (n 29) 362.
[50] ibid, 379–84.
[51] ibid, 384–86.
[52] ibid, 389. *cf* ibid, 397–401 (Judge Ajibola).

provide limited assistance to nationals, including arranging legal representation. No such notification was provided to the LaGrand brothers, however, who remained unaware of their rights under the VCCR throughout their trial and initial appeals.

Following their conviction and sentencing in 1984, the brothers commenced a series of appeals within the Arizona state courts. The Supreme Court of Arizona affirmed the earlier decisions,[53] with the Supreme Court of the United States denying *certiorari*.[54] A round of post-conviction relief petitions also failed.[55] By now it was 1991. At this point, the brothers learned of their rights under the VCCR through other sources—not through the Arizonan authorities, despite the fact that these authorities had been aware of their nationality since their arrest in 1982.[56] In June 1992 they contacted the German consulate in Los Angeles. In December 1992, and on a number of subsequent occasions until February 1999, German consular officials visited the brothers at the state prison complex in Florence, Arizona, and helped their lawyers investigate their childhood in Germany. They also provided advice on how to raise the issue of omission of consular advice before the US federal courts.

When challenging their conviction through *habeas corpus* proceedings in the federal courts,[57] the brothers asserted that their lack of consular assistance impeded their ability gather exculpatory or mitigating evidence. This argument was, however, rejected on the basis that it had not been raised in the earlier proceedings before the Arizonan courts—an application of the principle of procedural default.[58] The brothers' arguments that the failure to raise the point was caused by ineffective counsel or, alternatively, had resulted in a fundamental miscarriage of justice, were also rejected.[59] The US Supreme Court again denied *certiorari*.[60] On 15 January 1999, the Arizona Supreme Court set execution dates.[61] A final series of appeals on the basis that the gas chamber constituted a cruel and unusual method of punishment

---

[53] *State v LaGrand (Karl)*, 733 P.2d 1066 (Ariz 1987); *State v LaGrand (Walter)*, 734 P.2d 563 (Ariz 1987).

[54] *LaGrand v Arizona*, 484 US 872 (1987).

[55] *LaGrand v Arizona*, 501 US 1259 (1991).

[56] *LaGrand*, ICJ Reports 2001, 466, 477.

[57] 27 USC §2254.

[58] *LaGrand v Lewis*, 883 F.Supp 451 (D Ariz 1995); *LaGrand v Lewis*, 884 F.Supp 469 (D Ariz 1995); *aff'd LaGrand v Stewart*, 133 F.3d 1253 (9th Cir 1998). The nominal defendants/respondents were Samuel A Lewis, the Director of the Arizona Department of Corrections, and his successor, Terry Stewart. Stewart was one of the individuals responsible for re-establishing the Iraqi prison system—including the facility at Abu Ghraib—after the US invasion of 2003, though a Department of Justice investigation cleared him of any involvement with the abuses perpetrated therein: *A Review of ICITAP's Screening Procedures for Contractors Sent to Iraq as Correctional Advisors* (US Department of Justice, Office of the Inspector General, February 2005) 31.

[59] Absent demonstration of an external impediment ('cause') or prejudice to a state defendant, assertions of error in criminal proceedings must first be raised in the relevant state court in order to sound in federal *habeas corpus* proceedings: *Wainwright v Sykes*, 433 US 72, 81 (1977). *cf* TJ Foley, 'The New Arbitrariness: Procedural Default of Federal Habeas Corpus Claims in Capital Cases' (1989) 23 *Loyola LALR* 193; M Raker, 'State Prisoners with Federal Claims in Federal Court: When Can a State Prisoner Overcome Procedural Default?' (2014) 73 *Md LR* 1173.

[60] *LaGrand v Stewart*, 525 US 971 (1998).

[61] *LaGrand* [2001] ICJ Rep 466, 478.

within the meaning of the Eighth Amendment initially succeeded before the Court of Appeals for the Ninth Circuit,[62] but was overturned by the US Supreme Court later that same day.[63]

B. The International Proceedings and Provisional Measures

As mentioned, the German authorities had been aware of the LaGrand brothers' situation since late 1992. Until early 1999, however, they had been of the view that their cause would best be served without high-level intervention. Once the execution date had been set, however, German involvement in the case increased.[64] On 4 February 1999, the German Justice Minister, Herta Daeubler-Gmelin, urged Jane D Hull, Governor of Arizona, to show clemency. A few days later, Chancellor Gerhard Schröder wrote letters to President William J Clinton and Governor Hull, noting Germany's long-standing opposition to the death penalty, and asking that the brothers' sentence be commuted to life in prison. The German Foreign Minister, Joschka Fischer, wrote to Secretary of State Madeline Albright seeking her support. Finally, on 16 February 1999, Juergen Chrobog, German Ambassador to the United States, travelled to Arizona to reiterate the request for clemency in person. Despite these remonstrances, Karl LaGrand was put to death hours after his final appeal failed. The execution was denounced by the German government the following day.

Significantly, on 23 February 1999, Karl LaGrand's petition was heard by the Arizona Board of Executive Clemency. It was rejected. At that meeting, however, Pima County prosecutor Kenneth J Peasley admitted that the Arizonan authorities had been aware of the brothers' German nationality on their arrest in 1984.[65] Germany would later use this 'revelation', of which it claimed to be formerly unaware, as the basis for its escalation of the dispute on the international plane.[66]

Walter LaGrand's execution was scheduled for 3 March 1999 at 3pm MST. On 2 March 1999, at 7.30pm CET (11.30am MST), Germany lodged an application in The Hague instituting proceedings against the United States before the ICJ, and claiming that through Arizona's failure to inform the LaGrand brothers of their right to consular assistance, the US had breached VCCR Articles 5 (concerning general

---

[62] *LaGrand v Stewart*, 170 F.3d 1158 (9th Cir 1999); *LaGrand v Stewart*, 173 F.3d 1144 (9th Cir 1999).

[63] *Stewart v. LaGrand*, 525 US 1173 (1999).

[64] *cf* SD Murphy, *United States Practice in International Law: Volume 1, 1999–2001* (Cambridge, CUP, 2002) 33.

[65] Peasley was named 'Prosecutor of the Year' by the Arizona Prosecuting Attorneys Advisory Committee in 1994 and 1996, winning the award largely on his ability to secure the death penalty against defendants. He was disbarred in 2004 after being found to have intentionally encouraged and presented false testimony in the prosecution of two capital murder defendants: *In Re Peasley*, 90 P.3d 764 (Ariz 2004).

[66] There are questions over whether or not this was actually the case. The authorities' knowledge of the brothers' nationality was set out in pre-sentence reports that would have been available to the brothers' attorneys, with whom German consular officials were cooperating: *LaGrand* [2001] ICJ Rep 466, 486–87; *cf* ibid, 552 (Judge Buergenthal, dissenting).

consular functions) and 36.[67] The application also highlighted the Optional Protocol to the VCCR,[68] Article I of which provided that disputes concerning the interpretation and application of the Convention lay within the compulsory jurisdiction of the ICJ. The application was accompanied by a request for provisional measures, urging the Court to take immediate action under Article 41 of its Statute and order that the US use all means at its disposal to prevent the execution of Walter LaGrand.[69]

On 3 March 1999, at 7.00pm CET (11.00am MST) the ICJ awarded provisional measures. Significantly, the ICJ issued this order on the basis of the German application alone, and without the benefit of oral submissions from either side.[70] In so doing, the Court relied (over the protests of the US) on Article 75(1) of its Rules, under which it retained the capacity to award interim relief *proprio motu*.[71] The Court, noting the irreparable prejudice that would be occasioned to Germany were one of its nationals to be executed,[72] ordered that:

> (a) The United States of America should take all measures at its disposal to ensure that Walter LaGrand is not executed pending the final decision in these proceedings, and should inform the Court of all the measures which it has taken in implementation of this Order;
>
> (b) The Government of the United States of America should transmit this Order to the Governor of the State of Arizona.[73]

In the paragraph immediately preceding the formal order, the Court reminded the Governor of Arizona that she 'was under the obligation to act in conformity with the international undertakings of the United States'.[74]

Judge Oda appended a declaration to the order expressing some hesitations but ultimately siding with the majority.[75] President Schwebel entered a separate opinion agreeing with the substance of the order, but objecting to the use of Article 75(1) of the Rules. He further pointed out that had Germany brought its application upon first becoming aware of the alleged default under the VCCR (ie in 1992), the request for interim relief could have been resolved in accordance with the Court's ordinary procedure.[76]

---

[67] *LaGrand*, Germany: Application Instituting Proceedings (2 March 1999).

[68] Optional Protocol to the Vienna Convention on Consular Relations Concerning the Compulsory Settlement of Disputes, 24 April 1963, 596 UNTS 487.

[69] *LaGrand*, Germany: Request for the Indication of Provisional Measures (2 March 1992) para 8.

[70] Though Vice-President Weeramantry did secure the informal views of both parties in a meeting held at 9.00am CET on 3 March 1999: *LaGrand*, Provisional Measures [1999] ICJ Rep 9, 13.

[71] ibid, 14.

[72] ibid, 15.

[73] ibid, 16.

[74] ibid.

[75] Notably that the relief sought was designed to protect the rights of an *individual*, whereas the provisional measures procedure set out in Article 41 was designed to protect the rights of *states*: ibid, 19.

[76] ibid, 21–22.

C. The Supreme Court Declines to Intervene

The US Government transmitted the Court's order to Governor Hull shortly after it was issued.[77] The Governor, however, had earlier declared that she would not stay Walter LaGrand's execution unless ordered to do so by the Supreme Court.[78] Accordingly, Germany made an emergency application to the Court seeking the necessary stay.

The scenario would have proved eerily familiar to the bench of the Supreme Court—as indeed it would have to their counterparts in The Hague. In 1998, the ICJ issued provisional measures in *Breard*, a case based on an almost identical application by Paraguay under the same provisions of the VCCR.[79] This was made in support of a dual Paraguayan/Argentine national, Angel Francisco Breard, who was arrested for a murder and attempted rape in Virginia in 1992 for which he was convicted and sentenced to death in 1993.[80] As with *LaGrand*, the measures in *Breard* were communicated to the Governor of Virginia, James S Gilmore III[81] and an application for a stay made to the Supreme Court. In *Breard v Greene*, the Supreme Court dismissed the Paraguayan application on the basis that the US had not waived its immunity before its own courts.[82] The Court further had the benefit of an *amicus* brief from the Department of State, which contained argument on the question of whether the ICJ's provisional measures were binding. The brief made reference to the *Restatement (Third) of the Foreign Relations Law of the United States*, which (sensibly) reserved its position on the point.[83] Nevertheless, said the brief, based on the precatory language of Article 41 of the Statute, 'The better reasoned position is that such an order is not binding'.[84] On this basis, the Court said that whilst it was 'unfortunate' that the matter came before it whilst ICJ proceedings were pending, it was unable to assist: 'If the Governor wishes to wait for the decision of the ICJ, that

[77] The same afternoon, the US Supreme Court denied Walter LaGrand's final appeal which was, like his brother's, premised on the Eighth Amendment: *Stewart v LaGrand*, 526 US 115 (1999); *LaGrand v Arizona*, 526 US 1001 (1999).

[78] Murphy, *United States Practice* (n 64) 32.

[79] *Vienna Convention on Consular Relations (Paraguay v US)*, Provisional Measures [1998] ICJ Rep 248. Noted: MK Addo (1999) 48 *ICLQ* 673.

[80] The details of Breard's prosecution were set out in *Breard v Commonwealth*, 445 S.E.2d 670 (Va 1994). Further: 'Agora: *Breard*' (1998) 92 *AJIL* 666; Murphy (n 64) 27–31.

[81] Albeit whilst claiming that the ICJ's Order was expressed in 'non-binding language': Letter from Madeline K Albright, US Secretary of State to James S Gilmore III, Governor of Virginia, 13 April 1998, partially extracted in (1998) 92 *AJIL* 666, 671–72.

[82] *Breard v Greene*, 523 US 371, 377–78 (1998). Breard made a joint application on the basis of VCCR Art 36, which was rejected the basis that the consular notification point was procedurally defaulted and that, in any event, he could not demonstrate that the provision of consular assistance could have changed the outcome at trial: ibid.

[83] *Restatement (Third) of the Foreign Relations Law of the United States*, vol 2 (St Paul, American Law Institute, 1987) §903(e): 'The Court has not ruled on whether an order "indicating" provisional measures is mandatory on the parties. It is not clear what effect the failure of a state to comply with provisional measures has on the decision in the principal case.' Further: ibid, Reporter's Note 6. On the effect—and criticism—of the *Restatement* project generally, *cf* KD Adams, 'Blaming the Mirror: The Restatements and the Common Law' (2007) 40 *Ind LR* 205.

[84] Extracted: Murphy (n 64) 30.

is his prerogative. But nothing in our existing case law allows us to make that choice for him'.[85] This conclusion was staggering, if only because of the complete lack of comity demonstrated towards the ICJ.[86] Breard was executed on 14 April 1998. Paraguay subsequently dropped its case before the ICJ, and the matter was removed from the Court's list shortly thereafter.[87]

In *Federal Republic of Germany v United States*, the Supreme Court perfunctorily dismissed the German application by reference to *Breard v Greene*: the US had not waived its sovereign immunity before its own courts and that the VCCR did not permit a foreign government to assert a claim against a state of the Union. With the execution scheduled to take place the following day, the tardiness of the German claim was also mentioned.[88] Furthermore, as revealed by the dissenting opinion of Judge Breyer, the US Solicitor-General, Seth P Waxman, filed a letter with the Court stating, 'an order of the International Court of Justice is not binding and does not furnish a basis for judicial relief',[89] without so much as mentioning the equivocation of the *Third Restatement*.

Walter LaGrand was executed, in defiance of the ICJ's provisional measures, on 4 March 1999. In ordering that the sentence be carried out on schedule, Governor Hull also ignored a 2 March 1999 recommendation from the Arizona Board of Executive Clemency that Governor 60-day reprieve having regard to the ICJ proceedings: this decision was made, the Governor said, 'in the interests of justice and with the victims in mind'.[90]

IV. THE PROCEEDINGS AND JUDGMENT IN *LAGRAND*

A. The Pleadings

Walter LaGrand's death was immediately condemned by the German Foreign Ministry.[91] Unlike Paraguay, however, Germany did not drop its proceedings before the Court—rather, in its written and oral pleadings, it requested that the Court not only find that the US had breached the VCCR, but also that interim relief ordered under Article 41 of the Statute was binding, placing the US in breach of a further obligation.[92]

The written proceedings before the Court ably rehearsed the scholarly and judicial debate set out earlier in this chapter, with oral submissions largely a reprise.[93] The German memorial, in the relevant part, argued that institutional effectiveness,

---

[85] *Breard v Greene*, 523 US 371, 378 (1998).
[86] A-M Slaughter, 'Court to Court' (1998) 92 *AJIL* 708, 708; HH Koh, 'Paying 'Decent Respect' to World Opinion on the Death Penalty' (2002) 35 *UC Davis LR* 1085, 1113.
[87] *Breard*, Order of 10 November 1998 [1998] ICJ Rep 426.
[88] *Federal Republic of Germany v United States*, 526 US 111, 112 (1999).
[89] ibid, 113 (Judge Breyer, dissenting).
[90] *LaGrand* [2001] ICJ Rep 466, 479.
[91] Murphy (n 64) 34.
[92] *LaGrand* [2001] ICJ Rep 466, 473.
[93] *cf* Kammerhofer, 'Binding Nature' (n 15) 72–75.

'deduced from a general principle of law',[94] required that provisional measures be binding on the parties. A related point was the general rule of judicial symmetry between the final judgment and interim relief: since withdrawal of consent to adjudicate was not possible once the Court was seized, it followed that a party should not be able to take action *pendente lite* that would frustrate an opponent's claim.[95] The German memorial also addressed the textual arguments surrounding the Article 41 and the discrepancies surrounding the English and French versions of the same, as well as the other official translations of the provision, concluding that only the English and Russian versions could be interpreted as being 'open to a 'softer' meaning'.[96] In reconciling the two texts, the German memorial made reference to Article 33(4) of the Vienna Convention on the Law of Treaties[97] (VCLT), which provided that in such cases 'the meaning which best reconciles the texts, having regard to the object and purpose of the treaty, shall be adopted'.[98] Reference was also made to the earlier practice of the Court.[99]

The US counter-memorial began with an opposing textual analysis of Article 41, noting that if the parties to the ICJ Statute had wished to use more obviously mandatory language, this would have been simple to achieve.[100] The US also considered Article 98(1) of the Statute, arguing for the identification of the word 'decision' with 'judgment' and excluding by implication orders for interim relief.[101] The German assertions regarding institutional effectiveness were also rebuffed, and the Court's practice trawled for indications that provisional measures were not binding.[102]

B. The Judgment

In considering the binding character of interim relief ordered under its Statute, the Court began by addressing the wording of Article 41 and noted that the dispute 'essentially concern[ed] the interpretation' of the provision, affirming the view of Fitzmaurice and others that the debate insofar as the ICJ was concerned was fundamentally textual, rather than reflective of wider principles of international law.[103] In this respect, it expressly noted the importance of VCLT Article 31(1) as a rubric of interpretation, paying particular attention to the need for any interpretation to be conducted 'in good faith in accordance with the ordinary meaning to be given to [the words of the provision] in their context and in light of the treaty's object and purpose'.

---

[94] *LaGrand*, Germany: Memorial, para 4.125.
[95] ibid, paras 4.129–4.131.
[96] ibid, paras 4.149–4.150.
[97] 22 May 1969, 1155 UNTS 331.
[98] *LaGrand*, Germany: Memorial, para 4.150.
[99] ibid, 4.154–4.156.
[100] *LaGrand*, US: Counter-Memorial, paras 127–37, 142–48.
[101] ibid, paras 154–58.
[102] ibid, paras 159–65, citing, inter alia, the sources referred to in n 45.
[103] *LaGrand* [2001] ICJ Rep 466, 501.

The Court then turned to point out the discrepancy between the French and English texts of Article 41, in particular noting that the phrase '*doivent être prises*' bore an allegedly mandatory character, in contrast to the English 'measures suggested'.[104] Bearing in mind the equally authoritative character of both texts, the Court then applied VCLT Article 33(4) (reflective of custom),[105] which provided that in cases of continued doubt following the application of VCLT Articles 31 and 32 to the problem, a discrepancy between authoritative translations was to be resolved in favour of the interpretation that best reconciled the alternatives 'having regard to the object and purpose of the treaty'.[106] This, in turn, directed the Court to the object and purpose of the ICJ Statute, together with the context of Article 41. It found that:

> The object and function of the Statute is to enable the Court to fulfill the functions provided therein, and, in particular, the basic function of judicial settlement of international disputes by binding decisions in accordance with Article 59 of the Statute. The context in which Article 41 has to be seen within the Statute is to prevent the Court from being hampered in the exercise of its functions because the respective rights of the parties to a dispute before the Court are not preserved. It follows from the object and purpose of the Statute, as well as from the terms of Article 41 when read in their context, that the power to indicate provisional measures entails that such measures should be binding inasmuch as the power in question is based on the necessity, when circumstances call for it, to safeguard, and to avoid prejudice to, the rights of the parties as determined by the final judgment of the Court. The contention that provisional measures indicated under Article 41 might not be binding would be contrary to the object and purpose of that Article.[107]

The Court then proceeded to confirm this reading by reference to the preparatory materials of Article 41[108] (though, in light of its textual analysis, it pronounced unnecessary such an investigation) and the wider obligation of non-aggravation of disputes as set out by the PCIJ in *Electricity Company*.[109] It concluded its analysis by confirming that Article 94 of the UN Charter did not preclude provisional measures ordered under Article 41 of the Statute from possessing binding effect—although

---

[104] ibid.

[105] See also *Young Loan Arbitration (Belgium, France, Switzerland, UK & US v Germany)* (1980) 59 ILR 494, 547 (Arbitral Tribunal for the Agreement on German External Debts). On interpretation of plurilingual treaties more generally, see P Eden, 'Plurilingual Treaties: Aspects of Interpretation', in A Orakhelashvili and S Williams (eds), *40 Years of the Vienna Convention on the Law of Treaties* (London, BIICL, 2009) 155.

[106] *LaGrand* [2001] ICJ Rep 466, 501.

[107] ibid, 502–03.

[108] ibid, 503–05. In undertaking this analysis in this manner, the Court may be considered to have erred slightly. By its terms, VCLT Article 33(4) makes clear that it may only be resorted to in the event that the application of VCLT Arts 31 (the general rule of interpretation) and 32 (concerning supplementary materials such as *travaux préparatoires*) have not produced a satisfactory result. By considering the preparatory material of Art 41 *after* applying VCLT Art 33(4), the Tribunal undertook its interpretive task out of order—although it appears unlikely that correct application of these provisions would have produced a different result. On application of VCLT Art 33(4) to plurilingual treaties, see P Germer, 'Interpretation of Plurilingual Treaties: A Study of Article 33 of the Vienna Convention on the Law of Treaties' (1970) 11 *Harv ILJ* 400; P Eden, 'Plurilingual Treaties: Aspects of Interpretation' in Orakhelashvili and Williams (eds), *40 Years* (n 105) 155.

[109] *LaGrand* [2001] ICJ Rep 466, 503.

it left open the question of whether under Article 94(2) an order for interim relief could be considered a 'judgment' subject to Security Council enforcement.[110]

The majority opinion in *LaGrand* was accompanied by a declaration by President Guillaume that did not touch on the issue of whether provisional measures were binding.[111] A further separate opinion from Vice-President Shi expressed no disagreement with the proposition that provisional measures were binding.[112] Separate opinions by Judges Koroma[113] and Parra-Aranguren[114] were similarly in line with the majority on this point.

C. The Dissenting Opinions

Two dissents were appended to the Court's judgment. The first, by Judge Buergenthal of the United States, held that the entire German application should have been found inadmissible due to the delay in bringing the claim before the Court. As Germany had clearly known of Arizona's intention to execute Walter LaGrand for at least two years prior to the award of provisional measures in 1999, he said, its insistence on waiting until the day before LaGrand's execution before urging the Court to order relief *proprio motu* was abusive,[115] and further constituted a litigation strategy that was prejudicial to the US.[116] Notably, despite fulfilling the position of a national judge *qua* judge ad hoc for the purposes of the case,[117] he did not adopt in their entirety the US submissions on interim relief, and indeed voted in favour of the paragraph of the *dispositif* in which the Court held that the US had breached the provisional measures previously ordered.[118]

A more critical dissent was given by Judge Oda, who was the sole member of the Court to vote against its determination as to the mandatory character of provisional measures. He declared the extensive analysis undertaken by the Court to be a 'vain and unnecessary undertaking' designed not so much to establish interim relief under Article 41 to be binding, but rather to exclude any alternative view.[119] He further went on to say that determination of this general question was 'an empty, unnecessary exercise' before going on to note:

> I wonder what the Court really wants to say in holding than an order indicating provisional measures is binding. Is the Court trying to raise the question of responsibility of the State which allegedly has not complied with the order? The question has not arisen in the past jurisprudence of this Court. It suffices that provisional measures 'ought to be taken' or in

---

[110] ibid, 505–06.
[111] ibid, 517.
[112] ibid, 518–24.
[113] ibid, 541–43.
[114] ibid, 544–47.
[115] ibid, 552–55.
[116] ibid, 555–57.
[117] ICJ Statute, Art 31. On appropriate role of a judge *ad hoc*, see *Bosnian Genocide* [1993] ICJ Rep 325, 408–09 (Judge ad hoc Lauterpacht).
[118] *LaGrand* [2001] ICJ Rep 466, 516.
[119] ibid, 537–39.

the French '*doivent être prises*' ... Whether or not an order indicating provisional measures has been complied with or not is decided by the Court in its judgment on the merits.[120]

Judge Oda's criticism amounts to a point on judicial economy; as the Court would determine the dispute between the parties finally during the merits phase, there was no need to decide whether provisional measures had been complied with or, by extension, were binding on the parties. If this reading is correct, then Judge Oda conflated the question of enforcement of provisional measures with the question of their binding effect. Alternately, Judge Oda may simply have been saying that it was better overall if the Court left the question of binding interim relief unanswered— presumably on the basis that to do so would be to invite defiance of the Court in politically charged cases.[121] In any case, although he voted against the rest of the Court on this point, he did not take a clear position on whether compliance with provisional measures was mandatory.

D. VCCR Article 36 and Other Issues

Although this chapter is concerned with the contribution of *LaGrand* towards the concept of provisional measures, it is worth considering the Court's conclusions on Germany's principal submissions. In short, Germany asked the Court to declare: (a) that the failure of the Arizonan authorities to inform the LaGrand brothers of their consular rights under VCCR Article 36(1)(b) breached the Convention and prevented Germany from exercising diplomatic protection on behalf of its nationals, as well as preventing the brothers from exercising a right bestowed on them as individuals by the Convention; and (b) that the use of procedural default to prevent the consular assistance point from being argued before the US courts was in breach of VCCR Article 36(2), which provides that whilst the rights referred to in paragraph (1) of the provision are to be exercised in conformity with the laws and regulations of the host state, 'said laws and regulations must enable full effect to be given to the purposes for which the rights accorded under this Article are intended'.[122]

With respect to questions of jurisdiction and admissibility overall, Germany asserted that the Court's jurisdiction was founded on Article I of the Optional Protocol to the VCCR, providing jurisdiction over questions concerning the 'interpretation and application' of the Convention. The US asserted that the present dispute could not be so characterised, but the Court sided with Germany, accepting that Article I provided comprehensive jurisdiction for all claims, based on the 'general jurisdictional' clause of the Optional Protocol and the close relationship between the issues raised by the German application.[123]

---

[120] ibid, 539.

[121] *cf* S Oda, 'Provisional Measures: The Practice of the International Court of Justice' in V Lowe and M Fitzmaurice (eds), *Fifty Years of the International Court of Justice* (Cambridge, CUP, 1996) 541, 554–56.

[122] *LaGrand* [2001] ICJ Rep 466, 472–73.

[123] ibid, 482–85.

The US also raised a number of objections regarding the admissibility of the German claim, two of which bear closer attention.[124] In the first place, the US argued that the examination of the procedural default rule would effectively amount to the ICJ arrogating to itself the role of an 'ultimate court of appeal for national criminal proceedings'.[125] This was rejected by the Court on the basis that all that Germany had sought to do in bringing the proceedings was to do no more than assess the application of VCCR Article 36 in the context of domestic criminal proceedings—its extensive recourse to US domestic law in its pleadings notwithstanding.[126]

Another US complaint was directed towards Germany's application for provisional measures and consequential submissions regarding the breach of those measures. The US argued that the lateness of the application had prejudiced the US and constituted an unfair litigation strategy.[127] The Court also rejected this submission, noting that whilst the timing of the German application might be criticized, the irreparable prejudice to Germany (viz the death of Walter LaGrand) justified the award of interim relief, tardiness notwithstanding, and this same justification enabled the breach of those measures to be considered on the merits.[128]

With respect to Germany's first substantive submission on the proper application of VCCR Article 36(1)(b), the US conceded at the outset that the Arizonan authorities' failure to notify the brothers that consular assistance was available was a breach of the provision. But whose rights were breached? According to the US, the provision only set out state rights which 'may benefit individuals by permitting States to offer them consular assistance'.[129] The Court, however, agreed with Germany's assertion that the wording of VCCR Article 36 indicated the vesting of a right in an individual. In reaching this conclusion, the Court relied solely on the bare words of the provision itself, finding that 'viewed in their context [this language] admits of no doubt', and that the Court was accordingly under an obligation to apply the provision as it stood.[130] This was the subject of some querulousness by Judge Oda and Vice-President Shi.[131]

With respect to its submissions on the procedural default rule, Germany argued that the application of the principle prevented Germany from exercising diplomatic protection on the part of its nationals and further prevented the brothers from exercising their individual rights under VCCR Article 36(1). A key element of this position was the fact that the brothers were only made aware of their rights under the Convention *after* their options before the state courts had been exhausted, such that procedural default effectively rendered the point impossible to raise. This, Germany said, violated the US's obligations under VCCR Article 36(2), requiring that states

---

[124] The other two were dismissed with relatively little analysis: see ibid, 487–88 (regarding the local remedies rule), 488–89 (regarding equality of parties).

[125] ibid, 485.

[126] ibid, 485–86.

[127] ibid, 486–87.

[128] ibid, 487.

[129] ibid, 493.

[130] ibid, 494. The Court, however, left open the question as to whether the right set out in VCCR Article 36(1)(b) could properly be classified as a human right, a point argued by Germany.

[131] ibid, 520 (Vice-President Shi), 536 (Judge Oda, dissenting).

parties to the Convention give 'full effect ... to the purposes for which the rights accorded under [Article 36(1)] are intended'. The US responded that this submission 'went far beyond the wording of the Convention' and that VCCR Article 36(2) set out no requirement regarding subsequent review procedures before a court of appeal.[132]

The Court affirmed that the procedural default rule did not violate international law per se (a point conceded by Germany), but that, in the present case, it had an adverse effect on the rights of Karl and Walter LaGrand. The Court held that 'full effect' within the meaning of VCCR Article 36(2) required that the procedural rules of a state party be such as to allow detained individuals to 'effectively challenge' convictions and sentences based in whole or in part on violations of those rights. The fact that US law permitted procedural default to be circumvented within certain narrow constitutional parameters was insufficient to meet this threshold. Accordingly, in the case at hand, the use of procedural default to limit the LaGrand brothers' defence breached international law.[133]

Having found in favour of Germany, the Court ordered that the US provide guarantees and reassurances of non-repetition. Under this remedy, the US was required to allow, by means of its own choosing, review and reconsideration of convictions and sentences passed in violation of VCCR Article 36(1), with respect to any situation in which a German national was sentenced to prolonged detention or other severe punishment.[134]

V. THE AFTERMATH OF *LAGRAND*

The 'special significance'[135] of the ICJ's judgment in *LaGrand* was immediately acknowledged by commentators: scholars and observers referred to the case's 'far-reaching impact'[136] and 'well-reasoned and convincing'[137] conclusions, which 'significantly enhanced the [ICJ's] standing as the principal judicial organ of the UN'.[138] It was also apprehended that, its conclusions on VCCR Article 36 and associated issues aside, 'the Court's ruling on the legal effects of interim orders [was] certainly the most spectacular' element of the decision, justifying the appellative 'landmark'[139] in its own right. But although a substantial number of observers viewed *LaGrand* with enthusiasm, this reaction was elsewhere muted. Sir Robert Jennings proclaimed that whilst the technical issues of the case would be of interest to lawyers, the 'strong element of artificiality' (particularly with respect to the 'extreme urgency' that led the Court to rely on Article 75(1) of its Rules) that pervaded the case would diminish its practical relevance, possibly to the vanishing point.[140]

---

[132] ibid, 495–96.
[133] ibid, 497–98.
[134] ibid, 513–14.
[135] Aceves (n 5) 217.
[136] Yang (n 5) 441.
[137] Mennecke and Tams (n 5) 455.
[138] Stephens (n 5) 195.
[139] Mennecke and Tams (n 5) 454–55.
[140] Jennings, 'The *LaGrand* Case' (n 1) 54.

Those who had previously held forth with the view that measures ordered under Article 41 of the ICJ Statute could not be considered binding were unsurprisingly critical of the decision. Thirlway, with his characteristic fractal subtlety, undertook to dissect the Court's decision,[141] pointing out the Court's failure in *LaGrand* to consider the intertemporal aspects of the problem;[142] that is, that the model of international dispute settlement on which Article 41 was ultimately based was very different to that which the Court seemed to apply in its 2001 decision—the 1920 *travaux préparatoires* of the PCIJ Statute and the internal views of that Court indicated that Article 41 was not intended to possess binding effect.[143] Thirlway also pointed out that the previous decisions of the Court that could have pronounced on the binding effect of provisional measures—particularly the *Fisheries Jurisdiction* cases—avoided the issue entirely: if provisional measures were binding, Thirlway argued, why duck the question repeatedly? The answer, to his mind, was clear: the Court was well aware that measures ordered under Article 41 of its Statute were not mandatory, a view confirmed *sotto voce* in *Nicaragua*.[144]

Further arguments were also deployed: the Court's linguistic analysis of Article 41 was inadequate; the sense of moral force behind a non-binding order was sufficient to ensure compliance such that a mandatory order was not automatically congruent with the object and purpose of the provision; the principle identified the PCIJ in *Electricity Company* did not give the Court the power to make detailed orders controlling state behaviour *pendente lite*; significant differences between international and municipal law meant that concepts of binding interim relief in the latter could not be applied unthinkingly to the former; and the concept of binding interim relief undermined the fact that jurisdiction in international litigation rested on state consent.[145] But these comments notwithstanding, Thirlway nonetheless bowed to the inevitable: 'However unsatisfactory the reasoning of the decision may be, it has to be accepted that it is the established law as seen by the Court; and in this domain what counts it is how the Court, rather than the generality of States, sees the matter'.[146]

A more pressing concern, arguably, was how the United States would respond to *LaGrand*. In his initial response to the judgment, Aceves noted that 'past practice suggests that the US courts may not accord significant weight to the ICJ's ruling',[147] and pointing to the failure of the Supreme Court to intervene in *Breard v Greene* and *Federal Republic of Germany v United States*. With respect to the Court's conclusions on VCCR Article 36, the immediate reaction of the US courts was to accord *LaGrand* little if any value.[148] This position was soon to be tested.

---

[141] H Thirlway, *The Law and Procedure of the International Court of Justice: Fifty Years of Jurisprudence* (Oxford, OUP, 2013) 956–68.

[142] E Bjorge, this volume, ch 6.

[143] ibid, 960.

[144] ibid, 961. *cf* n 45.

[145] Thirlway, *Law and Procedure* (n 141) 963–66.

[146] Thirlway (n 141) 1807. Further: Kolb (n 2) 638–50; Rosenne (n 11) 34–40; Gemelmaz (n 11) ch. 4; Oellers-Frahm (n 22) 1062–69.

[147] Aceves (n 5) 218.

[148] *United States v Minjares-Alvarez*, 264 F.3d 980 (10th Cir 2001); *State v Issa*, 752 N.E.2d 904 (Ohio 2001); *State v Lopez*, 633 N.W.2d 774 (Iowa 2001); *cf Valdez v Oklahoma*, 46 P.3d 703 (Okla 2002). Further: SD Murphy, *United States Practice in International Law, Volume 2: 2002–2004* (Cambridge, CUP, 2006) 23–27.

On 9 January 2003, Mexico filed an application with the ICJ alleging that the US had failed to inform 54 of its nationals currently on death row in 10 different states of their right to consular assistance at the time of their arrest and subsequent trial. The case was given the name *Avena and Other Mexican Nationals*, with its namesake being Carlos Avena, a man arrested in Los Angeles, California in 1980, convicted of two counts of first degree murder in 1981 and sentenced to death in 1982 in the California Superior Court for Los Angeles County.[149] The application was accompanied by a request for provisional measures identifying three of the 54 Mexican nationals—César Roberto Fierro Reyna, Roberto Moreno Ramos and Osvaldo Torres—as facing execution within the next six months unless the ICJ were to take action *pendente lite*.[150]

Given the timeline of the executions, the Court was able to hear oral submissions from both sides on the question of interim relief. Mexico noted that the Optional Protocol to the VCCR furnished the Court with prima facie jurisdiction, directed the Court to its previous orders in *Breard* and *LaGrand*, provided citations as to decisions in which US courts declined to provide redress for VCCR Article 36 omissions to Mexican nationals and further stressed that, if interim relief was not provided, the individuals previously identified would be put to death.[151] On 5 February 2003, the Court ordered provisional measures, requiring that the US 'take all measures necessary' to ensure that Fierro, Ramos and Torres were not executed pending final determination of the merits.[152] The US response to this was muted: at the time, the Department of State merely commented that it was 'studying' the order.[153] Texas—the state in which Fierro and Ramos were incarcerated—was less reticent, with a spokesman for Governor James Richard Perry stating: 'According to our reading of the law and the treaty, there is no authority for the federal government or the World Court to prohibit Texas from exercising the laws passed by our legislature'.[154] Fire-breathing defence of state sovereignty notwithstanding, Texas and Oklahoma (where Torres was detained) did not set execution dates for the three men: the Court's order was obeyed, though whether out of coincidence, respect for international due process, a simple desire to avoid uncomfortable headlines or a combination of all three was unclear.[155]

---

[149] For the details of Avena's prosecution, see *People v Avena*, 916 P.3d 1000 (Cal 1996).

[150] *Avena and Other Mexican Nationals*, Mexico: Request for the Indication of Provisional Measures or Protection (9 January 2003) 5.

[151] CR 2003/1, 24–35 (Ambassador Oñate).

[152] It further held that as the other 51 individuals were not under threat of imminent execution, it would be inappropriate to extend the interim relief ordered to their cases: *Avena*, Provisional Measures [2003] ICJ Rep 77, 91–92. Noted: Aceves (2003) 97 *AJIL* 923. On the domestic legal effect of the measures, see RD Sloan, 'Measures Necessary to Ensure: The ICJ's Provisional Measures Order in *Avena and Other Mexican Nationals*' (2004) 17 *LJIL* 673.

[153] C Hines, 'Consular Rights, Station House Wrongs' (*Texas Chronicle*, 23 February 2003) <www.chron.com/opinion/article/Hines-Consular-rights-station-house-wrongs-2130760.php> accessed 18 May 2015.

[154] ibid.

[155] *Avena* [2004] ICJ Rep 12, 71–73.

The same obedience did not follow the ICJ's judgment on the merits in *Avena*. Over the arguments of the US that to expand the decision in *LaGrand* would result in the ICJ sitting in judgment over the entire US capital punishment system, the Court held that the Mexican nationals involved were entitled to review and reconsideration of their convictions. The US responded by withdrawing from the Optional Protocol to the VCCR, depriving the Court of jurisdiction in the event of any future claims along the lines of *Breard*, *LaGrand* and *Avena*.[156] Implementation of the *Avena* judgment was then largely denied by individual US states—a memorandum from President George W Bush urging compliance notwithstanding[157]—with the Supreme Court again refusing to intervene.[158]

This failure prompted Mexico to lodge a further claim with the ICJ under Article 60 of its Statute, seeking 'interpretation' of the *Avena* judgment.[159] Provisional measures were also sought by Mexico to safeguard the lives of five individuals: Fierro and Ramos, subjects of the original *Avena* provisional measures, and José Ernesto Medellín Rojas, Rubén Ramírez Cárdenas and Humberto Leal García.[160] On 16 July 2008, the ICJ granted interim relief, ordering that the individuals concerned not be executed until final judgment was given or unless or until those individuals received review and reconsideration of their convictions under the terms of *Avena*.[161] On 5 August 2008, the Supreme Court again declined to intervene in Texas' planned execution of Medellín.[162] He was put to death that evening, with a spokeswoman for Governor Perry declaring: 'The [ICJ] has no jurisdiction here in Texas. We're concerned about following Texas law and that's what we're doing'.[163] In its judgment on the merits, the ICJ again found the US—through Texas—to have executed Medellín in violation of its obligation of compliance with respect to interim relief and its obligations as set out in the *Avena* judgment.[164]

---

[156] JB Quigley, 'The United States' Withdrawal from International Court of Justice Jurisdiction in Consular Cases: Reasons and Consequences' (2009) 19 *Duke JCIL* 263. On the response to *Avena* in the US courts, cf Babcock, 'The Limits of International Law' (n 9) 187–95; Murphy, *United States Practice* (n 148) 33–38; C Galway Buys, 'The United States Supreme Court Misses the Mark: Towards Better Implementation of the United States' International Obligations' (2009) 24 *Conn JIL* 39. On the US as an international litigant more generally, cf M Feldman, 'The United States as an international litigant', in N Klein (ed), *Litigating International Disputes: Weighing the Options* (Cambridge, CUP, 2014) 106.

[157] Memorandum from President George W Bush to Attorney-General Alberto Gonzales, 28 February 2005, extracted in (2005) 99 *AJIL* 489.

[158] cf *Medillín v Dretke*, 371 F.3d 270 (5th Cir 2004); *Medellín v Dretke*, 544 US 660 (2005); *Medillín v. Texas*, 552 US 491 (2008).

[159] *Request for Interpretation of the Judgment of 31 March in the* Case concerning Avena and Other Mexican Nationals (Mexico v US) *(Mexico v US)*, Mexico: Application (5 June 2008).

[160] *Avena (Interpretation)*, Mexico: Request for the Indication of Provisional Measures of Protection (5 June 2008) 5.

[161] *Avena (Interpretation)*, Provisional Measures [2008] ICJ Rep 311, 331.

[162] *Medellín v Texas*, 554 US 759 (2008).

[163] S Goldenberg, 'Texas execution plan defies Hague order' (*The Guardian*, 5 August 2008) <www.theguardian.com/politics/2008/aug/05/justice.usa> accessed 20 May 2015.

[164] *Avena (Interpretation)* [2009] ICJ Rep 3, 21. Well into the administration of President Barack Obama, the ICJ's judgment in *Avena* was still regularly ignored by US courts: S Charnovitz, 'Correcting America's Continuing Failure to Comply with the *Avena* Judgment' (2012) 106 *AJIL* 572. The position presumably remains the same under President Donald J Trump.

By way of a final note, precisely the same question of the application of VCCR Article 36 was raised in the *Jadhav* case between India and Pakistan, involving the detention of a national of the former, accused of espionage and terrorism, by the latter. When the national in question was sentenced to death, India brought a case before the ICJ, seeking interim relief under Article 41 of the Statute, which was duly granted along exactly the same lines as seen in *Breard*, *LaGrand*, *Avena* and *Avena (Interpretation)*.[165] At the time of writing, the final result of the case—and the likelihood of Pakistan's compliance with the ICJ's measures—remains unknown.

VI. *LAGRAND* AND THE LAW OF PROVISIONAL MEASURES

In commenting on *LaGrand*, Thirlway was moved to make the following dark prognostication as to what the decision would mean for the Court as an institution:

> The *LaGrand* case, with its ruling that provisional measures create a binding obligation, will perhaps be hailed as a progressive step in the system of international judicial jurisdiction. On the contrary, it is submitted that it could well prove to have been a disaster for that system ... It is not ... surprising that the Court was willing to 'punish' the United States [for the execution of Walter LaGrand] by finding that its Order had created a legal obligation. There is no hint in the Judgment that it had thought through the consequences of such a finding of principle: the effect of an Order made in a case in which it is subsequently established that there was no jurisdiction, for example. Hard cases make bad law.[166]

This, emphatically, has not come to pass. Rather, the decision in *LaGrand* has prompted the further development of the ICJ's jurisprudence on provisional measures, likely as a response to sentiments similar to those expressed by Aceves: 'If states are required to treat provisional measures orders are binding, it creates a concomitant obligation on the Court to ensure that its provisional measures hearings and orders adhere to the same standards as its rulings on the merits'.[167]

A. The Development of the Law of Provisional Measures

At the outset, is important to note that the ICJ clearly considered its conclusions in *LaGrand* to be applicable to orders under Article 41 of its Statute generally.

---

[165] *Jadhav (India v Pakistan)*, ICJ, Order of 18 May 2017. Further: C Miles and S Ranganathan, 'Some Thoughts on the *Jadhav* Case: Jurisdiction, Merits and the Effect of a Presidential Communication' (*EJIL Talk!*, 12 May 2017) <www.ejiltalk.org/some-thoughts-on-the-jadhav-case-jurisdiction-merits-and-the-effect-of-a-presidential-communication> accessed 14 May 2017.

[166] Thirlway (n 141) 968. Some scholars have attempted to mollify Thirlway on this point by arguing that binding interim relief can only be awarded where Court's jurisdiction has already been established: K Oellers-Frahm, 'Expanding the Competence to Issue Provisional Measures—Strengthening the International Judicial Function', in A von Bogdandy and I Venzke (eds), *International Judicial Lawmaking: On Public Authority and Democratic Legitimation in Global Governance* (Berlin, Springer, 2012) 389, 404-07. Such arguments rely on a differentiated understanding of the Court's jurisdiction to award interim relief that is not recognized either on the face of the Statute or in practice.

[167] Aceves (n 5) 218.

The Court resisted a German invitation to confine the binding effect of provisional measures to cases involving risk to human life[168] (averting an undesirable sectoral fragmentation), and has since invoked the decision repeatedly to affirm the mandatory effect of Article 41 at large.[169] At the same time, however, a tightening of the Court's jurisprudence on provisional measures is observable.[170]

In the first place, the Court has added—or perhaps, elaborated—the prerequisites that must be met if interim relief is to be obtained. Since the *Border Area* case, it is now established that the rights with respect to which provisional protection is sought must be those which fall to be determined on the merits.[171] Although elements of this as a separate requirement may be seen in the *Arbitral Award* case,[172] the Court took the opportunity in *Pulp Mills* to recast the question, characterising it as contemplating 'the link between the *alleged rights* the protection of which is the subject of the provisional measures being sought, and the *subject of the proceedings* before the Court on the merits of the case'.[173] The Court defined the threshold as one of 'a sufficient connection with the merits of the case for the purpose of the current proceedings'.[174] As such, it is now clear that the Court does not require precise equivalence between the rights to be protected and the merits of the proceeding,[175] but merely that some relationship be observable.

In the same sense, the Court has further seen fit to develop a form of provisional merits review, previously absent from the ICJ calculus on interim relief. Following a powerful distillation of the issues by Judge Abraham in *Pulp Mills*,[176] the Court provided in *Obligation to Prosecute or Extradite* that, pursuant to Article 41, 'the power of the Court to indicate provisional measures should be exercised only if the Court is satisfied that the rights asserted by a party *are at least plausible*'.[177] This formula—along with the rider that the Court is not called upon to determine during the provisional measures phase whether such rights exist—has been adopted in

---

[168] CR 2000/26, 51 (Professor Dupuy).

[169] See, eg, *Application of the International Convention on All Forms of Racial Discrimination (Georgia v Russian Federation)*, Provisional Measures [2008] ICJ Rep 353, 397; *Certain Activities Carried Out by Nicaragua in the Border Area (Costa Rica v. Nicaragua)*, Provisional Measures [2011] ICJ Rep 6, 26–27; *in passim*, Provisional Measures [2013] ICJ Rep 354, 368; *Questions Relating to the Seizure and Detention of Certain Documents and Data (Timor-Leste v Australia)*, ICJ, Order of 3 March 2014, 53.

[170] *cf* B Kempen and Z He, 'The Practice of the International Court of Justice on Provisional Measures: The Recent Development' (2009) 69 ZaöRV 919; Y Lee-Iwamoto, 'The Repercussions of the *LaGrand* Judgment: Recent ICJ Jurisprudence on Provisional Measures' (2012) 55 JYIL 237.

[171] *Border Area* [2011] ICJ Rep 6, 18. Further: *Certain Activities Carried Out by Nicaragua in the Border Area (Costa Rica v Nicaragua)/Construction of a Road in Costa Rica Along the San Juan River (Nicaragua v Costa Rica)*, ICJ, Order of 22 November 2013, para 25; *Certain Documents and Data*, ICJ, Order of 3 March 2014, 23.

[172] *Arbitral Award* [1990] ICJ Rep 64, 70.

[173] *Pulp Mills on the River Uruguay (Argentina v Uruguay)*, Provisional Measures [2007] ICJ Rep 3, 10 (emphasis added).

[174] ibid, 10–11.

[175] See, eg, *Avena (Interpretation)* [2008] ICJ Rep 311, *Georgia v Russia* [2008] ICJ Rep 353, 388.

[176] *Pulp Mills* [2006] ICJ Rep 113, 140.

[177] *Questions relating to the Obligation to Prosecute or Extradite (Belgium v Senegal)*, Provisional Measures [2009] ICJ Rep 139, 151 (emphasis added).

subsequent cases, including *Border Area*,[178] *Temple (Interpretation)*[179] and *Certain Documents and Data*.[180]

Third, the Court has seen fit to impose new restrictions on the award provisional measures for the non-aggravations of disputes, as contemplated by the PCIJ's pronouncement in *Electricity Company*. In *Burkina Faso/Mali*, a Chamber of the ICJ held that the Court had the power to award such measures independently of measures for the protection of rights *pendente lite*.[181] The ICJ, however, retreated from this position in the *Pulp Mills* case, declaring that the 'power of the Court to indicate provisional measures can be exercised only if there is an urgent necessity to prevent irreparable harm to such rights, before the Court has given its final decision'.[182] As noted by Palchetti, two reasons may be identified for this *volte face*, both connected to the Court's conclusion as to the binding character of provisional measures in *LaGrand*.[183] First, and as seen in the ICJ's increased emphasis on the plausibility test, the Court has taken as a general rule a more stringent approach to the awarding of provisional measures so as to increase the legitimacy of any orders so given. Second, the contextualisation of provisional measures post-*LaGrand* has led the Court to reemphasise that the primary purpose of interim relief is the protection of rights *pendente lite*, with measures for non-aggravation assuming a correspondingly diminished role.

Finally, one may detect in the Court's jurisprudence an early regime for the adjudication of a breach of provisional measures. The Court has not been shy in determining that a breach of its orders has taken place,[184] though it might fairly be said that it is still finding its way insofar as an effective system of consequences for breach is concerned.[185]

---

[178] *Border Area* [2011] ICJ Rep 6, 19.

[179] *Request for Interpretation of the Judgment of 15 June 1962 in the Case concerning the* Temple of Preah Vihear (Cambodia v Thailand) *(Cambodia v Thailand)*, Provisional Measures [2011] ICJ Rep 537, 546.

[180] *Certain Documents and Data*, ICJ, Order of 3 March 2014, 26.

[181] *Frontier Dispute (Burkina Faso/Mali)*, Provisional Measures [1986] ICJ Rep 3, 9. The question was earlier raised, but not answered, in *Aegean Sea Continental Shelf (Greece v Turkey)*, Provisional Measures [1976] ICJ Rep 3, 12. The decision in *Burkina Faso/Mali* was reiterated in *Land and Maritime Boundary between Cameroon and Nigeria (Cameroon v Nigeria)*, Provisional Measures [1996] ICJ Rep 13, 22–23; *Armed Activities in the Territory of the Congo (Democratic Republic of the Congo v Uganda)*, Provisional Measures [2000] ICJ Rep 111, 128; *Certain Criminal Proceedings in France (France v Congo)*, Provisional Measures [2003] ICJ Rep 102, 111.

[182] *Pulp Mills* [2007] ICJ Rep 3, 13, 16.

[183] P Palchetti, 'The Power of the International Court of Justice to Indicate Provisional Measures to Prevent the Aggravation of a Dispute' (2008) 21 *LJIL* 623, 640–41.

[184] Most notably in the *Bosnian Genocide* case: [2007] ICJ Rep 43, 230–31. See also *Armed Activities (DRC v Uganda)* [2005] ICJ Rep 168, 258–59.

[185] Miles (n 10) Ch 7; Lee-Iwamoto, 'The Repercussions of the *LaGrand* Judgment' (n 170) 251–60; M Mendelson, 'State Responsibility for Breach of Interim Protection Orders of the International Court of Justice', in M Fitzmaurice and D Sarooshi (eds), *Issues of State Responsibility before International Judicial Institutions* (Oxford, Hart, 2004) 35.

B. *LaGrand* and a General Principle of Binding Interim Relief

Beyond the ICJ's elaboration of its jurisprudence under Article 41, it is clear that *LaGrand* has come to exercise a palpable influence on other adjudicative bodies.[186] The most immediate response has been in the context of tribunals convened under the auspices of the International Centre for the Settlement of Investment Disputes (ICSID).[187] Article 47 of the ICSID Convention was almost directly copied from Article 41 of the ICJ Statute.[188] Despite the fact that the decision in *Maffezini v Spain*[189] anticipated *LaGrand* in determining that provisional measures could be binding on the basis of wording similar to that of Article 41 of the ICJ Statute, it is *LaGrand* which has had the more enduring influence on ICSID jurisprudence. In *Casado v Chile*, the Tribunal justified its conclusion that provisional measures were binding by reference to both these decisions, with the Court's reasoning in *LaGrand* seeming 'manifestly to apply by analogy to Article 47 of the ICSID Convention'.[190] *Maffezini v Spain*, by contrast, was included almost as an afterthought.[191] Since that time, *LaGrand* has regularly been cited as upholding a general rule as to the binding character of provisional measures in ICSID cases,[192] such that it is now 'fully integrated into ICSID positive law'.[193] As a consequence, there is no longer any serious doubt that provisional measures ordered in the ICSID context are binding—though some individual arbitrators or tribunals express agnosticism[194] or contradiction[195] on this point. It has also been held that the provisional 'holding requests' (redolent

---

[186] CA Miles, 'The influence of the ICJ on the law of provisional measures', in M Andenas and E Bjorge (eds), *A Farewell to Fragmentation: Reassertion and Convergence in International Law* (Cambridge, CUP, 2015) 218, 258–67.

[187] Convention on the Settlement of Investment Disputes between States and Nationals of Other States, 18 March 1965, 575 UNTS 159.

[188] C Schreuer, L Malintoppi, A Reinisch and A Sinclair, *The ICSID Convention: A Commentary*, 2nd edn (Cambridge, CUP, 2009) 758–60.

[189] *Emilio Agustin Maffezini v Spain*, Provisional Measures (1999) 5 ICSID Rep 393, 394. Interestingly, prior to his elevation to the ICJ, Judge Buergenthal was a member of the Tribunal in *Maffezini v Spain*. His conclusions in that case may have influenced his overall agreement with the German submissions in *LaGrand*.

[190] *Victor Pey Casado and President Allende Foundation v Chile*, Provisional Measures (2001) 6 ICSID Rep 387, 394.

[191] ibid.

[192] See, eg, *City Oriente Ltd v Ecuador & Empresa Estatal Pretróleos del Ecuador*, ICSID Case No ARB/06/21 (Provisional Measures, 19 November 2007) para 92; *Perenco Ecuador Ltd v. Ecuador*, ICSID Case No ARB/08/6 (Provisional Measures, 8 May 2009) paras 75–76; *Tethyan Copper Company Pty Ltd v Pakistan*, ICSID Case No ARB/12/1 (Provisional Measures, 13 December 2012) para 120.

[193] A Pellet, 'The Case Law of the ICJ in Investment Arbitration' (2013) 28 *ICSID Rev–FILJ* 223, 239.

[194] *Millicom International Operations BV & Sentel GSM SA v Senegal*, ICSID Case No ARB/08/20 (Provisional Measures, 9 December 2009) para 49.

[195] *Caratube International Oil Company LLP v Kazakhstan*, ICSID Case No ARB/08/12 (Provisional Measures, 31 July 2009) 67 ('it should be noted that, according to Rule 39, the Tribunal cannot order, but can only recommend provisional measures in ICSID proceedings'); *RSM Production Corporation v St Lucia*, ICSID Case No ARB/12/10 (Security for Costs, 13 August 2013) para 16 (Arbitrator Nottingham, dissenting) ('No matter how many times it is repeated, an order is not a recommendation. Only in the jurisprudence of an imaginary Wonderland would this make sense').

of measures for non-aggravation) frequently issued by tribunals pending determination of an application for interim relief are also binding.[196]

Another court to respond positively to *LaGrand* was the European Court of Human Rights. In *Mamatkulov and Abdurasulovic v Turkey*, a Chamber of the Court overturned previous jurisprudence[197] on whether its provisional measures were binding, referring in part to *LaGrand*.[198] The Chamber reached this conclusion by various means, but *LaGrand* was held to be relevant inasmuch as its reasoning 'stressed the importance and purpose of interim measures and pointed out that compliance with such measures was necessary to ensure the effectiveness of decisions on the merits'.[199] This, it was said, had a bearing on the interpretation of the European Convention of Human Rights[200] (which lacked a provision analogous to Article 41 of the ICJ Statute) via VCLT Article 31(3)(c), requiring that where possible, treaties ought to be interpreted consistently with other principles of international law.[201] Evolutionary interpretation of the Convention was also held to be relevant.[202] Put another way, the Chamber perceived *LaGrand* as standing for the proposition that provisional measures were binding as a general principle of international law. An identical approach was subsequently adopted by the Grand Chamber in *Mamatkulov & Askarov v Turkey*.[203]

In light of such decisions, it now seems reasonable to speak of international courts and tribunals—absent a *lex specialis* to the contrary—as having inherent power to order binding interim relief, by way of a general principle of international law. To the extent that *LaGrand* may be said to have created a new *status quo* with respect to provisional measures, this is the principal legacy of the decision,[204] notwithstanding the fact that its reasoning largely concerns textual questions specific to Article 41.

VII. CONCLUSIONS

What, then, does *LaGrand* represent? In this chapter, I have endeavoured to show that it is indeed a landmark, and thus worthy of inclusion in this volume, even if

---

[196] *Perenco v Ecuador*, Provisional Measures, para 76: 'The Tribunal cannot accept that a request, formally expressed, may properly be regarded as of less binding force than a recommendation'. Whether this forms the basis of a new *jurisprudence constante* remains to be seen.

[197] See *Cruz Varas v Sweden*, ECtHR App 15576/89 (Judgment, 20 March 1991) para 98; *Conka v Belgium*, ECtHR App 51564/99 (Decision, 13 March 2001) para 11.

[198] *Mamatkulov and Abdurasulovic v Turkey*, ECtHR App 46827/99 and 46951/99 (Judgment, 6 February 2003) 103. Noted: CJ Tams (2003) 63 *ZaöRV* 681; C Brown (2003) 62 *CLJ* 532.

[199] *Mamatkulov and Abdurasulovic*, Judgment, para 101.

[200] 4 November 1950, 213 UNTS 222.

[201] ibid, 99.

[202] ibid, 93–105.

[203] *Mamatkulov and Askarov v Turkey*, ECtHR App 46827/99 and 46951/99 (Grand Chamber, 4 February 2005) para 117; *cf* ibid, paras 147–51 (Judges Caflisch, Türmen and Kovler, dissenting). *cf* the earlier decision by the Human Rights Committee in *Piandong v Philippines*, UN Doc CCPR/C/70/D/869/1999 (Decision, 19 October 2000) paras 5.1–5.4, in which it was held that the execution of relevant individuals by the Philippines in violation of provisional measures was a violation of its implicit obligation to cooperate with the Committee in good faith so as permit it to consider communications under the Optional Protocol to the International Covenant for Civil and Political Rights, 16 December 1966, 999 UNTS 17, preamble, Art 1.

[204] Tzanakopoulos, 'Provisional Measures' (n 15) 83–84; Brown, *A Common Law* (n 30) 146–50.

its core subject does not immediately evoke, for example, the Cold War frisson of *Nicaragua*,[205] or set out the form of the post-1945 international system in the same manner as did the *Early UN Advisory Opinions*.[206] Even then, one might expect a municipal lawyer to remember *LaGrand* as being primarily about the death penalty and its perception internationally. But whilst procedural law is often neglected amid the inter-state intrigues of international law, that does not diminish its importance overall as a guarantor of the rule of law and a guardian of the legitimacy of international adjudication. Beyond this, the story of the case is a compelling one, and one is struck by the contrast between the trench warfare conducted in the US courts by Karl and Walter LaGrand's defence counsel, as set against the more stately processes of the Peace Palace.

In this light, three things stand out in examining the legacy of *LaGrand*. In the first place, the Court resolved—at one stroke—the longest running procedural debate in international law, and did so in a way that was immediately accepted by the majority of states and commentators (even if some did have concerns as to its reasoning). In the second, it initiated a period of expansion for the Court's jurisprudence on interim relief—one that has still yet to run its course. Finally, the decision has been used as a standard for the concept of binding interim relief in international law more generally, enhancing in the process the capacity of courts and tribunals in a variety of systems to effectively insure their awards against party misbehaviour.

In this sense, *LaGrand* might best be considered as an investment by the ICJ in the infrastructure of international law: perhaps not the most headline grabbing or vote winning of developments, but one of vital necessity to the smooth running and evolution of the system as a whole. From a certain point of view, a well-made road can be as much a landmark as a dam,[207] or a wall,[208] or a smelter[209]—at least to those who can tell the difference.

---

[205] R Kolb, this volume, ch 15.
[206] T Grant and R Nicholson, this volume, ch 10.
[207] L Boisson de Chazournes and M Mbengue, this volume, ch 18.
[208] J Dugard, this volume, ch 22.
[209] D French, this volume, ch 8.

22

Legal Consequences of the Construction of a Wall in the Occupied Palestinian Territory (2004)

JOHN DUGARD

I. INTRODUCTION

THE DECISION OF the International Court of Justice (ICJ) in its 2004 Advisory Opinion on *Legal Consequences of the Construction of a Wall in the Occupied Palestinian Territory*[1] ('the *Wall*') is the only authoritative judicial statement on many of the controversial questions of law that characterise the conflict between Israel and Palestine over the former mandate territory of Palestine. While the Opinion focuses on the legality of the wall, barrier, or fence that Israel is building on Palestinian territory, it also pronounces on a wide range of questions of international humanitarian law and human rights law that give it a general importance. Its unanimous findings on the illegality of settlements and the application of the Fourth Geneva Convention and multilateral human rights conventions in the Occupied Palestinian Territory (OPT) are particularly significant. Although the Opinion of the Court was unanimous on many of the key issues it has failed to win the same measure of support from the international community of states as the Advisory Opinion of the ICJ in *Legal Consequences for States of the Continued Presence of South Africa in Namibia (South West Africa)*,[2] which also dealt with legal questions arising from a disputed mandate territory of the League of Nations. Hopes that, like the latter Opinion, the *Wall* would guide the political organs of the United Nations in their search for a just and peaceful resolution of the Israel–Palestine conflict have not been realised. Nevertheless, it constitutes a significant statement of the law and provides a normative framework for the settlement of the conflict between Israel and Palestine. Moreover, it has inspired civil society to take concerted action to enforce international law. It is a landmark decision and one that may yet chart the course of events in the Middle East.

---

[1] [2004] ICJ Rep 136.
[2] [1971] ICJ Rep 16. See further J Crawford and P Mertenskötter, this volume, ch 11.

II. HISTORICAL BACKGROUND

The conflict between Israel and Palestine in the former mandate territory of Palestine is characterised by legal disputation. The United Kingdom had been entrusted with the mandate over Palestine by the League of Nations. After it made it clear that it was unable to determine the future of the territory, the General Assembly of the United Nations, as successor to the League of Nations, recommended in Resolution 181(II) that Palestine be partitioned into a Jewish state and an Arab state, with Jerusalem as an international city under UN administration. Whether the General Assembly enjoyed the legal competence to make such a recommendation was disputed then and is still disputed.[3] A proposal that the question be referred to the ICJ for an advisory opinion was narrowly defeated.[4] Subsequent political developments involving disputed questions of law have not been referred to the ICJ. These include the unilateral declaration of the State of Israel in 1948; the Armistice Agreements of 1949 that brought the hostilities between Arab states and Israel to an end after this declaration of independence; General Assembly Resolution 194(III) of 1948 on the subject of Palestinian refugees; the question whether Israel acted defensively or aggressively in the Six-Day War of 1967; the exact meaning of Security Council Resolution 242 calling for the withdrawal of Israel from the territories it had occupied; the annexation of East Jerusalem in 1980 condemned as invalid by the Security Council;[5] the legality of settlements in the OPT; and the Oslo Accords of 1993. In 2002, Israel commenced building a wall mainly in Palestinian territory, ostensibly to protect Israelis from suicide bombers entering the territory in the course of the Second Intifada. It was only subsequently, in 2003, that the General Assembly, frustrated by Israel's apparent disregard for international law, decided to request an advisory opinion on a disputed question of law.[6] In order to understand the historical and legal context in which the decision to build the wall was taken it is necessary briefly to outline the history of Israeli–Palestinian relations.[7]

From 1949 to 1967 the mandate territory of Palestine was divided between Israel, Jordan and Egypt. Jordan was the occupying power of East Jerusalem and the West Bank, while Egypt occupied Gaza. In 1967, following the Six-Day War, Israel occupied the Palestinian territories of East Jerusalem, West Bank and Gaza. Although it purported to annex East Jerusalem in 1980 it made no attempt to annex the

---

[3] N Araby, 'Some Legal Implications of the 1947 Partition Resolution' (1968) 33 *Law and Contemporary Problems* 97.

[4] For a full account of the attempt to secure an advisory opinion, see V Kattan, *From Coexistence to Conquest. International Law and the Origins of the Arab–Israeli Conflict, 1891–1949* (London, Pluto Press, 2009) 148–51. See further the separate opinion of Judge Elaraby in *Wall* (n 1) 246–48, [1].

[5] UNSC Res 478 (1980) UN Doc S/RES/478.

[6] UNGA Res A/RES/ES-10/14 of 8 December 2003.

[7] For a historical account of the dispute from a legal perspective, see S Akram and M Lynk, 'The Arab–Israeli Conflict' in R Wolfrum (ed), *Max Planck Encyclopedia of Public International Law*, vol I (Oxford, OUP, 2011) 499. For more general histories, see M Tessler, *A History of the Israeli–Palestine Conflict*, 2nd edn (Bloomington, Indiana University Press, 2009); I Pappe, *A History of Modern Palestine. One Land Two People*, 2nd edn (Cambridge, CUP, 2006); A La Guardia, *Holy Land, Unholy War / Israelis and Palestinians*, 3rd edn (London, Penguin Books, 2007); S Ben-Ami, *Scars of War, Wounds of Peace. The Israeli–Arab Tragedy* (London, Weidenfeld & Nicolson, 2005).

West Bank and Gaza, which it administered as occupying power. Despite the prohibition of the transfer of parts of its own civilian population into the occupied territories contained in Article 49(6) of the Fourth Geneva Convention of 1949, to which it is a party, Israel proceeded to establish Jewish settlements in the OPT.

Israel's repressive occupation and its expansion of settlements resulted in the First Intifada of 1987–88. This spontaneous uprising, mainly on the part of young Palestinians, took the form of civil disobedience, demonstrations, and stone-throwing. The Israeli Defense Forces (IDF) responded with force. Some 1200 Palestinians and 200 Israelis were killed. This uprising prompted a revival of the peace process and the United States and the Soviet Union co-sponsored peace talks in Madrid and Washington. These negotiations failed, but in 1993 the Palestine Liberation Organization (PLO) and Israel met secretly in Oslo to reach agreement on the Oslo Accords, in which the PLO recognised Israel and Israel agreed to the establishment of Palestinian self-government over the West Bank and Gaza. This interim arrangement would continue for five years and lead to a final status agreement.[8]

Both Israel and Palestine were dissatisfied with the Oslo regime. Israel complained repeatedly that the Palestinian Authority under Yasser Arafat failed to prevent acts of violence committed by Islamic Jihad and Hamas (which had been formed during the First Intifada). The Palestinians were aggrieved to find that the construction of settlements continued unabated and found the checkpoints that regulated their movements humiliating and harmful to the economy. Moreover, agreements reached with Israel under Oslo in respect of a permanent settlement, the economy, the transfer of territory, and prisoner release were not honoured.

In the final months of the Clinton administration in 2000 serious attempts were made to implement a final status agreement. President Clinton called a meeting at Camp David in July 2000 in which he, Chairman Arafat, and Prime Minister Barak participated. But the talks broke down, mainly on the issue of sovereignty over Haram al-Sharif, which accommodates the al-Aqsa Mosque, Islam's third most sacred site, and the Dome of the Rock. This site is also of special significance to Jews as it is claimed to be the place on which the Jewish Second Temple stood. For Jews it is known as the Temple Mount. Neither side was prepared to compromise on this issue.

Negotiations between the Israelis, Palestinians and Americans continued at Taba in January 2001 after the failure of Camp David as all parties were aware of President Clinton's determination to secure a peaceful settlement in the last months of his presidency.[9] Parties came close to reaching an agreement but time ran out. President Clinton's term of office had come to an end and Israel faced an election in early February. On 6 February 2001 the Likud Party under Ariel Sharon defeated the Labour Party under Ehud Barak. Sharon announced that high-level talks between

---

[8] For an account of the adoption of the Oslo Accords, see M Abbas, *Through Secret Channels* (Reading, Garnet Publishing, 1995).

[9] See G Sher, *The Israeli–Palestinian Peace Negotiations, 1999–2001. Within Reach* (Abingdon, Routledge, 2004). See further on this period, AD Miller, *The Much Too Promised Land. America's Elusive Search for Arab–Israeli Peace* (New York, Bantam Books, 2009).

the Israelis and Palestinians would be discontinued. In the meantime the Second Intifada had started.

On 28 September 2000 Ariel Sharon, leader of the Likud Party, accompanied by a large party of Likud supporters, visited the Haram al-Sharif/Temple Mount. The ostensible purpose of the visit was to assert the right of Israelis to visit the Temple Mount, but it was generally believed that the main purpose was to show that under a Likud government the Temple Mount would remain under Israeli sovereignty. Reluctantly the Barak Government gave permission to Sharon's visit to dispel any suggestion that it was prepared to compromise Israeli sovereignty over the Temple Mount. Fearing that the visit would raise tensions among the Palestinians, Arafat and other Palestinian leaders called on Sharon not to go.

As predicted, the visit was followed by protests and demonstrations in the Old City of Jerusalem, in which seven Palestinians were killed and some 300 wounded. Spontaneous demonstrations erupted all over the West Bank and Gaza prompted by disillusionment over the Oslo Accords, the brutality and humiliation of the occupation, poverty and the miserable conditions in the refugee camps. Protests and demonstrations were soon accompanied by stone-throwing and lethal force. The response of Israeli Defense Forces (IDF) was to use tear gas, rubber bullets and live fire in a display of excessive force.

Whereas the First Intifada remained a popular uprising characterised by demonstrations, stone-throwing and acts of civil disobedience, the Second Intifada became a low-level civil war. Both sides employed armed force of different kinds resulting in thousands of deaths and injuries.[10] On the Palestinian side, suicide bombings resulting in the deaths of many innocent Israelis, stone-throwing, armed force and rocket fire from Gaza joined protests and peaceful demonstrations as features of the uprising. Over 1,000 Israelis were killed. The IDF, supported by settlers, responded aggressively. Ground forces confronted mass protests and demonstrations with live fire supported by F16 fighter aircraft and Apache gunship helicopters. Helicopters were used for targeted assassinations of militants with little regard for 'collateral damage' to civilians near to the selected militant. The Israeli human rights non-governmental organisation B'Tselem estimated that from 2000 to April 2008, when the Second Itifada came to an end, some 4,475 Palestinians were killed, of whom most were civilians. Thousands of Palestinians were arrested, detained and tortured. Over 4,000 houses were demolished, agricultural land was stripped of trees and crops, free movement was seriously restricted by checkpoints and curfews, the coast of Gaza was blockaded, and hospitals and schools were attacked.

Suicide bombers that struck in the cities of Israel, killing and wounding hundreds of Israelis, had a devastating impact on Israeli society.[11] Ostensibly in response to these bombings, Israel commenced construction of the wall.

---

[10] For an account of the Second Intifada, see A Bregman, *Cursed Victory. A History of Israel and the Occupied Territories* (London, Penguin Books, 2014) Ch 12–14.

[11] For an account of these suicide attacks, see Written Statement of the Government of Israel to ICJ in the *Wall* (30 January 2004) 40–55. Some of the worst suicide bombings are described by Bregman, *Cursed Victory* (n 10) 270, 275, 286.

III. THE CONSTRUCTION OF THE WALL

In 2002 Israel began construction of a wall or barrier to separate the West Bank from Israel.[12] When finished it will run for about 700 kilometres. In places, particularly in urban areas, the wall takes the form of an eight-metre-high concrete wall. However, most of the structure is a barrier some 60–100 metres wide comprising three fences, of which the outer two are protected by coils of barbed wire while the inner fence has electronic equipment which allows intruders to be detected. There are patrol roads on either side of the outer fence and a trace road, which is a strip of sand that allows footprints to be detected. Sometimes the barrier includes trenches. There are fortified guard towers at regular intervals. Israel describes the structure as a 'fence' while the UN Secretary-General preferred to use the term 'barrier'. Within Palestine it is known as the wall, or more frequently the 'Apartheid wall'. In its Advisory Opinion on the *Wall* the ICJ preferred to describe it as a 'wall' to conform with the terminology employed by the General Assembly.[13] I shall follow this terminology.

The declared object of the wall was to prevent suicide bombers from entering Israel, but the fact that the wall did not follow the Green Line—the Armistice Line of 1949—and instead entered the West Bank and encircled Israeli settlements, made it clear that the wall was intended to serve another purpose as well, namely the incorporation of settlements into Israel itself. It was, arguably, a pretext for annexation of Palestinian territory under the guise of security.

When the construction of the wall began I was serving as Special Rapporteur on the Human Rights Situation in the Occupied Palestinian Territories to the United Nations Commission on Human Rights (replaced in 2006 by the Human Rights Council). In this capacity I was required to visit the OPT twice a year and to report to the Commission itself and to the Third Committee of the General Assembly. I followed the construction of the wall from the very beginning.

In 2002 I was taken to see paint marks or rocks on hills near Qalqiliya and Tulkarm which had been made by Israel to indicate the course of the wall. In June 2003,[14] some 150 kilometres had been completed. At that stage it intruded six to seven kilometres into Palestine, but today it extends over 20 kilometres into Palestinian territory. Most of the wall is built in Palestinian territory, on the Palestinian side of the Green Line, the internationally recognised border between Israel and Palestine. It seizes over 10 per cent of Palestinian land, including some of its most fertile agricultural land and water resources. The wall incorporates most of Israel's settlements in the West Bank, with over 80 per cent of the settler population. It includes 42 Palestinian villages with a population of some 56,000 into the 'seam zone' or 'closed area', that is, the area between the wall and the Green Line. In some places it completely encircles Palestinian villages, separating them from the West Bank and

---

[12] For an account of the wall, its route, and impact, see *Wall* (n 1) 168–71, [79]–[85]. See too R Dolphin, *The West Bank Wall. Unmaking Palestine* (London, Pluto Press, 2006).
[13] *Wall* (n 1) 164, [67].
[14] See my report to the Commission on Human Rights, E/CN.4/2004/6 of 8 September 2003.

converting them into isolated enclaves. Qalqiliya, a city with a population of over 40,000, is completely surrounded by the concrete wall and residents are allowed to leave only through checkpoints.

Those living on the West Bank side of the wall require permits to access their own agricultural land on the other side of the wall in the 'seam zone'. Permits for farmers are not readily granted; the process of application is humiliating; gates are few and often do not open as scheduled; and those passing through the gates are subject to harassment and abuse.

Jerusalem has been radically affected by the wall. Many villages or suburbs previously within the Governate of Jerusalem are placed on the West Bank side of the wall, which means that Palestinians living in these villages can only access their schools, hospitals, universities and holy places through checkpoints. In some places the wall runs through Palestinian communities, separating neighbours and families. It is difficult to understand what security purpose could possibly be served by building a wall through a Palestinian community.

In 2003 I sought to draw public attention to the wall. In August, I wrote an op-ed for the *International Herald Tribune*[15] which stated that the wall was 'manifestly intended to create facts on the ground' and that it constituted an act of annexation. 'Annexation of this kind', I said, 'goes by another name in international law—conquest'. My written report to the United Nations of September 2003 was equally strong and declared 'that what we are presently witnessing in the West Bank is a visible and clear act of territorial annexation under the guise of security',[16] an accusation that was repeated in my oral report to the Third Committee in October. The Third Committee referred the matter to the General Assembly.

IV. REQUEST FOR AN OPINION AND PROCEEDINGS BEFORE THE COURT

Meeting in its Tenth Emergency Special Session, the General Assembly adopted a resolution demanding that Israel 'stop and reverse construction of the wall in the Occupied Palestinian Territory' on the ground that it constituted a departure from the Armistice Line of 1949 and was a violation of international law.[17] The resolution requested the Secretary-General to report on compliance with the resolution and on 24 November the Secretary-General reported that Israel had failed to comply. While I was in New York to present my report to the Third Committee I suggested to delegates that it might be appropriate for the General Assembly to request an advisory opinion from the ICJ on the legality of the wall if Israel failed to comply with the resolution of the General Assembly. I was later approached by Nasser Al Kidwa,

---

[15] 2–3 August 2003.
[16] E/CN.4/2004/6 of 8 September 2003, para 6.
[17] Res A/Res/ES-10/13 of 21 October 2003.

the Palestinian ambassador to the United Nations about the form the question to the Court might take. I advised him to formulate any such request to the ICJ along the lines of the question posed to the Court in the 1971 *Namibia* Opinion; that is, to stress the legal consequences flowing from the construction of the wall. On 8 December 2003 the General Assembly adopted a resolution which welcomed my report of 8 September 2003[18] and asked the Court to pronounce on the following question:

> What are the legal consequences arising from the construction of the wall being built by Israel, the occupying Power in the Occupied Palestinian Territory, including in and around East Jerusalem, as described in the report of the Secretary-General, considering the rules and principles of international law, including the Fourth Geneva Convention of 1949, and relevant Security Council and General Assembly resolutions.[19]

Forty-nine states and regional organisations made written representations to Court and 15 addressed the Court in the oral hearings. The United States submitted a written representation questioning the propriety of giving an opinion but with no comment on the merits. EU member states provided written submissions but did not participate in the hearings. Palestine was given permission by the Court to make a written statement and to address the Court in the oral hearings. Israel chose to ignore the proceedings after submitting a written statement in which it contested the jurisdiction of the Court and the propriety of giving an opinion. Although Israel chose not to appoint an ad hoc judge, Judge Owada expressed the view that it would have been entitled to do so, in which case considerations of fairness might have required Palestine to also make such an appointment.[20] Strangely, although the UN Secretary-General submitted a written statement to the Court, the Legal Counsel of the United Nations did not make oral representations to the Court, despite the fact that this had been done in the *Namibia* Opinion of 1971. This suggested that the UN Secretariat were unhappy about the decision of the General Assembly to ask for an Opinion. This was later confirmed by senior members of the Secretariat in private conversations.

On 30 June 2004, nine days before the ICJ handed down its Opinion, the Israeli Supreme Court, sitting as the High Court of Justice, gave its judgment on a number of petitions challenging the construction and routing of the wall.[21] This court held that while in many instances the IDF had routed the wall to cause disproportionate harm to the Palestinian population, some deviation from the Green Line was permissible. In so deciding the Court accepted that the military had acted rationally in order to attain the military objective of the wall.[22]

---

[18] E/CN.4/2004/6 of 8 September 2003.
[19] UNGA Res A/RES/ES-10/14. The United States, the Russian Federation and the European Union abstained from voting on this resolution.
[20] *Wall* (n 1) separate opinion [19].
[21] *Beit Sourik Village Council v Government of Israel* (2004) 43 ILM 1099.
[22] ibid, 1120, [57].

V. THE COURT'S OPINION

A. Jurisdiction

The Court had little difficulty in deciding that it had jurisdiction to give an opinion.[23] In a unanimous decision it found that the General Assembly was competent to request an advisory opinion despite the fact that the question of Israel–Palestine was before the Security Council as an attempt to persuade the Council to condemn the construction of the wall had been vetoed in October 2003 by a permanent member, the United States.[24] This meant that in terms of General Assembly resolution 377 A(V), the Uniting for Peace Resolution, the General Assembly was competent to take such action.[25] The suggestion that the matter involved a political dispute and not a legal question was also rejected.[26]

B. Propriety

Next the Court turned to a number of arguments that had been raised that it would be improper for it to give an opinion as this would be inconsistent with the Court's judicial function. First, the Court dismissed the argument that it was precluded from rendering an opinion because Israel had refused to consent to adjudication, holding that the request did not concern a bilateral matter between Israel and Palestine only but one of broader concern to the international community.[27] Second, it held that the Security Council's decision in Resolution 1515 (2003) of 19 November 2003 to empower a Quartet, comprising the United Nations, the European Union, the Russian Federation and the United States, to engage in peace-making in the region by means of a Roadmap to a Permanent Two-State Solution to the Israeli-Palestinian Conflict was not an obstacle to the rendering of an opinion.[28] Third, the Court rejected Israel's argument that the Court did not have sufficient information before it, especially in respect of Israel's security needs, to make a decision. Here the Court held that it had been provided with adequate information by the Secretary-General, UN special rapporteurs, and parties appearing before the Court.[29] Finally, it dismissed the arguments that an opinion would serve no purpose[30] and that Palestine had not come to Court with 'clean hands' as a result of its violent acts in the course of the Second Intifada.[31] By 14 votes to one (Judge Buergenthal of the United States

---

[23] For criticism of the Court's decision on jurisdiction, see J Alvarez, 'Interpretation and Change, the Limits of Change by Way of Agreements and Practice' in G Nolte (ed), *Treaties and Subsequent Practice* (Oxford, Oxford University Press, 2013) 127.
[24] *Wall* (n 1) 146, [20].
[25] ibid, 151, [31].
[26] ibid, 155, [41].
[27] ibid, 157–69, [46]–[50].
[28] ibid, 159–60, [51]–[54].
[29] ibid, 160–62, [55]–[58].
[30] ibid, 162–63, [59]–[62].
[31] ibid, 163–64, [63]–[64].

dissenting) the Court found that 'there was no compelling reason' for it to use its discretionary power not to give an opinion.[32]

C. Merits

The ICJ has often used advisory opinions to consider and clarify legal issues that go beyond a narrow answer to the question asked. In so doing, it has contributed substantially to the development of the law. The advisory opinions on the *International Status of South West Africa* of 1950[33] and *Namibia* of 1971[34] are examples of such a broad approach to the advisory function. On the other hand, an opinion like *Accordance with International Law of the Unilateral Declaration of Independence in Respect of Kosovo*[35] confines itself to a strict and limited answer to the question posed. Although Judge Higgins accuses the Court of not having 'followed the tradition of using advisory opinions as an opportunity to elaborate and develop international law',[36] the *Wall* Opinion does do more than merely answer the question before it. In examining the legal norms that render the construction of the wall illegal, the Court elaborates on a number of issues that arise in the course of its reasoning. Some of these issues are dealt with thoroughly, others abruptly.[37] In the result the Opinion falls midway between the approaches adopted in *Namibia* and *Kosovo*.

The Court's Opinion is divided into two parts: a consideration of the illegality of the wall and the consequences of such illegality.[38]

The first part commences with an examination of the status of the Occupied Palestinian Territories which traverses the history of the OPT from the adoption of the Mandate for Palestine in 1920 to the Oslo Accords of 1993 and the Peace Treaty with Jordan of 1994.[39] This brief history falls short of the contextual history of the dispute pleaded for by Judge Higgins.[40] The Court then examines the construction, route and impact of the wall. In so doing it considers both the present structure of the wall and Israel's plans for the future course of the wall.[41]

After this introduction the Court turns to the applicable law. Here it considers norms contained in UN Charter, the General Assembly Declaration on Principles of International Law concerning Friendly Relations and Co-operation among States[42]

---

[32] ibid, 164, [65].

[33] [1950] ICJ Rep 128.

[34] *Legal Consequences for States of the Continued Presence of South Africa in Namibia (South West Africa) notwithstanding Security Council Resolution 276 (1970)* [1971] ICJ Rep 16.

[35] [2010] ICJ Rep 403.

[36] *Wall* (n 1) 212–13, [23].

[37] See I Scobbie, 'Words My Mother Never Taught Me—In Defense of the International Court' (2005) 99 AJIL 76, 80; D Kretzmer, 'The Advisory Opinion: The Light Treatment of International Humanitarian Law (2005) 99 AJIL 88; A Imseis, 'Critical Reflections on the International Humanitarian Law Aspects of the ICJ *Wall* Advisory Opinion' (2005) 99 AJIL 102,103.

[38] *Wall* (n 1) 164, [68].

[39] ibid 165–68, [70]–[79].

[40] ibid 210–12, [14]–[18]. This view is shared by Judge Kooijmans, 221, [7].

[41] ibid 168–71, [79]–[85].

[42] UNGA Res 2625 (XXV).

of 1970, international humanitarian law contained in the Hague Regulations of 1907 and Fourth Geneva Convention of 1949, and human rights law set out in the International Covenant on Civil and Political Rights, the International Covenant on Economic, Social and Cultural Rights, and the Convention on the Rights of the Child.[43]

The Court next considers whether the construction of the wall violates these principles.[44] Here it finds that the incorporation of Palestinian land and people into the 'seam zone' and the inclusion of Jewish illegal settlements in this area severely impede the exercise of the right of the Palestinian people to self-determination and therefore constitutes a breach of Israel's obligation to respect this right.[45] The Court notes Israel's assurance that the wall is only a temporary measure and does not amount to annexation but declares that it 'cannot remain indifferent to certain fears expressed to it that the route of the wall will prejudge the future frontier between Israel and Palestine, and the fear that Israel may integrate the settlements and their means of access'.[46] However, although it finds that the wall and its associated regime may create a *fait accompli* that could become permanent, and tantamount to annexation, it fails actually to find that the wall constitutes an act of annexation.[47] That the Court was reluctant to go so far as to find that the construction of the wall was an act of annexation appears from the separate opinion of Judge Elaraby in which he declares that the Court should have been more explicit on this subject which should have been reflected in a finding on the prohibition of annexation in the *dispositif*.[48] The Court's ambivalent statement suggests that at this stage, so shortly after the start of the construction of the wall, it was prepared to give Israel the benefit of doubt about its intentions.[49]

An examination of international humanitarian law leads the Court to conclude that the wall violates Articles 46 and 52 of the Hague Regulations of 1907 and Article 53 of the Fourth Geneva Convention requiring private property to be respected. Relying on UN reports, including my Special Rapporteur's report of 8 September 2003,[50] the Court finds that the wall results in the seizure of agricultural land and water resources, restrictions on freedom of movement and the right to work and denial of access to schools and health services in violation of the international human rights covenants. These measures violate the right to an adequate standard of living and result in internal displacement of the Palestinian people in violation of Article 49 of the Geneva Convention.[51] Such measures cannot be justified

---

[43] *Wall* (n 1) 171–81, [86]–[113].

[44] ibid 181–95, [114]–[142].

[45] ibid 183–84, [120], [122].

[46] ibid 184, [121].

[47] ibid. Judge Koroma in his separate opinion had no hesitation in describing the construction of the wall as an act of annexation: 204, [2].

[48] ibid 253, [2.5].

[49] See on the ambiguities in the Court's finding on annexation, Kretzmer, 'The Advisory Opinion' (n 37) 94, 96.

[50] E/CN.4/2004/6.

[51] *Wall* (n 1) 189–92, [133]–[134].

by military necessity or emergency measures.[52] Nor can Israel rely on self-defence under Article 51 of the UN Charter or on a state of necessity to preclude the wrongfulness of the construction of the wall.

The Court concludes by stating that it is not convinced that the 'specific course Israel has chosen for the wall was necessary to attain its security objectives'.[53] It finds that the wall seriously infringes a number of human rights of Palestinians living in the OPT and constitutes a breach by Israel of various of its obligations under international humanitarian law and human rights law.[54] On this basis it rules that Israel is obliged to comply with its obligation to respect the right to self-determination of the Palestinian people and its obligations under international humanitarian law and human rights law; to cease forthwith construction of the wall; and to make reparation for all damage caused by the construction of the wall in the OPT.[55] This decision was reached by 14 votes to one with Judge Buergenthal again dissenting.

Judge Buergenthal's dissent is based largely on the absence of sufficient evidence of Israel's security concerns. He acknowledges that Israel was itself mainly to blame for this by its refusal to cooperate with the Court in the provision of evidence but reasons that in advisory proceedings, unlike contentious proceedings, there is an obligation on the Court to satisfy itself that it has sufficient evidence on which to base an opinion.[56] Unfortunately Judge Buergenthal fails to address the generous finding of the Court that the construction of the wall did not constitute an act of annexation which was largely based on respect for Israel's statements, unaccompanied by evidence, that the wall was a temporary measure to combat terrorist attacks.[57]

The Court finds that Israel is obliged to comply with its obligation to respect the right of the Palestinian people to self-determination and its obligations under international humanitarian law and international human rights law.[58] The Court also holds that Israel is obliged to cease forthwith the construction of the wall and to dismantle all sections of the wall in Palestinian territory;[59] to make reparation to all property owners whose properties have suffered and to compensate all natural and legal persons for any form of material damage incurred as a result of construction of the wall.[60]

The Court finds that Israel has violated *erga omnes* obligations requiring it to respect the right of the Palestinian people to self-determination and certain obligations under international humanitarian law. This leads it to hold that:

> All States are under an obligation not to recognize the illegal situation resulting from the construction of the wall and not to render aid or assistance in maintaining the situation

---

[52] ibid 192–93, [135]–[136].
[53] ibid 193, [137].
[54] ibid.
[55] ibid, 197–98, [149]–[153]; 201–02, [163(3)] A–C.
[56] Declaration by Judge Buergenthal, especially 240–41, 243, 245, [1], [3.7], [10]). In his separate opinion Judge Owada suggests that the Court should have made an in-depth investigation *proprio motu* into the facts surrounding the wall: 270–71, [30].
[57] *Wall* (n 1) 182, [116]; 184–85, [121].
[58] ibid, 197, [149].
[59] ibid, 197–98, [151].
[60] ibid, 198, [152]–[153].

created by such construction; all States parties to the Fourth Geneva Convention relative to the Protection of Civilian Persons in Time of War of 12 August 1949 have in addition the obligation, while respecting the United Nations Charter and international law, to ensure compliance by Israel with international humanitarian law as embodied in that Convention.[61]

This decision was taken by 13 votes to two, with Judges Buergenthal and Kooijmans dissenting. Judge Kooijmans's principal complaints were that in this case the General Assembly had requested an opinion on the legal consequences of an act of a state and not, unlike the 1971 *Namibia* Opinion, an opinion on the legal consequences *for States* of the conduct of a state;[62] and that the finding of a duty not to recognise an illegal situation failed to specify what states were expected to do or not to do.[63] It is difficult to follow Judge Kooijmans reasoning. First, the legal consequences for *States* as a result of a finding that the wall was illegal was surely implied in the question put to the Court. Second, the duty of non-recognition coupled with the obligation not to render aid or assistance in maintaining the situation created by the construction of the wall makes it clear that states should desist from any action that might be construed as recognition of the wall or any consequences resulting from the construction of the wall.

Finally, the Court ruled by 14 votes to one (Judge Buergenthal dissenting) that the United Nations, and especially the Security Council and General Assembly, should consider what further action is required to bring to an end the illegal situation resulting from the construction of the wall.[64]

VI. SIGNIFICANT AND CONTESTED FINDINGS

The main focus of the *Wall* Opinion and its principal significance, obviously, is the finding on the illegality of the wall Israel is constructing on Palestinian territory. But, in reaching its conclusion, the Court examines a number of other issues, some essential for its finding and others, perhaps, only tangential to this finding. Some of these issues raise important questions of law that had been the subject of dispute for many years. All have important political consequences. The decision of the Court on these issues therefore adds to the significance of the Opinion.

A. Self-determination and Independence

The right of the Palestinian people to self-determination is today universally recognised. As the Court stressed in the *Wall*, even Israel recognises such a right.[65] The *Wall* Opinion therefore attaches great importance to this right which it describes

---

[61] ibid, 202, [163(3)D].
[62] ibid, [1], [39].
[63] ibid, [1], [44].
[64] ibid, 202, [163(3)E].
[65] ibid, 182–83, [118].

as a right with an *erga omnes* character.[66] All states, the Court declares, are under an obligation 'to see to it that any impediment resulting from the construction of the wall to the exercise of the Palestinian people of its right to self-determination is brought to an end'.[67] The importance of this right is echoed by several judges in their separate opinions[68] and by Judge Buergenthal in his declaration.[69]

But does the Court recognise that a necessary consequence of this right is an independent Palestinian state? Yes, say Judges Higgins and Elaraby in their separate opinions. According to Judge Higgins 'the Palestinian people are entitled to their territory, to exercise self-determination, and to have their own State'.[70] Judge Elaraby goes further and states that 'the United Nations is under an obligation to pursue the establishment of an independent Palestine'.[71]

The judgment of the Court is not so clear. In paragraph 88 of its Opinion the Court purports to cite with approval a passage from the 1971 Advisory Opinion on *Namibia* that in the light of developments in the past 50 years the ultimate objective of the sacred trust referred to in Article 22 of the Covenant of the League of Nations establishing the mandates system 'was the self-determination and *independence* of the peoples concerned' (italics added).[72] Yet in its citation of this dictum of 1971 in the *Wall*, the Court omits the word *independence* and simply states that the ultimate objective of the sacred trust in the mandates system 'was the self-determination ... of the peoples concerned'.[73] One can only assume that this omission was deliberate. But no reason is advanced for this omission. Was it because the Court was too timid to commit itself on such a controversial issue?

The statehood and independence of Palestine is disputed in some quarters.[74] The United States and Israel vehemently oppose such a notion, and most European States follow their lead. But over 130 states today recognise Palestine as an independent state and on 29 November 2012 Palestine was recognised an non-member observer state by the United Nations General Assembly by a two-thirds majority vote.[75] This resolution is generally regarded as recognition of Palestinian statehood, which has been confirmed by Palestine becoming a party to many multilateral treaties, including the Rome Statute of the International Criminal Court. Only the veto of the United States stands in the way of its admission to the United Nations. One can only speculate whether a bold assertion of Palestine's right to an independent state as a component of the right to self-determination in the *Wall* would have had any impact on Palestine's claim to statehood.

---

[66] ibid, 199, [156]–[157].
[67] ibid, 200, [159].
[68] ibid, Judges Higgins, 211–12, [18]; Elaraby, 250, [2.2]–[2.3]; Kooijmans, 228–29, [31]–[33].
[69] ibid, 241, [4].
[70] ibid, 211–12, [18].
[71] ibid, 251–52, [2.3].
[72] [1971] ICJ Rep 31, [53].
[73] *Wall* (n 1) 171–72, [88].
[74] See further on this subject, J Quigley, *The Statehood of Palestine. International Law in the Middle East Conflict* (New York, CUP, 2010).
[75] Resolution 67/19.

B. Fourth Geneva Convention

Israel became a party to the 1949 Fourth Geneva Convention Relative to the Protection of Civilian Persons in Time of War in 1951. Following its occupation of the Palestinian territories occupied by Jordan and Egypt in 1967, Israel refused to acknowledge the applicability of the Convention to these territories, preferring to view them as 'liberated', 'disputed' or 'administered' territories to which, as a matter of policy but not law, it was prepared to extend the humanitarian provisions of the Convention.[76] Although the political aspirations of those who yearn for a Greater Israel were largely responsible for this decision, there is no doubt that Israel was unwilling to commit itself to the obligation contained in Article 49(6) of the Convention to refrain from transferring part of its civilian population into the Palestinian territories. The political decision not to apply the Convention is backed by sophisticated legal argument. The principal argument maintains that Article 2(2) of the Fourth Geneva Convention applies the Convention only to cases of 'occupation of the territory of a High Contracting Party' and that the Palestinian territories were, prior to 1967, under the occupation of Jordan and Egypt and were consequently not the territory of a High Contracting Party. There was no sovereign power in the Palestinian territories to which the territory might be returned on the conclusion of a peace treaty.[77] A secondary argument, advanced by Stephen Schwebel, later to become President of the ICJ, was that the territories had been acquired in self-defence in the Six-Day War which meant that Israel's title was better than that of Jordan or Egypt which had occupied the territories unlawfully as aggressors in 1948. This gave Israel title by 'defensive conquest',[78] which could not be characterised as belligerent occupation. The Supreme Court of Israel carefully refrained from pronouncing on the applicability of the Fourth Geneva Convention.[79]

The Court dismissed the first of Israel's arguments after an examination of the Fourth Geneva Convention and the practice of states and international organisations. It emphasised that Article 2(1) of the Convention made it clear that all that was required to make the Convention applicable was the existence of an armed conflict between two or more of the contracting parties. (Israel, Jordan, and Egypt were all contracting parties.) In such a case the Convention applied in any territory occupied in the course of the conflict by one of the parties. The purpose of Article 2(2) was not to exclude from the scope of application of the Convention territories not falling under the sovereignty of one of the parties. Rather, the intention of the drafters of the Convention, said the Court, was 'to protect civilians who find themselves, in whatever way, in the hands of the occupying Power' regardless

---

[76] See D Kretzmer, *The Occupation of Justice. The Supreme Court of Israel and the Occupied Territories* (Albany, State University of New York, 2002) 32–34.

[77] See Y Blum, 'The Missing Reversioner: Reflections on the Status of Judea and Samaria' (1968) 3 *Israel Law Review* 279; M Shamgar, 'The Observance of International Law in the Administered Territories' (1971) Israel Year Book of Human Rights 262.

[78] S Schwebel, 'What Weight to Conquest?' (1970) 64 *AJIL* 344.

[79] Kretzmer, *The Occupation of Justice* (n 76) 54.

of the status of the occupied territories.[80] This interpretation was confirmed by the *travaux préparatoires* of the Convention and had subsequently been confirmed by states parties to the Convention, the International Committee of the Red Cross, the General Assembly and the Security Council.[81] The Court concluded that 'the Fourth Geneva Convention is applicable in any occupied territory in the event of an armed conflict arising between two or more High Contracting Parties'.[82] As Israel, Jordan, and Egypt were all contracting parties it followed that the Convention is applicable to the occupied territories to the east of the Green Line.[83] The finding of the Court on the applicability of the Fourth Geneva Convention in the OPT was unanimous.[84]

Israel's second argument based on 'defensive conquest' was not considered.[85] To do so would have required the Court to examine the history of the Palestinian territories between 1948 and 1967, which it had refrained from doing, much to the annoyance of Judge Kooijmans.[86] Was this a deliberate omission to avoid commenting on the reprehensible conduct of Jordan, which had tried unsuccessfully to annex the West Bank and East Jerusalem? Or did it wish to avoid challenging the view of a former colleague, Judge Schwebel, despite the fact that it was patently wrong. First, because his argument assumed that Israel acted in self-defence in 1967 in the face of much evidence to the contrary.[87] Second, because it failed to acknowledge that title to territory may not be acquired by the use of force, whether used defensively or aggressively.

C. Settlements

Article 49(6) of the Fourth Geneva Convention prohibits an occupying power from transferring parts of its own civilian population into territory it occupies. According to the *Commentary* of the International Committee of the Red Cross this clause was intended to prevent a practice adopted by some states during the Second World War of transferring their own population into occupied territory 'to colonize those territories'. Such transfers, said the *Commentary*, 'worsened the economic situation of the native population and endangered their separate existence as a race'.[88]

That Article 49(6) prohibits Israel from establishing settlements in the Palestinian Occupied Territories and from colonising such territories is accepted by the United

---

[80] ibid 174–75, [95].

[81] ibid 175–76, [96]–[99].

[82] ibid, 177, [101]. On the subject of the Green Line, see the separate opinion of Judge Al-Kwasawneh, 238, [11].

[83] ibid, 177, [101].

[84] For Judge Buergenthal's endorsement of the applicability of the Convention, see ibid, 240, [2].

[85] See Imseis, 'Critical Reflections' (n 37) 105.

[86] *Wall* (n 1) separate opinion, 221–22, [8]–[10].

[87] See J Quigley, *The Six-Day War and Israeli Self-Defense, Questioning the Legal Basis for Preventive War* (New York, CUP, 2013).

[88] J Pictet (ed), *Commentary, IV Geneva Convention* (Geneva, International Committee of the Red Cross, 1958) 283.

Nations, the International Committee of the Red Cross and states (including the United States).

Only Israel disputes the illegality of Jewish settlement in the OPT.

Initially Israel claimed that it had established settlements in order to defend its occupation of the OPT.[89] This pretext has, however, long been abandoned. Today settlements range in nature from small hilltop outposts to large cities with populations of many thousands, serving the needs of Zionists determined to occupy what they regard as Greater Israel—*Eretz Israel*—and ordinary civilians who treat settlements as towns and cities for suburban living, replete with schools, university, hospitals, supermarkets, sports grounds and parks. No longer able to justify settlements as a security measure, Israel has argued that it is not bound by the Fourth Geneva Convention and that, even if it were, these settlements are not prohibited by Article 49(6) as the inhabitants have moved voluntarily to the settlements and not been transferred by the government of Israel.[90] The Israel Supreme Court has studiously refrained from pronouncing on the legality of settlements.[91]

The ICJ had no difficulty in finding—unanimously[92]—that settlements in the OPT (including East Jerusalem) are illegal. In support of this finding it invokes repeated resolutions of the Security Council.[93]

D. Human Rights Conventions

The applicability of the Fourth Geneva Convention and a number of multilateral human rights conventions in the OPT is fundamental to the Court's Opinion, as the finding on the illegality of the wall is based on the violation of these conventions. Although Israel is a party to the International Covenant on Civil and Political Rights, the International Covenant on Economic, Social and Cultural Rights and the Convention on the Rights of the Child, it maintains, first, that these covenants do not have extraterritorial application to the OPT, and, second, that international humanitarian law is *lex specialis* governing the situation in the OPT to the exclusion of human rights conventions.[94]

Relying on its Advisory Opinion on the *Legality of the Threat or Use of Nuclear Weapons*,[95] the Court finds, unanimously,[96] that the three human rights conventions in question have extraterritorial application and do not cease in time of armed conflict, in which case they apply together with international humanitarian law.

---

[89] See the decisions of the Israel Supreme Court upholding. this argument, Kretzmer (n 76) 81–90.

[90] Y Dinstein, *The International Law of Belligerent Occupation* (Cambridge, CUP, 2009) 240, [576].

[91] Kretzmer (n 76) 77–78, 99; S Weill, *The Role of National Courts in Applying International Humanitarian Law* (Oxford, OUP, 2014) 105–21; *Mara'be v The Prime Minister of Israel* (2006) 45 ILM 202, 210, [19].

[92] See Judge Buergenthal's endorsement of the illegality of settlements, *Wall* (n 1) 244, [9].

[93] ibid, 183–84, [120].

[94] These arguments are set out clearly by M Dennis, 'Application of Human Rights Treaties Extraterritorially in Times of Armed Conflict and Military Occupation' (2005) 99 *AJIL* 119.

[95] [1966] ICJ Rep 226, 240, [25].

[96] See Judge Buergenthal's declaration, *Wall* (n 1) 240, [2].

The practice of the monitoring committees of the two International Covenants confirms this conclusion.[97]

E. Prolonged Occupation

International humanitarian law contemplates that a state of occupation will be of short duration. However, in 2004 the occupation of the Palestinian territories was already in its thirty-seventh year. In 2002 the Israeli Government had claimed that the prolonged nature of the occupation had resulted in fewer [or: less onerous] legal obligations for it as occupying power. In response, in my Special Rapporteur's report of that year, I had refuted this claim, arguing that the full protection of the Fourth Geneva Convention was still required.[98] The implications of the prolonged occupation were not raised in the proceedings before the Court in the *Wall* case. Consequently, the Court's strange pronouncement on this subject came as a surprise.

Article 6(3) of the Fourth Geneva Convention provides that:

> In the case of an occupied territory, the application of the present Convention shall cease one year after the general close of military operations; however, the Occupying Power shall be bound, for the duration of the occupation, to the extent that such Power exercises the functions of government in such territory, by the provisions of the following Articles of the present Convention: 1 to 12, 27, 29 to 34, 47, 49, 51, 53, 59, 61 to 77, 143.

In paragraph 125 of its Opinion the Court interpreted Article 6 to mean that all the provisions of the Convention remain in force 'during military operations *leading to occupation*' (italics added), whereas only the specified provisions of the Convention remain in force a year after this event. Such an interpretation, which introduces a qualification on military operations (see the italicised phrase above) not found in the Convention itself seriously 'reduces the scope of the protection that the population enjoys under the Convention'.[99] Inter alia, it precludes the operation of the enforcement provisions of the Convention contained in Articles 146 and 147. This interpretation takes no account of the fact that 'because of the sheer length of the occupation and the continued conflict in the region, countless military operations have taken place in the OPT, only one of which can actually be said to have led to the occupation of that territory (1967)'.[100] In the words of Professor Yoram Dinstein, it is a 'bewildering statement' as it 'suggests that the clock of the one-year rule of Article 6 (third paragraph) started ticking as soon as the Israeli occupation began, in June 1967'.[101]

---

[97] *Wall* (n 1) 177–81, [102]–[113].
[98] J Dugard, *Question of the violation of human rights in the occupied Arab territories, including Palestine*, E/CN.4/2002/32 (6 March 2002) 7, [7].
[99] Dinstein, *Belligerent Occupation* (n 90) 283, [679].
[100] Imseis (n 37) 108.
[101] Dinstein (n 90) 283, [679].

F. Self-Defence

Undoubtedly the most controversial part of the Court's Opinion is that dealing with self-defence. In a terse, unreasoned dictum, the Court dismissed Israel's argument that the construction of the wall was justified as self-defence under Article 51 of the UN Charter. First, the Court held that Article 51 recognises the inherent right of self-defence only 'in the case of an armed attack by one State against another State' and Israel 'does not claim that the attacks against it are imputable to a foreign State'.[102] Second, the Court held that because Israel exercises control over the OPT and the threat which it regarded as justifying construction of the wall originated from within that territory, the situation was different from that contemplated by Security Council resolutions 1368 (2001) and 1373 (2001) which Israel had invoked to support its argument of self-defence.

Neither of the reasons provided by the Court for rejecting Israel's argument is convincing. The first is incorrect. As pointed out by Judges Higgins,[103] Kooijmans[104] and Buergenthal,[105] and by academic critics,[106] Article 51 does not restrict the right of self-defence to attacks on a state by another state. The second reason hints at the correct reason but is side-tracked into drawing an unsatisfactory distinction between the situation in the OPT and that contemplated by Security Council resolutions 1368 and 1373. Resolutions 1368 and 1373, which were adopted in the wake of the attack on the World Trade Center on 11 September 2001, do not deal with an armed attack on the United States by another state. Instead they recognise the right of a state to respond in self-defence to acts of international terrorism without any suggestion that there need be an armed attack by a state. They are concerned with acts of international terrorism that constitute a threat to international peace and security. According to Judge Kooijmans, 'they therefore have no immediate bearing on terrorist acts originating within a territory which is under control of the State which is also the victim of these acts'.[107] This is the explanation for the Court's statement that the situation before the Court is different from that contemplated by resolutions 1368 and 1373 and why Israel may not invoke Article 51.

The real reason that resolutions 1368 and 1373 do not apply, unfortunately not mentioned by the Court, is that Israel is essentially engaged in a policing operation as occupying power of the OPT. Israel is not the victim of an armed attack that allows it to invoke Article 51 and the sympathy of the world. It is an occupying power that is building a wall to maintain its occupation. This is made clear by the

---

[102] *Wall* (n 1) 194, [139].
[103] ibid, 215, [33].
[104] ibid, 229–30, [35].
[105] ibid, 242–43, [6].
[106] R Wedgwood, 'The ICJ Advisory Opinion on the Israeli Security Fence and the Limits of Self-Defense' (2005) 99 *AJIL* 52, 58; S Murphy, 'Self-Defense and the Israeli *Wall* Advisory Opinion: An *Ipse Dixit* of the ICJ?' (2005) 99 *AJIL* 62, 64. For a contrary academic opinion, see O Corten, *The Law Against War: The Prohibition on the Use of Force in Contemporary International Law* (Oxford, Hart, 2010) 196.
[107] *Wall* (n 1) 230, [36].

Supreme Court of Israel in its two major decisions on the legality of the wall—*Beit Sourik Council v Government of Israel*[108] and *Mara'abe v the Prime Minister of Israel*.[109] Both these decisions hold that international humanitarian law allows Israel to construct a security wall to protect its army and settlers as part of its duty as occupying power to maintain order in the occupied territory.[110] Moreover, both decisions acknowledge that the legality of the wall and its route are to be judged by the rules of international humanitarian law, as found by the ICJ.[111]

There is a reluctance on the part of states to treat the occupation of Palestine as an occupation similar to other occupations in history.[112] Had Germany built a wall between itself and France in response to the 'terrorist activities' of the French resistance, it is unlikely that Germany would have justified its action as an act taken in self-defence. It would rather have seen such a wall as part of its actions to maintain control over an occupied territory whose citizens had resisted the occupation by violent means.

VII. AFTERMATH

The *Wall* Opinion was handed down on 9 July 2004. On 20 July the General Assembly adopted resolution ES-10/15 by 150 votes to six with 10 abstentions. Member states of the European Union and the Russian Federation voted in favour of the resolution while Israel and the United States voted against. The resolution 'acknowledged' the Opinion, 'demanded' that Israel 'comply with its obligations as mentioned in the advisory opinion', called upon member states to 'comply with their obligations as mentioned in the advisory opinion' and requested the Secretary-General 'to establish a register of damages caused to all natural or legal persons' by the construction of the wall. Since then both the General Assembly and the Human Rights Council have regularly passed resolutions approving the Opinion and calling for its implementation.

The Security Council has neither acknowledged nor approved the Opinion. Since November 2003,[113] when it endorsed the creation of the Quartet, comprising the United Nations, the European Union, the Russian Federation and the United States, to pursue a solution to the conflict in the Middle East premised on a Roadmap for peace, the Security Council has largely left the conflict between Israel and Palestine to this Quartet.[114] The Quartet issues regular press statements, addressed to the

---

[108] (2004) 43 ILM 1099, 1107, [23]–[25].

[109] (2006) 45 ILM 202, 207–16, [14]–[30].

[110] See further Scobbie, 'Words My Mother Never Taught Me' (n 37) 82–83.

[111] *Wall* (n 1) 189–92, [133]–[134].

[112] See the separate opinion of Judge Elaraby, ibid 254 I, [3.1].

[113] UNS Res 0 1515.

[114] See further on the Quartet, J Dugard and A Vermeer-Kunzli, 'The Elusive Allocation of Responsibility to Informal Organizations: The Case of the Quartet on the Middle East' in M Ragazzi, *Responsibility of International Organizations. Essays in Memory of Sir Ian Brownlie* (Leiden, Martinus Nijhoff, 2013) 261; K Elgindy, 'The Middle East Quartet: A Post Mortem', The Saban Center for Middle East Policy at Brookings, Analysis Paper No 25, 8 February 2012.

President of the Council about its concerns relating to events in the Middle East. It has only once mentioned the *Wall* Opinion and not suggested that it might be a useful guide to peace in the region.[115] This is due to the pivotal role in the Quartet played by the United States, which has made it clear from the outset that it was opposed to the Opinion and would ensure that it was not implemented.[116] The member states of the European Union, the Russian Federation and the United Nations have all expressed support for the Opinion in some way but they are powerless to persuade the Quartet to approve or to implement the Opinion.

An advisory opinion is by definition advisory. Clearly the opinion itself is not binding on states.[117] On the other hand, states are bound by the Fourth Geneva Convention, the Hague Regulations of 1907, the International Covenants and customary international law upon which the Opinion is based. While not bound by the Opinion itself, states, including Israel and the United States, are nonetheless bound by the obligations upon which it relies. The Opinion has simply elucidated and confirmed these obligations. It is not therefore correct to describe the Opinion as 'merely advisory' as far as sates are concerned.

Predictably, the Israeli government rejected the Opinion. This was followed by a decision of the Israeli Supreme Court in *Mara'abe v Prime Minister*[118] which ruled that the construction of the wall within Palestinian territory was justified as a security measure to protect both Israel itself and the safety of Jewish settlers. The Court held that the ICJ's opinion was flawed by reason of its failure to have access to the full facts surrounding the wall and accepted without serious examination the assurances of the Israeli military that the wall was constructed for security purposes.[119] My view that the wall also served a political purpose, namely to seize land and to incorporate settlements into Israel, was expressly rejected.[120] The court accepted that settlers were entitled to protection but refused to consider the legality of settlements![121]

States in the main have not complied with the obligations found by the Court to be binding on them in the *Wall* Opinion. Most recognise the illegality of the wall; but, under the influence of the United States, accept that Israel will be allowed to retain Palestinian land incorporated by the wall that accommodates Israeli settlements in any future peace agreement. In these circumstances it is hard to say that states have refused 'to recognize the illegal situation resulting from the construction of the wall' or that they have not rendered assistance in maintaining the illegal situation created by the wall—as required by the Court.[122] Moreover, states parties to the Fourth Geneva Convention have not put pressure on Israel to comply with the provisions of humanitarian law embodied in that Convention. On the contrary,

---

[115] Statement of 23 September 2004 (SG/2091).
[116] See Elgindy, 'The Middle East Quartet' (n 114) 46.
[117] *cf* R Ago '"Binding" Advisory Opinions of the International Court of Justice' (1991) 85 *AJIL* 439.
[118] (2006) 45 ILM 202.
[119] ibid, 226–29, [62]–[65]; 231–32, [70]–[74].
[120] ibid, 221, [43]–[44]; 22–227, [61], [63].
[121] ibid, 210, [19].
[122] *Wall* (n 1) 202, [163 D].

Israel persists in its argument that it is not bound by the Fourth Geneva Convention and no meaningful steps have been taken by state parties to ensure compliance. At the same time Israel continues to maintain that human rights conventions do not apply in the OPT.

Much has been written about the legal consequences for states of advisory opinions in the light of the fact that only judgments in contentious proceedings are designated as binding by Article 59 of the Court's Statute, and enforceable in terms of Article 94 of the Charter. On the other hand, Shabtai Rosenne maintains that the 'practical difference' between the two is 'not significant' as both depend on the *auctoritas* of the same court.[123] If there is little 'practical difference' between the consequence of judgments in contentious proceedings and advisory opinions for *States* there should be no difference at all as far as the consequences for the *United Nations* are concerned. After all, the ICJ is the judicial arm of the United Nations and it would seem that the organisation must be bound by an advisory opinion requested by one of its own organs and approved by that organ. In the words of Sir Hersch Lauterpacht, an opinion requested and approved by the General Assembly is 'the law recognized by the United Nations'.[124] Despite this the Secretary-General and the Secretariat of the United Nations have done little to ensure compliance with the *Wall* Opinion.

That the Secretariat was unenthusiastic about the request for the *Wall* Opinion was confirmed in private meetings I held with senior members of the Secretariat in my capacity as Special Rapporteur. This is reflected in the failure of successive Secretaries-General to express any support for the Opinion in the statements issued by the Quartet. They have simply acquiesced in the determination of the United States to kill the Opinion. Further evidence of this lack of enthusiasm is provided by the delay in the establishment of the office to handle the Register of Damages mandated by the General Assembly in resolution ES-10/15 of 20 July 2004 and the failure to authorise this body to secure compensation for those who have suffered damage as a consequence of the construction of the wall.

The Secretary-General has been encouraged to do nothing by his legal office. On 10 August 2004 Ralph Zacklin of the Office of the UN Legal Adviser gave an opinion to Kieran Prendergast, Under Secretary-General for Political Affairs, which declares that Secretary-General need not take action on the Opinion because the Secretariat 'is not a direct addressee of any of the legal consequences determined by the Court to arise from the construction of the wall'[125] and 'the Advisory Opinion itself is not binding'. Whether the Secretary-General should take action to implement the Opinion was a political decision which 'was legally ... not called for'.[126]

---

[123] S Rosenne, The Law and Practice of the International Court, 1920–2005, vol 3 (Procedure), 4th edn (Leiden, Martinus Nijhoff, 2006). See, too, K Keith, The Extent of Advisory Jurisdiction of the International Court of Justice (Leiden, AW Sijthoff, 1971) 221–22; M Pomerance, *The Advisory Function of the International Court in the League and UN Eras* (Baltimore, John Hopkins University Press, 1973) 371.

[124] Admissibility of Hearings of Petitioners by the Committee on South West Africa [1956] ICJ Rep 46.

[125] See J Dugard, 'Advisory Opinions and the Secretary-General with Special Reference to the 2004 Advisory Opinion on the *Wall*' in L Boisson de Chazournes and M Kohen, *International Law and the Quest for its Implementation. Liber Amicorum Vera Gowlland-Debbas* (Leiden, Brill, 2010) 403, 409.

[126] ibid.

Israel, states and the United Nations have not heeded the call of the ICJ for respect for humanitarian law and human rights law in the OPT. This has allowed Israel to proceed with the construction of the wall and the expansion of settlements. In 2004 the length of the wall was 180 kilometres.[127] Today it is over 500 kilometres long. In 2004 the settlement population numbered some 400,000.[128] Today there are almost 8,000 Jewish settlers in the West Bank and East Jerusalem: 400,000 in the West Bank and over 300,000 in East Jerusalem. (Israel withdrew its settlements from Gaza in 2005.) The settlement of Beitar Illit has grown to become a city with a population of 45,0000, while Ariel has a population of 18,000. Fifty-six settlements, accommodating nearly 80 per cent of the settler population, are in the 'seam zone' between the Green Line and the wall. Not only has the United States blocked compliance with the *Wall* Opinion; it has also prevented action from being taken to curb the expansion of settlements: in February 2011 it vetoed a proposal to condemn the construction of settlements in the OPT. On 23 December 2016, however, the United States abstained from voting on Security Council Resolution 2334 condemning settlements.

The colonisation of the West Bank and East Jerusalem continues unabated and increasingly it is argued that Israel's settlement enterprise has resulted in a system akin to that of apartheid in which a discriminatory legal order favours settlers above Palestinians.[129]

That the wall will annex Palestinian land taken by the wall is no longer seriously contested. The United States, the principal 'peace broker', accepts that the wall will in large part become the future border between Israel and Palestine and has given assurances to Israel that it will be allowed to keep settlements encircled by the wall.[130] Israeli politicians now openly assert that a future border will follow the route of the wall. The claim that the wall is designed to serve as a security wall has become secondary. In 2005 the Minister of Justice, Tzipi Livni, declared that the wall would serve as 'the future border of the state of Israel'.[131] This prompted the Israeli High Court to express concerns that it had been misled by the government on the purpose the wall was intended to serve.[132]

The wall has become a *fait accompli*. The opposition of the United States to the *Wall* Opinion, the failure of the Quartet to make any attempt to secure compliance with the Opinion, the readiness of European states to fall in line with the United States on this issue, and the reservations of the Secretariat of the United Nations mean that the wall has ceased to be a matter of contention between the international community of States and Israel. If world politics is defined in terms of relations between states and the actions of international institutions, the *Wall* has been a political failure. The manner in which states and the United Nations have ignored

---

[127] *Wall* (n 1) 170, [82].

[128] See Report of Special Rapporteur on Question of the violation of human rights in the occupied Arab territories, including Palestine, E/CN.4/2004/6, [37].

[129] See J Dugard and J Reynolds, 'Apartheid, International Law and the Occupied Palestinian Territory (2013) 24 *EJIL* 867.

[130] Bregman (n 10) 295.

[131] Y Yoaz, 'Justice Minister: West Bank Fence is Israel's Future Border', *Haaretz*, 1 December 2005.

[132] *Head of the Azzun Municipal Council, Abed Alatif Hassin and others v State of Israel and the Military Commander of the West Bank*, HCJ.2733/05.

the Opinion has undoubtedly affected the credibility of the Court. This does not appear to trouble those states which most strongly express respect for the Rule of Law in international affairs.

Any peaceful settlement of the seemingly intractable dispute between Israel and Palestine will have to be guided by international law. The *Wall* Opinion provides a normative framework for such a resolution of the conflict. This is realised by civil society which has invoked the Opinion as its lodestar for action towards the just settlement of the conflict. *BDS*—boycott, divestment, and sanctions—a civil society initiative to boycott Israel along the same lines as apartheid South Africa, was started on 9 July 2005, exactly one year after the *Wall* Opinion was handed down, invoking the Opinion as a justification for its action. Other civil society action is also premised on the Opinion. The decision of the European Union to require goods produced on settlements in the West Bank to be labelled as coming from the West Bank and not Israel[133] is based on the illegality of settlements confirmed by the ICJ in the *Wall*. In the short term the *Wall* Opinion may have been a failure. The long-term implications of the Opinion are probably still to be felt.

---

[133] *New York Times International*, 12 November 2015, 1.

23

Jurisdictional Immunities of the State (Germany v Italy; Greece intervening) (2012)

OMRI SENDER AND MICHAEL WOOD

I. INTRODUCTION

THE 2012 JUDGMENT of the International Court of Justice (ICJ) in *Jurisdictional Immunities of the State (Germany v Italy: Greece intervening)* is not groundbreaking in substance and not yet advanced in age, yet there are good reasons to consider it a 'landmark'. In testing the old international legal rule of state immunity before foreign courts against contemporary calls for reform, the Court affirmed that the rule still stands as an important tenet of international law, applying also in respect of acts which constitute grave international crimes. As the judgment illuminates not only the international law of state immunity, but also the ICJ's judicial approach and methodology more broadly, its impact is bound to reach well beyond the specific contours of the case. The present commentary seeks to explain this, detailing the origins of the dispute brought before the Court as well as the legal proceedings that ensued and their outcome.

II. THE LEAD-UP TO THE ICJ CASE

The wounds of the past were still festering in southern Greece in 1995, when relatives of the victims of a massacre committed during the Second World War by Nazi armed forces in the Greek village of Distomo brought a claim of indemnity against the German state before the local court of Leivadia. More than 215 civilians were murdered by the Waffen-SS in just a few hours of 10 June 1944, a reprisal for the actions of Greek resistance fighters that was deeply engrained in Greek national consciousness. Germany did not take part in the Greek proceedings, having notified the Greek Ministry of Foreign Affairs that the suit infringed upon its sovereign right under international law to jurisdictional immunity before foreign courts. But the Greek court held in 1997 that a state loses its right to invoke sovereign immunity where its acts amount to a breach of peremptory norms of international law (*jus cogens*), and ordered Germany to pay the successors in title of the victims approximately €28 million in damages.[1] Germany's appeal against that judgment was dismissed in May 2000 by the Hellenic Supreme Court (*Areios Pagos*), which held that organs of the Third Reich had abused sovereign power by committing 'hideous murders that objectively were not necessary in order to maintain the military occupation of the area or subdue the underground action'.[2] Being in violation of *jus cogens*, such crimes could not be considered as sovereign acts to which the privilege of immunity ought to be accorded.[3]

It was not long before Italian courts followed suit, embracing such an exception to state immunity in civil claims for damages brought against Germany by Italian nationals who had also suffered at the hand of the Nazis. Among such claimants was Mr Luigi Ferrini, a native of Tuscany who was deported to Germany in August 1944 to work as a forced labourer in the armaments industry following Italy's surrender to the Allies and declaration of war on Germany. Ferrini filed a lawsuit against Germany in 1998 in the Court of First Instance of Arezzo, which dismissed his claims on grounds of Germany's jurisdictional immunity under customary international law. The Court of Appeal in Florence agreed, but the decision was reversed in March 2004 by the Italian Court of Cassation (*Corte Suprema di Cassazione*), which held that immunity could be overridden when the act complained of amounted to an international crime.[4] Even if no definite and explicit customary rule to that effect was yet in existence, the Court reasoned, since international human rights 'are at the top of the international legal order' and prevail over other rules of international law, they must have priority over any rule of sovereign immunity, which should not allow a state to escape its responsibility for gross violations of fundamental human rights.[5] Two Orders issued by the Court of Cassation in May 2008, in other cases involving Italian civilians or members of the Italian armed forces who were denied prisoner-of-war status and were deported to Germany for use as forced labour, confirmed that Italian courts had jurisdiction over such claims brought against

---

[1] *Prefecture of Voiotia v Federal Republic of Germany*, Case No 137/1997, Court of First Instance of Leivadia, 30 October 1997 (ordering Germany to pay 9,448,105,000 in Drachmas). See also the case note by I Bantekas (1998) 92 *AJIL* 765. A similar ruling was delivered by the Court of First Instance in Tripoli (Greece) in Case No 59/1998; on the other hand, Germany's immunity was recognised by the Court of First Instance of Larissa in entertaining comparable claims (Case No 93/1998, NOMIKO BHMA 1098 (1998)).

[2] *Prefecture of Voiotia v Federal Republic of Germany*, Case No 11/2000 (4 May 2000), 129 ILR 513.

[3] ibid, 519–21; see also the case note by M Gavouneli and I Bantekas, (2001) 95 *AJIL* 198–204. A forceful dissenting opinion by five judges argued that no such customary restriction of sovereign immunity was (at least as of yet) in existence.

[4] *Ferrini v Federal Republic of Germany*, Decision No 5044/2004 (2004), (2004) 87 *Rivista di diritto internazionale* 539, 128 ILR 658. See also M Iovane, 'The *Ferrini* Judgment of the Italian Supreme Court: Opening Up Domestic Courts to Claims of Reparation for Victims of Serious Violations of Fundamental Human Rights', (2004) 14 *Italian Yearbook of International Law* 165–93; and the case note by A Bianchi, (2005) 99 *AJIL* 242–48. The Court referred Ferrini's case back to the Court of First Instance of Arezzo, which dismissed it again as time-barred; this judgment was reversed by the Court of Appeal of Florence, which in 2011 ordered Germany to pay Mr Ferrini damages and legal costs.

[5] ibid, [9]. The Court did not explicitly employ the term '*jus cogens*', but did refer to 'norms from which no derogation is permitted, which lie at the heart of the international order and prevail over all other conventional and customary norms … [being of] the highest status'.

Germany.[6] The *Ferrini* reasoning was again reaffirmed when the Court of Cassation rejected Germany's argument of lack of jurisdiction in an appeal against an order by the Military Court of La Spezia (upheld by the Military Court of Appeals in Rome) that Germany pay compensation for the massacres of Italian civilians committed by occupying or retreating German armed forces in Civitella (Val di Chiana), Cornia, and San Pancrazio.[7]

The decisions of the Italian courts paved the way for dozens of additional claims by Italian citizens against Germany, including through class actions. They did not go unnoticed by the Greek claimants in the *Distomo* case, who now turned to the Italian judiciary after their attempts to execute the 1997 judgment of the Leivadia court were rejected by the Greek Minister of Justice (whose consent to carry out a judgment against a foreign state in Greece is required under Greek law) as well as by the European Court of Human Rights and German Federal Supreme Court (*Bundesgerichtshof*), each of which considered that Germany's entitlement to state immunity in that case had been breached.[8] In decisions rendered in 2005 and 2006 the Florence Court of Appeal declared the *Distomo* judgment of the Leivadia court enforceable in Italy, leading the Greek claimants to inscribe in 2007 a mortgage on Villa Vigoni, a property of the German state located near Lake Como and dedicated to fostering cooperation between Germany and Italy in the fields of scientific research, higher education and culture. Germany's appeals against the decisions of the Florence Court of Appeal were again rejected by the Court of Cassation, which in May 2008 extended its *Ferrini* reasoning to immunity from enforcement measures.[9]

The German Government was not alone in its surprise and dismay in the face of these Italian judgments. Italy's Government, too, seems to have been taken aback by the willingness of its courts openly to disregard a basic rule of international law. The Italian Executive agreed with Germany that it was entitled to state immunity under international law, no doubt aware that, given its past, Italy too could be exposed to massive claims if the view of its courts on state immunity were to prevail. But all efforts by senior state attorneys to persuade the judicial branch to give effect to Italy's obligation to accord immunity to Germany under customary international law (applicable directly within the Italian legal order by virtue of the Italian Constitution)[10] were in vain. Extensive negotiations between the two Governments

---

[6] Orders of 29 May 2008 issued in the *Giovanni Mantelli and Others* case (Order No 14201, *Foro italiano*, Vol 134 (2009) I, 1568) and the *Liberato Maietta* case (Order No 14209, (2008) 91 *Rivista di diritto internazionale* 896), rejecting Germany's interlocutory appeal requesting a declaration of lack of jurisdiction.

[7] The *Max Josef Milde* case: see (2009) 92 *Rivista di diritto internazionale* 618.

[8] See *Kalogeropoulou and others v Greece and Germany*, Application No 59021/00, Decision of 12 December 2002, ECHR Reports 2002-X, 417; *Greek Citizens v Federal Republic of Germany*, Case No III ZR 245/98, Judgment of 26 June 2003, (2003) 42 ILM 1030.

[9] Order No 14199 of 29 May 2008; Judgment No 11163 of 20 May 2011.

[10] The *Procura Generale della Repubblica presso la Corte di Cassazione* made a submission to the Court of Cassation on 22 November 2007, advising that 'it is not at all easy to contend that in the international legal order conventional or customary rules have emerged pursuant to which the jurisdictional immunity yields if the civil responsibility of the state for the commission of international crimes is invoked', and concluding that the Court should determine that the Italian courts lacked jurisdiction in the case under consideration. The *Avvocatura Generale dello Stato* made an additional submission to the Court of Cassation, arguing that the Court's stance did not seem to be in line with the current position under international law.

in order to reach a diplomatic solution, with Germany urging the Italian authorities 'to see to it that the erroneous course followed by the Italian judiciary be halted',[11] proved futile as well. As more and more cases were building up against Germany, recourse to the ICJ must have seemed like the only option left.

III. THE ICJ PROCEEDINGS

It was presumably with great reluctance that Germany decided to institute proceedings in The Hague in late December 2008. Only when the damage that would be done by hundreds of further cases against it was deemed greater than the damage to its image caused by asserting state immunity in respect of Nazi atrocities, did Germany turn to the ICJ as 'the only remedy available to [it] in its quest to put a halt to the unlawful practice of the Italian courts, which infringes its sovereign rights'.[12] Although in form a unilateral application to the Court, it seems that the two Governments had both agreed to present their differences to the Court. Some five weeks before the lodging of Germany's Application, Italy stated in a Joint Declaration of the two Foreign Ministers that it

> respects Germany's decision to apply to the International Court of Justice for a ruling on the principle of State immunity. Italy, like Germany, is a State party to the European Convention of 1957 for the Peaceful Settlement of Disputes and considers international law to be a guiding principle of its actions. Italy is thus of the view that the ICJ's ruling on State immunity will help to clarify this complex issue.[13]

Echoing the political sensitivity, Germany acknowledged expressly before the Court that its responsibility for the grave violations of international humanitarian law committed by the Third Reich was undisputed.[14] Its only objective was 'to obtain a finding from the Court that to declare claims based on those occurrences as falling within the domestic jurisdiction of Italian courts, constitutes a breach of international law'.[15] Jurisdictional immunity, it said, 'belongs to the core elements of the

---

[11] Application instituting proceedings, filed with the Registry on 23 December 2008 (hereafter: 'Application'), 4.

[12] ibid. Germany brought the case under the European Convention for the Peaceful Settlement of Disputes of 29 April 1957, to which Italy was also a party and according to which (in Article 1) disputes among the states parties regarding questions of international law would be submitted to the ICJ.

[13] ibid, 20: Joint Declaration, Adopted on the Occasion of German-Italian Governmental Consultations, Trieste, 18 November 2008. In April 2010 the Italian Government, followed by the Italian Parliament in June of the same year, adopted legislative measures suspending until the end of 2011 the execution of all Italian judgments ruling against Germany pending the decision of the Court.

[14] Germany further clarified that it was not acting 'in the exercise of its right of diplomatic protection in favour of German nationals' but rather on its own behalf, since its own 'sovereign rights have been—and continue to be—directly infringed by the jurisprudence of the highest Italian courts that denies Germany its right of sovereign immunity' (Application (n 11) 12). It told the Court that 'We cannot undo history. If victims or descendants of victims feel that these mechanisms [for compensation and reparation, put in place after WWII] were not sufficient, we do regret this. However, the mechanisms for compensation and reparation are not the subject of the present dispute': CR 2011/17, 12 September 2011, 18–19, [12] (Wasum-Rainer).

[15] Application (n 11) 10.

relationship between sovereign States'; dismissing it as Italian judges had done was not only unlawful, but would 'have far-reaching repercussions in vast areas of international law'.[16]

More specifically, Germany argued that, under firmly established rules of customary international law, a state is immune from civil proceedings before the courts of another state in respect of the exercise of sovereign powers (acts *jure imperii*, as opposed to acts *jure gestionis* of a private-law nature). It sought to demonstrate that state practice leaves no room for doubt on the matter, highlighting that even the decision of the Greek Supreme Court (*Areios Pagos*), which set in motion the series of proceedings against it in Italian courts, had soon thereafter 'lost its underpinnings' when Greece's Special Supreme Court (*Anotato Eidiko Dikastirio*), charged by the Greek Constitution to settle controversies regarding the content of generally recognised rules of international law, held in 2002 that Germany was indeed entitled to immunity.[17] Employing the concept of *jus cogens* in deciding the procedural question of immunity was wrong, as 'the substantive primary rules and the applicable secondary rules must be carefully distinguished': the basis for state immunity was not to be found in the character of the legal norm which was allegedly violated, but in the character of the act as an act of state that cannot, as such, be subject to the jurisdiction of another state. Germany also claimed that the mortgage registered on Villa Vigoni violated the immunity from enforcement to which it was entitled under customary international law, and noted that the Italian Government had itself opposed the inscription of this judicial measure of constraint. While there could be no doubt as to the good intentions of the Italian Court of Cassation, said Germany, 'judges are not legitimated to place themselves at the forefront of processes of change' of the law.[18]

Germany further argued that the Italian rulings jeopardised the entire reparation system put in place after the Second World War, which was effected by a classic inter-state model under which it had already paid millions of dollars.[19] It recalled that Italy had agreed under the 1947 Peace Agreement with the victorious Allied Powers to renounce 'on its own behalf and on behalf of Italian nationals' all claims against Germany and German nationals, and that despite this express waiver the

---

[16] Memorial of the Federal Republic of Germany, 12 June 2009, 69.

[17] ibid, 41; see *Margellos v Federal Republic of Germany*, Special Supreme Court 6/2002, 129 ILR 526.

[18] Memorial (n 16), 55, 38. In the UK House of Lords, Lord Hoffmann had referred to a suggestion that the Italian court in *Ferrini* had 'given priority to the values embodied in the prohibition of torture over the values and policies of the rules of State immunity', and continued: 'if the case had been concerned with domestic law, [this] might have been regarded by some as "activist" but would have been well within the judicial function ... But the same approach cannot be adopted in international law, which is based upon the common consent of nations. It is not for a national court to "develop" international law by unilaterally adopting a version of that law which, however desirable, forward-looking and reflective of values it may be, is simply not accepted by other states': *Jones v Ministry of Interior Al-Mamlaka Al-Arabiya AS Saudiya; Mitchell and others v Al-Dali and others and Ministry of Interior Al-Mamlaka Al-Arabiya AS Saudiya* [2006] UKHL 26, [63].

[19] See also R Hofmann, 'Compensation for Personal Damages Suffered during World War II' in R Wolfrum (ed), *Max Planck Encyclopedia of Public International Law* (Oxford, OUP, 2013), <opil.ouplaw.com/home/EPIL>.

German Government was prepared in the 1960s, as a voluntary complement to this scheme, to provide reparation to Italian victims of Nazi persecution. Germany also insisted that persons injured were in any event able to bring their claims before German courts, and that such claims would be examined on the merits.[20] If the Italian courts were allowed to have their way, the consequences would be severe: all past and future inter-state peace settlements concluded after an armed conflict would be endangered, and new disputes and legal disorder would soon follow.

Italy, as respondent, found itself arguing in support of the position taken by its courts, even though it had acknowledged that that position was not in accordance with existing international law.[21] It claimed, in its defence, that its courts were 'faced with a clear dilemma: to condone a blatant denial of justice or to render justice to victims of heinous crimes'.[22] The real subject matter of the case, Italy added, was 'not just immunity ... but also, and above all, the ongoing non-compliance by Germany with its obligations of reparation for the egregious violations of International Humanitarian Law ... committed in the final years of the Second World War against Italian victims by the Third Reich'.[23] The origin of the dispute thus lay not in the recent series of Italian judicial decisions, but rather in the 'sad story of protracted denial of justice' by Germany.[24] Refusing to accord immunity to Germany in such circumstances was justified in law, Italy asserted, as 'immunity cannot mean impunity'.[25]

While conceding that every state is generally obliged to recognise the immunity of foreign states with respect to acts *jure imperii*, Italy argued that even for such acts, immunity cannot be regarded as absolute. Just as state practice (and consequently, customary international law) had progressively restricted the scope of the once absolute state immunity by differentiating between *acta jure imperii* and *acta jure gestionis*, it was now time to recognise a further exception concerning torts committed by one state on the territory of the forum state.[26] Even if such an exception was not yet a rule of customary international law, its existence ought clearly to be inferred from the contemporary position of international law, in particular the recognition of the existence of international rules having a *jus cogens* character; the formation of a body of rules criminalizing the conduct of individuals responsible for specified

---

[20] Germany also expressed willingness to continue making 'symbolic gestures' to commemorate the Italian victims (Application (n 11) 16).

[21] According to Bothe, 'When Germany brought the case against Italy before the ICJ, the Italian government was in a somewhat awkward position: it had to defend the position of its courts despite that it had and probably still espoused a different view and had said so before its own courts ... [nevertheless] the academic agents did a very good job in defending the positions of the Italian courts': M Bothe, 'Remedies of Victims of War Crimes and Crimes against Humanities: Some Critical Remarks on the ICJ's Judgment on the Jurisdictional Immunity of the State', in A Peters, E Lagrange, S Oeter and C Tomuschat (eds), *Immunities in the Age of Global Constitutionalism* (Leiden, Brill Nijhoff, 2015) 99, 101.

[22] Counter-Memorial of Italy, 22 December 2009, 6.

[23] ibid, 13.

[24] Written response of Italy to the questions put by Judge Simma, Judge Cançado Trindade and Judge ad hoc Gaja at the end of the public sitting held on 16 September 2011 (23 September 2011).

[25] Counter-Memorial of Italy (n 22) 80.

[26] Italy remarked, in this context, that 'domestic courts have always had a major role in contributing to the evolution of the law of State immunity': ibid, 42.

international crimes; and the increasing acceptance of the existence of a right of access to courts by individuals. Germany was not entitled to immunity because the acts attributed to it involved the most grave violations of rules of international law of an intransgressible character, for which no alternative means of redress were available.

Italy argued, moreover, that it had never absolved Germany from liability for the egregious breaches of international humanitarian law committed against its nationals during the Second World War, and that it could not have done so in any case given that such liability rests on non-derogable principles of international law. The 1961 German–Italian agreements on reparation were a confirmation that Germany recognised it was under an obligation to offer compensation to Italian victims; yet a very large number of these remained uncovered and had never received appropriate reparation. Italy stressed that German judges had consistently held, on the merits of cases brought before them by such victims, that state responsibility did not apply to military conduct in armed conflict, and that responsibility for violations of international humanitarian law in any event did not give rise to individual reparation claims. A particular source of aggravation was the fact that the Italian soldiers interned by Germany during the War were not included in any existing reparation schemes, including the 'Remembrance, Responsibility and Future' Foundation set up by the German Government in 2000.[27] Italian victims were thus left with no choice but to come before the Italian courts; all other avenues had been exhausted to no avail.

Italy also submitted a counter-claim to the Court, arguing that Germany had violated an obligation under international law to make reparations to Italian nationals as victims of war crimes and crimes against humanity committed by the Third Reich. It asked that Germany be ordered to cease such wrongful conduct and offer appropriate and effective compensation to the victims. In its Order of 6 July 2010, however, the Court found the counter-claim inadmissible *ratione temporis*.[28]

The written pleadings were already concluded when, in January 2011, Greece applied for permission to intervene as a non-party, seeking to inform the Court of its legal rights and interests so that these would remain 'unfettered and unaffected'.[29]

---

[27] The German federal law of 2000 that established the Foundation generally excluded from the right to compensation those who had had the status of prisoner of war (since, as the commentary to the draft legislation explained, it was thought that prisoners of war 'may, according to the rules of international law, be put to work by the detaining power'). German courts held that even if Italian internees were denied the status of prisoners of war by the German Reich, that could not effectively change their status as such and thus they were ineligible to receive any benefits under that law.

[28] See *Jurisdictional Immunities of the State (Germany v Italy), Counter-Claim, Order of 6 July 2010*, [2010] ICJ Rep 310. Judge ad hoc Gaja, appointed by Italy, voted with the majority to reject Italy's counter-claim, remarking only, in a brief Declaration appended to the Order (398), that in applying its Rules to decide whether Italy's counter-claim was admissible, 'an oral hearing would probably have helped the Court' to identify more precisely the relevant facts (as opposed to deciding the issue on the basis of the parties' written observations alone).

[29] Application for permission to intervene by the Government of the Hellenic Republic, filed in the Registry of the Court on 13 January 2011, 6. Greece made clear that 'its intention is to solely intervene in the aspect of the procedure relating to judgments rendered by its own (domestic—Greek) tribunals and courts on occurrences during World War II and enforced (*exequatur*) by the Italian courts'.

Faced with Germany's longstanding rejection of the possibility of holding bilateral discussions on war reparations, Greece's interest in intervention may have been to have the ICJ officially recognise that the settlement of reparation claims should be the subject of further negotiations. Broader political considerations may have also motivated the Greek move, which was announced by Prime Minister Papandreou at a time of severe financial crisis and growing public outrage at Germany's unwavering stance towards Greece in the then-ongoing negotiations within the European Union on economic recovery measures. The ICJ's decision in July 2011 to permit Greece to intervene as a non-party 'in so far as this intervention is limited to the decisions of Greek courts'[30] was presented in Greece as a great victory, allowing the country's voice finally to be heard.[31]

IV. THE ICJ JUDGMENT

The ICJ handed down its judgment on 3 February 2012, finding for Germany on virtually all counts. The Court held (by 12 votes to three) that Italy had violated its obligation to respect the immunity which Germany enjoyed under international law by allowing civil claims to be brought against it based on violations of international humanitarian law committed by the German Reich between 1943 and 1945. It further held (by 14 votes to one) that Italy had violated its obligation to respect the immunity from enforcement which Germany enjoyed under international law by taking measures of constraint against Villa Vigoni; and (also by 14 votes to one) that Italy had violated its obligation to respect the immunity which Germany enjoyed under international law by declaring enforceable in Italy decisions of the Greek courts based on violations of international humanitarian law committed in Greece by the German Reich.[32]

After setting out the historical and factual background, delimiting the subject matter of the dispute and confirming its jurisdiction, the Court turned to examine, first, whether the Italian courts acted in breach of international law by exercising jurisdiction over Germany in the proceedings brought by the Italian claimants. It began by deploring the acts of the German armed forces and other organs of the German Reich

---

[30] *Jurisdictional Immunities of the State (Germany v Italy), Application for Permission to Intervene, Order of 4 July 2011*, [2011] ICJ Rep 494. Judge ad hoc Gaja voted against the Greek Application, stating that the fact the Italy had held the Greek judgments to be enforceable in Italy did not amount to the required 'interest of a legal nature which may be affected by the decision in the case' (531–32). In his separate opinion, Judge Cançado Trindade hailed the Order as being 'of historical importance' and as showing 'that intervention in contemporary international litigation is alive and well: it has at last seen the light of the day. What we behold today, here at the Peace Palace, is a true *resurrectio* of intervention in present-day international litigation; its *resurgere* from its long sleep may come to satisfy the needs not only of the States concerned, but of the individuals concerned as well, and ultimately of the international community as a whole, in the conceptual universe of the new *jus gentium* of our times' (505, 530).

[31] Germany did not formally object to the Greek Application being granted (although it did argue that the Application did not meet the criteria set out in the Court's Statute for purposes of intervening); nor did Italy object. After receiving permission to intervene, Greece submitted a written statement (to which Germany and Italy responded in writing) and appeared at the oral hearing.

[32] *Jurisdictional Immunities of the State, (Germany v Italy: Greece intervening), Judgment* [2012] ICJ Rep 99, 154–55, [139].

against Italian men and women in 1943–45, asserting that 'there can be no doubt that this conduct was a serious violation of the international law of armed conflict' applicable at that time.[33] The Court then clarified that the sole question before it was 'whether or not, in proceedings regarding claims for compensation arising out of those acts, the Italian courts were obliged to accord Germany immunity'.[34]

Observing that any entitlement to immunity as between Germany and Italy could (in the absence of an applicable treaty) be derived only from customary international law, the Court then sought to determine, in accordance with Article 38(1)(b) of its Statute, whether a general rule of 'international custom, as evidence of a general practice accepted as law' conferring immunity on states exists, and if so, what its precise contours were. In the analysis that followed the Court noted, based on the actual practice of states, that 'whether in claiming immunity for themselves or according it to others, States generally proceed on the basis that there is a right to immunity under international law, together with a corresponding obligation on the part of other States to respect and give effect to that immunity'.[35] It added that 'the rule of State immunity occupies an important place in international law and international relations. It derives from the principle of sovereign equality of States, which ... is one of the fundamental principles of the international legal order'.[36] But another fundamental principle, the Court observed, was also at play: 'This principle [of sovereign equality] has to be viewed together with the principle that each State possesses sovereignty over its own territory and that there flows from that sovereignty the jurisdiction of the State over events and persons within that territory. Exceptions to the immunity of the State represent a departure from the principle of sovereign equality. Immunity may represent a departure from the principle of territorial sovereignty and the jurisdiction which flows from it'.[37]

Before moving on to define the scope and extent of the rule of State immunity, the Court recalled that the law of immunity is essentially procedural in nature, and is 'thus entirely distinct from the substantive law which determines whether [a particular] conduct is lawful or unlawful'. It noted, moreover, that the case before it concerned *acta jure imperii*, for which both parties agreed that states are generally entitled to immunity. The question, then, was whether an exception existed as regards acts committed on the territory of the forum state by organs of a state in the course of an armed conflict,[38] and to this the Court replied in the negative. Surveying extensive state practice, it rejected Italy's argument that customary international law had evolved to a point where such an exception to sovereign immunity exists. '[C]ustomary international law', the Court held, 'continues to require that

---

[33] ibid, 121, [52]. As the Court made clear, the unlawfulness of such conduct was not contested by Germany.

[34] ibid, 122, [53].

[35] ibid, 123, [56].

[36] ibid, 123, [57].

[37] ibid, 123–24, [57].

[38] The Court did not find it necessary to address the wider question of whether a territorial tort exception exists as a general rule, preferring to focus on the context of the claims before it (ibid, 127–28, [65]).

a State be accorded immunity in proceedings for torts allegedly committed on the territory of another State by its armed forces and other organs of the State in the course of conducting an armed conflict'.[39]

The Court next addressed, in turn, each of the three strands of Italy's second argument, according to which the denial of immunity was justified on account of the particular nature of the German acts and the circumstances in which the claims before the Italian courts were made. None were found, of themselves, to justify the action of the Italian courts. Customary international law, as demonstrated by a substantial number of instances of state practice and other evidence, was not found to treat a state's entitlement to immunity as dependent upon the gravity of the violations of international humanitarian law.[40] Even if the rules violated by Germany were *jus cogens*, the Court continued, the rules of state immunity were procedural in nature and could thus neither bear upon nor conflict with the substantive nature of the conduct at issue. The Court referred in this context to domestic court decisions that rejected the argument that *jus cogens* may have the effect of displacing the law of state immunity (and noted that no national legislation has accepted it), once again isolating the practice of the Italian courts as the single (and misbegotten) outlier. Finally, the Court could not find in customary international law that the entitlement of a state to immunity is dependent upon the existence of effective alternative means of securing redress, rejecting the 'last resort' strand of Italy's argument. Even if viewed together, the Court added, the three strands of Italy's argument could not justify the denial of immunity: state practice was not found to lend support to such an approach, and the recognition of state immunity was in any event to be determined as a procedural matter at the outset of legal proceedings, and not on the basis of a balancing exercise of the various specific circumstances at hand.[41]

Making clear, again, that its ruling on immunity 'can have no effect on whatever responsibility Germany may have' for the atrocities committed,[42] the Court thus found that the action of Italian courts constituted a breach of the international obligation owed by Italy to Germany. Stressing that it was not unaware that the state of the law may preclude judicial redress for the Italian nationals concerned, it noted that it was a matter of surprise and regret that Germany decided to deny compensation to the Italian military internees, and that compensating them and others whose claims

---

[39] ibid, 135, [78].

[40] ibid, 135–44, [80]–[104]. The Court also noted that 'the proposition that the availability of immunity will be to some extent dependent upon the gravity of the unlawful act presents a logical problem. Immunity from jurisdiction is an immunity not merely from being subjected to an adverse judgment but from being subjected to the trial process. It is, therefore, necessarily preliminary in nature. Consequently, a national court is required to determine whether or not a foreign State is entitled to immunity as a matter of international law before it can hear the merits of the case brought before it and before the facts have been established. If immunity were to be dependent upon the State actually having committed a serious violation of international human rights law or the law of armed conflict, then it would become necessary for the national court to hold an enquiry into the merits in order to determine whether it had jurisdiction. If, on the other hand, the mere allegation that the State had committed such wrongful acts were to be sufficient to deprive the State of its entitlement to immunity, immunity could, in effect be negated simply by skilful construction of the claim' (136, [82]).

[41] ibid, 144–45, [105]–[106].

[42] ibid, 145, [107].

have not been settled 'could be the subject of further negotiation involving the two States concerned, with a view to resolving the issue'.[43]

Turning next to the mortgage registered in Italy against Villa Vigoni,[44] the Court observed, first, that immunity from enforcement and immunity from jurisdiction are governed by different sets of rules that ought to be applied separately.[45] The legality under international law of the measure of constraint could thus be assessed without considering the legality under international law of the Greek court decisions themselves or the Italian decisions declaring them enforceable. The Court then confirmed that, in accordance with well-established state practice, customary international law did not permit imposing any measure of constraint against property belonging to a foreign state without its consent if the asset was used in pursuit of governmental non-commercial purposes. Since Villa Vigoni was used for purposes falling within Germany's sovereign functions, the registration of a legal charge on it was in violation of the immunity owed to Germany.

Finally, the Court addressed the decisions by Italian courts that declared enforceable in Italy the decisions of Greek courts upholding civil claims against Germany. In such cases where a court is seised of an application for the execution of a foreign judgment rendered against a third state, the Court explained, that court must ask itself whether, in the event that it had itself been seised of the merits of a dispute identical to that which was the subject of the foreign judgment, it would have been obliged under international law to accord immunity to the respondent state. It followed that since the Italian courts would have been obliged, under customary international law, to grant immunity to Germany if they had been seised of the merits of a case identical to that which was the subject of the decisions of the Greek courts, they could not grant *exequatur* without violating Germany's jurisdictional immunity.[46]

Italy having lost on all these counts, the Court found that it 'must, by enacting appropriate legislation, or by resorting to other methods of its choosing, ensure that the decisions of its courts and those of other judicial authorities infringing the immunity which the Federal Republic of Germany enjoys under international law cease to have effect'.[47] On the other hand, the Court declined Germany's request that it order Italy to take any and all steps to ensure that in the future Italian courts do not entertain similar legal actions against Germany. The Court explained that 'as a general rule, there is no reason to suppose that a State whose act or conduct has been declared wrongful by the Court will repeat the act or conduct in the future,

---

[43] ibid, 144, [104] and 143, [99].

[44] Although Italy suspended this measure of constraint after the ICJ proceedings had begun, did not seek to justify it before the Court, and indicated its lack of objection to any decision ordering it to ensure that it is cancelled, the Court considered that a dispute on the matter did formally still exist and thus proceeded to rule on it.

[45] The Court clarified that 'Even if a judgment has been lawfully rendered against a foreign State, in circumstances such that the latter could not claim immunity from jurisdiction, it does not follow *ipso facto* that the State against which judgment has been given can be the subject of measures of constraint on the territory of the forum State or on that of a third State, with a view to enforcing the judgment in question' (*Jurisdictional Immunities of the State, Judgment*, (n 32) 146, [113]).

[46] ibid, 149–52, [121]–[133].

[47] ibid, 155, [139].

since its good faith must be presumed'; there was 'no reason to believe' that special conditions existed which would have justified such an order either.[48] Hardly anyone, including Mr. Ferrini, who passed away only weeks after the judgment, could have anticipated what would then happen.

V. DEVELOPMENTS AFTER THE ICJ JUDGMENT

Germany was careful not to trumpet a great victory following the ICJ judgment. Its Foreign Minister, Guido Westerwelle, remarked that the clarification of the state of the law by the Court 'was not only in the interest of Germany but also in the interest of the international community. It is good and it serves all to have legal certainty now'.[49] No doubt there was relief in Germany that the ruling, which was widely considered to be legally sound, would stem the flow of cases against it. At the same time, some in Germany (as elsewhere) may have felt that the judgment was unsatisfactory in moral terms.

While there was naturally some regret at the judgment in Greece, there was also a feeling that it might encourage bilateral talks on compensation. The Italian Government did not seem too disappointed either; indeed, it was reported that it was 'secretly pleased' with the judgment.[50] Be that as it may, it acted swiftly to abide by it. In what has been described as a 'model of compliance',[51] Italian courts soon aligned themselves with the ICJ, including the Court of Cassation that *en banc* reversed its own position and declared in 2013 that the doctrines put forward by it in the *Ferrini* case 'have remained isolated and have not been upheld by the international community, of which the International Court of Justice is the highest manifestation. Therefore, the principle [of an exception to jurisdictional immunity in the case of war crimes, and related responsibilities of the German State] can no

---

[48] ibid, 154, [138].

[49] L Watson, 'Germany is safe from being sued by victims of WWII Nazi atrocities after world's highest court throws out claim from Italian held as a slave in 1944', *The Daily Mail* (4 February 2012) <www.dailymail.co.uk/news/article-2096306/Germany-safe-sued-victims-WWII-Nazi-atrocities-ruling-worlds-highest-court.html>. According to the report, 'Westerwelle stressed that Germany's decision to go to court was not aimed at diminishing the country's responsibility for Nazi war crimes: "The (German) federal government has always recognised their pain," he said'.

[50] H-J Schlamp, 'War Crimes Ruling: Human Rights Take a Back Seat to Sovereignty', *Der Spiegel* (3 February 2012) <www.spiegel.de/international/world/war-crimes-ruling-human-rights-take-a-back-seat-to-sovereignty-a-813226.html>. See also M Krajewski and C Singer, 'Should Judges be Front-Runners? The ICJ, State Immunity and the Protection of Fundamental Human Rights' (2012) 16 *Max Planck Yearbook of United Nations Law* 3, 4. Italy's Agent before the Court, Ambassador and State Counsellor Paolo Pucci di Benisichi, reportedly said that the result helped clarify the limits of states' legal immunity, adding that 'We are not disappointed ... Of course, I would have preferred a judgment that was closer to our line of defence': Associated Press, 'Court confirms German immunity from claims by Nazi victims', *The Guardian* (3 February 2012), <www.theguardian.com/world/2012/feb/03/german-immunity-nazi-victims-claims>. On 25 November 2014, less than two years after the judgment in *Germany v Italy*, Italy for the first time made a declaration recognising as compulsory the jurisdiction of the ICJ under Article 36(2) of the ICJ Statute.

[51] G Nesi, 'The Quest for a 'Full' Execution of the ICJ Judgment in *Germany v Italy*', (2013) 11 *Journal of International Criminal Justice* 185, 187.

longer be applied'.[52] The Italian Parliament approved 'with unusual promptness' the 2004 United Nations Convention on Jurisdictional Immunities of States and Their Property,[53] and Italy acceded to it in May 2013. The legislature also enacted, in January 2013, a law mandating Italian judges to declare *ex officio* (at any stage of legal proceedings before them) a lack of jurisdiction for war crimes committed by the Third Reich, and providing a ground to invalidate final judgments that conflict with the ICJ judgment.[54]

Then came a bolt out of the blue. On 22 October 2014, the Italian Constitutional Court held that this primary legislation, together with a provision in a 1957 Law incorporating into the Italian legal order the UN Charter obligation to comply with decisions of the International Court of Justice (ICJ), was unconstitutional.[55] To implement the ICJ's 2012 judgment, asserted 13 judges at the *Palazzo della Consulta* notwithstanding the arguments of the Italian Government, would be incompatible with the supreme principle of judicial protection of fundamental human rights guaranteed by the Italian Constitution. In cases such as the present one, they added, 'it is up to the national judge, and in particular to this Court, to exercise the constitutional review, in order to preserve the inviolability of fundamental principles of the domestic legal order, or at least to minimize their sacrifice'.[56]

The Constitutional Court emphasised that it was not seeking to review the ICJ's judgment: 'It has to be recognized that, at the international law level, the interpretation by the ICJ of the customary law of immunity of States from the civil jurisdiction of other States for acts considered *jure imperii* is particularly qualified and does not allow further examination by national governments and/or judicial authorities, including this Court'.[57] Another matter, however, was resolving 'the envisaged conflict' between the customary rule (which was incorporated into the Italian constitutional order by a provision stipulating that the Italian legal system conforms to the generally recognised principles of international law) and other

[52] Judgments Nos 32139/2012 (9 August 2012) and 4248/2013 (21 February 2013).

[53] See E Lamarque, 'Some WH Questions about the Italian Constitutional Court's Judgment on the Rights of the Victims of the Nazi Crimes' (2014) 6 *Italian Journal of Public Law* 197, 203.

[54] Law No. 5 of 14 January 2013 (Accession by the Italian Republic to the United Nations Convention on Jurisdictional Immunities of States and their Property, signed in New York on 2 December 2004, as well as provisions for the amendment of the domestic legal order).

[55] Judgment No 238/2014 (case referred to the Constitutional Court by the Tribunal of Florence, which raised the question of constitutionality of the aforementioned legislation when seised with additional cases seeking to obtain compensation from Germany for damages suffered during World War II but requested by Germany to apply the judgment of the ICJ of 3 February 2012). The Court did clarify that the unconstitutionality of the latter provision was made 'exclusively to the extent that it obliges Italian courts to comply with the Judgment of the ICJ of 3 February 2012', stressing that in any other case 'it is certainly clear that the undertaking of the Italian State to respect all of the international obligations imposed by the accession to the United Nations Charter, including the duty to comply with the judgments of the ICJ, remains unchanged' [5]. The Court did not touch upon questions relating to immunity from enforcement, dealing solely with immunity from jurisdiction.

[56] ibid, [3.1]. The President of the Constitutional Court, who also acted as Judge Rapporteur for the case, was Giuseppe Tesauro, and the judgment came very near the end of his short, three-month term as President (30 July–9 November 2014).

[57] But the Court did note that its President, as Judge Rapporteur for the case, had opined that it was doubtful whether 'the immunity of States (European Union States in particular) still allows, by effect of international customs existing prior to the entry into force of the Constitution and of the Charter of

constitutional principles, 'to the extent that their conflict cannot be resolved by means of interpretation'.[58]

In seeking to resolve this 'conflict', the Constitutional Court stressed that the commission of atrocities by the German Reich on Italian soil was uncontested, and that the ICJ had itself acknowledged that upholding Germany's immunity implies for those claiming reparations an unqualified denial of access to judicial remedy. It reiterated that the constitutional principle of absolute guarantee of judicial protection is 'a supreme principle of the Italian constitutional order', and asserted that the incorporation of a rule of international law into the Italian legal system must be precluded in so far as it conflicts with inviolable principles and rights enshrined in the constitution.[59] While foreign states enjoy immunity in Italian courts for their 'typical exercise of governmental powers', the wide scope of the customary rule of state immunity as defined by the ICJ 'entails the absolute sacrifice of the right to judicial protection', which in the Italian legal order no overriding public interest was found to justify. The Court concluded that in Italian courts jurisdictional immunity may thus not shield states from accountability for war crimes and crimes against humanity that 'as such are excluded from the lawful exercise of governmental powers'.[60]

The Constitutional Court recalled that it was by virtue of national jurisprudence, mainly by Italian judges, that international law had progressively evolved since the early twentieth century to recognise that state immunity was not absolute so far as acts *jure gestionis* were concerned. While it acknowledged that its judgment related to the Italian legal system alone, the Court went on to say that, as state practice, the judgment 'may also contribute to a desirable—and desired by many—evolution of international law itself'.[61]

Fundamental Rights of the European Union, for the indiscriminate denial of judicial protection of fundamental rights violated by war crimes and crimes against humanity'. For President Tesauro, immunity could not entail that individuals affected by such atrocities are also denied the possibility of judicial examination and remedy: 'Italian courts cannot leave the protection of individuals to the dynamics of the relationship between the political organs of the States involved, since these organs have not been able to come up with a solution for decades' [1.2]. See also C Tomuschat, 'The National Constitution Trumps International Law' (2014) 2 *Italian Journal of Public Law* 187, 188 ('The [Constitutional Court] confines itself to applying Italian domestic law ... However, it indirectly criticizes the ICJ for not rising to the level of human rights protection which, according to its view, is required within the famous group of '*nations civilisées*' in accordance with Article 38(1)(c) ICJ Statute').

[58] Judgment (n 55) [3.1].

[59] See also A Peters, 'Let Not Triepel Triumph—How To Make the Best Out of Sentenza No 238 of the Italian Constitutional Court for a Global Legal Order', *EJIL: Talk!* (22 December 2014) <www.ejiltalk. org/let-not-triepel-triumph-how-to-make-the-best-out-of-sentenza-no-238-of-the-italian-constitutional-court-for-a-global-legal-order-part-i> ('The Italian *controlimiti*-approach to European or international court decisions is by no means an outlier. Quite to the contrary, the *Sentenza* No 238 is just one more building block in the wall of "protection" built up by domestic courts against "intrusion" of international law, relying on the precepts of their national constitution. Ironically, this front of resistance (which now deploys effects "against" Germany) had been spearheaded by the German Constitutional Court (*Bundesverfassungsgericht*, BVerfG)').

[60] Judgment (n 55) [3.4].

[61] ibid, [3.3]. The Constitutional Court claimed that its own case-law had led the Court of Justice of the European Union to change its jurisprudence on judicial protection; and that the latter had itself annulled, for being incompatible with fundamental human rights, the European Community regulation seeking to implement UN Security Council resolutions (the *Kadi* and *Al Barakaat* cases): see [3.4].

One of Germany's Agents before the ICJ has written that the Italian judgment came 'as a shock to the international community' and set the Constitutional Court 'on a course with unforeseeable consequences'.[62] Others have criticised the judgment not only for its outcome of 'a shattering schism between internal and international law',[63] but also for the quality of its reasoning: 'More than the outcome, it is the poor reasoning behind it that is striking', argued an Italian jurist who represented Italy before the ICJ.[64] Still others (though mainly not international lawyers) could not hide their satisfaction. 'Europe is beginning to listen to America', hailed one American commentator, drawing a comparison between the Italian Court's defiance of the ICJ and the United States Supreme Court decision in *Medellín v Texas* (2008).[65] But Italy's international legal obligation to implement the ICJ judgment remains unaltered, as national law cannot be invoked to evade international obligations.[66] While Rome and Berlin continue to discuss potential legal

---

[62] Tomuschat, 'National Constitution' (n 57) 187.

[63] R Kolb, 'The Relationship Between the International and Municipal Legal Order: Reflections on the Decision No 238/2014 of the Italian Constitutional Court' (2014) 2 *Questions of International Law* 5, 6.

[64] P Palchetti, 'Judgment 238/2014 of the Italian Constitutional Court: In search of a way out' (2014) 2 *Questions of International Law* 44 (adding that 'Given the complexity of the case, one would have expected the Court to engage in a thorough assessment of the weight to be given to the competing interests at stake in the light of the concrete circumstances of the case. By balancing such interests, the Court could have helped to shed some light on the leeway afforded by the Constitution to the political organs in order to find a way out of this situation'). See also A Tanzi, 'Un Difficile Dialogo tra Corte Internazionale di Giustizia e Corte Constituzionale' (2015) 70 *La Communità Internazionale* 13–36 (arguing that the Court did not strike an appropriate balance between the right to judicial redress and compliance with international law, which was also required under the Italian Constitution); Lamarque, 'Some WH Questions' (n 53) 200 ('Such a black and white solution is unworthy of the elegant balances that the Italian constitutional case law usually produces').

[65] E Kontorovich, 'Italy adopts Supreme Court's view of ICJ authority', *The Washington Post*, 28 October 2014 (In *Medellín v Texas*, it was held that neither the ICJ's *Avena* judgment nor President George W Bush's Memorandum committing US domestic courts to give effect to it constituted directly enforceable law in the United States.) Somewhat prophetically, in 2010 (then) ICJ President Owada said that 'the Court had recently been faced with some increasingly complex questions concerning specific details of compliance ... when the Court rendered a judgment which must be implemented in the domestic legal order of a State, it might happen, depending on the legal system in force in that State, that the latter encountered difficulties in implementing the judgment. In the *Avena* case, the Government of the United States of America had in fact tried to implement the judgment of the Court at both federal and state level, but that had not been possible because of both the federal system in the United States and its constitutional system, in which the doctrine of "self-executing" treaties had prevented the executive branch from implementing the decisions of the Court at state level ... That type of question could arise in other States; the problem was how to harmonize the international legal order and the domestic legal order' (UN Doc A/CN.4/SR.3062: Provisional summary record of the International Law Commission's 3062nd meeting, 9 July 2010, 6). Also noteworthy is that in response, the German member of the Commission remarked that 'Germany also had a federal system, but fortunately a chamber of the German Constitutional Court had interpreted the Constitution as requiring that judgments of the Court were to be duly implemented by the domestic courts. He was concerned that the United States approach might become the model and had cited the above example to show that there were other ways of dealing with the Court's judgments' (11). More recently, Russia's Constitutional Court has ruled in 2016 that it was 'impossible to implement' the final judgment of the European Court of Human Rights delivered on 4 July 2013 in the case of *Anchugov and Gladkov v Russia*: see N Chaeva, 'The Russian Constitutional Court and its Actual Control over the ECtHR Judgment in Anchugov and Gladkov', *EJIL: Talk!* (26 April 2016) <www.ejiltalk.org/the-russian-constitutional-court-and-its-actual-control-over-the-ecthr-judgement-in-anchugov-and-gladko>.

[66] See *Vienna Convention on the Law of Treaties*, Article 27; International Law Commission's *Articles on State Responsibility*, Article 3 and Article 32. In the 2015 provisional measures hearing in the *"Enrica Lexie" Incident (Italy v India)* case, India referred to the Italian Constitutional Court's judgment and raised doubts as to Italy's capability of fulfilling its international obligations (see ITLOS/PV.15/C/24/2,

avenues for defusing the Constitutional Court's ruling, legal proceedings have resumed against Germany in Italian courts,[67] which on a number of occasions again ordered Germany to pay reparations. It remains unlikely, however, that claimants would be able to force Germany to pay.[68] And Germany has informed the Italian Government that if necessary, it stands ready to bring another case against Italy in The Hague.[69]

VI. *JURISDICTIONAL IMMUNITIES OF THE STATE* AS A LANDMARK CASE

While the benefit of hindsight is still limited, it seems clear that *Jurisdictional Immunities of the State* has given rise to issues that go to the heart of, and challenge, the role of international law in today's world. Although the response to the ICJ's judgment by the Italian Constitutional Court and its aftermath shake the very foundations of international law, it is to be hoped that these are temporary setbacks that will in due course fade into the background; they are not what makes the case a

---

40–42; ITLOS/PV.15/C/24/4, 13; ITLOS/PV.15/C/24/4, 15-16; ITLOS/PV.15/C/24/3, 19). Judge ad hoc Francioni stated in response that '... any reference to the recent decision of the Italian Constitutional Court is misplaced and ill-conceived. This is so because that decision concerned a case of undisputed war crimes and crimes against humanity committed during the Second World War which could not be more far removed from the present case, which concerns a conflict of jurisdiction over a maritime incident. Further, the judgment of the Italian Constitutional Court shows exactly the opposite of what India has tried to infer from it. Contrary to India's regrettable and repeated assertion that Italy's promise is tainted by an alleged disposition to shun compliance with international judgments, the case shows that Italy not only promptly complied with a decision of the International Court of Justice (*Jurisdictional Immunities of the State, Judgment* (n 32) ICJ Rep 99), but went as far as to adopt ad hoc legislative measure in order to ensure effective implementation of such decision in its internal legal order. Further, even after the Constitutional Court's decision affirming the inalienable right of access to justice for victims of international crimes, legislative measures have been adopted in order to ensure that no enforcement measures are taken with regard to foreign states' assets in violation of the decision of the ICJ in *Jurisdictional Immunities of the State* (see Law, fn 162, 10 November 2014, Art 19-*bis*), which was not mentioned by counsel for India, either intentionally or for lack of adequate information. Italy's trust in international adjudication and its commitment to fully comply with international decisions is further confirmed by its filing on 25 November 2014 of a declaration of acceptance of the compulsory jurisdiction of the ICJ under Art 36, paragraph 2, of the Court's Statute': '*Enrica Lexie' Incident (Italy v India), Provisional Measures, Order of 24 August 2015*, ITLOS Reports 2015, 182, declaration of Judge ad hoc Francioni, 221–22, [10], [15].

[67] It is understood that Germany has been transmitting to the Italian courts a *Note Verbale* addressed by the German Embassy in Rome to the Italian Foreign Ministry setting out its position and asserting its rights notwithstanding the judgment of the Italian Constitutional Court, and warning that a resumption or continuation of cases based on breaches of international humanitarian law by the German Reich would once again violate the state immunity of Germany. The lawyer for the Italian Government (*Avvocato dello Stato*) appears to urge the courts to uphold international law as decided by the ICJ. For more on the aftermath of the Constitutional Court's judgment in the Italian legal system see K Oellers-Frahm, 'A Never-Ending Story: The International Court of Justice—The Italian Constitutional Court—Italian Tribunals and the Question of Immunity' (2016) 76 ZaöRV 193–202; G Boggero, 'The Legal Implications of *Sentenza* No 238/2014 by Italy's Constitutional Court for Italian Municipal Judges: Is Overcoming the "Triepelian Approach" Possible?' (2016) 76 ZaöRV 203–24.

[68] On the paradoxical possibility that the 'most logical inference to be drawn would be for the Italian State to pay financial compensation to all those who feel that they have a legitimate claim against Germany' see Tomuschat, (n 57) 194.

[69] Other possible options available to Germany include recourse to the Security Council under Article 94(2) of the UN Charter (though this route is improbable).

landmark. Rather, it is as a key decision on the law of state immunity, and the light it sheds on international law more broadly, for which the judgment's significance 'reaches beyond predictions on the future for state immunity to the structure, subjects and systems of international law as a whole'.[70] Space does not permit a detailed analysis of all the reasons for this, but four points seem worth highlighting.

First, *Jurisdictional Immunities of the State* is, and is likely to remain for some time, the leading international case on the law on state immunity, which 'Until recently … relied virtually exclusively upon domestic case law and latterly legislation'.[71] In affirming that sovereign immunity continues to occupy an important place in international law the judgment holds unequivocally that state immunity is not, as some have suggested, merely a matter of comity. It furthermore clarifies the nature of state immunity as being essentially procedural, and provides coherent guidance as to its consideration and application. The ruling also settles for now the debate, intense but largely confined to academic commentators, as to whether states are entitled to jurisdictional immunity under international law in cases involving allegations of serious human rights violations (or international crimes),[72] providing an authoritative and orthodox statement of the *lex lata*.[73] It is noteworthy, however, that the Court narrowly circumscribed the issue before it, avoiding a decision on whether there is a 'territorial tort exception' to state immunity applicable to *acta jure imperii* other than those committed during an armed conflict, and expressly distinguishing the separate question of the immunity of state officials from foreign criminal jurisdiction.[74]

---

[70] L McGregor, 'State Immunity and Human Rights: Is There a Future after Germany v Italy?' (2013) 11 *Journal of International Criminal Justice* 125, 145. See also B Nussberger and V Otto, '*Jurisdictional Immunities of the State (Germany v Italy: Greece intervening)*' in R Wolfrum (ed), *The Max Planck Encyclopedia of Public International Law* (Oxford, OUP, 2016) opil.ouplaw.com/home/EPIL.

[71] MN Shaw, *International Law*, 4th edn (Cambridge, CUP, 2015) 507. See also J Crawford, *Brownlie's Principles of Public International Law*, 8th edn (Oxford, OUP, 2012) 488 ('the law developed primarily through domestic case law and limited treaty practice, supplemented more recently by comprehensive legislation in certain states'). Other international courts have touched on issues of state immunity, both before and after 2012, including the ITLOS (in *ARA Libertad*) and ECtHR (in *Al Adsani, Jones*). But it is the ICJ in *Jurisdictional Immunities* that has confirmed basic elements of the international law on state immunity.

[72] See also A Bianchi, 'On Certainty', *EJIL: Talk!* (16 February 2012), available online at www.ejiltalk. org/on-certainty: 'At last we have certainty. After almost twenty years of heated debate … we now know. States cannot be sued for serious human rights violations before the municipal courts of another state'; C Espósito, 'Of Plumbers and Social Architects: Elements and Problems of the Judgment of the International Court of Justice in Jurisdictional Immunities of the State', (2013) 4 *Journal of International Dispute Settlement* 439, 455 ('Perhaps the greatest achievement of the Court's judgment in Jurisdictional Immunities of the State is its lack of ambiguity').

[73] Other courts confronted with the issue have followed the ICJ's lead. In *Jones and others v The United Kingdom*, the European Court of Human Rights stated that '*Germany v Italy* … must be considered by this Court as authoritative as regards the content of customary international law' (Applications Nos 34356/06 and 40528/06, Judgment of 14 January 2014, [198]). The Dutch Supreme Court took a similar approach in *Mothers of Serbenica Association et al v The Netherlands and the United Nations* (10/04437, Judgment of 13 April 2012), [4.3.10]–[4.3.14]; as did the Quebec Court of Appeal (*Hashemi v Iran* (2012) QCCA 1449, 154 ILR 351, 159 ILR 299) in a judgment that was upheld by the Supreme Court of Canada.

[74] *Jurisdictional Immunities of the State, Judgment* (n 32) 128, 139, [65], [91]. The Court also found it unnecessary to consider the general regime of immunity from enforcement under customary international law (147–148, [115]–[118]).

Second, the judgment is instructive for what it says about *jus cogens*. In particular, the ruling further clarifies the nature of *jus cogens* as a category of substantive law and illustrates its position in relation to rules of international law that are procedural in character (such as the rules of state immunity). Relying on its previous jurisprudence in the *Armed Activities* and *Arrest Warrant* cases, the Court declined to recognise a possible conflict between these two sets of rules, explaining that:

> A *jus cogens* rule is one from which no derogation is permitted but the rules which determine the scope and extent of jurisdiction and when that jurisdiction may be exercised do not derogate from those substantive rules which possess *jus cogens* status, nor is there anything inherent in the concept of *jus cogens* which would require their modification or would displace their application.[75]

While the concept of *jus cogens* appears by now to be beyond dispute, such authoritative pronouncements on its essence and consequences remain highly valuable.

Third, *Jurisdictional Immunities of the State* resonates as a landmark not only for the points of law it spells out, but also for the judicial reasoning by which these points are developed and adopted. Most notably, in the tradition of the *Nuclear Weapons* and *Barcelona Traction* cases,[76] the Court showed unwillingness to accept a claim which, however morally appealing, did not accord with the law in force. Grappling yet again with the strain between traditional concepts of a state-centrist legal system and the contemporary pull of individual (human) rights,[77] the Court saw its role as being to decide the case before it on the basis of the existing law rather than as a campaigner or legislator.

---

[75] ibid, 141, [95]. It has been argued that this approach 'supports a very limited scope of peremptory norms' that was instrumental to corroborating the result that the Court was aiming to achieve (C Espósito, 'Jus Cogens and Jurisdictional Immunities of the State at the International Court of Justice: "A Conflict Does Exist"' (2011) 21 *Italian Yearbook of International Law* 161, 162–63); see also the dissenting opinion of Judge Cançado Trindade at 282–86). But see S Talmon, '*Jus Cogens* after *Germany v Italy*: Substantive and Procedural Rules Distinguished' (2012) 25 *LJIL* 979, 1002 ('The criticism of the 'substantive–procedural' distinction in international law as too formalistic and technical may be answered by noting that law, by its very nature, is formalistic and technical. These traits contribute to clarity, certainty, and predictability—also 'values' not to be discarded lightly'); C Tomuschat, 'The Case of Germany v Italy before the ICJ', in A Peters, E Lagrange, S Oeter and C Tomuschat (eds), *Immunities in the Age of Global Constitutionalism* (Leiden, Brill Nijhoff, 2015) 87, 91 ('The concept of *ius cogens* is not a magic wand that would transform all traditional rules into a new ethereal substance, immune from any controversy, as soon as touched by it').

[76] *Legality of the Threat or Use of Nuclear Weapons, Advisory Opinion*, [1996] ICJ Rep 226; *Barcelona Traction, Light and Power Company, Limited, Judgment* [1970] ICJ Rep 3.

[77] See also V Gowlland-Debbas, 'The ICJ and the Challenges of Human Rights Law' in M Andenas and E Bjorge (eds), *A Farewell to Fragmentation* (Cambridge, CUP, 2015) 133–35; SD Murphy, 'What a Difference a Year Makes: The International Court of Justice's 2012 Jurisprudence', (2013) 4 *Journal of International Dispute Settlement* 539, 552 ('International law has increasingly become attuned to the rights of persons as against the power or States and international organizations, but the traditional processes of international law pose difficult and sometimes insurmountable hurdles to persons in effectively vindicating those rights'); J Klabbers, 'The Curious Condition of Custom', (2002) 8 *International Legal Theory* 29, 34 ('With respect to prescriptions of moral relevance (think in particular of human rights), the traditional concept of custom has lost plausibility').

Several writers have, predictably enough, expressed deep disappointment with what they have labelled as a conservative judgment, 'a kind of Westphalian atavism where the ICJ placed the values of sovereignty over those of humanity'.[78] To them, 'the Court missed a double opportunity: to contribute to the development of international law by interpreting the rule on sovereign immunity in harmony with international human rights law and its dynamics, and to finally serve justice for the victims of war crimes'.[79] By so doing, it is argued, the Court had 'neglected fundamental requirements of the legitimacy of the international legal order'.[80] But such writers concede, even if reluctantly, that the judgment did in fact reflect existing international law, and that for the Court to find in Italy's favour 'would have meant a certain amount of creativity'.[81]

The Court, whose function 'is to decide in accordance with international law such disputes as are submitted to it',[82] thus in this case fulfilled its function. Had it decided otherwise, against the law, it would have been acting outside its mandate. Moreover, to disregard the jurisdictional immunities of the state, as some have suggested it should have done, would have had serious repercussions on international relations and cast doubt on international law as a whole. In pronouncing in favour of immunity the Court was therefore not a guardian of the status quo,[83] but rather of the international legal system that it serves.

Also unconvincing is the criticism that the Court has set international law back many years by interrupting the development of a rule of more limited sovereign

[78] R Howse, responding to an *Opinio Juris* blog entry: <http://opiniojuris.org/2014/11/19/guest-post-tearing-sovereign-immunitys-fence-italian-constitutional-court-international-court-justice-german-war-crimes>. The late Professor Benedetto Conforti, who had long opposed the orthodox position, and whose views may well have influenced the Constitutional Court and its President Tesauro, was a virulent critic: 'The Judgment of the International Court of Justice on the Immunity of Foreign States: A Missed Opportunity', (2011) 21 *Italian Yearbook of International Law* 135, 136, 137 ('There is no sign of progress in this judgment ... The lack of willingness to provide elements for future exceptions to this immunity from jurisdiction of foreign States lends the judgment an air of strong conservativism'); O Bakircioglu, 'Germany v Italy: The Triumph of Sovereign Immunity over Human Rights Law', (2012) 1 *International Human Rights Law Review* 93–109.

[79] S Negri, 'Sovereign Immunity v Redress for War Crimes: The Judgment of the International Court of Justice in the Case Concerning *Jurisdictional Immunities of the State (Germany v Italy)*' (2014) 16 *International Community Law Review* 123 (adding that 'the International Court of Justice deliberately chose to abdicate its recognised role as authoritative law-maker, restraining itself to a strict computation, and maybe short-sighted interpretation, of the data provided by State practice, regardless of the new trends and dynamics of international law ... in marking the triumph of judicial self-restraint over judicial activism, the judgment no doubt represents a missed opportunity to re-interpret the scope of the immunity rule in harmony with the evolution of human right law' (137)).

[80] Bothe, 'Remedies' (n 21) 100. Human rights organisations, too, admonished the judgment as a disappointment; Amnesty International, for example, described it as an 'astonishing ruling ... a big step backwards in [the protection of] human rights' (<www.amnesty.org/en/latest/news/2012/02/un-court-ruling-nazi-war-crime-victims-deplorable>).

[81] ibid 111 (explaining that 'The Court would have contributed to the development of the law by promoting a norm which may still be *in statu nascendi*').

[82] Statute of the International Court of Justice, Art 38.

[83] KN Trapp and A Mills, 'Smooth Runs the Water where the Brook is Deep: The Obscured Complexities of *Germany v Italy*' (2012) 1 *CJICL* 153, 168; Krajewski and Singer, 'Should Judges be Front-Runners?' (n 50) 34; Bakircioglu, 'Germany v Italy' (n 78) 108.

immunity.[84] To begin with, the Court took care to note that it was applying customary international law 'as it presently stands'.[85] More importantly, the judgment afforded states a specific opportunity to react and, if they so considered, to express an opinion that the law of sovereign immunity as applied by the Court was or should be different: if they had done so, that might well have led to a change in the law.[86] But states, who remain the principal source of legitimacy in the international legal system, seem to concur with the Court's view of the law. Again, then, the criticism seems misdirected. As a former President of the Court has remarked, 'Activists have the wrong target in their sights. They should bring pressure to bear on States, rather than berate the Court for conservatism'.[87]

Finally, the Court's analysis in determining the existence and scope of the customary rule at issue provides an instructive example of how such a task is to be carried out by those called upon to advise on or apply customary international law. In addition to reiterating the need to establish the existence of 'a settled practice' together with acceptance as law (*opinio juris*),[88] the judgment illustrates how in each case the underlying principles of international law that may be applicable to the matter ought to be taken into account; how the evidence is to be adjusted to the situation, with certain forms of practice and evidence *opinio juris* possibly being of particular significance; and how all available practice of a state must be assessed 'as a whole'.[89] The extensive review of relevant materials, also acknowledged by Judge Ad hoc

---

[84] See, for example, Bothe (n 21) 113; Krajewski and Singer (n 50) 10, 30.

[85] *Jurisdictional Immunities of the State, Judgment* (n 32) 139, [91]. See also Judge Koroma's separate opinion: 'Given that the Court's task is to apply the existing law, nothing in the Court's Judgment today prevents the continued evolution of the law on State immunity … The Court's Judgment applies the law as it exists today' (159).

[86] See also G Gaja, (2012) 364 *Recueil des Cours* 44 ('much as the Court's vies on the existence and content of principles and rules of general international law are highly regarded by all States, there is an ultimate test of acceptability of these views which may affect their impact in practice'). But see D Bethlehem, 'The Secret Life of International Law' (2012) 1 *CJICL* 23, 31–33 (on the difficulty for states in reacting to legal pronouncements not directly opposable to them).

[87] R Higgins, 'Equality of States and Immunity from Suit: A Complex Relationship' (2012) 43 *NYIL* 129, 146. See also S Rosenne, *The Law and Practice of the International Court of Justice 1920–2005*, vol I, 4th edn (The Hague, Martinus Nijhoff, 2006) 3 ('The Court's status as a principal organ of the United Nations, itself above all a political organization, emphasizes that the judicial settlement of international disputes is a function performed within the general framework of the political organization of the international society'); Gowlland-Debbas, 'The ICJ' (n 77) 144 ('The ICJ, an institution established at a time when bilateral and subjective relations between States based on the golden rule in *Lotus* prevailed, cannot always respond to expectations when faced with human rights cases. The requirement of a jurisdictional link and the fact that its decisions bind only the parties and its advisory opinions are just that, sits uneasily alongside the development of an international public policy in which subjective interests must give way to collective values and interests'). One of Germany's agents before the Court remarked that 'Careful analysis of the empirical background should precede any attempt at reforming the law as it stands. It is not helpful for international law to postulate rules which under the test of empirical practice prove to be purely utopian, without any real chance of becoming operative. Human rights law should be real law and not only a playground for activists where enormous resources are being squandered uselessly': Tomuschat 'The Case of Germany v Italy' (n 75) 98.

[88] *Jurisdictional Immunities of the State, Judgment* (n 32) 122, [55].

[89] ibid, 123–24, [55], [57]; 134, [76].

Gaja in his dissenting opinion,[90] not only served to show that the Italian practice did not gain support among other states; it also counsels more broadly on how treaty texts may be utilised in seeking to identify customary rules, and how domestic court decisions may be examined both as state practice and as subsidiary means for determining the law.[91] At a time when the International Law Commission has taken up the topic 'Identification of customary international law' to assist practitioners and others in such a task,[92] the judgment is a further important contribution by the Court to those seeking guidance on the matter. Whether or not the substance of the law on state immunity will eventually change, this methodological direction will surely have a lasting impact.

[90] ibid, 309, [1] ('The Court's argument is well built and includes a wide survey of relevant State practice'). Some have argued that the evidence relied on by the Court does not clearly provide sufficient foundation for its conclusions: see Judge Yusuf's dissenting opinion 291, 297–98 ('Would it not have been more appropriate to recognize, in light of conflicting judicial decisions and other practices of States, that customary international law in this area remains fragmentary and unsettled?'); Trapp and Mills, 'Smooth Runs the Water' (n 83) 156 (concluding that 'The most that can be said here is that state practice is mixed—and that the Court's selectivity in its examination of that state practice is potentially misleading', 158); Conforti, 'A Missed Opportunity' (n 78) 138–40; R Pavoni, 'An American Anomaly? On the ICJ's Selective Reading of United States Practice in *Jurisdictional Immunities of the State*' (2011) 21 *Italian Yearbook of International Law* 143, 144 ('It is the specific use or omission by the ICJ of certain significant manifestations of practice that lends itself to criticism and justified perceptions of biased, policy-driven conservatism. Most importantly, it weakens the persuasive force of the Court's findings'); Negri, 'Sovereign Immunity v Redress for War Crimes' (n 79) 132.

[91] ibid, 127–30, [64]–[69]; 131–35, [72]–[77]; 137–38, [85]–[87]; 138–39, [89]; 141–42, [96]. See also C Greenwood, 'Unity and Diversity in International Law' in M Andenas and E Bjorge (eds), *A Farewell to Fragmentation* (Cambridge, CUP, 2015) 50–51 ('Although the Court did not expressly make this point, it is clear that it examined the decisions of national courts for two distinct reasons. Those decisions were, of course, part of the State practice on which the customary international law of State immunity was based. As such, they were important for the Court's analysis irrespective of the quality of the reasoning on which they were based. Yet the Court also considered that reasoning in order to see what guidance it gave, in the same way as it examined the reasoning of the European Court of Human Rights in the judgments which that Court had given regarding State immunity. While the reasoning in some of those judgments was very brief, in others ... there was a detailed examination of the issues on which the Court placed a degree of reliance'); I Wuerth, 'International Law in Domestic Courts and the Jurisdictional Immunity of the State Case' (2012) 13 *Melbourne Journal of International Law* 819.

[92] See UN Doc A/71/10: *Report of the International Law Commission, Sixty-Eighth Session (2 May–10 June and 4 July–12 August 2016)*, 75–115, containing the Commission's 16 draft conclusions, with commentaries, adopted on first reading in 2016; a second reading is expected in 2018.

Index

Printed in the USA
CPSIA information can be obtained
at www.ICGtesting.com
LVHW070238040124
768061LV00006B/740